MAJOR FOREIGN POWERS

Fifth Edition

Major Foreign Powers

Fifth Edition

Gwendolen M. Carter

Northwestern University

John H. Herz

The City College, The City University of New York

Harcourt, Brace & World, Inc.
New York / Chicago / San Francisco / Atlanta

Preface to the Fifth Edition

"To write a book on comparative government at a time like the present is, in many respects, a foolhardy enterprise"—so began the preface to the first edition, and the statement remains as true today. The rapidity with which events develop makes difficult the long observation and mature analysis so important for the evaluation of institutions and policies. If the political systems of the two postwar Germanies have proved more stable than many people predicted, that of postwar France has gone through a major metamorphosis as a result of internal and external pressures. While the facilities for careful observation are still somewhat restricted in the Soviet Union, there can be no question that the transition from Stalin to post-Stalinist and, subsequently, post-Khrushchev leadership created problems of far-reaching consequences, the impact of which has not yet ended. And even though Great Britain has absorbed the results of its radical experimentation at the end of World War II and turned once more to its traditional slow and gradual political development, its economic problems nevertheless keep that country under constant strain. Thus, in this fifth edition, as in earlier editions, extensive changes have been necessary in every section of the work.

Yet the conditions that make difficult the writing and rewriting of this book are the very ones that make it most important for Americans to understand the politics of major foreign powers. The pleasant times of peace and stability, when it is easiest to prepare such studies, are also the times when foreign events have less effect on American life. But these times seem to have gone forever. We live in permanent crisis, and it is in such times that it becomes essential for Americans to have the widest possible knowledge of conditions and developments in important countries abroad.

Major Foreign Powers

The four countries dealt with in this book are of unquestionable importance to the United States. The Soviet Union and the United States are the world's two "super-powers." Great Britain and France still retain both influence and prestige, despite their diminished power. The fourth country, Germany, has been a great power and is again playing a significant role in international affairs. All four countries afford a wealth of political material of profound significance for the study of government.

To concentrate on these countries is not to suggest that others are lacking in political interest. Sweden and Switzerland, for example, have engaged in political and economic experiments of great interest for the Western democracies; so too have such overseas members of the Commonwealth of Nations as Canada, Australia, and New Zealand. India's courageous experiment with political democracy, Japan's attempt to build free government, the changing political forms of Africa's newly independent countries, and developments in the long-established states of Latin America demand our attention. So do conditions in Communist countries outside the Soviet Union, especially China. Both in the extended introduction and in the conclusion we shall refer to such countries, as well as to our major powers, in order to develop a broad framework of government and politics in the twentieth century. But such a framework needs to be combined with a thorough study of the institutions and politics of the four countries we deem most significant to Americans both as

v

factors in international politics and as political laboratories.

Approach to the Subject

Few books on comparative government are truly comparative. In most of them, each country is treated as a unit in itself, and there is little attempt to use a knowledge of the practices and institutions of one country to illuminate those of another, or to draw the many enlightening and suggestive comparisons that bring fresh insight to the reader. We hold comparison to be a major tool for understanding. We have therefore attempted from the very beginning, in our discussion of British politics, to draw comparisons with those American organs and procedures with which the reader may be expected to be familiar. Similarly, in the section on France, we make constant comparisons between the presidential-parliamentary government of its Fifth Republic and the parliamentary system of Great Britain. West Germany offers still a third variant in parliamentary and executive practice. The Soviet Union, of course, provides the most striking contrasts to the other three major powers. Naturally, however, there are marked similarities as well as differences between the Soviet Union and the Communist-controlled German Democratic Republic, which is treated in the German section.

Throughout, we have tried to depict governments not as casual or arbitrary collections of institutions existing in a vacuum apart from the people who have produced them, but rather as living complexes of activities and arrangements that change and develop in response to the character, needs, desires, and purposes of human beings. Thus, in the sections devoted to each country (with slight changes for Germany, because of the variety of its political experience), the first chapter discusses the nature of its people: their national, economic, religious, and geographic divisions, together with the organs of public opinion through which these diverse interests are expressed or controlled. The second chapter deals with those historical influences and political ideas that have been important in molding the institutions of government. The third turns to political parties as the agencies through which the people, or a dominant portion thereof, most directly influence or control the government. The fourth chapter is devoted to representative bodies which, in general, have the special function of reflecting popular interests. The fifth is concerned with the executive and the nature of political leadership (and for Germany also with the administration). The sixth (except for Germany) is concerned with national and local administration. The seventh chapter (for Germany, the sixth) turns to the administration of justice. The eighth (for Germany, the seventh) surveys the range of experiments and activities that promote the public welfare. (The eighth chapter of the German section deals with Berlin, both West and East, and with the German Democratic Republic, thereby facilitating comparisons with the Federal Republic and providing a unified treatment of a Communist regime outside the Soviet Union.) The ninth chapter in each section considers the position of the country in the world today.

The work opens with a consideration of the most significant issues for modern government and points up the contrast between democratic and totalitarian forms. The conclusion picks up general issues raised in the introduction and seeks to extend the comparisons of structure and function handled in the body of the work. It is our hope that together they will serve both as a synthesizing review and as an aid to understanding the most significant forces and problems affecting contemporary politics and government.

In writing this book, we have had in mind the reader who is seeking an introduction to the politics of the major powers rather than the scholar who has already specialized in the field. Wherever possible, therefore, we have dispensed with the top-heavy apparatus of scholarship which requires a footnote for every statement and thus diverts the reader from the principal train of thought. Where it is important for the reader to know the source of a particular statement, we have tried to introduce that information into the text itself. The reader who wishes to pursue subjects further will be able to do so by using the comprehensive bibliography of relevant books and articles in English, prepared by Professor Louise W. Holborn of the Radcliffe Institute for Independent Study, who has contributed helpfully to all editions of the book.

The first edition of this book was the result of close collaboration between Miss Carter and Mr. Ranney. Following Mr. Ranney's untimely death, the subsequent editions were prepared by Miss Carter and Mr. Herz. Miss Carter has been responsible for the sections on Great Britain, France, and the Soviet Union and Mr. Herz for the section on Germany, which was added in the second edition. The two authors jointly prepared the introduction and the conclusion and at all times have worked closely together to maintain the unity of the work.

The Authors' Personal Position

Each of the major foreign powers today is the focus of great controversy, and an author inevitably finds himself involved in questions that go beyond a mere description of political institutions and processes. Once one has ascertained as accurately as possible how an institution works, how power is exercised, how rulers are chosen, how elections are arranged, or which interests rule, the further question arises: Does the institution work well or badly, is the system good or bad?

In many cases, the answer to this question will depend upon one's personal set of values or standard of judgment. The person who thinks of poverty or unemployment as the greatest evil may well come to a different conclusion from the person who hates political tyranny above all else; the person who worships efficiency will look at the same institution in a very different light from the person who thinks it most important that men should base all their institutions upon voluntary consent.

It has therefore seemed well to the authors to do two things. First, we have tried to explain in our discussion of the politics of each country the nature of the ideas, the aims, and the traditions that have had a dominating political influence, so that it will be possible to judge the institutions of each country in the light of its own standards and beliefs. But we have also thought it important, on issues that are controversial, to make our own point of view perfectly clear—both because it should be more stimulating for the reader to see the issues discussed

frankly, even when he might himself disagree, and because it would be deceptive in any case to evade value judgments at a time when even to avoid an issue is to take a position. We therefore have not tried to conceal the fact that we share the political beliefs of liberal Americans. To us a society is bad that lacks the traditional democratic freedoms of thought, speech, press, and association. But a society is not good that is marked by poverty, ignorance, unemployment, or social and racial discrimination. Like most Americans, we would like to make the best of both worlds: to see the good political and spiritual life combined with the good material life. And it has seemed to us important to discover to what extent any one of these major foreign powers has succeeded in combining these ideals.

Acknowledgments

At the conclusion of so extended a survey, the authors are bound to think with special gratitude of the very many people who have given them assistance in reading and criticizing parts of the manuscript, in providing information, and in helping with the innumerable technical jobs involved in the preparation of a book. None of them, of course, bears any responsibility in the proper sense, but they are largely responsible for whatever merit the book has.

Although lack of space prevents us from again mentioning individually those who gave both advice and criticism in the preparation of earlier editions, our sense of gratitude to them remains keen. For helpful suggestions and counsel in preparing the fifth edition, the authors extend their special appreciation to Dr. Anthony King of the University of Essex, England; Professor Henry Ehrmann of Dartmouth College; Professor Ossip K. Flechtheim of the Free University of Berlin; Professor Harold Berman of the Harvard Law School; Professors Samuel Beer, Stanley Hoffman, Adam Ulam, and Karl Deutsch of Harvard University; and to those other individuals, too numerous to mention, who in one way or another have helped during the preparation of this edition. We also thank the British and French Information Services for their help.

The authors wish to make special mention of

their indebtedness to the inspiration offered, to the end of his life, by Otto Kirchheimer, scholar and friend. His untimely death, in November 1965, deprived the author of the section on Germany, in particular, of unflagging and invaluable advice and encouragement. He was one of the few bright lights illuminating the entire European comparative government scene. He will be sorely missed by all workers in that field. We dedicate this volume to his memory.

GWENDOLEN M. CARTER
JOHN H. HERZ

Evanston, Illinois
Scarsdale, N.Y.

Contents

III
THE GOVERNMENT OF GERMANY

by John H. Herz

IV
THE GOVERNMENT OF THE SOVIET UNION

by Gwendolen M. Carter

Charts and Maps

xi

SOVIET UNION

Introduction

CONTEMPORARY GOVERNMENT AND POLITICS

At no time has it been more important for Americans to understand the governments and politics of other nations. For better or for worse, the fate of this country is now tied to that of the rest of mankind. Our future more and more assumes the character of a common venture, either through peaceful coexistence to heights as yet unimagined, or toward doom through suicidal nuclear conflict.

The Degree of Diversity

To study foreign governments and politics poses major problems. In the first place, there are now many more independent states than formerly. Half a century ago there were fewer than fifty sovereign nations. Today there are over a hundred, with more to come. No one can hope to study them all. Nor are their numbers the only difficulty. When Aristotle prepared what became the first great treatise on government and politics, he is said to have put his graduate students to work to analyze some hundred and fifty constitutions. But his task was easier than ours. Compared to the systems within the relatively close world of the ancient polis, the present variety of the world's political units is vastly broader. Not only is there a sharp contrast between the systems within what we call the free world and those of totalitarian dictatorships, but there are also important differences among the countries within each group. Nor is this all. In the forms of government in such relatively unfamiliar but increasingly important areas as the Middle and the Far East, Africa, and Latin America, we are confronted with a colorful diversity that is constantly increasing as more and more countries acquire their independence.

As we look at the developing countries, we find some states with advanced forms of organization either patterned on Western models as are India and Jamaica, or operating as "one-party democracies" like Tanzania and the Ivory Coast, or, increasingly, under army rule as in the Congo, Pakistan, and Nigeria. We also find a continuing heritage of the "premodern" age. Some countries, in fact, are still in the primitive stage of civilization, with nomadic forms of life and feudal or absolutist institutions. Even within one region such as the Middle East, countries of this type, such as Arabia and Yemen, lie close to advanced states such as Lebanon and Israel. Moreover, the degree of governmental control may range all the way from the regulation and organization of almost all aspects of life to a bare minimum of government and administration.

Pressures to Uniformity

Despite these differences, we should not exaggerate the degree of diversity. Beneath the surface appearance of great variety lie trends toward much greater and rapidly increasing uniformity. As Samuel P. Huntington has said, "Undoubtedly the most significant difference between modern man and traditional man is in their outlook on man in relation to his environment. . . . Change is absent or imperceptible in traditional society because men cannot conceive of its existence. Modernity begins when men develop a sense of their own competence, when they begin to think that they can understand nature and society and can then control and change nature and society for their own purposes."

Today the outlook of traditional man is yielding almost everywhere to that of modernity. And thus the participation of all states in a common process of "development" is as inevitable as it is relentless. Later we shall have more to say about how the process of acceleration affects the "developed" countries and their societies. What concerns us here is that this drive for modernity is found on a world-wide scale that also encompasses premodern, traditional societies. Traditionalism is bound to give way with the "revolution of rising expectations." Its universal desire for the fruits of affluence and its demands for the better life that can be expected from scientific thought and industrial technology, inevitably penetrate into areas in which the traditional, fatalistic outlook used to make people shun the very idea of change. Once the expectation of rapid advance becomes prevalent, it cannot be stopped by inherited political institutions or processes. Nothing distinguishes our age more sharply from preceding ages than the rate at which change is taking place. Thus the technological-civilizational process that sweeps the planet may result in a more homogeneous mankind, with its previous, abundantly diverse forms of culture and civilization and its widely varied stages of development merged into a controlled, organized, and largely man-made cosmos.

Before this happens, however, the developing world will be faced with tremendous problems of transformation and adjustment. There are three dominant reasons why this is so. The first is the rapid rate of development. Whereas most of the so-called developed countries of the West had centuries in which to achieve the transition from premodern to modern society, the new countries strain to achieve it in a matter of decades. Second, the radical nature of the change compels the developing countries to leap from primitive conditions to the jet age. Third is the urgency of some of the basic problems, particularly the problem of raising living standards for an exploding population.

Hence, in order to achieve political modernization, it is likely and understandable that the new countries will often use forms of government, administration, and law that are different from standard Western models. (*Western* in this context refers to communism as well as democracy, since both owe their basic principles to Western civilization.) The emerging African version of the one-party state, for instance, may turn out to be equidistant from the two-party or multiparty model of democracy and the Communist-totalitarian state-party model. Nonetheless, it may well fulfill the needs of a transitional, developing society. These new African states may also develop quite unorthodox procedures and institutions to achieve such familiar results as the protection of individual or family rights and interests. Although Americans tend to feel that such protection requires a Western-type court system, other systems like that in Tunisia may reach a similar goal by another, seemingly more authoritarian road.

In one respect, however, it is likely that the brave new modernized world of the future will be uniformly democratic. There are many contrasting and in part contradictory definitions of *democracy*, but if, for the moment, we take equality as a criterion, we may say that equality of people in the face of technology and science, regardless of race, nationality, or religion constitutes the metapolitical essence of democracy today, because science and technology are based on common experience and common talent. Technologically trained man is exchangeable. With the technological approach it makes little difference whether a problem is researched in the United States, Argentina, or Japan. The technical rules for establishing an up-to-date atomic pile or a system of pest control or a linear programing system are the same, whether applied by people of white, Negro, or oriental extraction, by persons living under communism, fascism, or liberal democracy.

Hence, egalitarianism, as distinguished from a more subtle and comprehensive concept of democracy, underlies modernity. This fact is not denied, but, on the contrary, it is strongly emphasized in doctrine and in practice even by those political systems which otherwise fail to meet the requirements of democracy: that is, the Communist ones. Even in South Africa, which so exceptionally illustrates the countertrend, i.e., the counterpolicy of inequality, the technological facts of life have rendered complete apartheid (racial separation) impossible in practice because of the need for African workers in industry.

Generally, of course, egalitarian aspirations have had their strongest effects in the last decades in Africa, Asia, and other parts of the world where the vast majority of mankind had been living under colonial systems. The process of emancipation, in the sense of eliminating what the modern mind sees as irrational inequalities based on group, class, caste (as of slaves or serfs), religious or racial differentiation (as of Jews or Moslems), or on sex, seems to follow the same curve of acceleration that characterizes other developments.

Apart from this, however, it is far from certain that what emerges from the process of political modernization will turn out to be democratic in the sense of liberal Western democracy.

There was a time when we took it for granted that an advanced industrial country would be a democracy. Our experience since the end of World War I, however, has shattered this belief. Since that time, totalitarianism, both fascist and communist, has made deep inroads into regions where democracy seemed firmly established or seemed at least to have a chance. Indeed, communism has emerged as *the* great alternative to liberal democracy in the transformation of "backward" societies into modern ways of life. The trend toward uniformity, then, is not toward a single model of political organization; it is primarily toward two opposing models, the liberal-democratic and the Communist-totalitarian, if it is not toward something distinctively different from both.

Neither of the dominant models, of course, has only one form, but since democracy is distinguished from systems of constraint by its liberal openness to experimentation, there is a particularly wide diversity of governmental forms within the free world. In particular, there are certain departures from the American pattern of government and politics that can be extremely instructive to a citizen of this country who may expect this familiar pattern of democracy to be repeated elsewhere. The student of British, French, and West German governments and politics, for instance, learns of varieties of democratic life that contrast sharply with the institutions and procedures that he accepts as normal and natural.

Four Major Powers and Systems

There are strong reasons for approaching comparative government through studying the systems of four major powers, Great Britain, France, Germany, and the Soviet Union, while keeping constantly in mind that of a fifth country, the United States, both for comparison and for contrast between the familiar and the less familiar. These four countries are selected not because they are "the great" or even "great" foreign powers. Today the United States and the Soviet Union are, of course, the dominant world units in terms of power; other countries, such as Great Britain, France, Germany, and China, can no longer or not yet measure up to them. Great Britain, the Soviet Union, Germany, and France have been selected because they offer a variety of political experience and a range of governmental institutions that are representative of those of many other countries. In one way or another, these four (or with the United States, five) powers have influenced governmental forms and practices throughout the world. Understanding their systems helps in understanding those of countries as varied as Chile and China, Italy and Senegal.

Great Britain, of course, developed earliest

and perhaps most successfully that form of representative democracy, the parliamentary system, whose close interrelationship and coordination of legislative and executive contrast most vividly with the American pattern of separation of powers. The impact of British parliamentary institutions on the independent states that were formerly its colonies has indeed been remarkable. Rarely have institutions resembled so closely the parent stock as those of Canada, Australia, and New Zealand. While it is perhaps not so surprising to find British institutions and traditions operating in the older parts of the Commonwealth, it is remarkable to find some of its newer members, such as India, Malaysia, Zambia, and Trinidad, experimenting with British-type representative and parliamentary institutions despite their differences from older Commonwealth members in historical background and tradition, standards of living, degree of literacy, size of the middle class, and other economic and social conditions.

But the parliamentary variant of democracy is infinitely flexible. France, in its rather tortured and tortuous constitutional history, has presented us in the past with a second type of parliamentarism that has had variants in other Continental European countries. Its systems of administration and of local government and its codes of law have been widely copied. More recently French experience has illustrated one of the supreme problems with which nontotalitarian countries are faced: how to combine democracy with stability. Gaullist authoritarianism and the technocracy of the Fifth Republic are not only a new form for French "democracy," but have been widely copied—though with less successful results—in France's former African colonies.

In contrast to Great Britain and France, there is little in Germany except the concept of professional and expert civil service that has been an influence on or a model for other nations. Where it has so served to mold others, as during the Nazi tyranny, the influence was undesirable. But Germany is chiefly representative because of the range and variety of its political experience. The person who studies the radically different regimes that Germany has experienced can never again feel complacent about the universal applicability, even to Western countries, of the political principles and institutions to which he is accustomed. Basically, German experience illustrates one great problem of modern government: how to establish liberal democracy in a society which, though highly developed economically and educationally, has strong nondemocratic traits and traditions. As Germany's recent history shows, such an environment is open to the double perils of rightist and of leftist totalitarianism. Thus its repeated experiments in democracy are important for countries such as Japan with basically similar problems.

Not much, finally, need be said about the Soviet Union. The American who studies its government and politics inevitably becomes acquainted with an entirely new set of standards for judging political principles and political action. And the Soviet Union is, of course, the prototype in today's world of *the* other, the nondemocratic totalitarian trend. To be sure, China, Yugoslavia, and even Poland are in some respects markedly different from the Soviet Union; but the latter, though no longer recognized officially by other Communist countries as "leader," is still the model of socialist nations. There is also the likelihood and, from a Western viewpoint, the danger, of increasing Soviet influence in the underdeveloped world. In the light of the widespread competition between communism and Western democracy for the allegiance of the rest of the world, it is indeed vital for the West to understand the Soviet Union's politics and institutions.

When studying these four countries and their systems we shall not be interested exclusively, however, in their uniqueness and individuality. All organized society is today confronted with certain fundamental, overall problems, and it is one of the rewards of studying comparative government to observe how different systems cope with them. In the following pages, therefore, the most important among these problems will be considered under three headings: the increasing role of government among the institutions of society; the impact of a new international environment on domestic governmental and political systems; and the impact of doctrine, or "ideology." Each of these three developments poses particular problems for liberal democracy.

THE INCREASING ROLE OF GOVERNMENT

The distinguishing feature of modern government is that it is universally recognized and accepted as an active force in the shaping of economic and social conditions. Indeed, government is looked on as a major, and even the dominant, organizing power in society.

The Acceleration Process

What characterizes our world above everything else, as we have said before, is not merely change or transformation as such, but the speed of developments, the rate of change. The curve that reflects this rate of change rises slowly at first and then ever more rapidly and steeply; it also applies to more and more areas of human affairs. At the turn of the century Henry Adams, in one of his prophetic moods, suggested a law or a "rule of phase," according to which mankind goes through various "energizing" stages—a long religious stage, a somewhat shorter but still centuries-long mechanical one, followed by an even shorter but more high-powered electrical phase, and, finally, an "ethereal" (perhaps we should say nuclear) phase. Adams' exponential curve has proved more or less correct in the most varied areas of life: in the demographic history of mankind, where the rise was at first imperceptible and has now arrived at a population explosion; in the discovery, exploitation, and now, often, threatening exhaustion of such resources as oil and, indeed, water; in the development of the weapons of war and the increase in their destructiveness, from bow and arrow through gunpowder to H-bomb; in scientific discoveries and technological inventions; and in the means of communication and transportation (the so-called annihilation of time and space, or, better, of time and distance). In each and every case we find the same accelerating rate of transformation, with technology producing ever more change throughout society.

This is a change, moreover, that is unilinear, one-directional. We rush toward uniformity. Throughout most of history, the technological process did not vitally interfere with other processes—for example, the cultural, social, political ones—and thus left the world varied and diverse. Now it tends to swallow everything up that is not yet under its control, in favor of world-wide "modernization." Man's natural habitat is being replaced by a man-made, synthetic environment. It took man thousands of years to gain insight into the nature of his environment and to evolve means of survival in his struggle with hostile forces. It took hundreds of years to discover and explore the distant stretches of the globe. Now the whole surface of the earth is being transformed into a cultivated area, a "second nature" that serves exclusively to maintain human beings and provide the necessities of their life. At the same time, man is propelling himself into the universe, reaching for the moon and the stars. In a great paradox, this process of radical transformation is rendering the diverse ever more rigid and conforming. We rush into conformity. This cannot but have a profound impact on the functioning of government and the relation of man to his government.

The Emergence of Big Government

We have become so accustomed to government as an active, positive agent in the direction of our affairs that we often fail to realize the significance of the change this represents. Even autocratic government in the age of European absolutism was never as big and comprehensive as that of present times. It *could* not be so pervasive (even had it wanted to be), because the range of its activities was restricted by relatively undeveloped means of communication, transportation, and the like; the lord of a manor could therefore be more autonomous, even in a political sense, than the individual member of the "sovereign" people in a modern, integrated mass society. The government did not *need* to be so encompassing because of the less complicated nature of a numerically smaller society.

Numbers are all-important. In a small community, most affairs can be regulated by the voluntary cooperation of its members without the machinery of government—that is, administration, bureaucracy, and similar institutions. Larger units require much more organization. A school of thirty or fifty pupils can be run by a few teachers aided by a mother or two. One with a thousand students requires a higher proportion of teachers, a school board, and a school administration, including personnel services, a payroll office, and so forth.

In society at large the emergence of big government has been in essence a by-product of changes that were themselves of revolutionary character; primarily it has been a by-product of the industrial revolutions since the beginning of the nineteenth century. The French Revolution and the first industrial revolution gave rise to a profound change in attitudes toward the individual and his place within the community. The French Revolution preached the equality of individuals, a doctrine that directly challenged the long-existent, rigid social hierarchies of Europe; at the same time it aroused the sentiment of nationalism that exalts the community. Thus the individual was freed only to be merged into the group. But if the French Revolution provided much of the ideology and spur for social change, it was the industrial revolution that provided the new circumstances in which change became inevitable. The new industrialism with its new modes of production opened the way for individual activity and permitted social mobility to a degree never before seen. Yet while industrialism stimulated individualism, particularly in its early stages, its own inner logic was toward mass production, standardization, and vast economic units. Thus with industrialization as with the French Revolution the tendency was to free the individual from the restrictions of the past only to fit him into new and larger entities. Inevitably, the breakdown of traditional social and economic groupings produced the mass society characteristic of our time.

In the mass society created by the first industrial revolution the role of government by necessity changed. The state, the organized political community, needed to maintain a certain degree of stability in the social system in order to preserve its own equilibrium. It had to adjust the conflicting demands of different groups and classes. And it had to establish certain minimum standards of living and social well-being that were demanded by the new doctrine of equality. Thus government, as the agent of the state, was compelled to assume more and more responsibility for the creation and fair distribution of wealth. In so doing, government almost universally became big government, both in the scope of its activities and responsibilities and in the numbers of those it directly employed. Paradoxically, the two chief theories produced during, and in consequence of, this first age of industrialization—Marxism and liberalism—were both based on political expectations that were contradicted by what ensued in practice. The one forecast the "withering away" of the state, that is, of the coercive means of society; the other forecast that the state would be reduced to insignificance under conditions of *laissez faire*. What actually emerged was either totalitarianism or the rise of the giant welfare—and all too often warfare—state.

In our century entirely novel functions are being placed on government as a result of the process of acceleration we outlined above and as a result of the second (and third) industrial revolutions produced by that process. From the nineteenth century on, with the first industrial revolution, the state had to intervene to protect labor from exploitation, provide for social security, and so forth. Obviously these goals are still important (and, in many societies, still unachieved) today. But these functions must now be coupled with the "community" tasks that the technological process and ensuing modernity impose. Only gradually do the problems of the preservation of resources, natural as well as human, of land and landscape, of purity of water and air, of the protection of physical health (endangered as it is by pollution and chemicals) and of mental health (threatened by the new mechanized way of life) enter our consciousness. Most of these tasks can no longer be performed by small groups but must be undertaken by the "great society," or even through the cooperation of governments on a regional or global level.

Left alone, technological advance tends to become free-wheeling and unconcerned about community interests. By a kind of iron law of "technological conformism" man tends to be dragged by the scientific-technological development wherever the latter leads him. Without controls, there will be no limits on the speed of planes or cars (whatever the utility, or even profitability, of, say, supersonic planes) or the use of insecticides; no concern for priorities in the allocation of funds and resources for space exploration or highway building or for the production of luxury goods versus slum clearance or mass educational facilities. Especially in a competitive system rival big interests feel compelled to follow the trend of bigness, speed, etc., so long as it is profitable and permissible to do so. Hence, in non-Communist or nonsocialist states organized society must intervene to protect the public sector against the private sector and to oppose technological advance that is unconcerned with or even injurious to human interests. It must stop waste; it must establish priorities. In short, it must become the conscience of the community at large and the guardian of its long-range interests, as opposed to special and short-range interests.

But it is not only in competitive societies that the law of technological conformism applies. A recent news item from the Soviet Union indicates that there, too, "conservationists" have to fight the advance of industry which, unchecked, would pollute the lakes and the rivers. It is perhaps significant that it was a group of scientists, artists, and writers that called for government intervention to halt the process. It tends to show that all over the world, regardless of system, something like "technological disobedience," that is, a reversal of basic attitudes and, if necessary, organized protests and action, is needed to alert us to those outgrowths of the technological process that endanger the humanity of mankind. Only government is in a position to check the "big" interests in a pluralistic society or itself in a totalitarian one. In either case government must rely on the support of liberal (in the broad sense of the term) and individualist-humanitarian groups and trends.

Finally, government today cannot refrain from coming to grips with what, in the past, has rarely been a matter for public policy: the population problem. For government to interfere in this most intimate of human matters is distasteful to many, and yet it may have become government's most basic task. Where almost everything in the production and consumption of things becomes plannable and planned, the size of the underlying stratum of humans, for whom the planning and organizing are done, cannot remain uncontrolled. If it remains so, it tends to nullify the other efforts. The fact that population has so far not been controlled accounts for many of the political and general ills of the present-day world. Both types of government functions already identified—the social welfare and the "community" tasks—can be rendered fruitless when the number of people to whom they apply increases without control. Where population continues to explode, all efforts to aid the developing majority of mankind can assume the Alice-in-Wonderland character of running faster and faster only to stay in the same spot. All the efforts of the free world to extend its own ideals and institutions to the "third world" will remain illusory so long as billions of uprooted people fall prey to extremism. In the modernized world the wars against poverty and discrimination must come to naught unless this problem is tackled. Thus governmental means—preferably such means as taxation that increases with number of children, rather than more "Spartan" ones—are likely to be used more and more to extend human control over this last and most fundamental social frontier.

The Need to Limit Big Government

Can the increasing functions of government, lead to something like Orwell's "Big Brother," an all-powerful, all-encompassing state? The very listing of its powers shows the need for limitation and restraint. If the state is needed to restrain the technological process and those inclined to exploit this process to the utmost, the state in turn must be restrained from using its assumed powers in an arbitrary and uncontrolled fashion. Even the earlier welfare society and its government led to some misuse of power.

Any large-scale organization of the masses tends toward pervasive control, whether the organization is a large business corporation, a labor union, a farmers' association, or a government. This is because a huge and complicated agency can function only through coordination from one central place. But the power to control involves the danger of irresponsibility. Unchecked power of interference and regulation is the essence of totalitarianism, and large-scale mass society thus bears within itself a totalitarian trend.

These possibilities of domination have been vastly increased by the technological potentialities of the twentieth century. Hitler's and Stalin's setups for the annihilation and exploitation of millions of humans were only spectacular examples of what can be "technically" achieved through the modern means of organizing and controlling society and the human beings it includes. Nuclear weapons on one side, and "atoms for peace" on the other, are merely the ultimates in a vast range of powers and capabilities. There are others, equally foreboding. Science reveals more and more the social and mental malleability of man in mass society, and even the feasibility of biological transformation. These facts open up vistas of psychological manipulation and eugenic determination of inheritance that might change the very substance of man and mankind. Add to this the almost incredible instrusions that can now be made into the most intimate spheres of one's personal life—"bugging" a home or a place of work with electronic devices, for example—and one perceives the need for protection not only *by* government against private groups but no less for protection *against* governmental abuse. If the state does—and must—control such actions, who or what controls or restrains the state? Perhaps we already know too much for the safety of mankind. Since knowledge is power, the predominant problem is one of limits and limitations.

It is here above all that democracy and totalitarianism part ways. The distinctive feature of liberal democracy is that it is "limited government." What counts is not only the rule of the majority but even more the right, or at least the chance, for individuals and minorities freely to develop themselves. But any genuine freedom

in the personal and group spheres presupposes the placing of limits upon political power. It is only when there are limits on what government may do and on the way in which it may do it that citizens are free. Particularly in our mass societies, where the people at large can exercise at best only a limited control over crucial matters of domestic and foreign policy, the difference between free and totalitarian countries seems to reduce itself ultimately to two questions: whether the citizen can force a review of governmental processes and decisions before an authority—usually judicial—that stands above both; and whether or not there exists an inviolable sphere of privacy in which the otherwise organized, mechanized, ordered, and oftentimes bullied individual may yet proceed according to his will, whim, or fantasy, his beliefs or disbeliefs, in a socially useful and adjusted or an entirely useless and unadjusted fashion.

Requirements for Limited Government

But how is it possible to establish and maintain limitations when the technological and organizational trends of modern society—by their own force of gravity, so to speak—pull in the opposite direction? It seems so much easier and so much more effective to confer on those responsible for decisions the unhampered authority to do what they see fit to do. But the history of this century stands as a solemn record of warning that such handing over of authority may lead to the most cruel tyranny and inhuman abuse. If liberal democracy wishes to avoid this danger, its people must be eternally vigilant in safeguarding the liberties that are the rewards of restraint on government.

To ensure limited government requires a number of technical devices which, while seemingly of secondary importance as compared with general objectives and major principles, yet are vital for the successful operation of liberal democracy. To the person who is dazzled by the more dramatic conflicts in ultimate aim and aspiration among the world's leading political systems, the issue of political mechanics may appear drab and unimportant. Yet it is upon such "wretched technicalities" (to borrow the phrase of Ortega y Gasset) that the noblest political principles and aspirations depend. If the machinery is bad, the end, however magnificent, is bound to suffer.

What counts, however, in assessing these more technical devices and institutions, is not simply their existence in the written provisions of documents such as constitutions or statutes, nor their presence on organization charts. Indeed, the organization chart of the government in a country controlled by communism or some non-Communist version of authoritarianism may look quite similar to that of a Western-type democracy. What it does not show is, in the case of communism, the all-pervasive power exercised by the top level of the single party. Likewise, the written constitution of such a country may sound liberal and democratic, since it can contain, for instance, provisions safeguarding the freedom of the press or rules concerning debating, voting, and the opposition in an elected parliament. What these provisions do not tell us is that all newspapers are owned and controlled by the state, the party, or by party-dominated organizations, and therefore cannot voice independent opinions; or that genuine opposition, or even criticism, can hardly be expected from members of a parliament elected from a list of candidates, all of whom were chosen or approved by the ruling party, or from a "parliament" of hand-picked stooges of a military junta.

While we must not mistake a system operating behind a totalitarian or authoritarian façade for limited government, we must also be aware of the antidemocratic criticism often made of what we consider genuine liberal-democratic institutions and procedures. These criticisms are often strikingly similar to the ones we have just leveled against nondemocratic make-beliefs. Marxism and fascism, for instance, both claim that what we call freedom of opinion and of opinion-formation in the democracies disregards the fact that all or most of the press and other instruments of communication are controlled by powerful business and financial interests that are able to silence or crush any deviating voices; or that seemingly free elections can mean little where the voters have only a choice between two candidates whose positions are so alike that it means voting between tweedledee and tweedledum. We should not take such criticism lightly. In all big society, there is the

constant threat of "oligarchism," of concentration or petrification of power, and of manipulation of controls. Free institutions are constantly liable to be corrupted, and the façades of democratic institutions must be pierced to find out whether or not they serve genuinely liberal, that is, "limiting" and "delimiting," purposes.

There are four groups of questions to keep in mind when asking how, and to what extent, limited government functions in a specific instance. One set of questions concerns the instruments and channels of political information and expression; another asks whether and how the channels of political action are kept open and untrammeled; a third group is concerned with the influence of pressure groups on governmental and political life; and the last centers around how to keep the executive as well as the bureaucracy "responsible."

Freedom of Information and Expression

If the people, as voters, are to give meaningful direction to politics—that is, to choose between genuine alternatives—they must first of all have a chance to inform themselves freely about conditions and, in particular, about the various alternatives that exist. This implies, of course, that anyone with an idea or a policy to offer is given a chance to put it before the people and to have it freely discussed. For this reason, popular government can be little better than its sources of information. Freedom of information and expression of opinion require not only the absence of political intimidation but also a minimal economic chance to compete in the "market place of ideas." We have referred to the charge that even in liberal democracies the facilities for informing citizens and for expressing different opinions are inadequate and perverted. According to this accusation, owners of newspapers, for instance, are likely to be more interested in profits than in public service and to concentrate on those sensational features that will attract readers rather than on the task of political education. At worst it is charged that certain owners of newspapers deliberately distort the news and prejudice their comment in order to promote their own partisan political interests. In particular, where the press, the radio, and television have become big business, it is alleged that those who control them use their influence in behalf of the wealthier classes and leave the mass of the people without adequate channels of expression. On the other hand, where, as in de Gaulle's France, the press is free but radio and TV are accessible chiefly to the regime, the freedom to reach tens of thousands may mean little in comparison with the regime's power to reach tens of millions.

The free expression of opinion is more, however, than a question of formal channels of communication, serious though this question may become through the control of more and more of such channels in ever fewer hands. Equally important is the broader question of education, both of the young and of adults, and of creating and maintaining an interest in the great issues of the times. An educational system which, for fear of raising controversial issues, be it in the field of religion or the arts or in domestic or international politics, limits itself to the merely technical, dulls the mind, and eventually creates a "democratic" variant of the selfsame conformism that is both the hallmark and the effect of indoctrination under totalitarianism. And adults who hardly look at the headlines of articles on political news will not benefit from the most informative coverage of such news in the best papers in the world.

In this respect the growing complexity of issues in our age of modernity makes ever more difficult adequate provision of information for democratic opinion-formation. There is an ever increasing complexity in technical matters: Who, for instance, understands or even knows the technicalities of military defense and defense systems? Or in the economic sphere: Who feels at home with the technicalities of a large-scale budget or of the international payments problems? Or in matters of organization: Who understands the structure and functioning of even one of the large executive agencies of the United States government, let alone the overlapping setups in totalitarian countries? Moreover, the public is daily confronted with (or fails to face) a forever increasing number of issues, all competing for its attention. And there is the steady increase in the size of the audience whose views should be taken into consideration by the policy-makers who are supposed to be responsive to the public. Policy-makers are tempted to dis-

regard opponents or critics who are few in number so long as they can control or assuage the millions whose apathy they easily identify with consensus.

It is the distinguishing feature of liberal democracy that, despite all difficulties, it *can* cope with them; it is the test of those who live within such a system to see to what extent it does.

Freedom of Political Action

By freedom of political action we mean political activity beyond the reception of information and the expression of opinion. Even to voice opinion, or at least to make such voicing effective, people must be able to rally together and to organize themselves in movements, parties, or similar ways to exercise that influence which, in the mass age, can be exerted only by the many acting jointly. Here, again, it is frequently asserted that the channels of action are seriously limited. To cast a ballot once in two or four or more years seems to the critics a thin and not very meaningful form of political participation. The voter is free to join a political party; but the parties themselves, according to the charge, are far from democratic in their internal organization. A small elite of bosses or bureaucrats allegedly chooses the candidates and dictates policy. This tends to create apathy in the voter or party member outside the clique. Moreover, parties in representative systems are primarily used to elect the people's representatives to parliamentary assemblies. And here, again, charges are frequently made against the allegedly unrepresentative nature or the ineffective ways of using such instruments of representation. Thus, it is held that the parliaments in a democracy are a far from accurate reproduction of the sentiments of the voters, both in the strength of party representation and in the reflection of the economic interests and social divisions of the country as a whole. In those countries that have a two-party system, the strength of the larger party is likely to be greatly exaggerated; in those that have a multiparty system, parliamentary manipulation may result in a government very different from the one the citizens thought they were voting for. Moreover, the development of party discipline may oblige members of the legislature to vote in accordance with the orders of a small and unrepresentative group of party bosses against their own convictions and the desires of the people who elected them. Often, indeed, the popular impression of representative assemblies is one of a group of spokesmen of special interests battling and wrangling without thought of the common welfare of the country. It is popular to talk of the "decline of parliaments" and to suggest that the chosen representatives of the people are not capable of directing the work of government and that they must delegate their authority to the executive and civil servants. Regarding Continental-European systems, it has also become popular to talk of the "waning of the opposition," in the sense of the vanishing of parties offering meaningful alternatives.

These are charges to which we will be returning; until then it is important to keep in mind that such criticisms are not necessarily valid and that parties and representative assemblies, as in Great Britain, are usually alert to the needs of individuals and groups and may, indeed, be the best protection against injustice.

Freedom from Nongovernmental Pressures

We have just referred to the charge that in some situations special interests appear to dominate the battles of seemingly representative assemblies. Such interests may also exercise undue and disproportionate influence in other spheres of government and politics. They may control the press; they may censor other instruments of information or culture and stifle the free flourishing of entertainment; they may inhibit open discussion of issues in the schools or in the churches; and they may affect the policies of the government through their influence over the parties, over the choice of party candidates and their representatives, or through lobbies in parliament.

Moreover, interest groups may influence the executive and administration by bringing pressure to bear on officeholders and by staffing key positions with people who think that what is good for their respective group or class is good for the country. One of the decisive tests of a democratic regime is whether it can balance conflicting interests rather than be subject to any one interest or group.

Limiting Executive Power

Power in modern society may be too concentrated either within or outside the realm of government. In contrast to totalitarian regimes, with their characteristic concentration of power in party and government, democracies may appear particularly open to the dangers of nongovernmental, especially economic, influences and controls. Yet in an age of big and comprehensive government the opposite danger—of government itself growing too powerful—cannot be overlooked. We have seen how technological developments may provide the executive with powers of domination; we shall see below how international developments tend to strengthen the executive even more. Thus to place restraints on the use of executive power is the fourth important task of "limited government."

The problem here is how to restrain the executive without crippling it. Restraint at the top level might lead merely to enhancing the power and influence of that other portion of the executive branch, the bureaucracy, which, though legally and organizationally subordinate, yet possesses large and varied possibilities of independent action because of the vast and complex functions entrusted to it. Truman was once quoted as remarking when his successor was about to begin his job: "Poor Ike! He will sit there, and he will say: 'Do this, do that.' And nothing will happen." However exaggerated the comment, there are situations that render the top executive inefficient and leave the rest of the administration irresponsible. They lend themselves to the often heard charges that, at a time when government requires prompt, vigorous, imaginative, and decisive action, the democratic executive may be slow and bumbling, handicapped and weakened by systems of checks and balances, subjected to the pressures of special interests, corrupted by the requirements of partisan politics, and too inexpert to know the solution to the increasingly complex problems of modern political life. Equally it is suggested that the top executive is forced to delegate authority to a dominant and expert bureaucracy that was not chosen by the voter and that cannot be controlled by him; as a result, what with the immense complexities of modern politics and the infinitely varied devices for confusing and misleading the public, the voter cannot tell whom to blame for policies that he dislikes. The charge of executive inadequacy may be pushed to the point of insisting that democracy cannot even provide a stable government possessed of enough strength to enforce order, though this charge was more valid for France of the Fourth Republic than for any of the contemporary governments considered in this book.

At the same time, the top level of government has greatly increased responsibilities in such fields as defense and foreign policy. And even in free enterprise countries, there is an ever increasing degree of planning and regulation of more and more areas in the domestic field. It is often argued, therefore, that to subject the expert planners to control by the inexpert public would destroy the value of their plans. At least, planning requires a firm and stable government, it is said, for no plan can be effective if it can be remade or revoked each budget year, or if its sponsors are likely to be turned out of office at any moment and their policies reversed, or even if important modifications can be made by parliamentary vote. The very complexity and far-reaching character of the operations that government now undertakes can leave no one feeling entirely complacent about the degree to which popular control of public activities is possible.

But the test of limited government here, as elsewhere, is whether controls, popular or other, are available and how they are used. It is intriguing to study how different democracies have developed various procedures in this connection. To keep the bureaucracy responsible, such political devices as parliamentary control and criticism, ministerial and cabinet responsibility, and specific consent to appointments by parliament are commonly used. Other major devices to restrain the bureaucracy are through judicial means—such as appeals to ordinary or to special administrative courts staffed with independent judges—by persons claiming injury or violation of rights and interests by administrative action, or through an officer like the Ombudsman of Sweden, who investigates private complaints against official actions. In-

deed, it is this same roster of devices and procedures that lends itself to the enforcement of responsibility at the top level of government. Beyond this, of course, one chief means of keeping both the executive and the legislature limited in power is by limiting their tenure of office—that is, by holding periodic elections. In this way, the job of limitation reverts to the people.

THE IMPACT OF THE INTERNATIONAL ENVIRONMENT

Besides the problems that arise from the emergence of big government, there are even broader strains facing governments all over the world. One of the most persistent and least predictable arises from the international environment in which all countries must operate. Partly due to developments in science and technology (for example, nuclear weapons and space exploration), and partly to the emergence of new nations and power groupings, the international community is in a stage of rapid change. Indeed, the increase in the number of newly independent states almost suggests, again, the Adams curve of acceleration. In general, the international environment of nations has lately been characterized by the growing interdependence and integration of nations, although different countries and systems may and do react differently to new conditions and new needs.

From Self-Sufficiency to Interdependence

For some three or more centuries after the modern nation-state emerged, domestic affairs were relatively autonomous. Political institutions grew out of native soil, and changes, even revolutionary ones, were due to indigenous forces and indigenous movements. Foreign influences were not themselves without effect; but they were commonly transformed and shaped to fit the needs of the nation itself. Thus liberal democracy would change in coloring or even in meaning when exported from one environment to another. Indeed, throughout this period, domestic political forces and movements were less influenced by foreign affairs than they were themselves influences on foreign policies, as, for example, when Britain or the United States sided with liberal-democratic forces or when tsarist Russia backed the cause of absolutism on the Continent for its own internal political reasons.

We have now entered a period, however, of increasing impact of world affairs on internal politics and institutions. One chief reason for the change lies in the greatly diminished security of the nation-state from foreign attack. While it used to be a characteristic of the territorial state that it was a self-contained, closed, centralized unit that could provide its citizens with protection from outside control or interference, this situation has long ended. Industrialization transformed economic self-sufficiency into dependence on the world market and thereby enhanced the danger of defeat in war through blockade. But the decisive change has been in the nature of war itself. Air war and now nuclear war, by opening the way to vertical penetration, have meant the end of the frontier in its traditional function of protection. This development put an end to the sense of security that had aided countries in developing their own political institutions and ways of life.

One effect of the developments in new weapons has been the emergence of atomic superpowers and their blocs, compared with which even former big powers now occupy inferior status. One result has been a growing influence of the superpowers on the affairs of lesser nations and a competition for such influence between the two leading blocs. This competition is intensified by the ideological conflict and competition between the Western and Communist states. But such developments have also affected government and politics in the superpowers themselves owing to frequent emergency conditions created by nuclear bipolarity, cold war, and, indeed, the ever threatening danger of nuclear annihilation.

But it is not only in the area of power and of power relations that influences from nation to nation have grown. The world is shrinking so fast and its people and their needs are increasing so rapidly that cooperation and interdependence in such fields as trade and common markets, migration, and aid and development are by now as commonplace as the insistence on sovereignty and independent action used to be

in times of more autonomous units. In many cases this means less autonomy in individual policy decisions.

Relations Between Stronger and Lesser Powers

Inclusion in one or the other power bloc or defense system means adjustments of policy and sometimes of governmental institutions as well. The latter are most obvious in the relations of the lesser members to their Big Brother in the Soviet bloc. The initial copying by these then correctly so-called satellites of Soviet institutions and their ensuing subservience to Soviet policies—domestic as well as foreign—was primarily due to their common system of political belief but partly also to persistent pressures, especially under Stalin.

In the West, political ideals are sometimes less influential on institutions than one might wish them to be—dictatorships or otherwise authoritarian regimes, such as in Spain and Portugal, for instance, are not excluded from Western alliances—but even so the impact of the alignment is frequently powerful. This impact is felt first of all in the determination of objectives and the conduct of foreign policy. Once a Western orientation has been decided upon, anything but this orientation may appear "subversive"; major groups and parties must then agree on one and the same foreign policy. Such pressure toward foreign policy conformism may in due course affect matters of internal policy and domestic institutions as well. The leading power is constantly tempted—for what it may consider bona fide reasons of maintaining its own security and that of the alliance—to make sure that only "reliable" persons and groups are in control of its ally's government. It may then place pressure on that government not only to exclude Communists and affiliated groups from political power but also to keep out of positions of influence other parties and individuals suspected of, for instance, "neutralist" leanings. It may even go so far as to try to influence elections and election systems.

In the 1950's there was open use of American influence on behalf of both Italian and West German Christian Democrats. In the latter case, be it noted, there was no strong Communist party to be defeated but rather a Western-oriented but at that time still somewhat neutralist Social Democratic party. For similar reasons, the United States used its influence in Greece in favor of a change in its electoral system. More or less open armed intervention may even occur when there is a danger that a member of one's own system is defecting. This has been true not only in the Communist sphere, as in the cases of Hungary and East Germany, but also in the West, as in the cases of Guatemala, the Dominican Republic, and, to some degree, Cuba.

On the other hand, as the Dominican case shows, attempts to influence the affairs of less powerful countries too closely or too rudely are likely to backfire. In the 1960's, "allies" have often asserted their autonomy or independence more forcefully—in certain cases, indeed, such as those of China in the East and France in the West, so forcefully that there has been a breakup of bipolar power concentration in favor of an emerging multipolarity. In consequence, the influence exercised by the superpowers has tended to become more subtle and indirect. Even Soviet control of Eastern European allies, formerly exercised over the respective governments through Soviet army and Communist party control, has lessened to such an extent that it can hardly be compared any more with the dependency relationship that prevailed under Stalin. As a result, some of the Eastern European countries have begun experimenting with their own processes and institutions, especially in the cultural and economic fields. However, the basic decision in favor of the Communist type of economy, society, and government is still not an indigenous one. It is likely that the Hungarian Revolution and its defeat are still indicative of the limits set on the freedom of action of these members of the Soviet bloc.

In the West, interference of the type mentioned above has likewise become rarer. What remains is that in many cases foreign policy issues, and in particular the issue of orientation (that is, of more or less close alignment with the United States), not only tends to have a strong impact on internal policies and party alignments but tends even to overshadow what used to be considered the more vital domestic issues: socialism, the welfare state, and free enterprise. Thus in West Germany the foremost recent issue divided political leaders and the public into "Atlanticists," in favor of continuing the close lineup with the United States, and "Gaullists," favoring an autonomous Europe led by Germany and France. The issue rent the ruling CDU to such a degree that even its internal coherence was endangered. The chief opposition party, the SPD, on the other hand, which in the fifties had favored the assertion of independence, was now united in backing an "Atlantic" orientation. Thus the international situation influences the relations, alignments, and strength of those domestic political forces that used to be guided primarily by domestic issues.

In the case of the uncommitted countries it has not been so much through open control or intervention that either East or West has tried to influence developments. Both sides have been satisfied with any kind of system and type of government so long as they could hope to sway the respective unit to their side or at least to keep it out of the opponent's camp. As we have pointed out, Western-type, especially modified parliamentary, systems, parties, and elections are found in many of the newly independent countries as an outgrowth of their colonial heritage, but in the face of their strong nationalism this has not necessarily meant Western orientation or Western influence over domestic politics. Big power influence, where it does exist, is due rather to a sense of common objectives and to economic or technical or educational assistance. Beyond this, the influence of the regimes and institutions of the opposing powers often is in direct proportion to their developments at home and to their ways of life. Soviet successes in the industrial realm or in that of space conquest, or Chinese achievements or failures in the use of communes, may thus have a direct impact not only on the foreign policy orientation of an underdeveloped country but also on whether it decides to imitate one or the other of these economic systems and possibly also political institutions. Inasmuch as it actually practices democratic virtues both in its relations with the new states and at home, the West, on the other hand, may pull the developing states in the other direction. Thus it is not so much propaganda as it is the hard facts of actual practices (for instance, in the field of race relations, or personal and group liberties) which count. Beyond this, all depends, as we have observed before, on whether these nations will be able to cope with their great economic, social, and demographic development problems. Political and governmental chaos, or rapid succession of dictatorial regimes, are likely to ensue if they fail.

The Impact of Constant Emergency

The threat of nuclear annihilation, combined with nuclear bipolarity and the ideological split, has meant a constant emergency situation quite unlike the more secure periods of "peace" in former times. While totalitarian regimes are equipped to cope with such situations—one might almost define totalitarian rule as a perpetual state of emergency, or martial law—democracies, as limited governments, cannot but encounter serious problems in this situation. We have already spoken of the need for concentrating much power at the top for immediate and far-reaching decisions in order to cope with events. Another need is for secrecy, but this can go all the way to limiting the flow of public information to prefabricated official news handouts. An intelligence organization, such as the CIA, may engage in activities and actions that are far beyond the collection of information and that commit the nation. Thus both the necessity for quick decisions and limitation on providing information may reduce the realm in which the people at large or even their representatives can effectively participate in or consent to political decisions.

There are still more serious threats to liberal democracy. Apparent danger to national security may give rise to emotionalism or even a hysteria which, as in the United States at the time of "McCarthyism," tends to endanger free institutions as such. One recalls how the power of investigation, which for a time remained almost unlimited and unchecked, not only affected personal rights and liberties but also such constitutional principles as the separation of powers within the government itself. Thus it threatened at one point to subject lower and intermediate levels of the executive to control by members of the Congress, thereby undermining the hierarchy of the executive and the authority of its chief. An even more insidious threat lies in the trend toward conformity created under such conditions. The very existence of a totalitarian opponent tends to render dissent suspect. At such times, flight into political neutrality or indifference may characterize even those groups which, like labor, the churches, and university members, otherwise are often in the forefront of political action or influence.

There is, however, no inevitability in such developments. The British, for instance, have approached problems of internal security with both official and public restraint. Instead of flooding the country with loyalty investigations and subjecting the entire civil service to identical security standards, they have applied the latter to carefully selected sensitive agencies and only to positions where spies or subversives might do real damage. More important, they have never yielded to the frenzy of fear and suspicion that leads to the invasion of vital personal concerns with far-fetched charges, "faceless" accusers, and ostracism. And political involvement, especially on the part of the young, may still be strong, as evidenced not only in such diverse places as South Korea, Turkey, and Latin America, but more recently, and happily, also in the United States.

The Impact of International Organization

Despite the tremendous changes that have transformed a world of self-sufficient, separate nations into an ever more integrated whole, the powers have not seen fit so far to yield correspondingly large portions of their sovereignty to any world government. Ultimately, the nuclear dilemma as well as other increasingly urgent world problems (such as the one posed by the population explosion) may compel them to do so unless they are intent on suicide. But at present the direct governmental functions of international organizations are at best restricted to activities such as those of the United Nations' special peace-keeping forces in Palestine and Cyprus. Indirectly, of course, such agencies and their activities can influence countries and their policies in many ways: in foreign policies through pressures exerted in the Security Council or the General Assembly (as in the pressures on Great Britain and France, not to mention Israel, during the Suez crisis of 1956); and even on the development of domestic institutions and habits, where the newer countries, in particular, can learn much about the practices of more mature ones through contacts in the United Nations and elsewhere. Thus, for example, while equality of rights for women is not yet fully accepted in some Latin American, Asian, and African countries, is is difficult for them to withstand pressures at home to extend such rights when the latter are promoted on the international level. International cooperation can be expected to become more vital as well as more encompassing with the steady increase in urgency of those community tasks that result from the sweep of technology and modernization and that make the preservation of a common domain of mankind a common interest of mankind.

While the global sweep of nationalism renders nations reluctant to yield even fractions of their sovereignty to a formal world organization, they will do so, informally but increasingly, for practical reasons of common interests. Moreover, regionally, some nations have been ready to develop supranational institutions in limited areas to which they transfer quite considerable portions of what used to be under "exclusive domestic jurisdiction." In this regard Western Europe, with its manifold array of joint organizations, has set the pace, particularly with the Commission of the Common Market, of which France, West Germany, Italy, Belgium, Holland, and Luxembourg are members. Its existence affects the position and the policies of interest groups in the six member countries, and to some extent also those of their political parties and executive departments. Member-state politics cannot remain the same when basic economic, labor, and related affairs are decided on a higher level. There are beginnings of cross-national party relationships, although the jurisdiction of regional parliamentary institutions is still limited. On the other hand, the "European" bureaucracy at Brussels, the seat of the Commission, already shows the tendency of all bureaucracy to extend its influence beyond due limits. In this respect the existence of a court of the European Communities is important to protect those, like business corporations, that are under the rule of the communities and to limit regional governmental power. At this point we encounter basic problems of administration on a higher level than that of traditional government. The new arrangements of the Common Market may turn out to be of great significance for government and politics in the world to come. Their example may prove that gradual development toward genuine world government is possible through a process of step-by-step devolution of national sovereignty. And the example may be followed by groupings of the newly independent countries, many of which seem scarcely viable, economically and otherwise, as separate units.

THE IMPACT OF IDEOLOGY

Deeper than some of the challenges to liberal democracy already mentioned is another that is intimately connected with our constant state of emergency. The question is whether—in this time of international crises and internal strain, when the burdens of governments become complex almost beyond comprehension—human beings have the mental and moral qualities necessary for self-government. Democracy, to be successful, must stand on the assumption that men can think calmly, adjust their differences peaceably, consider other people's interests and ideas, make concessions and compromises, tolerate opposition and disagreement, and refrain from violence and the temptation to impose their will by force. Men suffering from anxiety, whether it is inspired by the dangers of nuclear holocaust or by the desperation of hunger or unemployment, find it hard to put public duty before private interest and to refrain from violence when it appears that violence will be effective.

What then, in such situations, can give people standards of stable and sober behavior in society? We are apt to forget, if we are living in relatively normal conditions, how large is the incidence of strain and emergency in this century. Especially for people and nations that lack a long and strong tradition of democratic life, what counts is how they act under strain.

It is then that their beliefs become decisive. What holds a political community together? What tends to weaken, to dissolve, to split, and even to destroy it?

We in the West have long ignored this problem, largely under the influence of that mainstream of modern social and political thought: individualism. We have assumed that political units like nation-states are founded upon, or could and should be founded upon, the free and voluntary association of self-determining, rational, enlightened human beings. But Burke pointed out that a country is more than a utilitarian or contractual association; that its cohesion rests less on interests and is less braced by reason than it is founded on custom and tradition; and that even prejudice may serve to preserve "the ancient order into which we are born."

"Anomie" and the Rise of Fascism

To talk of maintaining or even of instilling prejudices points up a basic dilemma in the relations between the individual and the community. We often forget that the attempt to render the individual autonomous and to make him the foundation of free communities and of limited government has been rare and recent in human history. For most of history, political communities have been kept together by an unquestioning, traditionalist allegiance of the ruled to the rulers. Generally, there was no conscious effort to indoctrinate the people, nor even to mold their attitudes and opinions through formal education; this was not necessary. It was the prevailing atmosphere, the transmitted value and belief systems that provided these standards. And it was in large part religion that provided whatever institutional and organizational apparatus was required to ensure their hold.

With the era of the Enlightenment came a change in attitude. To many people it seemed desirable to conduct human affairs on the basis of conscious, deliberate, and free acceptance of value standards, whether they then turned out to be religious or otherwise. Loyalty freely given provides a stronger and more democratic foundation of nations than does an enforced allegiance—or even a less consciously and more traditionally established allegiance. Thus such loyalty has become the truly democratic ideal.

Frequently, however, it is only the few who know how to develop their own personal beliefs and how to make these beliefs the basis of living together with others in political communities. This explains why it is that after traditional rulership has lost its grip, it is often a new irrational emotion, nationalism, which has ensured the cohesion of existing units or has made for the formation of new ones. When nationalism was simply a moderate and relatively calm feeling of belonging to that group that constitutes the nation, it could still be reconciled with a liberal-democratic individualism. But to the extent that nationalism became the substitute religion of those who needed or were instilled with more extreme and fervent feelings of attachment, it became a focal point for emphatic identification with one group and antagonism, even hatred, toward all others. Thus nationalism has all too easily been converted into an ideology of exclusivism and, in a variety of forms (racialism, bellicism, theories of imperialism, Social Darwinism, political romanticism), has eventually become the doctrinal foundation of various totalitarian movements of what, in a broad sense, may be called the "fascist" variety.

Fascism reflects that frustration of the individual in a society that has lost its ideological grip, which makes him look for new allegiance and identification through common hatred and enmity. The friend-foe relationship then becomes the underlying basis of all political attitudes and action. What particular group serves as a focal point matters little: it may be Jews, considered as a racial group, in the Nazi type of anti-Semitism; it may be Negroes, as in the racism of potential poor whites in South Africa, or in American southern states; it may be an ultra-nationalist syndicalism directed against both foreigners and domestic "exploiters," as in the earlier stages of Mussolini's or Franco's fascism or Peronism in Argentina; or it may be simply anticommunism of the McCarthy or Birchite variety. In any event, this approach reflects the *anomie* (the lack of basic rules or standards of value) of people lost in the maze of modern mass society who have become alienated from traditional ways of life and who try to find safe and absorbing new ones in movements and belief-systems of this nature.

The Appeals of Communism

Nationalism and fascism provide one kind of modern totalitarian ideology. Another kind is proletarian socialism, especially in the form of Marxism that in the nineteenth century brought a new creed and movement to rising and unattached proletarian groups. In many countries of the West, the "proletariat" was subsequently integrated, economically and otherwise, into existing society, and socialism then became modified into a movement of social reform not basically antagonistic to democratic institutions and politics. Movements such as that of British labor, in fact, have used such institutions to attain their social and economic ends.

But wherever industrial labor and other proletarian groups were neglected and remained economically exploited and politically oppressed outcasts of society, the philosophy of Marxism was supremely appealing as a creed which, by interrelating the station and fate of the exploited individual with the future destiny of all mankind, took care of their *anomie* as well as of their yearning for a coherent philosophy of government and politics. This rational or quasi-rational Marxist explanation of historical evolution and current conditions drew and draws to it many who would reject the irrational mysticism and racial or nationalist dogmas of fascism. This, above all, is still the integrating force of communism in that part of the world it now controls.

In its self-interpretation, communism is very different from simple rule by force. Concentration of power and all it involves appears as the means necessary to attain an ultimate and fixed end toward which history is moving. Everything that now happens is merely a transitional stage on history's inexorable path toward human emancipation and freedom. If opinion has to be controlled, it is only because portions of the public are still "backward" and have therefore to be educated by a vanguard that possesses full consciousness of what is historically necessary. If the members of this same vanguard have to exercise coercive and dictatorial powers, they do so as agents of a movement that fulfills the deepest yearnings of the masses; they thus act democratically, it is said, in a more profound way than do the "people's representatives" in the West who, according to this view, are mere self-seeking agents or stooges of business or other interests.

This Communist self-interpretation is most effective within the regimes under its control. In the non-Communist world, what impresses the half-starved, miserable individual affected by the "revolution of rising expectations" is the example of societies that have been able to pull themselves up by their own efforts from similarly miserable beginnings to their current levels of economic development and political power. If this can only be had at the price of a (so they are told) temporary sacrifice of liberties (whose value, in any event, is unknown to many of them), it may seem to them not too highly priced. The West can here hardly hope to compete successfully by merely opposing its own ideology of freedom; it must be able to promise, credibly, a better material future as well.

Confronted with the weakening of social ties that *anomie* represents, democracy runs two opposite dangers. If it sticks to its liberal ideal and leaves the individual free to choose among standards and causes without direction, the plurality of interests and creeds of modern society may lead to such disunity as to endanger the cohesion of the political unit. In the extreme case, it may even lead to the internecine warfare of armed ideologies. It may at least result in sheer political opportunism—likewise a doubtful basis for national cohesion. The other and opposite danger is that an effort may be made to instill loyalty from above, to indoctrinate the citizen and especially the younger generation with whatever "civil religion" seems appropriate. This obviously leads to the evils of conformity and to the undermining of the liberalism with which democracy is so intimately bound; in the extreme case it leads to a totalitarianism based on the ideology of anticommunism—the mirror-image of communism itself.

However, totalitarian regimes run into troubles of their own. There seems to be a law of diminishing returns in regard to indoctrination. Though individuals in mass society long for safe beliefs, they become satiated when doctrines are too frantically instilled or when, in the present conflict of systems and ideologies, one replaces another in bewildering sequence. This then may render the individual cynical or apathetic. He avoids taking sides or positions of responsibility—a common disease, especially in the East.

But the problem is an even more general one, affecting both West and East. The less the individual in mass society retains a chance to control events, the less he is politically *and* ideologically concerned, and—in an endless and vicious circle—the more frantic become the appeals of those actual or would-be rulers who feel the need for ever more fervent adherence.

We may expect communism to remain the great totalitarian challenge to the democracies for a long time to come. If so, the latter will naturally ally themselves with forces and movements opposed to any form of totalitarianism, that is, with churches and religions as long as they do not support fascist regimes or trends, and with those governments which, while not completely democratic according to the exacting standards of the older Western democracies, yet recognize some necessary restraints and limitations upon power in order to protect individual and group rights and liberties. Some of these latter governments, because of their authoritarian heritage, have failed thus far to live up fully to all the criteria established by British and American democracy. This is still true of Germany and likewise of Japan, whose modern political developments resemble those of Germany in so many respects and whose late industrialization and strong authoritarian traditions have so far hampered genuine democratization. Not all modernized countries have been fortunate

enough to enjoy the steady growth over several centuries of that incubator of liberal and democratic institutions, a rising middle class. The newly independent Asian, African, Middle East, and Caribbean countries have had an even more sudden break with the past.

Recognizing the existence of such handicaps to democratic development, nations committed to democracy might profitably draw a distinction between political democracy and liberalism and welcome as allies in the antitotalitarian camp nations and regimes which, while more or less authoritarian in their political institutions or in their approach to decision-making, are yet liberal in the sense of respecting and protecting the dignity of the individual and the free expression of personal and group interests. Wherever traditionalism does not exclude individual freedom and the development of personality, it may well constitute a bulwark against totalitarian inroads.

Keeping in mind the challenge of opposing and clashing ideologies and regimes, the dangers of an increasingly lethal world environment, and the more technical challenges to and requirements of limited government, we shall now study the individual governments of the four foreign countries we have selected. In doing so, we have not thought of ourselves as arguing a case; our purpose has not been to present a defense of democracy. We have tried to be fair, accurate, and complete and to avoid the delusions of wishful thinking. This, in itself, is an exercise in democracy that could not be performed by authors under totalitarian controls. Insofar, but only insofar, does the study of government involve commitment to a cause.

·I·

The Government
of the
United Kingdom
of Great Britain
and
Northern Ireland

1. The British People and Their Politics

1. THE CHALLENGE TO GREAT BRITAIN

The British [1] people today confront two great challenges: the need for economic revitalization and the need to build new relations with Europe and the nations beyond. No one doubts the soundness of British political institutions, the skills of Britain's people, or their deservedly high reputation for steadiness and sanity. But, as in World War II, Great Britain faces an international crisis, this time a crisis of external confidence in the willingness of the British people to make hard choices for the sake of their national economic survival in a highly competitive world. This time the sense of urgency must arise from self-criticism and self-discipline not, as in World War II, from response to a clearly perceived national danger.

In many parts of the world, economic crisis has led to authoritarian rule. Compensation for scarcity of resources has been sought in conspicuous displays, or foreign adventures, or even apathy. The British people have spurned such escapism, but they have not yet accepted in full the implications of the postwar world of technology, rationalization, mass production, and hard selling. Yet of all the countries in the world, Great Britain is the one that has the most vital need to compete successfully in world markets.

[1] *British* in this section refers to the inhabitants of the United Kingdom, although properly the term can be used also to refer to persons in other parts of the British Commonwealth and empire. *Great Britain* and *the United Kingdom* will be used interchangeably, though, strictly speaking, Great Britain includes only England, Wales, and Scotland. Northern Ireland, it should be noted, differs from the other parts of the United Kingdom in that its population is represented in a legislature of its own, in Belfast, as well as in the British Parliament.

Both of Great Britain's major parties recognize the urgency of coping with the country's economic need, but they differ in their approach to meeting that need. The Conservative party places primary emphasis on the enterprise of the capitalist class. Thus the Conservatives favor increased incentives to business and industry and maintain that the resulting expansion will encourage the renewal of outworn machinery and a spirit of active entrepreneurship in seeking and winning new markets. The Labor party, as an article of faith, emphasizes the vital role of the working class, the need for full employment, and the prosperity that can come from community action. Its realistic leaders, however, also stress the essential role of science in advancing production, preach self-restraint in labor's demands, curb inflation, and attempt to balance internal demands against external needs.

Both parties are committed to using the state's machinery and power as means of meeting economic challenge and social need. Both believe strongly in personal rights and the rule of law. Both are dedicated to the effective use of parliamentary institutions in the search for acceptable answers to complicated and delicate problems. Thus, in seeking economic renovation and wider associations, the British can draw on great resources of consensus on fundamental values and ways of action. In no other country has convention so strong a hold. Moreover, there is no country to which so many others look for an example of how individual freedom can be combined with effective government programs, and of how open discussion can be organized through channels that protect minority rights but facilitate majority action in response to accepted goals.

The Importance of Britain for Other Countries

British political machinery and experience have long had unusual importance for other countries, both because Great Britain has been one of the world's great powers and because British institutions have been imitated in many other lands. No people in modern times have been more fertile in the invention and adaptation of political institutions. And although the British have not always been conscious inventors, their slow evolutionary process has been conducive to political experiments from which many other nations have profited. Wherever men of British descent founded new governments in the last century and a half—in Canada, Australia, and New Zealand—they carried British institutions with them. Moreover, such countries as India, Kenya, and Jamaica, when they became independent, adapted British forms and institutions. On the continent of Europe almost every democracy has been strongly, if not always happily, influenced by the British example. The person who understands British government has a standard, therefore, by which to measure many of the world's democracies.

Similarities with and Differences from the United States

The British government, moreover, is sometimes held up as an example for Americans to imitate. Some of its more ardent admirers, it must be confessed, value it for different and even conflicting reasons, and some of them seriously misunderstand its character. Yet not infrequently the American people are urged to scrap some part of their constitutional machinery in favor of the British equivalent. It is all the more important, therefore, to understand the extent to which the two countries are comparable. The sharing of a common language and of common cultural, legal, and political traditions often encourages the assumption that the political outlook and conduct of the two countries must also be similar. Both nations take it for granted that peoples who are not "Anglo-Saxon" will differ from them in attitude and policy, but each is subject to a peculiar irritation when it finds its standards disregarded by the other. There is shrewdness in the comment that Great Britain and the United States are divided by their common language.

There are, in actuality, important political differences between the two countries, differences that stem in large measure from dissimilarities in geography, economic structure, class divisions, way of life, and even inherited political ideas. Anyone who is to understand British politics, therefore, must first of all know something about these differences.

2. THE ISLAND AND THE PEOPLE

The Island

Nothing has been more important in British history than the fact that Great Britain is an island. Only twenty-two miles of water separate the southeast shore of England from the European continent—and plans are now under way to build a connecting tunnel—but for many generations those few miles gave the British people something of the security that the Atlantic and the Pacific, until recently, gave Americans. It was not so long ago that the British equivalent of American isolationists seriously supported a policy of cutting themselves off from political and military struggles in lands across the Channel.

Today, air warfare and nuclear armaments have destroyed any such hope. If the Channel prevented Hitler's armies from conquering Great Britain, it could not keep the Allies from successfully invading France, and it could not keep German planes and rockets from devastating many heavily populated centers on the British island. Yet there are certain ways in which the earlier protective role of the Channel still influences British politics. During the critical centuries when Continental states developed great standing armies that became instruments of autocratic government, the British were relatively free from any corresponding threat. The British army, as the saying goes, was a navy; and a navy was hardly an asset in putting down popular resistance to royal authority on land. Security from invasion made it possible, in the seventeenth and eighteenth centuries, for the British to develop and consolidate free institutions of government at the very time that their neighbors across the Channel were submitting to absolute monarchy. Thus, though the Channel today has lost much of its defensive importance, the free institutions that it protected continue to exist.

Commercial and Military Position

Great Britain's geographical position has been important in another respect. So long as the Mediterranean was the chief path of trade, the island suffered commercially from its location on the fringe of the European world. But once America was discovered, the new trade routes turned the island into a center of world commerce. Great Britain pioneered the industrial revolution. Favorable conditions for importing raw materials and exporting manufactured goods made it the workshop of the world. Partly through the resulting capital accumulation, Great Britain became, too, the world's greatest banking center. If the island had remained purely agricultural, its population would necessarily have been small; but the profits from its industry, shipping, and worldwide investments made it easy to import the food and resources necessary to support a population larger than that of more self-sufficient France.

Moreover, Great Britain's very dependence on sea power encouraged the growth of a diverse and global empire, which ultimately became the British Commonwealth. Gibraltar at the mouth of the Mediterranean and the Falkland Islands off the southern tip of South America dominate the narrow seas through which passes much of the commerce of the world. Canada and Australia are vast areas that have been peopled largely from the British Isles, and, although they became self-governing in the nineteenth century, they still retain close links with the United Kingdom through the British Commonwealth of Nations. Other countries, such as Pakistan, Malaysia, and Nigeria, where the people are very different from the British in race, tradition, and conditions of life, also belong to the Commonwealth. During the nineteenth century the British Navy, unmatched in strength, provided what is often called the "Pax Britannica," which made possible an exchange of goods and services that helped both the overseas areas and Great Britain itself. Great Britain's vast international connections coupled with the resources of the empire and Commonwealth brought it power, prestige, and wealth.

Today this very dependence on foreign trade constitutes both a military and an economic liability. Because of its relative poverty in raw materials other than coal, Great Britain relies more heavily than ever on outside sources to maintain its factories; it needs vast quantities of oil from the Middle East, rubber from Malaysia, nickel from Canada, iron ore to make the steel with which to produce the locomotives and heavy machinery that form so substantial a part of its exports, and much besides. Although its foreign investments have largely been reestablished since the days they were liquidated to pay the costs of two world wars, Great Britain must still earn most of the money for food and raw materials by selling in foreign markets—often, as in the United States, in the face of protective tariffs. Forty percent of its total manufactures are exported, compared to 7 percent of those of the United States.

Since Great Britain remains predominantly a processing economy, failure to maintain its imports or its foreign markets can be disastrous. Both the United States and the Soviet Union have vast resources and markets at home; in an emergency they could support themselves to a considerable extent. But to Great Britain such an emergency might mean death. Thus, whereas the United States and the Soviet Union, in military terms, think first of all of security from attack against the homeland, Great Britain must think of the equally fatal effect of any serious interference with its commerce with distant lands. Moreover, failure to compete economically could also mean a kind of death by attrition.

Climate and Size

Another geographical consideration of great political importance is the smallness of the British island and the evenness of its climate. Great Britain (not including Northern Ireland, which has an area of 5,244 square miles) has an area of only 89,041 square miles, as compared with 3,022,387 for the continental United States. The island is twice the size of Pennsylvania but a little smaller than Oregon. Moreover, the major portion of its population (which by 1966 was

THE UNITED KINGDOM OF GREAT BRITAIN AND NORTHERN IRELAND

about 54.5 million) is concentrated in a relatively small area, since in the north and west (including most of Scotland and Wales) the country is hilly or mountainous. The climate, however, is remarkably even. There is somewhat more rain in the west than in the east and somewhat more sun in the east, but the winters tend to be mild, the summers cool, and the rainfall fairly well distributed throughout the year. There is nothing to compare with the great range of climate and the vast distances that encourage the distinctive outlook and individuality of different American regions. On the contrary, the great bulk of the people live within a few hours' train or motor ride of London, and the same newspapers can be read on the same morning throughout the island.

As a result, the Englishman is more likely than the American to think in national terms. Both in Scotland and in Wales there is still a strong local consciousness. Scotland has long had a Secretary of State of its own in the British Ministry and, especially under the Conservatives, is commonly represented in Parliament only by Scots. In the Churchill Cabinet of 1951 there was, for the first time, a Minister of Welsh Affairs (the office being combined with that of Home Secretary), and the Welsh also prefer Welshmen to represent them. Less than one-sixth of the British population is Scottish or Welsh, however, and the political importance of these groups is far from decisive. In England itself, where the overwhelming majority of the people live, there is little particularist feeling. There is considerable interest in local history and in regional variations in landscape, architecture, and dialect, but this interest is not reflected in a distinctive political feeling. Political parties can use the same literature and emphasize the same principles in Somerset as in London or Norfolk or Yorkshire.

Thus Great Britain's homogeneity and compactness have an important political consequence. In American politics little is more significant than the extent of political decentralization. Not only do sections of the country have distinct characters of their own, but each state has a complete government. The most important political organizations in the United States are state and local rather than national. No American party can win a national election unless it carries several of the great sections, and every party platform represents a compromise of rival sectional interests. Votes in Congress often run along sectional rather than party lines, and even the nominations for national office must take geography into account: if the presidential nominee comes from the East, the vice-presidential nominee must come from the Midwest, the West, or the South.

In England, in contrast, no one cares whether a party's leaders come from Durham or Devon or Essex. Unlike American practice, candidates for the legislature do not need to be residents of the constituencies for which they stand. Historically, the smallness of the island simplified the task of centralizing the government; and governmental centralization, reinforced by ease of transportation and communication, has fostered a well-integrated political and economic life. Apart from the strong sectionalism in Northern Ireland (which also has its own separate legislature) and some growing self-consciousness in depressed areas, the most important political issues in Great Britain are not primarily regional in character; statesmen are free to think in national rather than local terms.

The People: Nationality

In origin the inhabitants of Great Britain are both ancient and diverse, for the early history of the island is, almost to the point of monotony, one of invasion, conquest, and settlement by different peoples coming from a great variety of geographical sources. In later years Shakespeare could hail the "silver sea" surrounding the British isle and serving it

> . . . in the office of a wall,
> Or as a moat defensive to a house
> Against the envy of less happier lands.

But in prehistoric and early historic times, the seas often acted as a highroad bringing invaders and visitors from far places.

The first historical knowledge we have of the inhabitants of the island comes from a time when most of Great Britain was inhabited by Celts. By reputation they were a folk of imagination and quick intelligence, though somewhat lacking in discipline and emotional restraint;

and even today there is an amusing tendency to attribute any marked strain of individuality or lyricism in English writing, or any "un-English" political excitement among the masses of the people, to a survival of this Celtic element in the national character.

For a time, from the first to the fifth centuries, England and a part of Scotland were under the control of the Romans; but apart from their famous roads, a number of ruins, and some place names, few direct traces of Roman influence have survived. With the withdrawal of their legions early in the fifth century, the island was left open to the inroads of various Germanic peoples: Angles, Saxons, Jutes, and, later, Danes. As the invaders penetrated westward, it was only on the fringes of Wales, Cornwall, Cumberland, and western Scotland that the Celts continued to predominate.

The last great invasion of England took place in 1066, when the Normans gave the country, for a time, a ruling class which was French in customs, language, and manners, but which was not numerous enough to make fundamental changes in the composition of the population. Since that time there has been no successful invasion of the country. Moreover, except for the Celtic fringes of Wales (where about 30 percent of the people even today speak Welsh) and of Scotland (where a few Highlanders speak Gaelic), the Irish immigrants in a few large cities, and a wartime infiltration of Poles and Central Europeans, the population of Britain has long been exceptionally uniform in language, religion, and way of life.

Since World War II, however, the British have confronted something of a color and immigration problem that bears on their Commonwealth relations and their economic situation, as well as on their population structure. Immigrants from the West Indies and the Indian subcontinent had brought Great Britain's colored population to 800,000 by 1965, and their exceptionally high birth rate indicated the total would soon reach a million. Although these numbers represent only 2 percent of the population—as compared to the Negro 11 percent in the United States—some of the same problems regarding housing and employment have emerged in the United Kingdom. For the first time in British history restrictions were placed in 1962 on immigration from Commonwealth countries, thereby arousing ill feeling in some of the new members of that association. Despite strong official party disapproval, color was an election issue in a few local areas in 1964, though not in 1966. In 1965, the Labor government passed a renewed Commonwealth Immigrants' Act that maintained the restrictive Conservative limit of about two thousand work permits a month for Commonwealth immigrants, but it also passed an act prohibiting racial discrimination in "places of public resort" that is comparable to the public accommodations section of our Civil Rights Act of 1964. While the British are thus seriously attempting to prevent the growth, or at least the intensification, of color feeling and discrimination, important questions have been raised about whether limiting immigration in general, as has been done, to under 50,000 a year—compared to annual immigration figures for economically prosperous West Germany and Switzerland of between 350,000 and 400,000 Europeans a year, and for France of around 200,000—is consonant with the overriding British need to stimulate economic growth.

The People: Religion

Religion has had a greater influence on British politics than most of the British themselves realize. It is politically important, for example, that there is no great religious division and that, as a whole, the island's people are overwhelmingly Protestant. A few of the oldest and noblest families are Catholic, and recent immigration from Ireland has added significantly to this church's adherents in the poorest and least influential sections of society; but altogether only about 6 percent of the population in England and Wales and 9 percent in the United Kingdom are Catholic (compared with 20 percent of the population in the United States). Thus there is no basis whatsoever for a Catholic political party such as those that exist in France, Italy, and other countries.

Of greater political significance is the division that exists within the Protestant church. At present more than half the people of England are, at least nominally, adherents to the Church of England, that is, the Anglican Church, which corresponds to the Episcopal church in the United States; about a quarter are so-called Nonconformists, who are generally Methodists, Baptists, Congregationalists, or Presbyterians. In Scotland, however, the mass of the people belong to the Presbyterian church, which is the Church of Scotland, and in Wales most belong to Nonconformist denominations.

The Church of England

Because it is an established church, the Church of England is to a certain extent involved in politics. Its head is the monarch, and representatives of the Church sit in the House of Lords and help to make the law of the land. It was the Anglican clergy who performed the ceremony of crowning the present Queen; it is they who open Parliament with prayer. The highest members of the clergy are nominated by the Crown, and despite no fewer than nine commissions set up since 1870 to find ways for the Church to have more freedom in determining its own affairs, the Prime Minister makes the choice. Moreover, the creed of the Church of England is established by Parliamentary statute and may be changed only by Parliamentary action.[2]

More important than the present state of the establishment, however, is the historical influence of the opposition between the Church of England and Nonconformity. Authority in the Church of England, as just noted, traditionally has come from above, and it was natural for those accustomed to authority in the Church to support it in the state. Thus there has been a marked tendency for at least those of the upper class who are Anglicans in religion to be Conservatives in politics. And the Conservative party still considers itself, to some extent, the special defender of religion and the interests of the Church.

[2] Since it often happens that the Prime Minister is not himself an Anglican, there results an odd situation (and one which many Anglicans dislike) under which the highest clergy of the Church may be nominated by a Welsh Nonconformist like Lloyd George, a Presbyterian like Balfour or Bonar Law, or even—to achieve the ultimate in doctrinal incongruity—by a Unitarian like Neville Chamberlain. Moreover, many members of parliament are Nonconformists, Jews, Catholics, or members of no church at all. In 1927 and 1928, changes in the Prayer Book of the Church of England, requested by the representative bodies of the Church, were refused by Parliament partly because of the votes of Nonconformists and even—to the scandal of the devout—of one Parsee.

Nonconformist Influence

English Nonconformists, in contrast, have tended to be critical of state authority ever since their persecution in the seventeenth century.[3] The Congregationalists (who still call themselves "Independents") and Baptists practiced a peculiarly loose and individualistic form of church organization. Authority rested in the congregation, not in a clerical hierarchy, and members were free at any time to withdraw and form new churches. Such ideas, when applied in the political sphere, are closely related to those in the American Declaration of Independence (both denominations, of course, colonized New England) and provide grounds for questioning the legitimacy of any authority not based upon consent. Throughout the nineteenth century the Liberal party, with its emphasis on personal liberty and the limitation of state authority, drew its strongest support from these churches. Today there remains a large Nonconformist element in the Labor party.

It is still possible, in several important respects, to trace the influence of Nonconformity upon British politics. In the first place, the Nonconformists' demand for toleration of different religious ideas and organizations led naturally to insistence on respect for different political ideas and parties. In addition, Nonconformity is the source of the "Nonconformist conscience" (a first cousin of the "New England conscience"), which has come to be shared by a large section of the Anglican Church and which expects the conduct of the government, in foreign as in domestic policy, to be moral and Christian. For example, there was a vast outpouring of indignation within Great Britain itself against Eden's use of force in the 1956 Suez crisis.

Yet if the Nonconformist heritage has had an idealistic influence upon British politics, it has also had an intensely practical one. In some Continental Protestant churches, political action has always been suspect, but the British churches have encouraged a general interest and participation in politics. It used to be said in the nine-

[3] Although the Methodists, whose religious activity began in the eighteenth century, preached a doctrine of obedience and submission to state authority, they organized for vigorous political action on such issues as prison reform and abolition of the slave trade.

teenth century that every Nonconformist chapel was a recruiting station for the Liberal party. When the Labor party was founded, it was no accident that its party organization combined local democracy with a high degree of centralization, for many of its early leaders were themselves Methodist or Baptist lay preachers who could place both their eloquence and their practical knowledge of organization at the disposal of the new party.

In addition, the Nonconformist churches made their chief appeal to people in the middle and lower classes whom the established Church failed to reach. In countries such as Russia or France or Germany, where the church tended to identify its interests with those of the upper classes, it was natural to regard the church as an ally or tool of an oppressive state, an instrument for keeping the exploited in subjection. But in England the lower classes had a church of their own that was itself to some extent oppressed by and critical of state authority. Accordingly, there was no need, in attacking political injustice, to attack religion as well. On the contrary, religion played an important part in fostering both the trade union and the socialist movement in Great Britain. And since it is difficult to be both a Christian and a believer in the extreme doctrine of class war, religion contributed to the moderation as well as to the idealism of the Labor party.

Today all the British churches cooperate in programs of social betterment, and some of their most eminent members are advocates of radical economic reform. Moreover, by his formal visit to the Pope in 1965, the Archbishop of Canterbury supported the idea of wider associations, which are Britain's other greatest need.

Way of Life

In way of life, as in nationality and religion, the British people are exceptionally homogeneous. The sentimental American still likes to think of England as a "green and pleasant land" of villages, churches, and country houses, and the tourist still prefers a visit to the Lake Country or Stratford-on-Avon to an acquaintance with Manchester or Glasgow. But the unromantic fact is that Great Britain is heavily urbanized and industrialized; its population is one of the densest of any Western country. The

United States has about 50 people to the square mile; the United Kingdom has 552 and England and Wales 805. Sixty percent of the American population are classified as urban, but 80 percent of the people of England and Wales and 70 percent of the people of Scotland are so classified. In the United States 12 percent of the population are engaged in agriculture and 30 percent in industry, mining, transport, and so forth. In Great Britain only 4 percent of the population are farmers, and 44 percent work in industry, mining, and the like. Thus, where there are $2\frac{1}{2}$ urban workers for every farmer in the United States, in Great Britain there are 11.

The political consequences of this situation are very important. In the United States, quite apart from the strong influence of the farm states in the Senate, no national party appeals primarily to the urban workers. In Great Britain, however, such an appeal gives the Labor party a built-in basis of strength. Labor would win all national elections if it could gain all the votes of the urban working class. The fact is, however, that while class structure—whose influence is particularly pervasive in British life—has a great effect on individual decisions, a voter's perception of society may be very different from what might be inferred from his position in that society. Thus, whereas the steady increase in Conservative support through the 1950's was commonly explained in terms of the continual advance in living standards, the trend toward Labor in the 1960's indicates that floating voters are drawn from all social strata and make their electoral decisions on other issues: in particular, quality of leadership, soundness of domestic and foreign policies, concern for the interests of the community, and forward-looking plans.

Class and Mass

While British politics are increasingly influenced—as are American politics—by individual decisions and group pressures, class distinctions still pervade the tacit assumptions of most Britishers. Although income and occupation are important elements, British class distinctions also depend heavily on other considerations: tradition, education, behavior, manner of living, and even accent. In the past, people have generally been divided into those who are "gentlemen" and those who are not. The "gentlemen" were not identical with the nobility, although they included it; [4] and the important line of demarcation ran, not between the aristocracy and the middle class (as has often been the case on the Continent), but between the upper-middle class and the lower-middle class.

The most important factor in determining who fell on which side of the line was, and to some degree still is, education. Those who had been educated at one of the good public schools (a name which often confuses Americans because the British public schools are more or less the equivalent of our private preparatory high schools) were set apart from those who had not. In such schools the traditional aim has been to develop "Christian gentlemen" who are disciplined, loyal, and decent, who "play the game," bear pain and discomfort with a "stiff upper lip," and know how to wield authority and how to elicit respect from those they rule. In public schools that follow the inherited pattern, older students (known as prefects) rule over their fellows; both prefects and masters may deal out corporal punishment; participation in sports is considered of utmost importance; and religion holds a central place in school life. The chief educational concern used to be with the classics, although this is no longer true. The system has often been criticized for its lack of democracy and for its tendency to consider intellect less important than good sportsmanship and acceptance of the traditional code of behavior. Yet many foreigners as well as many Englishmen admire the type of citizen that results. Whereas upper classes in other societies have regarded wealth or military force as warrant for their power, the reputation of the British upper class for decency, dependability, and public service has helped preserve its political influence in an increasingly democratic age.

Part of the strength of this class came from the cohesion imposed by its way of life. Its members went to the same exclusive public schools, typified by Eton and Harrow, and to the universities at Oxford or Cambridge. They married among the same established families,

belonged to the same clubs, followed the same sports, mingled socially at the same houses, and generally followed the same professions: managing their estates or entering the army, the government, the law, or the Church. The old stereotype that a gentleman does not go into "trade" has long since died, however, and many members of the upper class are now to be found in commercial and financial enterprises. [5]

In any case, the barrier between the upper class and the rest of the population has not been rigid. On the contrary, the old ruling class has long prided itself on its ability to assimilate the more able and eminent of its fellow citizens born into other classes. In addition, higher education has become available to a much wider group. Members of the newer upper-middle class tend, however, to conform to the comfortable pattern established by the older aristocracy: they purchase country estates, abandon the Nonconformist chapel for the Church of England, seek admission to the right clubs, send their children to fashionable schools, and eventually themselves intermarry with the older families.

In the past, the prestige of the older families, combined with the wealth of the newer, enabled what is often now spoken of disparagingly as "the Establishment" to wield a political influence out of all proportion to its numerical importance in the country. Its members were heavily overrepresented in Parliament and were often accused of dominating the courts, the press, the Church, the armed forces, and the civil service, particularly the Foreign Office. There were times when the Cabinet itself resembled a reunion of Old Etonians (as under Balfour) or Old Harrovians (as under Baldwin). Even Macmillan's 1959 Cabinet included six Old Etonians. It is a mark of a new day in politics that Prime Minister Harold Wilson was educated at a grammar (in American terms, public) school and that the same educational background was a strong point in favor of choosing Edward Heath as Conservative leader.

It would be a great mistake, in any case, to assume that the broad distinction between class and mass represents the total picture of British class distinctions. Great Britain used to be termed a "nation of shopkeepers," partly be-

---

[4] In Great Britain, a title ordinarily descends only to the eldest son, while the rest of the children of a nobleman become "commoners." Thus a person may be closely related to a number of peers without having a title himself, and the distinction between the aristocracy and the upper-middle class is blurred.

[5] This is reflected in the table on the facing page.

cause of its great commercial and trading role in the world and partly because of the strength of its middle class of businessmen, shopkeepers, and professional men. With the continued growth of large-scale industry and an increasing emphasis on services, however, what is sometimes termed the lower-middle class became much more numerous. This class works for others, rather than owning its own businesses, and is composed of such groups as clerical workers, shop assistants, hotel and restaurant workers, and providers of private and public services. Harold Wilson came from this class, as did Lloyd George and Ramsay Macdonald.

Like the lower-middle class, industrial workers, farmers, and farm laborers are also each divided into many sectors, with their own predispositions, prejudices, and aspirations. Most British workmen are employed in relatively large workshops or factories, but there are also highly specialized workers in various fields. To count trade unionists as a single group is to overlook the basic differences between a factory worker on the production line and a white-collar or "black-coated" office employee. As for farmers, despite an increase in the number of independent owners, only one-third of the cultivated land in England and

Wales is under their care. Thus in contrast to the United States, where the small farmer who owns his own farm is of considerable political importance, the ordinary British farmer is a tenant, though often a prosperous one.

Thus easy assumptions about "who votes for what party" do not hold up. A striking fact is that the Conservative party has consistently drawn a large proportion of its electoral support from the working class. A 1964 survey by Robert McKenzie and Allan Silver confirmed estimates that one-third of the manual working-class electorate, including a large proportion of women and older men, commonly votes Conservative. Moreover, they found that Conservative values had spread more widely through the working class than they had expected. Thus, despite the fact that most British workers are in trade unions, they displayed considerable distrust of unions, on the grounds that unions are disruptive or officious. Working-class Tories showed themselves reluctant to extend nationalization, in favor of judicial flogging, opposed to colored immigrants, and convinced by the Conservatives' argument that they alone represented the whole country, not merely one segment of it. Among lower-income groups and women, support for Conservatives seemed to be associated

The Social Background of Some Contemporary Élite Groups

	1 Labor Govt., 1945	2 Labor Govt., 1951	3 Cons. Govt., 1951	4 Cons. Govt., 1960	5 Heads of Civil Service, 1958	6 Ambassadors and Ministers, 1953	7 Leaders of Industry and Business, 1950–55	8 Directors of large Insurance Cos., 1958	9 Directors of Bank of England and "Big 5," 1958	10 Army, 1953	11 Judiciary, 1953	12 Bishops, 1953
Aristocrats	2	3	14	15	—	—	3	—	—	—	—	—
Working Class	38	30	1	1	—	—	1	—	—	—	—	—
Etonians	5	5	24	17	3	—	8	46	50	—	—	—
Harrow, Winchester, Rugby, Marlborough	2	5	16	10	11	—	8	34	33	—	—	—
All Public Schools	15	23	52	48	—	65	29	—	—	} 21	{ 36	27
Sandhurst, Dartmouth, Woolwich	—	—	1	—	—	—	1	12	8 }			
Grammar Schools	} 11	16	8	18	{ —	—	15	—	—		—	—
"State Secondary Schools"					—	—	—	—	—	4	8	7
Elementary School only	30	22	—	—	—	—	1	—	2	—	—	—
Oxford or Cambridge University	15	23	40	46	50	—	22	57	83	—	—	—
Other Universities	9	8	3	3	15	—	8	10	14	—	—	—
Total in Category	66	66	65	66	73	75	65	149	166	34	58	43

Source: W. L. Guttsman, *The British Political Elite* (London: MacGibbon & Kee Ltd., 1963), p. 336.

with a deferential (but steadily disappearing) "they know best" attitude, which was also prevalent among farm laborers.

The turn in Labor's electoral fortunes, first in 1964, and more decisively in 1966, seems to have resulted in considerable measure from Wilson's ability to give his party a broader image. Mark Abrams has pointed out that a 1960 survey by Research Services Limited indicated that in the first three postwar elections (1945, 1950, 1951) Labor had secured the votes of slightly over 60 percent of the working-class electorate but just under 20 percent of the middle-class voters. This means it drew 87 percent of its votes from the working class and only 13 percent from the middle class. During the 1950's, Labor lost some of its already slight middle-class support and a small additional number of manual workers. Its revival of support appears to have come from both groups, and perhaps particularly from those manual workers who now regard themselves as middle class.

Group Politics

Politicians need support in their efforts to come into power and, once in power, in their efforts to govern effectively. For the first purpose, they appeal to the broad groups of consumers—for the second, to organized producers. Consequently, consumers of services and goods have their best chance to influence political decisions during an electoral campaign—organized producers, while government is being carried on. Naturally consumers and producers are not different sets of persons so much as different relationships to the economic process. Both are closely knit into the political process, because the government is so much involved in the economic system.

Consumers are principally interested in programs of service, rates of taxation, full employment, and the cost of living. Political parties stimulate and focus consumer demands through their programs, propaganda, and competitive promises, especially at election time. Great Britain is the original home of the cooperative movement, and about half the families in the island are members of consumers' associations. These associations run their own retail stores and in some cases own and manage their own factories. Most consumers' organizations are affiliated with the Cooperative Union. Another group toward which parties direct attention is composed of those receiving pensions, particularly the 4.6 million recipients of retirement benefits under the National Insurance system for whom the National Federation of Old Age Pensions Associations speaks. The closer the margin between levels of party support, the more important it is to attract the votes of this substantial group, whose interests are so singlemindedly concentrated on securing increased benefits.

The political concern with, and of, organized producers is somewhat broader. Samuel H. Beer, in *British Politics in the Collectivist Age,* divides organized producers into two groups— trade associations and trade unions. He points out that their opportunities to exert pressure arise from the government's need for advice, for acquiescence, and for approval. Advice includes the data, technical knowledge, and judgment provided by specialists from interested parties—that is, industry, business, and commerce—which are essential for supplementing the resources of government agencies. The Ministry of Transport, for example, consults with the Society of Motor Manufacturers and Traders, though more often on technical and administrative minutiae than on general policy. In addition, the kind of economic management assumed by modern government requires a broad basis of economic knowledge and market intelligence that in a nontotalitarian system can be secured only through close relations with private producers and trade associations. For example, when the Labor government after the war was seeking to increase Britain's export trade, it accepted the advice of the advisory committee of the Ministry of Supply to change the annual tax on cars to a flat rate in order to encourage the production of larger cars for the overseas trade.

Acquiescence commonly means cooperation, as, for example, when businessmen helped to implement the system of price controls, or when doctors agreed to participate in the National Health Service. The persistent opposition of steel producers to the nationalization of that industry by the postwar Labor government, on the other hand, threatened a stalemate that the government's public corporation might not have been able to break. (The Conservatives' return to office led to the denationalization of steel, but Labor is renationalizing it.) In practice, significant programs in the economic and social welfare fields require negotiation, not merely consultation, with the groups most affected.

The third level of interaction, approval, is an extension of acquiescence to the point of active endorsement. Agricultural price-fixing, for example, though announced by the government, was the result of annual negotiations with the National Farmers Union from 1946 to 1956, and levels were formally endorsed by that body. The same kind of approval has been sought by the Ministry of Health from the British Medical Association following controversies over pay scales. Such arrangements, Beer points out, reflect a view that those most affected by a policy, and particularly technical experts, have a right to participate in its formulation. This kind of functional representation or corporatism he finds prevalent in British political culture.

The growing participation of government in economic life, with the concomitant closeness of its relations with organized producers, has helped to stimulate industrial and trade associations. Concentration has gone further in industry than in commerce, the two being organized separately. By the 1950's, 90 percent of the larger firms and 76 percent of the smaller ones belonged to one or another of the 1,300 industrial trade associations. World War I had seen the formation of the Federation of British Industries (FBI, British style) and the National Union of Manufacturers (NUM). Another "peak" organization is the Confederation of British Industry, whose two hundred and seventy affiliates negotiate with 70 percent of the worker population. The FBI now represents six-sevenths of all industrial concerns employing more than ten workers. Some thirty or forty associations, each covering a total industry, seek with varying success to coordinate their interests when they consult with the relevant government department. Where there are a number of big producers, as in chemicals, iron and steel, and motor cars, coordination is much easier to secure than when many small firms are involved. In comparison with industry, commerce is more dispersed, although the Association of British Chambers of Commerce

(ABCC), founded in 1860, now has over a hundred constituent chambers, with some sixty thousand members. Many retail merchants who are not within the ABCC belong to the National Chamber of Trade.

Concentration of trade unions is no less striking. The Trade Union Congress, founded in 1868, has never had a rival, nor has it ever experienced a split such as that between the CIO and the AFL. By 1894, the TUC already represented 65 percent of all unionists and had a million members. Moreover, despite the phenomenal growth of trade union membership, the TUC by 1953 included 85 percent of all trade unionists—that is, 8,094,000 out of 9,524,000. By the end of 1962, the total membership of British trade unions was 9,870,000; the members were divided among 623 unions, but two-thirds were in the eighteen largest unions and just over half were in eight unions, each with more than a quarter of a million members.

Because of the special relation of the unions to the Labor party, both as constituent members and through their own sponsored MP's, much of their influence is exerted through the party. Even so, the TUC, like the big trade and producers' associations, maintains constant and close relations with the executive, both ministers and civil servants. Like other organized producers, trade unions share in the rough structure of functional representation that exists side by side with parliamentary representation, mainly through advisory committees. In addition, however, an almost constant series of less formal contacts goes on through visits and phone calls. What Beer calls "an intricate system of bidding and bargaining" proceeds constantly, linking parties and administration to the major interest groups of the country.

3. THE ECONOMY AND THE STATE

The Economic Problem

Today the British government faces an economic situation of great seriousness. More dependent on its own immediate productive powers than it was for a century before World War II, Great Britain must manufacture not only for its own needs but also for export—both to pay for the raw materials that it turns into manufactured products for itself and other countries and to pay for steadily (and dangerously) increasing imports for its own consumption. With its financial investments abroad largely depleted through the expenditures of two world wars, its share of the world's shipping lessened, and its relatively few remaining overseas possessions an economic drain rather than an advantage, Great Britain no longer possesses a cushion against a seriously adverse balance of payments. Thus, despite heroic efforts since World War II, the British remain in an unstable economic state, subject to international financial crises, threatened with inflation, in need of radical changes in employer-employee relations in crucial areas like those of the docks and shipping itself, and also in need of greatly increased productivity both to compete abroad and to outstrip spiraling wages and prices at home.

What makes the British economic situation so difficult to stabilize is not only its heavy dependence on external trade and confidence but the fact that a period of relative though misleading domestic affluence has followed the grim, sustained struggle for survival of the 40's and the uneven reconstruction of the 50's. The nearly six years of war in which Great Britain was literally on the battlefront were followed by five years in which the British, by a vast national effort, expanded their exports 70 percent above prewar levels through increasing production and, by local restrictions, through systematically exporting goods that were much in demand on the home market. Marshall aid made it possible to remove controls and stabilize the balance of payments, but almost immediately the Korean war and the need for rearmament in the face of threatening Soviet expansion diverted the most effective earners of overseas credits into defense production. Short periods of expansion have been followed by contraction—a pattern commonly stigmatized as "stop-go." Inflation has been curbed but not stopped. Most serious of all, particularly in relation to the persistent balance-of-payments problem, the British have not yet achieved, nor do they show signs of achieving, a rate of economic growth comparable with that of most other industrial countries.

Writing in January 1966, Mr. Angus Maddison, of the Organization for Economic Cooperation and Development, pointed out that British industrial productivity was below that of any Western European country north of the Alps and probably not very different from those of the Soviet Union, Italy, and Japan. His remedy, approved by *The Economist,* but not by all planners, was to increase productivity-raising investment and to reduce overseas defense spending and private overseas investment, thereby making possible, he believed, the National Plan target of a 3.4 percent annual growth in output per man. The Labor government is attempting a three-fold investment, prices, and wages plan, which has been endorsed by industry, commerce, and labor. But the plan has been very difficult to implement despite the drastic curbs on wages and prices instituted by the Wilson government in 1966.

Thus the British continue to be confronted by economic problems of major national importance. To meet them with even relative success requires harder and more productive work, better labor relations, more restraint in wage demands, and reduction in the consumption of imports—in sum, all the components necessary to balance imports with exports and to maintain its overseas credit. Entry into the prosperous Common Market might provide the incentives for new production by adding wider demands; even then, the pressures on the British themselves will remain heavy.

The Role of the State

Not only is the British government confronted by serious economic problems; it is also subject to a multitude of pressures from all groups in the community. First is the widespread expectation that the state must ensure reasonable standards of living for all its people. Organized workers have turned to the government for better working conditions, shorter hours, and higher wages. Manufacturers want subsidies and protection from foreign competition. The elderly demand pensions. And the great masses of the people—white-collar workers, skilled craftsmen, unskilled laborers—are eager not only for protection against the financial burdens of unemployment, ill health, and old age but also for government intervention to assure good housing, a decent diet, and satisfactory education.

That, despite notable advances, the British were far from satisfied with the components of their national life was reflected in the numerous committees of inquiry set up in 1960–61: on broadcasting, the railways, traffic and roads, secondary education, and higher education. Any adequate picture of the British scene, in other words, must take into account the dynamic change that is taking place in every sphere of life.

Looking from the outside, we must be careful not to oversimplify either British problems or British aspirations. What we are watching is the effort of a great country, once the foremost of world powers, to remain a major factor in international affairs and, at the same time, to establish conditions of social justice within its own boundaries. Even though the state must inevitably play a vast and pervasive role in the process, the British are determined to preserve the free institutions and the interplay of public and private interests that they have developed so impressively. The future of democratic government throughout the world will be much affected by the outcome.

4. ORGANS OF POLITICAL OPINION

Politics and Public Opinion

In studying the politics of any country, it is important not only to understand the nature of the social, economic, and other divisions of the population but to discover what organs of public and political opinion are available for the expression of these interests.

Experts still disagree about the exact meaning of *public opinion,* but no one today challenges the fact of its importance. In democracies it has long been assumed that governments ought, in general, to do what their people want them to do. And even in dictatorships the rulers, far from ignoring public opinion, have become proficient in the art of molding and manipulating it. In every modern country, regardless of form of government, the press, radio, and television are political weapons of tremendous power, and

few things are so indicative of the nature of a government as the way in which that power is exercised.

The Press

In a democracy like Great Britain the press, ideally, has three political functions: information, discussion, and representation. It is supposed to give the voter reliable and complete information on which to base his judgment, it should let him know the arguments for and against any policy, and it should reflect and give voice to the desires of the people as a whole, particularly in the relatively long periods between elections. In performing these services, however, the press may be restricted by action of the government or of private interests.

On the first score the British have had comparatively little to complain of. In the years before World War II, when the Conservatives were in power, there were occasional complaints that certain officials had tried to influence the press, the radio, and even newsreels in an attempt to prevent the publication of inconvenient news items or distasteful opinions. There was no open censorship, but tactful suggestions might be made to editors, reporters, or proprietors; and since proprietors often were Conservative in sympathy, and since editors and reporters might conceivably be reluctant to antagonize officials upon whom they were dependent for information, the suggestions may have had some influence.

During the war, the government acquired extraordinary authority under the Emergency Powers (Defence) Act of 1939 (not unlike its predecessor, the Defence of the Realm Act, 1914) to prohibit publications that were likely to cause serious public disorder or to promote disaffection. But these powers were exercised, on the whole, with laudable restraint and ended soon after the war.

The Structure of the British Press

Today, public concern and criticism are aimed not at the government but at the power of a few vast publishing empires. These empires, it is feared, might use their power to control the ideas and information reaching a large section of the British public or to influence the government itself. Unlike newspapers in the United States, the typical large morning newspaper in Great Britain has a national as well as a local circulation, which combined is far larger than that of any single American newspaper. This is partly because of the differences in size of the two countries but also because the British read more newspapers proportionately than any other people in the world.

In 1965 (at a time when almost no American paper, except tabloids, sold even a million copies) Beaverbrook Newspapers' *Daily Express* had a circulation of over 4 million; Lord Rothermere's *Daily Mail* (which incorporated the Liberal *News Chronicle*), some 2.5 million; and Cecil Harmsworth King's *Daily Mirror*, a popular pro-Labor tabloid, nearly 5 million, the largest of any daily in the world. In addition, Beaverbrook Newspapers controlled the *Evening Standard* (circulation 680,000), the *Sunday Express* (over 4 million), and a number of provincial newspapers; Lord Rothermere had the *Evening News* (1,278,000), the *Daily Sketch* (826,000), as well as provincial papers; and Mr. King (nephew of an earlier "press lord," Lord Northcliffe, and head of the International Publishing Corporation) controlled the *Sunday Mirror* (5,022,000), the *Sun* (1,361,000), the *People* (Sunday, 5,509,000), and the Fleetway publications. Mr. King's publishing enterprise actually governed twelve magazines with a total circulation of more than 13 million. Another chain is that of Lord Thomson, who in 1959 acquired control of Lord Kemsley's newspapers, of which the *Sunday Times* (1,250,000) is the best known. He also owns the *Scotsman*, the *Edinburgh Evening News*, and Scottish television; in 1964 he strengthened his provincial holdings by introducing the *Reading Post*, which has been widely publicized for its modern methods of production. In 1966, his financial backing was extended to the *Times*.

The concentration of control in the hands of a few (especially Mr. King) led the Conservative government to establish a Royal Commission to investigate the ownership, production, and sale of British newspapers and periodicals. Its 1962 report led to a provision that the Monopolies Commission, strengthened for the purpose with specialists, should investigate all transactions involving a combined circulation of 3 million. This provision does not operate, however, when a paper is about to close, as when the *Sunday Express* acquired the 150-year-old but deficit-ridden *Sunday Dispatch* in mid-1961, nor would it affect Lord Thomson's efforts to gain a regional monopoly in Scotland.

The problem is not simply one of concentration of control, although this is a major part of it; it is also a problem of ensuring adequate presentation of different points of view. On the whole, the structure of the press has favored the Conservative party—"wealth calls to wealth," as one person put it. In 1960, the *News Chronicle*, the outstanding Liberal newspaper, was absorbed by the *Daily Mail*; and the *Star*, the only non-Conservative evening paper, disappeared. The *Daily Herald* was bought by the *Daily Mirror* group after the Trades Union Congress relinquished its control. In 1964, however, it was replaced by a livelier paper, the *Sun*, whose appeal to the newer and younger Labor supporters has pushed circulation to 1.5 million, a quarter of a million more than its duller but worthy predecessor. The *Daily Worker* (Communist), founded in 1930, changed its name to *Morning Star* in 1966 and continues to sell about 60,000 copies.

In addition to the great newspaper chains, proprietors in Great Britain are organized for common action through the Newspaper Proprietors Association in London and the Newspaper Society in the provinces, while news agencies such as the Press Association and Reuters (which, in its collection and distribution of foreign news, has acquired the reputation of speaking for British interests and reflecting official British policy) are corporations. One obvious problem in getting free discussion of new ideas is the difficulty of breaking into this highly organized structure. When Lord Camrose's *Daily Telegraph* issued a Sunday edition, the *Sunday Telegraph*, early in 1961, it was the first new Sunday national newspaper since the *Sunday Express* appeared forty years before. The *Sun*, which replaced the *Herald*, was the first popular national daily launched since 1912.

The concentration of British journalism in London throws more power into the hands of a newspaper owner in Great Britain than is possessed by any in the United States. But the first Royal Commission on the Press, set up in October 1946 to investigate charges of "monopolistic tendencies in the control of the Press," found that there was "nothing approaching monopoly in the Press as a whole" and concluded that the British press has "high standards of public responsibility and service" and is "jealous of its own independence and reputation." At the same time, the Commission warned that "partisanship can and does on occasion lead to a degree of selection and colouring of news which can only be regarded as excessive."

It is difficult, of course, to tell just how much influence newspaper partisanship has on the British voter. Surveys of circulation indicated that the regions in which the *Daily Herald* predominated (South Wales, for example) tended to vote for Labor and that the *Daily Telegraph* and the *Daily Mail* predominate in the southern suburbs of London, Conservative strongholds. But it is at least as likely that readers choose the newspaper corresponding to the political convictions they already hold as that they acquire their convictions from reading the paper.

To safeguard the freedom of the press and to combat abuses of it, the Royal Commission on the Press recommended the establishment of a General Council of the Press. In July 1953, a council of twenty-five members, nominated by editors, journalists, and managers, began to respond to specific complaints against newspapers and tried to determine standards in controversial issues. Its first action was to rebuke the *Mirror* for running a poll on whether Princess Margaret should marry Peter Townsend; in 1963 it strongly criticized the imprisonment of two journalists who had refused to reveal their source of information in the Vassall spy case. Its annual reports show a keen concern for public as well as professional interests. On one issue the two interests clearly coincide: more freedom for the press to find out about local government affairs. On this issue the council succeeded in securing an act sponsored by a private member, which went into effect in June 1961. The council has found little evidence of undue influence by advertisers on the material printed by the press. It warns of another danger, however, to which the more serious press has also called attention: the great trend toward popularizing the press. This trend has turned many dailies, as well as Sunday papers, into news magazines with pictures, cartoon strips, and human-interest stories that detract from the primary purpose of providing and commenting on the news.

The Influential Press

Of particular importance, therefore, is the influence wielded by several national dailies of more limited circulation but of far higher quality than the giant newspapers. Among these papers, the Conservative *Daily Telegraph* has the highest circulation (just over a million and a quarter); the *Financial Times* (150,000) is widely read by business people; and the Liberal *Guardian*, formerly the *Manchester Guardian* (circulation 280,000), has an international reputation for the excellence of its news and editorial comment. The *Times* of London, however, is the most powerful of the island's newspapers. Although its circulation stays steady at a quarter of a million, its readers include the most eminent people in Great Britain: government officials, politicians, judges, diplomats, scholars, clergymen, officers of the army and navy, and the well-educated classes in general. Its reporting is noted for reliability and completeness, if not for liveliness; and, especially in foreign affairs, its reputation for reflecting or even anticipating government policy gives it an almost official tone. Perhaps its most famous feature is "Letters to the *Times*," which may provoke a national debate as effectively as might a speech in the House of Commons.

In addition to these daily papers, and to the *Sunday Times* and the *Observer*, certain weekly periodicals wield great influence. This is particularly true of the *Economist* (nonpartisan and widely read abroad as at home), the *Spectator* (moderately Conservative in tendency), and the *New Statesman and Nation* and the *Tribune* (which speak for Labor groups). Such publications make no attempt to win a circulation in the millions; they can afford to indulge in discussions of ideas and issues that require considerable intelligence on the part of their readers. It is in these periodicals, rather than in the daily press, that new and unorthodox ideas can best win a hearing. Their readers are, as in the case of the *Times* and the *Guardian*, men and women who themselves influence opinion and legislation; such publications, therefore, often exert a greater influence on politics than do newspapers with many times their circulation.

Radio and Television

Important as the press is in providing news and discussion, the growth of radio and particularly of television provides powerful means of capturing public attention. But while private enterprise predominates in the publishing field in Great Britain, radio broadcasting is a government monopoly, as was television until late in 1955. The British Broadcasting Corporation, a public corporation established in 1927 and financed by individual license fees, still provides all radio programs (except for competition from "pirate" broadcasters outside the three-mile limit and from continental radio stations), but it has long since been outstripped in the television field by commercial TV. The latter is organized in a very different way in Great Britain from the way it is organized in the United States. In 1954, the Independent Television Authority was established for an initial ten-year period—subsequently extended to 1976—to own and operate transmitting stations; the cost is met by private companies that provide programs, own the production studios and equipment, and reap the profits of advertising. The role of the ITA is to see that programs report the news accurately (in practice they have done so more attractively than has the BBC), preserve reasonable impartiality in controversial issues, and do not violate good taste.

The BBC, in the hope of adding to its slipping audience, was authorized (following the recommendations of the Pilkington Committee) to add a second TV wave band. It was opened in April 1964 on the newer ultra-high-frequency standard that is in general use throughout Europe. Existing services will ultimately be transferred to this wave band, and color will be introduced. Adequate funds are not available, however, to do as good a job as if it were commercially financed. With a view to extending educational radio and TV programs and bringing all standards to a common high level, proposals are being made that the BBC should get part of its income from advertisers (as does the Canadian Broadcasting Corporation) and that the ITA should receive a small basic income from the license fee so as to give it more independence in providing news and educational programs.

The BBC used to be criticized for the colorlessness of its news, but its current-affairs commentary these days is lively, topical, and occasionally brutal. What it must avoid, however, is obvious partisanship, so it cannot offer the kind of political commentary in which the weeklies excel. The BBC is also bound by a 1947 *aide-mémoire* that permits the opposition free time whenever a government broadcast is considered controversial. Prime Minister Wilson has accused the BBC of enabling the Conservatives, when they were in office, to make ministerial broadcasts with relatively little opportunity for Labor to reply, and of being less generous since his party came into office. The BBC has denied the charge and points to the phrase in the *aide-mémoire* which specifies that, if the government and the opposition reach no agreement on whether the broadcast is controversial, "the BBC will be free to exercise its own judgment."

In any case, radio and TV are playing an increasingly important part in bringing contemporary affairs to the general public. The old rule that radio and TV should not comment on subjects to be brought up in Parliament has been dropped. For the first time in history, the House of Commons was televised when the Queen opened Parliament after the 1966 election, and there is serious discussion—though also serious doubt—about the value of televising debates. The Lords, who surprisingly were the innovators in introducing a press gallery, microphones, and tape recorders, have suggested they should innovate television coverage also.

Radio and, particularly, TV have their greatest impact on public affairs at election time. In 1959 viewers of party broadcasts outstripped radio listeners—61 percent of the electorate watched at least one party television broadcast that year as compared to 27 percent who listened to a broadcast. Calculations for 1964 indicate that the total average audience during the campaign was 12,700,000 as compared with 8,900,000 in 1959. Political parties must be granted time on the air roughly in proportion to their number of candidates for Parliament. So far, the most dramatic of all electoral devices—a debate between the chief figures—has not taken place. In 1964, Mr. Wilson challenged

Sir Alec Home to such a debate; in 1966, Mr. Heath was ready for such a confrontation, but Wilson adroitly insisted that the Liberal leader, Grimond, would also have to participate. Heath rejected this proposal, since it would seem to place a major and a minor opposition party on the same level.

Adequacy of the Organs of Information and Opinion

The press, radio, and television in Great Britain offer suggestive contrasts both with each other and with the corresponding institutions in the United States.

If one takes as a standard the opening of channels for different views, for free discussion, and for reliable information, then the great American advantage is that there are many more such channels. While British national newspapers have tended to drive local papers out of business, most American cities still have daily newspapers of their own, making it easier for different regional views to be expressed. Yet even in the United States the growth of the chain newspaper has restricted this independence, while the decline in the number of cities with competing dailies is even more serious. Thus, while there are more daily newspapers in the United States than in Britain, there are many towns where the reader cannot choose among papers that reflect differing political outlooks.

In contrast, the great advantage of the British press is that the most powerful political movements in the country have their views expressed in organs of national circulation and that anyone on the island can choose among several, widely different national newspapers. The great disadvantage is that the extraordinary expense of starting and maintaining a newspaper means that the presentation of rival views in daily and Sunday papers depends on the press lords.

In theory, radio and television should in both countries provide notable instruments for political information and expression. Yet in the United States, although there is independence of ownership and a freer expression of opinion on controversial issues, the influence of advertising agencies and sponsors restricts the amount of time devoted to public affairs, while political comment tends to be one-sided and conservative. Still, the British experience hardly suggests that government ownership and supervision is the full answer.

To make the organs of information and opinion contribute helpfully to an enlightened public opinion is, in fact, no simple task. To place control in the hands of private owners is often to give a disproportionate voice to conservative political groups. To place control in such public organizations as political parties, cooperatives, trade unions, or business associations may give a wider representation to divergent views, but such organizations are likely to be even more one-sided than private owners in their presentation of the news. To place control in the government, quite apart from any danger inherent in official control of the sources of information, may be to achieve impartiality in reporting at the expense of the most fertile kind of political discussion and argument. To place control in the sort of trusteeship under which the *Times,* the *Guardian,* and the *Observer* used to be published provides greater personal freedom for editors and writers, but there was a possibility (happily avoided) of deterioration through lack of competition.

Increasingly it is suggested that the best solution lies in the simultaneous existence of a variety of forms. Thus, the competition of privately owned publications and commercial TV can act as a spur to those owned by public bodies or by trusteeships, while the existence of the latter can provide a check on the accuracy and completeness of the former.

2. The British Political Heritage

1. HISTORICAL BACKGROUND

Continuity and Change

Few things are more perplexing to the outside observer than the British habit of preserving the form of inherited institutions while modifying both their spirit and their function. Other great countries, such as France, Russia, and Germany, have altered their political systems openly, deliberately, and violently. But in Great Britain, with only one important interruption, political innovations have occurred gradually and at times almost imperceptibly. In many instances change has resulted not so much from logical forethought as from an almost casual blend of improvisation, expediency, and accident. And although the growth of British institutions can be traced through many centuries of history, this development has been so unmarked by precise and sensational innovations that frequently it is hard to tell exactly when a certain practice first appeared, or even to state with certainty what English political institutions were like at a given historical moment.

Origins of the Parliamentary System

The origins of the British Parliament often are traced to ancient Anglo-Saxon times when a council known as the Witenagemot (or Witan), whose composition and powers are still a matter of debate, used to be called together to advise the English Kings. With the Norman Conquest in 1066 the Witan disappeared; but William the Conqueror, while concentrating greater power in his own hands than the Saxon kings had known, summoned a *Magnum Con-*

cilium (Great Council) at regular intervals. At such times, according to *The Anglo-Saxon Chronicle,* the greatest men in England were with him: "archbishops, bishops, and abbots, earls, thegns, and knights." In the intervals between these meetings, a smaller *Curia Regis* (King's Court, or Little Council) remained to advise the King. The practical work of administration was carried on by the royal household.

In contrast to the Kings of France, whose authority continued to be challenged and limited by powerful nobles who commanded the allegiance of their tenants, William instituted a system of land tenure according to which the first loyalty of every landholder was to the King and not to a local lord. From an early period, therefore, England attained a degree of political centralization far greater than that on the Continent. Yet institutions of local government which had originated before the Conquest continued in existence and provided a limited experience in self-government.

It was William's great-grandson, Henry II (1154–89), whose reign (which followed a period of anarchy) marked the next great advance in English government. Traveling or itinerant justices now fostered the growth of a law common to all the land, while trial by jury replaced the earlier methods of trial by ordeal, battle, or compurgation.

Early Limitations on Royal Authority

If it was due to the strength of Henry II that an orderly and firm governmental authority was established, it was due to the weakness of his son John (1199–1216) that this authority was limited by Magna Charta (the Great Charter), the most famous if not the most effective of those restraints on political authority that are the essence of constitutionalism. Subsequent tradition has transformed into a charter of English liberty what was primarily a guarantee of the specific rights of English barons. Yet certain articles—such as the famous provision (Article 39) that no free man might be arrested, imprisoned, dispossessed, outlawed or exiled, or harassed in any other way save by the lawful judgment of his peers or the law of the land—lent themselves to a far broader interpretation and application than their sponsors imagined. The document was not democratic in any modern sense, but it reiterated the principle that the King was not unlimited in power and that abuses of power might be resisted. The legend subsequently attached to Magna Charta made it a powerful instrument for liberty.

The Growing Specialization of Function

With the passage of time, there was a tendency for judicial or administrative business, which required the continuous attention of some governmental body, to fall to the lot of the *Curia Regis*. As the amount of business increased and the members of the *Curia Regis* became more highly skilled and specialized, such subdivisions as the Courts of Exchequer, Common Pleas, King's Bench, and Chancery, which were the forerunners of the modern court system, split off from it. More purely administrative work was left to the royal household, to such institutions as the Exchequer and the Secretary of State, which developed out of it, and to the main core of the *Curia Regis*.

Somewhat later the *Curia Regis* itself developed into what was known as the Permanent Council; it was within this body that, in the fifteenth century, the Privy Council, a smaller and more efficient body, grew up and eventually assumed the powers of its larger and more unwieldy parent. In turn, a still smaller entity never defined in law, the Cabinet, grew up within the Privy Council in the eighteenth century. Today the Cabinet still formally legitimizes its acts through the Privy Council, although in practice it is the Cabinet that makes executive decisions.

The Rise of Parliament

The *Magnum Concilium* (Great Council) of the Kings of England was a meeting of the great nobles and ecclesiastics of the kingdom, somewhat resembling a modern House of Lords. From time to time, however, and generally for the purpose of winning popular consent to the levying of new taxes, Kings would summon representatives of the lesser gentry, who were too numerous to attend in person. In 1213, King John, in need of money, commanded the presence of four "discreet knights" from each county, and in 1254 (at a time when the Great Council was coming at to be known as Parliament) Henry III, also in need of money, summoned two knights from each county. In 1265, Simon de Montfort, who had led the barons in a temporarily successful revolt against the King, summoned a Parliament to which were invited not only two knights from each shire but two burgesses from each of those boroughs (towns) known to be friendly to his party. And although, with the reestablishment of King Henry's power, this practice was temporarily abandoned, the famous Model Parliament, held in 1295 by Henry's son, Edward I, included burgesses as well as knights, clergy, and barons.

At this time the privilege of attending Parliament was commonly regarded as a mixed blessing. Far from demanding the privilege as a right, people looked upon it with understandable apprehension, both because the journey to Parliament was expensive, uncomfortable, time-consuming, and, on occasion, dangerous, and because those summoned to Parliament were summoned to increase their own taxes. Thus attendance at Parliament was compulsory rather than the result of any demand for the right of representation. The lesser gentry and the burgesses were ordered to attend when they became prosperous enough to attract the attention of a government ever eager for new sources of revenue.

For a time Parliament met in three groups or estates: one for the nobility, one for the clergy, and one for the commoners. The lesser clergy, however, eventually withdrew; the higher clergy (who were themselves great nobles) met with the nobility; and the lesser barons or knights (who often were the younger sons of the nobility) sat with the commons, thereby helping to prevent the growth of a sharp political cleavage between the nobles and the middle classes. By the end of the fourteenth century, the system of two chambers, one for the lords and one for the commons, had taken shape. Moreover, early in the fifteenth century it came to be understood that proposals for grants of money should originate in the House of Commons and then win the approval of the Lords, an arrangement which, by centering the power of the purse in the House of Commons, enormously enhanced its authority.

During this period Parliament also acquired certain legislative powers. Earlier, individual commoners had had the right to present petitions to the King asking for redress of grievances, and eventually the Commons presented such petitions as a body. Successive Kings discovered that it was easier to persuade Parliament to grant new taxes if the petitions were granted first, and laws began to be enacted by the King at the request of the Commons and with the assent of the Lords. However, not until early in the fifteenth century did the laws always coincide with the terms of the petitions. Henry V (1413–22) agreed that nothing should be enacted that changed the substance of the petitions; and during the reign of his successor, Henry VI (1422–61), the formula came into use which is still followed: statutes are made "by the King's most excellent majesty by and with the consent of the Lords Spiritual and Temporal, and Commons, in this present Parliament assembled, and by the authority of the same."

Tudor Absolutism

Much of the fifteenth century was occupied by those struggles between rival factions of the nobility known as the Wars of the Roses. The ultimate victor in this conflict, Henry VII (1485–1509), was the first of the Tudor dynasty, a line of energetic monarchs who gave the country the firm and orderly government it wanted and so enhanced the authority of the King that the period is often referred to as that of "Tudor absolutism." Partly because of the effectiveness of the great nobles in killing one another off, Henry succeeded in concentrating great power

in his own hands. Parliament during his reign was the servant of the King rather than an independent force, and the real center of governmental activity was the Privy Council, a group of advisers chosen by the King and drawn from the middle classes rather than from the great nobility. Under the Tudors, too, greater authority in local government was given to country gentlemen (rather than nobles), who served without pay as justices of the peace and acquired both the political experience and the sense of public service that have been outstanding virtues of the British upper classes.

Although the power of Parliament declined under Henry VII, the struggle between Henry VIII (1509–47) and the Roman Catholic Church increased Parliament's prestige, not because Parliament failed to act as a docile instrument of the King but because the King made so much use of it as an ally in the struggle. Thus the "Reformation Parliament," which sat from 1529 to 1536, acquired a political experience and importance and enjoyed a degree of freedom of speech that set powerful precedents for later times. It was this Parliament that passed the legislation completing the breach with the Church of Rome and making the King the supreme head of the Church of England.

During the dozen years that intervened between the governments of Henry VIII and his daughter Elizabeth I (1558–1603), Edward VI (1547–53), a Protestant, and Mary (1553–58), an ardent Catholic, reigned over a country torn by religious controversy and plagued by bad government. Elizabeth, however, reestablished the Anglican Church of her father, with a ritual resembling that of the Catholic Church but with a creed that was more definitely Protestant than that of the church of Henry VIII. During her reign England came to identify itself with Protestantism in opposition to the Catholicism of its bitter enemy, Spain.

Elizabeth's government, like that of her father and grandfather, was firm and orderly, and it commanded the overwhelming support of public opinion. By this time members of the House of Commons, far from considering their duties a burden, had come to take pride in their growing political influence and to act with greater independence. Toward the end of Elizabeth's reign, the members (particularly those who were

Puritans, that is, belonged to the extreme Protestant wing of the Church of England) increasingly indulged in criticism; it was evident that, although the devotion of the Parliament to the Queen was very great, a tactless successor might find this body a source of serious opposition to his will.

The Limitation of Royal Authority

Elizabeth's successor, James I (1603–25), the first of the Stuart kings, was sufficiently tactless to precipitate precisely such opposition. Already King of Scotland, James I became ruler of the entire British island, although it was not until 1707 that the Act of Union formally united the two countries.[1]

In his native Scotland, James had already found the Calvinistic (Presbyterian) form of Protestantism far too democratic for his tastes; and the rapid growth of Puritanism in England provoked his opposition for similar reasons. His firm belief in the divine right of kings conflicted sharply with Parliament's conception of its own authority. From 1611 to 1621, with the exception of a few weeks in 1614, James actually ruled without any Parliament at all; and, when finally he was obliged to summon a new Parliament, its vigorous criticism led him quickly to dissolve it.

Far from ending with James's death, royal quarrels with Parliament grew more bitter. Charles I (1625–49) dissolved his first two Parliaments in rapid succession and resorted to highly unpopular forced loans in the absence of financial grants from that body. When Parliament was again summoned, in 1628, a Petition of Right (which ranks with Magna Charta as a charter of British freedom) was drawn up, asserting the ancient liberties of the kingdom and denouncing royal abuses of power. Charles was forced to accept this document.

Eventually, however, quarrels between the King and Parliament's Puritan members resulted in the Civil War which lasted from 1642 to 1649. In this struggle, which reflected a social as well as a political and religious cleavage, the majority of the peers, the Anglicans, and the

Catholics supported the King; the majority of the townspeople and the Puritans supported Parliament; and the landlords and country gentry divided themselves between the two parties. In 1649 the defeated King was executed, and in 1653 Oliver Cromwell, who as leader of the victorious parliamentary armies already held effective power, assumed the title of Lord Protector under the only written constitution England has ever had, the Instrument of Government. Yet Cromwell, like his royal predecessor, repeatedly disagreed with and dissolved Parliament, and his death in 1658 led quickly to the restoration of the monarchy with Charles II (1660–85) as King. The Instrument of Government vanished, the Anglican Church was reestablished, and all Nonconformists suffered serious restrictions upon their religious and civil rights.

In appearance Charles accepted the supremacy of Parliament; and although he disagreed with it from time to time and secretly longed for absolute power, controversy was never pushed to the point of endangering the throne. Charles's brother and successor, James II (1685–88), was less discreet. Even before his accession large numbers of "Petitioners" asked that he be barred from the throne because of his adherence to Catholicism, while "Abhorrers" of the petition upheld his right to the succession. Once he had become King, however, James's efforts to restore the Catholic Church enraged both Nonconformists and Anglicans (including many of the Abhorrers), and his quarrels with Parliament precipitated the Glorious Revolution of 1688, which drove him from the throne and transferred the crown to his daughter Mary and her husband William, Prince of Orange.

At the time of their accession, the quarrel between King and Parliament was finally settled. Parliament, in the famous Bill of Rights of 1689, listed the practices that had caused trouble during the previous half-century and forbade their revival in clear and unequivocal language. The legislative authority of Parliament was assured, the King was forbidden to levy any tax or impost without parliamentary consent, the regular convening of Parliament was guaranteed, and certain individual liberties were specifically confirmed. A few years later, in 1701, the authority of Parliament over the Crown was

---

[1] Wales had been added to the Crown by Edward I in 1284, and the fact that the Tudor dynasty was Welsh in origin later helped to reconcile Wales to this union.

established beyond all doubt when the Act of Settlement deliberately changed the order of succession to the throne, passing over the Catholic descendants of James II and providing that James's daughter Anne (1702–14) should be succeeded by the German, but Protestant, House of Hanover. British sovereigns, unlike those in certain Continental states where the official religion was that of the ruler, henceforth had to belong to the established church of their people.

The Rise of the Cabinet

The reigns of the first two Hanoverian Kings, George I (1714–27) and George II (1727–60) marked a further, if less dramatic, decline in the royal power as authority passed into the hands of the Cabinet, a small group of leading ministers who advised the King.

It had long been apparent that the Privy Council was too large and unwieldy a body to conduct public business, and smaller groups had already been used for that purpose. Charles II's famous group of intimate advisers, the Cabal, provided a precedent of sorts for the later development of an inner circle of ministers who consulted with the King and attempted to guide legislation through Parliament. However, so long as the Stuart monarchs remained on the throne, they maintained their right to choose their own ministers and to change them at will. The distinction between the legislature—Parliament—and the executive—the King and the ministers of his choice—was quite plain. During the reigns of William and Mary and of Anne, however, the distinction became less plain. Both William and Anne continued to choose their Cabinet ministers and to meet with them regularly, but it was obvious that their relations with Parliament were better when the Cabinet had the confidence of Parliament. Anne in particular disliked the idea of choosing her ministers from a single political party, but William experimented with such a ministry, and Anne herself eventually accepted one. Thus began the practice of choosing ministers who shared the same general views—and the views of the majority of the members of Parliament. There was no change in the law, but the dependence of the ministry upon the King less-

ened; at the same time, its dependence upon Parliament increased.

The first two Georges took a greater interest in Hanoverian affairs than in British. Far from trying to expand the royal prerogative, they let slip some of the powers that William and Anne had been careful to maintain. And since they had trouble understanding both the English language and English politics, they gave up the practice of presiding over meetings of Cabinet ministers.

From 1721 to 1742, both Cabinet and Parliament accepted the leadership of Sir Robert Walpole, who was First Lord of the Treasury and Chancellor of the Exchequer and who was in fact the first British "Prime Minister," a title that did not come into general use until much later.[2] When, in 1742, Walpole lost the support of the House of Commons, it was natural for him to resign his office, an act which implied that the survival of a ministry depended not upon the favor of the King but upon the acquiescence of Parliament. By the time George III (1760–1820) succeeded to the throne, the precedent of a strong Cabinet and Parliament and a weak King was well established, although not until the nineteenth century was the operation of Cabinet government clearly understood. George III himself did try, with some success, to recover the lost ground; but growing opposition in Parliament (as indicated by its famous resolution of 1780 that "the influence of the Crown has increased, is increasing, and ought to be diminished") and the insanity of the King during the last decades of his reign prevented the ultimate success of the effort.

The Rise of Parties and of Democracy

The growth of political parties in England was as gradual and unintentional as other changes in the government, but no change was of greater importance. Before the seventeenth century rival groups of nobles might contend for power, as in the Wars of the Roses, and there were adherents of different religious principles, but there were no political parties in the modern sense. The division in the Civil War, however, between the aristocratic, Anglican

---

[2] This title was first used officially in the Treaty of Berlin, 1878, but not in a statute until 1917.

Cavaliers who fought for King Charles and the middle-class, Puritan Roundheads who supported Parliament reflected a difference in religious and political principles as well as economic interests that prepared the way for future party alignments. With the Restoration of Charles II there appeared a clearer difference between the greater part of the land-owning gentry (the Tory squires), who upheld the authority of the King and the Anglican Church, and the alliance of powerful Whig nobles with the Nonconformists and the mercantile classes— a difference paralleling that between Abhorrers and Petitioners. When James II opened his attack on the Anglican Church, however, the Tories were torn between loyalty to the King and loyalty to the Church; some joined the Whigs in inviting William and Mary to take power, while others remained unreconciled to the change. Thus the Glorious Revolution, for a time, had the curious effect of making Whigs rather than Tories the chief support of the monarch, although William attempted, not always successfully, to draw his advisers from both parties. And for the first time the warring factions became political parties in the sense that each recognized the right of the other to exist and accepted the transfer of power from one group to the other without any attempt to destroy the opposing party by force.

With the accession of the Hanoverian monarchs, the Whigs (whose support of the Hanoverians against the Stuarts was wholehearted) entered upon almost fifty years of uninterrupted power. Later, George III, by the liberal use of patronage, succeeded in building a new Tory party of King's Friends. But their disastrous conduct of the war with the American colonies strengthened the Whig opposition, and in 1782 the King was obliged to accept a Whig ministry. The Tories came into power again in 1783, under the leadership of William Pitt the younger; but the King never recovered his personal authority. The issues raised by the outbreak of the French Revolution in 1789 caused a split in the Whig party, many of whose members, under the leadership of Edmund Burke, aligned themselves with the Tories; the result was that except for a short interruption in 1806, Tories remained in control of the government from 1783 until 1830.

Reform of the Suffrage

The Glorious Revolution had clearly established the principle of the supremacy of the House of Commons, but this House was far from being a democratic body. Property qualifications fixed in the fifteenth century still determined the vote in many areas, while the failure to redistribute seats in accordance with movements of population resulted in the growth of "rotten boroughs" (which had lost most of their population but retained their original representation) and "pocket boroughs" (which were under the control of landed proprietors who frequently sold the right to represent the borough in Parliament). Thus, in the Scottish constituency of Bute, only one of the 14,000 inhabitants had the right to vote, and he was therefore in a position to elect himself unanimously to Parliament. The constituency of Old Sarum had no residents at all, and Dunwich had sunk beneath the sea, but each was still represented in Parliament. In contrast, large towns grew up that had no representation.[3] Elections were notoriously corrupt, and the price of seats in Parliament was openly quoted. Many seats were controlled by members of the House of Lords, who appointed members to speak and vote in accordance with their instructions, and George III demonstrated that the King himself could play at the game.

For a long time there had been a demand for reform. John Locke at the time of the Glorious Revolution had denounced the abuses of the system of representation; and John Wilkes in 1776 had moved in the House of Commons "that leave be given to bring in a bill for a just and equal Representation of the People of England in Parliament." As the industrial revolution created a large class of well-to-do businessmen who were eager for a greater share of political power, agitation for reform increased. Yet the traditional ruling class clung tenaciously to power; resistance was bitter, and it was not until a Whig government came into office, late in 1830, that popular agitation met with a favorable parliamentary response. Even then it was necessary to dissolve the House of Commons and hold

---

[3] When Americans, in the years before their Revolution, complained of "taxation without representation," it was pointed out that English communities too were taxed without having any parliamentary representation.

a new election before a safe majority could be found for the bill reforming Parliament. The House of Lords continued its resistance until the King threatened to appoint enough new peers to assure a majority for the bill.

The Great Reform Act of 1832 marks the beginning of modern British democracy. It did not increase the electorate drastically (about half a million men, mostly drawn from the upper half of the middle class, gained the right to vote), but it did away with the worst inequalities of the old system, eliminating most of the rotten and pocket boroughs, consolidating or lowering the representation of the smaller communities, and giving new or increased representation to the large ones. What was most important, however, was the establishment of the constitutional principle that representation must approximate population.

In 1867 the electorate was almost doubled by extending the vote to about a million new voters, especially in the towns, and there was a further redistribution of seats. In 1884 the vote was extended in rural areas as well. In 1918 the vote was finally given to all male citizens of twenty-one and over and, with important qualifications, to women of thirty and over. In 1928 the suffrage was extended to women on the same basis as men. Thus the British achieved universal adult suffrage.

Change in Party Character

So drastic an increase in the number of voters inevitably had far-reaching effects upon the political system. During the first part of the nineteenth century both parties had drawn their support from the same well-to-do classes, and it was not at all unusual for leaders of the two parties to be intimately related through family and social ties. Even in policy, lines tended to be blurred. The Whigs were somewhat more willing to accept electoral reform and were opposed to high tariffs; but many Tories were in agreement with them, and in 1867 they "dished the Whigs" by themselves introducing the legislation that extended the right to vote. In fact, the Tories (who were, at this time, identified with the land-owning rather than the manufacturing element) were somewhat more willing than the Whigs to support measures of social reform, such as the protection of women and children in industry.

As the suffrage was extended under popular pressure, like that of the Chartist movement, the Liberal party (as the Whigs came to be called) grew to include several not altogether compatible elements: the old and conservative Whig aristocracy; the new and wealthy industrialists, who were opposed to high tariffs and any government interference with industry; the Nonconformist middle classes; and the majority of those workers who had the right to vote. The Tories, who now took the name Conservatives, also won the support of some of the urban middle and working classes, but the backbone of their strength was in the rural areas where the local squire and the Anglican parson exercised decisive political influence.

In the second half of the nineteenth century, and particularly in the years following the extension of suffrage in 1867, two exceptionally able and popular leaders, Disraeli and Gladstone, came to symbolize in their own persons the spirit of the Conservative and Liberal parties. With the increase in voters, party organization became more important for success in elections. And as voters increasingly chose their representatives in terms of party leaders and principles, the electorate began to replace Parliament as the real source of Cabinet powers.

The extension of the suffrage also encouraged a change in the class character of the parties. The old nobility, almost without exception, now passed over from the Liberals to the Conservatives, while the uneasy combination of workers and industrialists in the Liberal party encouraged, at the opening of the twentieth century, the formation of the Labor party, whose primary appeal was to the working classes. By the end of World War I, the Labor party exceeded the Liberal party in size; and although, during the 1920's, there were times when none of the three parties could win a parliamentary majority, the Liberals increasingly lost members at both ends, as the wealthy industrialists and merchants, no longer so distrustful of a high tariff and increasingly fearful of socialism, joined forces with the Conservatives, and as the working class came to regard the Labor party as the most effective advocate of its interests.

Reform of the House of Lords

The successive extensions of the franchise also brought a fundamental change in the position of the House of Lords. So long as the House of Commons remained unreformed, the influence of the Lords was very great, and it was not unusual for the majority of the members of the Cabinet, including the Prime Minister himself, to be members of that chamber. But as the right to vote was widened, so grew the prestige of the House of Commons as the spokesman of the electorate. Leadership in the Cabinet came to rest with men who could win elections and who were likely to be members of the House of Commons. Moreover, the opposition of the Lords to many of the political, social, and economic reforms accepted by the House of Commons led to increasing irritation; and when, in 1909, a struggle broke out over the Lords' financial powers, the way was prepared for the Parliament Act of 1911, which enabled the House of Commons, by complying with fairly rigorous conditions, to pass even nonfinancial legislation over the Lords' veto.

Thus, through a series of changes that were often inconspicuous and occasionally accidental, the British government developed from a highly centralized monarchy into one of the most advanced democracies in the world.

2. THE BRITISH CONSTITUTION

Form and Fact

The gradualness of this evolution, and the British habit of retaining traditional forms despite radical changes in the position of power, produced two characteristics of the British constitution that confuse most Americans: there is no single place in which the constitution as a whole is clearly and definitely written down, and those provisions of the constitution that do exist in writing often differ markedly from actual constitutional practice. A foreigner who reads the American Constitution will be misled about certain political practices (he will find, for example, no mention of judicial review, the Cabinet, or political parties, and the electoral college will seem much more important than in

fact it is), but in general he will find a not too inaccurate outline of the structure of the American government. In Great Britain, however, the form and the fact of the constitution sometimes seem to have very little to do with each other. Walter Bagehot could write, for example, in the introduction to the 1872 edition of his classic book *The English Constitution,* that Queen Victoria possessed the constitutional power to:

> . . . disband the army . . . ; she could dismiss all the officers, from the General Commander-in-Chief downwards; she could dismiss all the sailors too; she could sell off all our ships of war and all our naval stores; she could make a peace by the sacrifice of Cornwall, and begin a war for the conquest of Brittany. She could make every citizen in the United Kingdom, male or female, a peer; she could make every parish in the United Kingdom a "university"; she could dismiss most of the civil servants; she could pardon all offenders.

Yet any ruler who used his constitutional powers in this way, contrary to the advice of his Prime Minister and Cabinet, would find the entire country denouncing him for the unconstitutionality of his action. Nor is the confusion lessened by the fact that no law provides either for a Prime Minister or for a Cabinet. The fact is that, unlike the American, the British constitution is not a definable body of fundamental and mostly written rules. Rather, it is, as a parliamentarian has said, "a blend of formal law, precedent, and tradition." It is similar to the American Constitution, however, in that it consists of the rules that affect the working of governmental institutions. These rules are found in part in statutes but can be fully understood only through an examination of the institutions and procedures to be described in the following chapters.

Constitutional Sources

Great Documents

Among the sources from which the constitution is drawn are, in the first place, certain great charters, petitions, and statutes such as Magna Charta, the Petition of Right, the Bill of Rights, the Act of Settlement, the Reform Act of 1832, and the Parliament Act of 1911.

Most of these were acts passed by Parliament, but a document such as Magna Charta is considered to be part of the constitution simply because it represents a great landmark in national history, much as though Americans considered the Declaration of Independence and the Emancipation Proclamation to be part of their Constitution—as, indeed, they are part of the living tradition of American government.

The distinguishing thing about most of these charters and statutes is that they were the products of constitutional crisis and that they contain the terms of settlement of those crises. In the life of any great country certain issues arise that, like the controversy over slavery in the United States, cut to the foundations of the political system. In Britain, once such an issue has been definitely settled, either by the victory of one party or by a definitive compromise, the British consider that settlement part of their constitution. In spirit this practice is not unlike the addition of the Thirteenth, Fourteenth, and Fifteenth Amendments to the American Constitution at the end of the Civil War. But in Great Britain, since there is no written constitution to amend, the settlement generally takes the form of a law that looks like any other law passed by Parliament. What makes it a part of the constitution is the context of constitutional struggle within which it originated, as in the case of the great Reform Act of 1832 or the Parliament Act of 1911, and the fact that it shapes the character of some part of the governmental machinery.

Important Statutes

In addition to these more spectacular charters and statutes, there are certain other statutes that are significant, not because they mark the conclusion of a great constitutional struggle, but because they deal with subjects of such intrinsic importance as to place them automatically in a category above ordinary law. Into this category, for example, fall the laws extending the right to vote that were passed between 1867 and 1944 (when the local franchise was placed on the same basis as the national).

None of these laws aroused the excitement that characterized the Reform Act of 1832, but each of them, in its turn, was so important a step in the development of political democracy that any attempt to repeal them would now be regarded as an unthinkable attack upon the basic constitutional principle of universal suffrage. Yet, whereas in America the granting of the suffrage to women was embodied in a formal amendment to the Constitution, all these electoral reforms in Great Britain took the form of ordinary laws.

Judicial Decisions

A third important source of constitutional principles is to be found in court decisions. In interpreting the provisions of the charters and statutes that are part of the British constitution, judges have, to some extent, defined and developed its meaning much as the Supreme Court has clarified and expanded the provisions of the American Constitution. Even more significant, however, is the fact that some of the most important principles of the British constitution are principles of the common law—that is, principles not established by any law passed by Parliament or ordained by the King, but rather established in the courts through the use of decisions in individual cases as precedents for decisions in later cases. The first decisions often were based on common customs or usages; as these decisions "broadened down from precedent to precedent," there grew up a body of principles of general application that stands as a bulwark of British freedom and an essential part of the constitution. In particular, the civil liberties that in the United States are embodied in the Bill of Rights stem, in Great Britain, both from the good sense of the authorities in not enforcing the laws too strictly and from the contribution of the common law.

Today, according to the common law, the British subject has full freedom to say or write anything he pleases so long as it is not slanderous, libelous, seditious, obscene, or blasphemous; and public meetings may be disbanded only if the assembly becomes riotous or seems likely to commit a breach of the peace or a crime of violence. For the most part, such limitations do not constitute a serious interference with political liberty. *Blasphemy* and *obscenity* have little application to politics, and considerable latitude is given to strong political language before *libel* or *slander* can be invoked. *Sedition,* however, has at times received an unpleasantly broad and vague application, and the leeway that the police enjoy in determining what is a "breach of the peace" occasionally has aroused considerable concern. The subject is protected against serious abuse of authority, however, by his right to trial by jury and by the writ of habeas corpus (which prevents a person from being held in prison without trial). Both of these developed in the courts of the common law.

The Conventions of the British Constitution

Fourth, and most difficult for Americans to understand, is that part of the British constitution that depends on custom or convention. These conventions ordinarily are not embodied in written laws and thus are not enforceable in the courts. Moreover, since they constantly grow and change and adapt themselves to new circumstances, it is difficult to say at any moment exactly what they are. As our study of the growth of Parliament and the Cabinet has shown, such conventions usually originate in practices that are followed for the sake of convenience. But if such practices are followed for a long enough time, the person who departs from them will be denounced for the "unconstitutionality" of his action.

One of the accepted conventions of the unwritten constitution is that if a government resigns, the monarch shall ask the leader of the opposition to form a new government. Another (as the Preamble to the Statute of Westminster, 1931, declares) is that a law affecting the succession to the throne or the royal title shall require the assent of the Parliaments of the overseas members of the Commonwealth as well as of the United Kingdom. Although there is no recourse to law if these conventions are disregarded, such an action would be a profound shock to the public. Similarly, if a minister publicly disagreed with governmental policy and yet refused to resign his portfolio, or if the monarch refused to dissolve the House of Commons on the request of the Prime Minister or refused to sign a particular law, there would be a popular reaction at least as strong as that which greeted President Roosevelt's plan to modify the composition of the Supreme Court. So inevitable is this consequence, and so pervasive is the loyalty to constitutional practices, that such a course of action seems unthinkable. In this sense, the protection of the constitu-

tion is in the hearts and minds of the people.

There are, however, more practical sanctions. The conventions of the constitution usually exist because they serve a real purpose. To violate them is often to make the government itself unworkable. If, for example, the Queen began to act independently of the Cabinet, the Cabinet itself would resign, and the House of Commons would undoubtedly refuse to give its support to any new Cabinet—if, indeed, any members could be found to join such a Cabinet. The British government works only if the Cabinet and the House of Commons are in accord and if the Queen follows the advice of the Cabinet. To depart from these rules in any important respect is to interfere with the whole machinery of government.

If a convention of the constitution is violated, it can, of course, be enacted into law. For example, it was long assumed that, through lack of use, the House of Lords had lost its power to reject any financial measure passed by the House of Commons. In 1909, however, the House of Lords rejected the famous Lloyd George budget that threatened the economic interests of many of the peers by placing heavy taxes on land. The Liberal party, which controlled the House of Commons at this time, denounced the Lords' action as a breach of the constitution and succeeded, after a bitter struggle, in winning the passage of the Parliament Act of 1911. This act made it impossible for the Lords to delay money bills for more than one month. In this way, the written law restored a violated constitutional convention.

Such developments should not be difficult for Americans to understand. In the United States few constitutional practices are more important than the action of the Supreme Court in holding acts of Congress unconstitutional when they conflict with the Court's interpretation of the Constitution. Yet one may read the American Constitution through without finding any statement granting this power to the Court. Nonetheless, it has by now become so established a part of the American form of government that only the most extreme reactionaries would think of challenging it. The practice has become part of the living constitution if not of the written one. Similarly, it was once maintained that the custom of having no President serve for more than two consecutive terms had become an unbreakable precedent. In 1940, in fact, when President Roosevelt ran for a third term, his opponent, Wendell Willkie, actually charged that he was acting unconstitutionally—thereby using the word in its British rather than its American sense. The subsequent Twenty-second Amendment to the American Constitution, which limits the President to two terms, indicated that the convention was more firmly rooted than it at first seemed to be.

Sometimes a practice may be a matter of usage rather than of convention. We have seen that during the greater part of the nineteenth century the Prime Minister was at least as likely to be a member of the House of Lords as of the House of Commons. However, as the House of Commons gained prestige with the extension of the right to vote and with the curtailment of the power of the House of Lords, it became increasingly inconvenient to have the chief spokesman of the Cabinet in the House of Lords when the Cabinet's fate was being decided in the House of Commons. From 1902 on, Prime Ministers were regularly chosen from the House of Commons, and people wondered whether this practice would become part of the constitution. In 1923 what may well be the decisive precedent was established when the King, in appointing a new Prime Minister, passed over the most prominent Conservative, Lord Curzon, and appointed Mr. Stanley Baldwin.[4]

Later it was suggested that the same development was taking place in connection with the important post of Foreign Secretary. Here, too, there was a disadvantage in having a subordinate official explain and defend foreign policy in the House of Commons; the precedent seemed to be building up that only a member of the House of Commons might hold the post. In this case, the expectation proved premature, for Prime Minister Chamberlain appointed Lord Halifax to the position, and in 1960, despite protests, Prime Minister Macmillan chose Lord Home as Foreign Secretary.

[4] The fact that Mr. Baldwin was more acceptable to the rank and file of his party than Lord Curzon and the lack of representation of the Labor party—the official opposition—in the House of Lords may well have been the decisive reasons for the action; popular belief in the official interpretation, however, soundly established the precedent.

Because British government, like American, is party government—that is, carried on by whatever organized group has received majority support at the polls—it has been increasingly felt that the election returns should not only designate which party shall assume the responsibilities of governing but should also control, both negatively and positively, the program that it undertakes while in office. This view has given rise to what is called the "mandate convention," which assumes that the government should institute radical changes only if the electorate has passed on them at a general election. This view was a matter of considerable controversy after the Labor party's victory at the polls in 1945. It was noticeable, however, that the Conservative majority in the House of Lords, in the years immediately following 1945, approved bills instituting such measures as nationalization, with which it was out of sympathy, on the ground that Labor had received a mandate from the electorate. Moreover, when the Labor government decided in 1947 to reduce the length of time that Lords could hold up legislation, its action was bitterly attacked as a violation of the mandate convention, since this measure altered the balance of power between Lords and Commons and had not been submitted to the electorate. Further controversy raged over the Labor government's decision to make effective the nationalization of steel in 1950 despite its slim majority of seats in Parliament and its failure to win an absolute majority of votes in the February 1950 election. The Conservatives, after assuming office in October 1951, rescinded the nationalization, although they in turn could hardly claim a definite mandate for doing so. Thus it is clear that the mandate convention is not yet finally established. The very frequency of the references to it, however, indicates a growing tendency in the British constitution toward establishing some voters' control over major governmental decisions.

Constitutional Principles

We can now sum up the most important principles of the constitution.

The first of these is the *fusion of powers,* which means that the monarch must always take the advice of the Cabinet, and the Cabinet

the willingness of the Supreme Court
...r a broad interpretation of constitutional
...g rather than upon a deliberate decision
...electorate to change these words. Here,
...here is something to be said for a method
...ange whereby amendments may be made
...straightforward manner in time to meet
...ssential needs of a changing society, yet not
...l after much thought and discussion of their
...plications.

...n any event, the ultimate defense of any con-
...tution, whether written or unwritten, whether
...quipped with elaborate defense mechanisms or
...ith none at all, must lie in the devotion of its
...people. In this spirit of loyalty to their consti-
...tution, it would be rash to say that Britons in
...any measure yield to Americans.

H POLITICAL IDEAS

...rstand the attitudes of a people as
...e political programs of particular
...ecessary to know the political ideas
...med their allegiance, for nowhere
...ue than in politics that ideas are
...erunners and the outcome of action.
...se of the past hundred years, three
...nts of ideas have competed for the
...legiance of British citizens. In the
...the nineteenth century the principal
...were conservatism and liberalism.
...Tod...ey are conservatism and socialism. But
...lthough liberalism has declined as an independ-
...t force, its successful rivals have absorbed a
...gnificant portion of its content. As a result, it
...impossible to understand contemporary poli-
...in Great Britain without some familiarity
...h all three currents of thought.

sh Conservatism

...Great Britain, as in every other country,
...tural tendency of conservatives is to like
...onal institutions and political principles
...regard any far-reaching innovation with
...n, if not distaste. Established institutions,
...ink, rest upon the safest of all founda-
...at of experience. To desert them is to
...oneself to the uncharted seas of theoriz-
...speculation. Although change may be

necessary at certain times, it is not a good thing
in itself: thus it should be carried out in such a
way as to preserve as many as possible of the inherited institutions.

There are certain differences between British
and American conservatives, however, which
result from differences in the institutions they
have inherited. Where American conservatives
are devoted to a constitutional system that
places strong restraints upon the government,
British Conservatives trace their descent from
the Tory party, which stood for the authority of
the Crown against parliamentary limitation.
Although British Conservatives have long since
come to accept the supremacy of Parliament, the
fact that for so many generations the upper
classes controlled Parliament encouraged a
greater willingness to uphold the authority of
the state than seems natural to American conservatives.

The Influence of Burke

Somewhat paradoxically, the man who has
had the greatest influence on Conservative
thought, Edmund Burke (1729–97), considered himself a Whig. He defended the rights
of the American colonists at the time of the
Revolution, and he was devoted to the principles of the Glorious Revolution of 1688. To
Burke, however, these revolutions had been
fought in defense of the ancient constitution and
the inherited rights of Englishmen. The French
Revolution of 1789 seemed to him to have an
entirely different character. Its leaders frankly
proclaimed their intention of destroying or
remolding such ancient institutions as the
monarchy, the aristocracy, and the established
church; they proclaimed their belief in the
power of enlightened and reasonable human
beings to create new institutions and to remedy
ancient injustices. To Burke, the ancient institutions represented the accumulated wisdom of
the ages, and human reason seemed but a weak
and fallible guide in comparison with the lessons of tradition and experience. If new circumstances required changes in the inherited constitution, Burke wanted them to be made within
the spirit of that constitution and with as little
modification as possible of its inherited form.

Burke was appalled, therefore, when certain
Englishmen (like Dr. Price, an eminent Non-

must always have the support of the House of
Commons. According to this principle there can
never be, in Great Britain, the kind of prolonged disagreement between the executive and
the legislature that has occurred so often in the
United States. In the latter, it is not at all unusual for the President to veto legislation passed
by Congress or for Congress to refuse to pass
legislation recommended by the President.
There are times when the President belongs to
one party and the majority of congressmen to
the other.

In Great Britain, such disagreements are impossible. Before the days of disciplined parties,
it might have been a debatable point whether
Parliament controlled the Prime Minister and
Cabinet, or whether the Prime Minister and
Cabinet controlled Parliament. No one contested, however, the principle that they must
work in agreement. Today there is no chance
that the House of Commons would vote against
an important measure sponsored by the Cabinet
or pass a bill opposed by the Cabinet. Thus, in
sharp contrast to the United States, the executive and the legislature in Great Britain never
follow conflicting policies.

It is easy to misunderstand the nature of this
fusion of powers. Even Bagehot believed it
meant that the Cabinet is merely a committee
of the working majority of the House of Commons. On the contrary, although there is no
formal separation of executive and legislative
powers in the British parliamentary system corresponding to the somewhat artificial division
in the American system, there is a very real distinction between the Cabinet and Parliament. In
fact, the key to the British system of government is the continuously maintained balance between the Cabinet's executive and legislative initiative and the consideration of legislation and
ultimate control of it by Parliament. The Cabinet, or "government," makes appointments,
summons Parliament, initiates and organizes
the legislative program, decides on dissolutions,
all without consulting Parliament. In so doing,
it uses the inherent power of the Crown (which
it represents), a power vast in extent and still
not wholly defined in scope. Through this
power, and the strength resulting from a well-
disciplined party, the Cabinet provides positive
and effective direction of affairs. The function

of Parliament is not to weaken or supersede
this leadership but to make sure that there is
full consideration of all the issues introduced
by the government before it gives them its
consent.

A second and closely related principle is the
supremacy of Parliament. Supreme legal power
in Great Britain is exercised by Parliament (the
House of Commons, the House of Lords, and
the sovereign), which according to the old saying can do everything but make a woman a man
and a man a woman. In contrast to American
practice, there is no judicial review in the sense
of testing the constitutional validity of laws, and
there is no complicated process of constitutional
amendment. The veto power of the titular executive has lapsed through nonuse, and the King
will accept any measure passed by the two
houses of Parliament. No court would dare to
hold an act of Parliament unconstitutional, and,
theoretically, Parliament itself can change the
constitution at any time simply by passing an
ordinary law. Thus, it is sometimes pointed out
that Parliament could, quite legally, extend its
own term of office forever, depose the King
(who would have to sign the warrant), turn
England into a republic, make Buddhism the
established religion, or restrict the right to vote
to women of seventy and over.

Yet merely to say this is to point to the absurdity of the idea. Parliamentary supremacy is
exercised in the spirit of responsibility, and responsibility is to the nation as a whole, not just
to the majority in Parliament. There is a strong
sense of "the rules of the game." Profound psychological checks and voluntary self-restraints
come into operation when substantial changes
in the constitution are under consideration. Devices such as all-party conferences and royal
commissions, which will be considered in Chapter 4, can be used to secure agreement prior to
legislative action. Thus, although Parliament is
legally supreme, the key to its actions lies in
responsible self-restraint.

Theoretically there is a major difference between the American concept that legal authority
vests ultimately in the citizens, who confer it
temporarily on the President and on Congress,
and the British concept that legal authority inheres in Parliament and in the Crown (whose
authority is now exercised by the Cabinet). Ac-

cording to the British concept the British Parliament and Cabinet are two coequal, interrelated elements, each possessing and exercising an independent authority, not, as in the United States, an authority merely delegated by the voters.

But the distinction should not be pushed too far. Although *legal authority* rests in the Cabinet (using the authority of the Crown) and in Parliament, *political power* resides in the British people as it does in the American people through their right to vote for the representatives and government of their choice. Perhaps the greatest practical importance of the distinction regarding the ultimate seat of legal authority in the two countries, therefore, is in the attitude of the elected representatives: in the United States, members of Congress are likely to look on themselves as delegates from their constituencies; thus only the President represents the whole country. In Great Britain, on the other hand, members of Parliament, particularly the ministers, accept a primary loyalty to the House of Commons as an organ that must act on behalf of the country as a whole.

A third important principle is the distinction between the King as a person and *the Crown as an institution*. Regardless of the personal qualities of the individual, the institution of monarchy is the object of tremendous reverence, both because of its antiquity and because of the ceremony and pageantry of which it is the focus. Whatever changes may take place behind the governmental façade, the Crown continues to symbolize the stability and durability of British institutions and to command the loyalty and devotion of the British people.

In form, the powers of the Crown are very great. Every action of the government is carried out in its name. It is the Crown that makes appointments and assents to laws, that makes treaties and commands the armed forces. The not wholly defined prerogative powers inhering in the Crown can be used during emergencies. Moreover, as noted, *legally* the ministers derive their authority from the Crown and in this sense are responsible to it. But to say that the Crown has these powers and position is very different from saying that the monarch can make use of them independently. On the contrary, the ruler may exercise these powers only on the advice of his ministers, who, of course, are responsible *politically* to Parliament and the electorate. Except under the most unusual circumstances, the monarch may take no independent action of political importance. As Edward VIII discovered, the monarch may not even marry according to his choice against the advice of his Prime Minister. In short, the powers of the Crown are always used as the Cabinet, supported by Parliament, wants them to be used.

Finally, one of the fundamental principles of the constitution is the *rule of law,* according to which the government and its agents, as well as individual citizens, are subject to laws that are definite and known in advance and that can be modified only by act of Parliament. Thus, no citizen may be punished unless he has been found guilty of violating the law in a trial before a regular court whose procedure safeguards him against arbitrary conviction. Similarly, the courts will protect the citizen against government officials who interfere with his rights contrary to law. Thus both government officials and private citizens are equally subject to one body of law. and one system of courts.

As in the United States, the courts are the primary protectors in Great Britain of what we call "civil liberties": freedom of speech, freedom of association, freedom of assembly, and freedom from arrest and imprisonment "except," as Magna Charta stated it, "by judgment of his peers or by the law of the land." Historically, the common-law courts have been vigilant to stop the government from exercising arbitrary power. As noted, the courts devised the writ of habeas corpus centuries before Parliament passed the Habeas Corpus Act in 1679. They continue to ensure that executive authorities do not exceed the powers entrusted to them and do not deviate from the strict procedures under which they should act. On the tense issue of seditious conspiracy, the courts, through a long series of decisions, have established a balance between order and liberty: no one may use violence to change the laws or the constitution. Short of such action, however, almost any method of agitation may be used in the effort to change laws, policies, or institutions. Thus the King's Peace is preserved, but the popular will has ample channels for expression.

Civil liberties might be infringed, however, by statute or by administrative regulations that are still inside the law. The Home Secretary and Parliament itself are vigilant in scrutinizing laws, delegated legislation, and local bylaws in order to guard against such encroachments. In the words of one Home Secretary, laws should be passed "to promote liberty and not to restrict liberty." Such a view once led to the disallowance of a London bylaw forbidding roller-skating on the pavement!

But most important of all, perhaps, is the attitude of ordinary citizens, and of the police, toward civil liberties. Anyone who has listened to the explosive utterances of orators at Hyde Park Corner and watched their orderly audiences realizes the value of such safety valves. The story of the London bobby listening to a particularly inflammatory speech and finally drawling, "All those who are going to burn down Buckingham Palace make a line on this side," is not untypical. In such an atmosphere, civil liberties are not in danger, despite any absence of written guarantee.

The Value of the Constitution

Admirable as are the principles of the British constitution, however, Americans may be troubled by a number of questions that are variations on a single theme: with a constitution which is, in part, so vague and which can be changed so easily, either through the imperceptible development of custom or by the passage of an ordinary act of Parliament, how can anyone be sure that constitutional principles really will be maintained in times of special stress? In the United States the Constitution can be formally amended only by a long and complicated process, and Americans occasionally question the usefulness of the much-heralded rule of law if Parliament can change that law at any time.

As already pointed out, however, Parliament does not change the law lightly or without careful consideration. There is, in fact, a very real restraint upon its authority, although a different kind of restraint from that to which Americans are accustomed. The first defense of the constitution lies in the force of tradition and public opinion rather than in a court or a difficult process of amendment. The members of Parliament,

like most Englishme[...]
to believe in discussio[...]
viduals and minorities, [...]
serve the essential charact[...]
it would hardly occur to th[...]
assume the fantastic, they [...]
stitution, the revulsion of pu[...]
be so great as to destroy them[...]
that the same forces act in defen[...]
can Constitution, but in the Unit[...]
is more of an inclination to leave [...]
the Supreme Court. Yet there is som[...]
said for a system which makes it cl[...]
maintenance of the constitution is th[...]
bility of the people themselves.

In any case, it would be hard to pr[...]
liberty is any less secure in Great Britain [...]
the United States. If the Supreme Court [...]
United States has an excellent record[...]
protection of civil liberties, there have [...]
when, by its own confession, it has laps[...]
over, it takes a long time and a goo[...]
money to carry a case to the Supreme [...]
by the time a decision is rendered it [...]
late to remedy the damage. Hun[...]
who are the most likely to be opp[...]
not even be able to raise the necessa[...]

One advantage of a written consti[...]
sometimes said, is the greater ease w[...]
the ordinary citizen may detect an in[...]
its provisions. The lines are more [...]
drawn; it is not so hard to tell when[...]
steps over the boundary of constituti[...]
hibition; and there is a tangible [...]
around which public opinion can ra[...]
fact many issues touching civil righ[...]
from clear until after the judges h[...]
them.

Another claim is as debatable [...]
process of amendment, in the ca[...]
can Constitution, may give the[...]
warning about a contemp[...]
greater opportunity to thin[...]
and even a margin of time[...]
their minds and recover fr[...]
But the very difficulty [...]
process constitute an i[...]
tion. It is so hard to [...]
versial amendment a[...]
flexibility—particular[...]
government's econo[...]

pend o[...] to rend[...] wordi[...] of the[...] too, [...] of ch[...] in a[...] the[...] unt[...] im[...]

Brit

In the n[...] traditi[...] and to[...] suspici[...] they th[...] tions: t[...] abandon[...] ing and[...]

must always have the support of the House of Commons. According to this principle there can never be, in Great Britain, the kind of prolonged disagreement between the executive and the legislature that has occurred so often in the United States. In the latter, it is not at all unusual for the President to veto legislation passed by Congress or for Congress to refuse to pass legislation recommended by the President. There are times when the President belongs to one party and the majority of congressmen to the other.

In Great Britain, such disagreements are impossible. Before the days of disciplined parties, it might have been a debatable point whether Parliament controlled the Prime Minister and Cabinet, or whether the Prime Minister and Cabinet controlled Parliament. No one contested, however, the principle that they must work in agreement. Today there is no chance that the House of Commons would vote against an important measure sponsored by the Cabinet or pass a bill opposed by the Cabinet. Thus, in sharp contrast to the United States, the executive and the legislature in Great Britain never follow conflicting policies.

It is easy to misunderstand the nature of this fusion of powers. Even Bagehot believed it meant that the Cabinet is merely a committee of the working majority of the House of Commons. On the contrary, although there is no formal separation of executive and legislative powers in the British parliamentary system corresponding to the somewhat artificial division in the American system, there is a very real distinction between the Cabinet and Parliament. In fact, the key to the British system of government is the continuously maintained balance between the Cabinet's executive and legislative initiative and the consideration of legislation and ultimate control of it by Parliament. The Cabinet, or "government," makes appointments, summons Parliament, initiates and organizes the legislative program, decides on dissolutions, all without consulting Parliament. In so doing, it uses the inherent power of the Crown (which it represents), a power vast in extent and still not wholly defined in scope. Through this power, and the strength resulting from a well-disciplined party, the Cabinet provides positive and effective direction of affairs. The function

of Parliament is not to weaken or supersede this leadership but to make sure that there is full consideration of all the issues introduced by the government before it gives them its consent.

A second and closely related principle is the *supremacy of Parliament.* Supreme legal power in Great Britain is exercised by Parliament (the House of Commons, the House of Lords, and the sovereign), which according to the old saying can do everything but make a woman a man and a man a woman. In contrast to American practice, there is no judicial review in the sense of testing the constitutional validity of laws, and there is no complicated process of constitutional amendment. The veto power of the titular executive has lapsed through nonuse, and the King will accept any measure passed by the two houses of Parliament. No court would dare to hold an act of Parliament unconstitutional, and, theoretically, Parliament itself can change the constitution at any time simply by passing an ordinary law. Thus, it is sometimes pointed out that Parliament could, quite legally, extend its own term of office forever, depose the King (who would have to sign the warrant), turn England into a republic, make Buddhism the established religion, or restrict the right to vote to women of seventy and over.

Yet merely to say this is to point to the absurdity of the idea. Parliamentary supremacy is exercised in the spirit of responsibility, and responsibility is to the nation as a whole, not just to the majority in Parliament. There is a strong sense of "the rules of the game." Profound psychological checks and voluntary self-restraints come into operation when substantial changes in the constitution are under consideration. Devices such as all-party conferences and royal commissions, which will be considered in Chapter 4, can be used to secure agreement prior to legislative action. Thus, although Parliament is legally supreme, the key to its actions lies in responsible self-restraint.

Theoretically there is a major difference between the American concept that legal authority vests ultimately in the citizens, who confer it temporarily on the President and on Congress, and the British concept that legal authority inheres in Parliament and in the Crown (whose authority is now exercised by the Cabinet). According to the British concept the British Parliament and Cabinet are two coequal, interrelated elements, each possessing and exercising an independent authority, not, as in the United States, an authority merely delegated by the voters.

But the distinction should not be pushed too far. Although *legal authority* rests in the Cabinet (using the authority of the Crown) and in Parliament, *political power* resides in the British people as it does in the American people through their right to vote for the representatives and government of their choice. Perhaps the greatest practical importance of the distinction regarding the ultimate seat of legal authority in the two countries, therefore, is in the attitude of the elected representatives: in the United States, members of Congress are likely to look on themselves as delegates from their constituencies; thus only the President represents the whole country. In Great Britain, on the other hand, members of Parliament, particularly the ministers, accept a primary loyalty to the House of Commons as an organ that must act on behalf of the country as a whole.

A third important principle is the distinction between the King as a person and *the Crown as an institution.* Regardless of the personal qualities of the individual, the institution of monarchy is the object of tremendous reverence, both because of its antiquity and because of the ceremony and pageantry of which it is the focus. Whatever changes may take place behind the governmental façade, the Crown continues to symbolize the stability and durability of British institutions and to command the loyalty and devotion of the British people.

In form, the powers of the Crown are very great. Every action of the government is carried out in its name. It is the Crown that makes appointments and assents to laws, that makes treaties and commands the armed forces. The not wholly defined prerogative powers inhering in the Crown can be used during emergencies. Moreover, as noted, *legally* the ministers derive their authority from the Crown and in this sense are responsible to it. But to say that the Crown has these powers and position is very different from saying that the monarch can make use of them independently. On the contrary, the ruler may exercise these powers only on the advice of

his ministers, who, of course, are responsible *politically* to Parliament and the electorate. Except under the most unusual circumstances, the monarch may take no independent action of political importance. As Edward VIII discovered, the monarch may not even marry according to his choice against the advice of his Prime Minister. In short, the powers of the Crown are always used as the Cabinet, supported by Parliament, wants them to be used.

Finally, one of the fundamental principles of the constitution is the *rule of law,* according to which the government and its agents, as well as individual citizens, are subject to laws that are definite and known in advance and that can be modified only by act of Parliament. Thus, no citizen may be punished unless he has been found guilty of violating the law in a trial before a regular court whose procedure safeguards him against arbitrary conviction. Similarly, the courts will protect the citizen against government officials who interfere with his rights contrary to law. Thus both government officials and private citizens are equally subject to one body of law· and one system of courts.

As in the United States, the courts are the primary protectors in Great Britain of what we call "civil liberties": freedom of speech, freedom of association, freedom of assembly, and freedom from arrest and imprisonment "except," as Magna Charta stated it, "by judgment of his peers or by the law of the land." Historically, the common-law courts have been vigilant to stop the government from exercising arbitrary power. As noted, the courts devised the writ of habeas corpus centuries before Parliament passed the Habeas Corpus Act in 1679. They continue to ensure that executive authorities do not exceed the powers entrusted to them and do not deviate from the strict procedures under which they should act. On the tense issue of seditious conspiracy, the courts, through a long series of decisions, have established a balance between order and liberty: no one may use violence to change the laws or the constitution. Short of such action, however, almost any method of agitation may be used in the effort to change laws, policies, or institutions. Thus the King's Peace is preserved, but the popular will has ample channels for expression.

Civil liberties might be infringed, however,

by statute or by administrative regulations that are still inside the law. The Home Secretary and Parliament itself are vigilant in scrutinizing laws, delegated legislation, and local bylaws in order to guard against such encroachments. In the words of one Home Secretary, laws should be passed "to promote liberty and not to restrict liberty." Such a view once led to the disallowance of a London bylaw forbidding roller-skating on the pavement!

But most important of all, perhaps, is the attitude of ordinary citizens, and of the police, toward civil liberties. Anyone who has listened to the explosive utterances of orators at Hyde Park Corner and watched their orderly audiences realizes the value of such safety valves. The story of the London bobby listening to a particularly inflammatory speech and finally drawling, "All those who are going to burn down Buckingham Palace make a line on this side," is not untypical. In such an atmosphere, civil liberties are not in danger, despite any absence of written guarantee.

The Value of the Constitution

Admirable as are the principles of the British constitution, however, Americans may be troubled by a number of questions that are variations on a single theme: with a constitution which is, in part, so vague and which can be changed so easily, either through the imperceptible development of custom or by the passage of an ordinary act of Parliament, how can anyone be sure that constitutional principles really will be maintained in times of special stress? In the United States the Constitution can be formally amended only by a long and complicated process, and Americans occasionally question the usefulness of the much-heralded rule of law if Parliament can change that law at any time.

As already pointed out, however, Parliament does not change the law lightly or without careful consideration. There is, in fact, a very real restraint upon its authority, although a different kind of restraint from that to which Americans are accustomed. The first defense of the constitution lies in the force of tradition and public opinion rather than in a court or a difficult process of amendment. The members of Parliament,

like most Englishmen, have been brought up to believe in discussion, in the rights of individuals and minorities, and in the need to preserve the essential character of the constitution; it would hardly occur to them to attack it. If, to assume the fantastic, they did attack the constitution, the revulsion of public opinion would be so great as to destroy them utterly. It is true that the same forces act in defense of the American Constitution, but in the United States there is more of an inclination to leave this defense to the Supreme Court. Yet there is something to be said for a system which makes it clear that the maintenance of the constitution is the responsibility of the people themselves.

In any case, it would be hard to prove that liberty is any less secure in Great Britain than in the United States. If the Supreme Court of the United States has an excellent record for the protection of civil liberties, there have been times when, by its own confession, it has lapsed. Moreover, it takes a long time and a good deal of money to carry a case to the Supreme Court, and by the time a decision is rendered it may be too late to remedy the damage. Humble people, who are the most likely to be oppressed, may not even be able to raise the necessary money.

One advantage of a written constitution, it is sometimes said, is the greater ease with which the ordinary citizen may detect an infraction of its provisions. The lines are more distinctly drawn; it is not so hard to tell when someone steps over the boundary of constitutional prohibition; and there is a tangible statement around which public opinion can rally. Yet in fact many issues touching civil rights seem far from clear until after the judges have ruled on them.

Another claim is as debatable. The difficult process of amendment, in the case of the American Constitution, may give the public a longer warning about a contemplated change, a greater opportunity to think matters through, and even a margin of time in which to change their minds and recover from transitory hysteria. But the very difficulty and complexity of the process constitute an invitation to circumvention. It is so hard to get an extremely controversial amendment adopted that constitutional flexibility—particularly in the extension of the government's economic powers—has come to depend on the willingness of the Supreme Court to render a broad interpretation of constitutional wording rather than upon a deliberate decision of the electorate to change these words. Here, too, there is something to be said for a method of change whereby amendments may be made in a straightforward manner in time to meet the essential needs of a changing society, yet not until after much thought and discussion of their implications.

In any event, the ultimate defense of any constitution, whether written or unwritten, whether equipped with elaborate defense mechanisms or with none at all, must lie in the devotion of its people. In this spirit of loyalty to their constitution, it would be rash to say that Britons in any measure yield to Americans.

3. BRITISH POLITICAL IDEAS

To understand the attitudes of a people as well as the political programs of particular groups, it is necessary to know the political ideas that have claimed their allegiance, for nowhere is it more true than in politics that ideas are both the forerunners and the outcome of action. In the course of the past hundred years, three great currents of ideas have competed for the political allegiance of British citizens. In the middle of the nineteenth century the principal contenders were conservatism and liberalism. Today they are conservatism and socialism. But although liberalism has declined as an independent force, its successful rivals have absorbed a significant portion of its content. As a result, it is impossible to understand contemporary politics in Great Britain without some familiarity with all three currents of thought.

British Conservatism

In Great Britain, as in every other country, the natural tendency of conservatives is to like traditional institutions and political principles and to regard any far-reaching innovation with suspicion, if not distaste. Established institutions, they think, rest upon the safest of all foundations: that of experience. To desert them is to abandon oneself to the uncharted seas of theorizing and speculation. Although change may be

necessary at certain times, it is not a good thing in itself: thus it should be carried out in such a way as to preserve as many as possible of the inherited institutions.

There are certain differences between British and American conservatives, however, which result from differences in the institutions they have inherited. Where American conservatives are devoted to a constitutional system that places strong restraints upon the government, British Conservatives trace their descent from the Tory party, which stood for the authority of the Crown against parliamentary limitation. Although British Conservatives have long since come to accept the supremacy of Parliament, the fact that for so many generations the upper classes controlled Parliament encouraged a greater willingness to uphold the authority of the state than seems natural to American conservatives.

The Influence of Burke

Somewhat paradoxically, the man who has had the greatest influence on Conservative thought, Edmund Burke (1729–97), considered himself a Whig. He defended the rights of the American colonists at the time of the Revolution, and he was devoted to the principles of the Glorious Revolution of 1688. To Burke, however, these revolutions had been fought in defense of the ancient constitution and the inherited rights of Englishmen. The French Revolution of 1789 seemed to him to have an entirely different character. Its leaders frankly proclaimed their intention of destroying or remolding such ancient institutions as the monarchy, the aristocracy, and the established church; they proclaimed their belief in the power of enlightened and reasonable human beings to create new institutions and to remedy ancient injustices. To Burke, the ancient institutions represented the accumulated wisdom of the ages, and human reason seemed but a weak and fallible guide in comparison with the lessons of tradition and experience. If new circumstances required changes in the inherited constitution, Burke wanted them to be made within the spirit of that constitution and with as little modification as possible of its inherited form.

Burke was appalled, therefore, when certain Englishmen (like Dr. Price, an eminent Nonconformist clergyman) welcomed the French Revolution and proclaimed the right of men not only to establish governments of their own choosing but to choose their rulers and remove them for misconduct. These ideas (which, of course, were also present in the American Declaration of Independence) seemed to Burke to have no basis in English constitutional history. He denied the American belief that all men are created equal and are divinely endowed with certain natural rights. Human equality he called a "monstrous fiction" that made men discontented with their natural state in life. According to Burke, men possess only those rights that they have inherited from their ancestors: thus Englishmen have certain rights that Frenchmen have never possessed.

Burke also attacked the idea that a nation rests upon the voluntary agreement of its citizens. A nation, he said, is not a "partnership in pepper or coffee, tobacco or calico." It is a single organic entity, never young, never old, never middle-aged, in which one generation succeeds another in "a condition of unchangeable constancy." Far from being an association of people existing at any one time, it is a union of earlier generations with those of the present and with those yet to be born. Any sharp or sudden change is a threat to its life. New circumstances may require some modifications of the ancient constitution, but any changes should be made gradually and naturally. Thus the unplanned and almost imperceptible way in which the British constitution has adapted itself to new conditions embodies the conservative ideal of continuity, gradualism, distrust of reforms based on "theory," and confidence in only those changes that take place within the framework of inherited tradition.

Nineteenth-Century Conservatism

It was fortunate for the future of British Conservatism that Burke's teachings left the door open to change, for the nineteenth century transformed almost every aspect of British life. The rapid industrialization of the country and the growth of great cities brought insistent demands for extension of the suffrage and for governmental intervention to protect women and children in industry, to provide safe and healthful working conditions in factories and mines, and to regulate wages and hours of work. During this period the middle classes and, later, the working classes were fighting for the right to vote; if the Conservatives had refused to allow any change or concession, they might have precipitated civil war and perhaps their own destruction.

However, it has been typical of the best of Conservative leaders, such as Benjamin Disraeli (later Earl of Beaconsfield, 1804–81), and Winston Churchill (later Sir Winston, 1874–1964), that they have known when to yield to the demands of a democratic and industrial age. By making concessions before the accumulated pressure and irritation became too great, they not only retained a strong popular following but were able to make reforms in their own way, thus preserving much of the traditional order. Further, they were often able to determine the direction and the extent of the changes.

This adaptability to new circumstances has been easier for British than American conservatives, because the former have had no objection to state activity and have rejected both the doctrine of the right of the individual against the state and any belief in inalienable natural rights. Moreover, the most important reforms were directed against the new leaders of industry, who, until late in the nineteenth century, tended to be Liberal in politics in opposition to the Conservative landowners. Today, a Conservative spokesman, Quintin Hogg, regards certain principles, sacrosanct to American free-enterprise conservatives, as the core of the "liberal heresy." Partly because of this adaptability, partly because of the long, slow development of the British constitution, partly perhaps because the British tend to be empiricists rather than theorists, much of the conservative approach has deeply permeated British thinking and ways of action, even those of the Labor party.

Imperialism

In the late nineteenth century Conservatives became identified with another doctrine: imperialism. Earlier in the century many Englishmen, disillusioned by the loss of the American colonies and preoccupied with the industrial transformation at home, took little interest in the nation's overseas possessions. Disraeli himself could say in 1852 that "these wretched colonies will all be independent too in a few years and are a millstone around our necks." The empire continued to grow, but it grew, according to the famous phrase, "in a fit of absence of mind."

During the last third of the century, however, there was a remarkable change in the attitude both of statesmen and of the people as a whole. It was Disraeli who made Queen Victoria Empress of India and, with farsighted shrewdness, acquired for Britain the predominant control of the new Suez Canal, which so greatly shortened the route to India, Australia, and Hong Kong. As the economic competition of other countries developed, the possession of empire markets gained in significance. Moreover, the idea of empire began to exercise an almost magical fascination upon the imagination of the people. Stories of the adventures and conquests of empire-builders in distant lands had an enormous appeal for those leading monotonous lives in bleak industrial cities. The acquisition of an empire was a source of pride. Thus Joseph Chamberlain, who abandoned the Liberal party and became a great Conservative leader, proclaimed his belief that "the British race is the greatest of governing races that the world has ever seen," while another great Conservative, Lord Curzon, wrote that "the British Empire is under Providence the greatest instrument for good that the world has seen."

At its best, the doctrine of imperialism, far from preaching the exploitation of subject peoples, reflected a sense of responsibility for their development and welfare. Its close association with missionary activity should not be overlooked. But many imperialists thought of national profit or power before they thought of colonial welfare; and even at their best imperialists enjoyed a feeling of superiority that was not easily reconciled with a spirit of democracy.

At first there were many Liberal as well as Conservative imperialists, but with the passage of time (and partly because of the influence of the Nonconformist conscience) Liberals increasingly denounced the acquisition of territory by conquest and demanded greater rights for colonial peoples—a stand in which they were joined by the new Labor party. In contrast, Conservatives tended to resist the transfer of imperial power and the postwar transformation of the dependent Asian and African empire into part of a multiracial Commonwealth, but here, as elsewhere, they ultimately yielded to circumstances and helped to direct its final stages.

British Liberalism

The Influence of Locke

To the average American, the most familiar ideas in British politics are those associated with some of the early Whig thinkers. In particular the writings of John Locke (1632–1704), who wrote in defense of the Glorious Revolution of 1688, influenced the leaders of the American Revolution and found their way into the popular political vocabulary of the time. Thus, much of the American Declaration of Independence is simply a restatement of Locke's principles.

Locke taught that all men are naturally equal; that they possess a natural right to life, liberty, and property; that governments are voluntary associations formed to protect these rights; and that governments should be so organized and limited as to prevent an abuse of their powers. To that end Locke advocated a separation of powers between the executive and the legislative branches of government, and he denied the right of a government to injure the lives or property of its subjects, to tax or take property without consent, to delegate to other agencies powers granted it by the people, or to rule by arbitrary decree instead of by laws duly enacted by Parliament. If a government violated these principles, Locke believed that the people might recall their grant of power and set up a new government.

Much of the divergence between political thinking in Great Britain and the United States today can be understood in terms of the degree of rejection or acceptance of Locke's ideas. In the United States the success of a government founded upon these principles has seemed sufficient proof of their validity; but in late eighteenth-century Great Britain, Locke's belief in natural rights and the right of revolution came to be identified with the excesses of the French Revolution and the Reign of Terror and were regarded with a horror not unlike that aroused in the twentieth century by the principles of the Bolshevik Revolution in Russia. British

Liberals (and, today, many British Conservatives) continue to believe in limited government, but Liberal reforms would have been long in coming to Great Britain if they had had no other intellectual foundation than a belief in natural rights.

The Utilitarians

The man who, more than any other, provided a fresh basis for Liberal political action, Jeremy Bentham (1748–1833), was a Tory in origin. He had even less use than Burke for the doctrine of natural rights, for in his view the aim of government was not to protect men's "rights" but to promote "the greatest happiness of the greatest number." Every governmental policy was to be judged by its "utility," that is, by its tendency to increase human pleasure and to decrease human pain. Bentham worked out elaborate tables by which such utility could be judged; the policy that resulted in the greatest happiness was the policy to be followed.

There was nothing intrinsically democratic in this theory, except its emphasis on equality: but since Bentham was convinced that men are fundamentally selfish, he felt that only a government of the people would look out for the interests of the people.

The result was that Bentham, for reasons very different from those of Locke, came to some of the same conclusions. He did not think that men are equal because of a law of nature, but he did think that each man's happiness is as important as that of any other. Using this criterion, he subjected the inherited institutions of his time to a devastating rational analysis and advocated sweeping changes in such institutions as the electoral system, the law, the penal system, and the poor law.

Bentham's influence on the course of British Liberalism was prodigious. In place of the discredited school of natural rights, he offered a new program of practical political reforms that made a strong appeal to the common sense of the British people and that, it is sometimes said, helped to save Great Britain from the kind of violent revolution that afflicted the Continent. His influence, however, also helped to separate the main current of British Liberalism from the main current of American democratic thought. Whereas Americans continued to believe in the

existence of individual rights beyond the power of government and in the necessity of separating and balancing powers in order to control the government, Bentham saw no need to check government so long as it was promoting the happiness of the majority of the people. His "greatest happiness" principle provided a strong basis for popular government and majority rule though not for minority rights. Where many American liberals long clung to the idea that that government is best that governs least, Bentham and his followers (the Utilitarians or Philosophical Radicals) logically were bound to uphold governmental action aimed at the elimination of human misery. Thus Benthamite Liberals welcomed social welfare programs long before such programs became part of the creed of American liberals.

Economic Liberalism

Bentham himself did not foresee to what extent his ideas could be used to justify governmental action. In economic affairs, paradoxically, he accepted the teaching of Adam Smith (1723–90), who believed that there is a natural harmony of economic interests and that men, if not interfered with by the government, will unconsciously promote the interests of the community at the same time that they consciously promote their own.

According to Smith, the community pays its highest rewards to those who provide the services it most desires; and, since each individual wishes to earn as much money as possible, he will do exactly those things that the community wishes him to do. As a result, the government does not need to, and indeed ought not to, interfere with the economy but should limit itself to national defense, the protection of life and property, and the building of certain public works too costly for private individuals to undertake.

In the early part of the nineteenth century there was no apparent conflict between the ideas of Bentham and those of Smith. Merchants and industrialists supported the Liberal party as the agent of laissez faire and free enterprise at the same time that radicals supported it as the advocate of a broader suffrage and other democratic reforms. The advance of the industrial revolution and the growing demand for economic reform strained this happy partnership. Factory owners were bitterly opposed to many of the reforms that other Liberals advocated enthusiastically as the most effective way of promoting human happiness and eliminating human misery.

The Influence of Mill

To some extent this conflict in Liberal ideas was personified in the life of John Stuart Mill (1806–73). Mill's father, James Mill, had been one of Bentham's most able and intimate disciples, and John Stuart Mill himself grew up in the citadel of Benthamite ideas. As a young man, however, he began to question certain of Bentham's teachings. In particular, he placed greater emphasis upon the worth of the individual personality, and he thought the great objective of society to be not the happiness of the individual but his growth and development. Better, he thought, to be Socrates dissatisfied than a satisfied pig. Thus society should aim at the cultivation of those qualities that are peculiarly human and that distinguish men from animals: before all else the power to think well and to think for oneself.

Such a goal naturally led Mill to be suspicious of any state activity that would limit the freedom of the citizen or reduce his self-reliance. At the same time, however, Mill was well aware of the existence of economic abuses that only the state could remedy. In his famous essay *On Liberty* (1859) he tried to draw a distinction between those actions of the individual that concern only himself, with which the state ought not to interfere, and those actions likely to affect or harm others, which the state may control or prohibit. Thus the state might intervene to prevent the adulteration of goods or to force employers to provide healthful working conditions.

Mill also came to believe that political reforms of the sort advocated by many Liberals—the extension of the suffrage, and the reform of the law and of Parliament—though desirable in themselves would not produce a good society unless accompanied by far-reaching economic reforms. The fundamental problem of society, he wrote in his *Autobiography,* was "to unite the greatest individual liberty of action with a common ownership in the raw material of the globe and an equal participation of all in the benefits of combined labor." Thus Mill had, in fact, become a socialist in ideal—although a socialist who believed intensely in individual self-reliance and in freedom of thought and expression and who wished to combine this freedom with social and economic equality. He did not try to say in any detail how this change was to come about, but apparently it was his hope that through education and experience men might come voluntarily to "dig and weave" for their country as well as to fight for it.

Today British Liberalism is still struggling with the problem of how to reconcile individual liberty with social welfare. Many of the merchants and industrialists, who used to provide the party with its financial strength, have gone over to the Conservatives, and Conservative leaders often appeal to the rest of the Liberals to follow that example. Yet it is increasingly common today to hear Conservatives using the old Liberal slogans of individual freedom from government control.

Many Liberal voters have also turned to Labor —in some instances not because they approved of socialism in principle but because Labor's concrete program of social reform appealed to idealistic elements within the Liberal party. Moreover, as the Liberal party itself weakened, a vote for Labor often seemed the most effective way of voting against Conservatism and imperialism.

Today the Liberals, more than any other party, concern themselves with the protection of individual liberty. But they combine this devotion to liberty with what they call "a radical programme of practical reform." Thus it is characteristic of the present attitude of the party that Lord Beveridge, the sponsor of the famous Beveridge plan for security "from the cradle to the grave" was one of its conspicuous leaders.

British Socialism

Toward the end of the nineteenth century, as we have seen, the issue of economic reform was replacing political reform as the subject of greatest political controversy. To many reformers the obvious way of bringing about change was direct economic action by trade unions and consumers' cooperatives. But there were also those who believed that only political action could remedy economic and social injustice. Among them some, like H. M. Hyndman and the Social Democratic Federation, were under the influence of Karl Marx and believed that reform would come through class warfare and revolution. Others, like the members of the Independent Labor party, placed greater emphasis on winning seats in Parliament and local councils and concentrated on an ethical and democratic appeal which, in the Nonconformist tradition, had great influence on the British workingman.

The Fabians

Some of the most influential ideas, however, were those of the Fabian Society, which was founded in 1884. Unlike Marxian socialists, the Fabians opposed the doctrine of class warfare and advocated a policy of planned gradualism. As the saying went, they substituted evolution for revolution. Their motto was: "For the right moment you must wait, as Fabius did most patiently when warring against Hannibal, though many censured his delays; but when the time comes you must strike hard, as Fabius did, or your waiting will be in vain, and fruitless."

The membership of the Fabian Society has never exceeded a few thousand, but among its members have been men and women of the greatest ability and influence: George Bernard Shaw, Sidney and Beatrice Webb, H. G. Wells, Graham Wallas, Ramsay MacDonald; and in more recent years, Harold Laski, G. D. H. and Margaret Cole, R. H. Tawney, Leonard Woolf, Clement Attlee, and Hugh Gaitskell. When the Labor party came into power in 1945, the Fabian membership included 229 members of Parliament, several Cabinet ministers, and the Prime Minister himself. And if one hears little of the Fabians these days, and much more of the antidoctrinaire attitudes and impact of Hugh Gaitskell and Harold Wilson, this fact does not undercut the long-term, creative effects of the Fabian Society.

The aim of the Society, as stated in 1896, was "to persuade the English people to make their political constitution thoroughly democratic and so to socialize their industries as to make the livelihood of the people entirely independent of private Capitalism." Its method, in Shaw's words, was to give up "the delightful ease of revolutionary heroics" for the "hard work of practical reform on ordinary parliamentary lines." Distrusting theories and abstractions, the members devoted themselves to concrete social and institutional problems. "The competitive system," they maintained, "assures the happiness and comfort of the few at the expense of the suffering of the many. . . . Society must be reconstituted in such a manner as to secure the general welfare and happiness." However, this reconstruction of society was to be accomplished by specific and practical reforms which, little by little, would restrict the extent of capitalism and expand the amount of socialism. By raising wages, shortening hours of work, providing security in old age, ill health, and unemployment, and promoting public health and safety, they hoped to destroy or to reduce some of the worst evils of modern industrial society. By taxing inheritance, ground rents, and income from investments, they hoped to reduce the outstanding economic inequalities. And by increasing public ownership, local as well as national, of public utilities such as gas, water, electricity, and public transport, they hoped gradually to extend the amount of public ownership, to gain experience in the public management of property, and to prove the efficiency and practicability of such management. What was at first done on a small scale and in individual instances could eventually be expanded, they thought, into a completely socialized society.

The outstanding achievement of the Fabian Society undoubtedly was its influence on public opinion. The brilliant scholars, writers, and speakers who served it presented the results of their research in a vivid and effective way. Fabian pamphlets and Fabian lectures reached and influenced large numbers of people, especially in the middle classes, who would have been frightened by talk of revolution and bored by theory, but who could be convinced by hard facts and common sense. Particularly in the formative years, before the Labor party developed its own methods of mass propaganda, it was the Fabian Society which, more than any other group, gave the peculiar cast to British socialism that still distinguishes it from the more doctrinaire socialism of Lenin and the Communists.

In 1900 some of the trade unions, the Social Democratic Federation, the Independent Labor party, and the Fabians formed the organization that later became the Labor party and is today the political arm of British socialism. As a result, it is characteristic of British socialism that there is no one orthodox school of thought (as in the case of Soviet communism). Rather, a variety of ideas and many types of people are found within its ranks. Instead of formulating a rigid ideological program to which all must adhere, there has been a willingness, in a typically British way, to avoid ultimate theoretical issues while agreeing upon and striving for immediate and concrete goals. One consequence of this attitude is the fact that political controversy in Great Britain does not carry with it, as in some other countries, the danger of civil war. For the acceptance by the Conservatives of the constitutional tradition of parliamentary government and their willingness to endorse a wide measure of state activity and social reform, together with the determination of Labor to work for its changes gradually, peacefully, and constitutionally, means that there is a solid basis for cooperation and mutual understanding even when there is sharp disagreement on specific proposals.

3. British Parties and Elections

1. THE CHARACTER OF THE BRITISH PARTY SYSTEM

Without an understanding of the British party system, the most important aspects of British politics would seem inexplicable. It is largely because of the parties that the monarch is so weak and the Prime Minister so strong. Because of parties, the relation of Cabinet to Parliament has been almost completely reversed in the last eighty years. Even more fundamentally, the functioning of British democracy depends on the work of the parties.

Everyone agrees that in a democracy the government ought in general to do what the people want it to do, and everyone agrees that the government should be led by men whom the people themselves have chosen. But it is easier to say this than to discover a workable way of determining what the people want. The ordinary citizen, acting alone, is comparatively helpless when it comes to drawing up a complete program for his government. He lacks the time, the information, and the practical experience to work out the solution to political problems for himself, and as an individual he is too unimportant for the government to care very much what he may think. If he wants to influence the policy of his government, his best resort is to join with others who share his general views, to work out a common program with their help, and to run candidates for office who are pledged to put this program into effect.

This work of uniting, of organizing, and of agreeing on candidates is characteristic of political parties in all democracies. For those citizens who want to participate actively in politics, parties provide the natural channel for action. For the rest of the community, they offer a choice of candidates and policies. The ordinary voter, instead of having to determine his personal attitude on every issue, has the far easier task of deciding which of two or three broad programs suits him best. And the party that wins the favor of the largest number of voters, ideally at least, proceeds to carry out the program the voters have approved.

But if this is the ideal function of political parties, it must be admitted that it is a function often performed unintentionally or badly. Many men in any country join and work for a political party not so much because of their devotion to its public aims as because of their desire for personal power and the material advantages of office. Some parties may even be so organized as to impede rather than encourage political action by the ordinary voter. Thus, in judging the degree of democracy in and the effectiveness of any party system, it is necessary to ask several questions:

Does it offer the mass of the people a meaningful and an adequate choice both of policies and of leaders?

Does it reflect accurately the desires of the people and of the members of the parties themselves?

Is the internal organization of the parties sufficiently democratic to provide a channel for active political participation by the rank and file of the membership, not just in promoting the victory of the party, but in determining its policies and choosing its leadership?

Does the party system assist the process of arriving peacefully at a settlement of controversial issues, or does it exacerbate the differences among the different elements in the community?

Is the party system an effective instrument for carrying out the judgment of the voters once they have made a choice of parties?

The Two-Party System

In several ways the British party system is very much like the American. In both countries political parties are large popular organizations that try to win public office in order to promote policies in which they believe and also to enjoy the material privileges that go along with office. In both countries, ordinarily, there are just two large parties. Thus British and American voters, unlike Russian voters, have a choice between political parties that differ in policy and leadership. But, unlike French or German voters (whose votes are usually scattered among several parties), British and American voters are so restricted in their choice that an election generally (though not always) results in a clear-cut majority for one large party or the other.

Centralization

The greatest difference between the British and American party systems is in the degree of centralization. In the United States, power rests (if at all) with state and local party organizations, and no man can remain a leader of a national party unless he has the support of these organizations. Between elections, in the United States, the national party organizations almost disappear, but the local do not. They are built both on interest and on patronage. Many of the men who work for them do so because of the jobs and favors that they or their relatives get, or hope to get, from a successful machine. Work for the organization, therefore, is regarded as part of their regular job, and in a well-run organization it goes on continuously. But under such circumstances the workers are not primarily concerned with matters of principle and of national importance. To them and to the local bosses the important thing is not the principles the party holds but the offices it can win.

In Great Britain, in contrast, the leadership of the party and the money the party disburses are the chief concerns of the highly centralized national organization. And since a national organization is more likely to be concerned with issues of national importance, the British parties, in normal times, pay greater attention to matters of national policy and principle than do American.

This tendency is encouraged by the smallness of the country and the relative homogeneity of its population. In the United States, as we have seen, parties must appeal to a great variety of clashing sectional, class, and social interests, and they cannot appeal too wholeheartedly to one without antagonizing the rest. The party that stakes everything on the labor vote, for example, will probably lose the farmer and the middle classes. The party that devotes itself to the industrial East will irritate the West and the South. Any precise commitment to one group may mean a loss of votes from others. No party can win unless it has the support of a combination of groups and sections, and party programs tend to reflect this diversity. It is true that the Republicans emphasize business interests and the necessity of a balanced budget and are suspicious of the expansion of federal control, while the Democrats identify themselves with social welfare programs and do not hesitate to use national powers, financial and other, to aid underprivileged groups. In some measure, this difference between the American parties is sharper than that between the British, all of which accept the social welfare state. Nonetheless both Republicans and Democrats attempt to appeal to all groups in the community, and not infrequently each makes somewhat conflicting offers.

British parties are no less eager for victory than are American, but their job is somewhat simpler. Sectionalism is less important in England, and there are fewer issues to confuse the political picture. Although the class pattern is, if anything, more complex, a party can win a majority without combining so many incompatible groups. The consequence is a greater simplicity and clarity in party programs, resulting not from any special virtue in the British character but from an inherently simpler political situation.

Discipline

As a natural corollary of their centralization, British parties are more highly disciplined than American. Americans are accustomed to the idea that politics makes strange bedfellows, and in the past they have accepted without much question the alliance of conservative southerners with urban radicals in the Democratic party and the combination of eastern captains of industry with midwestern farmers in the Republican. One of the recurrent patterns of American politics has been the alignment in Congress of Republican and Democratic conservatives against Republican and Democratic liberals. In neither party have party leaders been able to impose discipline on their nominal followers.

There was a time, during the first part of the nineteenth century, when British parties also were strange and somewhat loose alliances and when advocates and opponents of free trade, imperialism, and progressive social legislation could be found within the ranks of both the Conservative and Liberal parties. This was a time, however, when comparatively few citizens had the right to vote and when, although the sources of their wealth might be different, all voters were drawn from the same well-to-do class. Members of Parliament could be acquainted personally with a large proportion of their electors and hold their seats on the basis of personal rather than party loyalties. There was little need for elaborate political organization.

Even after the Reform of 1832, many seats continued, to all intents and purposes, to be pocket boroughs of wealthy landholding or commercial families; and although some attempt was made to organize parties on a more popular scale, they continued to be somewhat unstable alliances of members of Parliament united on personal grounds rather than mass organizations of people bent on promoting some common policy.

It was the great extension of the right to vote in 1867 and later years that changed all this. Once the mass of the people could participate in elections, it was no longer possible for the parliamentary candidate to know most of the electors personally. He needed an elaborate organization to reach them, and he had to have money to pay for it. But he had no patronage of his own at his disposal, and, unless he was a very wealthy man in his own right, he inevitably turned to the national party for help. In the years after 1867, therefore, both of the large parties were obliged to build up organizations, and by the time of the Conservative electoral victory of 1874 it was clear that political success largely depended on the appeal of the party's program and leader and the effectiveness of the party organization. This was particularly true for Labor when it entered the party arena, for only by solidarity could it hope to match the greater resources of the older parties.

The building of effective party organizations had a far-reaching if unintentional consequence. Once the candidate for Parliament became more dependent for his success on the work and money of the organization than on his own efforts, his personal independence was seriously restricted. He could not vote against the party's leaders on important issues and then expect their organization to support him in the next election. Yet he could not win the election, in most instances, without such support. The result was that the ordinary member of Parliament could not, and cannot, vote against the leaders of his party with the casualness that characterizes much congressional cross-voting in the United States. The member of Congress is mainly dependent on a local party organization, and that organization may disagree with the national leaders or be indifferent to certain national issues. But in Great Britain only the man with exceptional personal appeal and extensive financial resources can face the prospect of having the national organization of his own party opposed to him.

The simplicity and discipline of the British system are objects of admiration and even of envy to many Americans. Yet a similar degree of discipline would scarcely be practical or desirable in the United States. In Great Britain, with its greater homogeneity and smaller area, it is possible to have a large measure of discipline without grossly misrepresenting the country as a whole. But in the United States, two centralized and highly disciplined parties could never do justice to the great diversity of elements and interests in the population. If the American parties lack cohesion and uniformity, it is because the nation itself lacks these qualities; and if the consequence is a certain ineffectiveness in government, it is the price of protecting important political and sectional interests.

Importance of the Leader

Probably no contrast between British and American politics is more striking than the relatively greater authority enjoyed by the party leader in Great Britain. It was quickly discovered when the vote was extended in 1867 and 1884 that issues had to be dramatized if they were to arouse the interest and suit the intellectual level of the masses. The essential element in drama is personality. Men who could never have followed the complexities and intricacies of Liberal and Conservative policy could understand a conflict between two leaders such as Gladstone and Disraeli. Just as a Roosevelt or a Kennedy in the United States could typify an attitude far better than any Democratic platform, so Gladstone and Disraeli could humanize abstract issues and appeal to loyalties that even the most cogent statement of principle could not arouse on a mass scale. As a result, a man no sooner becomes leader of his party today than every device of publicity is used to make him appear a noble and inspiring leader, if possible, but in any case a likable and trustworthy one.

The power of the leader is augmented by the nature of the British electoral system, for in Great Britain it is impossible for the ordinary citizen to cast his vote directly for the Prime Minister. The Prime Minister is only one of more than six hundred members of the House of Commons, and only those voters who happen to live in his constituency see his name on the ballot. In all other constituencies, the only way to vote for a particular Prime Minister is to vote for the local parliamentary candidate of the party of which he is the leader. In 1966, for example, those who supported Harold Wilson for Prime Minister had to vote for the local Labor candidate for Parliament, whatever they might think of his individual ability or personality, for only if a majority of the members elected to the House of Commons were Labor could Wilson be returned as Prime Minister. In the United States, as the 1960 election demonstrated, it is quite possible to vote for a Democratic presidential candidate and a Republican congressional candidate on the same ballot. In 1956 the leader of the Republican party, General Eisenhower, was President even though the Democrats had a majority of the seats in Congress. But in Great Britain, with different rules, the successful candidate for Parliament knows that it is far less his own personality that attracts the voters than it is the personality of his party's leader. He knows, too, that if ever he fails to follow his leader, he may very well lose his seat.

Party Discipline

The dependence of the candidate for Parliament upon his party's machine, program, and leader would appear intolerable to the average member of the American Congress. The latter likes to think of himself as a free man, capable of making up his mind on each issue as it arises and of voting as he thinks right, regardless of his party leader or even of his party platform. To him the restrictions on the British member would seem to destroy an element of personal freedom essential to democracy.

Many members of Parliament would agree with this analysis. But some of them would undoubtedly point out that the freedom of the member of Congress is sometimes purchased at the price of political ineffectiveness and party irresponsibility. For a party that cannot control its representatives in the legislature is in no position to make promises to the voters. Moreover, if a party cannot carry out its promises, it is very difficult for the voter to make an intelligent and effective choice. In Great Britain the voter knows that if the Conservative party is successful in an election, it will have the power to carry out its program; and the same is true of a Labor victory. But in the United States, because of congressional cross-voting, the election of a Democratic Congress is no guarantee that the advice of a Democratic President will be followed or even that the Democratic platform will be carried out.

Thus the party systems of Great Britain and the United States are based on different conceptions of what is most important in a representative democracy. To the British voter the important thing is the program and leadership of the party rather than the independence, personality, and ability of the local candidate. To the British voter it would seem a real defiance of the popular will for a candidate, elected as the representative of a party, to refuse to support an important item in that party's program. For the voters, in choosing him, have really chosen to support that program, and any departure from it would make the election meaningless. The closer the two parties come in numerical strength, the greater the tendency to stress party discipline.

To the American voter the essence of democracy is not for a representative to vote according to the dictates of party leaders but to vote on each issue as he thinks the voters in his own district would want him to vote or as his conscience and judgment direct him to vote. Thus the American voter, presumably, is choosing a man whose general attitude and judgment he trusts. If he dislikes the record of his congressman, he will vote against him in the next election. But if he votes against him it will be because he dislikes the congressman's record and not because the congressman fails at times to support his party's leaders. President Roosevelt's inability in 1938 to secure the defeat of Democratic congressmen who had opposed his policies is indicative of the dislike of American voters for "dictation" to their representatives even on the part of a very popular party leader.

Class Character

Finally, the division of parties in Great Britain has a different foundation from that in the United States. In recent years, it is true, the more prosperous classes have tended to vote Republican and the less prosperous together with organized labor to vote Democratic; yet there are many conservatives, especially in the South, who vote Democratic, and there are a number of labor leaders who have voted Republican. Neither party has any official connection with a trade union, and each party includes important elements from all income groups.

The class basis of British political parties is less sharply defined, as we have seen, than the

names of the parties suggest. The working-class Tory [1] and the Conservative-oriented farm laborer do much to underwrite the Conservative party's claim that it represents all classes and not just "the Establishment" and the middle class. Labor has a strong hold on the professional classes, although the Liberals and Conservatives take their share. The Liberals, as we shall see, won an increasing number of votes, though relatively few seats, in the transition period between Conservative and Labor control, indicating how support fluctuates between the two major parties. Yet despite all this, it is still easier to guess a man's political allegiance in Great Britain from his social status than it is in the United States. The trade unions are integral parts of the Labor party. The Conservatives have a built-in base of support among the titled, the upper classes, and the wealthy. It would be hard to name a British industrialist who votes for Labor or the head of a British union who votes Conservative.

Some of the distinctions between the British and American party systems, it must be admitted, seem oversimplified if not misleading in the light of recent elections. Goldwater and Johnson represented two much more sharply differentiated philosophies in 1964 than did Home and Wilson, or Heath and Wilson in 1966. Both of the present Labor and Conservative leaders are attempting to shed the class stereotypes that have been attached to their respective parties. It seems likely that the Republicans and Democrats will also come closer together once again in their efforts to appeal to all elements of the population. Yet there remain major differences in approach, organization, and objectives between the British and the American party sys-

---

[1] In a sample of five hundred working-class men and women, who by industry, trade union membership, sex, age, and membership in employer-run superannuation schemes matched the total adult working-class population of Great Britain, only 56 percent said they were working class, 40 percent described themselves as middle class, and the remaining 4 percent refused to consider themselves part of any class group. Thirty-eight percent of those describing themselves as working class, and 16 percent of those calling themselves middle class, supported Labor. Twenty-two percent of those who described themselves as working class, and 24 percent of those calling themselves middle class, supported the Conservatives. Their answers on political aims are listed in the table on page 66.

tems, many of which we have already spelled out in general terms. A detailed consideration of the British party system in action will make these differences more apparent.

2. HOW THE PARTIES WORK

In Great Britain, as in the United States, there is a good deal of political romanticizing about the way in which the people rise in their majesty every few years and march to the polls to determine which policies and which men shall govern them. The implication is that the voters have an infinite choice of men and policies, but the fact is that the ordinary voter, in the normal constituency, has a real choice between just two men who have already been chosen for him by the Labor and Conservative party organizations. (The Liberal party has been running an increasing number of candidates, and occasionally a candidate may run as an Independent; but the chances of such candidates being elected are slight in most constituencies.) Thus, any study of the roots of British democracy must dig behind the apparatus of voting and elections and examine the internal organization of the two major parties themselves.

Answers of Manual Workers to the Question:
"Which four of these do you consider most important for a good political party?"
(in percent)

Political aim	Self-described working class		Self-described middle class		All manual workers [1]
	Support Cons.	Support Lab.	Support Cons.	Support Lab.	
Would make country more prosperous	45	45	49	28	41
Would do most for world peace	56	50	45	44	47
Would do most to prevent nuclear war	47	45	45	49	45
United team of top leaders	36	22	34	22	25
Raise standard of living of ordinary people	30	42	29	43	35
Clear-cut policy	16	19	25	16	21
Fair treatment for all races and creeds	29	30	22	45	29
Respects British traditions	14	9	21	16	14
Out for nation as a whole	26	16	20	15	19
Chances for person who wants to better himself	22	19	19	12	19
Extend welfare sources	18	22	18	24	19
Try to abolish class differences	11	14	11	20	15
Satisfying for man with ideals	5	4	8	5	7
Stands for middle class	2	5	7	4	5
Stands for working class	12	25	7	41	20
Helps underdog	5	12	4	8	7

[1] The five desiderata for an ideal political party receiving most support were (in percent):

Would do most for world peace	47
Would do most to prevent a nuclear war	45
Would make the country more prosperous	41
Is out to raise the standard of living of ordinary people	35
Believes in fair treatment for all races and creeds	29

The five to which least importance was attached were (in percent):

Would try to abolish class differences	15
Really respects British traditions	14
Is most satisfying for the man with ideals	7
Is out to help the underdog	7
Stands for the middle class	5

Source: Mark Abrams, "Social Class and British Politics," *Public Opinion Quarterly,* 25 (Fall 1961), pp. 342–50.

The Labor Party

The Labor party differs noticeably from American parties in the depth of conviction and idealism it can still arouse. Its members occasionally still refer to it as the "Cause," although this fervor has declined with the increasing size of, and noticeable divisions within, the party. But it is significant (and this helps to explain why the feeling persists) that members of the local party organizations are expected to give devoted and unpaid service in a measure that is seldom matched by ordinary members of American parties. Americans, of course, have at times shown great political devotion, but it has usually been attached to individual leaders, like the Roosevelts, or Eisenhower, or Kennedy, or to a particular candidate, rather than to a political party as such. Loyalty to the Labor party, however, transcends any loyalty to its leaders; and service to the party is not restricted to a few weeks during election campaigns. Often it is a matter of consistent, devoted, dogged effort over a long period of years.

A second characteristic of the party is reflected in its title: it is the organized workers who provide the solid core of Labor party strength. In some ways this is a weakness, as we have suggested, for it may discourage support among the middle classes and even among farmers. The party leaders, particularly Wilson himself, are trying to give the party a broader base of support without impairing the strength of working-class support.

Party Structure

The Labor party's organization is one of the most complicated designed by the mind of man. From the time of its foundation the party has been composed of a number of autonomous organizations that have allied themselves for political purposes; in allotting each organization its appropriate representation in the general framework and in balancing the different, and sometimes jealous, groups against one another, simplicity and clarity of structure were early casualties.

Four types of organization have combined to make the Labor party: socialist and other societies composed for the most part of intellectuals and professional men; trade unions; cooperatives; and local and regional organizations of the Labor party.

SOCIALIST AND OTHER SOCIETIES In the first group are the Fabian Society, the Socialist Medical Association, the Jewish Socialist Labor party, and the National Association of Labor Teachers. In numbers these organizations are very small, and the terms of membership in the party now make it impossible for them to develop programs and policies of their own. In the past, however, as the history of the Fabian Society has indicated, they had a distinguished part in the development of the party's philosophy, and their research facilities and professional services still contribute new ideas and useful reports.

TRADE UNIONS The most striking feature of Labor party membership, at least to an American, is the predominance of trade unionists. The long alliance between the Labor party and the bulk of British trade unions has rested on a deeply felt identity of interest and on mutual confidence. Trade union participation in politics has always been looked on as subsidiary to collective bargaining, and its importance to the unions varies in proportion to the effectiveness of the party in furthering their interests. The unions have never depended wholly on the Labor party for support of their political interests, but they obviously play a more direct role in politics when Labor is in office. Although the Labor party has suffered from public reaction against unofficial strikes and the Communist infiltration of some unions, much of its stability comes from the solidarity of the unions. From the other side, affiliation with the Labor party has brought the trade unions a sense of social purpose they would otherwise lack.

The unions furnish the bulk of the Labor party's members—some six million out of nearly seven million in all—and also the bulk of the party's annual income. Through a curious, partly personal, partly union arrangement, a so-called political levy goes automatically from each worker's wages into his union's political fund unless the worker signs a statement opposing the contribution. (In 1927, following the general strike of the year before, the Trades Dispute Act required workers to volunteer to pay the political levy. The Labor government reversed the process in 1946.) The fee (amounting to about thirty cents) is a little less than half that paid by individual constituency members. Oddly enough, each union can decide the number of its members on whom to pay affiliation fees to the party. Since votes at the annual party conference depend on how many affiliation fees are paid (one vote for every five thousand paid-up members), union leaders must decide between their desire for votes and for funds for their own election budgets.

Union election budgets are particularly important for those unions that sponsor their own parliamentary candidates. Union candidates[2] generally stand for relatively safe seats, and in 1964, 120 of their candidates won, out of the 138 seats they contested. As usual, the Mineworkers secured the largest share, 28, but the Transport and General Workers Union took 21, and 26 other unions shared in union-sponsored parliamentary representation. Trade unionists have rarely been influential M.P.'s, because they are often selected more as a reward for past services than for their brilliance or eloquence. The Wilson Report after Labor's defeat in 1955 criticized the unions for not contesting or at least supporting campaigns in marginal seats, and the unions did more in this regard in 1964. Trade unions also contribute substantially to special election funds.

THE COOPERATIVES   The cooperatives, in contrast to the trade unions, have been a disappointment to Labor. Nearly two out of every three families belong to societies engaged in cooperative trading and manufacturing. Their active support could represent an enormous addition to the party's strength, both in money and in membership. But only the Royal Arsenal Cooperative Society, with 25,450 members, has affiliated with the Labor party at the national level. Moreover, since 1917, the cooperatives have had a political party of their own: the Cooperative party. Although this party has refused to affiliate nationally with the Labor party, it encourages local constituencies to run joint candidates—usually known as "Coopera-

[2] It is a party rule that every Labor candidate must belong to a union appropriate to his occupation, if there is one, but this affiliation is often merely nominal.

tive and Labor" candidates—both in local and in national elections. M.P.'s so designated must vote with the Labor party even if they differ, as they occasionally do, from Labor policies. Such an arrangement is obviously not conducive to an enthusiastic partnership.

LOCAL ORGANIZATION: THE CONSTITUENCY PARTIES   If the trade unions provide most of the membership and the money, the Labor party's local organizations provide most of the energy and do most of the work. Membership in these organizations is open to anyone who formally accepts the party's program by signing a membership card and paying a small monthly fee. Some people who already belong to the party by virtue of their membership in trade unions or socialist societies also enroll as individual members of the constituency organizations.

The most energetic, the most sincere, and the most ideologically inclined are likely to be found within the constituency members. It is the party militants who collect the party's dues, sell and distribute its literature, organize entertainments and bazaars in order to raise money, and do the hard work of electioneering. As a consequence, friction sometimes arises between the constituency party members, who feel they do most of the work, and the trade union representatives, who cast most of the votes at party conferences.

Since World War II, however, the obvious divisions in the Labor party have been less between local militants and unions than between leaders and followers. The leaders, whether in the parliamentary Labor party or in the unions, are likely to be cautious, moderate, and concerned with the party's appeal in the country at large. But the followers feel committed to the achievement of a socialist society and have often been rebellious at what seem to them expedient or halfway measures.

Both over tactics and attitude there are important differences within the party between the moderates and the socialist radicals. Most labor members, coming from a liberal, Christian, and humanitarian tradition, are bitter enemies of poverty and social injustice. Their first concern, however, is with the liberty and growth of human beings. But other members look on human liberty as less important than a profound modification of the capitalist system. Those in the first group feel the party should aim primarily at winning elections and should therefore appeal to the middle class with a moderate outlook characteristic of a prosperous society. The militants, in contrast, believe it is essential to stick to the socialist dogma even if its appeal is waning. In foreign policy, the first group feels a deep sense of mutual commitment with the United States, while the second group is often highly critical of what it terms American capitalist imperialism. Neither group, however, has sympathy for the totalitarian dictatorship of the Soviet Union; whenever the proposal has been made to admit the Communist party into the Labor party, it has been overwhelmingly voted down.

The Party Machinery

Federal structures are always complicated, and the Labor party is no exception. Its most representative organization is a party conference which meets every year and which elects an executive committee. Ultimate control over party decisions, however, rests with the parliamentary Labor party, which elects the leader of the party. A minor role is played by the National Council of Labor, which brings together representatives of the executive committee, the parliamentary Labor party, the trade unions, and the cooperatives.

THE CONFERENCE Unlike American party conventions, the Labor party's conference meets every year whether or not there is an election in the offing. Each of the member organizations holds one voting card for every five thousand paid-up members or fraction thereof. In addition, Labor members of the House of Commons and the House of Lords and endorsed party candidates for Parliament are ex officio members of the conference.

Two things are interesting about this system. It makes for a better representation of rank-and-file party members than is true in America, where delegates to political conventions are often hand-picked by local machines. Its emphasis is on serious and vigorous debate rather than on the nomination of candidates and the spectacular activities that characterize American conventions. Each affiliated organization

(that is, each union, socialist society, constituency organization, or cooperative) may propose one resolution (and, later, one amendment to a proposed resolution) for discussion. The organizations know, before the conference is held, which issues will be taken up, and they may discuss them in advance and instruct their delegates; in this way discussion of issues in local meetings may contribute significantly to the political education of the members.

It is often charged that the conference cannot function democratically because the large trade unions usually are in a position to dominate it. Ordinarily two or three of the largest unions cast more votes than all the constituency parties put together (the unions possess about five-sixths of all votes, though usually they send fewer than half the delegates). Also, each constituency party votes independently of the others, with the result that some of their votes offset others. The big unions, however, even when they contain large dissenting minorities, cast their votes as though their membership were unanimous. Thus, if a comparatively few unions come to an agreement with one another, as they are likely to do, their votes can control the conference. Moreover, since the rank and file of the unions' membership take less interest in the party, it is sometimes possible for a few "trade union bosses" to swing great blocks of votes and thus dominate the conference.

There is also a certain amount of dissatisfaction over the shortness of time at the delegates' disposal. The conference meets for only five days (even this long a meeting is a serious drain on the financial resources of the delegates), with the result that not very many subjects can be discussed, and these not very thoroughly. The leaders of the party in Parliament and on the national executive committee use much of the conference's time to expound their policies, and a disproportionately small amount of time is left for discussion by ordinary delegates. Critics of the policies of the party's leaders often find themselves limited to a series of five-minute speeches.

But if the party system is not perfectly democratic, it marks an advance over the degree of intraparty democracy in the United States. Any important issue is sure to be aired in the conference, and the five-day meetings are rarely dull. The leaders of the party are called upon to explain and defend their policies to the rank and file—in itself an important check—and even when they are sure of winning a large vote of confidence, they are bound to be influenced by the vigor and force of the criticism directed at them. If most of the votes support them, some of the most brilliant speeches may point out weaknesses in their policies and exert a moral and psychological pressure for which there is no American equivalent.

That serious problems can also arise from this situation became apparent in 1960. The Labor party was badly split over unilateral nuclear disarmament. The party leader, Mr. Gaitskell, opposed this policy but was defeated in the annual conference when two large unions threw their votes in support of it. Moreover, the day before, on October 4, 1960, the conference passed by 3,586,000 votes to 1,874,000 a resolution declaring that the policy of the party in Parliament "on questions of principle, shall be determined by the annual conference." But the parliamentary leaders, who are bound to ask whether a controversial resolution will appeal to the independent or nonaffiliated voters whose support is necessary for victory in a national election, firmly refused to accept either the nuclear disarmament resolution or the general principle that they should be bound by conference votes. Thus, though the leaders of the party treat the conference and its opinions with the utmost seriousness and make every effort to win its voluntary support, they have not been willing to accept it as a final authority.

THE NATIONAL EXECUTIVE COMMITTEE During the period between conferences, the management of party affairs and the direction of its head, or central, office are in the hands of the executive committee. In form and in theory the conference gives orders to the executive, but in practice and in fact it is often the executive that takes the initiative in determining policy.

In any contest within the conference, in fact, the executive is likely to win, a reflection of its composition. Of its twenty-eight members, twelve are elected by the trade unions, one each by the socialist, cooperative, and professional organizations, and seven by the local parties; five women members and the party treasurer are elected by the conference at large. The Labor party's leader in Parliament is a member ex officio. Most members of the executive are reelected from year to year, and the contests and the number of votes received give a good indication of the rising or waning popularity of particular figures.

The executive committee meets once a month for two or three days. The meetings are conducted by a chairman, who is chosen by seniority, but only for one year. In 1954 the committee formally committed itself to abide by majority decision. Under these circumstances the executive committee is unlikely to be outvoted at the annual conference because union representation is so strong in both. The startling 1960 vote overriding the committee's position on unilateral nuclear disarmament was reversed, it should be noted, at the 1961 conference.

In addition to directing policy for the extra-parliamentary party, the executive committee controls the central office (often called Transport House, from the building in which its headquarters are located) and the machinery of party organization. Thus it maintains contact with and guides the local organizations, provides speakers, arranges conferences, carries on research, edits party publications and propaganda, trains and examines the "agents" who direct local campaigns, organizes branches of the party in new constituencies, and manages the party funds. All these activities provide effective means for maintaining the accepted line in party affairs and are essential for electoral success.

The executive committee has two additional sources of influence. Its endorsement of Labor candidates for Parliament enables it to maintain party discipline. K. Zilliacus, a left-wing critic of Labor's foreign policy, has twice been refused endorsement. The Labor party (in contrast to the Conservatives) also runs an official Labor candidate against an unendorsed one.

The executive committee also has the authority to expel individual members or to disaffiliate organizations, although such action may be challenged at the party conference. Disaffiliation means in effect that the local party loses the financial support of the local branches of the trade unions, and few constituencies can afford such a loss.

STRUCTURE OF THE LABOR PARTY

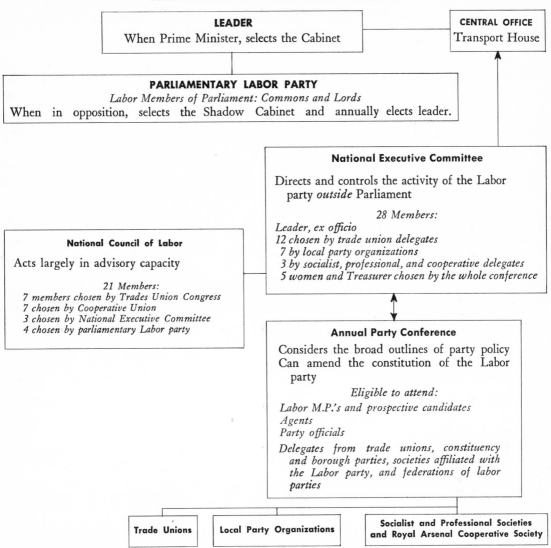

LEADER
When Prime Minister, selects the Cabinet

CENTRAL OFFICE
Transport House

PARLIAMENTARY LABOR PARTY
Labor Members of Parliament: Commons and Lords
When in opposition, selects the Shadow Cabinet and annually elects leader.

National Executive Committee

Directs and controls the activity of the Labor party *outside* Parliament

28 Members:
Leader, ex officio
12 chosen by trade union delegates
7 by local party organizations
3 by socialist, professional, and cooperative delegates
5 women and Treasurer chosen by the whole conference

National Council of Labor

Acts largely in advisory capacity

21 Members:
7 members chosen by Trades Union Congress
7 chosen by Cooperative Union
3 chosen by National Executive Committee
4 chosen by parliamentary Labor party

Annual Party Conference

Considers the broad outlines of party policy
Can amend the constitution of the Labor party

Eligible to attend:
Labor M.P.'s and prospective candidates
Agents
Party officials
Delegates from trade unions, constituency and borough parties, societies affiliated with the Labor party, and federations of labor parties

Trade Unions

Local Party Organizations

Socialist and Professional Societies and Royal Arsenal Cooperative Society

THE PARLIAMENTARY LABOR PARTY Although the extra-parliamentary organization of the Labor party is the major channel through which the opinions of its members can be expressed, it is the parliamentary Labor party that is the real center of power within the party. This is because only the parliamentary members of the Labor party can directly affect national policy. Moreover, it is the parliamentary Labor party that elects the party leader; if the party is out of office, it reelects him annually. This is commonly by acclamation, although there was an unprecedented contest in 1960 in which Harold Wilson unsuccessfully challenged the incumbent, Hugh Gaitskell—whom he succeeded after the latter's death in 1963. The constitution and the formal organization of the party emphasize the importance of the decisions made by the annual conference and the executive committee. But the fact that when the party is in power its leader is the most powerful political figure in Great Britain gives him at all times an extraordinary degree of influence and authority throughout the whole party.

At the same time, Labor leaders are expected to listen to criticism, both within the party as a whole and within the parliamentary Labor party, and to provide personal leadership on all occasions. Thus, party leaders always attend the sessions of the annual party conference, direct discussions, and reply directly to questions. When the parliamentary Labor party is in a minority in Parliament, meetings of caucus—which is made up of all Labor members in both the Commons and the Lords—are held at least once a week to discuss and decide party policy, and these members elect the shadow cabinet that occupies the front opposition benches.

When the Labor party is in power, however, its leader, who as Prime Minister selects his own Cabinet, enjoys great independence, both in relation to the annual conference and to the parliamentary Labor party. According to British constitutional tradition, the Cabinet is responsible to the House of Commons as a whole, and not merely to one political group. Moreover, there is a strong feeling that vigorous, effective, and prompt action by the Cabinet should not be hampered by the necessity of winning the prior approval of the rank and file of the party's members in Parliament.

Even when the Labor party is in power, however, special care is taken to consult party members outside the Cabinet. A liaison committee composed of some backbenchers, the chief whip, the Lord President of the Council, and one representative of the Labor peers acts as intermediary between the Cabinet and the party. The parliamentary party as a whole continues to meet at least once every two weeks for policy discussions in which the Prime Minister and Cabinet members frequently participate. Groups set up in 1945 to discuss particular subjects and special areas have proved useful. Often more influential than the formal groups, however, when the party is in power, are the informal groups within the parliamentary Labor party that represent particular interests, such as the trade unions and the miners, as well as groups with a special, usually leftish, ideological slant.

The parliamentary Labor party can expel M.P.'s from the parliamentary caucus (the technical expression is "to withdraw the whip" —that is, not to send notices of party meetings). The most notable dissident, Aneurin Bevan, was temporarily expelled on several occasions.

But, in general, whether the party is in office or out, unity is maintained in the parliamentary Labor party less by rewards and punishments than by an inner sense of cohesion and by an awareness that only a united party can hope to gain and maintain parliamentary power.

THE NATIONAL COUNCIL OF LABOR   Compared to the organizations already described, the National Council—though it is sometimes called an executive of executives—is of relatively little importance. This organization has twenty-one members: seven from the Trades Union Congress, three from the Labor party executive, four from the parliamentary Labor party, and seven from the Cooperative Union. Its monthly meetings may help develop mutual understanding of the needs and attitudes of these different organizations. Only occasionally, as during the Spanish Civil War, does the National Council of Labor develop an influential stand on policy. Its particular function, normally, is to help bring the Trades Union Congress into the area of political responsibility.

Intraparty Democracy

Critics have charged that the source of power and thus of control in the Labor party is in the hands of the trade unions. The unions provide the bulk of the membership and the money, as we have seen, and they have most of the votes in the annual conference.

Yet the potential power of the unions is restrained by a crucial consideration. Even if the unions were to use their control of votes in the party conference to try to force a self-interested policy upon the leadership of the party, they could not reinforce it politically. Though they provide a majority of the members of the Labor party, they do not cast anything like a majority of votes in a national election. The party must appeal to the whole spectrum of uncommitted voters—unorganized workers, consumers, housewives, the lower-middle classes, professional workers, farmers—and if these groups were antagonized, the party would be a worthless asset to the unions. The party is important to them only to the extent that it can win powerful support among the people as a whole. In order to do so, it must have a broad program acceptable to the majority of the British voters.

Another charge, made primarily by Conservatives, is that the Labor party, both inside and outside Parliament, is run by a clique of party bosses at Labor's head office. But this charge leaves out of account the vitality of Labor's annual conference and the fact that ultimate authority must rest in the hands of the party's leaders in Parliament. The annual conference may vote against a major policy supported by the party's leaders, but only if, as in 1960, the party is badly split on the issue. It may narrowly support its leaders, overriding left-wing Bevanite and substantial union opposition, as in 1954 over German rearmament. Much more commonly, it may give them a strong vote of confidence after lively discussion. But, alert though the parliamentary Labor party must be to the opinions of the rank and file of the party organization outside Parliament, it is ultimately responsible to the electorate on which it depends for whatever success it may gain in the next election. Thus no unrepresentative group of party managers, any more than the trade unions or even the mass of party followers, can take away from the party's parliamentary group its responsibility for and direction of party policy.

The Conservative Party

In principle the aim of the Conservative party is to preserve the best in the nation's political tradition while adapting that tradition to the demands of changing times. As the ancient defender of the monarchy and the Church, the party has always rallied against a threat to either of these institutions. But the monarchy and the Church are no longer vital issues, and the chief problem of the contemporary party has been to devise a way to meet the appeal of Labor.

"Tory democracy," preached in the nineteenth century by Disraeli and by Winston Churchill's father, has increasingly been accepted as the party's philosophy and appeal. The party is still hierarchically organized, hardheaded, and concerned with individual enterprise, in contrast to Labor's equalitarianism, but many feel it fits the accepted British social structure better than does the Labor party. Contemporary Tory democracy includes social and economic reform, governmental responsibility for health, education, and social security, and a considerable measure of economic planning.

The publication in 1947 of the Industrial Charter, which accepted the need for central planning, and the strong endorsement of this document by the Conservative conference of 1947 were decisive steps in the party's acceptance of the need to compete with Labor. At the same time, the Conservatives, especially their right-wing members, have shown a particular tenderness for the protection of private property.

Contrasting themselves with the Labor party, the Conservatives claim that they represent the nation as a whole rather than a single class within the nation. Every effort is made to attract voters from all sections of society, and great care is taken at party conferences to grant a conspicuous place on the program to workers and housewives. We have seen that, in fact, the Conservatives receive many votes not only from the middle classes but from the working classes as well. However, if we look at the party's leadership, the charge that the Conservatives are the party of the upper classes gains in substance. Not until 1955 did the Conservatives elect their first manual worker to Parliament, while for many years men of great wealth have been conspicuously present on the Conservative benches. Before World War II, about 40 percent of the Conservative members of the House of Commons possessed hereditary titles or were related to the nobility, while still more were directors of business enterprises. Since the war there have been many company directors among the successful Conservative candidates. The change in the party's top leadership in 1965 from Sir Alec Home (who had renounced his peerage in 1961 to stand for the House of Commons after succeeding Macmillan as Prime Minister) to Edward Heath, who like Harold Wilson is a self-made man, was epoch-making.

To some extent the overrepresentation of privilege in Conservative ranks had resulted from the strong feeling of obligation, among aristocratic families, to accept the burdens of public service. But as the government has intervened more and more drastically in economic matters, there has also been a strong inducement for great financial and industrial interests to take the lead in the battle against "socialism," both by contributing heavily to the Conservative party and by winning seats in Parliament for their spokesmen. In this way men of wealth have come to occupy a position of influence inside the Conservative party not unlike that of the "trade union bosses" in the Labor party.

In recent years the Conservatives have become increasingly sensitive, however, to the charge that they are a class party. The practice of local Conservative associations of choosing candidates who could pay their own campaign expenses and contribute heavily to the party funds came in for particularly serious criticism. In 1948, the Conservatives accepted the far-reaching recommendations of the Maxwell Fyfe Committee on Party Organization (which were much more comprehensive than those of Labor's Wilson Committee of 1955, which also followed a shattering party defeat). The Committee recommended that candidates should be relieved of all election expenses and that members of Parliament should not be permitted to contribute more than £50 a year to their association, with candidates contributing no more than £25. Thus, although the Conservatives almost certainly spend at least twice as much as does Labor on their permanent organization and commonly outspend Labor in the constituency campaigns, the question of finance, paradoxically, now plays a less important role in the selection of Conservative candidates than of Labor candidates.

The Party Machinery

In one respect, the Conservative party's organization is simpler than that of the Labor party, because it contains no autonomous organizations like the trade unions and the socialist societies. Nonetheless, its extra-parliamentary structure is complex and vast. The National Union of Conservative and Unionist Associations is a federal organization to which are affiliated some 542 constituency associations with somewhat under 2.5 million members, few of whom take any active role or interest in its work. The most broadly representative gathering is its annual conference.

THE CONFERENCE Conservatives claim that their organization is not only simpler than Labor's but that it is more democratic. In the first place, the Conservative constituency unit is said to have more autonomy of action than the comparable unit in the Labor party, which is looked upon as the local branch of the national organization. Moreover, the representatives of Conservative associations at the annual conference are "free to speak and vote according to their own consciences." In addition, each constituency organization is given equal representation regardless of size. If this arrangement seems to discriminate against the larger organizations, it also ensures that no delegate is in a position to cast a great block of votes comparable to those controlled by some of Labor's trade union leaders.

But if the Conservative conference is in a certain sense more democratic than the Labor conference, it has had a far less significant role. Whether or not the decisions of the Labor conference are in practice binding on the party organization, the discussions have always provided significant indications of the strength of feeling among the members, and the leaders have made every effort to sway the conference to their way of thinking. But in the Conservative conferences, the party's leader formerly did not even appear until after the discussions were over, and then only to deliver a carefully prepared speech that had little to do with what had been said by the delegates. In 1965, however, Heath inaugurated the practice of attending the whole conference, answering even sharp comments, and speaking to those points most at issue in the minds of conference members.

Heath and the Conservative Central Office also have plans for a radical reappraisal of the future role and organization of the party's annual conference. Rather than have the officers of the National Union become automatically the officers of the conference, the proposal is to have the four thousand conference representatives elect their own chairman, vice-chairman, and conference management committee, much as happens at the annual Labor conference. The objective is to attract more distinguished persons to public roles at the conference, thereby securing more public attention for those meetings and also providing a greater sense of intra-

STRUCTURE OF THE CONSERVATIVE PARTY

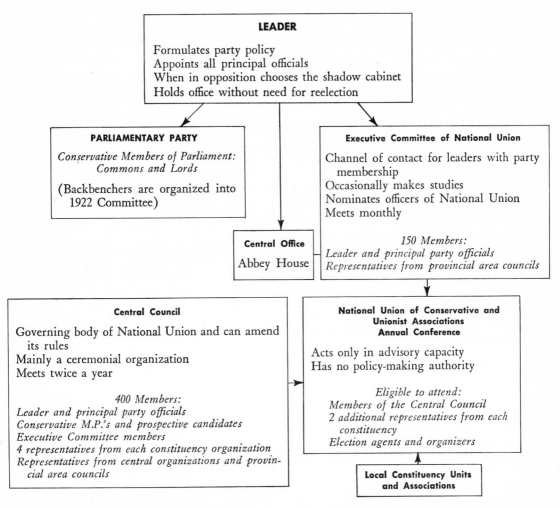

LEADER

Formulates party policy
Appoints all principal officials
When in opposition chooses the shadow cabinet
Holds office without need for reelection

PARLIAMENTARY PARTY

*Conservative Members of Parliament:
Commons and Lords*

(Backbenchers are organized into
1922 Committee)

Executive Committee of National Union

Channel of contact for leaders with party
  membership
Occasionally makes studies
Nominates officers of National Union
Meets monthly

*150 Members:
Leader and principal party officials
Representatives from provincial area councils*

Central Office

Abbey House

Central Council

Governing body of National Union and can amend
  its rules
Mainly a ceremonial organization
Meets twice a year

*400 Members:
Leader and principal party officials
Conservative M.P.'s and prospective candidates
Executive Committee members
4 representatives from each constituency organization
Representatives from central organizations and provin-
cial area councils*

**National Union of Conservative and
Unionist Associations
Annual Conference**

Acts only in advisory capacity
Has no policy-making authority

*Eligible to attend:
Members of the Central Council
2 additional representatives from each
  constituency
Election agents and organizers*

**Local Constituency Units
and Associations**

conference democracy and responsibility. Since such a change would end the century-old control of the National Union's officials over the conference, there is, not surprisingly, considerable hostility from that quarter, which claims that it represents "the entire voluntary organisation of the party."

THE NATIONAL UNION, THE CENTRAL COUNCIL, AND THE EXECUTIVE COMMITTEE The character and history of the National Union hardly support so impressive a claim. When the National Union was founded in 1867, it was intended to be "a handmaid to the party." Whereas the Labor party in its early period was intended to be the servant of the Labor movement *outside* Parliament, the extra-parliamentary Conservative organization was established to be the servant of the Conservative party *inside* Parliament. In particular, the purpose of the National Union was to win the adherence of those classes the Tories themselves had enfranchised in 1867, especially the working classes. Despite numerous reorganizations, however, the National Union has never become more than an electoral machine and a channel of communication—almost entirely one-way—between the parliamentary leaders and their followers.

The Central Council, the National Union's governing body, meets only once a year; in practice, it is a smaller but more vocal version of the annual conference. It acquired some fame in 1934 by hotly debating though finally approving the government's proposal for Indian constitutional reform, but this degree of controversy was unique. The question has been raised, however, of whether Conservative leaders would continue in office if the right-wing members of their party should defeat them in the Council on a crucial issue.

The Executive Committee (which normally meets every second month), its General Purposes Sub-Committee (which meets monthly), and a host of advisory and central committees and boards act "on behalf of the National Union," which in practice means on behalf of the parliamentary leaders, or leader. The first two are composed of representatives of the areas into which the constituencies are grouped (there are twelve areas in England and Wales). The Executive Committee has the power to approve or withdraw approval of the admission of associations and to settle disputes between constituency associations. Among the special bodies is the Advisory Committee on Parliamentary Candidates, which, it was decided in 1935, would have to approve constituency nominations in order for the candidate to receive "a letter of commendation from the Leader of the Party," a supply of parliamentary speakers, a financial grant for electoral expenses, and Central Office assistance—a powerful combination. This role of the Advisory Committee in endorsing candidates before they are adopted by the constituencies was underlined in the Maxwell Fyfe Report. In practice, however, the national organs of the Labor party play a more prominent role in the selection and adoption of parliamentary candidates than does the National Union or the Central Office. Moreover, the Conservatives do not run an official candidate (as does Labor) in the rare instances in which constituencies insist on a candidate who has been denied official recognition.

Whatever the provisions, the real function of the National Union, the Council, and the Committee is to provide means by which the leader can keep in touch with all sections of the party. Through them he can learn of any discontent or special currents of feeling among ordinary members of which he ought to be aware, and through them he can communicate his decisions and policy to the party membership.

THE CENTRAL OFFICE   As one might expect, it is the leader and not the Executive Committee (as in the Labor party) who controls the Conservative central office. The party chairman, who heads the central office, is appointed by the leader, as are its vice-chairman and treasurer. The principal administrative official, the general director, is responsible to the chairman.

Like Labor's Transport House, the Conservative central office, Abbey House, organizes local party groups, prepares propaganda and publicity, raises money, draws up lists of recommended candidates, and oversees the general efficiency of the party organization. It works closely with area and constituency organizations and with the National Union, trying to guide and mold them to its policies. One of the most significant developments in party organization is the extended use by the Conservatives of paid professional agents. These agents are career officials, trained, examined, and certified by the party's central examination board, which provides experienced and skilled supervision in constituency campaigns. Largely by the use of these party agents, and recently by tightened national party control, the Conservatives have developed in many places constituency organizations that are more efficient and more continuously operative than those of Labor.

No less important is the vast expansion of Conservative party propaganda since the war. In a startling change from earlier types of party publicity, this propaganda has been aimed at a mass audience, and with remarkable results: the Industrial Charter, for example, sold over two and a half million copies in three months. The party also uses such media as popular tabloids to put across its appeal. Since 1945 the central office has also contained the Conservative political center, which concentrates on special publications for active party members and is closely linked to the party's Research Department, which, especially when the party is in opposition (and therefore without civil service help), engages in long-range research to aid in the formulation of party policy.

Both the Conservatives and Labor have had aggressive, forward-thinking "ginger groups" outside the official party structure, but they commonly absorb the brightest members of these groups in due course. The Bow Group, which was formed in 1951, shot into prominence as a result of its criticism of Eden's Suez policy and its support for the policy toward former dependencies embodied in Prime Minister Macmillan's famous "winds of change" speech to the South African Parliament in 1961. The group contributed fifty-seven candidates to the 1959 election, of whom ten were successful, and placed fifteen in Parliament in 1964. The Bow Group's fervor thus diverted, its place was taken by a group of young, outspoken, left-wing Conservatives called Pressure for Economic and Social Toryism (proudly bearing the initials P.E.S.T.); P.E.S.T.'s publications appeal for "modern Toryism" and attack the "one class" image of the party in a manner reminiscent of the *Universities and Left Review,* which used to needle the Labor party with its arguments for unilateral disarmament. Neither compares with the Bow Group's magazine, *Crossbow,* nor produces the latter's workmanlike independent research pamphlets, which more closely resemble the work of the Fabian Society.

THE PARLIAMENTARY CONSERVATIVE PARTY Within the parliamentary Conservative party, the leader commonly has the same overriding personal power that the formal organization of the party provides him, but he is subject to much more ultimate restraint. Unlike the Labor leader, the Conservative leader chooses his own shadow cabinet when out of office. When the party is in power, Conservative ministers do not even attend the meetings of Conservative backbenchers. The leader alone determines how the party whip is to be used or whether a member is to be expelled from the party. Moreover, the formulation of party policy is officially the leader's prerogative.

Yet the name given to the meeting of Conservative backbenchers, the "1922 Committee," carries a moral that few Conservative leaders can overlook. It was the famous Carlton Club meeting of Conservative M.P.'s in October 1922 that led to the downfall of Austen Chamberlain, leader of the Conservative party in the House of Commons. The organization of private (that is, non-officeholding) Conservative M.P.'s into the 1922 Committee followed almost immediately thereafter. Contrary to Labor party practice, ministers may attend the meetings of this group only by invitation. This is true also of the specialized committees of the Conservative parliamentary party, which have no fixed personnel, as is common with Labor. Thus there is a significant degree of organization among the Conservative private members that exists apart from ministerial direction and influence. And while the 1922 Committee is the parliamentary equivalent of the National Union—that is, it is a sounding board of sentiment, not a policy maker—the leader can remain such only if he retains the confidence of his parliamentary members.

It is this fact that explains the apparent paradox that three Conservative leaders, Austen Chamberlain, Neville Chamberlain (to make way for Winston Churchill's leadership in 1940) and, though less obviously, Sir Alec Home in 1965, have found themselves compelled to give up their office. It is worth noting that the Labor party has displayed more loyalty to its leaders and less ruthlessness than the Conservative party. Despite widespread dissatisfaction with Ramsay MacDonald's attitude toward socialist goals, it was his decision to form a national government in 1931 that precipitated the break. (The Labor party maintained a solid front against participation.) When George Lansbury in 1935 confronted an irreconcilable conflict between his party's support of sanctions over Italy's attack on Ethiopia and his own pacifism, it was his decision to resign. Despite Gaitskell's unpopular attacks on clause four of the party's constitution, which pledged the party to try to establish a society based on "the common ownership of the means of production, distribution and exchange . . . ," and despite his opposition to unilateral nuclear disarmament, which the party conference approved by a narrow margin in 1960, Gaitskell was reelected party leader in the unprecedented contest with Wilson later the same year.

Although Sir Alec Home lost the basic confidence of his party in his ability to win a future election, he established two important innovations: the presence of the leader throughout the annual conference (although, as we have seen, Heath was the first to implement the practice); and a formalized procedure for the selection of the Conservative leader. Secrecy and agreement on a particular individual by certain Conservative "notables" (sometimes called "the magic circle" or "country house politics" or, more elegantly, the "customary processes of consultation") had played a disproportionate and subsequently bitterly criticized role in the selection of both Macmillan in 1957 and Home in 1963.

The new procedure, approved by the National Union Executive and other relevant agencies, was formally announced in February 1965 and was thus available, after Home's subsequent resignation, for the election of Edward Heath later that year. It is similar, though not identical, to the procedure used by the Labor party. In the event that there are more than two candidates, though this has never yet happened, Labor has an eliminating ballot in which all members of the parliamentary Labor party can vote. The decisive contest is between two names, as in Wilson's hard-fought and closely won battle with George Brown for the election in October 1963.

The Conservative procedure, followed only when a new leader is needed, provides for three ballots, with the voting limited to Conservative M.P.'s in the Commons. The chairman of the 1922 Committee of backbenchers directs the process. Nominations are published, though the names of proposers and seconders remain secret; to win on the first ballot a candidate needs to get both an overall majority and 15 percent more of the votes than any other candidate, a stiff hurdle. On the second ballot, fresh nominations are required (providing scope for further consultative processes), but an overall majority is sufficient. If a third ballot is needed, a preferential voting system is used to bring the new leader a decisive majority. Once this crucial stage of selection has been completed, the choice is presented to the traditional party meeting in Church House, numbering 1,076 persons in 1965, made up of Conservative members of the Commons and Lords, candidates for election, and the 134 nonparliamentary members of the National Union Executive. Although in a

fifty-year period the name proposed to this final party meeting has never been challenged, the process would begin all over again if such were to happen.

In practice, the new Conservative process for selecting the leader worked smoothly and quickly following Home's resignation on July 22, 1965. The first ballot results were: Heath, 150 votes; Maudling, 133; and Powell, 15. Both Maudling and Powell withdrew, and Heath was unanimously accepted at the traditional meeting on August 2, 1965. Not only had the Conservatives used a new and open process for choosing their leader, but Heath was the first Conservative in over forty years not to become both party leader and Prime Minister at virtually the same moment. The subsequent defeat of his party in 1966 and its opposition role in Parliament confront him with greater difficulties in reknitting the party's unity and developing its forward look than faced his predecessors.

The Minor Parties

The Liberal Party

For many generations, until Labor took over this role, the Liberal party (and its predecessor, the Whig) was one of Great Britain's two major parties. Today many of the most important and constructive ideas in British politics—for example, entry into the Common Market—still come from its ranks. The ambition of the Liberals is to form a new reformist center party, and their supporters have worked devotedly for this objective. Yet despite the substantial number of votes that Liberal candidates receive—18.7 percent of the vote in the 168 seats they contested in 1964—these are spread so evenly that in the five general elections since 1950 the party has been able to win only between 6 and 12 seats, several of them in Wales. Moreover, the Liberals' ability to draw votes from both the right and the left, probably in a 1–2 proportion, handicaps their bargaining powers (discussed widely while Labor had a precarious majority between 1964 and 1966) with either of the two major parties. This fact also increases their influence, however, insofar as neither Labor nor Conservatives are willing to adopt policies that would alienate voters to whom the Liberals appeal.

The Liberals have pioneered an organizational innovation—the Liberal Party Committee—representative of the party organization both inside and outside Parliament, which is designed to keep their leader, Jeremy Thorpe, closely in touch with party sentiment. The main extra-parliamentary organization consists of: the annual conference, called the Assembly; the Council, an Assembly in miniature that meets quarterly; the Executive Committee, appointed by the Council; the central office, directed, as in the Labor party, by the Executive; and the Organizing Committee (appointed, like other committees, by the Executive) that plans party strategy. While this structure and its activity attest to the vitality of the party, any greater electoral successes in the future seem unlikely.

The Communist Party

The Communist party in Great Britain, as elsewhere, has followed so opportunistic and shifting a policy that it has disillusioned many of its former supporters and remains in a weak position. It is chiefly of interest because of its efforts, now largely repelled, to infiltrate the leadership of certain unions and to place a few "crypto-Communists" among Labor M.P.'s. In its relations with the Labor party, the Communist party has alternated between scurrilous attacks and efforts to affiliate. These efforts have invariably been rejected, and under present party rules they cannot even be considered.

The Communist party, by itself, is extremely weak numerically, although its members to some extent make up in enthusiasm and unquestioning devotion what they lack in numbers. Since the 1945 election, when the party won two seats, the Communists have not succeeded in placing a candidate in Parliament. They put up a hundred candidates in 1950, in their first and only attempt to fight an election on a national scale, between ten and eighteen in 1951–59, thirty-six in 1964, and fifty-seven in 1966. All their candidates lost their deposits (which are forfeited if the candidate does not receive one-eighth of the total vote cast) in 1951, 1964, and 1966, and virtually all in the intervening elections. Their percentage of votes is so small, therefore, as hardly to be worth noticing, except as an indication of discontent in one or two industrial districts.

3. PROGRAMS AND ELECTIONS

The Party Programs

Americans who look at the British party system are sometimes tempted to think of the country as divided into two hostile camps, one fighting for the maintenance of capitalism and vested interests and the other determined to destroy them. Some English writers, too, have encouraged the belief that between the two camps there can be no compromise and that the struggle can end only in the triumph of one or the other.

If one is looking for dramatic conflicts, however, a reading of the party programs is a disillusioning experience. The differences in position are far less extreme than one might expect, and on some points the positions of the two parties are practically indistinguishable. For this phenomenon there are several explanations. It is true, for example, that the Labor party, according to its constitution, is socialist in principle "and proud of it." The constitution demands "the progressive elimination from the control of industry of the private capitalist, individual or joint-stock; and the setting free of all who work, whether by hand or by brain, for the service of the community, and of the community only." But the party's socialism has been neither radical nor doctrinaire, and its leadership has never suggested that the changes for which it is working should take place other than gradually, constitutionally, and practically. The policy of the Labor party has been to concentrate on individual reforms: to work for the nationalization of certain key industries; for specific improvements in working conditions; for protection against ill health, unemployment, and undernourishment; for education; and for security "from the cradle to the grave." The Conservatives (and, of course, the Liberals) realize that they also cannot win an election without appealing to the same middle-class and lower-middle-class voters who have been attracted by much of Labor's program. Thus they too affirm their support of social security and full employment.

The party in power emphasizes what it has accomplished. "We stopped the inessential, we postponed the less essential, and we went right ahead with our priorities," boasted Labor in 1966. But both parties, in their manifestoes, concentrate on what they plan to do in every sphere of life. Thus Labor wrote in 1966 in its manifesto, *Time for Decision,* that it would help to modernize and strengthen British industry, expand agriculture, build houses and new towns, clear slums, coordinate transport, provide jobs for all, reconstruct social security, expand higher education, protect tenants against eviction, reorganize Whitehall, modernize Parliament, and play a key role in the preservation of peace. The Conservatives, in their manifesto, *Action Not Words,* promised to "run the country's affairs efficiently and realistically so we achieve steadier prices in the shops and a really decent standard of social security," get taxes down, improve industrial relations, provide better transport, help agriculture, provide more generous pensions, establish better education, accelerate housing, check the crime wave, deal with immigration problems, provide more recreation facilities, bring new prosperity to Scotland and Wales (known to be heavily oriented toward Labor), and strengthen the Commonwealth.

Both manifestoes were also specific about certain controversial policies. On public ownership, Labor affirmed its intention of nationalizing steel, taking a public stake in the aircraft industry, removing statutory restrictions on the activities of nationalized industries, and creating a National Freight Authority to coordinate road and rail transport and publicly owned port authorities under regional management. The Conservatives took a tough-with-labor line by warning that they would introduce legislation to forbid the closed shop, to compel unionists to work with nonunion labor, and to give employers the opportunity to seek injunctions against restrictive labor practices "obviously contrary to public interest." Neither, however, spelled out in any detail the way in which it intended to establish the stable income policy or to accelerate economic growth, to which both committed themselves.

On external policies, the two parties differed noticeably both on entering the Common Market (with the Conservatives much more enthusiastic) and on Rhodesia (with Labor's firm stand against accepting the seizure of unilateral independence by that country's white minority contrasting with the Conservatives' emphasis on negotiating with Ian Smith without prior commitments).

Naturally, each accused the other of having left undone those things it ought to have done, as well as doing those things it ought not to have done. Labor harked back to 1964 and the economic crisis it inherited and accused the Conservatives of "tired and discredited policies" and of "backward-looking complacency in industry and commerce, of reliance upon individual and group selfishness as the main motive for change." It appealed for "ending dominance of vested interests, liberating the forces of youth and building a New Britain." The Conservatives, in turn, described Labor's record from 1964 to 1966 as "a depressing catalogue" and asserted they would break away from "the growing constraint of socialism and the dreariness which stems from it." Thus each party claimed that it alone had the true interests of the nation at heart, while the other would sacrifice these interests to those of its dominant group: according to Labor, the "hardfaced" men in the Conservative party who exploit others, and according to the Conservatives, the "socialist bureaucrats" of the Labor party. Thus the stereotypes persist and, indeed, have enough validity in the differences between Labor's equalitarianism and the Conservatives' hierarchical predisposition to carry weight.

Elections

Elections in Great Britain may occur with very little warning, and British parties are therefore obliged to adopt a strategy quite different from that of American parties. In the United States, of course, anyone can predict the date of presidential elections for generations to come. The Constitution requires that the election be held every four years, whether it is convenient or not: candidates may announce their availability a year or more in advance, and there is active competition for delegates to national conventions in the winter and spring preceding an election. The nominating conventions themselves are held during the summer; September and October are dedicated to campaign addresses; by the time the voters make their decision early in November, they have been exposed to many months of electioneering.

In Great Britain, in contrast, the Prime Minister may advise the Queen to dissolve Parliament and ask for new elections any time he desires. Elections are supposed to be not more than five years apart (though because of the war there was no election in Great Britain between 1935 and 1945), but within this five-year period the Prime Minister has complete freedom to set the time of voting. Thus it would be perfectly possible for several elections to take place within a single year, though the cost, inconvenience, and public irritation work strongly against over-frequent elections. A Prime Minister with a strong majority in the House of Commons will probably wait four years. In the course of the fourth year of office, however, he and his colleagues will begin to look for favorable issues on which they can "go to the country," and when they have found such an issue and when the time seems appropriate, the Queen, on the Prime Minister's advice, will dissolve Parliament. Naturally, the Prime Minister attempts to select a moment favorable to his own party's electoral chances, but, as the 1950, 1951, and 1964 elections demonstrated, it is difficult in a complex political situation to be sure to whose advantage the time will work. In any case, except in extraordinary circumstances, the power to dissolve has only a marginal effect on the outcome of the election.

The time between dissolution and election is very short. On the eighth day (not counting Sundays and holidays) after the Royal Proclamation of Dissolution, candidates must have filed their nomination papers, and nine days after that (again excluding Sundays and holidays) the vote is taken. The Conservatives waited until almost the last possible moment in 1964, with the announcement on September 15, dissolution on September 25, the closing of nominations on October 5, the election on October 15, and the opening of the new session on November 3 (the mandate of the old Parliament would have expired on November 5).

Sometimes it is possible to guess in advance when a dissolution is likely to take place, but rumors can be exceedingly deceptive (Labor expected a spring election in 1964). Even under the best circumstances a party must concentrate into three or four weeks a campaign that in America would occupy at least as many months. This means that any party that waits until dissolution to prepare its organization suffers an impossible handicap. To be successful, it must be ready to fight an election at any time. The candidates must be selected and made known to their constituencies, their programs must be worked out and publicized, and every effort must be made to dramatize issues in advance. Foreigners sometimes have the impression that Great Britain is in the midst of a never-ending election campaign, and they are not altogether wrong.

The Constituencies

Candidates for the House of Commons are elected from geographical areas that should be roughly equal in population. This requires periodic redrawing of the boundaries of constituencies; since 1944, this has been done separately for England, for Scotland, for Wales, and for Northern Ireland by permanent commissions composed of five members, mostly civil servants, and presided over by the Speaker. The first general review of boundaries since 1918 resulted from the Representation of the People Act of 1948 (amended slightly in 1949). Since the population had shifted substantially in the intervening period, an almost entirely new electoral map resulted. The total number of seats for the House of Commons dropped from 640 to 625 (largely due to the abolition of the two remaining forms of plural voting: the business premises vote and the university graduates vote [3]); only 80 constituencies retained their former boundaries; and many of the rest were so extensively redrawn as to be new in fact, if not always in name. A further review of constituency boundaries in 1954 was less drastic in results, but it led to the abolishing of 6 constituencies and the creation of 11 new ones (all in England) and brought the membership of

---

[3] The business premises vote was relatively insignificant except in the City of London and a few other constituencies in the larger cities, where it has traditionally been a Conservative asset. There were 12 university seats, however, of which about half were generally held by distinguished Independents, such as Sir A. P. Herbert and Sir Arthur Salter. None of the university seats was ever held by Labor.

the House up to 630. The next redrawing of boundaries will be in 1970.

The British are not wholly satisfied with their current process of revising constituency boundaries. Frequent review of boundaries means continual disturbance not only to party organizations but to those persons who are shifted from one voting area to another. On the other hand, to leave them untouched as long as was common in the United States is to court serious distortion.

Whatever points of criticism there may be, the British process of redistribution is impressive in its impartiality. Moreover, British constituencies have far smaller numbers of people than do American—about 80,000 as compared to 350,000—while the latter vary widely in size within and among states and between urban and rural areas.

At one point it seemed as if there was an anti-Labor bias in representation, both because Labor's strength is so concentrated in urban areas and because rural areas generally have slightly more representation per voter than city areas. The 1964 results seem to contradict this assumption, however, since Labor won that election with a smaller number of votes than it received in 1959. Thus other factors, such as levels of voting in particular areas, may be at least as important in determining results.

The Voters

Any person who is a British subject, twenty-one years of age, and not subject to any legal incapacity is entitled to vote in any election in the constituency in which he resides. Each constituency has a register of those entitled to vote, and it is the responsibility of the government (not of the voter, as in the United States) to see that the register is kept constantly up-to-date.

What are the decisive influences on voters? It has long been customary to say that the personality of the leader, the platform of the party, and the appeal of the local candidate are the major factors. In recent elections, however, there has been a flood of nationally produced propaganda, partly through radio and, even more, through TV, and partly through the press. Increasingly this material is the result of carefully designed surveys of public opinion, particularly among the "Mugwumps"—that is, the target, or floating, voters. It is even said that the local campaigns of candidates have only about a 15 percent influence on the outcome of an election. Thus a great deal more attention than in the past needs now to be paid to the parties' use of public opinion polls and advertising.

Opinion Polls and Propaganda

Opinion polls shot into public prominence between 1959 and 1964 as the best, indeed the only, continuously available evidence of public sentiment. They have been used to predict the results of all postwar British elections and have done so with almost invariable accuracy.[4] National Opinion Polls, a subsidiary of Associated Newspapers, began regular political polling in 1961, thereby providing Gallup with a worthy com-

[4] **Accuracy of the Polls 1945–64**

(Winner and percentage margin of victory)

Year	Actual result (G.B. only)	Gallup percent	Daily Express percent	Research Services percent	National Opinion Polls percent	Average error percent
1945	Lab. 9.8	Lab. 6.0	—	—	—	3.8
1950	Lab. 3.3	Lab. 1.5	Lab. 0.5	—	—	2.3
1951	1	C. 2.5	C. 4.0	C. 7.0	—	6.0
1955	C. 1.9	C. 3.5	C. 2.7	—	—	1.2
1959	C. 4.2	C. 2.0	C. 3.7	—	C. 3.9	1.0
1964	Lab. 1.9	Lab. 3.5	C. 0.8	Lab. 1.0	Lab. 3.1	1.6
Average error		2.5	2.5	4.7	0.8	2.5

[1] In 1951 Labor won 1.5 percent more votes in Great Britain, but the Conservatives won a parliamentary majority.
Source: The *Times* (London), March 9, 1966.

petitor for public attention. With the apparent resurgence of the Liberals after 1959 and the growing possibility that Labor might oust the Conservatives in the next election, the succession of election-oriented polls provided a sense of continuous excitement. This continued between 1964 and 1966 because of Labor's slim majority. As a result, poll watching had considerable impact on both the style of the election campaigns and the morale of the participants.

To pick an election winner from public opinion polls requires translating attitudes to parties, policies, and political leaders into a relationship between votes and parliamentary seats. This poses major difficulties. It requires in the first place random sampling over a wide area, particularly in those places that are most decisive in an election—that is, those that are outside the safe seats.[5] A further problem is that the Labor party has traditionally "wasted" votes by building up larger majorities in its safe seats than the Conservatives do; hence there appeared a bias in the electoral system that gave the latter more seats for their votes. Thus in 1951, the Conservatives won a working majority in the House of Commons although Labor secured more votes. Had the same bias appeared in 1964, the Conservatives would have won again. The public opinion polls (except the *Daily Express* poll) predicted correctly in 1964, however, because the 1951 bias did not again operate on the electoral results. In 1966 there were no doubts.

Poll results are watched carefully by politicians who are seeking a favorable moment to call an election. The results may encourage emphasis on particular topics, and they undoubtedly create dismay or elation among party workers, depending on which party is reported ahead. Party members have always had their own unofficial ways of testing public opinion, usually by talking to persons from a wide range of occupations. In 1956, Labor commissioned a private poll, and two years later the Conservatives sponsored a local survey after the Rochdale by-election. Only after 1959, however, did Labor in particular begin seriously to take advantage

of polling techniques and of the associated publicity.

Labor's earlier refusal to employ market research and public relations techniques stemmed from an ideological resistance to accepting middleman "interference" between them and their constituents and from objections to what were called "highly paid motivational persuaders." The party's conversion to the use of private polls—and propaganda—was undoubtedly associated with the facts that both Gaitskell and Wilson had training as economists and were therefore familiar with statistical methods and that the Conservatives had used advertising with such marked success in the 1959 election. In 1960, *Socialist Commentary* commissioned Dr. Mark Abrams of Research Services Ltd. to conduct a private poll that was subsequently printed as a Penguin Special, *Must Labour Lose?*. This study brought startling evidence that Labor had lost touch with younger people and had acquired an image "increasingly obsolete in terms of contemporary Britain."

From 1960 on, Labor's publicity campaign paid special attention to transforming Labor's image among "uncommitted electors in uncommitted constituencies" into that of an united, energetic, and go-ahead party. By the time Wilson became party leader in 1963, expenditures on advertising and public relations had trebled since 1959, and the money was being spent much more thoughtfully and selectively. Major press campaigns, the concentration of television time on economic and other domestic problems, and the direction of special attention to white-collar workers and youth evidenced that Labor was responding to the kind of information that polls revealed about voter interests. More professionalism and better coordination were developed between Transport House and party leaders, even though Wilson insisted on keeping personal control of the day-to-day running of the final election campaigns, and on dominating them both in 1964 and 1966.

The Conservatives had less need than Labor to be converted to advertising and the usefulness of polls, but their splits over party leadership and their dispiritment over the party's slipping popularity led them to make less effective use of both after 1959 than did their opponents. More than is generally realized, the

[5] No polling group samples opinion in Northern Ireland (commonly an overwhelmingly Conservative area) because its party divisions differ from those of the rest of the United Kingdom.

Conservatives focus a great deal of their election planning on their manifesto. But in 1964 the knowledge of concealed economic crisis, and in 1966 the fact that the party was just beginning to pull together again under Heath's leadership, made its preparation less an exercise in unity than it had been on earlier occasions. Before 1959, the Conservatives had "prosperity," "good government," and "Mr. MacWonder" (i.e., Macmillan) to promote. Thereafter they failed to find such attractive themes. Moreover, they had difficulty popularizing Sir Alec Home in 1964, especially over television, and relatively little time (though he was a better subject) for popularizing Heath in 1966. In the future, however, the Conservatives can be expected to use modern techniques to the full, and with great effect.

The Candidate

Although some constituencies—for example, Manchester—prefer to be represented by local men, candidates for Parliament in Great Britain are not required by law or custom, as in the United States, to be residents of their own district. This fact makes it possible for the central office to find safe seats for candidates whose talent makes their presence in Parliament desirable but who would never be elected by, or who have actually been defeated in, their own place of residence. In the United States the wisest Democrat in the country might live in Vermont and the ablest Republican in Mississippi, but neither is likely ever to sit in the House of Representatives or in the Senate. In Great Britain, as long as candidates are citizens and of age and as long as they do not fall in the rather oddly juxtaposed categories of criminals, bankrupts, lunatics, peers, and clergymen of the Roman or the established church, they may run in any constituency in the realm.

According to British electoral law, anyone—excepting these few—may become a candidate for Parliament who, on nomination day, files papers signed by two registered electors (who are called nominators) and by eight other registered electors who "assent" to the nomination. Sometimes candidates secure large numbers of assenters to show the breadth of their support. There are no primaries, as in the United States, since in practice the decision on the candidate is made, as we have seen, by the local party organization. In addition, the sum of £150 must be placed on deposit, the money to be forfeited if the candidate does not receive one-eighth of the total number of votes cast in the election. This financial provision is intended to restrict frivolous candidacies; actually it has the effect of strengthening the official party organizations, which can more easily provide the money and ensure a sufficiently large vote. For a candidate to "lose his deposit" is something of a political disgrace, and on the morning after an election there is considerable curiosity to see which candidates have undergone this humiliation.[6]

The initiative in selecting candidates for the major parties belongs to the constituency organizations. As one would expect, the local organization of the Labor party (whose general management committee must include representatives of local trade union and other affiliated organizations) is more complicated than that of the Conservatives. Both parties, however, have small executive committees that hold the real power. Often the group asks, and acts upon, the advice of the central office, and in both parties the candidate chosen by the executive committee is presented for formal approval to a general meeting of party members. In the Labor party the candidate must also win the approval of the national executive committee, and he must be a dues-paying member of the party and, if eligible, of a trade union. Since 1945, as we have seen, the Conservative central office has similarly insisted on national endorsement of candidates.

Long before he files his nominating papers, an official party candidate begins to "nurse" his constituency, showing himself in public as much as possible, joining local clubs, meeting the voters, and generally making himself well known and popular. Conservative candidates, who often have considerable personal wealth, discover that every charitable organization in the constituency expects a financial contribution; and although Labor's less affluent candidates can hardly hope to win popularity in this fashion, they compensate for their handicap by

---

[6] In 1966, 237 candidates lost their deposits: 3 Labor, 9 Conservative, 104 Liberal, 57 Communist, 10 Scottish National, 18 Welsh National, 1 Irish Republican, and 35 others.

the assiduity with which they visit, advise, and help the residents of the district, often becoming a combination of errand boy and father confessor whose time and services are expected to be at the disposal of every voter.

Once a general election has been called, this activity is intensified. The candidate shows himself as widely as possible; if he cannot call personally on every voter in the district, he is at least likely to do so in strategic places. Often he tours his district in an open car, stopping in each city street and in each country village and speaking with the aid of a microphone, while his party workers ring doorbells and bring the voters out to hear him.

The Agent

In addition to a candidate, a well-organized constituency has an agent, whose job it is to know the intricacies of the election law and to see that his party does not violate it, to direct the work of fighting a campaign, and, between campaigns, to build an organization and prepare the strategy for victory. During an election he is the nerve center of the party organization, assigning workers to the places where they can do the most good, watching the plans and activities of the opposing parties, sensing the feelings of the voters, discovering the greatest threats to victory in time to meet them, and generally keeping all the threads of party organization and activity in his hands. The agents are really professionals, trained by their parties and having their own professional associations. A successful agent may be promoted to a job in a better-paying constituency or in the party's central office. Candidates are dependent upon agents for advice on their campaign activities (although an occasional candidate attributes his political success to the flouting of his agent's instructions), and it is the agent who must plan meetings and arrange and supervise the collecting of signatures and the filing of nominating papers, the securing of committee rooms and meeting places, and the printing and distribution of publicity and advertising.

The extensive use of trained constituency agents has been a striking development in party organization since the war. The Conservative party has by far the largest and best-trained group of agents. Moreover, as the Wilson Report pointed out after Labor's 1955 defeat, some safe Labor constituencies have agents simply because local unions support them while marginal constituencies, which really need them, often lack funds to support an agent. Since then, both parties have worked harder on the marginal and even on their opponents' traditionally "safe" seats.

Election Expenses

The amount of money that can be spent in the election period by any candidate in any constituency is limited by law, the exact figure depending on whether the constituency is rural or urban and on the number of voters it contains. New and lower limits of expenditure were established between the 1945 and 1950 elections, the result of an earlier all-party agreement, but it is generally admitted that these limits are too low, particularly in view of the great increase in printing costs. In any case, no limit is placed on the amount of money that can be spent before an election is called.

In addition to the limitation on actual election expenses, there are heavy penalties, including forfeiture of election, for bribery, "treating," exerting undue influence, declaring false election expenses, and incurring expenses without the authority of the candidate or election agent (a device that prevents private persons from spending money to help their candidate, thus evading the restrictions). There are lighter penalties for paying to convey voters to the polls, publishing propaganda without an imprint, paying for music, banners, ribbons, and other marks of distinction, paying private electors for advertising, publishing false personal statements about a candidate, and disturbing election meetings. Party agents receive elaborate instructions from headquarters warning them of all the pitfalls. The services of bands may be accepted only as a free gift, and even a cup of tea at campaign headquarters must be paid for to avoid a charge of "treating." A 1949 restriction on the number of cars that could be used to transport voters to the polls was removed before the 1959 election without noticeable advantage or disadvantage to either party.

It is even being questioned whether restrictions on election period expenditures serve much purpose. If the candidate with the most money at his disposal (and this usually means the Conservative candidate) has an advantage, this cannot be removed regardless of the restrictions imposed during the limited period of official electioneering. More significant than amounts spent may well be the distribution of resources so as to ensure their most effective use, and the spirit that animates local campaigns.

The Local Campaign

The foundation of the local parliamentary campaign is the canvass. It is the aim of each party to call on every voter in the district, both to give out literature and to learn, if possible, how he will vote. Elaborate and secret records are then compiled, on which the party bases its campaign. No party wastes its time on those who are going to vote for its opponent, but the parties do need to know who their supporters are so that they can be sure to get them to the polls; and they want to know who is doubtful so that they can tell where to concentrate their energy.

Much of the work of canvassing and compiling records is done by women. The Conservatives profit from the leisure of women in the upper classes; but even in the Labor party women often have more time than their husbands and are better able to find a free hour or two in the afternoon to attend meetings, work at headquarters, canvass, or collect dues. Regular meetings are held to keep them informed of current events, and such meetings may perform a social as well as an educational and political service. It is noteworthy that all parties have large women's organizations and that Labor has five women on its national executive committee.

The most effective events in a campaign used to be the formal meetings addressed by candidates and prominent party leaders. Political use of television and other forms of national propaganda have added a new and powerful dimension to campaigning. What has surprised both parties, however, is that far from reducing interest in meetings, television appears to strengthen it, although the older type of formal session is much less popular than more spontaneous street meetings. And if at such meetings there are fewer bands and less ornate decorations than at American party rallies, in one

sense the meetings are livelier than their American counterpart. Heckling has been turned into a fine art, and the candidate must expect to be harried and interrupted by sharp, witty, and inconvenient questions. The test is often one of his good humor and presence of mind rather than of his principles, and a quick and clever response can sometimes do the candidate more good than the most carefully prepared speech.

The best picture the voter receives of the candidate's position is contained in the "election address," a pamphlet of three or four pages mailed to the voters post free. The pamphlet usually contains a picture of the candidate, a statement of the principles and issues in which he is interested, and the events that have distinguished his career. Sometimes the candidate's wife adds a message to the women of the constituency. ("We may not know anything about politics, but we *do* know the price of butter" is typical.) A photograph of her is often included as well. According to the Gallup Poll, these personal manifestoes have been read widely

Election Geography

In any election, each party has certain strongholds that it is almost sure to carry. Labor's greatest strength, as one would expect, is in the working-class districts of the big towns, in some of the smaller industrial towns, and in mining and industrial areas such as South Wales and the northern lowlands of Scotland, Lancashire, and Yorkshire. From 1945 on, Labor has carried every seat in the county of Durham.

The Conservatives are strong in the residential districts of the large cities (for example, the West End of London), resort towns such as Bournemouth, and the southern suburbs of London, Sussex, and Surrey. Surrey has given all its seats to the Conservatives since 1945.

The Liberals receive most of their support from the "Celtic fringe" of Cornwall and Wales, where, among other considerations, the Nonconformist vote is still strong.

Yet these data indicate a much simpler election map than actually exists. The fact is that in almost every area, even those regarded as impregnable strongholds of one party or the other, there is a very sizable group of voters supporting the opposition. Thus in 1959, when the Conservatives increased their majority in the House of Commons for the third time in succession, the only area in Great Britain that cast fewer than 25 percent of the votes for Labor was Devon (22.3 percent), where 25.8 percent went to the Liberals. In the same election, Labor did not poll less than 30 percent of the vote in any of the nineteen largest cities of the country and less than 40 percent in only two. The Conservatives, in turn, secured less than 40 percent of the vote in only one large city, and less than 30 percent in the east end of the County of London.

In 1966, when there was a 3 percent swing to Labor for the second election in a row, the Conservatives similarly held their own in county averages. In only eleven constituencies in the whole of England did the Conservative vote fall below 20 percent and in fifty-five others below 30 percent. On the other hand, those cities that had below-average swings to Labor in 1964 compensated with above-average swings in 1966. Although it is particularly difficult to measure the swing within a social class, computer analyses indicated that the swing to Labor in 1966

Geography of a Typical British Election (1959) [1]

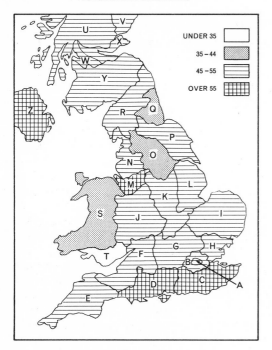

PERCENTAGE OF VOTES CAST FOR
CONSERVATIVE CANDIDATES

UNDER 35
35 – 44
45 – 55
OVER 55

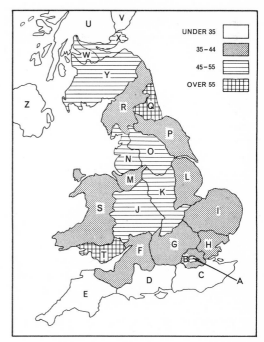

PERCENTAGE OF VOTES CAST FOR
LABOR CANDIDATES

UNDER 35
35 – 44
45 – 55
OVER 55

Important cities are in parentheses. **A** County of London **B** Suburban Boroughs **C** Southeast **D** Wessex (*Portsmouth*) **E** West of England (*Plymouth*) **F** Severn (*Bristol*) **G** South Central **H** Outer Essex **I** East Anglia **J** West Midlands (*Birmingham, Coventry*) **K** Northeast Midlands (*Nottingham, Leicester*) **L** Lincolnshire **M** Cheshire **N** Lancashire (*Liverpool, Manchester*) **O** West Riding (*Sheffield, Leeds, Bradford*) **P** East & North Riding (*York, Hull*) **Q** Northeast England (*Newcastle*) **R** Border **S** Rural Wales **T** Industrial Wales (*Cardiff, Swansea*)
SCOTLAND **U** Highlands **V** Northeast **W** Clyde (*Glasgow*) **X** Forth (*Edinburgh*) **Y** Lowlands
NORTHERN IRELAND **Z** (*Belfast*)

[1] The areas are those used by David E. Butler, *The British General Election of 1959*, p. 190.

was slightly better than average in middle-class seats, including seaside towns and commuter constituencies.

No party has won an absolute majority of votes since 1935. Labor's 13,064,951 votes in 1966, 47.9 percent of the total cast, marked the highest number and highest percentage it had ever won. It secured a substantial majority in the House with its 363 seats. The Conservatives, with 11,418,433 votes, won 41.9 percent of the poll and 253 seats. The Liberals, with 311 candidates, secured 2,327,533 votes, 8.6 percent of the returns. Their intervention resulted in 183 seats being won on a minority vote: 129 Conservative seats, 43 Labor, and 11 of the 12 Liberal seats. Forty-six candidates were elected with a majority of less than 1,000 (20 Labor, 25 Conservatives, one Liberal). The lowest majority, three votes, was secured by a Conservative. Thus in many places the scales were more evenly balanced than appears from the final result.

4. EFFECTIVENESS OF THE BRITISH PARTY SYSTEM

By now it should be possible to hazard certain answers to the questions asked at the beginning of this chapter.

Choice of Candidates and Policies

In the first place, certain critics charge that the choices offered by British parties are narrow and unnatural. Human interests and human desires, they point out, are almost infinite in their diversity; to force them all into one of two molds is to destroy the representativeness of the system and to oblige people to vote, not in favor of a program for which they feel genuine enthusiasm, but against the program they dislike the more. Particularly among the middle classes, men complain that they are compelled to choose between a party pledged to the interests of big business and a party pledged to the interests of organized labor, and that such a choice is a mockery.

Paradoxically, other critics make exactly the opposite complaint. Extreme Conservatives and Laborites protest that the programs of the two parties, in appealing to the uncommitted voter in the middle, have become so similar that each has sacrificed its essential beliefs and made any real choice impossible. Left-wing Laborites, as suggested, feel that their party is too lukewarm in its socialism, that it makes too many concessions to the middle-class element, and that left-wingers are compelled to vote, on election day, not for the radical program they would prefer but for a milk-and-water reformism that completely misrepresents their attitude. Similarly, many an old-line Tory of the Colonel Blimp vintage finds himself horrified at the Conservative party's movement toward a collectivist program. Yet, since there is no way in which he can vote clearly and unmistakably for the old England of the ruling classes and the vested interests, he votes reluctantly for a program in which he does not believe. Both of these groups would charge, in short, that everybody in England is obliged to accept the kind of program that appeals, in particular, to the lower-middle classes.

Party Representativeness

Another paradox arises when one questions the representativeness of the parties. As already noted, it is the extremists and the militants—that is, voters who are not typical of the electorate as a whole—who are most likely to join a party organization. Thus the party that is most representative of its rank and file is less likely to work out a program that is representative of the community in general. In this sense, extreme democracy inside the party may be a handicap to democracy outside, and the giving of authority to a party's leaders may actually increase the representativeness of the party's program. For it is the extremists who find it most difficult to compromise and who are most willing to take a noble, unyielding, and doctrinaire stand. But the responsibilities of the party's leaders are considerably broader. They are expected to lead the party to victory, and for this they have to win the support of those who are not party members. The party members will vote for them anyway: they have nowhere else to go. It is the uncommitted voter who must be won. Thus the party's leadership is more concerned with finding a program that can attract the support of the community in general; it will stop only at that point where a loss of enthusiasm on the part of party workers will provide a counterbalancing threat to success in the election.

Intraparty Organization

It is natural, however, for members of both great parties to complain about the lack of democracy in party organization: in the Conservative party, it is charged, the leader and his chosen associates make the crucial decisions, and the rank and file are free only to cheer and to "recommend"; in the Labor party, it is charged, the trade union bosses dominate the party conference, and the parliamentary leader is free from effective party control. No system, say the complainants, so undemocratic in its foundations can possibly be democratic in its results.

To some extent, the Labor party has worked out more democratic procedures than the Conservative. There is more, even if still not enough, participation in local organizations. Moreover, through the mechanism of the party conference the rank and file have an opportunity to challenge party policy, to cross-examine party leaders, and to take part in a vigorous debate that has a powerful psychological influence. At the same time, through its customary control of the less active but more numerous trade union votes in the conference and through the relative freedom of the parliamentary Labor party, the leadership can usually prevent the party from taking action that would alienate a large number of uncommitted voters. Thus the leadership is held responsible to the rank and file of the party not in the sense that it is likely to be outvoted but in the sense that it is forced to listen to criticism and to justify its policies. This is the case also within the parliamentary party, where backbenchers discuss issues freely and often critically with their leaders, even when the latter are in office.

In the Conservative party the balance is different: the personal power of the party leader is greater, and the prestige of the party conference is less, although the leadership is now beginning to undergo the kind of cross-examination and to participate in the kind of debate that characterize a Labor conference. Yet, as we have seen, the parliamentary party can be ruthless in deposing a leader if he appears out of

step or ineffective. Thus if immediate checks on the leader are less obvious in the Conservative party, the ultimate controls tend to be more drastic.

Interparty Compromise

Perhaps the greatest advantage of the British party system, as a two-party system, is the extent to which it facilitates political compromise. Some observers, both native and foreign, used to consider Great Britain a likely prospect for class war and violent revolution on a Marxian pattern. Nowhere else had industrialism developed so extensively, and nowhere else was it possible to find the bulk of the people falling into such distinct and apparently innately hostile classes: workers on the one hand, and "exploiters" and their retainers on the other.

Yet the underlying assumption of democracy is that free men can find a peaceful solution of their differences, determining what reforms are necessary and carrying them out without resort to violence and in such a way as to satisfy, not just a bare majority, but the good sense of the preponderance of the community.

What strikes the foreign observer of British party politics is the extent to which both parties, in appealing to the voter who is not pledged to either party, have had to moderate the prejudices of their own extremists and, by so doing, to work out a program that is far less distasteful to the opposition. Labor can find in the Conservative program many points with which they agree, even if the program does not go far enough and shows too much tenderness for vested interests. And the Conservative can find in Labor's program moderation and respect for common sense and constitutional procedure, not to mention a similarity to some of the points in his own program.

Party Effectiveness

One last paradox concerns the effectiveness of each party in carrying out its program, for here too a restriction on democracy within the party may be said to contribute to democracy on a national plane. The high degree of party discipline, as exercised over members of Parliament and also over constituency organizations, often leads to charges of intraparty dictatorship;

yet it is only a disciplined party which can ensure that the promises given the voter by the party's leaders (promises which presumably have attracted the voter to support the party) are going to be respected. Freedom for each party representative to follow his own conscience or whim may mean the failure of the party as "an effective instrument for carrying out the judgment of the voters once they have made a choice of parties."

In making the parties such an effective instrument, the two-party system performs an essential function. The voter could make a more accurate choice and one closer to his own ideas if there were a greater variety of major parties representing each gradation from reaction to revolution. But there would be no guarantee, and in fact the probabilities would be all against the possibility, that any one party would receive a majority of the seats in the House of Commons and thus be in a position to carry out its program. Accordingly, the voter would never have the satisfaction of voting for a definite program but instead would be voting for a party whose general attitude pleased him. Moreover, it would be harder for the voter to choose among the parties, for their records would be more obscure; no party would exercise control, and no party could be blamed or praised for what resulted. Under a two-party system, however, so long as a party is well disciplined, responsibility cannot be evaded. If a party has a clear majority, it has no excuse for not carrying out its program. Without a clear majority, even the clearest program is meaningless, because the party lacks the strength to put it into effect.

Thus one runs into the paradox that clarity of choice must be modified in the interest, not only of compromise, but even of giving the voter any choice at all. For the only effective choice the voter can have depends upon reducing the principal positions to two.

Conclusion

By this time it should be evident that many of the criticisms made of the British party system cancel one another out and that it is impossible for this system, or any system, to meet some of the criteria of an effective and democratic system without simultaneously departing from others. In achieving a balance of the various desiderata, however, the British have not been unsuccessful. The choice presented to the voter, even if a moderate one, is clear and real, for there are significant differences in the programs, similar though they may be in many respects. Moreover, the programs, in attempting to attract as many voters as possible, tend to be representative of the desires of the electorate as a whole even when they depart from the desires of the most militant party members. In neither party do the rank and file have direct control over the decisions of their leaders; but in both parties, and especially in the Labor party, channels have been developed for applying great pressure upon the leaders. And finally, the two-party system, by ensuring that one party will win a majority of the seats in the House of Commons, provides that party with the effective power to carry out the program the voters have approved.

4. The British Parliament

1. THE HOUSE OF COMMONS: REPRESENTATION

The House of Commons is that part of the British government which, more than any other, is expected to represent all the elements and parties that make up the British people. But *representation* and *people* are both vague words; they give rise to a host of questions relevant to the role of a member of Parliament. Should a representative put the interests of his constituency first, or should he concern himself primarily with the interests of the whole country? Should he feel bound by instructions from his local party or a larger group of his constituents or interest groups of particular importance to his area, or should he make up his mind on each issue according to his own convictions and to the evidence presented in Parliament? Should he be bound to follow the policies of his party only when they adhere to what was presented in its election manifestoes, or should he support his party leaders and organization at all times?

A century and a half ago, Edmund Burke rejected the contention of his constituents in Bristol that he should act in accordance with their instructions and successfully asserted his right to make decisions as a representative for England rather than for Bristol. As with so many of Burke's views, this concept that a member of Parliament is a national representative first, and a local representative second, has had a deep influence within Great Britain. Both Parliament and the Cabinet, as we have seen, look on themselves as representative of all the people. But it remains true that an M.P. has, in addition, a special relation to his constituency and to his party. If he is less constantly concerned with special favors for his constituents than is a member of the United States House of Representatives, he still has an obligation to help them when he can and, still more important, to keep them informed about currents of public policy and to explain the reasons for his speeches and votes. Moreover, as a member of a party, he has an obligation to weigh carefully any proposed changes of policy and to help to modify them if he feels this necessary, but only rarely to oppose them—only, in fact, when his conscience is at odds with party decisions.

To say this is not to underestimate the difficulties of balancing the three roles that every member of Parliament must fulfill: as local representative, party member, and national representative. Later in this chapter, we shall explore some of the problems of the M.P.; in the meantime it is important to see what kind of person is selected as a representative in Great Britain. For however much a concept of representation may influence a man's approach to an issue of policy, his background, education, profession, and way of life also affect his political behavior.

Members of Parliament

Exhaustive studies of British elections prepared under the auspices of Nuffield College from 1945 on reveal the great variety of experience represented in the House of Commons, and that there are striking and continuing differences between the training and occupations of Conservative and Labor candidates for office. Over the years, the professional element in both parties has been enlarging. Labor M.P.'s have increasingly better schooling. It is still true, however, that the preponderance of Conservative M.P.'s, but relatively few Labor M.P.'s, have attended public schools (by British terminology) and Oxford and Cambridge. Nonetheless, in 1966, a higher number of Labor M.P.'s than Conservatives had attended universities.

A study of approximately equal numbers of Labor and Conservative members (256 to 257) in the 1964–66 Parliament for whom such information was available reveals sharp differences in occupation as well. The most noticeable difference was between Labor's 45 industrial workers and miners, and its 43 trade union officials, and the Conservatives' 2 industrial workers and one union official. Whereas Labor had 36 businessmen and no farmers or landowners, the Conservatives had 97 businessmen and 43 farmers and landowners. Labor had many more teachers—46 to the Conservatives' 6—but fewer lawyers—40 to the Conservatives' 77. Only the number of journalists and writers was relatively even: 40 Labor and 31 Conservative.

This difference in composition of the Conservative and Labor parties illustrates one of the most interesting changes in the character of the Commons. Before the great extension of the suffrage in 1867 and before the rise of the Labor party, most of the members of the House of Commons were gentlemen of means. Some of them received their income from landed property and some from commerce and industry, but both types were present in both parties, and they were almost uniformly the products of a similar education and a similar way of life. Many of the members were related to members of the opposing party, and political opposition was mitigated by a common class background and code of conduct. An effect of the predominantly wealthy membership was that salaries for members were not introduced until 1911. (In 1957 they were raised to £1,750 [$4,900] a year and in 1964 to £3,250 [$9,000] a year.) There are still no offices for members in the Houses of Parliament, no routine typing or clerical assistance, and no private telephones; the visitor often sees M.P.'s sitting on the stone benches in the antechambers dictating to secretaries who must be paid out of that share of their salary that income tax authorities allow for expenses. Thus the past continues to affect the operations of the present—and to handicap those without personal or organizational facilities.

The rise of Labor introduced into Parliament something of the class division that prevailed in the rest of the nation. The Conservative benches continued to look like those of the old House of Commons, but on Labor's benches sat manual workers who had themselves known economic hardship and who had had little education and little time to acquire the refinements of life. Especially in the days when the middle-

Educational Background of M.P.'s and Cabinet Ministers 1918–55

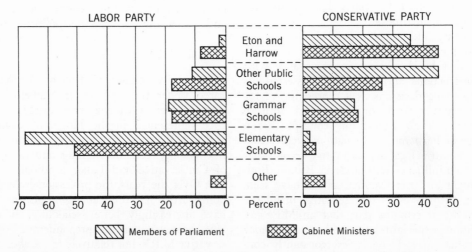

Source: W. L. Guttsman, *The British Political Elite* (London: MacGibbon & Kee Ltd., 1963), p. 96.

class element in the Labor party was small, observers noticed a striking difference between the two parties as the tall, smartly dressed Conservatives filed into their lobby to vote and as their shorter, more roughly clad opponents filed into theirs.

So striking a class distinction might seem at first to have challenged the survival of the parliamentary tradition of peaceful discussion and compromise. Much of Parliament's effectiveness had depended on the mutual respect and friendship, the common code of manners, and, to a large extent, the common political aims that were fostered by a common class origin. It was long popular to say, with Lord Balfour, that parliamentarism was a form of government in which people were so thoroughly in agreement on fundamentals that they could safely afford to bicker. But as the House of Commons came to include men who differed widely not only in education and occupation but in class origin and political philosophy, it was natural to wonder whether they would not disagree so sharply on fundamentals that parliamentary government would be stultified.

Such fears were excessive, for on one fundamental the two leading parties have always been in agreement. Both accept the parliamentary system itself; and that system assumes that while the voters may put in power any party they choose, that party must allow its opponents full freedom to criticize, to organize, and to persuade the voters to vote in their favor at the next election. Thus neither party fears that its opponent will try to restrict its activities or interfere with the free and public working of the system.

Practical Experience

An important consequence of the wide occupational distribution in the House of Commons is the fact that so many members have had some direct personal experience with many of the problems discussed by that body. In the American Congress most of the members are lawyers, and it is obvious that the duties of the lawyer and those of the legislator are easily combined; yet in the House of Commons lawyers form less than 20 percent of the membership. Organized interests in Britain do not limit themselves to attempts to *influence* members of Parliament; they see to it that some of

their own members *become* members of Parliament. American labor groups let rival candidates compete for their support, but the British trade unions have their own members sitting and voting in the House of Commons and contributing their personal experiences as miners or metal workers or transport workers. And whereas the National Association of Manufacturers in America usually brings pressure to bear on congressmen after they have been elected, the Federation of British Industries has its own members sitting in the House of Commons, as do the National Union of Ratepayers' and Property Owners' Association, the National Farmers' Union, the National Union of Teachers, the British Medical Association, the Central Landowners' Association, the Newspaper Proprietors' Association, the Cooperative Union, and the Brewers' Society, not to mention the armed forces, the banks, and the insurance companies. When a technical subject such as the condition of the cotton industry is discussed, both the workers and the factory owners are on the floor to take part in the debate. Party discipline, it is true, generally is strict enough to oblige party members to vote with the party even when its decision runs contrary to the desires of the pressure groups they represent or to their own personal interests; and the pressure group that is to be effective must concentrate on influencing the Cabinet rather than individual members of Parliament. But the House of Commons prides itself on the special attention it renders speeches based on personal knowledge and experience, and the presence in the House of men having expert knowledge on a great variety of subjects means that carelessly or inexpertly prepared legislative proposals are subject to devastating criticism.

2. THE HOUSE OF COMMONS IN ACTION

Ceremonies

The average visitor is likely to be deeply impressed by the amount of ceremonial in the House of Commons. Most afternoons at 2:30 and Friday mornings at 11:00, as the House convenes, the Speaker in wig and gown marches in in solemn procession to the shout of

"Hats off, Strangers!" With him go the chaplain in his robes, the sergeant-at-arms bearing a sword, and the mace bearer with the mace and a long staff decorated with gold leaf and topped by a gilded crown—a much venerated symbol of royal protection, which Cromwell once referred to as "that bauble." The Speaker ascends his canopied throne, the chaplain reads the 67th Psalm and three short prayers, the doorkeeper shouts, "Mr. Speaker at the Chair," the mace is laid on the table (indicating that the House is in session),[1] and as those members who feel less need of divine guidance stream into the room, the House begins the business of the day.

This procedure is a daily event. When a new session of Parliament opens (generally once a year), there are additional ceremonies. Before a Speaker is elected, the Commons, as they assemble, are summoned to the Lords' chamber by the "Gentleman Usher of the Black Rod," a messenger from the House of Lords bearing an ebony rod with a golden tip. There they are directed by Lords Commissioners in scarlet robes and cocked hats to proceed to the election of a Speaker. The Commons then troop back to their own House, elect their Speaker if it is a new Parliament, and report their choice. Finally, Black Rod summons them again to hear the speech from the throne—a speech that, in appearance, is solemnly delivered by the Queen to her loyal subjects in Parliament, telling them what her policies will be during the coming sessions and what legislative action she will ask them to take. In reality, however, as everybody knows, the speech is prepared for the Queen by her Cabinet and represents its plans and policies, not hers. Nonetheless, the Commons return to their own chamber to debate in all seriousness a motion returning "humble thanks" to Her Majesty for her "Gracious Speech."

Before the discussion begins, one more tradition must be complied with: the House must listen to the first reading of a bill "for the more effectual preventing of Clandestine Outlawries" —not because the danger of clandestine outlawries is so great that action must be taken before the Queen's message can be attended to,

but as a sign that the Commons have the power in their own right to proceed with legislation without the Queen's recommendation. In fact, so slight is the pressure for the bill that it is then and there abandoned, to be introduced again in identical form at the beginning of the next session. The House in the meantime moves on to debate the reply to the "Gracious Speech."

Customs of Debate

During its debates the House observes certain characteristic customs. Members never address one another directly or call one another by name. All remarks are addressed to the Speaker, and other members are referred to as "the honorable Member for South Hackney" or the "honorable Member for Bootle" or whatever the member's constituency happens to be—unless, indeed, there is some additional distinction. Thus members of the Cabinet and of the Privy Council are referred to as "the right honorable gentleman, the Member for Limehouse," or Woodword, or Warwick and Leamington. Lawyers are "honorable and learned" gentlemen, officers are "honorable and gallant", and lords and ladies are "the noble lord" or "the noble lady."

Whenever a new member makes his maiden speech in Parliament, he humbly asks the forbearance of the House, and at the close of his speech the next speaker (who is generally a member of the opposing party) congratulates him on the success of his effort, assures him that, although he does not necessarily agree with all of it, he has listened with great interest, and expresses the hope that there will be many times in the future when the House may have the pleasure of hearing him on subjects in regard to which he has special competence. Similarly, when a new Cabinet minister makes his first speech, the next speaker for the opposition congratulates him on his appointment and on the success of his speech before he proceeds to attack the points that the minister has just made.

When the debate is over, the House of Commons also has its peculiar way of taking votes. If there is any doubt in the Speaker's mind as to where the majority lies, or if the minority demands a "division," bells are rung and the policemen in the lobbies and corridors shout, "Division." After two minutes the Speaker puts

---

[1] While Parliament is in session the flag flies from the Tower and at night a light shows.

the question again, two tellers come forward from each side, and the members rise from their places and march into the lobbies. Those who vote "aye" go into one lobby, and those who vote "no" go into another. Six minutes are allowed for late arrivals from smoking room, writing room, restaurant, and corridor. Then the doors are locked, the members are identified and counted, and the tellers come forward to report the result to the Speaker, those representing the majority standing on the right facing the Speaker and those representing the minority on the left.

The Case for "Quaintness"

To foreigners the daily ceremonial, the pageantry of the opening session, the trooping back and forth in response to the summons of Black Rod or to the cry of "Division," the fictions concerning the Queen's speech, the exaggerated courtesy with which members are referred to, and even the invariability with which all maiden speakers, good and bad alike, win the compliments of the House—all these may appear either quaint or ridiculous, and in either case useless.

Nothing could be further from the truth. The ceremonial and courtesy have a tremendous influence on the work of the House—an influence that can be understood by anyone who has read Hitler's contemptuous description of his visits to the Austrian parliament in *Mein Kampf*. For no parliament can retain the respect of its people—and indeed no parliament can transact business—if it is in constant uproar, with members hurling insults at their opponents across the floor, with the opposition determined to do everything possible to disrupt a sitting and to block the Cabinet's program, and with hatred and bitterness making impossible any achievement of the democratic ideal of government by discussion, cooperation, persuasion, and reasonable compromise.

The elaborate ceremonial and the exaggerated deference and courtesy contrive to impress the member and to introduce into his attitude an element of respect and even awe that keep him from indulging in disrespectful or disorderly conduct. On the first day of a new Parliament the occasion is seized, while the Speaker is being elected, to warn new members of the conduct expected from them in the House. So greatly do the ceremonial and pageantry exalt the authority of the Speaker that ordinarily a gesture from him is enough to quiet the House. If a disturbance breaks out, the Speaker simply rises from his seat, and the bickering members subside and seat themselves. If one of them continues to be obstreperous, the Speaker "names" him, and the House (including his own party) votes immediately for his expulsion. Older members of the House like to talk of times when its peace was shattered by strange and shocking episodes, when Speakers were shouted down or members engaged in fisticuffs. But it is because of their rarity that such memories are cherished. The "quaint" and "ridiculous" proceedings make for an order and efficiency that are, or ought to be, the envy of more modern and rationally organized bodies. Even the parading through the lobbies to vote has been praised for its power to soothe ruffled tempers and to cool off the House when feeling is running high.

This does not mean that the discussion is a lukewarm, milk-and-water affair. Courtesy and formality are thoroughly compatible with aggressiveness, sharpness, and vigor; and understatement can be as telling as overstatement. The art of the graceful taunt has been highly developed, together with the art of the witty but cutting rejoinder. Moreover, members are aware that the eyes, if not of the country, at least of the press are upon them, and when they wish to hit, they hit hard. The fact that they call one another "honorable" and congratulate one another on their delivery does not prevent the most vigorous criticism—yet it keeps the debate on the level of rational discussion and good humor and prevents it from degenerating into a purposeless row.

The Speaker

To understand the role of the Speaker of the House of Commons, it is just as well to forget about the Speaker of the American House of Representatives. In the United States the Speaker is a leader of the majority party of the House of Representatives. Once elected, he continues to be a leader of his party and to help in winning the approval of the House for its program. He takes part in conferences on party strategy, and he may use his powers to favor his own party.

In Great Britain, in contrast, the Speaker's prestige depends on his impartiality. When a new Speaker is chosen, he is placed in nomination, it is true, by the majority party's leaders; but he has usually not been an active partisan during his service in the House, and ordinarily he has already prepared himself for the office by presiding over the House in Committee of the Whole or over one of its committees. The opposition is always consulted before his name is proposed, and if the opposition objects, his name is withdrawn.

An almost unprecedented contest over the selection of a new Speaker took place in 1951 after the Conservatives were returned to office. The Labor party did not object to the Conservative candidate for the office but proposed that the former Deputy Speaker was more suitable because of his greater experience. The House voted on the candidates, and the Conservative nominee was elected. In 1959, in a still more unusual development, the Conservatives offered Labor its first Speaker but named the one individual they would support. Labor rejected the offer but subsequently protested the choice of Sir Harry Hylton-Foster because he had been a member of the previous Conservative government. Labor did not vote against him, however, as they were not prepared to put up another candidate. On Hylton-Foster's death in 1965, there was a unanimous election of Dr. Horace King, the first Labor Speaker of the House.

Once selected, the Speaker rises above the parliamentary battle and breaks his ties with his own party. If a new election results in a victory for the opposition, he continues in office (in the United States he would be replaced); and he is proposed for reappointment by the leaders of the party to which he does not belong. In fact, once chosen, the Speaker retains his office until death or voluntary retirement.

For a long time, there was also a tradition that the Speaker of the House of Commons should be reelected without opposition. In 1935, and again in 1945, however, the Labor party, to maintain the vitality of its local constituency organization, contested the reelection of the

Conservative Speaker in his own district, but with notable lack of success. In 1950, no official Labor candidate opposed the Speaker, and an Independent Labor candidate who ran against him was overwhelmingly defeated. In 1964, both the Labor and Liberal parties ran candidates against Sir Harry Hylton-Foster but again without success. It seems, therefore, that the electorate is as determined to maintain the tradition that the Speaker should be reelected to the House as the parties have been to maintain the tradition of reappointment within the chamber.

It is difficult to exaggerate the importance of the Speaker for the functioning of the House of Commons. He regulates debate through the power to select amendments; protects minorities, since closure of debate requires his approval; maintains strict adherence to the rules; and develops a sort of case law of procedure through his rulings. In the words of Colonel Douglas Clifton Brown in 1945: "As Speaker, I am not the Government's man, nor the Opposition's man. I am the House of Commons' man and I believe, above all, the backbenchers' man." As the executive has become more and more powerful, the Speaker has stood out ever more prominently as the defender of the rights of the House, sometimes, as Gladstone once said, defending the House against itself. At a time when party discipline controls voting so rigorously, the Speaker's encouragement of wide-ranging discussion is the most important means of assuring that Parliament fulfills its primary function of airing all aspects of an issue.

The Whips

The effectiveness of the parliamentary system is almost as dependent on the party whips as on the Speaker. It is the business of the whips of each party to keep in touch with party members, to inform them what business is coming up and when a vote is going to be taken, and to see to it that they are present to vote as their leaders want them to. The chief whip of the majority party is the parliamentary Secretary to the Treasury (sometimes still referred to as the "patronage secretary," although patronage is not what it once was or what it still is in the

United States). Three or more Lords Commissioners of the Treasury assist him, as do the comptroller and the vice-chamberlain of the royal household. All these officials draw a salary from the government, and there may, in addition, be a number of unpaid whips. Opposition whips work without official pay.

Reputation to the contrary, it is more important for the whips to be tactful, sympathetic, observant, and likeable than to be fierce. They must know what the private members are thinking, for the whips are the principal channel through which the party's leaders learn of the feeling of the rank and file. They must identify the rising young members of their party. They try to keep the members in line through good temper and reasonable appeals rather than threats and a display of force; but they also know how to suggest to the erring member the perils of party unorthodoxy. They must know what the opposition is likely to do next and what tactics will be most successful in getting business through the House with the least expenditure of energy and risk of embarrassment.

The word *whip* is also used for the notice sent to each party member listing Parliament's business for the week. If an item in this list is not underlined, there is no special reason for the member to be present; and if it is underlined only once, the matter is not very pressing. A *two-line whip,* however, means that the business is really important; and if an item is underscored three times, nothing should keep the member from voting. The party whips will be watching, and a failure to vote will be regarded as a serious sign of disloyalty, particularly since in cases of illness it is now possible to vote by proxy.

Informal Agreements

Gladstone once commented that the British constitution "presumes more boldly than any other, the good faith of those who work it." And it is, in fact, chiefly through voluntary and informal agreements, based on this good faith, that the House decides on its business and gets it done. What efficiency the House has is mainly the result of the ease with which the opposing parties enter into arrangements "behind the Speaker's chair" and "through the usual chan-

nels" to determine what shall be discussed, when it shall be discussed, and how much time shall be allotted to the discussion. Any breakdown of this system of voluntary agreement would be fatal to the working of the parliamentary system as a whole.

Under this method of arranging matters informally, the whips of the opposing parties (who are the "usual channels") consult with the leaders of their parties and then with one another "behind the Speaker's chair." The opposition whips may agree to the speeding up of the debate on certain measures the Cabinet wishes passed if the majority's leaders in turn agree to find time to discuss certain topics in which the opposition is especially interested. There thus exists a paradoxical situation (and one quite incomprehensible to any Communist or authoritarian) in which a Cabinet, which has the necessary votes to force its measures through, voluntarily sets aside time so that the opposition may attack it on the very points the opposition most wants to criticize and on which the Cabinet is most vulnerable.

Without arrangements of this sort, Parliament might have the best rules of procedure in the world and still be an outstanding failure. When a select committee of Parliament investigated the procedure on public business in 1931, the then Prime Minister, Ramsay MacDonald, told its members: "I must pay my tribute to the 'usual channels.' They are simply admirable. Whenever a reasonable arrangement can be made it is made. . . . I do not know how you could do your work in this House without the 'usual channels.' "

The Chamber

If the House of Commons in action is ceremonious, it is also extremely intimate. The room in which it meets is a small one: there are seats for only 346 members on the floor, although in normal times there are somewhat more than 600 members; there is no space even for desks. At one end of the room is the Speaker's throne, and in front of the throne sit three clerks, in wig and gown, at the head of a long table holding books, documents, and two dispatch boxes. Five benches run along either side of the Speaker, the table, and the center aisle. On the Speaker's right sit the members of the majority party, with their leaders (the Cabinet ministers) occupying the front bench, which is called the Front Treasury Bench. Directly opposite them, on the other side of the table, the shadow cabinet (the leaders of the opposition) occupies the front opposition bench. There is no gradation or middle ground. One's position must be taken frankly, for or against the Cabinet.

On ordinary occasions there may be only forty or fifty members in the House (a quorum is only forty), and the front benches may be relatively empty; but at question period and for great debates members flock into the chamber, fill the seats, overflow into the gallery, and stand about the sides, lending a feeling of excitement and drama, of history in the making, which is most impressive and which makes the speakers themselves eager to rise to the occasion.

The smallness of the House has an important influence on the nature of the debate. In such a chamber it would be foolish to engage in oratorical pyrotechnics. The members are on the same level with one another—there is no platform from which to harangue the assembly. If they speak from the front benches, half of their audience is behind them. If they speak from the back benches, half of the audience has its back toward them. The opposition sits only a few feet away: there is no need to shout in order to make it hear. Indeed, the leaders of either party can address one another almost in conversational tones across the table. They may, upon occasion, strike the table or the dispatch box for emphasis, or indulge in a restrained gesture, but there is little temptation to play to the grandstand. It is easy for members to make interjections, ask questions, and carry on a running debate that is serious, intimate, and not devoid of flashes of wit.

There is, in fact, a much admired and carefully cultivated "House of Commons style"—easy, casual, conversational, characterized by presence of mind and equability of temper. Occasionally, as in the case of Lloyd George or Winston Churchill, brilliance in speech will win great admiration; but in general the House prides itself on giving its attention to men who may be clumsy in their expression but who are deeply sincere or thoroughly competent to speak of the subject in hand. The members themselves know the tricks of addressing crowds in their own constituencies, and they have no desire to listen to an eloquent windbag. The man who can impress them is the man who knows his business. No audience, in short, could give

Floor of the House of Commons

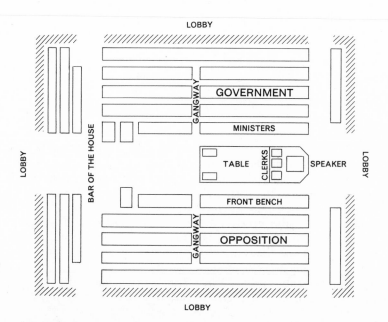

less encouragement to tub thumping or rabble rousing, and any speaker who indulged in such practices would find his listeners shifting their feet, rattling papers, interjecting sarcastic comments, and generally constituting the most difficult of all assemblies to address.

This is an atmosphere and an attitude, it is worth noting, which the House is eager to preserve. When its chamber was destroyed by enemy action during World War II, it was willing to permit changes and expansion in the galleries; but the floor of the House had to remain the same as ever, far too small to accommodate all the members but quite large enough for the kind of debate in which it excels. As Winston Churchill explained in his famous speech of October 28, 1943, when the rebuilding of the House of Commons was under discussion:

> If the House is big enough to contain all its Members, nine-tenths of its Debates will be conducted in the depressing atmosphere of an almost empty or half-empty Chamber. The essence of good House of Commons speaking is the conversational style, the facility for quick, informal interruptions and interchanges. Harangues from the rostrum would be a bad substitute for the conversational style in which so much of our business is done. But the conversational style requires a fairly small space, and there should be on great occasions a sense of crowd and urgency. There should be a sense of the importance of much that is said and a sense that great matters are being decided, there and then, by the House. . . .
>
> We wish to see our Parliament a strong, easy, flexible instrument of free Debate. For this purpose, a small Chamber and a sense of intimacy are indispensable.

The House as Political Educator

It would be hard to imagine an assembly better calculated to make the business of government vivid and comprehensible to the masses of the people. Here the greatest statesmen of the realm—the men whose pictures are in every paper and whose names are on every tongue—face one another in one small room, their followers drawn up behind them, attacking and defending, asking each other pointed and difficult questions, and debating the most controversial issues.

Such a scene is not a daily occurrence: there are many times when the debate is long-winded and dull, when most of the members take refuge in lobby, writing room, or smoking room, and when the leaders busy themselves with committee or administrative work and stay as far away from the House as possible. But on important occasions, when there is a motion of censure or when a highly controversial bill is under consideration, the reality comes close to the ideal. And if this sort of thing happens only occasionally in Parliament, it never happens in the American Congress. There is no way (except briefly on television during the 1960 campaign) in which the presidential candidates of the two great parties may be brought face to face, regularly and naturally, to prove their mettle, a visible symbol of the conflict of ideas and interests. The President appears in Congress only to deliver a message but never to take part in debate, to be cross-examined, to explain his intentions, or to defend his policies before the sharpest minds of the opposing party. Indeed, many of the best minds and most popular leaders of the two parties do not even sit in Congress. There was never a time, for example, under the Eisenhower administration, when he and the greatest members of his party appeared in Congress to be confronted by a Democratic "front bench" composed, let us say, of Adlai Stevenson, John F. Kennedy, Harry Truman, Averell Harriman, Sam Rayburn, and Lyndon Johnson. Three of these gentlemen were not even in Congress, and there was no pressure upon them to work with one another as a daily matter, to adopt a common attitude, or even to arrive at any attitude at all on the most pressing questions of the time. If their views on any subject became known to the public, it was generally the result of carefully framed statements given to the press or delivered in an occasional public address, not of daily political activity carried on in the full glare of public attention on the floor of Congress.

Thus the American who takes his civic obligations seriously and who tries to follow the policies and the leaders of the different parties must have his attention fixed in part on the White House and the Cabinet, in part on each of the two houses of Congress, and in part on the state capitols. He is likely to be all the more confused by the fact that the leaders of the same party may be advocating incompatible and conflicting policies. In Great Britain, however, there is only one place to watch. The Prime Minister and the greatest men, both of his party and of the opposition, sit in the House of Commons (only rarely is an active leader a member of the House of Lords). There they confront each other, not occasionally or on isolated issues, but regularly, week after week, on every issue of any importance. The leaders of the party must come to agreement on what the party's attitude is to be, and there is no way of dodging the issues. The party's record, as well as the record of all its leaders, is open and uniform on every subject that is debated and voted upon.

If effective popular participation in democratic politics depends upon the ability of the ordinary citizen to understand the political events of his day, then there could be no simpler way of conveying to him the rival attitudes of the great parties and their leaders than by this constant, dramatic, and simple confrontation of the two groups at all times. Even the method of voting by walking into different lobbies is a conspicuous way of encouraging parties to act as a unit and of putting the vote of each member on the record—for the man who "crosses the floor" into the lobby of the other party is always a marked man.

The drama and ceremony of the House of Commons have one other consequence. In the heyday of fascism it often used to be said that democracy was drab, colorless, and almost impossible to understand. Dictatorship could, on the contrary, provide spectacles to satisfy the popular need for excitement and emotion, and no form of government could be easier to understand than that of one man ruling over others. In Great Britain, however, such criticism loses much of its point. Parliament, unintentionally perhaps but nonetheless effectively, has made itself both colorful and comprehensible. Systems of checks and balances and divisions of powers in other countries may make democracy too complex for the ordinary citizen to follow or understand. In Great Britain the organized conflict of unified parties makes this task easy and even exciting.

Nothing could better convey the hold of the House of Commons on the emotions and imagi-nation of the British people than Winston Churchill's speech in Parliament on October 28, 1943:

> . . . the House of Commons is much more than a machine; it has earned and captured and held through long generations the imagination and respect of the British nation. It is not free from shortcomings; they mark all human institutions. Nevertheless, I submit . . . that our House has proved itself capable of adapting itself to every change which the swift pace of modern life has brought upon us. It has a collective personality which enjoys the regard of the public and which imposes itself upon the conduct not only of individual Members but of parties. It has a code of its own which everyone knows, and it has means of its own of enforcing those manners and habits which have grown up and have been found to be an essential part of our Parliamentary life.
>
> The House of Commons has lifted our affairs above the mechanical sphere into the human sphere. It thrives on criticism, it is perfectly impervious to newspaper abuse, or taunts from any quarter, and it is capable of digesting almost anything or any body of gentlemen, whatever be the views with which they arrive. There is no situation to which it cannot address itself with vigour and ingenuity. It is the citadel of British liberty; it is the foundation of our laws; its traditions and its privileges are as lively to-day as when it broke the arbitrary power of the Crown and substituted that Constitutional Monarchy under which we have enjoyed so many blessings. . . . I do not know how else this country can be governed other than by the House of Commons playing its part in all its broad freedom in British public life.

The Work of the House

It is customary to say that the principal job of the House of Commons is to make, to support, and to overthrow ministries. Strictly speaking, a ministry consists of about seventy offices of ministerial rank filled by members of the party that has the confidence of the House of Commons. About twenty of the most important ministers comprise the Cabinet, and the decisions of the Cabinet are binding on all ministers. The British also use the word *government* much as Americans use the word *administration* when they speak of "the Johnson administration" or a "Republican administration." Thus, in practice, the terms *ministry, Cabinet,* and *government* tend to be used interchangeably.

According to Bagehot's classic work on the English constitution, "The House of Commons lives in a state of perpetual potential choice: at any moment it can choose a ruler and dismiss a ruler." Today, however, this statement has lost its meaning. With the extension of the suffrage from 1867 on and the growth of party organization and party discipline, the occasions on which the House of Commons is in a position to expel a majority government are virtually nonexistent. Only in those exceptional cases when no party controls a majority of the seats in Parliament (as in 1923–24 and 1929–31) is the ministry unstable; and even then it is not necessarily unstable, for divided opponents are unlikely to wish to force an election. Labor's slim majority between 1964 and 1966 placed its members under great strain but did not prevent it from executing major and extensive legislation. It would take a major crisis, and, indeed, a split within the party itself, to force the resignation of a government composed of the leaders of a party with a majority.

The days are gone when Bagehot could write, "Nowadays, the power of leaders over their followers is strictly and wisely limited: they can take their followers but a little way and that only in certain directions." Actually the reverse is far closer to the truth. Through the party machinery the leaders control their followers and take them pretty much where they will. Usually they are careful to avoid policies that are so unpopular as to split the party, and they may shut their eyes to deviations by their followers on matters of lesser importance. But if the leaders are determined to carry out a policy, even one that is unpopular among a large proportion of their followers, they are almost certain to get their way. If one looks for a peacetime example of a ministry that came to office with a firm majority and that resigned simply because of a hostile vote by the House of Commons, one must turn back to 1885. Consequently, in normal times the ultimate check upon the power of party leaders is not the fear of a defeat in the House of Commons but the fear that the policies they favor will split their party or that these policies will lose them the next election. Thus it is not so much the House of Commons

that chooses and dismisses ministries as it is the people as a whole when, at a general election, they give a majority of the seats to one party.

What, then, is the principal business of the House of Commons? The fact that it is a "legislature" suggests that it makes laws. The fact that it is a house of "Parliament" suggests that it talks. And the latter impression is the more nearly correct. The chief business of the House of Commons, undoubtedly, is to talk—in a variety of ways and for a variety of purposes.

The Function of Criticism

The most important of these purposes is to criticize the ministry, a form of talking which is the special function of the opposition. It can even be said that the most important part of Parliament is the opposition—without it the open criticism which is the health of the system would not exist. This is, indeed, so generally recognized that the leader of the opposition is paid a salary by the government so that he can devote all his time to organizing his attack upon it—an arrangement that must bewilder the citizens of those totalitarian states where the fate of an opposition leader is prison or the firing squad rather than an official income.

To the outsider the job of opposing might appear a thankless one. Week after week, month after month, the leaders of the opposition prepare an attack upon ministerial positions. Each legislative proposal and each administrative action is scrutinized, in principle and in detail, for possible weaknesses. Week after week, month after month, attacks are made and votes are taken. And week after week, month after month, the ministry marches its well-disciplined majority into one lobby, the opposition files into the other, the votes are counted, the opposition suffers another defeat—and the next day the warfare begins all over again, again to end in apparent futility.

In reality, however, there is nothing at all futile about the proceeding. The Cabinet may know perfectly well that it is going to win whenever a vote is taken, and the ministers who are responsible for the legislation or the policy under attack may know perfectly well that they have the votes to sustain their action. But there is slight comfort in this knowledge if, in the meantime, the opposition is sharply and devastatingly castigating their intentions and their competence and if reporters are looking on from the press gallery while the ministers try to find an adequate defense.[2]

The opposition is not talking under the illusion that it may persuade enough of the Cabinet's supporters to cross the floor and overthrow the Cabinet. It is talking to the country at large, and it is trying to make the Cabinet appear to the public eye either incompetent or vicious or, if possible, both. Great Britain, it must be remembered, is in something of a continuous election campaign. The opposition does not know at what moment the Cabinet will ask for a dissolution of Parliament and call for a new election— and the three weeks of the campaign are far too short a time to prepare a case and convert the people of the country to the opposition's point of view. The campaign, therefore, must go on constantly, and the people must be made to see that the opposition is alert, intelligent, public-spirited, and constructive, in contrast to a doddering, blundering Cabinet. Every issue must be explored to see whether it may not be the one on which the opposition can ride back into power. And there is no better way of achieving this goal than by holding the Cabinet and its supporters up to attack and ridicule in the House of Commons on every conceivable point—for there they

must sit and listen to and cross swords with the opposition. There is no evading it. And if no single encounter will destroy the Cabinet, the cumulative effect may be successful.

When a minister finds himself obliged to defend a policy, safe though his party's majority may be, he knows that he will be subjected to the full fire of the opposition, penetrating, sarcastic, shrewd, and witty, sometimes talking in pity and sometimes in wrath, but always searching for the chink in the Cabinet's armor that will reveal that many factors have been ignored, that incredible blunders have been committed, that its understanding is weak and its intention bad. If the minister shows an inadequate grasp of figures, if he errs in his facts, if he is weak or apologetic, he will face the jeers, the interruptions, the interjections, and the shouts of his opponents—and if he allows himself to become rattled or disconcerted, their glee will know no end.

Under the circumstances it is little wonder that the minister and his subordinates, in preparing their legislative proposals and their administrative rulings, try to foresee all the possible objections and criticisms of the opposition, to plug the gaps before the opposition can take advantage of them, and to take every human precaution to make their proposals as foolproof as possible. Nor could anything be more desirable. Changes that the opposition could never achieve on a formal challenge are often anticipated by the Cabinet itself. And if it becomes apparent in committee or even in debate that there is a real weakness in the government's proposals, it is not unusual for it to accept amendments or even to withdraw proposals rather than to press things through to a certain but Pyrrhic victory. Let no one say that debate and criticism are without a very real effect.

The System of Debate

According to the custom of debate, the party that is presenting a motion or a piece of legislation decides who shall introduce the debate and who shall sum up its case. The party that is opposed to the motion or bill decides who shall lead its atack and who shall conclude its argument. The Speaker learns of their identity in

[2] As late as 1771 it was illegal to report debates in the House of Commons. To evade punishment, editors disguised their parliamentary reports under such titles as "Proceedings of the Lower Room of the Robin Hood Society" or the "Report of the Senate of Lilliputia," while the names of participants were altered in a recognizable fashion, so that Sir Robert Walpole might become "Sir R-b-t W-lp-l" or "Sir Rups Walelup." Attendants were bribed to give reporters information concerning the speeches, and Samuel Johnson (who attended the House of Commons only once) composed reports of parliamentary speeches that were considerably more elegant and effective than the originals, but in which he took care that "the Whig dogs" should not get the best of their opponents.

Early in the nineteenth century, however, William Cobbett began to print parliamentary debates as a supplement to his *Political Register;* in 1811 the work was taken over by his printer, T. C. Hansard, who published *Hansard's Parliamentary Debates;* and today, although the government itself now publishes the text of the debates, this record still goes by the popular name of Hansard. If few people read the verbatim text or even a very complete account of the discussions in Parliament, a far larger proportion have a general idea of what is going on and of the attitudes of the opposing parties than is the case in the United States.

advance through the "usual channels," and he learns, either through the usual channels or from the members themselves, the names of others who would like to participate in the debate. In theory the Speaker recognizes anyone who rises and "catches his eye," in the order in which they catch it. But in practice he already has in mind, on important occasions, the names of the people by whom he will allow his eye to be caught. After the spokesmen for the leading parties have had their chance to speak, he is likely to look to the minor parties and to members with differing opinions inside the major parties, or to members representing different interests or geographical areas. The debate proceeds in an orderly fashion, generally a member on one side of the House being recognized and then someone from the opposite side, so that contrasting views follow one another and so that each side may reply to the arguments of the other. Finally, leaders of the two chief parties sum up the case for their side and against their opponents. The Speaker is careful to give proper, and even excessive, attention to the views of the minority. Since the mass of the members of the great parties are ignored in favor of their leaders, the best way to be heard frequently in the House is to belong to a small group which, because of the distinctiveness of its outlook, contributes to every debate. The Speaker also insists that members speak directly to the resolution, so that, in marked contrast to debates in Continental legislatures, which may spread ever more widely from the point at issue, discussions in the House are sharply focused. The result is an orderly, pertinent, and comprehensive debate which, in spite of much unavoidable dullness, generally makes more lively and coherent reading than the equivalent debates in the *Congressional Record.*

Opportunities for Criticism

The debate on specific bills introduced by the Cabinet gives the opposition an opportunity to attack individual legislative proposals. But many of the subjects which are most important, and on which the Cabinet is most vulnerable, have nothing to do with new legislative proposals. One of the biggest jobs of the opposition is to criticize matters of administration and policy-making: to question the foreign policy of the Cabinet, to defend the civil liberties of the subject against governmental interference, to check up on inefficiency or blundering on the part of the bureaucracy, to attack the way in which legislation is being administered, and especially to oversee the general trend of governmental policy in its larger aspects and to make the government defend both its intentions and its practice.

The opposition has its best opportunity to criticize governmental policy as a whole when it debates the reply to the Queen's "Gracious Speech" (which is, of course, a review of the Cabinet's position and a statement of its general program) and during both the general debate on the budget and the series of more specific debates on the departmental estimates. Technically, of course, the latter debates should be concerned with financial matters; but it is customary for the opposition to use this opportunity to criticize the policy of the different departments which are asking for appropriations. If the opposition dislikes the Cabinet's foreign policy, it can use the debate on appropriations for the Foreign Office to attack, not the way in which money is being spent, but the policy pursued toward American involvement in Vietnam, for example, or toward the Soviet Union. Such debates may be introduced by a motion on the part of the opposition to cut the department's appropriation by some trivial sum—perhaps £100; and the "usual channels" are used to determine which departments the opposition most wants to criticize and to apportion a major part of the debate to these particular matters.

In addition to these regularly scheduled debates, the opposition may ask for special facilities to attack the Cabinet's policy in general or to discuss some especially important issue. If the opposition "demands a day" for a *motion of censure,* the Cabinet will find time for a debate in the near future. On such occasions each side brings forth its biggest guns. The Prime Minister and the leader of the opposition take a prominent part in the debate, and the country as a whole has one of its best opportunities to size up the two parties and compare the effectiveness of their leadership. Both parties know that the press and the public will watch closely for some indication of the relative competence of Cabinet and opposition, and each is eager that the verdict of newspapers and political commentators on this particular skirmish be rendered in its favor.

More limited subjects, or those that do not warrant a full-dress debate, may be brought up on the *motion for adjournment* at the close of the day's business. At such times short speeches may be made criticizing or questioning the Cabinet's attitude on particular matters, such as its policy toward Rhodesia or its infringement of civil liberties at home. In unusual and rather spectacular instances, a member may, as soon as the House meets, move to adjourn to discuss "a definite matter of urgent public importance"— the Speaker being the judge of whether the matter fits the definition. If forty members support the motion, the ordinary timetable of discussion is suspended, and later on the same day (when the Cabinet's spokesmen have had time to inform themselves on the subject) a full debate may be held.

What is important about this provision is that even a Cabinet with an overwhelming majority supporting it in the House of Commons cannot prevent the immediate ventilation of any important grievance. The weakest opposition has at least forty votes at its disposal, and once the Speaker has agreed that the matter is definite and urgent, the debate is assured.

The Question Period

Perhaps the most effective check on the day-to-day administration of the government is the question period, an institution with no equivalent in the United States, although to some extent the President's press conferences offer a somewhat comparable source of information. There is never a set time, however, when leaders of the American government are questioned as to their policies, intentions, and the administration of their departments by members of the opposing party in Congress. Four times a week, at the beginning of the sitting of the House of Commons, ministers devote almost an hour to answering questions that have been put to them, in writing and in advance, by any member of the House. Occasionally, members ask questions, even when they already know the answers, in order to attract the attention of the country to an urgent matter. Ministers themselves have been known to inspire questions so that the public might be informed of certain matters.

The questions are numbered, printed with the Orders of the Day, and distributed to the members. As soon as the question period starts, the first questioner rises and begs "to ask question number one," and the appropriate minister replies. The questions are classified so that different ministers can answer a series of inquiries on the same day. As a result, in a comparatively short time, forty or fifty questions, covering the greatest range of topics, may be taken up.

There is considerable art both to asking and to answering the questions. The opposition tries to make things as difficult for the ministers as possible; the ministers often try to make the opposition look as foolish as possible. The questioner must give warning of his question in writing, but he, or other members, may and usually do ask "supplementary questions." Sometimes an initial question, completely innocent in appearance, is asked simply to provide an excuse for springing a trap of carefully planned supplementaries. The minister must know when to give a full and detailed answer, when to avoid the question, when to state bluntly that he has nothing to add to information already available, and when to pass the question off with a joke at the expense of the questioner. A question which is too obviously disregarded or evaded may cause more unpleasantness than a slightly damaging answer and a promise of reform; but there are times, too, when it is better to anger the questioner by evading the question than to make a serious admission. The minister who is clumsy may precipitate a host of supplementaries and a debate on the very subject he would like to avoid; the minister who is pleasant and quick-witted may win the House to his side. Something of the proper tone is suggested by the reply of a minister who, upon being asked in a supplementary question why English bricks were being sent to Scotland, made no attempt to defend the transaction. "The answer," said he, "is a simple one. The English are a simple, kindly, generous people."

Control of the Civil Service

The questions constitute a particularly effective check on the administration and the civil service, as well as the ministry. One of the commonest forms of question begins, "Is the Minister aware that . . . ," followed by an account of some error or inefficiency on the part of a government agent or agency, and ends "and what action does he propose to take?" The fear of this kind of question has a powerful effect on the civil servant and his superiors, who know that any misdeed or mistake, deliberate or otherwise, may be exposed in the light of Parliament and by a person who has no interest in minimizing its seriousness.

Some people suggest that the result is to make the civil service unduly cautious and reluctant to display initiative or imagination and that far too much of its time is wasted in hunting up the answers to questions for the use of the minister who must reply to them. But it would be hard to deny that the system makes for responsibility in two ways. In the first place, the parliamentary heads of the departments or their representatives are on the floor of the House to answer for the errors of their subordinates—so that the administration is itself held in line promptly and effectively. But the opposition itself must also act responsibly, for the administration has its ministers on the floor of the House to defend it with detailed facts.

In Washington, unjustified and inaccurate attacks are sometimes made on the floor of Congress against administrative officials who have no opportunity to defend themselves with equivalent publicity; the opposition in Great Britain, on the other hand, is promptly answered by the very people who are in the best position to refute any charge that is, intentionally or not, unfair.

The Defense of Civil Liberties

Even more important than this check on the civil service, however, is the protection afforded civil liberties by the question hour and the debate on adjournment. There is something both moving and impressive in this spectacle of the highest officials of the kingdom, including the Prime Minister himself, accepting the obligation to answer questions and to provide time to discuss any violation of the rights of the humblest of their fellow citizens. In the United States, a person whose rights are infringed must look to the courts for protection, and in many cases he must engage in long and prohibitively expensive litigation. But in Great Britain, without loss of time and without expense, the subject who feels himself wronged can find a member of Parliament who from zeal for justice or simply an eagerness to embarrass the government will be delighted to cross-examine the most important ministers in order to bring all the circumstances into public view. It is at such times that one has the sensation, increasingly rare in modern times, that the ideal of government as the servant and not the master of each individual human being is being realized in practice.

Moreover, if there seems evidence of an abuse of power, the question can lead to an adjournment debate which thrashes out the issue in the fullest detail and publicity. A question regarding the use of third-degree methods on an American woman, for example, led to such a debate and, in the end, to far-reaching new instructions to the police to be more scrupulous in their investigations.

There are important defects in the British Parliament, as the following sections will indicate, but among its virtues none is more important than its proof that democratic government can be simple, understandable, often interesting, at times dramatic, and a vital means of popular political education and protection of individual rights.

3. THE HOUSE OF COMMONS: LAWMAKING

Any description of Parliament that gives first place to its work as critic, educator, and defender of civil liberties inevitably surprises many readers. The House of Commons has enjoyed the reputation for so many generations of being the greatest lawmaking body in the world that there is something disconcerting in the discovery that, today and normally, it has very little to do with legislation in the sense of thinking up laws, writing them out, and determining what precise provisions they shall contain. It would be an oversimplification to say that laws are thought up by parties, pressure groups, or civil servants; that they are framed by civil servants; and that they are formulated into a program by the Cabinet. But such a generalization is closer to reality than is the contention that Parliament makes the laws.

What Parliament really does is to consent to laws. Even this consent, however, is largely the result of pressure brought by leaders of the majority party on their more or less docile followers in the House of Commons. In fact, the decisive point in the enactment of any law is not the moment when the House of Commons gives its consent but the moment when the leaders of the majority party (who, of course, comprise the Cabinet) decide to give their support and approval to the bill. The House of Commons is not a cipher. There are various ways in which it influences the final form of legislation; for example, significant amendments can occasionally be made to Cabinet proposals—if the government permits. But control rests firmly in the hands of the majority party's leaders. Without their consent no legislation may be adopted; and any legislation that is passed has first received their tacit or explicit endorsement. So obvious is this control today that even in normal years seven-eighths of the time of the House of Commons is devoted to business planned by the government. Occasionally the government may take for its use all the legislative time that the House of Commons has at its disposal, and the opposition and private members may not even be allowed to introduce bills of their own.

The "Decline of Parliament"

The government's control over legislation has resulted in much talk of the "decline of Parliament." Young men of ability and ambition, it is often said, no longer think of Parliament as offering an adequate outlet for their talents. The essential decisions are made outside its halls and, under the strict regime of parliamentary discipline, the private member has little to do except vote as his party's leaders tell him to vote. On the opposition benches, it is true, a newcomer may distinguish himself by his ability to harass

the government; but on the government benches even an able speech tends to be regarded as an unnecessary hindrance to the speedy passage of legislation for which the majority party has ample votes. In neither major party is there much admiration for independence of thought or conduct, and in neither party is the newcomer likely to have an opportunity to pass into law bills of his own invention or to induce a major change in the legislative proposals of others.

If Parliament is declining as a legislative body, there are two major reasons for the decline. The first of these is lack of time. There may once have been a period of "inactive government," when Parliament could concern itself primarily with constitutional issues, foreign policy, or taxation. But today even the most conservative government is expected to enact social and economic legislation of the most varied and voluminous nature. Health, education, security against old age and unemployment, the regulation of working conditions and wages, and the supervision and promotion of industry are the normal work of governments in all modern countries. The result is that every legislative body is confronted with many more demands for legislation than can possibly receive adequate discussion and investigation. If every member of Parliament had the right to be heard on every important section of every important piece of legislation, it would be impossible to pass more than one major measure a year. Yet even a Conservative government in "normal" times has much more on its legislative program than that; a government that has sweeping promises of reform on which to make good faces an incomparably more difficult situation. Under any circumstances it is impossible to devote more than a few days of debate to any measure, however technical and elaborate. The lion's share of the time is pre-empted by ministers who explain the bills and by opposition leaders who attack them. The ordinary member of Parliament is only too likely to be passed over. The inevitable result is a feeling of frustration and discouragement on the part of the private members and even a lowering of the quality of debate, as shortness of time prevents searching analyses of the details of a bill.

The second great problem is lack of expert

knowledge. The type of social and economic legislation that occupies more and more of the time of the House of Commons is highly technical. The ordinary member of Parliament may understand the purpose of the legislation, but often he is quite incompetent to understand the technical means needed to achieve this purpose or the effect that such means will have on other legislation or on other interests of society. It is one of the advantages of the House of Commons that so many of its members have had some firsthand experience with problems that come before it for discussion; on any single problem, however, there are likely to be very few who are able to understand, let alone to formulate, the intricacies of the legislation under discussion. It is reported that only two members of Parliament understood the Local Government Bill of 1928-29, and one of these was the minister who presented the bill and who had been very carefully instructed by the civil servants who drew it up. Under such circumstances, the parliamentary process loses much of its significance, and there is an understandable feeling that it is the experts in the civil service who do the real work of legislating while the members of Parliament go through a series of colorful but essentially meaningless motions.

This problem is enlarged by the fact that an important part of the work of Parliament is not merely to pass legislation but to supervise the way in which it is carried out and, in general, to oversee the work of the administrative departments of the government. The head of each department is a minister sitting in Parliament, and through him each department is supposed to be under direct parliamentary control. But the ordinary member of Parliament is as incapable of understanding and directing the detailed and technical work of the expert administrators as of framing their legislation. If ever he has suspicions and criticisms, he may ask questions or speak on the motion for adjournment, but he is likely to lack both the information and the experience to cross swords successfully with a minister who has been properly coached by the expert staff. Furthermore, administrative action, to be effective, must often be taken promptly, and there is no time to wait for parliamentary debate or decision on the matter at hand. At such times, Parliament is presented with a *fait accompli,* and although it may criticize and question, it is too late to prevent or alter.

Limitations on Debate

Parliament has developed a variety of devices for meeting, or mitigating, the problems of time and expertness. In particular, in order to conserve time, it has introduced rigorous controls over debate that are intended to prevent filibusters and other time-consuming attempts to delay or obstruct legislation and to concentrate debate on the most important aspects of legislation.

Some of these controls are informal and voluntary; some are decidedly coercive; but in either case they raise a serious question for democracy. Discussion is generally regarded as the heart of democratic government; to restrict it is to restrict the possibility of information, understanding, and voluntary agreement concerning the points at issue. Moreover, restrictions on debate may be used to oppress or suppress a minority. Yet it is also important that some conclusion be reached and that the desires of the majority be safeguarded against the obstruction of a willful and vigorous minority. The parliamentary problem, then, is to provide for the adequate expression of all important views without permitting the final decision of the majority to be thwarted.

Of the formal devices used by the House of Commons, the most important are various forms of *closure.* Any member may at any time "move the previous question," and, if the Speaker is willing to entertain the motion, the House of Commons must vote immediately and without further debate on the question of whether or not it desires an immediate vote on the subject under discussion. If at least one hundred members vote in favor of the motion, and if they constitute a majority of those present and voting, debate is halted and a final vote taken. Of course, a majority party always has one hundred votes at its disposal, and the provision would be open to serious abuse were it not for the fact that the Speaker refuses to accept such a motion until the opposition has had a fair chance to present its case.

There are several refinements of the closure procedure. A *guillotine* resolution may be adopted, assigning a certain amount of time in advance for the debate on a specific measure. At the conclusion of that time, regardless of where the debate stands, the guillotine falls and a vote is taken. In order to prevent such a procedure from concentrating debate on the opening provisions of a bill, the device of *closure by compartments* may be used to divide a bill into a number of sections, assign a certain amount of time to each, and arrange for the guillotine to fall as each subperiod of time elapses. In addition, through the use of the *kangaroo,* the Speaker may arrange to concentrate the debate upon those proposed amendments that are most important or most controversial, hopping over those that are of less consequence. Increasingly, the Cabinet has tended to invoke these devices as part of the regular process of debate rather than as emergency measures to be used under exceptional circumstances. As this tendency has grown, the Speaker has acquired an ever heavier responsibility, for his discernment, judgment, and impartiality are now the chief institutional safeguard against their abuse.

The informal devices for limiting debate receive some of their effectiveness from the knowledge that, in case of failure, more formal methods of closure may be invoked. The strength of the majority's powers renders the minority more willing to arrive at agreements "behind the Speaker's chair." The whips of the two leading parties are likely to work out together a timetable for debate according to which each side agrees to restrain its own spokesmen in return for concessions from the other side. As a result of such agreements it usually happens that the leaders of both of the great parties, together with representatives of the minor parties, have ample opportunity to present their cases; but the opportunities of the rank-and-file backbenchers are drastically limited. Thus the Speaker, at the beginning of the debate, may make this sort of announcement:

I have worked out a list of about 30 names covering, I hope, most interests and, geographically, most areas, but that leaves something over 70 who will be disappointed. Naturally, in these circumstances, I have had to disregard, to a great extent, the claims of maiden speeches, and I am sorry to say, too, that I have had to disregard many old Members who have not spoken yet in this Parliament, but I really could not work them in under the scheme that I have adopted. I am sorry that 70-odd Members will be disappointed, but I simply cannot help it.

Such restrictions are loudly deplored by ordinary members of Parliament, but the whips and the leaders of the great parties insist that only through such limitations can the parliamentary machine be made to work.

Leadership

The concentration of greater power in the hands of the leaders of the majority party (that is, the Cabinet) has offered a second method both of saving time and of introducing greater expertness into the legislative process. The leaders' firm control of the House of Commons, based as it is on party discipline, is the real force behind the different devices for limiting debate. It is easier, of course, to work with the cooperation of the opposition, and the leader of the House has a particular responsibility for consulting with its leaders and for planning the parliamentary program so that the opposition feels it is given adequate opportunities for its attacks. The Speaker may prevent any attempt to abuse the closure powers. But in the end the majority's leaders, when they use their powers to the full, can determine what shall be discussed by Parliament, when the discussion shall take place, how long it shall last, and when the vote shall be taken.

The fact that most (and in some sessions all) of the legislation enacted by Parliament is sponsored by the Cabinet and that the Cabinet has access to expert assistance not available to the ordinary member also means that legislation is far more carefully and competently framed than is most of the legislation adopted by the United States Congress. The normal procedure is that a legislative proposal which the Cabinet intends to sponsor is submitted to all the governmental departments concerned for study and comment by the permanent officials of the civil service. The various interests that will be affected may be called in for consultation, and outside experts may be asked for their opinion. On the basis of this information, the Cabinet makes its decision to submit the proposed legislation, and the office of the parliamentary Counsel to the Treasury undertakes the highly technical job of drafting the precise terms of the legislation—for there are innumerable opportunities for the layman to blunder by overlooking the effect of the new legislation on laws already passed, by using words that will have a legal effect quite different from that intended, or by using words that will not accomplish the purpose intended.

Thus the bill that goes to Parliament may be the result of promises made in the party platform, of influence exerted by a powerful pressure group, or of suggestions from the permanent staff of one of the government departments; but whether the inspiration is expert or amateur, the bill has been subjected to the scrutiny of men of experience and technical capacity in the field concerned. Even these men are fallible, of course, and the great burden of legislation and administration forces them, too, to act in haste and without sufficient consideration. The private member of Parliament, because of his own knowledge or because of the protests of outside interests, is sometimes able to point out flaws in the measure as submitted. Yet the Cabinet, because of its control of the majority party, is obliged to accept only those amendments that it wants to accept, and there is no danger that the expertly prepared legislation will be mutilated by the host of hasty, irrelevant, incompatible, ill-considered, or badly drafted amendments that threaten official proposals in the United States.

To the private member this fact brings little consolation. He likes to think that he was elected to Parliament to do something—to share in the making of legislation or at least to play an active part, as a critic, in modifying it. The concentration of authority in the hands of the leader, and the lack of alternative sources of expert information by which to judge the legislation, inevitably encourage a feeling of frustration and the impression that party leaders think of him simply as a "brute vote" whose opinions, if any, are at best a nuisance. To the private member, then, it is likely to appear that expertness is being won at the expense of responsibility.

Committees

The committee system offers a third method of conserving time and increasing expertness.

Bills that are accepted by the House of Commons in principle (that is, given second reading) are sent to a committee for more detailed consideration. In some instances the committee is simply the House of Commons itself sitting under a different name, *Committee of the Whole House,* and at such times the Speaker leaves the chair, and a chairman presides over the meeting from a post at the head of the table. Procedure is simpler than in a regular meeting of the House: motions need not be seconded, and the same person may speak repeatedly in the same debate. It is this committee that considers all money bills (that is, all revenue and appropriations measures); it is known as Committee of the Whole on Supply and on Ways and Means. Justified traditionally by the argument that all M.P.'s should be able to contribute at every level in such a vital field, this procedure is, in practice, not only time-consuming (a survey of a recent ten-year period revealed that one-fifth of the working time of the House had been spent in Committee of the Whole) but self-defeating. Even the cautious *Report of the Select Committee on Procedure, 1959,* considered ways whereby much of its work could be "sent upstairs," that is, to smaller committees. Only three types of bill, in fact, are particularly suited to Committee of the Whole: those that are uncontested or, because of their simplicity ("one-clause" bills), do not need detailed committee examination; those that have to be passed with special speed; and those of "first class constitutional importance," such as the Statute of Westminster, 1931, or the Parliament Bill of 1947 affecting the powers of the House of Lords.

STANDING COMMITTEES In most instances, however, a bill is referred to one of the *standing committees.* These committees often meet simultaneously (in the afternoons as well as the mornings if the House is not considering important business), and it is possible for them to consider several times the amount of legislation that could be taken up by the Committee of the Whole House. Furthermore, a larger number of members have an opportunity to speak. In contrast to the United States and to Germany, where all legislative committees concentrate on special subjects, such as foreign affairs or finance or labor, the House of Commons refers most issues to one of five general committees known simply as A, B, C, D, or E. In addition, there is a committee to deal with private members' bills and another called the Committee on Scottish Affairs. The latter is composed of the seventy-one members from Scottish constituencies and between ten and fifteen non-Scottish members. All Scottish matters are sent to these members for what approximates a second reading (unless ten members of the House object). This concession to Scottish nationalism does not contradict the general practice of nonspecialization, however, for Scottish affairs may include a wide range of subjects related only in their application to that particular area. The same variety exists in regard to private members' bills.

Some members of a House of Commons standing committee, however, have specialized knowledge of the subject with which they are dealing. The appointments are made by the Committee on Selection, which not only provides a government majority on each standing committee but tries to appoint members who are particularly qualified to deal with that bill. Moreover, the membership may change as a committee undertakes a new type of measure. Thus, the personnel of British standing committees differs considerably from bill to bill, and there is much more expert knowledge available in committee sessions than the system might appear on the surface to provide. In other words, as K. C. Wheare points out in his excellent *Government by Committee,* the essential difference between the American and British committee systems as far as expertness is concerned is that in the former the bills go to the members with specialized knowledge and interests, whereas in the latter the members with such knowledge and interest go to the bills.

A more significant difference between the two systems is that in the United States measures go to a committee before being given second reading by the legislature as a whole; thus the principle of the measure may well be changed by the committee before the legislative body has a chance to consider it, if, indeed, it ever gets that chance. In Great Britain, committees are always looked on as secondary amending bodies, committed to the principle

approved by the executive and adopted by the House at second reading. Moreover, standing committees cannot receive evidence from outside interests, as is done so often in the United States; nor can government officials speak or be questioned in committee sessions, though they are present in the committee room to advise the minister. It is the latter who provides the leadership in the committee, piloting the measure under consideration through the detailed examination, clause by clause, which it receives from the opposition. The chairman of the committee, a backbencher from either party, acts, like the Speaker (by whom he is appointed), as an impartial presiding officer who protects the minority's right of debate and yet can expedite the discussion at his discretion.

K. C. Wheare shows that the extended use of standing committees has made it possible to pass a large number of important and controversial bills that the House could not otherwise have handled without some new forms of closure. He feels that these bills received careful examination in committee and also, with rare exceptions, adequate discussion in the House as a whole. He even recommends—as a time-saving and efficiency measure—that standing committees be entrusted as well with the fourth stage of legislation, the report stage, which follows consideration in committee, since this stage deals with technical matters of detail that a relatively expert body is better equipped to handle, in his opinion, than is the House as a whole.

But are standing committees as expert as they should be? And is the scope of their work adequate? The 1959 Select Committee on Procedure suggested abolishing the former core of twenty general members and this has been done. The 1965 Select Committee on Procedure recommended the establishment of specialist committees to examine the administration of government departments so as to enable M.P.'s "more effectively to influence, advise, scrutinise, and criticise." The development of more specialized committees and the extension of their competence to examining administration as well as legislation in a particular field, as do American committees, might enable Parliament to scrutinize and criticize executive action more adequately. But the Labor Cabinet is reluctant to countenance much challenge to its administrative and legislative authority, and the two specialist committees for agriculture and for science and technology set up late in 1966 are circumscribed in membership and scope.

SELECT COMMITTEES Select committees were originally distinguished from standing committees not only by their concentration on a particular subject matter and by their power "to send for persons, papers, and records" and to sift evidence, but also by the fact that they were appointed to deal with particular circumstances and could be expected to terminate their activities when they completed their reports. There are still select committees of this kind. The House may set one up at any time to examine a particular public bill prior to the normal committee stage. But there are also some perennial select committees—the Committee of Selection, which nominates the members of the standing committees, the Committee on Privilege, and, on a more mundane level, the Kitchen and Refreshment Rooms Committee—which deal with procedural or domestic matters of concern only to the House itself. More noteworthy, four important select committees—on public accounts, estimates, statutory instruments, and nationalized industries—are now set up every session and exercise direct scrutiny and control over the operation of departments.

The most important of the four is the Public Accounts Committee, first set up in 1861, which investigates the accounts of the ministries. To ensure rigorous examination of departmental spending, its chairman is always a leading member of the opposition. The Committee's work is immensely aided by an official known as the Comptroller and Auditor-General and by his large and expert staff, who are unique among administrative officials in being directly responsible to Parliament and not to the executive. The Public Accounts Committee deals only with past expenditures. The Estimates Committee, in contrast, considers current expenditures. But it is handicapped in so doing by its lack of independent experts comparable to those of the Comptroller and Auditor-General and still more by the assumption that it cannot challenge the government's financial policies but can only suggest economies in specific estimates.

The third select committee that exercises scrutiny over the departments is the Statutory Instruments or Scrutiny Committee, which will be considered in detail in the next section on delegated legislation. The fourth, the Committee on Nationalized Industries, is considered in Chapter 6.

Taken together, these committees demonstrate (as does the work of certain—though not all—American congressional committees) the value of a concentrated role for M.P.'s of energy and skill, both to make their work meaningful and to provide adequate supervision of the activities and decisions of the executive and administration.

ROYAL COMMISSIONS While much of the important legislation of the nineteenth century was drafted as the result of the reports of select committees, it is now more common to undertake such investigations through a Royal Commission, an executive rather than a parliamentary agency. Royal Commissions are generally composed of experts or interested persons known to be open-minded on the subject under investigation. The purpose of the Commission is not only to marshal facts but also to evolve a policy. There have been Royal Commissions on the coal mines, local government, the civil service, population, the press, and a variety of social welfare problems. Though the reports of such committees are not binding on the executive body, they have had exceptional importance, not only in influencing members of Parliament, but in informing and educating public opinion in general; in certain instances the published reports of Royal Commissions have become best sellers in their own right.

Delegated Legislation

A fourth way of providing time and expertness is for Parliament to pass bills in general outline, at the same time delegating to government officials the power to make rulings and regulations that will achieve the intent of the bill in specific cases. Thus Parliament sets the general purposes of the legislation, but expert administrators work out the technical details that Parliament has neither the time, the information, nor the skill to anticipate. If changing circumstances or unpredictable developments make certain rules inappropriate or obsolete, the administrators are free to make new regulations to carry out Parliament's original purpose, and Parliament itself need not be troubled to pass new legislation.

Such a delegation of legislative authority has obvious advantages in achieving expertness and flexibility, and every advanced industrialized country has had to resort to delegated legislation in order to prevent the legislative machinery from breaking down in the face of the volume and technicality of laws demanded by the public Many have charged, however, that delegated legislation forms a serious threat to the legislative authority of Parliament and to popular control of governmental action, particularly when there is subdelegation (for example, when a statute permits an order in council, which in turn authorizes a ministerial order, which may authorize an official regulation, and so forth). One of the most violent of these attacks was made by the Chief Justice of England and Wales, Lord Hewart, in a book entitled *The New Despotism* (1929), which charged that delegated legislation coupled with administrative adjudication (whereby officials determine whether a rule has been broken in a particular case and, if so, impose penalties) had brought Great Britain under "the new despotism" of the public service.

Lord Hewart's book, which created a sensation in Great Britain, led to a careful study of the situation by the Committee on Ministers' Powers. The Committee came to the conclusion that delegated legislation is inevitable under modern conditions and that, in fact, the power had not been abused. Certain specific safeguards, however, were suggested. First, legislation should be drafted carefully and accurately. Second, the "precise limits" of administrative discretion should be laid down in the legislation, and courts of law should have the right to determine whether government officials overstep their authority. Third, a standardized procedure was proposed under which administrative regulations applying a particular law would be publicized in Parliament.

Since June 1944, a select committee of Parliament called the Statutory Instruments or Scrutiny Committee has considered all statutory rules and orders and has decided whether or not they should be drawn to the special attention of the House. Only some 3 or 4 percent of administrative rules and orders must be affirmed by Parliament; others lie before the House for forty days and are then considered approved if there has been no negative prayer (that is, appeal) against them. Sometimes the House is not even aware an administrative rule is on the table unless the Scrutiny Committee makes a special report on it. In order to determine whether it should do so, the Scrutiny Committee can call departmental witnesses to explain what has been done, but it is sharply limited in checking or criticizing such action and in asking why it has been done. Moreover, despite the fact that the committee is expected to investigate "unexpected" or "unusual" use of powers, it is not allowed to question the relevant minister, on the grounds that this is the prerogative of the House as a whole: a curiously rigid and restrictive view of ministerial responsibility.

It is doubtful that this procedure provides adequate parliamentary control of administrative rules, but at least it combines general supervision with conservation of parliamentary time and energy. To prevent negative prayers from being used as a means of obstruction (attempted by the Conservatives in 1951 in an effort to wear down the Labor government's small majority), the Speaker is empowered to secure a vote on such a prayer at 11:30 P.M. (they are commonly brought up at the end of government business at 10 P.M.) unless, in his judgment, further debate is essential. Thus in yet another instance the Speaker is the guardian of both the liberties and the effectiveness of the House.

In the United States, there is no requirement that Congress must review administrative orders, unless it is written into legislation as in the Administrative Reorganization Act of 1946, which authorized the President to propose plans for reorganization of an executive department or agency. These plans are transmitted to Congress; if they are not rejected by Congress within a prescribed period of time, they go into effect. Any other administrative order can only be challenged in the courts—which are used more widely than in the United Kingdom—to determine whether the rule is within the delegation of power and whether proper procedures have been observed. The distinctive American answer to the problem of delegated legislation, however, is the regulatory commission. In the United Kingdom, it is felt that such institutions would violate the close relation between the executive and legislature. Thus such safeguards as exist against the possible abuse of delegated legislation are kept largely within the parliamentary system itself.

How Bills Are Passed

Different kinds of bills are treated in Parliament in different ways, the chief distinction being between *public bills* and *private bills*. Public bills are those that are of general importance to the country as a whole; private bills concern a special locality or person or body of persons. A measure to set up a national health service or to nationalize the steel industry is a public bill, but the Manchester Ship Canal Bill or the North Devon Water Board Bill is private.

A public bill may be introduced by any member of Parliament, although only a minister may introduce a money bill. If a public bill is introduced by a minister, it is called a government bill. When a private member introduces it, it is a *private member's bill* (not to be confused with a private bill).

Public Bills

Regardless of its source of inspiration, every bill must be sponsored by a member of Parliament who gives notice of his intention to introduce the bill and, at the proper time, gives the bill (or a dummy containing its title) to the clerk, who reads the title aloud. This proceeding is known as the *first reading,* and the bill is then printed at government expense and distributed to the members.

The crucial stage in the life of a bill, however, is the *second reading.* The first reading is automatic: there is no debate, and there is no vote. But on the second reading the fundamental principles and purposes of the bill must be explained and debated; and, understandably, the House will not consider the details of the bill until it is certain that it approves of its broad intent.

Most of the bills discussed on second reading are government bills—that is, they have been approved by the Cabinet and framed with the expert help of the civil service. The motion that they be read a second time is made by a minister, who opens the debate with an explanation and defense of the main provisions of the bill; and the debate then proceeds in accordance with the pattern already described. In conclusion, a leader of the opposition usually sums up the case against the bill, and a minister makes a closing speech in reply to the attacks.

The vote that is then taken could be crucial not only for the bill but for the life of the Cabinet itself. For if an important bill sponsored by it should be defeated on second reading, the House would thereby indicate its lack of confidence in the Cabinet. If the Prime Minister considers the issue a matter of confidence, he will be obliged either to resign or to ask the Queen to dissolve Parliament and call a new election. Thus the debate attracts the greatest attention both within Parliament and without; it is on this occasion that the House of Commons comes closest to fitting the traditional picture of a great legislative assembly.

The private member, either of the majority party or of the opposition, has much more difficulty than the Cabinet in getting a bill read for the second time. Not only does he lack the disciplined following that would assure him a majority, but it is unlikely that he will even be granted the time necessary for the discussion of his bill. The Cabinet, of course, through its control of the majority party can control the timetable of the House, and it sets aside the time needed to consider the bills which it itself sponsors. But even at best there is comparatively little time provided for the consideration of private members' bills, and occasionally the Cabinet takes for its own proposals all the time available.

As a result, even when time is set aside for private members' bills, it is impossible for every member who would like to introduce a bill to do so. Members have to ballot for the privilege of introducing a bill; and although 250 members may take part in drawing lots, only those few with the highest numbers have any hope of introducing their bills. The others must try again the next year, and probably the next and the next and the next.

Those who are fortunate enough to win in the drawing are only at the beginning of their troubles. The whips of their party may insist that they introduce bills that the party's leaders wish to have considered. If the member has a bill of his own and persists in introducing it, he must somehow or other manage the technical job of draftsmanship, and he must act as his own floor manager—persuading enough members to attend the discussion of his bill, both on the floor and in committee, to maintain a quorum, and persuading enough members to vote in favor of it so that there will be a majority. Finally, he must be assured of the approval— or at least the benevolent neutrality—of the leaders of the majority party, for only those bills can receive the approval of the House that the leaders are willing to see approved.[3]

Once a bill has been approved on second reading, it automatically goes to a committee. In the United States, in contrast to British procedure, this stage precedes the second reading, so there is no general discussion or approval of a bill before it is sent to committee. Consequently, many more bills are considered, and it is a common practice for committees to bury or pigeonhole many of their bills, intentionally or otherwise. In the United Kingdom, however, once a bill has been approved on second reading, committees are under obligation both to consider and to report out the bill.

In contrast to the debate on second reading, which focuses on the principle of the bill, the debate on the *report stage* is intended to let the House consider the details of the bill. It is at this time that it may be most necessary to invoke the various closure procedures in order to get through the mass of detailed and technical amendments that may be proposed. This is why K. C. Wheare suggests leaving this stage to a committee. The House as a whole has a chance to consider the bill when the motion is made that it be read a third time. On *third reading,* however, no changes other than purely verbal ones may be proposed: the bill must be voted on as it stands, and passed or rejected.

Once accepted by the House of Commons, the bill is sent to the House of Lords, or, if it has already passed the House of Lords in the same form, to the monarch, for approval. If the Lords reject the bill or make amendments that the House of Commons is unwilling to accept, the bill is not necessarily lost. By persisting in its original intention, the House of Commons may, after some delay, enact the legislation in spite of the Lords' disapproval.

Private Bills

Individuals or groups who desire the enactment of a private bill (as distinguished from a private member's bill) simply file petitions with an official in each House called the "Examiner of Petitions for Private Bills" and with the government department most directly concerned. Persons whose interests are affected by the bill are notified, and when these conditions have been complied with, the bill is read a first time and ordered to be read a second time. Following the second reading, those bills that are unopposed go to a committee on unopposed bills, while the others are sent to a private-bills committee that holds elaborate hearings in which each side is represented by paid counsel, and witnesses with an interest in the bill are brought in to testify. The committee members act as impartial judges, and their report to the House of Commons is almost invariably adopted without discussion.

Regardless of whether it is opposed or not, the passage of a private bill is an expensive proposition. Both houses impose high fees related to the amount of money the bill proposes to raise or expend, and it is necessary to pay fixed parliamentary agent's fees as well as printing bills for the draft statute and the eight advertisements that must run in the local press and London *Gazette* before consideration. Thus, even if the procedure is straightforward, the cost may give a local authority pause.

Such committee action saves parliamentary time, however, and time is also saved by the device of granting power to government departments in certain classes of cases to issue "provisional orders" giving local authorities the type of permission that would otherwise require a private bill. These are then grouped in *provisional orders confirmation bills*, which follow

---

[3] These are only the major pitfalls that the private member must avoid. One can find an elaborate and grimly amusing description of the others in Sir A. P. Herbert's book, *The Ayes Have It,* which recounts the author's own difficulties in winning acceptance of a bill for divorce reform. In spite of his exceptionally good luck, it is worth noting that even one so blessed in friends and ability could not get his bill accepted without considerable assistance from the government of the day.

the same procedure as ordinary bills but which are sent to Committee of the Whole House rather than to other committees.

Financial Legislation

Control over the public purse strings is the great traditional weapon of popular defense against executive tyranny, and according to constitutional custom, as reinforced by statute, this power belongs exclusively to the House of Commons. All money bills must be introduced in this House, and since the constitutional crisis of 1911 the House of Lords has had no power to reject a money bill passed by the Commons.

In practice, however, the House of Commons has yielded its financial power to the Cabinet. According to the Standing Orders of the House of Commons, the House may consider no proposal for the expenditure of money that is not recommended by the Crown (that is, the Cabinet); and any proposal to reduce expenditures is considered an indication of lack of confidence in the department whose appropriations are attacked. (In fact, as we have seen, the opposition often turns the debate on appropriations into a debate on policy by proposing that the grant to that department be cut by some insignificant sum.) Thus, unless the Cabinet itself is willing to propose an increase in expenditure or to accept a proposal to reduce appropriations, the budget as originally proposed is adopted unchanged. So strong is the presumption that the budget will be approved in the form presented by the Chancellor of the Exchequer that the provisions are put into effect immediately following the speech in which the Chancellor "opens his budget." The Chancellor and his colleagues are bound by so strong an obligation of secrecy before the delivery of the speech (in order to prevent the possibility that someone might profiteer from the possession of inside information) that, in the fall of 1947, even the inadvertent revealing of certain budgetary proposals a few minutes before the speech entailed the prompt resignation of the Chancellor, Hugh Dalton. A graver indiscretion by James Thomas, Chancellor of the Exchequer in 1936, abruptly and permanently terminated his parliamentary career.

The consequence of this system is to ensure the enactment of an expertly prepared budget at the price of effective parliamentary participation in its formulation. All financial proposals are carefully planned by government experts, and although proposals for expenditure and for raising revenue are considered separately in Parliament (expenditures are considered in Committee of the Whole on Supply and the raising of revenue in Committee of the Whole on Ways and Means), the two types of proposal are coordinated in advance and are enacted in an Appropriation Act and a Finance Act that have been planned as part of a single financial program.

This procedure can easily arouse considerable envy in the breasts of American officials. In the United States, as in the United Kingdom, the executive may prepare a careful plan for balancing revenue and expenditure, but the United States Congress is its own master in budgetary as in other matters. Once the President's financial proposals have been set adrift on the legislative sea, they are at the mercy of the winds of congressional prejudice and special interests. Unpopular taxes may be cut; special expenditures demanded by powerful pressure groups may be added; executive departments that have incurred congressional wrath may find their appropriations drastically reduced; and the most carefully laid plans of the administration may be disrupted. During the debates on the budget many an executive agency lives in a condition of the tensest anxiety, wondering whether it may be eliminated entirely through the loss of its appropriations—a situation that is hardly calculated to encourage able men to enter public service. And there are times when any resemblance between plans for expenditure and plans for revenue seems to be little more than coincidental.

But if Americans sometimes look at the British system with envy, a considerable number of Englishmen are far from sharing their admiration. Undoubtedly, one of the most important elements in the "decline of Parliament" is the removal of this critical subject from effective parliamentary control. Debate on the budget loses much of its point when the major provisions are predetermined; and as the debate shifts from finance as such to a discussion of the policy of the departments asking appropriations, the ordinary member is deprived of an opportunity to acquire a clear understanding of financial policy in general.

The Private Member

The combination of party discipline and effective rules of closure makes Parliament a remarkably efficient body in the sense of getting work done. And the most vaunted advantage of the British parliamentary system is its freedom from the sort of deadlock between executive and legislature that occurs so frequently in the United States. A good many Englishmen, however, believe that the efficiency of Parliament is purchased at too high a price. It is possible—as it is not in the United States—for the government to draw up a coherent and well-planned program of legislation in the knowledge that it will pass through the legislature without serious mutilation. But the immunity of such legislative proposals is possible only because of the relative impotence of the ordinary member of Parliament.

Because of limitations on time, the average member has no opportunity to introduce a bill of his own, and his chances of participating in an important debate are slim indeed. Moreover, the ties of party discipline are so tight that only the exceptional member dares to disregard the prescription of the party whips, and it is the exceptional issue on which the party whips have nothing to prescribe. One of those rare occasions came in 1964, when the House of Commons on a free vote on a private member's bill to abolish capital punishment demonstrated, as it had already done in 1956 under similar circumstances, its opposition to the death penalty. (The House of Lords, which had vetoed the measure in 1956, finally acceded in mid-1965.) The very rarity of the free vote—for which individual members must often yearn—makes it clear that parties hardly ever now accept the Burkeian view that the exercise of individual conscience adds to rather than detracts from the authority of a vote.

Occasionally a member may deviate from party prescription with impunity, particularly if the matter is one of conscience and if there is no question of loyalty to the party's purposes in general. Large numbers of Labor members have on occasion ostentatiously abstained from voting on a matter involving nuclear armaments without suffering penalties. Even then, however, it is safer to refrain from voting altogether than to walk into the lobby of the opposing party. Of the eight Conservative "rebels" who voted against the government's Suez policy in 1956, none again won seats as Conservative members. The member who deviates frequently or on a crucial issue must prepare to meet a stern challenge. In consequence it is the norm for party lines to hold firm in every division and for members to troop obediently into the proper lobby in response to the summons of the whip.

The Bases of Party Discipline

There are several reasons for this remarkable discipline. In the first place, the party member who regularly and intentionally defied the leadership of his party would almost certainly lose the support of the party organization in the next election, and he might be formally expelled from his party. Here it must be remembered that the ordinary member is elected, not only because of his own qualities or virtues, but still more because he belongs to a particular party and is a supporter of its leader. If he is expelled from the party, his local organization is almost certain to turn against him and to choose a more obedient candidate. Even if a rebel is supported by his own constituency, if he is a Laborite his party will enter a candidate against him, thereby splitting the party's normal vote and almost certainly guaranteeing him defeat.

Behind the cruder weapons of party discipline, however, there are certain psychological considerations that exert a strong influence upon the private member. Thus he knows that if he votes against the policy of his party when it is in power and if enough of his fellows join him, the party will be defeated and will be forced, according to constitutional convention, to resign or to dissolve Parliament and call a new election. Neither alternative is attractive. A new election would oblige the member to fight for his seat all over again, and elections are expensive and victory far from sure. Moreover, a party that is obliged to fight an election as the result of a split in its forces in Parliament is in an extremely vulnerable position. Its members are likely to attack one another more vigorously than they attack the opposition, and only the opposition profits. The Liberal party lost its power largely because of repeated splits in its ranks, and Labor's disastrous defeat of 1931 followed a similar cleavage in the party.

But if the prospect of a new election is bad, the prospect of a Cabinet resignation usually is worse. A member of a party may disagree bitterly with his leaders on one issue or even on four or five, but that is a very different thing from wanting the opposition to take over the government. If he disagrees with his own party on even 20 percent of its policies, he probably disagrees with the opposition on 90 or 95 percent. The discontented members of a party are usually those who are on the extremes furthest away from the principal opposition. Thus the most disgruntled members of the Conservative party are generally the reactionary Tories who may dislike the moderation of their own party but who turn apoplectic at the thought of bringing Labor into power; and the most dissatisfied of Labor's followers are the ones who are most radical and who would die before they would help to establish a Conservative government. Even if they disagree with their party leadership on an important issue, the knowledge that a serious defection would cause its resignation and bring the hated enemy into power is enough to make most of them swallow their scruples and go into the correct lobby.

Often, of course, if there is an important amount of resentment in party ranks, the leaders will be warned by the whips and some concessions may be made. Resentment in the party may be an indication of resentment among the public at large, and the party's leaders are always concerned with success at the next election. But if the leaders decide to hold firm, they can do so.

For those few members who are able to vote against the leaders of the great parties without losing their seats, the path of opposition is a lonely one. It sometimes leads to great personal distinction, but it rarely leads to power. The independent generally condemns himself to a life passed in the wilderness of the back benches where his voice, however eloquent, is disregarded. Only in exceptional circumstances

(there have been a few) will he be invited to take a position in the Cabinet, and ordinarily the price of such an invitation is a return to complete party orthodoxy.

Yet the man of ability and ambition is impressed by the relative futility of a role in which he is always in opposition and always outvoted, in which he is perpetually the critic and never the leader. He would like to try his hand at framing legislation and at directing an important government department. Such work, however, is the preserve of Cabinet ministers, and for most men the road to the Cabinet is the road of conformity. Because he had been a vigorous critic of party policy, it took a major war to bring Winston Churchill into the Cabinet; and for those lacking Churchill's talent, prestige, and family connections, the moral seems obvious

Is the private member therefore condemned to complete impotence? Not exactly. In form he will rarely be able to speak against his party leaders or to vote against them, but in practice his party's leaders are concerned with his opinion, not because he may vote against them, but because he may represent a wider popular resentment and because a loss of morale among private members might be a serious threat to victory in the next election. It may be the job of the whips to see that the members go into the right lobby, but it is also their job to let the party leaders know what the members are thinking. And if discontent is sufficiently widespread, important concessions or modifications of policy may take place—not in the public glare of the House of Commons but in the privacy of party conferences and Cabinet meetings. Thus in 1935, a Conservative Cabinet commanding an overwhelming majority in the House of Commons abandoned the Hoare-Laval plan for the partition of Ethiopia—although not the attitude that lay behind it; in 1947, the Labor government modified its Conscription Bill because of pressure from its backbenchers; in 1956, the Conservatives finally agreed to introduce equal pay by stages; and in 1960, the Bow Group of young Conservatives almost certainly influenced official policy in favor of increased political power for Africans in territories with resident white populations.

In this sense, then, the anxiety or views of private members, particularly when there is reason to suppose that their attitudes reflect an important sector of public opinion, may have a real effect upon legislation and policy.

Pressure Groups

English commentators used to note with satisfaction the absence from British political life of those pressure organizations that so frequently are charged with dominating and corrupting American politics—a conclusion that inevitably seems strange to the American who observes how largely the British House of Commons is populated by representatives of trade unions, cooperatives, the Federation of British Industries, and many smaller groups. The fact is, of course, that pressure organizations exist in Great Britain as in the United States, but their legislative influence is exercised in a different manner and with very different results.

In the United States the President's scant control over his own party in Congress and the weakness of party discipline make it possible for pressure groups to approach congressmen one by one and persuade them that the support of their group is indispensable for reelection. And since the congressman is dependent upon his own efforts or upon a local party organization for reelection, he is tempted to listen to the spokesmen of pressure groups even when they oppose the policy of his party's leaders. In Great Britain, however, the ordinary member of Parliament knows that the most important element in his election is the fact that voters approve of his party and its leadership, and no pressure group can provide sufficient support to compensate for the loss of a party label and the endorsement of the party's leader. If he has to choose between antagonizing an interest group and antagonizing the national party organization, he may be unhappy about the necessity of choosing, but the choice is not hard to make. Even if the pressure group should succeed in defeating him, the national party organization can find him another constituency in which to run.

The result is that the pressure group that wants to get somewhere in Great Britain does not waste its time trying to persuade individual members to revolt against their party's leaders.

Instead, it tries to convince the Cabinet and the leaders of the party organizations that the party as a whole cannot win an election unless it satisfies the pressure group. This is a much harder task. The party, obviously, is far more powerful than the individual member and far more difficult to intimidate. The pressure group quite possibly may need the party's support far more than the party needs the support of the pressure group. And, as American experience has shown, it is far more difficult for a pressure group to influence a national election than to influence a series of specially selected local ones.

Of course, some pressure groups are so strong that even a powerful British party will listen to them. But it is in this matter of degree that the great difference between the two countries lies. In the United States small and insignificant groups, making no pretense of representing a majority of the voters, may exert considerable influence; but in Great Britain only the most significant interests, in terms of voting power or financial resources, can achieve the same result. The Cabinet can always declare that an issue is a matter of confidence; and, as we have seen, only rarely will a member desert his party at such a time.

But if this seems to make pressure groups and political parties antagonistic, the impression is incorrect. Pressure groups play an even greater legislative role in Great Britain than they do in the United States. S. E. Finer, in *Anonymous Empire: A Study of the Lobby in Great Britain,* and Samuel H. Beer, in his penetrating study of group politics referred to in Chapter 1, make it clear that in contrast to the situation in the United States, the pressure groups in Great Britain are "domesticated." They work more closely with political parties, with the legislature, and, above all, with the government departments. If they also act more soberly and responsibly, it is largely because they are more closely tied in with the normal process of government. They have no need to exert public pressure unless they are in obvious opposition to the government's policies.

What, then, is the normal relationship of an interest group, or lobby, to legislation in Great Britain?

In the first place, the lobby is quite likely to provide a good deal of the detailed material that goes into a party program, simply because it is an easy source of reference, once the party has decided to espouse that particular cause—but not before. In other words, the lobby does not determine what the party will support, but once that decision is made it can do a good deal to shape the detailed application of a particular principle.

Second, and still more important, a lobby has a major opportunity when the victorious party is ready to turn a part of its party platform into legislation. The lobby is commonly consulted when the minister is ready to prepare his bill; if the provisions do not satisfy the lobby, it is likely to exert continuous pressure seeking this or that amendment. In fact, one of the important purposes of both the committee and report stages of a bill is to provide interested groups with opportunities to propose changes that they feel to be necessary.

In the third place, the lobby is alert to the administration of the new law. When the relevant department finds itself obliged to draft an ordinance implementing some feature of the law, it commonly consults with the interested parties. In fact, it is unusual if there has not been continuous contact between the department and the lobbies concerned with its subject matter. If the administration of the measure is causing difficulties, the affected groups complain directly to the ministries. An adjustment is then usually made either through another ordinance or even through an amendment or a supplementary act. Legislation initiated by civil servants and interested parties is so common as to be known as "official" legislation. When it deals with minor matters, it tends to go particularly swiftly through the legislature, and many of the laws passed each session are of this type.

This integration of pressure groups into the process of government is not an abdication of responsibility by popular and administrative government agencies. It is, rather, a sensible accommodation between those agencies that are entrusted with the responsibility for formulating and carrying out public policies, and those that represent the wide variety of interests that comprises the nation. Some of these interest groups are obviously more closely aligned to one of the major political parties than the other. Some are courted by both. But, in general, it is not difficult for a lobby to find an articulate spokesman within Parliament to present its case. Only if it feels foiled within Parliament does a British lobby take its case over the heads of the members of Parliament to their constituents, or to what Americans call "the grass roots." When the Cotton Board failed to get what it considered adequate attention to its plea for protection against Indian and Hong Kong imports, it engaged in a nation-wide campaign with full-page advertisements in the daily press. Normally, however, the lobby finds adequate channels open to it within the regular processes of government.

All this means that British pressure groups attract far less attention than do American pressure groups, but not that they are less influential. In practice, although their efforts are less spectacular, they are probably more consistently effective—and, in general, to the advantage of all concerned. When a pressure group goes over the heads of political parties and government officials to swing opinion on a particular issue, it tends to undercut the position of what should be the responsible groups. But when, as happens so widely in Great Britain, the pressure groups and the responsible officials work together smoothly to develop laws and ordinances that fulfill useful public purposes, then responsibility is left where it belongs, and the pressure group becomes an adjunct to the political party itself as a means of determining public needs and attitudes.

Parliament as a Representative Body

Whom, then, does Parliament represent?

One thing, at least, is clear. The member of Parliament has to consider much in addition to his own judgment and conscience. There are rare occasions (as in the vote on the abolition of capital punishment) when his party leaves him free to choose for himself; furthermore, he will often agree wholeheartedly with the decision of his party. But if his conscience should lead him into frequent disagreement, and if he should follow his conscience rather than his party, it is extremely unlikely that he will retain his seat.

It is, obviously, only in an attenuated sense that the private member can be said to represent first of all the voters in his local constituency. In any conflict between party decisions and local opinion, he will almost certainly go with the party—for, if worse comes to worst, it can provide him with another constituency, and it is an unusual local issue, in any case, which will defeat a member of Parliament if his service is satisfactory in other respects. Moreover, the fact that legal authority is vested in Parliament itself means that members of Parliament feel more responsible to that institution as the organ of the whole people than to their own constituencies. That their responsibilities to Parliament are expressed in line with the will of the party reflects the fact that political power is ultimately in the hands of the electorate at large.

Private members, however, tend to represent their constituents in another sense, by rendering a great variety of service. Members like to list in their campaign literature testimonials from their constituents to the effectiveness of their help with income tax or pension problems. Many are assiduous in investigating local or individual grievances or complaints. And once the pattern has been established, they may be asked for advice on everything from matrimonial difficulties to the choice of a profession.

To some observers this type of service represents a great decline from the former lofty position of the M.P. as a lawmaker of the nation; and certainly there is little to be said in defense of the errand-boy member of Parliament. Much, however, can be said for the presence in the government of someone whose task it is to be interested in the grievances of even the humblest citizen of the smallest village and to protect his rights and welfare against official infringement, administrative inefficiency, or error.

The House of Commons can be the protector of individual rights only if private members remain alert to possible injustices. Regardless of the type of issue or circumstance, they may raise questions in the House of Commons unhampered by the need to ask permission of anyone. It is at this moment perhaps more than any other that they fulfill the Burkeian role of national representatives.

A second and still more effective means whereby a backbencher can play an independent role is during an adjournment debate, which,

as we have seen, comes at the end of all other parliamentary business. Whereas a parliamentary question is generally limited to one minute, the member allotted the adjournment has fifteen minutes, while the minister has an equal length of time to reply. Publicity accorded the adjournment debate is often disappointing, since the debate takes place after the first editions of the London papers have closed. As a means of turning the minister's attention to some precise point he has overlooked, however, it is the backbencher's best opportunity to speak for what he believes is the national interest.

Thus the member of Parliament really represents, in his conduct and voting practice, a variety of groups and interests whose relative importance cannot be precisely assessed. If his party's leaders are determined to enforce discipline, he will vote with them. But party policy is itself an interesting balance of intraparty pressures and drives and the interests of those external groups whose support is essential to electoral victory. The result is that the individual member of Parliament is probably less representative of the voters in his local constituency than is the individual congressman in the United States. Parliament as a whole, however, is more likely to follow a policy that reflects the desires of the nation as a whole than is the American Congress, mainly because centralized party discipline prevents national interests from being lost sight of in the struggle of an enormous variety of local and special interests.

4. THE HOUSE OF LORDS

The House of Lords has long been the subject of bitter political controversy, not so much because of the ardor of its defenders as because of the difficulty of agreeing upon a substitute body. Today few people would defend the traditional form and powers of the House of Lords; but any proposed alternative opens the road to infinite disagreement. To understand why, it is necessary to know something of the House of Lords as it has existed in the past and as it functions in the present.

Composition of the House of Lords

Most of the popular criticism of the House of Lords has risen from the anachronistic position of so aristocratic a body in a progressive democracy. The overwhelming majority of its 1,000-odd members hold their seats not because of any popular demand for their services, nor because of any marked capacity for legislative work, nor even because of any outstanding personal achievement or intelligence (although some of the peers are extremely able and intelligent). Rather, most of the members hold their seats as the result of chance: the typical peer, who represents 90 percent of the membership, simply happens to be the eldest son of the eldest son in a chain reaching back to an ancestor who was first created a nobleman. Personal intelligence or stupidity and a devotion to, neglect of, or complete indifference toward the public welfare have not been criteria of eligibility.

The greatest outcry in the past against the inevitability of hereditary succession came from rising young politicians, like Quintin Hogg and, even more strenuously, from Anthony Wedgwood Benn, whose efforts to renounce his seat in the Lords in order to be able to hold one in the House of Commons were long rebuffed. Finally, in 1963, the Peerage Act permitted the disclaimer of peerages, an opportunity seized by both Hogg and Benn. The measure also permitted the Earl of Home to become Sir Alec Home, leader of the Conservative party and for a short while Prime Minister after Macmillan's resignation.

In addition to some eight hundred and fifty hereditary peers, the House of Lords includes princes of the blood royal; twenty-six lords spiritual of the Church of England; sixteen peers representing the peers of Scotland; the five survivors of the twenty-eight representative Irish peers who held seats in 1922; nine lords of appeal in ordinary (the "law lords," whose seats are held for life and may not be inherited); and about a hundred life peers, appointed under the Life Peerage Act of 1958.

Among right-wing Conservatives it is natural to regard such a House as one of the glories of British government. To them the peers, as the descendants of the men who made Great Britain great, are the living symbol of the finest traditions of national history. Their family interests and heritage are supposed to be identical with those of the nation; their prestige and wealth place them above those temptations and selfish ambitions that harass ordinary mortals; and they have been reared in a tradition of service and devotion to the public welfare that renders them peculiarly qualified to act as trustees of the nation as a whole.

In attacking this picture, Labor's spokesmen like to point out that relatively few peers are descended from Great Britain's ancient noble families. Almost half of the peerages have been created since 1906; only one in fifteen dates from 1689; and only one in fifty from 1485. Moreover, a "boom in barons"—forty-six new peers in the last six months of 1964 to increase Labor and Liberal representation in the Lords —created an unprecedently rapid increase in numbers, although Pitt had created fifty in five years, Lloyd George a hundred and fifteen in six years, and Attlee ninety-eight in six years.

More than a few of the newer peers have won their titles, however, through distinguished service. Most Prime Ministers, for example, are offered peerages when they retire from party leadership, and, although Churchill refused, Attlee accepted an earldom. Moreover, diplomats, administrators, generals, poets, scholars—indeed, anyone who has contributed to the glory of the British name—may receive a peerage. Thus Lord Beveridge, author of the famous social insurance report; Field Marshal Montgomery; and Lord Lindsay, Master of Balliol College, Oxford, and a distinguished political scientist, were all "Lords of the first creation."

The Life Peerage Act of 1958, introduced by the Conservatives and opposed by Labor on the ground that it was designed to perpetuate the hereditary chamber, has been used to bring in additional nonparty persons of distinction and some members of the Labor party. Paradoxically, although there are twenty-four peeresses who since the 1963 Peerage Act sit in the Lords, the first women to be admitted were those appointed under the 1958 Act, of whom the most distinguished have been Barbara Wooton, the economist, and Dr. Edith Summerskill, a former Labor minister.

Criticisms of the Composition of the House of Lords

Despite this recent addition of outstanding men and women and the deliberate attempt to increase the number of Labor and Liberal spokesmen, most of the members of the House of Lords have a very different kind of background and attitude. It used to be charged rather freely, in the opening decades of the present century, that many men were raised to the peerage actually, if not overtly, because of generous contributions to the campaign funds of the Conservative or Liberal parties. Today no one is allowed to offer to buy or sell a peerage or other honor, and a committee of the Privy Council inspects the names of those to be honored for political services. But if the "sale" of peerages has ended, the names of wealthy men have not disappeared from the honor lists. On the contrary, those honored during the past quarter-century have included a large number of captains of commerce and industry—bankers, brewers, mine-owners, press lords, ship-owners, railroad directors, and manufacturers of automobiles and chemicals.

A chamber so constituted, it is often said, is bound, consciously or not, to be a prejudiced body. It is not so much that it *represents* wealth and privilege as that it *is* wealth and privilege personified. Most of the great landowners and big businessmen who comprise the vast majority of its members do not look on proposals for radical social and economic reform with conspicuous sympathy. Even the House of Lords' traditional opposition to temperance legislation seems not totally unconnected with the presence in its ranks of representatives of the great brewing interests (often called the Beerage).

The most serious grievance of the critics is that the overwhelming majority of the peers are not just Conservatives, but right-wing Conservatives. Thus no matter how the popular vote goes in any election and no matter which party controls the House of Commons, the Conservative party and, significantly, its more reactionary members, command most of the votes in the upper house. When the Conservative party is in power, its legislative program meets no interference from the upper house.

But, prior to 1945, whenever the Liberal or Labor party formed a Cabinet, its policy found a serious obstacle in the House of Lords. And although it was possible to argue for or against the general desirability of a second chamber, it was difficult to justify a second chamber that acted as a check only half the time and only when certain parties were in power.

Powers of the House of Lords

The power of the House of Lords to refuse its consent to legislation meant that here alone, in the British system of government, was there any real possibility of deadlock. If the Cabinet and the House of Commons disagreed, one or the other had to give way, either through resignation of the Cabinet or election of a new House of Commons. But if the peers disagreed, little could be done about it: they could not be forced to resign, and (with the exception of the Scottish peers) they were not dependent upon election. Only if the monarch agreed to appoint enough new peers to override their opposition could they be forced to submit; and this was too drastic a solution to be appealing.

Because of this danger of deadlock, several restrictions, formal and informal, grew up. It was understood, in the first place, that no defeat in the House of Lords could force a Cabinet out of office. Secondly, it was long understood that the peers should not reject or modify financial legislation contrary to the desire of the House of Commons. When, in 1909, the peers did reject the famous Lloyd George budget, the resulting constitutional crisis brought about the Parliament Act of 1911, according to which no money bill could be rejected by the House of Lords. A money bill that did not receive its approval merely lay on the table for one month and then was sent to the King for signature just as though it had been accepted.

A more general limitation was also incorporated in the Act of 1911, through the provision that the House of Commons could override the opposition of the Lords by passing the bill in question three times in three successive sessions in not less than two years—a provision that substituted a power of delay for the earlier power to defeat legislation.

In addition to the formal limitations of the

Act of 1911, there was an understanding that the House of Lords ought not to defeat a measure that had received the explicit endorsement of the people at the preceding election—that is, for which there was a "mandate."

The Lords and the Labor Party

The Labor party remained suspicious, however, that these restrictions were more apparent than real. Thus when it triumphed in the 1945 election, it gave notice that the rejection by the Lords of any important part of its legislative program would precipitate a violent constitutional crisis. The Conservative leader in the House of Lords agreed that "it would be constitutionally wrong, when the country has so recently expressed its view, for this House to oppose proposals which have been definitely put before the electorate."

By 1947, however, the situation was becoming more strained. As the Labor government's term of office lengthened, less was heard in the Lords about its "mandate." There were threats of delaying tactics and unpopular amendments. When the Labor party decided to nationalize the iron and steel industry, it determined to clear the way for passage of the measure in the fourth year of the Labor government's term of office by cutting down the length of time during which the Lords would have a suspensive veto.

The outcome was the Parliament Act of 1949 (introduced in November 1947 and passed over the Lords' veto two years later), which modified the procedure of the Parliament Act of 1911. A bill may now become law despite the opposition of the House of Lords if it has been passed by the House of Commons in two successive sessions (instead of three, as in the 1911 act), and if one year (instead of two) has elapsed between the date of the original second reading in the House of Commons and the final date on which the bill is passed by the House of Commons for the second time.

The furor that greeted this measure for further reducing the influence of the House of Lords on legislation led to a fresh attempt to reform a chamber that everyone admits is an anachronism in a modern democratic state. The Parliament Act of 1911 had been passed, in fact, on the assumption that the Lords would

be replaced by "a Second Chamber constituted on a popular instead of hereditary basis." But the Bryce Committee on the Reform of the Second Chamber, which reported in 1918 after a careful and detailed inquiry, found itself in the dilemma that still confronts reformers: the composition of the second chamber can hardly be changed radically without giving it a more intelligible basis of membership and making it more active, and both moves would tend to make the Lords a greater rival of the House of Commons than it is. Thus proposals for powers that the conservatives criticized as inadequate were already rejected by the progressives as too great; while the indirect method of election proposed by the Bryce Committee would have produced members whom conservatives scorned as not aristocratic enough and progressives termed undemocratic.

The all-party conference of 1948, which met under the chairmanship of the Prime Minister, Mr. Attlee, reached a measure of agreement on the character of a reconstituted House: no one party should have a permanent majority; the members, called Lords of Parliament, should be drawn from the hereditary peers or commoners created life peers; appointments should be on grounds of "personal distinction or public service"; women should be allowed to serve; members should be paid salaries (they subsequently got three guineas [$8.50] for each day of actual attendance, an amount raised to $4\frac{1}{2}$ guineas [$12.50] in 1964, and intended as reimbursement for expenses and obviously not as remuneration); those members who neglect their duties should be disqualified; and those peers who were not Lords of Parliament should be free to vote at elections and to stand for the House of Commons. It was also agreed that "the Second Chamber should be complementary to and not a rival to the Lower House." But on the fundamental question of the exact powers of a reconstituted House of Lords, it proved impossible to secure an agreement.

Functions of the House of Lords

To understand the basis of disagreement it is necessary to consider the existing functions of the House of Lords.

In the first place, the House of Lords is the

highest court of appeal in the Kingdom (a fact whose significance is described further in the chapter on the courts). During its sittings as a court, however, only the nine law lords, the Lord Chancellor, and any members who hold or who have held high judicial office take part in the proceedings.

In addition, the House of Lords performs several services of great usefulness to the House of Commons: its private-bills committees (whose work, of course, is judicial rather than legislative) relieve the Commons of the work of considering many private bills, and it also assists in the work of considering provisional order bills and special orders. Furthermore, the House of Lords conserves some of the Commons' time by initiating bills that are more or less noncontroversial in nature and that can be passed through the House of Commons with little discussion if they have been thoroughly discussed and put into shape by the Lords.

However, the House of Lords has four functions of considerably greater parliamentary significance. Its action in examining and revising bills passed by the House of Commons has gained in significance as the Commons have become more seriously pressed for time and more highly disciplined. Among the Lords are men with experience in earlier Cabinets and in the House of Commons or men who have served as diplomats and administrators or have had great practical experience in business and industry. The pressure on their time is not nearly so great, nor do they need to worry about impressing their constituents or appeasing party whips and playing to the galleries, since, in any case, their seats are safe. They can, accordingly, engage in intimate, practical, and highly intelligent discussion and criticism. Particularly at a time when the amount of technical legislation prevents the House of Commons from giving adequate consideration to the bills it passes, the House of Lords has proved extremely useful as a chamber of revision.

The same qualities of experience and independence make the House of Lords an excellent body for the discussion of legislative issues that the Commons are too busy to discuss or that party leaders may consider too explosive to touch. Thus the Lords may anticipate important questions, prepare the public for their consideration, and educate public opinion on the merits of different positions. Their debate in May 1952 on commercially sponsored television, for example, admirably prepared the way for its introduction. Strikingly, in the past few years the Lords initiated progressive bills on homosexuality, abortion, and Sunday observance.

In two potentially significant respects, the House of Lords has powers as great as those of the Commons. It can reject or withhold consent from the statutory rules and orders through which the broad principles of legislation are given detailed application. These rules and orders form the major means, in fact, through which government is carried on. As a Conservative spokesman pointed out in 1948, a full use of this power by the House of Lords "could reduce government to a nullity." The Lords could also throw out a private bill, leaving its promoters, and the Commons, helpless.

Controversy has centered, however, on the fourth of the legislative functions of the House of Lords: its power to interpose delay in the enactment of legislation. No one questions that one of the fundamental purposes of a second chamber is to slow up the passage of legislation in any instance in which the other house seems to be acting without popular authorization or in opposition to public opinion—"to provide a breathing space to enable the British people to make up their minds," as the Marquis of Salisbury once worded it. But for how long should the House of Lords be able to hold up legislation passed by the House of Commons, and under what circumstances? Mr. Churchill maintained that all controversial legislation should be passed in the first two years of a government's term of office, and that thereafter the House of Lords should act as a brake to radical change (such as nationalizing iron and steel), until such time as the "engine of the popular will is refueled by popular election." Mr. Attlee retorted that this would mean that "the engine had to go to be repaired every five years for a Conservative government and every two years when a Labor government was in power."

In the all-party conference, the Conservatives insisted that as a minimum the Lords should be able to interpose eighteen months' delay after the second reading of a measure; this amount of time, they felt, was essential if the House of Lords was to retain its function as a balancing force in the constitution. Thus they refused Labor's compromise suggestion of nine months from third reading (which frequently occurs more than three months after second reading). Labor then returned to its original proposal and insisted on no more than one year's delay after second reading. Should the Lords exercise a veto on current Labor legislation, there seems little doubt that their delaying powers would be further curbed or eliminated—a fact the Lords know and take into account.

Thus the House of Lords remains its old self, except that its suspensive veto on legislation has been shortened in time and largely nullified in practice. In one of the most advanced democracies of the day, a body based on what everyone agrees is an indefensible principle continues to share lawmaking functions with the House of Commons. Its functions of review and revision have been retained, while the likelihood of its thwarting or even seriously delaying action desired by the government has been virtually eliminated. And though neither Conservatives nor Labor wholeheartedly approve this compromise, they at least agree there must be no changes that might enable the second chamber to compete with the House of Commons.

5. The British Cabinet, Prime Minister, and Monarch

1. THE CABINET

The Cabinet is one of the typical anomalies of British politics. It is the center of governmental authority, the body that controls the House of Commons and that directs the administrative apparatus of the state. Yet one can search the law through without finding more than incidental references to it or to its leader, the Prime Minister. Its power arises not from any formal delegation of authority but from its ability to force those who do hold legal power—the Parliament, the monarch, the Privy Council, and the permanent administrative staff—to do what it wants them to do.

In form the Cabinet is a group of royal advisers that grew out of the royal household and the Privy Council, much as the Privy Council itself descended from the Great Council of the Norman Kings by way of the *Curia Regis* and the Permanent Council. Every Cabinet minister is appointed to the Privy Council. Since membership in the Council is for life, the Privy Council is a very large body that includes both former and incumbent Cabinet members, together with certain high administrative officials, leaders of the Church of England, and a number of writers, scientists, and others who have been honored by appointment to the Council. The Council as a whole never meets except for purely ceremonial occasions. But there are many occasions when three or four members of the Cabinet come together, usually at Buckingham Palace and ordinarily with the Queen in attendance, and transact business in the name of the Council as a whole. Its most important function is the issuing of "orders in Council," a great variety of executive orders many of which are a form of delegated legislation representing an exercise of general authority granted by act of Parliament.

What the Cabinet Is

If in form the Cabinet is a group of royal advisers, in practice it is a very special kind of group. Far from having a free hand in appointing its members, the Queen must choose as Prime Minister the leader of the party that commands a majority in the House of Commons; and the remaining Cabinet appointments are made according to the advice of the Prime Minister. Once appointed, of course, it is the Cabinet that decides policy, and the Queen must always follow its advice.

It is sometimes said that the Cabinet is really a committee made up of the leaders of the majority party in the House of Commons together with a few members of the same party who sit in the House of Lords. As already pointed out, however, this is a misconception. The Cabinet advises the Queen to summon and dissolve the body from which most of its members are chosen; it initiates and organizes the legislative program; and, in effect, it controls the House of Commons instead of being controlled by it, since its members control the party that controls the House of Commons. In short, a group that appears dependent upon the Queen and the House of Commons in fact dominates them both.

Clearly, then, the position of the British Cabinet is very different from that of the American

Cabinet. In the United States few Cabinet members are ever chosen from Congress, and those who are must resign their seats in Congress. Once in the Cabinet, they are responsible only to the President. Congress may reject their proposals and attack their policies, but if the President is contented with their work, they remain in office. Indeed, the President and the majority of Congress may belong to different parties; but Congress has no way, short of impeachment, of forcing either the President or his Cabinet out of office. It is possible for the Congress and the President to continue in a deadlock for months on end. In the United Kingdom, however, such a deadlock would be resolved immediately either by resignation of the Cabinet or by a new election. In short, while the American Cabinet is dependent upon the President, the British Cabinet is not dependent upon the Queen; while the American Cabinet does not control, and is not controlled by, Congress, the typical British Cabinet has complete control of the House of Commons.

The Membership of the Cabinet

When a new Prime Minister is appointed, he has to fill about seventy posts, major and minor, which together make up the "ministry." About thirty of these appointments are ministers, but not all the ministers are in the Cabinet. In fact, there are three possible types of Cabinet: the large, or full, Cabinet of prewar days, which might number as many as twenty-three, as in Mr. Chamberlain's Cabinet of 1939; the small, coordinating Cabinet, such as Mr. Churchill's War Cabinet of eight members, or the still smaller Cabinet of five members recommended by Mr. Amery in *Thoughts on the Constitution;* and the medium-sized Cabinet of sixteen to eighteen members common since World War II. While Cabinet positions are not always the same, the Prime Minister himself, the Chancellor of the Exchequer, the Home Secretary, the Foreign Secretary, the Secretaries for Commonwealth Relations, the Colonies, and Scotland, the Lord Chancellor, the President of the Board of Trade, and the Ministers of Defense, Labor, and Agriculture and Fisheries generally will be among them. Men of great political importance but lesser administrative ability, elder

statesmen, or men whose time should be free for committee work and the integration of policy may be given positions whose duties are light or nonexistent: Lord President of the Council, Lord Privy Seal, or Minister without Portfolio. Ministers charged with matters that are temporarily of first-rate importance may become members of the Cabinet as the need arises and may be dropped when the need is over. After the election of 1945, for example, the Minister of Fuel and Power (who was to direct the nationalization of the coal mines), the Minister of Education (who had to put the new education law into effect), and the Minister of Health (who had to take action to meet the housing crisis) were added to the Cabinet, although they had not been in the Cabinet in the preceding ministry. The Minister of Fuel and Power was subsequently dropped from the Cabinet in 1947 after nationalization of the coal mines had been carried through.

In addition to those ministers who are members of the Cabinet, certain ministers may be designated as "of Cabinet rank," which means they are invited to attend Cabinet meetings when the affairs of their departments are under consideration.

Finally, there are certain parliamentary undersecretaries and other ministers: the Undersecretaries for Home and Foreign Affairs, the Parliamentary and Financial Secretaries of the Admiralty, the Parliamentary Secretary of the Ministry of Health, the Junior Lords of the Treasury (who act as party whips), and others. The holders of such posts often are younger men whose ability is being tested in preparation for higher posts. Similarly, parliamentary private secretaries, though of course not in the ministry, get a chance to demonstrate their capacity for higher offices.

Appointment of Members of the Cabinet

The Prime Minister's task in choosing his Cabinet is very different from that of the American President. In the United States the President may choose whomever he pleases, subject to confirmation by the Senate. It is unusual to have more than one or two of the most conspicuous and popular party leaders in the Cabinet, and a large majority of the Cabinet, when first appointed, may be relatively unfamiliar to the public at large and also almost unknown to one another, a fact that makes it difficult for them to work together as a team. It even happens sometimes that Cabinet members belong to the opposition party, as in the case of Robert McNamara, a Republican who has been Secretary of Defense under both President Kennedy and President Johnson. Thus the field from which they may be drawn is so large and the President is so little restrained in his selection that speculation about the composition of a new President's Cabinet is a popular sport of political analysts and gossip writers after every change of administration.

In Great Britain there is far less opportunity for this pastime. In form, the Prime Minister has complete authority to select whomever he pleases, since the Queen will make appointments upon his advice alone. But in practice, every outstanding leader of the majority party who holds a seat in Parliament expects, and is expected, to be in the Cabinet. Its membership includes not only the important and influential but usually also representatives of differing points of view and political outlooks, so that, in this sense, the Cabinet becomes a microcosm of the party. Thus anyone can tell, before a British election, the names of at least half a dozen men in each party who inevitably will be in the Cabinet if their party wins. Most American political leaders consider the governorship of a state or a seat in the Senate to be a position of greater power and prestige than membership in the Cabinet; but the political authority of the British Cabinet makes it the logical goal for every ambitious statesman, and to keep an able and popular leader out of the British Cabinet would be to encourage dissatisfaction and even dissension within the majority party.

The Prime Minister's power is considerably freer when it comes to deciding which man shall receive which post, although even here a few men may be important enough to insist on specific appointments. The Prime Minister also has a relatively free hand in deciding which of the party's less conspicuous or younger men shall receive posts in the government. Thus any announcement of Cabinet appointments or changes is likely to include several surprises.

In choosing members of the Cabinet, several qualities have to be considered. The man who is to head a department should have had considerable experience in the House of Commons and should have demonstrated his ability to take care of himself in debate and during the question period. Much of the government's success in the next election will depend upon its ability to meet the constant, varied, and vigorous assaults of the opposition on the floor of Parliament. In addition, however, the direction of a department calls for considerable administrative capacity; and the man who has already distinguished himself in an earlier ministry as undersecretary of an important department may well look forward to promotion to a higher post. Occasionally, however, a party has been out of office for a long time, or (as was the case with the first Labor government in 1923) has never held office; it is then necessary to take a chance and later to redistribute posts, perhaps several times, as members reveal their respective talents and shortcomings.

Collective Responsibility of Cabinet Members

The presence in the British Cabinet of the outstanding leaders of a party is perhaps less remarkable than the fact that these leaders subordinate their personal views to a common policy. Americans are so accustomed to seeing the widest, and occasionally the bitterest, disagreement among leaders of the same political party that they would have difficulty imagining that a Cabinet which included the leaders of all important party factions—let us say a Republican Cabinet composed of Nixon, Rockefeller, and Goldwater—could submit to this sort of discipline. Yet in Great Britain such agreement is the essence of Cabinet responsibility. As Lord Grey (who was Foreign Secretary from 1905 to 1916) once stated, a Cabinet member should work heartily for Cabinet decisions, should not insist on his personal views in nonessential matters, should argue for the substance of a proposal rather than its form, and should look for ways in which his ideas can be reconciled with those of others. He ought not to sacrifice what he thinks essential to the public interest, but he should be more seriously interested in getting the Cabinet to agree than in winning a personal victory. Once a decision is reached, he should never threaten to resign unless the matter is of vital importance and unless he intends to carry out the threat. Thus there may well be serious disagreement and a great deal of discussion before the sense of the meeting becomes apparent; but once there is preponderant opinion in favor of a certain course, the Cabinet as a whole is expected loyally to support that policy.

This ideal can be achieved more readily in Great Britain than in the United States because of the greater homogeneity of the island and the absence of so great a diversity of conflicting interests and attitudes. Further, British party leaders generally share sympathies and outlook. Among the leaders of the Conservative party the emphasis that public school education lays on loyalty, discipline, and teamwork is important. Among Labor's leaders the experience that many have had in trade unions imposes a belief in the kind of absolute solidarity that wins strikes and makes collective bargaining possible. Similarly, the fact that the party leaders have had long service together in the House of Commons means that they have had to learn to cooperate closely in the planning of common party strategy and that, from their earliest days in the House of Commons, they have been accustomed to act as a coherent party unit, as symbolized by the disciplined procession into the proper lobby on every important vote. Disagreement may well exist among different wings of the party, but it is the sort of disagreement that finds its full expression in party meetings or within the secrecy of Cabinet discussions and rarely in the public glare of parliamentary debate.

In the United States, no one would expect the Secretary of Labor to resign because he disagreed with the policy of the Secretary of State. If the Department of Agriculture embarks on an unpopular policy, no one supposes that the Secretary of the Treasury is to blame. In fact, the President himself is under no obligation to consult with his Cabinet before deciding on the gravest issues; he may even make a decision to which his entire Cabinet is opposed. But in Great Britain, whether consulted or not, every minister must accept his common responsibility as long as he retains his post.

It is, clearly, only upon this assumption that the British Cabinet system makes sense. Unless the entire body has accepted responsibility for the policy, there would be no point in forcing a whole Cabinet out of office if the House of Commons defeats the government on one major issue on which it is willing to stake its existence. And there would be little meaning and much confusion in the voter's choice if he were asked to pass on a party's record and program when prominent leaders of the party accept neither the record nor the program and feel under no obligation to abide by either.[1] Under the system of collective responsibility, party leaders cannot pass the buck or disclaim personal responsibility for mistakes on the grounds that they lack political control. The control is there, and when an individual minister acts or fails to act, the voter can with justice blame the Cabinet as a whole for the minister's conduct as long as he remains a member of the Cabinet.

Thus it is understood that whenever a Cabinet member makes a statement on any important political problem, whether it concerns his own department or not, he is speaking for the Cabinet as a whole. And it is especially important, therefore, that members should agree in what they say. Lord Melbourne, Prime Minister in 1834 and from 1835 to 1841, is supposed to have put his back to the door, at the end of a Cabinet discussion on the duty on corn (that is, wheat) and to have said: "What are we to say? Is it to make our corn dearer, or cheaper, or to make the price steady? I don't care which: but we had better all be in the same story." The rule still holds.

What the Cabinet Does

The Cabinet, according to the Report of the Machinery of Government Committee, 1918, has three main functions: (a) final determination of the policy to be submitted to Parliament; (b) supreme control of the national executive in accordance with the policy prescribed by Parliament; and (c) continuous coordination

---

[1] In 1932, the Cabinet, which at that time included members from several parties, a situation that is characteristic only of times of extreme national urgency, announced its famous "agreement to differ" on the issue of free trade and permitted some of its members to vote against the policy of the government. It was commonly noted at the time that if this practice were to become general, the basis for the Cabinet system of government would be destroyed.

and delimitation of the authorities of the several departments of state.

The Cabinet as Legislature

The first of these functions is, obviously, largely a matter of legislation and constitutes a recognition of the fact that, in a time of voluminous and highly technical legislation, the 630 members of the House of Commons constitute too large a body to work out a comprehensive and consistent program. It is up to the Cabinet necessarily to plan an overall legislative program, deciding which measures shall occupy the time of Parliament, and in what order, and ultimately approving the form in which these measures shall be submitted.

Inevitably, then, the Cabinet becomes something of a little legislature; and as its legislative load has grown, it has come face to face with problems of procedure that have confronted Parliament itself, and it has resorted to some of the same remedies.

The demands upon its time are, of course, very great. Its members must be present in Parliament, at least when matters concerning their own departments are under discussion. Their load of departmental work may be very heavy, and they may be expected to spend long hours in committee meetings. Yet they must also find some time for the consideration of problems of overall policy and for the discussion of those proposals which the government intends to introduce into Parliament.

Ordinarily, the Cabinet as a whole meets only twice a week for a period of about two hours, and its work must be organized with extraordinary efficiency if it is to be well done. Until World War I, however, there was considerable reluctance to recognize this need, and procedure in Cabinet meetings was quite informal. There were frequent occasions when Cabinet members disagreed over what had been decided, and in some cases they had no memory at all. Thus Lord Hartington's private secretary could write to Mr. Gladstone's: "There must have been some decision. . . . My chief has told me to ask you what the devil *was* decided, for he be damned if he knows."

Today, as in the House of Commons, activities are better organized. The proceedings of the Cabinet still are secret, but the Cabinet Secretariat, or Cabinet Office, under the direction of the Prime Minister, organizes the agenda for meetings, keeps a careful record of the conclusions, and circulates them to the ministers. A few days before each meeting the agenda must be sent around so that each member will know what is to be discussed. Careful memoranda describing and explaining the measures under consideration are supposed to be circulated at least two days before proposals are discussed. A short summary familiarizes the minister who is bogged down in departmental duties with the major points in the argument. In addition, copies of Foreign Office telegrams and dispatches are sent to the members of the Cabinet to keep them informed of day-to-day developments in foreign policy. All departments directly concerned in a measure (including the Treasury, if there are financial provisions) are expected to consult with one another and to work out an agreement for presentation to the Cabinet before the matter is placed on the agenda and the memorandum circulated. Once these departments have come to an agreement, the Cabinet can often dispose of the matter with comparatively little or even no discussion.

It is possible to discern other ways in which the organization of the Cabinet's legislative and policy-making activities have led to devices similar to those developed in the House of Commons. In both bodies the agenda is carefully prepared, and control over the agenda is concentrated in comparatively few hands. Just as the Cabinet and the whips (in consultation with the opposition) prepare the program of business for the House, the Prime Minister, with his secretariat, and in consultation with individual ministers, works out the program for the Cabinet. The Prime Minister as an individual has just as much control over the Cabinet's agenda as the Cabinet itself has over that of the House.

In addition, the Cabinet, like the House of Commons, delegates much of its work to committees. Some of these are standing committees, and some are temporary. Their character and use depend on the legislative program and on the Prime Minister's view of the best way to handle its manifold aspects.

In comparison with House committees, Cabinet committees are more varied in composition, number, and importance; moreover, the public knows little about them until after an administration has gone out of office. In such areas, however, as new education programs and the Common Market, where vast quantities of information are essential, R. A. Butler (now Lord Butler), who was a Cabinet minister for over seventeen years, tells us that in his experience all the basic work was done in the relevant departments and coordinated in a Cabinet committee and that only the ultimate policy implications were decided by the Cabinet as a whole. Indeed, he found that most of his own work as Minister of Education had been done outside the Cabinet and was hardly referred to it at all. Moreover, he maintains that the necessity for secrecy requires the budget to be the virtually exclusive province of the Chancellor of the Exchequer, although, of course, the Prime Minister is fully informed. To this degree, therefore, the pressure of government business and the character of particular aspects of it have reduced the comprehensiveness of the Cabinet's decision-making to ultimate and vital political decisions.

The Cabinet as Administrator

The second big job of Cabinet members and other ministers is to supervise the carrying out of legislation that has been passed by Parliament and to determine policy where there is no legislation to furnish guidance. This is the traditional function of the executive, but it is also a function which has become far weightier in recent years. As legislation has become more voluminous and more technical, Parliament has more frequently passed laws in skeleton form, leaving it to the Cabinet or the minister to decide on the precise rules, orders, and actions that will give effect to them.

This practice immediately raises the question of whether the ordinary minister is himself capable of making these rules. His presence in the Cabinet often is not so much the result of his technical competence as of his ability to win votes, to speak effectively on the platform or in Parliament, and to plan party strategy. He may have technical competence as well—indeed, there are always some Cabinet members whose presence in the Cabinet is a mystery to those who do not understand that it is due to great

administrative capacity rather than to effectiveness on the floor of Parliament. But it is still the exceptional Cabinet member who is a first-class administrator as well.

Under the circumstances, the charge is often made that real power has passed from the Cabinet to members of the permanent civil service—on whose advice Cabinet members are largely dependent. The ordinary ministerial head of a department, it is said, is unlikely to be an expert in the field assigned to him; what information he acquires comes to him through the permanent staff; and it is the rare, if not the rash, individual who would override its recommendations. Some departments are even accused of having a "department policy" designed and carried out by the permanent staff, regardless of who heads the department or which party is in power. Under such circumstances, the official government would be little more than a puppet, and the real government would be the civil service.

Actually, such a picture is badly exaggerated. In addition to those ministers who combine parliamentary and administrative ability, the system of appointing younger men as junior ministers provides an opportunity, as we have noted, for promising parliamentarians also to be trained in administrative work in preparation for later advancement to major posts. Far more important, however, is the fact that the minister need not be an expert (in the sense of understanding all the technical details of the work of his department) so long as he has access to expert advice, drawn, if possible, from a variety of sources. What is required of the minister, rather, is that he should have good judgment both of issues and of men, that he should be able to select the essential elements of a proposal, that he should be able to make up his mind quickly, and that he should be able to foresee the political consequences of his department's policies.

This is a job, moreover, which an experienced parliamentarian should be able to do very well. A man who has taken a leading part in the work of Parliament for several years is already a man of broad political experience. In earlier years, as a leader of the opposition, he may have helped to work out its policy in opposition to that of the Cabinet of the day. If he is a person of ability, he will have learned what type of action is likely to anger the House and what type of administrative ruling will be difficult to explain or justify. Indeed, if there is any subject on which he can qualify as an expert, it is the gauging of public opinion. The member of the civil service is also likely to be constantly in touch with many interest groups, so he too can often gauge what the reactions will be to particular measures. But it is not his responsibility—nor in a sense his right—to make decisions on this basis, though his advice would always be welcomed. He and his fellow civil servants are chiefly responsible for outlining alternatives and for describing the practical consequences of particular programs.

But a miscalculation of public sentiment is likely to be fatal to the career of the politician; in nursing his constituency and, on a higher level, in sensing the mood of the people's representatives in Parliament, he gains a knowledge of popular desires and reactions which is invaluable in the work of administration. In the words of Sir William Harcourt, a Liberal M.P. who repeatedly held Cabinet office in the late nineteenth century, "The value of the political heads of the departments is to tell the permanent officials what the public will not stand." If a government is to be truly democratic, it would be hard to overestimate this function.

The political head of the department is essential to satisfactory administration in another respect. So far as the ordinary citizen is concerned, the civil servant is "un-get-at-able." He is not elected by the voter, and he will not be discharged because a voter, or even a majority of the voters, dislikes what he does. The ministerial head of a department, however, is "get-at-able" in at least two ways. He must submit regularly to the questions of members of Parliament, and he must keep his eye on the next election. By making the Cabinet member responsible for what goes on in his department, it is possible to make the department itself responsible. If a civil servant abuses his powers or is negligent in his duty, if he injures an ordinary citizen or engages in an unwise or unpopular policy, the minister at the head of his department will have to answer parliamentary questions of a decidedly unpleasant nature. If the action under criticism is a serious one, there

may even be a special debate on the subject. The opposition may present a motion of censure, and the whole country may be roused by the event. In extreme cases the government may even have to worry about winning the next election. Under the circumstances, the minister who must answer the questions in Parliament, who finds himself pilloried in debate and in the press, or who finds the hive of public resentment swarming about his head will call his departmental subordinates into line and force them to modify the policy that has aroused the storm. Far more frequently, the knowledge that such a storm is possible will prevent the policy from being inaugurated in the first place.

The Cabinet as Coordinator

In any country in which so many matters are subject to administrative intervention or control, there is always danger of the growth of those evils commonly subsumed under the term *bureaucracy*. The action of one department almost inevitably affects the work of others. A ruling about health may affect education, labor, agriculture, and still other departments. Two departments may make inconsistent rulings. Conflicts of jurisdiction may arise. Activities may duplicate one another or overlap. The principles and policies upheld by one department may be in flat contradiction to those of another.

Most serious of all, departments may be left to compose their differences with other departments without any serious consideration of whether the resultant overall policy is a policy at all and, if it is, a desirable one.

The Cabinet is not well suited to the task of coordination. There are too many members for effective discussion, and its members are often too preoccupied with the problems of their own departments to see policy as a whole. The Prime Minister himself is so busy and, particularly in the past, possesses such inadequate sources of information that he has often seemed an arbitrator between departments rather than an initiator of broad governmental policy.

Whether or not it takes official form, there is a strong—and constructive—tendency for a small number of Cabinet members, together with the Prime Minister, to form a kind of "Inner Cabinet" to consider basic policy and to arrive at a general agreement before the Cabinet as a whole meets. This procedure also speeds the transaction of business.

In consequence of such developments there has appeared something of a hierarchy within the ministry, three or four levels of which may be distinguished: the members of the "Inner Cabinet," who often coordinate the work of several departments; the other members of the Cabinet; ministers "of Cabinet rank" who do not regularly sit in the Cabinet; and the remaining ministers. But most observers praise this system as a means of achieving a broader understanding of policy and a higher degree of integration than would be possible if each Cabinet member concerned himself only with his own department and if an undifferentiated group of eighteen or more Cabinet ministers had to work out a general program. Some critics point out that the added authority of the Inner Cabinet has at times decreased the prestige and importance of the rest of the Cabinet, and some suggest that the smaller body should be the Cabinet with the rest coordinated through it. It is also possible, though rare, that the existence of the different levels may encourage a consciousness of rank, a rivalry for power, and a tendency to pay attention to the views of an individual less because of their intrinsic merit than because of his exalted position.

"Cabinet Dictatorship"?

Americans who look at the Cabinet system in operation sometimes conclude that Great Britain lives in fact under a Cabinet dictatorship. The firm control that the Cabinet exerts over the House of Commons means ordinarily that legislation it is determined to pass is passed and that legislation it opposes is lost. It is difficult for public opinion to bring effective pressure to bear on individual issues; and the voter ordinarily must wait until the next election—which may be two or three or four years off and which may involve a great many different issues— before he can register his disapproval. Thus it is sometimes charged that Great Britain practices a form of "plebiscitary democracy" in which people vote "yes" or "no" on the record of the government in general but are deprived of any share in the formulation of individual policies.

The system has even seemed to facilitate the violation of electoral pledges. Perhaps the most glaring example occurred following the election of 1935, in which the Conservative party won a heavy majority in the House of Commons on a platform that called for vigorous support of the League of Nations and the system of collective security. During the next few months, however, the government followed a policy that helped to undermine the power and prestige of the League and eventually accepted the conquest of Ethiopia by Italy in direct violation of the Covenant of the League. But though the government thus departed from its platform within a few weeks after its great electoral victory, it was under no necessity of calling a new election. Despite the defection of a few critical members, the government's overwhelming majority and party discipline prevented any effective challenge.

In contrast, Americans are likely to think of the fight over reform of the Supreme Court early in 1937. In the election of November 1936 President Roosevelt had been returned to office with a spectacular majority of the popular vote and with a strong Democratic majority in both Houses of Congress. Yet, when a short time later he proposed to modify the composition of the Court, popular opposition was so strong that the proposal could not be carried through Congress. The lack of discipline in the American party system and the vulnerability of individual congressmen to popular pressure meant that the voters could influence Congress to resist the President; in an analogous situation British voters could hardly have brought the House of Commons to resist the Cabinet.

Cabinet Responsibility

It is often said that the British government is more efficient than the American because there can never be any danger of the kind of deadlock between the executive and the legislature that haunts the American system. But as a result of such occurrences, it has also been said that the American system is more responsible because the President cannot force through a policy to which public opinion is opposed.

Actually, such a statement is a great oversimplification. Even if the Cabinet is not, as a rule, overthrown by the House of Commons, it is subject to considerable pressure. The ever present readiness of the opposition to exploit any weakness, the constant search by the press for an exciting issue, and the knowledge that within five years at most a new election must be held are all serious limitations. The government may disregard public opinion on a few issues so long as it knows that the public approves its record in general. But if there is widespread public revulsion, and if large numbers of members of Parliament report that their seats may be endangered in the next election, the government is quite likely to make concessions. In addition to all these reasons why the charge of Cabinet "dictatorship" is not justified, the British executive has traditionally acted with admirable restraint in its use of power, recognizing that the key to the successful functioning of the parliamentary system is that the House of Commons should have ample opportunity to criticize its policies, and that, in this sense, the House should be the mouthpiece of public opinion.

In any event, there is a certain superficiality in speaking of responsibility only as the ability of the people to prevent the government from doing what the people do not want it to do. At least as important is the government's ability positively to do what the people want it to do. And here the difference between the two systems is more clearly marked. If the British and the American executives were equally bent on pushing through a policy desired by the majority of the people, the British executive would be far more likely to succeed. Under the American system of separating governmental powers —and checking and balancing them—and with the laxness of party discipline, Congress often responds to the efforts, not of a majority of the people, but of a minority. All that a minority group need do to check legislation is to control a single house of Congress or, in some cases, a single committee, in particular the Rules Committee, of the House of Representatives. In Great Britain such a situation would be inconceivable.

The issue may be summarized thus: Is it better to have a government capable of carrying out the will of the people—but also capable of carrying through something the people do not will? Or is it better to have a government so checked and balanced that it is not likely to

push through an unpopular program simply because it cannot overcome even minor opposition? In a period of relative calm there may be something to be said for the second alternative as a way of forcing divergent groups to compose their differences and work out a generally acceptable program. But in times of crisis, which these days seem omnipresent, the government that cannot take decisive and prompt action is in danger of losing important opportunities. Ordinarily when need is great, the American Congress has been willing to support many of the President's measures. The British executive, however, has the great advantage of being able to plan a comprehensive and coherent program and to ensure its enactment under virtually all circumstances, while the American executive frequently has his proposals rejected by a Congress unable to develop a comprehensive policy of its own.

Here, too, however, one has to be careful not to push the parallel too far. Great Britain, it must be remembered, is a country in which there are few important minorities and in which there is less danger of majority tyranny. But in the United States, with its great sectional, racial, religious, and other diversities, it is important that a minority have the power to defend itself. The process of working out a democratic agreement, through discussion and consent, is inevitably a more complicated and difficult matter in a country such as the United States; and to say that the American system works less vigorously and effectively under normal circumstances is not to say that it is less well suited to the needs of the American people.

2. THE PRIME MINISTER

The Prime Minister and the Cabinet

The Prime Minister has been the principal beneficiary of the Cabinet's growth in power. In former days he used to be, in Lord Morley's phrase, *primus inter pares,* first among equals. Today any such designation would be far too modest. Differences in the personalities of different Prime Ministers make generalization dangerous: what is true of a Churchill in time of war is not necessarily true of a Home or a

Wilson in time of peace. Nevertheless, all modern Prime Ministers have the determining voice in policy.

The Prime Minister still is not the master of his Cabinet that the American President is of his. The Cabinet of the President is essentially a group of advisers whose advice the President is free to take or to leave. It is the persuasiveness of the arguments of the members of the Cabinet that is important, not their votes. Lincoln could say, at the end of a Cabinet discussion: "Noes, seven, Ayes, one: the Ayes have it"; and his successors retain this power. In fact, the President is not even obliged to consult his Cabinet before embarking on important measures. As we have seen, the majority of the members of his Cabinet are likely to be relatively obscure politically. They are not the greatest leaders of their party, and in most cases they cannot threaten the President with any serious loss of support if he enters into open conflict with them. But a British Prime Minister is expected to include in his Cabinet his party's most important leaders, and he can less easily brush their opinions aside.

This limitation, however, has not prevented the Prime Minister from gaining greater and greater ascendancy over his colleagues. One can understand, of course, why a man with the experience and personality of a Churchill should dominate his Cabinet. What is remarkable, however, is that even before the war Chamberlain, who had far less popular appeal, held a similar ascendancy over his Cabinet. With the aid of a few advisers chosen from the Cabinet and the civil service, he decided upon and carried out his own policy, not only in the field of foreign relations but in domestic policy as well. There were times when the Cabinet was not consulted on important matters; and ministers who disagreed with him, such as Eden and Duff-Cooper, could resign without shaking his authority.

Chamberlain's two predecessors, Baldwin and MacDonald, exercised similar authority. If Baldwin was somewhat less energetic in pushing his personal views, it was he nevertheless who dominated whenever there was serious disagreement. MacDonald had a more active interest in directing policy, and he has been accused of using his authority over the Cabinet's agenda in an arbitrary way to determine what should be considered in Cabinet meetings and to veto items that displeased him. Attlee as Prime Minister aimed at winning agreement among his colleagues rather than at imposing a decision upon them. Frequently, he was criticized for "not giving a stronger lead." Yet in his sincere, unspectacular way, Attlee was not only decisive but, on occasion, ruthless. After an initial period of weak leadership, Eden also came to dominate his Cabinet, particularly (and unfortunately) in foreign affairs, a fact which suggests that the office itself creates a certain pattern of behavior for even the most quiet personality. If Home appeared less forceful than Macmillan, he introduced some major changes into Conservative procedures. Since Wilson's succession to office, there has been no question about the dominance of the Prime Minister.

The Sources of the Prime Minister's Strength

There are several considerations, other than personality, which help to determine the Prime Minister's position inside his Cabinet. For one thing, as the work of administration has become increasingly heavy, Cabinet members have often been so preoccupied with the duties and problems of their own departments as to leave general policy to the Prime Minister and his chosen advisers. In addition, particularly in the Conservative party, the exalted position of party leader gives the Prime Minister a prestige far greater than that of any other individual in the Cabinet; and in the case of the Conservative party it also gives him control over the party's organization and funds, weapons of decisive power against any challenger. For both parties, the prestige of the Prime Minister and the party are so closely intertwined that any attack on the Prime Minister is bound simultaneously to discredit his party and to give ammunition to the opposition, and few of his colleagues would risk such disaster in order to defeat one of his policies. For that matter, the constant publicity given the Prime Minister because of his position is likely to give him a prestige and a popular following greater than that of any of his colleagues.

Popular Leadership

No less fundamental, however, is the increasing habit of looking to the executive for leadership, not only because Parliament is less and less able to work out a coherent policy or to frame technical legislation, but also because of the belief that the Prime Minister is more likely than Parliament to think in terms of the general interest. Parliament is largely made up of competing interests: the trade unions have their representatives and so do the big industrialists and financiers. The Prime Minister, however, is not pledged to any special interest. His position is high enough so that he needs no man's favor; on the contrary, he has a very considerable number of posts and other rewards at his own disposal. His position politically is so strong that he can afford to think of the public interest at the expense of private and selfish interests. He may not be able to ignore the most powerful of the special interests, but he is in a far stronger position to resist a selfish minority than is the ordinary legislator. Indeed, to some extent his position encourages him to do so because, even when he thinks of the next election, he must think not in terms of any single interest or constituency but in terms of winning a majority of votes in the country as a whole. Any too evident devotion to any special interest (even to the trade unions in the case of Labor or to big business in the case of the Conservatives) may antagonize enough marginal voters to lose the election.

What the Prime Minister Does

The perfect Prime Minister would have to be an unusually versatile man, for he must combine the talents of the leader of a great political party with those of the chief of government officials. The success of his party at the polls may depend upon his ability to appeal to the popular imagination and to sense the desires and the needs of the mass of the people. He ought, like Stanley Baldwin and Clement Attlee, to have the sort of character and appearance that inspire trust and confidence. He ought, like Winston Churchill, to be able to speak directly to the hearts and minds of his countrymen, so that through his words political issues may become clear and political needs comprehensible. It is up to him, more than any other elected figure, to give the human touch to government and to make the ordinary citizen feel that he is in some direct and personal contact with the issues that are being decided.

But the Prime Minister must do more than play a great role before the public as a whole; he must also act as leader of his party in that narrower community, Parliament. Here a quite different set of qualities is required. An expert platform manner is less important than judgment, understanding, and the ability to grasp the essential points of the issues under discussion and to display a command of the technicalities involved, to sense the feeling of the House, and to adopt the proper strategy. Cogency of argument and skill in debate now become important, for the House of Commons is not a place where eloquence can be substituted for competence or where impassioned oratory can compensate for ignorance of the facts.

Then, too, the Prime Minister is head of the Cabinet. This role requires that he be a good judge of men, for, apart from those few who "choose themselves," he must select his colleagues. When he presides over the formulation of policy, he must function as "the good chairman," the man who can see the main issues and the questions of principle, who can arbitrate between different views, who has common sense and good judgment, who can guide the discussion toward a definite conclusion, and who can get the Cabinet team to work together harmoniously and efficiently.

Moreover, with the growth of the government's administrative functions, there is the need for "the good administrator" who can comprehend the overall pattern of the government's responsibilities, who can bring the incredible variety of governmental policies and activities into reasonable relationship with one another, and who can act as manager-in-chief of the government's business.

And finally, the Prime Minister must maintain particularly close relations with the Queen, for it is the Prime Minister alone and not the Cabinet who advises her on such matters as appointments and dissolutions and who must keep her informed on governmental decisions. The monarch, of course, accepts the advice of the Prime Minister on any significant issue, but assent is not always a mere matter of form. The tact and perception of the Prime Minister is an important element in their personal relationship; and the effectiveness of this relationship can have far-reaching consequences, as was clearly demonstrated at the time of the abdication crisis in 1936.

Obviously, no one man is likely to combine all the qualities needed for this job. A great popular leader may be a failure in the give-and-take of parliamentary debate, or he may be quite inadequate in the less public but vitally important work of chairman, coordinator, and administrator. More than one government has been wrecked by a Prime Minister who was as colorful and brilliant a leader as Parliament or the country could desire but who lacked the respect and even the trust of his colleagues and could not direct a Cabinet discussion toward definite decision or action on the issues before it. Yet the qualities required for the different functions are not necessarily incompatible. Good judgment, both of men and of issues, is essential to the leader of the party in Parliament as well as to the chairman of the Cabinet. So are a grasp of the most important issues and principles and the ability to keep a group of men—larger in one case than in the other—working together in harmony and, if possible, with enthusiasm.

Training

In this sense, the training that all British Prime Ministers must receive is more demanding than that of the typical American President. The man who can sustain the crossfire of Parliament over a period of years and who can lead his party successfully both in debate and in strategy must be a man of considerable ability. The competition for leadership is rigorous; the aspirant is constantly sized up against the leaders of his own party and those of the opposition, and the sizing up takes place within a single chamber. In the United States there is no comparable device for the testing and winnowing out of the ablest leaders.

Some people fear that this kind of training may prevent the development of great leaders in the future. If the House of Commons is the only path to political leadership, and if the

House is itself dominated by the machines of the great parties, there may be less opportunity for the man who is brilliant but unorthodox to rise to the top. It is sometimes suggested that a Lloyd George or a Winston Churchill starting on a parliamentary career today would never be allowed to emerge from the wilderness of the back benches—if, indeed, he could win election to Parliament in the first place. The man who is too independent or too imaginative will hardly win the approval of the party whips, and leaders are likely to regard as a troublemaker the young man who opposes their ideas or flirts with dissident groups. It took imminent military disaster to put Winston Churchill in the Prime Ministership, and short of such exceptional aid, the road of the independent is a hard one.

Yet if the restrictions on personal independence seem to be growing, there is considerable hope for the undisciplined in the fact that the Cabinet formed by the well-disciplined Labor party in 1945 contained three men—Sir Stafford Cripps, Aneurin Bevan, and George Strauss—who had been expelled from the party in 1939 for advocating a Popular Front with the Communists, and who, though they had since returned to the fold, owed much of their prominence in the party to their earlier obstreperousness. Paradoxically, the British Parliament, in practice, seems more often to provide important opportunities for political mavericks than does the American Congress.

The Prime Minister and the American President

In comparing the power of the Prime Minister with that of the American President, the President appears to have two advantages. He has, first of all, a fixed term of office—four years —and no matter how unpopular he may be with Congress or even with the majority of the voters, he has the constitutional right to hold onto that office until the next quadrennial election. The Prime Minister, in contrast, has no certain tenure. If the House of Commons no longer threatens his tenure of office, public sentiment or some unexpected development may drive him to resign or call for a new election.

The second apparent advantage is that the President is supreme within his Cabinet and may act against its unanimous opinion, while the Prime Minister must carry with him a Cabinet that contains men of greater political stature than does the Presidential Cabinet, and men with whom he must share his power.

Both these advantages, however, lose something in practice. The Prime Minister who enters office with a safe party majority is, to all intents and purposes, as sure of his five years in office as the President of his four. Moreover, he can call for an election at the time he feels it will be to his party's advantage, something quite impossible for the President. If the Prime Minister is more seriously restricted by his Cabinet than the President by his, there is no doubt that the Prime Minister is frequently in a position to dominate it to a significant extent.

The decisive advantage that the Prime Minister has over the President is his control of the legislature. The tightness of party discipline is a weapon for which the President has no equivalent. Congress is an equal partner with the President, and it is inclined to feel jealous of his authority. It is under no obligation to accept his recommendations; any legislative program that he submits is likely at best to be modified and at worst to be mutilated, rejected, or ignored. The President's chief weapons are his power to appeal to public opinion, the judicious distribution of patronage, and the veto. As Franklin D. Roosevelt demonstrated, a public appeal can have great effect if the issue can be dramatized and if the President has the right personality and knack. Even Roosevelt, however, could not swing public opinion, much less Congress, on an unpopular issue, and no President can weary the public with too many appeals or it will fail to respond. Patronage is now of limited extent, and after the first six months of a new administration the President is not likely to have a great deal at his disposal. The veto is a negative power; it is not of great help in pushing for the enactment of a positive program.

In contrast, the Prime Minister's legislative control is almost beyond challenge. He is, in fact, more likely to have difficulty in getting his ideas accepted by the relevant minister than by the House of Commons. As long as the majority of Commons belong to his party, the House of Commons will not obstruct him; on the contrary, it will follow his instructions, not as an equal partner in the government, but as an assembly under his control.

Limitations on the Prime Minister

Does this mean, then, that the Prime Minister is not a dictator in his control of the Commons only because he personally chooses to avoid dictatorship and not because of any effective restraint upon his will? The answer is: not in any realistic sense. The Prime Minister holds his power for a definite period of time. Except for national emergencies there must be a free election at least once in five years, and at this time the people are perfectly capable of turning out both him and his party. This is an eventuality which no dictator contemplates or permits. Moreover, no dictator tolerates an active opposition, but the Prime Minister is always subject to the most searching cross-examination and the most vigorous denunciation by his opponents both in Parliament and in the press.

In addition, the spirit of the British constitution acts as a telling restraint. Anyone who succeeds in becoming Prime Minister must have served a long apprenticeship in a tradition that takes for granted the rivalry of two powerful parties, the exuberance of criticism, the existence of a vigorous opposition enjoying special privileges, and the voluntary yielding of office when a vote in a general election goes against the government of the day. The Prime Minister may at times use his power in an autocratic fashion, and he may show his irritation at criticism, but fundamentally he recognizes that he is the servant of the people, that they have the right both to criticize and to discharge him, and that if he wishes to do his duty and to keep his job, his will must be subject to theirs. This is, of course, an attitude no dictator can comprehend.

3. THE MONARCH

The Monarch and the People

In ordinary times the British monarch is more conspicuous than powerful. The coronation is the occasion for an unparalleled demonstration of popular and patriotic devotion; and the monarch's drive to the Houses of Parliament to open a new session is lined with throngs of faithful and admiring subjects. Indeed, crowds of people will gather to watch any member of the royal family—whatever he does—who would scarcely turn their heads (save in time of grave national crisis or during a bitter political campaign) to catch a view of the Prime Minister. Newspapers and magazines chronicle in detail the activities of royalty: Prince Charles has a birthday, Princess Anne visits the theater, or the Queen opens a flower show, and the papers give as much room to pictures and descriptions of the event as they would to most political developments abroad. (If the activity is of major interest, such as Princess Margaret's marriage, political events may indeed be driven off the front page.) A Prime Minister may make a significant political decision without one-half the fanfare that accompanies a royal visit to a Welsh or Scottish village. Indeed, one of the classic methods of calling attention to some worthy cause, whether it be the restoration of the cathedral of Canterbury or, in time of war, the conservation of bath water, is to have the royal family engage in some symbolic gesture to publicize the need.

Yet in spite of the ceremonial and the excitement, the Prime Minister and the Cabinet rule; the monarch, in any political conflict, must submit. The monarch is not totally devoid of power, but royal powers tend to be informal, contingent, and often highly speculative. In fact, the position of the monarch has undergone a paradoxical development. Royal popularity has grown enormously at the very time that the personal power of the monarch has declined. Nor is this change a matter of coincidence. The popularity of the royal family today is largely due to the fact that it takes no part in politics, wields no open political power, takes sides publicly in no political controversy, and therefore makes no political enemies. Today it is rare when any important British organ of public opinion criticizes the Queen or her immediate family. The monarch can literally do no wrong. And if this is because, politically, the monarch can do nothing at all, royal popularity does not suffer thereby.

The Loss of Royal Prestige

To anyone who notes the general tone of reverence adopted by the popular press in England and the deep feeling with which large masses of people regard the Queen, it seems incredible that the monarch should ever have commanded anything less than this general regard. But as Kingsley Martin points out in his penetrating and entertaining book, *The Magic of Monarchy,* such was once the case. In the seventeenth century the people of England cut off the head of one King and deposed another. William of Orange and, later, George I and George II were, to a greater or lesser extent, suspected and even disliked as foreigners. They were objects of active hatred on the part of those who were loyal to the old Stuart line. If George III was hailed as a real Englishman and a "patriot King," his insanity later in life scarcely added to the credit of the monarchy; and the reigns of his sons, George IV and William IV, obviously reduced the royal prestige. To those familiar with the press's present deference to royalty, it is something of a jolt to read the comments of the *Times* on the death of George IV: "There never was an individual less regretted by his fellow-creatures than this deceased King. What eye has wept for him? What heart has heaved one sob of unmercenary sorrow?" To compare this comment with the widespread and genuine grief at the death of George VI is to become aware of a vast change in British public sentiment toward the monarch.

Recapture of Royal Prestige

This change in the monarch's position occurred during the reign of Queen Victoria, who as a young ruler was herself subjected to serious criticism. As late as the 1870's there was a flourishing and noisy republican movement. Later, however, the new imperialistic spirit helped to turn the Queen into a symbol of Empire and as such to kindle public enthusiasm. Moreover, her very longevity commanded respect. A new generation grew up which remembered nothing of earlier royal scandals and which felt respect and even affection for the venerable matriarch. The ultrarespectability of her private life appealed to the politically powerful middle class. And if Victoria was at times very active politically behind the scenes, her avoidance of overt political action rendered her, so far as the vast public was aware, immune from partisan attack or criticism.

Victoria's son and successor, Edward VII, played a useful but unspectacular role. It was her grandson, George V, who established the monarchy still more firmly. The decency of his private life and the conscientiousness with which he performed the taxing duties of his office won him a respect and a freedom from criticism that set the pattern for the present time. So immune to criticism did the royal family become that, at a time when it was widely known in the United States that Edward VIII was contemplating marriage with the twice divorced Mrs. Simpson, no British newspaper— not even the *Daily Worker*—dared mention the affair, partly because of the law of libel, but chiefly because of fear of the reaction of readers who had been brought up to think the King above reproach. Moreover, the editors themselves had a well-developed habit pattern that made them renounce the scoop of the century rather than depart from their customary standards. Partly as a result of this reticence, George VI was able to succeed with noteworthy ease to both his brother's title and his father's prestige. Under his daughter, Elizabeth II, who ascended the throne in 1952, the monarchy has become even more popular.

The Bases of the Monarch's Prestige

Several considerations help to account for the popularity of the monarchy. For one thing, it answers a need for color and drama, for great spectacles and pageants, which too often is left unsatisfied in modern society. Especially in an age when life for large numbers of people is drab, monotonous, and uneventful, the need for diversion and for some emotional outlet is a serious one—and one which, incidentally, explains some of the appeal of the uniforms and parades of fascist movements.

The royal family, moreover, introduces an element of human interest and warmth into the lives of many who are poor, lonely, and frustrated. The individual who, in a highly urbanized society, misses the gossip and friendliness of village life and feels uprooted and alone can find some substitute in news of the royal family. Many details of their lives are carefully related in the public press, and he can take a personal interest in their clothes, their diversions, their trips, and their romances in a way that parallels, to some degree, the insatiable curiosity of many Americans about the lives of their favorite motion-picture stars. Undoubtedly many people, consciously or unconsciously, identify themselves with individual members of the royal family and find some release from the limitations of their own existence. Moreover, Elizabeth II, with her close family life, her youth, charm, and deep sense of responsibility, not only provides a pattern of life that many try to emulate but also awakens a spirit of chivalrous devotion that contributes a new element to royal popularity.

Limitations

But if such factors contribute to the monarch's prestige, it is clear that both prestige and power depend upon satisfying the urges that contribute to royal popularity while at the same time keeping out of politics. If the monarch ever became an open partisan of one party and an enemy of the other, the party opposed would inevitably be driven both to criticize and to attack. And since in a democracy the opposition sooner or later comes into power, the time would come when the monarch would be obliged either to work with ministers who had made the attack or to abdicate. Indeed, the leaders of a party that the monarch publicly opposed probably would refuse to hold office while that person retained the monarchy, and they might abolish the monarchy altogether.

In short, the price of the monarch's popularity and position in Great Britain is his abstention from politics. Edward VIII, during the depression, visited one of the most poverty-stricken areas of Great Britain and, on viewing the shocking conditions, made what would seem the obvious comment that something must be done. In Great Britain, however, the comment aroused considerable discussion. The question of help for the depressed areas and of relief in general was a political question, and it was suggested that the King had uttered a political opinion. People wondered whether the King intended actively to do something to implement his opinion and, if so, what action could be taken that would not violate the constitutional tradition. Altogether, the flurry of speculation that could arise from such a remark indicates one reason why the present rulers of Great Britain generally limit themselves, when they talk with their subjects, to statements and questions of the most innocuous character.

As royalty must be free of political bias, so must it be free from scandal, for it is hard to combine reverence for the royal family with disapproval of its private life. As long as the monarch leads a conventional life, his job is a good one. But any unorthodoxy, although it may exhilarate a small elite, will blast the illusions of the masses of the people. The monarch who is to remain in office must be reconciled to a responsible and conscientious existence, must be willing to be bored interminably by long-winded if well-intentioned speeches of welcome and gratitude, and must maintain an air of interest and even of pleasure at innumerable and exhausting public ceremonies. Regardless of weather, the show must go on. The crowds must not be kept waiting, and they must be able to take their fill of the sight of a gracious, kind, conscientious, understanding sovereign. The King or Queen who is not ready to pay this price had better imitate Edward VIII.

The Monarch's Powers

So much for the psychological aspects of the monarch's position. What are his real powers?

There is no simple answer to this question. In general, the monarch's job is simply to do what the responsible ministers decide. When an election is held and the former government has resigned, the monarch customarily sends for the leader of the victorious party and asks him to form a government. As long as the House of Commons is willing to follow this leadership (and this means until the next election), the Cabinet stays in office. The monarch makes the speeches the Cabinet desires and signs the legislation Parliament passes under the Cabinet's leadership. If that government is defeated in an election and resigns as a result or if it meets an adverse vote in the House of Commons, the monarch calls on the leader of the new ma-

jority party and takes orders from a new master. The result is the kind of paradox one finds in a Gilbert and Sullivan operetta. The Prime Minister kisses the monarch's hands when he takes office, and he addresses him with the utmost deference. But the facts are all the other way around. It is the Prime Minister who tells the monarch what to do, and if there is any conflict of wills, it is the Prime Minister who is in the dominant position.

What influence the monarch has, in short, depends on personality rather than on formal power. He has the right to be informed and to be consulted. The Prime Minister must always tell him of Cabinet decisions and must be ready to explain the reasons for any policy. The monarch can, in the words of Bagehot, encourage and warn; and if he is intelligent, these powers may be important. For the monarch is in an unusually advantageous position. In the course of a normal reign many governments come and go, and there are close contacts with the leading statesmen of the age. It is not difficult as a result to acquire considerable political knowledge and experience. And since the Prime Minister must discuss his policies with the monarch, speak of new developments, and listen to what he has to say, the latter is in an excellent position to influence the man who has the power to decide on policy.

Few people really know, until long after the monarch has died, how much of a part he has played in politics. Queen Victoria, for example, was a woman of decided opinions. In the great rivalry between Gladstone and Disraeli, she was heart and soul with Disraeli. Repeatedly she took action behind the scenes to help her political friends and to impede her enemies. But the public at large was quite unaware of her activity. Again, in the reign of Edward VII, the King's hostility toward Germany and his support of the French alliance are credited with having had considerable importance. George V is reported to have acted as something of a brake on the Liberal government that was in office when he succeeded to the throne.

Exceptional Circumstances

In addition to whatever informal influence the monarch may have, there are certain exceptional times when he may seem to exercise real power. If one party has a clear majority in the House of Commons and if one person is clearly the leader of that party, the monarch must ask him to become Prime Minister. But there have been times in the past when no party has had a clear majority in Parliament or when the majority party had not yet designated its leader. At such times the monarch may appear to make a personal choice. Even in such cases, however, he is careful to follow the course least likely to arouse criticism. If there is no obvious leader of the majority party, it is highly important to find out who is most acceptable to the party's leaders in general. Queen Elizabeth apparently acted on the advice of Sir Winston Churchill and Lord Salisbury, as Conservative elder statesmen, when she asked Mr. Macmillan to be Prime Minister following Sir Anthony Eden's resignation in 1957. This procedure was acceptable to the Conservatives partly because such informal means were customary and partly because there was a general consensus on the succession. The Labor party declared publicly in 1957, however, that if it were to be in a similar situation the monarch should take no action until after the parliamentary Labor party had met and chosen a new leader. Subsequently, when the Queen chose Home under circumstances similar to those in which she had chosen Macmillan, she did not escape criticism. That the Conservatives have now established their own formal method of selecting a new leader demonstrates that both parties clearly wish the responsibility of choice to be in their own hands, not in those of the monarch.

If there is no clear majority in Parliament, then the monarch turns to the party that is best able to form a government that is in accordance with the verdict of the last election or that is most likely to receive the support of the House of Commons. If a Prime Minister should be defeated in a vote on a significant issue in the House of Commons and should prefer resignation to dissolution, it is customary for the monarch to send for the leader of the opposition, even though the opposition does not have a majority. If, however, as in 1931, the government resigns without having been defeated, the monarch is somewhat freer and may consult anyone—including the leaders of all the political parties—in attempting to work out a satisfactory solution. Thus George V, as we now know from Harold Nicolson's biography, urged Prime Minister MacDonald, following his resignation in 1931, to form a new Cabinet made up of leaders of the other parties and persuaded the leaders of the other parties to concur. But there is still complaint, particularly from Labor, that the monarch in so doing, exceeded his constitutional powers.

It is now difficult to imagine a situation in which the monarch would exercise independent initiative in a political matter. The crucial point is that so long as he follows the advice of the Prime Minister, royal prestige cannot be affected; if the consequences are unfortunate, the fault is the Prime Minister's. But if the monarch acts independently, direct criticism can be expected. And the road of least criticism is the road for the monarch.

Evaluation of the Monarchy

What then, in sum, is the contribution of the monarchy to Great Britain? It is a popular symbol of national unity, a possible source of sage and experienced advice to the Prime Minister, and (though only in very exceptional circumstance) a possible means of helping to break a political log jam.

Some observers like to point out that in the United States a citizen is torn by conflicting desires. He wants to admire and revere the President as chief of state and leader of the country; but often he wants to hate him as the leader of the party to which he is opposed politically or as the author of policies that seem to him disastrous. In Great Britain the strain is considerably less. The ordinary citizen can love the monarch and at the same time denounce the Prime Minister.

Appeal to the Irrational

British writers often praise another aspect of the monarch's position. Ever since the rise of fascist governments roused general fear that democracy might not be able to compete with various leader-worshiping cults, many people have noted the highly effective, if unintentional, way in which the monarchy has diverted potentially dangerous inclinations into relatively harmless channels. In the monarch the people have a leader who is far more colorful and the center of far more ceremonial than Adolf Hitler at his best. As a person and through the royal family, the monarch is the incarnation of national history. Thus he excites a respect that cannot be commanded by ordinary human beings. Few people are likely to turn to a Führer while the monarch affords so exceptional an outlet for the irrational feelings that occasionally menace democracy. Yet—and this is the beauty of the system—the monarch is politically powerless. The people may give adoration to their heart's content in almost perfect safety. Their trust cannot be abused, because the monarch lacks the power to abuse it.

Democracy and Royalty

Intellectuals in the Labor party sometimes have pointed out that the monarch's circle of personal friends and companions is, almost inevitably, limited to the upper classes. Such men and women are unlikely to have had any personal experience of poverty and deprivation. Most of them are likely to be, not only Conservatives, but right-wing Conservatives. Thus what advice the monarch offers can be expected to be Burkeian rather than socialist in emphasis. Nonetheless, most Labor party members are strong supporters of the monarchy in its strictly constitutional and ceremonial role.

The American may be more seriously impressed by another criticism put forward by certain British critics to the effect that the monarchy is a bulwark of the class system and that this system is incompatible with democracy. So long as a court exists, the charge runs, and so long as men of title play a dignified and colorful part in the national life, so long as there is rivalry for invitations to a royal garden party, there exists an official institution for the effective, if unintentional, encouragement of social snobbery. While monarch and court exist as living reminders of hierarchy, title, and class, the path toward social equality cannot be completely smooth. And although it is debatable whether political democracy is dependent upon a large measure of social democracy, those who believe it is may regard the monarchy as one of the liabilities of British democracy.

The Monarch and the Commonwealth

Whatever one may say of the role of the monarch within Great Britain, there can be no question of its extreme importance within the Commonwealth of Nations. In a very real sense the Crown is the symbol that holds that association together.

Colonies, of course, can be governed as effectively by a republic as by a monarchy. But it was of crucial importance in the evolution of British colonies from a position of dependence on Great Britain to one of independence within the Commonwealth that there was a monarchy to act as a formal and sentimental link between them; for thus, although they had no common Parliament or Cabinet, they had a common sovereign.

Today the Queen of the United Kingdom is at the same time the Queen of Canada, of Australia, and of New Zealand of the older Commonwealth, and, among its postwar members, of Ceylon, Sierra Leone, Jamaica, Trinidad, and Tobago, Malta, Guyana, Gambia, Lesotho, Botswana, and Barbados. Although the other members of the Commonwealth are republics, they acknowledge the Crown as the symbol of the free association of the Commonwealth nations and, in a similarly symbolic sense, the Queen as "head of the Commonwealth."

Particularly among those of Anglo-Saxon descent in the overseas parts of the Commonwealth, there is a somewhat romantic and emotional, but patriotic and powerful, loyalty to the King or Queen which helps to hold these areas close to the people of the United Kingdom. Thus George VI's visit to Canada in 1939 helped to consolidate the sentiment that brought that country united into World War II. Still more dramatic have been the royal tours of unprecedented extent that Elizabeth II and her husband, Prince Philip, have taken to overseas parts of the Commonwealth. Some of the bonds of the Commonwealth are bonds of tradition, and many are bonds of self-interest; but the person of the Queen or King fills an essential place by providing a visible, easily comprehensible symbol of unity. In this sense, the monarch is irreplaceable.

6. The British Administration: National and Local

1. THE RANGE OF PUBLIC RESPONSIBILITIES

In the past century no development the world over has been more spectacular than the increase in the scope of government activity. In the early nineteenth century the major responsibilities of government were to provide peace and order and to make it easy for private enterprise to do the rest. But the growth of heavy industry and crowded cities following the industrial revolution created problems of health and exploitation that individual efforts could not solve. One after another, each group in the community turned to the state to provide protection or aid, and each new demand added to the work of government.

Thus in the early nineteenth century the danger of disease and epidemics in Great Britain's overcrowded communities brought a demand for compulsory rules of sanitation and for the establishment of public health services. Public outcry against the widespread use of child labor in cotton mills and coal mines resulted in restrictive legislation while, more positively, the state also assumed responsibility for providing public education. Labor sought protection against dangerous work conditions and later won the right to organize and bargain collectively. Industry, in turn, as it came to be challenged by the competition of other countries, asked protection through tariffs and sought positive public aid in reequipping itself for greater productivity. British farmers, long neglected in the national concentration on industry, ultimately secured benefits of govern-ment-sponsored research and price supports. And finally, individuals, at first the aged, the destitute, and the unemployed, and since World War II also the sick, families with more than one dependent child, and, in fact, all those who have exceptional need, have received government support in one form or another. In responding to these and other demands, the British state became a "service" or "welfare" state, committed to creating favorable conditions of life for all its people. And although in so doing, the state through its agents increasingly intervenes in the affairs of the community and the lives of individuals, the public remains confident of the reality of popular control.

Nationalization

The most striking expansion of the functions of government in Great Britain resulted from Labor's program of nationalization after World War II. Nationalization substitutes public for private ownership so that, in place of the more traditional responsibilities of regulating and promoting private enterprise, government itself undertakes production and distribution. Labor's nationalization program brought under public ownership significant productive enterprises that were in a strategic position to exercise control over the rest of the economy.

Public ownership was not new, of course, either in Great Britain or in the United States, for in both countries many municipalities have long owned electrical supply or gas works, run streetcar lines, or operated docks (for example, Port of London or Port of New York Authority). In Great Britain three large-scale public enterprises were established in the interwar period (the first two by a Conservative government): the British Broadcasting Corporation, which provides all British radio and part of television broadcasting; the Central Electricity Board (now absorbed in the general nationalization of electricity), which built and operated four thousand miles of high-voltage transmission wires, known as the Grid, which cover Great Britain with a network of power; and the London Passenger Transport Board (now under the Transport Commission), which operates various forms of transportation in the vast London area. What was new about the Labor government's nationalization program was its basis in socialist theory, its scope, and the potential power it placed in the hands of the government.

During its first session the Labor government nationalized the Bank of England, the coal mines, and telecommunications, and consolidated national control over civil aviation. All electric power supply and transmission were nationalized in 1947. The railways, road transport, London transport, and docks and inland waterways came under national control at the beginning of 1948. The nationalization of gas supply and some parts of the iron and steel industry rounded out the program.

Some of this program, such as the nationalization of the Bank of England and of Empire and Commonwealth communications, was not a subject of dispute. Moreover, it was commonly accepted that the coal mines were so badly depressed that only public ownership could tackle the monumental job of modernizing them, while the coal resources themselves had been declared public property in 1938. In addition, apart from iron and steel, every area of nationalization had some basis in a Royal Commission or other public report. Nonetheless, the program was contested, and some of it hotly. Although the railways needed new equipment, particularly after the strain and damage of the war, many would have preferred to give public aid for this purpose to the existing four large private railway companies rather than to nationalize them. Still more concern was shown over public control of road and inland water transport. The Conservatives denationalized long-distance road haulage in 1953, although they left most of road transport under the British Transport Commission.

Most controversial of all was Labor's nationalization in 1950 of large parts of the iron and steel industry, a vigorous, articulate semimonopoly, with its own plans for reorganization and development. Like long-distance road haulage, the iron and steel industry was formally denationalized by the Conservatives in 1953, a process aided greatly by the fact that alone among the nationalized industries, the Iron and Steel Corporation was a holding and financing concern, not an operating one. Despite this denationalization and the sale back to private hands, by 1955, of more than half of the steel-producing concerns, the Conservatives retained a large measure of public control over the production of iron and steel through the Iron and Steel Board, which is rather like an American independent regulatory commission. Labor's renationalizing of steel was fought long and skillfully by the Conservatives.

Although denationalization and renationalization are possible, they create obvious economic and political uncertainties and problems. The Conservatives pointed out officially in their 1947 *Industrial Charter* that industrial recovery might be "indefinitely delayed if every change in the majority of the House of Commons was followed by a complete reorganization in certain of the basic industries." They have fully accepted the nationalization of the coal, electricity, gas, and rail-transport industries. But steel is a source of particular concern to Labor's left-wing, while opposition to change in the industry's organization is strong among the Conservatives. In any case, large-scale public ownership will continue to occupy a prominent place in the British economic structure.

Economic Planning

More significant both for the responsibilities of government and for the future of the British economy is economic planning. Spurred by the striking results of French planning since World War II, the British are again experimenting seriously with means of stimulating, if not directing, the economy along paths that will better answer national needs. Their task is more difficult than that of the French, however, since they start from an advanced and developed position and therefore must adapt an economic structure that is already functioning rather than, as in France, more or less building anew. The British must also change the focus of their economic planning from that of the immediate postwar period, which was dominated by the emphasis on social security and full employment (even the Churchill administration in 1944 declared, "The Government accept as one of their primary aims and responsibilities the maintenance of a high and stable level of employment after the war"), to the dominant current national need to develop a high rate of growth in industrial output.

Great Britain, as we have seen, is in a precarious economic state; its existing standard of living depends on its being able to pay for its imports by expanding the flow of exports in an increasingly competitive world. Despite the Conservatives' general lack of interest in economic planning, which resulted in their giving it relatively little attention after they assumed office in 1951, the economic pressures of the 1960's—when the index of British industrial production ceased rising—led them to establish two bodies in 1962: the National Economic Development Council (NEDC, commonly known as "Neddy"), an advisory body to make reports on problems of economic growth and suggest ways of avoiding unevenness in the process of growth; and the National Incomes Commission, to review claims for wage increases of particular importance or difficulty. The fact that these bodies were merely advisory, however, made their effect somewhat problematic.

The Labor government, with its greater commitment to planning, moved quickly on its return to office in 1964 to establish more machinery and to outline a national economic plan. The Department of Economic Affairs, established in October 1964, took over from NEDC the preparation of the plan. The NEDC, reorganized in November 1964, still provides the principal channel through which representatives of government are associated with both sides of industry in formulating and ultimately implementing the plan.

Since the Secretary of State for Economic Affairs is the chairman of the NEDC, the two are closely tied together. Other ministerial members are from Labor, Technology, and the Board of Trade. The council has its own Director-General and staff (who are not members of the civil service). The exchanges among industry, labor, government, and specialist economists in the frequent meetings of the Council lead to a broadening of views on all sides. In addition, a series of economic development committees have been set up that are concerned with particular industries and consist of the same cross section of interests represented in "Neddy."

The National Plan published in September 1965 outlined the hoped-for lines of economic development between 1964 and 1970. The objective is a 25 percent increase in national output during this period. Out of an analysis of the prospects for growth of some 50 different sections of industry, it was estimated that 800,000 additional workers would be needed to achieve the necessary annual growth rate of 3.8 percent. Economic crisis has seriously impeded this progress.

On the regional level as well, a new concern for development has become apparent in the 1960's. There were two reasons: pressure from the depressed area of northeast England, and the general concern over industrial growth. Nothing quite so definite has been done for England and Wales as the establishment, in 1962, of the Scottish Development Department to take over the work of the old Home Department for electricity, roads, and industry and supervision of local government. Economic Planning Councils—composed of twenty-five part-time, regionally knowledgeable persons—were set up in 1965 for a number of regions, but they are merely advisory. Regional Economic Planning Boards composed of civil servants are to prepare draft plans.

But what kind of planning can best accelerate economic growth? The Soviet Union, of course, uses coercive punishments coupled with differential rewards to secure adherence to its plans, but such means are out of the question in a democratic country. The French have stimulated growth through pouring investment into selected sectors of the economy. British planning has not yet clearly developed either its incentives or its sanctions. Presumably the existence of nationalized industries makes planning easier, but the high percentage of private economic activity makes public-private interaction essential as well as characteristic. Basically the problem is one of willingness. Is the government prepared to develop not only a plan but vigorous enough leadership to convince the British people that national survival as a great country depends on dedicated and directed effort aimed at national economic growth, regardless of whether it impairs the position of particular industries? Unless it is, the National Plan will remain no more than an aspiration.

2. THE ORGANIZATION OF NATIONAL ADMINISTRATION

In response to the vast increase in public services to the community, government, both in Great Britain and the United States, has become the nation's biggest business. Since World War II the British national administration has employed nearly a million people and is spending over £3 billion annually, more than a quarter of the national income. The ordinary citizen living under an inactive administration a generation before might have felt little concern over administrative organization and personnel, but today the welfare of the country and of the citizen is greatly affected by both.

In order to judge the way in which government handles its business we must break the issues down into several specific questions: What methods of direction and control are used by government officials? How are government officials themselves kept under control, and what safeguards are there for individuals and private groups? How effectively can the public participate in setting the goals and the methods of government action?

The answers to these questions must be sought in a study of the ways in which public administration is organized and operates, of the forms of administrative action, and of the way in which public servants are chosen and carry on their duties.

The Basic Units: The Ministries

The backbone of the administrative structure in Great Britain is provided by the ministries, or departments. The distinctive feature of a ministry is that it is organized hierarchically under a minister who assumes direct responsibility in Parliament both for the general lines of departmental policy and for the detailed actions of his subordinates.

At first glance, British administrative organization appears confusing, because there is little uniformity in the titles either of the ministries or of those who head them. In the United States all administrative departments are created by act of Congress, and each is under a single head known as the Secretary (except in the cases of the Department of Justice and the Post Office). In Great Britain the ministries have had a variety of origins that is reflected in the variety of their names. Some ministries, such as the Treasury (the descendant of the Exchequer, which evolved from the royal household), stem from great offices of an earlier time; others, such as the Foreign Office, War Office, and Home Office, have evolved from the ancient office of secretary of state (for which reason each is capable legally of performing the duties of all the others, except in cases where special responsibilities have been defined in legislation); only the more recent ministries were created by act of Parliament. In addition, some ministries were established under boards or commissions, as in the cases of the Treasury and the Board of Trade. However, it was discovered in time that such ministries were more efficient if authority were concentrated in a single person. Although there is still a Treasury Board, it never meets; the real head of the Treasury is the Chancellor of the Exchequer (not the Prime Minister, although he has the title of First Lord of the Treasury). The real head of the Board of Trade is the President of the Board of Trade. Thus, despite seeming differences in organization, each of the British ministries (except for the Post Office) has a single head. Increasingly also their specific functions are defined in legislation.

Internal Organization of the Ministries

Immediately below the minister in a British ministry is the permanent secretary, who is both chief adviser to the minister and chief administrative officer of the ministry. In an American department, the top offices nearly always change hands when a new administration comes into office, but not in the United Kingdom, where experience and continuity are weighted more heavily than is sympathy with a particular political program.

The permanent secretary and the undersecretary, if there is one, must be constantly available for consultation with the minister, particularly when Parliament is in session; thus, the detailed control of administration is mainly in the hands of the assistant secretaries who head the several divisions into which a ministry is divided. Each of these divisions deals with a particular activity or area, and their work is coordinated through the higher officials in the ministry and by use of intra- and interdepartmental committees.

It is sometimes charged that high civil servants are the real power in government—in other words, that they are the managers of our modern political-economic society. The permanent secretary, as the link between the rest of the ministry and the minister, inevitably has a great deal of discretion, of course, in determining what material to lay before the minister. Even more important is the fact that he may have a much wider range of experience than the minister himself in the subject matter of the ministry, particularly when the minister has recently come into office. In practice, however, the relative importance of the minister and the permanent secretary is likely to be a matter of personality. Inexperienced and weak ministers may be swayed consistently by their advisers; but any minister who has a definite conception of what he wishes to accomplish can carry it through. A high civil servant may, and should, put before a minister his best arguments in favor of one course of action. If he is overruled, the ethics of the service demand that he carry out his minister's policy loyally and as effectively as possible. And in the end, since it is the minister who must stand before Parliament and assume responsibility for what his department has done, the minister will want to be convinced of the soundness of an important policy before he undertakes to support it publicly.

ADVISORY BODIES   Government departments that deal with the public, or that need expert advice, nearly always have advisory councils or committees to undertake research, provide insight into the sentiments of the groups affected, and otherwise aid public officials in determining the character, scope, and most feasible means of implementing government policy. In some cases, the minister is obliged by statute to consult a standing committee; in most cases, however, the minister appoints a committee because he recognizes the value of its advice. In all, there are several hundred of these advisory bodies which provide the recognized structure of communication between the public and private sectors. As we have seen, however, there is a constant interchange which may use but is not restricted to these bodies.

The membership of advisory bodies varies widely according to the nature of the work performed. Some are expert bodies that give scientific counsel; others associate civil servants with representatives of industry, labor, and specialists of different types drawn from the universities or professional bodies. Some committees span central and local government organs. The characteristic feature of advisory committees or councils is that they associate interested parties in the formulation of policy, good evidence of the kind of group politics so prevalent within the British political system, and a wholesome means of helping to keep all sides informed about critical issues and prevailing trends of opinion.

The Work of the Ministries

Partly because the British government has assumed so many responsibilities, but more particularly because the British do not like the "holding company" type of department (such as the American Department of Health, Education and Welfare, with its many divisions and bureaus), there are a good many more ministries in Great Britain than there are federal departments in the United States. Moreover, the number of ministries changes more frequently, since new ministries are established when new needs arise. Sometimes, however, distinct though related fields of work may be grouped together in a single ministry, as in the Ministry of Agriculture, Fisheries, and Food.

British ministries may be grouped roughly into five categories: defense, external relations, internal order, economic and social matters, and finance.

DEFENSE In April 1964, the largest administrative merger in British central government made the three service departments—the Admiralty (given precedence because of the nation's age-old dependence on the Navy), the War Office (Army), and the Air Ministry—integral parts of the Ministry of Defense. Previously they had only been coordinated through it. The year before, the service departments had lost most of their public works sections to the Ministry of Public Building and Works in an arrangement parallel to that under which the Ministry of Aviation serves as a defense department with "civil" functions.

At the head of the Defense Ministry is the Secretary of State for Defense, who is ultimately responsible to Parliament for the members and operations of the armed services and also for 109,000 nonindustrial and 176,000 industrial civil servants. The services remain separate, however, and each has a Minister and a parliamentary Under-Secretary of State. A new Defense Council (chaired by the Secretary of State and including the three Ministers of Defense, the Chiefs of Staff, the Chief Scientific Adviser, and the Permanent Under-Secretary of State) directs high defense policy, which is closely coordinated with a Cabinet Committee on Defense and Overseas Policy chaired by the Prime Minister.

EXTERNAL RELATIONS British external relations are carried on through two departments, of which the Foreign Office is the major one and the center through which relations with foreign countries are conducted.

Working closely with the Foreign Office is the Commonwealth Relations Office, which conducts relations with the overseas parts of the Commonwealth: Canada, Australia, New Zealand, India, Pakistan, Ceylon, Ghana, Nigeria, Cyprus, Sierra Leone, Malaysia, Tanzania, Jamaica, Trinidad and Tobago, Singapore, Uganda, Kenya, Malawi, Malta, Zambia, Guyana, Gambia, Lesotho, Botswana, and Barbados.[1] The Commonwealth Relations Office

passes on to these governments the salient features of the information flowing into the Foreign Office from its foreign and consular services; the overseas members reciprocate with any special information that their own foreign and consular services may have secured. Until 1966 the Colonial Office supervised the administration of Great Britain's remaining colonial possessions, almost all of which are now islands or ministates, but these responsibilities were transferred to the Commonwealth Relations Office that year.

As colonies become members of the Commonwealth, and as relations with the latter become more like those with friendly foreign states, the separation of the two offices has grown increasingly artificial. In 1964 the Plowden Committee on Representational Services Overseas recommended that the Foreign Service, the Commonwealth Relations Service, and the Trade Commissioner Diplomatic Service be merged as H.M. Diplomatic Service. This recommendation was carried through on January 1, 1965. Although the Plowden report pointed out that it would be "a rational and useful development" to amalgamate all external relations under one department, it did not explicitly so recommend, lest it "could be misinterpreted as implying a loss of interest in the Commonwealth partnership." This is the best, perhaps only, justification for the maintenance of present arrangements.

The Ministry of Overseas Development conducts the British aid program, which has special but not exclusive Commonwealth aspects. Under it, the Commonwealth Development Corporation provides capital for such basic projects as roads, docks, and schools. The ministry also negotiates bilateral and multilateral arrangements, participates in United Nations technical assistance, and handles issues concerned with UNESCO, FAO, and the United

[1] Although Ireland officially left the Commonwealth in 1949, relations with that country are still handled through the Commonwealth Relations Office, as have been those with South Africa since it withdrew from the Commonwealth in 1961. From March 1962 to April 1964 a special Central African Office concentrated on that area during

the breakup of the Federation of Rhodesia and Nyasaland. Rhodesia (formerly Southern Rhodesia) was then returned to the Commonwealth Relations Office, which had previously dealt with this autonomous but not independent territory. On November 11, 1965, Rhodesia's small minority white governing group unilaterally declared independence to maintain its control over the majority African population. This unconstitutional act led to international sanctions under the leadership of the Labor government to secure a guaranteed transition over time to African majority rule and an agreed means of securing Rhodesian independence constitutionally.

Nations Trade and Development Corporation.

The ministries engaged in defense and in external relations (with the exception of the Ministry of Overseas Development) have one important feature in common. They are working to a great extent with material that is confidential in character and of vast importance to national security. It is thus much more difficult for Parliament to maintain a check on the work of these departments than on those concerned with purely internal affairs. The defense ministries tend to present block estimates with relatively few details on which parliamentary scrutiny can fasten; a defense minister's reply in Parliament that "it is not in the national interest" to give certain information is usually sufficient to satisfy a questioner. On the other hand, both the Foreign Secretary and the Prime Minister are expected to give fairly frequent and substantial surveys on foreign affairs to the House and to permit debate on general policies. When issues are critical and controversial, political leaders have not hesitated to call for votes of confidence on their foreign policies.

INTERNAL ORDER   The responsibilities of the Home Office are varied, since it is a kind of "residual legatee" that performs all the work of the ancient secretariat of state not parceled out to the other secretaries of state. Its general supervision over law and order leads to its control over the police, insofar as such control is not vested in the hands of local authorities. Thus the Home Office has jurisdiction over the metropolitan police of London and, because the national government gives grants-in-aid to local police services, the right to establish standards of organization, discipline, and equipment for the police elsewhere. It supervises measures relating to juveniles and regulates the conduct of elections, immigration and naturalization, civil defense, and fire services. The Home Office can also decide whether to permit or disallow the bylaws passed by the major units of local government.

There is no ministry in Great Britain exactly comparable to the United States Department of Justice, although, as we shall see, the Lord Chancellor performs many of the functions of a Minister of Justice. The Home Office appoints the paid police magistrates (known as stipendiary magistrates) who are found in London and a few other big cities, and makes recommendations to the Crown for pardons.

ECONOMIC AND SOCIAL MATTERS   As one might suspect, the largest number of British ministries are concerned with economic and social matters. Some, like the Post Office (which manages not only mail but also telephone and telegraph services), provide direct services. The Ministry of Labor runs employment exchanges; the Ministry of Pensions and National Insurance administers the social security services (see Chapter 8) and pensions; the Ministry of Housing and Local Government supervises the operations of local government and of town and country planning and housing; and the Board of Trade keeps statistics and regulates patents, insurance, shipping, and overseas trade.

Others, such as the Ministry of Health, the Ministry of Agriculture, Fisheries, and Food, the Ministry of Land and Natural Resources, the Ministry of Technology, and the Ministry of Education and Science (which joined two earlier ministries in 1964), are chiefly concerned with research, with drawing up programs, and with inspection to see that standards are maintained by local authorities who provide the services in these fields in accordance with local conditions but under the supervision of the central departments.

A third group of ministries in this general category includes the Ministry of Transport, the Ministry of Aviation, and the Ministry of Power, which work closely with the public corporations that administer services or industries in their special fields. Thus for the most part, their work is also in the field of research, supervision, and inspection.

Today the work of most British ministries is no longer strictly confined, as it once was, to Whitehall (the street on which many of the central offices are located). Most ministries have regional offices, offshoots of the self-contained regional organizations established during World War II when it was feared that government services might be disrupted by the rain of bombs on London. These offices have now become a permanent part of British administrative arrangements and provide a healthy deconcentration of authority.

Popular control of ministries dealing with domestic affairs is not hampered by secrecy restraints on parliamentary questioning. But popular control is made difficult by the technicalities and complexities of the functions under the control of these ministries. The minister himself often is less familiar with the minutiae of the work of his ministry than is his colleague in the Foreign Office. Thus he is more dependent on his permanent officials both in day-to-day departmental work and in responding to parliamentary criticism. However, he is not often so cogently criticized as his Foreign Office colleague, for only the most expert or experienced private member can hope to master the details of a soil-conservation or public-health program sufficiently to dispute its technical or technological features.

Such a statement does not mean, however, that popular control must be ineffective in a technical field. Long ago Aristotle pointed out that the guest who eats a meal is as good a judge of its flavor as the cook who prepares it. Parliamentary scrutiny of administrative work concentrates normally not on the details of the program but on its effects, for the citizen can tell whether or not he is well governed even when he does not know the technical remedy for administrative errors or abuses. It is up to the minister to explain why things have gone wrong and what is being done about them.

Interministerial Coordination and Control: The Treasury

All the ministries that have been described so far have one thing in common: they are *line agencies,* a term that means they deal directly with the public. Some agencies, whose work is wholly or in part on behalf of other ministries, are known as *staff agencies.* They include the Civil Service Commission, which sets the tests for selecting public personnel, and the Ministry of Public Building and Works, which looks after the maintenance of public buildings (and also regulates the building trades).

The most important staff agency in Great Britain and also the most important of all the ministries is the Treasury, which is responsible for finance. The British Treasury combines the staff functions of the United States Bureau of the Budget (which prepares the President's budget and supervises the expenditures of departments) with the line responsibilities of the United States Treasury Department. And since the British Treasury not only keeps close financial control over all other departments but also supervises the standards and conditions of work of all civil servants, it is the major administrative agency of interministerial coordination and control.

This coordination and control by the Treasury is exercised at every stage of departmental policy. No ministry may make a proposal involving expenditures or present a financial estimate to the Cabinet without first receiving Treasury authorization. Thus, if a ministry wishes to expand its activities, it must persuade the Treasury that such an expansion is necessary and that it does not involve duplication of a task already performed by another agency. Since the Treasury is likely to be far more open to a projected expenditure if the reasons have been carefully explained in advance and if it has been consulted early in the development of the project, there is a strong incentive for representatives of other ministries to keep in constant touch with the Treasury in order to win a sympathetic comprehension of departmental needs. In this way, Treasury officials acquire an overall picture of the plans and activities of all ministries, which is of the greatest assistance in integrating and reconciling their multifarious activities.

In preparing the budget the Treasury must judge the best way of utilizing the financial resources of the government and must decide which of the rival claims on the available revenue are most important. The decisions of the Treasury can be overruled only by the Cabinet, and even here the Treasury occupies a commanding position, since its head, the Chancellor of the Exchequer, is looked on as second in importance only to the Prime Minister. It takes an unusually persuasive minister with an unusually persuasive case to overbalance the Chancellor's arguments.

Moreover, there is no chance that Parliament will override the Treasury in the interests of a particular ministry, as happens so often in Congress. In the United States the President proposes the budget but the Congress disposes of the money, often in a fundamentally different way from what the administration had planned. In Great Britain there is never any doubt that the major recommendations of the budget, which is a closely knit financial plan, will be accepted exactly as proposed. In any case, no estimate for a ministry may be increased by Parliament.

The Treasury also controls the collection and expenditure of public money. All government revenue, which is collected for the Treasury by the Board of Inland Revenue, the Board of Customs and Excise, the Post Office, and the Commissioners of Crown Lands, goes directly into the Consolidated Fund, which is deposited in the Bank of England. About 15 percent of national expenditures fall in the category of permanent charges, which are not voted annually. These include the interest on the national debt, the salaries of judges, and the Civil List, which covers the expenditures of the royal family—all matters that it is felt should be kept out of politics. All other matters, including the expenditures of all ministries, must be authorized by annual statutes, the parliamentary check upon the financial system. This check is reinforced by the semi-independent Exchequer and Audit Department under the Comptroller and Auditor-General, an important nonpolitical officer, who is quite independent of the Treasury (though he works closely with it in checking expenditures by the ministries) and who makes an annual report on withdrawals of public money directly to the highly important parliamentary Public Accounts Committee.

Even after their estimates have been voted, ministries are not free to spend their appropriations as they wish. They can draw their money from the Consolidated Fund only through a requisition by the Treasury, countersigned by the Comptroller and Auditor-General, and this is normally issued for only one-quarter of their appropriations at a time. Moreover, any increase in the number or salaries of officials in a ministry has to receive Treasury approval, even if the ministry has enough money on hand to provide for it.

By virtue of its responsibilities the Treasury is economy-minded, as evidenced by the famous comment of one Permanent Secretary of the Treasury that he "could not sleep for thinking of the defenseless condition of the British taxpayer." Line agencies are naturally more concerned with securing money for carrying on their services than with curtailing their expenditures, and it is highly important that a ministry like the Treasury scrutinize the agencies' requests and demand rigorous accounting of their expenditures. At the same time, the Treasury has not infrequently been accused of being narrow in vision, traditional in methods, and reluctant to adjust to changing conditions. That the Treasury had done little to keep administrative organization within the ministries up-to-date became apparent under the strain of World War II. The Organization and Methods section of the Treasury was staffed by only two members at the outbreak of war, although it rapidly expanded to forty-eight in response to obvious need. Organization teams were sent into different ministries to advise on methods, and subsequently each large ministry established its own Organization and Methods division, which has worked with the Treasury division in devising better methods.

The relation between personnel and pay has also given the Treasury a commanding position in regard to the civil service. The Permanent Secretary of the Treasury is often spoken of as the "head of the civil service," and the Treasury has authority in such all-important questions as salary scales (subject to arbitration in cases of dispute between the Treasury and the staff), reorganization plans, and superannuation allowances.

The Public Corporation

Although the ministries are the basic units of public administration at the national level, the new responsibilities of government for the direct administration of sections of the economy are not handled directly by these units but by public corporations established for this particular purpose. In other words, when the British government enters the field of business and industry to manage broadcasting services, distribute electrical power, and run the coal mines, it entrusts the operations, not to a departmental, but to a typically business structure.[2] Except for public ownership and the consequent necessity of ensuring ultimate parliamentary responsibility, such a corporation is organized like a privately owned corporation or joint-stock company. It stands outside the regular ministerial structure and in its day-to-day operations is responsible not to a minister or to Parliament but to a board holding office for a fixed term and with responsibilities defined by statute. The board itself is appointed by a minister and works closely with the appropriate ministry. Nonetheless, within the limits laid down for it by Parliament, this board is empowered to recruit a staff and plan the operation of the corporation. In an age when the increasing concentration of economic power in the hands of government arouses considerable concern, the public corporation provides a device for decentralizing authority and removing certain enterprises from the direct control and political pressure of the party in power.

Although the public corporation may be organized and operated in a manner similar to that of the ordinary joint-stock company of private capitalistic management, its basic purpose is quite different. Whereas the private company is operated to make a profit, the public corporation is expected to provide the maximum service at the minimum cost consonant with self-support. Although some public corporations have made a profit, it is not part of their responsibility to do so. They are expected to use the techniques of efficient business for the purposes of community service. "The public corporation," wrote Herbert Morrison, to whom this institution owes much of its present form,

"must be no mere capitalist business . . . even though it will, quite properly, be expected to pay its way . . . its Board and its officers must regard themselves as the high custodians of the public interest."

The justification for using the public corporation rather than the orthodox ministerial structure lies in the character of the work undertaken. A successful business must plan development over a long period, undertake experiments, and organize research. But such flexibility cannot be maintained under a fire of constant criticism that obliges officials to justify every step they take. The ministerial structure is designed to centralize responsibility in a minister who can constantly be held to account in Parliament. Such control, however, makes for caution and dependence on precedent, and although such qualities may be desirable in administering legislation, they are less appropriate for some of the government's new activities. The carrying on of business demands a business structure.

Although the advantages of the public corporation are obvious, there nevertheless remains the serious problem of how to combine autonomy in the day-to-day operations of the public corporation with ultimate public responsibility. Some degree of public control is effected because, as already noted, the board of each public corporation is appointed by a Cabinet minister with whom it works closely in carrying out the functions laid down in the law that established the corporation. Parliament receives detailed annual reports and, of course, may debate them as well as ask searching questions at any time on general policy. In the case of the British Broadcasting Corporation (though of no other corporation) there is a review of the charter at ten-year intervals.

Whether or not these means provide adequate public control we will be in a better position to consider after looking in some detail at the work and organization of two important public corporations: the British Broadcasting Corporation, one of the earliest of these bodies, and the National Coal Board, which was established after World War II with the most staggering responsibilities of any of the public corporations.

[2] Public corporations may be said to fall into three types: the industrial or commercial corporation that runs an industry or public utility; the social service corporation, such as the National Assistance Board or the New Town Development Corporation; and the supervisory public corporation, such as the Iron and Steel Board. Only the industrial or commercial corporation is described here, though the BBC is sometimes said to stand in "a sort of no-man's land" between the social service corporations and the nationalized industries. The ordinary social service corporation has less independence than the industrial corporation from ministerial control, because its purpose is to provide a particular social service on behalf of a government department.

The British Broadcasting Corporation

The BBC, as we have seen, provides all British home and overseas radio broadcasts and instituted British television, though it now has severe competition in the latter field. In place of the vast number of programs interspersed with commercials that crowd the American wave lengths, the BBC has three programs daily: the Light Program for popular entertainment, the Home Program for more serious fare, and the Third Program. The last, created in 1946 for the thinking public, is the most daring of the BBC's efforts to improve public taste. Half the program is devoted to classical and modern music; during the remaining portion there may be plays by Shaw, Racine, Euripides, T. S. Eliot, or Sartre, or discussions and lectures that explore fundamental subjects. Many of the best-known intellectuals in England—G. M. Trevelyan, G. D. H. Cole, Lord Lindsay, Julian Huxley—have been heard on this program. That it has not shied away from controversial subjects was illustrated by a brilliant hour-long debate between the atheistic philosopher Bertrand Russell and a Jesuit monk on "The Existence of God."

The BBC is also the largest overseas broadcaster in the world, sending news abroad in forty-five languages. During the war it beamed directly to the undergrounds of occupied Europe and since then has remained a substantial force in British influence abroad.

The BBC is under the general direction of a seven-man Board of Governors selected for five years by the Prime Minister on the recommendation of the Postmaster-General, who is the minister responsible for broad issues of policy and finance under the charter of the BBC. The governors are expected to personify broad representative views, but until shortly after World War II, when some new appointments were made, it was generally felt that the choice of governors had been too much influenced by political considerations and that the appointees were both too old and too conservative. Under its first director, Sir John Reith, the BBC built up a competent body of experts to direct programs but showed some of that lack of initiative and response to public demand that might have been expected from its monopoly position. Since the war, however, and particularly since its TV programs have been challenged by those of the Independent Television Authority,[3] it has embarked on more imaginative programs and has been rewarded by wider popular support.

The BBC permits no advertising and must finance its home service through an annual fee (£1.5 [$3.50] for sound alone and £5 for combined sound and television) which is paid to the Post Office by each radio owner. (The government gives a grant for the overseas services.) Under its charter, the BBC must broadcast government announcements, for example, police notices, and agricultural bulletins (it may specify at whose request the notice is being given); it must not send out information which the Postmaster-General bans (so far he has never exercised this power); and in time of emergency the government may assume complete control of the BBC. One of the few prohibitions is the ban on the expression of editorial opinion. But none of these provisions has inhibited its independence of action.

What is perhaps most surprising to Americans about the BBC is the extent of its monopoly position. British broadcasting became a monopoly almost by accident, in fact, largely due to the preference of the Post Office for dealing with a single company. The whole question of whether or not the BBC should retain its monopoly was examined in a report issued in 1951 by a special commission, the Broadcasting Committee, under the chairmanship of Lord Beveridge. At that time there was a good deal of public criticism of the monopoly. But despite that criticism, the Broadcasting Committee so warmly endorsed the monopoly of the BBC in radio as to suggest that it should never come into question again. At the same time it proposed various safeguards against the dangers of monopoly: strengthening the Board of Governors vis-à-vis the permanent officials; more decentralized control of regional programs; more independence for overseas broadcasting, within the general framework; and a more effective system of advisory committees.

[3] For a lively account of the establishment of I.T.A. see H. H. Wilson, "Pressures on Parliament: The Commercial TV Affair," in *Politics in Europe,* edited by Gwendolen M. Carter and Alan F. Westin (New York, Harcourt, Brace & World, 1965), pp. 1–35.

It seems hardly likely, however, that the Broadcasting Committee said the last word on monopoly in British broadcasting; not a few hope that the experience of competition in commercial television may lead in time to a combination of private and public broadcasting in Great Britain like that in Canada and South Africa. There is a sense, of course, in which the planned British programs provide more rather than less variety than do the programs in the United States. Americans are likely to say that their radio programs give the people what they want (but certainly not all the people), while the British programs give them what the BBC staff thinks they ought to have. But few people in Great Britain want to give up the present guarantee of a large number of well-designed programs on radio and television and to depend wholly in either or both on the mercies of private companies and advertisers.

The National Coal Board

The National Coal Board, on January 1, 1947, acquired control of some 1,500 coal mines and collieries, a large number of related undertakings such as coke ovens, brickyards, and wagon repair shops, and thousands of acres of land, together with nearly 150,000 houses. It became the employer of some 800,000 people. Nearly one-third of the mines were so small that they were left in the hands of private operators who work under license from the Coal Board; their total output represents no more than 1 percent of Britain's coal production. All the other coal mines in Great Britain are operated by the Board (except for open-cast mining, which is carried out by special contractors). The Board must also market all coal both in Great Britain and abroad and, when necessary, arrange for imports. Without doubt, it has faced the most important and most difficult tasks of any public corporation, both because of the variety and magnitude of its holdings and because of the key position of coal in the whole British economy. Moreover, the Board inherited an unenviable situation, for the industry had long been notorious for its outdated machinery, severe labor troubles, and generally depressed condition.

The National Coal Board, therefore, has faced problems very different from those of the BBC. Rather than taking over in the early stages of development, as did the BBC, the National Coal Board has had to reorganize, consolidate, and modernize one of the largest and oldest of British industries. Although public funds met the initial costs of modernization and government bonds provided the compensation (determined by independent bodies) to the former mine owners, the mines are expected to earn their own running expenses. Above all, it has been hoped that national control of the mines would result in a new spirit of cordiality between management and workers and that this spirit, together with technological improvements, would lead to a greatly increased output of coal.

These hopes have not yet been fulfilled to any major degree, and as a result the National Coal Board has been the target for more persistent criticism inside and outside Parliament than any other public corporation. Output of coal has not kept abreast of Britain's increased industrial needs, and, in consequence, there have been a number of serious fuel shortages since the war. Moreover, although coal was once Great Britain's greatest export, that country now must even import coal on occasion, though net imports have not yet reached the level of net exports. Part of what seems to be a growing shortage results from the inevitable wastage of a natural resource and the speeding up of British industrial production; the British are already planning a farsighted program of atomic energy plants through which they expect ultimately to replace much of the country's dependence on coal for producing electricity. But it has also been apparent that labor relations in the coal industry have not noticeably improved, that the all too small number of technical specialists in the coal industry were not always being used to maximum efficiency, and that there was relatively little public understanding of what the Coal Board was trying to do for the industry. As a result of these lacks, and of a number of detailed, impartial investigations, the National Coal Board has undergone a series of reorganizations aimed at providing more coordinated and effective leadership for the whole industry.

The Coal Board, appointed by the Minister of Power, was originally a body of nine full-time experts chosen for their knowledge and experience in such fields as coal mining, fuel and power, marketing, accountancy, and science. Thus, in sharp contrast to the BBC practice of having a board of "amateurs" supervise its experts, the Coal Board was a body of specialists. These specialists were to form both a policy-making board (as in some industries nationalized later) and a managerial board, with each member acting as head of the appropriate department. Several reorganizations were necessary, however, before a balance was secured between managerial and policy-making responsibilities. The Board, increased to twelve members, has a chairman, deputy chairman, six full-time members, and four part-time members. Each of the full-time members now directs a major segment of the work of the Coal Board: production, marketing, finance, scientific work, staff, and industrial relations.

Throughout its history, the Coal Board has been a highly centralized structure, markedly so in comparison, for example, with the gas industry, which has twelve autonomous area boards that are advised and coordinated but not managed by the Gas Council. Most published studies of the organization of the Coal Board propose, in fact, that there should be a great deal more decentralization of authority. They point out that bigness is not necessarily an advantage for efficiency, unified control, or even accountability. They note that the eight divisional boards (each of which operates the mines in a particular area) have felt too tightly controlled, that the forty-eight area offices under the divisions have also sometimes been restive under control from above, and that the colliery managers, in particular, have complained that they are slighted, or undercut in authority, by the increased use of technical specialists and labor officers. The Acton Society Trust reports on the coal industry come to the general conclusion, however, that decentralization is "a problem of the adjustment of human relationships" rather than of bestowing more autonomy on the divisions by legislation. The Fleck Committee seems to have adopted the same general view in recommending that all major elements of policy—wages, prices, marketing, investment, and so on—be settled centrally as before but that overall direction be firm rather than autocratic.

Part of the answer to developing better relations within the coal industry is also to get better-trained colliery managers and have closer working liaison all through the organization.

The basic and most difficult problems of the coal industry still remain: how to stop its shrinkage of labor, how to improve morale among the miners, and how to replace the old friction between miners and management with understanding and cooperation. It was hardly surprising that the Board's necessary use of so many of the former colliery managers led the miners to feel that the "same old gang" implied the same old policies. An Acton Society Trust investigation in one particular coal-mining area found that the miners retained a deep fear of future unemployment, a belief that they were despised by others in the community, and a deep-seated dislike and distrust of management at every level. It found, too, that while the miners were well versed on wage questions, they knew nothing about the Board's plans for reorganization of the mines, about mechanization and its relation to the use of manpower, or about the particular contribution to industry of administrators and technicians. The report concluded that the miners needed to be given more intelligible information about the industry, that such information should help to transmit the notion that a nationalized industry belongs to its workers as well as to management, and that, above all, positive means should be developed to give the miners a sense of participation in the decisions and workings of the industry.

It is true that there is a series of consultative councils at every level of the industry's structure. The National Consultative Council originally met monthly (more frequently than any other comparable body in nationalized industry) and discussed a wide range of subjects. The colliery consultative committees can discuss anything connected with the pit, though naturally they must not interfere with operations. In these committees, at every level, the National Union of Mineworkers has a strong influence; it has the exclusive right, for example, to nominate the candidates for the local consultative committees, a right not possessed by any other union in nationalized industry. The NUM also appoints the nine worker representatives on the twenty-seven-man National Consultative Committee. Partly, perhaps, in consequence of this union dominance of worker membership on the consultative machinery, but more particularly because there is too little direct relation between local demands and the activities of these committees, they have only rarely aided the exchange of views between management and labor; more commonly, management has seen the committees as potential threats to its authority, while labor has tried to use them only for its own ends. The unions, for example, have shown almost no interest in the vital issues of recruitment, training, and education. It must also be said that their desire to have uniform standards throughout the whole industry often leads to such a long-drawn-out process of consideration at each level of the consultative machinery that the men at the local colliery inevitably feel either that they have no direct participation in decisions or that their requests are not being considered seriously.

The consultative machinery with consumers works not much better than that with labor. There are two central bodies, the Industrial Coal Consumers' Council for those using coal for industrial purposes, and the Domestic Coal Consumers' Council for those using it for domestic purposes. But thus far the reports of these councils have sounded more as though the councils were apologists for the Coal Board than defenders of the public interest.

Evaluation of the Public Corporation

The experience of the Coal Board demonstrates that nationalization alone is no answer to the problems of an industry. It also demonstrates that public corporations are fairly flexible organizations; that they have welcomed and even invited impartial, outside examinations of their structure and working; and that it is far easier to publicize their errors of judgment or management than it is in the case of private industry. Nonetheless, this still leaves a good many questions still to be examined: in particular, the type of board and of board members, the power of the minister who is responsible for the particular industry, and the general issue of accountability to Parliament.

Three possible types of board can be used in nationalized concerns: the board that represents all the interests involved, as used by the Port of London Authority; workers' control boards, which the Trades Union Congress rejected as an objective in 1944; and the so-called efficiency board, which is the type that has been adopted for reasons already indicated. Those who fear the power of the manager in modern life might well be alarmed at the immense potential control vested in the relatively small number of persons who are on the boards that run the nationalized industries. Relatively few have been drawn from the professions, the universities, or from scientific enterprises. Contrary to some prevailing impressions, however, the boards have not been dominated by civil servants, retired union members, or retired army personnel; moreover, their members have been independent of politics and of private business. What criticism can be made of them is not of their competence, impartiality, or hard work, but that they have been more concerned with output than with building a spirit of industrial democracy within their enterprises and have been much better at business than at public policy.

All of this leads to the question of whether the minister is the best person to appoint the members of the board of the nationalized industry for which he is responsible. Would it not be better, as the Acton Society Trust suggests, to leave appointment of board members to a small permanent committee with its own staff? This committee could examine the whole field of potential candidates, keep permanent records, and be much better equipped than any single minister to determine on which board a particular person would be most useful.

The minister plays a crucial role because of his responsibility for appointing the board members and because he is accountable for the public corporation to Parliament. Once again, as in connection with his department, it is the minister who is "get-at-able." But whereas everything a department does may normally be questioned in Parliament, one of the reasons for putting the nationalized industries under public corporations rather than departments was to provide them with administrative and financial independence in day-by-day operations.

To draw a definite line between matters of administration, for which the Board is responsible, and general policy, for which the minister is jointly responsible with the Board, has been more than difficult. All ministers have refused to answer questions on trade union negotiations, for example, or subordinate organizations within the public corporation, or salaries (except of Board members). But there is a zone between administration and policy where the minister is free to decide whether or not to answer.

What is perhaps most difficult from the point of view of accountability to Parliament is that there is no way of determining whether a minister is actually responsible for a particular decision or not, unless he is willing to volunteer the information. It is true that the Coal Board and the Minister of Power must jointly decide on the target for coal production and the prices to be charged for coal, and that the minister may therefore be held accountable for these decisions. But, in general, ministers seem to attempt to influence boards by informal pressure rather than direct orders. Both Conservative and Labor members have criticized the reluctance of ministers to use their statutory powers to give direction to the boards, charging that the ministers thereby escape their due responsibility to Parliament.

Although questions in Parliament can be useful, it is primarily in debate that issues are thoroughly ventilated and decisions reached. Since the nationalized industries give annual reports to Parliament, there is material for thorough discussions. But a major problem here is to find time for such discussions in the always crowded parliamentary schedule. The Coal Board was the subject of five general debates in the first four years of its existence; civil aviation is usually well debated every year. But it seems almost impossible for Parliament to debate all the major nationalized industries as often as once every year; even if it could, a short debate could cover only a relatively small portion of relevant ground; and beyond this is the fact that in debating the reports, Parliament is dealing with past history whereas often it is present policy that needs the most attention.

It is sometimes said that the work of the nationalized industries is too technical for Parliament usefully to consider. Yet it is the accepted axiom of parliamentary government that a representative body of amateurs can decide

better on matters of public policy than an irresponsible body of specialists. Few would propose that parliamentary control of public corporations should be dropped, but many feel that it should be aided or supplemented through closer scrutiny by a more specialized body. Proposals have run the gamut from an economic or industrial Parliament—a third house primarily concerned with economic matters but ultimately responsible to Parliament—to a much more limited representative or supervisory commission for each nationalized industry. One of the most useful suggestions is to establish a specialist quasi-judicial body to deal with technical matters like price fixing in the same way as the Transport Tribunal establishes railway rates for the public in Great Britain, and the Interstate Commerce Commission for interstate railway travel in the United States. The proposal that the Conservative government adopted in 1954, however, was to establish a new select committee to report periodically on the affairs of the nationalized industries.

It may be asked why it was necessary to set up a new parliamentary committee to supervise the nationalized industries when public corporation reports and accounts are already subject to scrutiny by the Public Accounts Committee. (The air corporations, BOAC and BEA, are supervised, in addition, by the Select Committee on Estimates, since they receive government subsidies.) Experience had shown, however, that the Public Accounts Committee already had more than enough to do with its responsibilities for departmental accounts. Moreover, what Parliament really needed, in the view of many people, was something much closer to an efficiency audit, so that it could judge whether a nationalized concern was providing the best possible service and, at the same time, producing as cheaply as possible.

The Select Committee on the Nationalized Industries established in 1955 was originally so restricted in gaining information that it reported it could not be "of any real use to the House." Subsequently, it has become a very much more effective instrument of Parliament. Its 1961 report, made after an eight-month scrutiny, on how the nationalized gas industry could be reorganized to provide more effective service proposed alternative plans to those of the

Ministry of Power and of the Gas Council itself. In addition to the work of this Select Committee, however, it is hard not to feel that, as Herbert Morrison had originally proposed, there should be periodic "stock-takings" of the place of the nationalized industries in the economy as a whole, as well as of their particular structures.

3. LOCAL GOVERNMENT

As the public administration has had to assume new and ever widening responsibilities, it has become increasingly important to secure effective means of decentralizing its activities. The public corporations, as we have seen, relieve the central ministries of a particular type of technical and administrative work that the ministries are not equipped to handle and that might well overstrain their organization to the point of breakdown. Another highly important way of relieving the central ministries of the burden of day-to-day administration is through local government. Local government is important not only for this reason, however, but also because it enables the people of local communities to take an active share in managing their own affairs. Thus they can gain useful political experience in matters they can easily understand. Moreover, local self-government can also act as a helpful counterbalance to central control.

Local autonomy was established early in England and Wales,[4] but local self-government is relatively recent. From the time of the Tudors, justices of the peace, appointed by the Crown and selected from the local gentry, exercised a benevolent direction as judges, legislators, and executives in county areas, while local oligarchies ruled in the ancient but antiquated boroughs or towns. The dominance of both groups was not undercut until the nineteenth century, when the industrial revolution and the resulting increase in governmental activities laid responsibilities on local areas that they were obviously incapable of handling. The

first shift in authority, however, was to a series of boards and commissioners, established one by one as local areas assumed new tasks in regard to public health, highways, public assistance to the poor, and elementary education. Since each of the new authorities was usually provided with a new set of areas within which to carry out its work, England and Wales became a bewildering network of sanitary districts, poor law districts, conservation districts, and so forth, whose boundaries rarely coincided. Only through a series of local government acts, extending to 1894, was order brought out of this chaos. In a parallel development, governing power was transferred gradually to elected councils, first in the boroughs or towns (1835), then in the counties and the newly created county boroughs or cities (1888), and finally in the subdivisions of the counties, the districts and parishes (1894). Thus by the end of the nineteenth century, local self-government had been established as the rule throughout England and Wales.

Though local self-government is still cherished in Great Britain, it is becoming more and more difficult to speak of a separate sphere of local action clearly set off from national government. Certain services once looked on as purely local have steadily taken on more national significance. The local school is part of a national educational system; public assistance is no longer a community task but a national responsibility; even gas and electricity, once characteristically municipal services, have now been nationalized.

Facilitating the rapidity of this change is the fact that in Great Britain there is no constitutional division of powers such as that existing between the national and state governments in the United States. There are only two levels of government in Great Britain—national and local—instead of the three levels of government in the United States—national, state, and local. And the British Parliament has authority over both the organization and the powers of local governments in the same way as American state governments have authority over the local governments, like cities and counties, within their boundaries. It is true that there is no more chance that England and Wales would wipe out local self-government by legislative action than

---

[4] There are slight, though not essential, variations in the forms of local government in Scotland and Northern Ireland. The institutions described are those of England and Wales.

there is that Massachusetts would do so. But since World War II, local authorities have been increasingly concerned with administering national programs at the local level. At the same time, they can, of course, always raise their standards above those which are required and, in addition, undertake particular projects selected by their own governing bodies.

This senior-junior partnership in central-local relationships extends also to financing local services. Local councils impose *rates,* or taxes, in proportion to the annual rental value of property in their areas; they also gain revenue from license fees, rental of municipal property, and so forth. But more than half the money spent at the local level comes from *grants-in-aid* by the central government—which meet, for example, about 50 percent of the cost of local police forces, and 20 to 75 percent of the cost of roads—and from *exchequer equalization grants,* which are provided on the basis of need to poor areas, so that the services they can provide do not fall too far short of those established by wealthier communities.

Local Government Councils

The organ of self-government in every unit of English local government, no matter what its size may be, or whether it is rural or urban,[5] is the council. Not only is there far less variety in the structure of local governments in England than in the United States (where county and city governments differ widely in form, and

where there are a number of different types of city government), but there is also no separation of powers in English local government such as is common in American city government. Thus the local government council in England has both executive and legislative powers, decides matters of policy, passes ordinances, fixes the budget, considers the way in which programs should be carried out in detail, and selects and works with the permanent officials who run the local services.

Most of the members of a local government council are elected for three-year terms; some, called aldermen, are chosen (or, to use a more technical term, co-opted) by the councilors themselves. Since property qualifications for voting in local government elections were swept away in 1945, anyone who can vote in a parliamentary election has also the local franchise. One result is that local elections have taken on the character of miniature national elections, with Conservatives and Labor working hard to gain control of local councils, both to demonstrate their political strength throughout the country and to consolidate their influence in the organs that administer so many national programs. This more active participation in local elections by national parties may have shifted attention from local issues, but it has heightened interest in the contests and led to a larger turnout of voters than during the period between the two World Wars, when the percentage voting was often even smaller than in comparable American elections.

The Council at Work

Once the councils are elected, party politics are less dominant than in the national sphere, although Labor claims there is more drive behind programs for social welfare, recreation centers, and housing when Laborites control a council than when the Conservatives do. The councils perform immensely important services, spending more than £500 million a year on new schools, houses, roads, clinics, sewage, and the like. Government grants now finance more than half the net expenditure by local authorities; a grant is paid according to a formula based mainly on size, population, current rate of expenditure on services, and the need for de-

---

[5] English local government areas are somewhat confusing. There are sixty-two administrative counties (often, though not always, identical with historic counties like Devon and Hampshire), and eighty-three county boroughs, which include all the important cities in the country except London, for which there are special arrangements. Administrative counties are composed of noncounty boroughs (consisting of towns not big or important enough to rank as county boroughs), as well as urban and rural districts. The districts, which are subdivided in turn into parishes, share their powers and responsibilities with the administrative county and also share the money they collect in rates. Many noncounty boroughs seek the more independent status of county boroughs, that is, the right to keep all the money they collect and to administer all their own services in their own area, but a change in status can be made only through an act of Parliament. In February 1966, a Royal Commission was established to undertake a searching countrywide review of local government organization and functions.

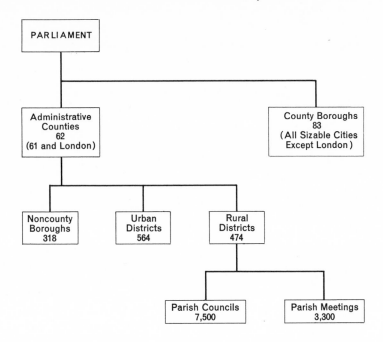

veloping services. But while the council as a whole determines the general outlines of a local program, most council work is administrative and is carried out by committees. These committees function wherever local government has responsibilities. They inspect schools, hire teachers, work on plans for roads, parks, and sewerage systems, or discuss specifications for the units in new housing developments, working closely at all times with the members of their permanent administrative staff. As a result, members of the council acquire a practical experience in governmental problems and administrative work for which members of Parliament have no equivalent. Though the very fact that so much of the work of local government is administrative leads to great dependence on the advice of the local civil service, in the end it is the council that makes the decisions. Moreover, though local administration must fit within the overall pattern of central administration, it is the council that determines the way in which this is done. Thus, despite the pervasive influence of national and local administrative officials, local self-government is still a reality in Great Britain.

4. THE PUBLIC SERVICE

The success of any organization depends on the people who do its work. This fact is particularly true of the public service, which demands of its members not only efficiency but also devotion to public purposes. To the extent that the public servant acts in an official capacity, he must be perfectly neutral toward the aims of the government. He must be willing to serve with equal energy and devotion the purposes of a Conservative government when it is in power and of a Labor government when it is in power. If his private opinions are opposed to public policy, it is the public policy that he must serve, conscientiously and wholeheartedly.

To state this principle, however, is not to determine, in every instance, the best way of realizing it in practice. Both Great Britain and the United States have had to find practical answers to a long series of subsidiary questions: What training and what qualities are most important for the public servant who is to be both expert and responsible? To what extent can public servants be allowed, in private life, to engage in partisan political activity? To what extent may they enjoy the right to strike or (especially in business enterprises run by the government) the right to a closed shop? How representative should the public service be in the sense of having its personnel typify a cross section of the people whom it serves? Is it more desirable for the highest public servants to be professional in the sense of having permanency of tenure or to be active supporters of, and to change office with, the government of the day?

The Civil Service

Great Britain developed one set of answers to these questions in the middle of the nineteenth century that still dominates the methods of selecting people to staff its ministries. Reform of its government service arose out of Great Britain's own particular type of spoils system: not, as in the United States, one in which new administrations regularly replaced government officials with their own appointees, but one in which government offices had become the preserve of the sons of noble families who could not make a living elsewhere. Thus the principal need was not, as in the United States, for permanence of tenure, but to secure people of ability and appropriate training.

At that time most government work was paper work—that is, it consisted mainly of collecting material, keeping records, and writing reports for the use of ministers. The work of the public service seemed to fall, therefore, into a great number of routine jobs that could be done by people of average ability, as long as they were careful and well supervised, and a very much smaller number of positions at the top that demanded great insight and judgment. When Lord Macaulay undertook the task of "housecleaning" the service, it was decided that recruitment for both lower and upper positions should be by merit. For the top key group of officials Macaulay had the example of the training instituted somewhat earlier at Haileybury for the recruitment and selection of young men for the Indian service, a selection avowedly designed to secure the type of able, cultured English gentleman who would best maintain British prestige abroad. Such men were the products of the English universities of the day; it was

therefore not surprising that the tests designed for recruiting the home civil service were likewise geared to the educational system. Those who wished to become high administrators had to demonstrate their ability through tests similar to comprehensive final examinations at a university, while the army of clerks was recruited on the basis of examinations similar to those in secondary school.

To make sure that the tests were administered fairly, a Civil Service Commission [6] was established in 1855, and, since 1870, open competitions have been the normal means of entry to the British civil (as contrasted with the military) service. Success in these competitive tests is necessary both for positions within the United Kingdom, that is, the Home Civil Service, and for the senior positions in the Diplomatic Service. Those who receive a certificate of qualification from the Civil Service Commission are ranked as part of the established civil service and have long enjoyed permanent tenure.

Selecting Civil Servants

The present structure of the British civil service and the present means of choosing its members differ little from the original pattern set up in the mid-nineteenth century. At the base of the 700,000 nonindustrial members of the service are the two clerical classes, the *subclerical* and the *clerical,* numbering over half a million, whose members perform the simplest work among the nonprofessional, nontechnical classes, which altogether comprise more than four-fifths of the established civil service. Much of the work is repetitive, or performed under orders, and can be handled by people brought into the service at sixteen or seventeen with good standing in the first years of secondary education.

If members of the clerical classes show re-

[6] The British Civil Service Commission is composed of three members who are appointed by the Cabinet after consultation with high Treasury officials. Unlike the United States Civil Service Commission, whose three members are generally chosen from outside the service, the British commissioners are nearly always persons of long experience in the British civil service and hold office until eligible for retirement under regular civil service rules. Since the British commissioners almost never have had active political experience before appointment, there is no rule in Great Britain (in contrast to the United States) that only two of the three members of the Commission may belong to the same political party.

sourcefulness, initiative, and judgment, they may be promoted to the *executive* class, which has some 77,000 members. The executive class may also be entered directly by eighteen- or nineteen-year-olds who have completed secondary school, passed an examination, and had an interview. Members of this class perform as important tasks in the civil service as noncommissioned officers perform in the army. They undertake preliminary investigations and sometimes collect data for the answers to parliamentary questions. They may also have full responsibility in questions of minor importance. Often they become specialists in fields like taxation or accounting. Ultimately they may acquire responsibilities in the organization and control of their departmental sections and carry out important decisions.

The most distinctive class in the British civil service is the so-called "permanent brain trust," the 2,300 members of the *administrative* class. On this group rest the responsibilities for formulating policy and for controlling and directing departments. The top members of the administrative class are the advisers of ministers, and insofar as the civil service wields political influence, it is through this group. We have seen that a minister in the British system is first and foremost a political figure and only secondarily an administrator, and that he therefore depends a great deal on the chief officials in his department to organize and direct its work and also to provide him with information and advice important for political decisions and for successful debate. Carefully chosen from the cream of university graduates between the ages of twenty-two and twenty-four, the members of the administrative class are men (and, increasingly, women) who can meet the outstanding members of any profession on equal terms.

One of the major differences between the British and American civil services lies in the fact that the former is a career service in which the members of the administrative class have a chance for promotion to the highest administrative positions in the department, whereas in the United States the top departmental offices nearly always change hands when a new administration comes into office—not simply, as critics sometimes suggest, in order to provide

political spoils for the electoral victor, but because of the belief that the policies of the new administration will be carried out most effectively if those responsible for their administration are actively in sympathy with them. The vigor and imagination with which some political appointees tackle their jobs gives support to this view, and some observers have suggested that the British system, by forcing a high civil servant to subject his own political beliefs and prejudices to those of the government that happens to be in power at a given time, may well substitute experience for a dynamic enthusiasm. The British view, however, is that men of the highest caliber will not enter the civil service unless they can look forward to positions of great responsibility in which they will share in the making of policy.

The desire to attract people of great ability into the civil service at an early age explains the British practice of recruiting for broad grades or classes at sharply defined ages and on the basis of general tests similar to those in the educational system. The American service, in contrast, more often selects people for particular positions and places great weight on practical experience and specialized knowledge, without regard for age. The American practice makes possible a readier exchange between government and other occupations and helps to keep the civil service in touch with developments in private business or in the law, and the British now make increasing use of this approach in selecting specialists. For their general administrators, however, they still maintain the traditional system.

TESTS FOR THE ADMINISTRATIVE CLASS How can one predict that a twenty-two- or twenty-three-year-old will develop the qualities of political acumen and administrative skill necessary in order to become a sound political adviser; or the ability to carry out administrative programs, for example in housing or public health, in such a way that the public will not be antagonized? The British believe it can be done through written tests and an interview, which are the customary means of selection.

The competitive *written examinations* generally cover eight subjects. Three of them: English, contemporary affairs, and some general topic, are uniform for all candidates. The other five may be chosen from a list of nearly sixty subjects, including obscure and technical ones. In the United States the examinations designed for college seniors interested in entering the public service lay emphasis on special subjects at least somewhat relevant to the work they will perform; but in Great Britain an examination in Sanskrit will be weighted as heavily as one in economics. The judges are concerned primarily with the candidate's ability to express himself and to handle material with which he is familiar. They also try to avoid having their tests influence the educational curriculum.

Of increasing importance in selecting candidates is the *interview,* which is designed to give the examiners an indication of the candidate's ability to meet people and to respond quickly and decisively to a challenge. Originally, the interview was largely unplanned in character. "You may ask him almost anything that occurs to you, to find out what his interests are and how he reacts to other people and other things," said a former member of the Civil Service Commission in describing the older interview technique. "It is as wide as we can make it. Of course you ask him about his games and sports; everything under the sun, really." Such comments suggested that the public school boy had a particular advantage in the interview, partly because he was likely to have had a richer variety of experiences both in education and in travel than the product of the ordinary secondary school, and also because he was likely to have superior poise, manners, and appearance.

To make sure the interview gives a well-rounded picture of the individual, it has now been increased in length from the former fifteen minutes, and more systematic techniques are used for gauging qualities of adaptability and leadership. Since 1920, the interview has been the chief means of selecting scientific, professional, and technical officers whose professional qualifications are established by their certificates. After World War II, when the civil service considered many veterans who were outside the normal age limits, it used qualifying examinations in conjunction with intelligence tests and extended interviews. This practice developed finally into a whole battery of tests conducted over a period of two to three days for a group of about twenty candidates at a time. The Diplomatic Service now commonly uses this latter technique of testing, but it is only one of several means used for the Home administrative class. The final selection board in the latter class still uses its own interview in addition to the reports and examination results in making its decision.

THE BACKGROUND OF THOSE SELECTED   What kind of people do these tests bring into the civil service? Contrary to popular belief, the 2,300-odd members of the administrative class of the Home Civil Service are not drawn exclusively from the privileged classes. It would be even less accurate, however, to suggest that they represent a cross section of the nation as a whole. Few of the higher civil servants are aristocrats or men of great wealth, but even fewer are drawn from the working class or the lower-middle class. The great majority have come from that part of the upper-middle class that must work for its living but that shares the manners and the outlook of the "ruling class." Comparatively few of them have attended the most exclusive public schools, but a high percentage have attended Oxford or Cambridge (often with the help of scholarships).

Two developments have tended steadily to break down the class character of the administrative class: the more liberal program of promotions developed after World War II, and the widening of general educational opportunities. Special competitions limited to established civil servants permit members of the clerical and executive classes to be promoted to the administrative class; even before the war almost a quarter of its members were drawn from the service itself by promotion and examination. But there is still some feeling that a reinvigorated Civil Service Commission could usefully widen the sources of selection: in particular, by recruiting more from outside Oxford and Cambridge and the liberal arts.

THE DIPLOMATIC SERVICE   Although the Home Civil Service has never been the preserve of the wealthy and aristocratic, the same could not be said in the past of the Foreign Service. Until 1943, candidates had to be approved by a board of selection, which was likely to be influenced by a noble name; in addition to the regular tests for the administrative class, knowledge of foreign countries and languages was required that assumed extended study abroad. Successful candidates now receive an eighteen-month period of study abroad at public expense, and the special knowledge and language tests come only after this period has ended. Greater equality of opportunity has also resulted from the reorganization and consolidation, already noted, of the former overseas services into the Diplomatic Service. Some people regret, however, that so sharp a separation remains between the Home Civil Service and the Diplomatic Service and feel that greater interchange of personnel would be healthy for both groups.

PROFESSIONAL, TECHNICAL, AND SCIENTIFIC PERSONNEL   Criticism is also leveled at the often rigid separation of administrators and specialists. The government service has great need of professional, scientific, and technical personnel: doctors for public health work; engineers for building bridges; economists for statistical work; and physicists for atomic research. Many feel it would be more sensible to put both administrators and specialists in a single Senior Civil Service with more scope for interchanges. Moreover, they believe the constant interaction between the public and private sectors and the rapid advances in new techniques, particularly in private industry, should be reflected in easier secondment to and from outside occupations. More use of specialists and of outside research, and less secrecy, especially in discussion of long-range policy issues, are also recommended. Finally, it is recommended that specialists have direct access to the minister instead of having to transmit their ideas through the permanent secretary.

Training Administrators

Perhaps the greatest weakness in the British system is in training. Having deliberately placed its emphasis on capacity rather than experience, in the belief that people of intelligence will be able to learn whatever they need to know after they have entered the service, the civil service has done relatively little to provide systematic training thereafter. The French have a well-planned three-year course that combines study

with practical experience, but neither Great Britain nor the United States has anything comparable.

All the larger ministries have short-term training divisions for all grades, which operate under the general direction of the Treasury. These, however, do not begin to meet the objective, recently publicized, of a School of Administrative Studies which would recruit from a wide field and possibly provide staff for nationalized industries and for public agencies as well as the administrative service. Related is the proposal to supervise more carefully the relatedness of the jobs through which a young administrator moves, so that he will retain his zest and constantly broaden his experience. With this progression could then be associated mid-career training. On this matter, a good start has been made in the seven-week course (fourteen weeks for those from the economic departments) through the Center for Administrative Studies (established in 1963) for specialists and administrators in their third year of service. The trend is in the right direction, but a more carefully planned and extensive program of training at an earlier level could do much to make the civil service more attractive and better equipped for its vast and varied responsibilities.

Employer-Employee Relations

When government becomes an employer, it faces many of the same problems of labor relations that private business encounters. There is one major difference: strikes by civil servants, though not illegal in Great Britain (they are punishable in the United States under the Taft-Hartley Act, 1947), are not considered an acceptable form of pressure. But neither in Great Britain nor in the United States are government employees below the administrative rank restricted in their right to form unions. Moreover, British civil service unions (like those in the United States) have been allowed to affiliate with ordinary industrial unions since 1946, when Labor repealed the ban on affiliation enacted by the Conservatives following the General Strike of 1926.

WHITLEY COUNCILS   The normal channel, however, for consideration of all questions affecting employment in the civil service is the Whitley Council, a joint negotiation board on which members of the higher civil service and representatives of civil service unions are represented equally. Their joint considerations are expected to end with a general agreement acceptable to both sides.

Organized on every level of the civil service, Whitley Councils act on problems appropriate to their various spheres. The National Whitley Council consists of fifty-four members, of whom the twenty-seven official members are appointed by the Chancellor of the Exchequer (evidence of Treasury control), while the twenty-seven staff members include leading officials of various civil service associations, many of them professional, full-time trade union workers. It lays down the general principles governing conditions of service and proposes legislation affecting the conditions of civil servants. About seventy autonomous councils operate on the department level and are concerned with the application of particular rules. In some cases there are also district and local Whitley Councils, and every ministry with a large number of industrial employees, like the Board of Trade, has a Joint Industrial Council that deals with any matters outside wages and trade questions.

Some of the most important reports on which changes in the civil service have been based (including recruitment after World War II and equal pay for men and women in the nonindustrial civil service) have been drafted by the National Whitley Council. Nonetheless, many staff members feel that they have too little influence on decisions at the national level. This is hardly surprising, for the official members of the National Whitley Council can only meet staff demands within the limits established by the Treasury and ministers. A public recommendation by the National Whitley Council means in fact a policy already approved by the Cabinet.

Whitley Councils have much to commend them. They regularize contacts between higher and lower civil servants and provide for frank exchanges of views; they help employees to see the purpose of new plans and training programs; and they help employers to understand better the effect of what they do. The Councils cannot provide for joint management of the ministries, for the latter are not business enterprises but the staffs of politically responsible ministers. But the Councils do a great deal to fit rules to individual situations and to stimulate good relations.

As far as salaries and wages are concerned, the Treasury negotiates with the staff associations, or trade unions, to try to find a settlement satisfactory to both sides. If this is not possible, however, the government long ago committed itself to the principle of arbitration. For nonindustrial civil servants, the Civil Service Arbitration Tribunal (of which the Treasury names one member, the unions another, and the Minister of Labor the chairman) provides awards that the government accepts as binding under normal circumstances. Disputes affecting industrial personnel are settled by the Industrial Court, which is made up in a similar manner. Thus one of the most likely causes of friction between the government and staff can be assigned to a court of reference, which, unlike the Whitley Councils, stands higher than either.

Internal Security in the Civil Service

Perhaps the most difficult and certainly the most delicate problem faced in recent years within the British civil service has been to establish an adequate program of internal security in a climate of opinion that abhorred the excesses of McCarthyism in the United States. It has been the misfortune of both the Labor and the Conservative governments to find out too late that valuable information had been transmitted to the Soviet Union by supposedly responsible government servants. The Profumo case that rocked the Conservative government had strong implications for security as well as morality. Thus, a progressively tighter security program has been instituted within the service, though without changing its essential features.

The British security program aims at excluding possibly disloyal persons (that is, with either Communist or fascist associations) from sensitive areas; it operates without publicity; and as far as possible people are transferred within the service rather than discharged. All civil servants engaged in work related to defense contracts are required to state specifically whether they fall within the purview of the security program, and they are automatically disqualified for security posts if they acknowledge having had such connections. Moreover, in certain sensitive areas investigation is automatic. Although the investigations of the security services necessarily remain confidential, a civil servant under suspicion receives full opportunity to reply to the charges of unreliability and, if he so desires, to have a personal interview with his immediate superior, with the minister, and with a specially constituted advisory body.

The British have handled their security program with great quietness and apparently with efficiency, and without disrupting the morale of the service. Periodically, cases arise such as the Vassall spy case or that of Maclean and Burgess. Both Maclean and Burgess were members of the British Foreign Service who had been under surveillance by security services but who nonetheless were able to flee to Moscow after transmitting secret information to the Soviet Union. Such cases raise grave questions regarding the adequacy of security arrangements.

But while the British may find themselves forced to intensify and extend their security checks, they insist on taking into account not only the risk of treachery but also the protection of individual liberty. It might even be said that the British are prepared to take certain risks with security (though they are trying hard to avoid them) rather than with their cherished principle that a man must be assumed innocent until he is proved guilty.

Local Government Officials

Local government, as we have seen, carries a substantial part of the responsibility for administration at the local level. In their work, the local councils depend not on nationally appointed public servants but on officials selected and paid for by themselves. In fact, local government authorities employ over a million people (more in normal times than the national government), about one-quarter of whom are teachers and over 100,000 of whom do administrative, technical, and clerical work. Much of the importance and independence of local governments, in their day-to-day working with the national government, arises from this control of their own officials.

On the whole, the highest local officials are of outstanding ability, partly because the national government has established standards for most professional positions, and partly because of the high professional ideals maintained by the National Association of Local Government Officers, a voluntary organization with steadily increasing influence. In contrast to the general practice in the national administration, the permanent heads of departments in local governments are chosen because of their special training in health, housing, road building, and so forth, and are trained doctors, engineers, or other experts, not general administrators. Some observers consider this unfortunate, believing that it often turns a good doctor into a bad administrator, and that local government would be better advised to recruit general administrators from the universities, as is done in the national government. But there are others who feel that local government could teach the national government a good deal about the administrative usefulness of the expert. Newcastle's innovation in 1965 in making a former Ford executive Britain's first city manager (thereby adopting an American device) may also carry useful lessons.

At least there is general self-congratulation that the English local government service escaped the spoils system that has haunted so many American cities and counties. Nor have there been experiments in electing local government officials, and thus there has been no counterweight to the authority of the council. In fact, English government officials, on the whole, are loyal to their councils to a fault, even when their own farsighted plans are crippled by too parsimonious councilors.

The major problems in local government service are found at the lower levels. Emphasis on professional qualifications for high officials means that opportunities for promotion from lower (and less specialized) levels are much more restricted than in the national civil service. In addition, local councils often try to balance the cost of hiring well-trained professional men by employing inadequately trained people in lower positions. Until after World War II, junior clerks were sometimes brought into the service at an immature age and without good records in secondary education. Training plans were lacking. Only recently have Whitley Councils become common at every level of local government service. Thus there is still much to be done to develop the uniformly high standards in the service on which the excellence of local government programs must depend.

Staffing the Nationalized Industries

Since government entered the fields of industry and business, it has faced new problems in selecting and managing personnel. Because so much of the work of the public corporations is technical in character, they have preferred not to use civil service tests for recruiting their staffs. Neither have they adopted the practice of the TVA, however, which has an excellent merit system of its own. Thus the public corporations are still undertaking their own recruitment without having developed fixed standards for doing so.

Those who support full freedom for public corporations in securing their own staffs argue that government must adopt not only business methods when it enters the field of private enterprise but also business standards. Also they feel they may secure more imaginative persons to cope with the new types of problems. There is no danger of patronage, they point out, when so many positions must be filled by people with technical qualifications. Moreover, they maintain that the need to compete with private industry for trained personnel makes it necessary for the public corporations to set their salary scales by industry's levels rather than by those of the civil service.

This latter point, not surprisingly, is a particularly sore one for the civil service. Yet, in light of the increasing difficulty of attracting an adequate number of first-class candidates for the administrative class, it may be that the answer is to give the civil service, too, the standards of pay common in private enterprise.

Whether adjustment of salary scales is the way to secure it or not, there are obvious advantages in being able to interchange certain types of personnel between the civil service and public corporations. It would help to keep the civil service more alert to current economic developments and the public corporations more responsive to the demands of their public posi-

tion. If these advantages are to be secured, however, the public corporations must establish some type of merit system, either one that is similar to that of the civil service or one that is geared specifically to their own recruitment needs.

Unions in Nationalized Industries

The new nationalized industries also face problems in employer-employee relations. Workers in nationalized industries continue to be represented by the same unions that had represented them in their dealings with private employers. The government, however, is in a far stronger position than any private employer, particularly where it is virtually the only employer, as in the coal mines. Accordingly, some of the smaller unions originally feared that the government might impose a closed shop—that is, grant exclusive bargaining privileges to a single union and compel all workers in the industry to join that union or else give up their jobs. Such a ruling applied to an entire nationalized industry might completely destroy certain unions. But while the Trades Union Congress has agreed not to push for the closed shop at the expense of unions not affiliated with it, it does demand that workers in government-owned industries belong to some union. Moreover, government naturally appreciates the greater ease and simplicity of negotiations carried on with a single union instead of several.

The unions themselves have faced a new problem as the result of government ownership. In the past many restrictive practices (such as limiting the production of any one worker and requiring the employment of a minimum number of workers on certain types of jobs) were adopted as ways of preventing men from being overworked and exploited by their employers and as methods of increasing employment. But now that the government is the employer, the restrictions on production, instead of hurting an individual employer, hurt the community as a whole. Certain labor leaders have already urged workers to change their earlier outlook, identify their interests with those of the community, increase individual production, and drop their old methods of "spreading the work around." But the habits of many years are hard to change; and it remains difficult, as we have seen, to convince the ordinary worker in a nationalized industry that he should work harder simply because there has been a change in the form of ownership, or because he has been told, for example, that "the mines are his."

How Satisfactory Is the Civil Service?

Although the British may criticize their civil service, they will rush to its defense if other people attack it. On the whole, it commands respect and possesses far higher prestige than the American civil service. The average member of the administrative class is neither a "philosopher king" nor a daring innovator, but he is competent, wide awake, and responsible. He enters the service through tests that emphasize clear, logical thinking and expression and ability to view situations objectively. In the service he works on important problems during most of his life. Moreover, he is schooled throughout his career in its professional ethics, according to which he must put public interest above personal advantage.

The civil servant is expressly forbidden to put himself in a position where duty and interests conflict. "The public expects from them a standard of integrity and conduct not only inflexible but fastidious," stated a report of 1928. The permanent secretary of the Air Ministry was dismissed in 1936 for using his knowledge of public negotiations for his own private advantage, a rare example of violation of the primary rule of the civil service code.

In recent years there has been some concern over the number of members of the administrative class who have resigned to take positions in private industry, carrying with them, of course, the specialized knowledge they had acquired within the service. However, the drain from public to private employment does not begin to parallel that in the American service, where the higher members of the internal revenue bureau, for example, are under constant inducement to take private positions with the very firms whose accounts they have been scrutinizing. This use of public experience for private advantage cannot be guarded against entirely; but better salaries in the public service are one answer, while the possibility of loss of pensions on resignation has also acted as a strong deterrent to mass transferals. Temporary secondments might be a mutually helpful alternative to permanent withdrawal.

The second major rule in the civil service code of ethics is the ban on direct political activity. "The step from the civil service politician to the politicized civil servant is but a short one," a Royal Commission warned. Though other elements of the code are embodied in Treasury minutes or departmental codes or enshrined in custom, this prohibition is embodied in legislation.

As the number of civil servants increases, however, there is increasing concern over the extent to which a large and exceptionally intelligent part of the electorate is prevented from making its contribution to political discussion. It would, of course, be wrong for civil servants to use information acquired through their work as a weapon against the government of the day; and it would be impossible for a minister to work with men who were actively and openly his political opponents. But it is harder to see why an employee of the health service should be prevented from stating his views on foreign policy or local government issues. Some staff groups have already appealed to the Cabinet to reconsider the extent of the restrictions on the political rights of civil servants, particularly those below a certain level. In 1961, local governments lifted the ban on national political activity by their officials. This is the more useful because it is conceivable that in a semicollectivized society the rule against political activity would deprive a large part of the electorate of the freedom of political speech and action essential to a healthy democracy.

It is less the rules, however, than the general attitude of the service that provides its distinctive stamp. When the President's Committee on Administrative Management in the United States recommended in 1937 that the President should have more executive assistants, it wrote that these aides should have "a passion for anonymity." Most higher civil servants in Great Britain possess this quality. They serve without thought of particular gain (though they have comfortable salaries) and they have a high sense of responsibility.

Yet in 1954 the British people received an uncomfortable reminder that officialdom can also be inefficient and insensitive and that official decisions, regardless of their merits or lack of them, are extraordinarily difficult to overturn. The Crichel Downs case, which became a byword throughout Great Britain, concerned an estate in Dorset that had been requisitioned by the government in 1937 as a bombing site. When it was no longer needed for this purpose, its hereditary owners tried to buy it back, but their offer was curtly rejected by the Ministry of Agriculture, which planned to use the area as a model farm. Only because of remarkable persistence and vigor were the former owners finally able to secure a public hearing of the issue, and only thereafter were they allowed to regain their land. But the case proved to have other equally justified consequences: after a shake-up of permanent officials within the ministry, the minister himself, in an unprecedented action, formally resigned on the floor of the House in acknowledgment that, regardless of the virtual impossibility of knowing all the ills of so large a department, his had been the ultimate responsibility for this lack of concern for the legitimate claims of private persons.

The Crichel Downs case highlighted the problem often subsumed under the general heading of bureaucracy, a problem ever more serious as the laissez-faire philosophy of the middle-class state gives way to the demands for a planned society. Nothing but public and parliamentary alertness and a deep sensitivity to human values on the part of civil servants and ministers can be an adequate protection against the possible arbitrariness of officialdom.

There is another problem raised by the vast increase in governmental responsibilities: Can public servants give the government that measure of wholehearted zeal and devotion essential for tackling successfully the overwhelming problems of today unless they have the same general philosophy on the country's needs as that held by the political authors of policy? This is a question raised particularly in the past by Labor, for it is obvious that higher civil servants commonly are closer akin in background, education, and associations to the Conservatives than to their opponents. Yet the way in which British civil servants have thrown themselves with energy and zeal into Labor's plans for development (plans for which, in some instances, they themselves had long been pressing) has done much to convince any doubters that the civil service has great capacity for imagination and change.

Higher civil servants are sometimes spoken of as "statesmen in disguise." In the new activities of government, it may well be that the civil service also needs "men of push and go," to quote J. Donald Kingsley in *Representative Bureaucracy*, "energetic innovators and hard-driving managers." Yet civil servants must also be responsive to public purposes, as well as to ministerial direction. Perhaps above all, one might say after studying the Crichel Downs case, civil servants need an ever deeper awareness of human needs and values as the essential corollary to their steadily increasing influence in modern life.

Conclusion: Public Administration and Popular Control

The government of every democratic country faces the problem of combining technical expertness with responsibility to the voters and their representatives. The outstanding characteristic of the expert is that he knows more about his special field than does the layman; but the outstanding characteristic of democracy is that the government (including the public service) must, in general, be accountable and responsive to the public. To subject the judgment of the expert to the direction and control of ordinary citizens may seem to the expert to destroy the value of his expertness. But to free the expert from this control is to destroy democracy.

Fortunately, the problem is not quite so difficult as these statements would make it appear. The expert is generally an expert in the methods of achieving a given purpose, but the purposes are those of the citizen. The expert knows how to build a bridge; it is the citizen who wants to get to the other side of the river.

One of the most striking aspects of British public administration is the variety of forms used to combine efficiency with public responsibility. In some areas there is full dependence on the ordinary departmental structure; in others, the public corporation is combined with ministerial direction; while in others still, the central departments work closely with popularly elected local councils that hire and pay their own staffs, with whom they work on terms of extraordinary intimacy compared with anything found at the national level.

When the whole complicated structure of public administration is surveyed, it may well seem that neither coordination nor popular control is particularly effective. It is true that much governmental activity necessarily depends on the caliber of the people who staff a particular agency, a fact that points up the importance of the selection, training, and standards of the public service. But at the same time it must be emphasized that there is no public agency able to act in an arbitrary fashion and apart from the rest of the administrative system. Though government uses a business form for public enterprise, each public corporation works closely with a minister. Economic planning also makes the ministers more and not less important. Moreover, the ministries continue to provide the backbone of the administrative structure and through the ministries, the boards, committees, and corporations are linked to the Cabinet and to Parliament. If this at times seems an exceedingly long and slender link, it is nevertheless the one that makes public control possible.

7. English Law and Courts

1. ENGLISH COMMON LAW

The traditional association of law and liberty is so intimate that, particularly in Anglo-Saxon countries, what is called "the rule of law" is looked on as the essence of free government. According to this concept, every individual in the community has certain rights that should not be infringed upon by other individuals or by government officials. Independent courts are available to which he may appeal if there is any interference with these rights. The rule of law means too that if an individual is accused of failing to do his duty or of committing an injustice, he cannot be punished until after he has had a public hearing in the courts and a formal verdict, based on a specific and known body of law, has been made against him.

Certain additional features of the rule of law are equally important as safeguards of individual liberty. Thus the rule of law (sometimes spoken of as "government under law") implies that the powers of the government can be extended or changed only through regular and accepted political processes that result in publicly known legislation. This is particularly important at a time when government is assuming so many new responsibilities that directly affect the community, for otherwise people might be punished under rules of which they were unaware, as was true in Nazi Germany and has been so in the Soviet Union. In Anglo-Saxon countries the rights and duties of the government and the relations between the government and private individuals within the state are defined in what is called *public law*. Because the powers of government are defined, government officials are limited to those actions for which they have specific authority, and a private individual can check a particular action by asking the courts to determine whether it is justified by the provisions of the law under which the official is acting.

The law (which may be defined broadly as a known body of rules related to general principles that the courts use in deciding specific cases referred to them) and independent, impartial courts are as important in ordinary social relations within the community as they are in preventing arbitrary action by the government and its agents. By defining individual rights and duties the law removes uncertainties regarding the rules governing daily conduct and renders unnecessary recourse to violence to settle disputes. *Private law* is concerned with the relations between private persons (for example, husband and wife or partners) and with questions relating to private property or to one's own person, such as contracts, trespass, and torts (for example, slander, deceit, and assault).

Most of private law falls into the category of *civil law,*[1] which concerns itself with the rights of individuals looked on merely as individuals. In civil law, individuals have to take the responsibility for bringing cases before the courts. But if there is a very serious violation of the rights of one individual by another, the case comes under *criminal law,* which is public law and for which the government assumes responsibility. The acts with which criminal law is concerned are those considered to be a threat to public order and therefore the responsibility of the whole community. While trespass, for example,

---

[1] The term *civil law* is also used in quite a different sense to distinguish jurisprudence based on Roman sources from the jurisprudence of Anglo-American countries, which has its roots in common law. For the former, see Chapter 7 in the section on France and Chapter 6 in the section on Germany.

is a civil offense because it affects only the person whose property has been interfered with, murder is a criminal offense because it robs the community of one of its members and, by example, may threaten the security of others. There are also many other acts, not bad in the sense of threatening the security of the community, but in the sense that they violate certain standards established by the government (for example, maximum hours of work, safety conditions in factories, and so forth), which the government prosecutes under criminal law.

The exact content and relationship of the various bodies of law change and develop with changing conditions. Otherwise they would put society in a strait jacket. The economic and social needs of society have been affected so vastly by industrialization, for example, that what was once considered to be a matter that only affected the individuals immediately concerned (for example, child labor) has become a matter of concern to society as a whole. Moreover, as some individual rights are curtailed (for example, that of employers to determine the conditions of work for their employees), new rights, such as the right to benefits under social security and workmen's compensation for injuries, are extended.

Ideally, therefore, the law should meet two criteria. It should be certain and precise so that it provides known standards for action. At the same time, it should be flexible enough to meet new conditions.

The peculiar pride of the Anglo-American legal system lies in its ability to combine a high degree of certainty as to legal rules with striking adaptability to changing conditions. This characteristic has been demonstrated in the long continuity of the English common law, extending over eight hundred years. During this time the English have developed a national system of law characterized by a complex interweaving of written statutes and unwritten custom and precedent. The adaptability of this system of law has been demonstrated not only in England but, under different conditions, in all the English-speaking countries, including most of the newer members of the Commonwealth.[2] While the

United States diverged sharply from English practices in establishing its political institutions, the American legal system was built directly on English legal rules, practices, and institutions. And though American law and courts have developed their own distinctive features, it is still true that precedents are occasionally exchanged across the Atlantic.

The Strands of English Law

The characteristic features of the English common law system were molded by experience and can scarcely be understood apart from their historical development. The legal system of England and Wales,[3] though well integrated, is made up of three separate strands: *common law, equity,* and *statute law*. A judge may well draw on all three in making his decision in a particular case, and, although he will differentiate among them in so doing, he will suggest that they are part of a single system of law. Yet historically, common law, equity, and statute law have separate roots and functions.

Common law and equity are often spoken of as "unwritten law," because they developed out of the decisions of judges; statute law is "written law" made by the legislative process. We are inclined to think that all law is written law, but in fact the unwritten common law and equity were not only the first to develop historically but in many fields are still the most fundamental. If all legislation in England and the United States were suddenly declared null and void, there would still be a body of common law and equity on which to depend, though the rules and remedies would in large part be strange and archaic. If, on the other hand, common law and equity were suddenly swept away, the basic foundation in both countries for the rules governing such matters as contracts, wills, trespass, or libel would be missing, except insofar as the rules in these fields have been embodied in legislation.

---

[2] Ceylon has Roman-Dutch law, for historical reasons, as do Rhodesia and South Africa, formerly in the Commonwealth.

[3] Scotland and Northern Ireland have their own legal rules and institutions, which differ in part from those of England and Wales. Scottish law, in particular, has been more strongly affected by Roman law than has English law. They also have separate court systems and slight differences in their legal professions. Everything in this chapter, therefore, refers only to England and Wales.

The Common Law

The common law developed in the first centuries after the Norman Conquest. Previously, there had been local courts administering the local customs that had been handed down for generations. But in the twelfth century, as a measure for centralizing authority, the King sent out traveling judges who listened to cases in the local courts and applied the customs they found in various places. Gradually, by the process of unification, they forged a law that became "common" to the whole realm and was used in deciding the cases that came before the new royal courts at Westminster.

The judges whose job it was to assemble and reconcile regional rules had to use their own knowledge and judgment to make the law uniform. In theory they were "discovering" the existing law; in practice they were discreetly selecting those rules that could be applied in the future. In this sense, therefore, it is true to say that the common law was "judge-made law," or "found in the bosom of judges," as an old Latin phrase expressed it.

This method of making the law uniform ended about the middle of the thirteenth century. At that time, the great exposition of the common law by Henry of Bracton, himself a judge, marked the conclusion of its formative period. The common law was now looked on as a "complete" law, that is, judges were expected to be able to draw decisions in all kinds of cases from it. Thereafter, the common law developed through the decisions of the central courts at Westminster.

The common law was both stable and adaptable. Stability resulted from an early enforcement of the rule of precedent, or *stare decisis*. According to this rule, once a decision had been reached by a superior court in a particular kind of case, all other cases of a similar kind had to be decided according to the same rule. No new principles were to be introduced that could not be deduced from earlier cases. But complete rigidity was avoided by the fact that every case had individual features and that there might be a number of precedents on which judges could draw in making their decisions.

Nonetheless, after the formation of the common law was completed, it became sufficiently inflexible as to give rise to serious complaints. Despite its completeness, there were in fact cases for which it could provide no remedy. Sometimes there were manifest injustices because of strict adherence to precedent. Moreover, feudal relationships were beginning to give place to those of a money economy. To provide remedies for deficiencies in the common law, there developed the second strand in English law: equity.

Equity

Equity was rooted not in custom but in conscience. It was based on the belief that law should correspond to the moral standards of the community. When the common law courts did not provide "equity" in the sense of a just redress of grievances, it was possible to appeal from the King's Courts to the King himself. Such appeals were referred to the Chancellor, "the keeper of the King's conscience," who after investigation could issue a special writ ordering the person against whom the complaint was made to perform the act necessary to secure justice.

Equity could provide remedies where the common law could only impose penalties. For instance, equity could force performance of a contract, whereas common law could only give damages for its breach. Moreover, equity, through an injunction, could prevent the commission of an act that would be damaging to property. If a house were to be destroyed to make place for a road, the Chancellor, like a modern court, could issue a writ under equity to prevent the action until the necessity for the road had been investigated. Common law, in contrast, could only award damages if the destruction of the house could be proved to have been unnecessary.

Another characteristic and important provision of equity was the "trust." Under common law, property transferred to another person became his own, even though he might be administering it for the benefit of a third person—for example, the infant child of the original owner. Under equity the Chancellor could not take away the right of ownership from the person to whom the property had been transferred, but he could order that person to use it for the purpose for which it had been given to him—that is, for the benefit of the child. Thus equity did not abolish rights that existed under common law but insisted that they be used in a just or equitable way. This notion of a trust allowed for many applications. In the form of settlements under wills or of charitable organizations or of industrial combinations the trust has been a central institution of English and American law of property.

Common law and equity have many similarities. Both were shaped by judges to fit the needs of the period in which they were formed. But those needs differed. Common law provided a basic system of law that conserved local customs but shaped them in terms of the new centralized royal authority. Equity supplemented its rules by drawing on some of the general principles of Roman law and on what one authority has called "the practice of the 'good citizen,' i.e., the really upright and conscientious person." Equity was thus complementary to the common law and never pretended to the completeness of common law. But gradually equity, too, became a system bound by precedent. In the eighteenth century, a great Chancellor declared that the doctrines of equity "ought to be as well settled and made as uniform almost as those of the Common Law."

Statute Law

The third strand in English law is "written," or statute, law—that is, legislation passed by Parliament or any one of the subordinate bodies to which Parliament has delegated lawmaking powers. This is by far the largest source of law in modern times. Until the nineteenth century, however, almost all private law, as well as almost all criminal law, was common law or equity. Even when much of the criminal law was embodied in statutes in the nineteenth century, together with much of the law governing trusts, partnerships, bills of exchange, and sale of goods and lands, the basis still remained common law. In the fields of private and criminal law, statute law, like equity, is supplementary to common law.

There is a major difference, however, in the relation between common law and equity and the relation between common law and statute law. Equity does not contradict common law but mitigates it or meets its deficiencies. Statute law overrides common law. In fact, the main reason for statute law in the field of private law is to alter rules that have been established by judicial decision but that no longer fit community standards (for example, the relations of parent and child). In case of a conflict between statute and common law, the statute is always upheld.

Compared to the long, slow process of change in unwritten law, statutes offer an easy and speedy means of changing the law. They substitute the legislator for the judge. Why then have statutes not entirely replaced the unwritten law? And what is meant by saying that England and the United States have common law systems despite the vast volume of legislation placed on the statute books of both countries each year?

The Characteristics of the Common Law System

One characteristic feature of the common law system is, as suggested, that fundamental principles are generally embodied in unwritten law and the exceptions are in written law, instead of vice versa. Codification of the law has taken place in some fields so that the general principles are embodied in statutes. In such instances the unwritten law fills in the gaps. In 1965, in response to an election pledge, a five-member law commission for England and Wales, and a similar one for Scotland, were set up by parliamentary act to modernize, simplify, and consolidate the law in the most thoroughgoing reform in English legal history. Even the codification of the general principles and rules in a given field, however, commonly reiterates principles of common law or equity or openly builds on them.

Another characteristic feature of the common law system is often spoken of as *case law*. In case law, judicial principles are worked out by the judges in the course of deciding cases; the opinions they give in support of their decisions become authoritative sources of reference for subsequent cases. Thus a judge places his chief dependence in interpreting a statute or a rule of common law on the opinions given in deciding previous cases of a similar kind, particularly those cases settled in higher courts. At the same time, whenever conditions make it necessary, it is possible, as Professor Geldart says in *Elements of English Law,* that "by a process of deduction, by argument from analogy, the existing principles may be made to yield a new principle, which is new because never explicitly stated before, but which in another sense is not new because it was already involved in what was already acknowledged." Thus stability is combined with flexibility.

2. JUDGES, JURIES, AND OFFICIALS

No one can overlook the importance of the judge in the English common law system, both for the development of the law and for the protection of individual liberty. Courts are judges sitting in their official capacities to consider and pass judgment in particular cases that have been referred to them. On the judges' knowledge, judgment, integrity, and independence depends the quality of the legal decisions that not only settle particular cases but also decide precedents for the future.

One of the great struggles for individual liberty in England centered upon the independence of the judiciary. The royal courts were originally set up by order of the King, but they quickly acquired a large measure of autonomy. Nonetheless, since the judges were appointed and dismissed at royal pleasure, the King possessed powerful weapons if he wished to bend the administration of justice to his purposes. Moreover, the King was the ultimate "fount of justice," and Stuart Kings maintained that this gave them the right to override the customary rules of law. As great a Lord Chancellor as Francis Bacon declared that judges should be "lions under the throne." But the judges of the seventeenth century resisted royal efforts to make their decisions serve royal purposes. The Act of Settlement, 1701, put the judiciary beyond fear of government pressure. Accordingly, English judges, though appointed by the government, came to hold office for life or until retirement, in the same way as do American federal judges.[4]

In addition to safeguarding the independence of their judiciary, the English put a high premium on specialized legal knowledge and experience. All English judges are drawn from the legal profession, so that, unlike the Continental system in which judges and lawyers belong to two separate, though similar, professions, English judges have a long background as practicing members of the Bar. Americans, too, draw their judges mainly from the legal profession; but in England there is a further restriction on the selection of judges unknown in the United States: English judges must come from that part of the legal profession whose members are known as barristers.

The Legal Profession

The distinctive feature of the English legal profession is that it is divided into two separate groups: solicitors and barristers. Insofar as this division finds a parallel in the United States, it is in the distinction between the office lawyer who prepares cases and the court lawyer who argues them. But in England the distinction is so great that solicitors and barristers receive their credentials from their own separate societies and cannot perform each other's functions.

The *solicitor,* the office lawyer who is consulted by a client, does not necessarily have any university training and becomes a member of the Law Society as the result of passing a series of special examinations. Although he may plead cases in the local civil and criminal courts, he may only prepare cases for the High Court.

To the *barrister* is reserved the right of "audience," or pleading cases in the higher courts, as well as the monopoly of judicial appointments. A barrister [5] is a member of one of the four Inns of Court, which are historic, self-governing voluntary organizations that combine the functions of a law school and a professional association and acting together form the Bar. The Inns of

---

[4] Most American states, in contrast to the British system of appointment, select the judges for the state judiciaries through direct election or election by the legislature. One argument in support of election is that the practice of judicial review gives the judges a political function, and that

therefore they should be kept responsive to public opinion. It is generally acknowledged, however, that the caliber of elected judges is less high than that of appointed judges.

[5] There are two ranks of barristers: "juniors" and Queen's (or King's) Counsellors. The latter, who are appointed by the Crown from among distinguished barristers, cannot appear in a case without a junior and are limited by rules to certain types of work, chiefly pleading in open court; but they are well recompensed by receiving fees double those of the ordinary barrister.

Court provide a corporate life for their members in historic buildings containing chapels, libraries, dining halls, and rooms for work and study. They train those who wish to enter the profession, test them through examinations, and decide whether they shall be admitted to the Bar. A barrister remains under the jurisdiction of his particular inn throughout his professional career and must maintain the professional standards of the Bar at all times on penalty of being disbarred.

The Qualities of the Judiciary

Drawing the English judiciary solely from among barristers has had certain consequences. For one, it has meant that English judges combine great ability and experience in interpreting the law with high standards of personal integrity. No suspicion of corruption touches even the lower levels of the judiciary, and much of the innate respect for the law in England comes from the distinguished service of generations of judges.

At the same time, judges have traditionally been drawn from the wealthy and privileged classes of society; as a result, the judicial system in England is occasionally stigmatized as a class system. Young barristers, since they depend on the work that solicitors give them, often have difficulty in earning enough to support themselves in their early years of practice. Thus, few enter the profession unless they have some outside support. But once they start earning, successful barristers receive some of the largest incomes in England. Thus the barrister is likely to belong to a well-to-do family and to have acquired large personal means and social prestige before he is invited to become a judge.

Some socialists in England maintained that so long as English judges were drawn from the ruling class, labor must expect to find that the courts, far from protecting their liberties, were actually conniving against them. But it is noteworthy that such accusations have faded away. There seem to be as many young Labor as Conservative barristers. Nor did the courts attempt to block any of Labor's measures. Experience tends to show that the class character of the English judiciary is far less marked now than it used to be and that the high standards of the judges ensure fair treatment for all groups in the community.

The Justices of the Peace

At one place in the English judicial system professional judges give way to "amateurs," the justices of the peace. The justices staff the local courts of criminal jurisdiction where all but 2 or 3 percent of criminal cases are settled. They are selected on the basis of personal qualities from among the local inhabitants of a district, receive a short course of training before starting their work, and serve without pay. The justices of the peace were originally (under an act of 1361) the King's agents in maintaining peace in the counties and were usually drawn from "the gentry." Their responsibilities are now limited to such minor criminal cases as cruelty to animals, stealing, and offenses by juveniles (that is, those under seventeen), but having J.P. after one's name still carries considerable prestige.

Throughout England and Wales there are now more than thirteen thousand male and three thousand female justices of the peace,[6] a striking contrast in numbers to the hundred judges who staff the country's higher courts. J.P.'s never act alone, except in granting minor appeals for bail. Because younger people can rarely afford to give so much time without pay, most of the justices of the peace are well over fifty. Following the recommendation of a Royal Commission in 1948, there is now an age limit of seventy-five (sixty-five on the juvenile court bench), which is gradually being reduced. It is sometimes charged that the privileged position of J.P.'s makes them unsympathetic to those whose offenses they judge and that they depend too much on the testimony of the local police. But the system has many advantages. The use of so many unpaid officials keeps the costs of criminal jurisdiction low. In the small cases with which they are mainly concerned, the local knowledge of the justices may enable them to

---

[6] As late as 1967, 2,250 of these justices had received this position by virtue of other offices but this practice is to end. In the County of London and a few large cities, there are stipendiary magistrates, some fifty in all, analogous to the police magistrates found in every American city. But there seems little demand to replace the justices of the peace by a wider use of paid magistrates, and there is even some criticism of having decisions made in a criminal case by a single person, as magistrates do.

impose particularly appropriate penalties or to temper justice with mercy. Perhaps the best feature of the system is that it strengthens the tradition that justice belongs to the people and is their responsibility.

The Jury

Another use of amateurs in the judicial process is in the jury. Traditionally, one of the most important rights of an Englishman or an American is trial by his peers. Taken together with the writ of habeas corpus, under which a person accused of a crime must be brought to trial or released within a limited period of time, the right to demand jury trial has long been looked on in Anglo-Saxon countries as a basic safeguard of individual liberty.

Jury trial has become far less common, however, than it was in the past. This is particularly the case in England, though it is also happening in the United States. The grand jury, still used in the United States to determine whether the prosecution has enough evidence to proceed with a trial, was abolished in England in 1933. The petty, or ordinary, jury of "twelve good men and true" is still used invariably in both countries in trying the most serious criminal offenses, such as rape, kidnaping, and murder. The jury makes the vital decision whether the defendant is guilty or innocent, although the judge, of course, decides the actual sentence. But jury trial is rare in English civil cases, much less common than in American courts. Still more surprising is the relatively small use by the English of juries in those criminal cases where the defendant is offered a choice between trial by a jury and a judge or by justices of the peace alone. Barely 10 percent of those who could have jury trial do so.

Part of the reason for not using juries in civil cases is that the litigants must pay the jury's fees. Defendants may decide against jury trial in lesser criminal cases because jury service, in practice, is mainly restricted to the well-to-do, who cannot be expected to have great insight into the problems of the poor. The most important reasons for the decline in the use of juries, however, seem to be the desire for speedy trials and the belief that—apart from cases involving public morality, such as libel or desertion of family

—the jury does not perform any service that the judge or justices cannot do as well alone. In consequence, judges and justices of the peace in England carry an increasingly large share of the administration of justice.

The Judicial Administrative System

English judges have a very large degree of independence in running the courts and are far from being subject to the control of a central administrative department such as the Ministry of Justice in France. The English system is highly efficient, however, since two important political figures, the Lord Chancellor and the Secretary of State for Home Affairs, have considerable authority in ensuring a smoothly working judicial system through their power to make appointments, draft rules, direct cases from one court to another, and maintain general supervision of all court business. The more important of these two from the point of view of the courts is the Lord Chancellor, who is always chosen from among distinguished senior barristers—a reflection of the strong feeling in Great Britain that the courts should be directed by legal experts. He is appointed by the Prime Minister and is a member of the Cabinet from the House of Lords. The Attorney-General and his chief assistant, the Solicitor-General, who give legal advice to ministries and represent the Crown in cases in which its interests are concerned, are members of the House of Commons.

No one person in the United States combines so many judicial offices and functions as does the Lord Chancellor. He presides over the House of Lords. He appoints all the justices of the peace, county court justices, and judges to the central courts, except for two—the Lord Chief Justice and the Master of the Rolls—who are appointed by the Prime Minister. He maintains general supervision of the whole court system and helps to keep the court structure efficient, up-to-date, and abreast of its work.

Most judges have life tenure (county court judges retire at seventy-two or may be dismissed, but this is very rare), and they usually remain in the same post to which they were originally appointed. Most administrative officials hold office under civil service rulings. Most court rules are traditional. Thus to a great extent the court system can be said to be basically self-operative.

There is no real parallel in England to the American offices of federal and state district attorney. The Director of Public Prosecutions may direct the prosecution in serious murder cases or offenses against the coinage or election laws, and he can always act in any case where it is felt that the public interest might not be upheld adequately without his intervention. His importance is chiefly as an example, however, for he enters an infinitesimal number of cases compared to those instituted by individuals.

It is hardly conceivable that it would be possible to carry out the vast law enforcement task of the federal and state governments in the United States with so small a percentage of public prosecutions as take place in England. The reason the system works in the latter country is that it is possible to depend so largely for prosecutions on the active initiative and sense of responsibility of private persons. Moreover, the number of serious crimes in England is still relatively less than in the United States.

3. THE COURTS

The central institutions of the judicial system are the courts. Courts can decide only those cases that are brought before them either by a private individual or a public officer. No matter how unjust a situation may be, the courts have no means of interfering unless a specific complaint is filed. But the character and accessibility of the courts have a good deal to do with the frequency with which they are used. If justice is to be easily available to all people, there must be local courts as well as national, their procedures must not be too technical, and the cost must be within the reach of persons of average means.

A century ago the English court system was a bewildering collection of separate courts. The royal central courts had been superimposed on the local courts. Different sets of courts administered common law and equity, and there was a constant struggle among and within the systems to acquire cases and thus the fees that litigants paid. Conflicts of jurisdiction were frequent, and the litigant who made a mistake about the court in which to start his case might find himself forced to begin all over again in another court after a long and expensive process in the first one. In addition, there was little uniformity of procedure. The complexity of court organization defeated the purpose of making justice easily available.

A determined effort to tackle this problem and bring uniformity into the court structure was made through the Judicature Acts between 1873 and 1876. The distinction between common law and equity courts was swept away, and all courts received the right, where necessary, to use both kinds of law. The central courts were combined technically into the High Court of Justice and the Supreme Court of Judicature, which, although they are only symbols of unity and not courts that ever meet, serve the purpose of preventing conflicts of jurisdiction among the separate central courts of which they are composed. As the chart on page 180 makes clear, each of the three divisions of the High Court of Justice specializes in a particular subject matter, but the fiction of maintaining that they are part of the High Court of Justice simplifies the transfer of cases from one to another if necessary.

At the same time, the respective jurisdictions of the central and local courts were clarified, although some overlapping of jurisdiction still remains. Although the English court system is not a simple hierarchy of courts forming a complete system within which there is no duplication of work, the degree of unification is sufficiently complete for many American observers to view it with envy.[7]

Differences Between Civil and Criminal Cases

The basic division in the modern English judicial system is into civil and criminal courts, each of which handles only the cases in its particular jurisdiction. Civil law, as we have

[7] There are, of course, fifty-two hierarchies of courts in the United States, since each state and the District of Columbia has one, and there is also the federal structure. The federal courts are well unified, much better than most state court systems. In general, there is little overlapping between the two systems, since the federal courts handle cases involving federal laws, and the state courts those involving state laws. If the litigants are from two different states, however, they have the choice of bringing the case before a state court or a federal court, the latter being permitted on ground of "diversity of citizenship."

COURT SYSTEM OF ENGLAND AND WALES

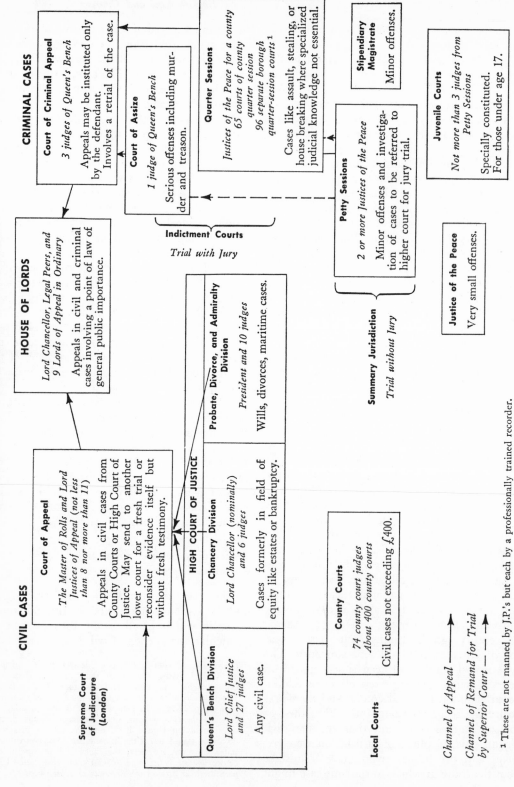

CRIMINAL CASES

Court of Criminal Appeal
3 judges of Queen's Bench
Appeals may be instituted only by the defendant. Involves a retrial of the case.

Court of Assize
1 judge of Queen's Bench
Serious offenses including murder and treason.

Quarter Sessions
Justices of the Peace for a county
65 courts of county quarter session
96 separate borough quarter-session courts [1]
Cases like assault, stealing, or house breaking where specialized judicial knowledge not essential.

Stipendiary Magistrate
Minor offenses.

Juvenile Courts
Not more than 3 judges from Petty Sessions
Specially constituted. For those under age 17.

Petty Sessions
2 or more Justices of the Peace
Minor offenses and investigation of cases to be referred to higher court for jury trial.

Justice of the Peace
Very small offenses.

Indictment Courts
Trial with Jury

Summary Jurisdiction
Trial without Jury

HOUSE OF LORDS
Lord Chancellor, Legal Peers, and 9 Lords of Appeal in Ordinary
Appeals in civil and criminal cases involving a point of law of general public importance.

CIVIL CASES

Supreme Court of Judicature (London)

Court of Appeal
The Master of Rolls and Lord Justices of Appeal (not less than 8 nor more than 11)
Appeals in civil cases from County Courts or High Court of Justice. May send to another lower court for a fresh trial or reconsider evidence itself but without fresh testimony.

HIGH COURT OF JUSTICE

Probate, Divorce, and Admiralty Division
President and 10 judges
Wills, divorces, maritime cases.

Chancery Division
Lord Chancellor (nominally) and 6 judges
Cases formerly in field of equity like estates or bankruptcy.

Queen's Bench Division
Lord Chief Justice and 27 judges
Any civil case.

Local Courts

County Courts
74 county court judges
About 400 county courts
Civil cases not exceeding £400.

Channel of Appeal ———→
Channel of Remand for Trial by Superior Court ——→

[1] These are not manned by J.P.'s but each by a professionally trained recorder.

seen, is concerned with the relations between individuals when no element of public security is involved. Disputes over contracts, boundaries, wills, the payment of debts, or suits for divorce are all typical subjects for civil courts. The person seeking redress institutes an *action* to right whatever wrong has been committed and often, in addition, to force the payment of a fine to the injured person.

Civil cases are expensive, especially for the loser. Since they are for the benefit of individuals, the government takes no responsibility for paying their cost, apart from the salary of the judge and the basic maintenance of the court. To meet the additional expenses of running the courts, litigants pay fees that are often quite high. Frequently these costs are added to the damages imposed, thereby making unsuccessful litigation an extremely costly process.

There are a number of ways in which criminal cases differ from civil cases. Since criminal cases involve acts that affect public order, they begin through *prosecutions,* instituted either by private persons or the police, but in either case in the name of the Queen.

Further, because criminal jurisdiction is concerned with acts that affect society as a whole, the costs of a criminal trial are borne by the public, and any fines imposed go into the public treasury. In such cases as assault, damages may also be awarded to an injured person; those damages are, however, usually collected through a civil suit conducted parallel to the criminal prosecution.

In both civil and criminal cases it is possible to appeal from the judgment of a lower court if permission is granted by the higher court. Only in exceptional cases, however, are appeals permitted on the ground that the facts elucidated by the lower court are in question—a rather common practice in the United States. In England, appeals are generally restricted to cases where the interpretation of law by the lower court is challenged.

The Structure of the Courts

The separation between the civil and the criminal courts is most rigidly maintained at the local level, where there are not only two entirely different sets of courts—the county courts, which deal only with civil cases, and the courts of the justices of the peace, which deal with criminal cases—but also no interchange of personnel between these two sets of courts.[8] The central courts are also clearly separated between those that handle civil and those that handle criminal cases, but the judges for the criminal courts at this level are drawn from the Queen's Bench[9] Division of the High Court of Justice, which is for civil cases. The only place where the hierarchies of civil and criminal courts officially merge is at the very apex, where the House of Lords provides the final source of appeal for both.

The House of Lords

Odd as it may seem, the highest court of appeal in England is the House of Lords. This court is a classic example of the continuity of English institutions: the historic right of the House of Lords to hear appeals dates back to the days of the *Magnum Concilium* of Norman times. But no less is this a classic example of the ability of the English to alter practice while retaining form: for more than a century it has not been the House of Lords as a whole that acts as a court but a very select group of its members, a group, in fact, that is elevated to the peerage for the sole purpose of performing this judicial function. In 1876, provision was made for the appointment of seven (now nine) Lords of Appeal in Ordinary (commonly known as Law Lords) who are paid professional judges with life peerages. Together with the Lord Chancellor and those peers who hold or have

---

8 This practice of having separate courts for civil and criminal cases finds no parallel in the United States. American county courts, for example, have extensive criminal as well as civil jurisdiction and are found in almost every one of the 3,050 counties into which the United States is divided. Many American states have a maze of local courts, in none of which is there so clear a separation of function as between the English county courts and courts of the justices of the peace.

9 The Queen's or King's Bench is a direct descendant of the old *Curia Regis* of Norman days, through which the King personally dispensed justice. Theoretically, the Queen's Bench still sits under the presidency of the Queen while it is in London and travels with her into the counties, though in practice the Lord Chief Justice represents the Queen in London and a Lord Justice represents her in the assizes in the counties. Its historical background explains why judges of the Queen's Bench undertake so many functions, including both original and appellate jurisdiction, and civil and criminal jurisdiction.

held high judicial office (such as former Lord Chancellors), they form the actual court of appeal. Thus, as other peers are excluded from participation, the appellate jurisdiction of the House of Lords in practice is that of a small group of highly trained legal experts. In a dramatic decision in July 1966, these judges declared they would not be bound by precedent if it hampered them in taking contemporary conditions into account in making a judgment.

The existence of this second appeal court is an expensive anomaly and its value has been challenged, particularly by the present Lord Chancellor, Lord Gardiner. At least it is used sparingly. Its chief function is to elucidate particularly difficult points of law, and it rarely hears more than fifty cases a year, of which very few are criminal cases. The House of Lords is the highest court not only for England and Wales but for Scotland and Northern Ireland as well; in this way it performs a distinctive function by providing a certain unification for the three judicial systems.

The Judicial Committee of the Privy Council

There is one other appeal body, the Judicial Committee of the Privy Council, which, strictly speaking, does not belong in the English judicial hierarchy, because it reviews cases appealed from courts in various parts of the British Commonwealth and empire outside Great Britain itself. Technically the Judicial Committee is not a court that renders decisions but a body that gives advice to the Queen on cases referred to it; in practice, however, the distinction is unimportant. Though the jurisdiction of the Judicial Committee of the Privy Council is very different from that of the House of Lords, its personnel is almost identical because, at the time when the Law Lords were created as salaried life peers, it was decided that they could carry the bulk of work in both bodies. Moreover, whoever else participates in the judicial work of the House of Lords is almost always a privy councilor and thus entitled to be a member of the Judicial Committee of the Privy Council. The main difference in the membership of the two bodies is due to the practice of adding, on occasion, one or more judges from the Commonwealth overseas to the Judicial Committee,

particularly when a case affecting a particular area is under consideration. Any independent Commonwealth country may eliminate or restrict the right of appeal to the Judicial Committee of the Privy Council, and most of them, except New Zealand, have done so. It still serves, however, as the final source of appeal for British territories that have not acquired full rights of self-government.

How Satisfactory Is the English Court System?

The court system in England and Wales is well organized to handle different types of cases according to their degree of severity and to permit appeals so that there can be a check on the judgment and reasoning of the judges in lower courts. The independence of the judiciary and the courts ensures freedom from political influence. But there are other questions that must be raised in determining whether or not English courts are adequate to their responsibilities. What is the atmosphere of the courts? Do the courts provide an opportunity for all aspects of a situation to be explored? Do they give private persons adequate protection in criminal cases when the resources of the government are behind the prosecution? Do the courts provide speedy, effective means of settling disputes? Is justice, in practice, open to all on equal terms?

The Atmosphere of the Courts

Visitors to English courts are impressed by the solemnity of the proceedings. Even lower courts have a dignity and formality which in the United States is almost wholly confined to the higher courts. Arrayed in wig and gown, the judge or judges sit above and apart from the rest of the court. The lawyers, also gowned, present the circumstances of the case and reply to each other's arguments in a restrained way that contrasts with the vehemence so often displayed by American lawyers. Witnesses are brought forward and questioned as to the facts, but there is no "bullying." The defendant and plaintiff may present their views. The judge listens attentively, giving the impression that every fact is important in making his final decision. Spectators are not permitted to make a noise or to indicate their sympathies. The atmosphere is that of a learned debate. There may be drama in a great lawyer's brilliant presentation of a case or in the manner in which he draws the facts from an unwilling witness. But the appeal is not to the spectators in the courtroom: it is to the judge, or jury and judge, who will make the decision. The presentation may be eloquent but to be effective it must be logical and based on a wide knowledge of legal practices.

Is All the Evidence Brought Out

The distinctive feature of a trial in an English or an American court, as compared with a trial in a Continental court, is that in the Anglo-Saxon system the judge looks on himself as an umpire before whom a case is argued, not as an investigator seeking to determine guilt or innocence. The English or American judge makes little effort to speed the proceedings. He leaves the major responsibility for bringing out the facts to the interested parties. During the trial the judge does not assume an active role in cross-questioning, as does a Continental judge, though English judges are apt to play a more decisive part in bringing out relevant facts than are American judges. In any event, the English judge makes sure that irrelevant material is excluded from consideration and that full opportunity is given to all sides to present their case. It is left to the parties, at least in a civil case, to make use of their chance.

Is Adequate Protection Afforded the Defendant?

The notion that a trial is a contest in which both sides should have an equal chance is maintained also in criminal cases, though here the prosecution, with the resources of the government behind it, has an obvious advantage. Much is done, therefore, to afford protection to the defendant. A person accused by the police of a breach of law must be immediately warned that anything he says may be used against him. Furthermore, in the trial, witnesses may not be asked leading questions (for example, not "Did you see a revolver in his hand?" but "Did you see anything in his hand?" and "What was it?"). Nor may evidence be introduced of previous misdoing calculated to prejudice opinion against the defendant.

Other safeguards guarantee that there can be no arrest without a warrant; crimes must be known to the law, that is, there can be no prosecution for an act that had not been declared to be a crime at the time it was committed; ignorance of fact is a complete defense—for example, in a case for bigamy, ignorance of the fact of a previous marriage. By these means the individual is given protection from arbitrary state action.

The Anglo-American system goes very far in giving defendants the benefit of every doubt. Yet the fact that serious crime rates are not high in England and Wales except in limited, overcrowded areas indicates that the standards of the community have not suffered because of this practice. That serious crime is proportionately higher in the United States than in England seems to result from inadequate enforcement of the law rather than from court procedures that protect defendants. As far as court action is concerned, the Anglo-American system seems capable of upholding community standards and at the same time affording the accused elaborate protection designed to give him the maximum chance to defend himself.

Do the Courts Provide Speedy Remedies?

Besides providing for careful consideration of cases and for elaborate protection of the rights of individuals, the English court system is also fairly successful in providing speedy, effective means of settling disputes—contrary to the situation in the United States, where many courts are years behind in their cases.

In English courts the rules of procedure are simple, straightforward, and effective. In the United States the rules are generally the result of legislative activity and are frequently unsuitable for their avowed purpose of aiding the execution of justice. English rules governing the giving of evidence, pleading, and so forth were originally developed by individual courts, but since 1873 they have been drafted by the Rules Committee under the Lord Chancellor. The work of this committee has been so satisfactory that there has never been a parliamentary veto of its proposals. As a result English legal procedures are marked by a minimum of technicalities. Only rarely are decisions reversed in England on a question of procedure, in contrast to the frequency with which this happens in the United States.

One difficulty in the way of speedy handling of cases, however, is the general lack of decentralization in the English court system: appeals must be heard in the central courts in London, and this makes for inconvenience and expense.

Are the Courts Open to All on Equal Terms?

Technically, of course, the courts are open to all on equal terms. Equality before the law and equality in having recourse to the courts are cherished rights of Englishmen. But in practice it is like saying that everyone has a right to buy a Cadillac. Court and lawyers' fees are so high in England (as well as in the United States) that people of moderate means cannot view the prospect of civil litigation without concern. Moreover, though there are no court fees to pay in criminal cases, legal aid is as expensive in this field as in civil cases.

The most substantial attempt in English legal history to meet the charge that the court system unduly handicaps the poorer litigants was made by the Legal Aid Act of 1949. Although since 1926 there had been an enlarged program of free legal aid for people who were entirely without means, the system had suffered from various defects, such as lack of publicity, no provision of aid in the county courts, and lack of relevance to the problems confronting those of moderate income. The Legal Aid Act of 1949 covers representation in all the regular courts and, in effect, provides that the very poor pay nothing for legal aid and that those of moderate income pay what they can afford. The Law Society and Bar Council administer the system of legal aid; the local assistance board investigates the question of means (a fact that restrains many people from applying for aid); and the Treasury finances the plan. Certain types of action, notably those that are open to abuse such as suits for libel or breach of promise, are not covered by the act.

Some people feel that even the provisions of the 1949 act do not sufficiently meet the criticism that the English court system unduly favors the wealthy. They advocate a national legal service, comparable to the National Health Service, under which lawyers would be organized for the service of the community. Others believe that the expenditures on trials should be compulsorily limited, as are the expenditures on parliamentary campaigns. Yet it is well to remember that very low-cost justice might be exploited by those who have nothing to lose by pressing dishonest charges. The method taken by the Legal Aid Act for making justice more accessible to all may well be the safest means of approach to a perennial problem.

Whatever changes may be undertaken to make English justice more easily available to the mass of the people, there is a universal desire to maintain the independence of the judges and the freedom of the courts from political control. The average Englishman believes these features essential for the individual rights he so dearly cherishes.

4. JUDICIAL CONTROL OF GOVERNMENT OFFICIALS

To judge the acts of government officials by the same rules of law and by the same courts as the acts of ordinary citizens has long been considered a major safeguard of liberty in Anglo-Saxon countries. One of the characteristic features of the "rule of law," declared Professor A. V. Dicey, a great nineteenth-century commentator on the British constitution, is that "every man, whatever be his rank or condition, is subject to the ordinary law of the realm and amenable to the jurisdiction of the ordinary tribunals"; and he drove this point home by declaring that "every official, from the Prime Minister down to a constable or a collector of taxes, is under the same responsibility for every act done without legal justification as any other citizen." Thus an official is no more above the law than anyone else and is equally responsible for justifying his actions in regular court proceedings.

Great Britain and the United States both continue to uphold the general rule expressed by Dicey and, in consequence, do not follow the Continental practice of having a separate system of administrative law to cover the relations between government officials and private individuals and a separate system of administrative courts for such cases. Nevertheless, there have been certain modifications of the rigid interpretation of the view expressed by Dicey. Thus in both the United States and Great Britain today there are a number of administrative tribunals that deal with certain types of complaints against official actions. Moreover, in the interest both of forceful governmental action and of effective recompense to individuals injured by the action of state officials, there have also been gradual modifications of the rule that government officials are personally liable for acts committed without legal authority.

Personal Liability of Government Officials

Part of the reason for this latter development lies in the danger that an official may not perform his duty according to his best judgment for fear of a personal suit for damages as the result of a decision taken in an official capacity. Or it could happen that the citizen who had been injured might well find himself unable to collect adequate recompense from the official personally.

Take, for example, the case of a sanitary inspector who believes he detects foot-and-mouth disease in a cow at the stockyards. He orders the animal to be killed at once. Subsequently it is found that the animal was not suffering from the disease. The owner attempts to get redress through the courts. If the judge agrees that the action of the inspector did not fall under the authority of the law, the inspector becomes personally liable for damages. On the other hand, if the judge finds the inspector justified in his action because the law provides him with a wide range of discretion, the owner of the cow is left without redress, so long as the state refuses to assume responsibility.

To meet such problems, both the courts and the government have gradually modified their stands. English and American courts usually uphold a government official in a private damage suit as long as there is no proof of negligence. In addition, both the British and American governments have made it easier to enter suit against the government itself in many types of cases.

It is still true that when the government is providing its basic services, such as maintenance of order, conduct of foreign affairs, and operations of the army and navy, it is not subject to suit. (Thus a bystander injured by a policeman in pursuit of a murderer may not be able to get damages.) But since the Crown Proceedings Act of 1947 it has been relatively easy to get redress for injuries suffered by individuals in the course of the non-law-enforcing operations of government.

The Crown Procceedings Act enables ordinary citizens for the first time to bring suit against the government in the same courts (for example, the county court) and in the same way "as if the Crown were a fellow citizen." Thus in the case of the sanitary inspector mentioned above, the owner of the cow could now collect damages from the state, while the inspector himself would be free from responsibility as long as there was no negligence involved. Moreover, the act makes government departments responsible not only for statutory duties but also for the common law duties imposed on ordinary employers, owners, and so forth.

At a time when the state is acquiring such extended functions of regulation, control, and operation of services, little could be more important than to establish the right of individuals freely to sue government agencies in case of injuries. In the words of an Attorney-General, this act ensures that "the rights of the little man are just as mighty, and are entitled to just the same protection, as the rights of the mighty state." What it recognizes, in fact, is that the cherished principle of equality before the law requires new procedures to protect the citizen in his relations with the modern administrative state.

The Parliamentary Commissioner for Administration

Still a futher means of safeguarding the interests of the citizen in relation to administrative actions is provided in a number of countries—Sweden, Norway, Finland, Denmark, and New Zealand—by an official known in Scandinavia as the Ombudsman, who undertakes his own investigations of complaints by private persons and reports to the legislature. To perform the same functions within the distinctive framework of the British government, Labor established in 1966 a Parliamentary Commissioner for Administration, an independent officer with security from dismissal except by parliamentary motion. To make sure that the Commissioner does not undercut or replace existing channels, any complaint of personal injustice has to be referred to the Commissioner through a member of Parliament and not directly. Thus Parliament has secured one more instrument, besides the question period, letters to ministers, adjournment debates, and debates on supply, through which to protect the individual from deliberate or accidental violation of his rights through governmental action.

Administrative Tribunals

Most of the supporters of the Anglo-American system oppose setting up a separate system of administrative courts for dealing with official acts. Yet increasingly it has been found useful, both in the United States and Great Britain, to set up what are called administrative tribunals. These tribunals share the characteristic features of courts of law: independence of the executive, the application of known rules, a certain formality in procedure, and binding decisions not subject to ministerial review or rejection. They are administrative only in that they are composed of administrators, not judges, and that they handle cases and questions arising out of administrative regulations.

In both countries there have long been commissions to consider railway rates and tax and patent appeals. Great Britain has special tribunals, both regular and *ad hoc* (that is, set up for a particular case), to which employers and employees may by agreement refer industrial disputes. Moreover, several British ministries have special bodies to deal with appeals on their handling of their particular responsibilities, among the most valuable of which are the local appeals tribunals on social insurance legislation and benefits, which are representative of the public, employers, and employees, and which provide a much needed human touch in a complex system.

There are several justifications for this development. In the first place, procedure in these administrative tribunals is direct, speedy, cheap, and easy for a layman to understand. Workmen's compensation cases, for example, used to be referred in England to the county courts where the procedure was time-consuming, tedious, and costly; now they are handled by an administrative tribunal that can adjust its procedure to the particular case, is not bound by rigid precedents, and yet strives to provide uniform rulings. In fact, just because there is a single central tribunal, there is more apt to be consistency of treatment and coordination of results. Further, administrative tribunals are staffed by experts who deal with subjects, for example, patents, that require technical knowledge. Administrative tribunals can be particularly useful in setting up new standards in a previously unexplored field, for example, town and country planning, which challenges private property rights, traditionally protected by the common law.

It is hardly surprising that the administrative justice provided by these tribunals has come under attack. Lord Hewart, who assailed delegated legislation in his book, *The New Despotism,* also had words to say against administrative tribunals. But the Committee on Ministers' Powers upheld administrative justice as inevitable in the modern state and highly useful so long as it is exercised within reasonable bounds. To aid in so doing, the Tribunals and Inquiries Act of 1958, which followed the report of the Franks Committee on administrative tribunals and procedures, set up a ten- to fifteen-man council, whose members, appointed by the Lord Chancellor and representing agriculture, trade unions, social services, industry, the legal profession, and public administration, review the working of tribunals in England, Scotland, and Wales and give Parliament an annual report.

In any case, administrative tribunals come under the control of the law courts through *review* and sometimes through *appeal.* Appeal is possible on a point of law from the majority of tribunals, a principle implemented by the 1958 Tribunals and Inquiries Act. There is also a general right of review by higher courts over the decisions of all lower courts, including administrative tribunals. Although administrative tribunals, because of their expert knowledge, are likely to be the best judges of the facts of a case, for example, the safety devices in a factory in a workmen's compensation case, it is a safeguard of individual liberty that the regular courts have the final decision on whether authorities are acting within their powers as laid down by statute and are strictly following prescribed procedures.

It would be a mistake to assume that the courts provide the only restraint on the public administration. Parliament and the Cabinet undertake general and sometimes very detailed supervision of the administration; government offices themselves, in particular the Treasury, keep constant check on administrative activities; and the press is constantly alert to publicize injustices to individuals. But the final protection of individuals, whether from arbitrary arrest or the negligence of officials or any other misuse of authority, lies with the courts. Only they can perform this service. For this reason it is not too much to say that independent and impartial courts are a decisive factor in maintaining a balance between the power and the responsibility of government.

8. Great Britain: A New Society?

The British have long practiced political democracy; they are now in the process of developing social and economic democracy. The effects of this newer trend on the character and working of government are likely to be no less than the effects of the earlier breaking down of political privilege. Social and economic developments not only increase the functions of government (as has been true in Great Britain for more than a century) but give government purpose and direction. Thus the British people as a whole are today facing two interrelated but very different demands: to provide more equality of opportunity and treatment; but also to accelerate economic growth both to support these ambitious programs and to maintain Great Britain's world position.

Modern Social Responsibilities

In the past, individual distress, whether caused by unemployment, sickness, or old age, was looked upon as a personal, not a social, problem. Private aid, often a matter of religious charity, met most of the needs of the poor. When it did not, the task was left to local communities. However, workhouses and poor farms were purposely kept as uncomfortable as possible to discourage people from resorting to them. Poverty was looked on as a disgrace resulting from sheer lack of initiative and unwillingness to work; hence public aid to the poor was both meager and grudgingly given.

More recently, men have placed the blame for poverty and mass unemployment upon the economic system rather than upon individuals themselves. They have seen that in a society dependent on mass production, the impact of

fluctuating demand and technological change is often felt far outside the particular industry involved. Moreover, the fact that the results of unemployment are far more disastrous in modern urban society than in older agricultural ones, where the land could help to provide a living, has brought a heightened sense of public responsibility.

Protection of the Weak

This new conception of state responsibility has been reflected in the belief that the weaker members of society must be protected from the worst effects of economic pressures and that village solidarity must be replaced by social solidarity—that is, by the support of the *whole* community. Between 1906 and 1911, almost thirty years before similar American action (though not as early as in Germany), the British government made spectacular advances in public welfare by instituting a "New Deal" which introduced national health and unemployment insurance for some groups, noncontributory old-age pensions, a national system of employment exchanges, and free meals for needy school children.

After World War I, maternity and child welfare services were extended, more adequate help was given to the blind, and unemployment insurance was broadened to cover about two-thirds of the wage-earning population. Since during the depression vast numbers of workers exhausted their unemployment benefits and others were ineligible for them, it became necessary in 1934 to establish an unemployment assistance service. In the interwar period, housing programs and slum clearance (made necessary by the enormous number of ancient slums and outworn buildings dating back to the beginning of the nineteenth century) vied with unemployment for first place in the attention of social welfare departments.

But despite the very real achievements of the welfare program (which included the rehousing of one-third of the British population between 1918 and 1939), the effects of the depression and of long periods of unemployment, particularly in depressed industries like coal mining, remained vivid in people's minds. During the Battle of Britain in World War II, the sacrifices made by all classes threw ordinary social and economic inequalities into sharp relief. Even a Conservative party report declared in 1941 that "the nation is less satisfied with its immediate past than it has ever been in its entire history."

National Minimum Standards

Under the spur of dissatisfaction with the past and with years of recurring depression, a new concept of public welfare began to appear. The older view—that public welfare should be primarily protective in character and limited to groups least able to take care of themselves—gave way to a newer view: welfare measures should not only be a support in time of need but should also provide positive means of improving the condition of the whole society. Where supporters of the older view feared a weakening of personal initiative if the state provided a basic minimum standard of living for everyone, and were even more concerned lest an extension of state responsibilities in welfare fields would place a crippling burden on the economy, the advocates of the new conception of welfare maintained that national minimum standards would not only leave room for initiative but would encourage it by restoring hope and health to the former underprivileged. The latter also believed that the increase of income in the lower brackets through a nation-wide social security program would help to maintain the demand for goods and thereby prevent unemployment.

The Beveridge Report

The extent of popular support for governmental action to produce economic security, health, knowledge, and general well-being became obvious with the instant acclaim of the Beveridge Report. It was the essence of the argument of Sir William Beveridge, the noted British economist, that five "giants"—*want, ignorance, idleness, squalor,* and *disease*—were preventing the attainment of the goal of "freedom with security." Although *want* was the "giant" with which Beveridge's report on *Social Insurance and Allied Services* was particularly concerned, he warned that all five had to be attacked simultaneously in order to defeat any one of them. Thus the battle required not only nation-wide social security but a public attack on unemployment, undernourishment of children, and menaces to health; and it involved governmental responsibilities for better housing, more town planning, and broader opportunities for education. Since December 1942 (when the Beveridge Report immediately became a best seller) measures for education, national insurance, health services, housing, and town and country planning have instituted striking changes in all these fields. Although the most far-reaching of these measures have been introduced by Labor governments, they have been in part the result of joint planning and in general, except for certain details, have commanded the support of every party and substantial group in the community. Thus though they are effecting a minor revolution in distribution of income and equalization of opportunities, they constitute a typically British revolution-by-consent.

1. EDUCATION

Basic to change in any society is the educational system, particularly in a country that seeks both technological advance and greater social equality.

Though the educational system did not create the class distinctions in England, it has been a powerful element in perpetuating them. Prior to the Education Act of 1944[1] fees were imposed for attendance at the secondary schools, which provided the only route to college and thus to a profession. Unless the children's par-

---

[1] Education in Scotland has always been more equalitarian than in England; thus a greater number of changes have taken place in the English educational system.

ents could pay these fees or the children could win scholarships, their education ended at the elementary level—at the age of fourteen—with no chance for them to enter the schools that would prepare them for college. Under this system, children of the poorer classes were not equipped even for most simple white-collar jobs. The educational system thus tended not only to perpetuate the class structure but also to stratify the opportunities for jobs.

Moreover, educational opportunities were further limited by the predominant position of the private preparatory schools (comparable to the private elementary schools in the United States), which had a virtual monopoly over entry to the great public boarding schools such as Eton and Harrow (called "public" because they are not run for private profit, though they are entirely or mainly independent of state aid or control, and are, in fact, like the American private preparatory schools), to which students normally go at thirteen. Only 5 to 10 percent of the schoolboy population entered the preparatory schools and the great public boarding schools, but the great majority of this group went on to a university, particularly to the most ancient and distinguished of British universities, Oxford and Cambridge. Although Oxford and Cambridge accounted for about one-quarter of all the university students in England and Wales before the war, only a small percentage of their prewar undergraduates had attended the state elementary schools, although half of the students at other British universities were trained at such schools.

Moreover, in contrast to the United States only a relatively small proportion of British youth attended college. With a population three times as large, the United States had twenty times as many students in colleges and universities in 1939 as had Great Britain (one million as compared with fifty thousand). It is true that socially and intellectually the American college, at least in the first two years, is more akin to a British secondary school than to a British university and that vocational and professional training in Great Britain is handled in other types of institutions. Also, in proportion to the total population, the number of university students in Great Britain had doubled since 1900. Nonetheless, only the relatively small

minority of one in a thousand enjoyed higher education in prewar Britain.

New Programs

The new educational programs do not seek to change the highly individualized methods of English education but rather to open educational opportunities to all students on the basis of intellectual capacity rather than of ability to pay. For this purpose the old division between elementary and secondary schools has been replaced by a unified free system that extends throughout the period of compulsory education, from five to (since 1947) fifteen (to be raised to sixteen by 1970) and, for the 15 percent who are specially gifted, to college age. On the basis of testing at the age of eleven, pupils now go to grammar schools which stress cultural subjects, or to technical schools, or to secondary modern schools which stress all-around education though with some vocational emphasis.

Side by side with the state-supported or controlled school system stand the separate church schools and the private (or, as the English say, public) schools. Under the 1944 Education Act, the state registers all separate schools and can insist that they meet adequate standards of instruction and accommodation. Most church schools now receive government grants-in-aid toward their expenses (increased in 1966 to 80 percent), and in return they must take up to one-quarter of their students from those awarded scholarships by local education authorities. The public schools, of course, fall in another category. The education they provide is the finest in England; they are wholly self-supporting and despite increasing tuition fees continue to have long waiting lists of applicants.

The Labor party, however, is not satisfied with the present system. It strongly favors having all secondary education carried on within comprehensive schools (combining grammar, technical, and modern school sections), since it disapproves, not of different types of education according to aptitude, but of separating children into different schools. It is also committed to abolishing the decisive examinations at age eleven on the ground that this is too early to determine aptitudes and capacity, particularly for children from working-class homes.

Labor has long been concerned about the separateness and the class implications of the public school system. In February 1966 the government set up the Public Schools Commission to examine ways in which public schools could be integrated into the state school system. Moreover, the Secretary of State for Education, Mr. Crosland, has been explicit that the 176 elite quasi-independent but direct-grant secondary schools must cooperate with local authorities and fit themselves into a total educational scheme. While school building needs are still so great that all available educational resources remain heavily taxed and to this degree somewhat insulated against pressures for change, Labor's drive for educational integration at the secondary school level has far-reaching long-range implications, perhaps greater than any other part of its program.

University education has also been the subject of reports and plans. There has been a considerable increase in the number of universities —there were 30 in 1965, of which 7 had opened between 1961 and 1965. Soon there will be 45, as Scotland adds 3 and as more colleges of advanced technology achieve university status. By 1965 the number of university students had increased to 168,000 (the figure in the United States was 5.4 million, with a population nearly four times larger). Nonetheless the British remained dissatisfied on several counts: not enough students remain in school who might prove to be university material (only 30 percent are still in school at 16 in Great Britain, whereas in France it is 50 percent and in the United States 90 percent); too few teachers are being trained either to meet current needs (60,-000 more are needed to eliminate oversized classes) or to prepare for raising the school-leaving age to 16 (that would require 20,000 more); and not enough scientists and technologists are being produced. The Robbins Report of 1963, accepted in principle by the Conservatives, called for a 10 percent increase in universities and colleges of advanced technology and for an increase of places in higher education to 558,000 by 1980–81. While these figures have not been formally accepted, the pressure for additional staff and buildings grows.

In 1963, many English universities joined in a "clearing house" scheme to simplify university placement. Since 1964 prospective candidates have been applying through the University Central Council on Admissions instead of to individual universities, and their applications are automatically passed on to the next university of their choice if they fail in the first one. Oxford and Cambridge joined the scheme in 1967, and Edinburgh (but not other Scottish universities) is a member. Unlike current American enrollments, men outnumber women in British universities by three to one. Disturbing in the light of the British need for technological advance has been the failure to fill available science and engineering places (there were 1,500 vacancies in 1966) at the universities. The blame has not yet been apportioned but the need remains.

Great Britain has worked out an extremely satisfactory means of providing state aid to its universities without in any way imperiling their independence. All British universities are privately run but receive block five-year grants (paid in annual installments) through the University Grants Committee on the basis of universities' requirements and plans. These grants amount to about 70 percent of the income and 95 percent of the capital needs of the universities. They have been the largest factor in changing British universities over the past two generations from strongholds of the privileged classes to institutions widely open to talent. Although fees still remain high, three out of four university students are on scholarships, which are sufficiently generous to make part-time work unnecessary.

Formerly acting on behalf of the Treasury, the UGC now reports to the Secretary of State for Education and Science, who appoints its sixteen members. They are drawn mainly from university staffs but also represent local education authorities and the grammar schools. Apart from a full-time salaried chairman, who has commonly had a distinguished academic career, the members of the UGC are part-time and are not paid. Much of the work of this remarkable body is done through subcommittees with co-opted specialists, but final allocations are the responsibility of the UGC itself.

The broadening of educational opportunities

at every level is crucial to Labor's equalitarian philosophy. It is acceptable also to Conservatives, because of its stress on ability. What is new in the approach is the deliberate effort to educate the whole people (the task to which American education is dedicated) instead of an elite. But the British are concerned to maintain the emphasis on quality that has marked their oldest universities and the stress on character that has been the great contribution of the public schools. Thus they seek to promote individual development as well as to respond to social needs, and to encourage diversity of personality and originality in a social order conditioned by the collectivist age.

2. SOCIAL SERVICES

Education seeks to develop the individual in terms of his capacities and inclinations and to make him aware of the cultural heritage and dominant ideas of his society, to the end that he may play an effective role in the community. Social security endeavors to prevent this contribution from being wasted through poverty or ill health.

Assistance (or relief, as Americans would say) and insurance are the two major approaches to social security. Assistance rises from the old concept of relief and is directly related to need. Because it has the advantage of being individualized, it is excellent for emergencies; but according to the modern view, it should be the exceptional and supplementary rather than the normal way of relieving poverty.

The basic form of modern welfare service is insurance. Social insurance is a great national plan for sharing risks and handling the problem of maintenance of income. It has two great advantages over assistance: it is simpler to administer, and the benefits carry no taint of public charity. Insurance thus meets common needs through a general plan, but local authorities in Great Britain still have responsibilities under the National Assistance Act for giving aid in cases of "sudden and urgent need."

The objective of social security is to ensure a "national minimum standard." The investigations on which the Beveridge Report were based indicated that between three-quarters and

five-sixths of the urban poverty in Great Britain was due to interruption or loss of earning power because of unemployment or illness. Much of the remaining poverty resulted from the fact that many families had more children than they could support on meager wages. Hence the plan for social security places its greatest emphasis on family allowances, health insurance to provide medical care, and national insurance to establish a minimum standard of living when unemployment, old age, or death rob the family or individual of normal sources of livelihood.

Family Allowances

In earlier times children were considered an important source of income to the family, and today in some countries in Africa and in Asia their labor is of great usefulness in the care of animals or cultivation of the soil. But because Western industrial countries forbid child labor and enforce compulsory education, children have become a drain on family resources, one of the biggest single remaining causes of poverty. The provision for children's allowances seeks to rectify this situation. Such allowances also simplify the national insurance problem, since without them "adequacy of provision" under national insurance would vary according to the size of the family. Although no allowance is made for the first child, a mother receives a small weekly allowance for the second child and, since 1956, for each subsequent child.

National Insurance

Social security for everyone "from the cradle to the grave" (or, more jocularly, "from the womb to the tomb") is the purpose of the British national insurance plan, incorporated in the National Insurance Act of 1946, and the National Insurance (Industrial Injuries) Act of 1946, which, with the National Health Service, entered into force on July 5, 1948. The former measure followed the original Beveridge proposals closely and combined existing social services into one plan to which all other new services are related.

The major criticisms of measures that antedated the Beveridge plan were that they excluded too many groups, omitted certain basic needs, paid too low benefits, and covered too limited a time. It was also felt that excessive commercialism and waste accompanied the activities of "friendly societies" that collected insurance contributions for funeral and death benefits. Moreover, the variety of unrelated social measures made for confusion that often lowered the quality of service.

The plan established to meet these criticisms has instituted national insurance for everyone. Contributors buy and stick a single stamp on a card once a week. Contributions differ according to whether persons are employed under a contract of service, are self-employed, or do not want a job (known as nonemployed, in distinction to unemployed). Housewives and the self-employed or nonemployed may contribute or, if they earn very small amounts, may be freed of contributions, but they then lose benefit rights. If persons are unemployed or incapable of work, are drawing pensions, or are pursuing full-time education or unpaid apprenticeship, they are credited with contributions but need not pay them. Otherwise everyone in Great Britain between school-leaving (that is, fifteen) and retirement age pays a weekly contribution to the nation-wide plan, and the rest is provided by employers in relation to their number of employees, and by the government.

Insurance Benefits

Once a person has made a minimum number of payments, he is entitled to benefits when he needs them, graded according to the number of his dependents. Benefits are awarded regardless of the cause of need, whether sickness, unemployment, or retirement (for which women are eligible at sixty and men at sixty-five). There are only two exceptions to this rule: the self-employed cannot draw unemployment insurance, and persons injured through industrial accidents receive more. (This is done to encourage workmen to enter hazardous occupations such as mining.) Special benefits also provided under the national insurance plan include maternity grants, widows' pensions, guardians' allowances (for orphans), and death grants to cover the cost of funerals.

The greatest triumph for Labor in the national insurance plan was the complete abolition of the "means test," under which personal re-sources were investigated before benefits were given. It was also looked on as something of a triumph that there is provision for indefinite national assistance under local control if unemployment should extend beyond the initial hundred and eighty days that insurance covers. Other benefits include provision for vocational training, under which higher allowances are paid to those taking approved courses. Hence the plan provides practical, intelligible protection for labor against modern industry's greatest hazard. But the provisions indicate clearly that an essential assumption of the plan is the avoidance of mass unemployment, for only a community with a high level of employment can support such a program. Indeed, rising costs have forced even Labor, as we shall see, to reconsider these original principles of the national insurance system.

National Health Service

The most radical of the measures to establish a national minimum standard for everyone is the National Health Service Act, which superseded a variety of health insurance schemes and entitled everyone in Great Britain to virtually free medical attention and hospital care. The principle, long accepted in education, that all persons should have access free of charge to specialized institutions and professional skill is thus extended to health.

Few topics are more controversial than socialized medicine. According to the most popular slogans of critics, "People don't appreciate what they don't pay for" and "Doctors won't be interested in their patients if they are just cases from the panel." Advocates of the system maintain, however, that its great achievement is to prevent illness as well as to cure it. They also maintain that long-established standards of professional ethics are unlikely to fall merely because physicians are placed in the same position as teachers in any state-supported school.

The major difficulty in establishing a national health service is, as Lord Dawson of Penn, the King's physician, once pointed out, "to combine socialism in its administration with individualism in its practice." Though many British doctors were convinced of the need for a national health service by the wretched facilities in rural areas (of which they first became aware during the war when they were bombed out of London with its excellent facilities), they long opposed the government's plan on the ground that they would lose their independence. Ultimately compromises have been reached, however, so that by most standards the British national health service provides a working arrangement that combines "socialism and individualism." It is based on three principles: health services are free and available to everyone; patients have a free choice of doctors and of hospitals; and participating doctors may have both public and private practices.

All hospitals are nationalized under the act, but there is a good deal of decentralized control: medical and dental clinics and health centers are under the direction of local government authorities and of executive councils nominated by local practitioners, local government authorities, and the Minister of Health. A large-scale, long-term program for hospital reorganization and development was launched in 1961. At first, prescriptions, spectacles, dentures, and wigs were free, but there have been small charges for dentures and spectacles since 1951 (increased in 1961) and, since June 1952, for medicine and certain appliances supplied to hospital outpatients, for dental services, and for day nurseries run by local health authorities. Labor has been critical of these charges and abolished the small prescription charge in 1965. In practice, there is still a considerable demand for private treatment by doctors, and for private pay beds in public service hospitals. Some of the costs of such private service are met by voluntary insurance schemes; there may also be some truth in the quip that the "obstinate desire of the upper income classes to pay fees may prove to be as long-lived in medicine as in education!"

The group most dissatisfied with the national health scheme has been the general practitioners. Partly because of a misguided decision in 1957 to cut the intake of medical schools by 10 percent, the average number of patients on a doctor's list—that is, those who turn to him for attention when they are ill—was 2,300 in 1965. A quarter of all patients, however, were on lists of over 3,000, close to the permissible maximum of 3,500 (or 5,500 for a doctor with an assistant). General practitioners have long complained that their remuneration is inadequate in relation to the pressure of work and their professional expenses, and that their status within the community is consequently suffering.

A series of efforts has been made to take doctors' pay out of politics, but none has been wholly successful. The original arrangement was through the Whitley Council system, which worked well for other staff but not for doctors. Direct negotiations between the minister and the profession were no more satisfactory. In 1952, both sides agreed to refer the issue to a Judge Adjudicator, who awarded a 25 percent increase. In 1956, recourse was had to a Royal Commission, which reported in 1960 that doctors stood fourth—after actuaries, barristers, and solicitors—in career earnings among the top professions. The Commission recommended a 23 percent increase and proposed a special Review Board to ensure "the settlement of remuneration without public dispute." In 1963, the Board gave a 14 percent increase that was to last three years. This award was immediately greeted with noisy objections from the doctors at the annual meeting of the British Medical Association, whose leaders then returned to the Review Board to request an increase of 32 percent. An interim award of a 9 percent increase was made in February 1965, with an additional £5½ million ($15,400,000) for general practitioners, intended especially to improve their premises and to secure more help in the surgery. Nonetheless, bitterness and unrest continued. The dentists also expressed dissatisfaction with their conditions of work. For a time, the health service appeared in peril.

Late in 1965, a report designed to resolve the threatened impasse addressed itself to several matters: the pay structure; the methods of payment; the need to provide remuneration for increased burdens of work, seniority, advanced study, and up-to-date equipment. Further, it recognized that family doctoring is a progressive career. The report, which was accepted by the doctors, encouraged group practices and envisaged new health centers with adequate staff and the latest equipment. Thus, despite strains arising from the pay freeze in 1966, the health service may be evolving a more satisfying, as well as a more satisfactory, national scheme for preventing illness from dragging families into poverty, and for maintaining British health at a higher level.

3. HOUSING, AND TOWN AND COUNTRY PLANNING

Social welfare involves not only "mind and body," but also "estate." Inadequate housing and overcrowded cities have been, and remain, two of Great Britain's major problems. Beveridge believed housing to be the most urgent and important domestic issue, because it reflected the greatest social and economic inequalities and therefore provided the greatest opportunity for raising the standard of living. Moreover, as he pointed out, good housing is an indispensable foundation for health, efficiency, and education. But housing in Great Britain has been a twofold problem: building in itself, and town and country planning, so that slums may be replaced by well-designed communities.

Subsidized Housing

The housing problem was particularly acute in Great Britain at the end of the war. Some four million houses had been destroyed or damaged by bombing and for six years no new houses had been built. Establishing rigid priorities in the use of materials, the Labor government sought primarily to provide houses for families most in need of them and for this reason entrusted the building program to local authorities under the belief that they would be more inclined than private enterprise to build houses to rent, rather than to sell, and that they would also pick those tenants whose need was greatest. Between 1945 and 1951, one million houses were built, 80 percent of them by local authorities.

The Conservatives, coming to office at a time when more materials were available, raised the building level to some three hundred thousand houses a year—that is, about six per thousand of the population. Their philosophy was different, however, from that of Labor. They emphasized houses for owners rather than for rent and encouraged private builders rather than local authorities. To free landlords from fixed rents, some of which were unjustifiably low, they abolished rent control in 1957 on all new lettings, and on older ones above £30 ($84) a month. The latter development in particular, however, gave rise to extensive property speculation, culminating in the Rachman scandal, and to an undue concentration on office blocks and luxury apartments.

Labor's return to office in 1964 led rapidly to a new Rent Control Act to provide greater security for tenants; to the Control of Office and Industrial Development Act, 1965 (extended first to London and Birmingham) to curb property and building speculation and to reduce demands on the construction industry; and to an increased building program that aims at half a million houses a year by 1970 (much closer to American, Swedish, and West German levels). While noting that the number of owner-occupied houses in England and Wales had risen between 1951 and 1964 from 31 percent to 47 percent (7,200,000 out of 15,370,000), the government's 1965 White Paper (Cmnd. 2838) also pointed out that it was the poorer families that were most in need of accommodations within their means and that only public sector building for rental could meet this need. By a judicious rearrangement of subsidies and licensing, it is hoped to direct both private and public construction to the areas and for the purposes most needed.

Town and Country Planning

Any large-scale program to improve and expand housing immediately brings up the closely related issues of urban renewal, the siting of industry, the building of new towns, and land values. These issues are particularly pressing in Great Britain, because, as one of the most densely populated countries in the world, it has many urgent and often conflicting demands on its land. Agricultural production is vital to British food supplies, forestry is necessary for timber reserves, town developments are desirable to draw people away from overcrowded areas, and factories are requisite to the acceleration of industrial production. Town and country planning aims "to secure a proper balance between the competing demands for land, so that all the land of the country is used in the best interests of the whole people."

A whole series of acts, based on searching and detailed reports, has established a framework for national planning of land use, decentralization of industry, and wider and simpler powers of purchase of land by local authorities. A major problem in town and country planning, however, has been to develop satisfactory systems both of compensating private owners whose land has been acquired for planning purposes or has deteriorated because of new planned developments, and of taxing increased values accruing from public development projects.

In certain respects, marked advances have been made in town and country planning since World War II. Fifteen new towns had been built by 1960, and ten of the projected eleven national parks, seven forest parks, and eighty-two nature reserves had been established by 1961. Control of land use was well in hand. But the age-old problem of collecting the fruits of betterment, acquired so unevenly by private owners through the mere chance of proximity to public or private (for example, industrial) projects for development, has continued to bedevil the government.

Labor's overambitious attempt through the 1947 Town and Country Planning Act to secure virtually 100 percent of the increase in land value led only to a freeze-up of the land market. The Conservatives went to the opposite extreme in 1953 by abolishing the system of development charges and permitting private sales of land to take place at market price while continuing to keep the price of publicly acquired land to existing-use value, thereby placing a heavy premium on sales to private interests. Labor, in 1965, introduced the relatively low provision of a 40 percent development charge (compared to a newly introduced 30 percent capital gains tax) but, to encourage sales of land, let it be known that the percentage was likely to rise. The government also established a Land Commission with power to accelerate compulsory purchases for public purposes and to provide much needed advice to local authorities for their redevelopment schemes. Thus a fresh effort is being made to tackle one of the knottiest of Britain's problems.

4. IS SOCIAL SECURITY COMPATIBLE WITH ECONOMIC GROWTH?

As the British face their two major demands —for social security and for economic growth— questions inevitably arise as to whether the two are competitive or complementary. The public popularity of comprehensive social security, including family allowances, the costly health services, and housing and building subsidies, is undeniable and to be expected. Every industrial country in the world, and many developing countries, assume major responsibilities for the welfare of their citizens. For the British to attempt to give up their welfare provisions is unthinkable.

It is equally obvious, however, that the burden placed on the public purse by current financial arrangements is increasing almost unsupportably. Although the principle of insurance is maintained to the extent of weekly contributions by employers and employees, only about 30 percent of the cost of social services comes from direct contributions. Unlike the American social security system, contributions from both private sources are on a flat rate rather than a percentage of wages or salary up to a set amount. Moreover, the American system is still far less comprehensive, since Medicare (hotly fought by the American Medical Association until almost the end) is only for those over sixty-five. Thus the cost of social security to the American government as distinguished from the contributions of private persons, employees, and employers is relatively small. In Great Britain, in contrast, it is approximately one-fifth of the gross national product. To be specific: in 1959, the consolidated current and capital expenditure on social services and housing by the public sector was £3,708.7 million ($10,384.36 million), and the gross national product was £21,376 million ($59,852.8 million). The respective figures for 1964—£5,725.2 million ($16,030.56 million) and £28,910 million ($80,948 million)—show an alarmingly high proportionate increase in costs to the Exchequer, which must be recovered through taxation. In essence, therefore, the social welfare program involves a vast redistribution of personal resources in Great Britain, leading to a far greater equalization of real income in that country than exists in the United States.

Confronting the progressive aging of the British population through longevity, and the likelihood of widespread shifts in employment patterns caused by rapid industrial and technological change in response to the pressures for economic growth, the Labor government is rethinking its philosophy of social welfare. High on its list of priorities is a national severance pay scheme to cushion the impact of redundancy on workers. While unemployment funds are currently adequate to finance such a scheme, its introduction may be followed by a shift from flat-rate contributions, and thus flat-rate severance benefits, to percentage of earnings for both. In the longer perspective, it may be advisable to expand graduated contributions from both employers and employees, and to replace the philosophy of right to receive benefits by one of relative need.

Two factors encourage thinking along these new lines: the overwhelming cost by the mid-1970's, when there will be nine million retirement pensioners as against six million in 1965; and awareness that, in practice, the present system has not overcome poverty. A sociological study comparing 1953 with 1960 has reported that the percentage of poor rose from 7 percent to 14 percent in that period. In 1966, a million men earned less than £11 ($30.80) a week; a quarter of a million households with an average of three children earned less than they would be entitled to under public assistance; one-fifth of all pensioners were still forced to rely on public assistance; and half a million or a million more were believed entitled to such help but were unwilling to ask for it.

What the British have accomplished in the postwar period is a far better indication of the country's capacity, however, than are the blemishes that still remain. Standards of health have improved, school and university enrollments have increased, and new houses and new towns have been built. Moreover, a great though peaceful revolution has been going on —and will continue.

This is not to say that Great Britain's middle class, which has long produced its leaders in industry, the civil service, and the law, as well as in art, music, and literature, will not long continue to do so, despite the fact that the economic position of this class is no longer nearly so favorable as before the war in relation to that of the working class. Even if the middle class no longer has the leisure to staff the great voluntary associations (for example, the Red Cross) as it did in the past, it has its inherited traditions, sense of values, and customs to support its retention of a predominant place in the professional world. One of the most significant observations made about expanded secondary education in Great Britain is that the children of the middle class not only often do better in the long run than those of the working class, even when their tested ability does not seem as high, but that there is far greater pressure for middle-class children to continue with education regardless of whether they have outstanding academic ability or not. Thus the infiltration into managerial positions from the working class is likely to be slow, though it will not be impeded by the fixed barriers of the past.

Britain needs the concerted efforts of all its people, as it did during World War II, to meet the challenges of the last third of the twentieth century. Its objectives are clear; the way to achieve them less so. How it meets its domestic and external needs is of deep significance not only to its own people but to everyone.

9. Great Britain and the World

By geography, Great Britain is a European country; through history it became a world power. In the nineteenth century it held a dominant international position by virtue of its industrial leadership, financial power, and naval supremacy. But today Great Britain is no longer preeminent in any of these fields. Moreover, as we have seen, it faces a domestic economic problem of grave dimensions. Thus the British face agonizing dilemmas over how far their international commitments should still extend, and what role they should now pursue in world affairs.

In each of the three great intersecting spheres of the Western world—the Atlantic community, Western Europe, and the Commonwealth of Nations—Great Britain possesses or seeks a distinctive position. Within the Commonwealth group of some twenty-five independent states scattered throughout the continents of the world, Great Britain as the senior partner enjoys a unique relationship based on history, interest, and a common acceptance of the Crown as the symbol of their unity. In the Atlantic community, Great Britain and the United States have an unshakable though not uncritical alignment. Only in Western Europe has Britain failed to achieve the integrated role that many feel should form the core of its economic relationships and political associations. This failure is commonly blamed on France's refusal to share its predominance in Western Europe, but it stems more fundamentally from basic differences between British and French objectives in international relations. The French seek to make Western Europe an independent third power in the world, free of American influence; the British seek to interrelate Western Europe with their other associations.

Before we attempt to analyze more fully the strengths and weaknesses of the British position in international affairs, we must consider in more detail the characteristics of the Commonwealth and the competing claims of Britain's relationship to that group, to the United States, and to Western Europe. Only then can we draw up a balance sheet that may indicate the direction of the future.

1. THE COMMONWEALTH OF NATIONS

The Commonwealth of Nations [1] is a remarkable and unique international grouping. Other countries such as France, Holland, and even the United States have been colonial powers and have advanced their colonies to independence. But only Great Britain has been able to maintain close, continuing relations with former colonies that have become independent both in theory and in practice. Moreover, apart from the importance of its historical development, the Commonwealth of Nations provides an example of close cooperation between countries of equal status but widely different strength. Thus observers often speak of the Commonwealth as a model for international cooperation.

The Commonwealth of Nations consists of Great Britain and those former members of the

---

[1] The older name "British Commonwealth of Nations" has generally been replaced by "Commonwealth of Nations" since 1949 when it was formally recognized that the accession of the Asian Dominions meant that the proportion of British within the Commonwealth was, in fact, small, French-Canadians and Afrikaners always resented the prefix "British." It is still used in Great Britain, however, and also in Australia and New Zealand.

British empire that have acquired full control over every aspect of their internal and external policies but choose to retain a special relationship with Great Britain and other members of the Commonwealth. The relationship was developed historically by Canada, Australia, New Zealand, and South Africa; it was extended in 1947 and 1948 to India, Pakistan (the Moslem part of the Indian subcontinent), and Ceylon; and from 1957 on it was extended to Ghana, Malaysia, Nigeria, Cyprus, Sierra Leone, Tanzania (the union of Tanganyika and Zanzibar), Kenya, Uganda, Jamaica, Malawi, Zambia, Gambia, Malta, Singapore, Trinidad and Tobago, Guyana, Botswana (formerly Bechuanaland), Lesotho (formerly Basutoland), and Barbados. In a time when the international trend has been toward nationalism and separatism, these countries of widely differing geographical position, size, natural environment, racial composition, and political power have distinctive political and economic relations within the Commonwealth of Nations.

The strength of the Commonwealth is the strength of the relationship existing between these countries and Great Britain. To understand the present bonds uniting the Commonwealth, we must see how Canada, Australia, New Zealand, and South Africa passed from a position of dependence to one of equality of status with Great Britain without an intervening stage of separation. It is necessary, also, to see why the other countries chose to be members of the Commonwealth when they acquired independence of Great Britain. The bonds of the Commonwealth come not only out of history but also out of present circumstances.

The Evolution of Commonwealth Status

The characteristics of the modern Commonwealth were shaped by history. Canada, Australia, New Zealand, and South Africa were British "colonies of settlement," although in Canada the original settlers were French and in South Africa (until 1961 a Commonwealth member) they were Afrikaners. (Those of British extraction are still fewer than the Afrikaners, and both are far outnumbered by the local Africans, Indians, and Colored.) But in all these countries, British institutions and traditions had a strong formative influence leading to a feeling of loyalty and common purpose with Great Britain, at least among those of British descent.

In its era of undisputed naval, economic, and financial dominance, Great Britain provided notable benefits for its colonies. The British Navy (to which the colonies contributed nothing except port facilities) ensured their defense. Free of the crippling burdens of armaments, the small populations of these huge areas could concentrate on developing their resources. Great Britain was their major market and source of capital.

But loyalty and material benefit would not have been enough to maintain the British connection if political aspirations had been disregarded. The reason the second British empire did not go the way of the first British empire, which split asunder in the American War of Independence, was that a way was found to enable colonies to develop self-government without ceasing to be British. This way was called *responsible government,* which stemmed from the famous report of Lord Durham who was sent to Canada following a rebellion in 1837. Durham recommended that decisions on policy in most fields be made by locally elected representatives and not overridden by the governor and Colonial Office. When small scattered colonies were consolidated into the larger units of Canada, Australia, New Zealand, and South Africa, the constitutional right to determine their own policies was called "dominion status." [2]

From the first, this right covered all internal matters, including tariffs and immigration regulations. Before 1914 Great Britain maintained ultimate control of foreign relations, and in World War I it declared war for the Dominions as well as for the rest of the empire. But the great wartime contributions freely made by

[2] The name "dominion" was first used at the time of Canada's Confederation in 1867. It was derived from the Biblical phrase, "Thy dominion shall stretch from sea to sea." It was long used to refer to any of the self-governing overseas members of the Commonwealth and took its meaning from whatever status Canada or Australia possessed at a given time. Thus it never had a fixed connotation that limited their development to full independence. Except for New Zealand, "dominion" is not an official part of the name of any Commonwealth country.

THE COMMONWEALTH OF NATIONS

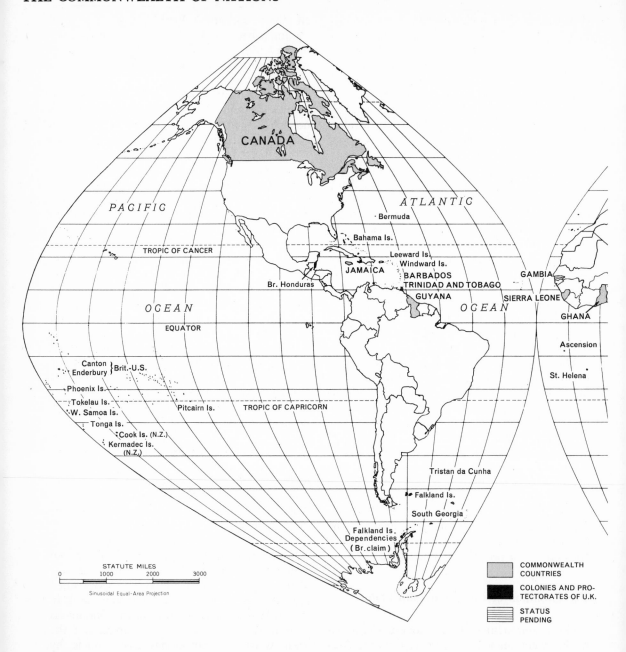

PACIFIC

ATLANTIC

· Bermuda

· Bahama Is.

Leeward Is.
Windward Is.
JAMAICA
Br. Honduras
BARBADOS
TRINIDAD AND TOBAGO
GUYANA

GAMBIA

SIERRA LEONE

GHANA

OCEAN

TROPIC OF CANCER

CANADA

EQUATOR

OCEAN

Ascension

St. Helena

Canton
Enderbury } Brit.-U.S.

Phoenix Is.

Tokelau Is.
W. Samoa Is.
Tonga Is.
Cook Is. (N.Z.)
Kermadec Is.
(N.Z.)

Pitcairn Is.

TROPIC OF CAPRICORN

Tristan da Cunha

Falkland Is.

South Georgia

Falkland Is.
Dependencies
(Br. claim)

STATUTE MILES
0   1000   2000   3000

Sinusoidal Equal-Area Projection

COMMONWEALTH
COUNTRIES

COLONIES AND PRO-
TECTORATES OF U.K.

STATUS
PENDING

Canada (which with only eight and a half million people lost more soldiers in the war than did the United States) and by Australia, New Zealand, and South Africa justified their claims to independence of action in this sphere as well as in internal matters. Moreover, traditional forms had to be brought into line with political realities.

In the interwar period the problem was worked out step by step. The Dominions became separate members of the League of Nations. Equality of status was recognized in the Balfour Report of the Imperial Conference of 1926, which declared Great Britain and the Dominions to be "autonomous communities within the British empire, equal in status, in no way

subordinate one to another in any aspect of their domestic or external affairs, though united by a common allegiance to the Crown, and freely associated as members of the British Commonwealth of Nations." The Statute of Westminster, 1931, drafted after consideration by political leaders from all parts of the Commonwealth, brought legal forms into harmony with long-

existing constitutional conventions by opening the way for Dominion parliaments to become formally supreme in their own jurisdictions.

The Statute of Westminster, 1931

The Statute of Westminster declares that no British law shall henceforth have effect in a

Commonwealth country except on request of that country, that British laws already having effect within it can be repealed by the legislature of that country, and that no power to disallow a statute inheres in the British government. Moreover, legislation of Commonwealth members thereafter had extraterritorial effect. This means that it can be enforced outside the particular country, for example, over its own merchant shipping.

The Statute of Westminster is a legal landmark in the history of the Commonwealth. The members of the Commonwealth themselves knew that informal constitutional arrangements had long approximated the legal situation inaugurated by the Statute. But in the eyes of the outside world the Statute of Westminster is the Magna Charta of the Commonwealth.

Not all parts of the Commonwealth welcomed the Statute of Westminster with equal enthusiasm. Ireland and South Africa adopted it immediately. Canada adopted it only after provisions were inserted at the insistence of the provinces to ensure that the act could not be used to change the balance of the federal system without their consent. But Australia and New Zealand were more reluctant to bring it into effect lest it suggest a change in their close feeling toward Great Britain. Australia finally adopted the Statute of Westminster in 1942 and New Zealand in 1947. Subsequent members of the Commonwealth inherited it automatically.

Abolishing Appeals to the Privy Council

The Statute of Westminster makes possible the abolition of appeals to the Judicial Committee of the Privy Council. Traditionally the Privy Council was the final court of appeal for all British subjects outside Great Britain, its position resting on an inherent prerogative existing since the earliest days of colonial government. Ireland and Canada began the process of abolishing appeals, which can now be made only from dependent territories and a very few Commonwealth countries. Even under the Statute of Westminster there is no uniformity of practice among the members of the Commonwealth. But what anomalies remain are due to individual choice. They could be changed at any moment if the country concerned wished to do so.

Independent Policies and Ultimate Unity

During the interwar period, legal and constitutional issues within the Commonwealth were satisfactorily solved. It was less easy to evolve a workable basis for policy that would harmonize the strictly limited interests of individual Dominions with the world-wide commitments of Great Britain. The basis finally reached combined a constant flow of information and much informal consultation among the different members of the Commonwealth with ultimate freedom of action on the part of each individual member. Such freedom of action was limited in practice by the recognition that, should trouble arise, only popular policies would be supported by other members of the Commonwealth. In the 1920's, for instance, Canada and South Africa disassociated themselves from British Middle East policies and at all times were less ready for the formal machinery of cooperation or for commitments to Great Britain than were Australia and New Zealand. Ireland withdrew from the Commonwealth in 1936. But from 1937 on, the threat of Germany and Japan drew the remaining members of the Commonwealth together. When war broke out in September 1939, Canada, Australia, New Zealand, and South Africa by their own acts entered the conflict in support of Great Britain and in opposition to aggression.

At the end of the war many people expected that the weakened position of Great Britain would lead to the breakup of the Commonwealth. On the contrary, the association has steadily expanded. As Great Britain's numerous colonies have achieved independence, most of them have chosen to be members of the Commonwealth. Burma decided not to do so when it became independent in 1948; and Sudan in 1956. British Somaliland joined with Italian to form the Somali Republic in 1960 and the Southern Cameroons became part of the Cameroun Republic in 1961. (Northern Cameroons became part of Nigeria.) Otherwise, as the dependent empire diminished (and diminishes) in size, so grew (and grows) the Commonwealth.

Republics in the Commonwealth

The importance of the Crown for the Commonwealth has already been emphasized. Yet beginning with India in 1949, many Commonwealth countries have decided to become republics. That a satisfactory resolution of this situation was quickly found is another evidence of the pragmatic flexibility of the association. In each case a specific request must be made to a Commonwealth conference that the state be accepted as a republic within the Commonwealth, but, except in regard to South Africa, no objection has ever been raised. The latter, smarting from criticism of its policies of racial discrimination, withdrew its 1961 request to be accepted as a republic and left the Commonwealth. All the others have been welcomed as Commonwealth members and have accepted the Crown "as the symbol of the free association" of the independent countries of the Commonwealth and, in a similarly symbolic spirit, the Queen as "the head of the Commonwealth."

Commonwealth Institutions

The Commonwealth has relatively little political machinery. It is indicative of the general informality of its relations that the Commonwealth's most important institution for formal exchange of views, the *Conference of Prime Ministers* (or the Imperial Conference as it used to be called) has no executive authority. As its name suggests, the conference is a meeting of the Prime Ministers of Commonwealth countries. It has been held frequently since World War II. Conference resolutions have no legal effect unless adopted by the individual countries, and the Conference of Prime Ministers is therefore a means of consultation, not a formal organ for reaching decisions. But the basic willingness of Commonwealth countries to work together stems in large measure from the frank conversations that these and other meetings make possible.

Conferences of Prime Ministers take place whenever there is an issue of general concern, like accepting republican India as a Commonwealth member in 1949 or considering the implications of the November 1965 unilateral declaration of independence by Rhodesia's white minority. Numerous other Commonwealth meetings have dealt with subjects such as trade, the convertibility of sterling, and economic aid to developing countries. There are also *ad hoc* conferences in many other fields of mutual interest, such as welfare, agriculture, and technology; constant exchanges among "opposite numbers" in particular Commonwealth countries; and meetings of Commonwealth representatives to the United Nations and other international gatherings.

The adequacy of such means of Commonwealth consultation has long been debated. Prime Minister King of Canada opposed additional machinery lest it formalize and thus make less satisfactory what he termed the "continuous consultation of cabinets." Prime Minister Curtin of Australia, however, who had suffered in the war from lack of information on British strategic decisions, favored establishing a permanent secretariat to prepare for Commonwealth meetings. Long after his proposal, such a secretariat was set up in London in 1965 under a Canadian Secretary-General, Mr. Arnold Smith. The Commonwealth Prime Ministers' Conference of September 1966 was the first for which the new Secretariat was responsible. At least its existence means that henceforth the agenda and arrangements for such meetings are in the hands of a body drawn from the Commonwealth at large and not the British Commonwealth Relations Office, as was common in the past.

The Bonds of the Commonwealth

It may well be asked: Why does the Commonwealth hold together? The machinery it has evolved for purposes of consultation does not bind individual members to a particular course of action. The symbol of a common Crown is not enough to determine policy.

It may also be asked, in the light of the frequency with which its members oppose each other in international conferences, whether the Commonwealth has any real value. That it is not an exclusive group is demonstrated by the close defensive arrangements existing between Canada and the United States. Why, then, does the Commonwealth continue to exist and what is its significance?

As a matter of fact, the very lack of exclusiveness is itself a source of strength to the Commonwealth. Membership in that body does not prevent a country from pursuing policies conducive to its particular interests. The only agreed-upon limitation is that it shall notify the other members before it undertakes such action. Thus Commonwealth membership involves few sacrifices except in moments of supreme crisis. On the other hand, it provides a number of advantages both to Great Britain and to its partners.

Strategic Ties

For Great Britain, the most important consideration is that twice in a generation the prompt and voluntary support of the older Commonwealth members has been a major element in supporting a British struggle for survival. During the year from the fall of France to the Nazi attack on the Soviet Union, Canada was Great Britain's strongest ally.

For the Commonwealth at large, however, there is no longer a defensive unity. Since World War II, the defense of the North Atlantic has become an international responsibility (safeguarded by the North Atlantic Treaty Organization) and no longer, as before World War II, chiefly a British responsibility. In the Pacific and Southeast Asia it is the United States on which Commonwealth members—particularly Australia and New Zealand—must chiefly depend, although the British still accept obligations to support Malaysia. The western Indian Ocean, long looked on as "a British lake" because of the number of bordering Commonwealth countries, lacks defensive strength. Even existing British military responsibilities "east of Suez" are strongly opposed by many of Labor's backbenchers, while the newer Commonwealth members are unwilling to provide bases for British forces. Thus it is chiefly the mutual sense of responsibility of the older Commonwealth members, and the lines of communication maintained by the Royal Navy and the Royal Air Force through scattered staging posts, that have strategic significance under present circumstances.

Economic Relations

Compared to the relatively informal arrangements in the strategic sphere, intra-Commonwealth economic relations are quite close and well integrated. Except for Canada, whose dollar is linked to the American, all the members of the Commonwealth are part (and by far the most important part) of the *sterling area,* made up of those countries within which the pound sterling rather than the dollar is the principal unit of exchange. Thus currencies are convertible, trade flows freely between these countries, investment operates easily, and settlers or travelers can take substantial sums of money with them—none of which is true between these countries and the United States. Moreover, some sterling countries pool their dollar resources, which are banked in London and distributed from there according to the agreed needs for withdrawal.

Intra-Commonwealth trade has long been encouraged by *imperial preference* under which Commonwealth countries extend to each other lower tariff rates than most favored-nation agreements provide. Americans used to charge that imperial preferences are discriminatory and a barrier to trade, but Commonwealth countries like New Zealand that are heavily dependent on trade with Great Britain feel they are necessary at least until there is more assurance of easier entry for their goods into American and European markets. In any event, currency restrictions, import licenses, and the like make imperial preference much less important today than in the past.

For the newer Commonwealth countries, with their fragile economies and high aspirations, the economic aid of the older members, particularly Great Britain, is of great importance. A Commonwealth program of economic aid and technical assistance for the Asian Dominions, known as the *Colombo Plan,* was launched in 1950. Subsequently extended to all southern and southeastern Asian countries, and with financial support from non-Commonwealth as well as Commonwealth countries, the Colombo Plan has achieved specific and noticeable results. In no other area has so substantial a program of Commonwealth aid been organized, but British financial and economic support for basic expenditures is extended to all the developing African and West Indian Commonwealth countries. Some of them also receive financial, economic, educational, or technical aid from Canada.

Citizenship

One of the historic advantages of being "British" has been the possession of a common nationality that opened the way for those from any part of the Commonwealth to travel freely in all other parts of the Commonwealth and empire and to gain the franchise and work permits more easily than was the case with citizens of foreign countries. Traditionally the United Kingdom interpreted most generously the original common law ruling that anyone born "in the King's Dominions" is a natural-born subject. In its Nationality Law of 1948 it provides that any citizen of the United Kingdom, its colonies, or a country of the Commonwealth is a "British subject" or (some people objecting to the term "subject") "Commonwealth citizen," the terms being interchangeable. This status provides material advantages such as (until the Commonwealth Immigration Act of 1961) the right to enter the country at any time and the right to qualify for the franchise, be a member of Parliament, or of the civil service (except in wartime). Other Commonwealth countries, each of which similarly defines its citizenship rules by statute, grant some, though ordinarily less extensive, privileges to citizens from other Commonwealth members.

The Balance Sheet of the Commonwealth

Most of the benefits of membership in the Commonwealth are mutual. All of them rest on the understanding of and willingness to work together for common purposes. The very flexibility of the arrangements makes them difficult for foreigners to understand and to evaluate; but flexibility and informality are at the heart of the success of the relationship for they permit adjustment to circumstances and quiet behind-the-scenes negotiations that may yield rich returns without acerbating domestic or foreign feelings.

Nonexclusive as the Commonwealth relation is, it yet offers an inner circle of friends whose interest and support are the more welcome in times of profound international tension. This fact was influential in the decisions of India and Pakistan and subsequently of other countries to remain within the Commonwealth. Not only does this interest and support extend to internal problems (most obviously with the Colombo Plan), but it means also that at international conferences these countries have a group (comparable to the inter-American group) on which they can always call, if not for votes, at least for exchange of views. Moreover, although most of the overseas part of the Commonwealth now have their own separate diplomatic services they gain useful additional information as well as services through the world-wide facilities of the British Foreign Service. A further advantage is that they can make their points of view known through British representatives at foreign minister or summit meetings with which they otherwise would have no direct contact. Perhaps most important of all is the balanced view of world conditions made possible by frank and free discussions among Commonwealth nations. Through such discussions, nations like Canada and Australia have gained new awareness and insight into Asian and African affairs.

It used to be said that the British Empire-Commonwealth, including about one-quarter of the people of the world and covering one-quarter of the earth's surface, was one of the great forces for maintaining world peace. Since World War II, the Kashmir dispute between India and Pakistan and the bitter attacks on South Africa's apartheid policies and Rhodesia's unilateral independence and white domination contradict this boast. Commonwealth countries traditionally never interfere in each other's affairs, and such issues are best placed before the United Nations.

Will the Commonwealth last? Prophets have foreseen its end before this and have been confounded. Will it retain its Asian, African, and West Indian members? In the long run perhaps only if the Commonwealth aids their nationalistic aspirations at the same time as it helps them mature as members of the international community. One of the positive features of the contemporary Commonwealth from the point of view of the rest of the world is that its older members have such a wide experience to share with its newer members and that, as a result of the continuous and intimate contacts it fosters, the latter may work more constructively in the international community. But this can happen only if there is conciliation and understanding on both sides. South Africa's and Rhodesia's racial policies are, of course, deeply resented in Africa and the West Indies, as they are in India and Pakistan. South Africa's withdrawal from the Commonwealth removed a constant irritant, and Rhodesia must change its policies or also cease to be associated. Only if the Commonwealth as a whole can adopt the nonracial outlook that should be the concomitant of its multiracial character will it retain its African, Asian, and West Indian members. Thus, in the future as in the past, the cohesion and strength of the Commonwealth will depend on the contributions it makes to the interests and development of its members and to their harmonious relations with the rest of the world.

2. INTERNATIONAL RELATIONS

The Commonwealth has long been considered the inner area of British international relations, providing built-in opportunities for influence and trade. But Great Britain's foreign policy must also take into account its relations with the United States and Western Europe. In addition, Britain has sought good economic and political relations with the Soviet Union and Eastern Europe and has tried to retain its influence with the Arab countries, without impairing its links with Israel.

If all these areas with which Britain is associated were friendly with one another, the historic position of the British in regard to each might provide them with unparalleled opportunities to act as a center of unity. But the harsh fact is that jealousy, rivalries, divisions, and even aggression between and within blocs have been more common in the postwar world than have friendship and cooperation. Moreover, Britain has sometimes acerbated its own problem by dealing with each of its associations separately and failing to fit the different parts of its foreign policy into a coherent whole.

Britain's most difficult problem has been its relation with Western Europe. It is drawn impellingly to that area by geography, military strategy, and, increasingly, by economic interest. Yet there are barriers of culture, language, and, most fundamentally, attitude that make close association difficult for both sides. The French, both before and under de Gaulle, desire a dominant position in Western Europe that they could hardly maintain if Britain were an active participant in all its programs. But beyond this problem is the inherent conflict between the

British world view, within which Western Europe becomes the more important the closer it is kept to the Atlantic alliance, and the French objective of pushing and keeping the United States out of Western Europe and making the latter an independent third force centered on Paris.

In the field of strategy and defense the British have committed themselves to certain solely European groupings, but always with the ultimate objective of associating the United States and Canada with them. Thus the British gave the lead to the Brussels Treaty of 1948 that pledged political, economic, and cultural cooperation among Great Britain, France, and the Low Countries—Belgium, Holland, and Luxembourg—and joint military action in case of attack. Most significant of all was the establishment of a single military headquarters at Fontainebleau, outside of Paris. The consummation of Britain's general objectives, however, was the North Atlantic Treaty Organization, established in 1949, in which the United States and Canada associated themselves in a vast system of mutual defense with the five Brussels Treaty powers, as well as Norway, Denmark, Iceland, Portugal, and Italy, and, after 1951, Greece and Turkey. Operating through unanimous decisions by the permanent representatives of the member nations, the NATO council proposes what each country should give to the common pool of men and arms. NATO forces are unified within a single overall organization (under which there are regional subdivisions like that of the Brussels Treaty group). There is also a supreme Commander in Chief (who has always been an American).

Despite the establishment of NATO, Western Europe still looked dangerously weak compared to a potentially aggressive Soviet Union. The first burning question was how to strengthen NATO by rearming and admitting Western Germany through means satisfactory to France. Plans for a European Defense Community failed, but in what was called the Western European Union Great Britain accepted military commitments on the Continent in 1954 that paved the way for a newly sovereign and rearmed Germany to enter NATO, into which its military forces were completely integrated. The second burning question has been how to persuade France, particularly under de Gaulle, to accept the American military presence in Europe that its Western European allies and Great Britain believe is the ultimate safeguard of peace. Despite their efforts, the French are now scarcely cooperating with NATO and have requested the removal of all American military personnel and materiel from French soil. Thus they have undercut longstanding unified military plans for the defense of non-Soviet-dominated Europe, possibly encouraged West Germany to establish an independent military force apart from NATO, and further irritated American policymakers.

Comparable British efforts to encourage close cooperation between Western Europe and the United States in the economic sphere have encountered the same kind of problems. The British are closely linked to, and increasingly dependent on, American financial power to underwrite the stability of the pound. As in military, especially nuclear policy, close economic relations with the United States constitute the prime principle of British policy. To extend this relation to Western Europe has been difficult. The British took the lead in organizing the plans for European self-help incorporated in the requests for aid under the Marshall Plan. They strongly backed the European Payments Union, established in 1950, to aid freer flow of trade and payments throughout non-Soviet-dominated Europe. They have participated vigorously in the Organization for European Economic Cooperation and its 1962 successor, the Organization for Economic Cooperation and Development (OECD), both concerned with development aid and trade policy, and they have done so with more enthusiasm since 1951, when both the United States and Canada became associated. But Britain has not been a member of the most significant functional organizations of Western Europe—the European Coal and Steel Community, Euratom (the atomic energy pool), and the European Economic Community, better known as the Common Market (which is discussed in detail in Chapter 9 of the French section).

Originally the British were reluctant to enter these functional associations lest they involve political consequences that might limit Great Britain's freedom of action in relation to both the Commonwealth and the United States. There was some internal controversy over possible British membership before the European Coal and Steel Community came into being in 1953; there was almost no public consideration of joining Euratom, which was established in 1958; and there was a formal decision not to sign the Rome treaties under which the nascent Common Market came into effect on January 1, 1958. Britain then hoped to be able to sponsor a wider and more compatible free-trade area. By 1961, however, after rounds of discussions with largely unenthusiastic Commonwealth countries and with its trading partners in the so-called "outer Seven"—Denmark, Norway, Sweden, Switzerland, Austria, and Portugal—of the European Free Trade Association (EFTA) that Britain had founded in 1959 largely as a bargaining counter in negotiations with "the six," the Conservative government decided to seek membership in the increasingly prosperous Common Market. But after extensive negotiations, conducted largely by Edward Heath, subsequently leader of the Conservative party, President de Gaulle exercised a unilateral veto in January 1963 on British admission. The Labor government attempted late in 1966 to reopen the issue, but the French response has not been encouraging.

Thwarted by France's determination to maintain its dominance in Western European organizations and to prevent the British from trying from inside to urge them into wider associations, particularly with the United States, Great Britain is inevitably left more dependent than ever on its close relations with the United States and with Commonwealth countries. And this fact confronts Great Britain with yet a further problem—British commitments east of Suez—that is the more serious because of the precariousness of its economic situation. The isolated position of Australia in the southwest Pacific, Britain's historic ties with Malaysia, and the reluctance of the United States to have Britain withdraw further from its commitments in Southeast Asia, all combine to demand a British military presence in that area. But as Labor backbenchers have pointed out cogently, British commitments east of Suez are a constant financial drain that Britain can ill afford. The futility of British efforts in South Arabia has led to a decision to withdraw from the Aden base by 1968, but Wilson supports the necessity of maintaining staging posts in the Persian Gulf and the Indian Ocean and a mobile force to protect British interests in Africa, the Arabian Peninsula, and Malaysia.

The breadth of Britain's historic commitments have made it—and in some areas still make it—singularly difficult for that country to withdraw without precipitating new conflicts. Without British support, coupled with the American presence in Vietnam, Malaysia could hardly have withstood Sukarno's pressures, nor could its 1966 agreement with Indonesia have been secured. Yet it is clearly in Britain's interest, as well as that of the rest of the world, that its overseas military commitments should be internationalized as quickly and smoothly as possible. The Cyprus crisis of 1963–64, with its bitter fighting between Greek and Turkish Cypriots, demonstrated that neither the Commonwealth nor NATO was adequate to the situation and that only United Nations auspices were acceptable for the peacekeeping force. Whether the crisis created through the unilateral declaration of independence by Rhodesia's small but dominant white minority can be met more successfully by United Nations action than by British-led sanctions against its regime is difficult to say, but at least the responsibility has been shared.

Great Britain's future is not wholly in its own hands. It is an important but no longer a decisive factor in most international negotiations. Of all the major countries in the world, Britain has the most to gain from global organization for military security and for the economic advance of developing countries. As early as 1907, at the height of British imperial power, a famous Foreign Office memorandum to the Foreign Secretary maintained that danger to British world-wide interests could be averted only if its policy "is so directed as to harmonize with the general desires and ideas common to all mankind, and more particularly that it is closely identified with the primary and vital interests of a majority, or as many as possible, of the other nations." This objective was never more important than it is today.

Conclusion

The American who tries to evaluate British political institutions runs a double risk. Before he praises or condemns, he must remember that the two countries are so different that the institutions of the one might well be catastrophic in the other. He must also remember that it is possible for reasonable and democratic people to disagree about the qualities most important in a democracy. Is it more important that the majority should have its way or that a minority should be able to maintain its entrenched interests? Is it better for government to be efficient or to be representative? If it is necessary to emphasize one or the other, is it preferable to have government by the people or government for the people?

To the person who accepts traditional American political values, there are three somewhat disturbing aspects to British government today: the continuing influence of the class system, the rigid discipline in political life, and the growing authority of the state.

THE CLASS SYSTEM

Americans generally accept (if they do not always practice) the principle that "all men are created equal." They may, therefore, be disturbed by the distinction of rank centering around a royal court, the power of an unrepresentative and unresponsible House of Lords to delay legislation, the advantages enjoyed by the upper classes in recruitment for the civil service and the courts, the financial handicap that often prevents poorer citizens from holding local office, and the advantage that the expensiveness of legal proceedings gives to the wealthy.

On several of these counts, especially the last ones, the English are not unconcerned. On the other hand they are also much more aware than Americans of the changes that are taking or have taken place. The monarchy has too great a hold on the popular imagination to be in any danger but, in any case, it now gives much less encouragement to social snobbery than formerly. Many Englishmen would point out also that social snobbery, class distinctions, and financial advantages are prevalent in the United States, even without the encouragement of a royal court. The House of Lords has been deprived of much of its power of delay, and the attack on the political and economic manifestations of social inequality is more effective in Great Britain than in the United States. It is even likely that British society has become more equalitarian in fact than American society, though hardly in form.

POLITICAL DISCIPLINE AND AUTHORITY

Many Englishmen see eye to eye with Americans on the dangers of unearned privilege; but intelligent citizens of the two countries are less likely to agree on the issue of party discipline and the subordination of the legislature to the executive. The ordinary American still likes to think of his representative as a man who is independent, who thinks for himself, who is more concerned with the desires of the people back home than with the demands of his party's leaders. And if the life of democracy is discussion and free participation in political action, then a political system that forces the representative to become something of an automaton,

209

voting always as his leaders desire, may seem to mean the death of the democratic spirit and system. Parliament itself may seem to lose its prestige and significance when debate is limited and all important legislative decisions are made by the Cabinet.

To this charge there are two answers the Englishman might make. The first is that freedom of action and discussion is not nearly so extinct as many Americans (and some British critics) maintain. Both major parties, in recent years, have had highly vocal rebels against party policy. Both parties have great freedom of discussion before decisions are made, though the whips try to insist on a united front when it comes to a vote, particularly in critical situations. And if it is true that the discipline is far more strict in Great Britain than in the United States, the Englishman might well say that there is also less political anarchy. Deadlock, irresponsibility, disunity, and incomprehensibility can be just as fatal to democracy as an excess of discipline.

To some extent the argument loses its point because the choice is not a rigid one between the defects of the two systems. It would be possible for Americans to introduce far more discipline into their political life without running any noticeable danger of making Congress a rubber stamp. And Parliament could offer considerably more independence and personal activity to the private member without incurring serious danger of anarchy.

One's judgment, in either case, will depend upon one's standards. The American will probably feel that unless the people and their representatives in Congress have an active part in molding legislation (and not simply in approving the plans of others) the qualities needed for self-government will atrophy. But many of the British will insist that it is more important for legislation desired by the people to be competently framed and promptly passed than for members of Parliament themselves to mold less expert laws. It is more usual for the American to be obsessed by the fear that political power will be abused (as is natural in a country where there are so many different types of minorities); and it is more usual for the Englishman to fear that excessive restrictions on power will permit a minority to obstruct the will of the majority.

Both countries, to be sure, succeed in enacting essential legislation, and both countries provide checks upon the abuse of power. But it is far easier for the British executive to win approval of its legislative proposals, whether good or bad. And it is far more difficult for the American executive to secure the approval of Congress even for proposals that have been expertly drawn and that have the support of a clear majority of the people.

PREDOMINANCE OF THE STATE

The political consequences of the growth in state activity in Great Britain are still a subject for speculation. Both of the major British parties now accept the fact that there must be a considerable measure of governmental planning and direction of the economy, although the Conservatives oppose and even some highly placed Laborites, including their leader, do not urge further government ownership, except in steel, of the instruments of production and distribution. Moreover, both parties accept the responsibility of the government to promote a society that is prosperous, healthy, well educated, and secure against the economic consequences of unemployment, ill health, and old age.

But this acceptance has presented a certain dilemma to democracy. The assumption of such responsibility calls for a tremendous expansion of government activity and for the concentration of enormous power in government hands. It also means the assumption of tasks so complicated and numerous that the ordinary citizen or member of Parliament cannot possibly direct or even understand them; at most, he can judge whether or not he likes the consequences. Two difficulties in particular have arisen since postwar nationalization programs: When the government itself has become administrator of so large a part of the economy and employer of so large a part of the working population, what adequate supervision can be maintained? And if certain people (for example, important unions) refuse to cooperate with those plans that the government considers essential to the well-being of the people as a whole (for example, the 1966 wage freeze), can they be compelled to do so without destroying the freedom essential to democracy? In a very real sense, the future of British democracy depends on its success in handling these problems. The British demonstrated great capacities for disciplined and effective efforts in their postwar recovery. They face now the still more difficult task of making maximum efforts, both on the national and international level, in a situation of relative affluence. The British have shown that they can voluntarily assume self-deprivation and "austerity" to rebuild their economy. Can they maintain the same unremitting effort without the same incentives? The test that British democracy now confronts is whether a free people, facing the competition of strong industrial countries such as the United States, the Soviet Union, and, increasingly, Germany, can so mobilize its technical ability and productive capacity as to maintain itself among the industrial leaders of the world and at the same time retain unimpaired its long-cherished traditions of individual liberty.

·II·

The Government
of
France

1. The French People and Their Politics

1. PARADOX AND PROSPECTS

That France has reestablished itself as a major international influence is a new factor in world affairs. Exhausted by war, torn by internal divisions, defeated in one colonial struggle after another, and hampered by an unstable political system, France in the fifties seemed to be sinking into insignificance. Even in that decade, however, France was making its way toward a healthy settlement with its former colonial possessions and was building a firm basis of political and economic cooperation with its Western European neighbors. Moreover, under the brilliant leadership of Jean Monnet, France was laying the foundations for the economic revival that has transformed the nation.

The de Gaulle Republic, under the direction of a highly competent bureaucracy, has pressed ahead the modernization of France's economy. To this economic revolution, the Fifth Republic has added a political one: the transformation of an unstable, Assembly-oriented system into a semiauthoritarian structure with strong executive leadership supported by a loose conglomeration of interests and groups committed to de Gaulle's leadership. Whether or not these political characteristics and alignments can be maintained, French politics can never return to what they were in the past. Nor can the French economy. This at least is predictable about France's future.

France and the World

What happens in France has a critical influence on the rest of the world. For many centuries *la grande nation* has been the most influential country of Western Europe. Its literature, philosophy, and political ideas have affected the thinking of civilized men everywhere. The triumph of revolutionary France in the late eighteenth century carried democratic ideals to much of the rest of Europe; in the mid-twentieth century the de Gaulle regime has given many former French African states a pattern for consolidating power under a strong president. France has played a crucial role in organizing Western Europe into a prosperous economic unit, and it is France that will decide whether the European Economic Community shall admit the United Kingdom into the Common Market. The United States and the United Kingdom often complain that France's external policies seem directed only by its leader's view of national interest—what is sometimes called "the cult of independence." Yet France's prosperity and renewed self-confidence have contributed notably to stability in Western Europe.

2. THE LAND AND THE PEOPLE

The Land

Geographical Influences

In comparison with the United States or the Soviet Union, France is small in area; yet it is larger than any other Western or Central European country. Its territory of 213,000 square miles (somewhat smaller than the state of Texas but almost two and one-half times the size of Great Britain) contains a population (in 1966) of just over 49 million people (in comparison with Great Britain's 54 million). Its climate is temperate, its landscape for the most part is gentle

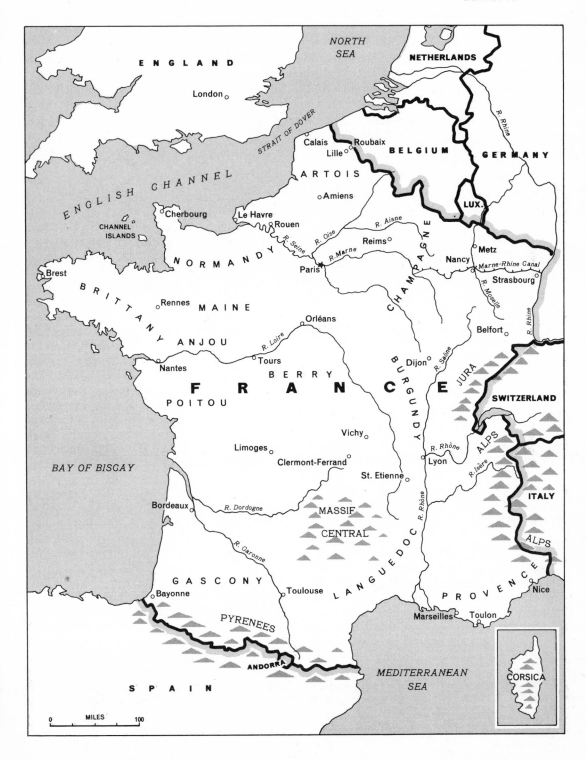

ENGLAND

NORTH
SEA

NETHERLANDS

London

STRAIT OF DOVER

Calais
Lille
Roubaix

BELGIUM

GERMANY

R. Rhine

ARTOIS

LUX.

ENGLISH CHANNEL

Cherbourg
Le Havre
Rouen

Amiens

R. Oise

R. Aisne

Reims

CHAMPAGNE

Metz
Nancy

Marne-Rhine Canal

Strasbourg

CHANNEL
ISLANDS

NORMANDY

R. Seine

R. Marne

Paris

R. Moselle

R. Rhine

Brest

BRITTANY

Rennes

MAINE

Orléans

Belfort

ANJOU

R. Loire

Dijon

JURA

SWITZERLAND

Nantes

Tours

BERRY

BURGUNDY

R. Saône

POITOU

F R A N C E

BAY OF BISCAY

Limoges

Vichy

Clermont-Ferrand

St. Etienne

R. Rhône

Lyon

ALPS

R. Isère

ITALY

Bordeaux

R. Dordogne

MASSIF

CENTRAL

R. Rhône

R. Garonne

LANGUEDOC

ALPS

GASCONY

Toulouse

PROVENCE

Nice

Bayonne

PYRENEES

Marseilles

Toulon

ANDORRA

MEDITERRANEAN
SEA

CORSICA

SPAIN

MILES
0   100

though varied, and its beauty and fertility have long been proverbial.

A variety of geographical influences have contributed to French national unity. At its farthest extremes the country is not much more than 600 miles across, and most of France lies within a few hours' train travel from Paris. With the exception of the Vosges Mountains (which separate Alsace from the rest of France) there are no barriers dividing one section of the country from another. On the contrary, the great river systems—the Seine, the Loire, the Rhône, the Gironde, the Garonne—link the coast with the interior regions and the different parts of the interior with one another. Certain uplands exist, as in Brittany and the *Massif Central* of south-central France, but they do not interfere with easy communication from south to north and west to east.

France's sense of national unity has also been encouraged by the existence of natural boundaries that cut it off from other lands. Of its six sides, three are bounded by water (the English Channel on the north, the Atlantic Ocean on the west, and the Mediterranean Sea on the south), and two by mountains (the Pyrenees in the south, and the Alps and the Jura Mountains in the east). Only on the northeastern frontier is there an absence of natural barriers. French history for centuries has been dominated by the struggle first to establish a northeastern boundary and then to maintain it against attack. On this frontier France has had to meet invasion three times in the last century. It is only in very recent years that firm cooperation between Western European countries has eliminated the fear of aggression.

Regional Variations

Despite its compactness, France is a land of many distinct regions and attitudes. Far more than in England, differences have survived in costume, dialect, and way of life. According to popular stereotypes, the dark-haired son of the Midi (the south of France) is noted for his eloquence, his excitability, his religious indifference, and his political radicalism; the blond Norman for his reticence, shrewdness, and conservatism; the Breton, for his mystical piety; and the Lorrainer for his steadfast patriotism.

More important are the political and economic contrasts. The north and northeast, where some 80 percent of French industry is concentrated, are politically conservative but economically progressive. The west, center, and southwest are politically to the left but slow in introducing economic innovations. But France's economic revolution is now bringing new industry to these latter areas, often under government stimulus, with a consequent lessening of the restrictive influence of small landholders and businessmen.

The People

Nationality

As in Great Britain, the earliest inhabitants of France of whom we have historical record (the Gauls) were Celts. As early as 600 B.C., however, the Greeks had founded a colony at Marseilles on the Mediterranean coast, and in the second and first centuries B.C. this region (whose modern name, Provence, is derived from the Latin word *provincia*) opened the way first to Roman influence and then to Roman conquest of all Gaul. But in contrast to Great Britain, where the Roman influence was neither profound nor permanent, Roman influence on France was both powerful and continuous. The Gallic peoples adjusted themselves to their conquerors with exceptional ease, and the impact of Roman language and law still is apparent. As a result, it is common to speak of France as a "Latin" country.

Early in the fifth century A.D. France was invaded and conquered by a succession of Germanic tribes—the Visigoths, the Burgundians, and the Franks—but the Teutonic conquerors did not, as in England, destroy the earlier way of life. The fighting in France between Celt and Teuton was less bitter than in England, and particularly in the southern half of the country the conquerors tended to accept the language, law, and religion of the people they conquered.

In the centuries that followed there were few infiltrations or additions of new blood. The Northmen who invaded Normandy quickly adopted the language and institutions of the natives, and only Brittany (which offered a haven to Celtic refugees from the British Isles) and Alsace (which was not acquired until the seventeenth century) contain a significant number of people who speak a language other than French. There are, however, a small Basque-speaking minority in the south and a small Flemish-speaking minority in the north. With the possible exception of Alsace (where the inhabitants, though generally loyal to France, continue to speak a Germanic dialect and at times press for a certain degree of autonomy), there is no problem in continental France of national minorities: the tension between people of different nationality, which has complicated the political life of such countries as Belgium, Czechoslovakia, Canada, and the Soviet Union, has no counterpart in French politics.

Population Trends

France's particular population problem has been its birth rate. In the days of Napoleon, France was the most populous European country apart from Russia. It was outstripped by Germany in 1870, by Great Britain at about the turn of the century, and even by Italy in 1930. While the rest of Europe experienced a phenomenal population increase, France suffered a steady decline in birth rate throughout the nineteenth century. To translate the end result into military terms: France, which had the same number of men of military age as Germany at the time of the Franco-Prussian War (1870), had less than half as many as Germany at the outbreak of World War II. Being also less urbanized and industrialized meant that France's economic power was much below that of its neighbor.

After World War II, however, the French population suddenly began to grow more rapidly than ever before in its recorded history—at a rate, moreover, considerably higher than those of several of its neighbors. The increase of 5 million from 1949 to 1954 was almost as great as the increase during the whole nineteenth century. By 1960 the proportion of young people in France had outstripped the proportion in West Germany—24.5 percent of the French population was under 15 as compared to 21.5 percent in West Germany. Indeed, even their numbers were greater. Today the increasing youthfulness of France's population is matched by the rapid modernization and rationalization of industry, a potentially powerful combination.

Religion

France, traditionally "the eldest daughter of the Church," is overwhelmingly Catholic. Of its 49 million inhabitants (1966), 40 million are, in some degree, attached to the Roman Catholic faith; fewer than a million are Protestant; some 300,000 are Jews; the rest are atheists or freethinkers. Potentially, at least, France provides a powerful basis for a political party promoting Catholic ideals and interests.

Yet if eight out of ten Frenchmen are Catholic in form, fewer than three in ten are deeply devoted to the interests of the Church. Most Frenchmen are Catholic in the sense that many Americans are Protestant: they attend the great church festivals, and they use their churches for baptisms, weddings, and funerals. But they resent the interference of the Church in politics, and it is not unusual for a Frenchman to be both Catholic and anticlerical.

Nevertheless, and in great contrast to Great Britain, where in recent generations religion has not been a major political issue, the position of the Catholic Church in France was until quite recently a subject of bitter political controversy. Before the Revolution of 1789 the Church was closely allied with the monarchical regime, which vigorously persecuted heresy (notably Protestantism) and religious and philosophical speculation. But this very persecution aroused the enmity of liberal intellectuals against the monarchy and against the Church as well. This enmity was slow to die. Restrictive pro-clerical measures under the Bourbon monarchy, a reaction to the excesses against the Church during the French Revolution, convinced many nineteenth-century Frenchmen that no one could be both a devout Catholic and a good republican. Although the latter years of that century saw a lessening of tension between the Church and the Republic, the Dreyfus Affair (see Chapter 2) and legislation separating Church and State revived the earlier bitterness. Thereafter and until World War II, the Church avoided overt political action. The fact, however, that Marshal Henri Pétain's Vichy regime, which appeared to collaborate with the Nazis, bestowed special privileges on the Church and that some of the highest church officials supported him again aroused republican suspicions.

Even after the war the relationship of the Catholic Church to French political life remained complex. With the liberation of France, Catholic leaders of the Resistance formed a new party, the *Mouvement Républicain Populaire* (MRP), of whose devotion to democracy and social progress there could be no doubt. Initially, the MRP captured over a quarter of the country's votes and was one of its three major parties. But the most troublesome of postwar religious issues, that of state subsidies to church schools (see Chapter 8), subsequently drove a wedge between the MRP and its natural allies on the left, helped to weaken the MRP itself, created crises in both the Fourth and Fifth Republics, and further complicated ideological divisions within France. Thus the religious issue in France in the past has disrupted the relations of groups with similar economic and social objectives in a way almost inconceivable to Americans or Britons.

The French Way of Life

Frenchmen are often portrayed as fiercely individualistic, argumentative and inflexible, bitter over distinctions of class and wealth, antiforeign, and resistant to change. André Siegfried wrote in 1930: "An anarchic individualism characterizes the Frenchman; he is hostile to the state; he is unwilling to associate himself with it; he does not want others to interfere with his affairs."

These characteristics have been somewhat modified by the recent impact of technology, radio and television, by growing affluence, the movement to the cities, increased travel, and the postwar flood of foreign products, which are still resented but universally displayed. Yet Frenchmen, and even more so, Frenchwomen, retain many of their traditional characteristics: their pride in France, particularly in French culture, language, art, and science; their independence, individual and national; their peasant mentality, which leads to an abhorrence of waste and a passion for concealing their wealth in order to avoid taxes; and their desire for perfection, whether in cooking, art, or the turn of a phrase.

Traditionally France has been a country of small farms and *paysans*. The 1962 census disclosed that 21 percent of the French working population were still farmers—as compared to 5 percent of the British and 6 percent of the American. Moreover, most French farms are still minute by American standards, with 79 percent under 50 acres and 56 percent under 25 acres; farms in the United States, in contrast, average over 300 acres. But the high costs of inefficient farming, coupled with the expansion of industry, are bringing to France the same changes that Great Britain and the United States underwent at an earlier period. Between 1954 and 1962, 1,300,000 Frenchmen left the land, reducing the percentage on farms from 28 to 21; in another decade it will be down to 15 percent. The few French farms over 1,000 acres in size and the 4 percent over 120 acres—those that can use mechanization efficiently and often draw cheap labor from Spain and Italy—are those that will reap the benefit of the great agricultural opportunities of the increasingly tariff-free Common Market of Western Europe (see Chapter 9). In the meantime, the French peasant protests, even riots against changes, but will soon no longer be the distinctive feature of French life.

This trend in agriculture is related to what is happening in industry. (Again we find similarities between what is taking place in France today and what took place earlier in the Anglo-Saxon countries.) The number of small craftsmen-employers in the towns has gone down by 25 percent since 1954. The number of independent traders is lower by 6 percent, although urban employment has increased by 9 percent. Between 1954 and 1962 those earning wages and salaries outside of farming increased by 1.6 million. At the same time there was a marked shift to employment in services (insurance, banking, trade) and away from traditional industries—like textiles, clothing and leather—and also, most dramatically, by 22 percent (204,000 workers) from mining to newer fields like building, chemicals and engineering, particularly electrical engineering.

These rapid shifts in occupation are a result of France's unprecedented economic growth after 1950. In the 12 years to 1962, total consumption (by 1956 prices) rose 76 percent, and consumption per capita rose about 57 percent. Since 1957, consumption has grown about 6 percent per annum. The transformation of French society is uneven, but it is clearly well under way. Moreover, the full impact on social mobility of the postwar population increase will be felt only in the coming decade.

Although France is being transformed from a semirural to an urbanized society, significant differences still persist between the character, size, and distribution of French cities and British cities. Few facts have affected French history more than the overwhelmingly dominant position of Paris, with its 8.5 million people (in 1965), almost 18 percent of the whole population. The other French cities are far less populous. France's second and third cities, Lyons and Marseilles, have just over 900,000 and 800,000 respectively; the next largest are Bordeaux and Lille, with under half a million. Only 12 other cities had a population greater than 250,000 in 1962. Thus there are no large cities outside the capital to act as counterpoles of attraction as there are in Great Britain.

As a result, Paris is the locus of a striking amount of the country's productive activity. Sixty-four percent of the country's companies have their head offices in Paris; one-quarter of all industrial workers, one-third of all college and graduate students, and 65 percent of all artists and writers are centered there.

Another marked feature of uneven distribution of wealth and activity in France lies in regional disparities: in particular, between the heavily industrialized northeast and the well-developed east on the one hand and the much less industrially advanced west, center, and south. The northeast has two advantages: its coal and iron deposits and its proximity to the heavily populated region around Paris. Within the northeast, which covers only 20 percent of the nation's territory, 38 percent of the population produces 46 percent of the country's industrial and agricultural output, and at a 25 percent higher productivity rate than the national average. In comparison, the western part of the country (the area west of a line drawn from Le Havre to Marseilles) is falling behind in agriculture and is experiencing relatively slight industrial development. The most recent French Plan (see Chapter 6) is intended to reduce this serious imbalance, but it will be a long-term process.

The political significance of France's uneven growth is masked by the diversity of support enjoyed by General de Gaulle. This support spans urban and rural areas and both the industrial northeast and the undeveloped west. The maps in Chapter 3 show some new voting alignments, but it is not clear how much these alignments result from the Gaullist mystique and how much from economic and social factors. Pockets of dissatisfaction show themselves from time to time in angry eruptions and demonstrations, almost always in the less-developed areas of the country, which were once staunchly Gaullist. In contrast, the Communists, who might be expected to thrive on discontent, continue to enjoy considerable support in sections of affluence and high development. In this period of political mobility, after the relative political apathy in the first years of the Fifth Republic, so many factors affect political attitudes that it is difficult as yet to generalize about the sympathies of its different groups.

Despite the rapid economic and social changes that are taking place in France, disparities in income and opportunity have not sharply segmented its population. In Great Britain the lines between farmer, worker, and professional and business middle class are relatively clear (though less so than they used to be). In France, however, many members of both the farming class and the working class are also middle class, in the sense that they own property, employ themselves, accumulate savings, and, unlike the workers to whom Marx appealed, have much more than their chains to lose. The ranks of the middle class also include the large number of Frenchmen who own their own shops and businesses, the professionals, and the increasingly large number of white-collar workers.

Clearly France, more than most modern countries, is dominated by a property-holding middle class, which, since the days of Aristotle, has been regarded as the foundation of social order and constitutional government. Thus, despite the response of one-fifth to one-quarter of all French voters to the appeal of the Communist party as a party of dissent (not only to those who are dissatisfied with their own lot but to those who cherish some high though vague goal of domestic or international perfection), France's unevenly developed but generally affluent society possesses great stability.

Interest Groups

To say that there is a strong middle class in France is not to say, however, that bitterness does not exist among and even within segments of society or that special-interest groups do not compete vigorously and often acrimoniously with one another. Frenchmen have a particular attachment, in fact, for whatever group they feel represents their own special interest or special point of view. This feeling has often led them, particularly under the Fifth Republic, to rely on pressure groups or their own direct action instead of what are demonstrably rather ineffective political parties. Thus latent tensions created by bitterness over inequalities in income between large and small businessmen, businessmen and labor, large farmers and landless tenants, or over policies toward Algeria have led from time to time to the sudden rise to prominence of such groups as the army, and to continuous pressure by trade unions, agricultural groups, and business associations.

The Army

The role of the army in France has been quite different from the role of the army in Great Britain or the United States. Either by active participation or by studious noninvolvement, the army has often turned the course of French history. The new national army of the Republic protected the nation from invasion, brought Napoleon I to power, and under his command marched across Europe imbued by ideological zeal. But under the Restoration and throughout the nineteenth century, the army was used to suppress social upheavals and became the guardian of order rather than the defender of freedom. Yet, though the army supported Napoleon III in his revival of the Empire, it did not promote General Boulanger's abortive attempt to overthrow the Third Republic in 1889 nor aid Marshal Pétain in 1940. In 1958, however, the army's open support of General de Gaulle was a major contribution to the demise of the Fourth Republic.

Humiliated and defeated in Indo-China by 1954, the army struggled for seven years to keep Algeria French. During those years, however, the French public became increasingly outraged by the brutality the army used against partisan bands and French liberals in Algeria. Many senior army officers, from their side, became infused with a political passion to keep Algeria French. When they realized that de Gaulle, far from advancing the purpose for which they had supported him, intended to give Algeria independence, they mutinied, in April, 1961. Later, others attempted de Gaulle's assassination. But even those who unwillingly accepted the army's withdrawal from Algeria to France posed a great danger to the nation, from which the military appeared to have become chronically alienated.

De Gaulle's foreign policy has been molded in large measure by the priority he has given to the task of controlling and then reintegrating the army into France. His reaction to the 1961 mutiny was swift, stern, and decisive. Nine generals and eight other high officers were tried and convicted by the High Military Tribunal. The Ministry of the Armed Forces was put under the direction of trusted Gaullists, and the General Staff was overhauled. But de Gaulle also believes that the only way to keep the army permanently out of politics is to preoccupy it fully with its professional task of protecting France. Hence he insists on equipping the army with the most up-to-date and powerful weapons, including the independent nuclear deterrent. Thirty years earlier General de Gaulle had written that the French army needed new morale, a precise function, and, the prerequisite for both, effective equipment. To provide them has been one of his most congenial tasks. Whatever the impact of this policy on international relations, it may have saved the unity of France.

Organized Labor

Compared to the dramatic role of the army in French politics between 1958 and 1961, the activities of more orthodox interest groups may seem tame. Yet in the postwar years these groups played highly influential roles in French life that at times seemed almost as decisive.

The leading organization of French workers has long been the *Confédération Générale du Travail* (CGT). Traditionally, this organization, in accordance with the independence that characterized the old French working class, had held aloof from politics and, unlike the British trade unions, had refused to identify itself with any political party. Instead, the union put its trust in "direct economic action," confident that the general strike, in particular, constituted a more effective weapon than any amount of parliamentary chatter. Following the foundation of a French Communist party in 1920, however, those workers who were under Communist influence seceded from the CGT and formed the *Confédération Générale du Travail Unitaire* (CGTU), which maintained an independent existence until 1935 when, as part of the Popular Front movement for common action of all leftists against fascism, the two labor organizations were reunited.

During the Pétain regime in unoccupied France from June 1940 to November 1942 (see Chapter 2) this organization like other workers' organizations was banned, but its members regrouped themselves underground and emerged after the Liberation, unchanged in name and with a larger membership and greater power than before. There was, however, an extremely important change in the nature of the resurrected CGT, for during its years as an illegal organization the Communists had succeeded in capturing control. Under their leadership, the union dropped its old attitude of noninterference in politics. Communist leaders explained that the economic powers of the government were now so great that the unions could not refrain from attempting to guide it. However, anti-Communists charged that another motive was at least as important: the desire to use the trade unions as a weapon for the Communist party's own political purposes.

At first glance, the relationship between the Communist party and organized labor might not seem very different from the relationship of the Labor party and British trade unions. In reality, there is a fundamental difference. The British trade unions look on the Labor party as an instrument for the peaceful attainment of economic reform; the party is useful to the unions only to the extent that it can persuade a large part of the electorate voluntarily to vote for its candidates and program. But in France the position of party and unions is reversed. The party controls the CGT and uses it as a weapon to coerce the voters who might not otherwise accept the Communist candidates and program.

In the fall of 1947 the Communist party called what was virtually a general strike, ostensibly to bolster a legitimate demand for higher wages, but actually to force a change in government and to prevent France from cooperating with the European Recovery Program as proposed by U.S. Secretary of State George Marshall. Only the government's decisive measures to maintain order, the good sense of French workers, and the opposition to the strikes by the moderate reformist wing of the CGT prevented the plan from succeeding. In December 1947 a large number of workers, including both those who were sympathetic to the Socialist party and those who wished to return to the old nonpartisan tradition, broke away from the CGT and formed a new organization, the *Confédération Générale du Travail—Force Ouvrière* (FO—Workers' Force). Nonetheless, the CGT at the behest of the Communist party launched a second crippling strike in October–November 1948, this time concentrated on the coal mines. Once again courageous action by the government, combined with the support of other workers, proved that the Communists could not dominate the nation's economy. But though this experience reduced Communist influence within France as a whole and particularly within the labor movement, the CGT has remained the dominant organization among industrial workers; in not a single basic industry has its supremacy been shaken.

The French trade union movement is now divided into one major, two minor, and several smaller groups. The CGT, with its nearly two million members (in 1946 it had 5.5 million), is by far the largest and, indeed, has more members than all French political parties put together. The much less numerous Catholic trade unions are strongest among white-collar workers in private industry. Originally united in the *Confédération Française des Travailleurs Chrétiens* (CFTC—French Confederation of Christian Workers), they are now split between a very small union that keeps the original name to preserve the reference to Christianity, and a larger union that has replaced the word Christian by Democratic (CFTD). Still smaller is the *Force Ouvrière,* which includes most unionized civil servants and state-employed workers. Both the FO and CFTD insist they are not allied to a particular political party, but they are inevitably associated with the Socialist party and the MRP respectively. Thus, in practice, they lose both the influence that British trade unions possess through affiliation and the influence that American trade unions possess through their political independence.

One of the most widely unionized groups in the country is that of the teachers, some 80 percent of whom are represented in the Autonomous Teachers Union. Between 40 and 50 percent of civil servants are unionized. But in total, and particularly when compared with Great Britain, France has a relatively small percentage of trade unionists. Moreover, the continued adherence to worn-out myths of class warfare, and the control of the CGT by the Communists, have led the workers' movement into an essentially negative role. Prosperity seems to have done little to change this situation. A new generation that is free of the historical stereotypes of exploitation may be necessary before French labor can assume the forward-looking attitudes now prevalent in so much of the rest of the economy.

Organized Farmers

In agriculture, traditionally a far more individualistic occupation, attempts have been made to produce a counterpart to the organization of industrial workers. Before World War II certain pressure groups promoted the interests of particular types of agricultural producers—winegrowers, sugar beet growers, and so forth—but there was no single powerful channel for the exercise of the farmers' political influence. Following the Liberation, an association of large farmers was formed under Socialist leadership; it became the postwar *Confédération Générale de l'Agriculture* (CGA). It had a brief political success in 1951 when 27 of its leaders were among the 59 farmers who became rightist deputies; the farmer-deputies temporarily occupied a strategic position from which they could control the destinies of any center coalition. By November 1951, however, the Peasant group had split, and its days of particular prominence were over. Less politically oriented than the CGA (which no longer exists) is the *Fédération National des Syndicats d'Exploitants Agricoles* (FNSEA), which is more important than was the former as a farmers' association but

takes no stand on other than agricultural issues.

Temporarily significant was the effort of the extreme rightists, the Poujadists, in the later years of the Fourth Republic to enroll small farm-owners and landless tenants in their protest movement against economic change. Changing their name from *Union de Défense des Commerçants et Artisans* to *Union et Fraternité Française,* the Poujadists posed briefly as champions of the more stagnant areas of French agriculture. Poujade's rapidly diminishing political influence coincided with improved agricultural conditions. But French agriculture is still far from healthy, and angry farmers often demonstrate fiercely against government policies to develop more efficient agriculture.

Organized Business

Much more united than French farmers, and even more so than French labor, are French employers. But the progression which led to the present efficiently organized employers association, the *Conseil National du Patronat Français* (CNPF), was a slow one. The ineffectiveness of the original employers association, the *Confédération Générale de la Production Française* (CGPF), established in 1919 in response to government urging, became obvious in June 1936 when political pressures from the Popular Front and a wave of sit-down strikes forced employers to conclude the humiliating "Matignon Agreement" with the CGT. This agreement transformed what had been technical rights into genuine protection of the kind normal in an industrial state: freedom for workers to organize and bargain collectively, minimum wages, the forty-hour week, and holidays with pay. Its disclosure of out-of-date working conditions, and the inefficiency of the CGPF, led to demands for tighter organization. Although it proved impossible to develop any genuine unity of policy among employers prior to the Fourth Republic, organized business was strong enough to prevent any further advances by labor before the war.

Scornful of the vacillations of parliamentary government in the Third Republic, the French business community as a whole supported the Vichy regime, particularly in its early stages, and approved its emphasis on labor discipline and a government-directed economy. As a result of this apparent collaboration with Vichy, organized business was virtually ostracized during the early days of the Liberation. The cohesion employers had developed during the war aided them, however, in organizing the CNPF in the first half of 1946, while their wartime experience predisposed them to a controlled economy dominated by businessmen.

The CNPF is a loose, decentralized federation of trade associations, but its executive body is capable of swift and decisive action in the interests of employers. Its tactics do not differ distinctively from those of other pressure groups. The CNPF has not demonstrated, however, such forward-looking attitudes as have either British or American employers' associations. It tends rather to act defensively and in short- rather than long-range terms. Thus, though French heavy industry and large-scale business have achieved a remarkable degree of prosperity and economic progress in recent years, there has been a continuation of the mutual suspicion of capital and labor that has long bedeviled French society and reached a stage of dangerous tension under the Fourth Republic.

The vigorous economic and financial policies of the de Gaulle government have built on the economic accomplishments of the Fourth Republic. Despite their efforts through the Poujadist movement, small, inefficient enterprises had proved unable to slow up the process of change, even though at times they threatened the political structure of the country. Today, even small business is convinced of the value of the freer economy of the Fifth Republic and the Common Market. It is doubtful that the growing sense of mutual interest between large and small enterprises, and between employers and employees, is yet strong enough to stand the strain of a serious economic reverse. Nevertheless, continued prosperity is likely to strengthen harmonious relations.

The National Economy

Despite strains, pressures, and disparities in growth among and within regions, the French national economy is remarkably strong. This is the more striking because it had been virtually static in the years before World War II. The original credit for the improvement must be given to Marshall aid. Subsequently, government planning for economic growth has been supported by its judicious injections of capital into selected areas of the economy. More recently the Common Market and other external arrangements have provided considerable stimulus. The results of these efforts and opportunities have been that industrial production has risen decisively, diversification has become common, French products can now compete with those of France's neighbors, and the nation enjoys a comfortable trade surplus.

France's large measure of self-sufficiency has made it easier for its government to plan for economic growth than it is for the British government. The French economy benefits from an unusual balance between industry and agriculture. In addition, France is rich in certain resources: it produces 9.7 percent of the world's supply of bauxite (the principal ore of aluminum); it is the world's third-largest producer of iron ore (after the U.S.S.R. and the U.S.); and it is the world's leading exporter of potash.

Despite these advantages and France's remarkable recent advances in production and distribution, there are still problems for its economy. A larger and better-trained labor force is needed. It is proving difficult to persuade backward areas of the country to accept new techniques and the dislocations that accompany them. What has already been accomplished, however, makes it clear that France's economic growth is sound and that French prosperity is likely to become more evenly distributed as industrialization proceeds.

3. ORGANS OF POLITICAL OPINION

The Press

In France, as in Great Britain, the chief source of political information and analysis is the press. In France, however, there is a sharper distinction between what is called the "press of information" and the "press of opinion." The former devotes itself ostensibly to reporting events, to entertaining its readers, and to providing literary and artistic criticism. The press of opinion, in contrast, consists of the journals of political parties and makes little pretense of being objective.

The Prewar Press

In the years before World War II the ethical standards of the French press were low. Many, indeed, attributed the collapse of French morale and of the government itself, in the summer of 1940, to the press's insidious work.

Unlike British newspapers, many of which (largely because of income from advertising) are highly profitable enterprises, the French press has always had difficulty supporting itself. In the prewar period many newspapers sought other sources of revenue. Large economic interests, such as the *Comité des Forges* (an organization of the great iron and steel manufacturers), subsidized individual newspapers. Foreign governments at times spent large sums to influence the French press in favor of their policies, and the French government itself was known to use "secret funds" to win the support of influential papers.

The Postwar Press

Following the Nazi victory in 1940, some newspapers ceased publication, some collaborated actively with the Germans, some tried to continue publication while cooperating with the authorities as little as possible, and some published underground. After the Liberation, those newspapers that had published beyond a certain date during the German Occupation were suspended or condemned, and a special commission was set up to lease their property to authorized newcomers. Moreover, in response to the urging of leftist parties that "the reign of money" must not be allowed to return, newspapers were restricted to certain forms of income. Political parties were allowed to subsidize newspapers, but nonparty newspapers were required to support themselves by sales, advertising, job printing, and similar methods.

For a time these restrictions plus the general interest in political events gave the party press the largest circulation. But as interest in politics diminished, the party press, especially of the left-wing, suffered. By the spring of 1948, four of the ten Communist dailies had ceased publication. In 1953 *Ce Soir* went off the stands, and

L'Humanité became the only important Communist daily left. The Socialists have had to struggle hard to save their great Paris daily, *Le Populaire*. The left-wing daily *Libération,* founded clandestinely in 1941 in Vichy France, closed in November 1964. *Combat,* the most brilliant journalistic offspring of the Resistance, has survived only because a group of businessmen took it over in 1961.

Though private money once more plays a significant role in the French press, France has few press lords in the British sense. Most of the money to finance papers comes from other sources. *France-Soir,* a Gaullist paper which has the largest circulation of all French dailies (1,250,000 in 1966) is associated with the firm of Hachette, the dominant distributor of papers and books. Two of the main Parisian dailies, *Le Figaro* (500,000) and *L'Aurore* (425,000), independent and moderate rightist respectively, receive support from the textile industry. Only with the greatest difficulty was *Le Monde* (300,000), the pride of French journalism, able to resist the efforts of a group of businessmen to take it over. By giving shares to the editorial staff, *Le Monde* now ensures its editor tenure for as long as his staff supports him.

Government pressures, and outright coercion, have also harassed the left-wing press and, under the Fifth Republic, the right-wing press as well. During the Algerian war the government frequently seized issues of dailies and weeklies that contained unpalatable comments or news. Between 1955 and 1962 there were over two hundred seizures in mainland France and many more in Algeria. The Socialist-led government of Guy Mollet (1956–57) attacked weeklies of the democratic left and even tried to put pressure on *Le Monde* by threatening to withdraw state-controlled advertising, a very significant source of revenue. The Fifth Republic has been no less restrictive, particularly by an unprecedented use of an old law that makes it possible to punish certain kinds of attacks on the head of state.

Whenever the press has stood together against government efforts to exert or extend control, the authorities have backed down. United press opposition stopped Premier Debré's attempt in 1960 to force the chief French news agency, *Agence France-Presse,* to submit to closer government supervision. At that time, following widespread protests, the government disavowed rumors of a "reform" of the press laws. But only *Le Monde* has consistently condemned seizures of newspapers, whether of the left or of the right, and not until March 1965 did the French Publishers' Association speak out against government censorship of books.

Although many Frenchmen read a wide range of newspapers, the total circulation of dailies is proportionately lower than in either Great Britain or the United States. Greater Paris, with its 8.5 million people, has 12 dailies with a circulation of just over 4.5 million. Metropolitan New York, with over 10.5 million people, has fewer dailies—four in all—but they have a total circulation of over 12.5 million. London far outstrips both. The provincial press in France, on the other hand, with its 95 dailies, some 20 of which cover large areas, is much more significant than is the provincial press of Britain and commands over 60 percent of the total daily circulation in the country. Most of the editorial matter in the provincial newspapers comes from Paris, it is true, but the Paris press itself is no longer so widely read as before World War II.

The Paris Press

In the shifting pattern of press popularity, the press of opinion, especially left-wing opinion, has suffered the greatest losses. *L'Humanité,* the official Communist newspaper, which had over half a million circulation in May 1946, had leveled off at about 180,000 by 1966. The Socialist journal *Le Populaire,* which sold a quarter of a million copies a day in 1946, has had a hard time maintaining a circulation of 13,000. Even *La Nation,* however, the organ of the ruling Gaullist UNR party, could sell only 20,000 copies a day in 1966, an indication that Frenchmen are tired of partisan papers. *La Croix,* a liberal Catholic paper, has fared better, but its circulation of 133,000 (1966) was below what it was in 1951.

Next in circulation to *France-Soir* in 1966 was *Le Parisien Libéré* (915,000), which is independent and right of center. It is followed by *Le Figaro* and *L'Aurore,* the Gaullist *Paris-Jour* (350,000), and *Paris-Presse* (97,000). Thus apart from *L'Humanité, La Croix,* and *Le Monde,*

the most substantial circulations are of rightist papers.

By far the most outstanding paper in France (some say in Europe) is *Le Monde,* the nearest equivalent to the *Times* of London. The completeness and accuracy of its news, its brilliant, sometimes witty, political analyses, its hospitality to nonconformist views, its restrained reporting of unpalatable realities, and the excellence of its foreign correspondents attract a wide group of influential readers. Half of its readers are said to be professional people, businessmen, high administrators, and political figures. Alone among Paris dailies, *Le Monde* has a substantial circulation outside the capital: some 80,000 in the provinces and 20,000 in North Africa.

Radio and Television

The brilliant use of radio and television made by the candidates in the presidential campaign in 1965 vastly accelerated the political and newscasting importance of these media. Though since mid-1964 they have been technically a public utility—*l'Office de la Radiodiffusion et Télévision Française* (ORTF)—the Fifth Republic, like earlier regimes, has used them without restraint to advance the purposes of its leaders. Thus it has staged presidential news conferences, or limited or ignored the speeches of opposition leaders, when these tactics suited government purposes.

As with party leaders in Great Britain, however, all the presidential candidates in 1965 were given radio and television time during the two weeks of the official campaign. Senator Jean Lecanuet, ex-President of the MRP, used his time to present the issues to the voters with such skill that he drew de Gaulle into an unplanned degree of active campaigning on these media. Moreover, after the election public figures from all the parties continued to receive an opportunity to present their special points of view.

Actively competing with the official French radio are Radio Luxembourg, the Saar's Europe No. 1 station, Radio Monte Carlo, and the BBC (which retains its wartime popularity, particularly in newscasts). These stations are said to have won over a high proportion of French listeners to their more popular programs. French television has a monopoly, however, and at least half the French population can be reached through the six million or more TV sets now in use.

The French government justifies its partisan use of programs by citing the press support enjoyed by the opposition. Yet the bias of the French media is in marked contrast to the political impartiality of British radio and television.

The Effect of French Organs of Opinion

A particular virtue of the French press in relation to democratic government used to be the fact that most of the major political groups and interests of France possessed their own organs of opinion. As a result, especially in Paris, the reader had a greater choice of papers and opinions than does the average Englishman. Foreigners were often bewildered and frustrated by the lack of objectivity of most French newspapers. The Frenchman knows, however, that party papers are political weapons and that he must adjust himself to the bias of the particular paper he reads.

Nonetheless, the sharp drop in the circulation of the party press suggests that Frenchmen became bored in their reading, as in their politics, by excessive partisanship. They also grew weary of the excessive conformity of the press. Yet there are encouraging signs in radio, television, and the press that these organs of opinion are responding to the new spirit of political questioning that appeared in the 1965 campaign for the presidency. Thus, as with so much else in France, the organs that mold political opinion are themselves being molded by change.

2. The French Political Heritage

1. ANTECEDENTS OF THE REPUBLIC

Perhaps the most striking difference between the political history of France since 1789 and that of Great Britain and the United States in the same period is the lack of constitutional continuity. Since the Glorious Revolution of 1688 Great Britain has had no political revolution and has made no violent change in its government. Since 1789 the United States has had only one constitution and has had no successful rebellion. But the story of modern France is largely one of recurrent revolutions and threats of revolution. In contrast to Anglo-American political continuity, France since 1789 has had eleven constitutions: three constitutional monarchies, two empires, one semidictatorship, and five republics. Moreover, most of these changes have been effected by violence. Thus it is not unnatural that talk of achieving further change by revolution seems far more realistic in France than in the United States or Great Britain, and that the French take their political institutions far less for granted than do the other great democracies.

Such frequent and drastic changes inevitably have had a profound influence on the nature of French politics. In order to understand contemporary France, therefore, it is essential to have some knowledge of the earlier regimes.

The Heritage of the "Ancien Régime"

Modern France's chief inheritance from the ancient monarchy is the tradition of a highly centralized, hierarchical administration, a tradition that is all the stronger because of the long and painful struggle required for its establishment. The power of the medieval Kings of France was far more severely restricted than that of their English counterparts. For many years the frequent wars with England (culminating in the Hundred Years' War, from 1337 to 1435) divided the country; and even after the invaders had been expelled, the French King was unable to exercise effective authority over such powerful nobles as the Dukes of Burgundy and Brittany. Louis XI (1461–83), through the skillful, Machiavellian use of his power, reduced their authority substantially. But throughout the sixteenth century great nobles (frequently identifying themselves with the Protestant party in the wars of religion) intrigued and fought against the royal authority. Only in the seventeenth century did a succession of great ministers of the King—Richelieu (who crushed the last vestiges of Protestant military power and political autonomy), Mazarin, and Colbert—unify the country politically and establish a centralized administrative hierarchy that was dependent solely upon the authority of the King. Today it is still popular to say that, whatever else has changed in France, the system of monarchical administration still is recognizable. That system has been transformed, however, under the Fourth and Fifth Republics into a modern, efficient technocracy.

The *ancien régime* also had an important negative influence upon succeeding governments by impeding and delaying the growth of a tradition either of constitutionalism or of parliamentarism. During the Middle Ages there had been a strong belief both in France and England that the King's power was subject to the inherited customs and law of the kingdom. But in the seventeenth century the Kings of France, partly through the use of the great military force needed to defend and extend the land frontier,

227

established the kind of divine right monarchy that the dazzled Stuart monarchs had tried in vain to introduce in England.

The Middle Ages had also seen the growth of an embryonic French parliament, the Estates General, representing the nobility, the clergy, and the growing middle class. This body, however, met only when summoned by the King, and from 1614 to 1789 it was not summoned at all. In consequence, when the French people finally overthrew the monarchy, they had none of the experience in the conduct of parliamentary institutions and in self-government that made possible the orderly supplanting of the royal authority in England. Early nineteenth-century attempts to introduce a parliamentary system based on the British pattern failed: the experience, customs, and habits of mind essential to the success of such institutions could not be carried across the Channel with them.

The keeping of social peace in France was impeded by another characteristic of the ancient monarchy: the maintenance of a sharp distinction between the nobility and the middle class. In Great Britain the younger sons of the nobility regularly became "commoners," and the most distinguished of the commoners often acquired titles. Consequently, the nobility and the upper-middle class were far from hostile. But in France, class lines were maintained with considerable strictness, and the privileges of the nobility (which seemed unjustified once the nobility abandoned the rigors of military service for a pleasant but parasitic life at court) aroused great resentment.

As the middle class grew more numerous, more prosperous, and better educated, it regarded with ever increasing animus the high taxes (from which the nobility were exempt), the financial ineptitude of the government, the class barriers to careers in the army and administration, the absence of organs for the representation and defense of their economic and political interests, the restrictions on industry and trade, the arbitrary exercise of the royal authority, and the limitations on freedom of thought, expression, and political action. Thus the Revolution of 1789 was a violent reaction of the middle classes against many of the outstanding characteristics of the monarchy—but a reaction which, by its very violence, produced what

has proved to be an enduring cleavage in French national political life.

The Revolutionary Heritage

The great French Revolution started out, in 1789, as an attempt to reform the monarchy; it ended, in 1792 and 1793, by abolishing the monarchy and executing the King. As the Revolution advanced, it was marked not only by foreign war and by civil strife between Royalists and Revolutionists but by a struggle among the Revolutionists themselves. A Reign of Terror followed in which the Revolution devoured many of its own children—first those who had been more moderate and finally the terrorists themselves. In 1795, in reaction against both the excesses and the idealism of the preceding years, power was entrusted to the five-man Directory, a government characterized by weakness, mediocrity, and corruption. There was little popular desire to defend so uninspiring a regime when Napoleon Bonaparte, one of the distinguished generals of the Revolutionary armies, attacked it, proclaimed the Consulate (with himself as First Consul) in 1799, made himself Consul for life in 1802, and established an empire (with himself as Emperor) in 1804.

But if the life of the First French Republic was short, agitated, and bloody, it had enduring consequences. The work of unifying the country was completed by sweeping away all internal economic barriers and by proclaiming the French Republic to be, in the famous phrase, "one and indivisible." Moreover, this unity found a powerful spiritual reinforcement in the growth of a fervent sentiment of national patriotism, symbolized in the *Marseillaise* and the deep attachment to the tricolored flag which, at least until the Popular Front of the mid-1930's, overrode the divisions of religion, class, political outlook, and economic interest.

In addition, the Revolution abolished the reign of privilege and established, as an enduring principle of French government, the "career open to talent." The partial destruction and division of the great estates of the nobility and the Church helped to create the powerful, property-owning rural middle class in which the Republic, in later generations, was to find its strongest support. And the noble, if unrealized, aspiration toward political liberty and self-government, as expounded in the Declaration of the Rights of Man and of the Citizen, provided an ideal and a precedent for subsequent, and more successful, struggles for human freedom.

The Influence of the Empire

Napoleon's success in destroying the Republic led to one stream of thought in France that was marked by the fear of any strong leadership and by a certain distrust of even the people themselves as a bulwark of democracy. Each of Napoleon's successive usurpations was ratified in plebiscites by an overwhelming majority of the people; and it was evident that the great majority of Frenchmen were ready to exchange a perilous liberty for personal security, political order, and military glory.

Yet if Napoleon destroyed the Republic, subverted political liberty, and concentrated unlimited power in his own hands (and in this sense was a forerunner of modern totalitarian dictators), it was not forgotten that he also maintained and consolidated many of the social and economic gains of the Revolution: the elimination of privileges based on class, the destruction of provincial barriers to trade, the freeing of the people from feudal tithes and duties, and the distribution of property among the peasants. Moreover, he added certain contributions of his own. His codification of the law and reorganization of the administration determined the form of two institutions that remained essentially unchanged through all the political vicissitudes of the coming generations and that have had a profound effect upon French political life. De Gaulle's semiautocratic leadership in the Fifth Republic has been both criticized and endorsed for much the same reasons.

Experiments with Constitutional Monarchy

The defeat of Napoleon in 1814 and 1815 and the restoration of the Bourbon monarchy under Louis XVIII provided France with its second opportunity to develop constitutional monarchy and parliamentary government on the British pattern. The ancient nobility and the higher clergy, however, were reluctant to adjust themselves to the new political code. The accession of Charles X in 1824 inaugurated an era of re-action that precipitated the revolution of July 1830 and the substitution of a new monarch, Louis Philippe of the House of Orleans.

The new "citizen king" was pledged to constitutional government and to moderate policies, but there was still no clear acceptance of the principle of ministerial responsibility and, therefore, of popular supremacy; further, the Orleanist monarchy's prosecution of its political opponents was taken as additional proof that monarchy could not be reconciled, as in Great Britain, either with political liberty or with democratic government. In 1848, with surprising ease, the King was dethroned and France began its second republican experiment.

The Second Republic

The life of the Second Republic was short and agitated. From the very beginning, there appeared a cleavage between the moderate men of the middle class who favored republican government but feared social upheaval, and the radical working class of Paris, which was primarily responsible for the Revolution. The two elements came to blows in the bloody "June days" of 1848, and the moderates, who controlled the government and who were supported by the provinces (which looked upon "red Paris" with great distrust), triumphed over their opponents.

Their victory, however, was short-lived. In the presidential election of December 1848 the candidates of both moderate and radical republicans were overwhelmed by the tremendous popular vote for Louis Napoleon Bonaparte, the nephew of the great Napoleon—whose orderly and glorious government appeared in retrospect as something of a golden age. Imitating his uncle, "Napoleon the Little" in December 1851 dissolved the legislative assembly, seized its leaders, and won the consent of the people (in each case by an overwhelming vote), first to an extension of the presidential term of office to ten years and then to the establishment of an empire to be ruled by Louis Napoleon under the title of Napoleon III.

Thus for the second time a Republic that lacked internal cohesion was overthrown by a strong, popular leader with monarchical ambitions.

The Second Empire

The first years of imperial government were marked by the vigorous persecution of political opponents and the concentration of great power in the person of the Emperor. Yet it was symbolic of the cleavage between those who were interested primarily in political liberty and those who were chiefly devoted to social justice that certain socialists supported the Empire in its early years in the hope that it would introduce economic and social reforms.

As popular dissatisfaction with the imperial government increased, an attempt was made to transform the regime into a "liberal empire," although the problem of whether a Ministry's first responsibility was to the legislature or to the Emperor was never clearly resolved. The disastrous Franco-Prussian War of 1870 intervened before the new constitutional experiment could be carried very far. In September a new revolt in Paris overthrew the government and established the Third Republic.

Thus the agitated years between 1815 and 1870 had brought no clear agreement on fundamental political principles and institutions; if anything, the political problem had grown more complicated. The supporters of both monarchical and republican government were divided among themselves into supporters of Bourbons, Orleans, and Bonapartes, those who favored a moderate republic, and those who favored radical social reform. Yet there was one gain: each of the different regimes had experimented with some form of parliament. Thus, even though the problem of the relation of executive to legislature had never been worked out, a considerable degree of familiarity with parliamentary institutions had been gained, and the new Republic could draw upon a valuable store of political and parliamentary experience.

2. THE POLITICAL HERITAGE OF THE THIRD AND FOURTH REPUBLICS

Early Crises of the Third Republic

For many years after the collapse of the Empire, the life of the Republic was anything but secure. The first elections actually resulted in the victory of a royalist majority; and it was only because the monarchists could not agree which king to restore that the Republic, more or less by default, was permitted to survive. In addition, in 1871, the city of Paris, which had precipitated every successful revolution since 1789, again revolted and established a government known as the Commune. This time, however, the revolt was mercilessly crushed, and the very vigor with which the provisional government suppressed the Communards reassured the mass of non-Parisian voters that a republican government could also be conservative and stable. Yet the new prestige of the Republic was purchased at the price of bitter hatred, and the memory of the martyrs of the Commune is still cherished by Paris workers.

It was not until 1875 that France acquired the makeshift constitution under which the country lived, somewhat to its own surprise, until 1940—a far longer period of existence than any other French constitution. The new constitution was really a series of three laws—on the organization of the public powers, the organization of the Senate, and the relations among the public powers—passed by a combination of republicans and moderate royalists who were tired of long delay, eager for some kind of definite political order, and willing to compromise on a set of laws that could easily be adapted to a restored monarchy. According to these laws, a bicameral parliament was set up consisting of a Chamber of Deputies to be elected by universal suffrage and a Senate chosen by indirect election. The two chambers meeting in joint session (under the title of National Assembly) had the power to elect a President of the Republic for a term of seven years. When each chamber had adopted a resolution to that effect, the National Assembly could amend the constitutional laws by a majority vote. Ministers were collectively responsible to the chambers for the general policy of the government, and individually responsible for their personal acts. With the consent of the Senate, the President could dissolve the Chamber of Deputies before the expiration of its term of office (four years) and call new elections.

The Sixteenth of May

It was not long before these laws met their first severe test. The President of the Republic, Marshal Marie de MacMahon, was a royalist and a strong partisan of the Church. When the Chamber of Deputies (of which the republicans had control) passed an anticlerical resolution, MacMahon rebuked the Chamber. On the famous Sixteenth of May, 1877, Premier Jules Simon resigned in protest, as MacMahon had hoped he would. When the President appointed a pro-clerical Ministry that lacked the confidence of the Chamber of Deputies, he was felt to have attacked parliamentary principles; and when he proceeded to dissolve the Chamber of Deputies, with the consent of a bare majority of the Senate, many believed that the Republic was in extreme danger. MacMahon's supporters were decisively beaten, and in 1879 the President resigned his office.

The episode had an enduring effect on the Third Republic. From that time on, the dissolution of parliament in case of disagreement between the Ministry and the parliamentary majority was not considered to be a normal part of the parliamentary process, as it has been in Great Britain, but rather as a weapon that would be used only by a potential destroyer of the Republic.

MacMahon's successor, Jules Grévy (1879–87), was authentically republican and sufficiently colorless to prevent anyone from fearing his aspirations. During his period of office the Republic further strengthened itself by instituting a system of universal, free, and lay education, which was intended to be secular and neutral toward religion. In practice, however, the teaching was ardently republican, and the survival of the Republic was often attributed to its prowess in the battle for the minds of the children.

The Boulanger Episode

The colorlessness as well as the corruption of the Grévy administration explain to some extent the phenomenal growth in popularity, in 1886, of General Georges Boulanger, the Minister of War, a young man of dashing appearance but questionable character. Having won dramatic expressions of support in different parts of France, Boulanger finally succeeded in sweeping the city of Paris, the old stronghold of radical republicanism. When his friends urged him to overthrow the government by force, however, his nerve failed, he fled the country, and in 1891 he committed suicide on the grave of his mistress. While this fiasco made Royalists and clericals appear absurd, good republicans shuddered at the thought of what an able adversary might have done with the opportunities Boulanger had squandered.

The Dreyfus Affair

In 1892 Pope Leo XIII called upon French Catholics to accept the republican government, but unfortunately such efforts at reconciliation (which might have simplified French politics by eliminating the religious issue) were doomed by the crisis known as the Dreyfus Affair.

A financial scandal involving high government officials and Jewish bankers had shaken the Republic and raised the issue of anti-Semitism. To this fire, fuel was added by word that a young Jewish army captain, Alfred Dreyfus, had been found guilty of selling military information to Germany and had been condemned to imprisonment on Devil's Island. By an extraordinary series of coincidences and accidents, however, Dreyfus' family and friends learned that top officers of the French army knew that the real culprit was not Dreyfus but probably a cosmopolitan adventurer, Major Charles Esterhazy, the nephew of General Walsin. Largely to conceal the corruption, intrigues, and chaos that ruled in the Ministry of War, officers had connived to suppress and ultimately to forge evidence against Dreyfus.

The charges against the army created a national crisis. Most royalists, clericals, militarists, and superpatriots, as well as those who hated Jews, Protestants, and foreigners, felt that an attack on the army was an attack on France itself, and that it was far better that an innocent Jew should suffer than that the integrity of military commanders should be questioned. Most of the staunch republicans, the anticlericals, and the socialists saw the struggle as one between intolerance and reaction on the one side, and justice and liberty on the other. Intellectuals like the writers Émile Zola and Anatole France and the painter Claude Monet, together with many scholars and teachers, deserted their studies and studios and joined with such practical politicians as Clemenceau and Jean Jaurès to clear Dreyfus' name.

Esterhazy and the forger, Henry, ultimately confessed, and Dreyfus was liberated and restored to the army. Even so, many anti-Dreyfusards refused to believe the evidence or insisted quite frankly that justice was less important than order and national power. Thus the case intensified divisions that had seemed on the point of lessening.

The Anticlerical Reaction

Some of the republicans who triumphed in the struggle over Dreyfus were as fanatical as their most reactionary opponents, and they now turned their fury against the Church. The Combes Ministry, which came into office in 1902 (Combes himself had been trained for the priesthood), led the attack. Government officials and army officers were discriminated against if they went to Mass or sent their children to church schools; and in 1905 the famous *Separation Law* not only revoked the government's power over the appointment of bishops (a change that the Church welcomed) but deprived the Church of all financial support from the government and vested ownership of all churches in the government, although religious congregations were permitted to continue to use them without payment. Although the government soon relaxed the rigidity of enforcement, the provisions of this law were bitterly resented and resisted by faithful Catholics.

The Interwar Period

World War I did not shake the stability of the Republic. Though the country passed through a series of financial crises from 1924 to 1928, it was not until the economic depression of the early 1930's coincided with the rise of fascism in Germany and with new financial scandals that the Republic again came into danger. In January 1934 the suicide of Stavisky, a Jew of Russian origin (and therefore an apt subject for anti-Semitic and nationalist propaganda), led to the disclosure of financial malpractices that could have been carried on only with the friendly tolerance of high government officials. The Cabinet of Premier Camille Chautemps, by trying to hush up the scandal, gave ammunition to those who charged that the government from top to bottom was corrupt and that it was conniving with swindlers and thieves. On February 6, 1934, a great mob, predominantly fascist, with a sprinkling of royalists and Communists, attacked the Chamber of Deputies. The police, with great difficulty, held the mob in check, but the Cabinet resigned.

The Popular Front

In the face of the depression and the menace of fascism, the three great parties and organizations of the left—the Radicals (the moderate lower-middle-class party, often called the Radical Socialists), the Socialists, and the Communists—drew together in the Popular Front of 1935. Forming a common front, they won a substantial though not overwhelming victory in the election of 1936, and León Blum, the leader of the Socialist party and a Jew, became Premier (a fact that gave further encouragement to anti-Semitism among the rightists).

The Blum government, concentrating at first on social reform, passed a series of laws providing for collective bargaining, the raising of wages, nationalization of the munitions industry, the forty-hour week, aid to farmers, and the reorganization of the Bank of France. In economic and social life it created a veritable watershed in French development.

But the reforms of the Popular Front took place in an atmosphere of great social tension, and the outbreak of the Spanish Civil War intensified the bitterness between the right and the left and to some extent revived the clerical issue. Despite its far-reaching program, the Popular Front developed serious cracks within a relatively short time and was obliged to resign after one year in office.

The End of the Third Republic

In the following months no government provided the firmness and leadership needed to meet the succession of crises that set in, and there was an increasing tendency for emergency powers to become a regular and necessary part of the political order. The most shattering evidence of cabinet instability was the parliamentary crisis in March 1940 (the month Hitler's armies invaded Norway). The country was on the verge of a second parliamentary crisis when the Germans invaded the Low Countries in May. Thus the government had neither the confidence nor the support of the country at the time of its greatest trial. France's subsequent military disaster was intensified by the absence of effective political leadership.

On June 16, 1940, a new Cabinet was formed under the leadership of Marshal Henri Pétain, a hero of World War I, who was looked on, even by the left, as a model military man. Only when in power did he display his clerical and authoritarian sympathies. Pétain promptly opened negotiations for an armistice with the Nazis. Signed on June 22, it divided France between an occupied northern zone and an unoccupied southern zone. The National Assembly (the Chamber of Deputies and Senate in joint session) convened at Vichy, the capital of the unoccupied zone, and by 569 votes to 80 gave "all power to the Government of the Republic under the authority and signature of Marshal Pétain." The Third Republic was at an end.

The Vichy Regime

Until November 1942 (when the entire country was occupied by German troops) France was thus divided. The German army occupied the northern half of the country and a strip along the Atlantic coast, while the remainder of the southern half (unoccupied, or Vichy, France) retained a semblance of independence under Marshal Pétain.

Pétain was supposed to frame a new constitution (to be ratified by popular vote) guaranteeing the rights of "work, family, and native country"—a vague but significant substitution for the traditional republican trinity of liberty, equality, and fraternity. But the constitution was never promulgated. Throughout the life of his government its only legal basis was in the provisional grant of powers. Pétain did, however, issue a series of "constitutional instruments" that repealed the constitutional provision for the election of a President, abolished the responsibility of the government to the legislature, and ended the latter's legislative powers. From this time on Pétain himself held all legislative power, and the ministers were responsible to him.

The announced aim of the Pétain government was to bring about regeneration and to free the nation of the vices that were thought to have destroyed France under the Third Republic. Masonic lodges (which were regarded as a republican political machine) were dissolved and their members deprived of government office. Organizations of workers and employers were disbanded, and state organization of industry was introduced under organizing committees, which rapidly fell under the control of big business. Attempts were made to introduce religious education into the schools, and subsidies were given to Catholic schools. In addition, under pressure from the Nazis, the government introduced anti-Semitic policies of such severity as to evoke formal protests from both Catholic and Protestant leaders.

The Resistance and the Liberation

From the moment of the fall of France, General de Gaulle, at the time relatively unknown to the masses of the French people, rallied a group of "Free French" in London and appealed to the people of his country to resist. At first he had little popular support, but as the Pétain government revealed its undemocratic character, as the Germans drafted labor for work in Germany, and as the stubborn British defense showed that the war was not over, the Resistance movement became stronger. Many young men escaped to join de Gaulle's army, and many more joined in the work of the underground. After the German attack on the Soviet Union in the summer of 1941, the French Communists took an outstanding part in the Resistance movement. The movement always included men and women of all political opinions, however, from extreme rightists to liberal Catholics and Socialists. Workers and members of the professions provided the most recruits.

The political and economic program of the National Council of Resistance (which combined all the leading resistance groups) called for a provisional republican government headed by General de Gaulle; the reestablishment of democracy with full freedom of thought, conscience, and expression; full equality of all citizens before the law; and the institution of social and economic democracy through the destruction of the great "feudal" economic and financial interests and through a planned economy under which private interests would be subordinated to the general interest. About the political ideas of General de Gaulle himself, there was considerably more doubt. It was known that he was a pious Catholic, and as an army officer he was naturally suspect to many good republicans. Yet he proclaimed his loyalty to the Republic, and as the day of liberation approached he came personally to symbolize the spirit of the Resistance.

With the Liberation of France in 1944, General de Gaulle became head of the provisional government. An assembly existed, but it was purely consultative. The Cabinet was chosen by de Gaulle and was responsible to him alone. Thus the regime in the first fourteen months following the Liberation was rightly called a "dictatorship by consent."

The Constitution of the Fourth Republic

It was obvious that France must have a new constitution, and when the first legislative assembly was elected in October 1945, the people, by a vote of 18.5 million to 700,000, decided that one of its tasks should be to frame such a document. Thus France was governed for several months by a combined legislature and constitutional convention known as the "Constituent Assembly."

But although the people were agreed on the need for a new constitution, they were not agreed on its nature. Conservative quarters called for a strengthening of the executive according to a somewhat incongruous blending of American and British practices. Most leftists, however, were opposed to any strengthening of the President or Premier and maintained that parliament alone should represent the national sovereignty.

The First Version

As a result, the first version of the constitution, a leftist draft that was presented to the voters in May 1946, placed almost complete authority in the hands of a single chamber called the National Assembly. General de Gaulle, who had resigned as President in January 1946 following a series of controversies with the left, maintained silence on the issue of ratification. But the Catholic MRP (*Mouvement Républicain Populaire*) and the few remaining Radicals, as well as the rightist political organizations, urged a negative vote. The Communists and Socialists naturally urged ratification, as

did the Communist-controlled CGT. To the general surprise, however, the constitution was rejected by a narrow margin—10,584,539 votes to 9,454,034.

The Second Try

In the new Constituent Assembly, elected in June 1946, the MRP replaced the Communists as the largest party, but the Communists and Socialists, when supported by deputies from Overseas France, were still able by a very slight margin to outvote their opponents. As a result, the second version of the constitution was very much like the first. Though a second chamber, the Council of the Republic, was added, power continued to be concentrated in the National Assembly, and the executive remained very weak. Nonetheless, the MRP (even while announcing its intention to seek amendments) decided to join with the Communists and Socialists in urging the voters to accept the constitution. General de Gaulle, however, demanded that it be rejected, and in this attitude he was supported by the Radicals and the parties of the right.

The results of the election were curiously indecisive. In the referendum of October 1946, 9,297,470 voters supported the constitution; 8,165,459 voted against it; and 7,775,893 eligible voters stayed away from the polls. Thus the constitution of the Fourth Republic came into being with what General de Gaulle and his supporters claimed was the support of only a little more than a third of the population.

The Balance Sheet of the Fourth Republic

The paradox of the Fourth Republic is that, despite the slim margin with which it came into existence, and the almost universal opprobrium with which it ended thirteen years later, it encompassed a period in which a newly vigorous France came into being. By 1958, France had its highest birth rate in a century; much of its industry had been modernized, and its industrial production had expanded since 1953 as quickly as that of Germany and far faster than that of either Great Britain or the United States. The French standard of living had improved markedly, partly because of economic growth and partly because of the enlightened social security system established after the Liberation. Moreover, France under the Fourth Republic undertook a farsighted and generally successful policy of closer relations with its Western European neighbors, culminating in the acceptance of the Common Market and Euratom in mid-1957.

Why, then, was the Fourth Republic written off as a failure in 1958, both at home and abroad? Partly it was because France's parliamentary regime had found itself increasingly handicapped by the presence on both the extreme left and the extreme right of large groups that rejected the parliamentary system in the form in which it existed and thus forced the moderate parties that lay between them into a constant series of expedients to maintain effective government. Because of this handicap, the Fourth Republic never succeeded in enforcing a genuinely equitable social distribution of the national income; it proved incapable of resisting the pressures of special groups (such as those producing alcohol); it failed to cope with the problems posed by the poverty of the Catholic schools in which one-fifth of the children of France were being educated; and it could not tackle effectively the urgent needs of tax reform and improved housing. But beyond this, the Fourth Republic was weakened irreparably by the dismal succession of defeats in France's overseas possessions and the costly and long-drawn-out war in Algeria. It was crisis in Algeria that brought de Gaulle to power once more in 1958 and led to the Fifth Republic.

The twelve-and-a-half-year period of de Gaulle's political semi-isolation saw shifting party alignments as confusing as those of the Third Republic. When de Gaulle resigned from office in January 1946, he had left the political field to three large, well-disciplined, but ill-mated political parties: the Communists, the Socialists, and the new socially progressive Catholic MRP. Their uneasy partnership lasted less than a year. In May 1947, the Communists voted against the government and were ejected from it; an ensuing wave of revolutionary strikes led by the CGT was ruthlessly broken. Already on the right had appeared de Gaulle's new political organization, the RPF (*Rassemblement du Peuple Français*), which he intended to be above parties but whose parliamentary representatives

were soon playing the parliamentary game. At first RPF votes combined with Communist votes to thwart the Socialist-MRP alignment, and the latter was forced to rely increasingly on the Radicals and Independents.

The new electoral law of 1951, by aiding electoral alliances, weakened the proportionate strength of the Communists and RPF in the Assembly. Coveting a share in power, many former Radicals and Independents, who had gained their seats as representatives of the RPF, now moved into the central coalitions. In 1952, the RPF split openly; in 1953, de Gaulle renounced it. In 1954, a new alignment of Radicals and Socialists helped Pierre Mendès-France displace the MRP and Independents. He replaced the latter's do-nothing policies with a whirlwind attack on France's major external issues. He settled the war in, and withdrew from, Indo-China; he gave internal autonomy to Tunisia; and he forced the project for the European Defense Community to a vote, in which, however, this was rejected. In the election of 1956, Mendès-France's new Left gained strength, the MRP and Independents held their own, and a new anti-democratic rightist group, the Poujadists, a protest movement of small shopkeepers and backward farmers against the dislocations of modernization, appeared in the chamber. But despite his apparent electoral success, Mendès-France was gradually isolated, and the Socialists and MRP combined under the former's leader, Guy Mollet. On February 6, 1956, however, Mollet capitulated to riots organized by French *colons* (settlers) against a liberal settlement of the Algerian question. In so doing, he made it virtually impossible for any other leader of the Fourth Republic to work out an acceptable solution in Algeria.

3. THE MAKING OF THE FIFTH REPUBLIC

The Fifth Republic was born out of violence and the need to reestablish political unity and stability. It has rightly been called the de Gaulle Republic, for de Gaulle has molded its constitution and its policies to his own view of the country's needs in a way no other Frenchman has been able to do since the days of Napoleon I.

Whether in so doing de Gaulle has provided the permanent base of stability in France that he seeks is uncertain. What is certain is that he has forced French politics and institutions into radically new patterns.

The war that destroyed the Fourth Republic was a colonial-type struggle, the Algerian revolt. Guy Mollet's swing to the side of the *colons* led to the pitting of 350,000 French soldiers against some 15,000 active Arab rebels. But as warfare descended into barbarism on both sides, the French became increasingly sick of the sacrifices, uneasy about the tactics, and insecure at home. In the autumn of 1957 there was no government for five weeks because none could secure a majority. When the government fell again in April 1958, it took a month to patch another one together. As Pierre Pflimlin prepared to present his Cabinet to the Assembly on May 13, the extremist Europeans in Algeria, fearful that he would propose negotiations with the rebels, broke into a frenzy. A self-elected revolutionary committee took office in Algiers under the benevolent eye of the army. Ten days later the extremists had seized control of Corsica. France itself appeared imperiled.

In fact, a stalemate had set in. Whatever the leaders of the army might have desired, it was questionable if the young conscripts would have marched on Paris. But the politicians in Paris were paralyzed. Only de Gaulle was clear about what should be done.

On May 15 de Gaulle publicly announced his readiness, if he was called upon, to assume power. After a tense period of waiting, President René Coty acted. Pflimlin resigned and de Gaulle was appointed Premier. On June 1, the Assembly accepted him by a majority of about a hundred, mainly from the right but including Radicals and Socialists. The Communists voted solidly against him. De Gaulle's condition for accepting office was the power to rule by decree for six months, at the end of which time he promised to propose a new constitution for the country's vote.

Those who supported de Gaulle in this time of crisis were motivated by various expectations. The Gaullists saw the chance at last for strong executive leadership; many who disliked de Gaulle's principles and personal authority saw them as the only way out of France's current im-

passe but looked on them as a temporary evil; those leading the revolt, especially the "colonels," could not believe that a general did not share their view of how to maintain the glory of France. Only the Gaullists were to be satisfied.

De Gaulle used the six-month period of decree power to push through a host of reforms. A new constitution was formulated, under the direction of Michel Debré. This constitution changed the balance of French political life. It vested legislative leadership in the executive and played down the role of the Assembly. It made a post in the Cabinet incompatible with membership in the Assembly. The choice of Premier henceforth rested with the President. The presidency, clearly designed for de Gaulle himself, emerged as the balance wheel in the constitutional system. Although the presidency was not yet the popularly elected office de Gaulle ultimately made it, the President in the Fifth Republic from the start was clearly intended to stand out as the representative of the nation selected, as he was, by a strikingly large and broad electoral college of local government representatives.

In September 1958, in a referendum in which the French territories in Africa and elsewhere as well as metropolitan France voted, the constitution of the Fifth Republic was accepted by an overwhelming majority of the voters—30,708,438 to 5,394,970. Metropolitan France voted 17,688,-790 to 4,624,511. The constitution of the Fourth Republic, as we have seen, had been greeted by marked lack of enthusiasm. That of the Fifth Republic, for all its novelty, or perhaps because of it, was launched on a wave of overwhelming approval.

The Political System of the Fifth Republic

The most striking characteristics of the Fifth Republic have been the length of time—from June 1958, when de Gaulle took over power, to December 1965, when he was forced to participate in a second ballot to win the first direct election for the President of France—that de Gaulle's dominant leadership received overwhelming support from the French electorate; the use of the referendum as an institution and source of authority; the emergence and apparent persistence of a Gaullist coalition or association that has produced a dominant, even majority party, the UNR (*Union pour la Nouvelle Republique*), in the National Assembly for the first time in the history of republican France; the new political personnel that has carried on and added to the technical revolution that has been transforming France; and the widespread character of social and economic change.

It is these facts, spelled out in detail in succeeding chapters, rather than the constitution itself, that are the significant factors in the making of the new France. Yet it has been the de Gaulle constitution, as modified at his own insistence, that has provided the framework within which the forces of contemporary France have been at work. It is necessary, therefore, to look at the constitution of the Fifth Republic, particularly in the perspective of those of the Third and Fourth Republics, to understand the France of today.

The Constitution of the Fifth Republic in the Perspective of Those of the Third and Fourth Republics

Partly by design, but partly also because of its dual parentage, the constitution of the Fifth Republic is a hybrid of presidential and parliamentary government. De Gaulle saw strong executive leadership as the primary objective and insisted that the President, far from being the choice of the legislative chambers and with no legislative role, as he had been under the Fourth Republic, should be a national figure both in manner of choice and in authority. But Michel Debré, with his training in law and political science and his experience in the Fourth Republic's second chamber, possessed the perspective of a parliamentarian and the temperament of a reformer. The structure he designed, therefore, was a reformed parliamentary system in which the former excessive power of the National Assembly and the consequent instability of the Cabinet would be curbed by constitutional restrictions.

The power to dissolve the legislature has always been looked on as a major means of maintaining executive leadership in a parliamentary system. It was determined that there should be a major change in the Fifth Republic in regard to the use of this power. We have seen

that after the MacMahon intervention on the famous Sixteenth of May, 1877, the use of dissolution had lapsed in the Third Republic; it was so hedged with restrictions under the Fourth Republic that it played little role. Thus the Premier was left at the mercy of the competing interests and ambitions of the members of the lower house, who, in contrast to the relatively clear-cut divisions characteristic of British and American politics, were divided into a spectrum of political ideologies and groups extending from the far left to the far right. French governments in the Third and Fourth Republics were always coalitions, therefore, that depended on the support of several parties, and often the withdrawal of a single parliamentary group would mean the fall of the Ministry. Whereas British Prime Ministers could commonly count on being in office for four or five years and could thus make long-range plans, a French Premier was lucky if he could survive for a year. While the same person often retained a ministry through several governments, top leadership was subject to frequent changes. Sometimes, as we have seen, the country was left for weeks on end without a Cabinet in office.

Under the Fifth Republic, the power of dissolution, as a reinforcement of executive leadership, was specifically written into the constitution. But rather than being at the disposal of the Premier, as in effect it is in Great Britain, the right to dissolve the French chambers is vested in the President, and in practice has been exercised at his discretion. Thus when Debré wanted the chambers dissolved at the end of the Algerian war in mid-1962, at a time when de Gaulle's prestige was particularly high, his request was refused. It was Debré himself who lost his position, being replaced as Premier in April 1962 by Georges Pompidou, who had never been even a member of parliament or of a political party.

This illustration of how de Gaulle as President overrode the advice of his Premier is characteristic of the way in which he systematically eroded the parliamentary features of the constitution in favor of presidential leadership. The constitution declares that the President is responsible for "the regular functioning of the governmental authorities, as well as the continuance of the state," and also for "national independence, the integrity of the territory, respect for . . . treaties." Under the Fourth Republic, the Premier and Cabinet were in control of foreign affairs, but from the start de Gaulle insisted on determining foreign policy. On May 15, 1962, for example, he publicly described his European policy even before informing the Cabinet, five of whose members, those from the MRP, promptly resigned.

Indeed, de Gaulle has maintained an important role in regard to all major policy decisions. He referred those concerning Algeria to referenda rather than the legislature. Despite charges of unconstitutionality he also insisted on a referendum on the issue of direct election of the President. Beyond these specific issues, de Gaulle has also molded those economic and social decisions, particularly of an unpopular character, for which the Cabinet has had to take public responsibility. Moreover, when the military putsch in Algiers took place in April 1961, he used his emergency powers to govern the country until the autumn, preventing the chambers either from legislating or introducing motions of censure against the government.

The greatest change in the functioning of the political system under the Fifth Republic has been the relative powerlessness of the chambers. For this situation there were many reasons. One dominant reason has been the personality and towering presence of de Gaulle, particularly in contrast to the transitory, often fumbling leadership of the Fourth Republic. The other was the awareness of the tightrope to be walked if the army was to be made to accept Algerian independence (which was not proclaimed until July 1962). Throughout, de Gaulle's position has been buttressed by the unswerving personal loyalty first of Debré and then of Pompidou, by the limited time—five and a half months in the year—in which the chambers can be in session, and by the remarkable strength of the Gaullist alignment in the lower chamber.

One cause of the instability of the Cabinet during the Third and Fourth Republics had been the divided and shifting character of the party system. On the left were three large parties: the Radicals (the loosely organized party of the anticlerical lower-middle class—that is, the small shopkeepers, the less successful professional men, and the small farmers); the better or-

ganized Socialists; and the tightly controlled Communists. In the Fourth Republic, as we have seen, there was also a new socially minded Catholic party, the MRP, which, except for its Catholicism, often seemed more to the left than the Radicals. On the right the political situation was less clear, for there the groupings were looser and the organizations less highly developed. In general, the right was conservative in economic matters but was divided between those who were anticlerical and strongly republican and those who were pro-clerical and socially conservative.

Under the Fifth Republic, the number of parties was no less (indeed a small new party, the PSU, appeared in 1958 between the Communists and the Socialists). But there was a decisive difference: the parties aligned themselves either for or against de Gaulle's policies instead of trying to devise policies of their own around which to organize enough support to control the chambers. The Communists have always been bitterly opposed to de Gaulle, but in any case their numbers in the National Assembly were reduced by a return to voting through single-member constituencies. The Socialists supported de Gaulle's accession to office in 1958 and endorsed the Algerian settlement, but they criticized almost everything else. The Radicals, the "vital center" in the Third Republic and a balance wheel in the Fourth, were decimated in the November 1958 Assembly elections although they retained strength in the Senate and in particular areas of France. The MRP supported de Gaulle during the Algerian war but broke with him over his European policy and his authoritarian attitudes toward parliament. The Independents (the term in France is synonymous with conservative) in the Assembly opposed the Algerian settlement, although their ministers reluctantly accepted it. Most significant, however, the amorphous UNR, despite its slight organization and program, began to bring France some semblance of a three-party system: the UNR, ordinarily with certain other support; the rest of the non-Communist parties; and the Communists, who formed a bloc of their own.

The National Assembly has not been acquiescent in the reduction of its status and authority. Even during the Algerian war, its deputies tried to resurrect the process of interpellation, which had been used with deadly effect under the Fourth Republic to destroy Ministries. The deputies were stopped in this effort only by the action of the Constitutional Council, the official guardian of the functioning of the constitution. Debré had to force bills through parliament four times by staking the life of his government on the outcome. In 1961, all parties except the UNR walked out of the Assembly in protest against the curbing of their legislative powers during de Gaulle's assumption of emergency powers. In 1962, as will be described in detail in Chapter 4, the "old parties" battled fiercely with de Gaulle, who not only overrode both the Assembly and the Senate but also the Constitutional Council and the Council of State (see Chapter 6) in his determination to take his own route to establishing the direct election of the President. Thus the opposition deputies have tried, repeatedly but unsuccessfully, to recapture the role the Assembly played in the past.

Basic to the realignment of executive-legislative relations under the Fifth Republic is the fact that the President, General de Gaulle, and not the Premier, controls the executive power. And the only way in which the Assembly can influence the President is through the Premier and the Cabinet. As Debré envisaged the government of the Fifth Republic, and indeed as it appears in the constitution, executive-legislative relations would be those of a traditional parliamentary system, except that the rule-making functions of the Assembly were restricted and those of the Premier and his Cabinet specified. Under those circumstances, the President would have remained above the political battle, in the role he himself once described as "a national arbiter far removed from political struggles." But circumstances—in particular the Algerian struggle and the dangers posed by an alienated army—and de Gaulle's determination to dominate policy have led the political system of the Fifth Republic to operate much more in presidential than in parliamentary terms.

Nonetheless, the provisions of the constitution, the ill-concealed impatience of the deputies over their subordinate role, and the renewal of political concern throughout the country suggest that the balance has not been established permanently. The surprising fact that de Gaulle had to enter a second ballot in the first direct election for the President, in December 1965, marked his first setback after a series of overwhelming plebiscitary victories. Despite his efforts and the great authority that has accrued to the presidency, it is not the role of the President as such but of President Charles de Gaulle that has molded the Fifth Republic. There is reason to wonder, therefore, whether the Fifth Republic, or the type of presidential leadership that distinguishes it, can survive its dominant figure.

Emergency Powers: Article 16

The most controversial clause in the constitution of the Fifth Republic is Article 16, under which the President can assume emergency powers at his own discretion. The constitution provides that he shall consult the Premier, the chairmen of the two chambers, and the Constitutional Council before declaring such a state of emergency. It defines the conditions that constitute a state of emergency as a threat to the institutions of the Republic, the country's independence, or the fulfillment of its international commitments. Nonetheless, the clause leaves the President full freedom to make the ultimate decision on his own judgment and thereby legalizes his use of full powers.

Behind de Gaulle's insistence on the insertion of this provision in the constitution was the break in the continuity of the French political system in 1940, with the Nazi invasion. It was not another war, however, but an ill-planned coup on the part of certain French officers in Algeria that gave rise to the declaration of an emergency in April 1961. No one in France disputed the need for and the use of these powers at that moment but the deputies of the older political parties grew restive and bitter over being kept so long from exercising their normal legislative functions.

The Referendum

While Article 16 permits the executive to bypass parliamentary procedures in times of extreme crisis, the process of referendum throws certain crucial decisions to popular vote. The constitutions of both the Fourth and the Fifth Republics were legitimized by being accepted by majority vote in a referendum. Indeed, the first draft of the constitution of the Fourth Republic was rejected by the voters on May 5, 1946, and the second draft was accepted five months later. The constitution of the Fifth Republic was accepted by referendum on September 28, 1958.

Whether other types of decision should be made by referendum has been a matter of controversy. The referendum has been a favorite means for General de Gaulle to capitalize on his popularity and on the widespread belief, particularly in the early days of the Fifth Republic, that he was indispensable. His use of the referendum to win support for Algerian independence was widely accepted as the best way of keeping this controversial issue out of the party arena. But there was great hostility on the part of the "old" parties and tacit, if not explicit, opposition from the Constitutional Council and the Council of State to his use of the referendum, rather than the regular amendment procedure, to institute the choice of the President by direct election.

De Gaulle justified the use of this procedure by referring to Article 11 (under which the referenda on Algeria had been called), which permits use of the referendum "on the proposal of the Government during sessions." His opponents pointed out with still more cogency, however, that Article 89 specifically provides for the amendment process and for the participation of the chambers therein. Whatever may have been the merit of instituting the process of direct election for the office of President, the fact that de Gaulle insisted on using a referendum on October 28, 1962, to validate the new procedure weakened its constitutional legitimacy and provided a somewhat dangerous precedent for the future.

The Constitutional Council

Neither in the Fourth nor in the Fifth Republic has the body set up to supervise the constitutionality of executive and legislative acts been effective. The Constitutional Committee of the Fourth Republic was created in 1946 to protect the second chamber, the Council of the Republic, from encroachment on its limited powers by the National Assembly. The Committee's jurisdiction was to determine the constitutionality of a measure challenged by a majority of the second chamber and the President.

On one occasion, but on one only, the Committee gave slight protection to the Council in a matter of procedure.

Little more useful has been the Constitutional Council set up under the Fifth Republic, even though it was supposed to have more responsibilities and more power than the earlier Constitutional Committee. The Constitutional Council must be consulted on whether organic laws and the standing rules of the Assembly are in conformity with the constitution, but the Council can do no more than give its opinion and leave action to the relevant body, the Cabinet or the Assembly. The Council has three other functions: to supervise elections and decide any disputes arising out of them; to advise the President on the existence of an emergency and the measures he should take to handle it; and, if asked, to give advice on the boundaries between executive and legislative competence, and whether proposed laws (other than organic laws) or treaties are in conformity with the constitution. But it is clear that the right to advise is far different from the power to decide—and that, in practice, the Constitutional Council is hardly more effective than its predecessor.

The Process of Amendment

The 1958 constitution, like that of 1946, has a relatively simple formula for amendment. The constitutional provisions of Article 89 are that the President, on the proposal of the Premier or a deputy, may make the initial proposal; the proposal must then be adopted in identical terms by both chambers and ratified by a referendum or, if the President so decides, by a three-fifths majority of both chambers sitting together. This procedure, if used, would provide the Senate with a greater role than did the procedure under the Fourth Republic, in which the Assembly could dispense with the consent of the second chamber if it had a two-thirds majority among its own members. Under the Fifth Republic, however, the amendment process has atrophied, partly because de Gaulle by-passed it when making the most decisive change in the constitutional balance of power, and partly because the sphere of the executive is so great, both through constitutional provisions and through deliberate enlargement by de Gaulle, that the presidency is the molding force in the regime.

4. FRENCH POLITICAL IDEAS

Far more than in Anglo-Saxon countries, political ideas in France have remained the fighting words of political action. While the Fifth Republic has been marked by a diminution of ardor in this respect, much of French thinking is still comprehensible only if one has some knowledge of the great rival political traditions of France.

The Ideas of 1789

The French Revolution, which provided French republicanism with its political creed, shared much of its political philosophy with the American Revolution. Some of its leaders, such as Lafayette, had fought for American independence, and many of its thinkers had been influenced by the Declaration of Independence and the Virginia Declaration of Rights. Both American and French liberals had read the writings of John Locke, and certain Americans, such as Thomas Jefferson, had formed close friendships with the men who prepared the intellectual program of the French Revolution.

The Enlightenment

In contrast to the United States, however, there were two distinct intellectual currents in the French revolutionary stream. The one that ran closer to American thought was that of the philosophers of the Enlightenment, a group of thinkers of the middle and later part of the eighteenth century who believed that man was a good and reasonable creature endowed with inalienable natural rights. According to their creed, man, by using his reason, could discover the principles of a just society and, being good, he would act upon them. Once he was freed from political and religious tyranny, there would be constant progress toward a perfect society. Thus the political philosophy of the Enlightenment was one of reason, individualism, humanitarianism, confidence in human progress and perfectibility, love of mankind, and hatred of religious superstition and political tyranny.

The Influence of Rousseau

The second current, which flowed from the thought of Jean Jacques Rousseau (1712–78),

was also characterized by a passionate hatred of tyrants. But where the philosophers of the Enlightenment exalted reason, Rousseau trusted to the uninstructed instinct of the ordinary citizen; and where the philosophers insisted upon the natural rights of the individual, Rousseau emphasized the interest of the community as a whole. Rousseau believed that the highest authority in any community was the *general will,* the content of which was determined by a direct vote of all citizens. Men were to vote, however, not according to their selfish interests but according to their understanding of the interests of the community. It was inconceivable to Rousseau that a community of free men (for Rousseau, too, believed in the natural goodness of man) should choose to pass tyrannical or unjust legislation. The ordinary citizen might be mistaken in his judgment, but he would always desire the welfare and freedom of all. Therefore, if ever a minority should differ from the majority, the minority should submit; and if the minority refused to submit, it should be "forced to be free." For Rousseau, unlike the authors of the Declaration of Independence, there were no "inalienable rights." Popular sovereignty (that is, government by popular vote) and the rule of the majority were the important considerations. Where the philosophers of the Enlightenment were chiefly concerned with political liberty and its protection against the government, Rousseau was chiefly concerned with political equality and the right of all men to participate in their government.

The Declaration of the Rights of Man and of the Citizen

The French Declaration of the Rights of Man and of the Citizen (1789)—the counterpart of the American Declaration of Independence—contained elements of both philosophies. The preamble, following the doctrine of natural rights, proclaimed that "forgetfulness or scorn for the rights of man are the only causes of public misfortunes and the corruption of governments." The first two articles maintained that "Men are born and remain free and equal in rights; social distinctions can only be founded upon common utility," and that "The aim of every political association is the conservation of the natural and imprescriptible rights of man;

these rights are liberty, property, security, and resistance to oppression."

Article 3, however, introduced a Rousseau-like element: "The principle of all sovereignty resides essentially in the Nation; no body, no individual can exercise authority which does not expressly emanate from it." Article 4 to some extent combined the two schools, declaring that "Liberty consists in being able to do everything which does not harm others: thus the exercise of the natural rights of man has no limits other than those which assure to other members of society the enjoyment of the same rights; these limits can only be determined by law."

Article 6 (apart from its provision for representative government) followed Rousseau: "Law is the expression of the general will; all citizens have the right to participate personally, or by their representatives, in its formation; it should be the same for all, whether it protects or punishes. All citizens, being equal in its eyes, are equally eligible for all dignities, positions, and public offices, according to their capacity, and without other distinction than that of their virtues and of their talents."

Other articles in the Declaration protected men from arbitrary arrest, imprisonment, and punishment; guaranteed freedom of thought, including religious thought; proclaimed "the free communication of ideas and opinions" to be "one of the most precious rights of man"; guaranteed to each citizen the right to "speak, write, and print freely"; and proclaimed property to be "an inviolable and sacred right." Except for the guarantee of property and of the "career open to talent" and a provision calling for popular consent to taxation, the concern of the framers of the Declaration was with political rather than economic rights.

During the French Revolution many of these rights were violated in the most flagrant way. But the "ideas of 1789"—liberty, equality, popular sovereignty, the career open to talent, government under law—remained the heart of traditional republican doctrine in France. The continuing importance of these ideas was indicated by the preamble to the French constitution of 1946, which began with the words:

> On the morrow of the victory of the free peoples over the regimes that attempted to enslave and de-

grade the human person, the French people proclaims once more that every human being, without distinction of race, religion or belief, possesses inalienable and sacred rights. It solemnly reaffirms the rights and freedoms of man and of the citizen consecrated by the Declaration of Rights of 1789 and the fundamental principles recognized by the laws of the Republic.

The Conservative Reaction

The Early Traditionalists

The French Revolution, with its culmination in the Reign of Terror, brought shock and disillusionment to many of the French people, and it was natural for a school of thinkers to appear who defended the monarchical tradition and challenged the political assumptions on which the Revolution had been based. Never very influential so far as the mass of the French people were concerned, certain of their ideas have nevertheless continued to dominate the thinking of leaders of the upper classes and of literary and intellectual circles.

The most prominent of the early traditionalists were the Vicomte de Bonald (1754–1840) and the Comte de Maistre (1753–1821). The former, challenging the idea that men desired "progress," insisted that their real desire was for the peace, stability, and order of a hereditary society. Men, he believed, were basically unequal. The happiest society is one in which the place of each person is determined by tradition and inheritance and in which each stays in that place. The best society is one in which a hereditary monarch wields the executive power; in which there are permanent social distinctions between a hereditary nobility and the commoners; in which there is an established church; and in which there is a harmonious balance between monarch, nobility, and independent judiciary. Order and authority he regarded as established by God. To revolt against the established order was to resist His will.

Maistre, the more influential of the two thinkers, attacked another pillar of the faith of the Enlightenment: the belief in the power of reason and in the ability of men to use their reason in order to plan and control their destiny. Like Burke he taught that inherited institutions and practices and even inherited prejudices represent a wisdom far greater than that attainable by the use of the human power of reason. Human institutions, instead of being shaped by men, are the product of many different social, economic, and political forces that men cannot control and that mold the minds of men.

In contrast to Rousseau's belief in direct popular government, Maistre maintained that in all governments it is the able and energetic few who rule. Monarchy he thought to be the best of all governments, and government he held to be naturally absolute and unlimited. "There can be no human society without government," he wrote, "no government without sovereignty, no sovereignty without infallibility." And although he agreed that temporal sovereigns, unlike the Pope, were not infallible, he thought a belief in their infallibility to be the only sound foundation for an orderly society.

The Newer Conservatives

Where the earlier post-Revolutionary traditionalists centered their loyalty on a hereditary monarchy, an aristocratic order, and an established church, the later traditionalists (while not necessarily rejecting these ideas) added an extreme nationalism as one of the essentials of the conservative faith. Maurice Barrès (1862–1923), one of the most popular of French novelists, continued the warfare against liberal individualism by insisting that the individual, far from shaping himself, is the product of his ancestry, his national traditions, and his native soil. The man who cuts himself loose from these influences is rootless and self-destructive, denying the core of his own being. Detesting and fearing foreigners, Barrès preached a doctrine of veneration for one's ancestors and one's dead, of reverence for the French language and the French earth. Men were to identify themselves with their families, their villages, and their provinces. Barrès' own affection for his native province of Lorraine, where repeated invasions had encouraged a particularly strong variety of patriotism, led him to believe that the road to French patriotism lay through devotion to one's locality. A religious skeptic, he nevertheless honored and defended the Catholic Church as the religion of his ancestors. In politics his only standard was that of unquestioning nationalism. Whereas the philosophers of the Enlightenment had preached the religion of humanitarianism, of love for mankind, of liberty, truth, and justice, Barrès judged all issues in terms of French power and glory. "Every question," he wrote, "must be solved in sole relation to the interests of France."

A somewhat different brand of nationalism was that of Charles Maurras (1868–1952). Unlike Barrès, Maurras was a native of Provence, that province of France in which the classic influence of Greece and Rome is still the strongest. To Maurras, France was the representative and defender of the classical spirit against the barbarians of the Teutonic and Anglo-Saxon world. Personally a skeptic (the Vatican eventually denounced both him and his organization, the *Action Française*) he saw in the Catholic Church, not the institution of "Hebrew Christianity" (which he detested), but the preserver of the classical tradition of ancient civilization. As opponents of this tradition, he attacked not only those Frenchmen of foreign descent (to whom he applied the Greek word *metic*) but Protestants and Jews as well. To him the Republic and the Revolution were something un-French, the product of a foreign and Protestant tradition (Rousseau had been, in origin, a Swiss Protestant from Geneva). He wanted to restore the old France of the monarchy, classic order, and authority. Stability was more important than justice. At the time of the Dreyfus Affair he declared, "Anything which disturbs the public order is an injustice, so that true justice is to respect public order." And when the army officer who had forged some of the evidence incriminating Dreyfus confessed and committed suicide, Maurras wrote in tribute: "Our bad half-Protestant education has kept us from estimating justly so much moral and intellectual nobility. . . . But your unlucky forgery will be recognized among your finest feats of war." The "unlucky forgery," Maurras insisted, could injure only the enemies of France. The Maurrassian doctrine of "integral nationalism" ("the exclusive pursuit of national policies, the absolute maintenance of national integrity, and the steady increase of national power—for a nation declines when it loses military might") made any conception of universal justice or morality a delusion if not an irrelevancy. Liberty, truth, and similar values became inconsequential in comparison with the worship of national power.

Maurras never commanded a popular following. But the beauty and clarity of his style and the force of his intellect won him authority in French intellectual circles. He lived long enough to be one of the supporters of the antirepublican and antidemocratic government of Marshal Pétain, paradoxically preferring defeat of the Republic to the victory of France, and he was imprisoned for his collaborationist activities. The successors of Maurras have never forgiven General de Gaulle for his opposition to Marshal Pétain, whom they regard as the symbol of religious orthodoxy, political order, and authority.

Socialism and Communism

Early Socialists

Although the industrial revolution came later to France than to England and was never so complete, socialist thought flourished in France from an early date. Before the general ascendancy of Marx, the influence of such thinkers as Saint-Simon (1760–1825), Fourier (1772–1837), Louis Blanc (1811–82), Blanqui (1805–81), and Pierre-Joseph Proudhon (1809–65) extended far beyond French borders.

The teachings of the early French Socialists were highly varied in detail, but the majority of them shared certain general characteristics. For the most part, they were true children of the Enlightenment, believing in reason, progress, and the goodness of human nature. They thought that social evils resulted from the wickedness not of men but of their institutions; yet, with the exception of Blanqui, they desired a peaceful reformation of society. All of them appealed to right and justice (although to Marxists these ideas were simply the reflection of a class interest), and in most instances their concern was with the building of a new society rather than with the violent destruction of the old. Often they believed that specific reforms (the introduction of social workshops as advocated by Louis Blanc, or the organization of model communities known as phalansteries according to the plans of Fourier) would provide the remedy for the worst social evils. Some of them were opposed to any growth in the authority of even a democratic government, and

Proudhon, whose influence was particularly strong among French workers, attacked Communist proposals for state planning and organization. He spoke of these as the "yoke of iron [which communism] fastens upon the will, the moral torture to which it subjects the conscience, . . . [and the] pious and stupid uniformity which it imposes upon the free, active, reasoning, unsubmissive personality of man."

Marxian Socialism

Even after Marxism, toward the end of the nineteenth century, had come to be the predominant type of socialism in France, there continued to be a strong humanitarian and reformist current in French Socialist thinking. Jean Jaurès (1859–1914), who more than anyone else personified French socialism, was ready to acknowledge in orthodox Marxian fashion that political developments were dependent upon economic ones, but he rejected the inevitability of class warfare. He was deeply concerned with the spirit and dignity of man as well as with man's material needs. He thought of socialism not simply as a response to certain economic conditions but as the culmination of all that was best in Greek, Jewish, and Christian civilization and in the thought of the Enlightenment. Economic forces were important, but they operated upon human beings who were infinitely diverse and who could not be understood in terms of a single mechanical economic formula. Rejecting the doctrine of a basic conflict of interests that could be resolved only through class warfare, Jaurès went so far as to recognize the good faith and idealism that had motivated the bourgeoisie (the bogey of all orthodox Marxists) at certain times. He believed that capitalists and workers shared certain interests in common that could be made the basis of a peaceful evolution toward the socialist society.

Jaurès was assassinated at the outbreak of World War I in 1914; in the later years of that great struggle the Socialist movement was seriously divided. Many Socialists supported the war as a battle for democracy, although an increasingly large minority became disillusioned and turned either to an absolute and extreme pacifism or, more significantly, to the belief, propagated by Lenin, that the international war must be turned into a civil war, a class struggle between the bourgeoisie and the proletariat. To this last group, the success of the Bolshevik Revolution in Russia was an inspiration and a source of tremendous prestige. In 1920 the left wing of the Socialists adopted the name of "Communists" and joined the Moscow-led Third International. Most of the leaders of the party, however, remained loyal to the old name and the old program, and in the following years they attracted a greater popular following than did their Communist rivals. This following, however, included not only workers but also a large part of the population of the small towns and countryside, as well as many members of the white-collar middle class, including a high proportion of government employees. As a result, there were several different "chapels," or what the French often call *tendances,* within the Socialist party: one that was devoted to radical social change and the interests of the working class, and commonly called the "doctrinaires"; one that was strongly pacifistic; and one that represented the progressive middle classes who desired moderate social reform within the framework of constitutional democracy. For a time, much of the popularity of the party resulted not from its desire for social reform but from its pronounced opposition to war—for France had almost bled to death in World War I.

Christian Socialism

Throughout the nineteenth century there had been some more or less isolated individuals in France who preached a doctrine of Christian Socialism, believing that democracy and social reform should be achieved through the application of Christian principles and with the help of the Catholic Church. So long as Pius IX remained Pope (1846–78) such movements were frowned upon by the Church; but his successor Leo XIII (1878–1903), while attacking Marxian socialism, urged the passage of social legislation to protect the working class. In France a large number of Catholics, particularly among the younger laity and the lower clergy, gave enthusiastic support to these ideas. Early in the twentieth century the movement known as the *Sillon,* led by Marc Sangnier, a young Catholic who believed devoutly in the Church's social mission, attempted "to place the social forces of Catholicism at the service of democracy." The group was condemned and silenced by the Vatican in 1910 not so much for the content of its social doctrine as for its claim to independence from the authority of the Church. But in the interwar period, a small party known as the Popular Democrats represented a continuation of the doctrine of a democratic and social Catholicism. Its leaders were prominent in the Resistance, and under the new name of the *Mouvement Républicain Populaire,* MRP, the group emerged as one of the strongest, and for a time most influential, parties of postwar France.

French Political Ideas in the Interwar Period

The years immediately before the outbreak of World War II forced a considerable readjustment in the French ideological pattern. Until this time, the parties of the right, in the spirit of Barrès and Maurras, had been identified with extreme nationalism, which often took the form of hatred of Germany, skepticism about the desirability or efficacy of international organization, and bitter opposition to social and economic reform. In contrast, the parties of the left (except for the Communists, who continued, with occasional intermissions, to work for international revolution) adopted slogans of peace and reconciliation, disarmament, and peaceful social progress. In 1933, however, an aggressive Hitler came to power in Germany at the very time when a disastrous economic depression had aroused a demand for sweeping social reform in France. A dilemma for both sides resulted: rightists had to decide whether they hated an aggressive Germany more than they feared social reform at home, and leftists had to decide whether they loved peace and social progress more than they hated Nazism. The result was a shifting of position and a split in both groups. A few rightists maintained the position of traditional French nationalism: Germany, whether monarchist, democratic, or fascist, must be kept powerless. A somewhat greater number, however, felt that France had been too corrupted by Marxism, anticlericalism, and lack of discipline to be able to fight successfully against the fascist powers.

Disunity on the left was just as serious as that on the right. The majority of Radical Socialists and Socialists reluctantly came to the same conclusion as their leaders Edouard Herriot and Léon Blum—that it was necessary to fight German aggression in order to save French democracy. But many Radicals were leaders in the effort to appease Hitler. And while at least half the Socialists resolutely opposed appeasement, most of their deputies voted for Marshal Pétain, though there were forty among them who refused to swing with the majority. The leaders of the Catholic progressives, the Popular Democrats, stood firmly for democracy and against appeasement. But the Communists, after being most vocal in the demand for resistance to Hitler, reversed their position in August 1939 when they received word of the Hitler-Stalin pact and actively opposed French participation in the war.

Finally, on the left, on the right, and in the center, there were masses of people who found it impossible, when confronted by a choice of evils, to choose either alternative with enthusiasm or even with firmness. The state of bewilderment and the lack of conviction of the ordinary Frenchman in 1939 and 1940 undoubtedly were important elements in the German triumph.

The Resistance

In its first months the Resistance movement lacked any clear political philosophy. Its leader, General de Gaulle, a devout Catholic, seemed to some to symbolize the militarism, nationalism, and clericalism which, to an earlier generation at least, marked an enemy of the Republic. However, as the Vichy government revealed its antirepublican and anti-trade union character, and as outstanding representatives of the Church and of big business collaborated with it, the Resistance movement became increasingly leftist in composition. Those Catholics who participated in it generally represented the Christian Socialist element in the Church. And in 1941, particularly after the invasion of the Soviet Union, the Communists took a conspicuous part in resistance activities. The program of the National Council of Resistance, which after 1943

combined all the major parties and organizations of the Resistance, called for radical social and economic reform. When a new constitution for the Fourth Republic was drawn up and ratified, its preamble, after reaffirming "the rights and freedoms of man and of the citizen consecrated by the Declaration of Rights of 1789," set forth a long list of social and economic guarantees.

But if the constitution, in this sense, represented a triumph for the socialist parties, whether Christian, reformist, or Communist, it would be wrong to suggest that traditionalism and conservatism had lost their power. Badly discredited at first by their association with the Vichy government, the conservatives steadily won new strength, partly as a reaction against growing Communist aggressiveness, partly by exploiting General de Gaulle, to his disgust, and partly perhaps because of the natural swing of the pendulum of political success.

In the Fourth Republic France was plagued both by colonial and by Communist problems. In many ways ideology was subordinated to the day-to-day efforts in solving these persistent threats to stability. No other nation in Europe, it may be noted, was faced with both problems at once: Great Britain had the colonial problem, Italy had the Communist problem, but neither had to battle simultaneously on two fronts. The Fourth Republic was able to cope with the Communist problem but not with the colonial one; that problem finally came to an end when the Algerian crisis was solved.

The process of decolonization (the battle in Algeria from 1954–62) led to de Gaulle's return to power in 1958. With his return, his supporters tried to revive Gaullism in a different form from that of the Resistance period. The Gaullists preached a "new France" devoid of the kind of political squabbling that had marked, and sometimes disgraced, the Fourth Republic. This "new France" was to play an important role in international politics and was to transform the nature of French administration at home. De Gaulle himself preached a new kind of nationalism that would restore France to its "rightful place" in the concert of nations: that of leader. To achieve that place, France would have to set an example for the "Third World": in foreign affairs it would be both anti-American and anti-Communist; at home it would evolve a society governed in an ultramodern fashion.

Before France could play the role in world affairs de Gaulle envisaged, he had to liquidate the Algerian war. By 1962 he had freed his hands and could embark upon his mission. His "neonationalism" prevented him from supporting the type of European Common Market that might subordinate France to countries which might be "tools of the United States of America." He thus became the target of the "Europeanists," who wanted France to take the lead in shaping a new European community.

De Gaulle also applied his ideas on government to the French civil service. He tried to popularize certain aspects of the "technocratic ideal." The National Assembly was no longer to play *the* important role in directing France; much more initiative was to be left to the technocrats or specialists who were needed to run the country. Thus he supported the ideology of "effective technocracy": a modern, efficient, active administration that could be trusted to run the country wisely and well.

Today, then, as in the past, there is a conflict of ideas in France. On the right, the bearers of the tradition of order and authority have added efficiency to make a new trilogy. On the extreme left, the Communists, while using the words *freedom* and *democracy,* interpret them in such a way as to justify the use of force and the suppression of the rights of political opponents. Between these two can be found every gradation of political view. In the center are those who hope to combine the philosophy of 1789 and a certain amount of freedom of enterprise with a moderate degree of social reform, and those who wish to combine social reform with loyalty to the Church. On the moderate left are Socialists who, in the tradition of Jaurès, hope to achieve social reform and a planned economy through the use of democratic methods without violating individual liberty. Each of these ideas is represented by an organized political movement or party. To understand both their present and their past appeal, it is necessary to look at these organizations in more detail.

3. French Parties and Elections

1. THE CHARACTER OF THE FRENCH PARTY SYSTEM

The French party system has long challenged the generalizations about political parties that Englishmen and Americans are tempted to make. To them it seems natural that there should be two large parties, that one should rule and the other oppose, and that every once in a while they should exchange positions. The rise of a third party has usually been regarded as a disrupting influence that upsets the entire system. Particularly in Great Britain, government seems possible and comprehensible only when one party is able to take the responsibility for political leadership, and when there is a united and forceful opposition prepared to take power whenever that party is defeated.

In France, however, none of these assumptions seems either natural or obvious. A two-party system, however desirable in theory, has appeared totally inadequate to represent the great variety of French political interests and principles. The characteristic multiplicity of parties in France has made, and still makes, difficult the development of a clear and cohesive majority and/or a responsible opposition. Moreover, the bitter opposition between the extremes of right and left and the antidemocratic tendencies at both ends of the spectrum have created a disturbing absence of the restraint and tolerance that mark the alternation of parties in Great Britain and the United States.

To the foreigner the French multiplicity of parties often seems unintelligible and chaotic. The French are accused of political fickleness and frivolity, with the implication that any solid and sensible people could organize a firm and simple party system. If anything, however, the French people have not been frivolous and fickle enough. The issues dividing them have had an ideological or historical base, and the party groupings reflect these divisive issues. Thus the French have rejected the sort of practical and facile compromise that can unite northern progressives and southern conservatives in a single Democratic party.

In sum, the reflection in the French party system of the cleavages in French society prevented it, prior to the Fifth Republic, from accomplishing what seem to Anglo-Americans the most important functions of a party system: to represent the opinions and desires of the voters, and to provide effective government.

It was to provide effective government that the Fifth Republic shifted from party government to executive government. Paradoxically, one result has been a far stronger trend toward large parties, or toward groupings of parties, under the Fifth Republic than ever before. One main reason has been a new source of division in French politics: that between those supporting and those opposing President Charles de Gaulle and his policies. But whether this new factor, consolidated in party organization, will permanently affect the French party system has yet to be seen.

The Party Systems of the Fourth and Fifth Republics

The party system of the Fifth Republic, like that of the Fourth Republic, is a multiparty system. There is little similarity, however, between the Assembly elected in 1946 and the Assemblies elected in 1958 and 1962. In 1946, the Assembly was dominated by three large, well-disciplined parties of the left: the Communists, the Socialists, and the MRP. There were two parties of secondary importance: the RGR, a union of republican leftists formed around the old Radical party, and the conservative PRL. The Independents were a small and apparently ineffective group. In 1958 and 1962, in striking contrast, two right-wing parties —the UNR and the Independents—won a dominant position in the Assembly, only seventy seats short of a majority in 1958 and eight more than an absolute majority in 1962. The once-powerful left was sharply reduced in strength and is still struggling to build itself into an effective opposition.

The transition from the 1946 Assembly to the 1958 one was less abrupt, however, than their juxtaposition here may suggest. The original coalition of the three leftist parties broke up in 1947 as the result of the intransigence of the Communists; thereafter a series of governmental crises encouraged splinter groups, revived the importance of the rightist parties, and, on occasion, made the votes of the Independents crucial, particularly during the curious situation created by the establishment in 1947 of General de Gaulle's organization, the RPF. The RPF claimed to be above political parties and, in fact, aimed at the total elimination or absorption of its opponents. After spectacular successes in the municipal elections and those for the Council of the Republic in 1947 and 1948, the RPF emerged as a full-fledged party. It contested the national election of 1951 with such effect that the RPF became the largest party in the Assembly.

The fact that the two largest party groupings produced by the 1951 elections, the Communists and the RPF, were the two most antagonistic to each other, and also to the parliamentary party system within which they found themselves, inevitably threw particular weight on the so-called center parties. Since, aside from the Socialists and MRP, these parties all had the loose organization characteristic of the parties of the Third Republic, the Assembly became once more the scene of shifting coalitions. This was still more the case when de Gaulle disavowed and, in a sense, disbanded the RPF in mid-1953, leaving its deputies free to participate in the struggle for political power.

Nor was the pattern changed by the 1956 elections. The RPF had disappeared, and its

place on the extreme right was taken by a far less disciplined group, the Poujadists, whose opposition to the parliamentary system was not tempered by the experience with its functionings that so many Gaullist deputies had possessed. The Radicals under Pierre Mendès-France temporarily took a turn toward the left and united with the Socialists to form a governing coalition called the Republican Front—a government held together less by internal cohesion than by pressures from the extremes and by fear of further crises. The political compromises, shifting party alignments, and parliamentary individualism that marked French politics thereafter paved the way for the collapse of the Fourth Republic, the reemergence of de Gaulle, and the establishment of the Fifth Republic.

The marked, though somewhat erratic, trend to the right in French politics was accentuated in the Fifth Republic. The explanation lies both in the continued (though by 1965 diminishing) dominance of President Charles de Gaulle and in the splintered character of the left. So long as the Algerian crisis persisted, de Gaulle received the support of the MRP (which, indeed, drew on a largely conservative electorate despite its socially progressive program), as well as of the newly formed and avowedly Gaullist Union of the New Republic (UNR) and the highly conservative Independents. Significantly, de Gaulle ostentatiously refused in 1958 to have his name associated with the UNR, since he recognized that many of his own supporters were also dedicated to keeping Algeria French. His major objective was to be free to handle the Algerian situation on whatever terms and with whatever timing he himself decided. Hence he kept the Algerian issue as far as possible out of electoral and legislative considerations and used public referenda to register support for his decisions.

In 1962, however, de Gaulle adopted another tactic:[1] a forthright attack on the old parties that were reaching toward a new, if tenuous, unity in opposition to his decision to have presidential elections decided by popular vote in-

[1] For a case study of these events see "Presidential Power and the Constitution: de Gaulle Appeals to the People 1962," by Stanley Hoffman in *Politics in Europe: Five Cases in European Government*, edited by Gwendolen M. Carter and Alan F. Westin (New York, Harcourt, Brace & World, Inc., 1965).

stead of by the indirect and traditional process of selection by persons already holding offices. (These were the deputies themselves in the Third and Fourth Republics, and a wide range of local representatives in the Fifth Republic). Declaring scornfully that "to confuse today the parties of yesteryear with France would be simply ridiculous," de Gaulle arrogated to himself in the legislative election of 1962 (as he had in the preceding, controversial referendum on direct election) the perception of France's "true will."

De Gaulle's actions in 1962, combined with the settlement in Algeria, sharpened the line of division between the UNR—Gaullist Independents and the rest. Seeking desperately to reestablish the old solidarity of the left, leaders of the opposition parties face the dilemma posed by the existence of the Communist party on the far left, which still polls some 20 percent of French votes. The Socialists, in particular, are constantly harassed by doubts about their relation to the Communists: should they align themselves with the Communists, as Guy Mollet decided to do in 1962, on the assumption that Gaullism was the greater peril? Or (as does the British Labor party) should they emphasize the difference between their evolutionary socialism and the more radical brand espoused by French Communists?

In addition, of course, the parties of the center and left have trouble even retaining their own cohesion. Yet this very difficulty provides insight into the pressures and trends of opinion within France. So do the sporadic activities (and somewhat diminishing enthusiasm) of the political clubs that sprang up during the early period of de Gaulle's undisputed leadership. Thus the spectrum of French parties is no less important an indicator of the character of French society now than it was in the days when parties played a more important role in shaping French policy.

2. THE PARTY SPECTRUM

Within the French multiparty spectrum, the crucial issue is whether the right, the center, or the left—non-Communist and/or Communist—

will form the nucleus around which majority legislative strength can be built. The majority position of the right—which was unprecedented from 1958 to 1966—appeared threatened by the growing strength of the opposition that unexpectedly forced General de Gaulle to enter a runoff ballot in the presidential elections of December 1965. His challenger, François Mitterrand, had wide support among the Radicals and Socialists, and also on the extreme left among the Communists, and oddly enough on the extreme right as well. Jean Lecanuet's brilliant personal success—although he finished third—enabled him to build the Democratic Center that balanced between a rightist and a center-left orientation. Thus the perennial French issues of "who should combine with whom" and "under whose leadership" continue to plague French politics. Thus all descriptions of party stands, organization, and alignment must be viewed as tentative.

The Right

The most significant change on the right during the early years of the Fifth Republic was the advance of the UNR and its allies, the dissident Gaullist Independents, and the resulting reduction between 1958 and 1962 in the strength of the Independents. The new Gaullist right absorbed much, if not most, of the traditional right. Moreover, it won its parliamentary victory in 1962 not only because of its close identification with de Gaulle but also because it appeared to represent a new modernism concerned with industrialism, urbanism, and technology. In contrast, the Independents, whose support dropped from 20 percent of the vote in 1958 to less than 10 percent in 1962, belonged to or represented local notables of a predominantly rural society that was rapidly being superseded in the "new" France.

Thus the basic questions about the future of the right are: Will the UNR's loyalty to de Gaulle provide it with sufficient popularity for it to maintain its dominant position? Will the economic transformation of France help the UNR to develop a greater rationale and cohesion of its own? Or will it be splintered by an opposition that is able to exploit the growing popular dissatisfaction with the authoritative policies of an entrenched executive working closely with a technically minded bureaucracy?

The UNR

The most paradoxical feature of the French party system in both the Fourth and the Fifth Republics is that the only man who can create a mass party drawn from all elements in the population, General Charles de Gaulle, does not believe in political parties, nor perhaps even in the representative system within which they play an essential role. When he formed the *Rassemblement du Peuple Français* in the spring of 1947, it was, he insisted, not a political party but above party, aimed at the political union of all French people. As it quickly gained phenomenal popularity, however, the RPF took on the form of a well-organized political party, and de Gaulle's followers sought ministerial offices as members of the RPF. Disillusioned, de Gaulle renounced his parliamentary followers in April 1953, leaving them free to engage in the parliamentary struggle for power from which he had tried so long to restrain them. Yet the end result was the disappearance not only of the RPF but of most of those who had swept into the Assembly in 1951 under its banner.

The *Union pour la Nouvelle République* was in a sense a reemergence of the RPF. It failed, however, to capture all the supporters of the earlier movement, and its leadership added to that of the former Gaullist groups some of the quasi-fascist elements that had engineered the overthrow of the Fourth Republic in May 1958. Though de Gaulle refused to lend his name to the UNR during the election campaign or to assume active leadership of it thereafter, its success in winning some 20 percent of the votes in the 1958 election and in capturing the major bloc of seats in the runoff contests was clearly attributable to his popularity. So was its even more striking success in the legislative elections of November 1962.

The major areas of Gaullist strength are western, northern, and eastern France; the areas of weakness are the center and the south. However, the Gaullist vote for deputies in 1962 was less decisive in the north than had been the vote for de Gaulle himself in the referendum on the direct election of the President. Nor was it nearly so decisive as was the voting for de Gaulle in the presidential election of December 1965, where again his support clustered in the northwest, the northeast, and the southeast. These areas form a curious melange, for they include both the underdeveloped west, where there have been many antigovernment demonstrations, and the highly prosperous northeast. Thus the voting for de Gaulle himself gives only a rough indication of the strength of the Gaullists.

The UNR prides itself on its loyalty to de Gaulle and publicly disavows any desire to have de Gaulle follow the policies its members most desire. This self-abnegation facilitated de Gaulle's settlement with Algeria, which many members of the UNR found distasteful, and subsequently kept them in line behind economic and social policies that are much more advanced than their conservative bias would suggest.

Few members of the UNR, apart from Michel Debré, are widely known either nationally or internationally. Neither de Gaulle himself nor Premier Pompidou owns a party card. On the whole, the UNR is not yet well rooted in the cities; it does less well in municipal than in national elections. Its success in replacing the Independents in so many areas rests on its position as the party of the government (which, in contrast to the situation in Great Britain, is quite different from being the governing party). Rather unkindly, the UNR has been called a claque rather than a political party. Americans find it easier to understand the party than do the British, for the UNR, like American parties, is a heterogeneous collection of groups of the right and center held together by their acceptance of the national leadership of an outstanding figure, and by their association with, though not possession of, political power.

Such organization as the UNR possesses does not extend beyond its small group of leaders, men like Debré, who are keenly aware both of the party's potential and of its deficiencies. In theory the party is strongly centralized, and its annual conference supreme in defining doctrine and program. A national council, made up of an equal number of persons inside and outside parliament, is said to assume responsibilities between the sessions of the conference. But in practice the secretary-general (there is no president), the twenty-member political committee, and, to a lesser degree, the sixty-member central committee make most of the decisions, including the selection of candidates, particularly for run-off ballots. Local organization is weak and shifting. At the national level, the philosophy of following rather than initiating means that policy decisions are left to the government.

The Independents

The Independents, who are what the French call moderate and what we call conservative, have had a checkered history. Like the UNR, they had predecessors under the Fourth Republic who benefited from the prevailing if uneven trend toward the right. These predecessors consisted of several rather ill-defined parties: the *Parti Paysan* (the Peasant and Social Action Party) and the *Parti Républicain de la Liberté* (PRL), in the First Assembly; the Independent Republicans for Social Action and the Independent Republicans, in the Second Assembly; and the Independents and Peasants for Social Action (IPAS) and the Social Republicans (the remnants of the RPF), in the Third Assembly. Under one designation or another, these groups held between seventy-five and a hundred seats in each Assembly during the Fourth Republic.

Broadly speaking, these rightist groups all stood for the traditional institutions of the family and the Church, urged support for church schools, and opposed nationalization and economic *dirigisme* (planning). Though they inclined toward the right-wing Radicals on economic policy, they were divided from them by the clerical issue. Despite, or perhaps because of, their lack of a precise program, they attracted considerable support. They provided (in March 1952) one of the Fourth Republic's most popular Premiers, Antoine Pinay, subsequently the formulator of the first programs of economic liberalism under de Gaulle. In the 1956 Assembly, however, their opposition to the economic programs of the left and center, and their hostility to concessions on Algeria, caused the fall of Ministry after Ministry and greatly contributed to the collapse of the Fourth Republic.

Nonetheless, in 1958, the Independents

emerged as the second largest party of the Assembly. For a brief span, it appeared as though they might realize their ambition to become the great conservative party of France. The Independents drew strength from small or large, rather than middle-sized communities, they appealed to persons of moderate but comfortable means, and they had the support of local "notables." But, like the Radicals, they were associated with the discredited Fourth Republic and with the values of what was rapidly becoming an obsolete, rurally oriented society.

Moreover, the Independents soon split over de Gaulle's leadership and policies. By 1962 they had disintegrated into three distinct groups: the pro-Gaullist Independents, who linked themselves with the UNR to form a parliamentary majority after the 1962 elections; an anti-Gaullist but constitutional group, which campaigned against de Gaulle's decision to have the President selected by direct election and suffered disastrously in the process; and an anti-Gaullist extremist movement, which bore some faint resemblance to the Poujadists.

Despite this splintering, the pro-Gaullist and the once anti-Gaullist Independents may have key roles to play in the future. Both groups compete with the UNR for the same conservative and clerical electoral support. The Gaullist Independents, led by Giscard D'Estaing, resist absorption but have no other place to go. The formerly anti-Gaullist Independents, however, under the sparkling leadership of Jean Lecanuet, have formed what is called the Democratic Center, which has obvious links through its leader with the MRP but has been tempted by the chance of sharing political power with the UNR.

The Center

The center parties—the *Mouvement Républicain Populaire* (MRP) and the Radicals, in particular—played a crucial role during the Fourth Republic by keeping the French government from falling under the control of either the extreme left or the extreme right. In so doing they frequently had the cooperation of the Socialists. The question continually faced, however, was where the center of political gravity was to be: in the non-Communist left, or the center, or the center-right. Complicating the establishment of any stable alliance was—and to some degree still is—the incompatibility between the traditional anticlericalism of the Radicals and Socialists, and the Catholic base of the MRP.

Under the Fifth Republic the center parties still face the same difficulties, though they have been somewhat ameliorated by a settlement of the issue of state support for parochial schools (see Chapter 8). But they have acquired an even more difficult problem: how to persuade pro–de Gaulle voters that they, rather than the UNR, represent the true center in French politics. The brilliant performance in the 1965 presidential campaign of Jean Lecanuet, ex-president of the MRP, brought the center into a new prominence. Although he finished in third place and was thus eliminated from the runoff election, Lecanuet has continued to exploit his popularity—his TV performances and publicity buildup have sometimes been compared with those of John F. Kennedy—in an effort to develop a cohesive center attractive to those from both sides of the spectrum. Although he has formally separated himself from the MRP, he can count on its continued support in his Democratic Center. This alignment can turn either to the right, as it showed signs of doing late in 1966, or to the center-left. Since Lecanuet refuses to work with the Communists, the possibility of any single anti-Gaullist alliance is eliminated.

The Mouvement Républicain Populaire

The *Mouvement Républicain Populaire* came into existence at the end of the war as one of the two largest parties in France. Its appearance constituted a double phenomenon: the emergence of a large and well-organized party capable of balancing the great parties that traditionally constituted the French left, and the creation of a large party able to combine friendliness to the Catholic Church with a democratic and semisocialist policy.

The leaders of the MRP—Georges Bidault, André Colin, Maurice Schumann, and Robert Schuman—had taken an active part in the Resistance movement, had an excellent record of opposition to fascism both at home and abroad, and were genuinely devoted to social and economic reform. They had joined with Socialists and Communists in drawing up the program of the National Council of Resistance, and they insisted that the MRP was itself a leftist party. Yet they also profited from the prestige of General de Gaulle, a Catholic, who, though conservative, was believed to favor them.

If the position of the leaders of the party was perfectly clear, however, there was considerable doubt about the nature of their following. In the first elections after the Liberation, the party received a tremendous popular vote, but much of this vote resulted not from desire for social reform but from fear of Communism or admiration for de Gaulle. Thus much of its earlier electoral support shifted quickly to the Gaullist RPF or to other conservative parties and never returned.

Yet this rapid drop in electoral support perhaps saved the MRP from becoming much more conservative than its founders desired. It has sought to reflect the progressive social conscience of the Catholic Church, so manifest after World War I, and to attract both the Catholic trade unions and young people. Like the Socialists, its leaders believe that the fullest development of the human personality demands proper economic and social conditions, but they emphasize social rather than economic reform. Like parties further to the right and in contrast to the Socialists, the MRP supports state financial aid for church schools. It has a sense of purpose based on an interpretation of life as concrete as that of the Communists.

It maintains contact with its constituents through Catholic trade unions (though the CFTU is no longer so close to the MRP as it originally was), youth groups (which help at election time), professional associations, and family organizations.

Around this program and through these agencies, the MRP built a mass party that polled between 14 percent and 25 percent of the votes under the Fourth Republic. Under the Fifth Republic its support and its importance have been much less. In 1958 it won fifty-six seats; in 1962 only thirty-six. Its growing disillusionment with de Gaulle—whose sharp words in May 1962 against European integration and the supporters of a supranational community precipitated the resignation of the five MRP ministers from the Cabinet—was matched by the shift of its voters to the right. In 1962 it won an even smaller percentage of votes than the Independents—8.9 percent on the first ballot and 5.2 percent on the second, as compared to the latter's 9.5 percent and 7.8 percent—though it won one more seat.

All during the Fourth Republic, the MRP was plagued by the fact that its electorate was more conservative than its leadership. When this division was compounded by the split between the anti-Gaullism of its leadership and the Gaullism of many of its natural supporters, the party's future was threatened. In May 1963 its annual congress even voted in support of merging its identity in a new opposition party, if such a party showed prospects of securing majority support. At the same time, the MRP explicitly rejected any notion of associating itself with the Communists. This stand seemed to indicate a hope that the MRP, the Independents, and the Radicals might form a strong enough center grouping to offer a hope of electoral success against the UNR. But since these three together polled less than a quarter of the votes and won less than a quarter of the seats in 1962, the hope seemed illusory. Moreover the chance of adding the Socialists to such a grouping was made much less likely by the explicit exclusion of the Communists.

In formal structure the MRP consists of sections united into federations that send representatives to an annual congress. There is also a national committee (which gives special weight to parliamentarians) and four executive organs: the president, the secretary-general, the executive commission, and the bureau. Under a liberalization of rules in 1959, the president, who is supposedly the leader in political matters, cannot be a cabinet minister, nor can he be reelected more than three times. The secretary-general, who handles organization matters, can stay in office longer. The bureau, some of whose thirteen members are now selected by the national committee, is the intermediary between the secretary-general and the executive commission. These changes were intended to keep the party leadership more in tune with the membership, but they do not solve the MRP's major problem: how to make itself a vital part of a non-Gaullist, non-Communist political grouping.

The Radicals and the RGR

From the beginning of the twentieth century until the election of 1936, the Radical party (*Parti Républicain Radical et Radical Socialiste*), often known as the Radical Socialist party, was more than any other identified with the Third Republic. It was the representative par excellence of the lower-middle classes, which held the greatest power: small shopkeepers, farmers, less successful professional men, and in general those who were suspicious of big men and big ideas and who were devoted to republican principles (particularly to anticlericalism) and to the heritage of the French Revolution. Inevitably, therefore, it suffered from the reputation of the Third Republic for inefficiency and corruption. Although its outstanding leader, Edouard Herriot, had a stainless record of opposition both to Nazism and to Vichy, the party as a whole was discredited. Loss of much of its press added to its weakness. In consequence, during the early years of the Fourth Republic the Radicals appeared in parliament only as a minor group. The center of a loose alliance known as the *Rassemblement des Gauches Républicaines* (RGR), it hoped to hold the balance of power between more powerful groups, although it seemed to have little hope of becoming a leading party itself.

In this perspective the role played by the Radicals in the Fourth Republic was almost as striking as the decline of the Socialists. As the balance of power shifted to the right with the ousting of the Communists in the spring of 1947, the votes of the Radicals became more significant. Before long, one of their top figures, Henri Queuille, formed a Ministry that turned out to be the only one in the course of the first Assembly to last longer than a year. By 1950 the Radicals had reestablished their local electoral machines, and in each subsequent election of the Fourth Republic they increased their representation in the Assembly till they ranked once more as one of the larger parties. Always a loosely united party, the Radicals were peculiarly susceptible, however, to internal divisions. In the early days of the Fourth Republic they split over the issue of whether to cooperate with de Gaulle or to work with the democratic parties to the left.

Still more serious was the ultimate effect of Pierre Mendès-France's efforts to reform the party structure and turn the Radicals into a disciplined national party. In his whirlwind attack on France's major problems during his premiership in 1954–55, Mendès-France achieved a settlement in the disastrous situation in Indo-China and secured economic sacrifices in the interests of strengthening France's economic situation. He was finally toppled from office, however, by the withdrawal of the support of the right-wing Radicals. Shortly thereafter, Mendès-France's group displaced the conservative party leaders and secured a seal of approval for a leftist emphasis in economic policy that recalled the early roots of Radicalism and heralded the possibility of an alliance with the Socialists. After the 1956 election, Mendès-France led the Radicals into a coalition with the Socialists (thereby reestablishing an anticlerical left—the Republican Front—for the only time in the history of the Fourth Republic). But the choice of Socialist Guy Mollet as Premier weakened Mendès-France's hold on his own party; he resigned from the Ministry in May 1956 without overthrowing the governing coalition. When, in 1957, he also resigned as leader of the Radicals, he had failed to break the local machines or to institute discipline among the party's parliamentary members. Moreover, the old members had been alienated, and the new ones he had attracted failed to remain constant. Thus the party suffered a striking defeat in 1958, despite the return to the *arrondissement* electoral system (see below) that had once been the basis of their strength.

In 1962, however, the Radicals held their own better than did either the Independents or the MRP. It seems likely, therefore, that the UNR's striking success in that election was largely at the expense of the other two. Moreover, although the Radicals and the other center-left groups of the *Rassemblement Démocratique* (Democratic Rally) associated with them polled fewer votes on the first ballot than the MRP, they gained more on the second ballot and managed to win forty-two seats, six more than the MRP. While this relative success strengthened the hands of those who were eager to

maintain their association with the left, the major objective of the Radicals is still to consolidate all non-Gaullist groups.

The unexpected emergence of François Mitterrand (whose UDSR—the Democratic and Socialist Union of the Resistance—has been loosely associated with the *Rassemblement Démocratique*) as de Gaulle's competitor in the second ballot for the presidency in December 1965 provided the kind of opportunity the Radicals and their associates have sought for their coordinating role. While Mitterrand's inclinations are toward the left rather than toward the MRP and Independents, he has sought associations in both directions. The Radicals would prefer such mobility but have found themselves increasingly impelled toward an alignment with the left.

Like other parties, the Radicals have their departmental federations, national congress, executive committee, bureau, and president. In 1959 the executive committee was cut in size from six hundred to two hundred, and inherited the power of a special group, the Comité Cadillac, to decide whether Radicals should participate in a ministry. The president, who has a two-year term, may now be reelected only once. But regardless of formal provisions, there is relatively little relationship between the party organization and the loosely organized deputies who call themselves Radicals.

The Left

Of all the general designations in French politics, that of "the left" is the most deceptive, the most confusing, and the most troublesome. Surprising to an American, French politicians find it an advantage for their popular image to belong to "the left." Thus center and even some rightist parties include some variant of left or democratic in their name and try to avoid the seats on the extreme right of the semicircular Assembly.

The fact that the Communists are at the extreme left of the political spectrum provides them with an aura unthinkable in most other democratic countries. The most serious weakness in the French party system in both the Fourth and Fifth Republics is that the Communists, an antidemocratic party, have consistently polled at least one-fifth of the votes in each legislative election. The number of seats in the Assembly that the Communists have won in different elections depends on the electoral system in force and the degree to which the non-Communist left and center hold together in run-off contests. But the continuing strength of Communist electoral support confronts the other left and left-center parties with a dilemma. They prove weak when they refuse to work with the Communists, and they face the danger of domination if they associate themselves with the Communists.

To draw distinctions between the Socialists and the Communists is as easy as to differentiate between the Socialists and the Radicals. Yet in both cases there are similarities as well as differences. The Socialists and Radicals are both left of center, and both are anticlerical. They differ sharply, however, in their approach to economic planning, which the Socialists support and the Radicals oppose. Both the Socialists and the Communists are Marxist in ideology, but only the latter are aligned to Moscow.

The Radicals, Socialists, and Communists formed the constructive Popular Front government of the mid-1930's that created decisive changes in France's economic and social structure. The tripartite relationship in which the Communists shared in the first year of the Fourth Republic left a less happy memory. Thus French politicians fear a Communist alliance but see its advantage for forming a strong opposition to the Gaullist UNR.

The presidential campaign of 1965 gave encouragement to those who favor such a left-center alignment. The refusal of Gaston Deferre, the wealthy, popular Socialist mayor of Marseilles, to accept Communist support in his candidacy for president so split his own party that he was forced to withdraw from the race. François Mitterrand, in contrast, although from a splinter center party, accepted Communist as well as Socialist support in his presidential campaign and won the run-off position against de Gaulle. Moreover, thereafter he formed the Left Wing Federation, which grouped together Socialists, Radicals, and political clubs, and opened talks with the Communists over tactics in the 1967 elections. Yet the old problems remain to haunt the Socialists. If they work with the Communists, this left alliance may so frighten the right and right-center as to consolidate the Gaullist majority. But if they ignore the Communists will they be able to gain a sufficient number of seats to play a distinctive role in the Assembly?

The Socialist Party

The tragedy of the Socialist party in France is that it has never been able to command the enduring allegiance of that kind of working-class organization that forms in Great Britain the bulwark of the Labor party. Immediately before World War II the Socialist party (which is often designated by the initials SFIO—*Section Française de l'Internationale Ouvrière*, or French Section of the Workers' International) was the largest of French parties. It had high hopes during the Resistance of becoming the strongest force in the revived French state, just as Labor became in Great Britain in the immediate postwar period, and with much the same kind of program. The first manifesto of the Socialist party announced a reorganization to make it a "great republican, democratic, and revolutionary force in the nation." Yet French Socialists have not been able to overcome the handicap of having a more dynamic group to their left, the Communist party.

In postwar as in prewar France, the Socialist party has been handicapped by the incongruity of its position and its following. In theory, it is a Marxist party, and as such it wants to be the representative of the working class. But, except in the northern regions, the industrial and mining departments of Nord and Pas-de-Calais, the SFIO has never satisfied the deeply felt class consciousness of the French workers, on which the Communists have capitalized so successfully. Fundamentally, French workers mistrust the bourgeoisie; but increasingly both the followers of the SFIO (in particular, teachers, professional and state-employed white-collar workers, and lower-grade civil servants) and its leadership are bourgeois. The British Labor party has been able to draw strength from its combination of working-class and middle-class support; the French Socialist party tends to fall between the two, not wholly trusted by either. Hardly less important is the Socialists' lack of appeal to youth and also, largely because of its anti-clericalism, to women.

Characteristic of the Socialist party is its division into *tendances,* or, as is sometimes said, into little "chapels" beside the big church, Communism. The two chief *tendances* are the doctrinaires, who press the party to adopt a more radical attitude, to return to the purity of Socialist doctrine, and to refuse to cooperate with middle-class parties; and the humanitarians, who emphasize human values and the importance of political and spiritual liberty and are ready to work with those who similarly prize them.

The great fear of French Socialists has been that, like the Liberal party in Great Britain, their support will be whittled away by the counter-attractions of the parties on either side of them. This fear has been intensified by the loss of much of their influence over the industrial working class (the *Force Ouvrière,* with which they have cordial relations, has limited working-class strength) and by the fact that they retain little significance apart from their role in parliament. During the Fourth Republic, the Socialist party alternated between sharing in Ministries—1946–51 and 1955–58—and deliberate self-exclusion from the Cabinet in order not to work with center and rightist groups. Thus the Socialists have been torn between their desire for political influence and their fear of falling into the kind of opportunism that ruined the Radicals in the late years of the Third Republic. Although the Socialists decisively supported de Gaulle in 1958, and although Guy Mollet, their secretary-general, was in de Gaulle's Cabinet until Debré's Ministry in January 1959, they have vigorously criticized all of de Gaulle's policies except his decision to give Algeria independence. Thus they early formed a part of the Gaullist opposition. Throughout the Fifth Republic, however, the Socialists have been more divided than ever, both internally and over their outside alignments.

A small new party that called itself the United Socialist Party (PSU) appeared between the Socialist party (SFIO) and the Communists early in the Fifth Republic. It drew support from both the SFIO and the Communists, from left-wing radicals and various small cliques. At its second congress, in 1963, no fewer than seven factions fell into dispute. The only point on which all its members agreed was that the PSU should try to reunify the Marxist left, particularly by encouraging the SFIO to cooperate both with themselves and with the Communists. The Communists, already wooing the SFIO, ignored the PSU. The SFIO, in turn, believed that the PSU was trying to destroy it.

These maneuvers would not have made so much difference if the SFIO itself had not been split internally between those following Guy Mollet, who favored the leftward alignment, and those who agreed with Deferre that the Socialists should reject the Communist alignment and work for an association with the Radicals and others of the left center. Mollet succeeded in developing an entente with the Communists in the 1962 election (which meant withdrawing competing candidates on the second ballot) that not only saved his own seat but won the Socialists thirty of their sixty-five seats, and the Communists twenty-two of their forty-one.

But while restraint under such circumstances could be mutually rewarding, only one candidate could successfully oppose de Gaulle for the presidency, and the Communists, as the price of their support, demanded a common program for the parties backing an opposition candidate. Deferre refused to consult them as we have seen, and temporarily won his party's endorsement for this stand at the 1964 congress despite Mollet's opposition. Failing, however, in his major effort to create a strong left-center grouping, Deferre retired. Mitterrand then succeeded in securing such support and thereafter built it into working arrangements for the 1967 legislative elections.

The local organizations or sections of the Socialist party are grouped in departmental federations. A federation that includes five sections, or a hundred members, can send representatives roughly proportionate to its members to the annual national congress, which defines basic doctrine and tactics. In the intervals between its meetings, the highest party organ is theoretically the national council, which is composed of one delegate from each departmental federation. The key authority in the party, however, is the executive committee, a body of forty-five members selected by the congress by majority vote (a process that under-represents minorities and entrenches the dominant group). The executive committee selects the five-man secretariat, the other center of power, and also the leader of the youth organization and the editors of the party's newspapers. The secretary-general (parliamentarian Guy Mollet since 1946) directs party organization and election strategy, but he has often not been able to persuade either the executive committee or the parliamentary members of the party to follow his lead. Moreover the party's local organizations often insist on nominating candidates who are not the first choice of the national leaders. Although this can be a source of weakness in its parliamentary representation, the very democracy this practice reflects can also be the party's proudest boast. Nowhere else in the French party system is there so decisive a control of party machinery by its rank and file and, as a consequence, so deep a feeling of genuine comradeship among many of its party members.

The Communist Party

The Communist party is quite unlike any other political group in France. This is partly because it is closely allied, or even perhaps subservient, to Moscow. But it is also true that its inner core of members regards the party as "the model-in-miniature of the new society" that it works to bring into existence, a society the more easily recognized because it already exists in the Soviet Union. Obviously, only a relatively small proportion of those who vote Communist, sign its petitions, and even speak at its meetings look on the Communist party in this light. Only the inner core provides both the strength and the essential characteristics of the Communist party. Whatever policies may be adopted as the result of tactics—and the party has followed highly flexible and varied policies since the Liberation of France—the overriding aim is to subserve the higher purposes of Communism.

Though the ultimate goal of the Communist party, as an exponent of the revolutionary Leninist school of Marxism, is social revolution, its tactics in France have been exceptionally opportunistic. On occasion, the party has promoted moderate and constructive policies aimed, not without success, at winning the support of small farm-owners as well as the landless and small businessmen as well as laborers. Though it tried to cripple the country with strikes from 1947 to 1950, it has more frequently—especially in 1962 and thereafter—bombarded the Socialists with demands for common action.

In the 1962 election, the Communists, through their party newspaper, *L'Humanité,* continually encouraged a rapprochement with the Socialists. Moreover, as we have seen, the Communists entered wholeheartedly into the bargain with the Socialists for mutual withdrawals and gained, as the Socialists did, from the arrangement. In January 1964, the Communists moved closer doctrinally to the Socialists by formally asserting that a one-party regime is not necessary "for the passage to Socialism" and that the transition to Socialism can be achieved by peaceful means. At the same time, the Communists revised their party statutes to provide that all party committees, except the all-important national Political Bureau, should be selected by secret ballot. In addition, under the Fifth Republic, the Communists have behaved in parliament in a much less obstructionist fashion than when they were in opposition in the Fourth Republic. Although they have been unwavering in their opposition to de Gaulle from the genesis of the Fifth Republic, they have demonstrated that opposition through legitimate parliamentary tactics and, on occasion, have even voted for proposals by the non-Communist opposition instead of restricting themselves to parallel action.

The Communist maneuvers over the 1965 presidential election provide a useful insight into their position and into their relations with other parties. Repeatedly they threatened to nominate their own candidate unless some agreement was reached on a common program for the opposition candidate. Thus they used their ability to split the opposition vote to win an affirmation of the acceptability of their support. Their continued opposition to Deferre was an influential factor in forcing his withdrawal, and their votes were important—they claimed decisive—in making Mitterrand's challenge to de Gaulle so effective in the 1965 presidential election. The dilemma of French politics of the left is, therefore, the indispensability of Communist support for electoral success coupled with the suspicion of other parties that any alliance will be turned to Communist advantage alone and that unscrupulous tactics will discredit those who worked with them.

It may be wondered why, in the face of such widespread suspicion of their motives, the Communists continue to poll such extensive support. One important reason is their control of the largest and most vigorous of the trade unions: the CGT. Through the CGT, the Communists maintain constant contact with a major group— the industrial workers—who commonly vote their ticket. They also include in their own estimates of membership civil servants, artisans, shopkeepers, agricultural workers, and teachers. In 1959, they disclosed that over half of their 200,000 to 400,000 members were over forty, and nearly four-fifths of them male. Perhaps only 70,000 of this total membership can be ranked as militants, but this hard core is devoted and disciplined.

The Communists can exploit real, as well as fancied, grievances of members of these groups. Moreover, as indicated, they enjoy an unjustifiable but no less real advantage as a result of their leftist position, which endows them with the aura of the French revolutionary tradition. In contrast to the other parties, with their shifting alignments, "flabby" leaders (to use the Communists' term), and internal splits, the Communists exude energy, and self-confidence. They are dynamic and aggressive, and they present a picture of unity, which sometimes cloaks their own inner struggles. There is no question to which they do not provide a clear and simple—and often destructive—answer.

Like other Communist parties, the French party has a highly disciplined hierarchical structure that gives supreme authority to those at the top. Its foundation is made up of cells of from three to eighty members. There are three types of cell: workplace, home, and rural. The workplace cells (forming 20 percent of the total number in 1955) are preferred for their effectiveness in developing class-consciousness and for being a potential basis for an underground organization. They are, however, difficult to organize in the face of employer opposition and shifting work schedules. The home cells (45 percent) are organized more loosely by streets or communes and thus have less revolutionary potentialities; the rural cells (35 percent) combine home and workplace.

The cells meet once a week or biweekly to consider national and international news in the light of party doctrine. They are autonomous, and each has its own bureau, or executive. Coordination is secured through the "section," which may include the cells in a large factory or those in a particular area. The sections, in turn, are grouped into departmental federations, one for each department in France. The federations send delegates to a party congress that meets, in theory, every three years and is technically the highest party authority. In fact, its role is educational: to present party orthodoxy to those present. Draft theses or motions may be circulated ahead of time and discussed vigorously in cell meetings, but there is no questioning or criticism at the congress itself.

The congress, again technically, elects a central committee of seventy-one members and twenty-two alternates who include the hard-core leaders of the party and its ancillary organizations, especially the CGT. The central committee selects from its own members a fourteen-man Political Bureau, which deals with day-by-day affairs, and a six-man secretariat, headed by a secretary-general. Despite the elaborate paraphernalia of elections on which this structure appears to rest, the leaders, in practice, are self-chosen. And it is they, and in particular the Political Bureau, who give the orders that the whole party must follow.

A particularly important and distinctive feature of the Communist party organization is the power of the Political Bureau to give binding instructions to the Communists who sit in the National Assembly and the Senate. In Great Britain not even a party congress, in either the Labor or the Conservative party, can do more than issue recommendations calling upon the party's members in parliament to take certain kinds of action. It is even more unheard of for the executive committee of a party to issue a parliamentary mandate. But French newspapers regularly carry items to the effect that "the Political Bureau of the Communist party met and gave a mandate to its parliamentary group" to vote in a certain way or to pursue a certain policy. Leaders of the Communist party may also be deputies, but it is their role outside the

Assembly that is all-important. Thus the Communist deputies as a whole have been chiefly significant in the eyes of the party as instruments for their opportunist policies: appealing to or embarrassing the Socialists, attacking the Gaullists, and supporting or discrediting the Assembly, whichever suits their purposes at that moment.

The Political Clubs

A phenomenon of the Fifth Republic, rather more important in its early years than later, is the political clubs. These sprang up in response, for the most part, to the diminution of the role of political parties and of parliament, as compared to the role of the executive, and to the shifting realignments of political ideologies during and after the Algerian war. In all, there are or have been about 120 political clubs, with a membership of between 15,000 and 20,000. One type of political club has been concerned chiefly with discussion and political education, either among those who held relatively similar views, or among those who held a wider spectrum of political opinion. The other type of political club has envisaged action as the end result of discussion, and their members have been commonly hostile not only to Gaullism but to the parliamentarianism typical of the Fourth Republic.

Perhaps the greatest significance of the clubs is that they have furnished a political forum for young people. Most of their members have been under forty. They formed, particularly just after 1958, a new force or "new strata" that sought new ways to infuse vitality again into French politics. Most club members are intellectuals, a more clearly defined and respected group in France than in British or American society, and almost all have tended toward the non-Communist left. A few of the clubs—like the left-wing Christian Democratic *Groupes "Esprit,"* whose members have been meeting since 1932 to discuss articles in periodicals, and the more typical and more important *Club des Jacobins,* which was established in 1951 to reinvigorate the Radical left wing—predated the Fifth Republic, but most were founded in the dark days of 1958 when it was widely feared that the Republic might collapse in chaos.

Though most of their activities are private, there have been times, particularly in 1963 and 1964, when groups of clubs have sponsored public conferences to give publicity to wide-ranging discussions. These discussions have sought to aid new political relationships and policies and, in particular, to spur a closer association or even unity of the non-Gaullist parties. Deferre's candidacy for the presidency received an early boost from the clubs. Subsequently they provided Mitterrand with his most consistent support within the Federation of the Left. Thus they added a more specifically political role to their earlier contribution of keeping alive a questioning spirit during the Fifth Republic's period of political apathy.

Pressure Groups

Pressure groups are commonly discussed in conjunction with political parties. But, since French pressure groups, particularly under the Fifth Republic, have been more concerned either with direct action or influencing the administration, they are considered both in Chapter 1 and Chapter 6. Much of the most effective pressure by French special-interest groups is exercised quietly but fairly continuously on the bureaus of the ministries, a process aided by the fact that administrative officials and the top staff of technical, commercial, and industrial concerns often share common training and exchange positions.

As in Great Britain, interest groups were long considered in France to be either insignificant or slightly disgraceful, and de Gaulle himself distrusts and dislikes them. Nonetheless, as will become clear in the description of the French administration, a structure of advisory committees has long provided private interests with a built-in means of exerting political influence. As power shifted from the legislature to the executive and the administration under the Fifth Republic, the latter area inevitably became the focus for pressures. Not until the French political parties and legislature win again—if they ever do—a powerful role in the formulation, if not the execution, of governmental policy, will it be appropriate to analyze the activities of pressure groups in connection with party politics in France.

Conclusion

The party system of the Fifth Republic is in flux, affected by two contrasting trends: the one trend working toward a two-party confrontation within the non-Communist parties consisting of the Gaullists and their allies on the one hand and the non-Gaullist, non-Communist parties on the other; but the other trend developing an association among the parties of the left and left-center. The Gaullists have demonstrated a surprising ability to command electoral support in France, and the natural result has been to spur their opponents to find some way of working together that will afford them a chance to share political power, or at least to influence the way in which it is used. The revival of political concern, particularly during the presidential election of 1965, opened the way for the succeeding electoral battle for the Assembly. But continuing to confuse and frustrate the efforts of each part of the non-Communist, non-Gaullist political spectrum to organize cohesive support around itself are the self-seeking efforts of individual leaders and political groups, the tendency to split over philosophies or personalities, and the prevailing fear of the Communists.

The strength of the executive in the Fifth Republic has relegated the legislature to a subordinate position, with a concomitant lessening of the role of the political parties. Yet the very strength of the executive has come from its ability to count on an acquiescent parliamentary majority. There is no doubt, therefore, that a great increase in the parliamentary membership of the non-Gaullist, non-Communist parties, or of a stronger, more cohesive left-center, would result in a very different type of interaction between executive and legislature. It is in this perspective that party maneuvers in France must be evaluated.

3. ELECTIONS

The Electoral System for the National Assembly

The French have shown a dismaying enthusiasm for new electoral systems. No other country has tried so many different ones—five distinct types, and fifteen with noticeably different features, during the past hundred years—or has made electoral change so much of a habit. Only once in that period, between 1889 and 1919, have the French used an electoral system for more than two elections in succession. If, as Peter Campbell demonstrates in his careful study, *French Electoral Systems and Elections, 1789–1957*, French electoral systems were not to blame for governmental instability, neither were they able, during that period, to create stable regimes. Thus the perennial search continued for an electoral formula that would help to reduce the number of extremists at either end of the political spectrum, or lessen the number of splinter groups, or in some other way produce a cohesive majority.

Most electoral changes in France have attempted to further partisan ends. They have been designed to work to the advantage of dominant groups, as in 1945 when the MRP, the Socialists, and the Communists endorsed proportional representation in the well-justified expectation that they would gain more seats than under the two-ballot system of single-member districts, which favored those parties (at that time the Radicals) with strong local machines. Or else they have been designed to answer particular emergencies, as when the system of *apparentement* (electoral alliances) was introduced in 1951 to strengthen the center parties against the Communists and Gaullist RPF, or as when the single-member district and two-ballot system was revived in 1958 for the twin purposes of weakening the Communists and aiding the conservative parties. However justified the reason may have seemed at the time, the frequency of the changes and the obviousness of the purposes behind them have impaired the sense of legitimacy of both the electoral process and its results and thereby have seriously weakened public faith in the democratic system.

The two most important electoral systems used in France have been those of proportional representation with a list system and the single-member constituency with two ballots. The former was used in two different forms under the Fourth Republic; the latter was characteristic of the Third Republic, except between 1919 and 1927, and has been adopted by the Fifth Republic.

Proportional Representation Systems and Their Consequences

The three elections held in 1945 and 1946 were based on strict proportional representation, under which each party received seats within a large electoral district (commonly the department) in accordance with the percentage of votes cast for it. In 1951, this system was replaced by a modified majority system in which all the seats in a department went to any previously announced alliance or coalition of parties that won more than half the votes. In case an alliance did not win a majority of the votes, the seats in a department were divided proportionately, as before, but the alliance secured the number of seats to which its percentage of votes entitled it and then divided them (as it did if it won all the seats in an electoral district) in proportion to the votes cast for the separate parties that formed the alliance.

Strict proportional representation gave a marked advantage to the parties with national strength. Since it tended to split the seats in each department between two or more parties, it penalized those regional parties that had previously been able to win all, or a majority, of the seats in a department in certain large sections of the country. A third, and perhaps more serious consequence, was that proportional representation with a list system provided strong control by party officials over the selection of candidates, since, unless more than half the voters insisted on a change, candidates secured seats in the order in which their names appeared on the ballot. Thus there was much less relationship between voter and candidate than in Great Britain, not only in the legislature but also at the time of the election.

The modified majority system opened the way for smaller parties to secure overrepresentation by uniting in alliances. Thus it worked—designedly—against the Communists and, in 1951, against the RPF. But of itself the modified majority system could do nothing to secure unity behind any given program. In 1951, the center parties in seventy-six districts formed alliances, none of them with the Communists but, because of local circumstances, thirteen of them with the RPF. In thirty-eight constituencies, an alliance won more than half the votes; in one constituency a single list did the same. But in 1956, the center parties formed competing coalitions, and in consequence only in eleven electoral districts did alliances win all the seats. In the absence of a general agreement among these middle-of-the-road groups to reduce their differences in the interest of excluding the non-democratic parties (the Communists and, in 1956, the Poujadists), the usefulness of the system was nullified.

The Electoral System of the Fifth Republic

The last Cabinets of the Fourth Republic and de Gaulle's Cabinet all revealed sharp differences of opinion over what electoral system should replace the discredited modified majority system. Since de Gaulle's government was specifically authorized to determine the electoral system while it still possessed full powers (though Parliament thereafter regained its customary right to revise the system or establish a new one), de Gaulle followed the majority view in support of the single-member district plus two-ballot system characteristic of the Third Republic, which also fitted his own desire for a system that could be easily understood by the voters. Election is for a five-year period unless there is a dissolution.

The Two-Ballot System

The two-ballot system provides that if no candidate should secure more than half the votes at the election, there will be a second election a week later, both held commonly on a Sunday. The week interval gives each party and voter an opportunity to decide whether to continue to support the same candidate as before or whether to support another candidate who has a better chance to succeed. Under the Third Republic, both left- and right-wing parties used to switch their votes to that candidate among their group who had the best chance to win. Moreover, new candidates could enter on the second ballot.

This latter practice was forbidden by the Fifth Republic, and any candidate receiving less than 10 percent of the vote (until November 1966, 5 percent) on the first ballot is not allowed to run on the second. These provisions operate deliberately to the advantage of those parties that have the largest base of support or that are prepared to combine behind the candidate most likely to win.

In 1958 the sharp division between the Communists and other left-wing parties effectively prevented them from yielding to each other on the second ballot except in a few instances where the Communists did not oppose persons who had voted "no" on the referendum. Since only thirty-nine candidates were elected on the first ballot in 1958, the second ballot was particularly significant. It was at that stage that the Communists suffered so greatly while the UNR gained its nation-wide victory. Fairly characteristic was the situation in the Goutte-d'Or district of Paris, where the wife of the secretary-general of the Communist party polled almost twice as many votes on the first ballot as the UNR candidate who came second, 11,455 to 6,786. But on the second ballot, when only the UNR and Socialists retained their candidates against her, she lost to the UNR candidate by 12,545 votes to 20,160 votes.

It was this kind of situation that led the Socialists and Communists to enter into the arrangement in 1962 for mutual withdrawals. As we have seen, this arrangement helped the Socialists to win thirty of their sixty-five seats and helped the Communists to win twenty-two of their forty-one seats. This temporary Marxist alignment frightened the conservatives into the arms of the Gaullists and led to the UNR virtually absorbing the right and right-center. Moreover, the arrangement between the Socialists and Communists threatened the former's fragile cohesion and alarmed the Radicals. Yet only a non-Gaullist, non-Communist centrist alignment or a left-center one including the Communists appeared capable of challenging the Gaullists in the next electoral contest for the legislature.

The Voter and the Candidate

Regardless of the changes in the electoral system, the conditions under which a person may vote and run as a candidate in France have remained approximately the same over the years. Candidates must be over twenty-three (voters over twenty-one), French by birth or naturalized for at least ten years (voters naturalized for five years), and free from any of the incapacities defined by law. These incapacities include such expected barriers as conviction for certain crimes. Since the days of General Boulanger, no one may run in more than one district. There is no positive residence qualification in France, but a negative provision exists under which prefects and members of the judiciary may not run in districts where they have served until after a designated time (between six months and three years, depending on the position) has elapsed.

The most significant innovation of the Fifth Republic is to require the nomination of a substitute who can fill a member's seat in the chamber should this member be chosen as a minister or accept an incompatible position— e.g., on the Constitutional Council or as a trade union official—or die. The position of the substitute is an anomalous one. He may or may not campaign, but if he does he has no financial responsibilities for the campaign. His name appears on the ballot along with that of the candidate, so that the voter is, in effect, selecting both; the voter's choice is complicated if he views the two candidates in a different light. And while the substitute assumes a parliamentary seat only if the member is unable to fulfill his own mandate, he is barred from opposing the member at the next election. The purpose of this provision is to keep ministers from moving in and out of the Assembly, but the character of Cabinets in the Fifth Republic has made it less important than was expected.

Candidates must announce their candidature at least twenty-one days before the first ballot, and, in a new effort to prevent frivolous nominations, each is required to deposit 1,000 new francs (approximately $200), which is not returnable unless the candidate receives at least 5 percent of the votes in either of the ballots.

Money in Elections

French political parties are under no obligation to publish the sources of their funds or their election expenditures. Moreover, no limit is set on spending in elections. In an effort to equalize the opportunities among candidates, the government reimburses everyone who retains his deposit for the expenses of certain types of publicity, including posters on official billboards and the printing and mailing of election addresses and cards. In theory, only this kind of propaganda is permitted; in practice, however, a good deal of unofficial material is circulated. With rare exceptions, French political parties and parliamentary candidates do not engage in the kind of splashy electoral advertising or gimmickry that often mark an American campaign. One candidate is reported to have spent the equivalent of $100,000 for spectacular self-advertising in the 1956 election, but the average total electoral expenditure for a national party is only two to four times this amount. Apart from unofficial contributions by trade union members to the Communists and the Socialists, most of the money contributed to electoral expenses comes from professional or from employers' groups, notably the CNPF (*Counseil National du Patronat Français*). These groups often support more than one party and may even contribute to a Socialist candidate if he seems likely to defeat a Communist.

Electoral Campaigns in the Fifth Republic

The 1958 Assembly Election

The 1958 electoral campaign was held in the shadow of the referendum two months before. Almost everyone, except the Communists, proclaimed his allegiance to de Gaulle. The UNR could claim most authentically, however, to be the Gaullist party, and it did so with the smooth techniques of modern publicity experts—with the added attraction of a series of well-known personalities who represented a variety of views.

Twelve parties or election coalitions presented the minimum of seventy-five candidates necessary to qualify for free radio and television time. The newest of the twelve were the UNR and the Union of Democratic Forces (UDF), which included the Mendès-France wing of the Radicals and François Mitterrand's wing of the UDSR. The political spectrum extended from Pierre Poujade's UDCA (Union for the Defense of Tradesmen and Craftsmen) to Maurice Thorez's Communist party. Noticeable were the splits in the Democratic Left between Guy Mollet's Socialist party and an Autonomous Socialist party made up of the dissident SFIO; among the Radicals, the Republican Center under André Morice, Felix Gaillard's Radical

Socialists, and the UDF; and between the democratic Catholics of Pierre Pflimlin's MRP and Georges Bidault's French Christian Democracy (DCF).

The Communists entered candidates in all districts on the first ballot and, despite their obvious isolation, optimistically avowed their intention of seeking a union of republican forces on the second ballot. The Socialists under Guy Mollet supported de Gaulle's policy in Algeria, the evolution of the Franco-African Community, economic expansion, and social progress. The UDF and Autonomous Socialist party called for negotiations with rebel and representative groups in Algeria and, on the home front, for more economic planning to secure full employment without inflation. Gaillard's Radical Socialists stuck to a more classic economic program but demanded a revolution in French education, particularly by making higher education more readily available to all, while André Morice's group supported a French Algeria. The MRP, badly shaken in morale, campaigned in support of de Gaulle's Algerian policy, European unity, and economic and social expansion. The Independents, in contrast to most other French parties, went all the way in support of the complete integration of Algeria and France, were skeptical about de Gaulle's policies toward the African territories, and favored an economic "liberalism" for France similar to West Germany's. The newly organized UNR took no precise stand on any issue and, despite the General's refusal to associate himself with any political party, stressed only its complete fidelity to him. Poujade sounded much more moderate than in 1956, though he assailed the Common Market. It was obvious, however, that his movement was at an end.

The Fourth Republic's adoption of the department as the electoral district had made campaigns less individualistic and elections no longer a matter of personality and camaraderie. But the return to the single-member district reintroduced most of the old campaign practices of the Third Republic. House-to-house canvasses replaced mass meetings in many places, though there were also a few well-publicized debates, notably between Mendès-France and his rightist and successful opponent, and between General Chassin of the Algerian ultras and the moderate

UNR Jacques Chaban-Delmas in Bordeaux. In general, however, the electoral campaign was less vigorous than were those of the Third Republic.

The 1962 Referendum and Assembly Election

The legislative election of 1962 followed so closely the referendum called to endorse direct election of the President that we must consider the two together. Despite widespread criticism and opposition from the older parties and, to a muted degree, from the constitutional bodies concerned, de Gaulle persisted in his determination to bypass the regular amendment process and refer the constitutional change to referendum. He so notified the chambers on October 2, 1962; the Assembly passed a motion of censure, bringing down the Pompidou government; de Gaulle dissolved the Assembly on October 6; and the fight was on.

THE REFERENDUM   The campaign before the referendum on October 28 was marked by high political tension but little popular excitement. Both sides redoubled the assaults (now written rather than verbal) that had already been in process before the Assembly was dissolved. It was apparent that the opposition's arguments were almost entirely negative, that the executive was prepared to exploit to the full the government's monopoly of broadcasting (each of the six parties received ten minutes, while de Gaulle and the ministers spoke at will), and that de Gaulle was determined to make the referendum a personal vote of confidence in himself. On October 18, he declared:

> If you answer no, as all the old parties would like so as to restore their regime of disgrace, as well as all the plotters who want to promote subversion, or even if the majority of "yes" is weak, mediocre, risky, it is obvious that my role will be over, immediately and forever.

Many were torn between their unhappiness over this use of the referendum and their unwillingness to indicate lack of support for de Gaulle. The outcome indicated their uncertainty.

The tally showed the lowest proportion of "yes" votes yet received in a referendum by de Gaulle: 74.95 percent of the registered voters (who numbered 28,185,478) participated, but only 62.25 percent of the valid ballots (which amounted to 21,125,054) supported him. Thus the "yes" vote of 13,150,516 was only 46.66 percent of the registered voters. In fourteen out of ninety departments the "no" vote exceeded the "yes" vote, the first time this had happened in any department in a referendum in the Fifth Republic. Twelve of these fourteen departments formed an arc stretching from southwestern France to the Italian border (except for Alpes-Maritimes at the southeast corner). In these the opposition was most marked in the villages and small towns.

The areas of high "yes" votes formed a somewhat paradoxical combination. Two—those of western France (Brittany and Normandy), and of eastern France (Alsace and Lorraine)—coincided with traditionally conservative strongholds; but in the third, the large industrial area of northern France, the left had formerly been very strong. Interestingly, there was a marked coincidence between the areas of high positive votes and high birth rate.

In 1958, the Socialists, the MRP, the Independents, and, more reluctantly, the Radicals (as well as the UNR) had supported de Gaulle. The referendum indicated that when these four opposition parties opposed him, they lost more than half their votes. Only the Communists had voted strictly according to instructions, while one-third of the Socialist voters, half the Radical and Independent voters, and some 85 percent of the MRP voters had voted "yes." Though *Le Monde* wrote that there had been "no winners, no losers," de Gaulle had, in fact, got his way. The long-range impact, however, would be largely determined by the results of the legislative election to follow.

THE ASSEMBLY ELECTION   In the campaign between the referendum and the election, the opposition showed itself as negative as ever and even more seriously divided. Since the constitutional factor was no longer at issue, it lost the support of certain professional groups and intellectuals. It found it difficult to answer the lofty Gaullist claim of representing order, efficiency, and rebuilding, and the charge that the old parties had brought France to stalemate and near-chaos. What may well have been deci-

Results of the Legislative Elections of November 23 and 30, 1958 [1]

	FIRST BALLOT		SECOND BALLOT	
	Votes	*Percent*	*Votes*	*Percent*
UNR or Gaullists	3,603,958	17.60	5,249,746	28.1
Communists	3,882,204	18.90	3,883,418	20.5
National Independents' Center	2,815,176	13.70	2,869,173	15.4
Socialists	3,167,354	15.50	2,574,606	13.8
Popular Republican Movement	1,858,380	9.10	1,370,246	7.3
Radicals	983,201	4.80	619,784	3.3
Moderates	1,277,424	6.20	570,775	3.1
Left Republican Rally	716,869	3.50	439,517	2.4
Republican Center	647,919	3.02	451,810	2.4
Christian Democrats	520,408	2.05	343,292	1.8
Extreme Right and Poujadists	669,518	3.03	172,361	1.0
Miscellaneous Left	347,298	1.04	146,046	0.8

[1] All percentages are based on the number of registered voters.

sive, however, was Guy Mollet's decision to form a negative electoral alliance between the Socialists and the Communists in which neither would compete with the other on the second ballot. This decision presented the right with a golden opportunity to flourish the Communist menace and further split the non-Communist opponents of Gaullism.

The first ballot, on November 18, had strange features. The total number of abstentions rose far above what it had been in any legislative election since World War II—31.25 percent. This may have been a mark of recognition that the Assembly had ceased to be the center of power. But the most important fact was that the UNR won 31.9 percent of the votes, a significant vic-tory. The UNR, together with its affirmed allies, the dissident Independents, polled 5,847,403 votes, about two and a half million more than in 1958. These votes were won largely, though not exclusively, from the Independents and the MRP.

The extreme right virtually disappeared. In contrast, the Communist vote went up slightly, to 3,992,431—21.78 percent of the total cast. This was an increase from the 18.9 percent in 1958, but it was markedly less both in total and per-centage than the more than five million votes and the 25 percent of those cast that were common under the Fourth Republic. The evi-dent trend was toward the moderate right.

Out of the 435 seats for metropolitan France,

Results of the Legislative Elections of November 18 and 25, 1962 [1]

	FIRST BALLOT		SECOND BALLOT	
	Votes	*Percent*	*Votes*	*Percent*
UNR	5,847,403	31.9	6,165,929	40.5
Communists	3,992,431	21.8	3,243,041	21.3
Socialists	2,319,662	12.6	2,304,330	15.2
National Independents' Center	1,660,896	9.1	1,125,988	7.4
Popular Republican Movement	1,635,452	8.9	806,908	5.3
Independents	798,092	4.4	241,853	1.6
Left Center	705,186	3.8	432,389	2.8
Radicals	679,812	3.7	635,712	4.2
Extreme Left	449,743	2.4	183,844	1.2
Republican Center	81,627	0.5	51,164	0.4

[1] All percentages are based on the number of registered voters.

a second ballot was necessary in 369 districts. In 227 of these districts, the competition was narrowed by withdrawals to a contest between right and left: Gaullist on one side and Radical, Socialist, or Communist on the other. The second ballot results showed a decisive increase in Gaullist votes to 6,407,782, almost a million and a half more in these 369 districts than on the first ballot. The traditional left—Radicals, Socialists, and Communists—also increased their percentage slightly, with the Socialists securing the major advantage. Both the Independents and the MRP, on the other hand, lost substantially, a further indication that the UNR was benefiting at their expense. Finally, as we saw earlier, the UNR and its allies obtained 249 seats, a clear and unprecedented majority of the members in the Assembly. De Gaulle had succeeded in his objective of turning the legislative election into a second and even more successful affirmation of personal support.

Elections for the Senate

The Senate is a weak body, much less important than the Assembly. It is elected indirectly, mainly by local councilors. Of the 108,266 electors in 1959, 53 percent came from communes with fewer than 1,500 inhabitants, 25.5 percent from towns with 1,500 to 10,000 inhabitants, and only 21.5 percent from cities with over 10,000 inhabitants.

Of the 307 members of the Senate selected in 1959, 255 were from metropolitan France, 32 from Algeria, 2 from the Sahara, 7 from overseas departments, and 5 from overseas territories; 6 were chosen by French citizens living abroad. The 60 senators from the seven most populous departments of France were elected by proportional representation. Those from France, Algeria, the Sahara (Algeria and Sahara were eliminated from subsequent representation because of Algerian independence), and four of the overseas departments were selected in the double-ballot system by department-wide electoral colleges. These colleges consisted of the deputies for the department, the department councilors, all municipal councilors for towns with over 9,000 inhabitants (with an additional delegate for each thousand inhabitants over 30,000), and 1–15 delegates for towns

and villages under 9,000, depending on their size. Though there was a slight additional representation for the more populous towns, since under the Fourth Republic one additional delegate was allowed only for each 5,000 inhabitants over 45,000, the overrepresentation of the rural areas remained marked. Since, in addition, the elections were for nine-year terms (one-third chosen every three years), as in the Third Republic (in the Fourth Republic for six years), and many of the electors were bound to have been selected several years earlier, there is a serious danger that the second chamber is always out of touch with public opinion.

While the Assembly elections of 1958 brought many new members into the chamber, the Senate elections in 1959 returned a high proportion of former senators and deputies. Eighty-four percent of those senators offering themselves for reelection were successful. Of the 85 new senators, 34 were former deputies. Twenty-five of these included such former leaders as Mitterrand, Edgar Faure, and Duclos, who had failed to secure seats in the Assembly the November before. On the overall results, the Communists lost only two seats and the Socialists five, as compared with their representation in the Council of the Republic of the Fourth Republic, while the Radical-oriented center won three more seats, the MRP eight more, and the Independents five more. In light of the expectation that the Senate would act as a brake on the National Assembly, it was particularly striking that the UNR failed by two to secure even as many seats as had been held by the RPF.

The campaigning for the Senate was restricted to negotiations between departmental party organizations. The UNR and Independents tended to work together, but their overtures to the MRP and other central groups were largely unsuccessful. Communist discipline held when the MRP retired its candidates in favor of Socialist or Radical candidates in over twenty departments on the second ballot (necessitated by the lack of an absolute majority on the first ballot). Noticeable was the contrast between the party representation from particular departments in the Assembly and in the Senate. Thus the hoped-for difference in the political complexion of the two chambers was achieved, but it was not the difference that had been desired.

The rural elements, which were out of touch with the new industrialization, were once more entrenched in the Senate. At the same time, some of the ablest parliamentary leaders of the Fourth Republic had seats in that body, while the Assembly had a majority of untried and inexperienced members.

In 1964, a new act instituted majority voting for party lists of candidates in all cities of more than 30,000 inhabitants (158 cities) in place of the existing system of proportional representation. The system had already been in effect for the 37,808 municipalities having fewer than 30,000 inhabitants. If a list receives a majority of the vote, it gains all the seats; if not, there is a runoff election between parties receiving at least 5 percent of the vote. In that case a plurality secures all the seats.

The government expected that this new system would polarize voting and force voters who had supported the center parties, which had done so well in 1959, to vote for either the Gaullists or the Communists. No clear pattern emerged, however, in the municipal elections of March 1965. If anything, the Socialists and Communists, working in each other's interests, emerged with an advantage. Otherwise the UNR would have won a majority in the Paris city council. In fact, the abolition of the proportional representation system in the larger towns, far from working to the advantage of the UNR, worked against it. The UNR won no seats in Marseilles and Lyons, the second and third largest cities in France, and lost Grenoble, Le Mans, and other smaller towns. On balance, the UNR held its own but made no noticeable impact at the grass-roots level. Of the towns affected by the change, only twenty-four changed hands, mainly to the advantage of the Communists. In the municipal elections, at least, and by projection in the elections for the second chamber, the UNR lacks the strength it evidenced in the Assembly elections of 1958 and 1962.

Elections for the President

The most dramatic and far-reaching constitutional change made during the Fifth Republic has been the change from indirect to direct election of the President. Controversial as was the process for winning support for this change, there is no doubt that it has revivified French politics. In the total picture of elections under the Fifth Republic, the election for the President in December 1965 emerges as the most significant, largely because it was marked by a type of political campaigning previously unknown under this constitutional system. Moreover it provided the most serious test up to that time of de Gaulle's popularity and, possibly, furnished the best indication of future developments.

The President of the Fifth Republic was always intended to be the key representative of the nation as neither the President of the Third nor of the Fourth Republic was supposed to be. There was therefore no intention of leaving his election to the two chambers (as had been the practice in the earlier regimes), particularly in view of the debacle of December 1953, when it took thirteen ballots to elect Senator René Coty, a moderate right-wing conservative. On the other hand, there was still too much fear of direct election in 1958 to entrust the choice of a President to the electorate at large. The compromise was to use an electoral college only slightly modified in composition from that which chose the senators.

A major difference between the electoral college for the Senate and for the President was that the latter included for this one time among its 81,764 members 3,643 of the elected representatives from the member-states of the Community, of which the President of France was ex-officio president. Another slight difference was that the electors from communes in France with fewer than 9,000 inhabitants were not special delegates; rather, the mayor and a designated number of councilors served as delegates. This change reduced the representation of villages under 1,500 people to 51 percent and of towns with between 1,500 and 10,000 inhabitants to 20 percent, while it raised only to 20 percent the representation of cities with over 10,000 inhabitants. This gave the rural elements the strongest voice in two of the three elected institutions of France.

In the first presidential election of the Fifth Republic, de Gaulle clearly chose himself for an office he had designed, and he subsequently made full use of its potential powers, as we have seen. Nominated by thousands of electors (at least fifty were necessary) from all the non-Communist parties except Mendès-France's UDF (which nominated Albert Chatelet, Dean of the Faculty of Science at the University of Paris) and the Communists (who nominated Georges Marrane, Mayor of Ivry), de Gaulle received 62,394 out of 79,470 votes cast—78.5 percent of the vote. The votes were cast on December 21, 1958, in the capital of each department of France and in the capital of each of the territories overseas. There was no stalemate, but there was also none of the glamour of the former electoral gatherings at Versailles.

The President is elected for seven years and may be reelected indefinitely. There is no provision (as there was in the 1946 constitution) limiting his terms. Although most people expected that de Gaulle would succeed himself, they were not prepared for the dramatic events of 1962 in which his attempted assassination (on August 22) was followed by his introduction of successful plans to provide for the direct election of the next President.

The present system of presidential elections was set up by the constitutional revision of October 28, 1962 (approved by the controversial referendum), the organic law of November 6, 1962, and decrees of January 25 and March 14, 1964. These provisions established that the election should take place by direct vote not less than twenty nor more than thirty-five days from the expiration of the presidential term (or the permanent incapacity of the President). Thus elections were due between December 4 and 19, 1965. Once again the process of second ballot was established so that if no candidate received an absolute majority of the votes on the first round, a runoff election would be held two weeks later between the two candidates receiving the greatest number of votes.

A candidate could be nominated by petition of any hundred members of parliament, of the Economic and Social Council, of General (i.e., Departmental) Councils, or elective mayors so long as they were drawn from at least ten different departments or overseas territories. A deposit of 10,000 francs (about $2,000) was re-

quired from each candidate; if he did not receive at least 5 percent of the vote, he forfeited his deposit. In that case, however, he was to receive an equal amount toward his expenses. A National Electoral Campaign Control Commission, composed of five high civil servants, was to supervise the campaign regulations, which provided for equal opportunity to use radio, TV, propaganda posters, and so forth, but only during the official campaign period, which was limited to fifteen to seventeen days.

First in the field was Gaston Deferre, Socialist Mayor of Marseilles, who was launched by the national weekly newspaper, *L'Express,* in September 1963 and officially announced his candidature as early as December 1963. Chairman of the SFIO in the Assembly, he also controlled the largest Socialist departmental organization in the country. But if his lack of dogmatism on Socialist doctrine and clericalism made him acceptable to the center parties, his forthright anti-Communism led to opposition, not only from the Communists themselves but also from the Mollet wing of his own party. In January 1964 Deferre won a grudging endorsement from the Socialists (and subsequently from the Radicals) while keeping a free hand for his campaign. He then established committees with a wide membership spanning the Socialists, Radicals and UDSR, Christian Democratic and Socialist trade unions, political clubs, and university professors. Thereupon he undertook a number of provincial tours. But though he attracted attention, Deferre gained little support. Public opinion polls in late 1963 and 1964 showed a two to one preference for de Gaulle over Deferre, a gap that widened when the polls included other alternatives. Nor did the chances appear more promising for two other early candidates, Jean-Louis Tixier-Vignancour, a right-wing extremist, and André Cornu, from the Radical grouping. When Deferre withdrew in June 1965, the only serious contender left was de Gaulle himself.

All the more remarkable, therefore, was the liveliness of the final campaign. Of the six candidates at the end, only three were of significance: de Gaulle himself, who majestically waited until the last moment to announce that he was running; Jean Lecanuet, ex-President of

The Presidential Election
December 5 and 19, 1965

Votes obtained by	Number	Percent of valid votes	Percent of registered voters
FIRST BALLOT			
Charles de Gaulle	10,828,523	44.64	37.45
François Mitterrand	7,694,003	31.72	26.61
Jean Lecanuet	3,777,119	15.57	13.08
Jean-Louis Tixier-Vignancour	1,260,208	5.19	4.35
Pierre Marcilhacy	415,018	1.71	1.43
Marcel Barbu	279,683	1.15	0.96
SECOND BALLOT			
Charles de Gaulle	13,083,699	55.19	45.26
François Mitterrand	10,619,735	44.80	36.74

the MRP and the center candidate, who had been virtually unknown before the campaign but soared up on the public opinion polls from 3 percent to 20 percent in the last month of the campaign; and François Mitterrand, from a small Radical-associated group, the UDSR, who also secured both Socialist and Communist support. It was Lecanuet's brilliant TV performances and modern campaign, his youth (he was 45—de Gaulle was 75) and good looks, and his pro-Europeanism, that sparked the official campaign period and brought a new concern for politics into French life. It was Mitterrand's solid support from the Socialists, Communists, and Radicals that won him second place in the polls.

The supreme surprise of the election was that in the heaviest polling in France's electoral history, with a turnout of 85 percent of the enrolled voters, de Gaulle received just under 45 percent, forcing him into a runoff election in which he won just over 55 percent. Although he was returned to the presidency for another seven years, de Gaulle had lost the mystique and the widespread sense of his indispensability that had dominated French politics since 1958.

The Geography of Elections

We have already suggested, in the preceding sections, the geography of voting under the Fifth Republic. The maps opposite show the areas from which the two most widely and consistently supported political forces in contemporary France—Gaullism and Communism—draw their major support.

4. HOW WELL DOES THE FRENCH PARTY SYSTEM WORK?

Any attempt to evaluate the French party system raises the same questions that arose in connection with British parties. The answers, however, are quite different.

In one sense, French parties offer their members and the voters a more accurate spectrum of political views and of leaders than does the British system, simply because the choice is far greater. Although it is often the despair of those seeking a broad association of political interests, it is also a matter of pride that any fervently held political view can be—and often has been—reflected in a particular political party. If the extreme right has been eliminated, as the 1962 election returns suggest, it is because France's economic growth is solving the problems that gave rise to it.

In another sense, however, the choice provided by the French political spectrum is less meaningful than the simpler British one. The very fact of the multiplicity of French parties makes it extremely difficult—one no longer says impossible—for any party to win a majority of

Geography of the 1958 French Election

PERCENTAGE OF THE FIRST VOTE
CAST FOR THE COMMUNISTS

PERCENTAGE OF THE FIRST VOTE
CAST FOR THE U N R

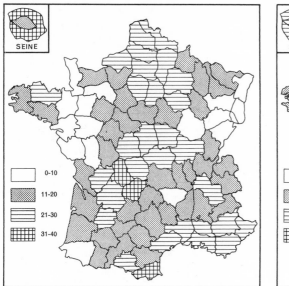

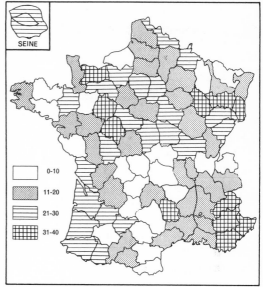

Source: Adapted from *Le Monde*, November 25, 1958.

The Referendum of October 1962

The Elections of November 1962

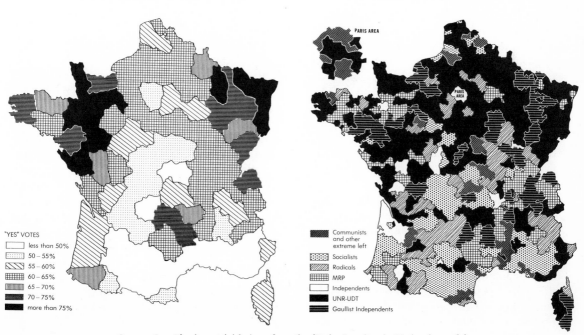

Source: Les Elections Législatives de 1962 (Paris, Imprimerie Nationale, 1963).

The Presidential Election December 5 and 19, 1965

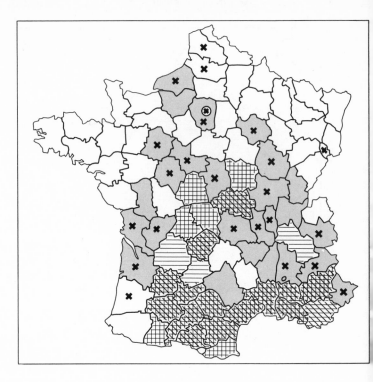

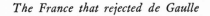

The France that rejected de Gaulle

	Departments voting NON October 1962
	Departments putting Mitterrand ahead December 5, 1965
	Departments putting Mitterrand ahead December 19, 1965

The France that accepted de Gaulle reluctantly

| | Departments giving him less than 45 percent December 5, 1965 |
| | Departments giving him less than 55 percent December 19, 1965 |

The France that remained loyal to de Gaulle

| | Departments giving him more than his national share of the votes in both rounds |

Source: Manchester Guardian Weekly, December 30, 1965, p. 4.

the votes and legislative seats. It is even more difficult to envisage any regular alteration of a governing and an opposition party as in Great Britain and the United States.

A major difference between British and American parties, on the one hand, and French parties, on the other, has to do with the period at which the process of mutual concessions and compromise takes place—a process that is inevitable if groups holding different views and possessing different interests are to be persuaded to work together. In Great Britain and the United States, the parties, in appealing to the uncommitted voter in the middle, tend to moderate their stands and achieve compromise *before* the election. In France, such compromise has commonly occurred *after* the election, through jockeying inside and outside the chambers. Thus the process is less the result of appealing to the voters than of bargaining among political leaders. It is noticeable, however, that the introduction of the direct election of the

President led to a franker and more broadly gauged appeal to voters than has marked legislative elections in the past.

It is now misleading to say, as we once could, that the French, unlike the British and the Americans, have no direct way of passing upon the principles or the officials that are to guide the government. French voters indicated both in 1958 and in 1962 that they support General de Gaulle and those politicians who are prepared to support his policies. But this is still not to say that French voters can yet choose decisively *between* two sets of political alternatives. British and American voters can choose their leaders and, to some extent, their policies, because each country has a basically two-party system, and only in such a system is one party *or* the other certain to win a majority. Many Frenchmen have been asking themselves whether France should not have a two- or at most a three-party system, and whether such a system would not give the people a much better opportunity to participate in their government.

Any two- or three-party system that France might develop, however, would almost inevitably differ fundamentally from the two-party system in either Great Britain or the United States. In both the latter, the opposing parties accept certain common political assumptions and values; neither party feels that the country is irretrievably lost if the other triumphs in the elections; and each party knows that there will be another election and another chance to win. In France the existence and the electoral strength of the Communists threaten this assumption. If they should ever turn out to be the dominant party of the future, the result might be not an advance toward democracy but an advance toward civil war. The conservative parties detest the Communist party, and they have no confidence that if it won power it would ever again yield it.

The great hope for French democracy must be, therefore, that the non-Communist parties, in cohesive groupings, will maintain or increase their electoral strength and legislative representation. The non-Gaullist, non-Communist parties are groping toward alignments that with or without the Communists could offer substantial opposition to the Gaullists. But will they succeed? Still more important: Will the UNR remain a major party after de Gaulle leaves politics, or will it split between those alignments toward which its non-Communist opposition is moving? The future of the French party system depends on the answers to these questions.

The 1967 Election

The 1967 election for the National Assembly —held March 5 and 12—resulted in a much reduced majority for the Gaullists but an alignment that will enable them to maintain their control of the chamber. The election returns indicated a turning away from the center in favor of either the Gaullists or the non-Communist and Communist left and thus a more definite division between two great forces than had previously appeared in French politics. The results for the 486 seats (16 of them overseas) were: Gaullists (the UNR together with the Independent Republicans under Giscard d'Estaing), 244; the Federation of the Left (a fusion of Radicals, Socialists, and splinter parties of the left under François Mitterrand), 116; Communists, 73; Democratic Center (under Jean Lecanuet), 27; various moderates, 15; moderate left, 5; extreme left, 5. The Democratic Center can be expected ordinarily to support the Gaullists rather than the left.

In the first electoral round on March 5, when it was necessary to secure an absolute majority of the votes to be successful, the Gaullists appeared to be doing well. They polled 37.75 percent of the vote, approximately the same as in 1962. The 79 candidates elected at that time included M. Pompidou, the Premier, and 10 of the 26 members of the government who stood for election. The Communists also increased their share of the votes, from 21.84 to 22.46 percent, while the Federation of the Left and, even more, the Democratic Center suffered reductions on their percentage of the vote.

In the second and decisive balloting on March 12, a major factor in the striking increase in seats received by the non-Communist left and the Communists was their adherence to their political pact to unite behind the candidate of either group who was best placed to win. Of the 18.7 million valid votes cast in the 397 districts contested on March 12, the results were as follows: Gaullists, 7.8 million (42.6 percent); the Federation of the Left, 4.5 million (24.1 percent); Communists, almost 4 million (21.4 percent); Democratic Center, 1.3 million (7.1 percent). Thus the balance had tilted toward the left. It remained to be seen whether the non-Communist left and the Communists would continue in the Assembly the cooperation they exhibited in their election pact.

4. The French Parliament

1. THE CHARACTER OF THE NATIONAL ASSEMBLY

The Powers of the National Assembly

Nowhere do the constitution and the practice of the Fifth Republic differ more markedly from those of the Fourth Republic than in the transformation of the National Assembly. Formerly the dominant agency of the government, it is now a representative body that is limited in authority, and controlled by, far more than it controls, the executive. In the Fourth Republic, the National Assembly was the center of power, and between elections it spoke in the name of the people of France. Under the Fifth Republic, there has been a strong move toward executive rule and, indeed, toward personal rule by the President.

Nonetheless, and according to the theory of the constitution, the Fifth Republic is a parliamentary regime, just as the Third and Fourth Republics were. In presenting the constitution, Debré declared that "the parliamentary regime is the only one suitable for France." In form, and to a certain degree in practice, the basic principles of parliamentary government persist, and the government is still responsible to the National Assembly, although the censure procedure for overthrowing it is a novel one. The distinctive change in the character of the French political system under the Fifth Republic is the increased prerogative of the whole executive—within which the dominant power exercised by President de Gaulle arises from his personal position, not from a constitutional base—and the fact that for the first time in French parliamentary history the executive is supported by an organized majority, the UNR and its allies, that underwrites the wishes of the executive. Should new elections change this situation, the interaction between executive and parliament would also change decisively.

The Composition of the National Assembly

The election of 1962 provided the UNR–UDT with more seats than any French party had ever had before in the Assembly—229 altogether, only slightly less than an absolute majority. With the 20 dissident Independents who were elected at the same time as avowed allies of the UNR, the executive could count on a clear majority in the house, an unprecedented situation in French parliamentary history.

This majority of seats had not, of course, been reflected in so decisive a majority of the votes. Rather surprisingly, the use of single-member constituencies and the two-ballot system created distortions in 1962, as it had in 1958, that were greater than those created by proportional representation under the Fourth Republic. Specifically, the UNR received only 31.9 percent of the votes on the first ballot in 1962 but received 46 seats, while the Communists won only 9 seats with 21.79 percent. On the second ballot, the UNR won 183 seats—making up its total of 229 deputies—with 40.51 percent of the votes, while the Communists, who retained 21.31 percent of the votes, virtually the same as before, won only 32 seats—making their total in the Assembly 41. The Gaullist Independents, whose support provided the UNR with its absolute majority of seats in the Assembly, received only 4.36 percent of the votes but 12 seats on the first ballot, and an insignificant 1.6 percent of the votes but 8 seats on the second ballot. Thus together the UNR

The French National Assembly

AFTER 1946 ELECTIONS

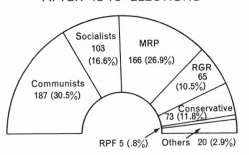

Communists 187 (30.5%)
Socialists 103 (16.6%)
MRP 166 (26.9%)
RGR 65 (10.5%)
Conservative 73 (11.8%)
RPF 5 (.8%)   Others 20 (2.9%)

AFTER 1951 ELECTIONS

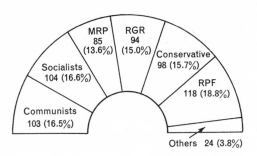

MRP 85 (13.6%)
RGR 94 (15.0%)
Conservative 98 (15.7%)
Socialists 104 (16.6%)
RPF 118 (18.8%)
Communists 103 (16.5%)
Others 24 (3.8%)

AFTER 1956 ELECTIONS

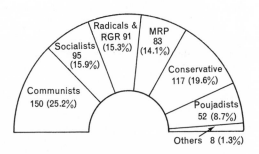

Radicals & RGR 91 (15.3%)
MRP 83 (14.1%)
Socialists 95 (15.9%)
Conservative 117 (19.6%)
Communists 150 (25.2%)
Poujadists 52 (8.7%)
Others 8 (1.3%)

AFTER 1958 ELECTIONS

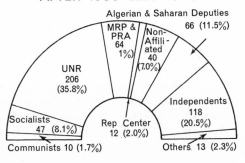

Algerian & Saharan Deputies 66 (11.5%)
MRP & PRA 64 (1%)
Non-Affiliated 40 (7.0%)
UNR 206 (35.8%)
Independents 118 (20.5%)
Socialists 47 (8.1%)
Rep Center 12 (2.0%)
Communists 10 (1.7%)
Others 13 (2.3%)

AFTER 1962 ELECTIONS

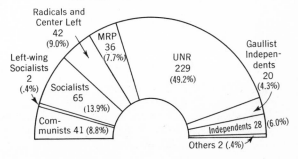

Radicals and Center Left 42 (9.0%)
MRP 36 (7.7%)
Left-wing Socialists 2 (.4%)
UNR 229 (49.2%)
Gaullist Independents 20 (4.3%)
Socialists 65 (13.9%)
Communists 41 (8.8%)
Independents 28 (6.0%)
Others 2 (.4%)

and Gaullist Independents totaled only 36.26 percent on the first ballot and 42.11 percent on the second and yet won 249 seats out of 464.

Interestingly enough, the 1962 election, like that in 1958 and in 1945, introduced many new faces to the National Assembly. In 1958 only 131 of the 552 members (including those from Algeria and the Sahara, which had become independent by 1962) had served in the previous Assembly, and only one-quarter of the deputies among the UNR, Independents, and MRP had had previous legislative experience. In 1962, 225 deputies were new to the Assembly, 121 of them Gaullist.

The Meeting Place

In contrast to the rectangular chamber of the House of Commons, the National Assembly meets in a semicircular amphitheater in the Palais Bourbon, which has close-packed benches rising sharply one above another. Members of the Ministry occupy special benches down front, where the representatives of committees may also sit when their topics are under consideration. In front of the auditorium is a high ornate desk, approached by a flight of stairs on either side. Here sits the President of the Assembly, flanked by secretaries at lower desks. Immediately in front of the President's desk is a rostrum, the "tribune," from which deputies may address the Assembly.

Parties are commonly grouped on the curved benches according to the shade of their political views. The left, of course, is the prized position, and almost any kind of maneuver will be made to secure some of its prestige. Despite the obviously conservative character of most of the UNR deputies, that party (which first favored the British system of seating the government across from the opposition) refused in 1958 to sit on the extreme right (forcing the Independents to sit there) and was ultimately given a center position from which it overflowed into areas commonly occupied by parties more suitable to those positions. In 1962, the elimination of the extreme right, and a vast reduction in the strength of the Independents, forced the UNR into the section on the right of the chamber. (The diagrams on page 275 indicate the relative strength of the major political groups following the elections of November 1946, June 1951, January 1956, November 1958, and November 1962. The diagrams, however, do not attempt to reproduce exactly the complicated and shifting groups or seating arrangements in the Assembly.)

The spirit of such an assembly differs fundamentally from that of the House of Commons. Instead of the sharp division between government and opposition—which forces every member of Parliament to take his position clearly on one side or the other and which makes any deserting member extremely conspicuous—the French arrangement has been one of slight gradations from left to right. Parties blend into one another, and deputies could formerly shift from one party to another with ease. Under the weak party discipline of the Third Republic, and the changing party alignments, especially on the right, of the Fourth Republic, the instability of governments was sometimes attributed to the facility with which a member could shift to the left or the right and vote with his neighbors against his own party. Winston Churchill expressed a typically British reaction to this situation when he told the House of Commons in his famous speech of October 28, 1943, that

> . . . the semi-circular assembly, which appeals to political theorists, enables every individual to move round the centre, adopting various shades of pink according as the weather changes. I am a convinced supporter of the party system in preference to the group system. . . . The party system is much favored by the oblong form of Chamber. It is easy for an individual to move through those insensible gradations from Left to Right but the act of crossing the Floor is one which requires serious consideration. I am well informed on this matter, for I have accomplished that difficult process, not only once but twice.

A more important consequence of the arrangement is the type of parliamentary oratory it permits. The French deputy who wishes to address his colleagues does not rise in his place, as in Great Britain, and speak in casual and conversational tones with courteous references to the honorable gentlemen on his right and left. He mounts the tribune, and often he orates. The speeches in the National Assembly frequently are more polished and brilliant than their Anglo-Saxon counterparts, but it is doubtful that they contribute as much to serious discussion and compromise. There is a great temptation to elicit cheers and applause from the close-packed benches and to impress or electrify an audience composed of connoisseurs of eloquence. The temptation is almost as great to provoke the fury of the opposition by the vigor of one's attack and the sharpness of one's taunts. Noble sentiments from the left are met with ironic laughter on the right; a particularly nasty taunt or insinuation provokes shouts of protest, and, in extreme instances in the past, deputies on one side of the auditorium have hurled themselves on their opponents, while attendants hastily intervened and the presiding officer suspended the session.

To attribute such episodes to the fiery Gallic temperament is a great oversimplification. In reality they reflect two great handicaps from which the French political system has long suffered. First, some political differences are so deep as to make it extremely difficult for men of the extreme left and the right to treat each other with the courtesy and forbearance that are so fundamental to the British parliamentary tradition. Second, and even more important, is the fact that on the extreme left (and earlier, on the extreme right) there is little if any loyalty to the institutions of parliamentary democracy as such. In Great Britain the first loyalty of almost every member of Parliament is to the constitutional system; very few would be willing to discredit the system in order to win an advantage over a political opponent. In France members at a political extreme may actually profit by making parliament appear ridiculous; they realize that the mass of the French people would turn to either a Communist or a fascist dictatorship only if they were convinced of the unworkability of democratic institutions.

The Organization of the National Assembly

The President of the National Assembly

The presiding officer in the French Assembly has always had a less honored position than has the Speaker of the House of Commons. Under the Fourth Republic, the lack of discipline and orderliness among the deputies made his office an extremely difficult one. There has been a noticeable change under the Fifth Republic. Now his audience is much less unruly, and issues rarely rouse the kind of tension so prevalent in the Fourth Republic, simply because the Assembly now has so much less power. The only occasion on which the Palais Bourbon, the "House without Windows," regained its old passionate atmosphere was during the one successful motion of censure of the Fifth Republic, that of October 4, 1962, over de Gaulle's decision to use the referendum to test opinion on the direct election of the President. That motion brought down the Pompidou government, but, as we have seen, it failed to change the course of de Gaulle's policy.

The President of the Assembly has certain new functions that increase his prestige and are intended to help him control the Assembly if control becomes a problem. He is one of those consulted by the President of the Republic on the existence of an emergency. He chooses three of the nine members of the Constitutional Council. Moreover, he may submit to that body a private member's bill that he believes constitutional but that the government questions. Under the standing orders, he can call deputies to order and force the closure of debate. Both these powers are subject, however, to practice, which, in the National Assembly, has characteristically developed out of action rather than rules. Although the President of the Assembly ranks fourth in precedence in the country, the Assembly's current lack of power suggests that, in fact, he occupies a position less important than that of his predecessor in the Fourth Republic, who had to attempt to keep that all-powerful body in check through personal persuasion.

The Groups

Unlike the Speaker of the House of Commons, it is not the President of the Assembly who allocates time in more important debates to the representatives of different points of view and who arranges for sittings. Rather, it is the *Conférence des Présidents*—the heads of recognized groups. Instead of allowing any group with at least fourteen members (as at the beginning of the Fourth Republic, although the number was later expanded to twenty-eight) to set up a formal organization and choose as its spokesman a president who enjoys special debating privileges, the Fifth Republic requires the group to have thirty members. Although this provision denied the Communists this opportunity after the 1958 election, all six major parties qualified (the Independents had twenty-nine seats) in 1962. Each group draws up a political declaration for its members to sign, and this declaration and the list of members are filed with the Bureau.

The Bureau

The Bureau is made up of the President of the Assembly together with its other officers (six vice-presidents, fourteen secretaries, and three questors). It handles not only the debates, but also the counting of votes, the drafting of minutes, and general arrangements. As was true in the past, positions on the Bureau are distributed among the party groups in proportion to their strength. Through the questors, the Bureau also handles the Assembly's accounts. Perhaps its most discretionary function is to determine whether deputies' bills are admissible under the restrictions of Article 40 on financial legislation. Between sessions, the Bureau protects the immunities of the deputies.

2. THE NATIONAL ASSEMBLY IN ACTION

Constitutional provisions have combined to make the National Assembly of the Fifth Republic an even less effective body in practice than is the House of Commons. In relation to the traditional functions of a legislature—making and supporting a government, criticizing and controlling that government, and shaping the laws—the National Assembly has been placed at a great disadvantage: it can overthrow a Ministry but it cannot create one. Unlike the

House of Commons, the tradition of the National Assembly has been one of power, not of criticism; it is not well fitted, therefore, to assume the role of critic.

The National Assembly and the Ministry

It is still common in parliamentary countries to say that the first duty of a legislature is to make and to support a government. In Great Britain, this statement has lost much of its point, since in ordinary circumstances it is the voters rather than the members of Parliament who decide which party shall be in power, that is, which members of which party shall constitute the Cabinet. In France, the Fifth Republic has removed from the Assembly what used to be a key power: the approval of the choice of the Premier.

It is true that after the Premier has been nominated by the President of the Republic, he presents his program first to the Assembly and then, through a minister, to the Senate. At this time the Assembly, by simple majority, can reject the Premier. It can also defeat his government by voting against any statement of policy or legislative text on which he demands a vote of confidence. Further, as we have seen, the Assembly can introduce a motion of censure if one-tenth of its members have endorsed it, and the government must resign if the motion receives the support of an absolute majority of the deputies. These, however, are negative provisions. Where the National Assembly used to be preeminently the maker of Ministries, it can now only dismiss them—and the one experience of 1962 suggests that the advantage is slight, if it exists at all.

It could be argued that the National Assembly has always possessed only a negative power over Ministries and that the decisive difference between its position under the Fourth and the Fifth Republics is the presence in the latter of the large bloc of UNR deputies who support the Premier whom the President has chosen. It is true, of course, that if the Assembly were subdivided into many small parties, the Premier would find it more difficult to secure the necessary support. But there are other factors that vastly strengthen the government in its relations with the Assembly. The incompatibility rule, which makes it necessary for a deputy to resign his seat in the Assembly if he becomes a minister, takes the maneuvering about places in a Ministry out of the realm of the parliamentary parties. The revived power of dissolution means that a vote of censure may, and experience suggests will, lead to new elections, which few deputies relish. Moreover, and still more important, the government possesses defined powers over the budget and over a segment of rule-making, powers that thus reduce the authority of the Assembly in these spheres. In addition, sometimes in the background but sometimes very much in the foreground, are the reserve and even the emergency powers of the President.

According to the constitution, parliament meets for two ordinary sessions a year beginning on the last Tuesday in April and the first Tuesday in October, respectively, and lasting a maximum of three months and two and a half months, respectively. In addition, it can be called into a special session of at most twelve days for a specific purpose by either the Premier or a majority of the Assembly. In March, 1960, 286 deputies requested a special session of the Assembly to deal with farmers' grievances. Though 286 deputies formed a clear majority of the members of the Assembly, de Gaulle refused their request. He argued that the proposal for the special session had been inspired by a professional group, the Farmers' Association, and was therefore from outside the Assembly, although this is not an unusual source of legislative proposals elsewhere. He pointed out that there had already been two special sessions (both of which, however, had been called by the government). Beyond this he questioned whether the Assembly could prepare satisfactory legislation on agriculture in twelve days, declared that the government was working on the subject but had not yet completed its proposal, and pointed out that any measure the Assembly might suggest would involve either decreasing revenue or increasing expenditures, both of which were outside its province. Thus de Gaulle assumed the right to decide whether action under a provision of the constitution was justified or not, and decided that it was not. He impaired, if he did not destroy, one of the safety valves of the regime. In doing so, he further weakened the position of the Assembly.

The Assembly still retains the power, of course, to defeat legislation proposed by the government. The struggle over de Gaulle's plan for an independent French nuclear striking force demonstrated, however, that the ability to force a vote of confidence on the life of the government places the latter in a strong position to force the hand of the Assembly. Late in 1960, for example, Premier Debré twice answered strong criticism of the measure from the left and center as well as motions of censure with a demand for a vote of confidence. Although the deputies were frustrated and angry at being denied the chance to postpone or modify a measure with such far-reaching and possibly negative implications for France's European policy, they were unwilling to take the supreme step of overthrowing the Ministry. Thus, in much the same way as a British Prime Minister is able to force through the House of Commons a particular measure that the House would not support on a free vote, the French Premier under the Fifth Republic is able to control and dominate the once uncontrollable National Assembly.

In the debate on nuclear policy, however, the Ministry and Assembly engaged in the kind of interaction characteristic of the parliamentary system in its classical form. The Assembly retained its right to withhold confidence, and the Ministry forced the Assembly to declare for or against its continued life. But this classic expression of parliamentary action operates in a less traditional milieu in France than in Great Britain and thus handicaps the Assembly in maintaining executive responsibility under normal circumstances. On the one hand, the President of the Republic not only has the constitutional functions of supervision and arbitration between government and parliament; in practice, he has assumed the right to intervene to the disadvantage of the Assembly. On the other hand, because of French political history and the multiparty system, the parliamentary procedures that keep a powerful executive alert and responsive to the criticism of private members and the community have never been developed in France. Thus the Assembly fails to exercise as much influence as it might otherwise do, even in its circumscribed role, as we will see in considering its work as a critic.

The Assembly as Critic

There are two particular ways in which deputies can criticize the government and check on its actions: through a vote of censure and through questions. Limits have been placed on both these techniques, however, to prevent them from being used to weaken the Ministry or to obstruct government business. Behind these limits lies the general conception, characteristic also of Great Britain, that the government should not be defeated on anything less than an issue of confidence. Unlike Great Britain, however, the tendency in France under the Fifth Republic has been to be chiefly concerned with numerical majorities (which the British party system almost always places at the disposal of a Ministry) rather than with the pertinence of the implied or explicit criticism.

The Vote of Censure

Votes of censure operate in two ways. If initiated by the deputies, each vote must have the signature of at least 10 percent of them to be brought to a vote; to succeed, it must receive an absolute majority of all the deputies. Moreover if the motion is lost, the deputies who signed the original motion lose their right to sign another motion of censure in the same session. These restrictions do not hold when the government attempts to force through a bill (to establish an independent nuclear striking force, for instance) by making passage a matter of confidence, since such a measure is automatically accepted by the Assembly twenty-four hours after the announcement if no motion of censure has been introduced in the meantime. Even if the motion of censure is introduced, it requires an absolute majority, and thus in effect the overthrow of the government, to defeat the measure.

Questions

The French have never used the parliamentary question with the same effect as the British do, partly, at least, because under the Fourth Republic the question had little political significance. In contrast, the *interpellation,* which was a request to a minister for an explanation of his actions, had a great deal of political significance, since it always carried the threat that it might be followed by a condemnation of the minister and thus of the Cabinet of which he was a member. By eliminating the interpellation and retaining only the parliamentary question, the Fifth Republic has drawn the sting from this procedure.

The British House of Commons sets aside the first period of its formal session for questions that may range over the whole gamut of administration and policy, but only Friday afternoon is reserved for questions under the Fifth Republic. A deputy may wish his question to be either "with debate" or "without debate," but the Conference of Presidents has the decisive word on how it shall be treated and may even decree a written rather than a spoken answer. After the answer to a question without debate, a deputy has five minutes in which to comment, after which the minister may reply. A question with debate is elaborated by the deputy in a fifteen- to thirty-minute speech; the minister may answer immediately or announce his intention to have a full debate within two days. If the minister replies immediately, a debate follows in which the time for expressing different points of view is organized by the President of the Assembly.

Written and oral questions remain largely what they were under the Fourth Republic: means of eliciting information, securing the interpretation of a decree, questioning an abuse of law, and, less often, raising issues of policy. Written questions have long been popular and might be still if ministers were more punctilious about answering them. They are published in the official record of the Assembly, and the reply is supposed to appear within a month; ministers may ignore questions, however, or declare that the public interest prevents them from replying. The postwar innovation of oral questions, a deliberate attempt to copy British practice, has not yet been molded to serve Assembly purposes of executive supervision.

The Assembly as Legislator

One of the sharpest innovations of the Fifth Republic is to restrict the legislature to certain fields of rule-making, while the rest are assigned to the executive. In the past the government has exercised wide powers through decrees, special

powers, and other instances of delegated legislation, but parliament remained the final judge of their extent and duration and parliament had the ultimate right of ratification. Under the Fifth Republic the legislature may make *rules* governing certain enumerated subjects—notably personal rights and civil status, electoral laws, creation of nationalized industries, the penal code, liability to taxation and national defense, amnesty, and declaration of war—and lay down general principles governing another list of subjects—education, labor, trade unions, social security, local government, national defense, property and commercial rights, finance (under conditions defined in an organic law), and long-term social and economic projects. The list is long, but it gives rise to as many, if not more, questions than it answers. How, in particular, is the line to be drawn between a legislative decision on general principles and its application, which is in the exclusive field of the executive?

In drawing the line between legislative and executive competence, use is made of a unique and impressive French institution, the Council of State (*Conseil d'Etat*) (which will be considered in more detail in Chapter 6), as well as of the Constitutional Council. In regard to all laws passed *before* the constitution of the Fifth Republic came into force, the Council of State determines whether or not they now come within executive competence; if they do, they may be modified by decree. The Constitutional Council makes the decision on the boundary between the two jurisdictions if the law was passed *after* the constitution came into force. But while the government can challenge the competence of the Assembly to deal by legislation with a particular subject, there are no comparable means by which the Assembly can question the government's use of the decree power.

As in so many other places, this strengthening of the hand of the executive in rule-making and the consequent curbing of the legislature may well have gone too far for the healthy interaction of the two. It is apparent that the legislature attempted to do far too much in the Fourth Republic and also that modern social and economic problems demand prompt handling by executive agencies rather than piecemeal treatment by a large and inexpert body.

Nonetheless the pendulum seems to have swung very far.

French practice in the making of legislation is to give the text to the President of the Assembly, who announces its receipt, has it printed, and, in contrast to British procedure (according to which the critical "second reading debate" precedes the sending of the bill to committee) but like American practice, assigns it to the appropriate committee.

The Committees

Major changes between the Fourth and Fifth Republics in the role and importance of committees mark yet another lessening of the influence of the deputies. In the Fourth Republic, nineteen specialized committees (or *commissions,* as the French call them) of forty-four members each, chosen according to the strength of party groups and with more or less permanent assignments, dominated the legislative work of the National Assembly and played a controlling role in both finance and administration. Under the Fifth Republic, there are only six standing committees. They have large memberships and shift their attention to whatever subjects the Assembly wishes them to consider. They were deliberately made rather unwieldy bodies in an effort to reduce their political importance. The change also enhances the importance of the *ad hoc* committees (which have no fixed membership and are elected by a majority of the Assembly), which are designed for use on particularly important questions or on matters that require speedy action.

Parliamentary groups—that is, those with at least thirty members—are allocated seats on the standing committees proportionate to their representation in the Assembly; debate is unrestricted; ministers may be questioned if they are willing (and they usually are) to appear; and decisions are taken by majority vote. Committee chairmen, who are chosen by agreement between the leaders of the major parliamentary groups, do not play the dominant role they do in the United States but have considerable responsibilities in guiding and even limiting the discussion of such large bodies.

The finance committee has more prestige than the others, although it enjoys nothing approaching its former power of investigating the budget of every department and interpreting finance as related to every aspect of policy. Under the allocation of responsibilities laid down in the constitution, the Assembly is not to reduce revenues or to increase expenditures. But by wily proposals balancing the two, the Assembly, on one occasion, managed to persuade the government to restore ex-servicemen's pensions and increase family allowances. Thus it demonstrated that constitutional provisions cannot necessarily withstand pressures exerted on representatives who are ultimately dependent on popular support for their election.

The final and conclusive factor reducing the importance of committees in French legislative procedure is that the ensuing debate on a government bill (*projêt de loi*) is not on the text of the measure that the committee has accepted but on the government text. Moreover, the Assembly may be required to vote on the whole of this text, or the text with such amendments as the government has accepted, or on specific clauses. Thus the sparkling and often dramatic role of the committee *rapporteur,* who used to open, and often dominate, the debate on a measure, is a thing of the past.

Apart from these major changes, the consideration of a bill is much the same after the committee stage as it used to be. Safeguards have been instituted, however, against dilatory motions that used to be so prominent in the past. Moving the "preliminary question"—that is, moving that the matter not be considered at all—can be done only once in the course of a measure; similarly there can be only one effort to prove the measure is incompatible with the constitution. Amendments can be made only to specific clauses of the bill. Thus speedy action on government legislation has become relatively common.

In sum, the Assembly lacks any decisive independent legislative power. A deputy may introduce a *proposition de loi,* but it must first secure the approval of the Bureau of the Assembly on its constitutional acceptability, then of the Bureau of the Finance Committee, and then of the government. Moreover, should a law be passed, the Assembly would still have no means of forcing the government to take action to implement it unless the government wished to do so.

Voting

Although the Assembly now has an electronic system of voting, installed in 1959, the traditional ways of recording opinion are still used first: a show of hands or, in case of doubt, a rising vote. Should an ordinary record vote be required, it can be done electronically from the seats of the deputies. If the machinery is not working, the time-consuming older process of the open ballot (*scrutin public ordinaire*) is still used, with ushers passing urns into which deputies put their personal cards: white in favor; blue opposed; red abstention. In the more formal record vote at the tribune, voting may be either electronic or by card.

The Fifth Republic has tried to introduce personal voting to replace the Fourth Republic's vote by proxy, under which, at times, one deputy (known as the "postman") would cast the votes for his whole party. But though there is now more restraint, the rule of personal voting seems honored in the breach rather than in reality. Thus do old habits persist despite new forms.

One further and unpopular innovation of the Fifth Republic is to provide an attendance bonus that is withheld if deputies do not attend and vote regularly. Absence without valid excuse (valid has been interpreted liberally) from three consecutive sessions of a committee means temporary loss of membership and of one-third of attendance pay; absence from more than one-third of the record votes in any one month entails loss of one-third of that month's attendance pay; absence from one-half the votes means loss of two-thirds of the month's pay. But Frenchmen are past masters at circumventing distasteful provisions, and it has yet to be demonstrated that this attempt to secure more regular participation has had a particularly useful effect.

3. THE SENATE

The Fifth Republic renamed the second chamber the Senate and provided it with power in legislation coordinate to that of the As-sembly. A smaller body whose members have a longer term of office than do those of the Assembly—nine years to five—the Senate might seem, therefore, to be a potential rival to the lower chamber, as it was at times during the Third Republic. Its indirect mode of election has always been designed to act as a counterweight to the base of universal suffrage of the Assembly. Yet within the generally weakened position of the legislature, the Senate plays a vastly subordinate role. Even so, de Gaulle has long talked of abolishing the Senate and replacit with an upper chamber composed of representatives of economic groups.

As elsewhere, the deciding factor in any disagreement between the Assembly and the Senate is the executive. The Assembly can no longer override the Senate on legislation as it did under the Fourth Republic, and, unless the government intervenes, a disputed bill can go back and forth indefinitely—in what is called "the shuttle" (*la navette*). In effect, then, the Senate can block legislation in which the government is not interested. But if the government so desires, it can promote procedures, either passive or active, that bring the measure to a vote. In the first instance, it can require the two houses to establish a fourteen-member commission, half from each chamber, to seek agreement on the bill, which is then brought to a vote, though only with such amendments as the government approves. Failing agreement, the measure may be dropped. But if the government is actively concerned with the bill, it can request each chamber to give the measure a further reading and then instruct the Assembly to vote either on the commission's draft or its own, and either with or without the Senate's amendments. In this latter case a simple majority vote by the Assembly is all that is needed to override the Senate.

A significant illustration of how the Senate's power in legislation can be nullified by the government and by an acquiescent Assembly was provided by the Senate's efforts to prevent the change from proportional representation to majority voting in the larger cities, as described in Chapter 3. Drawing its own electors from those selected by local elections, the Senate sought to preserve the system that had returned so many senators from the center parties.

The government hoped (as it turned out, vainly) that changing the system in the larger cities would benefit the UNR. The Assembly passed the measure on May 21, 1964; two weeks later, the Senate voted a bill that differed at key points from the government measure; the joint conference committee reached a stalemate. The government then moved to secure passage of its bill. On the second reading in the Assembly it cut off debate by calling for a "blocked vote," which requires the deputies to vote for the measure as introduced. The same procedure was required in the Senate, but there the bill was defeated. The measure was then returned to the Assembly, where it was reaffirmed in its original form at third reading. With the President's signature, the process was at an end. The Senate had failed to affect the character of a bill that changed the form of voting for its own electors.

But if the Senate cannot do more than suggest alternatives and temporarily delay the passage of a measure the government wants—thus performing the classic role of a second chamber —why does de Gaulle wish to abolish it and establish an economic upper house in its place? There are both personal and theoretical reasons. De Gaulle reacted bitterly to the sharp criticism he received from members of the Senate and, in particular, from its presiding officer, Gaston Monnerville, an able and popular Negro from French Guiana, on his use of the referendum rather than a constitutional amendment to test

opinion regarding the process of direct election for the President. De Gaulle even refused henceforth to receive Monnerville at the Elysée Palace or to let a senior member of the Cabinet go to the Senate. But under the constitution the President of the Senate acts as President of France if the incumbent is ever incapacitated. By transforming the upper chamber from a body that reflects local opinion to a super economic and social council (see Chapter 6), de Gaulle could serve two of his purposes: eliminate a body within which the opposition parties remain dominant, and establish a new kind of succession.

Beyond this largely personal objective, however, de Gaulle envisages a type of functional representation that would go well with his notions of technocracy. After his reelection as President, he began to speak of replacing the Senate with a purely consultative body that would draw its representatives not only from the municipalities and departments but also from the new regional assemblies and from economic organs. Such a body would fit his view that what France needs is to have its divisions—which he sees reflected in the political parties—overbridged by organs that stand for national unity. The Presidency is such an organ, and to make parliament more acquiescent he now proposes a consultative and composite body to replace the one part of governmental machinery that is still dominated by his critics.

5. The French Executive

The most striking feature of the Fifth Republic is the power and prestige of the President of the Republic and the unmistakable stamp of de Gaulle's personality on all domestic and international affairs. This is not only the dominant characteristic of the new regime; it also marks its sharpest contrast to the past.

The power of the executive has been a subject of perennial controversy in French politics. Generally speaking, the parties of the left have looked upon a powerful executive as a threat to democratic institutions, while the parties of the right have seen in a strong executive the only hope for political order and authority. The constitution of the Fourth Republic represented a clear victory for the parties of the left, with authority concentrated in the National Assembly. The constitution of the Fifth Republic is as strongly oriented toward a powerful executive.

In France the executive includes both the President, who like that of the United States is *not* responsible to the legislature, and the Premier and Ministry which, as in the United Kingdom, *are* responsible to the legislature. Whatever balance the constitution of the Fifth Republic intended, or suggested, between these two sources of executive power, there can be no doubt that the President has become dominant in every sphere of political activity. With a guaranteed term of seven years, a centralized administration and no federal division of powers, an acquiescent Premier and Ministry, and a curbed legislature, President de Gaulle possesses political powers that an American President might envy and that a British Prime Minister, regardless of the size of his majority, would never dream of using.

Contrast with the Past

This far-reaching and pervasive authority of President de Gaulle contrasts sharply with the situation prior to 1958. Under the Third Republic the President of France had acted as something of a nonhereditary constitutional monarch. He was a dignified head of state who could preside on ceremonial occasions, who stood above party, and who did not engage in partisan political activity. The rebuke given to Marshal MacMahon in 1877 and the forced resignation of President Millerand in 1924 for similar partisanship were warnings enough against making independent decisions.

Seldom have such rebukes been necessary. After the sad experience with Napoleon III, republicans were careful to see that no President should enjoy the prestige of popular election; and after the MacMahon crisis they took care to choose men who were colorless, reliably republican, and possessed of little popular appeal. Clemenceau's advice to Frenchmen to "Vote for the most stupid" may have overstated the matter, but of all the Presidents of the Third Republic only Poincaré could be considered a statesman of the first rank. Men of the prominence and ability of Clemenceau and Briand were regularly rejected.

As a result, the prestige of the French President stood much lower than that of the British monarch. He excited none of the reverence attached to the descendant of generations of Kings, and his personal abilities commanded little respect. Much of his work was purely ceremonial. He presided at official functions, received ambassadors, and represented the nation at diplomatic affairs and at ceremonies of all sorts throughout the country. Like the King of Great Britain, he was expected to lay cornerstones, open exhibitions, inspect hospitals, schools, and housing projects, attend peasant festivals, and tour the French empire as a symbol of the interest of the nation in its overseas possessions. At all times, he was expected to be good-humored, kindly, affable, gracious, and patient.

Though the makers of the constitution of the Fourth Republic deliberately tried to reduce the power of the presidency, the office actually gained more power than it had had before and provided the President with considerably more opportunity to exert influence than has the British monarch. Whereas the British King ceased to attend Cabinet meetings more than two centuries ago, the President presided over the meetings of the Council of Ministers and had the right to participate in discussions (although he could not vote). This role was of some importance, since in practice the Council of Ministers discussed certain issues of policy instead of restricting itself to formal action, as it had under the Third Republic. Moreover, when for the first time records were made of these meetings, the President of the Republic became their custodian. The President also had access to all important diplomatic papers, as was not always the case with his Third Republic predecessors.

1. THE WORK OF THE PRESIDENT

Under the Fifth Republic, however, all these possibilities for exercising influence have been turned into positive sources of activity and power. The many formal offices the President holds have provided him with unparalleled opportunities for keeping himself informed on the course of policy in all public spheres and for directing it when he wishes to do so—as increasingly he has.

The most important of these formal functions is to preside over the Council of Ministers, which has been turned into a forum for substantive debate on policy. In the first few years after de Gaulle succeeded to office in 1958, the Council of Ministers continued to act largely as a ratifying body for decisions reached jointly by the President and the Premier. By bringing policy discussions into the Council, however, as de Gaulle did after Pompidou replaced Debré as Premier, he has established direct and continuing relations with the ministers themselves and has made its sessions more nearly like those of a Cabinet, but of the American rather than the British type.

Other official duties of the President include presiding over the Superior Council of National Defense (a little-publicized, consultative body in an area in which de Gaulle takes particular interest and assumes particular responsibilities) and, rather more surprising, over the High Council of the Judiciary. In addition, he presided over the Executive Council of the Community (see Chapter 9) in the short period during which it functioned.

Unlike American presidential nominations of top administrative personnel, which must be ratified by the Senate, the French President's power of appointment is very wide and needs no formal ratification. While all French Presidents have had a role in proposing Premiers, de Gaulle is the only one who has determined who the Premier shall be. The acquiescence of the chambers in the leadership of Michel Debré, himself a parliamentarian and a believer in a "reformed" but functioning parliamentary system, is not surprising, particularly in the tense period succeeding 1958. But the measure of their docility has been their acceptance of Pompidou, who had never been in parliament or even a member of a political party, and who was obviously de Gaulle's lieutenant rather than a Premier in his own right.

The President also makes appointments to all state civilian and military posts, although the sheer magnitude of this task means that he must depend heavily on advice from the Premier and the Council of Ministers. The constitution specifically provides that the President appoint the members of the Superior Council of the Judiciary, a role shared under the Fourth Republic with the National Assembly (see Chapter 7). The President also has the right of pardon, although a pardon is supposed to have the countersignature of the Minister of Justice.

The role most congenial to de Gaulle is his position as commander in chief of the armed forces. The President is also empowered to conduct international negotiations and to shape and sign treaties, other roles into which de Gaulle has entered with satisfaction and vigor and without, so far as can be seen, being restrained by the constitutional requirement that his actions be countersigned by the Premier.

All decrees passed by the Council of Ministers must be signed by the President to become valid; so must all laws, within fifteen days after they have been passed. It is conceivable that the President might refuse to sign a law, thereby exercising a "pocket veto," but until the legislature reestablishes a separate authority of its own there will be no need for such tactics. Indeed, the President's use of his power to dissolve the legislature has already demonstrated that he will use his whip hand in case of a confrontation.

In the end, however, the power of the President, like that of any other chief executive in a nondictatorial state, rests on his ability to convince his country, or at least a voting majority, that he is acting in their best interests. The President's selection of the Premier, his leadership of the Council of Ministers, his ability to use the referendum (constitutionally, or even, as we have seen, unconstitutionally) to appeal to the people over the head of the legislature, and his right under Article 16 to declare a state of emergency for whatever period of time he deems necessary and for its duration to exercise ultimate power, have vested de Gaulle with the widest measure of individual power and discretion since the days of the Napoleons. France's continued trust in him suggests that, despite rumblings of protest from time to time, public confidence is still widespread. It is questionable, however, whether any other President could command the same measure of support or would be allowed to exercise the same degree of power.

The Staff of the President

The effectiveness of all executive work is determined in large measure by the efficiency of the organization and the personnel that underpin the making and the execution of deci-

sions. De Gaulle's military background and experience, coupled with his wide-ranging concern for all aspects of public policy, domestic as well as foreign, have led to a dramatic expansion of the presidential staff. Indeed, there has developed an administrative structure operating on behalf of the President that is parallel to and has sometimes been competitive with that of the civil service. Americans familiar with the White House setup find it similar in many ways to what has evolved under President de Gaulle.

The expansion of the presidential staff amply documents the revolution that has taken place in the presidential role. President Auriol's Elysée staff in 1953 included only two political counselors—one prepared his papers for the relatively infrequent meetings of the Council of Ministers, and the other handled relations with the press—and twenty-one officers of professional rank. The moment de Gaulle assumed office in 1958, he appointed seventeen political counselors, of whom four were assigned to Community affairs. This latter group, which had been enlarged by 1964 and had moved to offices outside the Elysée Palace, concentrated on France's relations with the former French African territories. By 1964 the other counselors had grown in number to twenty, and the total presidential staff, excluding secretaries and minor administrative personnel, to fifty-two.

De Gaulle's dislike of detailed administrative work means that his staff is responsible for summarizing reports and policy proposals coming from the Premier's office, or from ministers, for watching progress of policy matters in which the President is particularly interested, and for developing position papers on pressing policy issues and on matters on which de Gaulle finds ministerial action too slow. Two different approaches to reforming secondary education, for example, were produced by the Ministry of Education and by the education specialists on the presidential staff. Only after much publicity and considerable "in-fighting" of the type with which Washington is so familiar—and in which Whitehall engages only infrequently and discretely—did de Gaulle endorse the ministry's plans.

The potential, and occasionally real, clash between presidential staff and high civil servants was neutralized, and then virtually eliminated, by de Gaulle's practice of drawing his presidential aides from among the civil servants themselves, either on a temporary or permanent basis. Only ten out of the seventeen political counselors in 1958 were high civil servants; three were long-term Gaullists who had been put in charge of relations with parliament, political parties, and the press. By 1964, seventeen of the twenty top aides were high civil servants, and the other three were professors with special responsibilities for education and research. De Gaulle had retained no generalists or political figures in these roles.

The change reveals the enlarged focus of the President's activities. So long as the Algerian war dominated de Gaulle's concerns, he paid relatively little attention to domestic policies. But once that war was over, his impatience with what he called a "flabby" state machinery and his dominance of the working relationship between himself and Premier Pompidou—which contrasts sharply with Debré's partnership view of Premier-President relations—led to his increasing involvement in the everyday affairs of government.

The presidential staff has expanded not only in numbers but in influence. At the same time it has become more closely intermeshed in attitudes and personnel with the higher civil service of the ministries. The end result has been to lessen administrative rivalries but, at the same time, to make and keep the presidency the dominant force throughout the administration.

2. THE PREMIER [1]

From being the creature of the National Assembly of the Fourth Republic, subject to instant dismissal through the withdrawal of essential votes, the Premier in France seems to have become the creature of the President of the Fifth Republic. This was certainly not the intention of the framer of the constitution of the Fifth Republic, Michel Debré, who became the Republic's first Premier. Debré managed to combine an impressive loyalty to de Gaulle with an insistence on the rights (however circumscribed) of parliament and of himself as Premier. He also fulfilled the more traditional role of the French Premier, cajoling, threatening, and ultimately driving his program through the chambers. It is a mark of the new day in French politics that what overthrew Debré was not the withdrawal of support from within the Assembly but his dismissal by de Gaulle. Pompidou's self-effacing role vis-à-vis the President put an end to any attempt to maintain a dual executive on relatively equal terms.

It is not new for the role of the French Premier to be determined by the system within which he is working. Under the Third Republic, if anyone challenged the Premier's status as *primus inter pares* (first among equals), it was to insist that he was not even *primus*. His Cabinet was likely to include several men not only of equal but of greater political stature, including the heads of other political parties and former Premiers. Moreover, there was nothing to correspond to the British Cabinet's loyalty to a party leader, and the Premier lacked the prestige that an American President and a British Prime Minister enjoy because, in reality, they have been elected by the people and enjoy something of a popular mandate.

Those who drafted the constitution of the Fourth Republic intended to make the Premier a real leader on the pattern of the British Prime Minister—an innovation indeed. Formerly, the ministers had sent their bills directly to the Assembly; now they had to be signed by the Premier before they could be presented. Under the Third Republic ministers might call votes of confidence on their own initiative; now such votes could be called only by the Premier, after full Cabinet discussion. But while the drafters of the constitution of the Fourth Republic clearly hoped that these powers would give the Premier genuine authority and prestige, the fact that they were exercised jointly with others (that is, with the appropriate minister or, in the case of high appointments, with the President), combined with the existence of the multiparty system, largely undercut this hope. Thus, except in the rare case of Mendès-France, it was the conciliators like Henri Queuille, René Pleven, and Antoine Pinay who were the most successful Premiers, rather than dy-

[1] According to strict terminology, under the Fifth Republic the Premier is Prime Minister; the older term *Premier* has been retained, however, to avoid confusion with the British Prime Minister.

namic individuals with programs of their own.

But some may well feel that the Premier of the Fifth Republic has the most difficult task of all. He does not have to contend with individuals within his Ministry, who outshine him nor is his term of office so insecure. But no other Premier has had to work with a President who is far more powerful than himself. Thus, though his position in relation to the Assembly is relatively strong, he is far less independent as an executive than a reading of the constitution would suggest.

According to the constitution, the Premier chooses his own ministers, formulates governmental policy in conjunction with them, presents it to the Assembly, or, in case the response is slow, carries it out through the government's independent powers (especially over organic laws and finance policy). In practice, however, his activity has been limited to a joint formulation of policy with the President (in which the Premier has played an increasingly subordinate role) and to managing the legislature so that it will accept the government's program.

The Premier and the Cabinet

The role of the Premier under Debré differed from that under Pompidou for many reasons. The two men held different attitudes regarding their relations to the President, the ministers, and the Assembly. In addition, there was a sharp dividing line in the operation of the executive after the end of the Algerian war in mid-1962. De Gaulle was then left free to expand his concerns into all aspects of government, a role that he may not consciously have sought but was drawn into by the very interrelatedness of governmental activities and decisions.

Debré, strongly attracted by the role of the British Prime Minister, insisted on being the intermediary between his ministers and the President as well as the chief figure in dealing with the Assembly. Pompidou, in contrast, has not resisted de Gaulle's increasingly direct contact with individual ministers, holds infrequent Cabinet meetings, and uses interministerial committee meetings not as final decision-making sessions but in an attempt to secure agreement

before taking matters to the Council of Ministers. Nor does Pompidou seem to have resented de Gaulle's highhanded actions in amending the constitution to provide for the direct election of the President.

The position of the ministers has been strengthened by their immunity from parliamentary criticism, their long periods of office, their civil service orientation (most of them were civil servants and continue to concentrate on administration), and their increasingly close contact with the source of ultimate power, de Gaulle. Since, however, de Gaulle does not interfere with the details of policy so long as he is satisfied that the general lines are satisfactory and the activity sufficiently energetic, the ministers possess a great deal of responsibility. They and their staffs deal with the interest groups that, more effectively than the political parties, represent the dynamic forces at work within the country. By thus acting as the coordinator of policies rather than the driver of a unified political and administrative machine, Pompidou is probably contributing to the general effectiveness of policy rather than reducing it.

The Premier and the President

Though he acquiesces fully in de Gaulle's leadership, Pompidou feels that his particular responsibility is to reduce de Gaulle's work load. Thus, where Debré sought to share executive responsibilities and decisions and, indeed, virtually controlled all except foreign policy decisions, Pompidou, in the succeeding period of unified domestic and foreign policies under presidential leadership, has tried to simplify and focus those choices that are to be made at the highest level. As Premier he still performs the role of personal chief of staff for de Gaulle that he took over in 1958. At the more official level on which he now performs, he channels the business of government so that de Gaulle makes all final decisions in all fields, but in most cases only de Gaulle's acceptance or rejection is necessary. Only where agreement at lower levels cannot be secured is de Gaulle forced to concern himself with the arguments on both sides.

Despite Pompidou's self-effacement and self-restraint in his relations with the President, the constitutional provisions for the office of Premier invest it with some of the characteristics of the office of Vice President of the United States. As Premier, Pompidou makes important statements on policy to the Assembly and often to the press. Occasionally he has replaced the President at ceremonial functions. It is not surprising that some people have suggested that de Gaulle is grooming Pompidou to be his heir. Yet the very qualities that make Pompidou so admirable a chief of staff for a de Gaulle would be quite inappropriate for a de Gaulle-type President.

The Ministers

The Fifth Republic, in one of its most decisive breaks with the past, provided that members of parliament must resign their seats if they wish to accept ministerial office. In the past in France, with rare exceptions, and always in the United Kingdom and the older Commonwealth countries, ministers have been required to hold seats in parliament. The constant interchanges between ministers and backbenchers, and the ability of the backbenchers through questions or interpellations to keep the government constantly alert and responsive, have been among the most characteristic and most valued features of these parliamentary systems. By forcibly separating the legislature and executive through the incompatibility rule, General de Gaulle (on whose insistence it was introduced into the constitution) moved the Fifth Republic toward executive leadership of the American type.

A further similarity between current French and American practices is the lack of importance ascribed to the party experience and party identification of ministers. British Cabinet ministers, as we have seen, often choose themselves, in the sense that they are too important within the party to be overlooked by even an imperious Prime Minister. American Presidents, in contrast, choose members of their Cabinet from either party—Secretary of Defense Robert McNamara, for example, is a Republican—and from private as well as public life.

Yet the American Cabinet has never included any substantial number of civil servants, as have the Cabinets under the Fifth Republic. In the first Ministry of 1958, seven ministers were

civil servants. The practice thereafter has been to draw about one-third of the members of the government from the civil service, including the holders of such "political" posts as those of Finance, Defense, Foreign Affairs, and Interior. This significant role of high civil servants may, indeed, be a still more distinctive characteristic of de Gaulle's Republic than the incompatibility rule, which prevents ministers from holding seats in the legislature.

Whether France will continue both the incompatibility rule and the dominant role of high civil servants in the government once the de Gaulle era is over is open to question. De Gaulle's personality and prestige need no enhancement from either his Premier or his ministers. The chambers and the parties, as we have seen, react to President de Gaulle rather than to the Premier. But a lesser man in the presidency might well make necessary more colorful, more dynamic, and more representative figures in the Ministry if its interaction with the Assembly is not again to plunge into frustration and stalemate.

The Council of Ministers and Council of the Cabinet

The French government has always met in two different ways: as the Council of Ministers, and as the Council of the Cabinet. The former meets under the chairmanship of the President; the latter, under the chairmanship of the Premier, without the President. There have been major differences, however, in the role played by the two in the earlier Republics and in the present one. Under the Third Republic, the Council of the Cabinet, which was created to prepare for the meetings of the Council of Ministers, became the real policy-making organ, and the Council of Ministers merely a ratifying body. The same was largely true under the Fourth Republic, although in certain respects the Council of Ministers became more significant. Under the Fifth Republic, however, the significance of the Council of the Cabinet has been greatly reduced, and the Council of Ministers has become the decision-making body. Indeed, only fifteen meetings of the Council of the Cabinet were held in 1959–60, a time when de Gaulle was absorbed by the Algerian crisis, while there were a hundred sessions of the Council of Ministers. With de Gaulle's release from Algerian affairs, and with Pompidou's premiership, the Council of Ministers has become even more dominant.

The Government Secretariat

Until the Fourth Republic, informality and *ad hoc* decisions and organization were characteristic of the operations of the Council of Ministers and the Cabinet. Under the Fourth Republic, minutes of Council meetings began to be taken, and the embryonic secretariat established in 1935 was extended. Under de Gaulle, a still more extensive expansion has taken place. The Secretary General of the Government, who has been the head of the secretariat since 1947, and his staff prepare and circulate the agenda of the Council of Ministers, check the preparation of bills and administrative regulations, prepare the minutes for the President, and report on decisions and their implementation.

Like so much else under the Fifth Republic, the Secretariat General, which was previously of particular importance to the Premier and is still associated officially with that office, now also performs manifold coordinating tasks for the President, particularly in connection with the changed role of the Council of Ministers. Although the Premier has his own *cabinet*, or private secretariat, like other ministers, the Secretary General of the Government has long directed a considerable part of the Premier's staff and still provides the major preparation for his relations with parliament.

The Secretariat General also performs something of a general coordinating role. The Planning Commissariat, the Atomic Energy Commissariat, and the offices of the Delegates General for scientific research and the development of the Paris region are associated, though somewhat indirectly, with the Secretary General. Also attached, but with its own Director General, is the division responsible for the management of the civil service. The School of National Administration (*École Nationale d'Administration*) and the Center for Advanced Administrative Study (*Centre des hautes études administratives*) are also linked to the Secretariat, but the connection is tenuous. In the end, even the efforts of the de Gaulle Republic to secure executive supervision and coordination of the administration have not been outstandingly successful.

The Premier and the Assembly

However diminished the importance of the Premier vis-à-vis the President, and even vis-à-vis the ministers, there is no doubt that the Premier and his government have become a great deal stronger than ever before in their relations with the Assembly. The constitution of the Fifth Republic strongly tilted the balance of power away from the chambers and in favor of the government.

Among the new rights accorded to the government by the Fifth Republic are the right to the priority of government bills in the parliamentary timetable, the right to propose amendments to bills, and the right to open a general debate on a measure in either chamber. Thus deputies now hear the government's case on a bill before the *rapporteur* of the relevant committee can present his criticisms, and the debate takes place on the government's text, not on the text that emerges from committee. Moreover, the government has the right to reject amendments proposed from the floor after the committee stage, and also to force the chamber to vote either on particular clauses of the bill or on the bill as a whole. As we have seen, the government can also spur a decision on a bill over which there is disagreement between the Senate and the Assembly. What the government cannot do, however, is to secure the passage of a bill (unless it is on finance) that the Assembly refuses to approve.

In finance, the government has been given special powers to avoid a not uncommon situation of the past, i.e., having the deadline for the budget go by before it was voted. The constitution has provided a time limit for budgetary debates at the end of which the government can impose the budget by decree power if the Assembly has not voted it. The Fifth Republic also attempts to enforce more effectively the provision (which also existed under the Fourth Republic) that deputies cannot propose measures involving increases in expenditures.

But more significant than the constitutional procedures that have strengthened the hands of the government is the fact that the government has enjoyed majority support in the Assembly for its crucial policies—except over the direct election of the President, where the opposition clearly misread the temper of the public. So long as the Gaullists secure a majority of the seats in the Assembly and/or so long as the parties of the opposition fail to present a unified front that offers a credible alternative, the Premier and his ministers will have little difficulty ensuring the acceptance of the President's policies.

6. The French Administration: National and Local

1. THE CHARACTER OF THE FRENCH ADMINISTRATION

Changeable though the French political system has been, Frenchmen know that behind its vagaries and instabilities stands, and has stood since Napoleonic days, a centralized administration that deals efficiently, and usually justly, with the manifold problems of public concern. Far more of a technocracy than is the British and even more the American administrative structure, the French administration is often regarded outside as well as inside France as a model of its kind. What some call its impressive self-confidence and self-reliance, however, seems to others authoritarianism.

The tasks placed upon the French administration, both traditionally and now, have a collectivist flavor that helps to explain its pervasiveness. The state-wide administrative institutions that Napoleon consolidated have always undertaken certain social and economic activities aimed at national development. Some parts of the Third Republic, and much more of the Fourth, accepted the concept of the welfare state, with its correlative expansion of public responsibilities. Still more distinctive than its welfare programs have been the extent and success of French national planning since World War II.

Under the Fifth Republic the increased freedom of the executive from legislative supervision and control has given the civil service additional scope for action. While at times under the Third and Fourth Republics the civil service was the major, even the only, operating part of

government in the hiatus between Ministries, it always had to devote a good part of its energies to persuading politicians to support administrative projects. With the administration now so firmly rooted in the Cabinet itself and in the President's staff, it can often replace persuasion with action. There is thus some reason for calling the Fifth Republic a "civil service" or "administrative" state.

This is not to say, however, that France is being governed without reference to interest and pressure groups. Under the Third and Fourth Republics the establishment of numerous consultative committees was aimed at providing effective channels of influence for representative groups seeking special privileges and opportunities. So long as political parties were major factors in determining policy, interest groups divided their attention between these parties and the administration. As political parties and parliament became less important under the Fifth Republic for determining the character of policy—they have rarely determined its details—the interaction of pressure groups and the administration has become the more powerful determinant of public action. Groups within the administrative service itself have also sought to win recognition not only as representative bargaining agents, as in the Whitley Council system, but also as advisers on the form and occasionally the substance of public policy.

Such efforts to influence governmental action hardly contribute genuinely to the public interest. Nor does the pressure exercised directly by particular groups on administrative bureaus without having gone through the filter of a nationally organized political party. The tendency seems to be to pit special groups—farmers, railway workers, even postal employees—against an administration that believes less in compromise of the British type than in the existence of a "right answer" for every problem if only sufficient technical skill and know-how are available. In an expanding and prosperous economy, potential conflict—evidenced by angry protests, slow-downs, and strikes—tends to be neutralized, although post-Algerian France has had many such outbursts. More straitened circumstances, however, might provoke the very instability that the strengthening of the executive has sought to prevent.

The Public Sector

The French national government has always played a role in the economy, and this role has steadily increased. Nonetheless, neither the division between public and private activities, nor their association in "mixed" corporations, is clear-cut or logical. France, like some other Continental countries, has a number of long-established state monopolies: for example, the manufacture and sale of tobacco and matches. The state controls the production and distribution of fuel and power—electricity, gas, coal, and atomic energy—and has substantial interests in oil. The national government is dominant in transportation—railways, airlines, and two shipping companies—but private interests compete both in air and sea transportation and control most of the road transport. The state also engages in manufacturing; it controls most of the aircraft industry (a Popular Front development), about a third of the motor industry (which was nationalized because of the Renault plant's collaborationist activities with the Nazis), naval shipyards, some subsidiary production of refrigerators, tractors, and motorcycles, and the production of most fertilizers. Most surprising is the state control of insurance companies.

Much of this control developed by spurts rather than systematically. Under the Third Republic, state intervention was usually prompted by the economic difficulties of private enterprise. The persistent deficits of the railways, for ex-

ample, led finally to their being merged into a single government company in 1938 under a *mixed corporation*—that is, one whose board represents both public and private stockholders, and where public money indirectly subsidizes private activity. Broadcasting began in 1922 as a public enterprise, but private stations appeared later on. The manufacture of planes for maritime aviation was placed under a mixed corporation in 1933; in 1936 it was merged with the production for civil aviation under semi-autonomous mixed companies.

The postwar extensions of nationalization, though comprehensive, followed no planned program in France, as they did in Great Britain. True, the National Council of Resistance, leftist in orientation, formulated a program that looked to the day when the nation would take over "the fundamental methods of exchange and of production" and when the working class would share "in the conduct of the nation's economy." This program reflected a mistrust of private enterprise, a desire for better working conditions, and an awareness of the need for rapid reconstruction. But the Council had no clear plans for nationalization, and de Gaulle was unenthusiastic about such a development. Nonetheless, when he was succeeded in January 1946 by Felix Gouin, a Socialist, the rather tentative nationalization program of the first year of Liberation was extended and then brought to an end.

The Extent of Nationalization

Five nationalization projects were undertaken from December 1944 to December 1945: the coal mines in the north of France, comprising about two-thirds of those in the country; the Renault automobile works; the Gnôme et Rhône Airplane Motor Company; the principal airlines; and, most important of all, the greater part of banking and credit. In 1946 came the full nationalization of the coal mines (with minor exceptions), of the producers of gas and electricity (except for the natural gas industry and small gasworks and electrical companies), and of the thirty-four largest insurance companies, representing about 68 percent of the premiums paid in France. Further, the rules governing the Bank of France were extended to the Bank of Algeria. The assets and property of newspapers that had appeared during the Occupation were transferred to a national company. In all, about 20 percent of France's industrial capacity was nationalized, probably the highest percentage in any democratic country.

The French program of nationalization had certain marked similarities to that in Great Britain, but also significant differences. It was more empirical than the British and also more varied. Though the British went further in nationalizing inland transport, they have nothing comparable to France's partial nationalization of credit and insurance. On the other hand, British public ownership is more monolithic than is the French—that is, in Great Britain nationalization commonly extends throughout a particular field, whereas in France it tends to be limited, except in coal mining, to the largest companies in that field. A further difference is that the punitive motive for nationalization, which led the state to take over the Renault plants, the Gnôme et Rhône Airplane Motor Company, and newspapers issued during the Occupation because of their collaborationist activities, did not exist at all in Great Britain. Finally, nationalization ceased in France after the airlines, the two largest maritime shipping companies, and the Paris transport system were brought under public control early in 1948. The bill to nationalize the steel industry was never brought to a vote. Thus the French drive for nationalization came to an end earlier, but with more pervasive effect, than did the comparable drive in Great Britain.

Economic Planning

Although nationalization played a role in the recovery of France, the more decisive and long-range state contribution toward overcoming France's prewar stagnation and relatively low industrial capacity has come through France's own particular type of economic planning. Unlike the coercive and highly directive planning of the Soviet Union, French state planning operates by stimulating different segments of the economy toward accepted short-range goals. Thus it is commonly called *indicative* rather than *dirigisme*—that is, it indicates and stimulates lines of development rather than forcing them.

Characteristic of French planning have been its flexibility, its dependence on financial incentives, its emphasis on increasing the quantity of production, and its relevance to selected needs and goals. The emphasis of the first three Plans—1946–53, 1954–57, 1958–61—was on modernization and equipment. The first Plan concentrated on a few basic industries: coal, electricity, transport, steel, cement, and agricultural machinery. The second and third Plans concentrated on adjusting the economy to participation in the Common Market and on increasing exports and raising domestic living standards. The fourth and fifth Plans—1962–65 and 1966–70—have been more concerned with social and general economic development, the latter particularly in backward regions.

No one would claim that planning should receive the full, or even major, credit for France's current prosperity. Indeed there was considerable debate over whether the fifth Plan was even needed. There seems general agreement, however, that if government stimulus is no longer vital, except in stagnant areas, stabilization may be aided by the overall view of the economy that French planners try to provide.

2. THE ORGANIZATION OF THE PUBLIC ADMINISTRATION

In contrast to the relative independence of local government in Great Britain, and its self-assertiveness in the United States, the public administration of France is distinguished by its unity. French ministries occupy a position of dominance that has not been affected by the decentralizing (*decentralisation*) of particular functions to local bodies and public enterprises. Although these bodies and enterprises generally possess financial and administrative autonomy, they do not have the semi-independence of local government or public corporations in Great Britain. The French view the establishment of separate bodies in France as a delegation of state functions that does not impair the unity of all public services.

In general, the expansion of services in France

has led to the enlargement of the domain of the ministries. The nineteenth-century British theory of limited governmental responsibilities —laissez faire, or the public order state—never operated in France, nor has the British concentration of ministries in the capital city. In response to the monarchical and Napoleonic notion that government agencies operate their own services and are broadly responsible for the economic and social welfare of the community, French ministries have always maintained a network of regional and local branches and many functional agencies that keep the ministries in continuous and intimate contact with communities throughout the country.

The breadth of the functions of the ministries and the wide dispersal of their offices and staffs have made the problem of executive supervision particularly difficult, much more so than in Great Britain. Many of France's best civil servants, in fact, operate in supervisory roles. There is also a network of personal secretariats (*cabinets*) of ministers, inspectorates, and advisory committees undertaking supervisory work. In a very real sense, therefore, there are two levels of national administration: the active level (consisting of the ministries), and the supervisory. Each plays an essential role in the functioning of the French public administration.

The Active Central Administration: The Ministries

Contrary to what we might expect, the structure of ministries in France is far less coherent and uniform than in Great Britain. Ministries tend to be collections of units or services tied together very loosely under a single minister. Many of these units have long enjoyed considerable administrative autonomy and prestige of their own and have no intention of being dominated or submerged. Moreover, until the recent reorganization of regions, the external services of different ministries were not even planned according to uniform divisions. Thus any accurate description of the French national administration would have to be undertaken ministry by ministry.

Certain distinctive differences from the British administrative structure are, however, apparent. First, the British depend much more on semiautonomous local agencies and officials for the execution of national policies. In France, only a small proportion—less than 5 percent— of the central administration works in Paris; the rest are engaged in direct administration in the provinces. The direct external services provided by ministries are termed *deconcentration* as distinguished from decentralization, since the former involve field offices rather than separate local or corporate bodies. This practice of extensive field offices has always been characteristic of French ministries, whereas in Great Britain the practice was not introduced until after World War I and has never been extensive.

Second, technical personnel, in the broad sense of specialists, who are found in advisory roles in the British national administration, play a much more important role in France both in policy-making and in day-to-day administration. Indeed there is in France no class of general administrator in the British sense, since all French administrators receive specialized training. Because administrative law is so highly developed and important in France, legal training of a broad character is part of the preparation of almost all administrators. It is also true, however, that many specialists in more technical fields become general administrators at later stages of their careers. It is in this sense of "government by experts" that the term *technocracy* is used for the French administration.

Third, British ministries are more stable than French ministries. While both countries provide relatively permanent structures for foreign affairs, armed forces, interior, labor, agriculture, and the like, there is a great deal more reshuffling in France of particular services from minister to minister—a process even more evident under the Fifth than under the Fourth Republic —than there is in Great Britain. Moreover, some French ministries have short lives—as had the Ministry of Information and the Ministry of Repatriation—or else their functions are transferred to the Premier's office and then come under administrative agencies rather than ministers. This process is rather bewildering to the outsider, but it provides a great deal of flexibility and perhaps scope for useful experimentation.

Fourth, French ministries only rarely are headed by an official comparable to the British permanent secretary of a department. The chiefs of *directions,* units roughly comparable to British departmental divisions, are directly responsible to the minister, a practice incompatible with a coordinating civil service head. Moreover, the very variety of functions within single ministries makes such coordination difficult. (The only two ministries with a Secretary-General—that is, the French equivalent of a permanent secretary—are those with a clear unity of purpose: Foreign Affairs and Telegraphs.) Finally, ministers in the days of unstable Cabinets were reluctant to delegate coordinating authority to a permanent civil servant, preferring to entrust it instead to their own *cabinet* of personal aides.

The Supervisory Administration

The highly important and diversified supervisory administration in France has no obvious parallel in Great Britain, largely because the need that gave rise to it in France is satisfied by a different kind of structure in Great Britain. In France, the supervisory administration consists of a personal secretariat, known as the *cabinet,* attached to each minister, the inspectorates and advisory councils. Among the latter, the administrative section of the *Conseil d'Etat* is particularly important.

The Cabinet

A particularly sensitive and significant role is played in France, as in many Continental countries, by the minister's personal secretariat, or *cabinet.* Often called the minister's "eyes and ears," the members of his *cabinet* must share his political aims and yet also act as the administrative coordinators of his ministry. Originally, most *cabinets* were composed of political appointees, but increasingly they are staffed by technically competent high civil servants. One member, at least, usually concentrates on the minister's behind-the-scenes parliamentary business (there is no French equivalent of the British parliamentary secretary who can speak for the minister on the floor of the house) and may therefore be drawn from outside the service. The technical and coordinating functions of the *cabinet,* however, have made it advisable to draw most of the members from those whom the civil service will most respect—namely, the higher civil service itself.

Cabinets are limited to ten members (except for those of the Premier and the Ministers of Foreign Affairs, the Interior, and Finance) and are regarded as civil servants to whom most though not all the rules of the service pertain. Although their term of office in a ministry is commonly only that of a particular minister, members of a *cabinet* perform many of the functions of a permanent secretary, act as a brain trust, and speed along the minister's policy. Thus the overall working of the administration depends to a considerable degree on their tact and skill.

The Inspectorates

Inspectorates exist side by side with public services and expand with their growth. They may be concerned with all activities in a ministry, or they may concentrate on a particular activity. They exist within virtually all the ministries, except those of Foreign Affairs and Justice. They are flexible instruments of supervision, composed entirely of civil servants, and their members provide a pool of experience at the disposal of ministers for special administrative or advisory functions.

The most important inspectorate is that of finance. Together with the Court of Accounts (*Cour des Comptes*), a judicial body with powers and responsibilities roughly equivalent to those of the Comptroller and Auditor General in Great Britain, the Inspectorate of Finance audits all accounts on behalf of the Ministry of Finance. Its members possess wide powers of investigation, which extend to any matter affecting public funds.

In addition to this function, the *Inspection des Finances* comprises a special élite corps of the best graduates of the *École Nationale d'Administration,* the gateway to the higher civil service. Complaints are often heard that this inspectorate possesses a near monopoly of the best positions throughout the administration, particularly in financial and economic fields. This may be looked on as recompense for the fact that the most brilliant graduates are responsible for auditing, one of the most mundane though most essential tasks in the administration.

Advisory Bodies

Advisory bodies belong to two distinct groups: those composed wholly of civil servants, of which the *Conseil d'Etat* is the most famous and influential; and those of a representative character. The selection and composition of the latter vary widely, but most have a mixed membership of officials and representatives of interest groups. Eight out of nineteen ministries in 1959 had advisory councils concerned with all aspects of their work. Several ministries have a number of such councils. The Ministry of Health and Population, for example, has national councils for public health, public assistance, social work, and hospitals, as well as for doctors, dentists, midwives, nurses, pharmacists, and opticians.

The apex of the representative structure is the quasi-parliamentary Economic and Social Council (*Conseil Economique et Social*), a somewhat modified successor of the Economic Council of the Fourth Republic, which seems to be consulted somewhat more seriously in technical matters than was its predecessor. Composed of representatives of various organizations, persons of eminence in cultural, social, and economic fields, and with a strong official element, the Council gives advice both early and late in the formulation of the Plan. It has fifteen specialized sections to which nearly a hundred experts are co-opted, mainly from private enterprise, and it includes many of the same members as the somewhat less effective Planning Council.

How influential are the wealth of advisory bodies of various types that associate representatives of interest groups with the active administration is difficult to evaluate. Rarely do these bodies have powers of decision, although projects must sometimes be referred to them for comment. The effectiveness of their advice depends not on sanctions but on the weight of the arguments they put forward and often on the degree to which the minister is in sympathy with what they propose. Nonetheless, they provide a useful exchange of information that helps keep civil servants aware of currents of opinion in the country.

Although the advisory councils give interest and pressure groups formal access to the French administrative system, they find less formal channels even more effective, particularly under the Fifth Republic. It is often said that the prime stimulus of governmental action, outside that provided by de Gaulle, comes from the interaction of the representatives of pressure groups and members of the administration. And it is true that the natural role of political parties in focusing and cushioning the activities of pressure groups was greatly diminished in the early years of the Fifth Republic by the shift of power from the legislative to the executive and administrative branches. What the future holds depends on whether or not the political parties manage to return to the center of the stage. Whatever happens, however, is unlikely to diminish the importance of the most important general advisory body in France: the *Conseil d'Etat,* or Council of State.

The Council of State

Though technically the Council of State does not have direct responsibilities for administrative coordination and control, it is a body of confidential and trusted advisers that gives technical advice to ministries on the drafting of legislation (which in consequence is unusually polished) and also aids the executive in planning and preparing its legislative program. It has been traditionally responsible for checking the form and character of governmental decrees, and its role in this regard has been spelled out under the Fifth Republic. Article 38 of the constitution, which legalizes "special powers" under which the government can issue *décrets-lois* in matters normally within the sphere of legislation, also specifies that these ordinances must be examined by the Council of State.

By any standard the Council of State is a most remarkable institution, without parallel in Great Britain or the United States. Set up originally by Napoleon, its chief duties have always been those of planning, advising the executive, and resolving whatever difficulties may arise in the administrative field. Perhaps the most striking aspect of the Council of State is that it is composed of interrelated parts: an administrative body, which has the most intimate knowledge of the legislative program of the Cabinet, and a judicial body, which forms the supreme administrative tribunal of the country, as described in Chapter 7. The prestige and authority of the Council of State rest on its extraordinary independence in both its advisory and its judicial capacities.

The senior members of the Council of State are organized into five sections: four small administrative sections (of seven members each in 1962) that handle matters concerned with finance, interior, public works, and social affairs, respectively (they may meet together on matters of concern to several ministries), and a fifth, much larger (twenty-eight members) judicial section. The junior members of the Council, known as *auditeurs* (first and second class) and *maîtres des requêtes,* prepare reports for the consideration of the 58 *Conseillers d'Etat.* Promotion is from one grade to the next, and the total number of members of the Council in 1959 was 169, roughly equal in each of the three major groups. Particularly since 1963, the organizational division between the Council's administrative and judicial work has been overbridged as much as possible, to enable each to have insight into the problems and policies of the other. Thus every *auditeur* and *maître des requêtes* serves both in the judicial section and in one administrative section; *conseillers* may move from one to the other; and some members of each are always members of the other. Thus the two roles are intermingled and at the same time are kept rigidly separate in decision-making.

The legislative work of the Council of State has been more important under the Fifth Republic than ever before. The restriction on the legislature's power to amend government bills puts a heavy responsibility on the Council to give these bills their correct legal form and to alert the Cabinet to unintended consequences or potential illegalities. The Council of State is also expected to guard against the impetuous use of decree powers and to restrain the executive from unconstitutional procedures. Its position in the latter regard was weakened, and the constitutional standing of the regime impaired, by de Gaulle's disregard for the Council's strong majority opinion against using the referendum to amend the constitution to provide for the direct election of the President, and by his disregard also for the sizable minority opposition to the change on the ground that it distorted the balance between executive and legislature. Nonetheless, the Council remains the chief administrative restraint on executive action and is considerably more effective than the Constitutional Council (see Chapter 2). Unlike the United States Supreme Court, the Council of State exercises its restraint before, rather than after, the fact.

On all regulations of public administration— that is, the measures necessary to carry out a law—the Council of State must be consulted by the Premier, in whom resides the rule-making power in the Fifth Republic. Only in certain technical matters is the government forced to follow the advice of the Council of State, but in practice its advice is always influential. So too is the advice it tenders to ministries, on their request, concerning decrees, policy, and coordination. Although most of its work is necessarily unpublicized, the Council of State clearly enjoys general confidence and respect. It is the most distinctive and one of the most useful of French institutions.

The Organization for Nationalized Enterprises ("Établissement Public")

Nationalization in France is broad in scope and involves novel forms of representation. The mixed corporation, in which stock is held by private interests as well as by the state, has been used for the railways, the airlines, and two major maritime shipping companies. The French agencies are financially autonomous, as are British and American public corporations. Similarly, they are independent legal entities capable of suing and being sued; they are liable to taxation; and their employees are not subject to civil service rules, although they may enjoy comparable conditions of service. But the French nationalized enterprises are distinctive in two respects: they are looked on as part of a unitary state machinery, and they make wide use of the representation of special interests on their boards of directors (a device with which British and American public corporations have never experimented).

Under the formula of "industrialized nationalization" proposed by the *Confédération Gén-*

érale du Travail as early as 1918, most nationalized enterprises possess boards of directors composed of representatives of the state, the workers, and the consumers. This is known as tripartite representation. It provides for unsalaried boards (except for the chairman) in which the representatives of workers and consumers often predominate, in place of the British salaried boards whose members are appointed by the government. One further, though not surprising difference, however, is that the French boards of nationalized industries are at best advisory and supervisory rather than management agencies. They are particularly weak in influencing decisions when the chief executives of public enterprises work in close liaison with supervising ministries.

The chief difference between public enterprise in Great Britain and in France is that in France the officials in both the relevant ministries and the public enterprises tend to look on themselves as part of a single system. Although the directors of nationalized enterprises function with considerable independence, they have no more independence than does the chief of a division within a ministry. Since the crucial decisions—for example, on wages, prices, and investment—are made by the government, since the top personnel is appointed by the government and often drawn from the civil service, and since board decisions are subject to ministerial review, the issue of control, which is often so vexing in Great Britain, hardly arises in France.

It is true that the French have also experimented with other techniques for controlling public enterprises. Under the Fourth Republic both the National Assembly and the Senate had special committees to examine the records of public enterprises. These committees had far wider powers than their British counterparts or, indeed, than other French committees. There are no such committees, however, under the Fifth Republic. Public enterprises have advisory committees representing various interests, as well as the tripartite representation, on their boards. The Electricity and Gas Council, for example, has representatives from the legislature, ministries, local authorities, private and industrial consumers, the corporations themselves, and, perhaps most surprising, their own

staffs. But though this Council is supposed to be consulted on all measures concerning gas and electricity, this is not always done, its recommendations are not made public, and its quasi-judicial functions in case of disputes between corporations and local authorities are virtually ignored. Thus while there is a remarkable degree of formal representation of special interests throughout the system, there is no evidence that it challenges the ultimate unity and central control of the administration.

The Organization for Economic Planning

The great difference between French and Soviet planning is well illustrated by the contrast between the small, flexible staff of the French Planning Commissariat and the pervasive planning machinery of the Soviet state. Fewer than a hundred people form the Planning Commissariat, and many of these are clerical. Its dynamism comes from a relatively small group of very intelligent and, on the average, very young civil servants of varied backgrounds and skills who work through the ministries rather than trying to supersede them, and also through a large number of specialized committees representing special interests and special experience.

At the heart of the Planning Commissariat's imaginative drive has been a remarkable series of Planning Commissioners. The first of them, Jean Monnet, has a legendary reputation. Unlike most administrators, the Planning Commissioner is not responsible to any single minister. Rather, he is considered to be on the same level as a minister and even attends Cabinet meetings when appropriate. Indeed, Jean Monnet might be called the first nonpolitical minister, a forerunner of those so common under the Fifth Republic.

Although the Planning Commissioner has relatively little formal power, he has wide influence, partly through the network of agencies with which his staff is concerned, partly through his membership in key agencies like the National Credit Council, and partly through the widespread effects of the Plan. The Commissioner also participates in the work of various European and international organizations. It is not surprising that both Monnet and his successor, M. Hirsch (formerly Monnet's deputy), should have moved from the Planning Commissariat to direct the European Coal and Steel Community and subsequently Euratom, the European Atomic Energy Commission (see Chapter 9).

Each Plan specifies the segments of the economy to be stimulated by injections of public funds and the goals for increased production. The spadework for the Plan is done through specialized committees, which are set up afresh for each Plan. There were twenty-seven of these committees for the fourth Plan, twenty-two of them concerned with particular sections of the economy, such as steel, agriculture, and building schools and hospitals, and the other five with finance, productivity, employment, regional development, and scientific research. Almost a thousand persons, drawn from the administration, private industry, labor, and other specialized groups, served on these committees, and many of them were recognized leaders in their fields. The committees themselves divide into study groups, which include many more people with particular technical skills. This unusually broad and representative base has done much to bring a sense of democratic participation into the planning process.

The Planning Commissariat is particularly active during the earliest and later stages of the preparation of the Plan. At the start, it works with the economic research unit of the Treasury and with the Economic and Social Council to develop assumptions about the rate of economic growth and the desired direction of economic development. Once these are agreed upon, the specialized committees are called into existence and set to work. When the committees conclude their work, the Planning Commissariat takes their material, coordinates and refines it, refers a provisional draft of the Plan to the Economic and Social Council and the Planning Council (which is also representative of relevant interests but is less important than the Economic and Social Council), and presents it to the Cabinet for final retouching and approval.

Parliamentary consideration of the Plan has been relatively slight until recently. The first and third Plans were not presented to Parliament at all, and the second was presented only during its third year of operation. The fourth Plan consisted of a nine-line bill with five hundred and eighty pages of appendices: the kind of document that inevitably stultifies and makes worthless any general discussion. The fifth Plan received quite searching parliamentary consideration.

Despite the small legislative role in the preparation of the Plans, their ultimate form is the result of a broadly democratic process. Moreover, this process involves a systematic overview of the problems and prospects of the economy undertaken for the purpose of proposing governmental action. The public support accorded the Plans has come almost as much from the wide participation in the preparation of the detailed material on which they are based as from their obviously rewarding results. French postwar planning is the most distinctive and visible evidence of the constructive interaction of the public administration with private interest groups acting in the national interest. It reflects the far-reaching implications of state responsibility for the social and economic well being of the French people. It embodies an important dimension of the postwar trend in the French administration toward technocracy.

3. LOCAL GOVERNMENT

Local government is more important in France than in Great Britain or the United States, because it is an integral part of a hierarchy of national planning and operations. The most significant recent development in French local government—the administrative division of France into twenty-one economic regions, each under its own regional or "super" prefect—arose directly out of the need for units better related to economic realities and ministerial responsibilities than are the ninety-five (formerly ninety) departments. Indeed, if logic had been pressed to the full, France would have been divided into only nine economic regions, since there are only nine thriving commercial centers outside Paris around which to organize them. The decision to establish twenty-one regions may have been motivated by the fear that if there were fewer regions there might be a demand for popular assemblies in each, patterned on the council system in local government. Such assemblies might have won more authority than the local councils now possess and thus have established local centers of power that would have been anathema to the French theory and practice of centralized and integrated public administration.

Local government in France has a different meaning from what it has in Great Britain or the United States. In those countries, local government is prized because it encourages local participation in public affairs, roots many local decisions in local bodies with their own source of funds, and thus, so the theory runs, forms an important (some would say invaluable) counterbalance to the national government's control of so many aspects of life. Both in Great Britain and the United States many local services—including education, medical care, and public utilities—were first provided at the local level and were only subsequently integrated into a national system.

In France, however, both the process and the assumptions run the other way. The French have always taken a broad view, as we have seen, of the scope of national responsibilities. Since the days of Napoleon I, local representation and local responsibilities have been intermeshed with the integrated, national structure of administration.

French local government has alternated in practice between local control, prefectural control, and a balance between the two. The National Assemblies established a democratic and decentralized system of local government in 1789 and 1790. They set up elected councils in the *departments,*[1] the largest local subdivisions, and also in the *communes*[2] (including cities,

towns, and villages), and placed extensive powers in the hands of locally selected executives. Napoleon completely overthrew this system, however, and replaced it with a highly centralized administrative hierarchy, headed in each department by a *prefect* who controlled the communes in the area as well as the department at large and was merely "advised" by nominated local bodies and officers. Thereafter, continued efforts were made to increase local participation in deciding local affairs. Both the departments and the communes ultimately won back the right to elect their own councils. Moreover, each communal council achieved the right to choose its own executive officer, the mayor, who was vested with considerable power. The characteristic feature of a French department, therefore, is the cooperative relationship between the prefect and the locally elected bodies. Since national politics, and national politicians, often have their base in the local sphere, the interaction between the prefect on the one hand, and the mayor or even the chairman of the departmental council on the other, is not so one-sided as the unity of the French administrative structure might lead one to expect.

Scope and Resources of Local Administration

The administration of local services is chiefly through the field services of the ministries and the prefect. Purely local services are restricted to fields that the national government has not entered. In the nineteenth century local communities were forbidden even to establish local services such as gas, water, and garbage disposal in competition with private enterprise. Gradually, however, this rule was relaxed, and French towns now provide a range of local services that in some respects exceed those of British and American municipalities.

The major field in which local units provide supplementary services is that of relief and public welfare. Departments and communes have some mandatory responsibilities here—for ex-

---

[1] The basic units of French local administration are the ninety-five *departments,* of which the original eighty-three were established in 1790 by the Constituent Assembly, the rest resulting from subsequent additions to French territory. They bear no relationship to earlier historical divisions (as do many English counties), since they were deliberately designed to stamp out local particularism. Each department was kept small enough so that any person could make the round trip from his home to its governing seat in the course of a single day. A surprising feature to a foreigner is that the departments have included not only areas in Continental France but also in overseas territories. The administrative subdivisions of Algeria long formed three of the departments. In 1946 Martinique, Guiana, Réunion, and Guadeloupe became departments as a mark of close assimilation, indeed "oneness," with metropolitan France.

[2] The *commune* is the unit of local administration with the soundest basis in history and local sentiment and the greatest degree of self-government. Communes vary vastly in

size, however, and may be urban or rural. All cities, including Paris, are communes, but so are small rural districts, including sometimes only a score of houses.

There are two other units, the *arrondissement* and the *canton,* but they inspire little popular sentiment and lack important governmental functions.

ample, they *must* establish institutions for orphans, the insane and feeble-minded, and young delinquents, as well as schools for the deaf, blind, dumb, and subnormal. But they *may* also establish health and welfare clinics, and playground and sports facilities. Special aid for large needy families and expectant mothers is characteristic of the relief measures that local units extend on their own initiative. Public employment services are a postwar addition to local powers. More surprising is the provision by many towns of nursery schools and institutions for training in architecture, art, and technical fields.

Most French towns of any size now have municipal warehouses, markets, public baths, stadiums, botanical gardens, and libraries. More surprising to Americans, they also operate or finance municipal theaters, opera houses, and conservatories of music. The departments have no developments of this kind; their purely local activities are restricted to looking after their own public buildings and property.

The greatest weakness of French local government is its inadequate revenue. By law the independent income of French local units is limited to a variety of small taxes, a small fraction of some national taxes, the income on public property, and profits from municipal enterprises. Thus they have no single substantial source of funds comparable to the property taxes or rates collected by American or English local governments.

By far the greatest proportion of local expenditures are obligatory under national law, either as contributions toward national services or as outlay for mandatory local services. In return, the national government extends grants-in-aid of local services, which amount to about 20 percent of total local expenditures. But general financial arrangements have proved highly unsatisfactory and have all too often encouraged irresponsibility or curbed local initiative.

Organs and Officers

In England, as we have seen, there is only one main organ of local government in each unit, the council. But in the two most important local units in France, the department and the commune, there are three centers of authority:

the prefect, the locally elected council, and the council's own elected executive: president in a department, mayor in a commune. The mayor has a relatively strong position in his commune, but the president of the council in no way challenges the dominance of the prefect in the department.

The prefect is the titular head of the department and acts as such whenever the state is represented in its corporate capacity. In situations of disorder or danger, he has independent powers to act. His major functions, however, are administrative, and his supervision extends to any matter of national concern. In relation to the departmental council, the prefect possesses a power known as *tutelle administrative* (administrative guardianship), which he exercises mainly by reviewing decisions or insisting on the performance of required functions (for example, providing for mandatory expenditures). Still more important, however, is the reinforcement through a decree in 1964 of the prefect's position as director of all state activities in his department, except those specifically retained by the central administration (namely, armed forces, judiciary, education, finance, and the labor inspectorate).

The position of the prefect had been challenged by increasingly independent decisions made by the external services of the ministries. National deputies, who were also members of departmental councils (they have numbered at times between two hundred and three hundred), and members of the highly important "mayors' bloc" in the chambers who wanted particular types of policies or decisions, had found it easier to get concessions from ministries than from the prefect. But the 1964 reform has greatly strengthened the position of the prefect and his staff as coordinator of all national services in local areas of the regional, or "super," prefect in each region. The need to plan economic activity regionally, rather than departmentally, had been apparent since World War II. As early as 1950, private groups organized what they called Regional Economic Expansion Committees. In 1954 these committees were recognized by the government. In 1959–60, metropolitan France was divided into twenty regions, plus Paris (see accompanying map), and the capital of the largest department

The New Regions

in each of the twenty regions became the seat of an Interdepartmental Administrative Conference. The capstone of this development came in 1964 with the establishment of regional prefects assisted by small general staffs and by advisory committees of special interests. These advisory committees have been called regional versions of the Economic and Social Council.

The purpose of the regional organization is to coordinate the external services of the ministries at the regional level. Local jealousies have already shown themselves, and the present boundaries for regional action may not turn out to be satisfactory in the long run. What is particularly important, however, is that France's traditional administrative units at the local level

are not being allowed to hinder imaginative national economic planning. It is possible, also, that the kind of coordination being sought at the departmental and regional levels will have an impact on Paris and will produce more organizational integration both within the ministries and among them.

4. THE PUBLIC SERVICE

The quality of public service, like the quality of a private service, depends on the training, experience, character, and sense of devotion of its members. The French public service has certain distinctive qualities that arise out of the milieu from which its members are drawn, the type of responsibilities it carries, its traditions, its structural organization, and its career possibilities. In virtually all these respects there are noticeable differences between the public service in France and those in Great Britain and the United States.

We have already emphasized the pervasiveness and stability of the French public service and the degree to which it has been regarded as the stable element in French government. Despite the variety of regimes through which France has passed, the public service has always retained a strong sense of its own positive mission to provide administrative continuity under all circumstances, and to stimulate and even direct economic advance. Its impulse is not in any sense toward socialist or revolutionary goals (despite the syndicalist sympathies within its lower ranks) but rather toward capitalistic and national advance. It is largely due to the national public service that the foundations of France's present prosperity were so well established under the Fourth Republic.

Much more than the British, the French public service enlists recruits from all classes and from all regions of the country. The very pervasiveness of the national public service—so much greater than in Great Britain, where many tasks are performed by local officials (1,300,000 in the local government services in Great Britain, compared to 400,000 in France)—makes it both visible and attractive. As a result, there is keen competition to qualify for public service, particularly through the university-level technical schools which lead to the higher civil service. To graduate from one of these *grandes écoles* is to gain distinction useful in any walk of life, including business and commerce, and often leads to a career in business after the stated period of service to the state has been performed. An important by-product is that whereas in Great Britain the managers and directors of big business firms have their natural contacts with members of the Conservative party, those in France are more likely to share common interests and assumptions with high civil servants.

But if the *grandes écoles* produce graduates with certain common standards, they also foster particularism. Each of these schools has tended, especially in the past, to lead to a particular part

of the public service. The general civil service code, passed in 1946, was intended to unify the whole service by providing uniform conditions for its management and organization under a single body. This code, somewhat modified by practice and regulation, has done a good deal to blur the distinctions among different sections of the public service, but it has done little or nothing to bridge the sharpest division in the French public service, that between the members of the *grands corps,* who hold the highest posts, and the rest of the civil administrators. The former hold positions of power and prestige both within the service and within France itself. They are rarely, if ever, rivaled by their opposite numbers in Great Britain, and even less in the United States.

Organizing the Civil Service

Until the civil service code of 1946 was passed, the administration itself, and many individual ministries, defined their own conditions of service. The code is now assumed to apply to all except the judiciary, the military, and services or public corporations of an industrial or commercial character. Even within the public corporations, however, the code applies to those on salary; those who are paid hourly wages have comparable advantages to those of the civil service which are spelled out in special codes.

Modeled on the organization of the British civil services, three other reforms were introduced following World War II. A civil service division (*Direction générale de la fonction publique*), placed directly under the Premier, was created in 1945 to provide a hoped-for but not wholly successful unity of direction. A school of administration (*École Nationale d'Administration*) was set up the same year to recruit for the administrative class (executive and clerical staffs are still recruited by the department) and to develop post-entry training programs. And an overall structure established four general classes—A, B, C, and D—roughly equivalent to the British administrative, executive, clerical, and typist classes.

Despite these efforts to enforce uniformity throughout the civil service, the *grands corps* continue to maintain their distinctive position. Although in principle the highest posts are open to civil administrators (in particular from the specially created nonspecialized corps), in practice they tend to remain the preserve of the members of the *grands corps*. These are looked on as a pool of talent, and they may be moved to any section of the administration in which they are needed. They provide a sort of personalized unity, because of their common training, but not the overall organizational unity aimed at by the reforms of 1944–46.

Recruiting and Training the Higher Civil Service

Training is an integral part of the recruitment of higher civil servants in France. In Great Britain, as we have seen, the aim is to choose men of high intelligence and character for the administrative branch and to let them learn on the job. In the American service, recruitment is based either on academic capacity, tested by special examinations, or on experience. In France, however, stiff competitive examinations must be taken for entrance to a course of training. The *École Nationale d'Administration* (ENA) is the most important training school for higher civil servants, but certain ministries—Finance, Industry, Public Works and Transport, and the Armed Forces—continue to operate their own technical schools.

The French insist on impartiality in the selection of those who are admitted to the ENA. The *Conseil d'Etat,* ever vigilant for the rights of individuals, polices this rule and has refused to allow the government to reject candidates on grounds of political affiliation, since, in practice, this restriction would refer only to a connection with the Communist party. Neither religion, sex, nor residence can be taken into account. There has even been some reluctance to interview candidates, for fear personal bias might enter in. The impossibility of otherwise testing character, however, has led to the introduction of oral tests for entry to the ENA.

Since the major objectives in establishing the ENA were to draw the high civil service from a broader social base and to make it possible to abolish the separate examinations for the *grands corps,* one common examination was established. Moreover, half the places in the ENA were to be reserved for candidates already in the executive class (commonly recruited by de-

partmental competitive examinations and with training only on the job). Since the examination must be taken by age thirty, the latter provision produced a smaller number of applicants than was expected (in 1959, 99 civil servants applied, compared to 326 university graduates; only 14 civil servants were accepted, as compared with 46 university graduates). In any case, a proportionately high percentage of the civil service applicants turned out to be unsuccessful university candidates seeking a second try. The end result is that the French higher civil service, like the British, is still drawn predominantly from the middle and upper-middle classes, although there is now a sprinkling from the lower-middle class and the working class. Over 65 percent of the university graduates and 35 percent of the civil servants admitted to the school in 1959 came from the families of high civil servants or of men holding professional or managerial positions.

Examinations determine both whether an applicant will be admitted and what his future prospects will be. More than three-quarters of the common written and oral examinations test such subject matter as law, history, and economic geography. For the rest the candidate chooses one of the four main branches of administration: foreign service, general administration, or social or economic administration. The three-year training courses have many features in common and include both practical experience in a government department or a provincial prefecture and academic training. The decisive point for the student's future career comes at the end of the second year, when a final examination determines where he or she will be assigned: the fortunate few to the *grands corps* (*Conseil d'Etat,* Court of Accounts, finance inspectorate, or prefectoral corps), and the rest to the general corps of civil administrators. Once the die has been cast, specialized experience and training are provided in the section to which the students have been assigned.

Nothing in Great Britain or the United States parallels the rigorous training and controlled experience provided by the ENA. The internship during the first year enables the student to experience responsibility and authority in a significant situation where there is direct contact with citizens. Moreover, it is designed to provide "a new look" at life. Thus those from country districts serve in a city; those from the south serve in the north. Following the final examination, students acquire experience in private industry that will help them understand the problems of industrial management. Although the French have not been able to eliminate caste from their higher civil service, at least they provide their top administrators with well-rounded practical experience and theoretical training that any country can envy.

Conditions of Service

French civil servants enjoy far greater mobility both inside and outside the service than do their opposite numbers in Great Britain and the United States. They can move from one administrative section to another, and they may do so to secure promotion. They may take a post in a public corporation, a local authority, or an international organization without losing any of their rights, including their pension rights. More surprising, they may take leave and enter private employment without resigning, and they retain both their seniority and pension rights as of the moment of the change. Most startling of all, and in direct opposition to the situation in Great Britain, a civil servant may go into politics either as a member of parliament or as a minister. Indeed, as we have seen, one-third of all the ministers in most Cabinets under the Fifth Republic have been civil servants. Since there is no need for them to sever their connection with the service, the sharp distinction between politician and civil servant that the British maintain so carefully is blurred if not eliminated. This ability to move from public to private employment and back again, and from administrative to political roles and back again, reinforces and explains the key position of the higher civil service in France.

Every French civil servant is formally responsible under the law for carrying out the duties of his particular office; he must obey the orders issued by his superiors; and he must adhere strictly to all laws and executive orders. The responsibility of maintaining strict professional discretion is also emphasized.

Side by side with the duties for which a French civil servant is legally responsible stand the rights that he is assured. Among legal rights is protection by the government against suits for libel or attacks resulting from the performance of his duty and the long-existing right of a civil servant to take legal action over any violation of the personnel rules by a superior official, or over an administrative decision that might harm the collective interests of civil servants. Among economic rights is the right to receive a salary that is at least 120 percent of "the vital minimum," which is an officially endorsed subsistence wage. Among social rights are family allowances and other social security benefits of generous character. Most important in the view of many civil servants are the rights of association and representation, including the right to form and join staff associations, or *syndicats,*[3] and the right to have staff members on all administrative and technical commissions concerned with conditions of service.

Unions and Strikes in the Public Service

The most troublesome issue included in the definition of the status of civil servants is that of membership in *syndicats,* or civil service unions. The syndicats are the outgrowth of early staff organizations that fought for better conditions of employment. Strongly influenced by syndicalist doctrine, which proposed workers' control of all concerns, these staff associations sometimes aimed at controlling the work of their particular ministries (e.g., "The Post Office should be run by the postmen" was one slogan). In time the larger staff syndicats federated nationally into four major organizations —the General Federation of Civil Servants, the Postal Federation, the Teachers' Federation (primary and secondary), and the Federation of Public Utility Workers—which were more moderate than some of the earlier syndicats.

[3] The French make a distinction between *le droit syndical,* which is the right to trade union organization for the defense of common economic interests, and *le droit d'association,* which is a less far-reaching right to form an association with other persons for a common purpose. French civil servants have had the right of association for many years but although *syndicats* of civil servants have long existed *de facto,* the right to organize into trade unions was not officially recognized until the Law on the Status of Civil Servants of October 1946.

Nevertheless, the militant efforts and concerted pressures of the syndicats, coupled with their political agitation, roused fears that they might use their combined strength for purposes opposed to those of the government. For this reason, the right to affiliate with organizations such as the CGT has not yet been resolved *de jure,* though there has long been *de facto* affiliation.

Even more tension has centered about the use of the strike as a means of staff pressure. According to syndicalist doctrine, organized workers should use sabotage and the general strike as steps toward the overthrow of the capitalist order. In a modified form this ideology has been popular among the members of government unions, although strikes have been usually of restricted scope. A few serious incidents, however, have strongly affected opinion. In particular, the memory of the postal and railway strikes of 1909 and 1910 (the latter crushed by calling the strikers into the army and setting them to break their own strike) has persisted ominously on both sides.

Although the right to strike has not been defined, civil service strikes are not uncommon. When such issues have been referred to the *Conseil d'Etat,* it has generally opposed penalties for strikes. It has declared, however, that prefects, public prosecutors, the police, and higher civil servants cannot go on strike and that the services of key government departments and nationalized industries must be maintained at all times. A 1963 law provides that five days' notice of a strike must be given by all employees of central and local government and of public enterprises providing public service. To circumvent this minor restraint, however, dissatisfied unions, in particular that of the broadcasting service, took to delivering daily notices just in case!

Commissions Paritaires

The rank and file of the civil service have equal representation (*paritaire*) with their employers on the administrative and technical committees (*commissions paritaires*) that supervise the organization and functioning of the whole civil service. Although this machinery is not unlike that of the British Whitley Councils, the French system appears to give more weight to employee representatives.

The administrative committees, to which staff members are elected by their colleagues, consider recruitment, promotion, discipline, transfers, and other personnel questions. The technical committees, whose staff members are designated by the most representative of the unions, are concerned with practical problems of organization, efficiency, and reform that may be referred to them by the minister or by a union.

At the top of the system is the National Civil Service Council (*Conseil Supérieur de la Fonction Publique*), with twenty-eight members (fourteen from each side) chaired by the Premier himself. It hears appeals from the administrative committees, coordinates the work of the technical committees, and advises the Premier on administrative organization. Since 1959, each section has been able to meet separately. The Council meets only if the two do not agree; decisions are then taken by majority vote, with the Premier holding the deciding vote.

Neat as the system of consultation appears, neither side has been particularly helpful in making it work. Higher civil servants have tended to be uncommunicative about the reasons for their decisions, and the unions are sometimes intransigent on their objectives. At least, however, consultation has become the normal practice.

The Status of Employees in Nationalized Enterprises

In general, labor in nationalized enterprises occupies a position midway between the civil service and workers in private industry: it has a more effective share in management than the latter, and less limited union activity than the former. Most frequently, the rules governing recruitment, dismissal, and remuneration remain the same under nationalization as before. But special guarantees for union activity are provided by agreement (e.g., the union is guaranteed all material facilities, such as meeting halls, which it needs for pursuing its objects by legal means), and there is an absolute prohibition, embodied in law, against discrimination toward an employee because of union activity.

In addition, there are particular rules governing conditions of work and conciliation machinery for each of the nationalized enterprises. For example, the Miners' Charter (which takes the place of the collective agreement in private industry), includes provisions regarding pay, holidays, hours of work, social security, and so forth. Moreover, it establishes joint disciplinary and conciliation committees at the local, district, regional, and national levels. The first two levels of committees are particularly concerned with the enforcement of the Charter, but all may examine complaints and attempt to settle individual and collective disputes.

Local Government Officials

Because national supervision of their activities is so extensive and so detailed, local officials in France have somewhat less influence than in England. Nonetheless, the quality of local administration depends on their ability, and the general standards maintained throughout the local services compare favorably with those in England.

Since 1930 the national government has insisted that each local unit must either have its own merit system or accept the civil service rules designed for local administration by the Council of State. With the exception of a few executives at the top and the ordinary laborers at the bottom, all local officials are now selected by open competitive examination. These tests stress general educational qualifications and, in consequence, there is less differentiation between officials in the higher ranks and those in the lower than is true in English local government. Some observers believe that the emphasis on general educational qualifications rather than on specialized knowledge makes the chief official in the permanent service, the *secrétaire de la ville,* a more useful coordinator of local activities than is his opposite number in England, the town clerk. The effective coordination that exists is also due, however, to the unified control of the prefect over all departmental services.

The rules governing positions in local services are designed to provide security rather than to foster initiative or efficiency. Promotions and salary increases are too rigidly regulated to permit outstanding employees to advance quickly, but at least favoritism is no longer a factor. Strong staff organizations have instituted many other safeguards for the local employees, particularly in cases of disciplinary action, which must be considered by regularly constituted councils that can impose only a carefully specified series of penalties.

How Satisfactory Is the French Civil Service?

The French civil service has long been the underlying element of stability in the French governmental system. The rapidly changing Ministries of the past threw upon it not only heavy burdens but also a wide measure of power. By instituting a stable regime with centralized executive authority, the Fifth Republic has provided the civil service with long-needed coordination and control from above. This is particularly the case in regard to services demanding long-range planning and interrelation with other aspects of government.

The civil service has responded to this coordination more readily because the present Council of Ministers is oriented away from politics and toward the civil service's own interpretation of how the country should be run. If the regime is not strictly speaking a technocracy, it has certain elements of one. The most important ministries are headed by men who are themselves higher civil servants. General de Gaulle clearly favors continuing the practice of drawing the holders of these positions from this source.

Does this mean, then, that the civil service is less responsive to public purposes than before? Not necessarily. The group defining public purposes is now less subject to party pressures and maneuvering than before, but this development has freed it, as the British executive is free, to consider public purposes from a broader perspective. The situation is not without danger, since too much freedom from party control can lead to irresponsibility. But this danger is in the sphere of the executive, not of the civil service.

7. French Law and Courts

1. FRENCH CIVIL LAW

Much of the world has done French law the honor of imitation. English common law spread only to those countries colonized by the British, but French civil law became the pattern for many Continental European and Latin American countries. Even countries such as Iran, when they decide to supersede local customs by a unified national body of law, turn to the codes of French civil law, which are the product of a similar need.

The legislators of the revolutionary period in France expressed their common goal of national unity by creating an integrated, uniform system of laws. The mosaic of national, regional, and local laws existing in prerevolutionary France had led to utter confusion. In the south, the principles of Roman imperial legislation still prevailed in 1789, while in the north there were many systems of customary law embodying feudal and Frankish principles. Voltaire declared in the middle of the eighteenth century that a traveler crossing France had to change laws more often than he changed horses. A common national system of law seemed essential to bind France into a unified state.

The legislators of the revolutionary period had a further, equally imperative reason for restating legal rules and principles: they were carrying out a great social and economic revolution. The antiquated land laws, the privileged position of the Church, the hunting rights of the nobility had been swept away in an early outburst of democratic fervor. But the traditional criminal procedures, the penal code, and the rules governing the relations among individuals that remained were far from conforming to the statement of individual rights embodied in the Declaration of the Rights of Man and of the Citizen. Thus a drastic overhauling of legal rules and principles was imperative.

Overhauling and systematizing the legal rules affecting every aspect of life was a monumental task, however, and the legislators of the revolutionary period were able to make only a beginning. In 1791 they drafted a penal code; in 1795, a code of criminal procedures. They began work on a civil code, but by 1800 they had produced only three incomplete drafts.

The vast enterprise of consolidating all French law was continued by French jurists, however, often under the personal direction of Napoleon, whose administrative genius and, less fortunately, authoritarian views contributed to the final form of the codes. In 1804 the Civil Code appeared; in 1806, the Code of Civil Procedure; in 1807, the Commercial Code; in 1808, the Code of Criminal Procedure; and in 1810, the Penal Code. Together, they formed the *Code Napoléon,* a comprehensive, systematized body of laws covering all cases likely to be brought to the courts. As revised, supplemented, and enlarged in response to changing conditions, the Napoleonic codes constitute the law of France today.

Code Law

The characteristic feature of French law is its codified form. The requirements of the new society ushered in by revolution led to many new and advanced legal rules. But the principle of codification was not new. It had been embodied for centuries in the codes of Roman law, which were themselves the result of the work of generations of Roman jurists who transformed the ancient tribal laws of the city of Rome into a great unified body of laws, shaped by Stoic and Christian conceptions of justice as well as by the needs of a great empire. Roman law, which had been extended to France after the Roman Conquest, survived in the southern part of the country (as it did not in England) after the breakdown of Rome's political authority. French kings later found those parts of the Roman law that exalted the authority of the state and the ruler a useful weapon in their struggle to reduce the power of the Pope within France and to bring their own powerful vassals under control. And though the French Kings never succeeded in their efforts to establish a national law, they managed to enforce a number of royal ordinances throughout the country and to get most of the regional customs codified in the sixteenth century. It is not surprising, therefore, that when national law was established, it should have been presented in codified form on the pattern of Roman law.

Influence of Roman Law

Roman law influenced the substance as well as the form of the Napoleonic codes. Its emphasis on centralized authority rather than on the interests of the individual fitted the new French nationalism, though it might seem to conflict with French individualism. The paternalism so evident in Roman law was reflected in many of the provisions of the codes. The greatest influence, however, was the practice of relating the rules on particular subjects to general principles of justice. The judges who developed the English common law cited specific precedents rather than abstract principles of right as the basis for their decisions, however much they might privately be influenced by the latter. The jurists who prepared the French codes, like those who had prepared the great Roman codes, often prefaced the legal rules on a given subject by a statement of the basic principles on which they rested.

The Character of the Codes

The codes reduced and consolidated the laws to relatively small compass. The Civil Code,

for example, deals with civil status, marriage and divorce, ownership, domicile, guardianship, contracts, wills, torts (such as trespass, slander, deceit, assault), and so forth. It comprises 2,281 separate articles, each framed with a precision of language and clarity of expression so remarkable that one of France's greatest writers, Stendhal, is said to have read a few articles of the code every day as a lesson in style.

The articles of the codes provide the basis for judicial decisions: they are the fundamental source of reference for judges making a decision in any given case. This practice marks the fundamental distinction between "code law" and "case law." Even in interpreting a statute, the judges in Great Britain and the United States refer to earlier decisions of other judges in similar cases. In France, however, judges acting under code law are supposed to base their decisions on the code. But just as Anglo-American judges sometimes interpret earlier cases in a way that supports their own concept of justice, so French judges often are influenced by earlier decisions in their application of principles.

The codes cannot, of course, cover all eventualities. Conditions change, and new laws must be passed to bring the rules governing community action into line with community needs. Thus while the codes remain the basic statement of law in a particular field, a new statute must be given full weight as the most recent statement of law by parliament. A judicial decision will take into account, therefore, all the statutes in a given field, whether or not they are embodied in the code. Some of the advantages of code law disappear when there are many isolated statutes that must be taken into account in addition to the original codified statement of rules. As a result, trained jurists must sometimes undertake a rather extensive recodification, which is then passed by parliament in the form of a statute. The Code of Criminal Procedure, the Penal Code, and the bankruptcy provisions of the Commercial Code had to be reworked as early as 1832. Public standards changed markedly during the nineteenth century, particularly in these fields, and two more revisions of the criminal and the penal law were necessary before the end of the century. In March 1959, a new Code of Criminal Procedure came into operation that integrated many useful changes into the existing system.

The Civil Code was reworked and reissued in revised and extended form in 1904, on the hundredth anniversary of the original code. It is now somewhat dated, however, being better adapted to an agricultural than an industrial society. In particular it puts an exaggerated emphasis on the value of real estate as compared to other modern forms of wealth. The law of marriage settlements was reformed in 1961. Otherwise, no major reconsideration has been given recently to the Civil Code.

The Role of Jurists in Making Law

Code law appears to do away with the influence of judges in making law, because, apart from the interpretation of particular points of law made by the Court of Cassation (which in practice is accepted as binding), the decisions made by judges in particular cases lack the influence they have in Great Britain on the decisions of other judges. But since the most highly trained French jurists do the work of preparing and revising codes, France, in this sense, has jurist-made law.

The codes are laws, but even more than most laws they must be drafted with the greatest care. They are a distillation of the essence of the laws on a particular subject. They acquire the force of binding rules through the authority of the legislature and the executive, but they acquire their wording and emphasis from the jurists who prepare them.

The Advantages of Code Law

Code law has two obvious advantages: easy accessibility and uniformity. English and American common law must be sought in hundreds of volumes of law records and digests. French civil law is embodied in a comparatively small number of books. When the Shah of Iran telegraphed Paris to ask for the codes, a selection of commentaries, and a commission of French jurists, he was asking for all that was needed to establish a new system of national law for his country.

This does not mean that the ordinary citizen can apply the rules of the French codes as easily as a judge. The French have always maintained that only professionals should interpret legal rules; they have no group comparable to the unpaid and untrained English justices of the peace. The existence of the codes does mean, however, that it is not necessary to spend a lifetime studying earlier cases in order to become a judge. The English judiciary must be drawn from the comparatively restricted profession of barristers, because case law must be learned through long experience. Code law is so much more accessible that anyone with legal training can make use of it. This fact has a direct influence on the size and character of the French judiciary, which includes about 3,500 members, with ages ranging from twenty-five to seventy-five (in contrast, the English judiciary—apart from the justices of the peace and magistrates —numbers only about a hundred, all of mature age). The large size of the French judiciary means that French justice can be decentralized to a degree that contrasts sharply with the centralization of the English court structure in London.

The Disadvantages of Code Law

Code law does, however, have certain disadvantages. Most important is a certain lack of flexibility. The codes lay down rights, rules, and principles that should be applied under all circumstances. Case law, in contrast, modifies the judgment of parliament (which must deal with broad principles and rules) by the judgment of the jurist, who is dealing with cases that arise from day to day. The judge in the English legal system works from the particular toward the general; the judge in the French system works from the general to the particular.

Each approach has advantages for special types of cases. There are certain fields, such as contracts, promissory notes, and wills, in which written documents predominate. Here general and comparatively rigid rules can be applied over and over again without working an injustice. But in questions of personal relations and human conduct, flexibility, rather than exactitude, contributes to justice. To such fields the long, slow process of constant change characteristic of case law seems especially suited.

French and English law are not so different, however, as these comparisons might suggest. Both England and the United States have codified the law in particular fields, and they may extend the practice. And the regular French courts make use of precedents, though not to the extent of English judges, who observe the rule of *stare decisis* (that is, the binding force of precedent) much more rigidly than does the American bench.

Legal Systems as a Product of History

Both the English and the French systems arose historically and in response to particular conditions, not in response to abstract conceptions. England developed a structure of national law centuries before France. The English common law system was considered complete—that is, it could handle any kind of case—by the middle of the thirteenth century. The contributions of equity and statutory law were additions made as need arose, and they were woven into a system of laws that was unified despite its different strands. Since England already had a national legal system, there was no need to construct one in modern times.

France, however, lacked a national system of laws at a time when national self-consciousness coincided with revolutionary changes in economic and social standards. It had to create quickly what the English had built up gradually over hundreds of years. In this task the example of the Roman law was a signal help. By adapting its forms to their needs, France and other countries have built up the second of the great modern legal systems.

2. THE JUDICIARY

The English and the French judicial systems differ most sharply in their methods of selecting the judiciary and the relationship of the judiciary to its administrative officials. English judges are drawn from the legal profession, and only from that section of it that has been "called to the bar," the barristers—a fact that makes for close harmony between lawyers and judges. But in France a young man decides at the beginning of his career whether he will be a lawyer or a member of the judiciary, and in all likelihood he will remain in the role he has chosen.

To become a judge, a law graduate must pass the competitive examination for entry to the training school set up in 1958 for the judicial profession, the *Centre National d'Etudes Judiciaires,* and satisfactorily complete its three-year course. As soon as students enter the school, they become civil servants and are paid a salary; this is in an effort to raise the standards for recruitment and open the service to all, regardless of economic status. They spend the first year in some part of the judiciary; the second, in academic studies. Examinations at the end of the second year determine the type of court to which each will be assigned, and in the third year they concentrate on training for that particular work.

In England and the United States judges serve only on the bench, but in France members of the judiciary fall into two main categories: those who judge cases, known as *magistrats du siège* (that is, judges who sit on the bench); and the state prosecutors, who form the *paquet* or *magistrature debout* (that is, standing magistrates). The latter (and not the police, as in England) act on behalf of the state in criminal cases; they do not have the same independence as the judges on the bench, since prosecutors can be given orders and are ultimately under the authority of the Minister of Justice. Judges have security of tenure and cannot be disciplined by the government.

Since the judiciary is a career service, promotion has been a matter of concern. Under the Fourth Republic, promotion was determined by a body not under the influence of the Minister of Justice, the *Conseil Supérieur de la Magistrature* (*magistrature* means the collective body of the judiciary). Six of the *Conseil's* members were elected by the National Assembly (not from among its own members) and four by the judiciary itself. The Ministry of Justice never became reconciled to this system, however, and the eleven members of the High Council set up in 1958 are all chosen by the President from lists submitted by the judiciary; the President himself and the Minister of Justice are *ex officio* members. Moreover, under the Fifth Republic the High Council does not prepare the promotion list as it did under the Fourth Republic. Instead, it merely gives its advisory opinion on a list compiled by a special committee made up of seven members of France's highest court, the Court of Cassation, and six officials of the Ministry of Justice. Since the number of classes in the service was sharply reduced in 1958, from ten to two, and since salary increases have become virtually automatic, there is now less strain than there used to be over promotion and shifting within the service. Though the High Court now has less influence on promotions, it retains its control over the disciplining of judges, an important factor in their independence.

3. THE REGULAR COURTS

The French believed that justice is a service that should be provided conveniently and cheaply for everyone, much of the pattern of such services as the postal or the insurance service. Thus French law is administered by a network of centrally organized local courts that make justice easily available to every citizen.

Yet, though the French courts are organized under the Ministry of Justice, they are not simply another part of the administration. On the contrary, the most distinctive feature of the French court system is its division into regular and administrative courts; this distinction arises precisely from the fact that the French distinguish so sharply between the administration and the judiciary.

Because they were fearful that the courts would try to interfere with the social and economic changes they were introducing, the National Assemblies of the early revolutionary period specifically forbade the judiciary to limit or encroach upon the sphere of the administration. The constitutions of the subsequent Republics have included no similar prohibition. Nonetheless the courts in France have never adopted the practice of judicial review so significant in the United States, a fact that leads the French themselves to say that France has a truer separation of powers than has the United States.

Though there has never been pressure in France in favor of judicial review, French leaders recognized soon after the Revolution that the absence of a judicial check upon the actions of the administration was potentially dangerous. They met this danger not by expanding the powers of the ordinary courts but by developing a separate structure of courts, the administrative

courts. In France, therefore, any case that affects an administrative official or in which the state is a party (with the sole exception of criminal cases) comes before an administrative court. By excluding such cases from the regular court system, the French leave the latter free to devote their full attention to disputes between individuals (civil cases) and those in which an individual is accused of a breach of public order (criminal cases).

The Hierarchy of the Regular Courts

In 1958 the Fifth Republic reorganized the system of regular, or "ordinary," courts. The major casualties of the change were the three thousand professional *juges de paix* (so different from the unpaid, slightly trained English justices of the peace), who used to be found in almost every small canton and who concentrated on conciliation and minor civil cases. Modern transportation made such highly decentralized and numerous courts seem unnecessary, and the revised system reduced the total number by four-fifths.

The basic structure now consists of a lower court in each arrondisement and a higher one in each department. If a department is densely populated, more courts are provided—172 in all for 95 departments. The reorganization has made more judges available to serve in the higher courts.

The court structure is divided all the way to the appeal court level between courts concerned with civil cases and courts concerned with criminal cases. There is considerable difference in procedure between the two. But the appearance of separation in the court system masks a good deal of connection. Both civil and criminal courts at the arrondisement and at the department levels are staffed by the same judges and they use the same courthouse. Moreover, the twenty-five courts of appeal, and the Court of Cassation at the apex of the system, hear appeals from both civil and criminal cases.

The French facilitate the right of appeal but at the same time limit and structure it. Unless a case involves very minor sums, there is always a right of appeal except from the assize courts. Only one appeal can ever be made on matters of fact, however, and such appeals always go to

REGULAR COURT SYSTEM OF FRANCE

← Elective or Appointive Lines
Channel of Appeal →

Court of Cassation: Supreme Court of Appeal   (*Cour de cassation*)

*83 judges who work through five Sections: two civil (personal and family status, and property)
of fifteen members each; one commercial; one social; and one criminal
7 judges to a case (15 if a principle involved, and all members if a second appeal)*

Reviews interpretations of *law* in civil and criminal cases.
If the *Cour de cassation* quashes judgment, it sends case to another court at same level as
that from which case was originally referred. On second appeal gives authoritative interpretation that must be followed by lower court.

Appeal Courts (*Cours d'appel*)
*Several sections including one on social laws
3 to 5 judges*

Takes appeals on matters of *fact* from civil and criminal courts and retries case.
Prepares indictments for Assize Courts.

HIGHER COURTS

CIVIL CASES

Civil Courts—Superior
(*Tribunaux de grande instance*)

*172
3 or more judges*

Cases involving substantial sums, personal or
family status, or real property.
Unlimited jurisdiction (that is, can try any
case no matter how serious).

Courts of First Instance
(*Tribunaux d'instance*)

*455 (one for each arrondisement)
1 judge*

Minor civil cases.
Conciliation functions.
Settle election disputes.
Judge also presides over police court, family
and guardianship councils.

CRIMINAL CASES

Assize Courts (*Cours d'assisses*)

*95 (one in each department)
3 judges and jury of nine (verdict of guilty requires a majority of eight votes).*

Original jurisdiction for most serious crimes,
like manslaughter.

Criminal Courts (*Tribunaux correctionnels*)
*172
several judges*

More serious offences. Can impose prison sentences from two months to five years and
levy fines from two hundred francs up.

LOCAL COURTS

Police Courts
(*Tribunaux de police*)

455

Minor offenses. May impose penalties of one
day to two months in prison and small
fines.

Commercial Tribunals
(*Tribunaux de commerce*)

Members elected for two years by local businessmen.
Act in certain commercial cases defined by
law; appeal only if considerable sum involved.

Industrial Disputes Councils
(*Conseils de prud'hommes*)

Equal number of worker and employee representatives.
Chosen for six years (one-half retiring every
three years).
Arbitrate disputes arising out of industrial
contracts. Appeal only in more serious cases.

SPECIAL COURTS Appeal, when allowed, to Appeal Courts.	
Children's Courts (*Tribunal pour enfants*) One judge chosen from court panel for three-year term. At each seat of Superior Court.	**Courts of Farm Leases** (*Tribunaux paritaires de baux ruraux*) At each seat of Court of First Instance. To settle lawsuits between lenders and borrowers of rural funds.
Social Security Commissions (*Commissions de sécurité sociale*) One judge of Court of First Instance plus two representatives of interested parties.	**Court of State Security** (*Cour de sureté de l'Etat*) *5 members: 3 judges and 2 senior officers appointed by Council of Ministers* Crimes and indictable offenses against state security.

the appeal courts regardless of whether they come from the arrondisement- or department-level civil or criminal courts. If the appeal involves an issue of law, it goes to the Court of Cassation.

The Court of Cassation, which ordinarily acts through one of its five sections, does not retry the case, as do the courts of appeal. If it disapproves of the interpretation of law, it sends the case back to another court on the same level on which it was tried before. In the exceptional case of a second appeal, the Court of Cassation meets as a whole and delivers a mandatory judgment on the point of law that must be accepted by the third court at the original level to which it is then referred. This power of the Court of Cassation (defined in a law of 1837) is limited in theory to the particular case and the particular court. Obviously, however, it has wide influence, despite the French principle that precedent is not binding from one court to the next. A noteworthy example of this influence was a decision in 1896 that extended employer liability for industrial injuries far beyond the intention of the Civil Code.

The higher the place in the hierarchy of courts, the larger the number of judges assigned to a case. At the lowest (arrondisement) level, cases in the *tribunaux d'instance* (civil) and the *tribunaux de police* (criminal) are heard by a single judge, although there are several judges at each center to ensure that

cases are dealt with promptly. At the second (department) level of the *tribunaux de grande instance* (civil) and the *tribunaux correctionnels* (criminal), each case is considered by a bench of three judges. The appeal courts, which are divided into sections, have five judges to a case. The Court of Cassation, at the apex, has five sections of fifteen judges each, and seven must hear a case on first appeal. In the unusual situation of a second appeal, all seventy-five judges compose the bench.

In only one place—the assize court, which provides original jurisdiction in cases of serious crime—is a jury used in the French court system. The assize courts are held quarterly in every department (and almost continuously in Paris). The verdicts in the assize courts, as we have seen, are not subject to appeal, making the one exception to the general rule.

Special Courts

Two long-established special courts that operate wherever local interests ask for them are the industrial and the commercial courts. Both concentrate on conciliation; the industrial courts between employers and employees on such issues as disputed dismissals, and the commercial courts between merchants on disputes over sales or bankruptcy. By holding formalities to a minimum, by giving those concerned the right to elect their own judges from among their own members, and by being cheap and quick, these courts are justifiably popular and perform useful functions that are reflected in their place in the regular court structure. Appeals from their verdicts can be taken to the courts of appeal or the Court of Cassation. This possibility reflects the fact that industrial and commercial courts deal with subject matters that are handled in their absence by the ordinary courts.

Two other special courts, added after World War II, deal respectively with social security legislation and with disputes between tenants and landowners over rents. These courts differ from those described above in that each has a professional judge, commonly assisted by two elected judges, one representing each side.

The most controversial special court was designed to deal with threats to the security of the state. Following the attempted Algerian coup in 1961, General de Gaulle used his emergency powers to set up a special court to judge those concerned. This court was subsequently abolished, and his effort to establish a second, comparable court was quashed by the *Conseil d'Etat* as being outside his bounds of power. Finally, in January 1963, parliament established a permanent Court of State Security.

How Satisfactory Is the French Court System?

The structure of the French court system provides many advantages that are lacking in England. The fact that not only the courts of first instance but also the appeal courts are decentralized brings justice within the reach of everyone. Further, convenience, speed, and cheapness are enhanced by permitting only one appeal, instead of two or even three as is possible in England. Finally, the uniformity of the system means that the inhabitants of a southwestern city have exactly the same kind of courts of original jurisdiction and appeal as the inhabitants of Paris. In England, in contrast, not only are the appeal courts centralized in London, but the county courts, despite their concurrent jurisdiction in lesser cases with the divisions of the High Court of Justice, hardly rank on a plane of equality with the High Court in personnel.

A general evaluation of the French court system, however, requires consideration of the same questions that were raised in regard to the court system in England. What is the atmosphere of the courts? Do they provide an opportunity for all aspects of a situation to be explored? Do the courts give private persons adequate protection in criminal cases in which the resources of the government are behind the prosecution? Do they provide speedy, effective means of settling disputes? And is justice, in practice, open to all on equal terms?

The Atmosphere of the Courts

The sessions of a French court are likely to seem sober and even dull to an American, for there is much less use of oral evidence in a French court than in an English or American court. Witnesses are often questioned prior to court sessions and their information presented in writing, thus providing the same amount of information as in the Anglo-Saxon court system but in a less dramatic way. Moreover, while eloquence in an American or English court is often for the benefit of the jury rather than the judge, there is little chance for the French *avocat* to practice this kind of persuasion, since juries, as noted, are used in only one court in France, the Court of Assize.

Is All the Evidence Brought Out?

But at the same time, to a much greater degree than English judges, French judges take upon themselves the responsibility for seeing that all the evidence is brought out in a case. The judge in an English court looks on himself as an umpire before whom two parties argue out their case. French judges, even in civil cases, examine witnesses (often outside of court), question lawyers, and press proceedings in whatever direction they feel necessary to elucidate the facts.

Is Adequate Protection Afforded the Defendant?

It is partly this active role of the judges in a French court that makes Anglo-Saxon observers feel that defendants in a criminal case do not always have an adequate opportunity to defend themselves. Procedure in English criminal law emphasizes every possible safeguard for the accused, and judges are sometimes placed under considerable strain by their desire to provide fair play and at the same time prevent an obvious criminal from escaping the verdict he deserves. French judges labor under no such inhibitions. But the French themselves have been chiefly dissatisfied with the way in which their jury system has operated and with the manner in which the police conduct the unofficial inquiries that precede those of the *juge d'instruction*.

Under the belief that juries were afraid to convict lest judges award too severe penalties, judges and jury were associated in 1932 in determining the sentence. In 1941, the three judges and seven jurors were joined into a single body that determines both guilt or innocence, and the penalty. Under the Code of Criminal Procedure of 1959, the number of jurors is raised to nine, and there must be at least eight votes (thus at least five jurors) before a verdict of guilty is pronounced. The role of jurors has thus been transformed from what it is in England into that of lay assessors, partly at least because French magistrates, lacking the experience of the skilled barristers who become judges in England, were so much less adept than the latter either at guiding cross examinations or at giving oral presentations.

A more serious problem for French justice has been the preliminary investigation on which the state's case rests. Before a person accused of serious crime is even brought before the Court of Assize (there is no *habeas corpus* act in France), a careful and often long investigation under full safeguards has been conducted by a court official, the *juge d'instruction,* who has become convinced of the accused's guilt. What has disturbed French liberals is not this investigation but the unofficial inquiries made by the police prior to handing over the suspected criminal to the *juge d'instruction.* The police, who are known as *police judiciaire,* are considered to be outside the jurisdiction of the Council of State, which has authority over the administrative system, so no check is possible from that source. The 1959 Code attempts to prevent certain police abuses committed in the past by officially acknowledging, and then attempting to regulate, their *enquête préliminaire.* Detention is supposed to be limited to twenty-four hours, strict records of the inquiry are to be kept, and the detained person has a right, of which he must be notified, to medical examination. Unfortunately, the period of detention has been greatly lengthened in certain cases, especially those related to Algerian rebel activity in France, thereby largely nullifying a useful reform.

It is not true, as is so often said, that in France a person accused of a crime is considered guilty unless he can prove himself innocent. But because of the long preliminary interrogations, there is a presumption of guilt that is evident in the attitude of the presiding judges. English and American criminal procedures are mainly motivated by fear lest an innocent person be convicted, French criminal procedures by fear lest a guilty person escape.

Do the Courts Provide Prompt and Inexpensive Remedies?

The French court system, with its decentralization and its limitation to one appeal, provides justice noted for cheapness and speediness—except for occasional long delays in the Court of Cassation. The costs of a review by the Court of Cassation, however, are borne by the state. Local lawyers are used more often than in England, partly because the uniformity of the courts and the relative simplicity of the codes mean that the skill and training of the lawyers are not quite so important as in that country, and partly because no single place in France is such a center for the legal profession as London is in England. Moreover, though there is no statutory limit on the costs of legal aid, agreement on this subject is generally reached between lawyer and client before the case begins. On the other hand, this system is far from being so helpful to those in need as the legal aid now provided in Great Britain.

To Sum Up

The French court system provides justice in a convenient, inexpensive, and equalitarian way that cannot be rivaled by the English or American systems. While it is true that French magistrates are not so learned as English judges, this shortcoming is not serious, since their task of basing decisions on the codes is less difficult than the work of English judges in interpreting case law.

The major criticism to be made of the French judicial system is that the independence of judges is not safeguarded as well as it is in England. According to the constitution (Article 64), the President of the Republic is "the guarantor of the independence of the judicial authority." While this conception may well fit de Gaulle's view of his office as supreme arbiter between all other branches of government, it is anomalous to entrust judicial independence to an executive officer.

Apart from this fact, and French concern about arbitrary action by the police, the French are well satisfied with their judicial system. It is noticeable, in fact, that in certain ways the English system is moving closer to the French, notably in becoming more equalitarian in the sense of drawing judges from a wider social group, and also of bringing justice within the financial reach of persons of moderate means.

4. THE ADMINISTRATIVE COURTS

Side by side with the hierarchy of the regular courts in France exists a second hierarchy, the administrative courts, which operate to keep the agents of the state within their grants of power, and to give individual Frenchmen a remedy against arbitrary administrative decisions. Nothing exactly like the French administrative court system exists in England or the United States, though in both countries there is an increasing amount of administrative adjudication. Most Englishmen and Americans still feel that the best safeguard of justice is to have one law for everyone, rather than to have separate courts for examining the acts of officials. But the vast increase in the functions and powers of the administration in every modern state increasingly raises the question of whether the highly flexible, inexpensive, and all-encompassing jurisdiction of the French administrative courts does

not, in fact, provide a better protection of individuals from administrative arbitrariness than the much more cumbersome practice in England or the United States of bringing suit against officials through the regular courts.

Administrative courts (which are concerned only with civil cases) exist on both the local and national level in France. Centered in twenty-three regions and in Paris are the twenty-four *Tribunaux Administratifs* which, since 1953, have not only considered cases arising out of charges and claims against local administrations but also almost all the first-instance work transacted up to then by the Council of State (*Conseil d'Etat*). At the national level, the French administrative court system is headed by the *Conseil d'Etat,* which we have already considered in its role as an advisory organ and administrative agency, and which is one of France's most remarkable institutions.

The French administrative courts annul decisions or rulings that they decide are outside the grant of power or are otherwise invalid, but they do not substitute their own decisions or rulings. In other words, they act as a check on the administration's use of its authority, but they do not direct the administration along any specific lines. Moreover, the damages awarded by the administrative courts are paid by the government, not by the erring official. An individual could institute a case against a public officer in the ordinary civil or criminal courts, but it would be rather more difficult to secure damages than in Great Britain or the United States, where the doctrine of personal liability for abuse of power is much more strongly entrenched than in France.

The general distinction between cases that go to the regular courts and those that go to the administrative courts is drawn from the type and manner of activities, rather than the legal status of the body involved. Thus where public agencies act like private undertakings—for example, nationalized industries—disputes go to the regular courts. Where semiprivate committees have power to regulate industries, however, and impose penalties for violation of their decisions—that is, where they have powers that private bodies do not have—their actions are subject to review by the administrative courts.

Any controversy about whether a case belongs in the ordinary courts or in the administrative courts is settled by the *Tribunal des Conflits* (Court of Conflicts), which is composed of four members of the *Conseil d'Etat* and four of the Court of Cassation. In case of deadlock (which has occurred only ten times since 1872), the Minister of Justice casts the deciding vote. Thus the line of demarcation between the ordinary courts and the administrative courts is decided by a body equally representative of the highest body in each hierarchy. In practice, its decisions have not lessened the jurisdiction of the administrative courts.

Lower Administrative Courts

The *Tribunaux Administratifs* form the basic structure of general administrative courts. Since 1953, when jurisdiction over many overdue cases was transferred from the *Conseil d'Etat,* they have almost invariably acted as courts of first instance in cases dealing with official misuse or abuse of power—for example, an order that cattle be destroyed made on the incorrect assumption that they had foot-and-mouth disease, or a regulation for which there is no legal basis of power, or which is not being used for the purpose originally designated. (The latter goes beyond the powers of British courts.) The Administrative Tribunals also continue to deal with appeals over local tax assessments, claims for breach of contract by local public bodies, and cases involving public works, sale of government property, and even local elections.

An Administrative Tribunal has five members, a president and four councilors. They are recruited by competitive examinations, or from experienced members of the administration who possess law degrees. Their personnel thus combines wide practical administrative experience with rigorous intellectual training.

The procedure in the Administrative Tribunal is simple and straightforward. Appeals may be mailed and need include only a small fee, an official form on which the complaint is described, and the necessary supporting documents. While petitioners may be represented by counsel in public session, this is not necessary. The court (unlike a regular court) makes the investigation itself, rather like the Ombuds-man and his staff in Scandinavian countries, whose role has so much interested the British.

In addition to the *general* administrative tribunals, there are some forty different types of *specialized* administrative courts. The most important of these is the Court of Accounts, the supreme audit agency, but there are also many special courts. Sometimes, as in the field of public assistance (now known as social aid), these have their own network of lower and upper courts that reflect the wide scope of public intervention in and responsibility for the life of the individual.

All the specialized administrative courts as well as the general administrative tribunals come under the *Conseil d'Etat* as far as interpretation of law is concerned. Thus the *Conseil* occupies within the administrative court system the same place as does the *Cour de Cassation* in the regular court system.

The Council of State ("Conseil d'Etat")

The Council of State is by far the most important organ in the administrative court system. Moreover it has a high reputation both in France and abroad. In fact, of all French institutions, the Council of State, acting in its judicial capacity, is perhaps the only one that English and American observers feel might usefully be transplanted to their own countries. This is partly, as we have already suggested, because the particular problem on which the Council of State concentrates—administrative abuse or misuse of power—is increasingly significant in the modern welfare state, but also because the Council has proved itself in practice to be fearless, penetrating, and just in its operations.

To have administrative officials check other administrative officials might seem to make administrators judges in their own cases and so destroy the safeguards that the system is intended to provide. But the French believe that the more knowledge the members dealing with judicial matters have of administrative problems, the sounder their decisions will be. Thus deliberate efforts were made in 1963 to bring the administrative and judicial sides of the *Conseil d'Etat* still closer together. Members can move from one section to another, as we have seen, either through promotion or desire; nine members of the judicial section participate in the work of the full advisory body that counsels the government on bills and decrees; two judicial members are on the standing committee that gives advice on urgent bills and regulations; and, conversely, the administrative sections elect several of their members to sit on the judicial section. Thus the judicial section (*section du contentieux*), which has twenty-eight members, half the total membership of the *Conseil,* has an awareness and an understanding of current developments in the political and administrative spheres that no member of the judiciary in Britain or the United States can match.

The procedures of the *Conseil d'Etat* are similar to those of the Administrative Tribunals; indeed, they are very like those followed by such independent regulatory commissions in the United States as the Federal Trade Commission. The practice may be compared to that of a criminal court, except that the roles are reversed: the government official or agency is on trial on a charge made by a private citizen. At the level of the *Conseil d'Etat* the investigation is made by the nonjudicial members, the *auditeurs* and *maîtres des requêtes,* who are serving their apprenticeships and can expect at about the age of fifty to become judges. When presenting the issues of the case, following detailed investigation, the *maître des requêtes* is known as the *commissaire du gouvernement,* but he is an impartial examiner and his conclusions, usually though not always accepted, often condemn officials or agencies.

A well-known case in which individual rights were protected against a state ruling arose out of an appeal by five young men who charged that they had been excluded from the examinations for the *Ecole Nationale d'Administration,* the training center for the higher civil service, on grounds of political opinion—that is, that they were believed to be members of or associated with the Communist party. Meeting in plenary session on May 28, 1954, the *Conseil d'Etat* upheld the applicants and declared that the Secretary of State acting for the Premier (who by law had sole and unlimited authority to determine the lists of candidates) had no right to keep them from sitting for the examination, a decision whose broad implications have governed admission to these examinations ever since.

In a more recent case in which the Council of State acted in opposition to executive policy, it quashed the special court set up by President de Gaulle under his emergency powers and thereby forced the government to use parliamentary procedures to establish the Court of State Security.

A major criticism of the procedures of the Council of State used to be that, though introducing a case was simple and inexpensive, it often took years before the case came to trial. Decentralizing most cases to the Administrative Tribunals has made it possible for the *Conseil d'Etat* to concentrate on appeals, and in 1956 its number of subsections was increased. Cases are now commonly decided within a year or two.

How Satisfactory Are the Administrative Courts?

Experience demonstrates that the Council of State acts as guardian both of public interests and of individual rights. The justice it dispenses can be secured with relatively little trouble and at almost no expense. If a plaintiff's claim is upheld, he pays no costs; if it is denied, he pays only a nominal amount. Although a claim for money damages may make special court and registration fees necessary, the total cost of proceedings is too small to deter anyone who has a reasonable claim.

Moreover, as we have seen, the Council of State does not hesitate to hold high administrative officials to the strict letter of the law and to make them produce full evidence that the facts on which their action is based are exactly as the officials state them to be.

Beyond this, the Council is generous in awarding damages to be paid by the government to injured individuals. If it finds that a civil servant has been wrongly dismissed, it may order his reinstatement and also provide that he be paid a suitable indemnity for the prejudice and loss he has suffered. More unusual from an

English or American view is a case in which a man was awarded damages for injuries caused by a shot fired by a policeman at a mad bull. In another, a municipality paid damages to a man injured in a duck-shooting competition organized by the mayor, despite the fact that the mayor had been held personally liable by an ordinary court. In a third case, the Air Ministry was held liable for damages caused by the crash of a military plane.

It is thus apparent that the administrative courts are not in any way prejudiced in favor of the administration, either when considering the unexpected results of administrative action or when considering an issue concerning administrative discretion. On the contrary, the intimate knowledge of the inside working of administration seems to make the Council of State particularly sensitive to any abuse of power and alert to check it.

Do French administrative courts afford more satisfactory checks on the arbitrary action of officials and better safeguards of the interests of individuals than do the English and American judicial systems, with their practice of depending largely on the ordinary courts for redress?

There can be no question that a Frenchman can more easily secure redress for the unintended consequences of an official act than can an Englishman or an American. But it is also true that neither the English nor the Americans face such a serious problem in connection with official liability as do the French, since both in England and the United States administration is far more decentralized than in France, and in both countries local units of government have long been liable for damages in many instances where the central government was not. Moreover, both the American federal government and the British government now permit suit against the state in torts, so that in most cases the Anglo-Saxon can now secure relatively the same pecuniary redress for the results of official mistakes as can the Frenchman. Under present conditions, the main difference between the Anglo-Saxon and Continental systems in matters of financial redress is that in Great Britain and the United States the unexpected consequences to someone else of an act in line of duty are not usually indemnified by the government as they are in France (for example, bystanders injured by bullets fired by a policeman pursuing a murderer are not recompensed by the state in the United States or Great Britain but they are in France).

Advocates of the Anglo-Saxon system maintain that while the French system provides greater protection against pecuniary loss by individuals, the Anglo-Saxon system provides a stricter adherence to law. They believe that the very fact that the ordinary courts deal with cases affecting the administration side by side with other cases means that government officials are kept aware of the necessity of adhering to the regular laws of the land. They point out too that the Anglo-Saxon notion of personal liability for abuse of power, regardless of whether the act is committed under orders or not, places the weight of personal responsibility directly on every official and prevents him from "passing the buck" to his superior.

Yet no one who has followed the Crichel Downs case can feel very confident that the ordinary processes for checking administrative action in the Anglo-Saxon system are as satisfactory as they have been assumed to be. There is perhaps no public service in the world with standards as high as the British, yet unjustifiable official arbitrariness occurred in that case for which there was no obvious remedy. Only the most determined and lengthy efforts on the part of the former owners of Crichel Downs disclosed the inequities of that particular situation. In France, in striking contrast, the five applicants to the ENA could file a simple petition with the Council of State and have it result almost automatically in a searching examination of the reasons why the Secretary of State, acting for the Premier, had taken the course he did.

It has been the proud boast of the Anglo-Saxon system that the nation-wide tradition that every person, whether government official or not, is subject to the common rules of the law of the land, preserves liberty under the law in a way which no other system can match. With the all-pervasiveness of the modern administrative bureaucracy, it seems open to question, however, whether some special instrumentalities are not needed in Great Britain and the

United States to buttress their present systems by providing formal, inexpensive, and speedy investigations into charges of official arbitrariness or abuse of power. It is obvious that it is not the administrative court system as such, but the high standards of integrity and independence of the French Council of State, that have made it such an effective guardian of the public interest and of individual liberties. It seems not too much to anticipate, however, that if Great Britain or the United States were to set up an administrative body patterned on the Council of State, that body would operate under the same high standards by which the Council of State acts to check the French administration from abuse or excess of power.

8. French Society in Change

Paralleling the political changes that have transformed France's governmental institutions have been the economic developments that are creating a modern, industrialized, and increasingly affluent society. Economic modernization, new techniques in industry and agriculture, new concentration on the needs of backward regions, the impact of the Development Plans, and France's participation in European integration and the European Economic Community have all contributed to a more vigorous and more developed economy. Inevitably, economic progress has led to demands for wider educational and social opportunities. The French have not yet responded so effectively as the British to these demands, but they are experimenting with new programs, particularly in education. Twenty percent of the national budget for 1966 was allocated to education, where the pressures of numbers, particularly in secondary schools, have outstripped facilities. Thus France is wrestling with the problems of change in every sphere of life.

1. EDUCATION

The aim for French education is to develop a unified and democratic program through which all qualified students can move from the lowest to the highest level. In the past the different kinds of education received by the children of different social classes made the distinction between those who could continue to higher training and those who could not dependent on wealth and position rather than on ability. Higher education remains, in practice, the preserve of the upper and middle classes, but most of the barriers have now been removed at lower educational levels.

Lower Education

In the past, the bourgeoisie and the working class customarily sent their children to different schools. Working-class children attended the free municipal nurseries and then the primary schools (similar to American grade schools) until compulsory education ended at the age of fourteen. The bourgeoisie, on the other hand, had nearly always sent their children to the kindergarten and junior departments of the secondary schools, which were more like American private day schools. The junior departments of the secondary schools concentrated on preparing their students for the competitive examinations (taken at age eleven) that all candidates for the secondary schools had to take, while primary education was largely vocational. Thus, though it was always possible for an unusually able student of working-class parents to make the transition to the secondary schools, it was far more difficult than for those who prepared in the junior departments of the secondary schools.

This early educational segregation, and the consequent difficulty that the children of the poorer classes had in passing the competitive examinations for the secondary schools, were reflected in the relatively small number of students who continued with education at that level, even though France abolished fees for secondary education in 1933 (well before Great Britain).

The great importance of secondary education, apart from its mental discipline, is as the sole route to the *baccalauréat*. This examination must

323

be passed to qualify for many white-collar jobs or for entry to higher education required for professional positions.

The *baccalauréat* used to consist of a highly specialized series of written tests, given in two sections, a year apart. The program and format were changed no less than six times, however, between 1959 and 1966, sometimes quite drastically, in response to the pressure of numbers in the secondary schools and the demands of parents. Less stress is being laid on Latin and more on the sciences and the social studies, though not yet on economics, a subject still treated too theoretically and reserved at the university level for the law schools. In June 1966, for the first time, the *baccalauréat* was given as a single examination. These changes have had an unsettling effect on secondary-school children and have resulted in lower standards for access to higher education. A permanent form for the *baccalauréat* was promised for 1968. The growing democratization of French education to meet the needs of an increasingly complex industrial society is not without its problems, both in maintaining standards and in adjusting the curriculum to new social and economic needs.

Higher Education

Higher education in France is professional in character (as is the practice in Continental countries, in contrast to the more general education in English and American colleges) and is rarely completed before age twenty-three. It is provided not only in universities but also in a series of high-prestige, nonuniversity institutions, notably the *grandes écoles,* which are advanced professional institutes in which the best brains of the country are trained for careers in administration, education, industry and commerce, the armed forces, and so on.

In response to the vastly increased number of students now acquiring university entrance, the number of universities in France has expanded to twenty, plus a growing number of university colleges. The new institutions are in provincial towns and are becoming more popular because of their specialization in particular fields and because of the crowded conditions and high cost of living in Paris. Nonetheless, the Uni-

versity of Paris still possesses the highest prestige, particularly for a doctoral degree, and thirty percent of all French students—100,000 out of 300,000—still concentrate in the Paris area, even though facilities there are scarcely adequate for one-tenth that number. Despite the effort to encourage work in the faculties of sciences, their 129,000 students in 1964-65 were outnumbered by the 137,000 in the faculties of letters (two-thirds of the latter students were women).

A further problem for French universities is the overcentralization resulting from unified state control. Little can be done, and even less initiated, without official sanction, and the most vigorous young teacher-administrators spend much of their time and energy attempting to persuade officials at the Ministry of National Education of the need for new buildings and curricula.

Apart from a few nominal fees, French higher education is free. Nonetheless, some 65 percent of all university students in 1964-65 came from professional and executive families. The ingrained prejudice among the working class and farmers against higher education, coupled with poorer schooling in rural areas and the high cost of living in the cities, continues to perpetuate class distinctions and to prevent talent from being fully used. Within the universities, however, there is a spirit of friendship that produces strong bonds among students regardless of their backgrounds.

The cream of French talent, including some 4,100 students in 1966, is trained in the *grandes écoles*. The coveted entrance to these relatively independent establishments requires at least two years of training after the *baccalauréat* and success in stiff competitive examinations. The *grandes écoles* used to be looked on as potential threats to the Republic because their professional exclusiveness was combined with strong upper-class feeling. It was even said that their graduates constituted a "state within a state" because of their virtual monopoly before World War II of influential positions in education, diplomacy, the Council of State, and other government agencies. The graduates of the *grandes écoles* still occupy the highest position throughout France, both in public and private life. But their students are now fully supported by the state while they are training, thereby opening these opportunities far more widely to all classes in the community. *L'École Nationale d'Administration,* which has trained higher civil servants since World War II, as we have seen, is a good example of the reformed arrangements for the *grandes écoles.*

The New Educational Program

The pressure for admission to higher education—twice as many students now enter universities as in Great Britain—is the result of the reorganization of primary and secondary school curricula that, despite confusion and controversy, is developing a unified system. Primary teaching has become more democratic, and there is easier access for those of moderate means into secondary education. Apart from Sweden, France now has more children continuing from primary to secondary schools than any other European country.

In 1967 compulsory education was extended from age fourteen to sixteen. In 1900 there were 70,000 children in secondary schools; in 1970 there will be three million.

The 1960 reform aimed to give each child an education suited to his or her aptitude. The expectation is that children can be divided into three categories: those capable of abstract and theoretical studies, who should go through higher education; those who should have only a minimum of abstract and theoretical work but are capable of fairly extended education; and those who are unsuited to academic work and should concentrate early on practical training. Following a common elementary curriculum, there are two cycles of education, the first from age eleven to fifteen, and the second from fifteen to eighteen. During the first cycle, there are opportunities to move from one section to another according to demonstrated aptitude and accomplishments. The second cycle either ends with a certificate after two years or leads to the *baccalauréat.*

No phase of French education is yet settled permanently. Plans are under way for further changes in secondary and higher education. The excessive rigidities of the older system have been broken and the way opened to meet the needs of a dynamic economy.

The Catholic Church and Education

The sharpest controversy in French education has been over the influence of and, more recently, state support of private schools, a high proportion of which are parochial, or Catholic. Roughly speaking, one child in six attends a private primary school, and one in three a private secondary school. Since state facilities at both levels are already badly overtaxed, the facilities of the denominational schools are indispensable, particularly in the west of France. But long-standing hostility to religious influence in education has not yet abated, although one of the achievements of the Fifth Republic has been at last to provide badly needed state support for impoverished private schools.

This controversy has been one of the great divisive influences in French political life. It dates from the time when the Catholic Church was generally suspected of hostility to the Republic and when the republican government felt it necessary to restrict the Catholic teaching orders and to develop a system of free, public, lay education on the primary level. Fundamentally, the struggle was for the minds of the children. Republican statesmen were convinced that children educated by the Church would grow up to be supporters of the clerical and antirepublican groups and that only a school system that was republican politically and "neutral" theologically could create a generation of citizens devoted to the Republic. To the leaders of the Church, however, the "godless" schools of the Republic seemed anything but neutral, and every effort had to be made to restrict their influence.

During the late nineteenth and early twentieth centuries, when the Republic was struggling for its life, many of the public school teachers conceived of themselves as warriors in its defense. Often they looked upon the Church as the enemy of education and enlightenment, and, particularly after World War I, they were often socialist and pacifist in their outlook. In thousands of villages throughout France the opposition between left and right, between the Republic and the Church, came to be personified in the antagonism between schoolmaster and priest.

The poverty of the private denominational

schools forced the issue of state support on both the Fourth and the Fifth Republics. This issue had become the more controversial because Pétain's wartime regime extended financial aid to the parochial schools—an action that seemed to many staunch republicans new proof of the antidemocratic character of the Church. Despite the reluctance of the MRP, these subsidies were withdrawn when the Fourth Republic was established. However, despite prolonged and acrimonious debate, legislation following the 1951 election provided minimal aid for the denominational schools through a special allocation, which was made for each child in an elementary school and which was to be used to improve facilities and salaries. Their situation remained acute, however, because of the steadily increasing numbers in the schools. Premier Debré first provided emergency financial help to the Catholic schools in mid-1959 through an advance of the special allocation and then, despite the resignation in protest of his Minister of Education, a former Socialist, brought in comprehensive legislation at the end of that year that passed by a large majority, despite hot opposition by the anticlerical Radicals and Socialists.

This legislation offers the denominational schools a choice among four different relationships with the state. Two of these relationships represent extremes: complete integration in the public school system, on the one hand, or complete independence without government aid, on the other. The arrangement accepted by most Catholic schools is called the "simple contract," according to which the state pays qualified teachers on condition that the school meets national standards on the length of the school year (190 class days), number of students, and sanitary conditions. The fourth and less popular relationship is called a "contract of association," under which public school regulations and curriculum are fully instituted in the classes covered; the teachers, who are paid by the state, are drawn either from the state schools or through contract, and the state assumes all expenses of operating the classes. Either of these last two arrangements is undertaken on a nine-year basis and may be renewed under stated conditions.

Despite a threat by the Socialists that any parochial school accepting aid will be made a part of the state school system if the Socialists ever form a government, the arrangement is a reasonable resolution of a complicated problem. In keeping with the gradual transformation of the educational system as a whole into a democratic entity, the primary goal of the system is to maintain (or establish) standards and to remain responsive to the needs of France's people.

2. WELFARE SERVICES

There are major differences between Great Britain and France both in the organization and the coverage of their welfare services. France has no National Health Service, although its national insurance system provides for the reimbursement of certain medical expenses. Although the French government does not administer social services directly, it supervises the operations of social security organs (concerned with social insurance and family allowances) and local authorities (which provide public assistance, hospital care, and so forth). The end result is a complex series of agencies providing a wide range of relatively generous benefits, particularly in the form of family allowances. The system is, in practice, a unified one, despite the absence of a unitary authority.

The French have an exceptionally interesting and complicated system of social security, which has been strongly affected both by its historical development and by a basic concern for the family as a unit. Although it is less well integrated than the amazingly comprehensive but relatively simple system of social welfare established in Great Britain after World War II, the French system of social administration interrelates social insurance, family allowances, and public assistance with a wide range of preventive and welfare services. The unique feature of the French social security system is that it is administered by a series of private institutions called "the Funds," which have financial autonomy. Since, however, the Funds have the responsibility of directing important public services, they are supervised and ultimately controlled by government officials.

In some respects France was slow in introducing measures of social welfare, and there have always been powerful voices charging that the economy could not and should not stand the burden of such expenditures. Child labor was not curbed until 1874; factory inspection began some time later; and compensation for industrial accidents was only introduced at the turn of the century. Compulsory social insurance (including provisions for old age, sickness, maternity, and workmen's compensation) was first established in 1930, and then only for those earning less than a certain amount. Trade unions opposed the establishment of a state-administered system. Instead, a decentralized system of self-administered funds (*caisses*) was set up. Workers could join these funds directly or through mutual-aid societies. Employers and employees both contributed, and the government established scales of benefits for sickness and retirement. This system was extended in 1945 to cover most employed persons and their families, and it became part of the comprehensive Social Security Code of 1956.

The French social security system is in principle self-supporting, although the state aids certain classes of persons. Whereas in Great Britain there is a flat rate of contributions, in France they are graduated according to earnings. Employers must contribute approximately 10 percent and employees 6 percent of wages up to a maximum annual wage of about $2,000, and deductions are made at the source. Benefits include reimbursement of specified levels of medical expenses (official scales are established by a committee of civil servants set up in 1960; though they are published, they are not binding on doctors), sick pay, disability benefits, retirement and widows' pensions, and death benefits. In general, benefits are proportionate to earnings and do not cover full expenses or previous earnings. There is no provision for unemployment benefits, for which there has never been the pressing need in France that has existed at times in Great Britain.

Family allowances in France have a more important place in the social welfare system than in any other country. France was a pioneer in introducing family allowances, which date back to 1884 in private industry and were already a feature of public assistance before 1914. Family allowances were significantly expanded during and after World War I. They were made a charge on all employers in industry and commerce by a law of March 1932 and were further extended in 1939.

Although the French family allowance system is self-financing, the money comes entirely from employers, who contribute approximately 14 percent of their total wage bill. Allowances are not restricted to employees, however, but are available to everyone and are not related to income. They include children's allowances (the amount rises with the third and again with the fourth child) and allowances for the nonworking mother, for maternity, and for housing. Together with a wide range of advantages for large families in income tax rebates and reduced fares on public transport, the family allowance system is intended to encourage the rising birth rate and to provide social justice. While in Great Britain the social security system is primarily designed to provide protection during illness or unemployment, in France it is a major means of redistributing income. Indeed, for the less well paid, social security benefits may bring almost as much as their pay check and may be regarded as an integral part of their regular income. Social security charges, including those for family allowances, add approximately 30 percent to the total wage bill.

The general administration of the social security system is in the hands of the management boards of the Funds, which are found on the local, regional, and national level. Three-quarters of the members of the local social security boards are workers' representatives and one-quarter are employers' representatives; the ratio on the boards of the family allowance Funds is one-half workers, one-quarter employers, and one-quarter self-employed. Unlike the local and regional Funds, the National Security Fund is a public body. It includes, therefore, not only worker and employer members elected from the local and regional Funds, but also civil servants.

Candidates for these positions are put forward by trade unions and employers' organizations, but since there is so sharp and antagonistic a division among the French trade unions —the CGT, FO, and CFTC—the decision about who shall represent the workers in the social security boards is made by direct election. These elections, oddly enough, reflect political sympathies rather than different points of view on how the social security system should be run. The Communist-dominated CGT tends to obtain nearly half the employees' votes (44 percent in 1962, compared with 21 percent for the Catholic CFTC and 15 percent for the Socialist FO), and its representatives have used their position for political purposes. Such political abuse of board powers was curtailed in 1960 by an extension of ministerial control and by a sharper distinction between the functions of the boards and the managers of the Funds. The boards now vote the budget, supervise administration, and decide discretionary programs within prescribed limits. The director handles day-to-day administration and occupies a position roughly comparable to that of the managers of nationalized industries.

Conclusion

The French are still dissatisfied with certain rigidities and inequities in their educational structure and with certain injustices in the distribution of national income, both among groups within the population and among regions. Nonetheless they are making the most determined efforts in their history to develop a more open educational system and a more rational general social policy. A notable clause in the preamble to the 1946 constitution, repeated in that of 1958, declared that "every human being who, because of his age, physical or mental state, or because of his economic situation, finds himself incapable of working, has a right to obtain the means from the community for living suitably." The first three Development Plans concentrated on stimulating the economy, but the fourth and fifth Plans have deliberately associated social objectives with economic ones.

Since 1956, a summary of social expenses known as the "Social Budget" has been a regular appendix to the Finance Bill. In 1962, the social budget was more than 20 percent of the gross national product. Like its associates in the European Economic Community, France spends between 11 percent and 14 percent of its national income on social security benefits, and the expectation is that this percentage will rise. The process has been more halting and uneven than in Great Britain, but the objectives in France are also far-reaching and the achievements increasingly impressive.

9. France and the World

Largely ignored in international relations after World War II, France under President de Gaulle has become an influential, if controversial, factor in world politics. Though overshadowed in strength by the United States and the Soviet Union, France has reasserted its dominance in Western Europe, which it is trying to shape into an independent third force. Moreover, despite the loss of its colonial empire, France continues to possess great influence in former French Africa through its economic and educational aid.

1. FROM COMMUNITY TO AFRICAN INDEPENDENCE

When de Gaulle assumed power in 1958, France had suffered a series of humiliating defeats and withdrawals from former colonial territories, notably Indo-China, Morocco, and Tunisia, and was engaged in an exhausting struggle in Algeria. Moreover, the units of its empire in West Africa and Madagascar were pressing for further self-government.

De Gaulle himself had included representatives from French Africa in the Constituent Assemblies that drafted the constitution of the Fourth Republic. But despite the efforts of the native representatives and the parties of the left to establish a federal commonwealth through extending self-government to the various units of the empire, the 1946 constitution included three types of political arrangements for the African colonies that in the end proved mutually exclusive. Following the assimilative principle so strong in France's earlier relations with its empire, the African colonies sent representatives to the French parliament throughout the Fourth Republic, as Algeria and the old colonies (Martinique, Guadeloupe, Réunion, and French Guiana) had long done. In a quasi-federal move, a new structure, the French Union, was established, whose Assembly was composed of an equal number of representatives from overseas territories and from France. The third, and ultimately the most significant, feature was to provide each colony with a local representative body. Strong and skillful pressure by the African deputies in the National Assembly led to the 1956 *loi cadre*. This measure permitted local legislatures, elected by universal franchise and directed by local African leaders, to exercise limited autonomy by the time the Fourth Republic collapsed.

The Community

De Gaulle recognized the need to provide a new basis of relationship between the African territories and France. The means proposed in the constitution was the Community, which was the substitute both for the French Union and for the representation of the African territories in the French legislature. The constitution of the Fifth Republic acknowledged the right of the African territories to choose secession and independence but offered political, economic, and cultural association with France within the Community.

Each member state of the Community was recognized as self-governing; in general, their pattern of institutions was like that in France, though commonly they had only one party. But highly important matters were reserved to the Community: foreign policy, defense, currency, common economic and financial policy, the disposition of strategic raw materials, and (except by special agreement) control of higher education, the courts, and the general organization of interstate and foreign transportation and telecommunication. These latter subjects were managed by institutions established by and common to all members of the Community: the President, who was also the President of the French Republic in whose election the overseas departments and territories shared; the Executive Council, composed of the French Premier, the heads of government of the member states, and the ministers responsible for the common affairs of the Community; the Senate, composed of delegates from the legislative assemblies of France and the other member states, whose numbers were determined both by population and responsibilities in the Community; and a Court of Arbitration to settle disputes among members of the Community.

Despite the effort to establish common institutions, the Community was clearly presidential in character. The Executive Council, over which the President presided, was not responsible to the Senate, which, in fact, was purely consultative. During its short lifetime, the Community was run, therefore, by the chief executives of its various territories with only a slight check by popular representatives.

On the vote in September 1958 on whether or not to join the Community only Guinea voted no. It associated itself with Ghana. The twelve African members voted themselves the status of autonomous republics and sometimes adopted unfamiliar names such as Voltaic Republic instead of Upper Volta, the Malagasy Republic instead of Madagascar, and, still more confusing, Central African Republic for what was formerly Ubangi-Shari.

Temporarily Senegal and Soudan formed the Federation of Mali, but this union broke up in July 1960, partly over different political philosophies, partly over personal rivalries. The Soudan took the name of Mali. Houphouet Boigny of the Ivory Coast formed the Entente, an economic and cultural association between his wealthy country and the Voltaic Republic, Dahomey, and Niger. In early 1961, the "twelve" or "the Brazzaville group" established a loose association of six French-speaking states of West Africa (all except Guinea and Mali), the states of former French Equatorial Africa—Gabon,

Chad, the Central African Republic, and the Congo Republic (Brazzaville)—the Cameroun Republic (independent in 1960), and Malagasy. By 1965, this had transformed itself into OCAM (*Organisation Commune Africaine et Malgache*), which included also the Republic of the Congo (Kinshasa, formerly Leopoldville).

Though all the former French territories in Africa except Guinea voted for the Community (French Somaliland remained an overseas territory), Senegal and Soudan, in particular, wanted to turn it into an association more like the Commonwealth, with each state controlling all its internal and external relations. Under pressure, de Gaulle reluctantly agreed to this new form of relationship within the Community —which made possible separate representation in the United Nations for what was then the Federation of Mali. Fearing to lose the nationalist initiative, Houphouet Boigny (till then the strongest advocate of the Community in its original form and probably responsible for the relevant sections in the constitution), suddenly announced in July 1960 his intention of breaking the links of the Entente with the Community and immediately seeking United Nations membership. Thus the very attenuated membership of the Community consisted thereafter only of France, Senegal, the Malagasy Republic, Gabon, Chad, the Central African Republic, and the Congo Republic (Brazzaville). Since France's relations with each of its former African territories are now determined by bilateral agreements, the Community has ceased to have significance.

Despite this development, France maintains strong ties with its former territories in Africa. The economic aid it extends to them is greater in proportion to its national income (and used to be greater in extent) than that provided for Africa by Great Britain, the United States, or the Soviet Union. Aid includes general assistance, financing specific projects, and subsidies to maintain a high price for such African crops as coffee and cotton. All former Community members—and also the Congo (Kinshasa), Rwanda, Burundi, the Somali Republic, and Nigeria—have become associate members of the Common Market. The Common Market's European Development Fund has pledged aid to the Associated States, and France has a major share in determining how this money will be used. It still prefers bilateral programs.

Perhaps still more influential in maintaining French influence with its former African colonies have been the teachers, technicians, and administrators who have served, or continue to serve, in these countries. In their first years of independence it was common to have French civil servants playing a more decisive role in decision-making than did the African ministers. Many of the French administrators and technicians have now been withdrawn; so, too, have most of the French army units in Africa. But the number of French teachers serving abroad—more than 30,000—has increased. Five thousand teach in former French African countries; 12,000 in Algeria; and 12,000 in Morocco, Tunisia, Asia, and Oceania. More than 1.5 million students are enrolled in the more than 1,500 French teaching establishments abroad, and many of them take French as well as local examinations. The universities in former French African territories are part of the French university system. Over 40,000 foreign students are studying in France. Thus have the French been able to capitalize on the spread of their language and the high esteem for their culture.

2. INTERNATIONAL RELATIONS

Though de Gaulle devotes considerable attention to France's relations outside Europe, his primary concern remains its position on the Continent. In the past, French policy was dominated by the relation to Germany, by which it had been invaded three times in three-quarters of a century. Despite the destruction in Germany during World War II and its *de facto* partition between East and West, France cannot forget that there are still over seventy million Germans in Central Europe and only forty-nine million Frenchmen, and that Germany's natural resources give it a far stronger industrial capacity than France can hope to attain. To redress the balance, France has sought at different times to exercise some control over the Saar, the Rhineland, and the Ruhr, either directly or through a joint agreement, as in the Coal and Steel Community. France's purpose, of course, is to assure an adequate supply of German coke

for its own iron ore in Lorraine so that Germany will not have unrestricted use of the products that have contributed so directly to its military resources and heavy industrial plant. France has also sought to strengthen itself through alliances, in the pattern of its policy between the wars, and to coordinate and unify Western Europe under its own leadership.

Failing after World War I to secure either the strategic control of the Rhineland or a military guarantee from Great Britain and the United States, France sought security by insisting that Germany adhere to the letter of the peace treaty of Versailles, by building a network of alliances with the countries of Eastern and Southeastern Europe, and by seeking to strengthen the League of Nations. Relations with Great Britain, though close, were frequently strained by diverging views on the German problem and on the best way of organizing peace, as well as by rivalry in the Near East. As Germany grew aggressive under Hitler, France capped its alliance structure with the Franco-Soviet Treaty. But since it was weakened by internal division, France pursued a halting foreign policy, accepting or, as in regard to Mussolini's Italy, encouraging the British appeasement policy.

Feeling ignored during World War II by the three great powers that were carrying the burden of the fighting, France at de Gaulle's insistence sought to regain its place by building up its army, keeping its claims to the fore, and reestablishing the system of alliances. This time it began with the country with which ties had been established late in the interwar period, and toward which there was nation-wide gratitude for its part in the liberation of France: the Soviet Union. On December 10, 1944, de Gaulle signed with the Soviet Union a twenty-year defensive treaty that he hoped would put France in the position of mediator between East and West. But France, despite its alliance with the Soviet Union, was not represented at the decisive Yalta Conference a little over a month later. And in neither of the international conferences that France later attended, nor in its policy toward Germany, did France find the Soviet Union prepared to lend it much support.

In the light of this disappointment, the French turned back once more to the notion of an alliance in the West. On March 4, 1947, a fifty-year alliance with Great Britain was signed at Dunkirk to guarantee joint action in case of German aggression and to assure consultation in case Germany's economic obligations were unfulfilled. Agreements with Czechoslovakia and Poland and with Belgium and Holland were also discussed. Yet increasingly, French statesmen recognized the difficulties of bridging the gulf between East and West, and saw that the Soviet military position in Central Europe could offer a serious threat to France's own security.

Side by side with questions of political alignments in Europe went the problem of economic recovery. France originally blocked the economic coordination of the four zones into which Germany was divided at the end of the war and opposed the revival of the industrial capacity of the Ruhr. In the light of France's own economic problems, however, and its initial dependence on economic aid from the United States, French statesmen gradually modified their opposition to the economic recovery of West Germany so long as this area was considered an integral part of the program for Western Europe as a whole. France then embarked on a bold program of economic and political unification in this area, in particular through the Council of Europe, plans for a European army, and the Schuman plan for the European Coal and Steel Community. Of these three, it was the last that acted as pacemaker for the remarkable moves toward economic integration of "the Six": France, Germany, Italy, Holland, Belgium, and Luxembourg.

Established by international agreement in 1949, the Council of Europe, whose function is not to make policy but rather to develop a sense of community in Western Europe, operates quietly in Strasbourg through its Secretariat, its Committee of Ministers who represent the participating governments, and its Consultative Assembly whose members are drawn from all sections of opinion—except the Communists—in the parliaments of member countries. Frenchmen, but not de Gaulle, have been among its staunchest adherents.

In August 1954, France rejected the European Defense Community—an imaginative approach to the problem of German rearmament through establishing a supranational European Army with French, German, Dutch, Belgian, Luxembourg, and Italian units—which had been proposed by its own statesmen. But when the British Conservative government suddenly took on the far-reaching military commitments of Western European Union (see Great Britain, Chapter 9), France agreed in October 1954 to permit the newly sovereign and rearmed West Germany to enter NATO.

More influential than joint defense for progressively binding France and Western Germany together have proved to be supranational economic arrangements. Though the latter were originally designed to facilitate political integration, de Gaulle's insistence on national sovereignty has thwarted this potential by-product of supranational economic organizations. Nonetheless, the most far-reaching of Western Europe's associations, the Common Market (known more formally as the European Economic Community, EEC), has created bonds among its six members—France, Germany, Italy, Belgium, Holland, and Luxembourg—that are unprecedented in the history of Europe. To evaluate current French foreign policy, therefore, it is essential to know more about the European Coal and Steel Community, which was the first of Western Europe's supranational functional organizations, as well as about the other organizations that encourage integrated economic arrangements among the Six.

The European Coal and Steel Community

The European Coal and Steel Community, established on July 25, 1952, fuses the coal and steel production (the basis of military and industrial strength) of the same six countries—France, Germany, Belgium, Holland, Luxembourg, and Italy—under a common authority not subject to the control of any one government. Its basic purposes are to assure the efficient production of coal and steel at low cost, to organize the more than 130 million people of these six countries into a single competitive market for these products, and to pass on the economic advantages of so large a market not only to industrialists and governments but also to the workers in the form of improved standards of living. Its effect is to place under supranational control the production of the two key resources of an area as important strategically as industrially: the rich coal and iron triangle of Western Europe which, in an area only half the size of Alabama, includes Lorraine, the Saar, the Ruhr, and the Rhineland.

The supranational political structure of the European Coal and Steel Community is as complex as it is novel. The executive body is the High Authority, made up of nine members (selected by general agreement of the six governments) who are chosen not to represent particular countries or industries but "for their general competence" and who serve six-year staggered terms. The High Authority's decisions are by majority vote. It appears to have unlimited power to gather information, to prevent the growth of private cartels, and to prohibit and break up mergers that violate the nondiscriminatory aims of the treaty. It has considerable power in other areas affecting production. In practice, however, it works with the consent of its member governments rather than by issuing orders to them.

An elaborate structure of checks and balances to the power of the High Authority is provided through four other organs: the Council of Ministers, the Assembly, the Court, and the Consultative Committee. The Council of Ministers is the link between the governments and the High Authority; it consists of one member from each government, and its approval is needed for High Authority action in certain spheres defined by the treaty, notably the development of industry and the regulation of foreign trade. The Assembly (in which France, Germany, and Italy each have eighteen members, Belgium and Holland each ten, and Luxembourg four, elected either by popular vote or their national assemblies) meets annually to consider the High Authority's general report and has the supreme power of being able to force the resignation of the Authority by a two-thirds vote. The Court, composed of seven judges appointed for six-year terms by the governments acting jointly, is the final tribunal in all disputes between the Authority and governments or firms. It may order and restrain action by the High Authority insofar as empowered by the treaty. The Consultative Committee appointed by the Council gives producers, workers, and consumers equal representation, and provides advice on production programs and the "readaptation" of industry and labor to the new conditions of a larger market and more efficient organization of production.

Euratom

The second of the specialized functional agencies, Euratom, so quickly captured the public imagination that in July 1956, within a month of the drafting of the treaty, the French National Assembly approved joining the atomic energy pool, which was established in 1958. But current high coal stocks and low fuel prices have done away with much of the need for atomic energy (which seemed so urgent at the time of the Suez crisis). Euratom spreads the cost of nuclear research among a number of countries that could not afford it singly. But its importance is likely to be in the long run rather than immediately, since the high costs of production of atomic energy handicap it in competition with other types of fuel while Euratom itself faces stiff competition from the nuclear developments of Western Europe's private engineering industries.

The Common Market

Most significant and far-reaching of all Western European arrangements is the European Economic Community, or Common Market, which came into existence along with Euratom on January 1, 1958. The Common Market agreement ultimately aims to extend to the whole economy the principles that have been operating for iron and steel. The abolition of general restrictions on trade is naturally more gradual than those on iron and steel, but through extensive and often hard-fought negotiations the Six are moving toward a common external tariff and the abolition of internal trade barriers.[1] A major reason why the French economy is so healthy is that it has responded to the

---

[1] For a case study of how the basic agreement in agricultural policy was reached, see "The Common Market: Farmers and Foreign Policy: An Agricultural Agreement for Europe," by Michael G. Duerr in *Politics in Europe: Five Cases in European Government,* edited by Gwendolen M. Carter and Alan F. Westin (New York, Harcourt, Brace & World, Inc., 1965).

stimulus provided by the competition and opportunities offered by this larger area.

There are four institutions to manage the European Economic Community: the Commission, which is its permanent executive; the Council of Ministers, which makes policy decisions; and the Court of Justice and the Assembly (somewhat enlarged), which it shares with the Coal and Steel Community.

The extent of the authority of the Executive Commission, and particularly of its president, Walter Hallstein of Germany, has been a matter of dispute between de Gaulle and his five partners. They, like many of France's enthusiasts for European political integration, have welcomed for its political implications the prospect of independent decisions by the Commission. De Gaulle opposes the prospect for the same reason and would prefer to have the authority of the Executive Committee reduced.

The Common Market was scheduled to enter its third and final stage of economic integration in mid-1965, but France's insistence on the rule of unanimity plus a five- (rather than two-) year period of farm subsidies delayed the decision for a year, and temporarily threatened the future course of the association. The settlement in July 1966 protected France's *liberum veto* over decisions by the Executive Commission on the allocation of farm subsidies but opened the way again to continued elimination of tariffs within the area of the Six.

National tariffs on industrial products from other members of the Common Market had already been reduced by 1966 to one-fifth of their 1957 level and disappeared in 1967. Internal trade among the Six, aided by the elimination of import quotas, increased 168 percent between 1959 and 1966. Agricultural free trade within the Common Market, plus subsidies to enable the exporting countries' farmers (and especially those of France) to compete with lower world prices, resulted from the 1966 agreement. Thus France moved closer to a major objective: relative self-sufficiency in food supplies of Western Europe.

Basic to de Gaulle's economic, financial, and political policies is his determination that France shall be able to make its own final decisions on specific as well as general issues. Coupled with this overall objective are his efforts (which

run counter to what his Common Market partners desire) to reduce or eliminate American influence from Western Europe, where he insists France must be dominant. Both purposes are intimately bound up with de Gaulle's reluctance to admit Great Britain to the Common Market, for he recognizes that the British not only want the economic stimulus of association with the Six but also a closer relationship between them and the United States.

France and the World

In international affairs, de Gaulle bases his policies on the simple traditional principle that the world is composed of sovereign states. For France to play an independent role determined by its self-interest, requires, in de Gaulle's view, the executive's (in practice, his own) undisputed control of foreign policy. As far as international organization is concerned, he refuses to agree that the United Nations is more than a forum in which each state presents its own point of view and determines how far it will cooperate with other members. Thus de Gaulle not only refuses to participate in the peacekeeping operations of the United Nations but also to share in paying for them. At the same time he supports the admission of Communist China, regardless of its policies, because it is a sovereign and highly populous state.

On several counts de Gaulle pits France against the United States. First, he believes that France can dominate Western Europe only if American influence is neutralized or eliminated. Thus he has forced American troops and installations out of France, thereby impairing the strategic unity of NATO. Second, he resists American efforts to secure universal sharing of United Nations responsibilities and debts. Third, his insistence on converting American financial obligations into gold has complicated American monetary policy. Fourth, he capitalizes on opposition to American policies, for example, in Vietnam. Yet the instant support afforded the United States at the time of the Cuban crisis demonstrates that de Gaulle is not anti-American. His guiding rule is to put and keep France in the front rank of world powers. Thus he exploits every situation for France's interest, particularly those situations affecting the United

States and Great Britain, of whose ultimate support in time of need he has no doubt.

That de Gaulle refused to allow Great Britain to enter the Common Market is a further example of his determination to keep France the dominant influence in Western Europe. Whether he is making the right decisions to fulfill his purposes is another matter. A closer economic and political alignment with Great Britain might strengthen France and help to create a more stable third force by lessening British dependence on the United States. By weakening NATO and depending on Western European union and France's own nuclear *force de frappe,* he may be undercutting the strategic unity of the West. He might be mistaken in his estimates that the Soviet Union is no longer expansionist, that German reunification is not possible, and that Great Britain and the United States are basically his allies despite their irritation at his policies. But de Gaulle appears to have no doubts that his policies are the best for France, and the vast improvement in its international position since he assumed power in the Fifth Republic provides him with ample evidence that he is correct.

Conclusion

For the first time in half a century France is neither at war nor in fear of the coming of war. Coupled with the political stability and economic prosperity of the Fifth Republic, this freedom from fear has created a mood of confidence and security unknown to earlier generations.

The removal of the nightmare of an aggressive Germany, and of France's traditional fear of lacking essential energy resources, is the chief external factor creating the new spirit. The partition of Germany, plus France's close relation with West Germany in the Common Market, has eliminated the former anxiety. The development of hydroelectric power and the flow of oil from North Africa, supplemented by the arrangements of the Coal and Steel Community, have made France's scarcity of coal far less important.

Internally, the economic advance that is now spreading more evenly throughout the country has done much to reduce the former social barriers between the working class and the bourgeoisie. The modernization of agriculture and the consequent shift of peasants into industry have strengthened the equilibrium of French society. The newer industries—electronics, chemicals, and oil—into which many of the new workers have gone are those in which the influence of the Communist-dominated CGT is weak. Partly for this reason, though more because of prosperity, strikes have been relatively infrequent. Another reason for the unprecedented atmosphere of optimism in France is the increasing youthfulness of France's population, created by its high birth rate (higher than the German and above the European average).

The biggest question mark in France's future concerns de Gaulle. Rarely has a democratic regime in an established country depended so completely on a single individual. It is hard to imagine that the UNR would maintain its cohesion in response to another leader. Since the chances are slight that France can develop a two-party system apart from the Communists, the old problem of devising political stability out of disparate and antagonistic parties may return if the dominant force of de Gaulle leaves the scene. Yet perhaps the electorate has acquired more sense of responsibility for casting its votes for those who intend to work within the constitutional system and will also curb its anarchic tendency to support splinter groups rather than the larger parties that have a chance to support or constructively oppose governmental policies.

France has great elements of strength. It is well balanced between agriculture and industry, town and country. It is growing in numbers and output. It has an excellent civil service, technological competence, and useful experience in public planning for further development. More now than for many decades, France is in a position to make use of the great heritage it possesses.

·III·

The Government
of
Germany

1. German People and Politics

1. THE GERMAN PROBLEM

Germany is the one major foreign power that has been most troublesome and most problematic to the world and to itself throughout recent history. In two world wars, Germany was the major enemy of all or most of the other big powers. Defeat in the second spelled loss of power and loss of national identity, with the nation split into two political units with diametrically opposed political systems: the Communist-controlled German Democratic Republic and the Western-oriented German Federal Republic. The "German problem"—that is, the issue of partition and reunification—is one of the few great world problems over which a nuclear holocaust might involve the entire globe. Even short of such a holocaust, many Germans tremble lest a contest between East and West be fought over the German issue on German soil, with Germans fighting Germans.

Many people, however, especially outside Germany, would be less than enthusiastic about the peaceful reunification of all the Germans. West Germany alone today ranks second in world trade and third in industrial production and has risen to the status of the second strongest military power on the European continent. East Germany ranks eighth in world trade and is the second industrial power in the Communist world. What, then, might it mean for the world if the two were reunited?

This rapid rise, especially of West Germany, has been almost miraculous. But such radical transformation is not novel for Germany. Frequent and extreme changes have swung Germany from fragmentation and disunity (until 1871) to unification (after 1871), to the acme of centralization, under Hitler, and back to dis-

unity today. In foreign affairs, Germany has swung from impotence to commanding power; internally, from authoritarianism to democracy and back to totalitarian tyranny; spiritually and culturally, from the greatness of Kant, Goethe, and Beethoven to the moral abyss of the Nazi "annihilation camp." No wonder that to the world Germans have alternately appeared as good and bad in the extreme; even a more temperate judgment is likely to be called anti-German by some and pro-German by others. Whoever seeks to understand the Germans, rather than to idealize or to condemn them, appears biased to some.

Opinions about democracy's chances of survival in Germany are equally diverse. To some observers there is only one answer. Germans, they say, have been and always will be a prey to some sort of authoritarianism: old-style Prussian conservatism, recent fascist-type totalitarianism, Communist control as presently exists in East Germany, or a neo-Nazism that seems right now to be reviving in West Germany. Others believe that Germany can achieve democracy as easily as any other Western nation. The truth cannot be gained from preconceived ideas, but only from a study of those historical, geographical, and political forces that have shaped the present Germany. They show that Germany, politically as well as geographically, stands midway between the Western countries, with their longer and finer traditions of democracy, and Russia, with its almost complete lack of any such traditions. Western influence has been strong enough to give Germany ideas, movements, and sometimes institutions that were basically liberal and democratic. But—and this has been the tragedy of the Germans—such forces did not in the past prove strong enough to prevail against authoritarian counterforces. This does not preclude their victory in the future. It is precisely the present touch-and-go of democratic chances in West Germany that renders developments there so interesting to students of government and politics.

2. THE LAND AND THE PEOPLE

The Land

Germany is located in the heart of Europe and is bounded, roughly, by the Alps in the south, by the North Sea and the Baltic Sea in the north, by France and the Low Countries in the west, and in the east by whatever Slavic countries existed or now exist as political units. The vagueness of this description attests to the difficulty of defining Germany geographically. The map of Germany in different historic periods shows that until about a hundred years ago *Germany* was simply a geographical expression for the many territorial units into which the country was fragmented politically. After its unification in 1871, Germany reached from beyond the river Rhine in the west to far beyond the river Vistula in the east and was, with over 200,000 square miles, one of the largest countries in Europe; in addition, it held colonial possessions in Africa and the Pacific Ocean. These it lost in 1919 as the result of defeat in World War I; but even more important were its territorial losses at home. In the west, Alsace-Lorraine, gained from France in 1871, was lost again, and in the east much territory was ceded to newly established Poland, leaving one province, East Prussia, geographically detached from the main part of the country. Reaction came with a vengeance: Hitler, at the height of his power, not only controlled most of the European continent politically but actually incorporated into Germany vast areas, including Austria, Bohemia, and most of Poland.

Present Territory and Population

Today's map is different indeed. After the surrender in 1945, the victorious powers agreed that pending a peace treaty the frontiers should be those of 1937 (prior to Nazi expansion), but that large territories that were German at that time, namely all those east of the rivers

Oder and Neisse, should be administered by Poland, except for the northern half of East Prussia, which would be administered by the Soviet Union. These territories in fact now constitute integral parts of those countries, although most Germans, backed by the Western powers, maintain their claim to the 1937 boundaries.

Present German *de facto* territory thus has shrunk to about the smallest in Germany's entire history. Between the two world wars Germany comprised over 180,000 square miles, somewhat more than California. Today it comprises 136,000 square miles (about the size of Montana), divided between East and West Germany in the relation of about one to two. Within this rump Germany, however, there live as many people—about seventy-eight million— as inhabited the former, larger Germany. This is due to the westward shift not only of Germany's boundaries but also of its population. Most Germans formerly living in the detached territories of the East, as well as the ethnically German populations of such countries as Czechoslovakia, Poland, and Hungary, were forced into Germany as "expellees." Over ten million of them now live in West Germany and about three million in East Germany. Moreover, there has been a continual influx of refugees from the Soviet zone into West Germany, amounting, prior to the building of the Berlin "wall"— which stopped most of the influx—to over three million persons. Thus, in contrast to Britain's and France's approximately fifty million inhabitants each, there is a solid bloc of seventy-eight million Germans in the heart of Europe. Fifty-eight million of these live in West Germany, seventeen in the East, and the rest (about three) in Berlin.

Commercial Position and Resources

Geography has had a profound impact on German economic and political developments. When the main trade lanes went through Central Europe, Germany's location and system of rivers favored its economic development; but when the trade lanes shifted to the Atlantic during the age of overseas discoveries, Germany was left stranded in what became a backward area. This retarded the development of a German middle class. The advent of the industrial age, however, enabled Germany to become a great workshop for the industrially less-developed eastern and southeastern regions which it bordered and which exchanged their agricultural surpluses for German industrial products. Germany's industrialization was rendered possible by one major resource, coal, found in abundance in what became Germany's industrial heart, the valley of the river Ruhr (tributary of the Rhine in western Germany).

But like Britain, and unlike the United States and the Soviet Union, Germany has not been self-sufficient in most other basic resources, including agricultural products. While the climate is as temperate as that of France, the soil is in the main less fertile. Even when Germany still possessed its breadbasket east of the river Elbe, it had to import food. In addition, it had to import such basic industrial raw materials as rubber, cotton, oil, and ores. For a while, it is true, the possession of Lorraine (from 1871 to 1918) enabled Germany's heavy industry to draw from within its own frontiers both iron ore (from Lorraine) and coal (from the Ruhr, the Saar, and Upper Silesia). Steel mills arose near the coal fields, and many diversified industries (machinery, electrical, chemical, textile) were developed around Berlin and in such regions as the upper Rhine and Saxony. Germany's compactness, the absence of high mountain barriers, and its rich river system made possible a dense system of transportation by rail, water (canals connecting the main rivers), and highway.

But for Germany, as for Britain, it was, and still is, "export or die." The loss of the territories east of the Oder and Neisse meant the loss of the only region that had yielded a food surplus for the rest of Germany. Today, Germany must feed the people who have come from the lost territories out of more slender resources. Furthermore, dwindling trade between Eastern and Western Europe (and between the eastern and western portions of Germany itself) has deprived West Germany and its industry of important markets. While industry in East Germany is increasingly integrated with the economy of the Soviet bloc, for which it has become a major workshop, West Germany has had to compete for markets with the main Western powers—which it has done energetically and

with such success that Germany now ranks second, behind the United States and before Britain, in volume of world trade. Its exports in 1965 accounted for 20 percent of its GNP (as against 5.3 percent in the United States).

Thus, to the political miracle of West Germany's return to status and power among the nations must be added the economic miracle of a recovery and prosperity without equal in Western Europe. Credit for this must be given to an ingrained German urge to work—Germans simply cannot face disorder without doing something about it—and to an undaunted determination to rebuild what had been destroyed by Nazism and war. German workers, for instance, restrained their wage demands in order to enable German industry to compete in the world market. It is true, however, that Germans often forget the assistance lent them by others, especially by America, which poured billions into the German recovery effort. It must also be remembered that circumstances—and, paradoxically, those very circumstances that in the beginning seemed adverse—aided the German recovery. Physical destruction, which necessitated rebuilding from scratch, provided Germany with an up-to-date modern plant. Until the late fifties, the lack of an armament burden favored its budget, and demilitarization made it possible to concentrate on the manufacture of civilian goods. The influx of expellees and refugees, while at first a burden, provided a needed labor supply. And a trend toward "depolitization"—that is, a lack of interest in politics and public affairs, an aftermath of Nazism and occupation—allowed West German leaders to concentrate on economic affairs and Germans at large to immerse themselves in the task at hand.

Strategic Position and Sectionalism

Politically, Germany's central location and open boundaries have been both an opportunity and a temptation. In contrast to England, with its protected island position, Germany has been either a battleground for others—when weak—or a center from which to expand and conquer—when strong. As with France and other Continental countries, open land frontiers have made it necessary for the country to defend itself; this necessity led to the establishment of

D E N M A R K

BALTIC SEA

NORTH SEA

SCHLESWIG-HOLSTEIN

Kiel

Kiel Canal

Stettin

Hamburg

UNDER POLISH
ADMINISTRATION

Bremen

R. Elbe

LOWER   SAXONY

GERMAN

R. Oder

Hannover

Berlin

R. Weser

DEMOCRATIC

NETHERLANDS

HARZ

REPUBLIC

R. Rhine

NORTHRHINE-
WESTPHALIA

Kassel

Düsseldorf

R. Neisse

Cologne

FEDERAL REPUBLIC

H E S S E

ERZGEBIRGE

Bonn ★

BELGIUM

OF GERMANY

Wiesbaden   Frankfurt

Prague

R. Mosel

Mainz

R. Main

LUX.

RHINELAND-
PALATINATE

CZECHOSLOVAKIA

SAAR

Nürnberg

Saarbrücken

R. Rhine

Karlsruhe

B A V A R I A

Stuttgart

FRANCE

BADEN-
WÜRTTEMBERG

BLACK
FOREST

R. Danube

R. Danube

Munich

AUSTRIA

ALPS

SWITZERLAND

ALPS

ALPS

● LAND CAPITALS   ★ CAPITALS

MILES

0   100

the modern state with its standing armies and permanent bureaucracies. In contrast to France, however, Germany's boundaries, except for the sea in the north and the Alps in the south, have been ill defined and ever changing. This absence of natural frontiers has favored both foreign invasions and aggressive nationalism. Traditionally, German expansion was directed eastward (*Drang nach Osten*), but, as the wars of 1870, 1914, and 1939 showed, this did not preclude pressure toward the west.

If there are geographical causes of German nationalism, geography has also something to do with the opposite political phenomenon, sectionalism. The geography of Germany is diversified. Between the plains in the north and the Alps in the extreme south, more than half of German territory is uplands, crisscrossed by rivers, valleys, hills, and mountain ranges. In the absence of early political unification (such as France was blessed with), regional variation slowed down the process of unification of the numerous, often thousand-year-old subnationalities (*Stämme*), which in the course of history developed their own political ambitions. "Particularism" (as the Germans call this kind of sectionalism) has been as important as nationalism, and its existence has given rise to the recurring problem of German federalism—the problem of how to create *e pluribus unum*. Sectionalism in the narrow confines of Germany easily assumes the character of pettiness.

The People: Nationality

"Volk" and Race

Germans may be defined as those German-speaking people who do not claim allegiance to another nation. This is a problematic definition. As a nation the Germans are perhaps more difficult to identify than any other people. The German term for nation, *Volk,* is utterly vague.[1] Race was made the criterion of nationhood by the Nazis and other racialist Germans. But it

[1] *Volk* may refer to an organized community, in the sense of "nation," or "people" (as in "the American people"). Or it may have the political connotation of "the masses of the people," as opposed to ruling minorities (as in *Volkssouveränität:* popular sovereignty). Or it may signify in a social sense "the lower strata" or "the common people" (as in the term *Volkswagen,* for "the car of the common man").

is doubtful whether there are genuine European races in the sense of subraces of the Caucasian race that can be distinguished by origin and physical characteristics. Physically, Germans are much less uniform than the usual stereotype suggests. The blond, tall, blue-eyed type, though more prevalent than the shorter, dark-haired, brown- or gray-eyed type in areas of northwestern Germany, yields to the latter in many other regions of the country.

One problem, which German racialists turned into a race problem, hardly exists any longer: that of the German Jews. Prior to Hitler they comprised about 1 percent of the population (600,000) and, because of their tendency to adapt themselves through intermarriage as well as in customs and habits, they were on the way toward extinction by merger. The Nazis, considering them a dangerous group of alien race, eliminated them through enforced emigration and physical extermination. Today only a few thousand Jews survive in Germany.

"Volk" and Language

If we cannot define Germans by race, can we define them by language? Again we run into difficulties. For, while almost all inhabitants of what is Germany today speak one common language, not all German-speaking people in the world consider themselves Germans. Most Austrians or German-speaking Swiss, for example, do not consider themselves German in any more than a vague sense of cultural affinity. This merely reflects an historical process of continual "loss of national (that is, German) substance." Of the Germanic tribes that spread over Europe during the migrations of the fifth and sixth centuries A.D., many founded new nations (such as England) while others disappeared in non-Germanic populations. Those that remained in Germany after the disintegration of Charlemagne's Empire in the ninth century started a countermovement toward the east where, as far west as the Elbe River, Slavs had settled. They colonized goodly portions of Eastern and Southeastern Europe, generally, however, settling in mixture with the non-German populations. Thus, in what we today call Poland or Bohemia or the Baltic countries, Germans emerged as a ruling minority, with the original inhabitants as subject populations.

There, of course, they have now disappeared. In the west and south, on the other hand, groups that were originally German, such as the Franks (who founded France), the Swiss, and the Dutch, separated culturally and politically from Germany while the German character of others—the Austrians, for example—became uncertain.

Hence, in contrast to France and Britain, where early political unification created the nation, and to Italy, where political unification came late but where the language was an effective defining agent, Germans could never agree as to what constituted the German Volk. This uncertainty contributed to the difficulty of political unification. When unification was finally obtained, in 1871, it was on the basis of what was called the "Little Germany" solution, which left outside the *Reich* (the name of the political unit, Germany) many who considered themselves or were considered by Reich Germans to be national or racial Germans. No identity of Volk and Reich was achieved. On the other hand, the newly established Reich contained non-German national minorities, such as French in Alsace-Lorraine, Poles in the eastern provinces, and Danes in northern Schleswig, which created serious internal and foreign political problems. Between the two world wars, following the cession of Alsace-Lorraine to France and the eastern territories to Poland, few national minorities remained inside Germany; in Germany today there are hardly any, except for some Danes in Schleswig.

Thus today with the integration of Germans formerly living beyond the Reich frontiers, and with the recognition that Austrians are not Germans nationally, the nation for the first time can be defined more clearly as one bloc—the inhabitants of West and East Germany. The fact of their partition—involving a danger that they may eventually disintegrate into two not only politically but socially and culturally different nations—points up to Germans the urgency of reunification.

The Germans Today

In its population trends Germany has shown the characteristic effects of industrialization, urbanization, and modern hygiene. While in 1800 about twenty-five million inhabitants of what

later became Germany faced twenty-seven million Frenchmen, by 1900 the relation was fifty-six million to thirty-nine, a deeply disturbing fact to such French statesmen as Clemenceau, who spoke of "twenty million Germans too many." Yet even after the territorial losses incurred through World War I, Germany did not have the population density of Britain or Belgium. Today, despite the loss of over three million lives in World War II, there are, because of the influx of expellees and refugees, about five hundred persons per square mile, or about the same as in Britain. Expellees are mostly concentrated in West Germany, where they have, in the main, been well integrated into the booming economy. But the issue of their lost homelands still poses political problems with which we shall have to deal below.

War and its subsequent upheavals have had a profound impact on German age and sex distribution. In 1946 there were about 1,300 women for every 1,000 men; in the age group of 25 to 45, 1,640 for every 1,000. Since then the disproportion has been reduced, but there are still about a million war widows, and the proportion of women to men in the West in 1965 was still about 31 million to 28 million.

Within the German nation, the component subgroups are extremely diversified. Such major groups as Franks, Saxons, and Swabians divide into an indefinite number of subgroups. German popular dialects differ to such an extent that a German from the north speaking Low German and a German from the south speaking the Bavarian dialect can hardly understand each other. The common bond is the standard language taught by the schools and largely used in daily life. It is also the written language, which was established by Luther's translation of the Bible. Thus Germans, though religiously split because of Luther, owe to him a linguistic uniformity that has substantially contributed to national coherence.

Germans also differ culturally, in customs and habits, and in temperament. Even contrasts between neighboring groups, such as the almost Latin, lighthearted, and easy-going Rhinelanders and the heavy, stolid, brooding Westphalians, are striking. But the boundaries of the major German Stämme rarely coincide with those of the traditional political units in Germany (such as Prussia, Bavaria, and Württemberg). While the former were medieval in origin, the political units were established later through conquest, marriage, and dynastic rule based thereon. Contrary to common opinion, the typical Prussian was found only in some parts of Prussia, and even the typical Bavarian only in south Bavaria. The picture is further complicated by the addition to the indigenous populations of the expellees and refugees, themselves divided into Silesians, East Prussians, and so forth. This makes for occasional friction. Yet, like urbanization, it tends to result in greater uniformity through mixture.

The People: Religion

The impact of religious differences on German society and politics has been very strong. While the other major nations of Europe are denominationally more or less uniform, religion splits the German nation. This split has been more divisive in its effects than, say, in the United States, because it was accompanied and compounded by the territorial split of Germany into many principalities during the Reformation and Counter Reformation. At that time the rulers of the German principalities independently determined the religion of their subjects, and as a result the conflict between Protestants and Catholics went through the heart of Germany. Even today, after many shifts of population, this division is still largely territorial, with the north and east predominantly Protestant, and the south and west Catholic. In the southwest, however, early subdivisions tend to confuse religious lines. In Württemberg and Hesse, for example, there are more Protestants than Catholics, and even in strongly Catholic Bavaria there are some predominantly Protestant areas. In the unified Reich of 1871, Protestants outnumbered Catholics by two to one. Today, the loss of the eastern territories and the split of the remainder into East and West have left West Germany with the two denominations in the relation of about one to one (with Protestants having a slight edge), while East Germany is almost entirely Protestant (over fifteen of seventeen million).

This religious division has affected German society and politics because of the intimate connection between church and state. In some Catholic regions prior to the nineteenth century, high church dignitaries (bishops or archbishops) were often simultaneously the worldly rulers of corresponding "church principalities." In Protestant territorial states individual rulers became the highest church authorities. Luther himself agreed to the state's having authority over church affairs in return for the princes' protection of Protestantism. This meant subjection to worldly authority. Church organization became almost indistinguishable from state organization; in the eyes of the ordinary citizen, the Lutheran pastor became one of the persons representing state authority, the more so since the pastor received his salary through state subsidies granted to the churches. Thus Protestantism became a pillar of secular power, which throve, as in Tsarist Russia, on the alliance of throne and altar. The basically conservative influence of Protestantism in Germany was strengthened by the absence of Nonconformists. The partnership of church and state left antiauthoritarian groups, middle class or labor, liberal or socialist, without religious backing. Many were thus driven into antireligious attitudes. Marx, a German, considered religion to be the "opium of the people," a mere ideology to keep the masses subservient. Some non-Marxian Germans came to think similarly. Germans divided into (largely conservative) churchgoers and (largely socialist or liberal) nonbelievers.

The Catholic Church was basically as favorable to authoritarian tendencies as was Protestantism. After 1871, to be sure, it was driven to oppose the Prussian-dominated and thus basically Protestant new German state. Since Catholics were in a minority, and concentrated in certain regions, the Church developed what came to be known as "political Catholicism": a party (the Center party) to defend its interests, a press, and Christian trade unions. To retain its hold over the Catholic population, the clergy had to become politically active. Even today, Catholics on election Sundays are often advised in the sermon how to cast their votes. In most regions of Germany, primary education is denominational, even though it is given in public schools (which divide into those of Catholic character—with Catholic teachers, textbooks, and spirit—and those of Protestant character).

Catholicism still has to struggle for the continuance of this system, which is opposed by that of the nondenominational schools (see Chapter 7). Finally, the churches, Catholic as well as Protestant, have always depended on state subsidies.

For all these reasons, Catholicism has had as much interest as Protestantism in public affairs and in backing any government that did not threaten its interests and prerogatives. Its energetic participation in politics sometimes caused Protestants to suspect that Catholicism had a pernicious, Vatican-directed influence over German affairs. Catholics, on their part, suspected Protestants of discriminating against the Catholic minority in civil service personnel policies. Today, the Christian Democratic Union, or CDU—the main government party in West Germany—is backed by both Catholics and Protestants, and there is frequently anxious insistence on parity on the part of both groups.

The close association of state and church, as well as the general secular trends observable in most industrialized societies, have caused a good deal of religious indifference, especially among Protestants. Although 96 percent of Germans in the West are nominal members of a church, a recent survey showed that only 9 percent of Protestant young men and 15 percent of young women attended religious services regularly (the percentage is somewhat higher among older members). The corresponding figures for Catholics, on the other hand, were 55 and 63 percent respectively, indicating the greater hold of the Catholic Church over its members in general and over the workers in particular. Many of the nominally Protestant workers tend to be unreligious, whereas the promotion of social reform by important Catholic groups has strengthened the influence of the Church on workers professing Catholicism.

A striking new phenomenon in German Protestantism is the rise of a numerically small but elite group of "nonconformists." This group, which consists of both ministers and lay people, draws its inspiration from the stand taken by those Protestants who resisted Nazism. It discusses and radically questions domestic policy as well as such foreign policy problems as nuclear armaments and cold war. Whatever its (frequently ultrapacifist) illusions, it is one of the few groups in Germany today that radically challenge the prevailing conformity on questions of way of life and politics—thus encouraging something that is still woefully lacking in German life: democratic discussion of basic issues.

The People: Class Structure

To present a clear picture of German society is difficult. The East and the West of Germany grow ever farther apart in their social structure. East Germany has assumed the features of a Communist state, with its social structure more and more patterned after that of the Soviet Union. In West Germany no such radical transformation of society has occurred. There is still the familiar picture of workers and industrialists, traders and peasants, all competing for social and political influence through established institutions and channels, through trade unions, professional associations, organizations of businessmen, political parties, and above all through the bureaucracy.[2] Postwar developments have modified this picture slightly. Thus, there do exist groups of "have-nots" that are often overlooked in the prevailing prosperity. While in East Germany the expellees were readily absorbed during the general transformation of society, West Germany, with its established society, at first had difficulty in assimilating the newcomers, who amounted to one-fifth of the population. Although by now most have found work, many who used to belong to the upper strata have gone down in the social scale, sometimes to the level of unskilled workers. They consider themselves outcasts in an environment where all others, including the traditional proletariat, are lucky "haves."

There are other "pockets of poverty"—for example, among those who lost their property or their means of earning a living through the vagaries of war and the postwar period. One

[2] Over the last decade, the West German social landscape has been further enlivened by the influx of foreign workers—by now over a million of them, chiefly from Mediterranean countries—who, while not permanent inhabitants, have been creating all sorts of problems, from the political activities of Italian leftists to demands for housing, which is often woefully lacking. On the other hand, one group, formerly of great importance, has disappeared as a class—the feudal-agrarian big (and, for the most part, noble) landowners.

businessman or houseowner may have lost his property through bombing, while a neighbor or a competitor kept his; one German may have had property in the Eastern territories or the Soviet zone, out of reach now or confiscated, while another kept his property simply because it was located in West Germany. Some lost their jobs or their possessions because of former Nazi connections; others, as deeply or more deeply incriminated, escaped the penalties of "denazification" (see page 395). By and large, however, the effects of denazification were transitory, and the number of former Nazis permanently deprived of holdings or positions is small. The old business oligarchy, in particular, is still there. More significant was the impact of the currency inflation that hit Germany from 1945 to 1948. Those who lost their savings through inflation joined the ranks of the new "have-nots," and nothing much has been done for them. In general, however, the affluent society of West Germany has managed to indemnify or assist most of those who had been damaged by the war and its consequences, or by the Nazi regime, or in other ways; most of these people, including the expellees, founded or joined pressure groups that proved to be very efficient in extracting assistance and benefits from the government.

German Industrialism

German society has long been noted for its continuity, even rigidity. No change by revolution, as in France, has ever interrupted its steady development. Until about a hundred years ago, in contrast with Britain, Germany had been a predominantly agrarian country. It had played a relatively small part in the growth of commerce and trade in the West generally since the beginning of the modern age. Up to about 1850 the typical German social relationship, at least in the north and east, was still the feudal or half-feudal one of master and serf, of a noble landowner and an economically and socially dependent peasant; in the cities, handicraft, controlled by closed guilds, prevailed.

Then Germany became rapidly and thoroughly industrialized. As late as 1880, half of its gainfully employed people were in agriculture. After World War I, however, workers comprised almost half of those gainfully em-

ployed, while those in agriculture totaled less than a third. A tremendous migration from country to city took place in a brief period of time. New industrial centers developed rapidly. Today, one-third of West Germany's population lives in cities with over a hundred thousand inhabitants. Only 12 percent of gainfully employed West Germans still work on the land; 50 percent work in industry, 16 percent in commerce and transportation, and 22 percent in public or other services. Of the total working population, 56 percent are laborers. White-collar employees comprise 28 percent (including 5 percent public officials), so that over four-fifths of the working population consist of wage- or salary-earners. The remainder are self-employed, including independent businessmen, artisans, professionals, and farmers. West German society thus presents the features characteristic of other societies in the stage of "the third industrial revolution": The agricultural sector is steadily declining, and the "traditional" industrial sector, with its factory workers, declines proportionally in favor of the "tertiary" sector of—public and private—services, with its white-collar employees.

Not included in these figures are a large number of recipients of retirement and other pensions and similar fixed income. Germany, like other industrialized nations, consists of people who are increasingly dependent both economically and socially on jobs or similar security rather than on private initiative. Average income has been rising for all classes in the postwar period, but it is still significantly lower for workers than for white-collar employees and for many of the self-employed.[3]

Germany never had that broad basis of rising democracy, a large independent middle class. The tardy rise of German capitalism meant a jump from precapitalistic conditions into a developed capitalism, whose characteristic feature was the concentration of capital in giant corporations and combines, interlocked through

---

[3] While between 1950 and 1960, wages and salaries in the sum total of all incomes declined by 1.2 percent indicating a lag of 12 percent in the rise of fixed income compared to that of businessmen, the proportion has since been reversed with income from salaries and wages rising (in 1965) to about 65 percent of total income (1960:61) and that from independent work and assets declining from 39 to 35 percent.

cartel agreements. Small or middle-sized business establishments were disadvantaged through such events as the currency inflation of the early 1920's, the depression of the early 1930's, and Hitler's total war, and members of the lower classes never had much opportunity to rise socially. Germany has been characterized by slight social mobility, less, certainly, than in the United States, which was industrialized at the same time and with the same thoroughness. The Marxian terms *bourgeoisie* and *proletariat,* therefore, perhaps better fitted Germany than other industrialized countries: once born into either class one stayed there, and strong class-consciousness prevailed.

A Society of Status and Bureaucratic Rule

Such feeling for status and separateness is still characteristic of present-day West Germany.[4] The worker takes pride in his institutions—his trade union, his party, his adult educational organizations where he tries to make up for the higher education denied to him as a child. Such education generally distinguishes the member of the middle class not only from the proletariat but, within his own class, in multitudinous and minute ways from other middle-class members, whose higher or lower ranks are indicated by a wealth of titles, indications of status or occupation, and similar outward signs of social stratification. In all this, he patterns his behavior on that of a group that still enjoys high, if not the highest, prestige: the officialdom.

Although the German economy moved from feudalism to capitalism, the Germans themselves retained their earlier, semifeudal attitudes—not simply because the nobility for a long time maintained a key position in state and government, but because the spirit of status and rule from above remained the prevailing one in the caste of expert officials who ran, and still run, the country administratively. Traditionally these officials had been drawn from the nobility; and even when members of the middle classes

[4] For example, regarding the above-mentioned differentiation between employees and workers, recent polls revealed a higher social prestige of employees, even of those with lower income than workers, and the two groups rarely intermarry. That is, regardless of income, these two strata are still considered—and still consider themselves—as basically separate, as socially upper and lower.

were gradually added to its ranks, the official caste, instead of becoming imbued with the bourgeois spirit (as happened in Britain to a large extent), retained its old mentality, with its concern for prestige and distinctions of status, its exclusiveness, and its militaristic and conservative-authoritarian ideals. This class became the model for other strata of the population. Its mentality pervaded large parts of the middle class, and to some extent even the working class. In contrast to English and, above all, American society, participation in state power, rather than income or wealth, is the main yardstick of one's social status in Germany.

The People: Social and Political Attitudes

It has become fashionable of late among political scientists to study the behavior patterns of people by means of detailed, minute opinion and attitude surveys. The purpose is to derive reliable pictures of group and national characteristics and trends. While such survey research may, indeed, yield valuable insight, its evaluation requires that the results be placed in their historical context; without the historical dimension, the results are empty and may even be misleading. This applies especially to German affairs.

For example: A recent poll indicated that, while fifty-five of every hundred Germans have never met a Jew, fifty-four said they would never marry a Jew, and seventy-eight came out for the punishment of active anti-Semites. What does this prove about the causes of and the trends in German anti-Semitism? This anti-Semitism can be understood only historically—that is, we must know that German Jews, in contrast to British and French Jews, since their emancipation during the nineteenth century had found themselves by and large a "liberal" minority outside the authoritarian-conservative mainstream of German thought and attitudes. Many Germans thus tended to consider the Jews "elements of decomposition" and, through the educational establishment, handed on this distrust from one generation to the other.

Or, according to a recent study of national attitude patterns, a majority of Germans, in contrast to Americans, British, and Italians, do not believe that, as citizens, they can do much about social or political ills, expecting remedy rather from the action of public officials. Germany, according to the authors of this study, thus presents "an authoritarian subject culture, which involves imparting legitimacy to authority and bureaucracy, but not to political parties and competitive elections." [5] Again, this finding simply reflects historical experience—in this case, the tradition of the *Rechtsstaat* (see below). Unless we understand this tradition, we cannot assess the depth and stability of present attitude patterns and trends.

Can we generalize about German attitudes? Making history responsible for the emergence and development of so-called national traits precludes our considering them as innate, or immutable, or applicable to all members of the nation. National characteristics—that is, the image a nation presents to the outside world—change. The English, now thought of as stolid, phlegmatic, "muddling through," were regarded in the seventeenth century as turbulent and excitable. This reputation they lost to the French in the eighteenth century, at a time when the Germans acquired the reputation of being the nation of poets and thinkers, living politically in the clouds. A hundred years later the Germans had become, in the view of many, aggressors mainly interested in material goods, efficiency, power.

If the Germans changed radically during the nineteenth century, one reason may be that they achieved national unity and power through "blood and iron" rather than as the result of a popular movement. More important, perhaps, than such latter-day aggressiveness, have been certain long-standing traits that betray a worship of order over everything else.

Respect for Order and Rules

Experience—that is, German history, a history of disunity and disorder—produced this high evaluation of order. It showed Germans the danger in endless strife among *Stämme,* social groups, or religions. When Bismarck's strong-arm methods finally overcame political disorder, the ideal of order became coupled with that of authority. An ordered but free society seemed a contradiction in terms. An ordered society

must be established and ruled by those who know best, rather than by discussion and argument on the part of the many. [6] For every foreseeable situation there should be a rule, duly set by some authority with power to enforce it, and obeyed faithfully by the subjects. Germans prefer to deal with people under specific rules. Unused to taking the initiative to settle a public problem in an unregulated situation, many instinctively look for somebody to do it for them. This authority need not be legitimate or traditional. It was surprisingly easy for the Allies in 1945 to command the obedience of Germans and to restore order once they had laid down regulations in due form. But it had to be done by them.

This does not mean that the German is sheeplike. What makes German authoritarianism so difficult to understand is that it developed, not in a people who, like the Russians, were hardly awake politically, but in a highly educated and —outside the political realm—highly sophisticated people. There has been in Germany as much awareness and discussion of public affairs, grumbling about abuses, and complaint against authorities as anywhere else. The German is often even more impatient. But when it comes to standing up and defending his rights against authorities, the German with "civil courage" (as Bismarck called it) is the exception. This is why democratic institutions (which have abounded in Germany) are so rarely imbued with the democratic spirit.

Between Authority and Anarchy

This does not imply that all Germans exhibit an authoritarian mentality. On the contrary, the German has often been torn between the extremes of authoritarianism and anarchism. There is, for example, the typically German figure of Michael Kohlhaas, Heinrich von Kleist's hero, who in pursuing a claim defends the principle of individual justice to the point of violence, insurrection, and eventual self-destruction. Likewise, in their relation to the world, the Germans, as a nation, have been overbearing and egocentric, on the one hand,

---

[5] G. A. Almond and S. Verba, *The Civic Culture* (Boston, Little, Brown, 1965), pp. 173, 112.

[6] As late as 1957, a majority of Germans polled on the question of whether the will of the people should prevail, or whether the government should prevail "because it knows better," answered in favor of the government in the ratio of 49 to 35.

and on the other hand cosmopolitan to the point of being ready to lose themselves in the world. German nationalism has been coupled with an inclination toward self-pity, toward assuming too readily that injustice has been done to Germany, while injustice inflicted on others is less readily acknowledged or too readily forgotten. But this does not exclude an inclination to absorb foreign influence; Germany's "openness toward the world" enabled it to produce its great citizens of the world, its Goethe, its Kant.

Thus torn between extremes, the German is still searching for the golden mean of a free but ordered society [7] that recognizes the value of accommodation and compromise, discussion and agreement, civil rights and liberties, individual and group initiative. No German Dreyfus Affair ever established the primacy of individual liberty over *raison d'Etat*. Thus in Germany democratic attitudes failed to acquire the natural, spontaneous character that they have to some extent gained in the West. Here is the historic failure of Germany's elite, its educated middle class, its intelligentsia: by keeping aloof from active participation in political affairs, they prepared the way for the rule of the power-mad. Such distrust is still a chief obstacle in the way of a budding democratic spirit in postwar Germany.[8]

3. GERMAN POLITICAL IDEAS

The Importance of Political Ideas in Germany

On the surface, German political thought looks like that of the main Western countries. We can distinguish conservatism, liberalism, socialism. But political ideas are fertile only where masses, groups, and movements are in a position to give them effect. In Germany this has happened only intermittently. For political action, the impact of ideas on the ruling elite has by and large been more important than the political thought of the masses. Because the ordinary German was seldom allowed to put his ideas and ideals into practice, as a political theorist he tended to become an extremist. Not allowed to be radical in action, the German tended to be so in the realm of thought. There is some similarity here between the German situation and that of Russian intellectuals under the tsarist regime. Revolutions that other nations made in the realm of action, Germans performed in the realm of theory.

The lesser impact in Germany of political ideas on political action is also related to the absence of a great tradition of *political* thought, such as exists in Britain or France. German political thought, often cloistered and remote from the daily political scene, has been carried on in the main by philosophers and professors. It has thus easily assumed a metaphysical and abstract character. Great publicists and pamphleteers, who in the West utilized political theories as weapons in the political struggles of their times, have been conspicuously absent in Germany. Few Germans have had the sense of analytical criticism, psychological when referring to persons, social when referring to institutions, that exists in the Latin and Anglo-Saxon worlds. Exceptions, such as G. E. Lessing in the eighteenth century and Heinrich Heine and Friedrich Nietzsche in the nineteenth, were suspect to the average German; their criticism appeared to him merely negative. Even less refined types of thought had an uphill fight against the entrenched pattern of belief. As in the 1920's, the term *Links-Intellektueller* (leftist intellectual—as if intellectuals by definition had to be leftist) has become a term of opprobrium in West Germany again.

German Liberalism

Early Liberalism

In England all major schools of political thought are to some extent liberal, and liberal ideas predominate in the important classes and parties. In France, too, liberal-democratic thought has been the strongest ideological force in the last two hundred years. There was a time in Germany, also, at the end of the eighteenth century, when an entire generation was imbued with the ideals of the Enlightenment.

---

[7] Some such yearning is, perhaps, implied in former Chancellor Erhard's call for building a "structured society" (*formierte Gesellschaft*).

[8] "It is precisely among the elements which in most democratic countries tend to support democratic processes that contemporary Germany appears to have least support" (Almond and Verba, p. 111).

German philosophers, such as Kant and the young Fichte, and poets, such as Schiller and Hölderlin, greeted the French Revolution with enthusiasm. One young German, Wilhelm von Humboldt (1767–1835), in 1792 wrote what the English historian, Gooch, has called the "German equivalent of Mill's *On Liberty*." In his *Thoughts Concerning the Limits of State Action*, Humboldt restricted the government's legitimate function to the preservation of internal order and defense against foreign attack. While with Humboldt the accent was on individual freedom, with Immanuel Kant (1724–1804) it was on ordered freedom under law. In the realm of international relations Kant, in his *On Perpetual Peace* (1795), boldly proposed what at his time must have seemed utopian, a world federation of republican commonwealths. In his ideas on internal government he was more cautious, emphasizing the necessity of order and the citizen's duties toward society. Even more important for the development of subsequent German thought, however, was the emphasis in Kant's moral philosophy on man's rigorous duties under the moral law. The concept of moral duty later served Kantian philosophers (and the elite they influenced) to impress on Germans that obedience to the law as such meant the fulfillment of ethical postulates.

Kant's foremost philosophical disciple, J. G. Fichte (1762–1814), started out as an almost anarchistic follower of the principles of the French Revolution, but ended as an ultranationalist who proclaimed the unique historical mission of the German people, and as a champion of a planned economy and society in a strong welfare state. This surprising turn he shared with the majority of his compatriots, who, under the impact of the Napoleonic conquests, began to regard the philosophy of the Rights of Man as an alien ideology serving the French to deprive Germans of their freedom and independence.

Liberalism and Romanticism

Liberal-democratic ideas continued to be influential in one aspect of German life between 1815 and 1870: the German movement for national unification. Here, however, they took the peculiar form of political romanticism, an ideology that influenced many other movements, including authoritarian ones. Romanticism is the reaction to rationalism. It rejects general rules and universal principles derived from reason and worships, instead, the unique—that which distinguishes one phenomenon from the other and makes the world diversified. In Germany romanticism, in one of its implications, meant a radical individualism that proclaimed the supremacy of the unique personality over everything else. Thus, for Friedrich Nietzsche (1844–1900) romanticism meant the glorification of the "will to power" of the strong individual who fights both that "coldest of all monsters," the state, and the slave-morality of the masses protected by the state.

Because of this extremism, individualist romanticism either remained politically ineffective or was exploited for its own different ends by subsequent political movements (such as the Nazis' exploitation of Nietzsche's ideas). *Political* romanticism, on the other hand, insisting that uniqueness resides in collective entities, such as nationalities, rather than in individuals, became one of the main strands of German political thought. To an earlier representative of this thinking, J. G. Herder (1744–1803), all nationalities, each with its peculiar character and historical mission, were still equal in their rich variety; to subsequent German nationalists, however, the German nation assumed superiority over the others. Fichte has already been mentioned in this connection. In the German liberal-national movement the predominance of this thought meant that the "atomistic" individualism of the natural rights doctrine was rejected in favor of group supremacy over the individual. Germany was to be a democracy, but the individual was to be subordinated to the community and its will. The *Volksgeist* (spirit of the entire people or nation) was to be the regulative principle for ordering relations among groups, classes, and individuals in a nation, and old-established associations and groupings were to prevail over artificial institutions enforced from above.

The Rechtsstaat

Although the liberal-national movement was defeated, its ideals did contribute to German constitutionalism and the putting into practice of the idea of the *Rechtsstaat*. German constitutionalism, unlike that in the West, did not mean the embodiment of popular sovereignty in formal constitutional guarantees and processes. It meant, rather, a system under which the sovereign monarchical ruler allowed the people, organized in estates or classes, to participate in government within a circumscribed sphere, particularly in lawmaking. Similarly a Rechtsstaat (a state where law prevails), rather than guaranteeing the *political* rights of the people, guaranteed the citizen's legal security against executive arbitrariness. Its German promoters advocated above all the establishment of independent courts to protect the citizen against governmental encroachment. The establishment of the authoritarian Rechtsstaat in the nineteenth century sealed the alliance between a German middle class that obtained legal security and a ruling group that retained political power.

Germany and Laissez Faire

As French revolutionary social and political ideas came to appear alien to Germans, so in the field of economy did English laissez faire liberalism, chiefly because the German fledgling industry needed protection. Friedrich List (1789–1846) opposed Adam Smith and advocated protective tariffs, state intervention for the protection of industries, and a long-range political direction of economic developments. The idea of state intervention in the economy through subsidies, high tariffs, cartel arrangements, and similar restrictions of free enterprise remained strong in Germany long after German industry had outgrown its infancy. Here, too, liberalism remained ineffective unless adulterated with statism. One of the intellectual fathers of Nazism, Arthur Moeller van den Bruck (1876–1925), expressed a more general German feeling when he said that a genuine German political movement might partake of all kinds of political ideas, even socialism and democracy, but not of liberalism; the latter was only for wealthy "have" nations that could afford such a luxury.

German Socialism

Marxism and German Labor

The ideas of Karl Marx are described elsewhere in this book. But Marx and his friend and collaborator, Friedrich Engels (1820–95), were, after all, Germans, and it is in the form of Marxism that socialism gained the allegiance of the German working class. That Marxism prevailed, rather than socialist reformism or gradualism of the Fabian type, was the result of the failure of the ruling groups in Germany to assimilate the rising industrial proletariat. It remained isolated, an outcast group. Consequently, a doctrine of hostility to all existing institutions that predicted a workers' kingdom to come appealed to the workers more than did any movement of reform. A competing socialism, such as that of Ferdinand Lassalle (1825–64), which expected the worker to be emancipated by remodeling the existing state structure through parliamentary devices such as universal suffrage, had less appeal.

To Marx, there was no place for genuine freedom in any historic society; real freedom would come only after the great "leap" that would establish the classless society in which state and government would wither away. Any general theory of rights and freedoms in presocialist society was to him mere subterfuge to cover up class rule and vested interest.

Such negativism remained characteristic of German socialism even when, toward the end of the nineteenth century, certain practical reforms gave German labor some stake in society, and even when, after 1918, German socialists obtained a share in government. Despite all theoretical discussions within German socialism, and despite the actual split of the movement into two major political factions (Social Democrats and Communists), its basic attitude remained doctrinaire, even where in practice it became "reformist." Marx's *Kapital* remained the bible, and any adjustment to new situations had to be made by interpreting its dogma rather than by giving up old ideas and accepting new ones. German socialism until recently has been more dogmatic, less adaptable, and less pragmatic than either the French or British varieties.

Social Reform

If Marxism is the form in which socialism got hold of the German worker, other classes felt the impact of "socialist" ideas in a broader sense. After the foundation of the Reich in 1871, the ruling groups realized that if they were to avoid social revolution they had to grant social reform. Reform legislation was theoretically vindicated by a group of German economists whom their laissez faire opponents jokingly called "armchair socialists" (*Kathedersozialisten*), insinuating that theirs was a kind of ivory tower, professorial theorizing. The armchair socialists, however, proved to be more realistic than their dogmatically liberal opponents, whose theories never found full realization in Germany. Social reform thus started as something done *for* but not *by* the people, and to this day this is still the attitude of the major group that carried out reform—the bureaucracy.

German Conservatism

Legitimism

German conservatism existed in attitude long before its formulation in theory. Lutheran obedience to the powers that be became the basis of Prussian authoritarianism. When the latter was increasingly attacked by nineteenth-century liberalism and socialism, Friedrich Julius Stahl (1802–61) fashioned its theoretical defense. All authority derives from God, he declared, and the divine-right monarchy is bound by its own laws alone, not by any constitutions, institutions, or majorities. "Authority, not majority" was to be the right principle of legitimate government. But in this legitimism lay the main weakness of the theory. In a Germany still split into territorial monarchies, legitimism could not solve the problem of unification. It was hostile, or at best indifferent, to nationalism. Bismarck, when unifying Germany by the use of Prussian armed force against the other established monarchies, destroyed legitimism in practice. From then on, the major type of German conservatism was nationalist authoritarianism, born when national liberalism dropped its liberalism, and legitimist conservatism its legitimism.

Hegel

To this new conservatism the great German philosopher Georg Friedrich Hegel (1770–1831) contributed decisive ideas. His views on internal government may be called the conservative reaction to the ideas of the French Revolution. Hegel, in agreement with political romanticism, rejected all "absolute" principles, such as natural rights and individual freedom. Such principles are to be thought of merely as historical incidents in a larger pattern of evolution. Evolution, it is true, according to Hegel means the unfolding of the "world spirit" toward eventual freedom. But this freedom was not the freedom that liberal democrats or rationalist enlightenment philosophers had in mind. To Hegel the French Revolution embodied merely an extreme that was opposed to the antithetical extreme of absolute despotism. In Hegel's dialectic philosophy, opposite extremes, that is, forces and counterforces, always result in a subsequent "synthesis." He found the synthesis of absolute freedom and absolute despotism in an authoritarian Rechtsstaat. In this state there reigns neither liberal license nor reactionary compulsion. It is the ordered rule of an hereditary monarchy, acquiesced in and aided by the estates, or major classes, but primarily carried out by a class of expert servants of the state, the officials. Such a strong state regulates class and group conflicts of civil society in the interests of all. Only such a strong state can offer an abode to the highest manifestations of man: the arts, religion, and philosophy.

The state, superior to any rights of individuals or groups, was also the highest political institution externally. Between conflicting interests and claims of nations, only history passes judgment. Power, and ultimately war, decides which nation at a given period shall be the chosen instrument of the world spirit. Before its might all others legitimately perish.

The idea of the strong state exercised a tremendous influence in a Germany unified by force and trying for the first time in modern history to play its role as a world power. In the new Empire of 1871, German jurists (such as Paul Laband, 1838–1918, and Georg Jellinek, 1851–1911) and German historians (such as Heinrich von Treitschke, 1834–96) fashioned the theory of the state as essentially will and power, a legal and sociological person. This concept is as natural to a German as that of inalienable rights and freedoms of the individual is to an American.

Hegelianism has been responsible for yet another tendency of German political thought: to put social and political ideas and phenomena into the larger context of historical development. Everything in human affairs, according to this view, is part of one great historical process that determines all particular developments. Marx, in this respect, was Hegel's direct descendant. This tendency toward a uniform *Weltanschauung,* an overall world view or philosophy, easily leads to dogmatism. Different *Weltanschauungen* divide individuals, groups, parties, and movements more profoundly than do conflicting interests. The German habit of supporting such philosophies, added to religious, economic, and similar divisions, has often been a handicap in the development of democracy, which calls for adjustment and compromise.

The German Idea of the State

Out of this pattern of thought there developed under the Empire what may be called the dominant ideology of its elite—an ideology that also spread to large groups of the middle classes. This "German idea of the State" survived the Hohenzollern Empire and in two world wars was the basis for many Germans' conviction that theirs was the higher cause. According to this ideology, the type of state and society developed in Prussia-Germany is superior to Western liberal democracy because in the former "the best" rule with a sense of responsibility toward the many; social welfare is assured through efficient government by the expert; there is power enough to defend the community against threats from abroad, egotistic interest groups, and subversive forces; and, finally, all this serves to stimulate the higher cultural values of the arts, science, and philosophy.

Compared with this ideal of *Kulturstaat,* Western political systems appeared defective. In them, the community, a prey to individual or group egoism, is doomed to disintegrate. Where parliament is supreme, national interests become matters for bargaining, and factions haggle over the affairs of state. Where majorities decide, decisions are likely to be wrong, since, as Schiller had said, "Majority, that is nonsense; right reason has ever been known to only the few." But the abyss between Germany and the West was even deeper; it was, according to this ideology, the abyss between *Kultur* and mere civilization. Kultur is concerned with the higher values of religion and truth, arts and poetry, and with the state as their protector; civilization is concerned only with the satisfaction of material wants, with technology and industry. German Kultur is idealistic; Western civilization utilitarian. Concern with Kultur certainly was genuine with many Germans. But it also provided them with an alibi for not trying to achieve the level of social and political behavior that forms the essence of Western political civilization.

Twentieth-Century German Political Thought

When the powerful state of the Hohenzollerns fell before Western strength, traditional authoritarianism was temporarily discredited. But no single strong political philosophy took its place during the period of the Weimar Republic. Besides Marxism and Catholic Christian social thought, a large variety of often original, frequently extreme doctrines and systems emerged. Some tried to provide theoretical support for the new democracy. Thus Hugo Preuss (1860–1925), one of the makers of the Weimar Constitution, tried to fashion a kind of democratic pluralism out of Otto von Gierke's (1841–1921) *Genossenschafts-Theorie* (theory of associations, or corporations). Political life, in this theory, is not to be regulated from above, but is to be self-regulated by existing organic groups, and the state is to be the result of the integration of such groupings of the people into one nation. Hans Kelsen's (b. 1881) "Pure Theory of Law," on the other hand, dissolved the state, theoretically, into a mere system of legal norms. About the actual forms of state and society, theory could say nothing; they must result from the struggle of given social and political forces. To this concept of the state as pure law, Kelsen's antagonist, Carl Schmitt (b. 1888), perhaps the most original, certainly the most versatile of twentieth-century German political philosophers, opposed that of the state as the vessel of power politics. Schmitt's theory proclaims as sovereign not the people, not the individual, not the state as such, but the man who controls the state in periods of emergency—for all politics, internal and external, is warfare, a friend-foe relationship. This theory revealed real though often hidden power relationships in a state and among states. But if less legalistic and more realistic than other theories, it was also likely to serve dictatorial tendencies, particularly those antidemocratic forces that put an end to Weimar democracy under the cloak of emergency powers.

This diversity of theories left the German people without any accepted standards for attitude and action. The feeling of uncertainty about what to believe contributed to the rise of a new, dogmatic creed to which large masses flocked: Nazism. This doctrine was so closely connected with Nazi practice that it must be discussed where Nazi policy is treated (Chapter 2). After the breakdown of Nazism, the way was again open to free thought; so far, however, significant new theories have not appeared. One can observe a certain revival of the idea of natural law, that is, a higher law that binds even the sovereign state and its organs. This is in part connected with the postwar influence of Catholic thinking in West Germany, and in part still a reaction against a regime that had disregarded all standards of decency and humanity.

A tendency toward moderation has also become noticeable: Socialists, where they have not dropped Marxian doctrine altogether, are less dogmatically Marxian and more mildly reformist; rightists are less nationalistic, less authoritarian-minded, and economically more liberal in advocating a socially oriented free-market system (*soziale Marktwirtschaft*). This trend has brought German attitudes more in line with general Western trends of thought. However, among academicians, the conflict between a more democratically oriented group and one representing the authoritarian-Hegelian (and now Schmittian) tradition is as sharp as ever. It may be that the importation of academic political science from America into postwar Germany has favored the democrats somewhat, but the split still points up a basic dichotomy in German political philosophy and attitude.[9]

[9] Each of the two opposed groups of academicians has a periodical that serves as its chief theoretical mouthpiece: the *Politische Vierteljahrsschrift* (Political Science Quarterly) reflects the views of probably a majority of the political scientists; *Der Staat* reflects chiefly the views of public and constitutional law experts.

4. ORGANS OF PUBLIC OPINION

In our Introduction we stressed the vital importance of a lively system of communication media (press, radio, TV) as the basis for an informed citizenry in a democracy. In a traditionally authoritarian country like Germany it is necessary, in addition, that organs of opinion have a chance to scrutinize and, if necessary, criticize government—in particular, the executive. As we shall see, parliamentary opposition, which in a parliamentary democracy normally has that function, has frequently been weak or nonexistent in Germany; the job then falls to the press or similar media. How have German organs of public opinion coped with that job?

Earlier Developments

In the past, German organs of opinion fulfilled their task only up to a point. It was not that opinion was made exclusively from above. On the contrary, even under the Hohenzollern regime, a wealth of different views could be expressed by a rich and varied press. But the press hardly voiced an autonomous public opinion. It was rather the mouthpiece of established groups and parties with their rigid doctrines and fixed policies. It was, moreover, an "opinion" press, which made little distinction between reporting and editorializing. Also, many newspapers, especially the chains formed in the provinces, came under the control of business interests. Local diversity thus tended to vanish under the impact of opinion-making by large established interests. This system continued into the post-World War I period. People read the paper that voiced their line and confirmed their views. In a large city, for example, one was likely to find the official Social Democratic paper, the official Communist paper, the Center party paper, and later in the 1920's a Nazi paper. In addition—and probably with the largest circulation of all—would be a paper that claimed to be unpolitical (or unpartisan) but in reality was rightist-nationalist and an organ for business interests. There were, indeed, a couple of well-known liberal newspapers of high standards in Berlin (and a few also outside the capital, such as the renowned *Frankfurter Zeitung*), but they were usually to the left of general opinion and, as elections showed, without much influence on political attitudes despite their wide circulation. It was characteristically the other way round in France, where the big Paris press was to the right of public opinion. In contrast to France, the German press was not openly corrupt, although the influence of special interests, through ownership and financial control, advertising and party connection, was no less strong.

Public Opinion in West Germany

After twelve years of control of public opinion by the Nazis, the Germans in 1945 awoke with a burning desire for information in place of indoctrination. This gave the Allies a chance to utilize this desire in the interest of reorientation. Outside the Soviet zone, where Germans got a new type of indoctrination, they were quite successful in this respect. They avoided censorship but selected anti-Nazis as licensees of newspapers; these persons, in the main, proved to be free from political and doctrinal bonds. The new press adopted certain foreign features to make newspapers more genuinely free and representative, such as letters to the editor and more criticism of public authorities. In distinguishing reporting from editorializing, they provided a more objective kind of factual information. In this way the new press became a better instrument for democratization than a completely free, that is, unlicensed, press, with its inevitable Nazi and pro-Nazi tendencies, would have been. This suggests that democratization sometimes fares better under a purposeful management than under a hands-off policy of illusory freedom.

Since the termination of licensing in 1949 the press has been flourishing, but it has also experienced certain drawbacks.

Germans have ample opportunity to be well informed and to compare all kinds of opinion. West Germany stands high in regard to circulation as well as per capita ratio of newspapers. There are close to five hundred dailies with a circulation of over eighteen million, which compares favorably with Great Britain and France. They are widespread regionally, and in place of the Berlin papers—which, for obvious reasons, no longer circulate nationally—some excellent ones have also supraregional distribution—for example, the *Frankfurter Allgemeine Zeitung,* which, though it is politically rather conservative, is independent in its editorials and remarkable for both opinion and coverage. About two-thirds of the sales of the dailies are by subscription (in contrast to street sale), which favors more thorough reading. A city such as Hamburg has eleven newspapers, among them another one with national circulation, *Die Welt* (with, like the *Frankfurter Allgemeine,* a circulation of close to three hundred thousand). Other important dailies are *Süddeutsche Zeitung* (Munich), *Tagesspiegel* (West Berlin), *Frankfurter Rundschau,* and *Stuttgarter Zeitung.* In addition, there are several weeklies of considerable quality, such as *Die Zeit* (Hamburg, liberal), perhaps the outstanding German paper today, *Rheinischer Merkur* (Cologne, conservative Catholic), *Christ und Welt* (Stuttgart, Protestant), and *Welt der Arbeit* (Düsseldorf, organ of the German Trade Union Federation). In a class by itself is the Hamburg weekly *Der Spiegel,* patterned after *Time* magazine. Though it is often accused of sensationalism, it acts as a kind of private investigation committee and keeps the government on its toes by uncovering unsavory conditions, such as corruption in high places (on the *Spiegel* case, see below).

Among encouraging phenomena are also the small but influential quality periodicals (usually monthlies), such as *Frankfurter Hefte* (progressive Catholic) and *Der Monat* (liberal), which stress cultural and philosophical topics and are read by the German elite. There are also political cabarets, which provide needed criticism and biting humor in what is generally a stodgy political atmosphere.

But there are discouraging trends, too. The impact of the more serious press has been impaired by the steady rise of tabloids and illustrated newspapers—about a hundred of them, with a circulation of thirty-five million. (One of them, *Bild-Zeitung,* sells over four million copies daily.) Moreover, the newspaper empire controlled by one man has reappeared. Axel Springer, for example, now the biggest German press lord, owns serious papers, like *Die Welt,* and tabloids alike. When *Die Welt* came under his control, it changed from a vivid, critical paper to a rather tame, conservative one. This points up another danger: hidden partiality. The trend away from the compartmentalized, dogmatic party press of Weimar and earlier periods toward nonpartisan, independent newspapers has been all to the good, particularly inasmuch as extremist, radically leftist or rightist publications have all but disappeared. (Some remnants of rightist radicalism persist in the press of the expellee groups and self-styled soldiers' or veterans' organs.) Only a few papers today are sponsored directly by or admit being close to a particular political party. But such independence hardly means what it does to an American who is used to seeing his paper backing now one party and now the other, or even backing candidates of different parties during the same election. In Germany it usually means agreement with one party, or at least one "political orientation" (*Richtung*), and in fact, in most instances, it means being in close agreement with the government parties and their policies. This favors a noncommittal, colorless, and often accommodating journalism, a system in which only a handful of organs, more popular (like *Der Spiegel*) or more esoteric (like *Die Zeit*), fulfill the function of critical enlightenment.

Not as many shades of opinion as one might wish find expression, and government can afford to be less sensitive to public opinion than it could be with a more politically varied and critical press. Similar problems arise in regard to those media which, in Germany as elsewhere, tend to overshadow the printed word, namely radio and TV. German broadcasting, since its inception, has been less an outlet for public opinion or mere entertainment than a vehicle of culture, providing its audience with generally high-standard (though not necessarily highbrow) programs. Radio stations are under public ownership but are organized independently from government as public corporations on a regional or Land level; they are managed by mixed boards which are supposed to constitute a cross-section of society at large, with representatives of political parties, churches, educational institutions, trade unions and other occupational groups, and so forth. They are thus free from advertising (with the exception of a very short period—twenty minutes on weekdays, none on Sundays and holidays—of

commercials on TV) and from the ensuing bane of "lowest-common-denominator" entertainment based on rating, in return for which the German listener does not resent paying a few DM's monthly fee.[10] Most of the upkeep of radio and television, of course, comes from public subsidies. In return, the stations have to give free time to political leaders during election campaigns (which solves part of the problem of campaign financing) as well as generally to political parties, churches, and other agencies of different *Weltanschauungen*.

Until 1960 television shared a single network with the regional radio stations. In the early sixties Adenauer, aware of the political potentialities inherent in the control of a TV channel and perhaps inspired by the de Gaulle example in France, tried to create a second-channel network which was to be under the auspices of the federal government. Upon application by some Länder, the Federal Constitutional Court declared the plan unconstitutional as an invasion of the states' right to deal exclusively with these matters. Thereupon the second network was set up by the Länder which operate it jointly.

As in other European systems, avoidance of private ownership and management of radio and TV has not meant their control by either government or political parties. The autonomy of the respective setups and the participation of a large number of social groups in their management has so far prevented such a result. On the other hand, as compared with the corresponding American media, discussion of public and political issues has been generally less lively. It is true that some of the TV stations occasionally ventured into programing controversial issues, such as that of the Oder-Neisse line, or contacts with East Germany; they invariably ran into difficulties and in some cases were forced to fire the persons responsible for the programs. More significant, perhaps, has been the general avoidance of touchy issues, such as the trials of Nazi murderers. One positive political effect of the media, on the other hand, has been that their audience extends to the Soviet zone, whose inhabitants, though of course urgently admonished by their rulers to

[10] 2 DM per radio set, plus 5 DM per TV set. One Deutsche Mark equals 25 cents.

abstain from listening to and viewing Western stations, have this way a chance to keep in touch with life among their Western brothers.

On the whole, therefore, these media, in Germany, have been highly successful instrumentalities of mass education, devoting themselves to sponsoring music, theater, the arts, and so forth. But they have been less successful as instruments of public opinion, less so even than other organs of public opinion. Thus the German communication media have not yet played the role so vital in the older democracies: that of a fourth estate that checks public authority by constituting the voice of the people.

2. The German Political Heritage

1. HISTORY OF A DISUNITED NATION

"The legacy of German history is profoundly ambiguous. . . . It includes memories that counsel fear of remaining weak in a world of ruthless foreign interests, but it is also rich in memories of suffering and defeat following upon reckless bids for world power. It is rich in memories of success in fields requiring economic, technical and scientific performance; but it lacks memories of sustained political gains following upon peaceful development of democratic and constitutional practice. Dictatorship and war are remembered as terrible failures; but democracy and peaceful international relations are not at all widely remembered as successes." [1]

A recent comparative-attitude study revealed that Germans, with the aid of their rich system of communication media, follow political affairs at least as regularly as Americans and the British and are as well informed about government and politics. Yet few of them (7 percent, as against 46 percent in the United Kingdom and 85 percent in the United States!) take pride in any political or governmental institutions. This suggests, in the words of the authors, "alienation from the political system," an "interesting combination of high exposure and attentiveness to the political system, along with an absence of pride in it." [2] These findings

are perhaps not too surprising in view of the provisional and somewhat synthetic character of the present German political units. But they reflect also something deeper, something that distinguishes Germany most strikingly from the other major powers dealt with in this book: the absence of any well-established pattern of government and political way of life that can be used as a model for organizing the present and planning the future. The absence of such a clear image has meant not that historical experience is less important to the Germans, but rather that the Germans, not sure of themselves, tend to be influenced, either in imitation or in rejection, by the varying pattern of their past. It is particularly necessary, therefore, to understand German history, and particularly its recent phases, if one is to understand present attitudes and practices.

The Holy Roman Empire

For almost a thousand years Germany appears in European history as an empire claiming to be the successor to the Roman Empire and, as such, claiming supremacy over Western Christianity. Yet the Empire was never able to achieve the unification of Christendom. True, under Charlemagne (800–14) it approached genuine universality. It disintegrated after his death, however, and when it was refounded one and a half centuries later (in 962, by Otto I, the "Great") it comprised only the eastern half of

[1] Karl W. Deutsch and Lewis J. Edinger, *Germany Rejoins the Powers* (Stanford, Stanford University Press, 1959), p. 17.

[2] G. A. Almond and S. Verba, *The Civic Culture* (Boston, Little, Brown, 1965), pp. 64, 68. Only on the basis of such general low valuation of politics can seemingly more positive results of polls—for example, that over 50 percent of polled Germans think that "democracy is the best form of government"—be correctly assessed. We must exercise similar caution in assessing answers to such questions as "Which

German has done most for Germany?" (1952: Adenauer 3 percent, Bismarck 36, Hitler 9, Frederick the Great 7, as against 1963: Adenauer 28, Bismarck 21, Hitler 5, Frederick 4); or whether Hitler, if he had not led Germany into war, would have to be considered a great statesman (1959: yes, 41 percent, no, 42; 1961: yes, 30, no, 43): *Jahrbuch der öffentlichen Meinung* (1965), pp. 396, 397.

Charlemagne's Empire and had only the allegiance of German Stämme. The western portion of Charlemagne's Empire developed into what we call today a nation-state (France), but the eastern portion did not. Subsequently it came to be called the "Holy Roman Empire of Germanic Nationality," but the emphasis was on empire, not on nationality, and it continued to aspire to European leadership throughout the Middle Ages.

This universalism had much to do with the subsequent failure of Germans to become a unified nation. The Emperors' claim was contested by the Pope and by the rulers of other European countries, with the result that the Emperors became involved in unending and futile struggles outside Germany and were forced to grant ever more concessions to their powerful German vassals. Thus they lost their hold over Germany, which disintegrated into numerous territories. The grants of liberties to the nobles led to the emergence of the higher lords as rulers of territorial states.

The Territorial States

In England and France, medieval feudalism eventually gave way to a unified state that absorbed the feudal powers. In Germany, feudalism destroyed the old unity, so that public power had to be established separately in each of the territorial units where the higher lords now ruled. Thus the modern state, with its centralized state machinery, its triad of powers (standing army, bureaucracy, and taxation) and its triad of functions (lawmaking, administration, and justice) emerged in Germany separately in each of a number of units, which ranged all the way from big European powers (Hapsburg-Austria, and later Prussia) to middle-sized principalities (such as Bavaria, Saxony, Hanover) and to petty secular or ecclesiastical entities. The German dream of universal rule had led to fragmentation.

The old Empire, to be sure, continued to exist into the Napoleonic age, but its control over territorial rulers was nominal. Emperorship continued to be based on election, with the right to elect vested in the rulers of some of the main territorial states, the so-called electors. In practice, it became hereditary in the Hapsburg dynasty. The Emperor was powerful only because of his Austrian possessions. As Emperor he had to share whatever power he had with the imperial diet (*Reichstag*), an assembly in which the German "estates" (electors, other princes, and free cities), jealous of their individual sovereignties, were perennially incapable of common action. The Treaty of Westphalia (1648), terminating a war in which German princes, allied with outside countries, had fought each other bitterly and disastrously for thirty years, confirmed the estates' legal sovereignty.

Religious Split, Economic Backwardness

The Treaty of Westphalia also put the final seal on another German catastrophe. To the territorial cleavage was added the religious split. Germany, home of the Lutheran Reformation, had been unable to gain religious unity. Since each ruler determined the religion of his territory, Austria and parts of southern and western Germany remained Catholic, and most of northern Germany, including Brandenburg-Prussia, became Protestant. Religious schism intensified territorial divisions by creating contrasts. Lutheranism, with its principle of obedience to worldly authority, facilitated the rise of an efficient but austere absolutism in Protestant regions, especially in Prussia, while Catholic regions often developed a less rigid rule. Religion, of course, does not account for everything. Thus, the peculiar social-economic system of Germany east of the river Elbe, with its large estates owned by the nobility (the Junker class), which held its peasants in hereditary serfdom, contributed to authoritarian developments in Prussia. These contrasted sharply with the more relaxed, enlightened atmosphere in, say, the Rhenish archbishoprics or a southern "free" city, or the cosmopolitanism of the Austrians.

There was yet another cause of backwardness. In the sixteenth century, owing to the shift of European trade routes from the Continent to the Atlantic, the rise of a strong and prosperous German middle class that had begun in the later Middle Ages (when such cities as Augsburg, Frankfurt, and Cologne were centers of European trade) was suddenly arrested, and German economy remained chiefly agricultural up to the nineteenth century. This retrogression from trade and market economy to petty rural conditions was reflected in the realm of culture. Early in the sixteenth century the works of the great artists Albrecht Dürer and Hans Holbein still reflected the sturdy and solid culture of the late medieval German city. After them came a period of barrenness that lasted until long after the Thirty Years' War (1618–48), when another generation began to put its dreams into sublime music and metaphysics (Bach, Leibniz). Only toward the end of the eighteenth century did German culture have a general—and splendid—revival.

The Rise of Prussia

Thus political life in Germany came to center in the territorial states. And it was largely due to the rise of one of them, Prussia, that a unified Reich was eventually established. The rise of Prussia is one of the miracles of modern history. The Electorate of Brandenburg, named the Kingdom of Prussia in 1701, was remote from the centers of Germany and looked toward the Slavic East on the Baltic Sea. Who could have foreseen that it would become the most powerful of the German states and founder of the new Reich?

The Hohenzollerns

Unlike other German states, Prussia was in a way an artificial unit; it lacked Stämme unity and cultural tradition, a stable economic basis, and even geographical coherence. Its main territory was in the northeast, but other bits were scattered over the rest of Germany. Its rise was almost exclusively the work of its ruling dynasty, the Hohenzollerns, who built Prussia upon the sandy soil of eastern Germany by sheer will, energy, tyranny, and conquest. Frederick William, the "Great Elector" (1640–88), first in an almost uninterrupted hundred and fifty years' succession of brilliantly gifted rulers, defeated the feudal lords in his territory and then put them to work in his central administration. King Frederick William I (1713–40) built up the Prussian army as the foremost part of the state. Finally Frederick II, the Great (1740–86), in a series of diplomatic maneuvers and wars that rendered him famous for ruthlessness even in an age of Machiavellian power politics, es-

tablished Prussia as one of the recognized great powers of Europe.

Militarism

These achievements paralleled what Richelieu, Mazarin, and Louis XIV did for France, and, as in France, much of the administrative structure then established is still recognizable today. But while constitutionally Prussia was similar to France, the political climate was entirely its own. Since Prussia lacked the wealth and the skilled and dense population of other European nations, it could maintain itself by only two means: armed force, and an effective, thoroughly economical organization of state affairs. The army always came first. Militarism meant not only a strong army but the dominance of the military spirit, with the principles of discipline, hierarchy, and blind obedience invading nonmilitary fields. It meant that military affairs remained exempt from civilian control even when other affairs came to some extent under the control of parliament and parties. The Prussian officer became the symbol of social prestige, the German counterpart of the English gentleman or the successful businessman in America. To this day, military or government position rather than wealth, income, or birth is the measure of prestige in Germany.

Prussian Administration

In administration, too, Prussia developed its own climate. While in France and other countries the nobility flocked to the court, Spartan Prussia could afford no class of noble drones. The Prussian nobles formed the backbone of a bureaucracy whose capacity for hard work, efficiency, and discipline was unique among the countries of the *ancien régime*. This very fact created a sense of community between rulers and ruled. Prussia's kings considered themselves "first servants of the state," a phrase which Frederick II opposed to Louis XIV's *"L'État, c'est moi."* Glaring differences between rich and poor, capital and countryside, and the unmerited privileges of nobles living in luxury at the expense of the honest burgher, made a country such as France ripe for revolution. In Prussia the rustic way of life of rulers and Junkers (nobles) rendered more bearable the

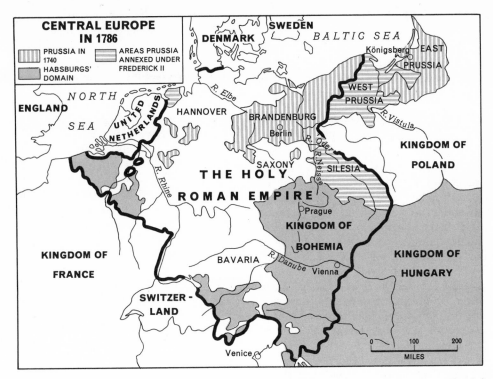

pitifully low living standard of the ruled. And the ruling groups, particularly the state officials, developed some sense of responsibility for their inferiors. There was to be no arbitrariness in the management of the affairs of state. Codified laws told the subjects what to expect, and law courts were established to protect them in whatever rights they were granted. Still, even though this was the beginning of the Rechtsstaat, everything remained based on the authoritarian principle of command and obedience. The few who by birth and ability were destined to rule did so efficiently, but no glimmer of freedom or political initiative penetrated into the garrison-state.

On this Prussian spirit was patterned much that still exists in German life and institutions. The family was authoritarian; pupils were in awe of their teachers. In the country, the Junker landowner held public (police) powers over those living on his estate; in business, the head of the firm became the master; even in such organizations as trade unions and political parties, which were formed later in opposition to the feudal-absolutist regime, functionaries domi-

nated the members. The state official became the model of management to such an extent that the very term *official (Beamter)* is often applied in Germany in fields of private management, for example, "banking officials."

Thus the rising middle classes in Prussia-Germany did not, as in other countries, replace the feudal-authoritarian pattern of life with a liberal-equalitarian one.

The First Defeat of Liberalism

Up to the time of the French Revolution, internal developments in Germany paralleled those in the other Continental countries. Not so in the nineteenth century: no liberal middle class arose then to replace the authoritarian rule of the old powers with a democratic system. In this, German developments paralleled Russian developments, except that Russia never knew a strong movement for liberal democracy. Germany did. The tragedy of her political history was that the liberal movement was unable to defeat its opponents. Instead, it was itself three times beaten.

Frustration of Early Reforms

The first defeat of liberalism occurred after a beginning of reform had been made in Prussia during the Napoleonic era. Defeat of Prussia at Napoleon's hands had shown up the weakness of her authoritarian rigidity as compared with the living forces of a nationalized and revolutionized France. Therefore, more farsighted leaders, foremost among them Freiherr vom Stein (1757–1831), contemplated a kind of revolution from above. Their idea was to modernize state and society by building up democracy from below, locally at first, and then regionally and nationally. All this was intended to give Germans a feeling of participation in public affairs and to make them capable of liberating themselves from the French yoke. Actually, the Prussian serfs were freed, and some measure of self-government was introduced in the cities. But the spirit of reform vanished after victory over Napoleon had been achieved (1813–14). The Prussians had fulfilled their duty on the battlefield, but the rulers forgot their word. The promised constitution never appeared. Reaction restored full rule from above. And while the peasant retained his legal freedom, he did not get land—any more than did the American Negro after his emancipation, or the Russian serf after 1861. There developed that contradiction between legal freedom and economic bondage that Karl Marx was quick to note and apply to his analysis of bourgeois society. The free but landless peasant migrated to the factories of the new industrial cities, where he was exploited to such an extent that the state eventually had to intervene. It did so when it appeared that, owing to the declining health of the urban proletariat, military conscription no longer yielded sufficient numbers of draftees. The King needed soldiers and factory legislation was therefore passed. In Prussia even social policies had a military foundation.

Frustration of Early Nationalism

Thus liberal-democratic hopes were dashed temporarily. So were national aspirations for unification. German nationalism, particularly among German middle-class youth, had emerged as a reaction to Napoleonic rule. Stein and others had the vision of a federated Germany built on a liberal-democratic foundation.

Napoleon himself had unwittingly created a precondition for national unification. At the time of his conquests, many of the smaller territorial states, including all the ecclesiastical principalities, had been consolidated into a number of larger units, and existing larger states had acquired new territory. Prussia at the Congress of Vienna (1815) got Rhineland and Westphalia in western Germany—an area including the potentially rich Ruhr. But, as with internal reform, reaction after 1815 prevented unification. The dynasties, and the nobles and officials allied with them, stood for the maintenance of the sovereign independence of the states. Instead of a unified Germany, a German Confederation (*Deutscher Bund*) was formed. It was a loose federation of German states without direct jurisdiction over inhabitants of member units. Its only organ, the federal diet, was not a representative body of the German people but an assembly of delegates from member states, a permanent conference of ambassadors that proved as incapable of action as had the diet of the defunct Holy Roman Empire. In practice it was chiefly used to suppress the liberal-national movement wherever it lifted its head.

The Second Defeat of Liberalism

The growth of national liberalism was not to be stopped, however, by suppression. With the beginnings of industrialization, agrarian Germany gradually modernized itself. The new industrial middle class demanded a share in government and clamored for national unity, especially since the many internal boundaries hampered trade. Economic unification of much of Germany was attained with the establishment, under Prussian leadership, of a customs union (*Zollverein*) in 1834. When German liberalism joined in the revolutionary tide that swept Europe in 1848, Germany at last seemed ready to join the trend toward constitutionalism and democracy. The failure of the Revolution of 1848 was, instead, the second disaster of German liberalism.

The Failure of 1848

At first, the revolutionary movement swept everything before it. The princes in the capitals were forced to promise constitutions; moreover, they were forced to agree to the convening of an all-German constituent assembly. Issuing from universal manhood elections, it was Germany's first real representative body. In its composition it was typical of German liberalism, which was a movement of the educated classes rather than of the masses. In St. Paul's Church in Frankfurt where the assembly convened, professors, poets, and intellectuals were as plentiful as lawyers are on Capitol Hill. With German thoroughness they began drafting a constitution. Instead of concentrating on setting up some kind of central government with real power and capable of resisting counterrevolutionary tendencies, they labored long over a catalogue of fundamental rights. After its adoption, while they quarreled over whether or not Germany should include Austria, whether it should be a monarchy or a republic, unitary or federalistic, the old powers acted. Armies and officialdom had in the main remained loyal to the dynasties. With their help the princes crushed the liberal forces in Vienna, Berlin, and elsewhere. The King of Prussia, to whom the Emperorship had finally been offered at Frankfurt, refused to accept a "crown of mud." Thereupon, the Frankfurt parliament was dissolved. The middle classes, frightened by the specter of social revolution (although at that time socialist and similar movements were still quite weak in Germany), gave in without further resistance. Those who could not reconcile themselves to a new era of reaction emigrated to America. As in a later period of oppression, Germany lost to other countries the cream of its freedom-loving elite.

The Third Defeat of Liberalism and the Founding of the Empire

Before the unity that German liberals had been unable to achieve was finally established through "blood and iron," liberalism was given another chance. Its failure has influenced the character of German government and politics ever since.

The Prussian Constitution

Among the reforms that had survived the defeat of 1848 were written constitutions, of which the Prussian Constitution of 1849–50 was one. This document reflected the peculiar German type of constitutionalism that has been mentioned before. It issued not from popular sovereignty but from the Crown that granted it. The Crown retained executive power; and while there was to be a parliament, that body had no control over the ministry, which was responsible only to the Crown. An upper house was composed of Junkers, appointed officials, and other dignitaries; a lower house represented the people, but in peculiar fashion: It was elected on the basis of a three-class system under which the handful of voters who paid the highest third of taxes elected one-third of the deputies, those who paid the second third again elected one-third, and the rest, about 85 percent of all voters, the remaining third. This system was devised to perpetuate the rule of the land-owning nobility allied with the wealthy upper bourgeoisie.

The "Prussian Conflict"

Still, the system offered an opening wedge for constitutionalism of the Western type. The test came when, during the European heyday of liberalism in the 1860's, a liberal majority was elected to the lower house in Prussia. This majority decided to establish once and for all its share in government power by rejecting a budget proposed by the conservative cabinet. Significantly, the issue was over appropriations for military service and the organization of the army. It thus affected one of the sacred principles of old Prussianism: the primacy of military affairs and their exemption from civil control. For a fleeting moment it looked as if this conflict between Crown and parliament might be solved as it had been in England in a similar situation two hundred years earlier. King William, unable to find a prime minister ready to fight it out with parliament, was on the point of abdicating when he found his man in the person of Bismarck.

Bismarck

Otto von Bismarck (1815–98) was that rare man who can see and weigh the real forces and chances in politics and use them in a realistic fashion without regard to personal or political prejudices or predilections. A Junker, he stood for authoritarianism. But, unlike his fellow nobles, divine right of kings, legitimism, and similar dogmas meant nothing to him; only power, not principles, counted. While his fellow nobles stood for Prussian sovereignty as against German unity, Bismarck realized that unity must inevitably come. If so, why not under Prussian hegemony? While others might hesitate to resort to force, scheming, and disregard of the law, Bismarck had no such scruples. He took up the fight for the authority of the Crown, ignored the parliamentary rejection of the budget, and enforced the Cabinet's fiscal program, all in violation of the Constitution. He had judged the situation correctly: officials continued to serve, the people continued to pay taxes and obey the laws, and thus the cause of parliament was lost. "Might made right," and this quite literally, for when Bismarck had concluded the struggle victoriously he forced parliament to give its retroactive sanction to his actions.

Unification

Bismarck now proceeded to forge German unity on the same iron basis on which he had reaffirmed authoritarianism. This meant fighting it out with the one power that opposed German unity under Prussian hegemony: Austria. The polarization of power in the German Confederation in two superpowers that dominated the smaller states as satellites could be settled, in Bismarck's view, only by armed contest. Once more disregarding a charter (this time that of the German Confederation), he took up the battle with its entire membership, and again might made right: After Austria's defeat (1866), a number of German states (Hanover, Hesse-Kassel, and others) were incorporated into Prussia. With the rest of the states in North Germany, Prussia now founded what amounted to a genuinely federal (not merely confederate) unit, the North German Federation. Its Constitution foreshadowed that of the second Empire. This Empire (*Deutsches Reich*) was soon established through the accession of the South German states to the North German Federation at the conclusion of the war against France (1870–71). German unity was finally achieved.

These events had a lasting impact on Ger-

mans. To many they seemed to prove the inherent weakness of popular forces and the invincibility of the established powers of army and state: force is what counts in history; without its use the cherished aim of national unity could not have been achieved. In exchange for unity, the German middle class reconciled itself to a continued lack of domestic freedom. Democracy now appeared as a mirage that for a while had misled Germans but in the long run had been unable to seduce them. The black-red-gold flag of the old liberal movement and of 1848 was remembered at best as a symbol of a romantic dream. Its place was taken by the black-white-red (in which the black-white of Prussia predominated) of the new German Empire. In the words of Golo Mann (Thomas Mann's historian-son), the Empire's "origin was violent, its constitution jerry-built, its society garrulous, its government cesaristic, with Power and Success its new Gods."[3]

2. GERMANY AS AN EMPIRE (1871–1918)

There are eras in the history of nations that particularly affect the character of their lives, of their societies, and of their political institutions. For the Germans such a period began when they achieved unity in 1871. That period constitutes a great divide. It was during those years that Western nations moved toward liberal democracy but Germany maintained and reinforced the authoritarian status quo. The Empire gave the Germans their first chance to live together as a stable, unified nation and to enter world politics as a great power. While in the same period Britain and France consolidated a pattern against which any antidemocratic tendencies and movements had to struggle, in Germany a pattern was set against which democracy had to struggle. This is what hampered Weimar democracy and to some extent still hampers that of Bonn. There is nothing to the stereotype that Germans are authoritarian by nature, but many were made so under and by the Empire. Hence its importance for present-day German conditions.

[3] Golo Mann, "The First Partition," *Die Zeit* (July 1, 1966).

Bismarck's Constitution

The imperial Constitution was unique in that it combined authoritarianism with federalism. That the Reich was genuinely federal, and not a loose confederation, appeared from the existence of central Reich organs and powers and from the fact that Reich laws were directly binding upon each citizen. But it differed from democratic federalism in that sovereignty, instead of residing in the people, rested with the princes of the member states, who were represented in the primary federal organ, the Federal Council (*Bundesrat*). However, being federal, the Empire could not be an autocracy. The Emperor (*Kaiser*), symbol of the Reich's unity, was checked by the Bundesrat, and also by the only democratic-representative institution of the plan, the Federal Diet (*Reichstag*). Thus the Constitution blended contrasting elements: federalism and hegemony, federalism and authoritarianism, and, lastly, authoritarianism and some measure of democracy.

The Reich and the Member States

Federalism was genuine, and states' rights were strong. Most of the administration of internal affairs remained under state jurisdiction, with the Reich's powers restricted to foreign affairs and certain economic matters. And even where the Reich had jurisdiction to legislate uniformly (for example, in civil, commercial, and criminal law), there was established a principle which to this day has been a peculiar feature of German government: The member states, generally, are in charge of the administration and execution of federal laws. Federal legislation thus does not usually require the establishment, as it does in the United States, of corresponding federal administration. To the ordinary citizen of the Empire, therefore, *state* still meant primarily the member state and its bureaucracy. But the tendency toward centralization, which characterizes modern federalism everywhere, developed in the Empire too. Financially the Reich, which at first depended on contributions from the states, grew gradually more independent, and this was the basis for more independence in everything.

But the increase in Reich powers meant little as long as Prussia played a dominant role in Reich affairs. The main body through which Prussian influence was exercised was the Bundesrat. This council was not a representative assembly with delegates elected by people or parliaments of member states (as, for example, the United States Senate), but consisted of delegates —usually high government officials—appointed and instructed by the governments (that is, the princes) of the member states. The votes of the twenty-five states were weighted, with Prussia having seventeen out of fifty-eight. Since Prussia could usually count on votes from smaller states, it held a strong position. Most important, it could block constitutional amendments, since fourteen votes sufficed to defeat an amendment. The council not only shared lawmaking power (with the Reichstag) but also had important executive functions, including the power to enact executive ordinances.

The Reich Executive

In the field of executive power, Prussia's influence was exercised through the Kaiser. Since the Prussian King was automatically the Kaiser, whatever powers he lacked as Kaiser he could indirectly exercise as King of the dominant state. As Kaiser, for example, he had no share in Reich legislation, but he could influence legislation through the Prussian votes in the Bundesrat. His other powers included foreign affairs, command of the armed forces, and appointing the Reich Chancellor.

The relation between Kaiser and Chancellor depended on their respective personalities. While theoretically the Chancellor was completely the creature of the Kaiser, who could appoint and dismiss him regardless of parties, majorities, or any other influences, as long as Bismarck was at the helm the relation resembled the British pattern, with Kaiser William I submitting to the political dominance of the Chancellor. The relation changed with the advent of William II (1888–1918). This capricious and egotistic monarch preferred pliable executors of his personal regime.

The Chancellor headed no cabinet of the British or French type but was rather chief of a number of secretaries who headed executive departments. His position thus resembled the relationship between an American President and his department heads, but with one crucial difference: the President's mandate issues from the electorate, while the Chancellor's mandate issued solely from his monarch. The Chancellor invariably was a high nobleman, officer, or official. The Reich bureaucracy, over which he presided, was staffed largely with Prussians. No party leaders, and very few representatives of other than the noble and official classes, could expect appointment to higher office. The Reich as well as Prussia was thus ruled by conservative forces. There *was* self-government in the cities, and some liberal, even parliamentary, beginnings in southwestern member states. But in the Empire as a whole the Conservatives were perennially in power.

Parliament and Parties

At face value, parliament (that is, the Federal Diet, or Reichstag) was a strangely democratic island in an authoritarian environment. It was exceptional in Germany (and in most of Europe, for that matter) in that it was based on universal manhood suffrage. Bismarck probably desired a strong popular symbol of German

unity against any too strongly particularist or even secessionist tendencies on the part of princes and member states. Also, he may have hoped that universal suffrage might turn out in favor of conservatives rather than liberals, since the Junkers controlled the rural vote.

The trouble was that the Reichstag's influence was slim, and chiefly negative. It had no power over the executive, and criticism and opposition were therefore pointless. It did have authority, with Bundesrat concurrence, to enact federal laws and pass the federal budget; to this extent, even a Bismarck had to have parliamentary majorities. Yet his (or his successors') position remained vastly different from that of a parliamentary prime minister. His mandate continued to issue from the monarch and not from the Reichstag. In only one instance did an adverse vote induce a Chancellor to resign, and that failed to become a precedent. To get the laws he wanted passed, the Chancellor simply manipulated the parties and their leaders. Bismarck, in particular, was a master at this sort of juggling. His task was made easier because

Reichstag Election Results Under the Empire

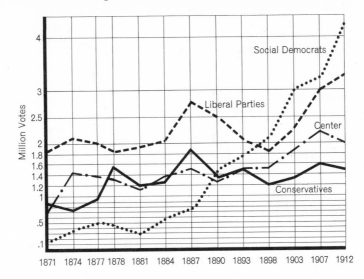

the parties, never being allowed to assume true governmental responsibilities, had little incentive to organize themselves into stable majorities or minorities in support of, or in opposition to, the government. Party leaders themselves could never hope to be called into responsible executive positions. To win them and their groups, handouts and concessions would usually turn the trick, and if worse came to worst, the Reichstag could be dissolved. Debates at times were furious, but usually futile. Under this system Germans had no chance to learn the ways of responsible government.

The Rulers

The success of a modern government may be measured by its ability to integrate economic and social classes into a nation. From this view the Empire was not an unqualified success. True, there was that admirable efficiency (the inheritance from Prussia) with which the state and everything within it was organized. This efficiency lent an appearance of strength and stability. But the Empire failed to integrate the forces that rose during its sway.

While at the time of its foundation the Reich was still more rural than urban, more small-town than big-city, more handicraft and small-factory than giant-enterprise, it soon changed into one of the world's foremost industrial, trad-

ing, banking, urbanized countries. Heavy industry based on coal and steel, and chemical, electrical, machinery, textile, and optical factories, changed the countryside; and the rise of the industrial classes, managers, white-collar employees, and, above all, industrial workers changed the social landscape. The class of big landowners (Junkers) lost proportionally in economic weight. But it did not lose its social and political power. That it could maintain that power into the industrial age was due to an arrangement between the old ruling powers and the bourgeoisie, under which the old powers retained political control, while the middle classes resigned themselves to the existing, authoritarian type of government in return for economic freedom and protection.

The National Liberals

This compromise, like the Constitution itself, was the work of Bismarck. After their defeat in the Prussian conflict, the middle classes in the main gave up the idea of constitutional reform. A split occurred in the political party that represented these classes, the Liberal party. Its majority became the National Liberal party, and an uncompromising left wing established itself as the Progressive party but subsequently failed to attain any large voting strength or influence. (It was this group, however, which guarded the tradition of 1848 and carried its ideas over into the subsequent, Weimar, period.) The National Liberals, on the other hand, represented that combination of economic enterprise and submission to established authority that became typical of German businessmen.

These National Liberals no longer had much in common with the liberal nationalists of the early nineteenth century. Nationalism had then meant unification; it now turned expansionist, imperialist, aggressive, and even racialist. The earlier political liberalism had been crushed. Bismarck thus could base the first decade of his rule over the Reich on collaboration with a chastened neoliberalism. It had adopted his political framework and now assisted him in his battle against political Catholicism and against Socialism (see below). Its reward was legislation that guaranteed legal security and freedom from executive interference in business activities.

Imperialism

But here difficulties loomed. Increasing competition from grain-producing countries overseas threatened German agriculture and therewith the economic basis of the Junkers. The Junkers clamored for protection. When the National Liberal bourgeoisie refused to yield to this demand, Bismarck, as suddenly as he had previously dropped conservative in favor of liberal backing, dissolved his liberal alignment in favor of renewed collaboration with conservatives. And again he split his adversaries: with protection for agriculture he combined protection for part of industry, mainly heavy industry. This economic alliance of Junkers and steel led to liberal-conservative reconciliation on the basis of high tariffs. Trading, especially export, interests were assuaged by the new imperialism, economic and political, which became the landmark of William II's era. William's naval program satisfied imperialists as well as those interests that throve on navy orders. In this way, most economic interests were satisfied on the basis of state intervention, protection, and expansion.

The chief dangers of this system arose in foreign affairs. German imperialism was clumsy in its diplomatic aspects; its emphasis on prestige and its aggressive temper antagonized major powers. The cautious and moderate policy that Bismarck had inaugurated after 1871 gave way to William II's swaggering foreign policy, which was largely influenced, or at least backed, by a nationalistic middle class, and provided this group with the vicarious satisfaction of political ambitions unsatisfied at home. Organizations such as the Pan-German League, which specialized in mass agitation for the new imperialism, were largely middle class in character and membership. When the danger became apparent, some among the middle classes began to voice opposition, but to no avail. William was protected from criticism, and his chancellors could not alter his basic policies.

Infeudation of the Middle Class

Internal political control was maintained by the authoritarian classes—the Junkers and their allies—partly through the Conservative party, partly, and more importantly, through a process that may be called the infeudation of the upper-middle class. The Conservative party, backed by nobility, army, officialdom, Protestant clergy, and part of the peasantry and of the middle classes, was merely the parliamentary arm of the ruling groups; it was grudgingly organized after 1848, when it appeared that nonconservatives had become politically vocal. Since the agrarian Junkers became numerically insignificant in the new industrial society, it was important to draw from other classes, particularly the upper-middle classes, sufficient numbers of people who would assist the nobles in ruling Germany through the army and the higher bureaucracy. To qualify, a nonnoble had to be imbued with the standards and prejudices of the old classes through a long process of "education to be a gentleman." He would first go through higher education at the *Gymnasium* (the high school for the upper and middle, not the lower, classes), and then enter a university and try to join one of the select fraternities. Equipped with a dueling scar, a commission as a reserve officer, and legal training, he would be ready for apprenticeship in administration or a similar field. To top it off, there might follow marriage into one of the old families. Promotion would likewise depend on these factors. At each step care was taken that only the right persons were selected. Catholics and Jews were seldom admitted, and none with unorthodox opinions. Prussians and Protestants were preferred.

The Ruled

The Proletariat

Within this pattern German society was deeply split. The average German during the Empire was prosperous, and the living standard of all classes was rising. The paternal state took care to provide some measure of security for those in distress. A comprehensive system of social security, including health and old-age insurance, workmen's compensation, and factory legislation, was devised in order to prevent social unrest. But it was a grudging paternalism. There was no question of admitting the lower classes to social equality, let alone allowing them to share in political power. The rising tide of the proletariat filled the ruling classes with fear, which was answered by sullen hostility on the part of the workers. Most of them joined the socialist movement through the Marxian Social Democratic party (SPD). Bismarck's attempt to suppress it after 1878 indirectly strengthened it. Driven underground, it now had its martyrs and it emerged into legality stronger than before. But, although it maintained an attitude of total opposition to the existing regime, its revolutionary doctrine slowly assumed the character of a "Sunday" creed, which was paid lip service at meetings and in publications. On workdays, however, Socialists were more interested in improving the worker's living standard through trade unions. The worker acquired a vested interest in society through what the state granted by social legislation and through what he wrested himself from the employer. He turned reformist, but socially and politically he remained an outcast.

Other Outcast Groups

Others besides the workers were forced into passivity or hostility. There were the tenants and agricultural workers on the eastern estates, many of them Catholic Poles, whose nationality and religion were two more reasons for discrimination. The Poles as well as the (likewise Catholic) inhabitance of Alsace-Lorraine were viewed with distrust. German Catholicism, a minority in the Reich, felt threatened and organized itself in the Center party. To Bismarck this seemed dangerous for the unity of the Reich. Backed by the National Liberals (who feared clericalism), he tried to destroy political Catholicism, but the Church and its organizations survived this culture struggle (*Kulturkampf*, as the anti-Catholics called it) as successfully as the Socialists survived Bismarck's anti-Socialist policies. Still, Catholics continued to be discriminated against in administrative appointments, and the interests of predominantly Catholic member states and regions were often neglected.

Toward the end of the Hohenzollern era, many Germans became aware of the cracks in German society and apprehensive of the danger into which the adventurous foreign policy of the regime was bound to lead them. As long as criticism was voiced only by leftists, the ruling class could allow them to complain, since it controlled the main instrumentalities of opinion, the schools, and the universities. But criticism became more ominous when it was voiced by Heidelberg professors, such as Germany's great sociologist Max Weber (1864–1920), or by rulers of big industrial combines, such as the industrialist and author Walther Rathenau (1867–1922). Such people realized the two-pronged danger inherent in foreign adventures and internal authoritarianism, and questioned whether it would be possible to steer the state through stormy waters while at the same time rejecting participation by the majority of the people. Toward the end of the era, responsible people began to think of constitutional reforms, especially the introduction of parliamentary government. But when it came, in the final stages of World War I, it was too late.

3. GERMANY AS A REPUBLIC (1918–33)

"Bonn is not Weimar," the title of a well-known book on present West Germany, points up the connection between the first German experiment in democracy and the current one. While it is true that the latter has tried to distinguish itself from the former by avoiding its mistakes, it is also true that much in the present setup can be traced back to the earlier one. The Weimar period provided the only democratic-parliamentary experience on which present

German democracy could build. Moreover, many problems that confronted the first German republic still seem to confront nations trying to solve burning questions of our time, such as capitalism versus socialism, or how to defend democracy against totalitarianism without destroying the bases of freedom itself. To analyze the Weimar system, assess its merits, and account for its failure is still of more than historical concern.

Emergence and Character of the Weimar System

In November 1918, under the impact of defeat in World War I, William II and the other princes abdicated, and a group of socialist leaders (right- and left-wing Social Democrats) proclaimed a republic and set up a provisional government. Following general elections a constituent assembly adopted the Weimar Constitution in the summer of 1919.

The choice of the Thuringian town of Weimar (from which came the unofficial name of

the republic) as meeting place of the assembly emphasized the difficulties as well as the hopes of the fledgling republic. The capital, Berlin, was found unsuitable for drafting a constitution because it was in the throes of bitter street fights between leftist radicals and their opponents, with the former opposed to constitution-making by parliamentary procedure. Weimar, the town where Goethe and Schiller had lived, was chosen instead, in hopes that a new spirit, symbolizing Germany's cultural heritage, might henceforth replace the spirit of Potsdam, residence of the Prussian kings.

The fulfillment of this hope presented a difficult task indeed. German democrats were faced from the start with a military defeat, a severe peace treaty (the Peace of Versailles, 1919), a deep social and political division of the German people, and ensuing internal disorder. They had to contend with Germany's isolation in foreign affairs, the vindictive attitude of her former enemies, a heavy financial burden caused by reparations, and an ensuing currency inflation that further increased internal dissatisfaction. Even more burdensome was the legacy of

authoritarianism. The old powers at first seemed discredited. But after a short time the memory of the previous regime's shortcomings faded, while the glories of the authoritarian past continued to be recalled. These glories were contrasted with present miseries, which, instead of being attributed to the failure of the previous regime, came to be blamed on the new one. German democracy thus was burdened both with the psychological handicap of being born of defeat in war and with economic conditions that compared unfavorably with those prevailing under the Empire. Thus it was exposed from the outset to merciless attacks from both the left and the right.

In fairness, the difficulties of those Germans who stood for Weimar should be kept in mind by those who would censure them for their eventual failure. At least they made a heroic effort. It was not, as has been sneeringly said, a "Republic without Republicans." And it would not seem that the experiment was doomed from the beginning. The Republic was heir to an important trend in German history, the trend that led from the early freedom movements of the Napoleonic age to 1848. Dormant under the Empire, this liberal trend now emerged as the untried alternative to a system found wanting. As in the case of France's Third Republic, there was no reason to believe that Germany might not have grown, under favorable circumstances, into habits of democratic government. But bad luck seemed to stalk it from its inception.

Democracy or Proletarian Dictatorship?

The Weimar system was not based on revolutionary action. The so-called revolution of 1918 meant simply the disappearance of the old powers (Emperor, princes, and their governments) without much pressure from the German masses. The old administrative machinery with most of its incumbents remained. Even the generals remained. There was left a political void now filled by the Republic. But what kind of Republic? Here the first problem arose. Revolutionary socialists, who formed the radical wing of the Social Democratic party and soon split away from it as Communists, wanted a proletarian dictatorship exercised by the councils of workers and soldiers, which had sprung up in Germany in the fall of 1918 and which

they hoped to control. The failure of uprisings they staged in the winter of 1918–19, however, showed that they did not carry with them the majority of workers, let alone the German people. The defeat of leftist radicalism opened the way for the second alternative: the establishment of a democratic republic.

Unfortunately for the future of German democracy, the Communists had been the only active revolutionary group. To beat them the Social Democrats had called upon generals and reactionary nationalist groups armed by the generals. Perhaps there was no alternative, since the republican masses were unarmed; yet the Social Democrats might have tried to arm these masses. In any event, it was a bad omen for the future of democratic government that it owed its birth to the intervention of its own rightist enemies.

Framing the Constitution

For the time being, however, the way was clear for the framing of a constitution. The Constitution, adopted by the Constituent Assembly at Weimar in 1919, was the work of three parties that together had obtained a large majority at its election: the Social Democrats, the Center party, and the Democratic party, heir to the Empire's Progressives and now the rallying point of the middle classes fearful of leftist radicalism. This election was important for two reasons. First, neither the radical left (the Independent Socialists, a split-off from the Social Democrats who subsequently rejoined them), nor the antirepublican rightists (chiefly the Conservatives, under their new label of German Nationalists) made a good showing. Second, the socialists (Social Democrats, Independents) failed to attain a majority. (The newly formed Communist party had boycotted the election.) Consequently, Germany's new structure had to be devised by a coalition of socialists and nonsocialists, workers and middle class. The German people had voted for "law and order." But what kind of law? What kind of order?

The Underlying Compromise

Bismarck's Reich had been founded on an understanding between the authoritarian forces, which would go on ruling politically, and the upper-middle class, which obtained freedom in the economic sphere. In similar fashion Weimar was based on a compromise, this time between the working class, as represented by Social Democrats and trade union leaders, and the middle class, acting through leading industrialists. The basis of agreement was the acceptance of the new, parliamentary-democratic framework of government. But it was an uneasy, and to some extent ambiguous, compromise. To the Social Democrats, for instance, a formal agreement between industrial and trade union leaders that had established the trade unions as equal partners in collective bargaining constituted the minimum from which to start in the direction of socialism. The entire Social Democratic program was predicated on the expectation that eventually there would be a chance to legislate socialism into existence. But to the industrialists this agreement seemed to be the maximum concession. Would they be ready to accept a contrary vote in good faith?

In addition, the underlying compromise was endangered from outside forces. Communist opposition from the left forced the Social Democrats to continue to stress full socialism as their final aim. This, in turn, frightened the middle class, with portions of it now joining the opposition from the right, which from the outset had been hostile to the new constitutional pattern. The Weimar system thus became ever more endangered from the right as well as the left. It was on this shaky and narrowing foundation that the Weimar Constitution rested.

The Constitution as such was one of the most progressive of its time. It provided for many procedures and institutions of democracy, and its liberal orientation was emphasized by its elaborate code of civil and political liberties. It established progressive standards for social and economic policies. Its main shortcoming was its eclecticism; the makers of the Weimar Constitution seem to have hoped for the best of all possible worlds. There were borrowings from America, Britain, and France, but they failed to blend. Instead of a simple parliamentary system, for example, there was a counterweight to parliament in the office of an independent president, but without clear indication as to whether the executive branch should be responsible to parliament or to the president.

Weimar Federalism: Reich and Länder

First on the agenda at Weimar was the problem of Germany's territorial organization. What was to become of the member states? The age-old particularistic traditions and interests prevented any dismemberment of Prussia or absorption of all states into a unitary state; the federal structure of the Reich was maintained. But in contrast to the Bismarck Constitution, the central government emerged with strong powers. There remained hardly a field in which the Reich (this term denoting central government, as contrasted to that of the states, now called *Länder*, or, in the singular, *Land*), could not exercise legislative functions if it so desired. To the Länder there chiefly remained administration of the federal laws. But even here many new Reich administrations with their own federal bureaucracies were set up.

The federal Constitution, moreover, prescribed that the internal structure of the Land governments would be republican and parliamentary. This did not mean, however, that Länder policies were always in agreement with Reich policies. Their political differentiation, rather than any pronounced sectional differences, made the Länder politically important during the Weimar period. Thus Prussia, in direct contrast to her Empire temper, became the stronghold of the moderate left, while Bavaria developed to the right of center.

A strengthening of central power also resulted from the abolition of Prussian hegemony. There was no longer a strong, Prussian-dominated army. What remained of the army was Reich-controlled. There was no Emperor through whom Prussia could exercise influence, nor was there a Bundesrat in which Prussia ruled. In the financial sphere, where the old Reich had been dependent on the states, the Länder now became dependent on the Reich, with its own major sources of income. The Reich government also possessed strong powers of supervision and enforcement. Its power to resort to sanctions against a recalcitrant Land was much used, and abused, whenever a Land government became too radically leftist. In cases of "rightist deviation" one was inclined to use milder methods.

A federal council (Reichsrat) was the organ

through which Länder interests were to be safe-guarded on the Reich level. Like its predecessor, the Bundesrat, the Reichsrat was composed of delegates instructed by the Länder governments. Since government in the Länder was now parliamentary, the delegates represented governing parties rather than the states as such. Yet, in practice, they acted chiefly as bureaucrats trying to bring Reich interests into accordance with those of the Länder. The Reichsrat's suspensive veto over legislation, which the Reichstag could override by a two-thirds vote, was seldom used.

Parliament and Its Powers

The old Empire had placed sovereignty in the princes, under Prussian leadership. The Weimar Constitution placed sovereignty in the people. But how is a modern, large-scale nation to exercise sovereignty? The classical European system is that of government by assembly: A representative body, issuing from a general election, acts as the sole mandatary of the people; all other organs of government must be under its control.

A Mixed System

The French have always been inclined toward such a system. The Germans feared it would mean government by parties and party bosses and therefore sought a compromise. This can be seen most clearly in the way in which they tried to solve the crucial problem of modern democratic government, the relation between parliament and executive. This relationship had seen three or four basic types of development in the West: the American system of presidential democracy based on the separation of powers; the British system of government responsible to Parliament, but with the Cabinet having the power to dissolve Parliament; the system prevailing under the French Third Republic, a parliamentary system in which the Cabinet did *not* have the actual power to dissolve parliament; and the Swiss system, under which the executive always follows the instructions of parliament and does not resign even in case of disagreement. Weimar chiefly followed the British system: The Cabinet was to be responsible

to the Reichstag, which, in turn, could be dissolved by the executive. In contrast to Britain, however, such parliamentarism in Germany, with its many parties, involved the danger of Cabinet instability of the French type. The Weimar Constitution therefore sought to render the executive strong and, to some extent, independent of the Reichstag; this constituted an American admixture. From the Swiss system were added certain devices of direct democracy, under which the people, through plebiscites, were to participate in legislation. In practice this device was chiefly used for purposes of demagoguery on the part of extremist movements.

Reichstag and Proportional Representation

Despite these restrictions, the Reichstag was the keystone of the arch. In it the will of the people was to be reflected from the broadest basis of election. Women were now given the right to vote. The voting age was lowered from twenty-five to twenty. And, most important of all, election was by proportional representation, with each group of voters given an equal chance of being represented according to its voting strength at the polls. Each 60,000 votes elected one candidate from lists submitted by the parties in large election districts; whether a party gained a majority in the district was immaterial. Each party got as many seats as resulted from dividing its number of votes by 60,000.

This system has been attacked by some as a main cause for the decline of the Republic. It is true that its virtue of representing relative party strength and political opinion more fairly than do other systems (which give political minorities less of a chance) was canceled out by its faults of favoring party bureaucracy—which made up the lists of candidates—rendering the individual candidate a mere number on a list, intensifying doctrinal differences, and making it easier for splinter groups to get representation in parliament. But even under the single-member-district system of the Empire, Germans had been used to voting for party rather than for individual candidates, and the system had produced about as many (and about the same) major parties as appeared under Weimar. Proportional representation can hardly be held responsible for customs deeply rooted in German history.

The Reichstag had comprehensive powers. It made the laws, adopted the budget, consented to treaties, and made continuance in office of the Cabinet and each minister dependent on its confidence. But its power was not unlimited. It was checked slightly by the devices of direct democracy, somewhat more by the powers of the Reichsrat, and most of all by those of the President (and of the Cabinet when availing itself of presidential powers).

The Executive

The Cabinet

The position of the Weimar executive (the Reich President and the Reich government, consisting of the Reich Chancellor and Cabinet ministers) did not seem to deviate much from the established pattern of parliamentarism. Chancellor and ministers were responsible to the Reichstag. The President's powers included representation of the Reich in foreign affairs, supreme command of the armed forces, and—the *raison d'être* of a presidency in a republic—appointment (and dismissal) of Chancellor, ministers, and other high officials. But all presidential actions needed the countersignature of the Chancellor or a minister. Since these persons in turn were responsible to parliament, presidential measures supposedly were within the range of parliamentary control.

Actually, during much of the Republic's life, and particularly in the "normal" period of 1924–29, the system functioned approximately as it was supposed to. The President used his powers sparingly and in political matters generally deferred to the Cabinet. The Cabinet depended on coalitions of parties which, among them, had a majority in the Reichstag. As in France, Cabinet policies were based on uneasy agreements between coalition partners; the Cabinet tended to be an alliance rather than a coherent unit, and to fall through internal dissensions more often than through outright defeat by parliamentary opposition. Cabinets therefore usually did not last long; but in personnel and composition the new Cabinet often resembled the preceding one. The Chancellor, no longer the autocrat as in imperial times, was supposed

under the Constitution to determine the general lines of the government's policies, but in practice he hardly did even that. His main concern was to keep the coalition going.

Parties and Bureaucracy

Real decisions were made in the party caucuses. The party bureaucracy, in contrast to the old Reich, was now in possession of the key political positions. But unlike their British counterparts, those manning the ministries were recruited, not from and through parliament as a school for political leadership, but rather directly from the ranks of party functionaries or related interest groups, such as trade unions and employers' associations. Great leaders, parliamentary or otherwise, were conspicuously absent. It was, by and large, honest government, but colorless, without vision or a long-range program, and unable to inspire enthusiasm. Moreover, it owed much of its efficiency to the permanent officialdom working under it. Party leaders holding ministerial posts were generally inexpert and therefore dependent upon the established civil service, where the unpolitical—meaning conservative or even reactionary—outlook prevailed. With certain exceptions (the Prussian police was one) the bureaucracy was not democratized. This would have required the gradual infusion of new blood and the elimination of at least the most stubborn reactionary officials. The wish not to have its efficient functioning impaired even for the sake of reform, however, prevented the Weimar Republic, as it did the Western Allies a generation later, from providing a new basis for a working democracy.

The Presidency

How, under this half-parliamentary, half-bureaucratic system, political authoritarianism eventually reemerged victorious is chiefly the story of the role played by the Weimar presidency. Even during the period of constitutional normalcy, until 1930, the President enjoyed considerable influence. Thus, although the small professional army (*Reichswehr*) which the Treaty of Versailles allowed Germany to have was supposedly under the civilian control of Cabinet ministers of defense responsible to parliament, in practice defense ministers, backed by the President as supreme commander, evaded parliamentary supervision. This was possible because of the widespread German desire for a President above parties and interest groups. His prestige protected authoritarian tendencies.

Two constitutional provisions contributed to this development. One was that the President should be elected by direct popular vote and for a period longer than that of the Reichstag (seven, as against four, years); the other concerned his emergency powers. Popular election meant giving the President a mandate independent from that of the Reichstag. This was hazardous in a country where the executive had traditionally represented antidemocratic groups. While in America the President often represents the commonweal as opposed to special interests entrenched in Congress, in Germany the election of a President (such as, in 1925, of Paul von Hindenburg [1847–1934], the old World War I hero) could appear as a sanction of conservatism and nationalism. Although Hindenburg waited five years before he showed his authoritarian predilections, little incidents early made clear the difference between his attitude and that of a head of state in Britain or France. For instance, when the left initiated a popular vote on the expropriation of the former princes' holdings, Hindenburg expressed his opposition in an open letter. Compare this public intervention in favor of one group of parties with British custom, under which the King may not even marry without the consent of the Cabinet.

Article 48 and Presidential Dictatorship

Many critics believe that Article 48 of the Weimar Constitution, which provided the President with emergency powers in case of constitutional deadlock, opened the way for dictatorship. This article was in fact used in the late years of the Republic to sidetrack parliamentary government in a way never attempted in Britain since the days of the Stuarts. But the existence of an emergency provision meant less than the circumstances that invited its misuse. Article 48 was even designed to prevent such misuse. Every emergency measure was to be communicated immediately to the Reichstag, which had the power to revoke it; it was to be a temporary suspension of ordinary constitu-

tional processes in order to save the Constitution as such.

But Article 48 was too broadly interpreted from the outset. Instead of being used as a safety valve, it served as an easy way out of ordinary difficulties. Economic or financial "emergencies" were construed as sufficient reasons to issue decrees instead of resorting to the enactment of ordinary laws. The time came when the President failed to obtain parliamentary approval for his measures. According to the Constitution he should then have yielded to the Reichstag. But the power of dissolution provided him with a way out. If he found a Chancellor ready to back him and defy the Reichstag majority (shades of William I and Bismarck!), he might dissolve the Reichstag and appeal to the people instead of canceling his emergency measures. What if the election failed to provide him with a majority? Could he keep his Chancellor in office and dissolve the newly elected Reichstag again? This obviously would mean flouting the will of the people and the sense of the Constitution, but that is what happened at the final stages of the Weimar Republic. In this way the chief executive's theoretical limitations were circumvented.

Basic Rights

The Constitution contained an elaborate catalogue of "fundamental rights and duties" that was meant to protect individuals and groups against the state.

The traditional political rights and freedoms, such as freedom from arbitrary arrest, of opinion, of the press, of association, and of assembly, were specified in the Constitution. But these rights were not protected, as they are in the United States, against infraction by law. Ordinary legislation, federal or Länder, could define, limit, or even suspend these rights. While in normal times these rights were respected, as they had already been to some extent under the Empire, there was little guarantee that they would be respected during the abnormal times that came to be more and more normal. Liberalism then vanished before "necessity of state."

In addition there was a catalogue of so-called social rights that was intended to solve some of the chief problems with which the Republic was faced: socialism versus private capitalism, secularism versus church influence, large estates versus land reform. However, the Constitution was drafted by a coalition of opposed interests whose agreements were mostly verbal and whose compromises really deferred decisions.

Thus, in the economic field, the Reich was accorded the right to nationalize industries, and the workers were assured of the right to participate in the regulation not only of labor conditions but of general economic issues. On the other hand, private property was guaranteed against expropriation without full compensation. In practice, there was no socialism through nationalization of industries, but rather private capitalism with some admixture of social reform; no workers' participation in planning or regulation of economic affairs, but only participation in the regulation of labor conditions through factory councils. There was no agrarian reform, no breakup or control of cartels, and no curtailment of the privileges of the bureaucracy or of the recognized churches. Not much had been solved; basic conflicts remained.

Social and Political Forces

During the more peaceful middle period of the Republic it seemed as if these conflicts might yet be solved gradually through compromise. In a period of prosperity and normalcy (1924–30), important sections of the population shared the fruits of a revived economy. The system of the middle 1920's was based on favors to industry, big landowners, and industrial workers alike. High tariffs, subsidies, and big profits (based in part on price fixing by powerful combines or cartels of industry) went hand in hand with an improvement of labor conditions through collective bargaining. But the lower-middle classes, the professions, the small savers, had lost their holdings during the galloping inflation of 1920–23. Little was done to help them. Their savings had enabled them to live better than the workers and to give their children a higher education. Now they were on the financial level of the proletariat, but they refused to consider themselves proletarians. They became hostile and frustrated, as did many small peasants, small businessmen, artisans, and shopkeepers.

Another inheritance from the years of post-war turmoil was nationalist activism. The defeat of the Communists in 1918–19 was credited to rightist action, rather than to the feeble Republic. Subsequently, the nationalist radicals posed as saviors of the national interest whenever anybody whom they considered treacherous appeared on the scene. They organized vigilantes, tried republican statesmen and others in kangaroo courts, and assassinated them. In ensuing court trials the judiciary often made a mockery of justice by letting rightist "patriotism" stand above republican legality.

The Constitutional Crisis

What social and political harmony there was under Weimar ended abruptly when depression struck Germany at the end of 1929. Industrialists refused to let the state intervene in order to provide employment. Even at the height of depression the orthodoxy of the balanced budget was preserved. By 1932 there were ten million unemployed in a nation of sixty-five million.

The economic crisis created a political and constitutional crisis. In the face of mounting radicalism on the right (Nazis) and on the left (Communists), the upper-middle classes turned right, believing that the way to cope with Communism was by force rather than by social aid and reform. Denouncing even moderately progressive and mildly liberal forces as "red," they calculated that only by establishing authoritarian government could they now hope to preserve the existing system of property. They desired to rule with the help of bureaucracy and military; instead they opened the gates to the flood of Nazi totalitarianism. Hindenburg, dismissing a Social Democratic chancellor who commanded a majority, and appointing a Center party leader of conservative leanings (Brüning) in his stead, inaugurated the system of presidential government (1930). But the election of 1930 showed that the masses in distress were no longer under the control of the authoritarians; they had turned to more radical movements. Nazi representation rose from twelve to a hundred and seven, that of Communists from fifty-four to seventy-seven. Yet there still existed ample opportunity to form a common front against these two extreme groups. Only after the July election of 1932 did Nazis and Communists combined have a so-called negative majority that could have stalled the parliamentary machinery. But the conservatives were unwilling to join forces with the republicans. They now ruled by decree, on the basis of Article 48, and the Social Democrats, still (with a hundred and forty-three deputies) the strongest party, backed them as the lesser evil.

Thus Chancellor Brüning even as late as 1932 had some kind of majority, although he refused to consider the Reichstag the real fountainhead of his authority. His authority, according to the new doctrine of the presidential system, lay in the confidence of the President. But when he was unable to persuade the Nazis to join the authoritarian regime, he was suddenly dismissed by Hindenburg, and a Junker, von Papen, was appointed. His "cabinet of barons" had not the slightest chance of majority backing in parliament. There followed the tragicomedy of repeated dissolutions and new elections, with the monarchist-feudal group temporarily in the saddle, trying to ward off revolution from left and right. The extreme groups organized themselves as states within the state, as "movements" with their own doctrines and loyalties and their own armed paramilitary formations, complete with emblems, slogans, and uniforms. To the right were the Nazis, with brown shirts and swastikas; to the left the Communists, with "red front" organization and hammer and sickle. On the defensive were the conservative nationalists, with a Steel Helmet veterans' organization and the imperial black-white-red flag symbol; and, belatedly and timidly, the Social Democrats and other republicans with their Reich Banner organization featuring, for once, the black-red-gold Weimar colors.

In the face of this pluralism the state was ever less able to control the antagonistic forces. As territorial powers in olden times had disrupted Germany, political factions now seemed to lead it to disintegration. An atmosphere of civil war prevailed. In the daily clashes between the armed gangs, the Nazis, usually the attackers, were openly favored by the authorities. The only force potentially still siding with the republican left was the Prussian police. The Presidential Cabinet, deposing the legitimate Prussian government with the help of Article 48, got control of this last bulwark of democracy. This outrage might have aroused the non-Nazi and non-Communist masses against the dictatorship, but their leaders instead appealed to the Constitutional Court. Industrialists, Junkers, generals, and officials, on their part, while at all times ready to fight Communists and republicans, were not ready to defend their own rule against the self-styled national opposition. Thus they induced Hindenburg to dismiss his last chancellor and to appoint Adolf Hitler. The 30th of January 1933, a day as fateful for Germany as it was for the world, was the end of Weimar. It was not, as the conservatives hoped, a return to Potsdam. No place name of German glory, cultural or military, can be associated with what now was to come: the badge of shame of Dachau and Auschwitz.

The Downfall of the Regime: The Question of Responsibilities

Structural Shortcomings

In dealing with causes and responsibilities for Weimar's failure one must distingush between the more technical-structural shortcomings of the Weimar government and the underlying political, social, and economic factors. Among the former the unresolved relationship between parliamentary and presidential authority was perhaps the major one. This division of authority was not harmful so long as the forces and interests behind both were broadly identical, that is, until 1930. It led to disaster when this identity ceased. In the ensuing conflict, the executive, which had the backing of the military, prevailed. Even the Nazis succeeded only when power was handed over to them by the President.

The decline of the Weimar system has been attributed to a number of additional structural shortcomings, but in a curiously contradictory fashion. It is alleged, for instance, that too much or too little attention was given to civil rights and liberties; that political parties were too powerful, or that the executive—chiefly through Article 48—enjoyed too much power. But these allegations will not really bear inspection. If it is charged that the Weimar Constitution granted too much liberty to political enemies of the regime, we find that in reality it was the unwillingness rather than any constitutional inability of the Republic to defend itself that helped the Nazis to rise to power. It knew how to defend itself effectively against its leftist enemies, the Communists. And if it is charged that Article 48 was responsible for the establishment of authoritarian government after 1930, it would be legalistic indeed to assume that antidemocratic forces would not have found ways to gain power even in the absence of such a provision.

Political Responsibilities

Real responsibility would seem to lie rather with certain social groups and political forces, and especially with their leaders. With the masses still too much inclined to follow their leaders, much depended on the emergence of democratic leadership, but in the main the cultural, intellectual, political, and economic elite were either self-seeking or filled with a generally authoritarian doctrinairism. This was true regardless of party affiliation.

Communists

The Communists were chiefly responsible for splitting what might have been a strong democratic labor movement into two warring factions. The Communists' insistence on control made cooperation with them impossible. Their utopianism consistently mistook "the fourth month of revolutionary pregnancy for the ninth." Their illusion of having the backing of the masses led them to denounce all others as fascists, particularly the Social Democrats. Not even at the height of the depression were they strong enough to take over, but they *were* strong enough to provoke, in real fascism, "the counter-revolution against the revolution that never took place." Unmasking democracy as veiled fascism, not ready to join forces with antifascists even after 1930, they in effect helped to usher in that real fascism whose difference from democracy they noticed when it was too late.

Socialists

The moderate socialists, the trade union heads, and so forth, sinned rather through omission. By and large they were honestly devoted to democratic principles. But they were not leaders. Their lack of militancy, their timidity and legalism were striking. Theirs was the main responsibility for the failure to insist on basic social reforms when the progressive tide was still high. Then, they might well have demanded reforms of the cartel system, broken up the Junker estates, democratized the civil service, Reichswehr, school system, and judiciary. Instead, they became concerned with petty favors. They possessed no vision commanding the allegiance of the young generation. When the danger from the right increased, there was no sense of what the struggle for power demands, no readiness to take calculated risks. They were not traitors, as the Communists charged, but self-betrayed. It is significant that the largest democratic group under Weimar did not produce one personality of the caliber of the Center party's Matthias Erzberger, the Democrats' Walther Rathenau, or the People's party's Gustav Stresemann.

Catholics

Catholic leaders had similar shortcomings. In the initial period, under the influence of their workers' groups, they developed some progressive zeal, but later they became representatives of an interest party like others, although the interest was religious-cultural rather than economic. Democracy for them was an instrument rather than an aim, discarded when its value as a tool became doubtful. Then, political Catholicism fell back into the authoritarian groove. It is true that a courageous minority resisted this trend, but in vain: eventually political Catholicism helped vote Hitler into total power, thereby committing political suicide.

Conservatives

Outside the Communist, Socialist, and Catholic elite most of the German leadership under Weimar remained reactionary. The more progressive leaders of the middle classes soon became officers without an army. Many of those who had joined the liberal-democratic camp deserted it, longing for the good old days before World War I and despising the less glamorous, defeat-born Republic. Theirs was a great responsibility as social and intellectual leaders of the middle classes, as teachers and professors, pastors and journalists. By ridiculing the new system, they stifled incipient republican enthusiasm. They advertised patriotism as they understood it: a mixture of old-fashioned authoritarianism, defense of vested interest, and nationalism. But their own reactionary credo was revealed as weak when most of them failed to live up to it and became followers of the Nazis. Among all those who contributed to the downfall of Weimar theirs was perhaps the gravest guilt.

Foreign Powers

Although it cannot provide Germans with an alibi, the responsibility of the other powers cannot be denied. Revengefulness and hatred prevented them from encouraging the fledgling Republic and its democratic forces when there was still time; blindness and plain cowardice induced them to appease and to yield when totalitarianism was in the saddle. Their intransigence kept the Republic in isolation and denied it the success in foreign policy without which it could not gain prestige at home. When a few concessions were made toward the end of the Weimar period, it was too little and too late. The nationalism of the victors had provoked that of the vanquished; and Briand and Stresemann, working for German-French reconciliation in the 1920's, could never entirely make up for what had been done in the crucial initial period. From the list of the gravediggers of Weimar the names of foreign statesmen can unfortunately not be left out.

It is true that much of what has been said about Germany applies to other countries, and yet they did not produce a Hitler. The split in the working class, the drab and sometimes sordid ways of parliamentarism and party politics, the authoritarian tendencies of the middle classes, the failure of the intelligentsia to provide progressive leadership—all these were not confined to Weimar Germany. There remains the question: Why did Germany, and not France, for instance, produce Nazism? The factors mentioned above may account for the weakness and failure of German democracy; they do not explain the rise of a totalitarian movement. At most, they provided a basis on which such a movement *could* rise. That it *did* arise

was due to something in addition: the emergence of a genius (an evil one, to be sure), who knew how to fashion a new creed and a mass movement under his leadership.

4. GERMANY AS A DICTATORSHIP

The Nazi Movement: Its Character and Its Rise

Even today it is difficult to approach the topic of National Socialism without emotion. Too profoundly has the fate of all of us been influenced by the rise of this movement and by the war it provoked. Neither can it be considered a dead issue. Fascism, of which Nazism was merely the German form, is still one possible alternative to democracy (the other one, of course, being Communism). And to the Germans themselves these twelve short years still constitute a largely unassimilated problem, "the undigested past," as it is sometimes referred to. Much in their future will depend on whether and how they will eventually come to terms with this greatest transgression in their history.

Adolf Hitler

Adolf Hitler (1889–1945) rose from complete obscurity. The son of an Austrian petty official, he flunked every chance of gaining access to a normal occupation. After he had dropped out of high school, a Vienna art school refused to accept him. To the end of his days Hitler was convinced that he had the talent and the temperament of an artist; this conviction led him to despise the "better," educated people who had entered upon civil careers through normal channels, as well as the expert, who could set his solid knowledge against Hitler's intuition.

In his youth, without education, degree, or training, Hitler sank down into the underworld, the lower depths of beggars, vagrants, and criminals, working occasionally but not regularly, envying those who did, and thus accumulating a tremendous store of hatred and frustration.

Hitler managed to identify his impulses with the cause of a group which, in his imagination, was like himself victimized, namely the Germans as a nation or a race. In Austria, in particular, he saw them outnumbered by non-German nationalities and by Jews. In the Reich they seemed to him threatened by foreign enemies intent on destroying German might. To him as to many, World War I was the way out of individual frustration. He enlisted in the German army; his life was now merged with a cause. But the defeat of Germany threw him into what became paranoic persecution mania. He would not admit that his cause had been defeated in honest battle. In his eyes the Germans had been betrayed by enemy propaganda, the front-line soldier "stabbed in the back" by Jews and Marxists. Since this was a world that did not appeal to Hitler, he had to change it; eventually, he had even to repeat the war, as would the boy who does not want his first defeat to count. He decided to enter politics.

There were many in Germany at that time to whom the disordered state of German affairs offered a chance to become adventurers in politics. Innumerable "folkish" groups were founded, many engaging in terroristic activities, all clothed in some mystical nationalist or racialist philosophy, all quarreling endlessly among themselves about fine points of their creed.

Hitler joined one of them. He discovered his gift as an orator. Unlike most leaders in the Weimar period, he knew how to stir the people's imagination and enthusiasm. He soon became the leader of the National Socialist German Workers Party, or NSDAP, which he used as a platform for his political career. In contrast to minor rabblerousers, he combined persistence with an ability to learn from experience. He would not make the same mistake twice. Defeated in his attempt to attain power by uprising (his "beer hall Putsch" in Munich, 1923), he realized the uselessness of direct attack on established authorities. From now on his movement would pretend to be legal. Employing entirely novel tactics, he would capture the state from within, through the organization of a movement with a political religion.

Organization and Rise of the Movement

The story of Nazism's rise is still of prime importance because it is thus far the only instance in which a totalitarian movement gained power in a long-drawn-out battle with an existing regime. Nazism, indeed, battled Weimar throughout the entire existence of the Republic.

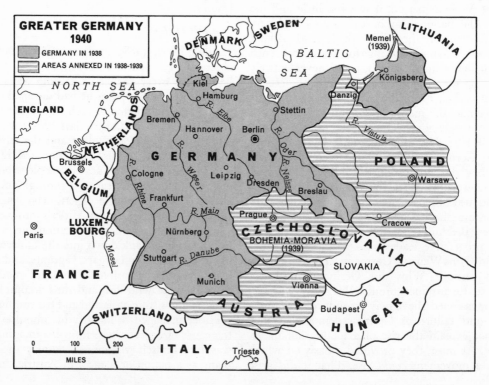

The very fact that most of the serious leaders and groups in Germany failed to take it seriously added to its strength. Hitler knew how to exploit such blindness.

From 1924 to 1930, the period of normalcy when most of the other ultranationalist groups were vanishing, Hitler devoted his efforts to building up the cadre of an organization by reorganizing the NSDAP on the basis of authoritarianism. He established the program of the party as incontestable dogma; he established himself as the infallible leader; he disciplined the rank and file; he selected a group of henchmen who unconditionally surrendered to his authority; and he relentlessly weeded out those who showed independence of mind or personal ambition. Democratic principles, such as voting, election of party functionaries, and accountability to the membership, were outlawed in favor of the "leadership principle." A hierarchy of ranks was established in the party, each member deriving his status ultimately from Hitler. Special formations were set up, such as the paramilitary Storm Troopers (SA), groups of brown-shirted, high-booted hoodlums who were to engage in brawls and street fighting in order to capture the attention of the public and to demoralize other groups. Finally, he established the doctrine of the movement—the "philosophy" that was to serve as basis for its propaganda.

The Nazi Doctrine

Ours is an age of political religions. The individual, lost in the mass, despairs of understanding his condition. Rational science no longer explains it in simple terms. He thus turns to creeds that offer easy explanations and seemingly firm values. Marxism, which started as a rational interpretation, has become a creed in its present form of Communist mass doctrine. Nazi doctrine did not even begin as an attempt to explain the world in rational terms. In Hitler's rambling and ranting *Mein Kampf* and in Alfred Rosenberg's book frankly titled *Myth of the Twentieth Century,* the doctrine was meant to be irrational myth, with racialism, social Darwinism, and political romanticism its chief ingredients.

It may seem wasted effort to present details of such crude and fantastic doctrine. Yet it would appear desirable to know the source of the intoxication that enabled human beings to commit with apparent good conscience crimes unequaled in human history.

According to this myth, world history is the struggle for survival and domination on the part of races. There are higher and lower races. Only the former, by subjugating the latter, are able to create culture. All high civilizations have been created by a superior racial group variously referred to as Nordic, Aryan, or Germanic. Thus, Greek and Roman civilizations were founded by tribes of Nordic stock. But the superior culture-creating minority is ever threatened with degeneration, especially through racial mixture with the masses of inferior breed whom they enslave. Aryan Vikings founded Russia; Franks, France; Saxons, England. But Germany itself scattered its forces. Its nobles degenerated; they imitated foreign ways and neglected the interest of the German racial community.

Subsequently the Germans encountered an even more mortal danger. The deadly enemy of all superior races, according to the Nazi myth, is a racial group sometimes characterized as a counterrace, the Jews, who are bent on destroying the inner strength of the peoples in order eventually to establish their own rule over the world. In this conspiratorial scheme they proceed with devilish cunning. To soften up organized communities, they preach individual rights, rule of law, checks and balances; they advocate formal democracy with its rule of the numbers, behind which looms their own rule. For, according to the Nazis, liberal democracy means either plutocracy, that is, "Jewish" economic exploitation of the Aryan, or Jewish Marxism, which divides the nations by preaching class struggle and results in Bolshevism, the victory of the "Jewish-led" proletarian masses. In either case it is World Jewry that triumphs.

Germany, as Hitler saw it in the 1920's, was the country on which Jewry was concentrating. Acting through plutocratic capitalism ("Wall Street") *and* Marxist socialism ("Moscow"), it was attacking what remained of inner strength in the German people, utilizing liberalism, pacifism, internationalism, humanitarianism, even political Catholicism, as disintegrating influences. But counterforces must needs reassert themselves. Led by a liberator, so Hitler predicted, Germany would establish its Third Reich. This Third Reich would be "a people's community," led by an elite entitled to rule for the benefit of all racial comrades. The welfare of the whole would be the guiding principle, with power concentrated in the hands of a leader acting as trustee of the entire community, unhampered by individual or group rights or by any other limitation of power.

Subsequently, the Nazis would proceed to reestablish the nation's greatness as a world power with a world mission. They would revive the spirit and instrumentalities of war, that is, militarism and armed forces. Regained military might would enable Nazi Germany to throw off the fetters of Versailles and to unite all racial Germans, such as the Austrians, in a Greater Germany. Then Germany would turn to the east, taking up where Germans left off in the Middle Ages, and acquire "living space" in those "vast open spaces." Before turning east, however, it would have to settle accounts with its hereditary enemy, France, the country that had always tried to prevent Germany from rising to greatness. After the defeat of the degenerate West, Germany would subdue eastern barbarism and in this way eliminate the world danger of Bolshevism. Eventually it was ordained to become master of the world.

Clearly, this doctrine would appeal to many. It would give them a sense of belonging to a community and the hope of becoming leaders in a group destined to rule; a sense of a task to be fulfilled not only in sordid self-interest but for coming generations; a sense of challenge and adventure, and particularly the German joy of marching again in uniform. It would resolve their worries and frustrations and give life a new meaning. It is obvious, too, that the doctrine fitted in with many a pre-Nazi ideal: authority and strong leadership; the rule of the best in the common interest; the idea of the *Volk* as the basic political unit, and of its mission in the world.

Nazi Propaganda

If the Nazi doctrine were all that Hitler had produced, he would now be as little known as any peddler of falsehood and hate. But he knew how to use his doctrine in order to build up what really counted—his movement. His was the first experiment in political mass propaganda, with all its now well-known implements: terror, violence, and brainwashing—in short, psychological warfare.

Hitler developed significant propaganda techniques. His propaganda, unlike that of ordinary political parties, was continuous, bombarding the people not just at election time, but day in and day out. The masses were showered with symbols: colors, display of flags, uniforms, insignia, the playing of anthems, the singing of songs, slogans endlessly repeated, an elaborate ritual. The tension was never relaxed.

Besides being incessant, Hitler's propaganda was primitive and emotional in its attacks on the instincts and sentiments of the masses. It made full use of stereotypes and prejudices. It was a concentrated offensive against one enemy in whom all evil and guilt was embodied. The attention of the masses was not distracted by multiple goals or multiple reasons. The Jew was *the* enemy. He was held responsible for everything adverse: for defeat in World War I and the peace dictate, for unjust reparations and the money inflation, for the depression and plutocratic exploitation, for class struggle and disunity.

All of this was combined with intimidation of dissenters, provocation of opponents, libel and slander. Hitler discovered that the lie, if only big enough and repeated often enough, was a potent weapon, since facts are usually not able to keep up with it. Nazis might be proved libelous in solemn trial, but some of the slander would always stick, and the trial itself would serve them as political forum. Thus they spread fear and terror, disrupted existing bonds and loyalties, and sowed confusion among non-Nazis. Many secretly joined the Nazi party as a means of political insurance. The Nazis managed to plant spies in government offices and agencies, to emerge, once the party was in the saddle, as the framework of Nazi government. They thus inaugurated what was to become known as fifth-column tactics, the tactics of boring from within, of forming a state within the state.

In contrast to the efforts of other parties,

Nazi propaganda was devised to appeal not to one particular group but to any and all (with the exception of Jews). To do this it had to be vague in order to bridge the great issues that divided the Germans. As one student of fascism has put it, "To be grandly vague is the shortest road to power, for a meaningless noise is that which divides us least." Nazi propaganda rejected plutocratic capitalism as well as Marxist socialism and stood for "genuine" national socialism. Under it the commonweal would prevail over private interest, but "justified" private initiative would not be destroyed and everybody would get his due. Parliamentary democracy as well as reactionary conservatism, republicanism as well as monarchism, were rejected in favor of an "ennobled democracy" where a people's community would be led by its elite.

This approach was most successful within social groups that were frustrated by failure and unsophisticated enough to fall for high-sounding generalities. It appealed to the small shopkeeper, losing ground in the competition with department and chain stores (the latter frequently Jewish-owned); the unsuccessful lawyer, resenting the success of Jewish (or other) colleagues; university graduates unable to find employment commensurate with their social status (the "academic proletariat"); small farmers, resenting exploitation at the hands of grain and cattle dealers (frequently Jewish); young people who throughout the depression had never had a job.

Nazi propaganda, however, was not equally effective with other groups. By and large, two groups withstood it best: the proletariat and the Catholics. Election figures prior to 1933 show that Socialists and Communists combined steadily maintained about 35 percent of the vote. Depression merely meant that Socialists lost and Communists gained. The Center party likewise withstood the Nazi onslaught, maintaining a steady 15 percent. The masses supporting Nazism belonged to the non-Catholic middle classes, whose parties, between 1930 and 1933, were practically wiped out. In addition, many new voters among the young voted Nazi. So did the habitual nonvoter, who, under the frenzy whipped up by Nazi propaganda, now went to the polls.

Besides the masses, it was important for Hitler to obtain the backing of the upper classes, especially those groups that alone were able to hand over state power to him. Gradually the rising tide of his movement persuaded important elements in the ruling groups, some industrialists, generals, officials, that his was the

Reichstag Election Results Under the Weimar Republic

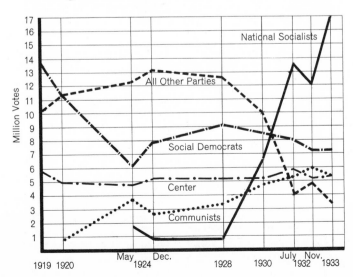

wave of the future and that they had to give him a share in power in order to maintain their own interests. Hitler now obtained financial subsidies from Ruhr industrialists. It was these groups that eventually persuaded Hindenburg to appoint Hitler chancellor. He neither had to gain a majority at the polls nor use force in order to obtain power. The national revolution, as the Nazis called their access to power, was neither national nor a revolution. It was victory by default.

Consolidation of Power

What followed was a lesson in how to consolidate power. The real revolution occurred only after the formation of the Hitler cabinet. In this cabinet the Nazis were still a minority, and the Junkers thought it possible to keep them prisoners of the majority. They were to be cruelly disillusioned. Hitler and his chief henchmen, Göring and Goebbels, using the strategic positions of which they had foolishly been put in command (such as the Prussian police and the agencies of propaganda), now prepared for a final election by terror and intimidation. An emergency decree gave them the power to suppress opposition meetings and publications, arrest opposition leaders, and put them into protective custody (Göring's new invention, soon to be known under the less reassuring name of concentration camps). Shrewd enough to proceed step by step, the Nazis first turned against the extreme left in order not to frighten the moderates, who were to be dealt with later.

Despite all this, the election (in March 1933) failed to produce the hoped-for Nazi majority; even with their conservative allies the Nazis did not get the two-thirds majority that Hitler needed to formalize his rule through constitutional amendment. But Göring, in his dual capacity of President of the Reichstag and chief of police, took care of everything. He excluded the elected Communist delegates from the Reichstag session. (Many of them, as well as some Social Democratic leaders, were already in concentration camps.) Still, outside help was needed. Partly through intimidation and partly through promises (to be forgotten as soon as the vote was taken), the Center party, along with some liberal groups, was induced to vote for the Act. Only the Social Democrats opposed

it. The Enabling Act of March 24, 1933, concentrated all power in the Executive (Cabinet), which could now legislate by simple decree and even amend the Constitution. The Reichstag and the parties had written their own death warrants. To be sure, the Act contained certain restrictions, for example, a guarantee of the existence of Reichstag, Reichsrat, and Presidency. But who was now to protest if these limitations were disregarded?

They were. After the emasculation of parliament the real revolution started. But it was a strange revolution. Afterwards no political institution resembled any previous one, and yet everything was achieved in a "peaceful" way, through a process of what was called *Gleichschaltung* (coordination, synchronization). The ever present threat of force, with the constant narcotic of propaganda, sufficed to stifle any idea of resisting. Thus, the Länder were coordinated, that is, provided with Nazi governments; so were the municipalities and other units of administration. All elected bodies in states, cities, and provinces were suspended. The civil service was purged of "politically unreliable" officials. Press, schools, universities, and the professions were coordinated; cultural and economic organizations and all other associations were put under the control of trusted Nazis. Labor was brought under control through the outlawing of the free trade unions. The political parties were outlawed one by one, proceeding from left to right, including those of the Nazis' own partners in the Cabinet.

Except for the army, the circles around Hindenburg, and the churches, total power was concentrated in Hitler's hands by July 1933. The revolution thereupon was declared officially terminated, to the dismay of a leftist wing in the party, which had expected more thoroughgoing action against plutocratic capitalists. Again taking the initiative, Hitler forestalled unrest by his blood-purge of June 30, 1934. Acting as prosecutor, judge, and executioner, he killed off the suspected radicals in his party and used the occasion to liquidate those outside the party suspected of conservative-reactionary opposition. By thus eliminating potential centers of resistance, he served notice on any and all that he meant business. Army, bureaucracy, big business, whoever might still have hesitated, now conformed. Thereafter no public purges were necessary. When Hindenburg, by this time senile and completely isolated, died on August 2, 1934, Hitler put the final touch to his rule: he merged the Presidency with the Chancellorship, and thereby assumed whatever powers had remained with the President. The main impact was felt by the army. With soldiers and officers now taking an oath of loyalty to Hitler as supreme commander, resistance from these quarters could henceforth be only scattered.

State and Society Under Nazism

Totalitarianism is characterized by concentration of all political power in one man or group and the use of such power for the complete control of society. The Nazis gained and maintained totalitarian control in five connected ways: (a) *by concentration of power,* that is, through organizing government in such a way as to allow no limitations of power, remnants of autonomies, or similar checks; (b) *by atomization of society,* that is, through dissolving existing groups so as to isolate individuals; (c) *by coordination of the individual,* that is, by then organizing these individuals in new groups established and controlled by the regime; (d) *by organizing and applying a system of terror* to maintain this control; and (e) *by propaganda,* that is, by maintaining a monopoly of information for the control of opinion and the indoctrination of minds.

Concentration of Power

The Leadership Principle

In the absence of any real limitations and delimitations of power, totalitarian government, considered as an organization, is simple. The Nazis did not even bother with the semblance of a constitutional document. The only constitutional principle in the Nazi state was the leadership principle, which meant that the will of the Führer (now Hitler's official title) was the highest law and the ultimate source of authority. Below the Führer, assignment and delimitation of jurisdictions were always provisional and revocable. The Reich Cabinet ceased to function as a body. Ministers, appointed and

dismissed by, and exclusively responsible to, the Führer, became mere technical experts, while decisions were made elsewhere, either by Hitler himself or by trusted lieutenants, usually high party leaders. After the Enabling Act most legislation occurred by decree, but it could also take other forms, such as the so-called Führer edict, a law issued by Hitler alone and sometimes not even made public.

As in other totalitarian regimes, there were some democratic trappings. "Elections" to a one-party Reichstag from a single list of candidates yielded the customary 99 percent majorities; so did so-called plebiscites. The Nazi Reichstag passed hardly any statutes, but rather served as an audience for Hitler's speeches, as did the annual party congress at Nuremberg. All this was devised to demonstrate to Germans and the world that the regime enjoyed the "enthusiastic backing of the people."

Centralization

Every totalitarian state tends to be unitary and centralized, outward appearance notwithstanding, for it cannot afford to grant autonomy to subdivisions that might become centers of emerging opposition. Thus the Nazis abolished the federal structure of the Reich, which became a unitary state. The Länder became mere administrative districts under the direction of a Hitler-appointed governor. But there was little left for the governors to direct, since most government activities were now handled directly by Reich ministries. Prussia was for all practical purposes abolished, its administration being merged with that of the Reich, while the other Länder at least retained their boundaries. On the local level, mayors and other officials were appointed and dismissed by the Reich minister of the interior, and municipal councils were appointive and advisory only.

Bureaucracy and Party

The Nazis were faced with a personnel problem with which all revolutionary regimes are confronted: whether to continue to utilize an existing, tested, and experienced but politically preregime bureaucracy, or to build up a new civil service from loyal but inexperienced followers. The Bolsheviks eventually chose the second alternative, as did the present rulers of

East Germany. The Nazis, however, were in a hurry. Preparation for the war that Hitler wanted was the all-important consideration; in order to put Germany on a war footing, the Nazis needed the services of the existing bureaucracy. But they took no chances. After an initial purge, they put the remaining officials on notice. The sword of dismissal hung constantly over the heads of officials who depended on their jobs for their own and their families' livelihood. Since they were specialists trained for this and no other profession, few dared not to conform.

Still, the old bureaucracy did not merge completely with the new party appointees. A dual system continued, with older professional civil servants and new Nazi appointees working together with varying degrees of friction, although all were equally under the control of the top echelon of the party. Key posts in the state were given to party members, who frequently held key party positions simultaneously. Thus, in contrast to Weimar, where the bureaucracy often cared little about its political superiors, the Nazis left no question that they meant to control the bureaucracy. On the other hand, the lower-level party organizations were not permitted on their own to interfere with the state administration. Both state machinery and party organization were thus separately kept under the control of the Nazi elite, which ruled supreme, using for its purpose now the state and now the party.

Supreme power thus rested with the Nazi leadership: with Hitler and with those on whom he conferred authority. Even this top group, however, remained unorganized and ever changing. Unlike Stalin and Mussolini, Hitler avoided institutionalization of authority even at the top—and with good reason, as was demonstrated by Mussolini's experience with his own Fascist Grand Council, which voted for Mussolini's dismissal in 1943. Nazi rule is a unique example of how an unorganized but strongly led gang can govern a modern nation.

Atomization of Society

If concentration of power and rule from above constituted the only criterion of totalitarian government, it would not, in principle, be different from other types of authoritarian rule with which history abounds. But while traditional authoritarianism, such as oriental despotism or the absolutist monarchy of the seventeenth and eighteenth centuries, was never entirely unrestricted by tradition, precedent, and customs, modern totalitarianism affects and molds everything. Society becomes the product of dictatorial policy alone; it is created and not creative. Existing groups and institutions are dissolved in a process that may be called the atomization of society. Totalitarianism exploits the fears and anxieties that go with freedom and individualism in order to enslave the individual. Severed from previous organic relationships, the citizen becomes dependent on the new regime. The usual bait is the promise of security. Thus many Germans sold their birthright of liberty in return for jobs under the Nazi armament program and for a stake in the glorious future that Nazism promised.

Eugenic Policies

The racial policies of the regime illustrate the extent to which the individual was rendered helpless. Extermination of non-Aryans was only one side of this picture. The other side was purification and strengthening of the "Aryan" race itself. Laws providing for sterilization and even castration of certain categories of people inaugurated a program of wholesale destruction of those found weak or obnoxious or merely useless. There were no guarantees against abuse; the individual was delivered to the tender mercies of those in power. The Nazi racial program culminated in a Führer edict (kept secret and communicated only to those directly in charge of its execution) for the "mercy killing" of inmates of asylums. How many thousands of "pure Aryan" Germans were thus put to death will never be known.

The Family

The fact that Hitler preferred to keep his mercy-killing decree secret shows that resistance against total atomization had not been completely broken. Such resistance was spearheaded by groups whose opposition was never entirely overcome by the regime. But the way in which the family, for instance, was attacked, indicated what might have happened eventually. Thus, it was the task of schools and Nazi Youth organizations to see to it that neither family nor

Church exercised non-Nazi influence on the youthful mind. No unsupervised leisure was allowed. Informing—telling on parents by children, on teachers by pupils, on priests by members of the congregation—was not a dishonorable act but a sacred duty. The corruption of moral standards that ensued can easily be imagined.

The Churches

Next to the family it was the churches which, with their own creed and attraction, seemed dangerous competitors for allegiance. With its glorification of non-Christian standards, of violence, and other bellicose virtues, Nazism was in essence pagan. But the Nazis were too clever to try to destroy the established churches outright. If by countenancing the traditional outward forms of religion they could obtain essential allegiance from the churches, this would constitute a greater victory for the regime than suppression.

The Nazis were never able to overcome completely the resistance of the churches. But the nature and extent of this resistance have sometimes been exaggerated. In the Protestant churches it was a minority of preachers and lay members who organized and formed the so-called Confessional church. The Protestant majority, however, complied with the Nazis, and another minority even became active Nazis, organizing themselves as "German Christians." In the Catholic Church, because of its authoritarian structure, there was no such split. But the spirit of resistance could not be translated into action as long as the Vatican authorized collaboration with the regime. The conclusion of a Concordat with the Holy See, in 1933, was Hitler's first triumph in foreign policy. The Church subsequently protested Hitler's systematic violation of its rights and interests, but neither the Confessional church nor Catholicism ever openly opposed Nazism—or the war it provoked—as a general and political system, although they did oppose policies that were irreconcilable with religious dogmas.[4] Their opposition thus was partial, and not a matter of total principle. Yet

they had their martyrs, and their defiance was a banner around which noncompliance could rally.

Army and Nobility

Army circles and the nobility offered another example of resistance to total atomization. Authoritarian though the philosophy of these groups had always been, it was a philosophy that still respected certain moral standards. Nazism restored their old status to them and revived the spirit of militarism. But their ultimate ideals differed. Fighting, to the Junker, still meant fighting for some cause—defense of the fatherland, of throne, or of altar. The Nazis' ideal was conquest of power for power's sake; in this battle, man was to become a morally insensible robot ready to commit any deed covered by "superior order."

When this became apparent, those officers and Junkers who were still imbued with their own standards of honor attempted to resist. But since they had allowed Hitler to assume complete control of the armed forces, resistance could only be carried on underground. The backbone of the resistance was broken by the blood-purge in 1934 and a subsequent purge in February 1938. We know now that a plan to overthrow the regime late in 1938 had to be postponed when the Western powers appeased Hitler in the Munich Agreement of September 1938 and thereby raised his prestige to its pinnacle. Not until the final stage of the war, when its loss was apparent, could a new attempt (July 1944) be undertaken. Its failure meant that even before postwar developments destroyed it economically, German Junkerdom lost its best members to the Nazi executioner.[5]

---

[4] Recent discussion of Rolf Hochhuth's play, The Deputy, and its indictment of Pope Pius XII's failure to speak out against the extermination of European Jewry on the whole has not disproved the justice of condemning an inactivity that prevailed whenever groups or interests outside the Church were involved.

[5] This is not meant to imply that some Junkers (and some priests) were the only "resisters" to the regime. On the contrary, what has since been dubbed the Resistance comprised a broad front, from army officers on the right, to officials and businessmen, to workers, trade unionists, and Communists. However, the Resistance remained scattered, a matter of individual persons and their moral decision ("the rising of conscience") rather than of organized groups. The latter-day claim of many Germans to have been members of the Resistance, if only passive ones, raises the problem of "collaboration," that is, at what point continuing in one's job, presumably to prevent worse things, turns into sharing responsibility and guilt. Neither in the German case, nor in that of French and other collaborators, nor in that of Stalinism, has a clear solution been found. However, it is likely that in most cases the genuineness of resistance was demonstrated by the claimant's exile, imprisonment, or death.

Coordination of the Individual

Party and Party Organizations

The atomization of society and the isolation of the individual were only means to an end—the total control of the individual through new groupings established by the regime. All organizations under Nazism became either controlling or controlled groups, and no individual or group was allowed to remain outside such organized control. This is what the much heralded "corporative" or "estates" structure of fascism (in Italy as well as in Germany) amounted to. It was not self-organization of the respective interests and groups, not pluralism, but merely a façade for totalitarian control. The main instrument for such supervision was the party itself, with its proliferation of affiliated and supervised party organizations. Frequently there were two organizations, controlling and controlled, for one and the same group or occupation. Thus, the Hitler Youth, an organization for every boy and girl, contained a select group, the *Stamm* (core) Hitler Youth, which was to be trained in special schools to become the future Nazi elite. As a result of these developments the party itself changed its character. The active "movement" of pre-1933 days was turned into an instrument as thoroughly manipulated as any other instrument of Nazi rulership. Only at its top level did it shade off into the realm of actual rulership.

Labor Under Nazism

How did the main economic and social groups fare under Nazism? Was it continued rule of capitalism, or was it the rule of a group hostile to private property, "brown bolshevism"? To begin with, labor was deprived of any influence. Its trade unions were suppressed, together with the political parties that had represented its interests; strikes were forbidden; advocacy of workers' demands, unless voiced by official party spokesmen, was interpreted as advocacy of class struggle and was considered subversive. The Nazi-sponsored Labor Front was a front to conceal actual Nazi control. Since it included employers, it was not supposed to represent specific labor interests, and even less to participate in the regulation of labor conditions.

As for these, the status of the workingman was one of complete regimentation. The state determined his wages, hours, and where and in what kind of occupation he was to work. But his job was secure in an economy with labor shortages. The average worker, comparing this situation with depression conditions, preferred job security to freedom plus unemployment. Although passively and often grumblingly, the German worker collaborated—an attitude that was not very surprising in a full-employment economy that promised him subsequent participation in the spoils of an entire continent. Longer hours, worsening living conditions, and scarcity of consumers' goods appeared as an investment that would pay off—cannons in order to get butter. Only when the cannons failed to procure the butter did the masses turn away from the regime. But one should not forget those workers—in particular, former Socialists, Communists, trade unionists—who took up the underground fight against the regime, with many becoming martyrs of the Resistance.

The Peasantry

Like the worker, the farmer was regimented; he was told what to plant and how much, what to deliver to the food authorities and at what price. Nazi agriculture was planned, though not collectivized. Under conditions of food shortage and rationing, the farmer was in a better bargaining position than the worker, and the regime treated him more gingerly. But there was no question of his belonging to, or being represented in, the ruling elite. Nazi Germany was as little a peasant's state as it was a worker's. Was it then the rule of the capitalists?

Business and Middle Classes

Nazism did not destroy capitalism as a system; it did not nationalize property. On the contrary, it made the owner "leader of the enterprise." He could now manage his affairs without fear of strikes or labor unrest. Nazism had released him from the fear of Communism and the necessity of dealing with organized labor as partner; it permitted high profits, strengthened cartel agreements, gave business a chance to profit from Aryanization of Jewish property and, subsequently, from the exploitation of conquered countries. This, however, was only one side of the picture. The other side was Nazi control of business. The "leader of the enterprise" was told what wages he had to pay, how many hours his workers had to work, even which workers he might hire. Almost everything concerning the management of his business, from the allocation of raw materials and credit to the determination of what to produce or sell and at what price, was dictated to him. The Nazi economy was a regimented war economy even before the war started.

As for the effects of this system, ironically enough, those who fared worst were the small businessman, the artisan, the small shopkeeper or trader—in short, the groups that had flocked to Nazism at its rise in the hope of economic salvation. They were sacrificed in favor of more efficient (and more influential) big business.

Big business fared well, despite controls. It shared in handsome profits and was permitted somewhat greater influence over the management of its own affairs: Its representatives in the estates (organs of "business self-administration") exercised more actual influence than did those other groups. They even had easier access to the highest leadership group. Big business was favored by the destruction of small enterprise and profited from the exploitation of cheap foreign and concentration-camp labor. Yet it operated in a system that gave it no influence over such crucial political decisions as the preparation for, and waging of, aggressive wars. It was, moreover, threatened by increasing state competition, as in the field of steel and chemical production, and it did not enjoy legal security. A system that can put anybody it dislikes into a concentration camp and that can confiscate property for any or no reason is scarcely the rule of "monopoly capitalism," even if it leaves monopolies temporarily intact and refrains from using the secret police against businessmen as long as they behave. The new Nazi elite saved big business for the same reason it hesitated to destroy the other old forces, like the bureaucracy and the Junkers. It needed them for all-out war. What would have happened if Germany had won the war is another question, but developments in the later years of the regime showed that the Nazis held the trump cards. If necessary, Hitler could always mobilize the proletarian elements in the party and play them off against recalcitrants.

Organization of the Terror

To some extent all organized society rests on compulsion. What distinguishes totalitarianism from free society is that it rests on terror *as an institution*. The individual is exposed to the permanent threat of forceful action against his possessions, his liberty, his life. When such organized violence is applied unpredictably, when its practitioners are free from supervision, there emerges the characteristic police-state atmosphere of all-pervading fear that leaves the individual with a sense of utter helplessness. This modern terror is distinguished from old-style coercion under despotism in three ways: (1) Its existence is never admitted. Officially, one lives in a genuinely free society, and anybody who dares intimate that terror exists is branded as subversive and is himself taken care of by the secret police. (2) It is systematized, that is, all institutions of state and regime are ultimately at its service. (3) It performs scientifically, using the refinements of modern psychology and other sciences for its purposes.

Nazi Law

The law, under this system, ceases to be a general rule defining rights and obligations, and becomes pure command and coercion, a means of mass manipulation by violence. As Nazi jurists put it, "Law is what is useful for the people," usefulness to be defined by the Nazis. Principles of ex post facto law and punishment by analogy were applied by judges who had lost their independence. Yet the Nazis found that many among the old judiciary could not entirely escape the Rechtsstaat spirit in which they had been trained. Hence Hitler's resentment against the judges, whom he accused of formalism. He established special courts, staffed with Nazi judges, picked from Nazi formations, and put them in charge of political crimes or the application of the racial and eugenic legislation. This explains the blood-justice of the People's Court at Berlin and similar terror institutions.

The Gestapo

But even special courts failed to be satisfactory as the main instrument of terror. They might, though rarely, acquit an accused. The regime needed an institution that was entirely free from remnants of formalism; it created it in the form of the Secret State Police, or Gestapo. The Gestapo was an agency with unlimited power over any individual and any group, against whose actions and decisions there was no appeal to courts or any other authority. Gestapo authorities could arrest anybody without a warrant and detain him indefinitely without further trial in their concentration camps. They could, and did, arrest a person just acquitted by a court because they still deemed him dangerous. They supervised the citizen in his daily life, watched his movements, tapped his wires, read his correspondence, overheard his conversation. With the help of the Security Service (SD), a vast network of voluntary informers, they scrutinized everybody's attitudes. Their tentacles extended even into foreign countries. No one could trust anyone else. Formation of opposition groups in this way was either prevented or nipped in the bud.

The Gestapo was closely linked with the party's SS (Protective Formation, as it was euphemistically called), which had emerged from the SA and become the backbone of the regime's terror machinery. Both SS and Gestapo were headed by Heinrich Himmler, a cold-blooded fanatic, next to Hitler the most powerful figure of the regime and later the most execrated name in all Nazi-dominated Europe. SS members, selected for fanatical devotion and capacity to inflict utmost cruelty if so ordered, staffed the Gestapo, guarded the concentration camps, and later formed the most frightful organization of all, the *Einsatzgruppen,* or Special Task Formations, which followed the victorious German armies all over Europe to hunt out and exterminate en masse Jews, Communists, and other marked groups. Thus the terror grew to the end.

In the concentration camp a new type of society spread over Europe. Paradoxically, it was the only institution with some self-government under Nazism. Internal management was usually left to a group of inmates, the ordinary criminals, whom the Nazis placed in the camps, along with vagrants and homosexuals, so as to be able to brand even the political inmates as criminals and perverts. Medical and other sadistic experiments performed on camp inmates were Nazi contributions to the study of how humans function under inhuman stress. Another contribution was the scientific development of mass extermination in gas chambers. It was no minor achievement, after all, to have "processed," within a few years, millions for the "final solution," requiring, as it did, the coordination of many thousands for the job of collecting, transporting, and killing the victims. But the bureaucratic genius of the Eichmanns assured success.

In the "ordinary" camps, meanwhile, the camp population swelled and came, toward the end of the war, to include many of the elite of Europe, from nationalists to Communists, from Catholics to Jehovah's Witnesses, officers and pacifists, Germans and non-Germans. Most of them perished, and many survivors were physically and mentally broken. From this loss Europe still suffers.

What rendered Nazi terror so frightful was its cold-blooded planning. Even what appeared as spontaneous mob violence (for example, the synagogue burnings of November 1938) was in reality carefully planned. Of perhaps more lasting importance, however, was the legalization of terror by administrative authority and bureaucratic procedure. Here the German tradition of obedience to authority paid dividends. Since all participants acted under orders, they all felt that their actions were legal—the judge inflicting the death penalty upon one who refused to inform; the police official assembling Jews for deportation; the doctors and nurses obeying the decree for mercy killing; managers of firms starving slave laborers or delivering incineration furnaces according to specification. The problem of how to treat such actions and their perpetrators was to become a legal and moral headache of post-Nazi regimes, and especially, post-Nazi Germany.

Jewish Persecution

Jewish persecution offers the prime example of how this bureaucratized terror worked. Without it even the Nazis might not have managed to kill six million "non-Aryans" within three or four years. The Nazis shrewdly started with "mild" measures: first exclusion of Jews from professions, then gradual destruction of their economic life, finally their deportation to Auschwitz and other annihilation camps in Eastern Europe where they were either worked or gassed to death.

Besides satisfying its racialist aims, this policy served the regime politically. It intimidated opponents, and it made allies of anti-Semites abroad who became the basis for fifth columns. It served as precedent for subsequent more general destruction of the rule of law. It was one (and almost the only) implementation of the original Nazi program, and this satisfied its earlier followers. In its confiscatory stage it appeared anticapitalist, but it also lined the pockets of those who could profit from Aryanization. It bound all participants in a common guilt with the Nazis and thus made jumping off the bandwagon more difficult. It would be wrong, however, to believe that it made all Germans Jew-haters. Some turned philo-Semitic under the impact of what they saw or learned, and even helped heroically. But the mass looked the other way, and many did not hesitate to profit. Like the Empress Maria Theresa at the partition of Poland, they wept but took.

Passivity and conformity were the main effects of the terror on the bulk of the population. If the average citizen did not "mix in things which did not concern him," he had a good chance of never being involved with the Gestapo. One should therefore not overestimate the impact of the terror on everyday life. The regime was satisfied if people knew in a vague and general way what threatened nonconformists. In this way resisters were isolated from their people even spiritually. It was different in occupied Europe, where the Nazis were the common enemy of resisters and the general population alike. For a German resister to work for freedom was to work for defeat of his country; this was the cruel dilemma into which Nazism had forced the decent German.

Propaganda and the Control of Men's Minds

Terror is one support of totalitarian power; the other is the organization of total allegiance or, at least, total conformity. While in pre-totalitarian societies, including the authoritarian ones, thought and opinion are to some extent spontaneous, totalitarianism strives to manipulate even this most intimate and personal realm. It monopolizes all channels of information and opinion and uses them for indoctrination.

The Propaganda Machine

This effort required: (1) the control not only of the traditional channels of communication but of everything that had any connection with thought, ideology, and opinion; (2) the distortion of information, research, and learning into indoctrination. Joseph Goebbels, as head of the Ministry of Propaganda, controlled not only press and radio but all cultural activities, the theater, films, music, the arts, and literature. Recalcitrants or suspects were condemned to economic death. Control extended into the schools, with their coordinated teaching staffs and Nazified curriculums and texts; into the universities; into the youth organizations. In a totalitarian regime everything has its propagandistic aspect, and life is permeated with the regime's slogans and doctrine.

Control of Culture

Thought control drew an Iron Curtain around the German people, cutting them off from all information detrimental to the regime. Newspapers, magazines, radio, all voiced the same line. Thought control further meant the suppression of anything opposed to the official ideals. History was rewritten and retaught in accordance with racialist doctrine; philosophy outlawed "liberalist" theories and "Judaized" thinkers; law repudiated the "formalistic" spirit of Roman law; art was purged of modernistic tendencies; literature was confined to writings extolling nationalism, militarism, heroism, and obedience. Nowhere else, perhaps, was the stultifying effect of conformity more apparent than in the cultural realm. Creative minds left Germany or withdrew into internal exile. The burning of books was the natural companion piece to the concentration camp.

Effects of Indoctrination

While the anticultural action of the Nazis alienated an intellectual and cultural elite, the average German cared little as long as the regime provided bread and circuses. This indifference did not mean, however, that indoctrination of the public was altogether successful. Nazi ideology penetrated German minds to a lesser extent than is commonly believed. The older generation was, for the most part, too deeply committed to pre-Nazi views to be easily won over by the new doctrine. Even the youth upon whose conversion the regime was banking emerged less Nazified in terms of doctrine than might have been expected. An overdose of indoctrination resulted in widespread skepticism or indifference, which, while in one way facilitating the task of post-Nazi re-education, also left a dangerous legacy of cynicism.

Thought control was more successful in the sphere of information proper, in the distortion and suppression of news. There was throughout the period of Nazism much grumbling; the political joke flourished (often tolerated by the regime as a relatively innocuous outlet); but correct information did not reach the masses. Gradually even what at first had been recognized as lie and distortion sank in. After the surrender in 1945, foreigners were amazed to find even genuine anti-Nazis believing that "the war had been forced upon us" because "the Poles started it." The story of Nazi propaganda shows that totalitarianism may be unable to instill permanent enthusiasm but may well succeed in giving the masses a distorted picture of the world.

Some Conclusions

Nazism failed internally and externally. It boasted that it had replaced the confusion and inefficiency of parliamentary democracy with a simple and efficient rule, but this was a myth. In actual fact, government, in becoming an ever more complicated mixture of old and new administrations, agencies, and jurisdictions, of party, state, estates, and armed services, became a maze in which the citizen was lost. Never before had there been so much red tape. Connections meant everything, not to mention outright graft, corruption, and favoritism on an unprecedented scale. Moreover, the seemingly monolithic state was not able to eliminate internal pressures and influences working at cross

purposes. Interests that in democracies operate more or less impersonally and openly (through parties, legislatures, and in similar ways) were here conducted backstage. While ultimate decision was always the Führer's, Hitler usually avoided taking sides, preferring to play off one faction against the other. Conflicts were thus solved through temporary arrangement and compromise (as they are in the despised democracies).

In one respect only could the regime claim success of a sort: the Führer's personal control remained unimpaired to the end. Struggle over succession, with the pretenders jockeying for his favor, caused some strains. Hitler vacillated. He first designated Göring and then demoted him. Himmler, next in line, also incurred his wrath, and the last days of the crumbling regime saw a dark horse, Admiral Dönitz, nominated successor. But this also demonstrated that the dictator's power remained unaffected. Not even his most powerful lieutenants dared to oppose him openly. And unless such rule is broken by the disintegration of the entire top organization (as in Italy in 1943), it cannot be overthrown from within. This was demonstrated by the fate of the German Resistance. Unable to organize mass opposition, it failed even in its broadest and most ambitious effort, that of July 1944, when there was a common front, except for the Communists, of representatives of all opposition groups, from trade unionists to Junkers. They failed to get decisive help from the army, and as a result the end of Nazism came only with military defeat and Hitler's death in his Berlin bunker.

This defeat sealed the failure of Nazi foreign policy. Nazism was unique in its singleness of purpose, with domination its objective and war its chosen means. Thus its fall through defeat in war was most fitting. But one should not forget how close it was to success (in 1940) and what its victory would have implied. Whatever form its hegemony would have finally assumed, its temporary New Order of Europe (1939–45) made it abundantly clear that to the doom of individual and group liberty there would have been added the doom of independent nations; to inequality within Germany itself would have been added the rule of Germany as a nation and the enslavement of all others. Perhaps there

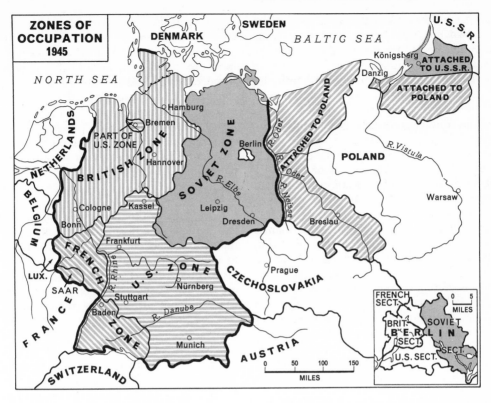

ZONES OF OCCUPATION 1945

might have been some gradation, with certain groups or countries given preference, but there would have been equal loss of liberty and extinction of ancient values for all. It is sometimes easy to forget, in the face of the Communist peril, that Nazi victory would likewise have meant the end of Western civilization.

5. POSTWAR RECONSTRUCTION

Germany in Defeat

A major military defeat in modern times has usually caused changes in the vanquished nation's political structure, as for example in Russia in 1917, or in France in 1871. The government of Germany was changed by her defeat in World War I, but the effect of the collapse of the Nazi regime in 1945 was more fundamental. Utmost concentration of totalitarian power suddenly gave way to virtual anarchy. The victors of World War II were thus faced with the collapse of an entire regime; their task was not

merely a matter of restoring what had temporarily broken down but of endowing a nation with a new type of society and public life.

This required temporary assumption of authority by the Allies themselves. Upon Germany's unconditional surrender in May 1945, the Allies allowed the territory east of the Oder-Neisse line to be placed under Polish administration, except for the northern half of East Prussia which was turned over to the Soviet Union. The remainder of Germany was divided into zones of occupation, with the Russians in eastern Germany from the Oder and Neisse to and partly beyond the Elbe; the British in the Northwest; the Americans in the South; and the French with territory adjacent to France and carved out of the British and American areas. The zonal lines between East and West, which had been drawn up well before the surrender, have now turned into political boundaries, forming, as in Korea, the Iron Curtain that separates the two main power blocs. If Western leaders are sometimes blamed for having granted Russia too much, it must not be forgotten that no one, when the zonal boundaries were drawn up, could be sure that at the time of surrender Russian troops would not be on the Rhine, instead of the Elbe.

The Allies then assumed "supreme authority with respect to Germany." This assumption of power, they further declared, was not meant to "effect the annexation of Germany," but, on the contrary, to prepare for eventual restoration of democratic government in a unified Germany. But the attempt to exercise joint authority through an Allied Control Authority soon had to be given up. For some time sovereignty then devolved upon the occupying powers separately in their zones, and there were four Germanies instead of one—not counting the city of Berlin, which had been exempted from the zones. This process of disintegration was succeeded by one of integration of the three Western zones, coupled with gradual restoration of German autonomy. By 1949 came the establishment of two German Republics, the German Federal Republic (*Bundesrepublik Deutschland,* BRD), comprising the three Western zones, and the German Democratic Republic (*Deutsche Demokratische Republik,* DDR) in the Soviet zone, with Berlin (likewise divided into Western and Soviet-controlled parts) formally attached to neither unit. How to fashion one sovereignty out of two—that is, how to reunify Germany— remained the overriding problem.

Failure to Establish German Unity

The Potsdam Program

The inability of the former Allies to restore German unity is explained by the estrangement between the Western powers and the Soviet Union and the ensuing cold war. Toward the end of World War II there seemingly was a good deal of agreement among the Big Three about the future of Germany. Early ideas of partitioning Germany into several independent states had been entertained by many, especially in France, but shortly after Yalta had been rejected in favor of German unity. The Allies had further agreed not to destroy German industry; the ill-famed Morgenthau Plan for rendering Germany more or less an agricultural country had been shelved before the end of the war. The Big Three at Potsdam (July–August

1945) decided to treat Germany as an economic unit, with common policies for the different zones. Eventually it was to have its own government. In order to make sure that it would be democratic, a gradual process of political reconstruction was to begin at the local level and proceed to the restoration of indigenous government at higher levels, but provision was made for the immediate establishment of central German agencies in fields such as economics, finance, and transportation.

Divergent Allied Approaches

Why did this program fail? The basic reason lay in the Allies' dissimilar conceptions of German reconstruction, which, in turn, went back to their disagreement about the nature of Nazism. To the Soviets, Nazism had been monopoly capitalism, the natural outgrowth of capitalistic developments; a non-Nazi Germany, therefore, had to be a noncapitalistic Germany, and the transformation of bourgeois society into a socialist one was considered a prerequisite of German democratization. To the French, Nazism had simply been another form of age-old German aggression, and any strong new Germany seemed to foreshadow a repetition of what they had experienced so often. Their aim, therefore, was to keep Germany as decentralized as possible and to forestall reunification as long as possible.

The Americans and British, in contrast, had no clear-cut interpretation of Nazism and therefore no clear-cut occupation policy. The British Labor government which had come into power in 1945 had some ideas about backing democratic socialism in Germany, and Americans were, to some extent, convinced that Germans needed liberal-democratic reorientation and reeducation. In actual practice, however, administration was put ahead of policy in order to provide Germans as soon as possible with a functioning government.

Disunity began with the Allies' failure, chiefly because of French objections, to establish the central German administrative agencies envisaged at Potsdam. But it is likely that mutual distrust would have driven the Allies apart in any event. In a cold-war atmosphere every step, every proposal, however innocuous and defensive, is interpreted as aggressive by the other

side. Inter-Allied negotiations on German unification showed that questions of detail might
well have been solved. Much-advertised differences over the political structure of a future
German government (which came to the fore
at the four-power conference at Moscow in
1947) in reality did not reveal fundamental disagreement. Major points of dispute, such as the
federal or unitary structure of government, were
close to being solved by compromise, when the
conference broke down because of the political
rift between the Allies. Willingness to come to
terms had diminished, since each side came to
believe that the presence of its own respective
Germany in its own sphere was more vital to
its security than the restoration of German unity.
Thus East and West were led into different
paths of political and general reconstruction.

The Failure of Democratic Reorientation

The success of such reconstruction depended
upon something more basic—a German reorientation that first of all presupposed repudiation of
the Nazi past. Any nation in whose name deeds
such as the Nazi crimes were committed must
cleanse itself of the past. A sound political community cannot be rebuilt if the most horrid
crimes remain unpunished and their perpetrators unmolested. The theory of the collective
guilt of the German people, which was current
around 1945, was nonsense, if only because it
would have involved all Germans in a common
guilt which, eventually, would have meant ab-
solving them all alike. But forgiveness for all
was equally impossible. The elimination of active Nazis and their major collaborators from
public life was necessary, not for reasons of
revenge but as a measure of precaution in building up a new society and government.

Denazification

In order thus to reconstruct German public
life, the Allies initiated a comprehensive program of denazification. In the East, it was instrumental in building up a new, undemocratic
system. In the West, where the powers did not
want one predetermined German group to assume control, it was a prerequisite of democratization. The failure of this effort still has its impact on German society and government.

The most consistent effort at denazification
was made in the American zone. What happened, and why the venture failed, can perhaps
be best understood by asking what should and
could have been done. First of all, denazification, if it was to be part of a process of reconstruction, had to be preventive, not punitive—
that is, its purpose had to be not trial and punishment (on the war crimes trials see Chapter
6), but elimination from positions of influence
of persons dangerous to democratic reconstruction. Second, such elimination should have been
limited to those Nazis who could be expected
to sabotage efforts at reconstruction if they remained in or were readmitted to positions of
influence in government, administration, industry, education, communications, and the like.
It should have stopped short of the masses of
Nazi followers who, for a variety of reasons,
had joined the party or its organizations without taking an active part in its policies. We can
now see that it would have been a practicable
though by no means easy job for Allied-Ger-
man cooperation thus to denazify by sifting the
basic local setups (such as a local police office,
a school, a university faculty) individually and
to weed out locally known real Nazis as well
as to see to it that none entered or reentered
subsequently.

Instead, the occupying powers undertook to
sift, question, categorize, and judge an entire
people—which would have proved technically
impossible even where political motives did not
enter. In view of the "universe of motivations"
upon which Germans had acted during the
twelve years of the regime, what were to be the
standards for dividing them into non- or anti-
Nazis, major offenders, lesser offenders, followers? How could a few lay members of German local boards hope to delve into the life
history of hundreds or thousands of persons,
most of them not locally known? (Most active
Nazis had shifted from place to place and zone
to zone, and most of them, especially those from
the East, had falsified their questionnaires.) The
investigation would have been difficult even
where pressure and intimidation did not occur;
and indeed pressures could hardly fail to develop where a majority of people were incriminated. A handful of nonincriminated Germans
could hardly be expected to resist them, espe-

cially since the Military Government (MG) failed to back them up.

The addition of punitive measures increased a tendency to sympathize with the victims of denazification. Insignificant though most of the penalties were (low fines that were paid in worthless currency), they gave credence to the propaganda that attacked punishment of mere political error. In the shuffle, the main issue —that of preventing dangerous Nazis from entering public life—was lost sight of. When procedures bogged down, wholesale amnesties and whitewashing of practically all nonamnestied persons closed the operation as ineffectively as it had been inaugurated. What had happened, seen in perspective, was that there had been an initial indiscriminate indictment and in many cases indiscriminate internment, followed by indiscriminate release, indiscriminate acquittal, and, finally, indiscriminate reinstatement. As came to light in all too many subsequent cases, no confidence could be had that even major Nazis had been caught in the proceedings. Thus the effects (such as suspension from office) were temporary at best, and ceased precisely at the time when elimination of Nazism would have been most necessary—that is, when the new administrative machinery of West Germany was established.

Reeducation

The failure of denazification affected German reorientation beyond the sphere of staffing agencies and filling positions; it rendered the Allied objective of reeducating Germans for democracy more difficult, since to many Germans democracy became identified with what the Western Allies tried to import or impose. As under Weimar, democracy had to establish itself in an environment of defeat, guilt, and distrust of foreign countries. In addition, there was partition; misery, increased by the refugee millions; vast destruction; and, as a legacy of Nazi propaganda, skepticism with regard to any creed old or new. Democracy was suspected of being just another propaganda slogan, this time used by the occupying powers for their own purposes.

Allied inconsistencies contributed to the growth of such cynicism. At first they tended

to treat all Germans, Nazis, non-Nazis, and anti-Nazis, as bad, charging them all with collective guilt, taking or condoning stringent measures that operated against all alike, such as the dismantling of factories or the expulsion of ethnic Germans from their homes into rump Germany under conditions of terrible hardship. This approach was gradually reversed to an equally unwarranted leniency, regarding Germans as decent fellows all. Anti-Nazis were then put on the defensive; they were suspected of radicalism or even Communism when they advocated mild reforms, while former Nazis recommended themselves as reliable anti-Communists.

Despite all this, there were beginnings of a liberal-democratic reorientation in West Germany. At the time of defeat, revulsion against the Nazi regime and all it had stood for had been general; and this was coupled with a yearning for freedom and political security. Allied reeducation efforts did help here and there, and not only in the reorganization of the more formal educational institutions, such as universities.

We have seen how the German press, free though licensed, stimulated democratic orientation. While the largest proportion of the people in the immediate postwar years were passive and bewildered, an active minority embraced the new-old democratic values. This led to a period in which Germans became so deeply divided in basic attitudes as almost to constitute two nations, with a minority devoted to the values of democratic freedom and a majority betraying an absence of political commitment and often a pronounced cynicism or opportunism. The attitude study that we referred to before found that far fewer Germans than English or Americans, though they were equally well informed, were ready to talk politics with others; most did not feel free to discuss issues; and many refused to reveal their party choice.[6] The latter attitude was probably a hangover from their experience under the Nazis as well as under denazification.

To an observer in the 1950's the split revealed itself perhaps most forcibly in German reactions to what had happened. To the "minority German" recent history began not, as it

[6] Almond and Verba, pp. 80–83.

did for the majority, in 1945 but in 1933. He was ready to admit the responsibility of the Germans for what had happened under Nazism and was concerned about remedies; he possessed firm moral views, abhorring totalitarianism, whether of the right or of the left. The "majority German" was not oriented in this direction. Although neither Nazi nor neo-Nazi—thus attesting to the relatively slight impact made by Nazi doctrine and propaganda as such—he failed to be impressed by the reprehensible character of Nazism; he was inclined, for instance, to deny that what the Nuremberg and subsequent trials of Nazi criminals had revealed had really happened. He developed the habit of repressing what he disliked to remember.

In this way Germans tended to become pragmatic, with at best a "show-me" attitude. In certain respects this caution was not unfavorable to reorientation: Ultranationalism, and the militarism and foreign-policy adventurism connected with it, were rejected by the majority as well as the minority; while with the latter this rejection was a matter of principle, with the others it reflected the experience of a lost war and postwar German weakness, and also the fear of endangering present prosperity. Remilitarization and regained power have since somewhat impaired this more reasonable attitude; but so far it has not led to an attitude of "revanchism"—a charge leveled by the East against West Germany, or, at least, against its rulers.

In the main, these attitude features of the fifties have persisted in the sixties. Almond and Verba are probably justified in saying that "theirs [the Germans'] is a highly pragmatic—probably overpragmatic—orientation to the political system; as if the intense commitment to political movements that characterized Germany under Weimar and the Nazi era is now being balanced by a detached, practical, and almost cynical attitude toward politics." [7] The dual structure of German society resulting from the split in basic values and, consequently, in attitudes can still be observed. Young Germans, however, are turning from apathy and cynicism to a critical questioning and even a moral con-

[7] *Ibid.*, p. 313.

demnation of their elders for their behavior under Nazism and after. After all, Germans under thirty-five experienced Nazism only as children, if at all; thus half of all the Germans alive today were not directly involved. Although young Germans have not been given a clear picture of what happened by either family or school (an indication of the failure of reeducation), they are generally free from bias and are ready to judge the merits and demerits of past systems objectively. With them, democracy, still weakly rooted, may have a chance that the older generation has denied it. [8]

These ambiguities in basic attitudes explain a good deal of what happened in West Germany in the postwar period, including shifts from neutralism and pacifism to brash assertiveness, and violent criticism of government contrasting with a defense of authoritarian outrages. Democrats are perhaps too easily inclined to discover neo-Nazism where there is frequently mere apathy and desire to be left in peace. But one cannot blame them too much for their suspicions if one takes into consideration a still widespread inclination to ridicule anything that is liberal or democratic; a tendency to admit unreconstructed Nazis to positions, while those who after the surrender had sprung into the breach are vilified or ostracized; the habit of making Yalta and Potsdam, that is, the Allies, responsible for everything adverse, rather than the war begun by Nazi Germany and of condemning in Nazism not its depravity but its failure to win the war; or the trend toward forgiveness of even those revealed as

[8] Shifts in attitude that perhaps reflect the rise and the different attitudes of the younger Germans are revealed in poll results such as these: To the question of who was responsible for the outbreak of the war in 1939, only thirty-two percent answered "Germany" and twenty-four percent said "others" in 1951, while in 1959 Germany was held responsible by 50 percent, and "others" by 11 percent. Different remembrance of conditions because of lapse of time explains the changed assessments in answers to questions like this: "When did Germany fare best?"

	1951	1963
today	2	62
1933–39	42	10
1920–33	7	5
before 1914	45	16

Source: Jahrbuch der öffentlichen Meinung, 1965, pp. 230, 233.

participants in the worst crimes. For it is one thing to forgive after judgment and repentance; it is quite another thing when forgiveness is claimed as a right by those who have failed even to admit guilt or error. These have been the great unresolved moral issues underlying German reconstruction. As long as they remain unresolved, rightist radicalism (as evidenced by the recent electoral gains of a neo-Nazi group) still has a chance to play on hitherto concealed ultranationalist and even Nazi-type prejudices.

Governmental Reconstruction in the Transition Period (1945–49)

The result of the territorial split and the failure of reorientation was a new totalitarian system in the Eastern zone and a democracy with strongly authoritarian features in West Germany.

Revival of Political Life

Revival of the procedures and institutions of political democracy started at an early point in all four zones. In agreement with the Potsdam program, elections were held, first for town and city councils, then for Land diets, in which parties all claiming to be democratic, from rightist Liberals to Communists, participated. Officials and cabinets, initially appointed by MG (the Military Government), were made responsible to such councils and diets, and government was organized in the Länder on the basis of constitutions adopted in more or less orthodox fashion.

Its Shortcomings

This democratization, however, was more a form (or, at best, a promise) than a reality. High voting figures made Allied officers assume that Germans now understood and underwrote the processes of democracy. In reality, Germans, hungry and miserable, simply did what they thought would please the occupiers and thus produce higher calorie rations. Moreover, local and regional autonomy meant little, since the reconstruction of a war-torn country like Germany required large-scale planning and central policy decisions. Activities that affected

the average German most vitally, such as rationing and price controls, food delivery quotas, and the amount of permitted industrial production, were outside German jurisdiction. Such matters were handled for entire zones, and even where the Allies used Germans on the zonal level, they were agents of the occupying power, not responsible administrators.

It is now clear that the introduction of formal democracy might better have been postponed until the Allies were ready to hand over genuine policy-making powers to Germans. The Allies themselves should first have undertaken those basic reforms (genuine denazification; democratization of the civil service; land, business, and educational reforms) which were the prerequisites of political democracy in Germany. This, it is true, would have had to be done by fiat of the victor, but it might have provided Germans with a sounder basis for subsequent reconstruction of democratic government. Instead, MG in the West divested itself of exactly those responsibilities that the Germans proved unready or unable to assume, while they were *not* put in charge of the more technical tasks (economic administration and so forth) which they were able to perform. In the Soviet zone, on the other hand, basic reforms *were* inaugurated by the conqueror's fiat but were not followed by anything approximating genuine self-government.

Economic Integration in the West

Faced with the impossibility of all-German unification, the Western Allies decided at least to unify their three zones. Economic preceded political integration. While the French balked, Americans and British merged their two zones economically in 1947. German bizonal agencies were fashioned into something resembling responsible government. There were an Economic Council, elected directly from Land diets and with legislative powers; a second chamber, representing Länder interests; and responsible heads of departments. In organization this foreshadowed the present Bonn government. In substance, it contributed little to democratization. Major jurisdictions were still reserved to the Allies, and even where Germans *did* have a free hand, actual power rested with the bureaucracy that staffed the new agencies, rather than with the people and their representatives. These officials considered efficient administration vastly more important for German reconstruction than submission to parties and diets.

Establishment of Eastern and Western Governments

Establishment of the present political German units of government—the Federal Republic of Germany and the German Democratic Republic —followed in 1949. In this the Western Allies took the initiative. The Soviets made it a rule always to trail the West by one step so as to shift responsibility for splitting Germany to the West and to appear as defenders of German unity.

The Western Allies had the more arduous task of first agreeing among themselves and then with the Germans. But the result was genuine German self-government. In the Soviet zone, Germans were ostensibly left free to draft a Constitution, but it was a foregone conclusion that the Socialist Unity party (SED) would act as the Soviet agent. The result was a puppet state, externally Soviet satellite and internally as pseudodemocratic as any other people's republic. In the West the Germans eventually became fully sovereign, and the framework in which government operates is that of constitutionalism and democracy.

On one point, however, both West and East German regimes agree. Both claim to be provisional, pending eventual German reunification, and each denies the other's popular mandate and legitimacy. Thus there now coexist two major though provisional units, and two minor units—West and East Berlin—a Germany in miniature. The boundaries are those of 1945, except that the Saar region, which was detached from Germany by the French after the war and set up with an autonomous government, was reunited with West Germany in 1957. There remains the territory east of the Oder-Neisse line, incorporated *de facto* into Poland and the Soviet Union. The question as to what all this constitutes legally seems as unanswerable as is the much-debated legal question of whether Germany, or one of its present units, is identical with the prewar Reich. The legal confusion is but a reflection of actual disarray.

West German Constitution and Government [9]

Drafting of the Bonn Constitution

Constitution-making in West Germany started with an agreement reached by six Western countries (United States, United Kingdom, France, Belgium, Netherlands, Luxembourg) in London on June 1, 1948. This agreement set the goal ("that the German people in the different states . . . establish for themselves the political organization and institutions which will enable them to assume . . . governmental responsibilities"); prescribed procedures ("the minister-presidents will be authorized to convene a constituent assembly in order to prepare a constitution for the approval of the participating states"); broadly defined the limits within which the Constitution-makers must work ("a federal form of government which adequately protects the rights of the respective states, and which at the same time provides for adequate central authority and which guarantees the rights and freedoms of the individual"); and put limits to future German autonomy through reservations concerning disarmament and the Ruhr. A further limitation, not mentioned in the London instrument, was contained in an Occupation Statute, which reserved important powers to the Allies.

The limitations concerning disarmament became pointless when integration of West Germany into the North Atlantic defense system shifted the accent toward rearming.[10] As for the Ruhr, the London agreement sealed the French failure to detach this industrial heart of Germany from Germany. An International Ruhr Authority, whose main function was to allocate Ruhr coal and steel to Germany and other countries, was soon superseded by the organization for pooling the coal and steel resources of Western Europe.

To avoid an impression of taking irrevocable steps toward splitting Germany, the minister-presidents of the eleven Länder—objecting to calling a "constituent assembly," to final popular

---

[9] On the East see Chapter 8.

[10] Certain limitations persist, however, such as the vital prohibition on production of ABC (atomic, biological, chemical) weapons. And with NATO now weakened, the question of whether to permit Germans to have an independent force has come to the fore again. (See Chapter 9.)

vote on the Constitution, and even to the term *constitution* itself—called a Parliamentary Council of sixty-five members, chosen by the Land diets on the basis of Länder population and proportional strength of parties in the diets. The Constitution was to be called Basic Law (*Grundgesetz*) and ratification was to be by at least two-thirds of the Land diets. The result was in fact a full-fledged Constitution, with the lack of direct popular participation in its preparation and adoption made up for by the subsequent election of the first West German parliament.

This Bonn Constitution (so called from the present capital of the Federal Republic) is the result of compromise between the Allies and the German parties. With both, the main issue was that of federalism, that is, states' rights versus centralism. Surprisingly, other basic issues, such as the type of parliamentary system to be set up, powers of the executive, and guarantees and restrictions of civil liberties, received relatively scant attention, although in these fields there are important innovations. Regarding federalism, the French and the Bavarian particularists favored a loose federation of autonomous states; the British and the Americans believed such a solution unworkable, and there was indeed, with the exception of Bavaria, no strong feeling for it in Germany.

Thus the loose federation idea was ruled out, and the issue was narrowed to the question of the second chamber (*Bundesrat*), which was to safeguard Länder influence in the central government. The Social Democrats wanted it to be elected by the *people* in the Länder (as Senators are in the United States), but the more authoritarian Christian Democrats wanted it to be a body of delegates appointed by the *governments* of the Länder (as under the Hohenzollern and Weimar systems). The Socialists wanted it to have a suspensive veto only, while the Christian Democrats wanted it to have equal powers with parliament. Eventually the Socialists conceded the bureaucratic type of council, while the Christian Democrats agreed to the suspensive veto.

Adoption of the Draft Constitution

With this problem out of the way, adoption of the draft Constitution proceeded smoothly.

The final vote was fifty-three to twelve, the minority comprising some Bavarians and a few representatives of smaller parties, among them the Communists. Social Democrats and Christian Democrats were able to agree on a constitution because workers as well as middle classes realized that German sovereignty on a non-Communist basis could be attained only through adoption of a democratic-parliamentary structure of government. The Basic Law was then approved by the three military governors and ratified by the Land diets, with all but the Bavarian diet voting for it. It was promulgated on May 23, 1949.

Elections for the Bundestag, the first free German election of a central parliament in seventeen years, were held on August 14, 1949. The two parties chiefly responsible for the Basic Law, Christian Democrats and Social Democrats, emerged as victors; their opponents, rightists as well as Communists, were soundly defeated. Although, strictly speaking, this was not a vote on the new Constitution, politically it meant confirmation. Bundestag and Bundesrat then convened, and with the election of a federal president and a federal chancellor and the formation of a Cabinet, the new government had started functioning by the end of September 1949.

Allied Reservations

Allied approval of the Constitution had been accompanied by reservations contained in an Occupation Statute promulgated by the three Allied military governors. Certain fields, such as demilitarization and security of the Allied occupation forces, were reserved to the Allies; in the fields left to the Germans, the Allies reserved the right to veto agreements between the federal government and foreign countries, and, in exceptional cases, to repeal any other German law; finally, the Allies reserved the right to resume "full authority" when "essential to security or to preserve democratic government in Germany or in pursuance of the international obligations of their governments." Ultimate authority thus still rested with the Allies. They exercised it through a civilian Allied High Commission, into which MG was transformed.

Subsequently these restrictions of German autonomy were whittled down; they were

STRUCTURE OF THE WEST GERMAN FEDERAL GOVERNMENT
According to the Constitution of 1949

EXECUTIVE

President

Elected for five-year term by federal Convention consisting of members of Diet and equal number of members elected by Land diets.

All acts must be countersigned by Chancellor or a federal minister.

Appoints and dismisses ministers on proposal of Chancellor, nominates Chancellor.

Promulgates laws, ratifies treaties, appoints federal officials.

Federal Cabinet

Chancellor

Nominated by President, elected by Diet.

Selects ministers, may request their dismissal.

Determines general policy.

May propose dissolution of Diet if Diet refuses confidence.

Ministers

Appointed and dismissed by President on proposal of Chancellor.

Responsible for direction of their departments.

Cabinet may request President to declare state of legislative emergency. Submits bills to Diet.

LEGISLATIVE

Diet

(Bundestag)

Elected by people of the Republic for four-year term.

Passes federal laws, including constitutional amendments.

Elects Chancellor.

May express nonconfidence in Chancellor, but only by electing a successor at the same time.

May be dissolved within twenty-one days after it has refused to vote confidence in the Chancellor, unless it elects a new Chancellor.

Federal Council

(Bundesrat)

Members appointed and recalled freely by Land governments; each Land has from three to five votes.

Initiates bills, scrutinizes government bills; suspensive veto over laws. Approval of constitutional amendments and of certain financial laws.

Right to approve declaration, by President, of state of legislative emergency; in this case, its approval of bills replaces that of Diet.

JUDICIAL

Supreme Court

Reviews decisions of lower courts, original criminal jurisdiction in treason trials.

Judges selected by federal Justice Minister and a committee composed of Land ministers of justice and equal number of members elected by Diet.

Constitutional Court

Decides on constitutionality of federal laws, on compatibility of federal and state law, other constitutional conflicts between federal government and Länder, complaints about violation of basic rights of individuals, outlawry of anti-democratic parties, impeachment of President and other cases.

Consists of members of Supreme Court and other law-trained members, half of them elected by Diet, the other half by Federal Council.

Other Highest Courts

(Special Courts)

---

scheduled to disappear with the establishment of the European Defense Community, but it took another couple of years after the failure of EDC to make West Germany fully independent. It became so in 1955 with the coming into effect of the London and Paris agreements of 1954. These, constituting an extraordinarily complicated network of treaties, protocols, and similar understandings of the Western powers with West Germany, in effect terminated an occupation regime still based on unconditional surrender.[11] The old regime was replaced with a regime under which Western rights in Germany,

[11] With the exception of Berlin, where, in principle if not in practice, the "four-power status" continues to this day. (See Chapter 8.)

and with respect to Germany, are retained with the consent of the Germans. This refers above all to the continued stationing of foreign troops on German territory. In domestic affairs the Germans were set completely free. Rule over a vanquished nation yielded to partnership.

The Structure of the Bonn Government

The Republic thus established is seemingly federal, liberal, and democratic. But Bonn federalism is tempered by strong central bureaucratic controls, and its democracy is balanced by authoritarian features. These are chiefly connected with the Chancellorship. In contrast to Weimar, the President is weak. He now is not popularly elected, and he does not have his own powers of dissolution or emergency. The Chancellor has emerged as the strong man. He cannot easily be deposed by the Bundestag, for, in order to avoid executive instability and frequent cabinet crises, the Bonn Constitution provides for the so-called constructive vote of nonconfidence—a vote which, to be effective, requires that a majority of the legal membership of the Bundestag simultaneously elect a successor to the Chancellorship. Thus the opposition must agree on a new cabinet before the overthrow of the old one. Once elected at the beginning of the legislative period, a Chancellor may thus be fairly sure of staying in office for the duration of a four-year term. This comes close to a Swiss version of parliamentary regimes, according to which the executive, once it has been established by the diet, continues to stay in office for the remainder of the parliamentary period. In countries with a firm parliamentary tradition, like Switzerland, the executive can be relied upon to follow the directives of the assembly. In Germany, with her authoritarian tradition, there is a danger that it will overshadow parliament. Also, the Bonn Constitution permits the Chancellor to appoint and dismiss ministers freely; he may even keep them in office in the teeth of parliamentary disapproval, since there is no provision for voting nonconfidence in ministers.

Possibly the effort to avoid executive instability has shifted the weight too much to the executive side. At any rate, it enabled Chancellor Adenauer to rule West Germany for fourteen years on a paternalistic pattern. Since his demise, the executive has been weaker, partly because of lack of strong leadership, and partly because of dissensions among and within the parties making up the majority. Still, the lengthy incubation period inhibited the rise of more democratic customs and habits.

In other respects, the Bonn system tries to strike an interesting balance between liberal principles and protection of state authority. Nazi experience produced a strong desire for guarantees of political liberty and personal security. Weimar experience, on the other hand, called for safeguards against misuse of liberty for antidemocratic ends. As a result, the Constitution goes far in defining rights and even protects some against suspension by statutes or constitutional amendment. On the other hand, there are provisions that permit far-reaching infringement of these rights, for example, those that allow the outlawing of parties that are hostile to "the liberal-democratic order" or seek "to jeopardize the existence of the Republic." We have here an attempt to cope with one of the most difficult problems confronting democracies faced with totalitarian danger: how to protect the constitutional order effectively without destroying the freedoms on which this very order rests.

On the whole, a valiant effort has been made in West Germany to lay the foundations of a working constitutional order. While democratic forces still face an uphill fight, there is at least a live and open issue as to how to win the fight. And in contrast to the closed system in the East, elections, votes in parliaments, competition among parties and among wings within parties are meaningful and relevant. In short, there is active political life; and democracy, while still frail, seems at least to have a chance. Bonn is a framework for an opportunity; nothing more—but also nothing less.

3. German Parties and Elections[1]

1. THE HISTORICAL PATTERN OF THE GERMAN PARTY SYSTEM

Background and Development

During the postwar period the British party system, famous for its stability and efficiency, has repeatedly yielded such flimsy parliamentary majorities that the continued existence of government depended on the health of one or two M.P.'s. During that same period the West German government, under what more and more resembles the British two-party system, has had the backing of clear majorities of parties (1953–57, even that of one party) and thus has been genuinely stable and efficient.

Does this indicate that Germans now have a sounder party system than the British? Before we jump to such a conclusion, we must understand the historical premises of the situation. While in the Western democracies parties have long embodied the chief political forces that carry on government, in Germany parties have usually been on the periphery rather than at the center of political life. Even today the average German does not like to be identified with a political party. More than eighty out of a hundred declared that they were unwilling formally to become members of a party; sixty out of a hundred expressed disgust with the idea of becoming politicians. In another poll, politicians ranked lowest (together with journalists and advertising agents) in their estimation of occupations.[2] When asked what party he belongs

to, the German is more likely than not to say that he is "above party." At the same time, however, he will admit to having close ties to one of the general philosophies, or world views, that underlie party programs. Thus the German has tended to be doctrinaire, with his opinion on all manner of specific problems determined by what the respective liberal, or socialist, or nationalist, or Catholic doctrine, to which he *and* his party adhere, has to say about the question. Thus he is partisan, sometimes in the extreme, in his general attitudes. This explains why what appear to outsiders as minor issues have been fought over in Germany as if they were matters of life and death. Only recently has there been some attenuation of this doctrinairism. At the same time, the German is inclined to despise "party wrangling" in diets and assemblies, that is, he tries to be "above party" in regard to the role assigned to parties in public life.

Contempt for political parties and strong doctrinaire attitudes are both rooted in German history. Parties arose in Germany after the state, with its authoritarian government, had long been in existence. In Britain and the United States parties were a part, and an essential part, of the state from the very beginning of modern government; in France they conquered the state. In Prussia-Germany they were imposed, like constitutions and parliaments, upon the pre-existing and stable organization of a bureaucratic-militaristic state. The essential business of state continued to be done without or despite them. Until 1918 the parties could be left to

---

[1] Chapters 3 through 7 will deal primarily with West Germany; the discussion of East Germany is reserved for Chapter 8.

[2] According to a 1965 poll, only 4 percent of adult Germans participate in some form of political activity; 11 percent said they would like to do so, but 78 percent were strictly

negative. Every fifth German did not know which parties were represented in the Bundestag—indeed, 13 percent could not name a single one of them; 70 percent did not know which parties made up the government.

bicker among themselves while stable government was guaranteed by rule from above. When responsibility to govern was suddenly thrust upon them, they were inexperienced, divided, unable to cooperate. Hence the failure of Weimar.

Germany's multiparty system was the result not of a peculiar election system but of Germany's authoritarian heritage, its lack of religious homogeneity, its regional diversity, and its deferred national unification. Different political movements originated in different parts of what later became Germany: democratic chiefly in the southwest, conservative mostly in the Prussian northeast, political Catholicism primarily in the Rhine region and Bavaria. Some of the resulting parties remained sectional parties, vestiges of which still survive. At the same time, classes, and the economic interests they represented, organized themselves as parties; and since they were not integrated into the state until after World War I they too tended to split into numerous groups, often representing petty special interests. Thus the average party remained a combination of "church" and pressure group. In the United States, pressures work from the outside on parties and their leaders and deputies; in Germany, such interests as labor or farmers have tended to organize themselves as political parties, trying to conceal their character behind an idealistic creed. In this they resemble French parties. But German parties, reflecting their society, have been more like centralized machines, without their members at large having much influence over organization and formulation of policies.

While this recalls the British system, in Germany there has more often been group leadership rather than individual leadership. Forceful leaders, such as Adenauer, have been infrequent in German party life. Local bosses in the American sense have also been the exception, all this mainly because of the low esteem in which the politician has been held in Germany. Since the most important positions in public life were in the hands of a permanent bureaucracy, the politician had little by way of spoils to distribute. His own job as a politician, even if he managed to be elected to some assembly, was unimportant before 1918 and continued to be regarded so under Weimar. Diets were considered mere "talking shops." This accounts for the failure of German party life to attract the forceful, ambitious, and broad-minded, and for the prevalence of the mediocre, elderly, and bureaucratic-minded.

Until recently, then, the German party system could be compared with the systems of the three main Western democracies as follows:

(1) It was a more-than-one-party system; that is, in common with the American, British, and French systems it was (except for the Nazi period) a system of genuine, freely organized, freely functioning, and competing parties.

(2) It was a more-than-two-party system; that is, like the French, and unlike the American and the British, the German party system did not produce two major parties that dominated the scene and alternated in government.

(3) It was a system without agreement on fundamental issues; that is, again like the French and unlike the American and British, German parties failed to agree on the essentials of a constitution. Fundamental problems of how to organize state and government remained party issues, and there was a tendency toward the formation of radical and extremist opposition parties.

(4) German parties, unlike those of the United States, and like those of France and Britain, represented specific social classes, reflecting specific economic interests, and having definite doctrines.

(5) German parties were centralized; like the British and unlike the other two, they were not grassroots parties but were dominated by, and were integral parts of, a central machine and its bureaucracy.

Recent Trends

Nothing is more indicative of genuine change in German political life and, possibly, even in German behavior patterns, than the changes that have recently taken place in regard to most of these points. The German party system now tends to resemble more the British, and even the American, system than the French. First of all, two major parties have tended to dominate the political scene, and since these two parties are moderate, there is today in West Germany more agreement on constitutional essentials than ever before. In addition, we discern a trend toward more forceful party leadership and even an increase in popular interest and participation. Doctrinairism is subsiding in favor of a more pragmatic approach to political issues, whether as an effect of re-education, Americanization, or a world-wide trend toward less interest in ideas and more in tangible things. It would, however, be rash to assert anything more than that the present system is in a stage of transition. It is too early to say whither it is bound and whether it will endure. While some cautious optimism is warranted, we must remember that much in the new system has been tied up with fortuitous circumstances, such as the emergence of one strong party leader, or general prosperity, or, indeed, national partition. It would be foolhardy to predict that it would survive radical change in these circumstances.

2. THE PRESENT PARTY SYSTEM

Postwar Reestablishment of Parties

The political reconstruction of Germany required the reorganization of political parties. But giving the Germans a free hand involved the risk that Nazis might revive their shattered organization. The solution resorted to by the four occupation powers was the licensing of a limited number of parties, with the Soviets taking the lead in their occupation zone and the other occupying powers following suit.

After importing exiled German Communists from Moscow and thus giving the Communist party (CP) a head start, the Soviet MG allowed the Social Democrats (SPD) to organize themselves; then, still expecting early German unification on an initial basis of "bourgeois" democracy, they licensed two middle-class parties, the Christian Democratic Union (CDU) and the Liberal Democratic party (LDP). This gave them the jump on the Western powers, which wanted the new parties in their zones to grow from the grassroots.

But the new parties in the Western zones failed to do so. Germans fell back into the habit of forming centrally organized parties. Surviving Weimar leaders filled the void and organized the four new licensed parties on the pattern

they had known. The masses, dazed and apathetic, took little interest. Only when full domestic autonomy was granted did more popular interest assert itself.

Party Trends

The initial trend was to the left. The Nazis and their rightist collaborators were discredited, more so than even the monarchists had been after 1918. The Communists, their brief defection of 1939–41 (the period of the Stalin-Hitler pact) forgotten, had gained prestige as antifascist resisters. The German worker seemed ready to back up the cooperation of all socialists. But the Soviets squandered this store of good will; their behavior in the Soviet zone destroyed the chance of genuine labor collaboration. Outside their zone the Communist vote declined rapidly. In Rhineland-Westphalia, for example, an area that includes the traditional Communist stronghold of the Ruhr, it went down from an initial 13.7 percent in 1946 to a mere 3.8 percent in 1954. In the last Bundestag election in which they took part, the Communists attained hardly more than 2 percent of the vote. In this respect West Germany contrasts strikingly with France and Italy, where the Communists emerged after the war as the stronger workers' party. In West Germany, on the other hand, the moderate socialists (SPD) have consistently enjoyed the support of the major portion of labor and in this way became one of the two major parties.

The other major innovation in the German political landscape has been the emergence of one strong middle-class party, the Christian Democratic, which now controls the other large bloc of votes. While this picture was perhaps somewhat deceptive in the beginning, since the parties that might have appealed to antidemocratic voters were not allowed to exist, it has since become clear that the trend has genuinely been one toward moderation. With the end of licensing, in 1950, it is true, there was at first a proliferation of other parties, including ultranationalist ones that enjoyed some regional success. But with the economic and foreign policy successes of the Adenauer government, the party system consolidated itself on the basis of two dominant parties.

This development raises two major questions.

First, is radicalism dead? Second, does West Germany now have, or is it approaching, a genuine two-party system?

Leftist extremism, in the form of communism, can be discounted as long as German partition and the resulting Communist control of East Germany endure. Communism had been strong in Weimar Germany because it appeared to a large segment of the working class as a genuine socialist movement. Since 1945, however, German communism has become identified with Soviet policies and with Soviet control of the Eastern zone. Thus one may even doubt the wisdom of the suppression (by verdict of the Constitutional Court, in 1956) of the Communist party as an "antidemocratic party." Its chances as a secret organization, aided and subsidized from the East, have hardly been diminished thereby, while in union and factory elections, where Communists frequently run as nonpartisan representatives of labor, they have from time to time been endorsed by politically non-Communist workers. But there remained, in 1965, an estimated mere six thousand to seven thousand (illegal) members and a radical-leftist party. The German Peace Union (DFU), founded in 1960 with Communist backing and partly infiltrated by the CP, polled less than 2 percent in 1961 and 1965, of which perhaps one-half was Communist. Thus West German communism at present seems doomed to insignificance, except as a tightly organized fifth column for propaganda and subversion.

Rightist radicalism is less easily discounted. True, the general climate of antiadventurism and moderation is genuine, but its roots have been largely pragmatic, if not opportunistic. As we have seen, a genuine reorientation toward democratic values has not been demonstrated by a majority of the people, and the continuance of moderation thus seems to be predicated upon continued prosperity on the one hand, and continuation of at least a "cold peace" on the other. It is true that until the mid-1960's neo-Nazi groups were unable to attract any significant number of voters. Among a bewildering number of forever splitting, merging, and reorganizing groups, one such group, the Socialist Reich party (SRP), with its unashamed and open neo-Nazi symbols and propaganda slogans (of the "a-pity-not-all-Jews-were-gassed" variety) had some success in the early 1950's but was subsequently suppressed as antidemocratic. Its successor, the German Reich party, likewise failed to find any considerable backing at the polls or otherwise. But in 1964 the various rightist splinters managed to merge, together with deserters from some more moderate parties, into one new organization, the German National Democratic Party (NPD). This party got a mere 2 percent of the vote in the federal election of 1965 but surged to approximately 8 percent in regional elections in 1966.[3] Its development, therefore, bears watching. Its successes indicate that rightist extremism, after failing to gain influence through infiltrating established parties, such as the FDP (Free Democratic Party, the name the party originally licensed as Liberal Democrats subsequently assumed), and two now almost defunct groups, the DP (German party, a small right-wing party) and the BHE (representing the expellees), has now some chance to reassert itself as a separately organized political force.

On the other hand, there is more to the problem of rightist radicalism than is revealed by voting and membership figures. In the main, the German mind is not yet stably moderate, let alone democratic. When we were discussing democratic reorientation, we discovered a strong tendency to repress the Nazi past and to apologize for it; later on, we shall encounter the sometimes strongly nationalist orientation of nonparty political associations. Frequently, a strange medley of contradictory attitudes characterizes the West German political atmosphere. In 1961, about two-thirds of those Germans polled came out for severe punishment of Eichmann; in 1965 two-thirds said that they opposed further prosecution of Nazi murderers. Often, a pronounced nationalism that is as strongly anti-Western (especially anti-American and frequently anti-British) as it is anti-Russian comes to the fore despite the nation's official Western orientation. Violent and sometimes irrational anticommunism seems to have taken the place of former anti-Semitism. Dreams of greatness and a hankering for strong, one-man leadership

[3] In Hesse: 7.9 percent; in Bavaria: 7.4 percent. In certain districts of these Länder they got considerably more.

Evolution of a Two-Party System in West Germany, 1949–65

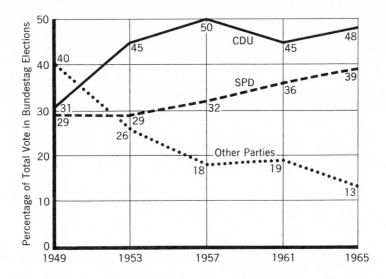

alternate with an insistence on moderation and on respect for individual rights and constitutional order.

In view of this ambivalence, much will depend on the development of more stable convictions among the followers of the major parties. Their present indifference toward party life and party politics suggests that they may become volatile should present conditions change—under economic stress, for example, or heightened international crisis. Much will also depend on the strength of democratic leadership. Adenauer's leadership was moderate but authoritarian and paternalistic, and his toleration of close aides with Nazi records hardly helped the task of reorientation. His successor, Erhard, lacked leadership capacity, and German ability to resist extremism may be determined by how successful the leaders of the "grand coalition" government, formed after Erhard's demise, will be in efforts to reassert democratic leadership and to combat the incipient rise of rightist radicalism.

Is there a trend toward a two-party system? There seems to be. The combined vote of the two major parties has risen steadily, from 60 percent in the first (1949) Bundestag election to 74 in 1953, to 82 in 1957 and 1961, and to 87 in 1965. However, if by a two-party system one

means that two parties alternate in office, with the one enjoying an absolute majority forming the government and the other the opposition, Germany does not yet have such a system. Even the Christian Democrats, who so far have always gained a relative majority, have never commanded more than 50 percent of the vote (with one exception, in 1953, when, however, they nevertheless formed a coalition government). Consequently, they always had to form a coalition with third parties, or with one third party, in order to gain the backing of a parliamentary majority. The third party in such circumstances holds the balance of power and wields an influence quite out of proportion to its relatively small voting base. Its influence on the composition of the Cabinet and, possibly, even the choice of Chancellor, may thus become decisive.

For many years the FDP enjoyed this favorable position. It was deprived of it only through the getting together of both major groups. This happened in 1966, when the CDU and SPD jointly established a government of the "grand (or great) coalition." But such a system, while constituting the acme of two-party *control*, can hardly compare to the classical two-party *system* (with one major group in office and the other one in opposition). Its danger lies in the vanishing of *any* opposition. Its weakness lies in the difficulty of agreeing on common policies and the likelihood of each encountering opposition in its own ranks against concessions to the coalition partner.

At the subnational, especially the regional, level of government the influence of third parties as well as that of the SPD has been more important. In the past, there were several smaller parties with regionally concentrated strength which thus would draw higher voter support in a given Land than their overall percentage in a national election. Although these regional parties are now disappearing even from the regional scene, the FDP has remained significant in a couple of Länder. The NPD, which in 1966 replaced the FDP in the Bavarian diet, may become so. Furthermore, Land elections falling between national elections show that the high vote rolled up by the CDU tends to decline sharply in the off years, usually to the benefit of the SPD. The table below shows the contrast

	BAVARIA			HESSE			LOWER SAXONY		
	1961	*Off-year Election*	1965	1961	*Off-year Election*	1965	1961	*Off-year Election*	1965
CDU	55	47	56	35	29	38	39	38	46
SPD	30	35	33	43	51	46	39	45	40

	HAMBURG			RHINELAND-PALATINATE		
	1961	*Off-year Election*	1965	1961	*Off-year Election*	1965
CDU	32	29	38	49	44	49
SPD	47	57	48	34	41	37

(Overall percentages in the federal elections were:
1961: CDU 45.3, SPD 36.2; 1965: CDU 47.6, SPD 39.3)

between votes gained by the two major parties in the Bundestag elections of 1961 and 1965 (percentages won by these parties in the respective Länder), and in the Land elections in selected Länder in off-year elections. Such figures show that the German voter has been sophisticated enough to split his vote; many of those voting CDU—which, for thirteen years, meant Adenauer—in Bundestag elections turned elsewhere, particularly to the SPD, in state and local elections. Certain states, and, increasingly, the major cities of West Germany have thus been controlled by the SPD rather than the CDU.

Thus present party trends are marked by

Three German Elections (Empire, Weimar, Bonn)

	1912	1928		1949
		All Germ.	*W. Germ.*	*W. Germ.*
SPD (Social Democratic party)	34.8	29.8	26.9	29.2
CP (Communist party)		10.6	8.6	5.7
Center [1]	16.4	15.2	23.3	34.1
Liberals [2]	13.6	8.7	8.9 ⎫	
Democrats [3]	12.3	4.8	4.6 ⎬	11.9
Conservatives [4]	12.2	14.2	9.5	
Others	10.7	16.7	18.2	19.1

[1] 1928: Including Bavarian People's party; 1949: CDU, CSU, Center party.
[2] 1928: German People's party; 1949: FDP.
[3] 1912: Progressive party; 1949: FDP.
[4] 1928: German Nationalists.

Bundestag Elections 1949–65

	1949	*1953*	*1957*	*1961*	*1965*
CDU/CSU	31	45.2	50.2	45.4	47.6
SPD	29.2	28.8	31.8	36.2	39.3
FDP	11.9	9.5	7.7	12.8	9.5
Block (BHE) [1]		5.9	4.6 ⎱		
DP [1]	4	3.3	3.4 ⎰	2.8	
CP	5.7	2.2			
Others	18.2	5.1	2.3	2.8	3.6

[1] 1961: All-German party (GDP).

three characteristics: (1) a flocking of voters to two major groups that are not too unequal in backing; (2) the continuing impact of smaller parties, especially the Free Democrats, and, more recently, the NPD; and (3) an uneven geographical distribution of votes, especially among CDU and SPD, with the former strongest in the Rhine region and Bavaria, the latter in Hesse and the North.

3. THE PARTIES AND THEIR POLICIES

We turn now to a consideration of the individual parties, beginning with the party that has dominated the federal government since its inception.

Christian Democratic (Christian Social) Union (CDU–CSU)

Background and Development

For the first time in the history of German parties there has emerged a nonsocialist party that rallies the largest proportion of nonsocialist Germans, especially the middle classes but also a significant number of workers. And since the Christian Democratic party has been *the* government party in West Germany at least from the inception of the Federal Republic to the end of 1966 (and even after that furnished the Chancellor to the "grand coalition"), its policy has had a decisive bearing on domestic as well as foreign policies. What kind of party is it?

The answer is not easy. Despite its forceful leadership, it has been and is many things to different people. Successor to at least portions of all the pre-Nazi rightist and centrist parties, it combines elements and trends of all of them. Most important, perhaps, is the heritage of the old Center party, the party of the Catholics which cut through all class lines and in program and policies reflected a merger of different social groups and economic interests. But the party is now more broadly Christian, that is, it joins Protestants and Catholics in its ranks. After World War II, large segments of European nonsocialists, liberated from or disillusioned with totalitarianism and unwilling to join rightist parties discredited by collaboration with fascism, favored a progressive movement based on Christian principles. Some of these nonsocialists genuinely embraced antitotalitarianism and democratic-social, if not socialist, ideals; others felt that this seemed to be the only effective way of stemming a more leftist flood. Hence the MRP in France and the Christian Democrats in Italy and Germany. Thus the CDU also fell heir to the former Conservatives (under Weimar, the German Nationalists, the representatives of the "old" ruling groups and classes) and to various liberal parties (the National Liberals, later the German People's party, which chiefly represented big business, and the Progressives, later German Democrats, which represented lower-middle and middle-middle-class elements). It is hard to state which force is dominant in this coalition of divergent forces. To a degree the party has succeeded in striking a balance, but over twenty years a trend can also be discerned that goes from more leftist beginnings toward a rightist and, in the socioeconomic sense, conservative orientation. But while it thus has assumed the place of an anti-

Geography of the 1965 Bundestag Election

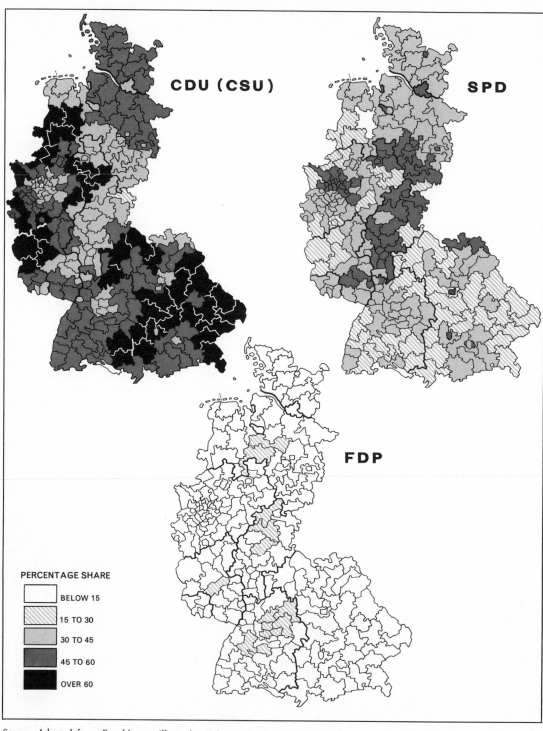

CDU (CSU)

SPD

FDP

PERCENTAGE SHARE

BELOW 15

15 TO 30

30 TO 45

45 TO 60

OVER 60

Source: Adapted from *Frankfurter Allgemeine Zeitung,* October 1, 1965, p. 4.

socialist conservative middle-class party, it cannot be completely identified with traditional German rightist parties, since it defends or at least accepts the present constitutional framework and stands for moderation in foreign policy.

Present Structure and Organization

The CDU was the last among the major parties to organize itself on an interzonal level. Its affiliate, the Christian Social Union (CSU) in Bavaria, still remains organizationally separate. The CSU is the successor to a Bavarian Catholic party, which during Weimar had split away from the center, being more agrarian-conservative and states' rights minded than the mother party. Representing the native Bavarian peasant and middle classes, the CSU is under conservative leadership and often experiences strong clerical influence. Although it forms a single parliamentary group (in Germany called a "fraction"; see Chapter 4) with the CDU in the Bundestag, it sometimes operates as if it were a separate party. Its present chairman, Franz Josef Strauss, has powerfully asserted its independence.

The CDU, on the other hand, though in theory it embraces states' rights principles, in practice has long been under centralized leadership. True, the statutes of the party provide for local and regional organization, but there is little apparatus of full-time party functionaries; the honorary, part-time functionaries, fearful of endangering their own positions, show little interest in party activities or efforts to increase party membership. On the top level there are: a Party Congress of about five hundred and fifty members (representing the regional districts in proportion to CDU membership there and last Bundestag voting figures); a somewhat smaller "little party congress" (*Ausschuss*) of about a hundred and sixty; a party executive of sixty-five, which includes the highest-level leadership; and the presidium, elected by the Congress and headed by the party chairman and a party manager. The 1966 Party Congress, revamping this top leadership at Adenauer's resignation as chairman, fixed the number of presidium members at eleven (including the party's chairman, three deputy chairmen, and a manager). Until March 1966 the chairman had been

Konrad Adenauer [1876–1967], one of the few forceful leaders ever produced in Germany, who could not be prevailed upon to give up his chairmanship even when, in 1963, he surrendered the governmental leadership (Chancellorship) he had held for fourteen years. So long as he was Chancellor, none of the party bodies or their leaders could, or cared to, challenge this one real center of power. Under him there was dissension, rivalry, jockeying for successorship; all this was ably exploited by the "Old Man," and talk of revolt or constitutionalization would regularly fizzle out after a while. When Erhard succeeded to the Chancellorship, factionalism and a good deal of infighting developed, which the Chancellor tried in vain to overcome. Adenauer, who had opposed Erhard from the outset, joined forces with younger, upcoming leaders, such as Rainer Barzel (chairman of the CDU/CSU parliamentary fraction), CSU leader Franz Josef Strauss, and regional party heads. One of the latter, Kurt Georg Kiesinger, backed and promoted by CSU leader Strauss, finally replaced Erhard as Chancellor in December 1966.

Membership and Policies

The CDU, like other middle-class parties in Germany, is distinguished from the SPD in that fewer of its followers are actually members who take an active part in party affairs. As against 700,000 SPD members, there are about 280,000 members of the CDU, constituting a little over 2 percent, as against 6 in the SPD, of those who vote for it. Thus the main problem is not to run the party—something that is done primarily by small groups of volunteers aided by party functionaries—but to keep the backing of the voters, that is, to maintain the allegiance of the different groups on whose backing the party depends at election time. (The pattern is reversed in the SPD, whose followers can be better relied upon to troop to the polls.)

Who are these groups? First of all, Catholics, who make up about 50 percent of the total West German population, about 60 percent of those voting CDU, and about 65 percent of the party membership. This has not meant, however, that the party is predominantly Catholic in outlook or policies. While clerical influence is noticeable here and there, there is a studious attempt to maintain "parity" between

Composition of Parties

	CDU/ CSU	SPD	FDP
Men	41%	56%	49%
Women	59	44	51
21 to 29 years	21	22	17
30 to 44 years	26	33	29
45 to 59 years	30	27	31
60 and over	23	18	23
Grammar-school edu- cation	74	88	56
High-school education	26	12	44
Workers	37	67	21
Employees	26	18	30
Officials	10	5	11
Businessmen	13	5	23
Professions	2	1	4
Farmers	12	4	11
Monthly income below 400 DM	14	10	9
400 to 599	25	31	20
600 to 799	26	36	23
800 to 999	18	15	21
1,000 to 1,499	13	7	18
1,500 and over	4	1	9
Protestants	40	63	69
Catholics	58	31	26
Others	2	6	5

is shown in the table on the left which also reveals the proportion of the parties' supporters in regard to age groups, sex, education, and the like. According to a poll taken in the summer of 1964 these groups backed CDU, SPD, and FDP in the percentages listed (each percentage group adding up to 100).

The CDU's diversity of backing has not led to confusion in policies. Adenauer saw to that. He represented the conservative wing of the party, and his rule reflected the victory of this wing over the left. The left wing is chiefly composed of the workers' wing of political Catholicism and its trade union arm, the former Christian trade unions (which are now absorbed into the overall trade union organization of Germany). The stronghold of this group is in the Ruhr, but its weakness is apparent in its failure to have even an attenuated program implemented. The wishes of this wing had been reflected in a platform of 1947, the so-called Ahlen program, which had gone so far as to advocate nationalization of coal and steel, participation of workers in the management of private industry, and dissolution of cartels and monopolies. But the actual policies of the party have favored protection of private property, free enterprise, and free trade. These policies enjoy the backing of major portions of Ruhr industry, the civil service (the federal civil service was established largely on the basis of Adenauer's patronage), and parts of the peasantry and the lower-middle class.

The party's left wing is now primarily represented through its "social policy committees" of CDU workers and employees on different party levels. The party's organization of about fifty thousand younger members (the Young Union), likewise tends to more progressive policies. Since the death of its most prominent leader, Karl Arnold, the left wing has been without forceful leadership, and on the whole the influence of the "big" interests has prevailed in questions of economic and similar policy. There has been tension from time to time, for example, over cartel legislation, between the party's outstanding economic leader, Ludwig Erhard, an old-fashioned economic "liberal," and Ruhr industry. On the whole, however, the spirit of big business has prevailed. In spite of this, prosperity has enabled the CDU

Catholics and Protestants in staffing party and state positions and in other personnel questions. Intraparty tension between socio-economic groups and interests is greater than that between the two religious portions of the party. Indeed, the party represents a delicate balance among four distinct sets of potentially conflicting interests: (a) Catholics and Protestants; (b) clericals and the more liberal (secular) minded; (c) industrialists and other big business interests, as against the employees and particularly the workers in the party; and (d) the sectional balance between the party's two chief strongholds, the primarily big-city area of the Rhine and the Ruhr, and the predominantly rural and small-town Bavaria (controlled by the formally separate CSU).

The relatively broad range of support for the CDU, in contrast to the SPD and the FDP, leadership to maintain its employee backing, and the foreign policy successes as well as the personal leadership factor contributed to its general success.

One of the party's most significant achievements has been its ability to obtain the backing of many Protestants, especially in the Protestant north. While for many Catholics the CDU is still the former Center party in a new guise, Protestants rally to it as to a more or less conservative middle-class party. While its Catholic element is more prominent in leadership and promotion, the Protestant vote is sufficient to make it broadly representative of a middle class to which have been restored profits, prosperity, status, and authoritarian values. It has thus become the party of "restoration." Even today, nothing is more revealing of its general stand and that of the masses of its voters, than its chief slogan in the 1957 election: "No experiments!"

Prospects

The future of the CDU as one of the big parties seems to depend on two things. One is whether its program and policies will continue to satisfy a sufficient number of supporters to enable it to pose as a true "people's party" drawing support from all major groups, in the American style. Representing, in the main, middle-class and, especially, business interests, it has yet to increase its appeal to the workers and other "lower" groups (as it must do if it is to gain absolute majorities). In the past, it has made regular handouts to the masses just prior to elections, in the form of increased social security benefits, reduced taxes on consumers goods, and so forth. In this way the CDU could appear as reformist and even progressive without jeopardizing the prosperity of the upper classes. Under less favorable economic conditions, however, occasional concessions may not suffice, and the party may then be faced with the dilemma of dissatisfying either the masses or the classes. Similarly, foreign policy reverses might split it into moderates (who still prevail) and more nationalist rightists (who might then come to the fore). Or the rightists might desert it and flock to the NPD.

The other major problem is that of leadership. While under Adenauer the CDU suffered from excessive control by one man, it now faces the opposite danger of dissension. From 1963 to 1966 the division of top leadership into party and government leadership in itself created serious problems, since it was contrary to the underlying idea of a parliamentary system in which the leader of the victorious party assumes control of government. Instead, Adenauer, unable to resign himself to Erhard's succession to the chancellorship, harassed him in every conceivable way—for example, by forming with Strauss and others a "de Gaullist" faction against the Chancellor and his Foreign Minister, Gerhard Schroeder. After Adenauer's resignation from the chairmanship, and Erhard's from the Chancellorship, much in the future of the party depends on whether its new leader will be able to create that minimum of party unity without which the party faces not only continual dissension but the very danger of disintegration.

The Social Democratic Party (SPD)

Background and Development

While the CDU is a new phenomenon in the history of German parties and politics, the SPD can look back on a hundred years' continuous development as *the* party of the German worker and, frequently, the strongest and potentially most powerful party of all. Even at a time when communism was a competitor, democratic socialism never lost the support of a majority of the working people. Its sustained strength, from the time when it emerged triumphant from Bismarck's antisocialist fight to the end of the Weimar period, and from 1945 onward when it again emerged from illegality, is thus hardly surprising. Its technically unsurpassed organization, the discipline and devotion of its members, its press, youth, and women's groups, and its close contact with free trade unions were envied and imitated by other socialist parties. Yet it has so far failed to have any considerable impact on German developments. When, after its long period of outsider status under the Empire, it at long last seemed to hold a commanding position (under Weimar), it failed even to preserve the constitutional framework of the new republican regime. And in the postwar period it was until 1966 condemned to play, in the main, the role of an impotent and frustrated opposition. What is wrong with the party? What are its chances, if any?

It is relatively easy to see why the SPD failed in the past. Under the Empire, when even moderately liberal groups were excluded from government, its role could only be negative, and its attitude the radicalism of its founders, Marx and Engels. The German proletariat, denied recognition by the ruling classes, developed a kind of "socialist subculture" of its own. But, gradually, the SPD veered toward a revisionism that held that the aims of socialism could and should be attained through democratic processes. When, in 1918, this opportunity seemed to have come, the SPD missed it, even in the moderate sense of laying the foundations of genuine political democracy. The causes of this failure—chiefly, the split of the workers' movement, the absence of imaginative leadership, the strength of authoritarian and reactionary forces —have been analyzed above.

After 1945 these causes were no longer present. The workers, like all others in Germany, were united in their stand against communism. Initially, at least, there was forceful leadership, and reactionary forces were unable to endanger the liberal-democratic framework of the new Constitution, so that the path toward the realization of the party's aims seemed open. Its lack of success so far may in part be explained by more "accidental" circumstances of an adverse nature: the separation from East Germany, a traditional SPD stronghold; the rise of an equally strong party as a competitor; and the emergence of strong leadership in that party. (Initially, at the first Bundestag election of a Chancellor, Adenauer defeated SPD leader Kurt Schumacher by only one vote!) But another part of the explanation lies in the party's own structure and policy.

Present Structure and Organization

Traditionally, the SPD has been the prototype of the strongly centralized German party, with a party machine that managed to control the membership at large. In contrast to the more rightist, middle-class parties, more of its followers are actual members of the party and take an active interest in its policies and debates. But the party machine (traditionally consisting of paid party functionaries, employees of such party enterprises as the party press, Social Democratic trade union officials, and Social Democratic holders of government positions) has always known how to form a self-perpetuating party elite. The machine has manipulated the elected party organs through devices well known to students of American party organization; thus the party executive has usually been the vantage point from which the leadership has controlled the party at large.

The party machine has traditionally been organized so as to place control of party affairs and policies in an executive that consists of both honorary and full-time paid members (about thirty in all). In 1962 a presidium of ten emerged as the top-level group in actual control. The executive has preponderant influence over the nomination of candidates for elections, controls the party's extensive properties and enterprises, appoints the permanent staff, and prepares the agenda of the party's "representative" body, the biannual convention, over whose deliberations it exercises great influence. A party council of delegates from the party's nineteen regional districts advises the executive. The convention, with some three-fourths of its roughly four hundred delegates representing the districts in proportion to their membership (the rest comprising members of the executive and other functionaries), is theoretically the highest organ. But the weight of the "apparatus" of the paid functionaries is felt everywhere.

For a time during the postwar period leadership was personal rather than oligarchic. In Kurt Schumacher the party for once had a chairman who, through his magnetic personality and his ability to appeal to the masses, held uncontested rule. But after Schumacher's death in 1952, the SPD reverted to group rule and the party chairman became again part of the machine. Erich Ollenhauer, well-meaning and honest but colorless and uninspiring, was no match for Adenauer in the two electoral contests of 1953 and 1957. Prior to the 1961 election, therefore, he was forced to abandon his role as candidate for Chancellor to a new standard-bearer, the young, vigorous, and popular mayor of West Berlin, Willy Brandt, who rallied a group of strong leaders around himself. After Ollenhauer's death, Brandt became chairman. The new leadership included [the late] Fritz

Erler, foreign affairs expert; Herbert Wehner, a former Communist but now at the right of the party; and, subsequently, Helmut Schmidt, who has become the party's defense and military expert, as well as some of the "territorial princes"—that is, government heads in SPD-controlled Länder, such as August Zinn in Hesse. Perhaps it was Brandt's second failure (in 1965) to lead his party to victory which, in 1966, persuaded the SPD leadership to enter a CDU-led coalition Cabinet. It remained to be seen how this first SPD participation in German government since 1930 would affect the party and its policies.

Policies and Programs

One of the reasons for the party's postwar lack of success was that Schumacher, in attempting to give it a new orientation free from its partly discredited tradition, based his new policy on wrong assumptions. One was in regard to nationalism. Socialism had been traditionally internationalist, which often earned it the undeserved stigma of being unpatriotic or even treasonable. The neonationalism of the postwar period with which the party appealed to the patriotic feelings of the German masses came exactly at a time when these masses, disillusioned with old-fashioned nationalism, were ready for some kind of supranationalist European regionalism. Moreover, with West Germany's rise to international stature, the party's criticism of the Adenauer regime as being remiss in regard to German national interests had little impact. Its orientation being necessarily Western, its differences with the CDU in the foreign field had to be over matters of detail, and even here Soviet policy, when turning against such SPD-backed proposals as reunification through neutralization, pulled the rug from under the party.

In the domestic field, too, the party's policy came close to a "me-too" attitude when Schumacher's other assumption, namely that Adenauer's free-market economy would fail in the absence of effective government controls, proved wrong. Its principal line became one of de-emphasizing its traditional goals, such as nationalization of industries, in favor of welfare state principles and demands. On some issues it actually became more liberal (in the economic

sense) than the officially liberal government parties, which have had to fight strong monopolistic pressures. By a similar paradox the SPD, the opposition party since the inception of the Bonn system, has been the most sincere defender of the Bonn type of democracy, while the other parties have been more tinged with authoritarianism. The moderation of the SPD on industrial issues did lead to victory in the question of codetermination (see Chapter 7), but this has hardly affected the West German social structure or even increased labor's influence in management. Divorcement from its previous close connections with the trade unions has not quite deprived the party of that powerful group's political backing; however, this has lost it important financial support (about two-thirds of the party's income now derives from membership dues alone, which are staggered according to the member's wages, but are generally small).

This trend to the right culminated in the adoption of the party's first new program in thirty-five years. The Godesberg Program of 1959 turns decisively away from Marxian principles. What it proclaims in relation to the churches, namely that "socialism is not a substitute for religion," applies to the new attitude in a general sense. Nothing could be more expressive of its shift from a past in which socialism was the quasi-religious creed of the proletarian masses. Now the party has become pragmatic. In economics the emphasis is on "market economy," that is, freedom of enterprise and freedom of competition. Planning and transfer of properties to public ownership are not ruled out but are considered policies of last resort rather than major policy objectives. Policy is "New Dealish" rather than socialist: control of overly powerful economic interests and of cartels, promotion of small business, and, of course, of labor's wage and similar interests. The formulation "competition so far as possible, planning so far as necessary" puts the accent neatly but elusively—depending, as it does, on a definition of what is possible and what is necessary.

Prospects

Postwar policy thus has tended to shape the SPD into a German version of the British Labor party. The question was whether it would be able to implement its policies through parliamentary majorities, which it can apparently obtain only by gaining the vote of nonlabor groups. The new program was clearly devised to attract such groups, as was the new leadership setup and the personalized, glamorized, and Americanized style of its campaigns. However, even with a sky-blue color replacing the traditional red of the party's campaign posters, the party still did not succeed in making the decisive inroads into the nonsocialist parts of the electorate that would have led it out of the "desert" where it has been condemned to control an insufficient 30 to 40 percent of the vote. The table on page 412 indicates that the SPD is no longer so exclusively a workers' party as it used to be, and its voting figures have been steadily rising. Still it remains doubtful whether, with its present policies, it will ever convince significant portions of the middle classes that their interests are better guarded by a party still suspected of socialism or, at least, "experiments," than by a party that so far has defended these interests so effectively. Under conditions of advancing living standards, when many of the demands of reformist parties seem fulfilled, such parties are faced with the problem of what they can still offer in competition with conservative parties.

It would seem that there do remain important tasks for a reformist party even outside the realm of economic and social improvement for the lower classes. In West Germany, there are two tasks: One, to counter those undemocratic authoritarian tendencies that are found everywhere, whether in the form of clericalism, attempts at censorship (of literature, arts, or political opinion), conferring far-reaching "emergency powers" on the government, bureaucratic high-handedness, or the class system of education. Second, to act as the protagonist of those policies that now loom even larger than those of economic welfare and social equality—namely, the protection of the human environment against the encroachments of an exploding technological civilization (the preservation of pure air, water, and soil, the planning of urban agglomerations, transportation, and so forth). This implies putting interest in the public sector

of the economy before interest in the private sector—an emphasis that would befit a formerly socialist party now in search of a meaningful program.

In recent years the SPD, though a bit haltingly, had placed emphasis on some of these programs. By entering a CDU-led coalition, however, it has—at least temporarily—given up its role as opposition. Its future as a meaningful party with a profile of its own would seem to depend on whether it is willing and able to fight for a specific program from the vantage point of a minority partner in government. Its dilemma is considerable: making the coalition work requires concessions. But if most of these concessions are made by the SPD, the party runs the risk—particularly in an economically and internationally deteriorating situation—of being blamed for a basically conservative policy, especially by its younger and more activist supporters who were opposed to the "grand coalition" from the outset.

The Free Democratic Party (FDP)

Background and Policies

The FDP, selected at the time of party reestablishment to be "the other" nonsocialist party, has actually proved to be the only third party with a continual nation-wide backing and the potential of influencing national policy. In this capacity, as we have seen, it may even emerge as "holder of the balance of power" between the major parties.

In regard to both program and policies, and to backing, the FDP is difficult to characterize. Successor to both previous liberal parties (Democratic and People's parties at Weimar), it is economically conservative, favoring an undiluted free-enterprise system without concessions to state planning or further social welfare steps. It stands for separation of state and church and favors interdenominational education; it is centralistic in the interest of national unity. Thus, in its combination of economic conservatism and cultural-political progressivism it resembles the traditional French Radical Socialist party.

In its backing, however, the party is less clearcut and homogeneous. It draws those voters from business circles to whom the CDU seems too much inclined toward the welfare state, but also from those, especially small traders and members of the professions, who consider the CDU dominated by big business. Part of its backing comes from Protestants fearful of clericalism. Nationalists (including former Nazis) to whom Adenauer's policy appeared overly dependent on foreign, especially American, influence, and neutralists to whom the Western alignment of the Federal Republic has seemed to involve too rigid and unyielding a policy also support the FDP. To complicate matters, the party's strength derives from very different strata in different regions. Its predecessors (National Liberals and Progressives) represented big business on the one hand and smaller trade and more enlightened burghers on the other. The latter group still backs the FDP in regions such as southwest Germany, traditional stronghold of liberal democracy. In other regions the party represents big business. But it can hardly be said that big business as a group is behind it; big business favors the CDU equally and is thus able to work through both at times and to oppose unfavorable trends in the CDU with the help of the FDP at others. Since the party, though centralist in its program, depends financially on its regional branches, of which the most rightist, that of Northrhine–Westphalia, contributes most, the party's policies, despite its liberal program, often reflect reactionary influences. While in the person of Theodor Heuss it presented Bonn with its first and genuinely democratic president, it has faced in two directions, as German liberalism has done so often.

Prospects

The future role and impact of the FDP seem to depend on two factors, one without, the other within, its sphere of control. The first is the strength of the other parties. If one of these controls an absolute majority of the Bundestag, the FDP confronts the danger of falling below the 5 percent of the vote needed for representation in the Bundestag, or at least the danger of internal dissension. This points up the second problem, namely, maintaining internal coherence and uniformity of policy despite the widely diverging forces that support it, some right of

the two major groups, and others left of the now no longer very leftist SPD.

Liberalism in Germany, as everywhere, has declined since pre-World War I days. From a prewar 25 percent, the combined vote of liberal parties sank to about 15 percent under Weimar, and emerged at about 12 percent after World War II. The FDP then entered a period of crises over leadership and policy. For a while it left and then reentered the government, with the warring factions eventually rallying behind a compromise figure, Erich Mende, the present party chairman. A native of Silesia and a former career army officer, Mende led the party to relative success in 1961 (with close to 13 percent of the vote) through strong appeals to nationalism.

Since then, however, the pull of the party has again decreased, not only nationally (with only 9.5 percent in 1965) but also in former regional strongholds. Indeed, in the Bavarian election of 1966, the FDP remained below the minimum required for representation in the diet. Apparently, most of its deserters went over to the NPD. The party thus faces the danger of being outcompeted by the more extreme right. An even greater danger threatens as a result of its opportunistic policy at Bonn. Its policy of playing both major parties against the middle backfired when the two got together, leaving the FDP out in the cold. Should the CDU–SPD coalition decide to change the present election system (see below) into one of single-member districts, this would be the FDP's death warrant. On the other hand, as sole opposition group at Bonn, the party has a chance to play a valuable and significant role if it is able to agree on clear-cut policies.

Other Parties and Groups

As mentioned earlier, neither the Communists nor rightist extremists or neo-Nazis played a significant role over most of the postwar period. In the mid-1960's, however, various small rightist groups merged into the National Democratic Party (NPD). In local and regional elections, this group managed to rally about 8 percent of the vote, which under German conditions had to be considered as significant.

The NPD

At the end of 1966 this party still constituted a coalition of neo-Nazis and traditional conservative nationalists who had come chiefly from the FDP and the DP (see below). As far as one could see, the neo-Nazis had managed to occupy the party's key positions and to control its finances. Many of its leaders turned out to have been more or less high functionaries in the Nazi hierarchy. Its highest voting figures were attained in small-town Protestant districts, ominously from exactly those lower-middle-class groups from which the Nazis had drawn support in the 1920's. The NPD vote was also high where military garrisons were stationed. Even in a big city like Nuremberg, the NPD obtained 13 percent of the vote. In its programmatic statements directed toward a more general audience (such as in election campaigns), its leaders voiced moderately conservative and nationalistic views, shunning Nazi trappings and denying being neo-Nazi. This was an obvious precaution, since the party must try to avoid falling under the constitutional ban of antidemocratic groups. In its "internal" propaganda, however—for instance, in its press, read chiefly by its members and supporters—there has been less restraint. There we find the complete Nazi litany, from unrestrained anti-Semitism (to the point of glorifying Nazi extremist Julius Streicher, to them one of the "Nuremberg martyrs") to xenophobia (especially in regard to foreign workers in Germany) and demands that "tribute" no longer be paid to the Americans, the British, and the Israelis. Racist nationalism is also apparent in their demands not to pay good D-marks for foreign aid to nonwhite peoples. Domestically, the chief butt of attack is the customary one on the part of German rightists: inefficiency of parliamentary government and corruption of parties.

Two other groups should be mentioned, although they are no longer as significant as they once were: the party representing the expellees and regionalist parties.

The All-German Bloc

Because the Military Government wanted to integrate expellees into the general party system, it did not license refugee parties. This policy failed, owing to the unwillingness of the old parties to take to heart the plight and the demands of the "disinherited." Still unintegrated into West German society and economy, the refugees in 1950 therefore founded their own party, the All-German Bloc.

This party was at first backed by one-half to three-fourths of the refugee population and was, of course, particularly strong in regions with large refugee elements. Subsequently, however, it lost its hold, drawing less and less of the refugee vote. This loss indicated the growing integration of refugees and the at least partial satisfaction of their demands through federal legislation (for example, the law on the equalization of burdens). The chief concern of the Bloc, therefore, evolved into making sure that this legislation was effectively administered and implemented.

Since it failed to surmount the 5 percent barrier of the federal election law (see below) in 1957, the Bloc decided in 1961 to merge with the German Party (see below) in a new "All-German Party" (GDP), in the hope—which turned out to be vain—thus to attain representation in the Bundestag.

Regionalist Parties

The German Party (DP) originated from an insignificant particularist movement of anti-Prussian Hanoverians. After 1945, it attracted the vote of the Lower Saxon farmer who was afraid of land reform that would favor the expellees. Success in Lower Saxony encouraged the DP to branch out into other regions, where its increasingly nationalist-reactionary attitude appealed to conservative middle-class elements as well as to former Nazis. Propped up by the CDU, it survived for a time as the former's coalition partner, but anxiety over reelection chances led the majority of its diet delegates to join the Big Brother. As mentioned above, the remainder of the party merged with the expellees' group—a somewhat strange union of opposites—to try its luck jointly at the 1961 election. The complete failure of the "All-German Party" at the polls (it obtained a mere 2.8 percent of the vote) sealed the fate of both refugee party and DP on the national level. In 1965 the GDP did not even run in the Bundestag election, and it seemed doubtful whether it, or its constituent groups (for example, the DP in Lower Saxony, or the Bloc in Schleswig-

Holstein), would be able to survive as a locally significant force.

A similar fate has befallen the DP's Bavarian counterpart, the Bavarian Party (BP). Representing the extreme particularism of Upper Bavarian farmers and small burghers, this group at first profited from animosity against refugees and Bonn centralism, but scandals and petty factionalism have condemned it to insignificance, even in its own bailiwick.

Nonparty Associations of Political Character

Political associations of a nonparty nature have commonly been a kind of substitute for Germans who wanted to be above the "ever-wrangling interest parties." These associations have often been more influential in German political life than parties proper. The Nazi party grew out of the folkish fighting associations of post-World War I times. Similar groups deserve careful watching now. With remilitarization, a revival of a spirit of militarism and ultranationalism is perhaps a greater danger than that of out-and-out neo-Nazism. A crop of veterans' organizations, former paratroopers or members of the *Waffen-SS,* run by former officers, try to pose as self-appointed guardians of German national interests. Potentially more influential are the nonparty organizations of refugees and expellees, which, organized according to origin (Silesians, East Prussians, etc.), draw more members from these groups than their political party, the All-German Bloc, had been able to. While the majority of their membership is more moderate in its attitudes, their leaders have frequently shown extremist tendencies. Their insistence on a legal "right to the homeland" (*Recht auf Heimat*) sometimes implies not only a right to "return home" but the right to reattach the "homeland" (which, in their view, comprises also the Sudeten area of Czechoslovakia) to a reunified Germany. Their political impact may be seen in the intimidating effect of their denunciation, in often vituperative language, of more moderate leaders and parties as "politicians of renunciation," reminding one of the defamations of Weimar statesmen as "traitors to the nation." Consequently, German leaders have so far been hesitant to come out for any territorial settlement short of the 1937 boundaries.

4. ELECTIONS

The Present Election System

Germans, with their traditional multigroup system, have usually considered elections as means to reveal the comparative strength of the different political groups rather than as a way to form a stable government. This accounts for their attachment to PR. In the old Empire, Reichstag elections had been single-member district elections, with run-off votes in case the first vote failed to give one candidate an absolute majority. Since Socialists were usually isolated in the runoff vote, they came to advocate PR as a progressive principle and introduced it into the Weimar system. There, as we have seen, it was blamed, perhaps unjustly, for the weaknesses of Weimar parliamentarism; as a result, after 1945 a mixed system was adopted for Bundestag and most regional elections, aimed at combining the advantages of PR (just representation of the various opinion groups) with those of the single-member system (more personal relation between voters and candidates and lessened party domination of elections). With slight variations in detail, the system works so that half of the deputies are elected from single-member districts by simple majority, the other half from Land lists set up by the parties. These lists make up for any losses a party incurs by not electing as many deputies from districts as would correspond to its overall strength in voting figures. Each voter thus has two votes: one cast for a candidate in his district, a second for a party list.

This system has had the following effects:

(1) It has personalized PR slightly by giving the voter a chance to vote for an individual candidate. The vast majority, however, have continued to vote a "straight ticket"—that is, for the district candidate belonging to their party.

(2) One main disadvantage of PR, splintering the vote, has been avoided. This has been chiefly due to an additional feature of the system, the "5 percent clause," according to which a party must obtain at least 5 percent of the nation-wide vote or win at least three seats in district voting in order to be represented in the Bundestag. This clause has eliminated from

the federal legislature by now all but the two major parties and the FDP.

(3) There has been consistently a rather high percentage of invalid votes. This cannot be due merely to the technical complications of voting under this system. Rather, it seems in part to express protest on the part of those who otherwise would vote for smaller (possibly more radically rightist or leftist) groups.

(4) The system has led to an intricate game of jockeying for position on the lists. These lists are made up by the regional party organizations, which determine who is placed on the respective party's list and in what place. A candidate running in a district can simultaneously be on the list, so that, in case he fails in his district, he may still enter parliament if he is in a safe, that is, forward, place on the list. The list, in turn, has to ensure that the party's representation is a rounded one, with representatives from the major groups (pressure and others) backing the party, experts in certain fields, some women (who usually are not run in districts), and those national leaders of the party who might be defeated, or do not care to run, locally.

The lists have given party bureaucracies a chance to make many deputies creatures of the machines. In the districts, of course, it is not so much the central machines and the larger pressure groups that influence selections, but rather the local groups. Still, the individual voter, who is not usually a party member, or even the ordinary party member has little influence over nominations. Although nominations must be made by conventions of elected party delegates in the districts, this is a far cry from direct primaries. In practice, leading regional party functionaries and interest groups do the determining, with the central party organization having an important voice though no veto. Candidates may be selected from outside the districts, which enhances party control even more.

Nevertheless, under present German conditions, this system seems preferable to the British or American plurality system, which, under German conditions, would mean the following: (1) With SPD strength, similar to Labor in Britain, heavily concentrated in the cities and that of the CDU more evenly spread, it might lead to a near-monopoly by the CDU and in practice inaugurate a one-party system. The dangers of such a system, in a country with an authoritarian tradition and a not too remote experience with one-party rule, need hardly be pointed out. (2) In any event, Germany might be divided politically into one-party regions, rendering the CDU a rural and small-town party and the SPD a big-city party, either one with correspondingly narrowed interests and representation. (3) The CDU would emerge as a primarily Catholic party and would probably lose its Labor following. (4) The FDP, which at present does not elect a single deputy in direct election to the Bundestag, would disappear. Yet, since the present election system is not anchored in the Constitution but can be revamped by ordinary law, such a death sentence for the third party could be easily inflicted by the two major groups working together. Late in 1966, when it appeared that the NPD might eventually replace the FDP as the third party, such a change was advocated by some. Yet it would be of doubtful utility, for, under conditions of increasing radicalization, a party such as the NPD might even win seats in single-member district elections. And, if successfully excluded, it might gain in extraparliamentary ways through posing as a victim of undemocratic maneuvers.

Campaigns and Procedures

In this field, too, problems have not been absent. On the whole, elections in Germany are carried out efficiently, and corruption, open or undercover, is not widespread, although there is little official regulation of electoral ethics. A usually high voting participation (around 80 percent) is facilitated by the absence of complicating procedures. No special registration is required; the authorities keep permanent lists of those entitled to vote; and rules for absentee voting are easy. There are no literacy tests or property qualifications, and residence requirements are liberal. Elections take place on Sundays with ample time for everybody to vote. The voting age is twenty-one, and women have been admitted since 1919. Women's suffrage in Germany has generally strengthened the Catholic and conservative parties as against the left; paradoxically—since the Socialists had always advocated women's suffrage—the CDU owes its superiority over the SPD to the female vote. For example, 52 percent of the female vote and only 42 percent of the male vote won in 1965 over the SPD, for which the corresponding figures were 36 and 44 percent. It has been traditional for the clergy to participate in the campaign, advising churchgoers on election Sundays on how to vote.

Lately, in addition to the more traditional means of campaigning through posters, ads in newspapers, and the like, radio and especially TV have become very prominent. Here, the public character of the media has saved the parties from the traditional American difficulty of "purchasing time." It's all free, and the free-for-all has been regulated by law in a way that combines the principles of equal time and proportionality to previous voting strength; in other words, the big ones are a bit "more equal" than the others when it comes to assigning time.

Nevertheless, and particularly in view of the absence of statutory limits for campaign expenditures, the problem of financing parties and elections in Germany, as elsewhere, is a serious one. While the SPD has traditionally depended on membership dues and other small contributions, the government parties and the CDU in particular for a long time enjoyed an organized, even streamlined, financing of their expenditures by the interests backing them, especially industry. Associations of employers, "promoters' associations," were set up by industry to centralize fund-raising by assessing individual enterprises and channeling the money to the major nonsocialist parties according to an agreed-on allocation. Up to 1958 tax exemption of such contributions meant that much of this financing was paid for by the taxpayer; in that year, however, the Constitutional Court outlawed such deductions as violations of the "equality principle" of the Constitution.

The fact that money from industry and similar large contributors was now less easy to come by led to new developments: In 1965, the major parties agreed to limit their campaign spending to specific amounts, which, though still considerable, were rather moderate in comparison to earlier elections. This, however, did not solve the larger problem of party financing in general. Therefore, the parties represented in the Bundestag began to vote themselves direct annual state subsidies. These payments were limited to the three parties represented in the Bundestag, distributed according to their proportional strength, and in recent years amounted to the not unsubstantial amount of 38 million DM per annum. In 1966, however, upon application by one Land and several of the non-benefiting smaller parties, the Federal Constitutional Court declared the practice unconstitutional; according to the judgment, such budgetary subsidizing of parties tended to render the parties dependent upon the state and endangered their existence as free instrumentalities of the popular will. Somewhat illogically, however, the prohibition was declared to affect only the overall activities of the parties and their general (for example, organizational) expenditures, while reimbursement of the costs of election campaigns was not to fall under the indictment (with the proviso that *all* groups participating in the campaign were to share in the benefits according to a reasonable key).

What this judgment presaged for the parties' financial and general future was doubtful. Perhaps the exemption of campaign costs was to prove broad enough to enable them to go on more or less comfortably. Perhaps they—and in particular the CDU and the FDP—would have to become dependent again on large contributions from big business. Perhaps the solution was to permit each citizen to make a limited, tax-deductible annual contribution to a party of his choice; a solution of this nature was advocated by many Germans who were interested in viable parties independent from government and big business influence alike.

The problems and developments connected with party financing attest to the urgent need for party regulation. The Constitution itself (Article 21) demands that the internal organization of parties and their financing be regulated by law. Such a law has been long in the making, but there has been no agreement on it so far. The chief stumbling block is party finances. The CDU majority has refused to agree to SPD demands that individual sources of party funds be revealed and that contributions by business corporations be prohibited. The law on parties might also embody more satisfactory rules on democratic practices within parties.

Even the SPD sometimes (for example, in regard to the expulsion of members) indulges in somewhat high-handed and arbitrary procedures.

5. EFFECTIVENESS OF THE GERMAN PARTY SYSTEM

Germans in the past have usually regarded political parties as divisive forces interfering with the legitimate tasks of government, an attitude that often rendered parties ineffective and allowed the executive to function outside their orbit. Rule by a party elite over the party as such, and the ensuing lack of influence by members or voters on party policies and management, contributed to the traditionally low prestige of parties. More recently, in addition, experience with Nazi propaganda has caused many Germans to feel that political promises and avowed political ideals are mere decoys set by self-centered and self-perpetuating politicians. Polls still reveal a good deal of such distrust and suspicion. For example, many Germans refuse to reveal their party preference, and only 42 percent of those polled even feel that election campaigns are necessary (as against 74 and 63 percent, respectively, in the United States and Britain), with a majority of educated persons among them.[4] A similarly low percentage (43) of respondents were able to name the deputy elected from their district.

In other respects, as we have seen, there has been some improvement. With the emergence of two major moderate parties, more Germans have come to think in terms of political alternation, compromise, and cooperation, instead of thinking primarily in terms of the doctrines, victories, and defeats of one or another political "movement." Yet, to the majority, parties are still identified with party leaders, and the leaders are considered as belonging to *die da oben,* those on top and in control, over whom the people at large have no influence. This is partly the parties' fault. Parties, even in their own self-image and behavior patterns, tend to be remote from the people, part of the official establishment that runs the nation. What might give the people more influence and render them more interested? A change in the party organization might help—for example, by making party membership less formal and more easy to obtain, as in the United States. At present, besides those few who are genuinely interested, most of the people who join parties do so because they expect rewards (for instance, candidates for office, or officials in search of promotion). Above all, there is need for more intraparty discussion of important issues and interparty debate about policies. Here, the growing similarity of two major parties, each desiring to become a "people's party" appealing to all strata, has had an inhibiting effect. One need not advocate a return to narrow doctrinairism to wish for more lively debate based on legitimate differences in principles and approaches.

In the absence of such revitalization, the role of parties is likely to remain small when decisions are made about the tasks to be performed by the inevitably expanding government of the future. The scientific and technological revolution will impose on Germany, as on other advanced nations, dimensions of planning (of environment, population, of science itself) unheard of so far. If these decisions are not made democratically by rejuvenated parties, they will be made autocratically by the traditional alliance of *die da oben*—that is, by bureaucratized and institutionalized parties in alliance with a governmental and scientific elite remote from the people. Only if and when more Germans realize that in a democracy the people must take the initiative in making parties and public life more expressive of popular desires will German parties implement democracy.

[4] G. A. Almond and S. Verba, *The Civic Culture* (Boston, Little, Brown, 1965), p. 108.

4. German Parliamentary Institutions

The meeting place of a representative assembly may be an index to its national importance. While Britain has the magnificent neo-Gothic structure of Westminster Palace, resurrected from World War II ruins in its old image, and while France has the classic Palais Bourbon in the very heart of Paris, the German assembly presently deserving the name of parliament still is housed in makeshift fashion in a sober office building at the "Federal Capital Village" of Bonn. No traditions surround it. The pompous Reichstag building in Berlin, like the diet it housed, more façade than substance, still stands as a burned-out symbol of Nazi incendiarism. Popular sovereignty in Germany is still in search of substantiation.

1. DEVELOPMENT AND CHARACTER OF GERMAN PARLIAMENTARY INSTITUTIONS

General Characteristics

The place of parliamentary institutions in German government is difficult to define. They have never had the power and prestige of parliaments in Western countries. But neither have they been (except during totalitarian regimes) the make-believe, pseudo-representative institutions often found outside Europe. They rather have expressed a middle condition reflecting a desire for genuine representative government continually thwarted by both authoritarian and antidemocratic tendencies.

The Reichstag of the old Empire, as we have seen, was not recognized as the equal of what Germans had come to regard as real government, the authoritarian executive. Even under Weimar, parliament was constitutionally checked by a semi-independent executive and proved unable, or was not permitted, to function when an emergency arose. Parliament is now reduced to a sham in the DDR. In West Germany, on the other hand, the Bundestag has emerged as a genuine representative institution. Bonn has given parliamentarism a second chance.

The German parliament has traditionally contained multiple political groups. They are seated in a semicircle (as in France), with govern-

West German Legislative Bodies, 1965

BUNDESTAG[1]

BUNDESRAT[2]

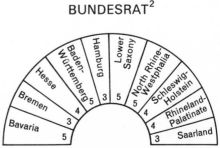

[1] PLUS 22 NONVOTING DEPUTIES FROM BERLIN (15 SPD, 6 CDU, 1 FDP)

[2] IN ADDITION 4 NONVOTING DELEGATES FOR BERLIN

mental representatives facing the deputies from raised seats (not, as in Britain, sitting on the front bench of one of the two opposed sides of the house). But, unlike France, the various parliamentary parties are separated from each other as organized groups. Consequently, there is no reorganization of party groups in parliament after an election. The parties are fixed once and for all, they move as separate armies into a new parliament, and even an individual deputy's crossing from one party to another is extremely rare.

Unlike the practice in Britain and France, there is in the German parliament little real debate or brilliant oratory (although recent borrowings from certain Anglo-American features, such as rising to question an orator, have added a bit of spontaneity to debate). Since deputies usually speak not for themselves but present an (often compromise) attitude or decision of their party, this lack of spontaneity is not surprising. On the other hand, disorder and use of strong language have been frequent, reflecting lack of respect for the institution of parliament. Occasional broadcasting and televising of debates have not altered a widespread German opinion of parliament as a place where interest groups wrangle and concern for the commonweal is lost. Many Germans still consider the existence of opposed and clashing views in parliament as something that is bad in itself.

Composition of Parliament

The table below reveals the wide spread of social classes and interest groups represented in parliament. Certain features are characteristic. One is that specific groups and occupations, though they send some direct representatives (farmers or bankers, for example), are also represented by the full-time officers of their respective interest organizations, such as the BDI (Federation of German Industry), farmers' associations, and so forth. In the table, these officers do not appear as such, but may be among those describing themselves as "top-level employees" or "farmers," or even "attorneys." Second, the relatively low number of "workers" indicates that they, too, are in the main represented by functionaries of their interest organization, the trade unions, and in addition by party functionaries and party journalists—persons who usually have workers' backgrounds but have become professional politicians. Thus, the lower classes are in general represented by those who have risen in social status.

Composition of the Bundestag [1]

	First Bundestag 1949–53		Fourth Bundestag 1961–65		Net change	1965		
						CDU	SPD	FDP
Public officials	69	16.8%	120	23.0%	+6.2%	60	48	12
Top-level employees	3	0.7	17	3.3	+2.6	9	5	3
Businessmen	37	9.0	58	11.1	+2.1	31	9	18
Small middle class	22	5.4	33	6.3	+0.9	21	8	4
Housewives	7	1.7	13	2.5	+0.8	6	6	1
Attorneys and accountants	32	7.8	39	7.5	−0.3	19	12	8
Trade union officials	41	10.0	50	9.6	−0.4	19	31	—
Farmers	52	12.7	62	11.9	−0.8	47	3	12
Workers and small employees	26	6.3	28	5.4	−0.9	10	16	2
Professions (including clergy)	31	7.6	32	6.2	−1.4	15	16	1
Journalists and publishers	35	8.5	36	6.9	−1.6	9	24	3
Party functionaries	55	13.4	33	6.3	−7.1	5	25	3

[1] Arranged in descending order of net gains (or losses) of each category.

Therefore a large proportion of German deputies are representatives in a double sense: they represent both the people who elect them and the great classes and interests that see to it that they are represented in parliament. So it is not surprising that cross associations (*Querverbindungen*) of deputies from different parties but representing the same interest frequently make common cause when their "cause" is at stake. (One slogan read, "Farmers of all parties, unite! You have nothing to lose but your subsidies.") Also, such a system renders the lobby, so far as it affects deputies, largely superfluous, since the chief interests are safely represented by the deputies themselves. At Bonn, the lobby chiefly addresses itself to the executive—in particular, to the ministerial officials in charge of drafting bills. Indeed, government bills are quite regularly discussed with (if they have not been initiated by) officers or agents of the respective interest groups before they are approved by the cabinet for submission to parliament.

Civil servants, as can be seen, are very numerous among members of German parliaments. When elected, they get leave of absence, with 50 percent or more of their salary paid. Every deputy receives sufficient though not overly liberal emoluments. German respect for education is apparent from the fact that a large percentage of the deputies have university degrees, many the doctorate. There are thirty-eight women in the 1965 Bundestag.

The Organization of the Bundestag

Fractions

The most important units in the Bundestag are the party groups called "fractions," each made up of the deputies of the same party. Thus, one speaks of the CDU/CSU fraction or the SPD fraction in a given Bundestag. Unless there is a subsequent schism or secession (something very rare in Germany), deputies belonging to the same party always constitute one single fraction, despite any political divergencies and wings that may exist within the party. The major reason for this cohesion is that fractions dominate parliamentary procedures, and fraction strength determines important rights. Fractions, for example, are represented in committees by members selected by them in proportion to their strength; time for debate is assigned to fraction spokesmen, often in proportion to fraction strength; only fractions may introduce legislative motions. If a group fails to attain, or loses, minimum fraction strength (according to Bonn standing orders, fifteen), it loses its influence in the Bundestag.

Fractions now, especially those of the combined CDU/CSU and the SPD, are so large that they constitute parliaments in miniature. On many issues, therefore, they must first come to agreement among themselves; officially, they vote, but in practice the "experts," represented in the "working committees" (which are set up corresponding to the various Bundestag committees) of the party, prevail—that is, the plenary party follows their suggestions. If conflict persists, the fraction leadership usually prevails. Once a fraction has made up its collective mind, strict party discipline is exercised, and the individual deputy is compelled to vote according to the line laid down. Otherwise he may be expelled from the party or lose party backing in subsequent elections. A study of voting in the Bundestag shows that over a given period fraction discipline was observed in the SPD in practically every case, in the CDU/CSU in nineteen out of twenty cases, in the FDP (here as in other matters less united) in nine out of ten.

Since campaign funds come from the party chest or from groups backing the party, for a deputy to disagree with the party over policies or program usually means the end of his political career. The professional politician in Germany—that is, one who devotes his career to politics—usually begins by running for election in a district, where he must be in the good graces of the local party. He then becomes a "backbencher" in his fraction. From that lowly position he advances to "expert" status in some specialized area (labor affairs, agriculture, criminal law, or whatever); as such, he has to prove himself to parliament at large. If he is successful, he may advance to fraction and party leadership (and hence, possibly, into the government). He remains, however, beholden to his party. All this, though detrimental to individual initiative, makes for coherent party action. In contrast to an American voter, the German voter, though he often does not know *whom* he is voting for, at least knows *what* he is voting for.

Speaker and Steering Committee

The Bundestag elects its speaker (President) and his deputies, who preside over the sessions. The speaker has important disciplinary powers. He may, for instance, exclude a deputy for thirty session days. But the most important body in organizing procedures is the steering committee (Council of Elders), on which the fractions are represented according to their strength. This committee prepares the calendar and appoints committee chairmen. In practice it also determines how much time will be devoted to a motion, and how such time is to be allocated to the various groups. While Bonn standing orders give each speaker, in principle, one hour, the pressure of work, as in other parliaments, demands restrictions, which may be voted by the Bundestag upon the proposal of the steering committee. Closure is by vote of the Bundestag upon motion of at least thirty members present, a procedure resembling that in the French National Assembly rather than that in the House of Commons.

2. THE GERMAN PARLIAMENT IN ACTION

The German parliament, like other parliaments, reflects that modern trend in government under which actual lawmaking, formerly first among the functions of representative bodies, recedes in importance before the function of controlling and supervising the executive. But this latter function has always been precarious in Germany. The crucial question, of course, is how to combine effective supervision by parliament with stability of government. Under Weimar, while parliamentary supervision at first led to Cabinet instability, the executive eventually emerged as the stronger power, destroying parliamentary control altogether.

The Bundestag and the Executive Under the Bonn System

Bundestag and Executive

The makers of the Bonn Constitution, drawing on the Weimar experience, strengthened the executive without conferring important powers on the President. Strong executive power is vested in the Chancellor. He is elected by the Bundestag, to be sure, but once elected he can be compelled to resign only by means of the so-called constructive vote of nonconfidence—that is, a vote by which the assembly simultaneously, and with a majority of its legal membership (as distinguished from a simple majority of those present), deposes one Chancellor and elects his successor. This is intended to prevent a situation where opposition parties on right and left could join to overthrow a government without being able to form a new one. The Chancellor's powers are further strengthened by the fact that he appoints and dismisses Cabinet ministers independently of the Bundestag; the latter cannot, as is customary in most other parliamentary systems, oust the individual ministers. The Chancellor, further, can ask the President to dissolve the Bundestag—though only when his demand for an expression of confidence has been rejected. His dissolution power is thus more restricted than that of the British Prime Minister. The Bundestag cannot dissolve itself. Nor can it *compel* the Chancellor, in order to have new elections, to ask the President to dissolve it (an inability that became crucial during the government crisis of 1966).

This peculiar relation between Bundestag and executive may conceivably lead to a constitutional stalemate if the Bundestag ever refuses a vote of confidence and yet is unable to elect a successor to the Chancellorship, while the Chancellor decides to stay and refuses to dissolve the Bundestag and hold new elections. Should the Chancellor, in this situation, manage to keep the other legislative body, the Bundesrat, on his side, he may try to rule under the "state of legislative emergency" provided for by the Constitution (see below). Otherwise, there would not appear to be a constitutional solution to such a conflict.

Questions and Interpellations

In its supervising functions, the German Bundestag has at its disposal the techniques customary in Continental parliamentary systems. Thus, as in France, there are interpellations and questionings. Interpellations, however, have to be signed by thirty deputies, and questions by fifteen; this means that criticism and control are functions of the parties, not of private members.

Thus the delays and the excessive demagogy that characterized the French parliament are avoided; but the initiative and independence of the individual deputy are stifled in favor of party controls. German parliamentary practice has so far failed to endow questions with the prestige that has rendered the British question period an effective check on the executive part of government, although questions have increased of late and are no longer considered as impudence by those being questioned. Bundestag standing orders have tried to encourage questioning by allowing a regular question period on the British pattern. Investigating committees, while provided for in the Constitution, do not usually play a significant role as a check on the executive. The minority (opposition party) has the right to have them established, but once they have been established the majority party is in control and can direct (or hamper) proceedings. Thus investigating committees have not proved very helpful as instruments of criticism. This merely reflects the larger problem of how in a democracy (in contrast to predemocratic systems, where the parliament as such is in opposition to government) parliament, whose majority is subservient to a powerful executive, can effectively supervise this self-same executive, especially when, as in West Germany lately, the opposition party fails to play its role wholeheartedly.

On the other hand, there has been one area in which the position of parliament as a supervising and criticizing body has been strengthened. When members of the armed forces file complaints about disregard of their rights and in similar matters, the Bundestag now has a kind of ombudsman on the Scandinavian pattern—that is, a parliamentary defense commissioner with quasi-judicial powers. The practice is an important experiment in a country where, especially in military matters, authority and the idea of unquestioning discipline have had priority over considerations of individual rights and human dignity.

Lawmaking

Ordinary Laws

In regard to legislative procedure, Germany stands between Britain, with its Cabinet control, and the former French system, with parliament in full control. In the federal government since 1871, and in the member states since 1918, the executive has had no direct powers over lawmaking, not even veto powers. But the trend toward increased influence of the executive over lawmaking is found in Germany as elsewhere. It appeared especially early in Germany, because of the traditional authority of the expert, and, particularly, because of the role played by the ministerial bureaucracy in the preparation of bills. To a higher degree than elsewhere, the drafting, processing, and execution of laws in Germany have been carried out by the bureaucracy. Consequently, the chief efforts of interest and pressure groups have centered on the bureaucracy.

Although bills may originate in the Bundestag as well as in the Cabinet, most of them are drafted in the ministries by expert officials. Of about 1,500 laws enacted between 1949 and 1961, about 1,100 bills were initiated by the executive, about 350 by the diet, and 21 by the Bundesrat. Deputies are at a disadvantage, because they have no legislative apparatus of their own; they are provided with no expert advisers or draftsmen and no legislative reference service.

Under the Bonn system, bills prepared in a ministerial department go to the Cabinet, which has to approve them, and from there to the Bundesrat. This body scrutinizes them thoroughly through committees staffed by high Land officials. In practice, informal contacts between these officials and the federal officials in charge of drafting precede this formal intervention of the Bundesrat in the legislative process, especially in cases where the legislation affects the Länder and has to be carried out there; the effect, as one has called it, has been "control of bureaucracy by bureaucracy," a more effective check on executive power than that exercised by the Bundestag.

After this first action by the Bundesrat (on its subsequent actions, see below), the bill goes to the Bundestag. There follow the usual three readings, with the second one the most detailed. Prior to the second reading the bill goes to committee; this stage is by far the most vital one. In plenary session, often only one member of each party discusses the bill, and possibly under time restrictions. In the committees, which are set up according to subject matter, the parties are represented by their respective experts, and it is here that important bills receive careful scrutiny.

Altogether, there are twenty-three committees in the 1965 Bundestag. Since the fractions send their respective experts into the committees, it is there that pressure groups and interest representatives have another chance to influence and shape legislation. Committee meetings are private, and deputies who are reluctant to advance their interests openly in the public plenary session may speak more freely here. There are no public hearings on the American pattern, so they do not have to contend with outside opposition. But they do have to contend with the ministerial officials who attend the meetings to steer their bills through. Their influence as real experts in the matter at hand is generally very great. Frequently, however, agreement in committee has been easy, because committee members, though of different parties, for the most part represent one and the same interest. Usually, the measures cleared by the committees are ratified by parliament. This kind of lawmaking amounts to logrolling on a grand scale by or on behalf of the most powerful interests in the country.

Financial Legislation

In financial legislation the German system lies somewhere between the British, where the Cabinet, and especially the Treasury, is in complete control, and the American, where Congress has traditionally exercised its discretion. In Germany there is a tradition of a comprehensive, well-prepared, and well-coordinated budget to be adopted annually in the form of a law dealing with both revenues and expenditures. Since the finance ministry is in charge of preparing the budget, the finance minister emerges as a very powerful figure. While this resembles the British system, there is more real debate and scrutiny of the budget bill in the Bundestag. The Constitution provides that budget increases proposed by Bundestag or Bundesrat require the consent of the government. This gives the government decisive powers, of which, it is true, it has made little use so far. The provision also highlights and tries to cope with a development under which, as elsewhere, the tendency

of modern parliament is more toward increased expenditures than toward scrutinizing, and possibly restricting, expenditures proposed by the executive.

Constitutional Amendment

Under the Hohenzollerns as well as Weimar, German Constitutions were flexible rather than rigid. Constitutional amendments could be passed by way of ordinary legislation through the regular legislative agencies. Under Weimar, such amendments passed with a qualified majority of two-thirds of both houses. Under Weimar, moreover, a practice developed of passing statutes that deviated materially from constitutional provisions without bothering to amend the text of the Constitution. Such laws were valid when passed by the required majorities.

Under the Bonn Constitution, as under Weimar, constitutional amendments can be passed by concurring two-thirds majorities in both houses. This is why it is important for a Chancellor to control not only a simple but a qualified majority. However, the Weimar practice of indirect or silent deviation from constitutional provisions is now prohibited. Amendments must expressly alter or add to the text of the Constitution, and certain constitutional provisions, such as those affecting the federal structure of government or certain basic rights, are exempted from any alteration whatsoever.

Decrees

Germany, a country where the bureaucracy is older than parliamentary institutions, has a long tradition of administrative legislation. When lawmaking became a function of parliament, this tradition was continued, with parliaments often passing mere framework laws that were implemented by executive decrees or ordinances. This delegation of lawmaking power to the executive has become more and more common with the extension of executive functions into all fields. Germans distinguish such decrees from mere internal directives in that lawmaking decrees bear on the rights and duties of citizens. The Bonn Constitution specifies the cases in which "lawmaking decrees" require consent of the Bundesrat. As a check on the ordinance power of the executive, German courts have always claimed the right, whenever an individual case came up, to review such measures to see whether they kept within the limits set by the framework law; if they were found *ultra vires* they were not applied.

"Legislative Emergencies"

Another type of decree at one time proved more dangerous to German democratic institutions than executive decrees—emergency decrees. Experience with Article 48 under the Weimar system led the authors of the Bonn Constitution to omit corresponding powers in the new document. But a watered-down version of emergency legislation was nevertheless retained. In case the Bundestag refuses to vote confidence in the Chancellor (without, however, expressing non-confidence by voting for a successor) and the President (acting on the Chancellor's advice) does not choose to dissolve the Bundestag, he may declare a "state of legislative emergency," after a bill declared to be urgent by the executive has been rejected by the Bundestag. The bill, as well as any other bill rejected within a period of six months after such declaration, then becomes law if it is approved by the Bundesrat. The Bundesrat, however, is not likely to be so different in political complexion as to be ready to play this game against a determined Bundestag. This fact, together with the time limit and a restriction that emergency legislation must not amend or suspend any part of the Constitution, renders the application of this provision unlikely.

More ominous, and of much greater political importance, has been a long-standing effort by the government to have the Bundestag enact a general emergency statute that would confer upon the executive sweeping powers, including the power to suspend basic rights and to use the military, in case of external or internal crises. The various drafts have differed in certain details—for example, whether parliament, or a smaller body established by parliament, shall have the right to find that an emergency exists and, if so, with what majority, and whether the right to strike can be suspended during the emergency. Although somewhat watered down over the years, the most recent draft still would make it possible that the Cabinet (or even some of its members only) would assume dictatorial powers, if necessary even on its own initiative.

Since this legislation, which would amend the Constitution, could not be enacted without the consent of the SPD, this party's attitude is critical. The SPD in principle agrees that emergency legislation is needed, but—primarily under the pressure of the trade unions—it has so far rejected the drafts proposed. Whether now, being in the government, it would go along, remained to be seen.

While some provisions for the event of genuine emergency are certainly legitimate, the risks to which too far-reaching legislation would expose German democracy are only too apparent. During the *Spiegel* case, we must remember, the Chancellor declared that "a vast abyss of treason" had placed the nation and, indeed, the whole NATO system, in gravest danger, whereas, as the highest court subsequently found, there was absolutely no basis for such fears and charges. Germans, particularly the bureaucrats, are too easily inclined to believe that, in the words of one minister charged with drafting such legislation, "Crisis gives the executive its chance." Once before German democracy committed suicide by permitting parliament to confer all power on the executive through an Enabling Act. Will the second German experiment in democracy be imperiled in similar fashion?

3. THE FEDERAL COUNCIL (BUNDESRAT)

Background and Character

Second chambers in modern times are usually one of two types: they may represent a special class or caste or they may represent the territorial units of a federally organized country. In Germany the second chamber, since 1871, has reflected the federal structure of the country. The German second chamber shares this function with corresponding bodies in other federal states, such as the United States Senate and the Swiss Council of States. The chief difference between these and the Bundesrat is that the former represent the people of the member units, while the latter represents the units as such, that is, their respective governments and administrations. While the non-German second chambers usually consist of representatives elected by the people of the states (or, sometimes, their diets), the German second chamber has always consisted of delegates *appointed* by the *governments* of the states and acting under their instructions. On the other hand, while non-German second chambers usually are based on the idea of equality of member states and therefore contain equal numbers of representatives from each, representation in the German second chamber has been weighted according to the size and strength of the member units, although not in exact proportion to their populations.

This has meant that, politically, the function of the Bundesrat has been less the parliamentary one of representing the people vis-a-vis the government than that of being another part of government, in charge of coordinating lawmaking with the execution of the laws. German administration is noted for its peculiar device of having the member states administer federal laws. The persons representing member-state governments in the council (essentially a bureaucratic group consisting of high state officials and ministers) have traditionally considered it their chief responsibility to coordinate central legislation with state execution and to see that no essential state interests were infringed upon by such legislation. To be sure, with Land ministers attending Bundesrat meetings themselves, party political issues sometimes come to the fore. Thus the existence of this body may serve to bring political constellations in the various Länder to bear upon politics at the central level.

Composition

The old Bundesrat was devised to perpetuate Prussian hegemony. The Weimar Reichsrat was devised to lessen Prussian influence. In West Germany today the problem of weighting voting strength has been facilitated by the demise of Prussia. But the Länder are still vastly different in size and population. The largest population is over fifteen million and the smallest little more than half a million. Consequently, the Constitution allows those with more than six million, five Bundesrat votes; those with over two million, four votes; and the others, three each. There are altogether forty-one voting members (plus four nonvoting members

from Berlin). Each Land may send as many delegates as it has votes, but it can cast its votes only uniformly. It is thus the individual (Land) cabinets that have to decide how, in a specific issue before the Bundesrat, the votes of a Land shall be cast. This may require a vote in the Cabinet, especially if it is a coalition Cabinet, and thus the policies of the Bundesrat are determined by which parties control the individual Land governments. In this way the party-political situation in the various Länder affects government on the central level. Frequently, however, the vote of Bundesrat members reflects the economic and financial situation of their Länder rather than their party or religious affiliations. Until 1966, with the CDU in control on the federal level, the Bundesrat, always counting a number of SPD-led governments among its members, has been that branch of government where opposition policy has occasionally had a bearing on national affairs. In the main, however, it has been the instrument through which Land bureaucracies defend state rights as well as the interests of the administrations they serve, and Bundesrat opposition or vetoes are usually encountered only when there is fear that the respective measure may prove onerous to the Länder, especially financially.

The Powers of the Council

Constitutionally, the powers of the Bundesrat lie chiefly in the field of lawmaking. As we have seen, it acts at an early stage of the legislative process when it scrutinizes a government bill before the bill goes to the Bundestag. It becomes active a second time after completion of the process in the Bundestag. When a bill has been adopted there, the Council in principle has a suspensive veto. (If the Bundesrat votes its objections by a simple majority, it can be overridden by a majority vote of the Bundestag; if the vote is by a two-thirds majority, a two-thirds vote of the diet is required.) In many cases, however, for instance, in financial legislation, the Bundesrat has more than a suspensive veto; it has to give its consent and thus becomes an equal partner with the Bundestag. The same applies to constitutional amendments (a two-thirds vote is necessary in each body). In practice, about half of all bills have required consent. In most instances, conflict between the two chambers is avoided by the employment of a procedure modeled on the American conference committee. This joint committee (so-called Mediation Committee) is composed of eleven members from each chamber, with the Bundesrat members free from instructions; in over 90 percent of the cases it has been successful in smoothing out differences. Since it is the Council, in this last stage of lawmaking, that can threaten to veto or to withhold its consent, it has generally succeeded in having its views prevail or at least its compromises adopted. Thus the freedom of action of the real parliamentary body, the diet, is once more restricted in favor of an essentially bureaucratic body.

Even within the Council itself, the weight of influence tends to shift from the politicians to the bureaucrats, for, while Land ministers attend the plenary sessions, permanent officials of the respective Land ministries (for example, financial or economic experts) attend those of the Bundesrat committees. The full session in practice ratifies committee recommendations; there is little chance of altering them, since the ministers, as delegates of their governments, are bound by the respective Land government's instructions, and the instructions (to vote for or against) must be based on committee recommendations.

On the whole, the Bundesrat has proved an important and effective part of the government. But its role is more technical than public. It has nothing to do with such political affairs as electing the Chancellor or criticizing the executive, and even in legislating it deals chiefly with the more technical aspects of the procedure. Consequently, its prestige, though considerable among those active in or concerned with government, is not significant with the public at large; indeed, it is hardly known there.

Conclusion

Present West German democracy has not yet found the happy medium between, on the one hand, party dominance over both parliament and executive and, on the other, executive irresponsibility. Party bureaucracies try to rule supreme through the Bundestag, while administrative bureaucracy uses the Cabinet and, within the legislature, the Bundesrat, as levers for its control. In the struggle between these forces the strong position of the Chancellor both constitutionally and, at least in the Adenauer era, through the impact of his personality, has favored the nonparliamentary forces. The resulting Cabinet stability has for the time being prevented the extreme of parliamentary control that was the bane of the French system. But it entails the opposite danger of dooming parliament to impotence or subservience. While the Bonn parliament has functioned smoothly in performing certain tasks, such as lawmaking, its role in supervising the executive through debate and criticism has generally been insignificant. The decline in the number of parties represented, though it has made possible the streamlining of procedures, has had an adverse effect, especially upon the chief government party. The CDU has been too strong in comparison with the other parties in the diet and too weak in its relations to the executive, of which at times it appears as a mere appendage. There has been, as German democrats complain, an absence of the "power instinct" of the diet as an entity intended to possess and defend rights of its own against the executive. In too many cases parliament has been satisfied to forego debating general policies for lengthy periods of time, especially foreign policy. A parliament that avoids such vital scrutiny relinquishes its most essential function. Whether the Bundestag will yet play the role of watchdog and echo the voice of the people will in large measure depend on whether parties and deputies assert themselves more frequently and energetically, as they did, by way of exception and prodded by public concern during the *Spiegel* case in 1962. Under a government of the "grand coalition," with only the smallest party in opposition, there is, of course, even more need of such assertion.

5. Executive and Administration

1. CENTRAL GOVERNMENT

A well-conducted government must have a system as well knit as any system of philosophy; all measures taken must be well considered, and finances, policy, and the army must move together toward the same purpose which is the strengthening of the State and of its power. Now, a system cannot emanate except from one mind; therefore it must issue from that of the King. . . .

These words from Frederick the Great's "Political Testament" set the theme that runs through the history of German political institutions up to our day: the ideal of service to the state and the idea that government must be streamlined under strong executive leadership. Whether such leadership has been vested in kings or emperors, presidents with broad powers, a fascist Führer, or an authoritarian Chancellor, and whether the source of its authority was found in divine grace or in real or alleged popular consent, matters less than the fact that Germany has traditionally expected its fate to be determined by executive leadership and not by representatives answerable to the popular will. Leadership until 1918 was in the hands of dynasties assisted by hereditary nobles and members of an infeudated middle class. After World War I, an attempt was made to entrust the state to representatives of the people. But a large proportion of the people had no faith that party leaders could fill the exalted place vacated by Kings; they chose as leader a general who considered himself the place-holder for the monarchy. Instead of a new William, however, the Germans got Hitler, tyranny, and defeat. Since the downfall of the Nazi system there has been more readiness to try democracy again.

The German ideal of centralized and coordinated leadership has been affected by two counterforces: first, the desire of various social groups and classes to make their influence felt and have their interests represented in the executive; and second, the federal organization of Germany. It is against this complex background that the problems of the executive in the West German government must be viewed.

The President

The Bonn Constitution, as has been shown, facilitates the emergence of a strong executive. But in contrast to Weimar, it is no longer the presidency from which authoritarian controls are likely to derive. The Federal President, unlike the Weimar President, is elected not by the people but by a joint parliamentary body called Federal Assembly, consisting of the members of the Bundestag and an equal number of members elected by the Land diets. While he has the customary representative functions of a head of state, he has little influence over actual government. Unlike the Weimar President, he cannot dismiss Cabinet or Chancellor, and he has no emergency powers of his own. Such acts as are formally his (for instance, appointment of federal officials, exercise of the right of pardon) must be countersigned by the Chancellor or the respective minister. This applies to control of the armed forces as well. His one important power is the designation of a Chancellor, but even here he can be overruled by the Bundestag. The question of whether he may *refuse* action proposed to him by the Chancellor or the Cabinet (for instance, appointment of a minister proposed to him by the Chancellor, or declaration of a state of legislative emergency) has so far not arisen. President Heuss, during his two five-year terms of office (1949–59), showed no tendency toward independent action. His successor, Heinrich Lübke, occasionally, especially when the new government was formed after the 1965 election, has shown inclinations toward independence. For example, he claimed the right to pass on the prospective Chancellor's candidates for posts in the Cabinet; he even came close to forming a faction with Adenauer at that time to prevent Erhard from becoming Chancellor; and afterwards he publicly stated his preference for inclusion in the Cabinet of the Social Democrats (the Great Coalition). Despite his success in the last-mentioned attempt, this has not created something like the Weimar dichotomy of power at the top. So far the President is still overshadowed by the Chancellor.

Chancellor and Cabinet

The government consists of the federal Chancellor and the federal ministers, but the Chancellor is supposed to be its moving power. A changing relationship between Chancellor and Cabinet reflects the history of German constitutional developments. In the Empire, the Chancellor was the only leader, and heads of departments had no part in the formulation of policy. Under Weimar, the Chancellor was to be responsible for the general lines of policy, while each minister, within these lines, was to direct his department independently.

While the provisions of the Bonn Constitution on the relation of the Chancellor to Cabinet and ministers are generally similar to those under Weimar, two significant differences have enabled the Chancellor to emerge as powerful in practice. The "constructive vote of nonconfidence" means that once elected by a Bundestag majority, he is fairly safe from dismissal during the legislative period, unless he loses the backing of his own party or unless the coalition forming his majority disintegrates (in 1966, both happened to Erhard at one and the same time).

Secondly, he is free to form and reform his Cabinet, over whose composition the Bundestag has no control. If he is also a strong personality, his office comes close to possessing the authority of the Hohenzollern Chancellorship; the danger of autocracy in such a case is undeniable. Konrad

Adenauer frequently ignored his ministerial colleagues in laying down policies or taking major political steps, denying them a chance to offer their advice and assuming major responsibilities himself, especially in fields where he was particularly interested, such as foreign affairs. Furthermore, he established the practice of dealing directly with the top representatives of the respective interests. On important economic questions he arrived at what might be called bilateral treaties, for instance, with the head of the German industrialists' organization or the leader of the farmers. Thus the respective minister and even the legislature were left to implement his decisions. He made his own office, the Chancellery, into a major top-level agency charged with checking on the ministries and occasionally even policy-making. No wonder that the head of the Chancellery, especially such a trusted and close adviser to the Chancellor as Hans Globke, came to wield vast power himself.

Adenauer's successor continued some of these practices, including the practice of dealing with interests over the heads of the respective ministries and the use of the Chancellery. On the other hand, Erhard had less of a "power instinct," and this way certain factors that hampered Adenauer only little detracted from his status. In coalition governments ministers who do not belong to the Chancellor's party are in any way protected from the threat of dismissal by the Chancellor so long as their party backs them, which meant that Erhard's control over FDP members of his Cabinet was limited; factions in the Chancellor's own party may back ministers belonging to a faction against a Chancellor whose personality is less forceful than was Adenauer's. Indeed, Adenauer himself, as party chairman, intrigued against Erhard. Here the system of manning party and government with different persons proved detrimental. In Britain, where the party leader becomes the Prime Minister, and in the United States, where the President becomes party leader, unity of policy is safeguarded. Erhard's election to party chairmanship, in 1966, came too late to restore party unity. His successor, presiding over a coalition of almost equal party strength (represented in the Cabinet in the relation of ten to nine) confronts an even more difficult task of leadership and coordination.

Responsibility to Parliament

A genuine parliamentary system, in the sense of enforceable responsibility of the executive to parliament, existed in Germany only as long as the Weimar Constitution functioned. At present, a parliamentary system can hardly be said to exist. The constructive vote of non-confidence required to force a Chancellor out of office makes such an occurrence an extremely remote possibility. And individual ministers can no longer be forced to resign; thus they are responsible to the Chancellor, not to the Bundestag. Although the Constitution is silent on this point, this has become an established practice. For instance, ministers belonging to parties that withdrew from the government coalition have frequently been kept in office despite their parties' protests. While in practice ministers now are always members of parliament, this means very little if parliament has no control over them once they become ministers. Under these conditions, Cabinet stability is hardly a problem; but responsible government, in the British sense, is.

Paradoxically, the influence of parliament may come into play more forcefully at a time when a newly elected Bundestag has not even convened—that is, during the coalition negotiations for the formation of a new Cabinet. These negotiations have sometimes been long protracted, with the minor parties or party, the FDP, or even the CSU, trying to lay down conditions. So long as there is no party in control of an absolute majority, there cannot be, as there so often is in Britain, a predetermined government, and the prospective Chancellor has to consider the various power groups in parliament. Once elected, of course, he is at least constitutionally free to reform his Cabinet.

Ministers and Bureaucracy

The loose relation between ministers and parliament has strengthened the association of the political executive and the permanent bureaucracy. Before 1918 the government was entirely a committee of the bureaucracy. Most ministers arrived at their posts through an official career; they were administrators, not statesmen.

Since democracy took over in Germany, the minister has had the dual function of representing his party and of directing his branch of administration. Combining these apparently contradictory functions is the art of ruling in any parliamentary system. But in Germany the minister has tended to be either an official who concerns himself chiefly with administrative tasks or a politician paying attention to party and group interests to the neglect of administration. The habit of making ministries the political caretakers of particular clienteles has gained ground. For example, the refugee ministry has been staffed chiefly with ex-Nazis from the East; similarly, departments such as agriculture have been "infiltrated" by the respective interest groups. Ministers often are top members of the respective social or economic group. Most ministers are legally trained. In the case of the CDU, their denomination is important, too, since "parity" is desired of the Cabinet as a whole.[1]

A German minister is more closely surrounded with bureaucrats than his French or British colleague. There is no Cabinet of the individual ministers as in France. Much of a minister's time is spent with the Bundesrat, itself a bureaucratic institution. Unlike his British colleagues a minister may be without much parliamentary experience. Thus the danger of his coming under the influence of his assistants is a real one, the more so because the ministries are staffed entirely with permanent civil servants except for political undersecretaries (in Germany called secretaries of state, usually one for each ministry). It is this unchanging ministerial bureaucracy, much more than the ministers themselves, which is in control of government and administration. The minister is generally little exposed to popular contacts and influences; what counts is to keep on good terms

---

[1] Sometimes the desire to balance the different denominational, sectional, and other groups goes to ridiculous lengths, reminding one of corresponding efforts in case of making up "tickets"—of presidential, vice-presidential, and similar nominees—in the United States. Thus—to give just one example drawn from the level of regional cabinet formation in Germany—in 1966 (then) Rhine-Westphalian premier Meyers was compelled to take on the ministry of justice in that Land in addition to his premiership because that minister, for reasons of balance, "had to be" a Westphalian protestant lawyer, and no qualified person combining these requirements could be found!

with the narrow circle of his party's leadership (to which he himself may belong) as well as with the representatives of the chief interests (pressure groups) which back the party. Popular forces and tendencies not thus represented are, for the most part, only dimly perceived from the heights where ministers dwell. Popular scrutiny and criticism—through debate and questioning in parliament, discussion in the press, press conferences, or similar devices that in the West have helped to ensure democratic control—have, at least so far, seldom been used to full effect.

Organization of Ministries

Ministries in Germany have always been organized functionally—that is, according to spheres of government and administration. The number of ministries varies slightly according to political requirements at the time of cabinet formation or reformation. There may be an occasional minister without portfolio, or a ministry may be established in order to provide some coalition party or pressure group with a portfolio. In 1966 there were about twenty ministries, and some writers have charged that about eight of them were "unnecessary." Usually, however, a ministry is in charge of a well-defined major field of government. This is more efficient than the somewhat untidy practice in Britain and the United States (independent agencies, boards, etc.). On the other hand, Germany's federal structure has rendered the distribution of functions between federal and Land ministries a problem. Central ministries are often nothing but agencies for the preparation of federal legislation, without administrative machinery and executive powers of their own, these being lodged with the different Länder and their ministries. For example, the justice and interior ministries under both Weimar and Bonn have functioned mainly on the Land level; and the respective central ministries, which exist side by side with the Land ministries, have been chiefly in charge of drafting uniform legislation in these fields.

In the Anglo-Saxon countries the administration with its executive activities is concentrated chiefly in the capital. In Germany, the state is more diffused throughout the country. There is hardly a town without a number of federal and state administrative offices or authorities side by side with municipal agencies; the bureaucracy thus permeates society. This decentralization of the executive keeps the central ministry offices, whether federal or Land, small and compact. They supervise offices and officials of their branch scattered all over the country. The authority of a ministry reaches down directly to its local agencies in the remotest parts of the country; there is rarely confusion of authority or jurisdiction. Even autonomous institutions under the jurisdiction of a ministry—for instance, the federal railways—enjoy little real autonomy in matters of policy or appointments. An exception has been the traditional autonomy of academic institutions (such as university faculties) in their relation to the education ministries of the Länder.

Each individual branch of administration is not only strictly organized; it has little relationship to any other. Departmentalization, as in France, characterizes German administration, and there is little interdepartmental coordination, such as that provided by the Treasury in Britain. The German executive branches form separate, parallel hierarchies, each with its own pattern of organization, rules of appointment, and so on. The problem of their coordination has become as acute in Germany as elsewhere.

Public Enterprises

The scope of general public activities, including publicly owned enterprises, has traditionally been greater in Germany than in Britain or France (not to speak of the United States); but most of this activity is handled on the local level, and the more recent central planning and administrative activities of Labor Britain and postwar France have been conspicuously absent in laissez-faire western Germany. Except for the traditional postal and railway administrations, there are few public enterprises on the federal or state level. The most important ones, such as the Volkswagen works, Lufthansa, and VEBA, a holding organization for electric power and mining, have been at least partly "privatized"; an attempt has been made to keep the shares widely distributed among low-income groups, with as yet uncertain success.

The German postal administration, as in Britain and France, also provides telegraph and telephone services, the technical part of radio broadcasting and television, and certain financial services, such as a savings institution. It is organized under its own ministry, with a separate budget and accounting system.

German railways have been public enterprises since Bismarck's time, when it was found advisable to build up the Prusso-German railway system to facilitate rapid mobilization. The railways were enterprises of the member states until Weimar, at which time they were consolidated under one Reich Transport Ministry, then the largest single transport enterprise in the world. Now, of course, they are divided into the West's Bundesbahn and the still so-called Reichsbahn of the East.

2. THE GERMAN CIVIL SERVICE

Asked for the most significant German contribution to modern government, a student of political institutions will probably answer: its civil service system. Asked to evaluate this contribution, however, the experts are likely to disagree. While some consider it an exemplary model for other countries, others hold it responsible in part for the authoritarian trend in Prussian and German history. There is some justification for both valuations. As a matter of fact, this German problem reflects a more general dilemma of modern government: whether it is possible to combine efficiency with democracy. Election of officials and rotation in office are means to a democratic civil service, but they also may open the door to spoils and incompetence. Career officials selected according to merit and appointed by the executive may be efficient, but they may also become a closed caste impervious to popular control. The American civil service reflects, in the main, the merits and dangers of the first alternative; the German system reflects the merits and dangers of the second.

Origins and Structure

The German civil service system is centuries old. Frederick William I of Prussia first defined the status, and especially the duties, of Prussian officials. Examinations governed appointment to certain categories of office; and to train candidates, corresponding professorships were established at state universities. Lower positions in the service were generally filled with ex-soldiers. This system, while regulating recruitment and duties, lacked well-defined rights. These were subsequently incorporated into the sum total of rules and regulations that became known as the "well-established rights" of civil servants. They include guarantee of life tenure, salary and pension rights, and the privilege of suing the state in the ordinary courts in case of financial claims. The Prussian model was imitated by the other German states, so that although there was no overall law regulating the service, there was uniform practice. The Weimar Constitution put all these rights and privileges under constitutional protection. Since the Nazi interlude—which politicized the system but did not abolish it—Bonn has reaffirmed the traditional system after attempts by the occupation powers to democratize it had failed.

Selecting Officials

As frequently happens in the history of social institutions, the Prusso-German civil service system has been improved upon by other countries that started by using it as their model, while in Germany itself the system kept its less progressive character. The recruitment of personnel, for example, has always been based on expert training and, to that extent, on merit, but it has also largely remained a caste system under which only the few had access to the service, particularly to its higher ranks. Recruitment has been geared to the educational system. Graduation from certain schools has been the chief requirement for admission to examinations, and since higher education in Germany has remained largely a class affair, selection for the higher service has been restricted to the sons of the upper classes.[2]

[2] The higher service in Germany may be compared to the administrative class of the British service, but the number of higher servants is much greater; in 1965, they amounted to about 10 percent of the total number of German officials (federal, state, and local): about 130,000. (The total of *all* members of the public service, officials, employees, and workers, was about 2.9 million, including close to a million in postal and railroad services.)

Admission to the higher ranks has been tied to particularly demanding qualifications. The usual entrance requirement for these ranks has been graduation from law school. Following an examination based on these studies, the prospective official has to undergo at least three years of in-service training. A successful second examination makes him eligible for appointment to the higher level of the service. It can easily be seen that only a lifetime career warrants such extended preparation (continuing to the age of twenty-five at least); that only parents of means can give their children such an opportunity; and that, once secured, a position will be anxiously guarded against competition from outside or from the lower ranks.

The service thus became a closed caste, with a large proportion of officials being sons of officials themselves. Advancement within the service usually required one generation, with the middle-rank officials trying, at great personal sacrifice, to give one son the education entitling him to enter the higher ranks. Social mobility thus has largely been confined to the caste itself. And while the original appointment is generally free from such considerations as religion or party affiliation, promotion, especially to the highest position, is frequently based on such factors. Personal pull likewise is important. It has always been useful to know the right people, to belong to the right student corps, to have the right political and religious affiliation.

Status of Officials

In return for a long and expensive training, the service has provided the German official with security and status. While salaries have always been relatively modest, they have been balanced by economic as well as social privileges. The official has lifetime tenure. This above all distinguishes him from the numerous employees and workers in the public services. He cannot be dismissed except for cause, and even then only by a judicial verdict in a special court. Detailed regulations define procedures before special disciplinary courts, whose members are the peers of the accused. There is thus full guarantee against arbitrariness. Except for dismissal for cause there is no way to remove even obnoxious officials. A politically objection-

able official, for instance, would not be promoted; he might be transferred to another office at equal rank and salary, but he could not be dismissed even if he affiliated with a party hostile to the state. Persons hostile to the state hardly ever infiltrated the service in monarchical times, but there were occasional Communists and, more frequently, National Socialists in Weimar times. So long as an official did not violate his official duties for political aims, he might belong to any party. This was particularly important for civil servants employed in the public enterprises (postal, railways), who, far removed from sensitive activities, actually performed the same functions as employees or workers in private enterprises. Under Bonn, however, membership in certain organizations (most of them Communist) has been made incompatible with official status.

In addition to salary and life tenure, civil service privileges include an elaborate system of pensions. The official, usually retired at the age of sixty-five, receives a generous retirement pension (up to 75 percent of his salary); there also are pensions for his widow and for surviving minor children. He is retired on pension in case of invalidism and is entitled to leave with pay during temporary illness. His salary is increased if he has minor children. Since the service in Germany comprises such large groups as teachers and postal and railway officials, a large proportion of the German people thus have security from the cradle to beyond the grave; on the other hand, since the official loses his pension rights if he resigns, the system ties him to his office and makes it easier for a determined regime (such as the Nazis' was) to compel political conformity.

Another privilege is the state's assumption of responsibility when damage is caused to an individual by a civil servant acting in his official capacity. To make the state liable protects not only the official (against whom, in case of major neglect, the state may take redress) but also the damaged citizen.

As highly cherished as material benefits are benefits having to do with status and prestige. They derive from an elaborate system of ranks and titles with which the service is endowed. Minute and, to a foreigner, often ridiculous distinctions and refinements form the basis not

only of job classifications but of the social standing of the official, his family, and the entire
caste. Thus titles may never be omitted in
talking to an official—not only when a non-
official addresses an official, but even among
the officials themselves, and then not only
when a lower official talks to a higher one but
also among colleagues of equal rank or when a
higher official talks to his subordinate. It is
never, as in America, "Ed" and "Joe," not even,
as in Britain or France, "Mister" or "Monsieur,"
but "Herr Rat" (Councilor), or "Herr Ober-
finanzsekretär." The civil servant's title is customarily extended to his wife ("Frau Rat"
means that not the lady but her husband is a
councilor) and is never omitted from his obitu-
ary. Such titles are imitated in occupations outside the bureaucracy (for instance in the professions, or among employees of larger private
enterprises); titles and the prestige they involve
still form the backbone of German social stratification.

Political and Professional Rights

With regard to the professional and political
rights and activities of civil servants, the German system is about midway between the severely limited Anglo-American type, and the
unlimited French. But to judge the implications
of this statement, one has to keep in mind the
caste character and conservative-authoritarian
background of the German service. Thus, the
right of professional association, in Germany,
would not usually mean formation of groups
affiliated with other workers' organizations and,
together with them, opposed to the state as employer. Although since 1918 German officials
have been free to join any professional association, only in the public enterprises (chiefly the
postal and railway services) have a majority
affiliated with the general trade unions. Most
officials have avoided any affiliation with ordinary workers and employees and have formed
separate interest organizations of their own.
In contrast to many groups of French officialdom (for example, teachers), even lower-rank
officials in Germany have no feeling of class
solidarity with workers and insist on their
special status. Their neutral associations, and in
particular the powerful and influential *Deutscher*

Beamtenbund (DBB), lobby against any infraction of the traditional privileges of their
members. They have been chiefly instrumental
in preventing any postwar reform.[3]

In relations between agencies as employers
and officials as employees, the right to strike has
rarely been claimed and never been conceded.
Until recently, Germans had nothing comparable to the British Whitley Councils; individual grievances were brought before the respective superior officer, to be handled under set
regulations. A law for Personnel Representation
now provides for personnel committees elected
by officials, employees, and workers in the various agencies, which take part in the issuance
and application of service regulations, the handling of individual grievances, and in certain
cases matters of appointments and promotions,
a step toward a less rigid and more humanely
organized civil service.

Although the German official is likely to pro-
fess that he is above parties, he may belong to
any party and engage in political activities. The
British and American occupants of West Germany, with their own ideal of an unpolitical
civil service, tried to impose on Germans a
system under which an official would not be
permitted to engage in political activities and,
in particular, would have to resign from office
when running for elective office. Germans disregarded the policy from the beginning, and
officials "on leave" abound in West German
parliaments.

How Satisfactory Is the German Civil Service?

The difference between the German and a
Western civil service system may be illustrated
by contrasting the German official with his
American counterpart, the government employee. The American comes and goes; the
German is there for life. He is not likely to be
on loan from some business firm or other
agency, or a "dollar-a-year man," or a consultant.
An American agency chief has to spend half

---

[3] While the DBB has about 700,000 members, the trade
union for workers employed in public service has fewer
than a hundred thousand officials among its close to one
million members. (In the postal and railroad services, however, most officials are organized together with those of
employee and worker status in the respective trade unions.)

his time justifying the agency to the public and to appropriations committees; German agencies labor (or thrive) under the opposite shortcoming of being practically unabolishable, and some continue long after their real functions have vanished. American offices must function under the glaring, though intermittent and erratic, light of publicity and investigation; German offices are protected from political interruptions but also from healthful criticism. The American government worker's job and salary are always under the threat of the congressional "meat-ax"; the German's are more secure than any business executive's. The American works at his government job as at any other job, loyally but without special devotion; the German feels that his service is an honor involving special duties and an allegiance originally owed to the King and now to that mystical higher entity, the state.

The German civil service has often been called too authoritarian. But every bureaucracy in a modern state must be based on the hierarchical organization and discipline that guarantee the efficient carrying out of directives from the top level. In Germany the advantages of such a civil service have been a sense of duty, industriousness, and, by and large, expert knowledge and probity. But the obnoxious features of both authoritarianism and bureaucratism have been equally present. Sense of duty has meant unquestioned loyalty to a central executive authority that could do no wrong. The service has been impartial to individuals but less so in regard to classes and general issues. Officialdom has consciously or unconsciously favored the upper classes from which most of its members have been drawn.

And in regard to the public at large, it has been haughty and supercilious. Morally, the tradition of unquestioning fulfillment of duties in the service of the state proved calamitous. While such an attitude may be a virtue in countries with stable and largely uncontested value systems (such as Britain and the United States), on the Continent, where no such common value standards exist, it implies either hidden partiality for one group and one philosophy or a readiness to serve with equal zeal any master whatever. It may then entail lending one's

services to the execution of any, even the most atrocious, policy. The Prussian Kings already had "regarded self-resilient initiative, let alone criticism of their orders, as an act of insubordination bordering on mutiny. Loyalty they confounded with unquestioning submission to the service code and unconditional subservience to the machine of compulsion."[4] Thus the service could be relied upon to put into practice with equal effectiveness a lofty program of social welfare and a program of exterminating Jews. It has been authoritarian when left alone; resistant when under democratic direction; and conformist when under the direction of a forceful though untraditional ruling group such as the Nazis.

As a bureaucracy the Prusso-German officialdom has lacked initiative and a sense of individual responsibility. "Centralization and militarization became the predominant characteristics of the Prussian civil service. Forms predominated over purpose; command over the substance of commands; hierarchy over colleagueship; discipline over free creation; routine over local and personal invention."[5] Their predominantly legal training, in particular, produced officials "more useful in a static than a dynamic state; excellent interpreters of the past but not inventors of the ways and means of the future; apter to explain than to evaluate; and inflexible in the power to make exceptions."[6] Their training became too bookish and too long, their career too specialized, their attitude too compartmentalized. It was to such office, and not, as in England, to politics and parliament, that the German elite was attracted. It was natural that a more authoritarian-minded and less independent and self-reliant type of man prevailed.

The "New" Civil Service

In 1945 the problem was twofold: first, what to do about those—probably a minority—who had penetrated the service as active and convinced Nazis; and second, how to "democra-

[4] Hans Rosenberg, *Bureaucracy, Aristocracy, and Autocracy* (Cambridge, Mass., Harvard University Press, 1958), p. 90.
[5] Herman Finer, *Theory and Practice of Modern Government*, rev. ed. (New York, Holt, 1949), p. 728.
[6] *Ibid.*, p. 802.

tize" German bureaucracy in the more general sense.

Reform Suggestions

The failure of denazification proved a great handicap to civil service reform. Since the denazified former officials could reclaim their positions by right, a considerable number of "unreconstructed" Nazis regained even sensitive positions. While this in itself was disturbing, an even longer-range effect of this failure was that a chance to make a large number of positions available to new and more democratically minded officeholders was missed. In the face of this situation the occupation authorities tried hard but futilely to convince Germans of the merit of measures designed to provide broader and more equal access to the service; to break down the traditional monopoly of the academically—and especially legally—trained officials who alone have access to the higher service; and to stimulate a spirit of independence and initiative within the service as well as among Germans in general in their dealings with, and attitudes toward, authorities.

In particular they suggested open competitions for all vacancies; legal training to be required only for positions of strictly juristic character; special examinations to enable non-academically trained lower officials to be promoted to the higher service; more persons with outside experience to be called into the service; and similar measures. In short, they aimed at introducing into Germany a system approximating the United States civil service.

Failure of the Reform Program

The fate of these suggestions illustrates the difficulty of transplanting institutions from one country to another with fundamentally dissimilar traditions. The Germans simply procrastinated until the powers of the occupation authorities lapsed and then enacted legislation continuing the traditional system of the German service with all its "established rights." Thus, while personnel committees have been established, they have been used to see to it that no outsiders are called into the service. Competition for vacancies means little, because of the strict training qualifications that are required; the monopoly of the legally trained,

in particular, is generally continued. From all this one may infer that Germans, as they see it, are disinclined to sacrifice efficiency for democratization. The problem is whether it is possible to *combine* efficiency and training with democratization. Civil service reform in Germany will have no real chance as long as higher training and education, which alone open the path to higher positions in the service, remain the monopoly of the upper classes. Extending higher education to qualified students from all social strata would be the first step toward reform, a German version of the merit system, the "career open to talent." But educational reform of this sort has run into problems of its own. (See Chapter 7.)

The New "Functionary" Type of Official

In one respect, despite the restoration of the traditional caste-type bureaucracy, present German officialdom significantly differs from the older pattern. It has been pointed out how the schism created in the German people by the experience of Nazism, dividing it into a democratic minority and a more unconcerned majority, cuts through the civil service as well. However, even among the majority the old-fashioned Prussian official with his conservative system of values and ideals has, in the main, disappeared. The typical German official no longer identifies himself with *any* political philosophy, conservative or otherwise. He is neither prodemocratic nor (on the average) neo-Nazi; he is not pro- or neo- anything, but merely serves whoever happens to be in charge. He belongs to a party, since this promotes his career; he certainly belongs to a church. But all this takes place without real commitment. Thus, from a genuine estate that knew what it wanted politically, and how to get it and defend it in the face of hostile parties and parliaments, German officialdom has turned into a group of functionaries. Sober and unromantic, the new official is primarily interested in his and his caste's security; warned by Nazi and post-Nazi experience, he avoids taking risks. He does as directed and shuns responsibilities. Thus he appears moderate. He rejects adventurism in foreign affairs and, by and large, backs the Bonn Constitution as well as the Bonn regime—which, after all, has put him into office, has reestablished the authority and the rights of his caste, and has generally, so far, ensured peace and prosperity. In this way one obstacle that handicapped Weimar democracy—political opposition of the civil service—has been eliminated at Bonn. The trouble is that this very fact implies the permeation of Bonn democracy with bureaucratic authoritarianism. The present alliance of the Bonn Constitution with the Bonn bureaucracy has rendered Bonn bureaucratic rather than the bureaucracy democratic.

3. STATE GOVERNMENT AND PROBLEMS OF FEDERALISM

France has been called "a republic at the top but an empire at the base." Germany, one might say, has been an empire at the top, with some democracy at the base. The German tendency toward an authoritarian centralism has been tempered by some dispersion of power and a degree of self-government in regions and local units. It is true that authoritarianism may prevail—and in German history has prevailed—in small units of government as in large ones. It was one of the errors of the Potsdam program to assume that decentralization by itself would cause democratization. In Germany, regional (state) units often were strongholds of reaction, while more progressive movements and policies were frequently national.[7] Yet whatever tradition of democratic self-government there was in Germany developed in local units (cities) at a time when most other government was authoritarian. Thus individual circumstances determine whether regionalism or localism in Germany is "progressive" or not.

It must be understood that German regional and local units are not only self-governing but also agents for higher authority. A mayor, for instance, is both a local and a state official, and in the relation between central and state government there has been a similar connection, with Land agencies in charge of executing uniform central laws. This meant that the central government had to have powers to supervise the execution of its laws by the states and has even meant granting the federal government powers of coercion against the states. To an American who thinks of states as sovereign, such a system will seem a far cry from genuine federalism. Still, there is a good deal to distinguish it from outright centralism, such as that enforced on the Länder (and lower units) during the Nazi period.

Territorial Structure

While the long history of German disunity produced that reactionary particularism under which vested regional interests, such as state bureaucracies, clung to their own interests and prerogatives, it has also meant an attractive variety of cultural life. Instead of one Paris or London, Germany has had a multitude of regional centers. To this cultural variety the German is sincerely attached. Something, he feels, would be lost if it should give way to the uniformity so predominant in modern civilization.

But while regionalism in Germany has had a real basis in popular sentiment, by the nineteenth century actual political units had largely ceased to coincide with cultural and traditional regions. Prussia, in particular, constituted the major obstacle to a more rational regional organization of Germany. With the elimination of Prussia, the postwar structure of Germany might have become a rational one if the newly established Länder had not had to follow the boundaries of the occupation zones. These boundaries were carved out of German territory with supreme disregard for traditional regions and boundaries. Thus the Länder, with the exception of Bavaria, at first commanded little genuine attachment, and there was a strong movement toward reorganization. Following the consolidation of three Länder in the southwest, however, opposition subsided, and the "cake of custom" by now has endowed the ten-Länder structure with some kind of general recognition.[8] But the problem of their economic

---

[7] In the following the terms *central* and *national* refer to the highest, that is, federal, level of German government; the term *regional* refers to that of state government, that is, the government of the Länder; *local* refers to the governmental units at the bottom (municipalities, and so forth).

[8] Of the previously existing Länder, only Bavaria and the two city-states of Hamburg and Bremen coincide with present units. The former Prussian provinces were made Länder. These include Schleswig-Holstein, which also includes the former city-state, Lübeck; Lower Saxony, made up of the old province of Hanover plus the former Länder of Braunschweig, Oldenburg, and Schaumburg-Lippe; Northrhine-

viability remains. The present units are clearly divided into "haves" and "have-nots," with the five financially stronger Länder, in order to avoid too much federal intrusion, even subsidizing the less industrialized ones to the tune of about two billion DM annually.

States' Rights and Powers

It is not only the territorial structure of the Länder that must be viewed as problematical. The distribution of powers between central and regional governments is likewise precarious and has indeed been one of the major problems of German federalism. In the Hohenzollern Empire, power still lay mostly with the member states. In the Weimar Republic there was a strong trend toward centralization, carried to the absurd length of totalitarian centralism by the Nazis. After the downfall of Nazism there was, understandably enough, a particularist reaction, which led to a postwar policy in favor of states' rights. But economic and political forces proved stronger than wishes and theories. In Germany as in every modern society fundamental economic and social problems tend to become national problems calling for solution on a nation-wide basis—particularly where, as in Germany, parties, trade unions, industrial associations, and similar groups are national rather than regional, and where the aftereffects of two world wars required a pooling of national strength.

The Bonn Constitution, to be sure, gives the Länder strong powers of legislation (as long as the federal government does not exercise its concurrent jurisdiction) and administration in many fields, such as interior and police, justice, and education. But the Länder have so far made

little use of their power to legislate; the federal level has preempted most fields, leaving to the Länder chiefly education and culture. As for administration, the financial viability of the regional units has been the crucial problem. The Bonn Constitution sought to guarantee the Länder a stronger position in this respect than they had had under Weimar. Income and corporation taxes, for instance, were in principle reserved to them. But the federal government, having the right (with consent of the Bundesrat, to be sure) to lay claim to part of these taxes, and having assumed the large expenses arising from war, occupation, and the new military establishment, began to claim an ever larger share. In order to avoid an annual fight over this issue, the federal portion is now usually fixed for several years ahead (for 1964–66 it was 39 percent).

Land Organization and Politics

The Länder in West Germany have more control over their internal organization than they had under Weimar. They are free to adopt their own election systems, and their constitutions vary from undiluted parliamentarism to Cabinet irremovability. All but the Bavarian (which has a consultative "senate") are unicameral. The Land executive usually includes such departments as interior, justice, finance, economics, agriculture and food, education and culture, labor and welfare. Generally speaking, the federal ministries are mainly concerned with the preparation of laws,[9] and the corresponding state ministries with the administration and execution of laws. The larger Länder also have agencies intermediary between the level of state government and local administration, such as districts (*Regierungsbezirke*) headed by state-appointed and state-directed district presidents in charge of certain police affairs, and so forth. The district is not a unit for self-government.

To some degree, politics in the Länder centers around national issues. Indeed, there is a kind of built-in nationalization of Land politics because of the impact Land elections and the en-

---

Westphalia, formed out of the former province of Westphalia and the northern, industrially most important part of the former Rhine province, as well as the former Land Lippe; and Hesse, comprising the former province Hesse-Nassau and most of the former Land Hesse. The remaining units are entirely new: Rhine-Palatinate, a merger of the southern portion of the former Rhine Province with some portions of Hesse and with the former Bavarian Palatinate; and Baden-Württemberg, the product of territorial reform, composed of the two old states Baden and Württemberg which, after 1945, were split into three units and, following two plebiscites in the area, consolidated into the present Land in 1951. To these nine, the Saar was added as the tenth Land in 1957. West Berlin, often referred to as an eleventh Land, is in a special position (see Chapter 9). For a map, see p. 341.

[9] Separate federal administrations, in the main, are limited to foreign affairs and defense (plus the more autonomous postal and railroad administrations).

suing formation of Land cabinets have on the composition of the Bundesrat. A further characteristic of politics in the Länder has been the unpredictability of cabinet formation after an election has taken place, even now when minor parties for the most part have disappeared. In the Länder, the FDP sometimes joins the SPD, and one finds even an occasional coalition of SPD and CDU.

"Nationalization" of Land politics stands in contrast to the dwindling political functions of Land diets and cabinets. There is less and less actual lawmaking going on in the Länder. The chief legislative function of the Land diets is to enact the budget. But even here, most of the expenditures are fixed, with over 50 percent being spent for personnel (since the main burden of administration proper is still with the Länder), and only about 10 percent remaining for discretionary purposes. Thus, in the face of quite different intentions, Bonn federalism has

left the Länder with not much more than administrative-executive functions. There remains some autonomy, and thus variety, in educational, cultural, religious, and similar fields. But even here there may be need for federal coordination, as for example over school systems, and in a growing number of increasingly important matters the Länder—sometimes jointly with federal agencies—have set up boards, for example, for stimulating and regulating scientific research.

The dwindling political functions of the Land diets are reflected in a generally lower voting participation (75 to 80 percent as compared with 85 percent or over in federal elections) and in the lesser interest (and, consequently, representation) shown in them by industrialists or functionaries of industrialists' organizations or of trade unions. Instead, there are more "small people" in the Land diets, and, above all, more officials. The table on the left shows the contrast between the Land diets and the Bundestag in these respects.

Comparison of Composition of Land Diets and Bundestag [1]

	Percentages in all diets (AVERAGES)	Percentages in the Fourth Bundestag (1961–65)
Public officials	31.8	22.3
Workers and employees	13.8	5.6
Farmers and officials of farmers' organizations	9.4	11.5
Lawyers and accountants	7.4	7.6
Business executives	5.7	6.5
Party functionaries	5.2	6.5
Trade union officials	5.1	9.6
Artisans	3.9	2.9
Journalists and publishers	3.6	6.9
Independent businessmen (large enterprises)	3.3	5.2
Small businessmen	3.3	3.1
Housewives	3.3	2.5
Professions (physicians, architects, etc.)	3.0	6.0
Functionaries of economic associations	1.2	3.8
Total	100.0	100.0

[1] Arranged in declining order of strength of the different groups in the Land diets.

4. PROBLEMS OF LOCAL GOVERNMENT

German local, especially city, government has generally been both popular and efficient. But it has not escaped the centralist tendencies that complicate the tasks of self-government in other modern countries.

Units of Local Government

German local government, like the British and unlike the uniform French, is a bewildering maze. The basic local government unit is the *Kreis* (county—literally "circle"). Larger cities (without, however, any strict delimitation) are known as city counties, which means that, there, county and municipal governments are identical. Rural and small-town areas are rural counties, traditionally headed by an official called *Landrat*. This may be compared to the British distinction between county boroughs and administrative counties. The average German rural counties are smaller than the British administrative counties, not to mention the large American counties. This makes it more difficult

Typical Land Subdivision

- - - DISTRICT BOUNDARY
——— RURAL COUNTIES
◆ CITY COUNTIES

Typical Rural County

◆ CITY COUNTY
——— TOWN OR VILLAGE
COMMUNITIES

for them to discharge tasks requiring large-scale planning and financing. In Germany, therefore, many such functions are entrusted to special authorities of the state, which, under the supervision of ministries and separate from county administration proper, function in the counties.

Development of Local Self-Government

It is in the individual municipalities, and especially in the cities, that the idea and practice of self-government took root in Germany. At the beginning of the nineteenth century Germany's liberal nobleman, Freiherr von Stein, remembering the medieval freedoms of German cities, hoped through self-government in the cities to teach the rising German middle classes to govern themselves in what he hoped would be a democratic nation of their own. This hope was not fulfilled nationally, but in the cities self-government began to flourish while state government was still authoritarian.

Municipal self-government was representative and autonomous, but only within certain limits. Representative institutions, until 1918, meant, not democratic government, but government by city patricians. This did give them administrative experience, however, which they could pass on to the lower classes when municipal government became genuinely democratic. The overlapping of state and local authority is also a part of this picture. Police affairs, for instance, were handled by local authorities, such as may-

ors, in the name of the state, and the state generally reserved the right to confirm appointments. Consequently there developed a system of collaboration between officials and citizens beneficial to both. Officials taught expertness and stability, and they learned how to share government with citizens and conduct themselves as responsible civil servants. Citizens learned the business of self-government in the numerous administrative committees (deputations) established to help administer schools, hospitals, and other civic affairs. The state, while not having a right of direction, reserved powers of supervision which, however, were used sparingly.

Within this general pattern, there developed a great variety of local government systems under different charters. Somewhat as in America, and in contrast to the uniform systems of Britain and France, the states (and sometimes individual regions within states) developed their distinct patterns. Common to all of them, however, has been the close relationship between an elected council and the mayor (or mayor plus executive associates, a body called *Magistrat*). This system taught the heads of local administration to blend political responsibility with executive power—something never learned by Germans on the state or national level. This feature of German local government distinguished it from the British system with its all-powerful council and its unpolitical executive staff, the French system with its party-

Authorities and Lines of Local Government Supervision

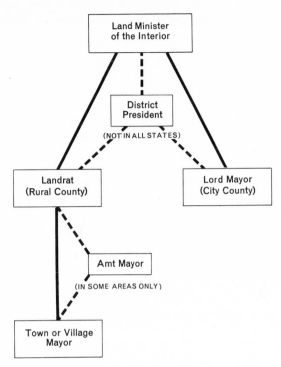

political, short-time mayor, and the American system with its separation-of-powers structure, its popularly elected mayors, its party patronage. In Germany, the mayor was usually elected by the council but for a term exceeding that of the council (usually twelve years), and, although party affiliation played a role, from among trained and qualified experts. He was actually a professional civil servant, and with his long-term appointment, was in a position to build up a staff of professional municipal officials to assist him.

Postwar Changes

There was no reason why after 1945 German local government could not have been rebuilt on the traditional pattern, but the Allies insisted on reforming it on the pattern of their own institutions. The questionable nature of such experiments is illustrated by what happened when the British introduced their system into their zone. They vested all power in a democratically elected council with its chairman as a

mayor, and they conferred executive functions on a staff of unpolitical civil servants headed by a director subordinated to the council. This was meant to revive grassroots democracy and to curb executive tyranny. But the resulting split between a largely ceremonial and powerless short-term mayor, as head of the council, and a long-term director, as chief of the administration, merely confused the Germans. In practice, they have converted the new system into their traditional one, with the director now almost undistinguishable from the previous mayor.

In the other former occupation zones pre-occupation systems have generally been restored, including the traditional state-local relation through mayor and *Landrat*. Yet, as an overall result, there are now altogether fifteen different systems of local government, a diversity that even Germans consider excessive.

Local Activities

An American might marvel at the wide range of activities in which German cities have for a long time engaged: economic and welfare services, public utilities, streetcars and buses, harbors, markets, slaughterhouses, pawnshops, swimming pools, parks, hospitals, housing developments, libraries, municipal theaters and opera houses, orchestras and concert halls, museums and art galleries, art schools, and sometimes universities. The few permanent opera houses in the United States find themselves in perpetual financial straits; performances of *Die Meistersinger* and *The Magic Flute* were given in the ruins of German cities in the winter of 1945–46. There are now over a hundred and fifty publicly owned and run theaters in some seventy West German cities, employing some twenty thousand persons. Many German municipalities have pioneered in city planning and public housing, and their record of rebuilding after 1945 was splendid. It is true that there were occasional scandals, but spoils and graft were generally small compared to that in many American cities.

More serious has been a tendency for the state (federal or Land government) to burden the municipalities with so many mandatory tasks that less and less remains to local initiative. Such fields as social welfare and housing have increasingly come under federal or state jurisdiction. With the increase in mandatory functions, cities are compelled to rely on the percentages of federal or Land taxes turned over to them, and the scramble for revenue among three levels of government has been continuous.

Municipal enterprises in Germany are organized in a number of ways: directly under a municipal department; indirectly as a separate public institution with its own boards and budget; or as an ordinary corporation under municipal or public-private ownership. It has been local government, *in addition to* state government, that made Germany a welfare state; it has been local government *rather than* the state that has promoted public management of economic affairs in Germany. The cities have furnished most of the gas, water, and power supply for the German population, and most of the local transportation. In rural areas, the counties have engaged in similar activities. Income from municipal enterprises constitutes one of the most important sources of income for local government.

Local Officialdom

Local officials resemble other public officials. They go through the same training and preparation for a career service, are divided into the same categories of higher, middle, and lower, enjoy the same privileges and acquired rights, and are paid on comparable salary scales. They share with state officials status as a group apart from the general public, but the slightly freer atmosphere of local government makes them somewhat less authoritarian and exclusive. There is a good deal of interchange among civil servants of different local units. Since the individual units of local government have to select their staff from a restricted group, there is more genuine competition for jobs here than in the state service. Competitive hiring, to be sure, has frequently meant selection on the basis of political affiliation, religious denomination, and similar criteria, but these factors have not usually overridden knowledge and training. Local administration thus demonstrates the more attractive features of German government.

6. German Law and Administration of Justice

1. NATURE AND DEVELOPMENT OF THE GERMAN LEGAL SYSTEM

Character of German Law

In the Anglo-American tradition the two bulwarks of freedom against the authority of the state are parliament and the common law. On the Continent, however, law is less a bulwark than an expression of the will of the organized community. At a time when English judges, armed with legal precedents and "right reason," protected the rights of the people from arbitrary authority, Continental jurists fashioned and codified the law as a body of rules for the ordered exercise of state authority over every subject. Judges and courts became a part of the state machinery thus established. In Germany, law is considered as state made, the court system as an integral part of the state organization, and judges, though enjoying independence, as state officials.

The German legal system thus resembles the French. First of all, it is code law, not case law. The statutory laws are supposed to provide a comprehensive source for the courts' findings. The German believes that it is one of the prerogatives of the state to regulate the citizen's activity through codified rules, and the prerogative of judges to see to it that these rules are correctly interpreted and applied. This attitude has produced an able but bureaucratic judiciary, controlling the public rather than protecting it against state bureaucracy. This does not mean that law and administration of justice are felt to be arbitrary. The German feels secure and comfortable under rules that are elaborate enough to govern his actions. Moreover, the circumstances of the individual case are not necessarily disregarded under this system, because codification does not exclude considerations of equity. On the contrary, the codes contain many rules that require the judge to apply what amounts to standards of equity. This gives him a good deal of discretion and enhances the role of precedent. Indeed, the growing emphasis on precedent in civil-law countries and on statutory law in common-law countries means that the two systems are gradually drawing closer to each other.

Emergence of a Unified Legal System

The history of German law reflects the country's political disunity. While Britain experienced early legal unification through precedents set by royal judges, and France, somewhat later, through uniform codes, German law remained splintered well into the period of the Hohenzollern Empire. It often lacked uniformity even within the same principality. Other German regions had only the unwritten, so-called common law. This was basically Roman law as rediscovered in the late middle ages and subsequently adapted to modern conditions by practice and custom.

The reception of Roman law into Germany served three purposes. It armed the rulers of the rising sovereign states with the Roman concept of state supremacy and thereby helped to eliminate the remnants of feudal public powers. Since it allowed only contractual rights to land, such as lease (outside of ownership proper), it made the feudal owner exclusive master of the estate and the peasant a mere tenant or laborer and thus destroyed in most of Germany the medieval remnants of free peasantry. Finally, since it acknowledged only a contractual type of work relationship, Roman law made the worker a mere party to a labor contract and thus destroyed traditional status relationships and the ensuing obligations of the employer. Roman law, in short, made the ruler sovereign, the Junker proprietor, and the employer master.

This law became the basis for nation-wide codification when the Reich was established in 1871 with federal power to legislate uniformly in fields such as civil and criminal law and procedure. So technically perfect were most of the resulting codes that even the Nazis, inveighing against their alien Roman features, did not see fit to abolish them. Any revision of their harsher and outdated features after 1871 was due to the efforts of progressive parties or individuals interested in legal reform and usually was accomplished by enacting statutes for the regulation of special fields, such as labor law, rent law, the law relating to matters of taxation or to social insurance, and so forth.[1] Law remained essentially Roman, logical, and deductive.

2. GERMAN COURTS

Despite its federal structure Germany does not have two parallel sets of courts, as has the United States with its federal and state systems. It has a single integrated system, with state courts on the lower levels and federal at the top. Although most courts thus belong to different member states, the system is rather uniform, because courts and procedures (like the bulk of applicable substantive law) are regulated by federal codes. Judgments and legal instruments are recognized and executable throughout the nation. There are, for instance, no stricter and easier divorce laws in one part of Germany than in another, no problem of nonrecognition of divorce decrees, and no necessity to extradite fugitives from justice from state to state.

Special Courts

On the other hand, German regular courts do not have the overall jurisdiction entrusted to courts in Britain and America. They rule in civil and criminal cases, while several sets of special courts deal with such matters as labor relations, suits against and among public authorities, and claims against social insurance institutions.[2] Thus labor courts, with local and appeal courts and a high court of legal review, decide lawsuits between employers and employees and cases arising out of collective labor agreements. They are staffed with learned judges sitting with lay assessors selected from and by employers and employees, and procedures are simplified, speedy, and inexpensive. Like France, Germany has a separate system of administrative tribunals that possesses guarantees of judicial independence and, by and large, has given fair protection against executive arbitrariness. The bulk of claims against public authorities, as well as suits between them, are handled by these tribunals. Judgment is rendered against the state and not against individual officials. The jurisdiction of German administrative courts has generally not been as broad as in France, where almost anyone can file a petition in the public interest, but it has now been broadened to include all cases where a person's rights are affected by an act of public authority. Legal unity in this field is now provided through a federal Supreme Administrative Court.

Regular Courts

The regular court system for civil and criminal cases has remained basically unchanged in the West since its establishment under the Hohenzollerns. There are four levels of courts:

---

[1] A bold revision of penal law, prepared during Weimar times, never came into force due to the advent of the Nazis; it might have become a model for any modern penal legislation. New, less ambitious, and much less progressive efforts in this direction have been facing endless delays in Bonn. With Social Democratic ministers of justice now in office at Bonn and in the key state of Northrhine–Westphalia, some progress may be anticipated.

[2] The jurisdiction of the regular courts now, however, extends to one area not usually covered by the regular courts in other countries. Jurisdiction over members of the armed forces has been vested in the regular courts rather than in courts-martial—a surprising and encouraging expression of civilian supremacy.

local courts, district courts, appeal courts, and the Federal Supreme Court, successor to the Reich Supreme Court, which watched over German legal unity before 1945.

Local Courts

Local courts are found in all larger and many smaller cities and towns. In the smaller towns there is often only one judge, who takes care of civil and criminal as well as probate and similar noncontentious matters (there being no one comparable to lay justices of the peace on the British or French pattern). In larger places a local court has several judges who divide the different categories of cases. They act as single judges in minor civil and criminal cases and in probate and similar matters. In somewhat more important criminal cases the judge is joined by two lay assessors who are chosen by lot from among the local inhabitants.

District Courts

District courts, which exist in all larger centers, are courts of primary jurisdiction as well as of review of local court judgments. They are staffed with a larger number of judges, who divide into sections (chambers) for different types of cases, and who always sit as collegiate bodies voting by majority. Their composition and jurisdiction appear in the chart on page 450. In contrast to Britain, to appeal in Germany means to take up a case anew and to consider the facts as well as the law. The assize courts deal with particularly grave crimes, such as murder, and have nothing in common with jury trial. The lay members of the assize courts sit, decide, and vote *jointly* with the learned judges—a system that gives preponderance in the procedures to the latter.

Appeal Courts

It is appropriate to use *appeal courts* to translate the German name of the next court level because, except for certain rare cases, they lack original jurisdiction. As in district courts, there are civil and criminal sections, here called *senates*. Criminal senates decide upon points of law only. The court may confirm a sentence, quash it, or order retrial by the lower court. It never tries the case itself.

The Supreme Court

The chief function of the Federal Supreme Court at Karlsruhe is to ensure uniformity of legal interpretation, which was especially necessary after years of legal confusion from 1945 to 1950. Besides deciding points of law in civil and criminal cases coming up to it from lower courts, however, it is also a court of first and last resort in political criminal cases (treason, subversion, etc.), where it frequently deals with East German agents and their Communist helpers.

The Supreme Court consists of civil and criminal senates. All appeal court judgments involving sums above a stated value, as well as all cases in certain defined categories, such as divorce cases, are reviewable by this court. Unlike the United States Supreme Court, the highest German court cannot select the cases to be reviewed.

Judicial Review and the Constitutional Court

Traditionally, German courts have had no power of judicial review. Such a power, which the French reject as an infraction of the people's sovereign lawmaking authority, Germans regarded as conflicting with the authority of the law-giving state. On American suggestion, however, judicial review was incorporated in the Bonn system, with the Constitution providing that a separate highest court, the Federal Constitutional Court, shall have the sole power of review. It decides cases in which ordinary courts have doubts about the constitutionality of a law, or upon application by a cabinet (federal or Land) or a Bundestag minority of at least one third of the legal membership. At first, misgivings were voiced by progressives who recalled that in the 1920's the courts had tried to check social legislation by assuming review power (producing a situation somewhat similar to that presented by the anti–New Deal United States Supreme Court of the mid-1930's). Ministerial officials, on their part, feared that review power would interfere with efficient lawmaking (understandably so, since they themselves were the chief drafters of bills).

Both fears have proved without substance. The Court, established in 1951, has acted with

REGULAR COURT SYSTEM OF WEST GERMANY

FEDERAL COURT

> **Supreme Court**
>
> Main function is to ensure uniformity of legal interpretation
> Cannot select cases to be reviewed
>
> | CIVIL SECTIONS | CRIMINAL SECTIONS | |
> | --- | --- | --- |
> | *5 judges* | *5 judges*
 Original jurisdiction | *5 judges*
 Revision |

CIVIL CASES

LAND COURTS

> **Courts of Appeal**
>
> *3 judges*
> Lack original jurisdiction
> Review district court judgments where district court had original jurisdiction

> **District Courts**
>
> Decide in all matters outside the jurisdiction of local courts and on appeals against local court judgments
>
> | SECTIONS FOR APPEALS | SECTIONS FOR ORIGINAL JURISDICTION |
> | --- | --- |
> | *3 judges* | *3 judges* |

> **Local Courts**
>
> *1 judge*
> Minor civil cases

CRIMINAL CASES

> **Courts of Appeal**
>
> *3 judges*
> Lack original jurisdiction
> Decide upon points of law in cases of local court sentences appealed to the district court

> **District Courts**
>
> Courts of primary jurisdiction and of review of local court judgments
>
> | SMALL CHAMBER | LARGE CHAMBER |
> | --- | --- |
> | *1 judge*
 2 lay assessors
 For lesser cases | *3 judges*
 2 assessors
 For appeals against local verdicts |
> | LARGE CHAMBER
 3 judges
 2 assessors
 Original jurisdiction | ASSIZE COURT
 3 judges
 6 assessors
 For grave crimes such as murder |

> **Local Courts**
>
> *1 judge*
> Minor criminal cases

> *1 judge*
> *2 lay assessors*
> More important criminal cases

circumspection and in a spirit of progressivism, and this is true also of the exercise of its other powers, which are substantial. It decides in cases of constitutional conflicts between federal and Land governments or among Länder, and also in cases of conflicts between the highest federal organs themselves. It fulfills part of the functions of the French *Conseil d'Etat:* any person claiming to have been deprived of a constitutional right by a public authority may appeal to it. It may outlaw parties as antidemocratic (as it did in the case of a neo-Nazi group and in that of the CP). Especially in the protection of the basic individual and group rights amply provided for in the Constitution (see below), the Court's activity has ranged far and wide. For instance, in regard to "equality" it has established new rules providing for equal rights of both parents in the education and care of their children and of political parties in connection with tax deductibility of contributions; on the other hand, the 5-percent clause in election laws was declared not to be in violation of the equality principle. Other important decisions have been mentioned in their proper places.

The Court's liberal attitude may in part be due to its composition and method of selection. In contrast to most German courts, its members are elected by parliament, and the majority of its judges are drawn from outside the career judiciary. There are two separate panels, or "senates," of eight judges each. All members must be trained in the law, and while some of them are selected from among the judges of the other federal high courts and enjoy life tenure, most of them are drawn from among professors and lawyers and are appointed for eight years. This diversity of background may be the reason for the general spirit of liberality found in the Court today.

Half of the membership of the Court is elected by the Bundesrat, voting by a two-thirds majority, the other half by a special committee of twelve electors set up by the Bundestag on the basis of proportional strength of Bundestag fractions, voting likewise by qualified majority (a minimum of nine out of twelve). In this manner no one party or party coalition can alone determine the composition of the Court.

3. THE GERMAN JUDICIARY

Judges, Prosecutors, Judicial Administration

The German judge is part of a bureaucratic setup. When he acts, the state acts through him. The judge remains anonymous even when he renders his judgment. He announces, for instance, that "the court" will take such and such a motion under advisement, and no dissenting opinions are made public.

The anonymity and formalism of the judge are the result of his training and the influence of his administrative superiors. Ordinarily—that is, in all Länder judiciaries—he is appointed and promoted by Land ministers of justice.[3] He is, to be sure, independent so far as his judicial decisions are concerned. The chief guarantee of his independence is his life tenure (which means irremovability except for cause) and his protection against being transferred against his will from one post to another. Like other high officials, future judges have to undergo specialized studies and training at universities and in-service training in courts. After the second examination, opening the way to judicial position, they must decide whether to enter the bar as practicing lawyers, or to choose the state service. Unlike British judges but like the French, German judges are not drawn from the bar but devote themselves from the outset to an official career. This not only shuts them off from the wider views that dealing with clients gives to the attorney, but also makes them conscious of being part of a specialized bureaucratic machine. Their large number (over twelve thousand in about a thousand courts) contributes to this feeling.

Prosecution is a separate operation within the machine of the administration of justice. Judges and prosecutors usually specialize. Thus both judge and prosecutor tend to become bureaucratic, bookish, and authoritarian-minded. This tendency is intensified by the influence of their superiors. Both hierarchies, courts as well as prosecutors, are under the ultimate supervision of justice ministers. In the judiciary, as in other bureaucracies, conformity and industry offer the royal road to success. The judge knows that if he continually renders decisions not liked by his superiors or decisions that are frequently appealed and reversed, or if he generally behaves individualistically and "uncooperatively," he can hardly expect promotion. The German judge is free of the pressure exerted upon an elected judge by public opinion, parties, and politicians—perhaps too free, for the drawback of the German appointive system lies in the influence exercised by the group, or caste, to

3 The relatively small number of federal judges in the federal high courts are selected in a procedure whereby the Bundestag acts in conjunction with the respective federal ministry (for example, minister of justice in case of members of the Federal Supreme Court, minister of labor in case of judges of the Supreme Labor Court, and so forth).

which the judge belongs.[4] His prestige consists in being a member of the group and depends on the rank he holds in it.

How Satisfactory Is the German Legal System?

It is sometimes said that in England and America, but not on the Continent, the judge is "king." We have seen that in some respects this assertion is valid. But in another sense a French or German judge dominates proceedings and trials to a much greater extent than his Anglo-American brethren ever do. For, while the British and the Americans look upon a lawsuit, and particularly a criminal trial, as a kind of duel in which the parties fight it out and the judge is a mere umpire to uphold the rules of the game, in Germany (as in France) the judge himself is entrusted with finding the truth, and the parties, attorneys, and prosecutors are simply aides in his investigation. In this sense, the law emerging from judicial proceedings is judge-made in Germany, while in Britain and the United States it is largely attorney-made. This has its advantages and its disadvantages. Highly formalized rules of evidence provide better protection for the defendant in Britain and America, but the lesser degree of formalism on the Continent permits more thorough investigation and avoids that abuse of formalities which is the bane of American trial procedure. In Germany there is little cross-examination of witnesses; the presiding judge examines them. He admits and excludes evidence. There is, of course, no truth in the persistent myth that the defendant is presumed guilty; he is presumed to be innocent unless the prosecution proves his guilt. But the defense (defendant as well as defense lawyer) has a difficult stand against the machinery of justice. The prosecution—as well as the police in preliminary proceedings, and the court itself—is less bound by formal rules. Preliminary proceedings are often long and drawn out, and release of defendants from arrest on bail is very rare.

On the other hand, there is little police brutality, and the curious discrepancy, known to American criminal procedure, between meticu-lously liberal court trial and frequently arbitrary and brutal investigation by the police is unknown. Arrest must be confirmed by a judge not later than the end of the following day, and detention prior to trial has to be reviewed periodically. Nevertheless, overly long periods of detention have been common, and a recent reform has therefore defined stricter prerequisites for such detention; it has also specified additional rights for defendant and counsel. No defendant is sworn in as witness in his own case, though of course he has the right to be heard. A defendant acquitted as innocent can claim indemnification for pretrial detention. The death penalty has been abolished in the Federal Republic. This has benefited many Nazi murderers (Eichmann, had he been convicted in West Germany, would still be alive). Few German prisons are as progressive as some of the best in the United States, but on the other hand there are no cruel methods of punishment as are still found in some American prisons.

Politically and generally, two areas of criminal law and procedure have proved particularly troublesome in West Germany. One is the area of treason and related offenses. Here the danger of having extremely loose and vague rules—providing, for instance, for "literary treason," which may be committed without criminal intent by the press—became very obvious in the *Spiegel* case. A similar danger lies in the possibility of invasion of privacy through wiretapping and the opening of letters (committed by, of all agencies, the Federal Office for the Protection of the Constitution, a kind of German FBI still staffed with many former Gestapo agents!). Here, traditional concern for state security still tends to outweigh concern for personal and group rights and liberties.

The German legal system is less weighted in favor of the rich than is the Anglo-American one. Appeals and revisions in civil cases, to be sure, often depend on a minimum money value of the case. But general costs are not high, mainly because, in civil cases, attorneys' fees are fixed at specific rates by statute. Impecunious parties or defendants are entitled to free proceedings (including the cost of witnesses and experts, in that case borne by the state) and the services of a court-appointed and

---

[4] This caste character is strengthened by in-breeding: Each fourth judge in West Germany is the son of a judge or a lawyer, each second the son of an official.

state-paid lawyer. Moreover, while in the United States a civil claimant often refrains from going to court because, even if he wins, he has to bear his own costs, German law provides that all costs are to be borne by the defeated party. Justice in Germany is thus relatively inexpensive; it is, moreover, accessible, generally fair, and not overly complicated. But it has been authoritarian, and has lately been encumbered with the awful legal legacy of Nazism.

4. THE LEGAL AFTERMATH OF NAZISM AND PROTECTION OF RIGHTS AND LIBERTIES

Perhaps no nation and no judiciary ever confronted legal problems as complex as those left to post-Nazi Germany as a legacy of the Nazi system. Unheard-of crimes had been committed, rights despoiled, new vested interests created in their stead. Many of these actions, moreover, had been carried out under statutes and regulations appearing in the form of law. Should all this now be left alone? Or should all of it be investigated, prosecuted, revamped? What was to be done about actions that the Nazis had made racial or political crimes and for which sentences had been passed? What, on the other hand, about acts that under the laws of the regime were not crimes, indeed may even have been legal duties, but that now appeared eminently punishable? What about Aryanized property of which Jews had been despoiled? What (to refer to a few particular cases) about the German soldier who, when all seemed over in 1945, deserted and went home? What about the judge who condemned him to death?

War Crimes and Their Prosecution

What, above all, about the enormous crimes committed in and outside of Germany, which were later to be known as war crimes or crimes against humanity (such as extermination of Jews and other groups, medical experiments on living persons amounting to torture, maltreatment of slave labor), whose perpetrators the Allies had vowed to "pursue to the uttermost ends of the earth" to bring them to justice?

It is true that Germans were at first spared

the trouble of worrying about these problems; the Allies took it upon themselves to deal with them before the Nuremberg International Military Tribunal as well as in courts set up by individual occupants in their zones. Some groups of major war criminals were tried in this way by the Allies and sentenced (most of them later to be pardoned). The Allies also enacted a number of laws dealing with such problems as restitution of despoiled property. But this still left to Germany the prosecution of all but the somewhat haphazardly selected cases dealt with by the Allied tribunals.

Coming to Terms with the Past

Through nothing else might Germany have more truly and more publicly purged itself than by the prosecution of such crimes. But the majority of Germans, as we have seen, failed to come to grips with the problem of what they refer to as their "undigested (or unresolved) past." This is perhaps revealed most poignantly in their attitude toward their own resistance: while some have come to recognize the Resistance fighters as genuine heroes who under most trying conditions fulfilled their patriotic duty, too many still see them as traitors and their persecutors as people who "merely did their duty." [5] And the long-drawn-out history of their attempts to cope with the problem of Nazi criminality reveals similar hesitation and confusion.

Here the failure of denazification, which reopened judicial and prosecution positions to former Nazis, has borne the bitter fruit of a biased or weak justice. Hardly anything was done to purge the judiciary itself, which during World War II had twenty-six thousand death verdicts to its account (as contrasted with less than three hundred in World War I). For over ten years, prosecution lagged; it was often a matter of sheer coincidence when crimes and criminals were detected. Even then prosecution and trial often turned out to be a farce. [6]

[5] Thus, in a 1960 poll, forty out of a hundred opposed the naming of a school after a Resistance fighter, while only twenty-five supported the idea.
[6] A particularly tragic case may be cited here as an example of the conditions described above. In the last days of the war, a few members of the Hitler Youth, children of fourteen or fifteen years who had been hastily armed without

Courts often accepted a defendant's assertion that he acted under duress or obeyed superior orders; sentences imposed often amounted to honorary acquittal. For a number of years Germans seemed to have solved the problem simply by ignoring it—until something happened to reactivate the issue. Among the prisoners returned by the Soviet Union in the late 1950's, there were found so many major Nazi criminals that the government decided to take more positive action. A central office was set up to collect evidence and coordinate the prosecution of all major crimes that could still be detected, and a number of spectacular trials began. The most spectacular (at least in the number of murders for which the defendants were indicted—millions) was the Auschwitz trial held at Frankfurt. These trials revealed not only what had long been known—the planned Hitlerite extermination of millions—but also that the "final solution" of the Jewish question had been accompanied by excesses surpassing even a Dantesque imagination.[7]

Tried in meticulously fair fashion, none of the accused could get worse than a life sentence. None of the accused ever expressed regret. Most felt that being brought to trial so long after the event was unfair. And that many Germans at large agreed with them is revealed by the general reluctance to have the statute of limitations (under which prosecution of criminals not discovered before the summer of 1965

would have become impossible) prolonged.[8] A law extending the period by four years passed the Bundestag only with difficulty; the entire FDP voted against it, and the FDP minister of justice resigned in protest. On the other hand, there have been expressions of shame and disgust, especially on the part of the young, to whom their elders had described these reports as "atrocity tales" or, in any event, as "gross exaggerations." Thus the soul of Germany has still not come to peace with itself.

Protection of Civil Liberties

A more welcome legacy of the Nazi period has been the greater awareness on the part of many Germans of the importance of individual rights, civil liberties, and their protection. The wholesale destruction of liberty under the Nazi regime, and the sense of utter insecurity it created, engendered a marked appreciation for the blessings of personal freedom and privacy. Traditionally, in contrast to Britain and France, the law in Germany has been not so much an instrument for the defense of individual freedom as one to maintain order and enforce individual duties. True, there has generally been less unofficial interference with liberties and the realm of privacy by pressure groups, such as has frequently developed in the United States (for instance, unofficial religious or political censorship of the press, theater, movies, and their employees). Public authorities, on the other hand, have been notoriously negligent in respecting such freedoms.

In this respect the postwar expansion of administrative jurisdiction and the liberal attitude of the Constitutional Court have added importantly to the protection of liberties. So have constitutional provisions, which, in contrast to the Weimar Constitution, give certain basic rights immediate applicability instead of leaving them as mere programmatic statements of aims. Thus the very first articles of the Bonn Constitution protect "the dignity of man" and the "free development of his personality." These some-

---

any training, were disarmed and sent home by the enraged inhabitants of a village through which they were passing. Discovering this "crime," an SS court-martial without further formality condemned to death the village mayor as well as another inhabitant, both of whom had courageously stepped forth and assumed responsibility. When one member of the "court" (the local Nazi leader) refused to sign the verdict, he was likewise condemned, and the three were put to the gallows on the spot, the population being forbidden to take the corpses down.

The trial of the guilty court members extended over eight years; it consisted of a series of acquittals by the assize courts, reversals of these verdicts by higher courts, and retrials by the assize courts. The final result of this tragicomedy was that one of the two lesser defendants was finally acquitted, the other got a light prison term, while the chief defendant died of natural causes during the last stages of the trial.

[7] The annals of humanity, or rather, inhumanity, should record such actions as the killing of newborn babies by smashing their heads against walls, or the way in which the commandant of the annihilation camp Treblinka used to kill inmates: He trained his dog, which he called Mensch (human being), to tear off human genitals; he would urge the dog on by shouting: "Mensch, get those dogs."

[8] At that time, about two thirds (according to one poll, about 60 percent—according to another one, about 70 percent) declared themselves opposed to further prosecution (apparently, even of those criminals already discovered).

what vague formulations have been used from time to time to preserve privacy by protecting personal secrets and private correspondence, by guaranteeing the right not to have one's name or picture used in films or literature without permission, and by prohibiting wiretapping. It is, of course, difficult to draw the line between the right of privacy and freedom of opinion, for example, the right of the press to report freely. A draft bill on "personality protection," which attempted to solve this difficulty but seemed to many to involve a danger of muzzling the press, has run into strong public opposition. Further rights, which show the progressive tendencies of the Constitution, include the right of asylum for any persons entering West Germany as political persecutees; the right of conscientious objection to military service; nondiscrimination not only in regard to sex but also in regard to race, religion, and political opinion; and prohibitions against the mental or physical ill treatment of persons arrested or detained. As one can see, many of these provisions reflect the adverse experience of Nazi totalitarianism.

As mentioned before, authorities still tend to disregard such rights. The way in which the now famous *Spiegel* affair was handled, and public reaction to it, are indicative of both dangers and hopes in the situation. The case, which involved the editors of a weekly whose revelations frequently had got under the skin of the government, in respect to the arrest and detention of the incriminated as well as to the government's response to criticism revealed clumsiness of action, disregard of rules and regulations, and even plain illegality on the part of authorities up to the highest level. On the other hand, criticism was voiced by many who showed genuine anxiety about infractions of basic rights; it led to the resignation of a minister and several high officials and compelled Adenauer to revamp his Cabinet. And it was the public at large, in particular the press, that prodded the Bundestag into more energetic action.

7. Problems of German Society

German society has long been characterized by its stability and even rigidity. Such stability was typical of all European society before the industrial age. But with industrial capitalism this static society became fluid; new methods of acquiring wealth altered established group and class lines; and the new principles of freedom and equal opportunity destroyed ancient privilege and allowed for social mobility, even a constant "circulation of the elite." German society, however, managed to order the new phenomena into a fixed system in which old and new classes had their assigned places. The bureaucratic caste, drawn mainly from the upper classes, continued to rule politically; business organized itself into cartels for the regulation of the market and into employers' associations to deal with workers and employees. The latter, largely prevented from rising to a higher status in society, organized themselves into trade unions. Hazards to economic and social stability were fought with an elaborate system of social security, particularly social insurance.

In the last forty years this system was shaken by a number of upheavals: inflation and depression, Nazi reorganization and disorganization, a war economy, the postwar influx of refugee millions, and the effects of currency reform and political partition. It is the more remarkable that after all these upheavals Germans have been able to preserve or restore the old social structure without basic changes; there is, to be sure, a bit more social mobility for individuals, and the workers' class is adopting middle-class habits of living, but collectively the rigid division of status and class is being preserved. Postwar prosperity made possible the integration of large groups (such as the expellees) that otherwise would have been forced to exist without status in society; it was effected by a coalition of bureaucracy, business, and peasantry, to which labor has been in only half-hearted opposition. It is this social structure that lends West Germany its significantly conservative character.

1. PROBLEMS OF EDUCATION

The Traditional System

No influence has been more important in maintaining the traditional class structure than the peculiar German system of education. It has divided Germans into two sharply defined groups: the educated (*Gebildete*) and those who have had no chance at more than a grade-school education. *Bildung* (inadequately translated as *education* or *culture*) has been the property of an elite, small as compared with the masses of the *Ungebildete*. Membership in this elite was attained not on the basis of selection of talent through equal opportunity but through the educational monopoly enjoyed by those financially able and, according to tradition and social status, obliged to send their children through the special institutions for higher education: the *Gymnasiums* (high schools) and the universities. The latter, in contrast to those in the United States, are not colleges for general education—which one is supposed to have acquired at the Gymnasium—but specialized and graduate institutions of learning. The Gymnasium at an early point branched off from the grade or "people's school" (*Volksschule*), which, providing elementary training, was the only school that most German children attended. They stayed there until the age of fourteen or fifteen, while the selected few were sent at about the age of nine to Gymnasium. After attending Gymnasium for about nine years, they would pass a final examination (*Abiturienten* examination), entitling them to enroll in a university. Thus the fate of a German child was determined at an early age and almost irrevocably by whether or not he belonged to the circle of those destined for higher tasks.

It is true that occasionally parents of lower status through great sacrifice managed to give their children a higher education. This was particularly true of lower- and middle-rank officials eager to see their sons climb to higher rank; but it was a rare occurrence for a child of a worker or peasant. On the other hand, the connection between money and the prestige enjoyed through *Bildung* was by no means automatic. Higher education has been demanding; and *Akademiker* (university graduates, enjoying, among the *Gebildete,* especially high prestige) have traditionally filled the higher positions in administration, justice, and education, as well as in the professions, positions with generally lower income but higher social prestige than business.

The traditional educational system was undemocratic not only in that it gave a small elite a monopoly of access to the leading positions in state and society, but also in that it instilled into Germans generally the attitudes of authority and submission. The structure of the German family (with the father dominant) has often been held responsible for the authoritarian atmosphere in which the typical German has been raised. But it was more likely the typical social institutions the young German came to know— the schools, the army, factory, or shop—which chiefly created this atmosphere. The German family did not remain authoritarian any longer than the family in other European countries; it ceased to be so after World War I. But in the schools the authoritarian spirit by and large continued to prevail: the student remained in awe of the teacher and professor. Since nearly all schools and universities in Germany are state institutions, the pupil encountered state authority at a tender age in the person of the teacher (usually male) at the *Volksschule.* Teachers belong to the state officialdom, and education thus never was a matter of cooperation between local community and school. There were, and are, no school boards or PTA's to alleviate this rigid system.

Problems of Educational Reform

Democratization of German society through educational reform was a chief concern of the Allies in the postwar period. It had two major aims: to eliminate Nazi influence (in teaching personnel, curriculums, and texts), and to abolish the class barrier. Texts and curriculums were revised, but the failure of denazification permitted the large majority of those who had been teachers under the Nazis to continue. Many of them were nationalist-conservative rather than Nazi, but the problem has been that they tended to avoid discussion of the Nazi past, so that German youth, in general, has either been left without knowledge of what happened under Nazism or has been given a distorted picture. This is a pity, because German postwar youth, as we have mentioned before, has been receptive to such information, even eager to get it. Young Germans have generally been receptive to new ideas and values that would fill the void left by Nazism, but there has been little attempt to fill this void with democratic values, especially in the universities, the training ground of the elite. Thus German students have become pragmatic, specializing for rapid career advancement, while their interest in general affairs, such as political matters, has been lagging.[1]

There has so far been little success in attempts to enlarge the social basis of education. Since education is under Land jurisdiction, reform measures have differed widely, with a few Länder extending the period during which all children attend *Volksschule* but most still having the short, four-year period. The Gymnasium is now attended by a somewhat higher percentage (about 13 percent) of the total school population. In part this still low participation reflects the financial inability of lower-class parents to support their children through long years of higher studies; but it also reflects a social-psychological difficulty on the part of workers

[1] In 1962, 60 percent of students in a poll declared that they were not interested in political matters.

and their children: a feeling of "not belonging there." This also accounts for the fact that the percentage of workers' children among university students (see accompanying chart) remains unchanged at 5 percent, whereas the previous high figure (about 50 percent) of sons and daughters of parents who are themselves academically trained (especially officials) has changed somewhat in favor of those without such training, especially white-collar employees. Thus the barrier is slightly pierced by these groups, but not by the lower ones. This change, however, has hardly meant a more liberal attitude. The exclusive corps (fraternities) have been revived; students join them less on their own initiative than because alumni in high positions make it clear to them that only in this way will they make the right connections for future advancement. Feudal customs (including dueling) and social snobbery are once again being instilled in many.

What can be done to improve matters? Abolishing the traditional dual system of education and substituting for it an American-type uniform system for all would probably prove im-possible, if only because there would not be enough teachers and facilities for the vastly increased numbers of children who would be going at least through high school. Extending the duration of *Volksschule* attendance by several years and reducing the length of study at Gymnasium correspondingly might be more feasible. But many Germans fear, and not without reason, that this might lower the standards of higher education. It can hardly be denied that mass education, whether totalitarian as in Communist countries, or democratic as in the United States, entails a danger of pseudo- or half-education. German (and British) education, while perpetuating a caste system, does ensure high standards, and it does preserve the foundations of culture in a world that is increasingly unaware of the importance of such preservation. German emphasis on presenting a coherent image of the world (especially through thorough study of history and the humanities at the Gymnasium), while easily taken advantage of by religious or political dogmatism, makes possible a deeper understanding than do courses in the "appreciation"

Social Background of West German University Students (1963)

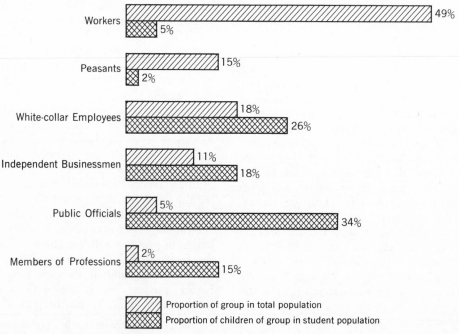

Workers 49% / 5%
Peasants 15% / 2%
White-collar Employees 18% / 26%
Independent Businessmen 11% / 18%
Public Officials 5% / 34%
Members of Professions 2% / 15%

Proportion of group in total population
Proportion of children of group in student population

Source: Gewerkschaftliche Rundschau, September 1965, p. 545.

of many scattered and unconnected fields. To this extent, German education does not compare entirely unfavorably with systems of mass education in which study and teaching may be held in low esteem and quality may suffer. But it has failed to give equal opportunity to the talented. This constitutes a moral failure. Moreover, it confronts West Germany with the danger of not having enough skilled and trained people, especially in technology and the sciences, for the increasing demands of a highly industrialized society.

With the number of Gymnasium graduates still as low as 6 percent of the respective age group of those eighteen or nineteen years old, West Germany ranks a mere eighth among Western European countries (and also, embarrassingly, much behind East Germany). For a highly developed country like Germany, the number of children attending "one-grade"—that is, one-room—*Volksschulen,* which still abound in rural areas, is a disgrace; quite generally, many children in such areas cannot attend Gymnasiums because the latter are concentrated in the cities. Much, therefore, can be done by creating better facilities for primary education as well as by facilitating and broadening access to higher education. Something might also be done by opening university study to selected outsiders (that is, persons who, while working, acquire the necessary knowledge through evening courses or similar sources). Compared with other developed countries, adult education in Germany has been lagging: whoever does not make it in his youth has no chance. Germans, though they have established a number of new universities, will have to invest much more by way of funds and commitment if they are to maintain the high standards and the prestige they have deservedly enjoyed in the areas of cultural and scientific achievement. By working at all three levels of education, Germans may gradually solve the problem of educational class segregation and discrimination without destroying the standards of which they are justly proud.

Of late there have been indications that Germans are becoming more generally aware of the urgency of the educational problem; their scientists and statisticians, in particular, have been telling them that they cannot expect to stay in the ranks of first-rate industrial nations if they fail to train a vastly increased number of scientists, engineers, doctors, and so forth. Maybe this pragmatic appeal will bear better fruit than reminding them of gaining traditional high cultural standards. At any rate, educational problems have suddenly become political issues, with the SPD, in particular, now raising the questions which, as agent of the lower classes, the party might have been expected to have raised for a long time. Its demands for a general leveling up of education can no longer be overlooked by the other parties when a growing number of parents who support them want their children to have better opportunities to compete with those of the traditional, small elite. A Council on Scientific Matters (*Wissenschaftsrat*) and a Council on Education (*Bildungsrat*) have been established to advise government on what to do and how to plan, especially in regard to finances.

Such leveling up might also in time eliminate what strikes the American most sharply when he meets Germans—their almost instinctive observation of the barriers between high and low, between educated and uneducated; it might gradually generate that feeling of being on an equal footing with everybody else which a society without educational monopoly, such as the American, has created despite all distinctions in wealth and income.

Religion and Education

Like France, Germany has been plagued not only by the problem of class education but also by that of the relation between churches and schools. There are no private denominational or parochial schools in Germany, since all schools (with the exception of a few private high schools) are run by the state. Religious influence, however, has been strong in those regions where *Volksschulen* are set up separately as Catholic or Protestant according to the faith of the pupils and teachers (*Bekenntnisschulen*). This means lowering of standards where one denomination is small (especially in rural areas, with one- or two-grade schools); it also tends to perpetuate the religious split of Germany by rooting it early in the mind of the child. The churches, however, defend the system and seek to extend it because it gives them influence over those children in particular whose families do not instill much religious feeling. Thus Catholic schools have been instrumental in holding German Catholicism together as a strongly integrated group. But the *Bekenntnisschulen* do not prevail everywhere. The high schools have never been divided in this manner. Also, there are many regions where even the *Volksschule* has been nondenominational, with students joining separate groups only for simultaneous religious instruction (*Simultanschulen*). This more liberal system has long been a major political issue, with Christian Democrats standing for separate schools, and with Socialists and Free Democrats opposed. Since decision is left to the Länder, the system of separate schools continues in such major areas as Bavaria and Northrhine-Westphalia. This struggle adds one more to the doctrinal issues dividing Germans.

2. LABOR AND SOCIAL SECURITY

German labor, in both its status and its policies, reflects the rigidity of German society. The educational monopoly of the middle class and the absence of an economic frontier in Germany prevented social mobility of the American type and froze labor at the lower level of society. Consequently, German labor developed class-consciousness and a *political* labor movement dominated by the Marxian brand of socialist ideology. German trade unions, unlike those in America, have not limited themselves to industrial activities but have tried (more in the British manner) to achieve gains for labor through influencing legislation and administration. Although (unlike British labor) German labor has not been strong enough to put a program of socialization into practice by gaining political control at the polls, it has been able—and is now satisfied—to make significant advances through labor legislation and social reform.[2]

[2] Those—chiefly trade unionists—who are dissatisfied with the recent, more moderate program of the SPD have of late been looking toward the unions as a kind of *Ersatz* leftist party to promote more socialist aims; some, like the metalworkers union, have actually gone in for more radical demands.

Social Insurance

Germany was one of the first countries to institute progressive labor legislation and social insurance. The period prior to Weimar was characterized by social reform measures granted from above. After 1918 gains were attained chiefly through labor's participation as a recognized partner in the regulation of labor affairs.

A comprehensive system of social insurance was adopted prior to 1918. This system reflected a traditional German concern for the social welfare of the masses not otherwise admitted to political or social standing. Compulsory health insurance was introduced in 1883, accident insurance (workmen's compensation) in 1885; disability and old-age insurance followed in 1891; unemployment insurance was added after World War I; and family allowances for each child after the first, after World War II. While the German system has not been so all-inclusive as the British cradle-to-grave system, it now comes pretty close to it. Four out of five Germans are covered by public health insurance (which also provides for pay during prolonged illness). Old-age and disability insurance now covers many groups besides workers and low-income employees; pensions may reach 75 percent of the worker's last earnings and have been made adaptable to a rise in prices ("dynamic pensions"). With modern economies forever beset by inflation, this seems to be the socially decent thing to do, and it is being imitated by other nations. Yet pensions paid to certain groups (for example, war disabled and war widows) are still much too low.

The system functions on the basis of rights acquired through contributions, amounting to about 28 percent of wages shared equally by employers and employees. As in France, it is administered on a functionally and geographically decentralized basis, with local and regional funds for the different branches and boards on which employers and employees are represented. By now, about 13 percent of the West German GNP is spent for social security, the highest percentage among Western nations.[3]

Since its inception this system has been one

[3] Figures according to Federal Ministry of Finance, 1964 (*Frankfurter Allgemeine Zeitung*, July 2, 1964).

of the most constant of German institutions. In its main features it is taken for granted by most Germans, despite the heavy financial burden it involves. Some maintain that the system has made the German too security-minded and that facilities such as the manifold benefits under health insurance have been taken advantage of; but it is hardly contested that public health has benefited, and even the average doctor, who first objected that the system destroyed the personal relationship between doctor and patient, gave up his opposition when, in financially difficult periods, he survived only owing to his *Kassenpraxis* (fees paid him for treatment of insurance cases). The problem of how to prevent abuses is, of course, a difficult one, particularly in health insurance. In Britain, doctors (in addition to a small salary) are paid according to the number of patients treated, with the danger that they may want to treat as many as possible as little as possible. In Germany they receive fees for each individual service rendered, with the danger of superfluous treatments and prescriptions. This problem has now been attacked through direct, though small, charges for certain services.

It may be that the social insurance system strengthens the German tendency to rely on others. But it is difficult to see how the average German worker or employee, who cannot manage to save much from his earnings, could be self-reliant. The alternative to insurance would be misery or, at best, reliance on charity or welfare, as in the United States. Insurance, with its contributions from the insured and its benefits thus earned by right, at least creates more self-respect than either of these alternatives.

Trade Unions and Codetermination

The more political aims of labor have traditionally concerned socialization, particularly the nationalization of key industries, and more recently a share of labor in management ("codetermination"). The latter implies at least a soft-pedaling of the former aim, because it means a share in the management of still privately owned enterprises. Actually, socialization, which had a chance in the immediate postwar years, lost that chance when the Allies delayed decisions until Adenauer took over; and the trade unions have since stressed participation in private management. Yet management, which right after the war was even resigned to some nationalization, now violently opposes union demands for extension of codetermination.

German trade unions used to be tied up with political parties, exercising their political influence chiefly through the SPD and the Center party; now, in West Germany, they are united in one overall and officially unpolitical German Trade Union Federation (DGB). This has meant drawing support from both the SPD and the left wing of the CDU (Communist influence is now negligible) and has required neutrality in political and party issues. Actually, neutrality has turned out to mean considerable support of and influence by the Social Democrats, whose relations with the Christian wing of the labor movement are hardly cordial. However, an often threatened schism has so far not materialized. As mentioned before, some unions now are politically even left of the SPD.

German trade unions have traditionally represented a large proportion of labor. The DGB has six and a half million members, 79 percent of whom are workers, 12 percent salaried employees, and 8 percent officials. (Employees are split, with many white-collar employees having a separate, non-DGB-affiliated union; officials, as we have seen, are likewise organized in large numbers in the separate DBB: seven hundred thousand of them, as against a hundred thousand in the DGB-affiliated public services union.) This reflects the attitude split of German higher strata from the workers. Even workers are unevenly organized, from miners (over 80 percent organized) down to agricultural laborers. On the whole, about one third of all workers and employees are organized in the DGB.

Among the DGB's federations, organized according to industries, the Big Five represent metal workers (with close to one third of total union membership), chemical, construction workers, those in public services, and miners. German unions traditionally have followed uniform policies rather than trying, individually or locally, to gain favors for this or that group of labor. But it has been the federations, rather than the DGB central organization, that have set the pace. When unions bargain collectively, their opposite numbers usually are not single employers but employers' organizations for an entire industry. They, in turn, are organized in one overall Union of Employers' Associations, so that two huge organizations of "social partners" face each other, and industrial relations, like other fields in Germany, are less a grassroots affair than one of arranging and organizing from the top.

German unions have been free from bossism (in the American sense); there has been no racketeering, and there are no prohibitive initiation fees. There is no closed shop.[4] Wildcat strikes are rare, and strikes organized by unions are disciplined. The unions employ thousands of paid functionaries and control large funds, used in part for educational purposes, including the training of a labor elite of union leaders, labor directors, works council leaders, etc.—thus offering young workers one way of rising socially outside the established German educational pattern.

German labor in the postwar period has been rather moderate in its wage demands in order not to endanger the reconstruction of the economy and, more recently, not to increase the inflationary tendencies of "overheated" prosperity. Its chief interest has been rather in *codetermination*. Codetermination had its origin in an older institution, the works councils (shop or factory committees) established in the Weimar period. These councils, which continue to exist, are elected by workers and employees in all larger enterprises (usually on the basis of party lists) and have as their main function participation in matters affecting workers directly, such as adoption of factory rules, dismissals, and so forth. Codetermination means extending such participation to general matters of management, at least in questions affecting workers and management alike, such as changes in the nature of the enterprise, mergers, and shutdowns. Following the pattern of MG,

which set up a temporary trusteeship management for the Ruhr industries, federal legislation first gave labor a codetermination right in the larger coal and steel enterprises and then, in somewhat different form, in all larger corporations in the Republic. Labor is represented on the supervisory boards of coal and steel on a fifty-fifty basis, on those of other joint stock companies by one third. In coal and steel companies it also sends a "labor director" as one of three members to the management board, or board of directors (the other members being the production and the business manager). The unions now demand adoption of this latter system by all larger enterprises.

Labor expected a new type of economy and society from this innovation. Management was apprehensive of losing its control over the direction of industrial affairs ("cold socialization"). Experience has shown that neither these fears nor labor's expectations were justified. Labor representatives bring the interests of workers or trade unions to bear on matters concerning labor more or less directly, and this has generally had a beneficial influence on labor-management relations. Beyond this, however, employers have remained masters in their own house. In the words of one American observer, Clark Kerr, codetermination in West Germany has proved to be "a sheep in wolf's clothing."

With the results of codetermination less impressive than originally expected, labor has shifted its aims and interests somewhat. One objective is to reduce the regular workweek to forty hours. Job security as such has become less urgent in a full-employment economy. Actually, labor shortages, though placing labor in a favorable bargaining position, have confronted the unions with a serious problem. Unions are less needed by workers who tend more and more to negotiate wages and other benefits with individual employers and who succeed in surpassing the standards laid down by unions and employers' organizations at large. Thus unions even have trouble recruiting new members. But they can be expected to be needed again in the years to come when Germany, because of automation, will have to grapple with the problem of under- or even unemployment instead of the present labor shortage.

[4] With benefits gained by unions extended to unorganized workers, union leaders have been clamoring for corresponding "contributions" from nonmembers (referred to as "solidarity contributions"), so far without success.

3. PROBLEMS OF BUSINESS AND AGRICULTURE

The Traditional System

Big corporations have dominated Germany's economic life for nearly a century. In its business structure, the German economy has been characterized by concentration of capital in giant enterprises (usually referred to as "trusts," or combines) and by restriction of free-market competition among them through cartel arrangements. Thus, in 1939, six big corporations controlled 95 percent of the Ruhr steel production and two-thirds of its coal through "captive mines"; the huge I. G. Farben combine had a near monopoly of German chemical production. The effect was not mass production for mass consumption but high prices for fewer buyers, a vested interest in armaments production and a consequent tie-up with militaristic and expansionist forces, and a fear of reform. In contrast to Britain and America, big business in Germany has traditionally backed antidemocratic forces and has used its economic power for a political defense of the business status quo. Government has generally supported this business structure. No inheritance taxes, or very low ones, kept large fortunes concentrated in a few families; cartels remained largely undisturbed, and the state assisted industry through subsidies.

Postwar Developments

Industry

West Germany has largely retained this essentially oligarchic structure of business. Allied policies did not affect its roots; although the Allies tried to deconcentrate industry by splitting up giant holdings, the long-term result has been the opposite: Deconcentration has yielded to reconcentration. In banking, the traditional Big Three are again predominant; so are Thyssen, Krupp, and two others in steel. Two percent of all German industrial enterprises, about a thousand, account for over half of German production and for 60 percent of German exports. While in the 1920's one-third of the employed worked in enterprises employing fewer than fifty, in 1960 only 10 percent did so, while 70 percent worked in units employing over two hundred. Favorable tax laws aid mergers. The results have been monopoly, or more often oligopoly, an ever tighter control over the economy by ever fewer corporations, and rising influence by corporations in political affairs.

The position of German industry is further strengthened by cartelization. Decartelization, as decreed by the Allies, yielded to recartelization. A law prohibiting cartels was enacted in 1957 (after endless wrangling in the Bundestag, in which the then minister of economics, Ludwig Erhard, was pitted against big industry and a large portion of his own party), but the outcome has been meager. Numerous qualifications and provisions allowing for exceptions have permitted the Federal Cartel Office to judge in favor of cartels rather than combat them, and there have been few decisions outlawing cartel arrangements. Hence it is not likely that the so far boldest venture in postwar West German cartelization, that of an almost complete cartel of the steel industry, extending to the setting of prices and almost everything else, which was announced in the fall of 1966, will run into legal difficulties.

Small wonder, then, that the influence of business organizations has been strong. Trade and industry as an interest group are now centrally organized in one Federation of German Industry (BDI), with thirty-eight member associations representing the main business activities; since voting is according to size of payroll, it is controlled by big business. As in the case of other interest organizations (for example, farmers and artisans), influence is exercised in the legislative field through much direct representation of business organizations in parliament and the strong influence of such deputies in the respective committees. In addition, pressures operate through direct contacts in the executive from the highest level down to the ministerial departments. Everything here is organized in expert, streamlined, and centralized fashion. Thus, like agriculture, labor, and the bureaucracy, business as an interest makes itself felt as one overall power group, leaving little leeway for the formulation and expression of local and individual trends and ideas. Like members of other groups, the individual businessman devotes himself to his own affairs; he leaves public promotion of his interests to others—professionals—just as he leaves politics to professional politicians.

Economic Policies

As for economic policies in general, the present West German government is wedded to the principle of a free economy and noninterference in economic affairs—that is, it avoids overall government regulation and centralized planning. This policy rendered possible the uninterrupted prosperity enjoyed since currency reform in 1948, with full employment, price stabilization (with the Central Bank of the Federation watching over currency stability), and a high annual growth rate. But one should not forget that this favorable development was due at least in part to other factors: the cancellation of German prewar debts; the absence of reparations; free postwar (Marshall Plan) aid; freedom, initially, from an armaments burden; and the willingness of the German worker to forego major wage increases. Although the living standards of all major groups have gone up, there still is great discrepancy between the upper and the lower strata. Moreover, while the average worker has shared to some extent in the general prosperity, certain groups (for example, those who lost their savings through currency reform) have been less fortunate. There is still a sizable stratum that resents the somewhat ostentatious luxury indulged in by the rich. "Reprivatization" of publicly owned enterprises has not meant that the masses have become property owners. According to a 1965 poll, almost half the population considers the present distribution of property unfair.

Agriculture

The absence of significant changes in economic structure and policies has been particularly striking in agriculture, where the Allies made a considerable effort to achieve long overdue reforms. This problem has been solved after a fashion in East Germany (see Chapter 8), but an alliance of vested interests and bureaucracy wrecked land reform in the West. Although the number of homesteads created for additional farmers has been inconsiderable, those existing have mechanized their production over the last fifteen years in remarkable fashion. The number of farms dropped by 25 percent, that of people working in agriculture, by 40 percent. Still, owing to poorer soil, this has not lowered the production costs of German agriculture sufficiently to enable it to compete with more effective neighboring countries, and it has continued to demand and receive the protection and subsidies traditionally extended to it in the past. Free-market principles do not apply to German agriculture. On the contrary, German refusal to reduce its agricultural tariffs to the level envisaged by the European Common Market for a while inhibited the tariff-cutting program of the Six. Only in 1966 a complicated system was devised, enabling the Common Market to be extended to agriculture by 1968. Thus, the German consumer still pays for maintaining a system that would otherwise be unable to compete with farming abroad.

Summary

The rigidity of society and economic structure that marked Germany in the past has not been basically affected by what has happened since 1945. While in East Germany the old structure has been replaced by a new manipulated society which is in the process of creating new class lines, in West Germany the lines for the most part are still drawn on the old pattern. An agenda of peaceful social change in the West might therefore include: first, giving a more equal share in the social product to those who through their sacrifices have rendered prosperity possible; and second, overcoming the old class or status lines, particularly since war and other upheavals have shifted many from one class to another. Political democracy, whose roots are still tender, would have a better chance to survive in times of stress in a Germany where the social product was more evenly distributed and where class and status distinctions were less acute.

8. Berlin and the Soviet Zone

1. THE GOVERNMENT OF BERLIN

The status of Germany's former capital mirrors not only that of the partitioned country but that of a world divided, a world whose problems—as is indicated by the term Berlin crisis—have frequently centered around this area where East and West have met so closely in the postwar period. Although its present fragmented, cut-off, forlorn position contrasts sharply with its glorious past, the more than three million inhabitants of Berlin have adjusted to a "life lived dangerously" in surprising fashion. What is Berlin's present status? How did it emerge?

Emergence of Its Present Status

It has been said that Berlin today offers "one of the strangest governmental phenomena of our times." Though it is no longer the German capital, one portion is headquarters of the government of one of Germany's two present units; ruled by two separate indigenous administrations and physically partitioned by a fortified wall, it is also under the authority of occupation powers; and its two portions are almost but not quite integrated into the two Germanies.

When the Allies, in September 1944, agreed on the zonal division of Germany, the area of Greater Berlin was exempted from the zones; it was to be occupied by the Allies and administered by them jointly through an interallied *Kommandatura*. In the summer of 1945, the four powers occupied their respective four "sectors" of the city and established patterns for their common rule. Under four-power rule, on the basis of a "preliminary constitution" issued by the Allies in 1946, Germans began to participate in government. But a major political problem, foreshadowing the subsequent split, arose even at this early stage. When the Soviets tried to force the two leftist parties to merge into one Communist-controlled "Socialist Unity Party" (SED), the Berlin SPD resisted the merger. (SPD membership in the three Western sectors—in the Eastern sector the vote was forbidden—voted against it by over 80 percent.) In the first all-Berlin vote, in October 1946, the SPD received 49 percent of the vote, the SED only 20 percent. A diet and a magistrate, the latter SPD-controlled, began to function and ruled Berlin freely for two years. In 1948, the diet was forcibly prevented (Soviet military police intervened in favor of Communist rioters) from meeting at its location in the Soviet sector and was shifted, with the remainder of the administration, to the Western sectors. After the failure of the Soviets to amalgamate the city by blockading it (the blockade was rendered ineffective by the American–British airlift), the split of Berlin into East and West was completed. West Berlin has operated since September 1, 1950 (on the East, see below) under a constitution patterned on Bonn parliamentarism. West Berlin is organized like a Land: it has a diet, elected for four years; a cabinet, called "senate" (thirteen members headed by a minister-president called "governing mayor"), responsible to the diet; administrative departments headed by senators; and twelve subdivisions called "districts," each with its separate organizational structure.

Status of West Berlin

Politically, West Berlin has been controlled by coalitions of the major parties (first SPD,

CDU, and FDP, then SPD and CDU, since 1963 SPD and FDP) even when—as now for over a decade—the SPD has had an absolute majority.[1] Under able and forceful mayors, from Ernst Reuter to Willy Brandt, West Berlin government has been both popular and effective.

However, the German attempt to have West Berlin incorporated into the Federal Republic as a full-fledged Land was thwarted by a veto of the Western Allies, who, though not interested in maintaining occupation rights per se, insisted on at least formal continuation of Berlin's occupation status. A change of that status might have given the Soviets a pretext to abrogate the Western rights of free access to West Berlin through the Soviet zone. Thus the tripartite Allied *Kommandatura* is still in control, although its actual powers have been gradually shifted to the Germans. In 1955, the year when sovereignty was granted to Bonn, a "Berlin Declaration" by the three commandants, while reserving certain ultimate rights, granted West Berlin "the greatest possible degree of self-government compatible with the city's special situation." Thus, day-to-day government and administration are entirely German. However, the Allies reserve the right to control the police, if necessary, or to nullify legislation in conflict with Allied rights. They also review international agreements concluded by Bonn that are to apply to West Berlin.

Actually, legislation by the West Berlin government proceeds in close alignment with Bonn federal legislation: Whenever a Berlin clause (that is, a clause declaring a statute to be applicable to Berlin also) is included in a federal law, the West Berlin legislature merely enacts a covering law stipulating the validity of this statute for West Berlin. At Bonn itself, the semi-inclusion of West Berlin in the Federal Republic is symbolized by the presence of twenty-two members from Berlin in the Bundestag and of four members in the Bundesrat. On Allied insistence, these representatives have no voting rights in plenary session, but they do vote in committees; on the other hand, the Bundestag members are not directly elected by the Berlin people but are selected by the Berlin diet. Also, West German high courts (with the exception of the Constitutional Court) have extended their jurisdiction to West Berlin, and a few even have their seat there.

West Berlin's economic ties to West Germany are as strong as its political ones. The city could hardly have survived without first American and then West German financial and similar aid. Financial aid, in the form of direct subsidies, tax relief, and the like, continues to the tune of about two billion DM annually. Almost all of its supplies (including such perishables as fresh vegetables and milk) come from the West by rail, road, or waterway; most of its exports go to the West;[2] its currency, of course, is the West German mark (DM). Within Berlin, on the other hand, there was until the summer of 1961 a strange but strong symbiosis of West and East; there were, for instance, about sixty thousand Berliners who daily commuted between their residences in East Berlin and their working places in the West (other thousands commuted in the opposite direction). And most means of communication and transportation operated on a city-wide basis. Now, however, a wall thirty miles long separates all.

On August 13, 1961, the East German regime built the wall that severed all communication between the city's two sections and thereby cut off East Berlin and the zone completely from the West. This action was followed by Soviet demands to terminate Berlin's occupation status and render West Berlin a special, third German unit without ties to West Germany and with a "free city" status; access to it would be guaranteed, but control of the access lines was to devolve on the DDR. Steadfast refusal by the Western powers to yield any of their rights led to recurrent crises, but the previous status of West Berlin has been left undisturbed. Passes agreed on by the two city regimes have enabled

---

[1] Election figures show the continued strength of the SPD and the insignificance of the Communist party, which, even after August 1961, was allowed, under the four-power status, to participate in West Berlin elections under the SED label.

	1948	1950	1954	1958	1963
SPD	64.5%	44.7%	44.6%	52.6%	61.9%
CDU	19.4	24.6	30.3	37.7	28.9
FDP	16.1	23.0	12.8	3.0	7.9
SED			2.7	1.9	1.3

[2] West Berlin, although comprising only part of Berlin's former industrial capacity, is still one of Germany's major industrial cities, with, for example, about 40 percent of West German electrical production.

West Berliners to pay periodic visits to relatives in East Berlin; these agreements have been renegotiated with increasing difficulty, chiefly because of Western fears of thereby lending implicit recognition to the East German regime and/or of implicitly recognizing a separate, "third-state" status for West Berlin.

East Berlin Government

The East Berlin government on the surface appears to be very similar to that of West Berlin in its close coordination with, but not complete inclusion in, its respective German unit. Politically and economically East Berlin is of course completely communized and, as seat of the DDR government, is East Germany's chief showcase. The East, nevertheless, has been as anxious as the West to observe the formalities of East Berlin's four-power status. East German statutes, for instance, do not automatically extend to East Berlin, the status of East Berlin members of the East German People's Chamber is limited, and there is a court system separate from, although similar to, East Germany's. In the organization of the government after the rupture in 1948, SED members of the old diet were simply supplemented with members from Eastern-style mass organizations (trade unions, etc.), and the new "diet" in turn organized a "provisional democratic magistrate." Subsequently, in 1953, a "Provisional Organic Law for Greater Berlin," the present basis of East Berlin government, provided for elected diet, magistrate, city districts, and a mayor. In practice, East Berlin functions as another District of the DDR. In regard to budget, economic planning, and enterprises it is treated entirely as an integral part of the Eastern Republic. The secret police includes it in its all-pervasive activities although, out of due regard for four-power sensibilities, persons condemned to death in Berlin are executed outside the city in the DDR!

It is understandable how embarrassing West Berlin, deep in Eastern territory, must have been to the East, and especially to the rulers of the DDR, as a symbol of Western-style political and economic way of life—freedom and prosperity—and, until August 1961, as the main escape hatch for Eastern refugees. Here, prior to the closing of that hatch, was a chance for many thousands of East Berliners, and even for many inhabitants of the Eastern zone, to visit daily a part of the free world, to mingle with their friends and relatives there—in short, not to be completely shut off in a totalitarian environment. And although West Berlin no longer fulfills that function, it still exists within the world of the East, and its presence continues to be heard (through the voice of its radio) and seen (through television). Hence the continuing insistence by the East to have Berlin's status changed from that of a Western-occupied area with accompanying Western rights to that of a "free city," which, in all likelihood, would no longer be as vibrantly free as it has been so far. Of course, there is no legal justification for the often repeated Eastern claim that West Berlin's location on East German territory makes it part of the DDR, with the effect that Western rights could be abrogated by treaty between the DDR and the Soviet Union. Legally, it forms an enclave not under the sovereignty of whatever territory surrounds it; its status can be changed unilaterally or bilaterally as little as other Western rights (for example, access rights) can be. But its legal and actual status is, of course, abnormal. If the West can avoid continuing crises, ultimatums, and danger of actual violence over the issue by arrangements which, while not sacrificing the basic freedom of Berlin and its inhabitants to whose protection the West is committed, would alleviate certain Eastern annoyances (for example, use of West Berlin as "propaganda center" or meetings of the Bundestag there), it would seem advisable to explore such possibilities carefully and patiently. Before 1961 the West did not sufficiently realize what has become so uncomfortably clear since then, namely, how numerous the means of harassment are that the East possesses; for example, communication and transportation between West Berlin and the Western sector of Germany by rail, road, or water, with the exception of strictly Allied military traffic, continue only by agreement with the East German authorities. So long as the East German economy still depends on trade ties with West Germany, East Germans can be relied upon to renew the transit agreements in return for renewed interzonal trade agreements; with increasing economic independence, however, they may be expected to turn the transit screw.

2. THE ESTABLISHMENT OF COMMUNIST CONTROL IN THE SOVIET ZONE

Imagine that after a disastrous defeat the United States was divided along the Mississippi, with the land west of the Rockies detached and its population expelled into one of the two remaining sections. Imagine further that a totalitarian regime was set up by an occupation power in one portion, while the other one was allowed to continue its traditional way of life. This, by and large, is what has happened to Germany; hence the urgency of the problem of reunification. Germans in the West not only long to see their brothers freed from oppression; they fear that, if partition is allowed to continue indefinitely, Communism might eventually succeed in making East Germany an alien nation separated from the West not only in its economic, social, and political institutions but in its general way of life.

The system established in the Eastern zone so far is based even less on popular backing or consent than was the Nazi regime, because its power basis is not even indigenous. If the flight since 1945 of about three million inhabitants to the West were not sufficient evidence, the events of June 1953—when workers and others rose against the regime—made it clear that only Soviet tanks saved a puppet government.

But this is not the only problem; if it were, there would remain only the diplomatic (or, possibly, military) problem of getting rid of Soviet and CP control. There is also a broader, politico-social problem connected with the economic and social changes that the regime introduced. The Nazi regime, while subordinating everything to its power rule, did not affect basic traditional institutions, such as private property in estates and industries, or the bureaucracy as such. Communism, by contrast, proceeded to transform class lines and society radically. It wiped out the Prussian Junkers and divided their estates among the peasants; it

destroyed the property-owning middle class and nationalized industrial and business enterprises; it replaced the old, authoritarian officialdom with public employees supposed to serve a society of free toilers and peasants. Initially, there was a good deal that was progressive in these measures: smallholders with too little land, as well as the landless agricultural proletariat and expellee settlers, got land; banking and industrial combines were deprived of their political influence; reactionary and Nazi officials were purged; war criminals were brought to justice. But no totalitarian regime does such things for their own sake; it builds on them its own control. If agrarian reform created a new class of smallholders, it did so only to absorb them subsequently through collectivization. If workers are no longer exploited by private employers, they are deprived of the right of collective bargaining and of the weapon of the strike and are forced to fulfill the norms of the plan set by the regime. If Nazi criminals were rightly convicted, trials were subsequently used to eliminate "class enemies," whether war criminals or not; if denazification effectively purged Nazis from office, it also, through trumped-up charges of "fascist collaboration," served to expropriate the middle classes (whether or not the individual concerned had been an active Nazi). Application for membership in the dominant party, on the other hand, would buy forgiveness for a doubtful past. A regime with a monopoly of political power could be lenient and could allow former Nazis in large numbers to hold or regain positions, as long as the regime controlled these positions.

Thus, whatever changes have occurred result not from the free play of social forces but from the policies of the one group in political control, the leaders of the Socialist Unity party (SED), acting under the guidance of Soviet Communists. A new class, which has absorbed many formerly independent businessmen, artisans, and members of the professions, now performs essential clerical, technical, and administrative functions for the state administration, public enterprises, and the party organizations. In return for these indispensable services, it enjoys social and economic privileges separating it from the other classes; it does not yet share in the elite's political power, although the tension between the ideologists and the experts seems to be assuming increasing importance with the growing numbers of the latter. So far, however, ultimate power still is jealously guarded by those in key positions in party and administration; they form a closed group, a group constantly purged, forever anxious to prove itself to its foreign masters. The way this group exercises control might well be discussed under the same headings as was Nazism. In East Germany as under the Nazis there is "coordination," only now under new management, with organizations such as trade unions, farmers' unions, and youth groups converted into SED-controlled "mass organizations"; there is the attempt to "atomize" society by undermining the family and battling the churches; there is the machinery of repression, first exercised by the Soviet MVD, and then by an indigenous, SED-run State Security Service (SSD); there is a propaganda machine that tries to capture the allegiance of the masses, this time with a *Weltanschauung* not racist but materialistic: the doctrine of Marxism-Leninism, whose concepts and slogans rule supreme. What has emerged is a thoroughly manipulated society.

Establishment of the German Democratic Republic (DDR)

Initial political measures in the Soviet zone seemed auspicious. Political parties were allowed to reorganize, and free elections to local assemblies were held. But democratization was abruptly halted when the Soviets realized that the Communists were unable to gain control this way. Their chief competitors, the Social Democrats, thereupon were forced to merge "voluntarily" with the Communists in a Socialist Unity party (SED). As the Berlin elections of 1946 showed, this shotgun marriage failed to convert the bulk of Social Democrats, but it destroyed them as a separate party in the zone. The two "bourgeois" parties, Christian Democrats and Liberals, at first profited from this, gaining even among workers and peasants, but they did not profit for long. They were gradually transformed into mere appendages of the SED, which itself was turned into an apparatus strictly controlled by its Communist top

leaders. Under the so-called "bloc principle," the parties would informally agree on presenting to the public a unanimous antifascist front before voting in diets or making any other decisions. "Unanimity" invariably meant that SED policy was accepted by the others. They were corralled into such conformity by purges in which the more independent leaders were replaced by compliant wielders of rubber stamps.

Under such conditions, constitution-making meant little. With the SED in control of procedures, it could act in pseudodemocratic fashion. A People's Congress of handpicked delegates in 1947 drafted a constitution primarily based on an earlier SED draft. In accordance with the Soviet policy of always trailing the West by one step, formal adoption of the draft was delayed until 1949 when a new slate of Congress delegates was submitted to East German voters for "democratic confirmation." Then occurred the only accident in an otherwise smooth procedure: A surprisingly high percentage of voters (38 percent) failed to endorse this list. Thereafter the regime dispensed with further democratic trimmings. The Congress proclaimed that the Constitution was now in force (October 7, 1949) and allowed a smaller group from its midst, the People's Council, to establish itself as the first People's Chamber, or parliament, under the new Constitution. This body in turn formed a Cabinet and, in conjunction with a Chamber of States (issuing from existing Land diets), elected a president.

This fraud was compounded a year later when the provisional parliament was replaced by the election of a definitive one (October 15, 1950). This election violated even the Eastern Constitution's own provisions, which prescribed elections by different parties under the system of proportional representation. Instead, the voter was presented with a single list of candidates. They were from different parties, to be sure, but the SED was careful to secure a majority for itself and its mass organizations on this list, while the CDU and the LDP together were allotted less than one third. All the voter had to do was to confirm the list; no competing slate was admitted. Since voters were "urged" to vote openly, the none-too-surprising result was endorsement by 99.7 percent of the valid vote. Subsequent elections have all been single-slate affairs, yielding similar results.

A frame of government was thus provided. But while the Bonn Constitution, despite undemocratic undercurrents, provides "rules of the game" allowing for genuine interplay of social and political forces, the Eastern Constitution is a façade behind which government proceeds according to its own rules. The German Democratic Republic (DDR) thus established is neither really German nor democratic. In contrast to other Eastern European countries, it is not a nation but part of one. Not only is power there exercised without popular mandate, but the unit in which this power operates itself is not legitimate in the eyes of its people.

3. THE CONSTITUTIONAL FAÇADE

Sovereignty

Like the Bonn government, the government of the DDR appears to be that of a sovereign and, according to its Constitution, even federal and liberal-democratic state. But appearances are misleading. As to sovereignty, the Soviets conferred a semblance of it upon the DDR at an earlier point and more fully than was the case in the West. In 1949, the DDR was granted international autonomy, including the right to have a foreign office, to establish diplomatic relations with countries that recognized it, and to conclude international treaties (such as the one with Poland, recognizing the Oder-Neisse boundary as definitive). The Moscow Treaty of September 1955 confirmed complete formal sovereignty, and an agreement of March 1957 transformed, as in the West, military occupation into contractual rights of stationing troops.[3] Actual Soviet control, however, is as firm as it is in any satellite, and by now even greater than, say, in Poland. General policies laid down in Moscow prevail. However, it is not necessary to assume that a simple command-obedience relationship exists; in the post-Stalin era, coordination has been chiefly through meetings of the respective top-party leadership or through multilateral CP meetings. But the Moscow line is invariably followed. Thus, in 1958, Khrushchev's new policy of decentralizing the economic administration was duly copied; so, in 1963 and thereafter, was the policy of freer economic organization ("Libermanism"). Soviet influence can be seen on two levels in particular: on the bloc level, for example, in bloc economic planning; and on the level of occasional Soviet intervention as an occupation power. Sometimes this intervention has concerned Germany as a whole, and sometimes it has concerned only the special situation of Berlin, in regard to which Soviet influence has at times even served to moderate the more bellicose tendencies of the East German regime.

Federalism

As in other respects, the 1949 Constitution followed the Weimar pattern by establishing Länder as federal subdivisions. But even then it was more centralized than Weimar; thus, the central government was to enjoy all important

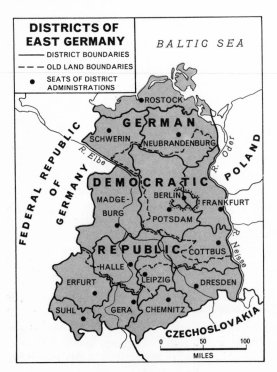

DISTRICTS OF EAST GERMANY
—— DISTRICT BOUNDARIES
– – – OLD LAND BOUNDARIES
• SEATS OF DISTRICT ADMINISTRATIONS

BALTIC SEA

GERMAN DEMOCRATIC REPUBLIC

FEDERAL REPUBLIC OF GERMANY

POLAND

CZECHOSLOVAKIA

ROSTOCK
SCHWERIN
NEUBRANDENBURG
R. Elbe
R. Oder
MADGE-BURG
BERLIN
POTSDAM
FRANKFURT
R. Neisse
COTTBUS
HALLE
LEIPZIG
ERFURT
DRESDEN
SUHL
GERA
CHEMNITZ

0   50   100
MILES

[3] A clause in this agreement provides, however, that the Soviet military may assume full governmental control "in the event of a threat to the security of the forces." There are 20 Soviet divisions, about 250,000 men, stationed in the DDR, in addition to close to 200,000 men of the indigenous NVA (National People's Army), which is integrated with the Warsaw Pact setup.

legislative power. A Chamber of States, through which the Länder were to participate in government on the central level, had a mere suspensive veto. Even this remnant of federalism, however, proved too much for a system that tended toward complete centralization. A reform did away with it (in 1952), replacing the five Länder with fourteen districts, which, as mere subdivisions of central government, cannot be compared to the previous Länder. The Chamber of States was officially abolished in 1958.

Democracy and Bill of Rights

The chief "democratic" feature of the Eastern Constitution is that all power is ostensibly concentrated in the popularly elected People's Chamber. Separation of powers, or any independent powers of executive and judiciary, are rejected as undemocratic. This system Communists had favored all over postwar Europe, in the hope that Communist control or influence would be unhampered by reactionary presidents or courts. The East German Constitution even extended the principle of proportional representation to the Cabinet, in which all parties were to be represented according to their strength in parliament. Under conditions of real democracy, this would constitute a novel experiment. In the DDR it simply served to strengthen the SED, since in this way the opposition was compelled to participate in government and, under the bloc principle, obliged to toe the SED line, with non-SED groups thus rendered prisoners of the "state party."

The East German bill of rights resembles that in the Stalin Constitution of the Soviet Union. Emphasis on "socialist" economic and social principles overshadows individual rights and freedoms, which may be limited or suspended by simple law. Control over the constitutionality of laws is vested in a committee of parliament, and not in the judiciary. All this matters little: What use are guarantees and procedures when laws reflect the fiat of the ruling group? What use is constitutionality when the Constitution can be amended by a two-thirds vote of an always unanimous parliament? Even these formalities are usually disregarded in practice. Provisions that require laws for infractions of individual liberties have been disregarded in favor of executive decrees not even formally authorized by legislation; important decrees are kept secret—that is, they are not known or knowable by the public at large, being issued as mere administrative instructions to the respective agencies. Thus, an internal directive may determine whether certain matters are handled by prosecutors and courts, or by the secret police; in this way questions of— quite literally—life and death for the citizen are left to the secret fiat of executive authorities. The bulk of the valid law is found in decrees, rather than in laws actually enacted by the legislature. In studying East German government, one must investigate actual powers and procedures rather than the ineffectual provisions of a merely ceremonial Constitution.

4. THE RULING PARTY

Development and Structure of the SED

Power in the DDR, so far as it is indigenous, is concentrated at the top level of the ruling party. Communism in East Germany is officially organized as the Socialist Unity party, the outgrowth of the enforced merger in 1946 of the Communist and Socialist parties. At first an attempt was made to have parity in leadership between Communists and Social Democrats and to have as broad a mass basis as possible. But when it appeared that the SED was unable to attract the rank and file of Social Democrats, parity was dropped, and the SED was transformed into an organization in which all key positions are held by Communists and the line of authority runs from top to bottom.

This self-styled "party of a new type" resembles in everything its big brother, the CPSU, whose statutes and programs those of the SED (1954, 1963) have copied faithfully. As in the Soviet Union, it is an exclusive order, with members carefully selected for loyalty and discipline. Acceptance is preceded by a one-year period of initiation, or candidacy. Membership represents about 15 percent of the electorate, which, compared with membership figures in free systems, seems high. But there is much pressure for membership, and many join for opportunistic reasons, so that probably not more than 10 percent of this membership, that is, about 1 percent of the population, consists of active and loyal adherents on whose backing the regime can rely. Moreover, it is now a party of functionaries. Workers, who once made up about half of the membership, now constitute only a minority, despite constant effort to infuse "new blood." [4]

As to organizational hierarchy, elected party organs such as the Party Congress (which meets only every four years) hold virtually no power. The decisive powers are the Central Committee, its Politbureau, and its Secretariat. The Central Committee, a body of about a hundred and twenty members plus sixty candidate members, officially elected by the Congress, is supposed to reflect society at large; it meets about once every three months, but it does not have the power to make genuine decisions. The Politbureau, the real policy-making top body of between fifteen and twenty party leaders, directly controls the corresponding party bureaus on the district and local levels. It meets about once a week. The Secretariat is a large body staffed with about a thousand full-time functionaries and organized in about twenty sections paralleling the chief ministries and other main state agencies. In charge of guiding these sections are from five to ten full-time party secretaries. On the lowest party level we find party groups consisting of from eight to ten members working in a shop or enterprise. While these units are, of course, without influence over party policy, they are important in that they are responsible for spreading the party gospel through the laity; they are the link that ties the supposed advance guard to its basis, the masses.

Actually, Party Secretary and Politbureau chief Walter Ulbricht, an old "Moscow Communist"—that is, a German Communist who went to Moscow rather than to a Western country during the Nazi regime—has survived all storms, crises, and purges and has thus been the uncontested leader since the inception of the regime. So long as he enjoys the backing of the Kremlin, he can be sure to continue in control. It is he who, through continuous re-shuffling of Politbureau members and Secretariat heads, determines top leadership under him.

Program and Policies

In program and policies the SED has followed the Soviet line in all its details and sinuosities. Its program echoes everything in this line from peace propaganda, anti-imperialism, and appeal to the desire for national unity, to social realism in art and literature. In respect to "liberalization," however, the regime has followed the Soviet lead only reluctantly. A regime based on so little popular acclaim is afraid of making concessions. Mutual fear between rulers and ruled still characterizes the DDR. In contrast to most Communist parties and regimes in the bloc, therefore, there has been no real "thaw." Those who seemed to see the new light after de-Stalinization in Moscow were purged. Another purge, affecting some of the highest party figures, followed the Polish-Hungarian events of 1958. Thus, in many respects (for example, in law enforcement and in the realm of culture) the regime has remained a Stalinist one.

National Front and Control of Puppets

In an effort to establish a façade of unity, the regime formed a National Front as front organization of all parties and groups extant in the Republic. In addition to the SED, a number of shadow parties actually survive, whose existence might mislead the uninformed into assuming that the DDR is a multiparty state. These parties are all subservient to the regime (in part even financed by it) and serve only to coordinate groups that otherwise might not be controlled so easily. Since the initial East zone CDU and LDP parties were brought under control through the bloc policy, through purges of their more independent leaders, and through the system of terror subsequently established in the zone, their present leaders have become puppets of the ruling group, whom they sometimes try to excel in "people's democratic" devotion.

In addition to CDU and LDP, which at least originated independently, two parties were created by mere SED fiat, a Democratic Farmers' party and a National Democratic party,

---

[4] Workers 1947: 48 percent; 1962: 34 percent. Peasants and agricultural workers 1947: 9 percent; 1962: 6 percent. On the other hand, white-collar workers (including party functionaries) 1947: 11 percent; 1962: 33 percent.

the latter with the officially avowed purpose of attracting former Nazis; both parties are dummies.

More important than controlling or organizing parties was the effort to coordinate the major social groups and interests through the establishment of so-called mass organizations; all of these are controlled by the SED through occupancy of key positions. Three main ones are: in the field of agriculture, the peasants' Mutual Aid Organizations; in labor, the workers' and employees' Free Trade Unions; and for youth, the Free German Youth. Thus the SED rules, not only the state, but all social activity.

5. GOVERNMENT AND ADMINISTRATION

Centralism

East German government is characterized by, first, the complete victory of centralism; second, the preponderance of the executive over every other branch of government; and third, the pervading control of the SED. Centralism is reflected in the concentration of governmental power and authority in the central government. The districts are merely administrative subdivisions without discretion of their own. Below them there are local and county units. All have elected diets and executive "councils" of partly full-time, partly honorary members officially elected by the diets. All of these are considered "organs of state power" and are under strict control from the central level. Thus, councils are allegedly under the dual control of the respective diet as well as of the next higher body (for example, a county council is under the district council; a district council is under the central ministry). The latter has the power to issue binding instructions to the councils; hence it is the decisive element. There are about a hundred thousand members of diets on the various levels—that is, about one for every hundred adult inhabitants of the Eastern zone; their function is, as in the Soviet Union, "educational." There are also so-called *activs* of inhabitants at large. These act as advisory groups to local and regional administrations and are used officially (and perhaps actually) to bring grievances to their attention. They are also used

to stimulate the fulfillment of plan figures, and so forth.

There is little room for local discretion. There are no legislative functions. Local and regional budgets are integral parts of the overall state budget, although small amounts (similar to the so-called directors' funds in enterprises) are left to the disposal of local authorities. It is to this streamlining from above that Ulbricht referred when he declared: "When we push that little button, the last village must report back within five minutes: Order executed."

An Executive-Controlled Parliament

It is in the field of elections and parliament that the fictitious or purely formal character of the Constitution reveals itself most clearly. Constitutionally, parliament controls the Cabinet and is supposed to be the sole lawmaker. Actually, it is a rubber stamp, whose eight fractions (five parties and three mass organizations) are coordinated through the bloc principle. When it meets, it functions more as a forum for government declarations than as a legislature. Even when it is permitted to enact statutes, its proceedings are distinguished by the absence of opposition, disagreement, criticism, or even debate. This is not surprising when one realizes that draft bills sometimes reach the proper minister only a few hours before he is supposed to lay them before parliament, and that deputies may get them only when the meeting begins. The majority of deputies consist of party functionaries and members of the Communist intelligentsia, behind whom rank workers and farmers.

Elections are by unity lists on which the groups constituting the National Front are represented according to a key giving the SED and the SED-controlled mass organizations a majority. There is a tiny residue of choice[5] in the occasional possibility of rejecting nominees in pre-election voters' meetings, but even here apparent popular rejection may be merely a means whereby the SED gets rid of an unwelcome nomination from one of the stooge groups.

[5] In local elections in 1965, for the first time, there were more nominees on the lists than seats to be filled, so that the voter could strike out unwanted candidates. There may here be a slight beginning of a more liberal election system.

Thus, elections are chiefly opportunities for rallying the people behind one or the other slogan for one or another of the forever changing "points of concentration" for which the propaganda machine is mobilized (for example, to raise agricultural productivity). The importance attached to elections is reflected in Ulbricht's statement: "We vote for one unity list because we are all united—that's why." To raise unity from a level of sullen apathy is the objective of all the regime's mobilization efforts: elections, National Front, stooge parties, and "operative brigades" formed for any imaginable purpose.

A Party-Controlled Executive

According to the Constitution, the executive part of government consisted of a largely ceremonial president and a responsible, coalition-type Cabinet. Following the death of the first and only president (Wilhelm Pieck) in 1960, the presidency was abolished and replaced by a twenty-four member Council of State, elected for four years by the People's Chamber. Besides ceremonial functions, it possesses powers to issue decrees with force of law and to lay down basic lines for defense and security. Ulbricht, who assumed its chairmanship, has here another vantage point for control. In the fall of 1961, the Council was granted practically unlimited emergency powers.

The center of governmental activity is the Cabinet, or rather, an inner cabinet called the Presidium of the Cabinet. This consists of the Premier and a number of deputy premiers as well as other ministers, altogether about fourteen. SED leaders make up a majority. Actual policy is made or coordinated at the Presidium level. The Cabinet at large never meets as a body; the Presidium meets regularly.

SED control of government is exercised in two ways: first, important measures for which the government is formally responsible are actually initiated and worked out at the top level of the party. Thus, decrees or draft laws may originate with the Politbureau; they are then dealt with in detail in the respective department of the Central Committee; thence they go to the ministry in charge, which makes the official draft and submits it to the Cabinet. Or, press directives come from the propaganda

(Agitprop) section of the SED Secretariat to the press office of the Minister-President.

The second means of control is through party leaders who simultaneously hold important government positions. There is now far-reaching personal identity between party and state leadership. Ulbricht himself, who was a mere deputy premier until he assumed the chairmanship of the Council of State in 1960, is now both actual and ostensible head of party and state. Likewise, the premiership, which until 1964 was in the hands of a former, "coordinated" Social Democrat, now is held by an SED man, Willi Stoph, heir-apparent of Ulbricht. The majority of the Presidium consists of Politbureau members. And district councils are headed or controlled by regional party leaders.

In addition to the ministries there exist a number of top independent agencies whose chiefs usually have Cabinet rank but whose main importance is in bringing party influence to bear on government and administration. Among these, a Workers' and Peasants' Inspectorate is charged with supervising the execution of laws on all levels, and with eliminating bottlenecks, preventing "sabotage," enforcing "discipline," and otherwise seeing that the economy functions properly. There is above all the State Planning Commission, a replica of the Soviet Gosplan, which is in charge of all planning activities for the planned economy, and in particular of working out Five- or, now, Seven-Year Plans; it is divided into departments, each of which is in charge of a major field. Major planning principles and policies derive either from SED leadership or, directly or indirectly, from the Soviet or Comecon level. Thus, here as elsewhere, actual (as distinguished from ostensible) lines of authority go downward rather than upward, and from party to government.

Administration and Civil Service

In the DDR the age-old problem of the German civil service has found a radical solution: the traditional service has simply been reformed out of existence. In order to do away with officialdom as a caste, public office was no longer to be differentiated from ordinary employment. This meant the abolition of the system of acquired rights and privileges: of guarantees of lifetime service, a special pensions system, and so forth. All public officials now have the status of workers and employees. They have ordinary employment contracts under the general social security system (under which, instead of retirement pensions, they receive much lower old-age "rents"), and they are affiliated with the general trade unions. In order to replace those, particularly in the higher ranks, who had fled or had been purged, rapid training courses were initially set up for candidates selected according to social origin and political progressivism. Now a special Walter Ulbricht Academy for Political and Legal Sciences trains an elite, class-conscious civil service of and for proletarian socialism.

But the problem of the cadres, that is, of having a loyal, reliable, and technically capable staff, continues to bother the regime. Replacement of the old pre-Communist intelligentsia by the regime-trained new intelligentsia proceeds gradually, and many years after the beginning of the regime, it had still to be satisfied with an administrative staff only 60 to 70 percent proletarian in origin. Selection for appointment and promotion is exceedingly thorough. Files, supplemented by personal interviews, contain data on the private lives and the political attitudes and performances of the personnel. These files form the basis for any action of the personnel offices, which are invariably staffed with reliable SED members. In addition, duplicates of the files go to the corresponding cadre sections of the party, whose consent is required for appointments. It is the public employees' duty to behave even in their private lives according to prescribed standards, to report on "unreliable" colleagues, and so forth. They are, of course, dismissible at any time for reasons of unreliability. Whether the system has created more than mere passive collaborators—excepting the few loyal followers—seems doubtful.

6. ADMINISTRATION OF JUSTICE

Law and "Socialist Legality"

Law, as under Nazism, has become chiefly an instrument of coercion. But since communism uses it to revamp society, it can be presented as a means for fighting the class enemy and building socialism. Serving to safeguard and enforce the varying policies of the regime, it is, as one observer has put it, "the respectable twin brother of terror." Actually, the regime has tried to dispense with terror whenever possible by substituting for it that engineering of consent—or at least an appearance of consent—that is also visible in connection with elections and operative brigades. There have been fewer show trials and similar open methods of legal intimidation than in some other satellites. And in the wake of de-Stalinization, there was some emphasis on avoiding arbitrariness in law enforcement and on at least applying the laws on the statute books without discrimination. But socialist legality, as this more liberal attitude was called, has yielded again to what is now considered the true way of law enforcement: observance and interpretation of all law in the light of the party line. An intended liberalization of the law of criminal procedure, that touchstone of liberalism, was given up, and punitive laws, especially in the field of political and economic crimes, were made even more stringent.

Only after the erection of the Berlin Wall did the regime apparently feel sufficiently at ease to enact a Law on Administration of Justice, which contains certain legal guarantees for an accused. It also transferred to a somewhat less autocratic body, the Supreme Court, some of the powers of supervision over the judiciary which the minister of justice had held previously. Further, instead of state courts, so-called conflict commissions, elected in enterprises but actually selected by the official trade union organization, are now in charge not only of labor conflicts but also, increasingly, of minor criminal cases in general. And informal "comradely courts," on the Soviet model, have been set up in neighborhoods to deal with law infraction in an allegedly less legalistic and more "social" manner, paying attention to social background, social damage, and the like. It may be asked whether this, instead of lessening fear, does not actually create more of a police-state atmosphere; especially when legal sanctions are replaced with "educational" measures (reprimand, obligation to apologize, and so forth) which may imply social ostracism.

Although, basically, pre-regime, even pre-Nazi, law codes are still valid, estrangement from the West German legal system is being widened by the enactment of special laws in areas in which the regime is especially interested —for example, in marriage and family law, and in labor law. Political partition is thus leading to increasing legal disunity.

Judiciary and Courts

"Judges of a new type," so-called people's judges, have by now completely replaced the former judiciary. They are trained not only in the technical details of the law, but also in the principles of Marxism-Leninism and their "social" application. Upon nomination by the justice ministry, they are officially elected by diets for four years, but they can be recalled for "serious violation of their duties."

Thus judicial independence has vanished. Judicial coordination is achieved through the criticism of judgments by higher courts, official indication in official journals of how laws are expected to be applied, inspectors sent down to the local level, and, even, official directives by the ministry to judges. The prosecutor's penalty demands are practically binding upon courts, and any objective attitude is condemned as objectivism—a serious deviation.

The court system consists of county courts, district courts, and a Supreme Court: in criminal cases the prosecution can freely determine which court shall hear a case. There is only one appeal (none where the Supreme Court has original jurisdiction); but even after a judgment has become *res judicata,* the Supreme Court, on its own or the prosecutor-general's initiative, may quash it as contradicting the principles and policies of the regime. Lay assessors are selected according to political standards. Attorneys are organized in lawyers' cooperatives, which assign cases and clients; however, their influence is dwindling. Execution of penalties (prison system, etc.) is under police administration.

Prosecutor-General

The power of the prosecutor goes far beyond what prosecution ordinarily implies. The prosecutor-general of the republic, who is the head of a centralized state agency of prosecution, is not subordinated to the ministry of justice, and has Cabinet rank; he resembles the public prosecutor of the Soviet Union in that he is supposed to watch over the proper execution of the laws, not only in the case of ordinary citizens but also on the part of any and all government agencies (including the ministries), all enterprises, and all their officers and employees. He and the members of his staff, whom he freely appoints and dismisses, thus exercise universal, police-type surveillance.

Secret Police

In this matter of universal surveillance the prosecutor-general seems to be in direct competition with another institution—the State Security Service (SSD)—which, like the Nazi Gestapo, is a separate police agency with a staff of its own and far-reaching powers. Whether the prosecutor-general or the SSD acts in individual cases seems to depend on secret regulations that may themselves be the result of a behind-the-scenes tug-of-war for power and influence.

Before 1953, the SSD, under one of the regime's most powerful figures, held a top status in the governmental structure. Subsequently, it has been downgraded and no longer plays an independent political role. However, it remains one of the chief enforcement agencies, and, while its detention camps have disappeared, it can arrest anybody. The sphere of its activity is apparent from the fact that about nine thousand persons were in prison in 1965 for political crimes. Its estimated fifteen thousand officials maintain a network of informers that numbers about a hundred thousand; frequently persons are pressed into such service through blackmail and intimidation, or in return for freedom from prosecution in cases where they have come under suspicion. On the whole, however, it can be said that in recent years the influence of the police has somewhat receded. As one observer has commented, "Terror and repression have largely been replaced by pressure, persuasion, and incentive." This holds for other areas of government and society too.

7. ECONOMIC, SOCIAL, AND CULTURAL PROBLEMS

With the social and economic revolution that was inaugurated in the zone in 1945, the economic and social rule of the two traditional ruling groups in East Germany, the landowning Junkers and the upper-middle class (industrialists and bankers), came to an end. It has been replaced by economic and social control on the part of the political ruling group; this was achieved through complete collectivization of agriculture and almost complete nationalization of trade and industry. Perhaps even more significant is the increasingly tight integration of the entire East German economy into the economic system of the Eastern bloc.

Agriculture

The most conspicuous of these transformations was the completion of land collectivization through a quickly launched, all-out campaign in the spring of 1960. But there had been previous revolutions in the countryside. The first distributed the large estates to smallholders and the landless. But farms allotted to peasants were generally so small as to make farmers dependent upon the state, with the latter's control exercised through compulsory delivery quotas and state-owned machine tractor stations. Then, in a first wave of collectivization in the early 1950's, the regime turned against the wealthier peasants, forcing many to flee to the West and consolidating their possessions in agricultural production cooperatives (LPG's), Kolkhozes on the Soviet pattern. A more lenient policy followed the uprisings of June 1953, but in 1958 a new wave began, which, by the end of 1959, had resulted in collectivizing about 50 percent of the land. We do not know what caused the regime, thereupon, to force a policy that had been supposed to extend over years to 100 percent completion within a few weeks. We know only the method. While there was no law compelling anybody to sign up, there was total mobilization of party workers, police, and other activists who descended in "brigades" on the countryside and relentlessly worked on each farmer until, worn out and intimidated, he saw no other way than to capitulate. Thus East Germany, alone among the satellites, can boast of complete "socialism in the countryside" as one of its achievements.

Collectivization has not yet reached the radical stage in which not only the land (as now) but also the cattle and individually owned im-

plements are commonly owned. There have been hints, however, that this "type III" stage (where everything except a small plot for vegetable planting and chicken raising is owned and managed collectively) is in the offing. The ultimate objective is the rural factory, where farmers are mere wage-earning laborers; they are now paid in "work units." The regime believes that all this is necessary in order to raise agricultural productivity in an overall scheme by which the East German living standard is to match and surpass that of West Germany. Actually, inefficiency and overbureaucratization have continually lowered agricultural productivity, making for shortages of consumers' goods despite conspicuous gains in the other sectors of the economy.[6] Here, too, the DDR's experience mirrors that of the Soviet Union.

Industry

Industry is completely planned and almost completely nationalized. At first, major enterprises were taken over directly by the Soviets and run as "Soviet corporations," although they were subsequently turned over to German ownership and management. This renationalization, however, has not prevented a growing coordination of the East German economy with that of the rest of the Soviet bloc, of which East Germany is now an important part.

East Germany, which was a victim of Soviet economic exploitation during the immediate postwar period, has since been transformed into one of the most important industrial units in the Communist world; as an industrial power it ranks ninth or tenth in the world, second (after the Soviet Union) in Comecon. It stands second in intrabloc trade and is the bloc's most important exporter of machinery. It further specializes in shipbuilding, tools, chemicals, and other products. It has become one of the heaviest Eastern traders with the underdeveloped world. Its economic growth, though initially it lagged behind that of West Germany (which was aided by Marshall Plan help while

---

6 Shortages of consumers' goods have been endemic in the DDR. In one story, a Leipzig man arrives home unexpectedly at noon to interrupt a tender scene between his wife and a strange man. Livid with rage, the husband roars at his wife: "How can you be wasting your time here when the grocer has lemons for sale?"

the East was squeezed by the Russians), has lately been as spectacular as that of West Germany. And the living standard of its people, though still lagging behind West Germany's, has also been rising.

While big industry has by now become completely nationalized, private ownership survives in some smaller craft and retail-trade establishments; but even there it is declining. Under a system of enforced state participation (a government "partnership" with the private owner) enterprises are taken over by the government upon the death of the owner. Handicraft is being collectivized in artisans' cooperatives. Only recently, and possibly temporarily, has a halt been called because of increasing difficulties in the supply of "little things."

Nationalized enterprises are organized as separate entities with separate budgets. Appointed directors, assisted by trade union–controlled boards, are responsible for their management and, especially, for the fulfillment of plan quotas. Since 1963, as in the other Eastern bloc economies, East Germany has tried, through a "New Economic System of Planning and Management" (NÖS), to reduce red tape and increase efficiency by giving plant managers more discretion in production, by permitting them to set prices calculated on the basis of actual production costs and market conditions, and by allowing for a certain amount of interfactory competition. With this development, the weight and influence of the technological and managerial elite, as against the ideological-political leadership, are bound to rise.

Labor

The fact that factory workers were in the forefront of the revolt in 1953 illustrates the paradox of a socialist regime that has not managed to command the allegiance of an appreciable part of the proletariat. This is the more remarkable in view of the improvement in living standards. Although wages and salaries in terms of purchasing power are still below the level of West Germany, there are certain compensations, including low-rent (though still crowded) housing, free medical services for everybody, free education, and retirement and disability pensions comparable to those of West

Germany. For certain types of work, especially that done by engineers, managers, functionaries, and outstanding (that is, politically deserving) intellectuals, salaries are much above the average.

But it is a managed system. Labor lacks means to defend its interests. Strikes are outlawed, works councils abolished, and work standards ("technically justified work norms") prescribed; often piece wages compel workers to work hard and long hours. The Free Trade Union Association (FDGB) is their only organization, but it is not really theirs. It is an SED-controlled, strictly centralized mass organization, with membership practically compulsory in all larger enterprises. Its chief purpose is to organize workers so as "to reach and surpass the norms of the planned economy." Similar to Soviet Union trade unions, the FDGB has some additional functions: one, to manage and control a social insurance system; and two, to supervise the observation of labor laws. The social insurance system, which has been set up as one huge, centralized system, comprises all the formerly separate branches of social insurance; it covers over 95 percent of the population, including public employees and students. It is financed by automatic deductions of 10 percent of all wages earned, a figure comparable to the West German rates. There is no unemployment. On the contrary, increasing labor shortages, due partly to the massive flight West (up to 1961) and partly to the low birth rates of twenty to twenty-five years ago, confront the East German economy with one of its primary problems. Thus the status and attitude of the masses are ambiguous: Driven and manipulated by what they still consider an alien and oppressive regime, they nevertheless get some sense of security and even some sense of pride from the economic consequences of their work. To stimulate the latter feeling at the expense of the former is the aim of the regime's efforts in the fields of propaganda and indoctrination.

Education and Culture

Culture has become the product of indoctrination and all cultural activity a manifestation of propaganda. The basis of this unending effort to indoctrinate and propagandize is dialectical materialism, the theoretical foundation of Marxist-Leninist doctrine. The German cultural inheritance, including classical literature and idealistic philosophy, is reinterpreted, and its creators and creations are either admitted as "humanistic" forerunners of socialism or else outlawed. Theater, music, science, arts are all under the direction of the culture ministry and thus coordinated. But intellectuals, writers, and artists who put themselves into the service of the new culture are not only well provided for materially but are extolled and honored, and this official promotion of culture cannot fail to make some impression even on the noncoordinated among a culture-minded people like the Germans.

Like culture, information and communication in all their channels—press, radio, TV, film—become means of propaganda and indoctrination. Daily directives are handed out by the press office of the Minister-President, and the official East German news agency is the only source of news reports. Therefore, he who reads *Neues Deutschland* (the central organ of the SED) has read them all. People are forbidden to read the West German press or to listen to any but the official broadcasting programs. But Germans have learned from Nazi experience how to circumvent such coordination, and since communication between the two worlds is not yet cut off completely, intellectual isolation has not become complete. There is, however, less interchange of ideas and persons than has developed of late between other Eastern countries and the West.

The Eastern regime is still suspicious of the possible effects of such interchange on the DDR population, as was clearly revealed in the summer of 1966, when an agreement with top SPD leaders to have them debate issues in public, televised confrontation in the East, while SED leaders would, in exchange, come to another such meeting in West Germany, was canceled by the latter on short notice.

Incompleteness of coordination can also be seen in the relation of the regime to religion. Its basic hostility is clear from its antireligious philosophy and is expressed in harassment of churches, clergymen, and those lay people who still cling to church membership and religion. Religious instruction has of course been eliminated from the schools and can be given only in private. Children insisting on communion or confirmation are threatened with obstacles to their future careers; a Communist "youth consecration" has been created as a competing institution. Thus, the regime sets itself up as a kind of atheistic counterchurch with the symbolism of special socialist ritual and ceremonies for births, weddings, burials, and similar occasions. Financially, the churches are dependent on the voluntary contributions of their members. But they have so far managed to subsist, and the regime has not dared to destroy them; they have even maintained some organizational and personal interconnections with the churches in the West. As under Nazism and, to some extent under the Soviet system, the churches remain the only recognized institutions not fully coordinated and thus the only ones able to continue some doctrinal opposition.

Winning over the younger generation has been a major "point of concentration." Education shows progressive and reactionary features all in one. It is free mass education on all levels, with a common "basic school" (*Grundschule*) of eight years, now gradually extended to ten, and with stipends for those who want to go on to university, where their number is proportionally larger than in West Germany. About 95 percent of all East German university students receive full "pay" (that is, tuition and living expenses) until they complete their studies. The old class system of education has been thus abolished. But, although children of bourgeois background are no longer discriminated against in favor of workers' and farmers' children in high school and university admission, as they were until 1959, examinations test "right" (that is, left) social and political attitudes, and students who are not doing well politically are weeded out.

The aim of East German education is to train the "polytechnical" man and prepare him for the practical occupations and professions needed by the regime's economy. Emphasis is therefore on mathematics, science, and technical preparation for work. One day a week there is schooling (or work) in an enterprise or on a farm (kolkhoz), and there is an ominous trend toward collectivizing the children's after-school time through compulsory attendance at organized activities. The young are thus steered toward what are considered socially useful or needed occupations, not toward development of their own personalities; they are groomed to become cogs in the production machine. Although, like their West German counterparts, they are basically pragmatic, they turn collectivist, developing little initiative and expecting directives.

Russian language is a compulsory course in high school and at the university, and all things Russian and Soviet are stressed in order to achieve a clear separation from the Western world, another prime objective of education. It is difficult to assess to what extent the regime is succeeding in these objectives. Judging from the difficulties it has had from time to time with groups of youngsters indicted for hooliganism or as degenerate beats, and even with its own Free German Youth, where it finds widespread cynicism and lack of political interest, one might conclude that youth is dissatisfied or, at least, uncoordinated. But the majority of students seem to go along with the regime more or less opportunistically, interested in passing their exams and adjusting themselves to the formal requirements of political organization and activity.[7] Since the regime badly needs young blood, desirable positions are open to the young more readily than in other countries, and many thus are bribed at least into passive compliance. Some are even sincerely devoted to what appears to them as an altruistic goal in life, such as working for socialism, world peace, and so forth. While most of the young in East Germany, and most of its people in general, hate the autocratic features of the regime, this by no means implies support of the way of life and the institutions of West Germany. All signs indicate that they are in search of a third way, something they vaguely describe as genuine socialism, that is, socialism minus the coercive aspects of communism. Thus they would not give up nationalized industry and planned economy for free enterprise, free education for a class system of education. This might indicate to the West that mere negativism is not enough to counter a regime whose propaganda can point to reforms which, if there were no totalitarian

compulsion, would be considered constructive by non-Communists.

Conclusion

What of the future? With Germany the birthplace of "scientific socialism," it is likely that communism looks upon the contest between a Communist and a non-Communist Germany with particular interest, perhaps perceiving a historical mission in the DDR's building what the Moscow conference of Communist parties in December 1960 called "the outpost of socialism in Western Europe." While it is unlikely—barring war or conquest—that communism will succeed in West Germany, there is a danger that it will succeed, given time, in establishing in East Germany a unit so deeply alienated from the West that it may emerge as an entirely different country. Many East Germans may even now be so alienated: we must not forget that all those below the age of thirty to thirty-five have never experienced liberal democracy or any other Western way of life; even the oldest among these have grown up under Nazism and then, almost without break, have lived under communism.

In addition, the massive flight from the Eastern zone drained it of those, such as teachers and doctors, who were wedded to Western ways, that is, of part of its most active opponents, as well as some of its most valuable and most urgently needed skilled manpower. This has confronted the regime with what continues to constitute its biggest problem, the problem of cadres, that is, of a trained elite. If the regime succeeds in solving the problem of recruiting and training a new intelligentsia, however, it is likely to survive present difficulties and eventually emerge as an economically flourishing and expanding unit whose Communist way of life may seem more and more natural to a majority of its inhabitants. Today, it is still a system of accommodation. Most of the people are still hostile to the bureaucracy, to indoctrination, to remnants of terrorism, and, above all, to being kept in a prison, unable to come and go where they like. But they are adjusting more and more to looking upon the DDR as theirs and not merely something transitory. Time is running out. Hence the stark urgency of the reunification issue.

[7] Thus, to the sorrow of the churches, over 90 percent of all children participate in the Communist "youth consecration." Generally, there has been a sharp drop in baptisms, confirmations, church weddings, and church funerals.

9. Germany and the World

History records few comebacks as staggering and as swift as Germany's in the postwar period—a comeback that is especially significant if one recalls how deep her fall had been and how determined the victors had seemed never to allow her to rise again. But if Germany seems to be once again "one of the big ones," one must specify in what respects. Germany today is neither "one" nor does she belong to what, in the nuclear age, has emerged as a new category of so-called superpowers. Not being one means that, in contrast to the other powers discussed in this book, her foreign policy cannot be treated as that of one. No longer being in the ranks of the foremost world powers implies that neither she nor her parts can any longer aspire to hegemony. Her still vital importance in world relations is intimately connected with the split of the world into nuclear power blocs. The cold war in the bipolar postwar world meant that Germany, located exactly where East and West have met and clashed in Europe, for reasons of geography, resources, economic strength, manpower, and military potential emerged as an essential factor in the buildup of either bloc. Each felt that Germany's presence in the other bloc would endanger the balance of power; each felt, therefore, that it had to keep under its control the area that it had occupied after the war, to build it up economically, to rearm it as an integral part of its defense system (NATO and Warsaw Pact, respectively), and to make it culturally and ideologically Western and Eastern, respectively. German partition, thus, has been both a cause and an effect of the world's split. Only against this world background can we hope to discuss in meaningful terms such problems as German reunification or West Germany's integration into Western Europe, or to assess proposed solutions. It is against the background of what has been said about German internal developments in preceding chapters that we must judge the desirability of such solutions.

1. GERMAN OBJECTIVES

A few years ago Karl Jaspers, a noted German philosopher, suggested that the Soviets might agree to free expression of the popular will in East Germany—that is, to renounce their control there—in return for a commitment by the West to continue the present separation of East and West Germany indefinitely. He advocated a solution under which all Germans would be free internally again, but at the price of national unity. Whether Jaspers' plan was feasible is not the point. What is significant was the public reaction to his suggestion: There was near-unanimity—from right to left, among spokesmen of all major parties, and in the press—in rejecting it. National unity, it was felt, should not be foregone at any price.[1]

This incident suggests that most Germans in the West (and probably still in the East) consider reunification as the chief objective of German foreign policy.[2] It is for them a natural

[1] In a poll taken shortly after Jaspers had raised the question, only 18 percent of those polled were ready to renounce reunification in return for a free Eastern zone.

[2] While economic improvement ranked first in public interest far into the 1950's, reunification has consistently taken first place since. About two thirds of those polled have held that reunification was the most important political question (for example, in 1963, it ranked before those who considered "no further inflation" most important). Over one half declared partition "unbearable." However, the percentage rose with rising age groups, from 44 percent among the young to 66 percent among those sixty and over.

objective, something never to be forgotten in the midst of the daily tasks and specific problems of West German policy, or, perhaps, in the pleasant life brought by prosperity. There may be some doubt about how much one should sacrifice for its sake; the public at large may seem at times a bit apathetic; CDU leaders may be apprehensive about how much the SPD would be strengthened in the event free East German votes were added to those in the Bonn Republic; Catholics may not like the idea of again becoming a minority in a predominantly Protestant Germany. But it is safe to assume that no regime and no statesman could survive politically while disavowing the primary objective.

Territorial Questions

Leaving aside for a moment the vital problem of whether and how reunification might be attained in practice, we turn our attention to more far-reaching objectives of German foreign policy—specifically, territorial objectives. It would not be surprising in view of the recent history of German expansionist aggressivism and the subsequent loss of territory, even of some that had been German for centuries, to find attitudes of extremism in this matter. Communist charges of West German "revanchism," indeed, assume its existence without further proof. In the face of this situation, present moderation comes as a pleasant surprise. In general, territorial, boundary, and nationality questions, which so often have led Germans into wars against the French, Danes, Russians, and Poles, play a minor role. Two lost wars have convinced most Germans that the problem of Alsace-Lorraine has been settled in favor of France. Most Germans accept the independence of Austria, a country whose union with a democratic Germany seemed close at one point after World War I—a chance undone by Hitler's insane policies.[3] The Danish frontier does not offer a serious problem as long as Germans grant decent treatment to a Danish minority of hardly more than a hundred thousand in North Schleswig.

But the Eastern question is still open, despite the fact that the lost provinces no longer contain significant German populations. As long as the West insists that the fate of these areas remains to be settled at the (however remote) German peace settlement, Germans are understandably reluctant to forego respective German claims. These claims sometimes extend even to areas outside Germany proper where German minorities once lived.[4] But it is indicative of present moderation that feelings of revenge, calls for reconquest, and demands for unconditional return have yielded to more sober attitudes even among the expellees. Those who still hope to "go home" some day expect to do so on the basis of a negotiated settlement, which, they realize, will require concessions by all concerned. As we have seen, there are radicals among the leaders of expellee organizations and among non-expellee nationalists or neo-Nazis who try to excite an extremist policy. So far the majority has rejected them.

Nobody can know, of course, how long today's spirit of restraint and antiadventurism will last. Some fear the effect of remilitarization. So far, however, rearmament (again contrary to Soviet charges) has not meant revival of militarism. West Germany is the only NATO power whose armed forces are fully integrated with NATO. The military has not regained the prestige it had in pre-World War II times. The young draftees are not particularly eager to serve, and the armed forces find it difficult, in competition with the civilian sector of the economy, to build up its professional officers' staff—certainly a far cry from the times when officers were at the pinnacle of German society in terms of status and prestige. Officers are now considered—and consider themselves—as primarily technicians, without the traditional, haughty *esprit de corps*. There have been abuses, chiefly of recruits by noncommissioned officers, but they have aroused public reprobation and have been dealt with in civilian courts. And civilian leadership has taken care that the military remain under civilian control and that the

---

[3] Austrians in their vast majority now want to stay independent; only eight out of a hundred Austrians polled still desire union with Germany.

[4] Thus, spokesmen for the expellees (and some professors of international law!) have asserted that the Sudeten area of Czechoslovakia is legally German, on the basis of the Munich settlement of 1938; this, however, is not the official stand of the West German government.

service be built up in a spirit different from Prussian authoritarianism. This concern is reflected in the cautious manner in which defense and army controls were distributed among various authorities: the President (certain appointment powers); the Chancellor (command in case of war); the defense minister (command in peacetime); a Bundestag defense committee for general supervision; and the "ombudsman" mentioned in Chapter 4—that is, the parliamentary defense commissioner who deals with individual complaints by members of the armed forces. All this testifies to a concern for civilian supremacy as well as to a desire to avoid overconcentration of power within the government itself.

That there still remain problems, however, became apparent when a military crisis broke in the fall of 1966. It is possible that the wholesale resignation, or retirement, of over one dozen top-level officers (including the highest, the "Inspector-General," as well as the commanders of the three main branches of the armed forces) reflected, in the main, dissatisfaction of the military with ministerial red tape, or an attempt to shift responsibility for mishaps, such as an amazing string of accidents involving the chief German air weapon, the "star-fighter." But it is likely that the conflict also reflected something more typical of traditional German militarism: objection to civilian control in the sense of ultimate power of command and decision-making and resistance to the idea of democratizing the military by treating the soldier as a "citizen in uniform" rather than continuing to inflict on him traditional "Prussian" discipline. If so, the replacement of the old group with, hopefully, less hidebound younger officers gives rise to satisfaction.

The turmoil, finally, may have some connection with uncertainty about the role of a nonnuclear military establishment in the defense of Germany and Western Europe. As long as the integration of the German forces into NATO lasts, an independent West German military policy is hardly imaginable. It might become possible should NATO disintegrate completely. It would be ironical, indeed, if de Gaulle's policy should make France responsible for the reemergence of a militarily independent Germany, a Germany which, France's *force de frappe* notwithstanding, would be the strongest military power in non-Communist Europe.

German Power Potential

That German territorial aims have been relatively moderate may be due, at least in part, to Germany's favorable power potential. The appearance of ruin in 1945 was misleading. There still existed most of Germany's natural resources, most of its industry, and above all the skills and the will to work of a highly qualified population. Disarmament and occupation hardly affected her permanent potential. Physical destruction, dismantling of factories, and similar measures to some extent proved a blessing in disguise, for the Germans were compelled to modernize their plant.

Thus, even in terms of West Germany alone, the effect of defeat on resources and other potential was less than it first appeared to be. The Saar region, with its coal and steel resources, was regained, and while the Upper Silesian mines and industries were lost, Germany's industrial heart, the Ruhr, remained intact. The Ruhr today is not only part of Germany's arsenal but a foremost part of the Western European Common Market.

The detachment of the Eastern zone and the loss of the territories east of the Oder-Neisse line have been more serious; above all it has meant loss of food-producing areas and hence West Germany's greater dependence on food imports. But greatly increased exports, made possible through a steep rise in her industrial productivity, have enabled her to solve this problem. As we have seen, East Germany has separately developed into one of the main economic strongholds of the Eastern bloc, and both Germanies have thus been able to overcome their truncated condition through economic growth. West Germany, in particular, has regained the strong competitive position in the world market that the high quality of German products, as well as its cartel arrangements, had traditionally secured for her. In war, of course, this means less self-sufficiency than ever before, but this, by itself, furnishes Germans with an additional reason for seeing the most promising future in peace rather than in conflict and war.

2. GERMAN ATTITUDES AND POLICIES

Background of German Foreign Policy

In contrast to the British, French, and Russians, with their long history as nation states, Germans have not even always been sure they should, or could, form a political unit. Centuries-old disunity drove some of them (including Goethe) to the pessimistic conclusion that they were incapable of ruling themselves as a nation. What would be the form and role of their state? Should it be a nation-state like others, or a Reich—with its mystical connotation of a larger unity of several nationalities—with a European "mission"? The medieval Empire was meant to integrate all Western Christian nations, but it was feeble; its modern revival, since 1871, had turned out to be intent on power politics and hegemony. The pendulum of attitudes had swung from an often utopian idealism (cosmopolitanism around 1800, pacifism after World War I, Europeanism after World War II), to cynical realism (*Realpolitik*). Few Germans had learned the more modest but also more difficult job of living as good neighbors among equals. True, such an attitude was rendered difficult by Germany's belated unification as well as by her geographical location in the heart of a continent that had been the center of world politics. This meant living between an East that had never known political liberties, and the liberal-democratic West. Germans have been periodically attracted and repelled by these poles, oscillating between authoritarianism and democracy, romanticism and enlightenment, pragmatism and mysticism. This oscillation has been reflected in Germany's foreign-policy orientation.

Eastern Orientation

The leading Prusso-German groups, in particular the Junkers, saw in the autocratic regime of the Tsars the backbone of order in Europe and ultimate protection against the "anarchic-liberal" West. In the nineteenth century this attitude was translated into first Prussia's, then Bismarck Germany's alliance with Russia. William II abandoned the "wire to St. Petersburg,"

and since he did not replace it with a Western alliance, this break with the East was later blamed by many for Germany's defeat in the two-front World War I. In the Weimar period an Eastern orientation, despite the transformation of Russian monarchical authoritarianism into Bolshevism, was advocated by influential rightist circles, including leading Reichswehr generals and diplomats who hoped to find in Russia the lever with which to raise a defeated Germany against a hostile West. Even among the Nazis a geopolitical school of thought dreamed of a huge Eurasian bloc, formed by Germany, Russia, and Japan, which would turn against the West and efface the Western empires. This policy, however, was submerged under Hitler's ambition to destroy both West *and* East.

Today Eastern orientation is representative of the DDR, whose rulers, of course, have little choice but to follow Soviet policy; only occasionally can they stress particular German interests. This subservience of the regime is illustrated by its conclusion of a formal treaty with Poland, recognizing the Oder-Neisse line as the definitive German boundary to the east.

Thus, it is only in West Germany that a genuine, spontaneous expression of foreign policy can be discerned, although East German policy is still important as a reflection of Soviet policy toward Germany. Germany lies at the very center of Soviet foreign policy, perhaps more so than does any other region of the world. Whether or not the Soviets still hope ultimately to control all of Germany, in practice their objective has been to keep Germany in its entirety from falling under the control of the West. They therefore at first proposed reunification under neutralization, intimating that they might trade control of their zone for such an arrangement. When the West rejected the proposal, they shifted their emphasis to building up East Germany as an economic workshop and a military bastion of the Eastern bloc.

Simultaneously, however, the Soviets have also established relationships with Bonn. Indicting the Western powers for their unwillingness to face "the facts," they claim that in fact there exist two German states with two different social systems, and that the world must deal with both of them. This two-Germanies policy (which would become a three-Germanies policy if the Soviets seriously advanced their claim to see West Berlin established as a separate "free city") reflects their realization that, on the one hand, the protracted East-West stalemate precludes any chance of Germany's being united under Soviet auspices, while, on the other hand, they think that yielding control over East Germany is too high a price to pay for getting West Germany out of the Western alignment. Thus, their less far-reaching short-range aim is to gain Western recognition of the DDR as an equal of the Federal Republic, a recognition that would include acceptance of its boundaries (that is, the Oder-Neisse line).

Hence, for the time being, the Soviets have shelved reunification as a task for the big powers. Instead, they propose that the two German governments solve this problem between themselves by at first establishing some kind of all-German confederacy, with an all-German council on which East and West Germans would be represented "by parity." The council would then prepare for unification by holding elections whose terms are left vague and whose free character in the Western sense can hardly be anticipated. So long as the West refuses to grant Ulbricht an equal voice in shaping Germany's future, this scheme has only propaganda value. In the meantime, the Soviets may be quite satisfied with the continuation of a state of affairs in which the West has to offer concessions if it wants a change, while the East can wait for changes in the Western setup or in Western policy that might break the present stalemate.

Western Orientation

Germans have never been more strongly Western-oriented than West Germans are today. The German alignment with the West was part and parcel of an overall Western policy which, from the late 1940's on, was based on the following assumptions: (1) East and West constitute two hostile camps, because (2) the East, by its very nature (with its Communist aim of world conquest) is and must remain expansionist. (3) The West, therefore, must be strong, especially militarily, in order to contain and then roll back the opponent. (4) The West has a chance

to do so because it will become stronger, while the East, based on a totalitarian terror system, will be weakened by internal crises and the absence of that freedom which is necessary for scientific-technological advance, especially in armaments.

On the basis of such assumptions a policy of strength seemed to promise success, either through "negotiating from strength" (Foreign Secretary John Foster Dulles' slogan, forever repeated at that time), or, should the Soviets be unwilling to make concessions in the course of such negotiations, through their military defeat. Hence there appeared to be realism in the West German alignment with the West, an alliance that to them seemed to open the way toward reunification and, possibly, the restoration of the frontiers of 1937 in return.

But just as the Communists' assumption that the West would "inevitably" decay through economic crises proved wrong, the West was mistaken in its basic assumptions concerning communism and the Soviets. Rather than proving expansionist and aggressive, the Soviets, at least for the time being, veered to a policy of maintaining the status quo. On the other hand, sputnik and, especially, their development of nuclear power—making them *the* other superpower—proved that totalitarian structure does not preclude technological prowess. Now the Western objectives, and in particular German reunification, were obtainable only through mutual concessions—unless one was ready to risk nuclear war. The policy of strength proved unrealistic but one would not admit it. Hence the protracted stalemate between East and West over the German question.

In all other respects, however, Western orientation proved a boon to West Germany. Economically, she became co-founder first of the Coal and Steel Community and then of the full-fledged Common Market (European Economic Community) which replaced it; thus she emerged as an integral part and a foremost member of a flourishing and mutually profitable European economic setup. As a member of the Council of Europe, she became a co-promoter of political and cultural integration. Politically, in particular, all this seemed to point to a Europe in which Germans, tired of narrow nationalism, might merge their allegiance with that of others, including the French. The Franco-German "friendship treaty" of January 22, 1963, capstone of Adenauer's fourteen years of pro-Western foreign policy, seemed to have buried an age-old enmity. A united Europe to replace obsolete nation states seemed in the offing, signaling a significant change in attitudes, particularly in that country whose middle classes for so long had rejected any nonhegemonial regionalism in favor of German nationalism. Strategically, as a member of NATO and the Western European Union, West Germany seemed protected as an intrinsic part of a strong alliance system in which she was the strongest European power in terms of conventional forces and armaments and in which she could avoid the dangers of militarism through full integration in a higher setup. Culturally and in internal affairs, finally, she seemed to be gradually accepting Western-style liberal democracy. In short, West Germany, claiming to represent all Germans, seemed to have emerged as a powerful and respected (and, by the same token, in Eastern eyes a feared and suspected) new member of international society.

By the middle 1960's this bright picture had grown dark. Grave problems had arisen, chiefly because "Western" orientation had failed to bring reunification or even to bring any hope that this seemingly insoluble problem would ever be solved, and because deep fissures had appeared in the Western camp.

The development of European regionalism was checked by the new nationalism of "European" nations, especially de Gaulle's France. This prevented the extension of the economic community of the "inner six" to Britain and others and thus split non-Communist Europe economically, rendering the Community a ground for the play of competing political and industrial ambitions rather than an arena for emerging "Europeanism." Above all, it checked the development of that supranationalism that was to become the basis of a regional political setup.

Whether the Germans themselves would have developed in time a new nationalism of the French type is uncertain, but events did pull the rug from under those who were ready to continue their struggle for a new "Europe." De Gaulle's policy of anti-Americanism, his new "European isolationism," now confronted Germans with a choice they had long hoped to avoid: Should they side with France or with Britain and the United States? German Gaullists pointed out that a break with France would not only destroy the political-psychological value inherent in the Franco-German alliance but might endanger the Common Market, in whose functioning German industry had invested a powerful economic interest. German "Atlanticists" (who include some CDU and most SPD leaders, and others) pointed out not only that there were equally powerful economic interests tying West Germany to the Anglo-Saxon nations but, above all, that the very existence of West Germany depended on continued political and strategic support by the United States.

Even strategically, however, the situation had become clouded. The chief problem was this: What would happen to German military forces and policies if NATO (of which West Germany is the only fully integrated member) should disintegrate further? In addition, there arose the problem of nuclear arms. After de Gaulle had started to build his *force de frappe,* Americans, anxious to stave off similar German demands, offered a plan for a multilateral NATO force in which Germans would have a share. This was to be a jointly manned fleet of submarines armed with nuclear weapons (over whose actual use the Americans reserved a veto). As long as the Russians did not possess retaliatory nuclear strength commensurate with the Americans, Germans had felt fully protected through the American deterrent. Now, however, their leaders split: The "Atlanticists," though they did not doubt—at least officially— that Americans would continue to be ready to use their nuclear force for the defense of Germany, saw some good in sharing in nuclear policy-making and strategy—that is, in determining what would constitute German "vital interests" in regard to targets to be defended, and so forth. German Gaullists, on the other hand, expressed doubt that Americans would be willing to risk their national substance for the defense of Europe; Germany, therefore, should rather look to the French for protection. They have not been able to explain, however, why the French should undertake risks that the Americans would not. Sensing this difficulty, perhaps, Gaullist CSU leader Franz Josef Strauss has proposed that a joint European nuclear force (that is, one excluding the United States) should be placed under the command of a politically united Europe (a proposal that is surely contrary to anything de Gaulle is ready to accept). These disagreements cannot but work in favor of those hidden and unofficial forces in Germany that would welcome revived German power. It would be ironical should French supernationalism push a non-aggressive and nonmilitaristic Germany back into traditional German nationalism and militarism.

In view of these developments, is West Germany likely to abandon Western orientation for a policy of independence? Dissatisfied with a role that Willy Brandt has described as that of "an economic giant but a political pigmy," might she try to establish an independent military setup and even ask for an independent nuclear deterrent? Might she try to use nuclear threats not only for deterrence but eventually for blackmailing the East in an effort to enforce reunification? Would she side with the United States in a bilateral alliance (something some claim to have existed *de facto* under the NATO arrangement since the days of the Dulles-Adenauer entente, when Germany frequently exercised a "veto" over American policies)? Or might she turn East and use her independence to close a "deal" with the Soviets? This has been the nightmare of the West, especially the Americans, since early postwar times. The fear is clearly unjustified so long as the Federal Republic is Western-oriented but would not be so if that orientation shifted. All these questions reflect the grave new problems that confront West German foreign policy and the foreign policy of the West in general.

Neutralism and the Policy of "Détente"

What do Germans chiefly want at this point? Western alignment has given them economic prosperity and at least a modicum of political and military security. But—and this is what distinguishes them from most of the major and minor European powers—they are "revisionist," not only in regard to the territories beyond the Oder-Neisse line but, above all, in regard

to partition. To many Germans, West Germany is "a fragment of a fragment." Despite Eastern charges, this does not—or does not yet—imply that they are "revanchists" plotting aggression. But their insistent demand for change has made, and keeps, Central Europe a major crisis area of the world. They are increasingly aware that the policy of trying to compel the Soviets to yield control over East Germany by Western "display of strength" has led to an impasse. Hence neutralism at first, and now a policy of *détente* toward the East, have been suggested by various groups as alternatives to standpattism.

Neutralism at one time seemed to offer some hope for attaining the goal of reunification. During the first postwar decade, when East Germany had not yet been fully integrated with the East, repeated offers from the East hinted at the possibility of reunification through free elections in the Soviet zone in return for some sort of neutralizing of all Germany. This, of course, would have meant West German renunciation of her alignment with the West, in particular, of membership and military integration in NATO. Adenauer, backed by the West, was fearful of the risks involved and decided that West Germany should first be made secure in a Western alignment. The SPD and others have since claimed that Adenauer (and his Western allies) might at least have explored the opportunities for a negotiated settlement and that failure to do so has given the East a chance to put the blame for the continued partition of Germany on the West. There is some validity in this reproach. But all that is past history. When the Soviets, in 1960, indicated that reunification had become impracticable for the time being, even the SPD was compelled to identify itself with the government's policy of Western orientation. The party then became more or less a "me-too" party in foreign affairs.

In the beginning, however, the SPD had not been alone in advocating neutralism. When rearmament began, large segments of the public outside socialism voiced resentment at the prospect of becoming new Hessians for yesterday's enemy. At that time neutralism found fertile ground in a Germany located—and divided—between East and West. Idealists of various sorts, including many in the churches (especially among Protestant leaders), as well as pacifists, socialists, and anti-Nazi democrats, all were fearful of the consequences of a new militarism. They hoped that through arrangements between the Western powers and the Soviets both Western and Soviet troops would be evacuated, and Germany reunited under a freely elected democratic government with an international status of neutrality that all powers would commit themselves to respect.

Various solutions were proposed in the 1950's by private groups and individuals (George Kennan, for one), political parties (the British Labor party, and the SPD, with its "Germany Plan"), and governments (Poland, backed by the Soviet Union, with the Rapacki plan). Some envisaged the complete neutralization and demilitarization of Germany (plus, possibly, some Eastern states); others proposed mere disengagement through the withdrawal of Soviet and Western troops, or a thinning out of forces, or denuclearization.

But the problems that reunification would raise were never discussed in detail. For example, would the East, if reunification were brought about through free elections, be willing to agree to economic unification and to give up their "socialist achievements" in the zone? Or, on the other hand, would the West guarantee the continuation of some of these reforms? Even more difficult, perhaps, than the internal questions that reunification would create would be the problem posed by the "neutral" international status of a reunified Germany. Both sides, of course, would require ironclad guarantees against any attempts to change this status by direct military intervention or internal coups (such as the one staged in Czechoslovakia in 1948). It might even happen that disagreement on whether some measure or policy (on the part of unified Germany or of the Powers) was in violation of the agreed-upon status would create more friction than is caused by the present status. And what about Germany herself, with her tremendous combined potential? Could she be kept demilitarized without endless intrigue and attempts at intervention? Could she be armed without again endangering the peace of the world? As (then) Prime Minister Macmillan said: "If Germany is to be neutral and unarmed, who is going to keep her unarmed? If she is to be neutral and armed, who is going to keep her neutral?"

These questions seem no longer of practical importance, however. Today, only a major imbalance of forces could compel one or the other of the two power blocs to yield its present position in Germany. The Soviets, in particular, having made their section an integral unit in their economic and political buildup, could hardly sacrifice it without a serious loss of power and prestige. It appears therefore that indefinite partition will be the price Germany will have to pay for continued peaceful coexistence among the power blocs.

In view of this deadlock on the major issue, reunification, and in view of the loosening of the Western alignment, West German opinion and foreign policy seem at a turning point in the later 1960's. All sorts of things that once were taken for granted can no longer be so taken (for example, West Germany's integration in, and protection by, one overall NATO defense system). New attitudes and approaches, therefore, seem possible. Among them are a new sense of independence, a desire to assert itself as a nation—in short, a new nationalism. It may be that, with the passing of one postwar generation, such self-assertion would have come anyway. But it is being encouraged by the weakening of regionalism and the slackening of the Western alignment.

Neonationalism is still somewhat ill defined, however, and it emerges in conflicting forms. One, already latent in earlier attitudes and policies, places its trust in a continued Western alignment, with Germany playing an increasingly powerful role, either as *the* major ally of the United States, or, as advocated by German Gaullists, as the leader of a Western Europe independent of United States dominance or even influence. According to another form of nationalism, Germany should aim at a capacity to play an independent role commensurate with her actual power, free from any ties East or West and hence in a position to play off the East and the West against each other, possibly even arriving at some Rapallo type of "deal" with the Soviets. Nationalism of this radical type is sometimes combined with demands for independent military, even nuclear, forces and policies. For some time it had been voiced by normally insignificant radical-rightist, neo-Nazi groups and parties. The recent emergence of a unified extreme right, however, gives some cause for concern. Nationalism, though voiced by certain groups in each of the major parties (especially the FDP), had so far been contained within them, so that extremism (for example, that of the spokesmen for the expellees in the CDU and SPD) had been canceled out by the more moderate attitudes. With the new uncertainties now besetting the moderates, however, nationalist demands may come to the fore within the major groups themselves, especially if they have to compete with the nationalism of a radical right.

Another alternative is a policy of *détente* vis-à-vis the East. This policy would make for greater independence than did the Western alignment, but it would be moderate rather than neonationalist and might even require some sacrifice of nationalist objectives. *De facto* recognition of the status quo would in itself lead to a lessening of tension between the two Germanies and between West Germany and Poland and other Eastern countries. Such a lessening of tension might create an atmosphere in which partition and the condition of the East German population would become more tolerable. Reestablishing some ties with the East has long been advocated by leaders of the FDP, the SPD (with qualifications regarding the status of West Berlin) and, of late, and somewhat hesitantly, even by some leaders of the CDU. At first this policy would call for West Germany to take little or medium steps, improving trade and cultural relations with the DDR, for example, or even establishing diplomatic relations with East European countries. Real *détente* might require *de facto* recognition of the East German regime and acceptance of the Oder-Neisse line. Such moves would abate the fear of revanchism now harbored by such countries as Poland, and would reduce the sense of isolation and frustration among the rulers of the DDR. Those rulers, with or without Ulbricht still at the helm, might then see fit to ease totalitarian controls and might even accept the gradual resumption of closer ties between the two Germanies. In time the "wall"

might become more permeable, and, with mutual suspicion lessening, a kind of federation might eventually be formed in which the two social systems could coexist, as Catholicism and Protestantism managed to do in Germany after the Confessional Peace of Augsburg at the time of the Reformation.

Such a policy might not be too high a price to pay for generally easing tension and for solving such vexing problems as that of West Berlin (which might gradually be merged again with its Eastern portion, with free access to it guaranteed). Actually, Bonn has been negotiating *sub rosa* with the DDR right along on such issues as interzonal trade and Berlin passes. To establish more formal ties would constitute neither moral and political approval of the Eastern regime, nor the recognition of partition, nor the sacrifice of reunification as an objective. Indeed, it might bring reunification closer to realization.

But such a policy would require giving up some cherished attitudes and policies that have sometimes assumed the form of doctrinairism. The so-called Hallstein doctrine, for example, has meant that Bonn would break off or refuse to have diplomatic relations with any country (except the Soviet Union) that recognized the East German regime. Such intransigence has hardly paid off, since it has embittered Bonn's relations with certain countries (including the Arab nations) but has not prevented them from dealing with the DDR through trade missions and in other ways. At the end of 1966, with the SPD in the government and Willy Brandt as foreign minister, it seemed that the ice was breaking. The perennial fear lest an East-West *détente,* by freezing the status quo, would inevitably be at Germany's expense appeared to give way to the realization that only in an environment of lessened tension might German objectives, including eventual reunification, have a chance. The Four Power Declaration by Britain, France, the United States, and Germany anent a NATO Council meeting in December 1966 called not only for the removal of "barriers to freer and more friendly reciprocal exchanges between countries of different social and economic systems" (meaning, primarily, the Eastern European countries) but also for moves to "develop human, economic, and cultural contacts between the two parts of Germany." If one remembers two decades of cold war recriminations, the winds of change were unmistakable.

Germany and the World

Little, medium, and even major steps in a policy of *rapprochement* between the two Germanies as well as between West Germany and the Eastern countries would constitute one way of reducing tension in Central Europe and thereby in the world at large. A second way might be for both East and West Germany to forgo nuclear armaments. Lately, the question of nuclear arms for Germans has been a major stumbling block in the world's search for arms control and disarmament. The Soviets have objected to plans like MLF and similar NATO or other group setups in which West Germany would share nuclear arms. Bonn, when it was granted sovereignty and the right to rearm, did forgo the right to produce nuclear weapons independently on its own territory, but this neither excludes West Germany from "nuclear sharing" nor, indeed, from getting her own separate force from others.

As we have seen, some nationalists in West Germany now urge that Germany become a nuclear power, jointly or independently. Their reasons may have to do with winning for Germany "big power status," or with ensuring that nuclear deterrence will protect vital German interests rather than those that Americans determine to be vital, or, possibly, with the more sinister purposes of exercising nuclear threats and blackmail. But if it is doubtful that France's *force de frappe* can deter a nuclear superpower, it is just as doubtful that a German force could do so. Moreover, the creation of such a force would of necessity appear as an act of provocation to the Soviets as well as to other European powers, whose fear of German military prowess is understandable in light of recent history. In the East, in particular, such a move would strengthen the ties between the Soviet Union and countries that have only recently emerged from satellite status—a result that would counter Western attempts to foster their growing independence. By the same token, German renunciation of nuclear yearnings, possibly combined with the denuclearization of Central Europe, would not detract materially from German security. That security would still be a function of the mutual deterrence of the superpowers. By eliminating obstacles to arms control, such a renunciation might contribute greatly to the peace of the world.

Indeed, the fate of the world might be in balance over the question of nuclear proliferation. In 1966, it seemed that such proliferation, without which avoidance of nuclear war is utterly unlikely, could be prevented by international agreement only if the West was ready to forgo plans of "nuclear sharing," such as MLF. Such plans, at that time, were still considered vital by the United States to stave off more radical West German demands for nuclear arms of its own. These considerations, as recent opinion studies have revealed, have been based on entirely wrong assumptions: Germans, elite as well as masses, in their vast majority were revealed as opposed to national nuclear weapons and not seriously interested even in sharing in a supranational weapons system.[5] Those German leaders, therefore, who have come out for a supranational plan—none so far have officially come out for national weapons—are not supported by public demands. Whatever German interest there is thus, paradoxically, seems to have been the product of American apprehensions that such interest would "inevitably" develop in the future. It would be tragic indeed, if the peace of the world would be jeopardized by insistence on satisfaction of nonexistent desires.

A third approach that might lead to the easing of tension would be a peculiarly German contribution: taking over increased responsibilities to raise living standards and improve con-

[5] See the report by Karl W. Deutsch on "Integration and Arms Control in the European Political Environment," *APSR* 60 (2) (June 1966), pp. 354 ff., which sums up his findings as follows: "There is striking consensus in France and Germany on the desirability of arms control and disarmament on a more than local or regional scale, and including further direct agreements between the United States and the Soviet Union. There is particularly strong consensus on the desirability of halting the spread of nuclear weapons to nations which do not now possess them. . . . There is strong opposition in Germany to the acquisition of national nuclear weapons, and there is no strong positive desire for any German share in a nuclear weapons system through some multilateral arrangement, such as the MLF project. . . ." (364)

ditions in the underdeveloped world. So far, German contributions in this area, though not negligible, have not been commensurate with American efforts or with the much greater French efforts. It would seem especially fitting for Germans to take a leading position in this respect among the nations of the West. They would thus repudiate, by deeds rather than words, their recent shocking digression from Western humanitarian ideals. Moreover, their present prosperity would enable them to do so without endangering their own living standards. By a strange quirk of fate, Germans, having had to relinquish their colonies after World War I, are considered "noncolonialists" by Africans and others, so that their aid would raise less suspicion and involve fewer political complications than that of other Western powers. With the fulfillment of the chief welfare state aims in the "home countries," contributions to the underdeveloped world would seem in any event to become the new version of the welfare state idea, with the "external" proletariat taking over the position held in former times by the internal proletariat. Germans, who in the best periods of their past have often led the world in social consciousness and responsible welfare policy, might in this way yet atone for the afflictions caused in their worst period.

Every nation needs a sense of role fulfillment. Germans stand in particular need of it, for two reasons. The first is that their history never provided them with a consistent national goal. The second is that what they want above all, unifica-tion, is unobtainable, at least for the near future, and they know it. If they are not to fall prey to prolonged frustration and thus become a constant source of unrest for Europe and the world, they must be given alternate objectives to strengthen their self-confidence.

In this their plight is not unique. Britain and France during the postwar period had to go through the pangs of being reduced from first-rank "world powers" to lower-rank countries. Such nations may experience crisis and unrest—as France did in the late 1950's—before finding compensation in different role fulfillment. It has been de Gaulle's great achievement to have given Frenchmen substitute goals, such as building a modernized economy and society, that reconciled most of them to loss of an empire. True, there will always be some whose frustration lends itself to rightist radicalism—in Germany perhaps more so than elsewhere. This simply means that its present leaders must strain all the more to give to the majority worthwhile goals. We have mentioned one: contributing, through development aid, to the solution of the great world problem of the future—overcoming the gap between North and South, the affluent and the destitute. Another one lies in solving, in Germany, the vast environmental problems that technology poses to the developed countries—the problems of metropolitan agglomerations, of clean air and water, of conservation of resources, and of preservation of landscape and cultural heritage. In this manner the Germans might find a role for themselves and, at the same time, furnish a model for others.

Conclusion

Inspired, perhaps, by American Presidents and their perennial proclamations of "New Deals," "Great Societies," and the like, Ludwig Erhard as Chancellor set for Germans the national goal of establishing a "Formed Society" (*formierte Gesellschaft;* in English this phrase might be better rendered as "structured society"). One should, perhaps, be glad to see Germans aim at a "formed" rather than a "uniformed" society. Yet the desire is not as innocuous as it may sound. If anything specific is meant by this vaporous term (and there have been doubts about what Erhard actually meant by it), it must be a desire to achieve a society in which people do not form one colorless mass but a society in which they are clearly divided into groups with their own significant purpose and status. Now it is true—as an able young German sociologist, Ralf Dahrendorf, has pointed out—that in contrast to a past when Germans were controlled by one class- and purpose-conscious feudal elite, present West German elites have been less coherent, less purposeful, even less conscious of being at the top. And this, in view of the traditional German habit of looking toward *die da oben* for standards and guidance, has created problems. Especially since the demise of the father-figure who, for a decade and a half, gave them the assurance of being cared for, there has been abroad a feeling of directionlessness and rulelessness which, as we have seen, is particularly poignant in matters of national image and foreign-policy goals.

In terms of liberal-democratic prospects, such weakening of the elites—even though it may make some Germans feel uncomfortable—should not be considered as entirely unfortunate. The "structured society" that Erhard put up as a goal in fact has long existed in Germany, although in the undesirable form of the traditional division of Germans through their class system of education. And, since traditional authoritarian patterns of behavior are still extant—even hardened under Adenauer's long and paternalistic rule—somewhat less emphasis on structure and more on social mobility, on "circulation of the elites," would seem to be called for. Such an emphasis would benefit democratic strivings. It would reduce the hold of authoritarian executives and officials on weak or inefficient parliaments. It would eliminate the caste character of the civil service (which is still overwhelmingly upper class in origin, with 50 percent of *Beamte* coming from *Beamten* families!). It would reduce the strong bureaucratic tendencies in most organizations, including the major political parties. In short, it would alleviate the rigid class and status lines of German society. West German society might thus distinguish itself from the extremely "structured" society of the East, which, though it is no longer based on educational monopoly and economic privilege, is an utterly rigid society in the control of a new, coherent, and self-assured political elite.

The same transitional state prevails in another area, that of liberties, freedom, and tolerance. A poll taken recently in the traditionally liberal city of Hamburg revealed that only 50 percent of those polled would allow an avowed atheist the freedom of voicing his convictions, and only 23 percent would consider him qualified to teach in public schools. Only 29 percent would grant freedom of speech to anyone who accepted the Oder-Neisse line, and a scant 18 percent would consider him qualified for teaching. On the other hand, only one out of three was ready to denounce a neighbor suspected of communism. This latter finding probably reflects the lasting effect of German experience under the Nazi regime. The *Spiegel* case, or rather, the public reaction to it, also reveals an encouraging trend toward a sense of what true liberalism requires.

Over against this, however, we find among many Germans a decreasing interest in public issues. This trend toward depolitization and privatization may be wholesome, in view of previous doctrinal divisions. But it involves a waning of meaningful opposition and opposition parties. As a result, minorities are driven toward extrapolitical groups and devices. The prevailing pragmatism threatens the very lifeblood of democratic life—a lively and sustained concern with vital public issues.

But not everything in German social and political life and institutions has been negative. The foregoing chapters have outlined what amounts to a mixture of assets and liabilities. We have just mentioned the major liabilities. Among the assets we would list a capable, well-organized, and uncorrupt administration; a flourishing, diversified local administration with a tradition of self-government; a system of social security that by and large has prevented distress; and an educational system of high quality.

In addition, there is hope in the younger generation. Twenty years after the demise of Nazism, the heritage of the past still hangs heavily over the German people. Some of the older Germans must continue to bear responsibility for its abominations, and the fact that others, though they were not directly involved, still try to cover up the past, adds to the nation's burden. But it is encouraging to see young people question their elders severely, and it would be unfair to condemn them for the sins of their fathers. Many young Germans reveal attitudes that were uncommon in the German past, such as openness to new ideas and untried ways of life. They are pragmatic, and while this may lead some into egocentrism and materialism, it may render others readier to experiment with more democratic devices in public life. Thus they may give another chance to Germany's humanitarian, liberal, and democratic potentialities, which have so often been stifled in the past.

Present moderation and absence of radicalism

make it possible to imagine a situation in which the assets could be used to westernize German public life without sacrificing what is valuable and sometimes unique in the German tradition. Doctrinal splits might be moderated into useful debates between government and opposition; rule-mindedness and authority-consciousness might be tempered by reasonableness; and class and caste exclusiveness might yield to preference according to merit. Experience with postwar occupation policies and experiments has shown that such developments, especially democratization, must remain basically a German task; these processes do not lend themselves to imposition from abroad. But it also shows that other nations can *support* good indigenous trends and forces by positive encouragement and, by discouraging hostile trends, help to defeat them.

Foreigners (and frequently the Germans themselves) have had three dominant though widely contrasting impressions of Germany: the Germany that is *Gemütlichkeit,* a certain homely way of life, often appealing to Americans who do not have it but who would like to have time for it; second, the Germany that means know-how and efficiency, appealing or disturbing to Americans, depending on how such skills have been used; and third, the Germany that is music, poetry, philosophy, a mainspring of culture and thought.

But Germany is not only beer gardens and pigs' knuckles with sauerkraut; nor is it only the Volkswagen and I. G. Farben, the Prussian general staff and the SS; neither can it be reduced to Schiller and Beethoven, Kant and Luther. A nation is not summed up so easily. And this is good, for even if Germany is a land of contrast and contradiction, that is better than if it were a country where all contrast and dissension were buried under enforced silence or conformity. The latter fate has been imposed on the Eastern portion of the country; whether the rest of the country will be able to escape that fate without plunging the world into war will depend on factors not controlled by Germans alone. Should they succeed in developing peacefully an open, free, and self-governing society, however, they will have gone far toward proving that democracy has a chance even under the most adverse conditions.

·IV·

The Government
of the
Soviet Union

1. Soviet People and Policies

1. CONTINUITY AND CHANGE IN THE SOVIET UNION

By any standard, the Soviet Union has had a striking and paradoxical history during the past half century. Born out of revolution and civil war, its regime has demonstrated remarkable capacity to resist internal pressures and external aggression. Largely composed of peasants when the revolution occurred, it has become the world's second strongest industrial power, with agriculture its weakest point. Flaunting a banner of liberation from tsarist autocracy, the Soviet regime has used violence, cruelty, and oppression toward its own people during crucial but extended periods. The public adulation of Stalin, who dominated the country far longer than any other Communist leader, was rivaled only by the virulence of the attack on his character and actions after his death. Long isolated by external hostility and self-denial from contact with outside countries, the Soviet Union now welcomes exchanges within moderate limits and, particularly in comparison with the Chinese philosophy of Communist revolution, appears to have become a proponent of stability in a turbulent world.

A study of the development of the Soviet Union naturally seeks to find out whether there was any clear line of continuity or whether it was chiefly molded by circumstance. Was the massive concentration on heavy industry in the 1930's under the Five-Year Plans a response to Marxist-Leninist concepts or a preparation to meet the Nazi attack? Was the post-Stalin "thaw" the result of Khrushchev's leadership or a step toward some long-range goal? Is the current bureaucratic regime fulfilling purposes foreseen in theory, or is it responding to pat-

terns already established by a highly centralized and hierarchical structure? Or are these alternatives too sharply posed, whereas in practice doctrine and empiricism have gone hand in hand?

The Soviet Union and the World

The answers we reach to these questions will affect the perspective within which we interpret current Soviet statements and actions. They may help us foresee the likely course of development in the Soviet Union's internal and external policies. And those policies are, of course, of vital significance to the United States, Great Britain, France, and Germany, not only because the Soviet Union is one of the world's great powers but also because of its influence on and relations with that very considerable proportion of the world that has accepted, in one form or another, the Communist ideology.

Since all Communist countries, and particularly the Soviet Union, avow their allegiance to the ideas of Marx and Lenin, it is essential to begin our study of the people and policies of the Soviet Union with an analysis of those ideas. We must also consider the ideas of the former Soviet leaders, Stalin and Khrushchev, and of the present ones, Brezhnev and Kosygin. Much of the conflict within the Communist world focuses—in words, if not always in reality—around interpretations of the Communist ideology and the rival claims of leaders and countries that they are correctly interpreting and promoting its true meaning. Much of the anxiety outside the Communist world is caused by fear of the implications of ideology for action, or its use as a cloak for national expansionism or for the subversion of other countries. It is essential, therefore, to have some knowledge of the doctrine.

The Ideas of Karl Marx

Any brief description of a doctrine as comprehensive and complex as that of Karl Marx (1818–83) [1] inevitably suffers from oversimplification and incompleteness. It is possible, however, to sketch out several leading ideas.

Historical Materialism

The first of these is the theory of historical materialism. According to Marx's own description in the Introduction to the *Critique of Political Economy* (1859), "the mode of production of the material life determines the general character of the social, political, and spiritual processes of life. It is not the consciousness of men which determines their existence, but, on the contrary, their social existence determines their consciousness."

In simpler terms, this statement means that the most important determinant of the character of any society is the economic factor: the way in which men produce and distribute wealth. Its assumption is that the actions of individuals and groups can generally be accounted for by their material interests; and, more than this, that political and religious ideas, concepts of justice and morality, forms of government, the customs of society, even art and philosophy, are largely determined by the forces of production and by property relationships. Only by understanding the economic conditions essential to production can one understand the law, politics, art, religion, and philosophy of a society.

For some periods this theory is not particularly satisfactory, but in the nineteenth century it seemed to explain an obvious phenomenon. At that time the industrial revolution was transforming the way of life of all Western Europe; it would be hard to name any aspect of human existence or thought that was not affected by the change. The rise of an industrial middle class went hand in hand with the extension of the suffrage and the expansion of political democracy. The growth of the cities, the tremendous increase in productive power, and the shift from farm to factory meant that vast masses of people were leading lives utterly different from those of their parents and grandparents. With the increase in education needed for an industrialized society, the reading public grew and culture became "popularized," while the machine provided both new means of artistic creation and new ideas of the beautiful and efficient. Even religious attitudes underwent fundamental changes as the machine gave man greater control over his world and turned his mind from the supernatural.

The doctrine of historical materialism assumes not only that the "economic conditions essential to production" are the most important influence in determining the nature of society, but that these conditions can be known "with the exactitude of natural science." As new forms of production appear in response to man's efforts to satisfy his needs, they conflict with existing property relationships; the result is a social revolution that transforms the institutions of society. According to Marxist teaching, the transformation takes place in conformity with definite scientific principles, and thus can be predicted with precision. Friedrich Engels, Marx's great friend and coworker, expressed the belief of the orthodox Marxist when he declared: "Just as Darwin has discovered the law of evolution in organic nature, so Marx has discovered the evolutionary laws of human history."

The logical consequence of this doctrine, obviously, was the belief that no significant change could be made in the social or political order that was not based first of all upon a change in the economic structure of society and, specifically, upon a change in its property relations. Such economic changes, however, were not the result of conscious endeavor: they were the inevitable outgrowth of the conflict between new productive forces (such as those of the industrial revolution) and an earlier system of production relations.

[1] Although Marx, a brilliant scholar, was born in Germany, most of his adult life was spent abroad, first in Belgium and France and eventually, for the last thirty years, in England, where the consequences of the industrial revolution were more apparent than in any other country. The *Communist Manifesto*, which he and Friedrich Engels published in 1848, became the platform of the First International, of which Marx was a leader during the last two decades of his life (while he was writing his monumental book, *Capital*).

Surplus Value

Marx's theory of surplus value has been used to explain the existence of great differences in income and, in particular, the fact that those who work hardest often receive the smallest incomes and that others who work not at all receive very large ones. This theory depended on several other theories popular among economists in the early nineteenth century. One of these, the *labor theory of value,* taught that the value of any commodity for which there is a demand depends on the amount of labor required to produce it. Those things that are difficult to procure or manufacture are expensive; those that can be acquired without work are cheap or valueless. But although value is determined by the amount of labor, those who labor do not necessarily receive payment equal to the value of their labor. On the contrary, the capitalists and the landlords (the *bourgeoisie*) who employ workers in their factories and on their farms pay them wages far lower than the value of their work and keep the surplus value for themselves. According to an *iron law of wages,* propertyless workers (the *proletariat*) are paid only the minimum amount of money needed to keep body and soul together. As Marx stated the doctrine, "The average price of wage labor is the minimum wage, that is, that quantum of the means of subsistence which is absolutely requisite to keep the laborer in bare existence as a laborer."

The industrialists are in a position to impose such conditions upon the workers because they own the instruments of production. The propertyless workers must have employment or they will starve. Yet there are more workers than there are jobs available (technological advances and the dispossession of many farmers by large landowners in England, where Marx did most of his writing, had created a large "reserve army" of unemployed who were competing with one another for jobs). Thus the man who wins a job under such circumstances is the man who underbids his competitors—that is, who is willing to work at the lowest wage needed to sustain life. As a result, the bourgeoisie accumulate more and more wealth (the *concentration of wealth*), while the proletariat become increasingly wretched (the *growing misery of the masses*).

Such developments, Marx taught, lead inevitably to a series of ever more disastrous economic crises. Since the workers with their miserable wages cannot buy the products they themselves produce, there are "epidemics of overproduction." The owners of the means of production must then acquire, through the use of economic or military force (*imperialism*), foreign markets in which to sell their goods. In addition, the less efficient or powerful employers are driven out of business by their competitors and themselves sink down into the proletariat. In a sense, capitalism destroys itself, for fewer and fewer people own private property, and more and more people become as destitute of private property as though they already lived in a socialist society. Moreover, in Marx's words, "the proletariat not only increases in number; it becomes concentrated in greater masses, its strength grows and it feels that strength more." Ultimately the proletariat uses this strength to overthrow the bourgeoisie, to "expropriate the expropriators," and to destroy the existing social system, for the injustices of surplus value can be destroyed only by eliminating private property in the instruments of production.

Class War

All history, according to Marx, is the history of warfare between classes, and it is the class struggle that is the bearer of change. Although in earlier times there were many different classes, in modern times the pattern has become simpler. In advanced countries, the slave and the serf have disappeared, and the nobility and the small property owner have vanished or lost their power. Increasingly there are only two classes of any significance, the bourgeoisie and the proletariat. Warfare between them is inevitable; the triumph of the proletariat is certain. It is the task of the Communists, who are "the most advanced and resolute section of the working-class parties in every country" and who have "over the proletariat the advantage of clearly understanding the line of march"—that is, the inevitable workings of the process of historical materialism—to educate, guide, and lead the proletariat and to prepare it for the violent seizure of political power. The state, according to Marx, is always "the organized power of one class for oppressing another," and the proletariat must seize control of the state in order to destroy the opposing class. "The Communists disdain," wrote Marx and Engels in the closing lines of the *Communist Manifesto,* "to conceal their views and aims. They openly declare that their ends can be attained only by the forcible overthrow of all existing social conditions. Let the ruling classes tremble at a Communist revolution. The proletarians have nothing to lose but their chains. They have a world to win."

The Tactics of Revolution

Marx and Engels were concerned not only to interpret the world around them but to change it. Their economic and social analysis was directed primarily toward determining when the final revolutionary assault could be made. Thus their "scientific" approach to social development was matched by a sternly realistic evaluation of strategy in relation to immediate circumstances. "The world commercial crisis of 1847 was the real cause of the February and March revolutions," wrote Engels. "A new revolution is possible only as a consequence of a new crisis." Thus economic crisis, revolution, and war were seen as essentially interrelated, while apt timing was seen as the major key to successful action. Moreover, in their view, developments in any single state were indissolubly interconnected with world politics, and military tactics thus became part of revolutionary strategy. Aware that the revolutions of 1848 had been defeated through armies recruited from the peasants, Marx and Engels saw the need to prevent that group from thwarting social revolution, particularly if there were to be a revolution in Russia, a possibility to which Marx gave increasing attention in his later years. The nation in arms through compulsory military service "surpasses general franchise as a democratic agency," declared Engels in 1891. "By 1900 the army, once the most Prussian, the most reactionary element of the country, will be socialist in its majority as inescapably as fate." In the short run, this statement underestimated the power of the army to mold its members rather than be molded by them; in the days of the Soviet Civil War, however, it seemed prophetic.

The Withering Away of the State

Marx was less explicit about what would follow the triumph of the revolution. At first, the Communist society would bear "in every respect, economic, moral and intellectual," the marks of the capitalist society from whose womb it had issued. Each individual producer would be paid in proportion to the amount of work he did. Only in a higher phase of Communist society —"after labor has become not only a means of life but also the primary necessity of life," and when the forces of production had increased and there was universal abundance—would the final Communist ideal be achieved: "From each according to his abilities, to each according to his needs."

During the early postrevolutionary period, the *dictatorship of the proletariat,* the power of the state would be used to destroy the bourgeoisie. The state, however, is useful only as an instrument for controlling other classes, and once the bourgeoisie had been destroyed there would be a period of transition. As the task of liquidating the bourgeoisie proceeded, the "government over persons" would be progressively replaced by the "administration of things," and the state as an instrument of coercion would "wither away." In the new society all would share in the products of the toil of all and there would be plenty and prosperity for everyone.

The Revisionists

In the late nineteenth and early twentieth centuries, many of Marx's contemporaries or followers suggested modifications in his doctrine. Certain of his predictions had not come true: the disastrous economic crisis he had foretold did not occur; the middle class, far from disappearing into the proletariat, became increasingly strong; and the workers, by using their new power to vote (the suffrage had been severely restricted when Marx first wrote) and their power to organize in unions and cooperatives, had greatly improved their bargaining position and their material prosperity. In many countries of Western Europe, members of other classes had helped in the enactment of social legislation: protection of women and children in industry, compensation for accidents, protection against dangerous machinery and unhealthful working conditions, limitations on minimum wages and maximum hours of work, and insurance against illness, unemployment, and old age. Marx himself had suggested that in advanced democratic countries, such as England, the United States, and Holland, the transitions to a socialist society might come peacefully. Socialist party leaders, such as Edward Bernstein, were deeply interested in winning higher wages and better working conditions. Increasingly, their real aim was to win a majority of the seats in Parliament and to introduce socialism through peaceful legislation rather than to prepare for revolution.[2]

The Ideas of Lenin

It was against this moderate or evolutionary tendency in socialist thought that Lenin revolted. He had been born in Russia in 1870 and belonged, somewhat paradoxically, to an intellectual middle-class family. His father was a civil servant, an inspector of primary schools, while his mother belonged to the lesser gentry. His older brother, whom Lenin adored, took part in a plot to assassinate the Tsar and was himself executed in 1887. In part from this experience (in part from his reaction to the failure of the moderates), Lenin could draw the practical lesson that a successful revolutionary movement must be based not on individual acts of

[2] The words *socialism* and *communism* are subject to some terminological confusion. At the time that Marx and Engels published the *Communist Manifesto* (1848), there were many different forms and prophets of socialism, and the word *communist* was used to distinguish Marxist socialists from others. Later in the nineteenth century, Marxism came to be the predominant form of socialist thought and, generally speaking, to be a socialist was to be a Marxist. The word *communist* returned to general use with the revolution in Russia. Up to that time the more radical wing of Russian Socialists had used the name Bolsheviks (derived from the Russian word for majority) in contrast to the more moderate Mensheviks (minority). Lenin, however, was eager to have a name more expressive of the doctrinal content of Bolshevik beliefs, and in 1918 the party officially adopted the name *Communist*. Lenin insisted that those parties in any country throughout the world that affiliated with the Russian Communists in the Third International must also adopt the name *Communist*.

In the Soviet Union the words are also used to mark the distinction between the first stage of communism (which is called *socialism*) and the second and higher stage (which is called *communism*).

Thus the words are used in a double sense: to mark a distinction between political parties, and to mark a distinction between different stages in the development of a Communist society.

terrorism but on the combined and disciplined efforts of an elite that should dominate and direct the masses. He became active in the Marxist movement in Russia, suffering both imprisonment and exile to Siberia; but from 1900 to 1917 he spent most of his life abroad, devoting himself to the building of a revolutionary movement.

The Party: The Instrument of Revolution

The restoration of violent revolution to a central place in Marxism, his grasp of the need for highly disciplined organization, and his ability to transmit his own enthusiasm for single-purpose action are at the heart of Lenin's work. He bitterly attacked those Marxists and Socialists who were not revolutionary. The Socialist periodical *Iskra* (the Spark), which was published by Russians in exile beginning in 1900 and of which Lenin was an editor, provided a vehicle for his ideas. Over and over again he insisted that the impetus for revolution must come, not from a mass organization that inevitably would include the lukewarm and waste its time debating, voting, and compromising, but from a small organization of professional revolutionaries, characterized by absolute obedience and relentless determination. Ties of friendship and individual rights must be sacrificed, he argued, if the success of revolutionary action were at stake.

Lenin foresaw that the masses would not instinctively follow the lead of the Bolsheviks. On the contrary, he declared, "The history of all countries shows that the working class, exclusively by its own efforts, is able to develop only trade union consciousness." Thus "our task . . . is . . . to *divert* the labor movement from its spontaneous, trade unionist striving to go under the wing of the bourgeoisie, and to bring it under the wing of revolutionary Social-Democracy."

Ripeness for Revolution

But if violent revolution was Lenin's aim, for what kind of revolution was Russia ripe? Orthodox Marxists believed that there could be proletarian revolutions only in highly industrialized countries where the majority of the people belonged to a class-conscious working class and where a bourgeois revolution (such as the

French Revolution) had already taken place. The evolutionary-minded Mensheviks preached, therefore, that the first step toward ultimate socialism was to aid liberal bourgeois forces in their opposition to autocracy. Trotsky, the most brilliant of the revolutionaries and originally a Menshevik, felt, in contrast, that the Russian middle class was too weak to carry through the cultural and political tasks that the bourgeoisie performed in Western Europe; thus he insisted that the bourgeois revolution in Russia could be made only by the proletariat and that there could be a direct transition to socialism and the proletariat dictatorship. Lenin accepted this view in 1917 and added the notion of "uninterrupted revolution" (what Trotsky called "permanent revolution"), the idea that once the proletariat seized power, it must use it to keep the revolution continuously in action until socialism had been firmly established both at home and abroad.

The Alliance of Proletariat and Peasants

Lenin was convinced that the proletariat would have to carry the burden of the bourgeois revolution in Russia. He formulated the still more striking and significant notion that the numerically weak proletariat must be originally allied with the peasants to provide the necessary mass base for action. The first step, he declared, was to establish "the revolutionary-democratic dictatorship of the proletariat and the peasantry" which could then carry through "the democratic revolution." Immediately thereafter, the proletariat would ally itself, in his view, with the rural poor and undertake the socialist revolution. Thus the small Russian industrial proletariat, led by the highly disciplined elite party, would be the driving force in both revolutions and would then continue to impose its will on the great majority of the population. The concept was strategically brilliant and, like that of the party, thoroughly Russian.

Imperialism

Most socialists continued to believe, however, that the proletarian revolution would take place first in a highly industrialized country; Lenin himself had declared in 1905 that "the *European-Socialist* proletariat" would have to come to the support of a revolution in Russia if socialism were to triumph. World War I seemed to offer the right opportunity. Bitterly disappointed when he found that far from uniting in proletarian comradeship, European socialists supported their national leaders at the outbreak of what was dubbed a capitalist war, Lenin reexamined the state of world politics in his *Imperialism, the Highest Stage of Capitalism.* In this book he argued that the concentration of production and capital had brought industrialized countries into the stage of monopoly capitalism. This stage was characterized by larger and larger monopolistic units within these countries, by the increasing control of the banks, and by the export of capital and the development of colonial and quasi-colonial empires, which served as places for profitable investment, as sources of raw materials, and as outlets for goods. This development inevitably led to rivalries, he declared, out of which wars were bound to grow. At the same time, this "internationalizing" of capitalism made it vulnerable to attack anywhere, and Russia was "its weakest link." The proletariat, urged Lenin, should do its best to "turn the imperialist war into a civil war." In 1917, events in Russia seemed a response to his challenge.

"The State and Revolution"

During the summer of that year while the Bolsheviks were preparing for the seizure of power, which actually took place in November (or, according to the old Russian calendar, October), Lenin found time to develop his ideas on the nature of the revolution and of the society that would succeed it, in an unfinished book, *The State and Revolution.* Here he challenged those moderate and reformist Socialists who, like the members of the British Labor party, believed that democratic states could introduce socialism peacefully and gradually. At the same time, he contradicted Marx on the possibility that England could make the transition without violence. Progress, he wrote, "does not march along a simple, smooth, and direct path to 'greater and greater democracy.' . . . No, progressive development—that is, towards Communism—marches through the dictatorship of the proletariat . . . ." Parliaments provided no real path to power. "The actual work of the

State is done behind the scenes and is carried out by the departments, the chancelleries and the staffs. Parliament itself is given up to talk for the special purpose of fooling the 'common people.'" Only by forcefully seizing control of the instruments of state power—the bureaucracy (the civil service), the army, and the police force—could a revolution triumph.

Moreover, once these instruments were captured, the proletariat itself must use them to destroy the former ruling classes. The "state" would still exist as an instrument of oppression, but now the proletariat would use it to suppress the capitalist class. The dictatorship of the proletariat, Lenin wrote,

> will produce a series of restrictions of liberty in the case of oppressors, exploiters, and capitalists. We must crush them in order to free humanity from wage-slavery: and resistance must be broken by force. It is clear that where there is suppression there must also be violence, and there cannot be liberty or democracy . . . . The proletariat needs the State, the centralized organization of force and violence, both for the purpose of crushing the resistance of the exploiters and for the purpose of guiding the great mass of the population—the peasantry, the lower middle class, the semi-proletariat—in the work of economic Socialist reconstruction.

As these purposes were achieved, however, the coercive apparatus of the state would become less and less necessary and could progressively wither away.

Communism: The First Stage

Lenin distinguished between two stages in the withering away of the state. During the first period, known as *socialism,* there are still certain resemblances to bourgeois society. The state as an apparatus of suppression continues to exist, but with the important qualification that "the organ of suppression is now the majority of the population, and not a minority, as was always the case under slavery, serfdom and wage-labor." It is no longer necessary to depend upon armies and the police for the job of suppressing, since "the majority of the nation *itself* suppresses its oppressors" and "in this sense the State begins to disappear." "The specific 'bossing' methods of the State," Lenin wrote, "can and must begin

to be replaced—immediately, within twenty-four hours—by the simple functions of managers and clerks—functions which are now already quite within the capacity of the average townsman and can well be performed for a working man's wage." Similarly, the old armed forces and the police will be supplanted by the armed masses of the working class, "a universal participation of the people in a militia."

During this first stage all the instruments of production will be socialized; the whole of society will become one great office and one great workshop. However, there will still be inequalities in income. Each man will be paid in accordance with the amount of work he does; certificates will be issued showing the amount of remuneration to which he is entitled. "The first phase of Communism," Lenin wrote, "still cannot produce justice and equality; differences, and unjust differences, in wealth will still exist, but the *exploitation* of one man by many will have become impossible, because it will be impossible to seize as private property the *means of production,* the factories, machines, land, and so on." It will even be necessary to retain a certain amount of bourgeois law, and there will continue to be "the *strictest* control, *by society and by the state,* of the quantity of labor and the quantity of consumption." But this control will be carried out, not by a government of bureaucrats, but by a "government of the armed workers."

Control over consumption is particularly important, because much of what is produced would have to be used, not for the immediate gratification of human wants, but for the expansion of the industrial plant. For this reason a reserve fund would have to be deducted from the quantity otherwise available for consumption.

Communism: The Second Stage

The second stage in the withering away of the coercive aspect of the state is a far freer one. It begins when socialism has been achieved, that is, when the hostile classes have been completely destroyed and when productive property has been completely socialized. As this stage advances it will be accompanied by a prosperity so great that it will no longer be necessary to calculate consumption carefully and to reward each person in proportion to his work. Instead there will be more than enough to reward everyone, not in accordance with his work (as under socialism) but in accordance with his needs.

In Lenin's words: " 'The narrow horizon of bourgeois law,' which compels one to calculate, with the pitilessness of a Shylock, whether one has not worked half an hour more than another, whether one is not getting less pay than another—this narrow horizon will then be left behind." Even the police force will no longer be necessary, for most crimes are the product of want, and once economic misery has been eliminated, the chief motive for crime will vanish with it. Individual persons may commit excesses, but the "armed nation" will handle such instances spontaneously, just as men separate fighters or protect women from insult without calling the police. "When people have become so accustomed to observing the fundamental rules of social life and when their labor is so productive that they will voluntarily work *according to their ability*," the state can wither away completely. Thus, where Marx was never very precise about the nature of the society that would be established by the revolution, Lenin set up a series of fairly specific standards and objectives by which the course and progress of the revolution might be judged.

Although the proletarian revolution took place almost exactly according to Lenin's specifications, he had to make many adjustments in practice thereafter that were not in accordance with what he had written in his book. In particular, he had to give up his idea that the state could be run by part-time citizens. In fact, the first years of Communist power were marked by warfare (both foreign and civil) and by the greatest destruction. But, as we shall see, Lenin showed striking ability in handling urgent practical problems, such as the role of the peasants in the new state, the role of the soviets, and the nationality problem. Thus he proved himself as significant a revolutionary strategist as a theorist. Even his New Economic Policy, which seemed to mark a general retreat from the Communist goal, proved to be an essential stage in dealing with Russia's industrial backwardness. Thus before Lenin died in 1924, he had laid practical as well as theoretical foundations for the Communist state in many spheres.

Lenin's Successor: Stalin

After the death of Lenin there was a struggle among his disciples for the honor of succeeding him as the living prophet of communism. Within a comparatively short time, however, it became clear that victory would rest ultimately with Joseph Stalin, the Secretary-General of the Communist party of the Soviet Union and a man who (although he had written on the problem of nationalities) was not so much a political theorist as an administrator and a man of action. His task was to determine the practical policies to be followed in a country where Communists already held power.

The two theories and, indeed, the practical policies most closely associated with Stalin grew out of the Soviet Union's position before World War II as the only Communist state in a capitalist world. Lenin himself had expected the revolution to be world-wide and had assumed that the socialist society would be achieved on an international scale. When it became apparent, however, that other countries, far from following the Russian example, remained bitterly opposed to its regime, Stalin maintained that it would be possible to build "socialism in one country." By imposing grinding sacrifices, Stalin forced a concentration on heavy industry that kept living standards low but immensely strengthened the Soviet economy, as was proved by its ability to withstand the Nazi onslaught. At the same time, Stalin justified strengthening the coercive aspects of the state—the army and the police force—and crushing internal opposition through instruments of violence—the secret police and methods of terror—by the doctrine of "capitalist encirclement," the view that outside powers not only threatened to attack the Soviet Union but fomented subversion within it.

To many old-line Bolsheviks, Stalin's abandonment of internationalism, his view that conditions had to get worse before they got better, and his fostering of personal adulation ran counter to what they had expected and fought for. So did his sacrifice of consumption goods to the needs of heavy industry, the growth of widely differing pay levels, social discrimination and stratification, authoritarianism, and the use of terror. Thus some of his most trenchant critics both inside and outside the country were men and women who felt deeply committed to the doctrines of Marxism-Leninism. Officially, however, the accepted doctrine of the period became Marxism-Leninism-Stalinism.

Stalin's unprecedented power rested on the high degree of centralization he imposed on the bureaucratic structure; on his own skill in balancing power groups within each organ—the secret police, Politburo, party, administration, and army—and in keeping them from coalescing against him; and on the obviousness of national danger from Nazi aggression and the desperateness of the struggle against it. Yet, paradoxically, the very success of the wartime military effort, the extensiveness of postwar reconstruction, and the necessary revival of the integrative functions of the party weakened Stalin's personal hold on Soviet institutions and life. His death in 1953 ended a dismal series of plots by which he had tried to recover his former authority.

Stalin's Successor: Khrushchev

Stalin's death opened a struggle for succession (as had Lenin's in an earlier period). Yet for all the shifts in power before Nikita Khrushchev emerged by 1957 as the undisputed leader (which he was to remain until his abrupt ouster from power in 1964), the transition was far smoother than after Lenin's death. Khrushchev acceded to power ostensibly to safeguard Stalin's emphasis on heavy industry and by exalting the power of the party *apparat*. To a major degree he retained these two emphases, promoting the primacy of the party over the state and economic bureaucracies, and emphasizing heavy industry and an extensive and imaginative though ultimately unsuccessful agricultural policy. What this period most strikingly evidenced, however, was a new style of leadership and new ways of attempting to secure response to the regime's purposes.

Immediately after Stalin's death, the dominance of the secret police was broken, and terror was eliminated. Law was gradually liberalized, and a greater emphasis was placed on "socialist legality." Moreover, in a general internal "thaw," Khrushchev sought to substitute "social organization" and social pressures for coercive state measures. Externally, apart from certain crises,

in particular those over Berlin and Cuba, a new moderation was evident, based on "peaceful coexistence" and a new concern for winning the support of "uncommitted" Asia and Africa, largely through economic aid.

The most startling manifestation of a new line after Stalin's death was Khrushchev's famous "secret" speech at the Twentieth Party Congress, February 1956. The two particular targets in his attack on Stalin and Stalinism were the "cult of the individual" and arbitrariness toward party organs and high party functionaries. By vilifying Stalin and blaming him for all the evils of the past, the new leaders sought to legitimize their own authority and to clear the way for new approaches.

Khrushchev's attack on the terrorist aspects of Stalin's rule stimulated a wave of revisionist comment that, particularly because it was phrased in Marxist terminology about "workers' control" and "the withering away of the state," forced the new Soviet leaders to formulate *their* view of the future in concrete terms. Not surprisingly, this future resembled a bureaucrat's dream. Communism will not follow the "vulgar" expectation of being "a formless, unorganized and anarchic mass of people," asserted Khrushchev firmly at the Extraordinary Twenty-First Party Congress in January 1959. "No, it will be a highly organized and arranged cooperation of workers. In order to direct machines, everybody will have to fulfill his functions as a laborer and his social duties at a determined time and in an established order." "Spontaneity is the deadliest enemy of all," Khrushchev told a meeting of the Party Central Committee in 1958. He pictured to *Pravda* (November 18, 1959) the Spartan bliss of Soviet life: "Just like bees toiling from dawn to dusk, creating a new building and filling it with honey, so our people fulfill their obligations and functions in society."

Khrushchev's major ideological innovation dealt with the enticing prospect that the coercive aspects of the state would wither away. He produced a deceptively simple conception that substituted society for the state. He condemned Stalin's justification of the continued duration and indeed expansion of state forms of coercion because of internal enemies (a doctrine somewhat rehabilitated at the time of the Hungarian uprising in the fall of 1956 and still available for use if needed) and acknowledged that "capitalist encirclement" no longer existed (although his references to "hostile blocs" implied that it did). He declared that "when the conditions for the transition to Communism have been created in our country, many administrative organs of the state will gradually die away." At the same time he affirmed that "the party has stronger foundations than the state organs. . . . Its development was called for by circumstances stemming from the political concepts of people . . . from principles of a moral nature. And mankind will always need moral factors." Subsequently methods of persuasion under communism were said to become "the sole regulator of relations among people."

By emphasizing *social organization*—a terminology that might be translated into *party* —the Soviet regime appeared to be reducing the dualism of party-state control; and by emphasizing persuasion rather than force, it was attempting to close the gap between the public and private spheres of life. The objective was to secure the results demanded by the regime through reawakening the early fervor of Leninist days. Billed as "totalitarianism without coercion" it appears more likely to have been—and to remain—totalitarianism through social pressures with the threat of coercion in the background to ensure the acceptance of persuasion.

In the realm of foreign policy, Khrushchev is most often associated with the doctrine of "peaceful coexistence" (somewhat tarnished at the time of the Cuban crisis). While agreeing that Lenin's theory of imperialism was correct for the earlier period in which Lenin wrote, he maintained that it was no longer true that wars are "fatally inevitable." Khrushchev also suggested that Communist parties might attain power in certain capitalist states in conjunction with the peasantry, intelligentsia, and "patriotic" forces and through parliamentary means.

The basic idea of peaceful coexistence was not, in fact, new. Lenin called it "parallel existence" and believed it essential for the survival of the Soviet state. Triumphing over the Trotskyite plea for a revolutionary strategy, Stalin told the Fifteenth Congress in December 1927 that "our relations with the capitalist countries are based on the assumption that the coexistence of two opposite systems is possible. Practice has fully confirmed this." What was distinctive about Khrushchev was that he used the doctrine to open the iron curtain, thus encouraging tourism, cultural exchanges, and trade expansion.

Khrushchev also turned "neutralism" into a doctrine of positive advantage to the Soviet Union. In replacing the former concept of "He who is not with me is against me" by the open-ended "He who is not against me shall be counted for me," Khrushchev created a much more complex and useful (to the Soviet Union) picture of the world. In this scheme of things, numerous states—from Sweden to Yugoslavia, through the Middle East and Africa to India and Indonesia—which were not specifically aligned with the West were included in what was called "the camp of peace." Inside this camp of peace was the "anti-imperialist camp" and still further inside was—and is—the "socialist camp" of Eastern European satellites. Regarding Stalin's doctrine of capitalist encirclement, Khrushchev once commented with perception, "At present it is not known who encircles whom." Thus coexistence became an instrument of foreign policy, since the possibility always exists of strengthening Soviet influence in the circles of "camps" toward which its diplomacy is directed.

Despite Khrushchev's emphasis on party primacy, his own reorganization of the party in November 1962 into two separate hierarchies— one industrial and the other rural—divided it institutionally and impaired its unity. As an unexpected consequence, the state bureaucracy reassumed some of its former integrative functions, thereby, as Zbigniew Brzezinski points out, restoring much of the institutional balance existing under Stalin but minus the balancer. Khrushchev, originally successful because he satisfied the dominant interests of the elite—the emphasis on the party, elimination of terror, and support of heavy industry but not of the economic bureaucracy—could not keep up with changing modes. Having neither ideological sophistication, personal charisma, nor great technical capacity, he tried to make up for them with crash programs, whirlwind tours, uninhibited outbursts, and calls for fresh intensity of effort. By replacing those who had previously been in office with a younger—and soberer—group of bureaucrats to whom, as it turned out, flamboyance was distasteful and orderliness essential, Khrushchev initially strengthened but ultimately destroyed his own position. By the time he himself had been replaced by this new generation of leaders, Khrushchev had become, to use Brzezinski's words, "an anachronism in the new political context he himself had helped to create."[3]

Khrushchev's Successors

Whether or not Brezhnev and Kosygin, who took over from Khrushchev, remain those on whom publicity centers, it appears that a new type of political leader is now in power in the Soviet Union. No longer are political leaders drawn from the generation that knew the revolution at first hand. Their experience is rather of the turmoil of the purges and of World War II. Thus their objective is stability; they are used to working together; and the smooth functioning of their complicated bureaucratic structure is more important than originality, personal glory, or ideological fervor.

Whether the new figures, with their penchant for what is called "collectivity of leadership," will carve a distinctive way for the Soviet Union is still uncertain. So is the question of whether some kind of alternation in office might become possible. For the first time, the dominant figure in the Soviet Union, the First Secretary, has been ousted from office by his associates. But the objective of replacing Khrushchev was not to assume his personal power and prestige but to secure greater depersonalization and efficiency.

Khrushchev had removed Stalin's supporters; with the turn of the wheel some of those he demoted were restored to authority. Others whom he favored have lost their posts. But this far less drastic type of purge, compared to those of the thirties, leaves open some chance that those currently in disfavor might have their day again.

Such possibilities of alternation could hardly spell stability under present circumstances.

Rather, they might lead to a "catch-as-catch-can." To avoid more serious and frequent upheavals, the Soviet Union may well have to institutionalize the means of integrating group interests and arbitrating group disputes. If it does not do so, it might well be threatened with degeneration or even a return to the use of terror. Yet before one considers such alternatives further, it is important to see in more detail what has already been accomplished by the Soviet state, the methods by which it has been done, and the setting within which it has been carried out.

2. THE LAND AND THE PEOPLE

The Land and Resources

The country in which the most crucial of Communist experiments is taking place is the largest in the world. Its population of 225 million is spread over an area of eight and one-half million square miles (the area of the United States is a little more than three million square miles)—one-sixth of the earth's land surface. From the Carpathian Mountains and the Baltic Sea on the western boundary to the Pacific Ocean on the eastern, the distance is as great as that from San Francisco to London. It is an area that includes both Arctic ice and the deserts of central Asia.

The natural resources of the Soviet Union are extremely rich and diversified. Official publications (which, in certain instances, represent rather optimistic estimates) claim for the Soviet Union first place in resources of iron ore, oil, manganese, water power, and timber; and second place in coal, lead, nickel, and zinc. Thus, in contrast to Great Britain, the Soviet Union's great problem has not been to obtain raw materials but to use the resources it already has.

One of the most startling developments of modern times has been the transformation of the Soviet Union from a relatively backward, predominantly agricultural country into the second most powerful industrial state in the world. Moreover, although the United States still outstrips it both in production of raw materials and of goods, the rate of expansion in heavy in-

[3] Z. Brzezinski, "The Soviet Political System: Transformation or Degeneration," *Problems of Communism* (January–February, 1966), p. 4.

dustry in the Soviet Union in recent years has been two to three times that of the United States.

Only by the most colossal sacrifices was the Soviet Union able to maintain this industrial pace. The Five-Year (once Seven-Year) Plans, which began in 1928, deliberately diverted raw materials from consumer goods to the production of heavy industry. Careful statistical calculations prove that in terms of food and other goods available in 1928, Russian workers suffered a 37 percent cut in real wages between 1928 and 1952. In a very real sense, therefore, the vast industrial revolution of the Soviet Union was financed out of the standard of living of its people. Moreover, since 1928 the Russian people have undergone some of the greatest mass migrations of history. These resulted not only from the impact of Nazi forces in World War II but, long before that, from the forcible collectivization of agriculture and the absorption of former peasants into the cities and factories. Beyond this have been the labor discipline used to keep workers at their jobs, the often inhuman pressure to increase output, the concentration on technical education to produce the skills needed for the industrial machine, and the ever increasing influence of the supervising officials and technocrats on whom the vast nation-wide development depends.

Geography and History

Although it is common to speak of European and Asiatic Russia, the country is, in fact, a geographic unit. The Ural Mountains, which are often called the boundary between the two continents, are no more of a division than are the Rockies in the United States. A central theme of Russian, as of American, history is the movement of population to the frontier (in Russia, to the north and east), and the progressive, if somewhat sporadic, expansion of Russian power over lands sparsely populated by backward peoples. To the west, however, Russia has bordered upon nations both populous and highly civilized; and on this frontier, where there is a lack of natural boundaries and natural defenses, there has been in recent centuries constant fear that invaders would follow in the path of Charles XII of Sweden, of Napoleon, and of Hitler. Whereas the United States has

been protected by the Atlantic and Pacific, Great Britain by the Channel, and France (except for the northeast frontier) by mountains and the sea, the western boundaries of the Soviet Union are a great plain, without any physical obstacle to stand as a bulwark against the rest of Europe. The result has been insecurity and suspicion that can only be compared to the French preoccupation with the securing of the northeastern boundary.

If the Soviet Union is physically a unit, its tremendous size has created serious problems in communications. The rivers of European Russia are an important means of transportation, but the links between European Russia and the Pacific depend largely upon man-made facilities. Like the United States and in contrast to Great Britain, the Soviet Union ,has had to develop land communications in order to make full use of the resources of its great empire. The sea is of little assistance. Although the country has one of the longest coastlines in the world (two-thirds of its boundaries are formed by the sea), many of the ports are ice-bound most or all of the year. Moreover, in the case of the Baltic and the Black Sea ports, other powers dominate the outlets to the great oceans of the world. One of the persistent elements in Russian history has been the effort to find free access to the sea. It is characteristic that Russia, under the Communists as under the Tsars, has constantly striven for control of the Baltic Sea and of the straits that lead from the Black Sea.

Although there are no outstanding physical barriers in the Soviet Union, there are fairly clear divisions into four great regions stretching from west to east: the frozen tundra of the north, the forest area immediately to the south (ranging from coniferous forests in the northern parts to a zone of mixed forests in the southern); the great steppe (or plain); and finally the semi-desert and desert regions of the south.

European Russia is a land of great waterways. It was on the famous "water road" of the Dnieper, the Neva, and the Dvina, which stretched from the Black Sea to the Baltic, that the first important Russian towns, Kiev, Smolensk, and Novgorod, grew up in the ninth and tenth centuries. It was not these towns, however, that formed the core of modern Rus-

NORWAY

SWEDEN

FINLAND

A R C T I C

FRANZ JOSEPH LAND

FED. REP. OF GERM.

GERM. DEM. REP.
Berlin

BALTIC

SEA

BARENTS

SEA

NOVAYA ZEMLYA

POLAND
Warsaw

LITHUANIAN S.S.R.
Vilna

Riga
LATVIAN S.S.R.

ESTONIAN S.S.R.
Tallinn

KARELO-FINNISH A.S.S.R.

Leningrad
Petrozavodsk

Archangel

NENETS N.A.

BYELORUSSIAN
S.S.R.
Minsk

Lvov

UKRAINIAN

MOLDAV. S.S.R.

S. S. R.

Kiev

Odessa

Kharkov

CRIMEA

Simferopol

Smolensk

Kalinin

Moscow

RUSSIAN

Gorky   Kirov

MORDOVIAN A.S.S.R.

MARI A.S.S.R.

CHUVASH A.S.S.R.

Kazan

UDMURT A.S.S.R.

SOCIALIST

KOMI
A.S.S.R.

Vorkuta

KOMI-PERMIAK N.A.

Perm

KHANTI-MANSI

N.A.

YAMALO

NENETS

FEDER-

N.A.

Igarka

R. Yenisei

BLACK

SEA

Rostov

R. Volga

TATAR A.S.S.R.

Kuybyshev

Ufa

BASHKIR A.S.S.R.

Oren-burg

Sverdlovsk

Volgograd

Magnitogorsk

TIUMEN

NOVOSIBIRSK

R. Irtysh

R. Ob

TURKEY

GEORGIAN S.S.R.

DAGESTAN A.S.S.R.

Astrakhan

CASPIAN

Omsk

Tomsk

ARMENIAN S.S.R.
Erivan

Tiflis

AZER-BAIJAN S.S.R.

NAKHI-CHEVAN A.S.S.R.

Baku

SEA

K A Z A K H

*Aral
Sea*

S. S. R.

Karaganda

Novosibersk

ALTAI

Novokuznetsk

Barnaul

OIROT

I R A N

Krasnovodsk

Ashkhabad

TURKMEN S.S.R.

UZBEK S.S.R.

*Lake
Balkhash*

Alma-Ata

Tashkent   Frunze

KIRGHIZ S.S.R.

R. Ili

Donetsk

TADZHIK S.S.R.

AFGHANISTAN

		UNION REPUBLICS OTHER THAN RSFSR
		AUTONOMOUS REPUBLICS WITHIN RSFSR
		NATIONAL AREAS

0   200   400

MILES

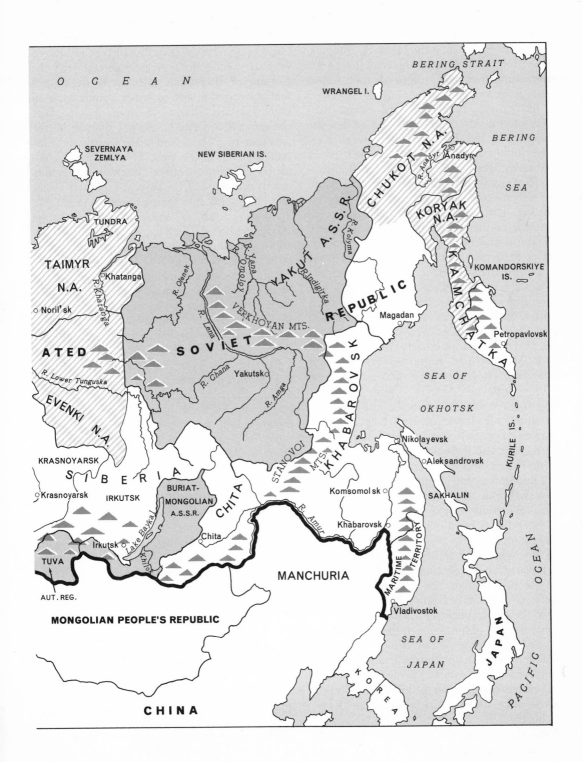

O C E A N

BERING STRAIT

WRANGEL I.

BERING

SEVERNAYA
ZEMLYA

NEW SIBERIAN IS.

CHUKOT N. A.

R. Anadyr   Anadyr

SEA

TUNDRA

KORYAK
N. A.

YAKUT A. S. S. R.

R. Kolyma

KOMANDORSKIYE
IS.

TAIMYR
N. A.

Khatanga

R. Khatanga

R. Olenek

R. Yana

R. Omoloy

R. Indigirka

REPUBLIC

KAMCHATKA

Noril'sk

Magadan

Petropavlovsk

ATED

R. Lower Tunguska

SOVIET

VERKHOYAN MTS.

R. Lena

SEA OF

OKHOTSK

EVENKI N. A.

R. Chana

Yakutsk

R. Amga

KHABAROVSK

Nikolayevsk

KRASNOYARSK

S I B E R I A

STANOVOI MTS.

Aleksandrovsk

KURILE IS.

Krasnoyarsk

IRKUTSK

BURIAT-
MONGOLIAN
A. S. S. R.

CHITA

Komsomol'sk

SAKHALIN

Lake Baykal

R. Amur

Khabarovsk

Irkutsk

Chita

R. Khilok

MARITIME TERRITORY

TUVA

MANCHURIA

OCEAN

AUT. REG.

Vladivostok

MONGOLIAN PEOPLE'S REPUBLIC

SEA OF

JAPAN

JAPAN

KOREA

PACIFIC

CHINA

sia. The steppes provided a peerless highway for a succession of invasions by nomadic peoples from the east such as the Huns, the Bulgars, and the Magyars. Following this road the Tartar hordes conquered and subjected the princedoms of Russia.

In the generations that followed, eastern Russia (including Moscow) remained under the domination of the Tartars, while western Russia (including much of the old water road) came under the control of Poland and Lithuania. Not until the eighteenth century were these regions completely reunited with the rest of Russia. During the period that intervened, the people of the western regions (particularly the Ukraine and Byelorussia) took on characteristics of their own that distinguish them from the so-called Great Russians of Russia proper.

When a new Russian realm arose, then, it was not on the western river road nor on the open southern steppe but in the region of mixed forests around Moscow. Even under the Tartar yoke, in the fourteenth century, the grand princes of Moscow had begun to expand their power. Ivan III (1462–1505), who assumed the Byzantine title of "Autocrat," pushed his territory to the Arctic Ocean in the north, and in 1480 threw off Tartar control. Ivan IV, "the Terrible" (1533–84), expanded his territory in both the east and the west, conquering the Tartars of Kazan and, with less success, fighting the Teutonic knights in the Baltic provinces. In 1547 he had himself proclaimed Tsar (or Caesar, another Byzantine title). At his death, his empire extended as far south and east as the Caspian Sea.

In the years that followed, Muscovy (Moscow) was engaged in almost constant warfare with the nations about it—a warfare that built a sense of national solidarity but that also required the development of a national army and a concentration of authority in the hands of the Tsar, which became a powerful force in the building of Russian absolutism. Indeed, the long history of foreign wars and invasions did much to convince the Russian people that only the strictest unity under a single leader could save the country.

Until the middle of the seventeenth century the chief expansion of Russian territory was to the east and south, at the expense of the disinte-

grating Tartar power. Russian colonists reached the Pacific Ocean as early as 1643, and Peter the Great (1682–1725) and his successors moved west as well. Peter's greatest success was the winning of the famous "window on the Baltic" that opened the way to easier communication with Western Europe. A few decades later Catherine the Great (1762–96) joined in the partition of Poland and added vastly to Russian territory in the west. Her successors completed the conquest of the Caucasus in the nineteenth century and by 1885 had pushed southward from Siberia to conquer central Asia.

Russia's defeat in World War I cost it the Baltic provinces (Estonia, Latvia, and Lithuania), Finland, Poland, and Bessarabia. The settlement after World War II, however, pushed out its boundaries to include all the Baltic provinces, Bessarabia, a small part of Finland, a large part of Poland (whose inhabitants were for the most part Ukrainians and Byelorussians), and parts of Slovakia and East Prussia that had never before belonged to Russia.

For the past two centuries at least, Russia has had considerable contact with the West; during the nineteenth century, in fact, there was a great intellectual battle between the Westernizers and the Slavophils—that is, between those who wanted to pattern Russia on the West and those who wished their country to concentrate on its own distinctive characteristics. But Western influences never sank deep, partly because of Russia's almost constant fighting with its western neighbors, and partly because the Russian people (who had been converted to Christianity by way of Constantinople in the tenth and eleventh centuries) belonged to the Russian Orthodox church, which had no affiliation with either Roman Catholicism or Protestantism. Moreover, the modern ideological disagreement with the West has heightened the historic sense of separateness and impeded the political and economic cooperation that, geographically, would seem obvious and natural.

The People: Nationality

The inevitable consequence of so long a history of invasion, conquest, and war was the building of an empire almost as varied in climate and type of civilization as was the modern British empire. The fact that the Soviet Union is a continuous land mass conceals this situation to some extent, but the Tsars were almost as adept in conquering peoples of other nationalities and colors as were the best of British imperialists. As a result, the rulers of the Soviet Union have been confronted with a peculiar combination of two problems, imperialism and nationalism, which more than almost any others have contributed to international unrest. In this sense the Soviet Union has had to experiment in its own territory with solving the same problems with which the colonial powers had to wrestle after World War II.

In contrast to such countries as Great Britain and France, which are largely homogeneous in population, the Union of Soviet Socialist Republics contains almost two hundred separate nationalities speaking a hundred and fifty languages. Only about sixty of these, however, include more than a few thousands of people; only a dozen include as much as 1 percent of the population. Since slightly over half of the population is Russian or "Great Russian" and since, according to the 1959 census, there were also thirty-seven million Ukrainians and eight million Byelorussians, nearly 75 percent of the population is Slavic. The remaining 25 percent includes everything from Eskimos to what were only recently nomadic desert tribes, and from Lutheran Protestants in the Baltic provinces to Moslems in the Turkish-Tartar regions. In culture they range from the most primitive peoples to the most highly civilized. While the Great Russians have produced outstanding works of literature and science, some of the lesser nationalities have not even had a written language.

Under the Tsars the existence of minority nationalities was regarded as a source of weakness. Vigorous efforts were made to discourage their languages, cultures, and religions, to "Russify" them, and to convert them to the Orthodox faith. Even when oppression was not violent, there was steady discrimination against members of the minority groups; it was natural for them, therefore, to retaliate with a burning hatred of the tsarist government. Many of the leaders of the revolutionary movement were drawn from these groups.

Communism and the Nationality Problem

There is something ironical in the fact that the first country in which the working class triumphed should have to meet the nationality problem in so extreme a form. According to Marxist thought the workingman has no fatherland. In every country the bourgeoisie exploit the workers, and the worker can be free only when he realizes that his real enemies are at home, not abroad. Once the international revolution has taken place and exploiters everywhere have been destroyed, there can be a world state in which all men live together in peace, equality, and happiness; for loyalty to the working class will have replaced any loyalty to national groups.

Even before the revolution Lenin had made up his mind to fight off all tendencies to organize the country on nationality lines. His view was that "A conscientious proletarian will always fight for a large-scale State." Stalin, who as a Georgian belonged to one of the minority nationalities and had written a book on the nationality question in 1913, was given the task of developing Bolshevik theory on the subject. In his *Report on the National Question* (1918) he wrote, "The principle of self-determination must be an instrument in the struggle for socialism and must be subordinated to the principles of socialism."

At the same time, both Lenin and Stalin were aware of the propaganda value of the slogan of self-determination. With the Revolution, Stalin became Commissar of Nationalities, and a "Declaration of the Rights of the Peoples of Russia" was published. This Declaration proclaimed the equality of the different nationalities and the abolition of all national and religious privileges of one nation over another and promised the free development of all national and ethnic groups.

Naturally, the more advanced nationalities—the Poles, Finns, Estonians, Lithuanians, and Letts—interpreted self-determination as separate national status. When they proved able to protect their separate identity under their own bourgeois leaders, the Bolsheviks reluctantly accepted their new status. But although Lenin had always conceded the "right to secede," he also exalted where possible the "right to unite" with other nationalities under the leadership of the local Communist parties that were coordinated through the central party structure in Moscow. Thus, Red Armies subdued resistance in most of the provinces of the former tsarist empire—including the Ukraine, with its highly developed sense of nationality—and forced them into the Union. In appearance, the Ukraine and other units such as Byelorussia, Georgia, Armenia, and Azerbaijan had their own separate state organizations subsequently known as union republics; in practice, "socialist unity" prevailed.

Aside from the Ukrainians, who were culturally and economically as advanced as the Great Russians, the other nationalities that ultimately became part of the Soviet Union were economically and socially backward. Most were Asiatic rather than European; many of them were still nomadic with little more organization than a primitive tribal structure. Their relation to the central unit was closer to that of colonies than of minorities in the Western sense. The Communists, however, have always closely associated "national" and "colonial" questions. The political arrangement devised for the Ukraine was extended in a somewhat modified form to these areas also.

It is in the political sphere that it has been most difficult to reconcile the national self-determination guaranteed by the Constitution with unity. On the face of things, the minority nationalities were given the fullest equality, including separate political units, the right to vote, and the right to hold public office, both local and national. Today photographs of the delegates to the Supreme Soviet (the Soviet parliament) often make a point of showing the great variety of racial types composing that body. But from the beginning, there were two factors that made the self-government of the nationality units illusory: their lack of experienced personnel for the jobs of government, the most important of which were thus held by Great Russians, and, still more important, the unified, centralized Communist party with its controls radiating from Moscow. Though the highest offices in the union and autonomous republics are regularly filled with local persons, the minority people have exercised little if any control over their own political affairs. The achievement of formal equality provided prestige and satisfaction for those nationalities that used to suffer from overt discrimination; nonetheless, the lack of effective power has created tensions from time to time that were similar to those exhibited by the intelligentsia in colonial areas.

Moreover, the Soviet government has reacted sharply against any manifestations of a consciousness of a distinct national heritage and destiny (technically known, in official publications, as "bourgeois nationalism"). In 1930, for example, the All-Ukrainian Academy of Science was suppressed, and in the great purge the casualties among the leading figures of nationality republics were particularly high.

It was often said during World War II that the Soviet Union had no quislings or fifth columnists. And yet at the outbreak of war the Volga Germans (a self-conscious, long-established group still speaking German) were scattered throughout the interior lest they form a fifth column with the Nazi advance. Certain other nationality groups—the Crimean Tartars, the Karachai, the Balkars, the Chechen-Ingush, and the Kalmyks—were dispersed at the end of the war as a punishment for acts of disloyalty. Many "nationality deviationists" were dismissed in a postwar purge that affected the top leadership in the Georgian, Uzbek, Karelo-Finnish, Estonian, Latvian, Byelorussian, Kazakh, and other nationality republics.

The revolutionary character of Communist policy for the nationalities lay in the economic and social sphere. Here, as in political affairs, the keynote of the policy was not liberty, but equality; and equality was interpreted to mean the equal distribution of productive capacity throughout the whole of the Soviet Union. Rather than adopting the notion of colonial territories as suppliers of raw materials, the Communists deliberately promoted both the building of industries and the collectivization of agriculture in their underdeveloped areas.

In part, this effort to transmit to backward groups the skills of an advanced civilization is inspired by the desire to create an urban working class that will be firm in its support of the Soviet system; in part it stems from the belief that once the different nationalities are on the same material level they will share the same political ideas and loyalties; above all it results from the necessity of industrializing the country as a whole and increasing agricultural productivity everywhere in order to realize the revolutionary promise of material prosperity. Regardless of motivation, however, the practical effect has been to open economic opportunities, to raise standards of living and health, and to eliminate much of the backwardness that used to keep the minorities in a subordinate position. Side by side with this economic transformation has gone a no less influential educational revolution, partly to teach the technical skills needed for industry and agriculture, partly to transmit the ideas of Marx and Lenin.

The People: Religion

In the years before the Communist revolution the great majority of the Russian people were adherents of the Russian Orthodox church. Other religions, in particular Roman Catholicism, which was allied with the Greek Catholic church of the Ukraine, were persecuted by tsarist officials eager to "Russify" the country as a whole. The Tsar himself directly controlled the Orthodox church, and it proved a docile instrument in support of his policy and power.

The triumph of the Communists in the revolution, therefore, inevitably presented a problem, for on a long series of issues there was a fundamental conflict between the church and the new government. Marxism maintained that religion was the opium of the people. By promising the miserable of this earth a heavenly reward, the church was accused of diverting the proletariat from the revolutionary action needed to remedy existing injustices; by teaching the Christian virtues of humility, obedience, and nonresistance to authority, the church deprived men of the weapons with which they could right their wrongs. Priests and ministers, to the Bolsheviks, were servants and agents of the ruling class. The alliance of throne and altar was regarded as the foundation of Russian absolutism.

Marxism and Religion

Even if no such practical considerations had existed, there would have been an inevitable hostility between communism and religion. Marxism is an all-embracing philosophy whose basic principle—materialism—and whose basic method—the scientific approach—are held to be in direct conflict with the spiritual values of the church—that is, with its dependence on revelation and faith. In addition, communism is a doctrine that demands the wholehearted, undivided loyalty of its adherents.

It is also true, however, that the Soviet state established freedom of conscience immediately after the October Revolution. Despite bitter attacks by the Communist party on all religious beliefs, there is a constitutional right to freedom of religious worship. So long as the churches keep to the narrow limits that the state permits and do not stray into education, social work, welfare, and social activities, they are tolerated, though at times there is vigorous antireligious propaganda. Up-to-date figures suggest that there remain sixty-five million believers in the Soviet Union.

Partly because the Russian Orthodox church patriotically supported the Soviet war effort, partly because militant atheism proved to have little appeal, the state and church reached a formal *modus vivendi* in 1943. The church agreed to place both its organization and its personnel under party supervision; in return, it is permitted to carry on its purely sacramental functions virtually unhampered, to train priests, and to issue religious publications for its own members. The practice of these activities, however, is permissive, not guaranteed, and restrictions can be imposed at any time. In 1962, for example, the penal code was extended by the Supreme Soviet to make punishable practices that may injure health, like long fasting (particularly relevant to Moslems and Catholics). Thus the needs of efficiency have primacy. The price of toleration is rigorous conformity to the provisions established by a regime committed to atheism.

The degree of toleration extended to the adherents of the Russian Orthodox church has been largely absent in the attitude of the Soviet regime toward "cosmopolitan" influences, such as those of the Roman Catholic church. (The powerful Greek Catholic Uniate church in the Western Ukraine was forcibly detached from its allegiance to the Vatican during the war and was crushed as an independent force.)

Most severe, however, have been the pressures against Jews and Moslems. From the "anticosmopolitan" drive in 1948 until Stalin's death in 1953, the Jews of the Soviet Union, the second largest Jewish community in the world, lived in a state of terror. Virtually all their cultural institutions had been abolished by the end of 1948; even organized Jewish religious observances have met constant harassment. Although great efforts continue to be made to maintain Jewish cultural and religious identity, Hebrew and Yiddish cannot be taught, and the one Yiddish publication still permitted has a precarious existence. Thus the forced assimilation of the Jewish people is far advanced.

The far more numerous Moslems (of whom there are between 20 and 30 million, as compared with 2.2 million Jews) have suffered an almost equally thorough Russification: their literature and language have been drastically modified by Russian forms; they retain only one training center for their mullahs (priests) (the Jews have none); and Moslem law has been superseded by Soviet law. Moreover, in Central Asia, where two-thirds of the Moslems are found, there are now millions of Russians directing industrial development and dominating the character of life. Thus, those groups in which a separate sense of nationality and a distinctive religion reinforce each other have suffered the greatest pressures to conform.

The People: Way of Life

The vast industrialization of the Soviet Union has necessarily created equally striking changes in the way of life of the Russian people. In 1961, for the first time, the urban population slightly outnumbered the rural—indicating a tremendous shift in both locale and population. In 1913 industrial workers had comprised less than 17 percent of the population, 65 percent were peasants, and 16 percent were either large farmers or members of the bourgeoisie. By 1939, the number of industrial workers had risen sharply to 32.2 percent of the population, collective farmers comprised 44.6 percent, while peasants farming individual holdings totaled less than 2 percent. The middle-class group of the large farmers and the bourgeoisie had been replaced by an almost equal number (17.5 percent) of office workers, clerks, and so forth. Of these enumerated groups, Molotov told the Eighteenth Party Congress in 1939 that 9.5 million—

that is, 13.5 percent—were intelligentsia, a category that covers all white-collar workers whether they be clerks, factory managers, scientists, teachers, artists, or army officers.

These figures represent not only great shifts in occupation but also a tremendous movement from the countryside to the city. In 1913 only 15 percent of the people lived in the cities; by 1961 about 51 percent of the population was urbanized. This does not mean, however, that the Soviet Union has yet achieved the mature economy of the United States or northwestern Europe in which agriculture and industry are so developed and so balanced that the interplay of community needs can be the determining factor in the distribution of labor. Although the total labor force is just over 25 percent more than that of the United States, the Soviet Union still has three-and-a-half times as many people —nearly half the population—employed in agriculture. Even with the current attention and aid to agriculture, the peasantry is still a relatively depressed group.

Social Structure

According to official publications, the class structure of the Soviet Union is a very simple one. With the liquidation of the exploiting classes and the collectivization of the farms, only two classes survive: workers and collective farm peasants. Between these classes there is no "class struggle." They are "friendly" classes whose interests are so harmonious as to require no distinct party representation. The third group, sometimes termed the "working intelligentsia," is called a "class stratum," that is, it consists of those of high status within the community. This intelligentsia makes up the ruling group in Soviet society.

Few developments have been more dramatic than the rise to power of this group. When the revolution took place, the workers took over the factories, but their inexperience and lack of skill soon led this temporary dictatorship of the proletariat to be replaced by the dictatorship of the party. But the party was no more able to run the factories, or subsequently to mechanize agriculture, than were the workers. It turned, perforce, to the technical specialists. In the 1920's, some of these specialists of bourgeois origin supported the regime and were handsomely rewarded. In the 1930's, the Soviet-trained intelligentsia became party members. Gradually the whole high-ranking group—party and government officials, managers and technicians, scientists and engineers, professors and army officers, teachers, doctors, lawyers, and playwrights, poets, and novelists as well—began to coalesce. Technically, they received a status in the Party Statutes of 1939 equal to that of the workers and peasants; in practice, they had already received one that was far superior. It is this group that provides the all-important party-political leadership and directs the successful industrialization of the country; and social prestige and power go hand in hand with indispensability.

The most significant division within the elite is between those who are responsible executives of the Communist party and those who are not. Industrial and scientific personnel play essential roles whose importance has vastly increased with industrial expansion, but they are less closely tied into the political system than is the party bureaucracy, whose members either organize activity within the party itself or direct the various segments of social and economic life.

The party leadership consists of three major groups. At the top are the full-time professional officials, the *apparatchiki*, or party apparatus, who provide the direction of the party, and of economic and cultural agencies, at every level: central, regional, local, and primary. By 1962, this group was thought to include between 100,000 and 200,000 members (the total party membership in 1966 was reported to be 12,471,000). The next level consists of the functional specialists who relate party policy to particular areas of the economy, or of the army, or of social or cultural activities. The third level consists of what Stalin once likened to the noncoms in an army, working under the two top levels, the generals and the officer corps. Many of those at the third level—secretaries of party units, for example—work only part time for the party and have other occupations as well.

Economic and Social Differentiation

Although these groups share in varying degrees in the directing power in the Soviet Union, only those in the elite strata secure special educational advantages, prestige, and high standards of living. One of the apparent contradictions in Soviet society has been that, with its advance into what appears to be the second stage of communism, there is more rather than less inequality in income between groups. Lenin, of course, anticipated that the differences in income persisting in the first stage of communism would become progressively less during the second stage; in particular, government officials were to lose their favored position and to receive a reward no greater than that of the average workman. As early as 1934, however, Stalin bluntly repudiated what he called "petty-bourgeois equalitarianism," which he termed "leveling down." In place of the goal of equality of income, he put equality of opportunity to develop the skills needed in an industrial society. Side by side with this emphasis has gone the notion of proportional rewards in relation to the value of the individual's contribution to the building and direction of Soviet society and strength.

Most unskilled or semiskilled workers are poorly paid, and, as far as possible, they are paid on the basis of piecework. In contrast, the Stakhanovites, who strive for a high rate of production, receive a great deal more in monetary rewards and a special social status that reflects their advanced position within the proletariat. The lower ranks of the white-collar workers are not much better paid than the ordinary manual workers. The next rank in this stratum—secondary and technical school teachers, medium-rank government officials, military officers, and technicians without managerial responsibilities—has a standard of living little if any better than that of the skilled worker. Above all these, however, is the group that enjoys a standard of living that is high by any scale: the top party, government, and trade union officials; the managers of factories, mines, and state farms; the generals, admirals, and air marshals; the top scientists; and, interestingly enough, the leading writers, ballerinas, and artists. Often managers and special literary and other favorites are also provided with apartments, cars, and other luxuries.

Differences in income in the Soviet Union are far greater than are common in Great

Britain. This fact does not disturb those who direct the Soviet state. Differential rewards not only produce the social stratification that is so noticeable in Soviet society but also help to produce conformity to the purposes of the regime. They have become even more important now that terror has ceased to play a prominent part in securing obedience. Managed inequality and differentiation, and competition for the good things of life, are thus encouraged. Indeed, although old-line Bolsheviks believed that the elimination of the exploiting classes would of itself lead to spontaneous effort and growth, Marxism-Leninism recognized that communism would require not only "an abundance of material and cultural benefits, but also a new attitude to labor—its conversion into a prime vital need. Until this is so," it declared, "people's labor requires a material stimulus, i.e. in the first place differential payment." Thus the day of "to each according to his needs" is likely to be a very long way off.

3. MASS COMMUNICATION

In few areas is there a sharper difference between Western and Soviet views than there is in attitudes toward the purpose of mass communication. In the United States, Great Britain, France, and Germany, it is taken for granted that news should be—though it rarely is—presented as impartially as possible, that different approaches to current issues should be encouraged, and that government policy is not immune from criticism. Government officials explain policy in those countries, but their words are accepted as information, not as dogma. It is accepted that writers and artists express their own inner urges—or produce what they think will sell. Scientists and other researchers are expected to publicize the results of their work and to let their theories and conclusions compete in the open.

None of these attitudes is necessarily acceptable in the Soviet Union. An orthodox Communist believes that truth and morality are relative to the interests of a society. His interpretation of all forms of expression in a capitalist society is that they reflect capitalist ideas. In a Communist society, he believes that all means of communi-

cation should deliberately contribute to the success of Soviet endeavors. And since the direction of these endeavors is in the hands of party leaders, all media of communication should contribute in their own way to the basic purposes determined by those leaders.

To uphold such a goal is not necessarily to force the expression of opinion into a single mold, although there have been periods in Soviet history, notably under Stalin, when a dead and deadly uniformity infused most media. Even then, it was possible by very careful examination to detect certain trends of opinion on particular issues. In times when leadership was not settled, however, as between 1953 and 1957—that is, between Stalin's death and Khrushchev's emergence as undisputed leader—different publications reflected different approaches to matters at issue between rival groups. Thus the Soviet's two most prominent newspapers, *Izvestia* and *Pravda,* participated in the heavy-light industry debate between Khrushchev and the "antiparty" group. In general, moreover, Khrushchev encouraged a livelier presentation of news and a freer literary expression. Even before he was ousted from office in 1964, however, a greater emphasis on orthodoxy had emerged. It has been pressed harder by his successors. Thus behind the alternations of "freeze" and "thaw" lies the will of the party.

In part, the work of directing public opinion is the negative task of preventing the publication of "wrong" ideas. For this purpose there is a government censorship office (*Glavlit*) that must give its approval to all material distributed in the USSR, not to mention that which is sent outside the country. Far more important, however, is the work of spreading "right" ideas; and this task falls preeminently to the Communist party's department of propaganda and agitation (*Agit-prop*), which is attached to the party's Central Secretariat and which, either directly or through the action of similar departments in regional and local organizations of the Communist party, appoints newspaper editors, supervises their editorial policy, determines what films may be produced and exhibited, criticizes the work of authors and artists, and directs hundreds of thousands of "agitators" or "political enlightenment workers" in their work of molding public opinion.

Propaganda and Agitation

The Communists make a clear differentiation between propaganda and agitation. Communist *propaganda* is said to be the "intense elucidation of the teachings of Marx, Engels, Lenin" and of the history of the Bolshevik party and its tasks. Through this elucidation in schools and universities, retraining courses, and constant planned discussions, party and government officials, directors of industries, and intellectuals are "armed" with knowledge of the "laws" that govern the development of society and political conflicts.

Agitation, in contrast, is the process of explaining to the masses the government's decisions and policies, and of mobilizing their efforts to carry these out. Thus, while propaganda is directed chiefly at the more advanced strata in Communist society, agitation is aimed at the great mass of the people.

Propagandists and Agitators

A colossal number of persons are engaged in the incessant propaganda and agitation that pervade every aspect of Soviet life. In 1953, estimates F. Bowen Evans in his *Worldwide Communist Propaganda Activities* (1955), there were 375,000 full-time and 2,100,000 part-time propagandists working in the Soviet Union. Today, over 6,000 schools, with a total enrollment of some 200,000, exist for the sole purpose of training expert propagandists; above these, in turn, are many regional propaganda colleges. There are also a dozen institutions that give the most advanced training in propaganda techniques, not only to the cream of Russian propagandists, but also to Communist leaders from all parts of the world.

In their unceasing efforts to mold the thinking of the Russian masses, the Communists put their heaviest emphasis, however, on daily face-to-face contacts between the agitator and those to whom he must explain the party lines and the current state of affairs. More than 2,000,000 agitators are engaged constantly in this work, and there are many more who undertake such activity in addition to their regular jobs.

The agitator is the major link between the party leadership and the masses. Selected and trained by local party units, the agitators are bright, young, and ambitious. They are constantly at work to explain in the simplest terms the reasons for the party's decisions or shifts in emphasis, and to make clear where the individual workers fit into the overall Soviet plan. In brief but frequent sessions of ten to fifteen persons held in every village, every shop, and every place of work, the agitators constantly exhort their listeners to ever more intense efforts. Thus they bring propaganda down to the grass-roots level and link it directly to the efforts and output of those people on whom production ultimately depends.

Not surprisingly, it is not always easy to secure an adequate number of agitators. It is preferable to have an industrial worker or a peasant on a collective farm act as agitator in his own unit. But because the agitator must always have an answer to criticisms and questions, and also urge his comrades to harder and harder efforts, he often finds it difficult to combine this role with good relations with his fellow workers. Hence managers are also used as agitators. But since their prestige hardly makes up for the quality of personal relationship gained through rank-and-file agitators, both sources are tapped in the unending effort to urge Russian workers to contribute their maximum efforts to production.

The Press

In addition to verbal exhortations, the Soviet people receive a constant stream of party-selected information on domestic and foreign events. Daily and weekly newspapers, magazines, wall newspapers, posters, electric signs, public loud-speakers, all pour out what party leaders wish the people to hear. The flood of propaganda is like commercial advertising in the United States (except that it is noncompetitive), and it probably makes much the same impact.

No publication can appear that has not passed the government censor; all are dependent on government-released supplies of paper. Moreover, the government has a full monopoly over publishing and news-gathering agencies. Thus it is easy to alter the interpretation of events, to withhold information, or to publicize an event or view throughout the country.

Nonetheless there is an extraordinarily large

number of newspapers in the Soviet Union, between seven thousand and eight thousand, and thus inevitably there is some variety in news and interpretations. There are three main types of publication: organs of the Communist party; government dailies published by national, regional, provincial, and city administrations; and specialized papers reflecting the interests of every organized group in Soviet society. Nothing illustrates better the degree to which the regime uses the printed word as a means of propagating its ideas and programs.

The most important of the Communist party's publications is the newspaper *Pravda* (Truth); but there are also special publications for party youth (in particular, *Komsomolskaya Pravda*). The leading government publication is *Izvestia,* which carries the texts of laws and decrees as well as a wide range of news. In addition, individual ministries have newspapers and magazines of their own; the Red Army, for example, publishes *Red Star,* and the Ministry of Agriculture's daily is said to have a circulation of a million. Among the publications of other organizations, the trade union paper *Trud* (Labor) is particularly important. *Pravda* and *Izvestia* have their own foreign correspondents; other publications are supplied by Tass, the government news agency.

Pravda is easily the most important of these publications, since it is the organ of the party. Even though the USSR is a much larger country than the United States, *Pravda* has a nationwide circulation; mats are flown daily from its publishing house in Moscow to other cities, where local editions are put out. Its own circulation in 1966 was 6.7 million, while that of *Izvestia* was 5.6 million. Moreover, *Pravda* editorials and news items are reprinted in regional and local newspapers throughout the country. In one way *Pravda* is the most powerful newspaper in the world, for there is no source within the USSR from which its pronouncements can be questioned.

But though policies themselves are above criticism, this is far from true of the administration of policies or the administrators themselves. One of the activities of newspapers is to use thousands of worker and peasant correspondents throughout the country to investigate instances cited by their readers of slackness, inefficiency, discourtesy, and stupidity on the part of administrators, factory directors, and public servants generally. Such criticism can be highly useful to the regime in checking the lesser bureaucracy and in pointing out bottlenecks. In some measure, it also acts as a safety valve by turning discontent against those who are immediately responsible for the execution of policies. With all its limitations, it is one of the more substantial links between the masses of people and the top party leaders; at the same time, it provides some encouragement for the ordinary citizen to look at authority with critical eyes and to indulge in a type of freedom of speech.

Radio and Television

Widely regarded as the supreme media of mass communication, radio and television, like the press, are directed by the party and the government. In addition to the 13.5 million radio receiving sets in the Soviet Union in 1964 (there were 183 million in the United States in 1964), and the 7 million TV receivers (the United States had 60 million), there were 30.5 million loud-speakers in streets and in meeting places operating much of the time. Unlike the press, radio and television concentrate chiefly on entertainment (80 percent of the programs, it is said, are music and drama), with political propaganda inserted much as are commercials in the United States. When the regime wishes to make important announcements, however, it has at hand the public broadcasting system, which cannot be turned off if the audience gets bored.

Artistic Expression

In the battle of ideas, the stage, the screen, poetry, fiction, painting, and even music have been used, in addition to the mass media, as weapons for indoctrinating and inspiring the masses. Although there have been artistic "thaws" since Stalin's death when socio-critical novels and plays about life in the Soviet Union appeared and were read avidly, there remains an ultimate control over works and authors whose material or slant is considered "anti-Soviet," particularly if it is so labeled in the West. What is remarkable is that despite curbs and, at times, brutal punishment, satirical works appear, dissent and criticism are expressed, and some of the finest writing of the day continues to come from Russian writers.

Widely publicized was the Soviet response to Boris Pasternak's *Doctor Zhivago,* which was selected for the 1958 Nobel prize for literature. Refused for publication in the Soviet Union because it was critical of the Bolshevik Revolution, strong though unsuccessful Soviet pressure was exerted to prevent it from appearing in Italy. Thereafter, Pasternak was forced to refuse the Nobel prize. Mikhail Sholokhov, a highly conservative author, best known for his *And Quiet Flows the Don,* published in 1928, was allowed to receive this award in 1965, a reflection of the current official attitude to literature.

Particularly startling have been the punishments meted out to dissident intellectuals. Two writers, Esenin-Volpin and V. Tarkin, were committed to mental institutions, an experience unforgettably described by the latter in the novel *Ward No. 7.* The Leningrad poet, Joseph Brodsky, was given eighteen months of hard labor in the far north. Still more severe were the sentences imposed on two unusually gifted writers, Andrei D. Sinyavsky, a frequent contributor to the literary journal *Novy Mir* (New World) (which has been aptly described as "the most constructively disruptive force in Soviet intellectual life"), and Yuli M. Daniel. The "crime" for which they were condemned by the Soviet Supreme Court in February 1966 was putting into print and publishing abroad clandestinely books including "beliefs and ideas that could be used profitably by enemies of Communism." The punishment for Sinyavsky was seven years, and for Daniel five years, in a forced labor camp.

Science

Scientists are also expected to serve the Soviet state, and a party orthodoxy in regard to scientific conclusions may be established by party fiat. Nevertheless, as with artistic expression, a party-supported interpretation in science may also be overthrown by party fiat.

The most striking example of this process has been the genetics controversy between the adherents of the almost universally accepted Mendelian theory of heredity and an older, so-called Michurian concept. According to the Michurian concept, upheld by the Soviet scientist Lysenko, acquired characteristics are inherited through a cumulative process. The controversy was carried on by geneticists, but the decision in Lysenko's favor in 1948 was made by the Central Committee of the Communist party. In favor throughout Stalin's lifetime, Lysenko's crop rotation system, which promoted the use of feed grasses rather than grain, was employed by Khrushchev, though with increasing skepticism, in his drive to open up virgin lands in the Soviet east. Demoted in April 1956, Lysenko subsequently returned to a position of some prominence, from which he was only finally removed after Khrushchev's downfall in 1964. In mid-1965, Soviet biologists joined in Mendel's centenary celebrations and vowed to redouble their efforts to make up for the time lost through following Lysenko's concepts.

However surprising this controversy may appear, it is obvious from Soviet space exploits that most of its science has not been affected in this manner. Moreover, for all the apparently uninformed dogmatism of certain party decisions in the scientific realm, it would be rash to underestimate either the active discussion that precedes them (and that often continues quietly in the hope of recovering favor for the opposing point of view) or the vast encouragement given at all times to scientific education and research in the interests of Soviet advance. Compared to other aspects of life, scientific work enjoys not only relative freedom within the Soviet Union but also constant encouragement both in postprimary education and through continuous government support. Even though no Russian scientist since Pavlov has produced a major new scientific theory, there are many whose applied science has produced outstanding results, particularly in militarily significant fields such as space and nuclear research.

Though Marxism-Leninism is the theoretical orthodoxy of the Soviet Union, Soviet leaders have not allowed dogma to interfere with the interests of their state. Stalin had a particular contempt for what he called the "Talmudists" who stuck by the "sacred" writings rather than face practical realities. Nothing illustrates this better than the linguistics controversy in which he overthrew the teachings of N. Ya. Marr, who had maintained that language was an element of the superstructure created by the economic basis of a given period of history. Marr declared that there must be a separate language for each of the economic stages Russia had experienced: that is, there must be a feudal, a capitalist, and a socialist language. Stalin, perhaps influenced by the Great Russian nationalism stimulated during the war, but more genuinely by practical considerations, flatly denied this theory in June 1950 in an article titled "Concerning Marxism in Linguistics," in which he declared that language "is not created by one class but by the whole society, by all its classes and by the efforts of hundreds of generations." This sounds more like Burke than like Marx, but it served the purpose of ending controversy and avoiding unnecessary change. Thus theory was kept in its place not as a master but as a guide to the leaders by whom alone it can be modified and adapted.

Education

It is the particular distinction of the Soviet regime that it has placed such great emphasis on education. Illiteracy, which ranged from 55 to 65 percent during tsarist days, has been virtually stamped out. In 1930, four years of primary school were required for all children; today, eight years of schooling between the ages of seven and fifteen are compulsory. Students are usually encouraged to take three further years of schooling to train themselves for productive work in the Soviet economy. The Soviet Union, we are told, is now producing twice as many engineers and technical specialists as is the United States.

Education is the most powerful solvent of traditional ways of life and the most promising means whereby the gifted can rise to positions of prestige and power. At the same time, education, like everything else in Russia, is geared to the needs of the regime. It not only produces the technical experts demanded by industrialization but is also, of course, a powerful instrument for the inculcation of the proper social and political attitudes. It is the duty of teachers to develop those qualities of cooperation and responsibility necessary for life in a collectivist

society: a recognition of the duty to work and a devotion to the common welfare. It is also their duty to build a "hot love for country," a "flaming hatred of her enemies," and those qualities of discipline, obedience, endurance, and courage that are necessary for victory in war.

This constant indoctrination of the children in allegiance to the Communist party, its leaders, and the tenets of Marxism-Leninism has far-reaching political consequences. In the absence of other sources of information and of the tradition of political questioning and criticism in which American, British, and French students are raised, there is a strong tendency to accept the orders of Soviet leaders as necessary and wise. Yet it also appears that there is more questioning in Soviet schools and colleges than we might anticipate—questioning that arises out of inconsistencies between slogans and practice. While such questioning offers no threat to the regime, it keeps alive the spirit of inquiry that dictators are loath to see.

The Suppression of Opposition

The positive function of developing enthusiasm for and devotion to the Communist way of life belongs to the schools, the press, and other instruments for communicating ideas; the negative function of suppressing opposition belongs to the political police.

The political or secret police played a decisive role in the Soviet Union from the first. It was obvious to Lenin that the enemies of the revolution had to be crushed pitilessly whenever they appeared. When he declared in 1921 that "terror cannot be dispensed with," he gave the key to what long remained an essential feature of the Soviet regime. Under one name or another—Cheka, OGPU, NKVD, MVD (Ministry of the Interior), MGB (Ministry of State Security), or, since 1954, KGB (Committee of State Security)—the political police has survived to the present time. It still has extraordinary powers of arrest, examination (in order to extract confessions), and imprisonment far beyond anything possessed by the police in Western democratic countries. Its prisoners long constituted the largest labor force in the country. Since the execution of its chief, Beria, in June 1953, the police has been neither above the state, nor even a state within the state, but it still remains a significant arm of the party and the ultimate recourse if persuasiveness fails to achieve the goals of the regime.

By 1936, all hostile classes at home were supposed to have been liquidated; from the mid-thirties, however, the secret police continued to act against deviationists, lax party members, and other obvious adversaries. Moreover, they conducted the pre-trial investigations for the great 1936–38 purge in which perished the "old Bolsheviks" who were not staunch Stalinists. The most significant feature of this action was that terror, which until 1934 had been used almost exclusively against factions or groups outside the ruling elite—that is, against Trotskyites, right and national deviationists, and the bourgeois intelligentsia—was turned against important segments of the ruling class itself in the interests of the party and of Stalin's own undisputed rule.

If terror is used indiscriminately or so widely as to shatter normal expectations of stability, it defeats its own purpose of acting as an ultimate regulator of the society. Recognition that such a situation had developed lay behind the new emphasis on legality that Stalin's successors proclaimed in deed and word. Within a month after Stalin's death they had freed the Kremlin doctors whose arrest on charges of hastening the demise of high Soviet officials had set off the last Stalin purge; also, as we have seen, Khrushchev outspokenly denounced Stalin's unpredictable actions toward high party members. Yet terror has not been forsaken in the Soviet Union. It is used much more discreetly, but it remains.

That there are dissatisfactions and tensions in the Soviet Union is undeniable. But that they are strong enough to imperil the regime in any way is highly unlikely. Propaganda, persuasion, improving standards of living, and the possibility of terror in the background are a powerful combination, particularly for people who have never known the type of life existing in the West. Coupled with a high degree of organization under the centralized direction of the Communist party, these factors provide strong and persistent means of control and stability.

2. The Soviet Political Heritage

1. HISTORICAL INFLUENCES

No aspect of Russian history is more marked than the persistent tradition of absolutism in government, the recurrent dependence on revolutionary violence to solve political problems, and the lack of experience with democratic institutions and constitutional procedures. Neither the Byzantine nor the Tartar influence (and these were the two civilizations with which the Russians were in closest touch before the sixteenth century) fostered a tender regard for individual liberty or popular government. The domination of the country by the Tartars for two and a half centuries effectively halted whatever native development there might have been toward self-government and cut Russia off from any liberating influences from the West. The princes of Moscow first established their power through the favor of their Tartar rulers. The almost constant warfare through which they enhanced their power increased the need for leadership and a concentration of autocratic power at the same time as it maintained the barrier against Western influence.

With few exceptions, the story of modern Russia, from its development out of the Muscovite princedom to the present, has been a story of arbitrary power arbitrarily exercised. The very name of Ivan the Terrible (1533–84), the first of the Tsars, is (outside the USSR) a byword for the most depraved and revolting cruelty. And although Ivan lived in an age when the England of Henry VIII and the France of the St. Bartholomew Massacre hardly qualified as examples of enlightened humanitarianism, neither English nor French history offers any parallel to the bloody and disordered political history of the following centuries: the succes-

sion of palace revolutions, murdered rulers, and civil strife between rival claimants to the throne. In contrast to Great Britain, where the outstanding characteristic of the constitution has been its slow, gradual, and continuous development, political development in Russia remained disordered and subject to repeated swerves. Even after the establishment of the Romanov dynasty in 1613, there was little of the regular continuity of government that permits free institutions and a constitutional tradition to arise. Whoever had the power seized the throne, and the people submitted.[1]

The Autocratic Tradition

Although the nineteenth century brought a more orderly succession to the throne, Russia remained, for the rest of the world, a symbol of tyranny, absolutism, backwardness, and reaction. Alexander I (1801–25), who had at first been influenced by liberal ideas, ended in the camp of reaction from which his brother and successor, Nicholas I (1825–55), never emerged. Nicholas I's son, Alexander II (1855–81), a conservative but no tyrant, introduced important reforms, notably the freeing of the serfs in

---

[1] Thus, after the death of Peter the Great in 1725, there was no clear succession to the throne, because Peter, like Ivan the Terrible, had slain his heir. Peter's second wife, Catherine (who had been a Lithuanian servant girl and who had no personal right to the throne), seized power by force and held it until her death in 1727. The crown then passed to Peter's young grandson, Peter II (1727–30); then to Peter's niece, Anne (1730–40); then to Anne's infant grandnephew, Ivan VI (1740–41), who was dethroned and later murdered in prison by Peter's daughter Elizabeth (1741–62). Elizabeth's nephew Peter III, a German prince, was dethroned by his wife, Catherine the Great (1762–96) and, like Ivan VI, was killed in prison. Catherine's son and successor, Paul (1796–1801), an unbalanced eccentric, was strangled by his own officials.

1861. For a time there was hope of a more liberal government. An attempt at assassination in 1866, however, precipitated a period of reaction and another (and successful) attempt in 1881 ended whatever hope there was for the peaceful development of a constitutional regime. The last two Tsars, Alexander III (1881–94) and Nicholas II (1894–1917), were determined to rule as autocrats. Under the pressure of the short-lived "Revolution of 1905," which was occasioned by the disastrous war with Japan, Nicholas II was forced to authorize, for the first time, a representative assembly on the Western model, the Duma. But as soon as possible he restricted and undermined its power.

None of these sovereigns was ever subject to effective constitutional limitations. Until the nineteenth century even the most powerful subject lived in danger of arbitrary arrest, imprisonment, and execution; and even during the nineteenth century the Tsar's police and censors kept the closest guard against any symptom of political liberalism.

The people, it is true, were not always completely docile. From the sixteenth century on there were frequent peasant revolts, some of which covered great areas and threatened the state itself. Yet the participants in these revolts did not think of themselves as fighting against the Tsar. The evils they suffered were blamed upon his favorites or subordinates, and the Tsar was even thought of as a protector standing above local oppressors. Sometimes it was charged that the true Tsar had been dethroned and that an imposter reigned in his stead (a long series of pretended Tsars won great followings among the masses). But the tsardom itself, among the peasants, was beyond challenge.

What opposition there was to tsarist autocracy came rather from certain segments of the upper or the middle classes. The first serious revolt against autocratic authority, the famous Decembrist uprising of December 1825, was the work of a small group of enlightened army officers who had been converted to the liberalism of Western Europe. They had no popular following, and their revolt was easily suppressed. More significant were the intellectual ferment among the intelligentsia throughout the nineteenth century and the efforts by some of them, especially the populist-minded Narodniks, to improve the condition of the peasants by working among them. It was not until late in the nineteenth century that the slowly growing urban middle class, which provided the impetus for parliamentary democracy in the West, sought liberal reform, and then rather for the sake of trade and profit than for liberty as such. The bourgeoisie remained dependent on the state as well as on the aristocracy as their best customers and, especially after the unsuccessful revolution of 1905, looked to the Tsar to keep the industrial workers in their place. There was widespread criticism, however, among the bourgeoisie of the economic burden of the tsarist bureaucracy and, because of the poverty of the peasants, the smallness of the internal market. The landed nobility remained the chief social and political support of tsarism. Even the liberal gentry, who worked for improved health and education for the peasants and supported parliamentary government, were not ready for drastic reforms such as the redistribution of the land. A wide gulf remained at all times between the intelligentsia and the illiterate masses of the peasantry. When, finally, a successful revolution did occur, those who sympathized with the liberal form of democracy that prevailed in the West were easily swept aside by the more ruthless supporters of Lenin.

Lack of Experience in Self-Government

Perhaps the most serious consequence of the tradition of autocratic government was that the mass of the people were left without experience in governing themselves. Democratic government, at least in modern times, is difficult government. It is easy enough for one man to rule over others, but for the people themselves to rule requires qualities of understanding, knowledge, experience, and confidence—qualities that are not innate and that can be developed only through use.

It was the tragedy of the Russian people that when the opportunity for self-government finally arrived they lacked the preparation. As late as 1913, as we have seen, two-thirds of the people were still illiterate, while there had been only the flimsiest precedents for popular participation in government. There was an early tradition that the people should gather in Moscow's Red Square and should endorse the choice of a new Tsar; but the people proved ready to cheer any Tsar who seized authority. (The story is told that Boris Godunov, in 1598, would not accept the crown until a great crowd knelt before him and moaned their prayer that he become Tsar—and that those who did not moan loudly enough were beaten.)

There were also times when it seemed possible that representative institutions of a sort might develop. Ivan the Terrible in 1550 had established a national assembly, the Zemsky Sobor. At first it could consider only those questions submitted to it; but later, during the "Time of Troubles" (1584–1613), a period of almost constant disorder and civil war, its power grew. It elected Boris Godunov Tsar, and in 1613 it chose the first Romanov as Tsar. Yet its powers and method of procedure were never clearly worked out, and its authority declined. No Sobors were held from 1654 to 1682, and after 1698 Peter the Great and his successors summoned no Sobors at all.

At times it also seemed possible that, as in England, the great nobles might take the first effective step in limiting the power of the ruler. The princes of Moscow had always had a Duma of Boyars (Council of Nobles), and during the Time of Troubles this institution also gained in authority. Peter dispensed with it, however, and although the older nobles gained some power in the Supreme Secret Council established by Catherine I (1725–27), their authority was short-lived. When, in 1730, there was a dispute over the succession to the throne, the Supreme Secret Council offered the crown to Peter's niece, Anne (whose title was particularly weak and who might therefore be expected to be dependent on them). They offered it to her on condition that she accept serious restrictions on the two traditional foundations of absolute authority, the purse and the sword. Once in power, however, Anne tore up the conditions in a dramatic scene, disbanded the Council, and restored autocratic power.

The Zemstvos

Another possible source of popular participation in government appeared in 1864 when there was a reorganization of the institutions of local government. The provincial and district councils (*zemstvos*) were elected popularly, although the voters were divided into three classes and the peasants chose their representatives indirectly. Control rested in the hands of the gentry, many of whom were progressive in their political and social ideas. The powers of the zemstvos were never very clearly defined, however, and, particularly under Alexander III (1881–94), their activities were severely restricted. In 1890 election by the peasantry was almost completely eliminated.

In spite of these handicaps, the zemstvos did notable work in the fields of health, education, and scientific agriculture. Through them, in addition, the liberal and professional classes received a certain amount of political experience. The All-Russian Union of Zemstvos organized the relief of the sick and wounded during World War I, and its president, Prince George E. Lvov, became the first head of the provisional government after the abdication of the Tsar in 1917. Yet for all their popularity among liberal and professional groups, the zemstvos commanded little support among the population in general.

The Duma

What appeared to be the most promising foundation for popular government was the Duma. Under the pressure of revolutionary agitation occasioned by the unsuccessful war against Japan, the Tsar in the "October Manifesto" of 1905 agreed to the establishment of a popular assembly, the Duma, which was chosen by universal suffrage. Several political parties participated in the elections, the two most prominent being the Octobrists, a conservative party that took its name from the Manifesto; and the Constitutional Democrats or "Cadets," who represented the progressive middle class and desired a constitutional government patterned after those in Western Europe. The Socialist Revolutionaries, a radical peasant party, and the Mensheviks, who were revolutionary in temper but objected to Lenin's methods, both officially boycotted the election. The Bolsheviks also refused to take part.

The Duma was balanced in its authority by an upper chamber, the Council of State (first established in 1825), one-half of whose members were nominated by the Tsar himself; there was accordingly no danger that legislation distasteful to the ruler would be passed. Moreover, when the first Duma, which was overwhelmingly liberal in composition, engaged in conflict with the Tsar's ministers (who were responsible only to the ruler), it was dissolved just ten weeks after its first meeting (1906). An ensuing appeal by some two hundred of its members for widespread passive resistance had no effect. The second Duma (1907) was somewhat more radical than the first, and it too was dissolved. Before new elections were held, however, the Tsar arbitrarily changed the entire basis of representation. He disenfranchised large areas of the country, reduced sharply the representation of the peasants, and increased that of the big landowners and the wealthier inhabitants of the cities. Thus the third Duma (1907-12), despite the Bolsheviks' participation in this and the succeeding election, was much more conservative and much less representative than its predecessors.

Even a conservative Duma, however, was more progressive than the Tsar and his ministers, and from 1908 on the Duma began to win admiration, particularly among the middle classes, for its restrained but telling criticism of the inefficiency of the government. Foreign observers had high hopes that it would develop into a truly effective and powerful constitutional instrument. In fact there was a real chance on the eve of World War I that the tsarist autocracy might have been transformed more or less peacefully into a liberal capitalist structure. But there was too little time for such an evolution, particularly since many of those (such as the Socialist Revolutionaries) who preferred other methods had become convinced by tsarist inflexibility that only violence would be effective. The widespread yearning for change created a dynamic that could be turned all too easily to the purposes of revolutionary extremism.

2. THE COMMUNIST REVOLUTION AND AFTER

The Seizure of Power

Yet in 1917 few people guessed how easily Russia would submit to a Bolshevik Revolution. To most observers the very fact that Russia was overwhelmingly agricultural—that its industrial development was still in its infancy—seemed to rule out the possibility. It was commonly noted that in countries such as Great Britain and Germany the farm vote was a conservative vote, and Marxists themselves had taught that the Communist revolution would occur, first of all, in a highly industrialized country.

The Peasantry: A Revolutionary Element

Such observations, however, represented a misunderstanding both of Russian agriculture and of Russian industry. Far from being a conservative force, the Russian peasantry was an unstable and even a revolutionary element. Much of the land in Russia still belonged to large landholders; the peasantry coveted this land with all its will and imagination. Though the great reforms of the 1860's had begun the process of land redistribution, they had also heavily burdened the peasantry with redemption payments. And while there was considerable private ownership and hereditary use of lands owned by the peasant community (the *mir*), the latter remained an important collectivist form of land tenure. Thus the peasantry was in a transitional stage that contributed to its instability and enormous hunger for land.

Workers and the Middle Class

Similarly, the nature of Russia's industrial development was such as to encourage revolution. Although Russia was not a highly industrialized country in 1917, what industrialization there was had come in a forced and almost artificial way. It was largely financed by foreign capital, and instead of following the British and French pattern, by which small-scale enterprise, directed and financed by a native middle class, prepared the way for heavy industry, industrialization in Russia was on a large scale from the very beginning and was dependent on foreign investment and the sponsorship of the state. Ownership was largely absentee, and the native middle class was small and weak, but the workers were already living under conditions typical of an advanced stage of industrialization. Whereas, in 1895, only 10 percent of the workers in Germany (one of the most advanced industrial countries) were employed in factories having a thousand employees or more, more than one-third of Russia's industrial workers were employed in such plants. The result was a degree of organization and radicalism among workers and a readiness to resort to strikes and direct action far more highly developed than in countries that might have seemed much closer to the pattern prescribed for a Marxist revolution. The conspicuous weakness of the middle class, in contrast, meant that when the revolution occurred there was little to correspond to the large class of small shopkeepers, independent artisans, and property-owning farmers that made it possible for France to have a government that was neither reactionary nor radical.

Military Disaster

In so unbalanced a situation Russia's disastrous participation in World War I provided the final impetus needed to produce revolution. In the early years of the war, it is true, Russian soldiers fought with conspicuous bravery. Yet their weapons were inferior and inadequate, the system of supply was marked by incredible corruption and inefficiency, and repeated military disaster destroyed the hope of ultimate victory. Weariness and disillusionment resulted in a powerful desire for peace at almost any price.

The Tsardom

In addition to being confronted by such impersonal forces as war and the peculiar nature of Russian agriculture and industry, the elements opposed to revolution suffered a special handicap in the personality of their leaders. The last Tsar and Tsarina combined all the disadvantages of weakness, stubbornness, and stupidity. They had fallen under the influence of a corrupt and unscrupulous "holy man," Rasputin, who they believed had been sent by God for their guidance and whom they credited with miracle-working powers. As time went on, no ministry could survive without his approval, and even the most conservative circles and those most loyal to tsarist institutions were disgusted and alienated. The Tsar and Tsarina were left without the firm support of any class in society, and when Rasputin was finally assassinated, too late to save the monarchy, members of the Tsar's own family participated in the plot. Thus when strikes broke out in March 1917 because of the lack of bread and the high cost of living, the

tsarist government was unable to cope with them. The Tsar abdicated, and those who would have defended the tsardom were left without a monarch around whom they could rally.

The Provisional Government

Legal authority passed to a provisional government appointed by the Duma, but the moderate and well-meaning men who comprised the new government were not great popular leaders: they might have been highly successful statesmen in a peaceful parliamentary democracy, but they were not well equipped to cope with a revolutionary crisis. Moreover, even when Prince Lvov was replaced by Alexander Kerensky, a very moderate Socialist Revolutionary, the provisional government could not free itself from the old official class and administrative machine. Partly for this reason it refused to legalize land seizures, even though land reform was the most pressing need. Thus it alienated the peasants. Kerensky also refused to cooperate with even the proliberal elements in the army, thus rejecting another possible source of support. At the same time, the provisional government was under heavy pressure by the Allies to keep Russia in the war while everyone in the country was clamoring for peace.

With the success of the March Revolution, councils of workers' and soldiers' deputies (the "soviets") sprang up in imitation of similar organizations during the 1905 Revolution. And, although at first they had Socialist Revolutionary and Menshevik majorities that supported the provisional government, they could easily be swayed against it.

The Role of Lenin

It was Lenin's great achievement that he saw the opportunity provided by such a situation. Contrary to the popular legend, it was not the Bolsheviks who led in the overthrow of the Tsar. The Russian people themselves, without guidance or leadership, had made the revolution; the leaders of the Bolsheviks, like Lenin himself, were in exile or in prison at the time it took place. Most of the Bolsheviks, including Stalin, were content with the fact that the tsardom had been overthrown but hesitated to cooperate with the provisional government. But

Lenin (whom the Germans returned, with other Bolsheviks, in a sealed train in April 1917 in an effort to weaken Russian resistance in the war) saw that it would be possible to push the revolution further—that is, to overthrow the "bourgeois" democratic republic and to establish a dictatorship of the proletariat. Though the Bolsheviks had only a few thousand members, Lenin foresaw that they could win the leadership of the soviets if they offered the people what they wanted. During the late spring and summer of 1917, therefore, under the slogans of "Peace, Land, and Bread" and "All Power to the Soviets," the Bolsheviks prepared for the seizure of power.

Had the Bolsheviks been its only opponents, the provisional government might have been able to resist, but an attempt by rightists, under the leadership of General Kornilov, to overthrow the government in the summer of 1917 upset the balance. The Bolsheviks gained credit for their part in defeating the rebellion; when they themselves were ready to strike, the right was too feeble to reinforce the parties of the center. The revolution that took place in November [2] triumphed with the same ease as the earlier revolution.

After the Revolution

The Bolsheviks had gained power by seizing control of the soviets, themselves revolutionary bodies; but almost at once they faced the test of a nation-wide election. When the election returns were counted for the Constituent Assembly, the most truly popular body in the history of Russia, the Bolsheviks had received only 25 percent of the votes, while the more democratic parties had 62 percent. In the "supplementary revolution" of January 5, 1918, Lenin dissolved the Assembly in what he declared was a "frank and complete liquidation of formal democracy in the name of the revolutionary dictatorship." Though temporarily supported by left-wing Socialist Revolutionaries, Lenin established a one-party regime later in 1918. Outright conflict ensued.

[2] By the old calendar, the revolutions were in February and October, but the Bolsheviks soon adopted the same calendar as the West.

The Civil War and War Communism (1917–21)

Every party within Russia was soon engaged in active struggle against the Communist regime; from August 1918 on, the Red terror by the Cheka, the Bolshevik secret police, began on a mass scale. Soon it was matched by the "White" terror of the counterrevolutionaries. For a while, Socialist Revolutionary governments, such as that under Chernov in the lower Volga Valley, consolidated popular support through liberal reform policies. But they had nothing in common with the reactionary "White" armies, which, by restoring property to the landlords in the areas they controlled, antagonized the mass of the peasants who might otherwise have been their allies. These armies were supported, though ineffectually, by the British, French, Japanese, and American governments in the hope of reestablishing a second front against Germany (the Bolsheviks had made peace in the spring of 1918 by the notorious Treaty of Brest-Litovsk) and of preventing stores of munitions from falling into German hands. The anti-Bolshevik forces were so disunited ideologically, politically, and militarily, however, that the Bolsheviks were able to attack them one by one. By 1921 they won their victory against counterrevolutionary forces.

During the period of the Civil War, extreme economic policies had been put into effect. Means of production, land, banks, and industrial plants were nationalized, private trade was forbidden, and farmers' produce above immediate needs was confiscated. The result was economic chaos. Farmers hid their grain or refrained from planting. Factory production fell disastrously. And the government had increasingly to resort to forcible measures, both to combat its political opponents and to mobilize labor and collect grain.

Hostility to the rigid controls and party domination led to peasant revolts in 1920, followed the next year by the Kronstadt Rebellion, an openly organized anarchistic political opposition demanding "soviets without Communists" and "free artisan production with individual labor." The last significant outbreak of its kind under the Soviet regime, the Kronstadt Rebellion, together with the great famine of 1921, gave notice that some changes in policy must be made.

The New Economic Policy (1921–27)

Lenin was always ready to adapt himself to the inevitable—and to profit by it. To the amazement of many of his collaborators, and over the strong opposition of some of them, he introduced the famous NEP (New Economic Policy). The free market was restored for both the peasant and the worker. After paying a proportional tax, farmers were free to dispose of their harvest as they desired. Privately owned shops reopened, and a new class of individual entrepreneurs (popularly called Nepmen) made their appearance. Many observers hailed the change as a proof of the failure of communism and anticipated a complete return to the capitalist system. But the retreat, however spectacular, was only a limited one. Heavy industry and foreign trade remained nationalized, and the government worked actively to consolidate its position in other fields as it gave ground in the economic. It was at the very time that the NEP was being introduced that the church underwent its first heavy persecution.

Shortly after the introduction of the NEP, Lenin suffered the first of a series of strokes. For many months he was almost totally incapacitated, and in January 1924 he died. The economic breathing-space that he had introduced, however, fulfilled its mission. Agricultural production returned to its prewar level, and industrial production rose sharply—although the Soviet standard of living continued to be far below that of the Western European countries. In addition, to the distress of the Bolshevik leaders, many peasants expanded their property holdings and developed the attitudes of middle-class farmers. Nothing could have been more hostile to Communist principles.

The years following Lenin's death were also marked by a spectacular struggle for power in which the chief contenders were Joseph Stalin (who, as Secretary-General of the Communist party, was in a strategic position to dominate the party's machinery and personnel, but against whom Lenin cautioned the party in his political testament) and Leon Trotsky, after Lenin the most famous of the revolutionary leaders.

No brief description can do justice to the involved and shifting issues and alignments of the years of struggle. The three chief issues were: in foreign policy, the Trotskyite insistence on the active promotion of world revolution in contrast to the Stalinist desire to build "socialism in one country"; in domestic policy, the Trotskyite demand that there must be a new drive toward industrialization according to a comprehensive plan; and, in party affairs, Trotsky's pressure for "intra-party democracy," that is, discussion of decisions, in contrast to Stalin's insistence on unquestioning obedience to the party line. In effect, Trotsky wanted to push forward the socialist revolution at home and abroad, while Stalin temporarily supported concentration on the home situation within the framework of Lenin's NEP. Neither side was completely consistent, however, and the policies of both groups were marked by political opportunism in which former enemies might ally themselves against former allies, and in which allies, once the enemy was defeated, divided against each other. Once Stalin had triumphed over Trotsky and his current allies (in the Politburo, and subsequently in the Party Congresses of 1924, 1925, and 1927), he turned against the NEP with even greater vigor than the Trotskyites had demanded. Once the "Left Opposition" (Trotsky, Zinoviev, and Kamenev) had been driven from power, Stalin proceeded to eliminate his former allies (Bukharin, Rykov, and Tomsky—the "Right Opposition") as well. That the divergence in foreign policy was over tactics rather than objectives was proved by Stalin's subsequent support of revolutionary communism in China. Thus fundamentally the struggle had been over timing but, above all, it had been for power.

The Renewal of the Socialist Offensive (1928–36)

Stalin's consolidation of power was marked by a new drive for the realization of socialism. On the industrial front, the first of the Five-Year Plans was introduced, calling for tremendous increases in the capacity of heavy industry and in the production of coal, electric power, and other resources. On the agricultural front, there occurred a forced liquidation of the farms. The more prosperous peasants were deprived of their holdings, and the "middle" and poorer peasants were obliged to unite in collective farms. The widespread resistance to this policy, though resulting in a temporary relaxation of pressure, was effectively and brutally suppressed, and the overwhelming majority of the farms were collectivized.

The Period of the New Constitution (1936–41)

By 1936 the success of the new policy was great enough for Stalin to proclaim that the socialist stage in the journey toward communism had been reached. Hostile classes had been destroyed, productivity had been increased, and a new and apparently democratic Constitution was introduced. Somewhat ironically, however, the introduction of this Constitution occurred in the midst of the great purges that followed the assassination of Sergei Kirov (1888–1934), one of the leading members of the Politburo. The inauguration of democracy in form went hand in hand with the terrorization of opposition groups.

Of the seven men who were members of the Politburo at the time of Lenin's death, only Stalin survived: one member (Trotsky) was assassinated in exile, one committed suicide, and four were executed. Moreover, the executions followed a series of spectacular trials that riveted the attention of the outside world on the battle for power within the Soviet Union and produced furious arguments about the validity and meaning of the almost unbelievable confessions made by those on trial. The "great purge" not only struck at some of the foremost leaders in the country, however, but cut deep into the ranks of the party. Only a small minority of the members of either the Council of People's Commissars (as the Soviet Cabinet was then called), or of the Communist party's Central Committee retained their former posts. The carnage was particularly heavy among leaders of the minority nationalities who held high office in the union republics. For many months there was an epidemic of hysteria that led to universal denunciations, mass arrests, and the execution of thousands of people who had been active party members.

This is a period that is still the subject of much debate. To some observers it marked a "great retreat" from Communist principles, in

which the peasant was again allowed a limited amount of private property, in which striking differences in income supported charges that a new upper class was arising, in which family life and a high birth rate were officially encouraged, divorce was discouraged, education returned to traditional channels, religion met with more toleration, and national patriotism (at least among Great Russians) was encouraged. But to others it seemed clear that the essential characteristics of the regime were unchanged. The instruments of production were still nationalized or collectivized; no political challenge to Bolshevik principles was permitted; nationalist movements among the minorities were suppressed as ruthlessly as ever; the secret police and censorship remained as all-pervasive as in the early days of the revolution; and the Communist party showed no greater willingness to share power with other groups than it had in the bitterest days of the Civil War.

"The Great Patriotic War" (1941–45)

The German attack on the USSR in the summer of 1941 interrupted the third Five-Year Plan and turned all the country's efforts toward meeting the backbreaking military demands. Although the Soviet government had made a pact of friendship with Hitler in August 1939, it had also taken the precaution of removing armament factories from the vulnerable western area to the region beyond the Volga and the Urals, while new factories of military importance were rushed to completion.

Despite such precautions the Germans were successful for a time in occupying a tremendous territory (inhabited by eighty-eight million people). Before they finally were driven from the country they had wrought enormous destruction. Some twenty-five million people lost their lives; another twenty-five million were left homeless. Some of the USSR's greatest cities and thousands of its villages were devastated. Industry, transportation, and agriculture suffered alike.

So desperate a struggle inevitably introduced changes in economic and political policy. Workers had to work longer hours and were "frozen" to their jobs. Penalties for lateness and absenteeism were exceedingly severe. Every effort was concentrated on military production, while the country as a whole suffered from the lack of clothing and food. During this period elections and ordinary legislative activity were suspended. No congresses or conferences of the Communist party were held. However, hundreds of thousands of new members (including large numbers of war heroes and "heroes of production") were admitted to party membership, both to increase its strength and to heighten its prestige. National feeling reached new heights, while the church won a certain toleration and took an active part in patriotic appeals.

The postwar and the post-Stalin periods both brought their own particular kinds of change. Along with reconstruction following the devastation of the war and continued stress on heavy industry, Stalin attempted to maintain his personal control throughout the country. With his death on March 5, 1953, began a new emphasis on social legality, voluntarism, and greater equality of opportunities and, simultaneously, the steady advance of Nikita Khrushchev to supreme power. On October 15, 1964, after Khrushchev had been ousted from office by his associates, Leonid Ilvich Brezhnev became First (later General) Secretary. We turn now to the constitutional framework within which these developments took place.

3. THE SOVIET CONSTITUTION

General Structure of Government

Within the Soviet Union the Constitution of 1936 was hailed as the most democratic the world had ever seen. Where the earlier constitution had deprived many persons of the right to vote, had weighted the franchise in favor of urban workers, had provided for the indirect election of higher representative bodies, and had made no provision for secrecy of the ballot, the suffrage was now proclaimed to be universal, direct, equal, and secret.

In form the Soviet government looks very much like that of any Western European democracy. There is a national legislature, the Supreme Soviet, which is made up of two chambers: the Soviet of the Union (which contains one deputy for every 300,000 of the population) and the Soviet of Nationalities, in which the

various union republics, autonomous republics, autonomous regions, and national areas receive representation. In the intervals between meetings of the Supreme Soviet, a smaller group of its members known as the Presidium, which technically is responsible and accountable to the Supreme Soviet, performs many of its duties.

Executive and administrative power are vested in a Council of Ministers, which corresponds in form to the British Cabinet or the French Council of Ministers and which technically is also responsible to the Supreme Soviet or, in the intervals between meetings, to the Presidium. According to the Constitution, the Soviet Council of Ministers has vast authority over almost all areas of administration. What is important, however, is that all these organs are controlled in practice by the Communist party. Thus their operations and importance are entirely different from what they would be in democratic states.

The Federal System

There is also a federal system which, at first glance, looks like that in the United States except that it is much more complicated and seems designed to reflect the multinational character of the Soviet Union. Thus there are fifteen union republics [3] and, as further subdivisions for particular nationalities, seventeen autonomous republics, nine autonomous regions, and ten national areas (all lying within the boundaries of one or another union republic). But one of the union republics, the Russian Soviet Federative Socialist Republic (RSFSR), contains more than half the total population and almost three-quarters of the country's area. Moreover, although in form union republics have certain rights and powers that are greater than those of the American states—the theoretical right to secede and to conduct foreign policy (on which rests the claim of the Ukraine and Byelorussia to have separate representation in the United Nations)—in practice, federalism in the Soviet Union is a matter of administrative units,

[3] The Russian Soviet Federative Socialist Republic (which itself contains more than a hundred nationalities), the Ukrainian, the Byelorussian (or White Russian), the Azerbaijan, the Georgian, the Armenian, the Turkmen, the Uzbek, the Tadjik, the Kazakh, the Kirghiz, the Moldavian, the Lithuanian, the Latvian, and the Estonian Soviet Socialist Republics. The Karelo-Finnish Republic was abolished in 1956.

THEORETICAL STRUCTURE OF THE SOVIET NATIONAL GOVERNMENT

USSR SUPREME SOVIET

Soviet of the Union	Soviet of Nationalities
Elected by citizens of the USSR on the basis of one deputy for every 300,000 inhabitants.	Elected by citizens of the USSR voting by federal subdivisions.

Elected for a four-year term.
Exercises exclusive legislative power.
Elects the Presidium.
Appoints the Council of Ministers and holds it responsible.
Amends the Constitution by a two-thirds vote.

Supreme Court

Elected by the Supreme Soviet for a five-year term.
Supervises the judicial activities of all judicial organs of the USSR and the union republics.

Public Prosecutor

Procurator General

Appointed by the Supreme Soviet for a seven-year term.
Ensures the strict observance of the law by all ministries, officials, and citizens of the USSR.

Presidium

The Chairman of the Presidium of the Supreme Soviet is nominal Head of State

Convenes sessions of the Supreme Soviet.
Issues decrees.
Interprets laws.
Dissolves the Supreme Soviet in case of persistent disagreement between the two chambers.
In intervals between sessions of the Supreme Soviet, subject to subsequent confirmation, releases and appoints Ministers of the USSR on the recommendation of the Chairman of the Council of Ministers.
In intervals between sessions of the Supreme Soviet, proclaims a state of war in case of attack or to carry out treaty obligations.
Annuls decisions and orders of the Council of Ministers which do not conform to law.
Appoints and removes high military and diplomatic officials.
Ratifies and denounces treaties.
Orders mobilization and proclaims martial law.

Council of Ministers

The Chairman of the Council of Ministers is the Premier of the USSR

Responsible and accountable to the Supreme Soviet.
Coordinates and directs the work of the ministries and other administrative bodies.
Ensures execution of the national economic plan and the state budget.
Ensures the maintenance of public order and the protection of the interests of the state and the rights of its citizens.
Directs the conduct of foreign policy.
Directs the general organization of the armed forces.

Ministers

(All-Union and Union Republic)
AND CHAIRMEN OF STATE COMMITTEES

Direct state administration within their jurisdiction.
Issue orders and instructions in pursuance of laws in operation and decisions and orders of the Council of Ministers.

not of division of power. This is the inevitable result both of centrally directed and all-encompassing economic plans, and of the complete control in every area of the Soviet Union by the highly centralized and disciplined Communist party.

In any case, Soviet leaders look on federalism as a temporary expedient. Lenin characterized it as a step toward "the most solid unification of the different nationalities into a single, democratic, centralized Soviet State." While paying lip service to the principle of secession, so justified in their view when a national group secedes from, and thus weakens, a bourgeois state, Soviet leaders do not countenance the possibility of secession from the workers' state. Thus in the words of Stalin: "In concrete instances the interests of the part may conflict with the interests of the whole. If that is so, we must repudiate the part." Soviet federalism is no more, therefore, than a convenient myth that makes it possible to combine the forms of autonomy with the facts of centralization of power.

The Bill of Rights and Duties

No section of the Soviet Constitution has attracted more attention than its Bill of Rights. This document is so different in form, coverage, and meaning from the American Bill of Rights that it must be looked at with particular attention.

The rights listed in the Soviet Constitution include the customary ones specified by modern constitutions—freedom of speech, assembly, press, organization, and religious worship (also, uniquely, of antireligious propaganda)—and freedom from arbitrary arrest. The inviolability of the home and the privacy of correspondence are assured. Equal rights are guaranteed for both sexes, and there is to be no discrimination because of racial or national origin. The right of asylum is extended "to foreign citizens persecuted for defending the interests of the working people, or for scientific activities, or for struggling for national liberation."

The first, and more unusual, provisions of the Bill of Rights are certain social rights. These are so clearly intended to be by-products of developments in the Soviet state that the con-

ditions out of which they arise are spelled out in detail. Thus the "right to work" is said to be ensured by "the socialist organization of the national economy, the steady growth of the productive forces of Soviet society, the elimination of the possibility of economic crises, and the abolition of unemployment." The rights to "rest and leisure," maintenance in old age, sickness, or disability, and education are similarly associated with explanations of the means to be taken to assure them.

Although experience has shown that no individual right has been protected by the courts against what the regime considered to be the national interest, there is a division between those rights that may normally be expected to be enforceable in court and those that are not. The equal rights of women, and the right not to be defamed on grounds of nationality, have been upheld in the courts under legislation enacted in accordance with the constitutional directives. The Procuracy—an office somewhat similar to that of the Attorney-General of the United States—has successfully protested an administrative decree that discriminated against nonresident workers. But the right to work, for example, is not enforceable in court. This type of "right" is, instead of a guarantee, a declaration of aspiration and, indeed, of expectation, once the Soviet state has achieved the necessary level of growth.

Side by side with the statement of rights goes a listing of duties that forms a further innovation in such documents. Oddly enough, the framers felt it necessary to declare that it is the citizen's duty "to abide by the Constitution" and "to observe the laws" as well as "to maintain labor discipline, honestly to perform public duties, and to respect the rules of socialist intercourse." The following clause outlines the duty to safeguard "public, socialist property" and terms those who commit offenses in this regard "enemies of the People." Clearly this is a serious crime. Following the declaration that "universal military service is law," the last clause of the document affirms "the sacred duty" to defend the country and describes treason as "the most heinous of crimes" to be punished with "all the severity of the law"—that is, by the death penalty.

So different is this document from a traditional bill of rights that it is difficult to evaluate. The least that can be said is that it is a declaration of desire; the most is that the implementation of any of its provisions depends on the will of the regime. While the Bill of Rights and Duties has undoubtedly become part of the political ethos of the Soviet Union, neither it nor any other part of the Soviet Constitution possesses what Western democrats define as the essential of constitutionalism: respect by the people and by governmental and party authorities for rules that limit and direct the exercise of public power.

The Soviet Concept of Constitutionalism

This attitude toward constitutional provisions points up a crucial distinction between the Soviet Constitution and those of the Western countries. In the United States, Great Britain, Germany, and France, whether the principles of the constitution are written or unwritten, it is assumed that they stand above any ruler or government and must be obeyed by them. Formal guarantees of the supremacy of the constitution vary from country to country; but the most fundamental protection of the constitution, particularly in Great Britain and the United States, is the fact that people have been brought up to respect it and that any tampering with it would arouse the greatest public indignation.

The Russian people lack any corresponding tradition of respect for constitutional provisions; thus, a departure from the Constitution's principles or from its specific provisions does not arouse the same feeling. According to official statements, the Soviet Constitution, like other constitutions, establishes fundamental principles and procedures that any government is obliged to obey. There is, in addition, a provision for amendment by a two-thirds vote of each chamber of the Supreme Soviet. But since no vote in the Supreme Soviet is ever less than unanimous, and since the highly disciplined Communist party is always in control, there is never any doubt that an amendment desired by the country's political leaders will be adopted. The crucial point is that within the Soviet Union there is none of that subordination of political leadership to law that responds to one of the

deepest convictions of the Anglo-American peoples.

Soviet and Western Conceptions of Freedom and Democracy

In short, Communist and Western conceptions of freedom and democracy are fundamentally different. Communists look upon democratic constitutions in the West as little more than a screen for political control by the exploiting class. Western democrats, from their side, believe that the absence of judicial or political restraints on the operations of authority in the Soviet Union is incompatible with liberty. Each, therefore, regards the other's use of the word *freedom* as basically hypocritical.

Lenin maintained that democracy in capitalist society "is always bound by the narrow framework of capitalist exploitation, and consequently always remains, in reality, a democracy for the minority, only for the possessing classes, only for the rich. Freedom in capitalist society always remains about the same as it was in the ancient Greek republics: freedom for the slave-owners." "The dictatorship of the proletariat," he wrote, "the period of transition to Communism, will, for the first time, create democracy for the people, for the majority, in addition to the necessary suppression of the minority—the exploiters."

The characteristics of Soviet society that spell freedom and democracy to the Communist are its provision of: widespread and relatively equal opportunities for education (more striking in the perspective of prerevolutionary Russia than in the perspective of the United States); job security and protection of labor against abuses by management; scientific and technological successes; the ideal, and to some extent the realization, of ethnic equality; the breakdown of former class divisions and access through education and ability to the higher levels of society; and the cultivation of a strong sense of collective solidarity. These are impressive achievements. That they have been formulated and largely acquired through the leadership of men who claim to have a monopoly of "right answers" and are not subject to popular or judicial control is not a source of concern to most Soviet citizens.

In contrast, the Western belief in freedom of speech and organization is based on the assumption that no one is infallible, that there can be honest disagreement among reasonable men on the best way of promoting the public welfare, and that through discussion, compromise, mutual concessions, and the adjustment of conflicting opinions solutions will be reached that are closer to the general interest than those that any individual or party might dictate. These basic differences of approach complicate relations between the Soviet Union and the West. Nonetheless, since Western democracies now place a greater emphasis on social welfare, and the Soviet Union shows more concern for legality in all except top decisions, both sides have acquired more basis for mutual understanding.

3. The Communist Party

1. THE PARTY IN THE PREREVOLUTIONARY PERIOD

Judged by the standards of British and French party systems, the party structure of the Soviet Union is novel and perplexing. To understand it the foreigner must rid himself of almost every preconception about the purpose, the form, and even the spirit of party activity; it would, in fact, be far better if some word other than *party* could be used to designate the Communist organization.

The differences between the Communist party and Western parties are in part the result of historical circumstance. In part they are the response to a different kind of purpose. The immediate purpose of parties in Great Britain, France, and the United States is to win elections. But before 1917 the primary purpose of the Communist party (or, as it was then known, the Bolshevik wing of the Russian Social Democratic Labor party) was to make a revolution. The tsarist regime had no intention of permitting its political opponents to win control of the government peacefully, or to engage in the type of opposition and criticism characteristic of democratic countries; and even if the tsarist government had been more tolerant, the Communist party would undoubtedly have refused to become a purely constitutional party. Lenin and his supporters had nothing but contempt for "reformist" parties in the West which, like the British Labor party, hoped to win power and to institute changes through peaceful, democratic, parliamentary methods. If far-reaching social and economic changes were to be achieved, the instrument would be not the ballot but class struggle. Power, Lenin believed, could be won only by force. Once the revolution had triumphed, it would be easy enough to persuade a majority of the people to support it. But first of all there had to be a revolution, and the party had to recruit, not men who would vote for it, but men who would revolt for it. "Give us an organization of revolutionaries," Lenin declared, "and we shall overturn the whole of Russia."

The task of overturning Russia was one that called for a special kind of organization and activity. The party, first of all, had to be a party of professional revolutionaries. No organization of amateurs could make a revolution. Only those men could be successful revolutionaries who were ready to devote to their work not their "spare evenings" but "the whole of their lives." There was no place for the dilettante or for those who were halfhearted, squeamish, ridden by doubt, or prone to independence or insubordination. Such men might make a successful debating society, but a revolution required tougher qualities. The people who joined the movement knew that they risked their liberty if not their lives. They could not think in terms of moderation or compromise, of seeing the other person's point of view, or of deferring to individual tastes and peculiarities. An organization that presumed to overturn the Russian state had to have a discipline of an almost military character. It was not for the rank and file to judge its orders or to question party strategy. What Lenin demanded was a hardened, specialized, experienced core of men of personal devotion, undeviating discipline, and professional skill. And this, in the course of years, was precisely the sort of organization he built.

Smallness of the Party

Men of the quality desired by Lenin are rare, and an organization limited to them necessarily had to be small. Smallness, however, was not a disadvantage. It was, on the contrary, essential to successful conspiracy. When critics of Lenin urged that the party be "accessible to the masses," Lenin pointed out that such a party would also be accessible to the police. The party, he said, should not cut itself off from the masses. But instead of having the masses join the party, the party's members should join the organizations to which the masses already belonged. Within trade unions, student associations, and other large organizations the Bolshevik members would form a solid core or fraction, constantly working to win positions of leadership in these organizations and to guide their policy in accordance with the Bolshevik program. In that way the party could hope to win mass support for its policies without admitting the masses to membership in the policy-making organization. In accordance with Marxist theory the party was the "vanguard of the proletariat," but the masses were to be guided and educated by the intellectuals who constituted the self-chosen leaders of the party.

Absence of Internal Democracy

The leadership principle applied not only to the party's relations with other organizations but to the inner working of the party itself. A revolutionary organization, Lenin frankly said, could not be democratic. It could not run its affairs publicly, debating policy, electing officers, and consulting the rank and file on all questions without revealing its strategy, its leadership, and its membership to the police (who would, and did, place spies in the organization). Under tsarist autocracy only an incorrigible utopian would ask for a large organization with elections, reports, and universal suffrage.

But there were other reasons for an undemocratic organization. A revolutionary movement needed leaders of special skill. Such men are rare ("talented men are not born by the hundred"), the rank and file is not likely to choose them, and, once chosen, it would be wrong to subordinate their policies to the judgment of the less talented members of the party. Lenin was merciless in his attack on the "wiseacres" who cried out "with the profundity of fools" that "it is a bad thing when the movement does not proceed from the rank and file." The rank and file would be only too likely to elect demagogues instead of revolutionaries. Leaders, therefore, must be co-opted, that is, chosen by others who already were experienced and able leaders and who knew the qualities needed for successful revolutionary endeavor.

Thus, neither in spirit nor in organization was there a heritage of democracy to pass on to the postrevolutionary party.

2. THE PARTY IN THE POSTREVOLUTIONARY PERIOD

The absence of democracy was no impediment to success. On the contrary, the organization of professional revolutionaries made the revolution precisely as Lenin had predicted and desired. Making the revolution, however, proved to be only the beginning of its work. Party leaders explained that an even more important task was the consolidation of the revolution and the introduction of a socialist economy. For this task the continued leadership of the party was indispensable.

The Party as Defender of the Revolution

The first new task of the party was to defend the revolution both against its foreign enemies and against those at home. Even after the foreign armies withdrew and the anti-Bolshevik armies were crushed, the struggle had still to be carried on against "antagonistic classes" inside the country. The revolution aimed at a "classless society," and this goal required the eventual destruction of the remnants of the old ruling class—the nobility, the landlords, the bourgeoisie—as well as the priesthood and the intellectuals who were regarded as its dependents. Later, the war against the kulaks (peasant landowners who were forced into collective farms) called for even more vigorous measures of suppression.

By 1936, however, Stalin announced, as we have seen, that all hostile classes had been liquidated. Henceforth, the party's function as defender of the revolution at home was as watchman against the "spies, assassins, and wreckers" whom foreign enemies were accused of sending into the Soviet Union.

The fear of hostile classes at home had been intensified by the danger that they might co-operate with invaders from abroad. In the first flush of successful revolution, Lenin and his associates had expected the Russian Revolution to be only the first in a world-wide series. But until after World War II the Communist success in Russia remained unique; everywhere else the revolutionary attempts were defeated. Thus Soviet Russia stood alone in a suspicious capitalist world, and the Russian people were warned constantly of the danger of capitalist encirclement and invasion—a danger that became imminent when Hitler won power in Germany on a bitterly anti-Communist platform.

Germany's attack on the Soviet Union in 1941 seemed to confirm these fears, even though capitalist countries such as Great Britain and the United States, instead of joining the "crusade against communism," immediately extended help to the USSR. Moreover, although after the war the Soviet Union was insulated from Western Europe by its ring of satellites, there was no immediate statement that the danger of capitalist encirclement had ended. The "cold war" between the Soviet Union and the United States kept tension high. Even after Khrushchev developed his theory of "camps" (described in Chapter 1), reduced barriers to travel, and encouraged other intercourse between the Soviet Union and Western countries, suspicion remained that the capitalistic West might somehow imperil the revolution. Thus the Communist party was proclaimed to be as important as ever in the defense of the country against its enemies.

The Party as Inspiration, Example, and Educator

The second function of the party, in the words of the Soviet Constitution (Article 126), is to act as "the vanguard of the working people in their struggle to strengthen and develop the socialist system."

As we have observed, Marx and his followers had expected the revolution to take place first of all in such highly industrialized countries as Germany and Great Britain. In such countries a mere change in the form of ownership and the purposes of production was expected to achieve the prosperity of the people. In Russia, however, before the promised reign of abundance could come into existence, a revolutionary transformation had to take place. The devastation of the Civil War had to be repaired, an agricultural country had to be industrialized, and an illiterate and backward people had to acquire the technical knowledge and skills necessary for a twentieth-century economy. Moreover, at the very time that men were being shifted from agriculture to industry, the productivity of agriculture itself had to be increased. An economic development that had taken a century or more in the West was to be compressed into a few decades. The capitalist countries, it was constantly reiterated, had to be "overtaken and surpassed."

The result was a staggering, backbreaking task, calling for infinite fortitude, strain, sacrifice, and devotion. Attention could not be given first of all to the things that would give immediate satisfaction to the people—to the production of clothing and houses and other consumers' goods. Instead, heavy industry had to be built, natural resources had to be developed, and men and women had to be taught the technical skills of an industrialized society. Eventually these resources and factories and skills could be used to satisfy the consumer, but first there had to be a long period in which people would sacrifice and struggle without seeing any great improvement in their standard of living.

In this task the party member was, and is, indispensable. It is up to him to explain to the peasant or worker why it is necessary to toil and sacrifice. It is up to him to master the new skills and to teach them to the people. It is his responsibility at all times to set an example of earnestness and courage, of discipline and devotion. When workers are disheartened or lagging, he must rouse their enthusiasm and stimulate their effort by conveying some conception of the ideal by which he himself is motivated. And this is no easy task. Marxist doctrine, even in its most simplified, even oversimplified, form, makes considerable intellectual demands. There have to be teachers of ability if people are to be inspired to work and sacrifice in its name. Moreover, the party member has to teach by example. Whenever there is a difficult job to be done, he is to volunteer. He is to work harder and longer than others. His fortitude and devotion are to provide inspiration to all who work with him. His conduct is to win respect and admiration for the party. He is to guard against discouragement and opposition. At all times he is to be guide, watchman, teacher, and animator in exhorting the masses. In this way the party is to be an education and an inspiration to the whole of Russia.

The Party as Governor

In the third place, the party had, and has, the job of leading and directing the government. According to the institutions and procedures established by the Soviet Constitution of 1936, the Soviet Union is a political democracy. Without changing a word of the Constitution, the system could be made to work much as any parliamentary democracy. There is a popularly elected legislature, as we have seen, and there is a Council of Ministers chosen by and responsible to it. There is, in addition, a federal system in which the member republics appear to have great powers. By implication, it is quite possible for the two houses of the Supreme Soviet to disagree with each other, for the Supreme Soviet to reject policies and proposals of the Council of Ministers, and for the federal republics to pursue distinctive policies.

As a matter of practice, however, none of these things occurs. The popularly elected Supreme Soviet never criticizes policies of the Council of Ministers except in administrative details. The Soviet of the Union never disagrees with the Soviet of Nationalities. The Ukraine never differs in administrative policy from Georgia or Uzbekistan. Most remarkable of all, there is never a case in which any of these bodies acts other than unanimously. Every vote in the Supreme Soviet is a unanimous vote: a "loyal opposition" does not exist.

The explanation of this remarkable unanimity lies in the work of the Communist party. Every political institution—the Council of Ministers,

the two chambers of the Supreme Soviet, and the governments of the federal republics—is under its control. If, in form, the organization of the government is decentralized and permits of disagreement, the Communist party itself is highly centralized and permits of none. Both in legislation and administration, it is the party that controls at all times, deciding what is to be done, when it is to be done, how it is to be done, and by whom. The party, as Stalin used to say, is the "supreme guiding energy in the State." The Constitution states frankly that the party is "the leading core of all organizations of the working people, both public and state." In explaining the Constitution in 1936, Stalin made this position even more explicit: "I must admit that the draft of the new Constitution leaves unchanged the present leading position of the Communist Party of the USSR. If our venerable critics regard this as a shortcoming of the draft Constitution, this can only be regretted. We Bolsheviks, however, consider this as a merit of the draft Constitution."

In the same spirit Stalin could tell the Eighteenth Congress of the party in 1939 that the party cadres "constitute the commanding staff of the leading organs of state. After a correct political line has been worked out and tested in practice, the party cadres become the decisive force in the work of guiding the party and the State." They direct the work of the Soviet and other governmental organs, and it is their job to see that all mass organizations (trade unions, cooperatives, youth organizations, cultural organizations, and others) accept the party's leadership and carry out its instructions. Thus Stalin could write, ". . . no important political or organisational problem is ever decided by our soviets and other mass organisations without directives from the Party . . . the dictatorship of the proletariat is, *substantially,* the 'dictatorship' of its vanguard, the 'dictatorship' of its Party, as the force which guides the proletariat." And whereas Stalin was guilty of bypassing party organs, Khrushchev reestablished the situation Stalin had described, and his successors maintain it even more strongly.

Methods of Party Control

The party operates directly through its own activities. It also keeps the closest possible control over the other agencies through which power is exercised in the Soviet Union: the secret police, the police, and the army (sometimes grouped together as the agencies that use violence); the complicated series of organizations often termed simply the "Soviet apparatus," that is, the ministries directing the economic and the noneconomic spheres of life; the control agencies that supervise these ministries (for example, the Commission of Soviet Control and the Ministry of State Control); and the administrative hierarchy of the soviets.

The relation between the party and these other agencies is a peculiarly subtle one. In the early days of the revolution, the party openly established its own agents, the political commissars, to watch over the army command. Another set of agents was established to supervise the work of the technical specialists in the economy. With the growth of the Stalinist state, however, the top personnel, not only in government and the secret police, but also in the army and the economy, became members of the party. It might be thought, therefore, that there was no reason why the party should continue to operate as a separate entity of control, since its members were the key figures in every aspect of Soviet life. In fact, however, the watchdog activities of the party have remained openly acknowledged and institutionalized.

At every important administrative level—particularly in the union republics, the subdivisions known as *oblasts,* and the smaller administrative areas, the *raions*—there are groups of "powers" of considerable influence, checking and counterchecking each other. Usually, these powers consist of representatives of economic ministries, the secret police, and the army; they are, however, under the overall supervision of the party. The party has particular responsibilities for securing the pattern of conduct the regime desires. Thus, it directs education, propaganda, and the system of graduated incentives through which the mass of the people have their most immediate spur to activity. It also supervises the economic agencies concerned with organizing production and distribution.

When there is a shift in ultimate power, as after Stalin's death, there may be temporarily (as there was) an uneasy balance among the party, the government, the operational units of the economy, the political police, and the army. It was Khrushchev's major achievement that he secured the primacy of the party in so relatively short a time and brought the other agencies into positions in which they acted as arms of the party, not as challenges to its authority. The succession of Brezhnev and Kosygin in 1964 was both smoother and immediate. Under all circumstances, however, there is a constant checking and counterchecking that puts a premium on achievement and thereby tends to weed out the incompetent and the lazy. Moreover—and this is its greatest merit from the point of view of those who hold supreme power, this system keeps the party constantly informed about developments in every area of life and throws all the important decisions into the hands of the party's top leaders. In this way, the system of checking and counterchecking is itself a supreme agency of party control.

3. CHARACTERISTICS OF THE PARTY

Composition of the Party

With the triumph of the revolution, one of the outstanding reasons for keeping the party small disappeared. There were no longer the tsarist police to fear; and the need for professional revolutionaries had passed. Yet the conception of the party as a small organization of talented leaders did not change. Men with the devotion and talent needed to build a socialist society still were rare, and it was believed that only a small group could maintain the necessary enthusiasm and sense of mission. Thus Lenin was already complaining in 1922 that the party was too large, that it was being joined by opportunists and patronage-seekers, and that measures must be taken to limit its size and to improve its quality.

To the leaders of a political party in Great Britain or France it would be inconceivable for a party not to want to be as large as possible. But in the USSR, with an immensely difficult task of "socialist construction" to perform, ability and concentration were more important than numbers. Stalin could declare in 1924:

It is not given to everyone to be a member of such a party. It is not given to everyone to stand the hardships and storms connected with membership of such a party. It is the sons of the working class, the sons of want and struggle, the sons of incredible privation and heroic efforts who before all should be members of such a party.

And his words were still quoted with high approval at the Party Congress of 1939.

As a result, the party has, ever since the revolution, found itself in something of a dilemma. With the assumption of the direction and planning of all political, industrial, and agricultural activity, there has been a tremendous growth in the size of the bureaucracy. If the Communist party is to be the governing party, the highest positions in all these undertakings must be held by party members; and in carrying out each new plan there must be vigorous, loyal, and devoted party members to set the pace and provide direction. The demand for talent and skill is an endless one; and in recruiting as members the men and women to do this work, the party inevitably must grow at a spectacular rate.

Yet the opening of the doors means the possibility that opportunists may gain admission. Since the Communist party is the dispenser of important jobs in government and industry, thousands of those who did not share its early struggles or believe in its ideals can be expected to join from motives of personal ambition and aggrandizement. It is of the utmost importance to ensure that the members of the party are personally loyal to its supreme leader.

Its Size and Recruiting

As a result, there have been sharp changes in the size and composition of the party. On the overall view it has expanded greatly: from 23,000 members in March and 200,000 in November 1917 to 12,471,000 in March 1966—that is, about one in every twelve of the adult population. But during this period there have been repeated purges of the membership (here the term means purification as well as terror). In 1921 and 1922 more than a quarter of the party's members were expelled. There were other great purges in 1928–29 and 1933–38 interspersed with several minor purges. At the time of the Eighteenth Party Congress in 1939, the party was composed of 2,477,666 persons, a marked drop

from the total membership of 3,555,338 in 1933—an indication of the impact of the 1933–34 purge and the great 1936–38 purge. In the period between the Eighteenth and Nineteenth Congresses (in 1952), however, the party almost tripled in size, adding 4,404,000 persons. Between the Nineteenth and the Twentieth Congresses (February 1956) it increased only 4.8 percent to 7,215,505, but by the Twenty-first Congress (January 1959) nearly six years after Stalin's death, it had grown by 14 percent to 8,239,131 members and candidates. Despite the fact that over 200,000 persons had been expelled, the numbers by the time of the Twenty-second Congress (October 1961) were 8,872,516 members and 843,489 candidates, of whom more than one-third had been added since the Twentieth Congress. By 1966, it was almost half again as large.

Before 1939 there were special restrictions on certain types of members. Candidates for membership were divided into different classifications according to their occupation and "class origin." Those in the less favored categories had to serve an exceptionally long period of probation and to find exceptionally large numbers of sponsors. In 1939 the rules were made more uniform and in 1966 stricter. Candidates have to be recommended by three party members of at least five (formerly three) years' standing who have known the candidate at their place of work; those under twenty-three must join the Komsomol, the youth organization. Both before and after the year's probationary period as a "candidate member," the applications of prospective members are discussed in general meetings of the lowest local party units. The decision of this body must then be endorsed by the district or city committee. Prospective members are no longer required to "master" the party's program (which Stalin declared only "a tried and theoretically trained Marxist" could do): it is enough for them to "accept" it, and "to submit to the rules and discipline of the party." Each member, however, has to be admitted individually on the basis of his personal record and qualifications.

Its Present Character

Today the Communist party is a party of young men and women, but led by an elite of older and longer-active members. At the end of the war, 63.6 percent of party members were under thirty-five. In 1966, over half were under forty, and almost half of all party members had joined after Stalin's death. The number of women has increased: the first woman to become a candidate member of the party Presidium (now again called Politburo) was Mme. Ekaterine Furtseva, in February 1956. (She later became Minister of Culture.) On the whole, however, the present party apparatus has impeded the entry of young people into the higher offices in the party, presenting a potentially explosive situation.

The level of education of party members has constantly risen. In 1956, 22 percent had completed secondary education, and 14.7 percent had had at least some higher education, as compared with 11.8 percent in 1952. By January 1966, 30.9 percent had a secondary education, and 18.2 percent had higher education. In contrast, only one of the eleven full members of the Politburo had completed university training.

Of the white-collar employees, scientists, engineers, teachers, and other intellectuals showed the greatest proportional increase. There is no limit on the admission of specialists—which is natural when one considers the change in the function of the party from making a revolution to directing a highly industrialized state under a planned economy. About 10 percent of the total membership hold full-time jobs in the party bureaucracy.

The lowest representation is still from the rural areas. The number of party fractions rose from about one unit to every twenty collective farms in 1939 to a primary organization on almost every collective farm by 1958. This was due partly to the consolidation movement that reduced the number of collective farms from 254,000 at the beginning of 1950 to some 78,000 in 1958, and partly to the thousands of party members from the towns (30,000 in 1955 alone) who were sent to direct party organizations on collective farms. The full transfer of planning and control to the local party unit on each farm was signalized by the abolition, in 1958, of the Machine Tractor Stations, the administrative units that had controlled pools of farm equipment and also had served as party watchdogs in what were looked on, with some justification, as largely hostile rural areas. But despite such efforts the party has still not succeeded in winning much support in the farming areas.

Discipline Within the Party

With the suppression of opposition outside the Communist party, the only place where freedom of political discussion and opposition could appear was within the party itself; and although Lenin had insisted, in prerevolutionary days, on absolute, undeviating discipline, and although the rank and file of party members could not challenge the decision of the leaders, there were (and are) certain occasions when the leaders themselves disagreed. The official theory was (and is) that of *democratic centralism,* according to which there is freedom of discussion within the party until a policy is adopted but absolute obedience to that policy once it has been adopted. Freedom of discussion does not assume as in Western democracies that truth will emerge from the competition of ideas; it assumes, rather, that criticism should aid the achievement of unity. Thus Lenin wrote in 1906 that democratic centralism involved *"freedom of criticism* so long as *unity in a specific action* is not destroyed thereby—and the inadmissibility of any criticism *whatever* which undermines or makes difficult *unity* of any action decided on by the Party."

As far as organization is concerned, the party regulations (Article 18) adopted in 1939 state that democratic centralism means:

a. The election of all leading Party bodies, from the highest to the lowest;
b. Periodical reports of the Party bodies to their Party organizations;
c. Strict Party discipline and subordination of the minority to the majority;
d. The absolutely binding character of the decisions of higher bodies upon lower bodies.

In the years immediately following the revolution, the desperate urgency of the situation threw decision-making into the hands of Lenin and his closest associates. Whenever the ruling ideology provided an answer, they acted without consulting the party membership. Where they failed to agree on objectives and means, however, party meetings were characterized by considerable freedom of discussion, and it was not a foregone conclusion that the leader of the party would always have his way. Lenin, for example, was twice voted down by the Central Committee of the party in February 1918 on his proposals for peace with Germany, although he eventually won a majority to his side.

It would be wrong, however, to suppose that this freedom of discussion marked any lessening of party discipline. In 1921, at the Tenth Party Congress, Lenin presented a resolution on party unity (later adopted as party policy) which attacked "factionalism" within the party, that is, the development within its ranks of any "opposition" having its own platform and discipline. In the same spirit Stalin declared in 1924 that "the Party constitutes a unity of wills which is incompatible with any setting up of factions and any division of power."

Much the same emphasis, it may be noted, appears in No. 27 of the party rules adopted by the Twenty-second Congress, October 1961. This rule asserts that "broad discussion, especially discussions on an all-Union scale, of questions of party policy must be carried out in such a way as to . . . prevent the possibility of attempts to form fractional groupings destructive to party unity or of attempts to split the party."

The struggle for power precipitated by Lenin's death in 1924 was reflected in contests at the Thirteenth, Fourteenth, and Fifteenth Party Congresses, held in 1924, 1925, and 1927 respectively. At each of these Congresses, Stalin's opponents claimed that they were simply making use of their right of intraparty discussion, while his supporters accused the critics of creating a faction within the party and of refusing to abide by earlier Congress rulings based on the doctrine of democratic centralism. Since Trotsky also accepted the view that the party was the legitimate spokesman of the people (evidence of the importance of the theory of the party even for an oppositionist), he was handicapped in his efforts and Stalin triumphed. In 1930, he reported happily: "The Sixteenth Congress is one of the few Congresses in our Party at which there is no longer an organized and well-defined opposition, capable of putting forward its own particular policy as against the general policy of the Party."

Since that time, meetings of the Party Congress have usually been harmonious, at least on the surface. In 1956, and again in 1966, there were latent differences of opinion on broad issues that were to be fought out in smaller bodies. Once decisions are made, however, the party unites behind them.

The "Monolithic Party"

In practice, party unity and discipline have had two results: to eliminate the influence of the rank and file on major policy decisions, and to concentrate decision-making in the hands of a small group, the Politburo (called the Party Presidium from 1952 to April 1966). This is characteristic of the official Stalin conception of the monolithic party first enunciated in 1924 in the struggle against Trotsky. As this view crystallized, party dogma, as formulated by the Politburo, was elevated above criticism and extended into all spheres of life, cultural as well as political. When Lenin's assumption that there could be criticism of major ideas and policies by his party colleagues was replaced in time by the notion of the infallibility of the leader, Stalin, the monolithic party achieved in practice and theory its logical apex.

One of the most striking developments of the post-Stalin period was Khrushchev's stinging criticism of the "cult of the individual," of Stalin's mistakes as a war leader, and of his arbitrariness toward high party functionaries. The overthrow of this aspect of Stalinism was widely heralded and coupled with what was called a return to Leninism. This return at first involved the practice of collective leadership (still more marked after Khrushchev's overthrow in 1964) and a greater openness about high party discussions. It also marked a salutary end to the almost pathological secretiveness and arbitrariness of Stalin's later years. And yet it is as difficult to find any essential change in the concentration of power in the hands of the top leaders in the post-Stalinist period as it is to find precedents in Lenin for what a Westerner would call free or open discussion. Certain practices have been revived that were normal in the earlier days of the Soviet regime: party organs meet more often and more regularly, and there is more participation through discussion. There is no indication, however, that the final result is anything other than the same concentration of ultimate decision-making in the hands of the top leaders.

One rash experiment in party organization attempted by Khrushchev in 1962, which may well have been responsible for his downfall, was reversed two years later. In an attempt to make the party an instrument more capable of following the details of industrial and agricultural planning and progress, Khrushchev divided the party into two hierarchies, one for each of these fields. The results were conflicting orders, a disruption of the unity and morale of the party, an accretion of strength to the economic bureaucracy (which took advantage of party disunity), poor economic returns (particularly in the regime's Achilles heel, agriculture), and Khrushchev's ouster. Immediately thereafter, the parallel party and government organizations that Khrushchev had set up at the provincial, regional, and local levels were reunited, and the party was withdrawn from the supervision of detailed performance to the loftier and more essential task for which it is (or should be) best fitted: the role of inspiration and ideological creativeness and motivation.

Thus the party again acquired its traditional unified hierarchical structure. How well it performs its overall functions of providing goals and the stimulus to realize them in a period of great technological advance depends, however, not merely on organization and the structure of power but even more on the ability of party members, and particularly of the party's top leadership, to win and keep the respect of an increasingly well educated and competent people and, perhaps even more, the confidence of an advanced industrial and scientifically oriented bureaucracy.

Party Self-criticism

The party has always placed great emphasis on self-criticism or, as it is called, "Bolshevik self-criticism." According to this practice the party searches for and points out to itself its own weaknesses. To the foreigner, however, such criticism inevitably seems somewhat artificial. There is never any criticism of top leaders, or of their close associates, or of the current policy of the party, only of the way in which it is being executed. One of the leaders of the party may criticize a policy, particularly a policy associated with a leader out of favor, but this is already the equivalent of an announcement that the policy is being changed. In addition, leaders of the party often attack certain practices of subordinate officials; and once the signal has been given and the appropriate prey designated, ordinary party members join in the denunciation. This is a useful device for keeping subordinates in order and breaking up any local combination that might challenge the central party authorities. But the party's leaders and the party line are sacrosanct. Soviet leaders are never obliged to listen to, or reply to, the sort of attack to which the leaders of the Labor party in Great Britain or the Socialist party in France are subjected at their annual party conferences and congresses. But this may well be a weakness as far as gauging needs is concerned, rather than a strength.

Strains and Strengths

It would be absurd, of course, to claim that there are no stresses or rivalries within the so-called monolithic party. The very absence of effective channels for criticism or regular means of advancement necessarily creates an atmosphere in which intrigue thrives. Thus behind even the apparent solidity of the Stalinist regime, groups of local officials made mutually advantageous deals instead of checking each other, as the system would have had them do. Small officials attached themselves to powerful patrons, rose with them, or were shattered if they fell into disgrace. Rivalry between Malenkov and Zhdanov, before the latter's death in 1948, went deep into the party's membership, creating two blocs of power, each striving for supremacy and eager to destroy the other.

Stalin's death in 1953 unloosed fresh and even more significant struggles for power, both among individuals and among the three major power groups in the Soviet system: the party, the secret police, and the army. The first question was: Who would control the party? To this, two immediate answers were given: there was to be collective leadership by the small group of persons in the Party Presidium (as the Politburo was renamed in 1952), and the all-important First Secretaryship of the Central Committee of the Party (which Malenkov inherited from Stalin at his death on March 5) was taken over by Khrushchev on March 14, just nine days later—though not officially until September.

Already, however, the secret police under Beria had emerged as potentially the strongest power in the country. Beria, whose MVD had complete control in Moscow in the days following Stalin's death, became Minister of the Interior; moreover, all the powers of that ministry were joined temporarily to those of the Ministry of State Security. A countercheck to this vast police power appeared quickly, however, in the armed forces, which temporarily assumed a new and more independent role than under Stalin.

Beria either overreached himself or was outmaneuvered. On June 26 he was removed from his offices and arrested; in December 1953 he was executed. Moreover, the Party Presidium took good care to ensure that the Ministry of the Interior could no longer offer a threat to the regime: it demoted and curbed the political police, which since 1954 has been under the Committee on State Security. For the moment both the army and the party had gained in the overall struggle for power. At the Twentieth Party Congress, Marshal Zhukov became the first professional military figure to reach the ranks of the Presidium, and for a time Marshal Bulganin seemingly shared the first place with Khrushchev both at home and in their travels abroad. However, both Zhukov and subsequently Bulganin disappeared from top party circles.

In fact, from the beginning of the transition, the party held its dominance. Insofar as the political police retains real importance—and it still has an essential role in the Soviet state—it is as a special arm of the party. Throughout, though with increasing obviousness, the power of the Party Secretariat has been the key factor in control. After the death of Stalin, as after that of Lenin, the holder of the office of First Secretary—Khrushchev, like Stalin before him—became the dominant figure. When Brezhnev and Kosygin engineered Khrushchev's ouster, the former assumed the office of First Secretary, the latter the office of Premier.

What was remarkable in the succession after Stalin's death, and even more so when Khrushchev was replaced, is that there was so little violence—in fact, none at all in 1964. The Soviet system has its strains but it also has great strengths. The top membership of the party is drawn from men who occupy responsible and privileged positions in society and who have a strong vested interest in its power and stability. There may seem a vast wastage of human energy and creativeness in the obvious suspicion and jockeying for power among and within the groups that make up the Soviet power structure. But the struggle helps to forge the self-assuredness and the drive of those few in whose hands power ultimately rests. On them depends the cohesiveness that reknits Soviet society (which is deliberately kept atomized to prevent the emergence of competing power groups), and this cohesiveness commonly outweighs divisive factors, except in supreme moments of crisis.

4. THE PARTY ORGANIZATION

The organization of the Communist party is, in form, that of a great pyramid. At its base are the more than three hundred thousand *primary party organizations* which, according to party rules,

> . . . are set up in mills, factories, state farms, machine and tractor stations and other economic establishments, in collective farms, units of the Red Army and Navy, in villages, offices, educational establishments, etc., where there are not less than three Party members.

These primary organizations provide the front line of the party's contacts with the mass of the people. They are responsible for organizing agitation, political education, and self-criticism. Each primary organization meets once a month, but actual direction of its activities is carried on by a bureau if the organization has at least fifteen members; otherwise, it is carried on by the secretary alone. If the organization is large, it may have several full-time paid officials. But the key to the work of the organizations at this level, as at every other, remains the secretary.

The next level above the primary party organizations is the *city* or *district* (both rural and urban) *party committees;* these also elect the bureaus which, because of their larger areas, include three secretaries, one of whom is always

STRUCTURE OF THE COMMUNIST PARTY

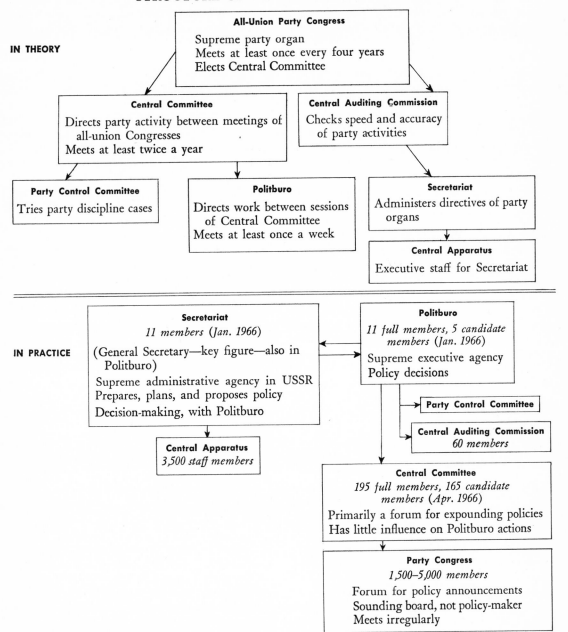

IN THEORY

All-Union Party Congress
Supreme party organ
Meets at least once every four years
Elects Central Committee

Central Committee
Directs party activity between meetings of all-union Congresses
Meets at least twice a year

Central Auditing Commission
Checks speed and accuracy of party activities

Party Control Committee
Tries party discipline cases

Politburo
Directs work between sessions of Central Committee
Meets at least once a week

Secretariat
Administers directives of party organs

Central Apparatus
Executive staff for Secretariat

IN PRACTICE

Secretariat
11 members (Jan. 1966)
(General Secretary—key figure—also in Politburo)
Supreme administrative agency in USSR
Prepares, plans, and proposes policy
Decision-making, with Politburo

Politburo
11 full members, 5 candidate members (Jan. 1966)
Supreme executive agency
Policy decisions

Party Control Committee

Central Auditing Commission
60 members

Central Apparatus
3,500 staff members

Central Committee
195 full members, 165 candidate members (Apr. 1966)
Primarily a forum for expounding policies
Has little influence on Politburo actions

Party Congress
1,500–5,000 members
Forum for policy announcements
Sounding board, not policy-maker
Meets irregularly

senior. All evidence points to the importance and difficulty of retaining adequate supervision of these secretaries. Their appointment must be confirmed by the regional, territorial, or central committee of the republic within which the city or district is located. The local committees are supposed to meet every month, obviously as a check on the secretaries' work, but even when they do so the discussions are often perfunctory. The city and district conferences, which elect the committees, are held only once a year and thus can have little effect.

Above the city and district committees are *area party organizations* on the regional (*oblast*) and union-republic levels. (The RSFSR is too large for an organization at the union-republic level, but a special Bureau of the RSFSR, directly under the Central Committee, was appointed in 1956.) In each republic there is a congress that meets once every two years (once every four years in the Ukraine, Byelorussia, Uzbekistan, and Kazakhstan), but policy as outlined by the leaders is always accepted unanimously, and, particularly above the city and district levels, actual power is exercised by the small executive organ, the bureau, and the three secretaries. In an area remote from Moscow, these secretaries and, in particular, the first secretary, may exercise a vast amount of power. One émigré described an *oblast* secretary as "on a small scale God and Tsar." The top party leadership obviously tries to keep these officials under its control, and the first secretary in these higher units is invariably a central appointee. The relatively high mortality rate among such officers illustrates the difficulty in keeping them tools of the Politburo (Party Presidium) rather than their own masters. At the same time their importance is highlighted by the frequency with which first secretaries of major cities and of union republics become officials in all-Union party organs.

All-Union Party Organs

At the top of the hierarchy stands the focus of power—the party organs of the USSR as a whole, which are themselves tightly integrated and directed by the small group of leaders in the Politburo. Technically, the supreme organ is the Party Congress; the Congress elects the Central Committee; and the Central Committee chooses the Politburo and the Secretariat. In practice, control operates in reverse.

Other organs are not particularly important. The Congress elects the Central Auditing Commission, which audits the party's accounts. (No accounts have been published since the revolution, but the 1956 Congress was told that 73 percent of party funds comes from party dues and practically all the rest from party enterprises, such as publishing.) The Central Committee appoints the Party Control Committee, which

enforces party discipline, but since 1956 there have been no local representatives on this body; it probably serves, therefore, only in cases of appeal from local party organizations or for higher party officials. The Organization Bureau was abolished in 1952. There is provision for a party conference to be convened annually between sessions of the Party Congress, but no party conference has been held since 1941.

In certain respects, this general organization does not differ sharply from the organizations of some democratic parties in Western countries. However, there is a vast difference in their spirit and operation. Under the conditions of democratic centralism, authority comes from above, not below. The very fact that the secretaries of the city, district, area, and higher party organs (the most important officials within the respective organizations) must be approved from above emphasizes that effective control rests with the leaders and not with the rank and file. The power of the leaders to direct or to prevent discussion, and the clear recognition in the party rules of "the absolutely binding character of the decisions of higher bodies upon lower bodies," shut out the possibility of any movement from below contrary to the desires of the leaders. In fact, a favorite comparison of the leaders of the party is that already cited between the party and an army, with the full-time professionals, the generals; the functional specialists, an officers' corps; and the secretaries of party units, the noncommissioned officers. It should be added that above them all is a general staff, the Politburo.

The Party Congress

The concentration of power in the hands of the relatively small group of men comprising the Politburo means that the All-Union Party Congress is a sounding board rather than a policy-maker. According to party rules the Party Congress is the supreme organ of the party, but it never engages in the kind of debate and criticism of its leaders so characteristic of the annual conference of the British Labor party. Each new Congress is supposed to elect a new Central Committee of the party, to determine the tactical line of the party on many questions of current policy, to revise and amend the program and rules of the party, and to hear and act on the reports of the Central Committee and other central party organs. In fact, however, the Communist Party Congress has never wielded the authority that these statements would suggest.

In the first place, the members of the Congress are chosen in accordance with rules laid down by the Central Committee and from known supporters of the leaders in power. In the second place, its meetings have been somewhat irregular. From the time of the revolution until 1925, meetings were held annually. Thereafter the interval between meetings grew progressively longer—a two-year lapse from 1925 to 1927, a three-year lapse until 1930, a four-year lapse until 1934, a five-year lapse until 1939, and then a thirteen-year lapse until October 1952, shortly before Stalin's death. Since then, there have been four Congresses, the regular Twentieth Party Congress in February 1956, the Extraordinary Twenty-first Party Congress in January–February 1959, the Twenty-second Party Congress in October 1961, and the Twenty-third Party Congress in March–April 1966.

The Party Congresses that follow a change of leadership are watched with special interest to see whether there are genuine debates on policies, criticism of leaders, or noticeable changes in the personnel of central party organs. Both in 1956 and in 1966, the rapid ousting of followers of the former leader and their replacement by the adherents of the new party leadership were very noticeable. So, too, was criticism of the weaknesses and faults of the former regime, although nothing said in 1966 rivaled Khrushchev's denunciation of Stalin in 1956. But divisions of opinion within the ruling top leadership were kept carefully muted on both occasions. In 1956, the trend toward greater liberalization seemed clear; in 1966, the conservatives dominated, even to the point of raising suspicions of a return to the firmer hand of Stalin. Ultimate direction, however, was left to whichever leader, or leaders, acquired or maintained control.

The Central Committee

Like the Party Congress, the Central Committee has usually had far less power or even influence than we might expect from reading the party rules. Important legislative measures are issued in the name of the Council of Ministers and the Central Committee, but the latter neither formulates nor reviews them. In any case, the size of the Central Committee limits the possibility of decision-making though not of debate.

In Stalin's later years, the Central Committee met only rarely. Brezhnev appears to have returned the body to an unimportant, perfunctory role. But Khrushchev used the Central Committee on at least two occasions to review issues over which the Party Presidium lacked its customary unanimity. The first occasion was in 1955, when Molotov disagreed sharply with other members of the Presidium over policy toward Yugoslavia and was overridden also in the Central Committee. The second resulted from the much more serious clash in June 1957 between Khrushchev and the antiparty group. Khrushchev was outvoted in the Presidium but hastily assembled the members of the Central Committee with the aid of the army and won majority support. His opponents—Malenkov, Molotov, Kaganovich, and Shepilov—were expelled from the Central Committee, and these four, along with Saburov and Pervukhin, were expelled from the Presidium.[1] It was out of these epoch-making actions that Khrushchev acquired supreme power in the country.

In the far smoother transition from Khrushchev to Brezhnev in 1964, Khrushchev and his supporters, including those in the army, were oblivious to what had been planned, and, indeed, some key figures, including Khrushchev himself, were out of Moscow when the decision on his ouster was made. When the members of the Central Committee were called in, Khrushchev's successors had already triumphed. They met with no resistance.

According to a new party rule adopted at the Twenty-second Congress, not less than one-quarter of the members of the Central Committee were to be "renewed" at each Congress; this rule was rescinded, however, by the Twenty-third Congress. But there is always a major turnover when new leaders come into office, since

[1] Molotov was for some time in what amounted to protective custody in Siberia. On September 5, 1958, Bulganin was also expelled from the Presidium. After a vehement attack at the Twenty-second Party Congress in October 1961 on the antiparty group, they seem to have been relegated to obscurity.

the First (now General) Secretary can make appointments to many posts that carry with them membership on the Committee. Forty-four percent of the members of the 1956 Central Committee—forty full members and seventy-one candidates—were new. (The change was almost as great as the one that took place during Stalin's great purge.) This fact was of great importance when Khrushchev appealed to the Committee in 1957 to override the Presidium.

The change of faces was no less evident after Khrushchev's replacement by Brezhnev. At least twenty members elected to the Central Committee in April 1966 (thirteen full members and seven candidates) came from Brezhnev's region in the Ukraine. The average age of Committee members is noticeably higher than in the body elected in 1961—nearly a quarter are over sixty while in 1961 only twelve percent were—and one-quarter of those selected in 1966 had served on the Committee under Stalin.

The Politburo

Authority rests in a much smaller body, the Politburo. This body makes the most important decisions on policy, and the greatest freedom of discussion within the party centers here. The greatest secrecy cloaks the number of meetings the Politburo holds and the character of its discussions.

At the close of the 1966 Party Congress, Brezhnev announced that the Politburo (just renamed) would have an inner cabinet of four members: himself; Kosygin, the Premier; Suslov, who is also a member of the Secretariat and is a specialist on ideological matters; and Podgorny, the new Chairman of the Presidium of the Supreme Soviet, often termed the President of the Soviet Union. All other members of the Politburo are in charge of departments that require detailed supervision, and it is presumed that the inner cabinet will devote itself to matters of general policy.

The inner cabinet of 1966 is believed to be divided fairly evenly between conservatives and those who are termed more radical. Brezhnev and Suslov are ranked as conservative, with Suslov the more so; Podgorny and Kosygin, particularly the latter, are thought to be more

ready for experimentation. Thus there appears to be a reasonable balance of attitudes.

Once a decision has been reached, every member of the Politburo gives it his complete support: the Politburo presents a solid front to the rest of the party (in this one respect not unlike the British Cabinet), and it would be unheard of for any other party organ to resist or reject its decisions. In this respect the present leaders echo Stalin's earlier warning: "We must never forget that we are a *ruling* Party. We must not forget that any open expression of our differences may reduce our influence in the country—

Dates at which members of the Politburo and Secretariat assumed their positions

Politburo
Members

Brezhnev, L. I.	June 1957
Kirilenko, A. P.	April 1962
Kosygin, A. N.	May 1960
Mazurov, K. T.	March 1965
Pel'she, A. Ya.	April 1966
Podgorny, N. V.	May 1960
Polyansky, D. S.	May 1960
Shelepin, A. N.	November 1964
Shelest, P. Ye.	November 1964
Suslov, M. A.	July 1955
Voronov, G. I.	October 1961

Candidate Members

Demichev, P. N.	November 1964
Grishin, V. V.	January 1961
Kunayev, D. A.	April 1966
Masherov, P. M.	April 1966
Mzhavanadze, V. P.	June 1957
Rashidov, Sh. R.	October 1961
Scherbitsky, V. V.	December 1965
Ustinov, D. F.	March 1965

Secretariat

Brezhnev, L. I. (General Secretary)	October 1964
Andropov, Yu. V.	November 1962
Demichev, P. N.	October 1961
Kapitonov, I. V.	December 1965
Kirilenko, A. P.	April 1966
Kulakov, F. D.	September 1965
Ponomarev, B. N.	October 1961
Rudakov, A. P.	November 1962
Shelepin, A. N.	October 1961
Suslov, M. A.	March 1947
Ustinov, D. F.	March 1965

to say nothing of the effect it may have abroad." It is true that Khrushchev lashed out even against members of the Presidium and that there were an unusual number of changes in its membership after the relatively stable early period of post-Stalin "collective leadership." Before the Twenty-second Congress, for example, there were fifteen full members; after the Congress there were only eleven. Moreover, the 1961 party rules provide that "as a rule" Presidium members will not be elected for more than three terms and that, as with the Central Committee, not less than one-quarter will be "renewed" at each Congress. Thus the old jest of Stalinist days is no longer valid: that the Politburo (Presidium) is a dead-end street from which there is only one exit, the grave. Even after Khrushchev's ouster, there was remarkable continuity in the membership of the party's top organ. In 1966, only four of the eleven full members and five of the eight candidate members of the Politburo acquired these positions after Brezhnev's accession to the office of First Secretary.

The Secretariat

The most important body in the USSR for preparing plans and proposing policy is the Secretariat of the Central Committee. It ranks second only to the Politburo in the making of decisions; and the fact that four Secretaries (in 1966) were also members of the Politburo provides an interlocking relationship. Where the Politburo is concerned with executive decisions, the Secretariat is the supreme administrative agency of the party. It is for this reason that Khrushchev's, and, after 1962, Brezhnev's position as First (now General) Secretary has been of such significance.

Though the Secretaries are formally elected by the Central Committee in plenary session, the latter's action is merely *pro forma* approval of a list already prepared by the top leaders. In the post-Stalin period, the number of Secretaries has varied between three (February to July, 1955) and ten (December 1957 to 1960). In 1961 there were five: Kozlov, Kuusinen, Mukhitdinov, and Suslov, working under Khrushchev—a number increased to nine after the Twenty-second Party Congress. (Mukhitdinov

lost his post here and in the Party Presidium.) In 1966, there were eleven. While arrangements seem fairly flexible, the allocation of responsibilities in December 1959 when there were still ten Secretaries suggests the major groupings: general supervision over the administrative staff of the Secretariat; foreign Communist parties; party and personnel matters; industry, transport, and political work in military organizations; culture, education, youth, and women's affairs; agriculture; Central Asian and Moslem affairs; and ideology, propaganda, and agitation.

Administrative Staffs

In supervising all activities in these varied fields, the Secretariat depends on administrative staffs which, not surprisingly, are organized very much like a government. The most important of these staffs is the Apparatus of the Central Committee, which assists all the top central agencies, but is directly responsible to the Secretariat. Its one thousand to two thousand experienced and particularly trustworthy Communists are responsible for overseeing all spheres of Soviet life; they have active field staffs, wide sources of information, and considerable authority.

Though shifts in organization are not infrequent, the work of the Apparatus makes certain divisions essential. In 1957, there were fourteen departments: Party Organs (divided into four territorial sections and four functional subsections); Propaganda and Agitation; Culture and Science; Higher Education and Schools; Agriculture; Transport and Communications; four for the main branches of industry; one for administrative organs; one for trade, finance, and planning; a foreign department; and an administrative department.

The Central Apparatus has particular significance not only because of its functions but also because it includes some of the most promising of the younger Communists—those most likely to be picked for the top organs. There are also apparatuses at the *oblast* and *raion* levels. But these are only some, though the most important, of the many administrative agencies of the party. All these agencies (which were staffed by some 240,250 paid officials in 1958) concern themselves not only with the party membership but with all aspects of life throughout the country. Looking at this vastly complicated mechanism of party control, which is superimposed on the ordinary agencies of government, it becomes strikingly evident that dictatorships have, in fact, far more intricate and overlapping organizations to manage than have democracies.

Youth Organizations

The Communist party has a special concern for securing the loyalty of young people, and a graduated series of youth organizations—the Little Octobrists, Pioneers, and Komsomols, or Leninist Communist League of Youth—associate a high proportion of those between the ages of eight and twenty-six with party programs and discipline. In the Little Octobrists, for children from eight to eleven, political education begins. From nine to fifteen, almost all urban young people are in the Young Pioneers, where political indoctrination is more intense, where there are any number of organized activities, and where "socially useful" work is encouraged, sometimes to the detriment of formal education. At fourteen, young people can become members of the Komsomol, where numbers are also an object. From a wartime high of fifteen million, membership dropped to between eight and nine million in 1948, but an all-out enrollment drive raised the figure to sixteen million in 1952, eighteen million in 1958, and twenty-three million in 1966. Not all those eligible, however, are members.

The Komsomols are organized on the pattern of the party and to a considerable extent carry on the same type of activities. Thus the young Communist is told that "all his life must be subordinated to the great aim—the struggle for Communism." He is trained in Marxism-Leninism, acts as an agitator, and is expected to provide an example of devoted work. The Komsomols, in fact, are supposed to aid production through exhortations and uncovering inefficiencies and to act as agencies of labor recruitment. For example, some 650,000 young people were sent by Khrushchev to the new lands he opened up in the East.

How devoted, in practice, are the vast majority of Communist youth? Probably there is a small group of activists in the Komsomols.

But for the most part the young people seem apathetic, the more so because there is little chance for them to assume initiative. The majority of the directors are professional bureaucrats; over 50 percent of the delegates to the Thirteenth Congress of Komsomols in 1958 were over twenty-six years old, the statutory age limit until that time for Komsomol membership (it was raised to twenty-seven). In other words, the Komsomols are not organizations run by young people themselves but the means whereby the party tries to capture and control the youth of the country.

5. SUCCESS OF THE SOVIET PARTY SYSTEM

If one were to repeat in regard to the Soviet party system the questions asked in earlier chapters about the effectiveness of the British and French systems, the Communist party would appear to be condemned on almost every point. The Soviet system does not give the people a "meaningful and adequate choice, both of policies and of leaders." It does not permit the reflection of the desires of the people and of party members when they are in conflict with the policy of party leaders. The internal organization of the Communist party is not democratic enough to provide a channel for effective participation in policy-making by the rank and file. If the party promotes the peaceful settlement of controversial issues, it is rather through the prevention or suppression of controversy than through the reconciling of divergent opinions. And if the party is an effective instrument for carrying out the judgment of the voters, there may be considerable question as to the significance of a judgment that is the result neither of discussion nor of free choice.

To make these statements, however, is to apply the standards of Western democracy to a system which, in spite of occasional nods to popular participation or freedom of discussion, is concerned primarily with other goals: the "defense of the socialist system" against its opponents, the education and inspiration of the masses, the stimulation for continued industrialization of the country and for improved agricultural production, and the forging of an instrument to animate and guide both the economic and political government of the country.

Judged by such aims, the Communist party has been a peculiarly effective instrument for the building of the Soviet state. The questions to be raised about its current and future performance are not related to the norms of Western democratic systems but to Soviet needs and the party's own avowed goals. Can it, in practice, provide leadership in a period of rapid and self-assured technological advance? Can it solve the knotty problem of agricultural production? Can it convince the youth of the country that to be a high-ranking member of the party is a more desirable career than is offered by other fields of life? Can it harness the brilliance of Soviet litterateurs to its own ideological purposes? Can it make Marxism-Leninism relevant to the last third of the twentieth century? It is in respect to these issues that the party appears least successful, and where its greatest challenges lie.

4. The Soviets

1. THE NATURE OF THE SOVIETS

Side by side with the pyramid of Communist party organizations in the USSR, and largely controlled by them, is a pyramid of governmental organizations known as the soviets—beginning with local soviets, which are roughly the equivalent of town or village councils in the United States, and culminating in a Supreme Soviet, which corresponds roughly to the United States Congress or the British Parliament.

Originally, however, the system of soviets was intended to be something quite different. It was regarded as an outstanding achievement of the November Revolution of 1917 that the soviets were substituted for legislative assemblies of the traditional type. According to Lenin and his followers, parliaments in Western countries were simply show windows to delude the masses. The representatives chosen by the people might talk to their hearts' content, but behind the scenes real power rested in the hands, not of the parliamentary talkers, but of the bureaucracy, the army, and the police force. Lenin could quote Marx to the effect that what was needed was "not a parliamentary but a working corporation, legislative and executive, at one and the same time." The masses, if they were to rule, must be the executive as well as the legislature. "Our aim," Lenin wrote, "is to draw *the whole of the poor* into the practical work of administration." The soviets were the instrument by which this objective was to be realized.

The word *soviet* in Russian is simply the word for council. It acquired special significance, however, during the revolution of 1905 when councils or soviets of workers' deputies sprang up spontaneously in many Russian cities and provided the leadership for the revolutionary movement. These were organizations of the workers themselves, and to Lenin they suggested both a pattern for future revolutionary action and a type of organization through which the mass of the workers might participate directly in political life. Moreover, the experience with the soviets of 1905 had captured the popular imagination. In spite of their suppression, the memory of their leadership persisted; and when the March Revolution of 1917 occurred, it was only natural for soviets of workers' and soldiers' deputies to be formed throughout the country.

Lenin, upon his return to Russia in April, vigorously supported this type of organization. "The Soviet of Workers' Deputies is the *only possible* form of revolutionary government," he told his followers. "To return to a parliamentary republic from the Soviet of Workers' Deputies would be a retrograde step." There must be "not a parliamentary republic . . . but a republic of soviets of Workers', Agricultural Laborers' or Peasants' Deputies throughout the country, from top to bottom." The slogan of the Communists was "All Power to the Soviets."

In part, Lenin's enthusiasm for the soviets resulted from tactical considerations. As the elections for the Constituent Assembly proved, the Bolsheviks could not hope to win control of a popularly elected parliament chosen by all classes of the population. But they could hope to win control of the soviets, since these were composed predominantly of the urban working class where the Bolsheviks had their greatest strength. By the time of the November Revolution the Bolsheviks had succeeded in winning majorities in the important soviets in Moscow and in Petrograd, of which the latter became the instrument of the seizure of power. They also won control of the All-Russian Congress of Workers' and

Soldiers' Deputies, which was made up of deputies from these and other local soviets. Thus they had powerful centers of influence from which to operate.

In particular, however, the soviets were hailed by Lenin as a special instrument, immensely superior to bourgeois parliamentarism for drawing "in the freest, broadest, and most energetic manner, all the masses into the work of government. . . . It is a power that is open to all, that does everything in sight of the masses, that is accessible to the masses, that springs directly from the masses; it is the direct organ of the masses and of their will."

The Soviets Before 1936

Almost immediately, however, the Bolsheviks faced the problem that has remained at the heart of their relations with the masses: how to win popular support and at the same time maintain party control. Concentration of authority in the period of War Communism meant similar concentration within the soviets also. Lower soviets were made responsible to higher ones; power came to be exercised by executive committees rather than by the members of the soviets as a whole. But it was still more significant that the Eighth Party Congress in 1919 decreed that party fractions under strict party discipline should be set up within each soviet with the aim of unifying and subordinating the whole structure of the soviets to the single will of the party. "The Russian Communist Party must win for itself undivided political mastery in the soviets," it declared, "and practical control over all their work."

Centralization of control led directly to a loss of mass support for the soviets, evidenced most forcefully by the Kronstadt Rebellion of 1921. Despite some relaxation of administrative controls during the 1920's, the soviets never regained their initial position as popular agencies. They provided no adequate contact between the party and the masses during the tense period of collectivization of agriculture. "The soviet organs of the proletarian dictatorship which ought to be in the center and provide the leadership of every revolutionary undertaking," it was declared in 1930, "drag at the tail of this vast movement of social change."

Thereafter the party embarked on a more active policy of stimulating, as well as leading, the soviets. Great emphasis was placed on getting the maximum number of people to vote in elections for the soviets; at least a minimum number of questions were required from the floor at soviet meetings. At the same time, party and administrative controls were tightened so that the soviets became, to a degree, an extension of the party administrative structure.

Though mass participation was one of the major purposes of the structure of the soviets, there were formal limitations on elections for the higher soviets until 1936. Election to the All-Union Congress of Soviets, "the supreme authority of the USSR," was indirect—that is, delegates were chosen as representatives of town and village soviets. Elections were also unequal: the town soviets sent one deputy for every twenty-five thousand voters, while the village soviets were limited to one deputy for every one hundred and twenty-five thousand inhabitants. Voting was public, by a show of hands, and class enemies (clergymen, employers of labor, those who engaged in trade or lived on their incomes, and former members of the tsarist police) were not allowed to vote. In addition, the Congress of Soviets met for only a few days every two or more years, a practice that left little opportunity for effective participation in government even by these indirectly chosen representatives of the masses. In the long intervals between meetings of the Congress, power was delegated to a Central Executive Committee that had two chambers, a Union Council and a Council of Nationalities. This body was supposed to meet three times in the interval between Congresses.

The Constitution of 1936

The new Constitution of 1936 introduced drastic changes as far as elections and organs were concerned. Stalin explained these changes by saying that the socialist system had now been unshakably established in all spheres of the national economy. The capitalist, landlord, and kulak classes had disappeared, and there was a new peasantry which, in its great majority, was a collective farm peasantry.

Under this Constitution suffrage became universal. With the exception of the insane and of criminals, who are deprived of electoral rights, every citizen over eighteen, regardless of social origin or past activities, is guaranteed the right to vote. Each vote counts equally—urban areas no longer have any advantage over rural ones. Moreover, the voting for deputies is both secret and direct. To emphasize participation through voting, elections are held at different times for local assemblies, republic soviets, and the Supreme Soviet, with those for the latter being, of course, the most important.

The Supreme Soviet consists of two chambers, a Soviet of the Union and a Soviet of Nationalities, the former representing the country by population and the latter giving special representation to federal areas. Both are elected at the same time and for four-year periods, beginning in 1946 after the wartime hiatus. All other soviets are unicameral.

If the changes in the Constitution were, in form, an advance toward democracy, they were also, somewhat ironically, a departure from the "soviet" ideal and a move in the direction of the parliamentarism and the separation of powers that Lenin had denounced. Whereas the Congress of Soviets and the Central Executive Committee had been described in the Constitution of 1923 as "the supreme authorities of the USSR," combining legislative, executive, and administrative authority, legislative power now was separated from administrative, the former (technically) exercised by the Supreme Soviet, the latter by the Council of Ministers. The same distinction is made in the case of the union republics; and it is only on the lowest levels of government organs, described under local government in Chapter 6, that the soviets of working people's deputies have administrative and executive responsibilities, largely through being themselves activists in the tasks of the Soviet state.

2. SOVIET ELECTIONS

When one reads the Soviet Constitution and electoral laws, there seems little difference between their provisions and those of Western democracies. The Constitution guarantees universal, direct, equal, and secret suffrage, regardless of race, religion, or sex. But so far, in prac-

tice, the right to vote in the USSR is the right either to vote for the only candidate on the ballot, or to cross out his name and vote for no one at all.

Before the name is placed on the ballot, however, a selection has been made by the electoral commission from among the many candidates who have been nominated by various organizations. Naturally the candidate who is finally registered is one who has been approved by the party, although he (or she) is not necessarily a member of the party.

The end result in the Supreme Soviet is, in part, a very unusual type of representation. There may be women tractor drivers, noted cotton pickers, and blast-furnace men. Men from Uzbekistan and Kirghiz with Mongol features and small skullcaps mingle with fairheaded Estonians and swarthy Armenians. Apart from these colorful Stakhanovites and nationality representatives, there is a fair cross section of the population: in 1962 the largest representation was of party career officials (224), government administrators (220), industrial workers (310), agricultural labor and collective farm peasants (220), and collective farm chairmen and state farm directors (118). The military, scientists, artists and writers, teachers, and physicians included between 47 and 60 members each. The basis of choice is not, however, to obtain a majority of people who will be able to discuss legislation wisely, since they will have no opportunity to do so in any case. The selection of deputies for the Supreme Soviet is chiefly an encouragement to themselves or to others of their kind; and their presence in that body—like the Supreme Soviet itself—is only symbolic.

The Electoral Campaign

But despite the fact that there is never any doubt as to who will win each election and that the results do not affect the government in any way, there is a vast amount of activity before the voting takes place. Speeches of prominent party leaders are broadcast and reprinted in millions of pamphlets. Campaign headquarters are set up in the voting precincts, replete with literature and lectures and entertainment. Organizations designate official campaigners to head their activities, to arrange meetings, and to direct the work of thousands of other campaigners who carry on a house-to-house canvass. These canvassers explain the structure of the government, the nature of its program, the technicalities of the election laws—and, of course, they get out the vote. On election day cars carry invalids to the polls, and precincts are set up on trains, ships, in hospitals, and in homes for the aged so that everyone may vote. Altogether it is not an exaggeration to say, in the words of the *Soviet Information Bulletin,* "No country of the world has known such election activity on the part of the voters as is manifested in the Soviet Union." Moreover, no other country has such an incredibly high poll—commonly over 99 percent. In fact, it takes great courage not only to vote against a candidate,[1] but not to vote at all.

If one asks why such apparently unnecessary activity is undertaken, the answer is that it serves very well the general purposes of the Soviet state. Elections provide an admirable opportunity for rousing popular enthusiasm and giving the people an outlet. The speeches of the candidates explain the purposes of the government. The voters see and hear the most important officials of the state. Mass meetings and mass propaganda are directed toward building a fresh loyalty to and confidence in the party and its leaders. The people are made to feel that their support is important and that the government is concerned with their approval. The elite receives reassurance and evidence of support with which to convince the doubter. Thus the campaign is, in part, an education for the voter and, in part, a device for demonstrating solidarity and devotion.

3. THE SUPREME SOVIET

The auditorium in which the Supreme Soviet meets (for the two chambers often sit together to elect officials, to listen to speeches, or to discuss proposals), like the rooms in which the British House of Commons and the French National Assembly meet, indicates something of the spirit in which the work is done. In the House of Commons, the rows of benches facing each other imply that there will always be two opposing groups, while the smallness of the chamber makes it easy to carry on discussion and to engage in a running debate marked by easy and informal participation from all parts of the room. In the French National Assembly, the fanlike arrangement of the amphitheater encourages the deputies to range themselves from left to right according to their political ideas. But the auditorium in which the Supreme Soviet meets allows no such differentiation. It is a large hall with many rows of desks and chairs. There is no sweep from left to right as in France; and there are no distinctive places for supporters or opponents of the government as in Great Britain. The members constitute a solid mass, as is appropriate in a country in which there is but one party and in which all delegates are assumed to be supporters of the government. Moreover, the delegates sit as an audience, ready to listen to and applaud the statements made by their leaders from the platform, not as an active group of legislators who may rise informally in their places to catch the eye of the presiding officer and take part in the debate.

That their function is to listen rather than debate is apparent from the infrequency and brevity of the meetings. There are never more than three sessions in a year; in fact, despite a provision for at least two sessions each year there is ordinarily only one. More significant is the fact that the sessions never last longer than twelve days, while the average session is five days. The British, American, French, and German legislatures, in contrast, sit about two hundred days a year and then can barely get through their work.

In the Soviet Union, however, members are expected to spend most of their time in their home districts, carrying on their regular occupations. Their function is not to explain the ideas of the people at home to the government, or to keep a careful check on what the government does, but to carry back to their neighbors

---

[1] On rare occasions a candidate does not obtain the necessary absolute majority of those entitled to vote. The election is then declared invalid, and fresh nominations are made. The total number of negative votes reported officially for recent Soviet of the Union elections was 247,897 in 1954; 580,641 in 1958; and 746,563 in 1962. In the same years it was 187,357; 363,736; and 464,115 for the Soviet of Nationalities.

the information they have received and, hopefully, to communicate to them something of the enthusiasm aroused in them by participation in the Soviet pageant.

Organization and Procedure

The Supreme Soviet is elected for four years, both houses at the same time. The Soviet of the Union has one member for each 300,000 of the population, the Soviet of Nationalities has 25 for each union republic, 11 for each autonomous republic, 5 for each autonomous region, and 1 for each national area. The total number of deputies in 1958 was 1,378 (738 in the Soviet of the Union and 640 in the Soviet of Nationalities). In 1962, the growth of population forced an increase to 791 deputies in the Soviet of the Union and 652 in the Soviet of Nationalities. Much of the time the two houses meet together, but this is optional. Laws are passed by a simple majority in each house and constitutional amendments by a two-thirds majority. Elaborate provisions exist in case the houses disagree, but, of course, they never do.

At the first session each house elects a chairman and four deputy chairmen; next, each elects standing committees—for legislative proposals, budget, foreign affairs, and, for the Soviet of Nationalities, economic affairs. These committees are working bodies and undertake what scrutiny is made of government policies. Thereafter, the Supreme Soviet proceeds to elect the thirty-three man Presidium, which holds office until the next Supreme Soviet is elected. Moreover, at the beginning of the sessions of a Supreme Soviet, the Council of Ministers of the USSR tenders its resignation but, naturally, is immediately reelected.

In the course of its three- to seven-day sessions (held from one to three times a year), the Supreme Soviet takes up pending legislation and the budget, hears a report on the activities of the government, and cheers its leaders enthusiastically. The greatest part of its very limited allotment of time is reserved for the budget; its provisions are explained by both the Minister of Finance and the members of the Supreme Soviet's own budgetary committee who, like those of the legislative and foreign affairs committees, ordinarily meet at least four times a

year and thus have somewhat more information at their command than the other members of the Supreme Soviet. When one realizes, however, that the Soviet budget takes in the entire economic life of the country, it is apparent that giving it the greatest proportion of time means only that the deputies are allowed a rapid (and not very revealing) look at the most important developments in store for their country. Moreover, the only criticisms that are ever uttered within the Supreme Soviet are about the workings of certain ministries that have not fulfilled their quotas or have an unusually high cost of production, and these criticisms quite obviously emanate from the government itself.

Education and Inspiration

One of the obvious purposes of the meetings of the Supreme Soviet is to inspire the delegates and to educate both them and their constituents. In addition to impressing those who attend from afar, the sessions provide an excellent forum from which the party leaders can address not only the delegates but the entire country. The press and the radio report faithfully and at length the speeches, the plans, and the discussion. During meetings of the Supreme Soviet the attention of the whole country is centered upon it, and the plans and purposes of the government in this way become familiar to the entire nation.

Education in this sense, of course, is very different from the education at which Western parliaments aim. It is like Her Majesty's "gracious speech" in Great Britain—with the discussion and debate cut off. It is not "education" in that the public is informed of a particular program through the clash—in debate—of its pros and cons. Rather it is a set of authoritative pronouncements that aim at publicizing the details of a program to which all citizens are expected to give joyful and unanimous support.

The Presidium

If the Supreme Soviet does not perform the law-making function in the Soviet Union, what body does? Its Presidium,[2] which functions as

---

[2] The Presidium has thirty-three members: fifteen vice-chairmen, who are the chairmen of the Supreme Soviets of the fifteen constituent republics; sixteen other members; and the secretary and chairman.

a collective executive under a chairman who serves as the nominal head of state, may exercise all the powers of the Supreme Soviet. Far more, in fact, is put into effect through the edicts and decrees of the Presidium than through the relatively small number of laws passed so perfunctorily by the Supreme Soviet. Yet, if one looks more deeply, it is clear that the Presidium, like the Supreme Soviet, is in turn subordinate to other agencies: the Council of Ministers and, still more, the Politburo and Secretariat.

5. Soviet Political Leadership

The men who head the government of the USSR must be leaders in two spheres: political and economic. Like the heads of Western governments, they must understand the nature of political power and they must know how to wield it. But in addition they must direct the industrial and agricultural production and distribution of the entire country. In this respect their job is far more demanding than any that Western politicians have to perform. They must have the qualities of captains of industry as well as of political leaders, combining in a sense the political talents of the Prime Minister of Great Britain with the administrative ability, let us say, of the president of General Motors or United States Steel.

There is one respect, however, in which the task of the highest Soviet leaders is easier than that of their Western counterparts. They need never worry over the criticisms of a hostile press or parliamentary opposition. They need never wonder, as must the American President, whether they can win the approval of the legislature for their program. They share none of the anxiety of French Fourth Republic Premiers as to whether they will be in office long enough to carry out their plans. They have none of the worries of a British Prime Minister over the outcome of the next election. They do not ignore public opinion, but they control the instruments that mold it, and they have the power to suppress those manifestations that they do not like. They can direct industry and commerce without regard for profits or public demand. They can change the direction of foreign or agricultural policy simply by determining to do so. In short, their position is something of a bureaucrat's dream: so long as they control the

Communist party, the Soviet leaders can concentrate on the job at hand, free from popular interference and opposition.

1. THE COUNCIL OF MINISTERS AND ITS PRESIDIUM

The Council of Ministers is the most important agency in the governmental structure for planning policy and implementing laws. Like the British Cabinet it combines executive and administrative functions, but its size makes it unlikely that it will debate and decide issues, as does the former. Though in theory the Council is "elected" by the Supreme Soviet, the latter gives automatic approval, as we have seen, to whatever list of members is decided upon by top party leaders. And while it is quite clear that the Supreme Soviet will accept any decision made by the Council of Ministers, it is equally clear that the Council itself will accept any decision of its own Presidium, which consists of eight members: the Premier, the Deputy Premiers, and certain designated ministers.

The Presidium of the Council of Ministers receives and coordinates plans from the different agencies of the government. Important plans are considered jointly with the Politburo. The Council of Ministers does not rank politically, however, with the top party organ. Very important differences of opinion on policy between government agencies go to the Politburo rather than being decided by the Presidium of the Council of Ministers. Issues that are not of such significance, however, are settled either by the relevant Deputy Premier or, if the problem affects several fields, by the Commission for Current Affairs, a subcommittee of the Presidium of the Council of Ministers or, more rarely, by the whole Presidium.

There is a close interlocking directorate at the top level of state and party leaders. Since October 1964, when Khrushchev was relieved of the post of Premier by the Presidium of the Supreme Soviet, Kosygin, who took over the office of Premier, has teamed with Brezhnev, the General Secretary, to make the most effective collective leadership the Soviet Union has yet seen. The two first Deputy Premiers, Mazurov and Polyansky, are also in the Politburo. Probably as a matter of procedural form, which is useful in personal exchanges with leaders of non-Communist states, Brezhnev became a member of the Presidium of the Supreme Soviet late in 1965, thereby following Khrushchev's 1958 example of combining party and state posts. Supreme polit-

ical leadership, in fact, resides in a relatively few persons, notably Brezhnev, Kosygin, and the other members of the Secretariat and Politburo not because they hold governmental office but because they head the countrywide network of the Communist party.

2. POLITICAL LEADERSHIP

The qualities required for political leadership in the Soviet Union are less easily defined than are those required in Great Britain and France. The most important man in the Soviet Union is not necessarily the Prime Minister, as in Great Britain, but the man who controls the Communist party. Only four men have held this position since the establishment of the Soviet Union: Lenin, Stalin, Khrushchev, and Brezh-

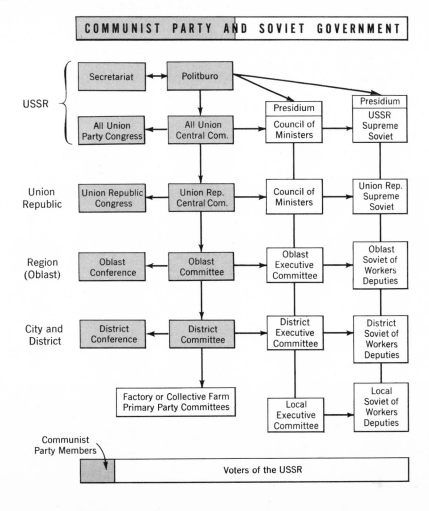

COMMUNIST PARTY AND SOVIET GOVERNMENT

nev. To these four should probably be added a fifth, Kosygin, because of the character of the current collective leadership.

The first of these, Lenin (who was never officially head of the party), acquired his importance when the Bolsheviks were only a conspiratorial organization of professional revolutionaries; only for a relatively short time did he control the government of the Soviet Union. We have already seen the powerful influence he wielded—and wields—in ideology and legend. The second, Stalin, held power for over a quarter of a century and built the USSR into the second most powerful country in the world. Few contrasts are so startling, however, as the contrast between the image of Stalin implanted during that period and the one held up before the world after his death—particularly after Khrushchev's "secret" speech at the Twentieth Party Congress, a speech that soon became known to party members and to countries outside the Soviet Union. The content of the speech was disclosed to the mass of Russians themselves only through the still more bitter attacks on Stalin made by Khrushchev and others at the Twenty-second Congress in October 1961. The third man to hold the top party office, Khrushchev, presented a striking contrast to Stalin in personality, style, and objectives. To him is due much of the liberalization of Soviet life. His successors, Brezhnev and Kosygin, are a different type again. Thus they are likely to perform somewhat different roles and pursue different aims. But the very fact of possessing the kind of power provided by mastery over the Communist party may demand and reinforce certain qualities that will turn out in the long run to be those essential for Soviet political leadership.

Stalin's Career

Stalin's career in the party began, of course, in the years before the revolution. Born in Georgia, the grandson of a serf and the son of a cobbler, he became an active leader in the revolutionary movement following his expulsion from the theological seminary in which he was a student. With the exception of a few short visits abroad, he spent all his time inside Russia and although (at the invitation of Lenin) he devoted himself to the development of a theory of nationality, it was as an active revolutionary rather than as a theorist that he distinguished himself. At the time of the revolution, he was less well known to the masses of the people than Lenin and Trotsky or even such leaders as Kamenev, Zinoviev, and Bukharin. His rise to power can hardly be ascribed to his personal fame or popularity. What was important, rather, was the fact that he was appointed, in 1922, to the position of Secretary-General of the party.

At that time the post was not particularly important, but Stalin saw its potentialities and made the most of them. In this position he held all the threads of party organization. The files and records of the party were in his possession; correspondence passed through his hands. The information on which the Central Committee or the Political Bureau acted in making appointments or promotions came from his office. His work brought him in touch with party officials throughout the country, and he acquired an unparalleled knowledge of the organization and its membership. Through this knowledge and through the powers of his position, he was able to win complete control of the party bureaucracy.

In a highly disciplined organization such as the Communist party, the control of lower organizations by the Secretary-General was not too difficult. The man who was patient, painstaking, persistent, and, upon occasion, ruthless could, almost imperceptibly, come to dominate it, and with it the country. By placing his supporters in such strategic positions as secretaries of lower organizations and as editors of the party press, it was easy, in later years, to inspire "spontaneous" resolutions from party organizations throughout the country in support of his position. He was able to evoke the simultaneous publishing of "spontaneous" editorials and articles praising his position and denouncing the principles and activities of his enemies, and to elect to Party Congresses delegates who were already committed to him and who would vote to uphold him, no matter how eloquent the appeals of his opponents. Lenin himself warned in his testament that "Comrade Stalin, having become Secretary-General, has concentrated an enor-

Interlocking Directorate—USSR Party and Government
(*January and April 1966*)

PARTY				GOVERNMENT	

Politburo	*Secretariat*	*Party Control Committee*	*Council of Ministers Presidium*	*Presidium of Supreme Soviet* (CEREMONIAL HEAD OF STATE)
MEMBERS	GENERAL SECRETARY		PREMIER AND CHAIRMAN	CHAIRMAN
Brezhnev [1,2]	Brezhnev [1]			
Kosygin [1]			Kosygin [1]	
Podgorny [1,2]				Podgorny [1,2]
	SECRETARIES			
	Andropov			
	Kapitonov		FIRST DEPUTY	
	Kulakov		PREMIERS	
Mazurov [2]			Mazurov [2]	
Polyansky [4]			Polyansky [4]	
	Rudakov		Brezhnev [1]	
Suslov [1]	Suslov [1]			
	Ponomarev			
Shelepin [5]	Shelepin [5]			MEMBERS OF
Kirilenko	Kirilenko	CHAIRMAN		PRESIDIUM
Pel'she [2]		Pel'she [2]		(33)
Voronov [4]				
Shelest [2]				
CANDIDATE MEMBERS				
Demichev [2]	Demichev [2]		DEPUTIES TO SUPREME SOVIET [6]	
Grishin [3]			Grishin [3] (Deputy, Foreign Trade)	
Mzhavanadze [2]				
Rashidov [2]				
Scherbitsky [4]				
Kunayev [2]				
Masherov				
Ustinov	Ustinov			

[1] The inner cabinet of the Politburo, April 1966. Podgorny was in the Secretariat in 1965.

[2] Brezhnev was chairman of the Party Bureau of the RSFSR, which was abolished in 1966; Mazurov was First Secretary in Byelorussia, Mzhavanadze in Georgia, and Rashidov of the Uzbekistan Central Committee. Shelest is First Secretary in the Ukraine, Pel'she in Latvia, and Kunayev was in Kazakhstan. Podgorny was First Secretary in the Ukraine, Demichev in Moscow, and Spiridonov in Leningrad.

[3] Grishin was Chairman of the Central Council of Trade Unions.

[4] Polyansky is Chairman of the Council of Ministers, RSFSR, and a member of its Central Committee Bureau. Voronov is first deputy chairman of the Bureau for RSFSR. Scherbitsky is Chairman of the Council of Ministers, Ukraine.

[5] Shelepin was formerly head of the Soviet security police. The Party–State Control Committee (see Chapter 6), of which he was chairman, was disbanded in 1965. Earlier he was head of the Komsomol.

[6] *All* members and candidate members of the Politburo are either officials or deputies of the Supreme Soviet.

mous power in his hands." Following Lenin's death, this power was used with devastating effect.

Stalin's Succession to Power

Lenin's testament threatened to place a block in Stalin's road to supreme power by suggesting his replacement as Secretary-General by a man with "greater tolerance, greater loyalty, greater politeness, and a more considerate attitude towards Comrades." (The testament was apparently read as a top secret document to the delegations at the Thirteenth Party Congress in May 1924 and became known abroad that summer. It was released to delegates at the Fifteenth Party Congress in December 1927 but was never published until it appeared in the Soviet Union in *Kommunist* in the summer of 1956 following Khrushchev's criticisms of Stalin at the Twentieth Party Congress.) Lenin also wrote that Leon Trotsky was "the most able man in the present Central Committee," and many foreign observers expected that Trotsky would become Lenin's successor. Although he had not joined the Bolshevik party until 1917, Trotsky had been one of the most conspicuous figures in the revolution, a writer of brilliance, an eloquent orator, and a military organizer who received much of the credit for the victories of the Red Armies in the Civil War. But Stalin proved a master at isolating his opponents, at fighting them on issues of policy rather than over the possession of particular posts, and at using his majority support at party meetings to shout down and outvote those holding different views.

The "Cult of the Individual"

By 1929 Stalin had succeeded in destroying the power not only of Trotsky but of every one of the great leaders of the revolution who did not give him unquestioning support. And it was only at this time, after the battle for power had been won, that Stalin seriously cultivated mass popularity and publicly accepted the homage that goes with the possession of power. His fiftieth birthday, in 1929, provided the occasion for an officially encouraged wave of adulation that carried his portrait or bust into every office and schoolroom in the USSR, made it customary thenceforth for every speech to contain lavish tributes to his genius and guidance, and evoked the constant public expression of an adoration that in another society would be offered only to a divinity.

This so-called "cult of the individual" was the subject of the most bitter denunciations at the Twentieth Party Congress; it was coupled with a devastating attack by Khrushchev on Stalin's wartime leadership, on his arbitrariness toward his foremost colleagues, and on the way in which he had bypassed party organs. But it is clear that the adulation of Stalin had served the regime in very practical ways. The Tsars, too, had been hailed as the fathers of their people and the chosen of God; to pay similar homage to the leader of the Communist party was using this tradition of devotion and reverence to consolidate support behind the people's new masters. Especially in the critical years of the First Five-Year Plan and the collectivization of the farms, it was claimed that a nation of uneducated peasants found it difficult to understand the objectives of the Communist party and thus would not sacrifice and struggle to put them into effect. Even in more advanced countries, a vigorous personality can often symbolize a set of political ideas and policies and make them understandable to the masses of the people far better than the program itself, no matter how simply and clearly stated. Moreover, the belief in the ruler as a good, wise, and all-protecting father corresponds to a very natural human desire for security amidst the perils and uncertainties of modern existence. Thus the freedom of action of Soviet leaders in the making of policy was facilitated by this all-pervading reverence and trust.

But there was another political consequence of such adulation, of which Stalin could not have been unaware. The leaders of the Communist party who hailed its head as "the towering genius of all mankind" or "the heart of the whole of progressive and advanced humanity" found it impossible to challenge him during his lifetime and difficult enough to diminish his stature thereafter. When Khrushchev was making his denunciation of Stalin to a closed session of the Twentieth Party Congress (it was published first in Western newspapers in June 1956), someone called out, "But why did you not kill him?" That simple agonized question expressed the horror both at the revelations and, one feels, also at the deception practiced by the whole group of party leaders who continued to the last possible moment to build up Stalin's public prestige.

Khrushchev

Stalin's successor in top party leadership had something of the same background. Khrushchev was born on April 17, 1894, into a poverty-stricken miner's family in the village of Kalinovka in Kursh province in south-central Russia; his grandparents were serfs. As a boy, Khrushchev worked as a shepherd and subsequently as a fitter and repair mechanic in factories and mines in the Ukraine. During World War I, he was apparently exempted from service as a specialist. He was not a trade unionist, and he did not join the Red Army and the Communist party until 1918, some six months after the November Bolshevik Revolution. He fought throughout the Civil War, however, and, at its end, enrolled in the Workers' Faculty of the Doniets Mining Technical School, which was one of the special workers' schools set up after the revolution to train party members who had had little schooling but who were needed as Communist cadres in "socialist construction." Immediately on his graduation in 1925, Khrushchev became party secretary in the Doniets Basin and in the same year a delegate to the Ninth All-Ukrainian Party Congress and also to the Fourteenth All-Union Party Congress, the scene of the bitter struggle over Stalin's concentration of power, which ended in the latter's triumph. That Khrushchev was on the right side of the struggle was evidenced by his promotion to a regional party office and his selection as a full delegate to the Fifteenth All-Union Party Congress in December 1927. (This was the Congress at which Lenin's testament was distributed to delegates but at which those in opposition at the Fourteenth Party Congress, who had not already been expelled or jailed, were ousted from the party.)

Though still a relatively unimportant party worker, Khrushchev had caught the attention of Lazar Kaganovich, Secretary-General of the Ukrainian Communist party. In 1929 Kaganovich arranged for Khrushchev to go to Moscow. His rise there was meteoric. Between January 1931 and March 1935, he moved from being First Secretary of one of the ten Moscow districts to become First Secretary of both the Moscow City Committee and the Moscow Provincial Committee. In February 1934, at the Seventeenth Party Congress, he was elected a member of the party's Central Committee; in 1938, an alternate member of the Politburo; and in 1939, a full member of that central policy-making organ of the party.

Khrushchev's elevation to the Politburo coincided with his transfer in January 1938 to Kiev and the Ukraine at the height of the great purge. In the triple roles of First Secretary of Kiev City, Kiev Province, and the Ukrainian Central Committee, Khrushchev in less than a year had purged most of the top party and government officials in the Ukraine, whose proximity to the border and separate nationality sentiments had aroused special suspicion. For a decade, he remained party head and from 1944–47 he was also head of the Ukrainian government. He directed the political assimilation of the western Ukraine when the Red Army invaded the eastern provinces of Poland in accordance with the Soviet-German Pact on the eve of World War II. He headed the "purification" of the Ukraine after Nazi forces were driven out. Through his supreme party and governmental control in the Ukraine, with its one-fifth of the population of the Soviet Union, and his membership in the Politburo, he exercised a type of power possessed by no one else in the country except Stalin.

In the immediate postwar period, Khrushchev also devoted the kind of attention to agricultural production in the Ukraine for which he was to be so well known after Stalin's death. Though drought conditions largely nullified his early postwar efforts and Kaganovich temporarily took over his control of the party in 1947, Khrushchev returned to direct a rapid forced collectivization, or recollectivization, in the Ukraine's western area and produced impressive industrial and agricultural totals before his mission in the Ukraine ended in December 1949.

From the Ukraine, Khrushchev went back to Moscow, but this time not only as First Secretary of the city and of Moscow province but also as one of the five secretaries of the All-Union Party Committee, with particular responsibility for agricultural affairs. He began the mergers of small collective farms and the emphasis on massive work teams, rather than small ones. This was the beginning of the tightening of party control over the farms—his major technique for directing agricultural policy. Opposition, voiced by Malenkov, to some aspects of this policy resulted in Khrushchev's transfer from agricultural to party organizational affairs in 1952. This was a move, however, that no doubt strengthened his strategic position within the party when the internal struggle for power began after Stalin's death on March 5, 1953.

Khrushchev's Succession to Power

The first listing of the ten-member Party Presidium on March 7, 1953, put Khrushchev in fifth place after Malenkov, Beria, Molotov, and Voroshilov and before Bulganin, Kaganovich, Mikoyan, Saburov, and Pervukin. Neither Khrushchev nor Voroshilov was included among the members of the Council of Ministers, whose Presidium was headed by Malenkov. Khrushchev retained his position as one of the secretaries of the Central Committee, however, and within nine days of Stalin's death had replaced Malenkov as First Secretary of the party, a post in which he was officially confirmed in September 1953.

It was Malenkov who led the Party Presidium in the condemnation of Beria, head of the secret police. Beria had seemed within striking distance of supreme power in the weeks following Stalin's death but was imprisoned in June 1953; it was Khrushchev who gained most from Beria's elimination. The brutal post-Beria purges in Georgia were on the pattern of those that Khrushchev himself had carried through in the Ukraine. Most significant, Khrushchev occupied the same key position within the party that Stalin had possessed when Lenin died.

While Khrushchev's steady advance from his position within the original "collective leadership" to undoubted primacy was not marked by the same obvious and open struggles and purges as Stalin's advance, there are interesting parallels in the way Khrushchev filled party offices with his own personal followers and then isolated one set of rivals after another. One-third of the members of the Twentieth Party Congress in February 1956 had achieved high party rank under Khrushchev; 44 percent of the members of the Central Committee elected by that

Congress were similarly new. Five of the six candidate members of the Party Presidium appointed at that time were Khrushchev supporters. In five years—that is, by March 1958, approximately the same time as it had taken Stalin, but with much less bloodshed and strife, Khrushchev achieved the full measure of command within the Soviet Union.

Before the Twentieth Party Congress no one could have called Khrushchev a theorist; yet in his opening speech to the Congress, as already described, he enunciated a number of doctrines that did much to free Communist doctrine from its previous inflexibility. Warning against any oversimplified view of the decay of capitalism, Khrushchev also urged that Western industrial achievements be examined closely for use in "the interests of socialism." Moreover, in emphasizing the doctrine of peaceful coexistence, Khrushchev relegated to its own historical period of imperialism Lenin's doctrine of the inevitability of war. Khrushchev declared that the stronger socialism became and the more effective its peace propaganda, the less likelihood of an attack by "imperialist states." At the same time, he made clear his faith in the ultimate triumph of world communism, which was to be advanced by every means, short of war, in the Soviet armory.

Not only internationally but also internally, Khrushchev held out the prospect of peaceful change to socialist control. Thus he suggested that in a number of capitalist countries the working class, the "toiling" peasantry, the intelligentsia, and "all patriotic forces" could capture a "stable" majority in parliament and thus transform the latter from an organ of bourgeois democracy into a genuine instrument of the people's will.

Such statements of policy belong obviously to a period in which the leaders of the Soviet Union feel confident of their country's strength. The policies are more flexible because there is less fear. In some respects, particularly the evaluation of Western industrial achievements, the new dogma rests on a more realistic appraisal of the outside world. Nothing in the new dogma, be it noted, suggests any compromise with the overriding objective of ultimate Communist domination nationally and internationally.

No less, perhaps even more, important for

Khrushchev than the enunciation of this more flexible line of policy was the tackling of the Soviet Union's vast agricultural problem. Faced with his country's great need for more food, he ordered the plowing up of huge areas in Kazakhstan in Central Asia, with far less successful results than he had hoped. He also continued the inexorable process of forcing the peasants, still the least amenable part of the Soviet population, into larger collective units and reducing as much as possible the private holdings to which they cling so strongly.

In one particular regard, Khrushchev varied his pattern greatly from that of Stalin. The old dictator rarely left the Soviet Union after he achieved power; Khrushchev traveled abroad almost incessantly to Communist countries, to the uncommitted countries, and to the West. He engaged in a type of personal diplomacy that Stalin undertook only occasionally—during and just after the war when the leaders of his allies sought him out. In contrast, Khrushchev saw other places for himself and engaged in outspoken propaganda.

The actual reasons for Khrushchev's overthrow are not clear. During the winter and spring of 1962-63, he is said to have been challenged by the "conservative" wing under F. R. Kozlov (whose chances for supreme power ended with a crippling illness) and to have survived largely because of support from Brezhnev and Podgorny. The situation in October 1964 did not suggest impending crisis, though there were reasons for dissatisfaction. It was obvious that Khrushchev had failed to meet his objectives in the agricultural field, and that the general advance in living standards was not sufficient to quiet discontent over certain shortages. Moreover, though industrial averages remained high, they were on a slight decline. In the foreign field, Khrushchev was blamed for the disintegration of the cohesion of the Communist world, in particular for the sharp division between the Soviet Union and China. This was rather an unfair charge, however, since, though Khrushchev increased the bitterness between himself and Mao through injudicious outbursts, the causes of division lay far deeper and have not yet been overcome. Even the division of the party into industrial and agricultural wings, quickly reversed by his successors, was inad-

equate reason to force Khrushchev out of all his offices.

Perhaps in the end what forced the *démarche* that burst on Khrushchev when he returned on summons from a holiday in the Crimea was the belief of his colleagues that he would continue to insist on making personal decisions in both the domestic and the foreign fields. The rest of the Politburo and the Secretariat felt that oligarchic solidarity and collective control were the more practical and intelligent sources of direction for the highly complicated mechanism of their advanced industrial totalitarian state. They may well have decided that the only way to secure such united and sober leadership was to rid themselves of their colorful, ebullient, but unruly master.

Khrushchev's Successors: Brezhnev and Kosygin

Both Brezhnev and Kosygin are the products of an industrial revolution. Both have had wide experience in administration. Both seem ready for a kind of teamwork, together and with their top associates, that has not been known before in the annals of Soviet leadership. Less ideologically oriented than Lenin, less masterful than Stalin, less dramatic and imaginative than Khrushchev, they may well be the type of new leadership the economy of the Soviet Union produces and needs in a period of technology. Whether they can match achievements to ideology, and competence to inspiration, remains to be seen.

Brezhnev was born in 1906 in Kamenskoye (now Dneprodzerzhinsk) in the Ukraine, of Russian parents. He enrolled in the metallurgical institute in his home town in 1931 and began work as an engineer in 1935 in an iron and steel works. His political career began in 1938 when he became secretary of a regional committee in the Ukraine. He first attracted Khrushchev's attention at that time. During the war, Brezhnev was a political commissar and attained the rank of lieutenant general. His progress in the party in the first years after the war was quite spectacular. After four more years as a party official in the Ukraine he became party leader in Moldavia. In 1952 he was made a member of the Central Committee, an alternate member of the Party Presidium, and a member of the Secretariat.

In the struggle for power that followed Stalin's death, Brezhnev temporarily suffered a setback and was dropped from the party Presidium. His rapid rise again to influential positions was the result of Khrushchev's support. He put Brezhnev in charge of converting the virgin lands of Kazakhstan in Central Asia into new farming areas and made him First Secretary of its Communist party. Brezhnev returned to Moscow in 1956 to be once more a member of the Secretariat, and after the ouster of the antiparty group in 1957 he became a full member of the Party Presidium.

When Khrushchev decided the Soviet Union needed an effective "President," the titular head of state, he turned to Brezhnev, who assumed this office from May 1960 to July 1964. During this period Brezhnev visited several European countries and took several trips abroad, to Africa, the Middle East, and India. In June 1963 he again became a member of the Secretariat and in July 1964 resigned as President to devote full time to being Khrushchev's deputy in the Secretariat.

Within the Party Presidium, Brezhnev was looked on as a Khrushchev supporter, and he echoed the latter's views so faithfully it was difficult to know which were his own. It may have been his desire for orderliness and joint decisions that led him to support what is said to have been the initiative of Mikoyan (the veteran leader who was unique in that he served successfully in top positions under both Stalin and Khrushchev) in organizing Khrushchev's ouster. Since he became First (subsequently General) Secretary, Brezhnev has developed more of a public personality, but he is still not well known outside the country.

Kosygin was born in Leningrad in 1904 and is thus slightly older than Brezhnev though he appears to have more energy. His father was a lathe worker. Kosygin joined the Red Army at fifteen and became a party member at twenty-three, but he continued to concentrate on his chosen profession of textile engineering. In 1938, however, at thirty-four, he was named Mayor of Leningrad. He was apparently well liked by Stalin and thus emerged unscathed from the period of the great purge. Acting as a troubleshooter in various posts, he became Finance Minister in 1948 and survived the purge in the Leningrad party organization in 1949–50. After Stalin's death Kosygin continued to hold senior positions, although he was not very close to party policy-making. He was head of the Gosplan, the economic planning agency, and in 1960 became a member of the Party Presidium and also one of the First Deputy Premiers.

Kosygin is primarily concerned with economic matters and is a supporter of economic reform and initiative. Within the inner cabinet, he is chief innovator. That he also has marked diplomatic skills became evident from his successful mediation between India and Pakistan in January 1966 at the Tashkent conference. While rumors have been plentiful that Brezhnev might not want to continue to hold his post or might be unable to do so, Kosygin's managerial skill and experience seem to have assured him a continued place in the direction of the Soviet state.

The Men Around the Leader

The passage of time has brought a marked change in the character of Soviet leadership. The men who led the revolution and who guided the Soviet government through its first years often were intellectuals of middle-class origin who were deeply interested in doctrinal controversy and who were experienced as conspirators and agitators. Once the work of socialization, collectivization, and industrialization had begun, however, it was obvious that many of them lacked the qualities necessary for leadership in the new society. The leaders of government had to direct industry, agriculture, and, above all, people; eloquence and a knowledge of Marxist dialectic were not particularly helpful in running railroads, increasing the production of iron and steel, or maintaining party discipline. Today the man who wins a position of leadership in the USSR is more comparable to the head of a giant American corporation or a national labor union than to a senator or the President.

Do the relations among known leaders now differ from the Stalinist and subsequently the

Khrushchev pattern of decision-making? If so, how does the system operate?

The prewar Politburo (nine members in 1939) was apparently organized around subcommittees and specialists. The latter operated under Politburo directives until new contingencies arose. If these were minor, they were settled by the appropriate subcommittee and its head, for example, the subcommittees under Molotov in foreign affairs, Mikoyan in foreign trade, and (until his death in 1948) Zhdanov in Comintern and subsequently Cominform affairs. If the issues were of major importance, they were referred to the Politburo as a whole. In reaching its decisions, the Politburo had at its command information not only from the ministries (from which the problems often came) but from its own party apparatus and from the secret police. Thus it had a variety of sources that it could check against each other in arriving at a relatively accurate picture of the situation.

Khrushchev's denunciations of Stalin indicate that this structure was bypassed consistently during the old dictator's later years and that decisions of major importance were taken without consultation with the appropriate member of the Politburo. Khrushchev spoke with particular bitterness of the fact that Stalin ousted Voznesensky from the Politburo without giving that body a chance to consider whether it should be done or not. The burden of Khrushchev's charges against Stalin, when examined closely, is not the character of Stalin's policies, nor even the brutality of his methods, but his failure to give due hearing to the specialists in particular areas and to have issues considered within the Politburo as a whole.

The practice in Khrushchev's time seems ultimately to have returned to what was normal in the Politburo in the 1930's. That there were violent disagreements among Party Presidium members over basic policies—for example, heavy industry versus consumption goods—in the period of struggle for power between 1953 and 1957 has already been mentioned. After the Party Presidium had been purged of Khrushchev's opponents, it apparently reverted to more peaceful discussion of major issues. Certain individuals were clearly designated as having particular responsibilities in special fields. Evidence that

there was wide sharing of responsibilities is provided by the fact that Khrushchev took so many and such long trips away from the country.

It was perhaps, however, the feeling of need for firmer, more constant direction of the party's chief organ that led to Khrushchev's dismissal. His ouster was also motivated in part, we can assume, by the recognition that the division of the party into an industrial and an agricultural hierarchy was undermining its unity. The emphasis on and the reality of unity within the party seem to have been by-products of the change in leadership.

Brezhnev has disclosed the fact that an inner cabinet of four members—himself, Kosygin, Suslov, and Podgorny—undertakes continual discussion of major policy issues. The other members of the Politburo (which in 1966 had, as we have seen, eleven full members and eight candidate members) have specific responsibilities for departments that require detailed supervision, somewhat on the pattern of the Politburo of the 1930's.

While it is always risky to suggest that some of the men around the leader are more important or are likely to become more important than others, there are a few names besides those in the inner cabinet that keep recurring. One of these is Shelepin, who was only forty-seven in 1966 and who had been successively head of the Komsomol, of the security police, and of the powerful Committee of Party State Control that was disbanded in 1965. As one of the four—Brezhnev, Suslov, and Kirilenko are the others—who are in both the Politburo and the Secretariat, Shelepin has an excellent organization base. He is said to be tough, ambitious, and forceful. Another figure frequently mentioned, though he is not in either the Politburo or the Secretariat, is Semichastny, who has followed Shelepin first as head of the Komsomol and subsequently as head of the security police. A third figure who is thought to be rising is Dmitry Polyansky, aged forty-eight in 1966, who was appointed one of the First Deputy Premiers (Mazurov is the other) in October 1965 and who has been a Politburo member since May 1960.

What separates men like this from the top leadership in the Soviet Union, or enables them to succeed to that eminence, is difficult to estimate. There have been vast differences among those who have wielded supreme power in that country and in the ways in which they have succeeded to office—and held it. It seems, however, that certain qualities and factors are present in each case, and to these we now turn.

The Bases of the Leader's Power

The power of the leader or leaders is based first of all on control of the party and administrative machines and, secondly, on prestige built up through every device of propaganda.

There is also a possible third foundation: the forcible suppression of any opposition. Lenin established the principle that terror must be used against any opponent of the Communist party. Within the party itself, however, during Lenin's lifetime the penalty for opposition was less severe. Even in the first years after Lenin's death, opponents of Stalin were demoted from positions of power or, as in the case of Trotsky, they were sent into exile instead of suffering execution.

But in 1934 the assassination of Sergei Kirov brought a sharp change in policy. Whatever the real explanation for the purges that followed, the consequence was to remove every Communist leader of any stature who was not ready unquestioningly to accept Stalin's leadership. Moreover, these purges went deep into the community, shaking it to its very core.

Though Khrushchev did not institute this type of purge, there were, nevertheless, wholesale ousters of officials after he became First Secretary and, in the early days, numerous executions both in the secret police and to a lesser degree within the party hierarchies, especially in Georgia. What was perhaps most remarkable was that Khrushchev did so much in so short a time, becoming master of the Party Congress and the Central Committee much more quickly than Stalin was able to do. But the very character of Khrushchev's succession to top power, and even more that of Brezhnev and Kosygin, reflects the fundamental change in the Soviet power structure since the industrialization and the large-scale bureaucratization of the whole system. Because of the resulting concentration of power in administrative hands, it is possible for a new leader to assume power with much less dislocation than in the past—simply by putting, or having, his loyal followers in the top positions. But this can be done only by someone with long experience with the party machinery.

Among the many imponderables in the situation, one fact stands out sharply: the age of the top leaders in the Soviet Union. Stalin was only seventy-two when he died in 1953, after more than twenty-five years in supreme power. In contrast, Khrushchev was almost fifty-nine when he became First Secretary in March 1953, sixty-five when he became undisputed leader, and just over seventy when he was dismissed. Brezhnev was sixty on December 19, 1966. For how long can a man endure the strain of this position?

Like all governmental systems, that of the Soviet Union demands that there be one person who must take ultimate responsibility. President Truman used to have a sign behind his desk: "The buck stops here." But far more than any Western democratic system, that of the Soviet Union tends to throw a whole series of decisions about people and policies into the hands of very few leaders—or even of one. Moreover, the very fact that there is no open organized opposition with its own highly important part in the government, as in Western democracies, and the additional fact that the government and party propaganda instruments can manufacture popularity for a leader instead of forcing him to win it himself, wipe out the restraints on the exercise of power that publicity and competing opinions always provide. The tendency is probably toward an ever increasing concentration of power in a single person. To maintain a workable balance within a dictatorial system requires self-restraint on the part of the leader, flexibility, and an ability to use the efforts of others in a way that contributes to their advantage, though never to the disadvantage of the man or men at the very top.

Very different qualities are thus needed by the leader in the Soviet Union from those demanded of Western leaders. He does not need personal popularity, at least initially, for he does not run for office; he does not need to be an effective parliamentary leader, for only within the Politburo will he have to defend his programs. To maintain his power it is necessary for him to control the only instruments that might deprive him of it—the bureaucracy, the army, and the security police; and he must be ready, if ever he finds that control threatened, to strike with the greatest promptness and ruthlessness and, if experience is any guide, without too great attention to individual guilt or innocence.

Both the threats to power and the methods of combating them, therefore, are fundamentally different from those in the West. In Great Britain and the United States and, to a lesser extent, in France and Germany, the head of the government need not worry about a political coup by the leader of the army or the civil service. What he has to worry about is the loss of an election or of a vote in parliament. This distinction marks an essential difference between the regimes. The Western statesman, in order to stay in power, must be able to persuade public opinion to support him or else adapt his policies to the demands of public opinion; but in the USSR the threats to power do not come from the electorate, the retention of power does not depend upon a popular vote, and the instruments of force upon which power really rests make it possible to a large extent to mold and direct the public opinion which, in other countries, is expected to direct the government. Because there has been more political struggle within the leadership since Stalin's death, practical politics and personal persuasiveness have become more important. These, however, must work within a closed context rather than in the open and must join with other potentially more threatening means of pressure; in the Soviet Union the key to power is to manipulate the sources of power so as to make them serve the purposes of the top man or group.

3. THE CHAIRMAN OF THE PRESIDIUM OF THE SUPREME SOVIET

In form, the Chairman of the Presidium of the Supreme Soviet, sometimes called the President, holds a position corresponding roughly to that of the monarch in Great Britain. His post has commonly been one of ceremonial importance rather than political power. As in the case of his foreign counterpart, the British sovereign, an important function has been to serve as a model of conduct and a human symbol of the government's paternal concern with the people's welfare.

The first holder of this position, Mikhail Kalinin, was invaluable as an embodiment of Russian virtues: a worker by profession, simple, friendly, and fatherly, listening to the complaints of the common people and receiving their petitions. His successor, Nikolai Shvernik, was also a man of the people. He was formerly the head of the Soviet trade unions and returned to that office when the aged and respected Marshal Voroshilov became Chairman of the Presidium. Another figure who fitted this pattern was Anastas I. Mikoyan, a veteran politician who survived remarkably long in more significant offices and crowned his career from 1964 to 1965 with this honorary one.

Much more surprising was that the office of Chairman of the Presidium was assumed in May 1960 by Leonid I. Brezhnev, who had already become a member of the Party Presidium in June 1957 and who was destined to replace Khrushchev as First Secretary after (with Kosygin) engineering Khrushchev's ouster in October 1964. Another surprising appointment made in December 1965 was that of Nikolai V. Podgorny, a former chief of the Ukrainian party and a Khrushchev favorite, once named by him as a possible successor, and after Khrushchev's dismissal thought to be a strong contender for top office in the party. Contradicting the assumption that Podgorny had been "kicked upstairs" is the fact that at the end of the 1966 Party Congress, Brezhnev listed him as being in the inner cabinet of the Politburo.

The Chairman of the Presidium of the Supreme Soviet is always either a candidate or a full member of the Politburo. It has sometimes been suggested that his wide contacts make him a useful link with public opinion. It is difficult to say whether the position is now looked on as purely honorary or as a waiting point for something higher.

6. Administration in the USSR: Planning and Controls

In the Soviet Union, public administration is not limited to only certain aspects of life as it is in democratic countries; it is all-pervasive. Most striking from a Western point of view is the fact that the state, through its agents, operates the whole economy. Thus in the Soviet Union, administration has a total (or totalitarian) scope, governing all of society in all its aspects—political, cultural, educational, social, and economic.

Great Britain and France have also engaged in economic planning, as we have seen, but there are vast differences between those countries and the Soviet Union in the extent and manner of handling such planning. In Great Britain and France economic planning has represented a late stage in governmental activity, superimposed on existing governmental machinery as fresh responsibilities have been assumed. In both countries industry developed under private initiative and economic planning is intended to provide no more than general direction for activities that are still predominantly in private hands. In the Soviet Union, however, economic planning has itself directed the growth of industry and now provides specific directives for the development of a state-controlled economy in which private ownership extends only to personal possessions. Thus economic planning in the Soviet Union is far greater in scope, more precise in detail, and much more authoritarian in character than it is in Great Britain and France. Stalin used to say that economic plans in capitalist countries are "prognoses" and "guess-plans," while in the Soviet Union they are *"instructions* which are *com-*

pulsory for all managements and which determine the future course of the economic development of our entire country."

1. MAKING THE PLANNED ECONOMY

Economic planning in the Soviet Union reached this degree of completeness, however, only by stages. Planning under central direction is not a Marxist concept;[1] it arose because of a national emergency, the Civil War. In that struggle, the Bolsheviks forced all the limited resources under their control into a single organization directed toward the one goal of survival.

The emergency did not end, in Lenin's view, when the Civil War was over. He was well aware of the hostility without and, to some degree, within the borders of the country. He did

---

[1] Marx wrote against the anarchy of production under capitalism, but he said little about production and distribution under socialist society. He had no conception of a group of planners molding economic life in any way comparable to the USSR's State Planning Commission. On the contrary, Marx had faith that society would be gradually transformed by a semideterministic "series of historic processes." When a socialist society was achieved, he believed it would be "organized as a conscious and systematic association" within which the producers themselves "would regulate the exchange of products and place it under their common control instead of allowing it to rule over them as a blind force." But this was no more than a vague idea that once the workers were in control they would organize themselves for the purposes of production and distribution and that they would know instinctively how to undertake these tasks. It might even be said to be a notion of laissez faire, which is the antithesis of planning.

not believe that security, either for the nation or for the workers' government, was possible without extensive industrialization. It was obviously not possible to borrow the necessary capital from outside: the country had to pull itself up by its own bootstraps. The sacrifices this involved would only be made, he maintained, if the productivity of agriculture and industry increased rapidly.

The Evolution of Economic Planning

Lenin did not envisage a nation-wide plan for the economy but the development of particular segments of it. With characteristic insight, he picked electricity as the key to the transformation of the national economy. A great plan of work to develop electric power throughout the whole country was important, he declared, not only economically but also psychologically. It "must be given at once, in a graphic, popular form, in order to captivate the masses by a clear and brilliant prospect (absolutely scientific in principle)," he wrote. "To work! and in ten to twenty years' time all Russia—industrial and agricultural—will be electrified!"

The State Commission for the Electrification of Russia (Goelro) was appointed in 1920 and expanded in February 1921 into the State Planning Commission (Gosplan). The task at this time actually was beyond either the skill or the resources of the country; it was even reported that the Commission's door bore the notice, "Please knock, the electric bell does not work." But the idea of planning was implanted and work had begun.

During the next few years transition was made from a series of projects, such as Lenin envisaged, to a centrally directed plan for an integrated national economy. In 1925, "control figures" were introduced that laid down the goals for industrial production in many fields. The key decisions to bend all efforts toward the industrialization of the Soviet Union and to concentrate on internal development ("socialism in one country") rather than on world revolution were made at this time. In 1927 a tentative Five-Year Plan was placed before the Fifteenth Party Congress. On October 1, 1928, the first official Five-Year Plan was put into effect. Since

that time the Soviet Union has operated under a series of plans that outline its goals for a period of time and give an account, more or less detailed, of how these goals are to be achieved. The first six plans were Five-Year Plans. In 1959 the span was increased to seven years overlapping the previous plan. The eighth plan, whose directives were formally approved by the Twenty-Third Congress in April 1966, is again for five years, 1966–70 inclusive.

The Character of the Plans

The plans are not fixed blueprints: they are economic budgets related to economic and social objectives. Like all budgets they are drawn up on the basis of detailed information, and they incorporate decisions about the services that will be provided in the next period. But, in contrast to British or American budgets, which cover only that part of the national income handled by the administration and contain a detailed statement of how the money will be raised, the plans[2] cover the whole economy, describe the division of productive national resources between capital and consumption goods, lay down wage and price levels, determine credit and currency policies, and in addition describe social and cultural goals.

The scope of the plans makes exact fulfillment impossible, and such fulfillment is not expected. The plans themselves are declarations of aspirations. More detailed information on how the goals should be fulfilled was originally incorporated in the "control figures" for different industries and from 1930 on in annual plans covering the whole economy. More specific plans are made for each quarter of the year, or in par-

[2] The published versions have varied in size. The First Five-Year Plan was printed in four volumes, the Second in two volumes, the Third in one volume of 238 pages, and the Fourth presented in a very condensed form as a pamphlet of 96 pages. Little specific publicity was given to the Fifth Five-Year Plan, but the Sixth Five-Year Plan was presented in great detail to the Twentieth Party Congress, February 1956. Khrushchev's Seven-Year Plan for 1959–65, which superseded the Sixth Five-Year Plan, was described in detail to the Extraordinary Twenty-First Congress, January–February 1959. An initial draft of directives for the Eighth Five-Year Plan was published preceding the Twenty-Third Congress and approved by it—as usual, unanimously—after some brief but pointed suggestions from the Congress floor.

ticular cases for shorter periods of time. More-over, there is a good deal of flexibility and ad-justment to circumstance. The figures for the more limited periods are governed both by the possibilities of a particular situation and by the overall objectives of the plan. For this reason, overfulfillment of a particular part of the plan is regarded with approval since the general ob-jective is a broad economic and social advance. Objectives often have not been achieved, but there is increasing precision both in the making and the execution of the plans.

The Concentration on Heavy Industry

In all the earlier Five-Year Plans the major stress was on the development of heavy industry. This concentration on heavy industry is the key to the economic history of the Soviet Union. It explains the relatively small amount of pro-ductive capacity devoted to consumer goods until recently. It led to the collectivization of agriculture under the belief that fewer peasants could produce enough food for the whole people if agriculture were mechanized and farmland aggregated into large units. This process also permitted manpower for construction work and for the production line to be drawn from the farms.

Economic planning involves the conscious making of choices between alternatives. The de-cision to concentrate Soviet resources on build-ing heavy industry was made at the very begin-ning of the Five-Year Plans—but only after a bitter struggle between Stalin and the "right deviationists," who believed that the standard of living of the people should be built up by production of goods for consumption before re-sources were used for large-scale construction projects. Stalin argued that sacrifice would per-mit the construction of heavy industry; heavy industry would provide for tractors and a de-fense industry; tractors would raise agricultural output; agricultural output would raise the stan-dard of living, and the defense industry would protect it; and the rise in the standard of living would end the era of sacrifice and lead to so-cialism.

The Argument of National Emergency

Stalin's determination to build heavy industry first was also motivated by the desire to be free from dependence on foreign countries and by the fear of foreign attack. On February 4, 1931, when the costs of the industrialization program were horrifying outside observers and causing serious dissension within the country, Stalin told a conference of factory managers that "To slacken the tempo [of industrialization] means to fall behind. And the backward are always beaten. . . . We are fifty to one hundred years behind advanced countries. We must cover this distance in ten years. Either we do this or they will crush us." When Hitler attacked in the summer of 1941, the words took on a prophetic significance and seemed to justify the enor-mous sacrifice and suffering of the preceding decade.

Building the Communist Society

Khrushchev maintained a similar stress on heavy industry despite his assurances that major attention would be paid to raising the standard of living. A major criticism of development in the Khrushchev period that Kosygin made to the Twenty-Third Congress in presenting the new Five-Year Plan was that "for many years the rate of production of consumer goods has lagged noticeably behind that of the production of the means of production." The new features in the Eighth Five-Year Plan are: a closer balance between the growth rate of consumer and producer goods; more investment in agri-cultural than industrial production; and intro-ducing the five-day week, raising the minimum wage, and cutting personal income taxes. Thus the emphasis in building the Communist society is no longer solely on the backbreaking task of attempting to catch up with and surpass the capitalist states in industrial production but also includes the creation of more pleasant condi-tions for farmers, consumers, wage earners, and pensioners.

The Balance Sheet of Economic Planning

The Soviet Union is still a long way from achieving either the industrial capacity or the standards of living in the United States. But compared with the position of the country when the Bolsheviks seized control, an unprecedented amount has been accomplished. The strains of violent and rapid change have been enormous and still continue; but planning in the USSR has succeeded in its major aim, that of transforming a relatively backward, predominantly agricultural country into a major industrial power.

It does not lessen the importance of this accomplishment to say that, contrary to the general impression, the Russian economic system was well adapted to planning when the Bolsheviks came into power. Industry did not develop in Russia, as in Great Britain, from indigenous, small-scale, and privately owned enterprises. Under the Tsars it was largely financed from abroad, was always on a large scale, and worked in close harmony with the state. Thus it was much simpler to adapt it to large-scale planning than would be true in a Western capitalistic country where private enterprise is naturally the chief adversary of government direction of the economy.

The magnitude of Soviet accomplishments can only be explained, however, by the "compulsory" character of planning in the Soviet Union, backed by the coercive authority of the state, and coupled with the psychological spurs of hope of improved living conditions and fear of external aggression.

The magnitude of the accomplishments is paralleled by the magnitude of the costs involved. The most striking evidence of cost was the forcible "elimination" of between four and five million kulaks during the First Five-Year Plan. But the continuation of low standards of living has involved a mass sacrifice.

Few countries have paid such a price for their industrialization. The United States was able to make use of outside resources of capital to establish the foundations of its present economic position. Great Britain, a pioneer in industrialization, presents more of a parallel to the Soviet Union since it, too, secured its basic economic plant at the expense of the living standards of its working people. But there were certain classes reaping prosperity in this early period of English industrialization, not only because the capitalist system enabled employers to exploit their workmen, but because England already possessed a well-developed, vigorous middle class, a body of creative artisans, and a productive agriculture. In the Soviet Union, it is true that many people of peasant and of worker origin have greatly enhanced their personal position through the extraordinary degree of social mobility possible through education and political advance. Moreover, there is today a considerable measure of prosperity. But for a quarter of a century the cost of Soviet industrialization was met by holding down consumption levels.

The overall industrial production of the Soviet Union now ranks second only to that of the United States. But the productivity of its labor is still below that of other heavily industrialized countries. Increase in per capita productivity, encouraged by incentives of all kinds, has been a major goal of all the Five-Year Plans since the first. So far, this objective and that of industrialization have overshadowed the other professed aim of the plans: the transition from socialism to communism so that everyone may receive according to his needs.

2. THE STRUCTURE OF ADMINISTRATION

Nation-wide planning of the kind developed in the Soviet Union involves administrative problems wider in scope and different in character from those in the United States, Great Britain, France, and Germany. Higher Soviet officials do not need the same tact in administering programs, since they are not subjected to the same restraints of public opinion. Yet if their work is easier in this respect, it is far more extensive in scope. Soviet administrators must handle not only the responsibilities normally carried by American or British public servants but also those undertaken by the managers and directors of all American or British industry, agriculture, transportation, and distribution services.

The Ministries, State Committees, and Regional Economic Councils

The basic work of direction and supervision is carried on through ministries, state committees, and other agencies, whose heads compose the Union Council of Ministers. These organs not only undertake functions customarily handled by Western governments but also those in the economic sphere that in the United States are mainly or wholly in private hands.

Ministries may be either "all-union" or "union-republic." The former directly administer all enterprises in their field throughout the Soviet Union; the latter direct the work of corresponding ministries at the union-republic level. Thus the difference is largely one of internal administrative organization and of the method of exercising control and does not represent any guaranteed division of responsibilities. Republic ministries without union counterparts also exist in certain fields such as local industry.

The Administration of Industry

Planning demands a vast series of economic decisions, ranging all the way from national goals for output in a particular industry to specific orders as to what an individual enterprise must produce. Since the tasks of planning must necessarily be divided, and since each set of structural arrangements has its own advantages and disadvantages, the Soviet Union has experimented widely with different schemes of organization.

Every plan of organization, however, includes several major aspects. First, the *industrial* sector is broken down into segments (for example, metallurgy, or textiles), and the plans for each industry must be determined and coordinated at the national level of government. Second, various *functional* bodies deal with such common needs as labor, investment, supplies, and transportation. Third, certain planning and operational powers must be decentralized *territorially*. The administration of industry at any given period is a combination of these three spheres, each of which necessarily interacts with the others.

No structure has been fully satisfactory. When Stalin drove hard-pressed executives to fulfill unrealistic targets through monetary incentives or fear of dismissal (or worse), they reacted with subterfuges or misallocation of resources. Particular economic ministries have sought to control sources of raw materials, fuel, and transport so as to be sure to meet their national demands—and in the process have robbed other ministries of essential supplies. Khrushchev attempted to extend mechanization from basic industrial operations, where it is well established, to auxiliary services, like repairs and transport, where manual labor is still common. His successors emphasize quality as well as quantity and continue efforts to lower costs and raise standards. Ministries are established or abolished, new committees are set up and old ones eliminated, and boundary lines shift between national and regional areas of primary responsibility. More important than the details of structure at a given time are the results, which are often uneven but which mark an overall advance.

The Administration of Agriculture

In contrast to industry, particularly heavy industry, where output is constantly rising and tensions offer no danger to the regime, agriculture has been widely known as "the Achilles' heel of Soviet Communism." It is the ultimate objective of the Communist party to organize agriculture on the pattern of industry. Step by step, through alternation of repression and incentives, the regime has moved toward its goal of eliminating private holdings in the rural areas where so many of the people of the Soviet Union still live. But no development has been so unpopular or has been resisted so fiercely. Despite all efforts, agriculture has not yet been forced into the pattern designed for it, nor has it reached the levels of production that can provide adequate food for the whole population (which is increasing at about the same rate as is agriculture itself, while the urban population is growing still faster). Neither does it have the necessary base for the expansion of certain types of light industry (for example, cotton for the clothing industry).

The peasants were originally won to the support of the Bolsheviks by the hope, so briefly realized, of owning their own land. When the peasant owners were forced into collectivized farms in the early 1930's, it was a revolution no less drastic in effect and much more bitterly fought than the revolution of November 1917.

After resistance was crushed by ruthless measures, including famine, the organization of the collective farms was stabilized, and mechanization became common. But the concentration of the Soviet system on industry has thrown an almost unbearable burden upon the peasants. During the earlier Five-Year Plans, the government had recruited nearly ten million peasants for industry, replacing them on the land by tractors and machines; during the later plans, only some three million peasants could be recruited, although an increased number of tractors was provided. Despite these machines, there was too little extension into agriculture of the growing efficiency of industry, and not much integration of rural life into the exchange economy. The government procurement system (which often works arbitrarily and ruthlessly, particularly when harvests are poor) takes a sizable proportion of each crop, thereby leaving individual peasants only a fraction through their collective "dividends" of what they produce.

No field is more difficult to plan than agriculture. Storms or drought can ruin the best hopes. Exaggerated expectations and unreliable reporting of the size of harvests encourage exorbitant demands. Particularly before 1953, but even under Khrushchev, there were inadequate incentives to the peasants to stimulate local initiative. Throughout, the administration of agriculture has been in the hands of industry-minded officials with little knowledge or understanding of the characteristic attitudes of farmers.

Two further problems have complicated the administration of agriculture. One is the division between the two types of approved ownership in agriculture: the collective farm or *kolkhoz,* and the state farm or *sovkhozy.* Until 1959, the collective farms were controlled by the Ministry of Agriculture and the state farms by the Ministry for State Farms. Even after the latter was abolished in 1959, another similar ministry was established to handle difficulties with the "virgin lands" project in Kazakhstan. The second problem is that the aura surrounding the institution of the collective farm leads political leaders to resist strongly, and sometimes brutally, the efforts of collective farm members to secure more private activity for themselves.

The collective farm is commonly organized as an *artel,* in which some possessions are owned by the whole group and some by individual households. Since the mid-1930's, individual households have been allowed to own their own house, a garden plot of about an acre (which has been stealthily increased in many instances), hand tools such as a spade, and some

animals, such as a cow and a few pigs, goats, sheep, and poultry. Individual surpluses, and those of the collective farm, may be sold on the local market. The work of the collective farm is apportioned in terms of an artificial unit called a "labor day," which is related to the amount of skill needed on a particular job. (Tractor drivers earn three to five labor days for one day of work, while ordinary chores yield only one-half labor day.) Each member of a household must provide a minimum number of labor days, which may total over one hundred and fifty. At the end of each month, the total number of labor days contributed to the farm is divided into the farm's collective net income—that is, after all its expenses have been paid—and each individual receives his share in accordance with the number of labor days he has contributed. This time-accounting basis is not only difficult to administer equitably but also patently inefficient.

In theory, the members of the collective farm "alone are the masters of their own farm"; according to the charter, they manage it through a general assembly that elects a chairman, an executive board, and a control committee. The amalgamations and federations of collective farms reduced the number of separate units from 250,000 in 1950 to 39,700 by the end of 1962 and increased the average number of households in each from 80 to 404. This more manageable number of units has made the farms more amenable to party control.

Few collective farms are now without party cadres, and a major effort has been made to strengthen the latter through party specialists. This has been particularly the case since the wholesale transfer of mechanized equipment from the state-run, party-controlled machine tractor stations to the collective farms. In line with more efficient management, labor compensation is being changed to piece rates, guaranteed minima, and money payments, and an effort is being made to bring collective farm prices into line with those of the state farms.

The state farms are large mechanized and state-operated units, each of which has a single director (as an industrial enterprise has) and is cultivated by hired labor. Organized from 1928 on in undeveloped land in the southern and southeastern parts of the country, the state farms had a checkered history initially because they were overlarge, overspecialized (sometimes they were known as grain or cotton "factories"), and lacked trained management. They were subsequently broken up into more manageable units, of which there were 8,570 in 1962.

For years the state farms had to receive a subsidy, but since 1956 they have sometimes made a profit, most of which they can keep. Looked on as ideologically superior to the collective farms, since peasants are wage earners on state farms, their numbers and land area are steadily increasing.

Administration of Foreign Trade

The Soviet government imposes the same rigid control over imports and exports as it maintains over internal industrial developments. It establishes foreign exchange rates, keeping them quite separate from the value of its domestic currency. All operations of foreign trade are in the hands of specialized corporations working under the Ministry of Foreign Trade. By maintaining this complete government monopoly and by putting the power of the state behind every commercial transaction (in other words, by state trading), the Soviet Union makes its international trade serve the purposes of its internal economic developments.

The Structure for Planning

All-pervasive in the Soviet economy is state planning and supervision. Whatever agencies are involved, the tasks of planning and supervision fall into three categories, each of them vast in scope. To prepare each Five-Year Plan, the planning machinery must bring up to date its estimates of existing material, labor, and financial resources in the country. To do so requires collecting and coordinating all the economic information it can secure throughout the Soviet Union. Second, it must prepare as detailed and as unified plans as possible not only for the whole economy but also for other related fields, such as education. Third, the structure for supervision must constantly check the performance of all the institutions involved in the plan, which means, in practice, all the institutions in the country.

As with industrial management, the agencies involved in these processes have changed several times in recent years. The Gosplan (the State Planning Commission or Committee) is always one of these agencies, but its functions have changed frequently. This is a source of considerable confusion to outside observers and perhaps to its own members. In 1955–56 the Gosplan was in charge of long-range planning while current tasks were under another agency; from 1957 to 1960 Gosplan was responsible for the overwhelming tasks of coordinating information, drawing up plans, and supervising their execution, though without any coercive powers; in 1960 long-range planning was transferred to another body, and Gosplan was left with its current tasks; in 1963 long-range planning was returned to Gosplan, and the supervision of implementation was given to the *Sovnarkhov* of the USSR. Both were made union-republic bodies with authority over identically named republic bodies. In March, 1963, a new agency called the Supreme Council of National Economy was established, but there is reason to suppose that this is the Council of Ministers in another guise—at least all decisions are issued as decrees of the Council of Ministers.

Preparing the Plan

When the Soviet Union first embarked on building a planned economy, the plans were little more than a series of estimates of production goals. Moreover, the plans for different parts of the economy were not interrelated until a late date, and, even then, often with unfortunate results. Sometimes there were not enough raw materials to meet the goals in particular fields, or skilled labor might be lacking. The comparatively haphazard results of the First Five-Year Plan indicate the weaknesses of this type of planning procedure.

This early planning procedure was replaced in the 1930's by the more accurate, though highly complicated, process of balanced estimates. Balanced estimates proceed on the basis of checking and counterchecking the resources available, the uses to which they can be put, and the effect of each part of the plan on every other part. The principle does not differ from that underlying the balance sheet of an ordinary business, although in the United States material and labor resources are generally translated into financial terms. To secure a balance sheet for an entire country, however, is a task of staggering dimensions.

Putting the Plan into Operation

The work of planning is not over, however, when the Five-Year Plan has been formulated, or even when it has been broken down into the more accurate and detailed annual and quarterly plans. Stalin once declared angrily, "Only bureaucrats can think that the work of planning ends with the drawing up of a plan. Proper planned guidance is developed after the plan is drawn up, after it has been verified locally and rendered more precise in the process of fulfillment."

Putting the plan into operation requires the adjustment of details to actual conditions. Where the plans appear to be workable when applied to a given situation, precise directives are issued. Where given circumstances make it impossible to carry out the plans, or where planning mistakes become obvious, means have to be devised to alter the plans and to take care of the effect of such changes on other parts of the plan. The relevant agency, or agencies, must have authority over the execution of the plan and exercise this authority on the spot. In this way it keeps aware constantly of every aspect of economic life throughout the country.

In coping with these huge tasks the machinery for planning draws on the resources of a vast network of planning bodies both in territorial areas and in functional divisions throughout the country. *Territorially,* there are planning agencies in every governmental area or subdivision, in particular the union republics, the regions, and the districts. *Functionally,* there are planning agencies in every ministry and department, and also in every trust, factory, and collective farm. The outside observer is inevitably impressed by the amazing comprehensiveness of the effort but is led also to question whether, in fact, it is possible to handle satisfactorily such enormous responsibilities.

This problem and its corollary—requests that industry, research, and other aspects of the economy be freed to some degree from the rigid dictates of the plan—have been considered increasingly since Brezhnev and Kosygin assumed the top offices in the Soviet Union. Since 1965, factories have been permitted to use part of their profits for social purposes, such as housing, and part to improve their efficiency. In at least one case individual farmers on a Siberian state farm have been allowed to experiment with their own plans for production on land placed under their control—and with impressive results. Open sale of surplus privately-grown produce, and planning by price adjustment rather than by directive, have been proposed. In fact, major changes in the price structure of heavy-industry products went into effect in mid-1967, but they were determined by the amount of capital and labor involved in production, not by the self-regulating levers of supply and demand that might have forced many concerns to close down. Thus change, where allowed, moves slowly and still within the established framework.

3. ADMINISTRATION AT THE LOCAL LEVEL

The functions of local government are as extensive and varied as those of Soviet government as a whole. Some of these functions, like traffic control, keeping public records, care of parks, and provision of local services, are similar to those in any modern country. In addition, local government in the Soviet Union maintains such public facilities as hospitals, schools, shops for retail distribution, markets, and repair shops. Local soviets also function as draft boards, recruiting those liable for military service. They are also charged with construction and small industry.

Local soviets lack adequate powers and resources, however, to handle these manifold tasks effectively. The pyramidal system of authority in the Soviet Union leaves each unit of administration subject to the one above. Thus all units have become to an increasing degree the agents of the centralized bureaucracy. Moreover, large industrial units often dominate the local communities in their areas, turning them virtually into company towns and usurping local government functions in road and bridge building, housing, and other services to meet their own needs. Vying with other comparable local units for a share of the resources doled out by higher agencies, competing with large-scale industry, and subject to sometimes conflicting orders from above, local administrations have retained little if any of the prestige and power they possessed in the early period of local autonomy.

The units of local government within the union republic are more complex than administratively significant. The nationality divisions —the autonomous republics, autonomous regions, and national areas—serve chiefly, as we have seen, to give the appearance of respect for nationality differences. The largest administrative division, the *krai* (territory), found only in the RSFSR, covers too much area to be particularly useful. The 160-odd *oblasts* (regions) into which the union republics are divided were once key economic units within which production was organized, but this is no longer the case. At the foot of the scale are the *raions* (districts), which are both urban and rural subdivisions. Despite their own present lack of power, the regions and districts form the territorial subdivisions within which information for planning is received and production is organized.

In form, of course, every administrative unit operates under the direction of the soviet for its area. The members of these soviets are elected directly by local voters for periods of two years. As in national elections, there is only one candidate at the time of election, but the percentage of nonparty candidates is far higher. In the RSFSR, industrial workers and collective farmers form the majority of deputies in the local soviets; in other union republics they may form over 80 percent of the members. This fact suggests that the primary function of the soviets is to recruit the energies of large numbers of persons.

This function helps to explain why the soviets have always had so many members. Such cities as Moscow and Leningrad have approximately a thousand deputies; even a hamlet of a thousand people has nine members, and slightly larger ones may have twenty-five. Moreover, the sections into which the soviets are divided

to deal with areas such as public health, education, local industry, and finance are also large. A section works alongside the administrative department in its field, both aiding and checking its work. But as an English authority once wrote, "The section recommends, advises, complains, and even demands. The *presidium* decides." Local departments also are subordinate to the relevant union ministries. Thus popular action is combined with retention of full power in executive hands.

The participation of a large number of people in public service has a good effect in itself. This can be seen also with the "activists," who are organized by the soviets to give help in local services in their spare time. Some of this activity results from public spirit that is not difficult to rouse over matters of such immediate concern to the community; some of it may be to attract attention that may lead to a job as an administrator or full-time agitator. In either case it helps to get necessary work done and to associate people with the purposes of the state.

But there is another advantage to the regime in the elaborate structure of soviets. It provides an outlet for grievances and thus a means for learning about administrative incompetence, or even concentrations of power. Even with all the listening posts provided by party members, the soviets may sometimes provide additional insights into the operations of local administration that may be extremely useful to higher authorities.

As far as the exercise of power goes, the soviets are controlled by their own executives, and behind these again are the real governors: the central administration and the party. A parallel may still be drawn, in fact, between the classic pattern of colonial rule and the operations of Soviet local government. The soviets are not unlike colonial assemblies in the period when they were allowed to talk but were given little share in political power. The Soviet central government and party correspond to the imperial authority that retained all the threads of power in its own hands. The analogy is most apt in Soviet Central Asia, where administration is mainly carried on by Russians who have little contact with or sympathy for the local inhabitants; but in essence it is applicable to all Soviet local administration.

POLITICAL SUBDIVISIONS OF THE USSR

	UNION REPUBLICS OTHER THAN RSFSR
	AUTONOMOUS REPUBLICS WITHIN RSFSR
	NATIONAL AREAS
---	BOUNDARIES OF REGIONS, TERRITORIES, AND AUTONOMOUS REPUBLICS
★	CAPITALS OF UNION REPUBLICS

BARENTS SEA

NENETS

YAMALO-NENETS

KOMI A.S.S.R.

SWEDEN

FINLAND

KARELO-FINNISH A.S.S.R.

Murmansk

Archangel

RUSSIAN SOCIALIST

BALTIC SEA

Helsinki

Petrozavodsk

FEDERATED SOVIET REPUBLIC

KOMI-PERMYAK

Tallinn

ESTONIAN S.S.R.

Leningrad

Vologda

Kirov

Perm

Sverdlovsk

Riga

LATVIAN S.S.R.

Pskov

Novgorod

Kostroma

Yaroslavl

UDMURT A.S.S.R.

LITHUANIAN S.S.R.

Velikie Luki

Kalinin

Ivanovo

Chelyabinsk

Kalinin-grad

Vilna

Smolensk

Moscow

Vladimir

Gorky

MARI A.S.S.R.

CHUVASH A.S.S.R.

Kazan

TATAR A.S.S.R.

Ufa

BASHKIR A.S.S.R.

Minsk

BYELORUSSIAN S.S.R.

Kaluga

Tula

Ryazan

MORDOVIAN A.S.S.R.

Ulianovsk

Kuibyshev

POLAND

Briansk

Orel

Tambov

Penza

Saratov

Orenburg

Lvov

Kiev

Kursk

Voronezh

Volgograd

KAZAKH S.S.R.

UKRAINIAN S.S.R.

Kharkov

MOLDAVIAN S.S.R.

Dnepropetrovsk

Rostov

Astrakhan

CASPIAN SEA

Kishinev

Odessa

RUMANIA

CRIMEA

Krasnodar

Stavropol

UZBEK S.S.R.

Simferopol

1. ADIGEI A.R.
2. CHERKESS A.R.
3. KABARDIN A.S.S.R.
4. N. OSETIN A.S.S.R.
5. S. OSETIN A.R.
6. NAGORNO-KARABAKH A.R.

BULGARIA

BLACK SEA

Grozny

DAGESTAN A.S.S.R.

ABKHAZIAN A.S.S.R.

GEORGIAN S.S.R.

ADZHAR A.S.S.R.

Tiflis

TURKMEN S.S.R.

TURKEY

ARMENIAN S.S.R.

Erivan

AZERBAYDZHAN S.S.R.

Baku

NAKHICHEVAN A.S.S.R.

IRAN

0	100	200	300

MILES

579

4. CENTRAL CONTROL OF THE ADMINISTRATION

Whatever may be the designated functions of local soviets or union republics, they do not limit the ultimate, all-pervasive control that emanates from the center. Through an intricate and intersecting network of agencies, all aspects of life are kept under constant supervision. Although on the surface there is an immense amount of popular participation and a framework of popular agencies, there is also what Merle Fainsod has called "a system of power founded on the institutionalization of mutual suspicion." [3]

Party Controls

The party, of course, establishes the framework of policy within which the administration must function. Practically all important administrators are party members, and sometimes party officials are transferred to industrial posts. Beyond this there is the work of the party fraction that exists in each enterprise and branch of the administration and not only works with management to ensure efficiency and top production but may also make direct reports to higher party officials. Thus within the party itself there is a whole series of channels for securing detailed information about the workings of the economy, and these channels check and countercheck each other, to the ultimate advantage of those at the very top.

The Secret Police

The second level of supervision is that of the secret or political police. The police plays a much less obvious role than under Stalin but it nonetheless remains significant. Like the party, the security organs operate as a unified system and are centralized under the Committee of State Security in Moscow. While the manager of an enterprise often works out a satisfactory *modus vivendi* with the party secretary in his enterprise, he almost always views the representative of the political police with suspicion

and fear. For this there is good reason. The secret police represents a punitive as well as an investigating body. It is the ultimate symbol of a system that institutionalizes suspicion and espionage within the administration as well as among its controlling groups.

Other Control Agencies

The third level of central control is exercised in part through the planning system, through the centralized supply of the most important materials and production, and through agricultural procurement. It is also exercised through finance and inspection. In this process, the budget is an important means of allocating resources among territorial divisions, as well as among sections of the economy. All funds must go through the State Bank, while all statistical data (except on the party) are collected and processed by the Central Statistical Administration. The efforts of the Party-State Control Committee (known before November 1962 as the Committee of Soviet Control) to eliminate inefficiency and waste in the public administration and state-owned enterprises have presumably been taken over by another central agency, since the Control Committee itself was abolished in 1965. As far as the legality of administrative and judicial actions is concerned, the central Procuracy (see Chapter 7) has full control. In other words, there is a network of agencies, of varying kinds and relationships but all of them centralized, through which constant and detailed control of the administration can be maintained.

The Role of Finance

It may seem strange that the Soviet Union depends so greatly on finance when production is according to plan rather than profits. In fact, though its use is very different from that in a capitalist country, finance is no less important. The plan is translated into financial terms that are used as a detailed check on its operations. Moreover, monetary incentives are widely used to stimulate output, while deliberately inflated prices curb consumption. Thus finance is rarely an independent factor but is used chiefly as an agency of control.

[3] Merle Fainsod, *How Russia Is Ruled,* rev. ed. (Cambridge, Mass., Harvard University Press, 1963), p. 388.

The Budget

The Soviet financial system and the annual Soviet budget are of major importance in the working of the planned economy. Few facts indicate so graphically the enormous growth of state power and activity as the sharp rise from the 23 billion rubles devoted to government expenditures in 1931 to 174 billion in 1940, 642 billion in 1958, and 82 (new) billion in 1962 (the equivalent of 820 billion old rubles). These expenditures include, of course, a wide variety of industrial and cultural activities that are undertaken in the United States by private sources. The Soviet budget for 1962 appropriated 36.2 billion rubles for the national economy, 28.9 billion for social and cultural services (that is, education, social welfare, and public health), and 12.7 billion for military defense. (Probably a considerable part of the money designated for the national economy goes into military expenditures.) These totals include the expenditures for all levels of government—local, regional, and union republic as well as national—making the scope of the budget as complicated as its total is vast.

The government, of course, can price goods at any level it wants so long as revenue meets the total cost of production plus sums adequate for replacements and further capital expansion. The sources of revenue open to it are the profits (in bookkeeping) of state enterprises (23.9 billion rubles in 1962, about 18 percent of revenue) and collective farms, and the direct and indirect taxes on individuals. By far the most important source of revenue, amounting in the 1962 budget to 32.9 billion rubles, well over one-third of the total, is the turnover or general sales tax placed on certain types of goods, mostly consumer goods. This is levied every time a producer or distributor sells a product— that is, when it goes from one enterprise to another in the course of production as well as when it is sold to the consumer; thus it vastly increases the cost of a product.

From 60 to 70 percent of the final retail price of such necessities as meat, butter, and soap may represent taxes—which means that the basic economic price may have been tripled. The prices of sugar, salt, and cigarettes are still more inflated by tax. This form of taxation is most convenient for the government, because the shopkeepers are turned into tax collectors and the public does not even realize why the goods are so expensive. Direct taxes, such as income taxes, on which the British and American governments depend so greatly, play a small role for the Soviet government (about six billion rubles in 1962) and may even be abolished as a propaganda measure. The turnover tax, of course, takes a very much higher proportion of the income of the poor than of the rich and is a major device for keeping their consumption down. It is also the chief means whereby the share of consumer goods in total industrial output is regulated.

5. THE WORKERS

The most colossal and in some ways the most decisive task in building the planned economy has been the mass recruitment of its workers. Probably three out of every four who were working in industry or administration by 1940 had been drawn into the system since the First Five-Year Plan.

The great majority of these workers came from the peasantry, always a source of supply for labor, and increasingly released after 1930 through the collectivization of the farms. From 1917 to 1962 the proportion of the peasantry in the population dropped from four-fifths to one-quarter.

High turnover and low discipline were the not surprising results of absorbing such huge masses of unskilled labor. There was so much demand for labor by different industries that it was nearly always easy to secure alternative employment. Out of this situation arose the present system, which still makes use of conscription for industrial training and work, of piecework and incentive payments, and of such disciplinary devices as labor books.

Labor Conscription

To ensure a constant supply of trained labor, the government in 1940 for the first time instituted labor conscription. In that year it organized the so-called Free Labor Force, or State Labor Reserves, by ordering an annual draft of eight hundred thousand to a million boys between the ages of fourteen and seventeen. Only students qualifying for higher education were exempt. As revised in 1947, the draft also included girls and provided that boys between fourteen and seventeen and girls of fifteen and sixteen should go to railway and trade schools for two years to train as skilled workers. Fourteen- to eighteen-year-olds of both sexes had to serve in factory plant schools for three to six months before being drafted into less skilled trades.

This compulsory drafting was replaced in March 1955 by voluntary recruitment. Nevertheless, during 1955–56 more than two-thirds of the young workers sent to the eastern regions to open up new lands had a one- to three-year period of labor conscription known as *orgnabor*. Otherwise organized recruiting in the villages for industrial and building purposes is now for volunteers.

Labor Incentives

Compulsory training has not been enough to answer the Soviet government's greatest concern: the relatively low productivity, which means that it currently takes three Soviet workers to produce the same unit of output as one American worker. Standards are set for most work, such as bricklaying or even typing, and additional percentages are paid for output beyond the standard. By 1938, only 16 percent of all workers and employees received ordinary time-wages; the rest were on piecework or received bonuses in addition to basic wages. Thus the "piece-wage," which Marx had declared to be "the form of wages most in harmony with the capitalist mode of production," was adopted by the Stalin regime as typically socialist.

The highest triumph of the piece-wage came with the Stakhanovite movement, which after 1935 replaced "socialist emulation" between collective groups. Under the earlier system, factories challenged each other to competition in production; the newer trend emphasized individual achievement. It took its name from a coal miner, Alexei Stakhanov, who hewed a record output of coal on August 30, 1935, introducing a new division of labor by separating the skilled from the unskilled parts of his work

and also by improving the tools he used and adapting them to the particular conditions under which he was working. Some of the production records set by the Stakhanovites were sheer publicity stunts, but the increase in individual quotas was sufficiently marked to provoke a definite hostility among many workers. This opposition was only stamped out in the great purge of 1936–38. Stakhanovism, described by Isaac Deutscher as a "mixture of progressive rationalization and old-time sweated labor,"[4] became the characteristic form of Soviet work.

The post-Stalin leaders have somewhat modified the essential characteristics of the system. They have simplified the piecework system by reducing the vast number of different categories by which pay rates are estimated. They have established minimum wages and have lessened the difference in the wage rates of the skilled and unskilled—chiefly through increasing production norms, which, in effect, means reducing the advantage of the skilled. Workers must still have a labor book, a passport, and police permission to settle in any major city. Since January 1, 1960, however, they can change their jobs without losing their sick-pay or temporary disability benefits and can retain their record of "uninterrupted service" if they start a new job within a month.

Thus definite efforts are being made to improve the conditions of the workers—efforts that have the more effect because they stand against the background of the stringent restrictions and punitive incentives of the Stalinist regime in the war and postwar periods. Although conditions remain hard by Western standards, post-Stalin leaders are obviously determined to make the workers feel that the regime is aware of their interests. This is evidenced by strikingly cheap bread and by low rents, though housing itself remains poor and scarce. Thus Soviet leaders are trying to depend as greatly as possible on persuasion rather than coercion.

Trade Unions

Naturally the concept of collective bargaining and the role of trade unions have been transformed within the Soviet state from what we

[4] Isaac Deutscher, *Soviet Trade Unions* (New York, Oxford University Press, 1960), p. 116.

know in the West. Trade unions were legal under the tsarist government, though often persecuted under trumped-up charges, but collective bargaining was virtually unknown in Russia until 1917. It disappeared again with the decree of June 17, 1920, which established state control over all wages. Though a measure of bargaining freedom appeared again under the NEP, it was soon apparent that the traditional concepts of trade unionism ill became the movement toward total economic control. To the trade union leaders it remained important for workers to secure shorter hours and higher wages, but to the government what was important was that the workers should contribute their energies to the country as a whole.

Equally important in creating conflict was the fact that once the workers' opposition had been suppressed in 1921, the trade unions remained the only organized force capable of competing with the party. The old leaders of the trade unions were therefore replaced by more docile officials. After June 1929 it was officially stated that the collective agreement was "to cease serving the immediate interests of the wage earners and become an instrument of rapid industrialization"; and after 1934, collective agreements were not renewed. When they were reintroduced quietly in February 1947, it was soon apparent that the move had little significance.

Since Stalin, some efforts have been made to broaden the responsibilities of labor unions. A decree of January 31, 1957, gave the unions a share in the settlement of labor disputes, which can never come, however, to the point of a strike or lock-out. A further decree of July 15, 1958, authorized the unions within enterprises to participate in the formulation of enterprise plans. More likely are requests for greater autonomy in regard to wages and work conditions if management can increasingly exercise its own initiative in the distribution of profits. Trade union members have been urged to criticize management when appropriate and without clearing their remarks through higher authorities, another example of encouraging "popular participation." At the same time, the chief purpose of the unions—to increase or improve production—and their close association with the party are reflected in the high salaries

of top trade union leaders and their prominent position at party congresses.

6. THE MANAGERS

In the Soviet Union there is no such distinction between the government official and the businessman as is familiar to Americans. Every industrial or business manager in the Soviet Union, as well as each of his workers, is a state employee. Every enterprise is as much a part of the government service as is a department in a ministry. Thus to describe the personnel of the public service in the Soviet Union is to describe the work of almost everyone in the country.

Since the energies of the Soviet Union are concentrated to such a vast extent upon industrial production, it is hardly surprising that the outstanding "public servants" in the country are the industrial managers. The distinctive characteristic of a manager is that, within the limits of the plan, he is entrusted with the operations of his own particular part of the public economy. A minister is considered to be a manager just as much as is the head of a factory, the difference in their work being one of scope rather than of kind.

As a result, there is much less difficulty in moving from a position as manager of an enterprise to an important position in a ministry than would be the case in the United States, Great Britain, France, or Germany. Former factory managers now occupy many of the highest administrative posts both in the Soviet government and in the Communist party.[5] Since the government directs industry, both governmental and industrial posts require much the same qualifications: technical knowledge of industry, efficiency in handling work and people, and a strong commitment to the purposes of the party and state.

The Evolution of Industrial Management

In the early days of the Soviet Union it was not easy to find people who had the necessary

---

[5] There are, of course, other types of positions, such as those in the diplomatic service, which are of very different character and hence require different training and experience. But the men in these positions are far fewer and of a less clearly defined type than those in industrial management.

knowledge of industry combined with loyalty to the regime. Nonparty specialists (who had received their training during the tsarist regime and who had belonged to the bourgeoisie) often were given responsible positions but shared their authority with less expert Bolsheviks. During the transition to the First Five-Year Plan, these nonparty specialists were sometimes accused of "wrecking" activities, a term that often meant nothing more than a failure to attain impossible goals with inadequate resources. But suspicions arising from their class origin led to the familiar round of purges and political trials. It led also to attempts to develop political loyalty and technical skill in the same person.

The "Red Specialists"

This new policy was applied in two ways. For one thing, the old Communist managers were given leaves of absence to get technical training. But even more effective were the technical schools, developed to train "Red specialists." Large numbers of workers were rushed through these schools in the hope of providing members of the proletariat with the training to enable them to assume managerial responsibilities.

Despite their proletarian background, the products of this training were more concerned with speeding production than with making conditions easier for the workers. Thus, in a Russian novel of the time, a manager declares that no effort must be spared in building a great industrial enterprise "even if the worker has it three times as bad as in the old days." Much was accomplished by the managers and technicians of the middle 1930's, though their work showed the lack of sufficient systematic training. During the purges of 1936–38, however, many of them suffered serious penalties, of which removal from office was one of the less severe. What was especially striking was the extent to which party members were the victims of this purge.

The New Technical Experts

The mass turnover in industrial management and administration after the Great Purge brought still another group into power. The new managers were usually young engineers, not long out of school, but with a much broader and more systematic training than the "Red

specialists." Though they had been brought up as members of the Communist party, their interest was in their profession rather than in political problems. They were unquestioning adherents of Stalin, to whom they attributed the progress of the industrialization program and the increased international strength of the Soviet Union.

The new managers were no more concerned about the low standard of living of the workers than their predecessors had been. "They were educated," writes an expert observer, "to the idea that a society with a developed industry and without a capitalist class corresponds, *ipso facto,* to the ideal of a 'classless society,' and that to strive for social equality would be mere 'petty bourgeois leveling.'" Their interest was in "a strong State to build a national economy."

This group of young engineers and technicians was first appointed to head or assist in industrial enterprises. Increasingly they have been picked for high posts in the ministries, which is why they are often said to be more like the general managers of big corporations than like civil servants. Thus, quite naturally, the managers of industry tended to become the leaders of the government that managed the economy.

This striking development marked a new series of relationships between management and the party, relationships that are still in process of evolution. It raises questions important not only for the Soviet Union itself but also for other countries. How are the managers recruited? What training and what incentives do they receive? Can supervision from above be combined with initiative at the local level? Are the managers a new and self-perpetuating elite in the Soviet Union? And what effect do they have on the role of ideology in the Soviet state and on the desire for stability, and perhaps even for democracy?

Selecting the Managers

There is a State Commission on the Civil Service in the Soviet Union that performs most of the functions handled by the Civil Service Commissions of Great Britain and the United States, except the important one of recruitment. Set up in 1935 as a part of the Commissariat of

Finance, the State Commission on the Civil Service became in 1941 an independent agency with responsibility to the Council of Ministers as a whole. Subject to its approval, and working closely with the Ministry of Finance, it establishes job classification systems and efficiency charts. Among its particular problems are keeping administrative staffs from becoming too large and shifting personnel from office desks to field work.

Actual recruitment is in the hands of the administrative agencies themselves but under the overall control of the hierarchy of party organs, each of which has its *nomenklatura* or list of specified managerial positions that can be filled only with that party organ's explicit approval. This practice is naturally unpopular among the economic bureaucracy. Safeguards against the favoritism that once turned departments, trusts, and even factories into strongly personalized organizations, particularly during the early Five-Year Plans, arise from the drive for efficiency, however, and the need for training and experience to cope with increasingly technical tasks.

Training for Management

The kind of training for management provided in the Soviet Union thus differs from that favored in the United States or in Great Britain. The Russians have little faith in the study of administrative techniques such as is provided in American courses or schools of public, personnel, or business administration. Still less do they favor the broad cultural training in the liberal arts on the basis of which the administrative class in Great Britain is selected. The Russians believe that training for management should be technical training, and that study of administrative organization and economics should be undertaken in close conjunction with the operations of a particular industry.

Many of the major administrative bodies in the Soviet Union now have their own training schools. In the Planning Academy of the State Planning Commission training is mainly in economics but is closely related to the technical problems handled by the Commission. Each of the agencies dealing with economic problems has an academy under its jurisdiction that gives technical training in its particular field (for

example, electricity, or machine tools) and combines it with administrative work.

The Stress on Specialization

The present type of manager is a product of Soviet education. He reflects its emphasis on technical equipment, its highly pragmatic character, its concern with theory only as an aid to practice. He is trained to become a production expert, and usually with considerable success. He is drawn either from those who have demonstrated their qualities of leadership on the job and are subsequently given technical training, or from the engineers and technicians who have proved their administrative capacities in the field of production. In either case, he is a specialist with technical training.

Management and the Party

But what about the relationship between management, whether in industry or in administration, and the Communist party? In 1929 the party itself declared that the manager was in sole and complete charge of his plant or office and that his "operational-economic orders" were "unconditionally binding" on all personnel "regardless of what posts they occupy in party, trade-union, or other organization." But party organs in particular enterprises still watch all details of administration within the plant and, as the Party Conference of February 1941 described it, "systematically 'bore into' the affairs of industrial plants . . . and help directors in their daily work of industrial management."

There is one radical difference, however, between the supervision of management by local party members before 1929 and since the plans have become well established. In the early period party members in a particular enterprise kept a close political and ideological check on managers, who often were not party members and whose "class origin" frequently laid them open to suspicion. Today party organs check only on the practical working of the enterprise, thus acting as a means of administrative control, not as a special watchdog of orthodoxy. This is because the managers themselves are now not only members, but often prominent members, of the party. They are prominent because of their unquestioning loyalty to the regime and also because of the deep concern of the party itself for production. Party and administrative controls are often exercised by people of relatively similar background and training who change from one sphere to the other at different stages of their career.

The very nature of the Soviet planned economy and the emphasis on continued heavy industrialization continue to place industrial managers in positions of leadership. Their characteristics coincide with at least two of the criteria laid down for Western bureaucracy by Donald Kingsley in *Representative Bureaucracy:* (1) they are deeply committed to the general purposes of the regime, at least so long as the regime continues its policy of reward according to achievement, and (2) they are men of "push and go." There is little evidence, however, that they are men who put the immediate welfare of the common people higher than the particular objectives of the ruling group.

Conclusion

One further question relates to ideology and party control. Managers and administrative personnel seek stability not only for personal reasons but because the production process operates most smoothly under such conditions. Yet there is constant interaction between those immediately responsible for production and those who persistently "needle" and coerce the administrators. That there are less obvious signs of strain at present than in earlier periods suggests that a relatively satisfactory balance has been established. Yet in the end there must always be tension between those whose primary objective is to achieve success in their own area of production and to improve their own economic position and those to whom the overall development of the country is the supreme objective. The party has ultimate responsibility for this wider sphere.

7. Soviet Law and Courts

1. SOVIET LAW

Both the Soviet Constitution and individual statutes and decrees abound with the phrase "according to the law." But the Soviet conception of the nature and function of law differs sharply from that held by Western democratic states. The latter look on law as a body of rules, equally binding upon private persons and government officials, administered by independent courts, and amendable only by regular and accepted political processes. Moreover, in countries such as the United States and Great Britain, which have a common law system, rules of law are modified by judicial decisions, based on precedents and justified by logical legal argument. In the Soviet Union, however, public interest (which usually means the interest of the ruling group) is always superior to the interests of individuals. Thus in cases involving public interest, law is determined by the will of the government at the particular moment and is not an impartial standard by which the acts of individuals and government agents can alike be judged.

It is the official assumption in the Soviet Union that the state, as a proletarian state, embraces all the interests of its members and is the chief means through which these interests are advanced. Thus, if the policy of the state should conflict (in a given situation) with what a particular law defined as the "right" of an individual, state policy would be assumed to be superior since it would be the more dynamic reflection of "the will of the working class." As a natural consequence, the Soviets reject the belief of the Western democratic states that the individual should be guaranteed a certain sphere of activity free from interference on the part of the state.

The characteristic notions of Soviet law have developed out of the prerevolutionary Russian legal tradition and also out of Marxist ideology. But law in the Soviet Union today is far more important than Marx and Engels ever conceived it would be—an indication of how different the Soviet Union is now from the state Marx and Engels envisaged.

Marx's Conception of Law

The views of Marx and Engels arose naturally out of their reaction to the societies within which they lived. Both men were highly critical of the laws that existed in bourgeois states. When other writers maintained that the laws governing society were the reflection of principles of universal justice, Engels replied that "the jurist imagines he is operating with *a priori* principles, whereas they are really only economic reflexes." Marx and Engels believed that law was only a tool of the state, which in turn was the instrument of the dominant group in society. The law of the bourgeois state, declares the *Communist Manifesto,* "is but the will of your class made into law for all, a will whose essential character and direction are determined by the economic conditions of existence of your class."

Both Marx and Engels were equally critical of the way in which laws were administered in bourgeois states. Marx considered that the notion of equality before the law was a cloak for actual inequality, because of the cost of legal proceedings and because he believed that judges were predisposed to the interests of property.

Marx's criticism of existing states and existing laws led him to believe that the ultimate goal was a society where coercion would be unnecessary. In the advanced stages of socialist society, the absence of economic exploitation would leave everyone free to act according to his own interest, which would be the interest of the whole group. Thus the oppressive functions of the state would "wither away" as people began voluntarily to perform the acts they had previously performed perforce. Laws would therefore become unnecessary, Marx and Engels believed, and fixed rules governing conduct would be replaced by the power of public opinion.

At the same time, they foresaw that the state "as an organization of coercion distinct from society," and laws as fixed rules according to which conduct would be measured, would be useful to the working class in their struggle to expropriate the bourgeoisie and to smash its resistance after the revolution. During this period Marx foresaw that it would be necessary to change the laws so that they would not favor the interests of property, to change the personnel of the judiciary so that it would be sympathetic to the interests of the working classes, and to eliminate the procedural intricacies that provided lawyers with the chance to find loopholes through which to protect property against the claims of "simple justice." However, he believed that this period would be short and that coercion could begin to disappear as soon as the exploiting classes were eliminated.

Lenin's Views on Law

Lenin had already made some modifications in Marx's views on law before the revolution took place. He foresaw that there would be a long period between the crushing of the bourgeoisie and the achievement of a prosperous Communist society and, in the interval, he believed it would be necessary to retain some bourgeois law. He felt, too, that though most crimes in bourgeois society resulted from economic conditions that would be removed when communism was achieved, there would still be individual excesses in the intervening period of the socialist state. Hence, he believed that coercive law would be necessary throughout this period to enforce labor discipline, to regulate the unequal distribution of the products of society, and to curb individual excesses.

The Evolution of Law in the Soviet Union

The Period of War Communism, 1917–21

When the revolution broke out in 1917, Lenin pressed for "revolutionary legality"—that is, that the organs of the new regime should not act arbitrarily but observe the rules that the government adopted. But the rapidity of the changes, the circumstances of civil war, and the great decentralization of activity meant that law quickly lost the element of predictability and uniformity. Punishments inflicted by the courts were determined "by the circumstances of the case" and by "the Socialist consciousness of justice." The rules enforced were a blend of party programs, individual interpretations of socialist needs, and existing laws, of which only those passed by the Soviet government were officially binding.

All prerevolutionary courts were abolished en bloc. But it was more difficult to establish alternative organs. The decrees affecting the People's Courts changed their structure with bewildering rapidity but, in any case, were not enforced. While some local courts that were composed of nonprofessionals existed, they handled only minor cases. Criminal offenses were dealt with by the Cheka (secret police) and by revolutionary tribunals, which acted without regard for legal processes. Thus there was little, if any, machinery for protection of private rights.

This period of War Communism (1917 to 1921) saw the establishment of certain important principles of the Soviet State: its exclusive ownership of basic economic resources (land, water, industry, and so forth), the monopoly by the government of major economic activities (banking, insurance, foreign trade), and ultimate governmental authority over such private property as was still permitted. But economic conditions were still too chaotic to be reduced to law except in the broadest terms.

In regard to the personal relations of citizens, some decisive steps were taken, such as the civil registration of marriage and the divorce law.

Because of this, Rudolf Schlesinger, in his book entitled *Soviet Legal Theory,* has called the effective changes in this period those of a "great bourgeois revolution with the principles of 1793 adapted to twentieth-century conditions."

The New Economic Policy, 1921–28

The period of the New Economic Policy saw the organization of the new court system and the promulgation of basic codes of law. The People's Courts, with one judge and two assessors, regularized the use of nonprofessionals in the lower courts. These courts were to apply the decrees of the "workers' and peasants' government," or if these did not cover the situation, to use "the sense of justice of the working class." Superior courts were set up with power to review the decisions of lower courts.

All courts were dependent, however, on the state organs that passed the laws; and the chief result of establishing superior courts was to secure greater central control of local jurisdiction. Thus the courts were subject to considerable control by the administrative branch of government.

The Civil Code issued in 1922 was patterned to some extent on the most advanced of Western European codes, the German and Swiss, but shaped by the "revolutionary consciousness" of the period of War Communism. Although the New Economic Policy appeared to accept private enterprise, it was in this period that the foundation for Soviet law in the economic sphere was laid. Private enterprise was permitted, in fact, only to the extent that it did not interfere with the state's program of nationalization. The first article of the Civil Code declared that "Civil rights shall be protected by law except in instances where they are exercised in contradiction with their social-economic purpose." This provision justified in the Soviet view the withdrawal of all rights from the "Nepmen" once they were no longer useful to the state. Thus social purposes were elevated far above any individual rights.

A similar disregard of individual rights appeared in the extensive use of the rule of analogy, which nullified the Western principle of "no penalty without a law" under which ex post facto laws (that is, laws with retroactive effect) are forbidden. The rule of analogy, as used in that period in the Soviet Union, meant that any act that a judge considered to be similar to a punishable action was *ipso facto* a crime. Under this rule, acts were punished that had been committed under legal orders in the prerevolutionary period. Moreover, current crimes and penalties were determined according to particular circumstances, to the views of the judges, and to the relation of the act to the policy of the regime. Thus a member of the Communist party might be punished more severely for a breach of labor discipline than an ordinary citizen, just because he was a member of the ruling group, while kulaks suffered more than peasants for hoarding or overcharging just because they were a potential threat to the ultimate socialist purposes of the regime.

Despite this use of law as a flexible instrument for the purposes of the regime, the tendency under the New Economic Policy was toward codification of law and a more systematic organization of the courts. With the steady advance of socialization, however, the questions Marx had raised became more pressing. Had law a place in a socialist society from which capitalist elements had been eliminated? And if so, what character would it assume?

The First Five-Year Plans, 1928–37

The first Five-Year Plans provided part of the answer to these questions. They constituted the second great revolution in the history of the Soviet Union, a revolution caused by economic planning.

Whereas War Communism had been the result of spontaneous action by numerous local groups that received little government direction, the revolution of the Five-Year Plans was instituted and carried through by the Soviet government. This latter revolution required, therefore, a certain measure of formal legality. Rights exercised under the NEP were withdrawn or abolished by decree. Similarly, the conditions under which the new collectivized agriculture was to function (for example, the organization of the collective farms and the distribution of their products) were prescribed by decree.

But if one looks beyond the mere matter of form, it is clear that such violent, ruthless, and radical changes as were involved in the elimination of the kulaks were revolutionary in character. In the words of Rudolf Schlesinger, they "lacked the elements of generality and certainty demanded of any law in an established social system." Even official apologists admitted that the legal system had been broken in order to meet this problem of revolutionary transition. The justification was the customary one: the needs of the socialist society were superior to any laws it might have established.

Not surprisingly, some Soviet theorists were now convinced that, since capitalist elements were being eliminated from the Soviet state under the Five-Year Plans, there would no longer be any need for law and judicial proceedings. In other words, law as an essentially bourgeois institution would "wither away." They believed that the great revolution of the First Five-Year Plan marked the end of Marx's initial stage of socialism and that "public opinion" would henceforth be the regulating force in society.

But this view soon lost official favor. The more changes there were to make, the greater was the emphasis on legal rules backed by coercive penalties. Even when the new economic forms in agriculture took definite shape and social relations arising out of nationalized industry and collectivized agriculture became more stable, there was no change in official attitude and policy. Law was declared to be the instrument of organization of the socialist society. Like the state, law became accepted officially as normal in the socialist stage of development.

Law in the Socialist Stage of Development

Soviet laws and procedures, as exemplified by the 1936 Constitution and subsequent laws, decrees, and practices, are a curious mixture of Western concepts and distinctive Soviet features. The Soviet Constitution, as we have seen, includes two types of rights: those that are enforceable in court, such as the equal rights of women, and those that are not enforceable, such as the right to work, but are an objective of public policy. Another novel feature is that the same chapter that enumerates the rights of Soviet citizens includes also a statement of their duties.

Limitations have been imposed on the great freedom originally encouraged in personal relations. In 1944, divorce ceased to be a matter of right and became dependent on a court ruling; moreover, only children born of a registered marriage now have rights to inheritance. Where originally there was total confiscation of the estate of a deceased person, inheritance of savings and personal possessions is now permitted without restriction; wills have binding force, except that minors cannot be disinherited.

The Operations of Criminal Law

A strongly marked characteristic of Soviet criminal law has been the principle that an act affecting the interest of the state is considered more serious than one that infringes upon the interests of a private citizen. Thus there are not only very severe penalties in cases involving breaches of public rules but also some remarkably lenient penalties in cases of assault and even murder.

The most disturbing feature of Soviet criminal law was the way in which its procedures left few if any safeguards to the accused and often made the outcome of the trial a foregone conclusion. Marked changes have taken place. In 1953 the special boards of the MVD (Federal Ministry of the Interior) were abolished, and in 1960 the Ministry itself was replaced by analogous ministries in the fifteen constituent republics. These bodies have issued new criminal codes and codes of criminal procedure based on the fundamental guidelines published in 1958. These principles include the necessity for a court trial before punishment, and prescribe that punishment can be only for acts designated as crimes in the Criminal Code. They also provide certain rights to the accused, particularly during the preliminary investigation, remove slight administrative offenses from the realm of criminal law, and eliminate use of the doctrine of analogy (this doctrine had not been used for a number of years). All these developments help, of course, to make criminal law operate more nearly in the Soviet Union as it does in Western states.

Barriers to Stability

Because it has taken all spheres of life under its control, the socialist state depends even more heavily than the capitalist state on positive law.

Moreover, custom and tradition are much less strong than in Western states. Stalin's successors have attempted to stress persuasion and social pressure, rather than coercion, hoping that people will learn to act in a "socialist way." But their very notion of "social legality" is ambiguous, since it implies not only lawful, orderly processes but still more the absolute authority of the Communist party over all aspects of life and its drive to transform the Soviet Union into a new form of social organization called communism. Thus there is a continuous tension between the notion of legality and the philosophy of socialism.

To a considerable extent coercion has been replaced by public supervision of private actions undertaken under broad and vague provisions or directives. There are antiparasite laws directed against "useless" members of society but not necessarily restricted to them. Voluntary militia units are exhorted to enforce socially acceptable actions. But unless this intensified social pressure operates within a known framework, it is hard to anticipate the evolution of the kind of legal stability that is necessary if conduct is to be a response to custom rather than to rules.

Soviet law still retains a "revolutionary" character. There has been no convincing evidence as yet that individual laws or the new revised codes might not be changed abruptly if the regime should feel the need to do so. Indeed law is clearly intended to implement policy and could never restrict the ruling Communist party that determines that policy. Even constitutional laws are frequently changed. Thus law in the Soviet Union continues to lack that degree of certainty that makes it the bulwark of Western liberties.

2. THE JUDICIARY AND THE COURTS

The administration of law, like the work of local organs of state power, combines widespread popular participation at the lower levels with central control. People in Soviet towns and villages share in the decision of cases in informal gatherings and in the courts to a degree far exceeding the participation of Americans and Englishmen in judicial action through the jury system. At the same time, as one would expect, the Soviet court system does not possess the independence from party and political control that characterizes the court systems in Western countries.

Outside the judicial structure, and directed against the "parasites," are "public meetings," at which a minimum of a hundred people can by majority vote impose a sentence of two to five years exile if the local soviet's executive committee subsequently approves. There are also informal comradely courts, which can be set up in industries, educational institutions, apartment buildings, and so forth, wherever a collective exceeds fifty persons. The forerunners of the comradely courts, from 1919 to 1923 and 1928 to 1940, were concerned almost entirely with enforcing labor discipline. After 1940, severe labor measures made them superfluous. Revived under Khrushchev, comradely courts can impose minor penalties for "wrong behavior"—for example, falsehood or rudeness in housing disputes. Their work is looked on as educative rather than coercive.

All major and more serious minor crimes and disputes between citizens are dealt with by the regular courts. The lowest of these, the people's courts, each with an elected judge[1] and two elected lay assessors,[2] also have a highly informal procedure, a characteristic feature of lower Soviet courts from the beginning. Witnesses interrupt each other and shout lustily when passions are running high. Decisions, which are reached by majority vote of the bench, are argued over like those of football games. Since these courts deal with simple, everyday matters, they have considerable independence in practice, despite the fact that all Soviet courts are subject to supervision and review from above.

Not surprisingly, there is none of this liveliness and sense of popular participation in the higher courts at the regional, territorial, and union-republic levels, in the Supreme Court of the USSR, or in special tribunals. Most of these courts also use one judge and two lay assessors if the case comes to them for its first trial; otherwise there are three or more judges. Above the level of the people's courts, however, the elec-

[1] All judges serve five-year terms.
[2] All lay assessors are chosen for two-year terms by local citizens, but none serves more than ten days a year.

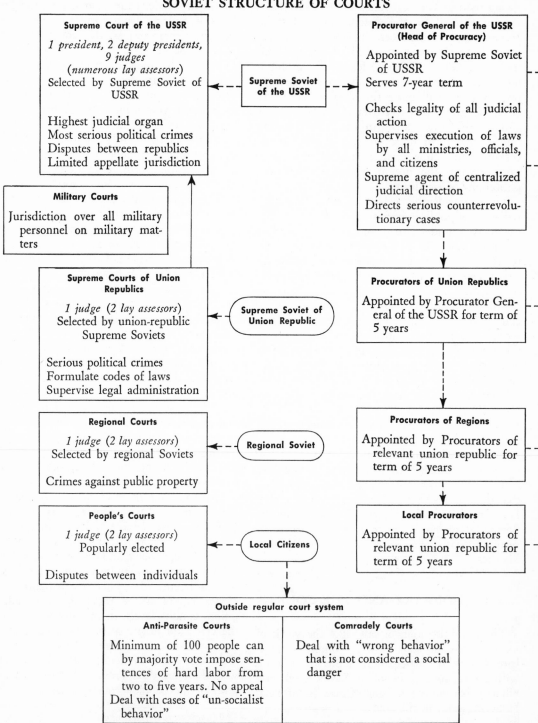

Elective or Appointive Lines – – – – →
Channel of Appeal ————→

SOVIET STRUCTURE OF COURTS

Supreme Court of the USSR

1 president, 2 deputy presidents, 9 judges
(numerous lay assessors)
Selected by Supreme Soviet of USSR

Highest judicial organ
Most serious political crimes
Disputes between republics
Limited appellate jurisdiction

Procurator General of the USSR (Head of Procuracy)

Appointed by Supreme Soviet of USSR
Serves 7-year term

Checks legality of all judicial action
Supervises execution of laws by all ministries, officials, and citizens
Supreme agent of centralized judicial direction
Directs serious counterrevolutionary cases

Supreme Soviet of the USSR

Military Courts

Jurisdiction over all military personnel on military matters

Supreme Courts of Union Republics

1 judge (2 lay assessors)
Selected by union-republic Supreme Soviets

Serious political crimes
Formulate codes of laws
Supervise legal administration

Supreme Soviet of Union Republic

Procurators of Union Republics

Appointed by Procurator General of the USSR for term of 5 years

Regional Courts

1 judge (2 lay assessors)
Selected by regional Soviets

Crimes against public property

Regional Soviet

Procurators of Regions

Appointed by Procurators of relevant union republic for term of 5 years

People's Courts

1 judge (2 lay assessors)
Popularly elected

Disputes between individuals

Local Citizens

Local Procurators

Appointed by Procurators of relevant union republic for term of 5 years

Outside regular court system

Anti-Parasite Courts	Comradely Courts
Minimum of 100 people can by majority vote impose sentences of hard labor from two to five years. No appeal. Deal with cases of "un-socialist behavior"	Deal with "wrong behavior" that is not considered a social danger

tion of members of the bench is by the appropriate soviet, including the Supreme Soviet. Political reliability is scanned with special care, since these courts may deal with cases in which the state has special concern.

In the general reorganization of 1957, the appellate jurisdiction of the Supreme Court of the USSR was formally restricted to the review of cases where the decision of a union-republic court violates all-union law, or the interest of another union republic. At the same time, the union republics were given jurisdiction over judicial organization and power to formulate codes of laws and the competence of the union-republic Supreme Courts was enlarged to include almost all phases of legal administration in their territory. The ministries of justice in the republics were subsequently abolished, as a symbol of the desire to maintain the autonomy of the courts. Their remaining functions, such as supervision of the bar and systematization of law, were transferred to the Juridical Commission of the respective Councils of Ministers.

The Procuracy

Although the Soviet Supreme Court no longer issues binding instructions to lower courts on the interpretation of laws, the Procuracy retains its dominant position in the judicial and administrative system. Far more important in the Soviet system of government than the Attorney-General is in the American government, the Procurator General heads an organization of some six thousand persons who serve as watchdogs on behalf of ordinary citizens, as well as the top leadership, against administrative abuses. Professor Harold Berman compares the work of the Procuracy favorably with that of the Ombudsman and points out that the Procuracy examines administrative abuses on a far wider scale. The Procuracy checks the legality of all administrative and judicial actions. Each of the union republics and its districts also has a procurator, but the union-republic governments have no say in the work of the Procuracy. It is thus the supreme agency of centralized direction in the judicial system. It also investigates thousands of complaints every year.

In practice, therefore, the Procuracy tends to be all-pervasive and virtually omnipotent. Its top office is always held by a high-ranking member of the Communist party (technically appointed by the Supreme Soviet for seven years) since it is the crucial place from which control is exercised over the bureaucracy. A procurator in the Soviet Union is concerned not only with the interests of the prosecution (whether on behalf of the state or of a private individual, as in a case of murder) but still more with securing a judgment that is "just" in terms of general, as well as particular, interests. The Procuracy also deals with the organization of the courts, the rules of law in current use, and their "strict execution" by government officials, institutions, and citizens (Article 113). It also questions the actions of officials, institutes proceedings, and generally watches over administrative regulations to ensure that they are not contrary to law.

Thus in a system governed by an autocratic central authority that has used its power to crush human rights, there is also in the Procuracy an effective system of control over abuses of human rights by ordinary administrative officials.

Revolutionary Justice

"Revolutionary justice"—that is, the imposition of punishment in a nonjudicial procedure—long played an important role in Soviet life. "The Courts shall not do away with terrorism," stated Lenin; "to promise such a thing means either to cheat ourselves or other people."

The tribunals that used to administer "revolutionary justice" were the special boards of the Ministry of the Interior (MVD), which were abolished in 1953. Exile to a specific locality, banishment from other localities, or service for up to five years in a labor camp were called "normal" penalties; any of these could be indefinitely prolonged. From all reports, physical punishment and death from hardship were far from infrequent.

Theoretically, "revolutionary justice" was supposed to deal with "counterrevolutionary activity." In an earlier effort to stabilize law, the Supreme Court of the Union declared in 1938 that no one should be convicted of counterrevolutionary activity unless his intention to overthrow the Soviet regime was proved. But it was apparent that the secret police dealt with a great many offenses—such as criticism, failure to meet quotas, or outward expressions of religious or nationality sentiment—which few people outside the Soviet Union considered dangerous to the security of the regime. As long as this continued it was apparent that the Soviet Union had not yet passed out of the period of revolution. One of the most important indications that the post-Stalin regime is genuinely seeking stability is the degree to which it has curbed revolutionary justice and brought punishable offenses before the regular courts.

Evaluation of the Soviet Legal System

Law and the courts are highly important in the socialist society, for they provide the chief means through which conduct is regulated in every field. Moreover, as is obvious, this involves a much wider range of activities than in the United States or Great Britain. Law, enforced by coercive action, can be a spur to the laborer as well as a deterrent to the thief.

It is not the national control by the state of the economy, but rather the attitude of the governing group, that ultimately determines the characteristic features of Soviet courts. The present Soviet government has moved away from arbitrary action, but it has not yet firmly established the guarantee of the rule of law that exists in democratic states: the principle that the state machinery, in general, and the judiciary, in particular, are bound at all times to respect and uphold the law. The Procuracy does a great deal to check the abuses of administrators. Minor officials are prosecuted for negligence or "overzealous" action; workers appeal penalties and are sometimes upheld. But if an issue of political loyalty is raised, it overrides every other consideration.

The courts in the Soviet Union accept the notion that the rules of law are relative to the circumstances and aims of the socialist state at a given time. The basic policies of the leaders of the state cannot be challenged. Moreover there is a disturbing encouragement of "popular justice" exercised without regard for fixed forms. Yet since Stalin's death terror has largely been eliminated, and laws and procedures have been reformed. There is indeed a constant tension between the desire to make law a fixed and certain norm and the unrestricted power of the will of the Communist party.

8. The USSR: A Workers' Society?

It is characteristic of the Soviet planned economy that the Five-Year Plans provide as precise goals for education and social security as for heavy industry and consumer goods. The two types of goals, in fact, are closely interrelated. Economic planning presupposes social aims, such as education, the improvement of the living conditions of the workingman, and the material prosperity of the whole society. Even more important is the fact that at each stage of Soviet development, its economic and industrial objectives are dependent upon the training and incentives provided for the Russian people. The keys to understanding the educational and social programs in the Soviet Union must be sought, therefore, not only in the broad objectives of the socialist state but also in the economic and political needs of its particular stage of development.

1. EDUCATION

There are few achievements in which the Soviet government takes greater pride than in the advance in education. Under the tsarist regime it is estimated that 55 to 67 percent of the population was illiterate;[1] now illiteracy is rare and found only among those over fifty.

There have been four major objectives of Soviet education: a literate intelligent population, economic specialists, political indoctrination, and mass training for industrial work.

Lenin pointed out, "You cannot build a Communist state with an illiterate people." The liquidation of the bourgeoisie and the rise of the proletariat were dependent on transmitting the simple conceptions of political ideology to the mass of the people. To accelerate this process there was a wide use of vernacular languages and of striking and easily mastered posters, headlines, pamphlets, and wall newspapers. Once a person could master a headline, he was no longer illiterate; the first step in the political-educational aim had been taken, and grounding in political grammar could follow.

The Russian people's vast eagerness for knowledge, so apparent even before the revolution, led citizens of all ages to respond to the opportunities for education with enthusiasm and persistence. Anyone who could read was set to teach those who could not. Simplified textbooks expounded "the faith." The impact of the new (if still very elementary) learning was revolutionary, particularly in the undeveloped areas of the Soviet Mideast and East.

Mass manual training had no less spectacular effects than mass mental training. If anything, it was more important both socially and economically. It was the great leveler among urban and rural peoples and a major factor in putting women on a real plane of equality with men. The great and immediate need of the industrialization program was rank-and-file workers. Short-term training for mass-production jobs and for improved workmanship had developed in special industries before the First Five-Year Plan. But the new goals for industry required immensely accelerated training. Under the direction of foreign specialists and of engineers

[1] The educational experience and the system of schools that the Bolsheviks inherited were not inconsiderable. Peter the Great established the first Russian university; Catherine the Great, a system of free elementary and secondary schools open also to women. But before the Soviet period, education touched only a minute proportion of the peasants. For the relatively small numbers who attended, tsarist universities were centers of liberalism, and during periods of repression their students worked for radical reform.

trained under the old regime, the new workers were taught on the job and in factory schools. Workers' universities, such as Khrushchev attended, enabled people of little or no previous education to combine their technical training with some general education. An abundance of educational opportunities coupled with the attraction of the new industry resulted in a remarkable social as well as physical mobility.

Yet the pressures of the industrial program soon introduced a new rigidity and stratification. The demand for skilled laborers, technicians, and managers intensified the concentration on specialized types of training and thus replaced the emphasis on full and open opportunities for further education. As specialization developed, schools became more highly selective in their choice of students; it became much more difficult for workers to acquire either the general or the special education that would enable them to prepare themselves for higher positions. During the later 1930's it was comparatively rare for managers to be drawn from the ranks of the workers. It also became much less common for workers' children to acquire the kind of training that would equip them for such positions.

Transitions in Education

As in so many other places, post-Stalin changes in the educational system have greatly limited the social differentiation so noticeable under Stalin; these changes have also tied schooling and work much more closely together. Under Stalin, seven years of education were supposedly compulsory, although only some 80 percent of the students completed them. At the end of this period, the student had four alternatives: to take a job, to go to a labor reserves school for two years of training in minor skills, to attend a three- or four-year technical school (*tekhnikum*) leading to highly skilled and some non-manual occupations, or to continue with the higher grades of the ten-year school whose predominantly academic training was the route to higher education. Fees were charged in the *tekhnikums,* the ten-year schools, and the higher institutions; there were no scholarships to the ten-year schools. In consequence, the latter

tended to be filled by the children of the "elite," administrative, economic, and military, as were the academic institutions preparing for professions. This was the more so since their parents often used their influence to secure places for their children. In contrast, the children of the workers and peasants were increasingly limited to the kind of training that fitted them for the same type of jobs their parents held.

The Nineteenth and Twentieth Party Congresses endorsed the ambitious plan of free universal ten-year education but with no increase in the number of institutions of higher education. Though the curriculum of the ten-year schools was modified to include more practical subjects, with the obvious intention of directing many of their graduates into technical schools, the students and their parents resisted on the ground that they had a right to enter higher education. In the face of a labor shortage accentuated by the low birth rates of the war years, Khrushchev made the decisive changes of reducing the number of school years from ten to eight, of insisting that this education should be largely vocational, and of demanding that every student take a full-time job at the completion of the eight years. Thus he sharply reduced the labor shortage and at the same time undercut the notion of the "right" to higher education.

Students who had completed their eight years of compulsory schooling were encouraged in the Khrushchev period to add three years of secondary school. This training consisted chiefly of preparation for vocational work, and only the very gifted were trained in liberal arts as preparation for higher academic study. In 1964, the three-year period commonly devoted to secondary school was reduced to two years on the grounds that many professions could be mastered in the shorter time and that longer training, as, for example, for a librarian, can be given in a *tekhnikum.* Ten years of compulsory education will again be instituted in 1970 but without changing the objective of maintaining close links between learning and occupation.

All higher education in the Soviet Union—whether in secondary or more advanced institutes—has this strong vocational cast. It is designed to produce the specialists needed by the Soviet state. There is no real equivalent, therefore, to the general education of an American liberal arts college. The vast majority of students pursue narrowly specialized courses in one of 700 technical institutes and take only such theoretical material as is relevant to their specialization, plus the required course on Communist ideology and a foreign language. Even the forty Soviet universities, which enroll some 10 to 15 percent of those in higher education, limit their students to one field in the social or natural sciences or humanities. Nearly half of all students in higher education are enrolled in some branch of engineering.

Many Soviet students take their courses in higher education on a part-time basis or at night school. Daytime enrollments have scarcely increased since 1955. The advantage of part-time or night-school work is that it can be carried on "without interruption of [industrial] production," to cite the words of the prevailing concept. It is more questionable whether quality can be maintained under these circumstances.

Surprising is the high percentage of women in higher education—62 percent in 1964—and in the professions. They formed 74 percent of the doctors (including dentists) in the Soviet Union in that same year, 59 percent of the economists, statisticians, and commodity specialists, 32 percent of the lawyers, and 31 percent of the engineers. Far more than in the United States, the Soviet Union draws on the capacities and labor power of both sexes.

Except for kindergartens and boarding schools, all education in the Soviet Union is free. Most students in full-time specialized secondary schools and institutions for higher education receive stipends. This equalitarianism does not quite outweigh, however, the elitism of the strong preference for white-collar jobs.

Evaluation of Soviet Education

Education in the Soviet Union, particularly in the initial eight-year compulsory period, is essentially different in aim from liberal education in the United States and Great Britain. Where the avowed aim of liberal education is to teach students to think for themselves, the Soviet education system aims at indoctrination in "Marxism-Leninism" and the purposes of the state. For in the Soviet Union, to a far greater extent even than in France, the schools are regarded as an essential weapon in the battle for the minds of future generations.

Liberal education aims to develop the native abilities of individuals without conscious reference to a preconceived social pattern. In contrast, Soviet training avowedly seeks to develop the skills necessary for the planned society at a given stage of development. With the strong equalitarian bias in early training goes also the heavy emphasis on technical and scientific training that enables the USSR to develop a far higher number of scientists and engineers than does the United States. Thus the educational program to foster a "classless" society is mated to the production of those particular skills that are necessary for the continuing expansion of heavy industry and for keeping the Soviet Union in the forefront of scientific achievements.

2. THE POSITION OF WOMEN

One of the most publicized features of Soviet society is the degree to which men and women perform similar tasks. Even before women were drafted for national service following the Nazi attack, there were more than thirty million of them working in the Soviet Union, nineteen million on the farms and eleven million in industry, with many famous women Stakhanovite workers among them. Part of the program for increasing labor resources is to attract still more women to the workbenches by increased provision of kindergartens and canteens, shortening the working day, and raising the wages paid at the lowest level at which most women are employed. Some women are also elected or selected for public offices, from trade union committees to the Supreme Soviet. A woman, Furtseva, was selected as a candidate member of the Party Presidium in 1956, although subsequently dropped late in 1961.

Equality for Women

The first fundamental changes in the status of women were brought about by the revolution of 1917. Before that time a woman had no separate rights and was subject to the will of her husband. The revolution established the equality of men and women and abolished the special privileges of husbands. Concurrently, women were placed under the same obligations as men to provide for the support of the family. Both shared equally in the support of children, and each was responsible for looking after the other in case of incapacity. "A spouse incapable of work and lacking a subsistence minimum is entitled to support by the other spouse if the latter is in a position to give it," reads the law of 1918. Thus the removal of disabilities because of sex was coupled with provisions that made self-supporting work a necessity even for married women, since private property had been abolished and individual wages were low.

In 1919 Lenin declared, ". . . to draw woman into socially productive work, to pull her out of domestic slavery, to liberate her from submission—degrading and stultifying—to the sterile and exclusive surroundings of kitchen and nursery—that is the main goal. This means a long struggle that requires fundamental remodeling of social techniques, and morals as well. But this struggle will end in a complete victory of communism." Thus the new position for women was identified with the ultimate purposes of the regime.

Women in Industry

But up to the middle of the First Five-Year Plan there was comparatively little change in the attitude of discrimination against women in industry. In 1930 only about three million women were wage earners in industry, agriculture, education, and public institutions—a smaller percentage than during World War I or the Civil War.

The change came with the pronounced labor shortage that developed after 1930. *Pravda* declared in December 1930, "The labor reserves are exhausted. . . . But there are tremendous reserves of female labor. Suffice it to say that in our cities alone about six million housewives are wasting their energies in the kitchen, in laundering and the like." The emergency, rather than any theoretical conceptions, was responsible for the use of women's labor and the consequent

necessity of developing measures of communal feeding, day nurseries, and so forth. As a Soviet periodical stated, "The last and most backward sphere of individual economy, the household, must be *collectivized*."

The demand for women in the factories met a more willing response from the women because of their need to supplement their husbands' inadequate wages. To some extent, the work was fitted to their special capacities; in certain positions, such as locksmiths and fitters, women were given preference over men; and a certain proportion of places was reserved for them in the technical and vocational schools. But women also had to join men in heavier occupations. In 1939 women were widely employed in underground coal mining and on nightwork.

By November 1939 women comprised 43.4 percent of the manual workers of industry, as compared with 28.8 percent in the much less developed industry of 1929. The number of women wage earners had risen to well over nine million by 1937, and the Third Five-Year Plan regarded them as its chief source of labor supply. Unlike any other country in the United Nations, the Soviet Union trained its women in peacetime to replace men in heavy production work so as to free the latter for the army, a factor of great importance in the resistance to the Nazi invasion.

The Role of the Family

The Soviet Union has been more consistent in its policy toward women than was Nazi Germany, which first insisted that women's work was to look after children and cooking and then later brought large numbers of women into its war industry. Even so, Soviet policies affecting women have varied from time to time.

This has been particularly true in regard to family relations. An essential part of the liberty and equality that the Bolshevik Revolution brought to women was to be freedom from irksome family ties. Either partner to a marriage could obtain a divorce simply upon application and without the consent of the other partner. In addition, the state itself provided abortion clinics for women who did not wish children.

Since the middle 1930's, however, the official attitude has changed. The government has undertaken an active campaign to raise the birth rate. The campaign has been so successful that housing, schools, and other facilities are now overstrained. Moreover, every effort has been made to strengthen family ties. Divorce is now more difficult to secure in the Soviet Union than in most capitalist countries, and communism was characterized in 1960 as fostering "consistent monogamy."

According to theory, the household functions of the family are gradually to be replaced by public restaurants and laundries, while formal training for children is to be transferred in large measure to the expanding network of boarding schools. Nonetheless, it is said rather vaguely that the family will retain its "moral and educative" functions. For the foreseeable future, however, women will continue to perform their customary tasks as well as provide nearly half the total labor force (more than half the doctors, as we have seen, are women). The problem of combining their two roles is, to a large extent, left to the women themselves.

3. SOCIAL SERVICES

The Soviet Union provides its urban wage earners with a complete and unified system of social security, except for unemployment aid, which is said to be unnecessary because of the collectivized nature of the Soviet economy. Some benefits have also been extended recently to collective farms, though peasants also organize assistance on a self-help basis.

Soviet social services contrast with social security provisions in other countries. They are looked on as part of the worker's real wages: Stalin said in 1927 that they added one-third to a worker's pay. Beyond this they serve not only as a protection for workers but also as an incentive to effort. Eligibility for benefits of special types is reserved for those doing particularly arduous tasks or those of special value to the regime. Social security is thus the positive side of labor discipline: the reward for conformity, as contrasted with the penalty for deviation.

All doctors, dentists, specialists, and hospitals are under centralized state control and are financed by the state budget. The funds allocated to these services constantly increase. Medicines, however, must generally be bought by the patient. Although equipment is still antiquated and drugs often scarce, there is an extraordinarily high proportion of doctors—one to every 550 persons in 1961. (The highest is in Israel, where the proportion is 1 to 420. In the United States it is 1 to 790.) This is largely because only doctors can give the certificates for treatment or sick leave that in industry, as in the army, are necessary to permit absence from normal duties.

The Soviet Union provides all the social services that are fairly common in Western countries: children's aid, disability and maternity benefits, socialized medicine, survivors' insurance for needy dependents of deceased workers, old-age pensions, and also rest homes, sanitariums (and travel expenses to reach them), and funeral allowances.

The absence of unemployment aid in the Soviet Union since 1930 both results from and aids its drive for full urban employment. Critics charge that, since the average worker earns too little to save much from his pay, the lack of unemployment aid gives managers great control over their employees. Even with the present absence of formal restraints on changing jobs, substantial pressures still operate to prevent workers from being long without employment.

Social services in the Soviet Union also differ from those in Western countries in another way: they are not provided on a basis of insurance. Workers contribute directly only through their trade union fees; enterprises are taxed by the government in proportion to their number of workers; and the total costs are items in the state and trade union budgets. Since social services are not on an insurance basis, benefits cannot be claimed as a matter of right. Moreover, benefits are usually higher for trade unionists than for others; they are graded according to earnings; and the amount is influenced by the length of service in a particular enterprise. For example, if a trade unionist has served more than 12 years, he receives 90 percent of his wages as sick-pay, but, if less than 3 years, only 50 percent. Those who are not members of trade unions get an established minimum up to half these rates. Stakhanovites and shock workers (who differ from the former by exceeding standard requirements through physical effort rather than by changing the production process) receive additional bonuses.

Except for health services and old-age pensions (which are under the Ministry for Social Assistance and were raised materially in 1956) the social security system is administered by trade unions under the overall direction of the All-Union Central Trade Union Council. Every factory and place of employment has a social insurance council set up by the local trade union committee. Unpaid "insurance delegates" check on malingering and supervise the rest homes. This process gives the impression that the workers' own organization controls most social services and makes it possible to tap a wide source of voluntary aid, a particular objective of the Soviet regime.

Conclusion

It seems paradoxical that, while Great Britain is seeking to establish a national minimum, the Soviet Union has combined its emphasis on equality with a strong stress on individual achievement. In education, in the position of women, and even in social security, the Soviet state rewards the intelligent and the skillful and those who endure long periods of service and produce much. In the process, a new social stratification has threatened to develop in the Soviet Union, whereas in Great Britain and France the trend has been toward blurring traditional class lines.

Economic and social changes in the post-Stalin era have provided a general widening of opportunities and marked improvement in basic conditions of work. The 1966 Party Congress and Five-Year Plan affirmed special concern for agricultural prices and work conditions. But it remains true that collective farmers still receive much less proportionately than industrial workers from the Soviet state and seem unlikely to gain much more until they too become wage earners on state farms. Most women continue to receive the minimum returns for their work, partly, at least, because of their other responsibilities. The educational system aids mobility, however, and persuasion and an emphasis on voluntary effort have replaced the earlier stress on coercion, although the latter is in reserve if needed.

Policies in the social sphere are as much instruments of the Soviet regime as are its economic policies. The official assumption that there is an identity of interest between the people and the government justifies the latter, in its own view, in using any means to achieve its most pressing purposes. Thus education and social services, which Western countries believe should be primarily for the development and protection of the individual, are officially directed in the Soviet Union toward producing specialists and the high production levels that remain the chief objective of the regime.

9. The Soviet Union and the Outside World

The outstanding feature of international relations since the end of World War II has been the existence of only two super-powers in the world: the United States and the Soviet Union. The predominance of both countries rests on their industrial strength and their strategic position, the one dominating the Americas and the other holding the central place in the Eurasian land mass. Though each has a long history of expanding influence, only since World War II have the interests of the two countries begun to touch all over the world. Neither country, moreover, had been accustomed to taking a leading part in international relations, since the United States pursued an isolationist policy during most of the interwar period, while the Soviet Union was excluded from international society because of its political unorthodoxy. Thus both were relatively unprepared for the positions of leadership forced on them by the outcome of the war.

The dominance of two powers that are so far apart ideologically has vastly complicated the problem of world peace. The United States, as the last powerful representative of nineteenth-century liberal capitalism, is the leading defender of that free enterprise of which the Soviet Union is the most vigorous opponent. And though both countries proclaim their devotion to democracy, the senses in which they use the word are so different as to constitute an added provocation.

The problems arising from the difference in the political and economic aims of the two countries are complicated by fear and suspicion on both sides. Americans have long seen a dual drive behind Soviet policy: the ambition of a new imperialist power following in the footsteps of the Tsars or trying (like Hitler) first to dominate Europe and then the world; and the drive of what is still the most powerful Communist state toward world revolution in accordance with Marxist-Leninist teaching—by sponsoring in non-Communist countries Communist parties whose ultimate aim is to overthrow their respective governments and establish Communist states. In both respects, the Soviet Union has seemed a menace to the survival of the free world and thus to the United States.

The Soviet Union, on its side, has similar fears. Twice since the revolution its territory has been invaded by anti-Communist foreign armies. Hitler's invasion left permanent scars; but the Soviet leaders have also not forgotten the earlier British, French, and American intervention in support of the White Russian armies. They still fear that Western countries might undertake an anti-Communist crusade. Behind such apprehensions lies the theory of Marxism-Leninism that the foreign policy of non-Communist countries is dominated by greedy capitalists and imperialists who are determined to encircle and crush the Soviet Union, the "standard bearer of socialism." Though Soviet leaders now maintain that war is not inevitable, they believe this is only because the Soviet Union has become too strong to be attacked with impunity. Even so, there remains a latent fear that the United States, the symbol of bourgeois capitalism, might attack the Soviet workers' state. It is also possible that present Soviet leaders, like Stalin in the past, find an atmosphere of international crisis useful from time to time to justify both their authority and their demands for sacrifices.

Tension Since World War II

Events after World War II provided ammunition for a steadily rising barrage of mutual accusations. Western countries looked at first with tolerance on the efforts of the Soviet Union to ensure that each of its neighbors would have a friendly government as a safeguard against another invasion. But the devices used to ensure "friendship" on the part of these countries soon proved to be those traditionally used by imperialistic nations to extend their power: the use of fifth columns, military occupation, puppet governments, and even, in certain cases, outright annexation. Moreover, in the Eastern European countries under Soviet control, opposition was increasingly repressed with a cynicism and ruthlessness paralleled only by similar action in the Soviet Union itself.

In Yugoslavia and far more so in China, the success of indigenous Communist movements vastly increased the number of persons within Communist-controlled states. Indeed, it has been in the Far East—an area increasingly influenced by Communist China—that conflicts, in Korea and Vietnam, have developed.

The countermeasures that the United States and its chief allies have taken have been said by Soviet leaders to prove the warlike intentions of the capitalist countries. The Truman doctrine of support for Greece and Turkey, which were under heavy Soviet pressure, was labeled profascist. Even the Marshall plan for the economic reconstruction of Europe, from which the Soviet Union and Eastern European countries were excluded only by Soviet decision, was called a plot of American capitalism to ensnare the European countries. The North Atlantic Treaty Organization was greeted as a sinister plan to create a military alliance against the USSR; so too was the South East Asia Treaty Organization (SEATO), the much less successful effort to organize a consolidated front against Communist expansion in that area. Still more violent criticism, as well as arms for North Vietnam, has followed American intervention in South Vietnam. Thus each action has called forth its reaction.

The Soviet "New Line"

The accession to power of new Soviet leaders after Stalin's death led—at first hesitatingly but by 1955 on a large scale—to measures obviously designed to reduce international tension. In 1955 the Austrian peace treaty was signed at last, and Soviet troops were withdrawn from that country; diplomatic relations were established with the German Federal Republic; Porkkala was returned to Finland, and Dairen turned over to Communist China (so that the Soviet Union no longer holds any bases outside its own territory); new disarmament proposals were put forward; and Soviet leaders attended the "summit" conference at Geneva that established personal relations among the leaders of East and West, if no more tangible results.

The broad conceptions behind these policies appeared in the speeches at the Twentieth Party Congress in February 1956. During its sessions, Khrushchev and highly regarded party theorists like Suslov enunciated three principles underlying the "new line" in Soviet policy: that wars are not inevitable; that peaceful coexistence is not a temporary but "a basic principle of Soviet foreign policy"; and that there are many forms of transition to socialism. Underlying the first two points is the argument that the new factor in the international situation is the growth in the strength and size of the Communist bloc, now numbering some nine hundred million people. Soviet leaders still maintain basically that "the capitalist and socialist outlooks cannot be reconciled," and that ultimate victory belongs inevitably to socialism "as the higher, more progressive, social system," but they no longer maintain the inevitability of conflict.

The contemporary Soviet line in foreign policy appears much more flexible and far less openly aggressive than it used to be. Despite obvious hostility to United States involvement in Vietnam, Soviet-American lines of communication have been kept open. Although continued influence over East Germany is at the heart of the Soviet Union's European policies, it has also established relations with West Germany and has responded to French government overtures for more extensive contacts. President Podgorny paid an official visit to the Pope early in 1967. Moreover, the Soviet Union maintains and sometimes expands its influence with some of the most important uncommitted countries of Asia, the Middle East, and Africa through provision of economic aid, including food, and through its spectacular scientific achievements.

Is this change in tactics a probing at the unity of the free world? Is it a reflection of the Soviet Union's flexible internal policies and assured leadership and thus the technique of a self-confident regime that finds endless opportunities to harass the West and that sees time on its side as it continues the massive industrialization of its country? How far is it a response to the severe split in the Communist world between the Russians and the Chinese? And can this line be maintained in the face of Communist China's pressures for more aggressive policies against the West?

Before attempting to answer these questions, or to suggest what policies the United States should follow in response to current Soviet foreign policies, it is important to consider in more detail the character of those policies since World War II. In so doing, we shall consider (1) the policies the Soviet Union has pursued toward the Communist countries in Eastern and Southeastern Europe; (2) its policies toward Yugoslavia, China, and the Communist parties in non-Communist countries; and (3) its general international relations.

1. SOVIET RELATIONS WITH EASTERN EUROPE

Immediately after World War II, the Soviet government's chief concern was to strengthen the European position of its country. Between 1939 and 1947 the Soviet Union reestablished the main lines of the European frontiers of Russia as they had been forged by a succession of Russian rulers since the time of Peter the Great, and as they existed when the last of the Romanovs was killed in 1917. Latvia, Lithuania, and eastern Poland were reacquired directly and Estonia indirectly in accordance with the German-Soviet agreements of 1939, and by Soviet military occupation in 1940. The transfer was confirmed by the Soviet-Polish Treaty of August 1945. Moreover, the Soviet Union also acquired certain areas in East Prussia, Bukovina, and the Carpathians that had never belonged to the Tsars. Germany had agreed in 1939 to the cession of Bessarabia to the Soviet Union; the transfer took place through the Soviet-Rumanian Agreement of June 28, 1940, which was

explicitly confirmed in the Rumanian Peace Treaty of 1947. The Finnish Peace Treaty similarly reestablished the former Russian positions on the Baltic and in the Arctic. Only at one point, the Dardanelles, did the Soviet Union fail to attain the territorial goals that its predecessors had established.

These new boundaries reflect both historical considerations, especially the previous Russian control of the Baltic states, and nationality considerations, as in acquiring that part of eastern Poland inhabited by Ukrainians and White Russians. More particularly, however, they reflect the strategic consideration of securing the maximum protection for the triangle formed by the Soviet Union's three chief European cities, Leningrad, Moscow, and Kiev. This means safeguarding the three main routes through which an invasion can be launched from the west against this strategic triangle. Napoleon's armies took the northerly route through the endless northern forests when they marched on Moscow in 1812. Hitler's armies launched their attack through the center route across the plain south of the great Pripet marshes. Soviet strategy seeks to guard not only these two approaches but also the more southerly route from the Danubian Basin. At the same time the Russians wish to place the Soviet Union itself in a position to direct offensives in these directions if it should feel the need to do so.

Its Boundary Zone

Strategically, the Soviet Union depends less on a fixed boundary line, however, than on a *boundary zone* made up of Southeastern and Eastern European countries: Rumania, Bulgaria, Hungary, Czechoslovakia, Poland, and East Germany. This boundary zone, which was once called the Soviet "empire," was brought under Soviet control through the Red Army, but relations are now chiefly maintained through liaison with the local Communist parties that control the "people's democracies," and through close economic relations.

Although the Red Army made Soviet control in Eastern Europe possible and both in East Germany (in 1953) and in Hungary (in 1956) has crushed uprisings against local Communist rule, the former quasi-feudal relationship no longer exists. But there is still a considerable

SOVIET EXPANSION IN THE WEST
SINCE 1939

- USSR IN 1939
- AREAS ANNEXED BY USSR SINCE 1939
- COMMUNIST, IN ALLIANCE WITH USSR
- COMMUNIST, NOT ALLIED TO USSR
- BOUNDARIES OF 1939

Petsamo

NORWAY

SWEDEN

FINLAND

Porkkalla

Leningrad

Tallinn

SOVIET

ESTONIA

BALTIC

LATVIA

Moscow

Riga

SEA

NORTH SEA

DENMARK

LITHUANIA

Kaunas

UNION

Königsberg

Minsk

GERMAN

Berlin

Warsaw

NETH.

FEDERAL

DEMO-
CRATIC

POLAND

BELG.

REPUBLIC

Kiev

REPUBLIC

Prague

LUX.

Lwow

OF GERMANY

CZECHOSLOVAKIA

FRANCE

BUKOVINA

BESSARABIA

SWITZ.

AUSTRIA

Budapest

HUNGARY

Odessa

RUMANIA

Belgrade

Bucharest

YUGOSLAVIA

BLACK SEA

ITALY

BULGARIA

Sofia

ALBANIA

GREECE

TURKEY

0   100   200   300
MILES

degree of cohesion induced by a judicious mixture of influence and pressure.

The local Communist parties in these states often began as minority participants in united-front coalitions, but by the time the coalitions acquired governing power, the Communists had generally seized their leadership through control of the key instruments of force: the police and the army. Thus the stage of the united front rapidly gave way to the regime known as the "people's democracy." This was characterized by the ruthless wiping out of all non-Communist elements in the government and throughout the country, and was said to mark a transitional stage from capitalism to socialism. Eastern European countries have varied forms of constitutions today, but each has effective party control of whatever instruments of government are used.

What practical coordination of policy now exists between the Soviet Union and its neighbors is facilitated by a network of official and unofficial agencies. Local Communist leaders make frequent trips to Moscow; Soviet diplomatic representatives, especially in Bulgaria and East Germany, have an unconcealed special relationship to the regimes to which they are accredited.

Political and Economic Domination Under Stalin

Formerly, under Stalin, the representatives of the Soviet secret police and the Soviet Communist party, unknown to the public and apparently sometimes even to each other, sent a constant stream of information to the Soviet Committee of State Security and Politburo. An interlocking series of alliances pledging mutual assistance provided the military counterpart of the close political arrangements.

No less complete than this political surveillance of the Soviet Union over Eastern Europe in Stalin's day was its economic dominance. Beginning first by demanding heavy indemnities in payment of wartime losses and by taking over former German assets in countries such as Hungary and Rumania, the Soviet Union increasingly geared the economies of its neighboring states to its own. Unlike Nazi Germany, however, which had dominated the economies of these countries before World War II and used them as an outlet for its industrial goods, the Soviet Union encouraged or even forced the industrial development of its neighbors, mainly so that it could draw upon their industrial production. As a consequence, Eastern Europe underwent much the same kind of expansion of heavy industry at the cost of living standards that the Soviet Union had endured, but with particular stress on those products useful to the Soviet Union's own development.

Eastern Europe After Stalin

Startling as was the impact within the Soviet Union itself of the denunciations of Stalin at the Twentieth Party Congress, the effect threatened to be still greater in Eastern Europe. While the Russians had been under Communist control for nearly forty years and could remember nothing else, the Eastern Europeans had experienced it for little more than ten years. It is true that a political and economic revolution had been wrought within them in that time and that control was apparently firmly centralized in the hands of their ruling party bosses; but the revelations about Stalin in February 1956 and the fierce attack on one-man rule were sufficient to topple the Bulgarian dictator, Chervenkov, in April 1956 and soon afterward the still more redoubtable Rakosi of Hungary. In addition, they touched off a series of self-criticisms by local Communist parties and rehabilitated some famous "Titoists"—that is, Communists who sought to follow a national line of development instead of a Soviet-dominated one.

Thereafter East European states began to experiment with different roads to national development. The sharp reactions to the Polish and Hungarian revolutions of 1956 (of which the latter caused a major refugee movement to the West) made it clear that the Soviet Union forcefully opposed multiple parties, defection from the bloc, or even neutralism. Nonetheless, Eastern European countries have developed a wide diversity of forms of socialism, strongly influenced by the stages of economic development through which they are passing.

Bulgaria and Czechoslovakia stand at two extremes of economic development, the former at the early stage of industrialization where simple, authoritarian methods are adequate, and the latter with a complex industrial economy needing the same flexibility as the Soviet Union itself. Poland, which seems closer to Yugoslavia outside the bloc than to the centralist states inside the bloc, has granted a long lease to individual property in agriculture and permits open expressions of criticism both inside and outside of parliament. The regimes throughout Eastern Europe are now accepted for the degree to which they are, or appear to be, national, rather than for their orthodoxy to Marxism-Leninism or their loyalty to the Soviet Union.

Various factors have helped to bring about these changes. Important was the length of time it took to complete Khrushchev's succession to ultimate power, and the more open-ended policies thereafter. Still more influential is the split in the Communist camp between the Soviet Union and Communist China. The latter's outspoken ideological line has been the more striking because the Soviet Union itself has been modifying and in some cases basically altering concepts and policies established under Stalin. Lacking the willingness and the ability to maintain its former dominance in Eastern Europe, the Soviet Union has adjusted to changing conditions. Thus its relations to Eastern European countries have changed almost as radically as have those of Great Britain and France in regard to their empires.

2. RELATIONS WITH OTHER COMMUNIST COUNTRIES

A major problem confronting the Soviet Union in the postwar period has been to determine its relations with other Communist countries, notably Yugoslavia and China, which established their regimes through their own efforts. The basic question throughout has been: Can the common acceptance of Communist ideology provide a basis for working together despite divergent tactics and even goals?

Yugoslavia was the first to emerge of the independent postwar Communist states. When major efforts failed to force it to accept the Soviet Union's leadership, Yugoslavia was expelled from the Cominform in June 1948, ostensibly for deviations in policy but actually for its independent policies. The effect of the Cominform declaration, however, was to strengthen rather than weaken Marshal Tito's position in Yugoslavia. Though originally reluctant to embark upon controversy, Tito gradually took up a position of opposition to the Stalinist leadership, challenging its overcentralization of power and maintaining that Yugoslavia, not the Soviet Union, possessed the true Marxist orthodoxy. In this conflict, in which armed intervention by the Soviet Union was always a possibility, the United States and Great Britain lent moral, economic, and even military support to Yugoslavia.

In May 1955 Khrushchev and Bulganin visited Belgrade and signed jointly with Tito a communiqué that recognized that different countries could reach socialism in different ways. Since that time, Soviet-Yugoslav relations have alternated between cordiality and tension. While attempting to limit Yugoslavia's influence on Eastern European countries, like Rumania, with its own independent policies, Soviet leaders know that Yugoslavia continues to be closer to the "socialist camp" than to the West.

The Rise of China

With China, the relationship has been far more difficult, though until 1961 there were less obvious signs of strain. China's great population and its geographical separation from the Soviet Union give it a strength and independence that Yugoslavia could never achieve. But originally China was more closely tied to the Soviet Union than Yugoslavia has been. Where the latter has had American and British material aid and moral support in its efforts to maintain its separate line, China has isolated itself from the West. The United States, from its side, has tried to exclude Communist China from the international community and has not extended recognition to its regime. Thus, in its efforts to press ahead its industrialization, China has had to rely heavily on Soviet material aid.

In the first years of Communist China, when Stalin was still in control in the Soviet Union, his ideological leadership was openly acknowledged by the Chinese Communist leaders. Khrushchev hinted in March 1956 that Stalin had dangerously strained Sino-Soviet relations by trying to control both the Chinese Communist

SOVIET EXPANSION
IN THE EAST
SINCE 1939

USSR IN 1939
AREAS ANNEXED BY USSR
SINCE 1939
COMMUNIST, IN ALLIANCE
WITH USSR
COMMUNIST, NOT ALLIED
TO USSR

ARCTIC SEA

BERING STRAIT

SIBERIA

SOVIET UNION

SAKHALIN

KURILE IS.

TANNU TUVA

Irkutsk

Harbin

Vladivostok

JAPAN

MONGOLIAN

Ulan Bator

PEOPLE'S REPUBLIC

Mukden

NORTH
KOREA

PACIFIC OCEAN

Tokyo

Peking

Port Arthur

Seoul

SOUTH
KOREA

PAKISTAN

CHINA

Nanking

Shanghai

TIBET

OKINAWA

NEPAL

BHUTAN

Chungking

SIKKIM

TAIWAN

INDIA

PAKI-
STAN

Canton

BURMA

Hong Kong

PHILIPPINES

LAOS

THAILAND

N. VIETNAM

0   200   400   600

MILES

CAM-
BODIA

S. VIETNAM

Party and the Chinese economy. If so, such efforts ceased with Stalin's death. In 1956, in fact, Chinese leaders somewhat reversed the process by actively intervening in the Soviet bloc when revisionism threatened to sunder its cohesion. Spurred by the revisionist reaction of their own intellectuals, Chinese leaders adopted a rigid ideological orthodoxy that stressed central controls, speedy and drastic social change, and active policies to further world revolution.

This forceful and distinctive Chinese line has confronted the Soviet regime with a challenge to its leadership of the Communist world. It provided alternative lines of policy to follow at a time when Eastern European states were seeking their own resolution of the struggle between centralism and revisionism. It has placed pressure on the Soviet Union itself to adopt more extreme positions than its leaders have been anxious to pursue. Thus, until its own internal struggle over ideology and leaders at the start of 1967, China had achieved an ideological initiative that threatened Soviet leadership in this sphere. Even thereafter it seemed unlikely that the Soviet Union could ever recapture its former dominance.

Relations with Local Communist Parties

The Soviet Union long had the particular advantage in its dealings with the Western democracies that in almost every one of the latter there is a local Communist party which, in practice, acted as the defender and supporter of the Soviet Union's foreign policy. This meant that propaganda in favor of Soviet aims and methods did not emanate from the Soviet Union alone [1] but was carried on within foreign countries by naitve citizens who had become vigorous and devoted adherents of the Soviet cause.

The Comintern

Throughout the interwar period, the outstanding evidence of joint action against the capitalist states was the Comintern, or Third

[1] As early as 1921 Great Britain concluded an agreement with the Soviet Union whereby the latter agreed not to promote propaganda within the British empire. American recognition of the Soviet Union in 1933 was made conditional upon a similar pledge, but no effective way has been found to enforce such an agreement.

International, an international revolutionary body organized by Lenin and his followers late in 1918 to unite the forces of communism in all countries and to aid the progress of world revolution. (The two earlier international workingmen's associations were quite different, the Second International being an organization of evolutionary socialist groups that broke down in 1914 but was reestablished after World War I.) The headquarters of the Comintern was in Moscow, and particularly after 1929 when Stalin had consolidated his position within the Soviet Union, both the international organization and the national Communist parties followed whatever line of policy the Kremlin decided. Thus foreign countries looked on the Comintern as the foremost instrument of the Soviet Union in promoting universal revolution and, as such, a menace to their domestic institutions. Much of the fear and suspicion in the interwar period arose from the belief that the Soviet Union was using the Comintern (and thus national Communist parties) to foment trouble in other countries and to overthrow their governments.

The formal dissolution of the Comintern in May 1943 made it easier to build the successful wartime coalition among the United States, Great Britain, and the Soviet Union. Stalin declared that the dissolution "exposes the calumny . . . to the effect that Communist parties in various countries are allegedly acting not in the interest of their people but on orders from outside." However, national Communist parties continued in existence, and there was little evidence that the disappearance of the Comintern brought any change in their dependence on the Soviet Union. On the rare occasions when an outside Communist party took a different line from that of the Soviet Union on a question of great national interest, there was considerable evidence to indicate that the "disagreement" was adopted for tactical purposes with the prior consent of Moscow.

The Cominform

To spur and coordinate the activities of Communist parties, a new organization, the Cominform, was organized in October 1947. Composed originally of the Communist parties of only nine states (the Soviet Union, Poland, Czechoslovakia, Bulgaria, Hungary, Rumania,

Yugoslavia, France, and Italy—of which only the latter two did not have Communist governments), the Cominform quickly developed an extensive system of centers throughout the non-Communist world from which it spread propaganda and tactical directions. Though its official headquarters was outside the Soviet Union (being established first in Belgrade, Yugoslavia, and subsequently in Bucharest, Rumania), the Cominform was obviously an agency for Soviet direction of outside Communist activities. While officially its tasks were "to organize and exchange experience and, in case of necessity, coordinate the activity of Communist parties on foundations of mutual agreement," the Cominform's continued though ineffective efforts to force Tito's Yugoslavia to follow Soviet leadership demonstrated that it was looked on as a high organ of orthodoxy. After Stalin's death, however, less and less was heard of the Cominform. The formal demise in April 1956 of both the Cominform and its newspaper, *For a Lasting Peace, For a People's Democracy,* was not unexpected.

International Communism Today

After Stalin, most local Communist parties within the Western countries found it essential to free themselves from suspicion of Soviet domination lest they lose their "national" appeal. Soviet or Chinese influences have had greater impact within some of the developing states of Asia, Africa, and Latin America. Though nationalist forces within these countries are often suspicious of the intentions of local Communists, the latter are quick to seize opportunities offered by the presence of obviously corrupt, authoritarian, and unpopular regimes, such as Batista's in Cuba, or by internal division and lack of national spirit, as in much of Southeast Asia.

As long as the Soviet Union was the undisputed leader of world communism, Communist parties in developing states such as India and Ceylon tended to contain their own internal divisions. With the emergence of China as an ideological rallying point, however, the splits already existing in local Communist parties have widened and have become more obvious. In India, for example, where the Communist party

is the second largest in the country (though far smaller than the ruling Congress party), the Communists have a "left" pro-Chinese group, a pro-Soviet group, and a third group that attempts to remain neutral between them. Even in Cuba, there appears to be a potential left-right split over the speed with which the revolution should be carried through, a point on which there remains a major division of opinion between Soviet and Chinese leaders. In both kinds of situation the Soviet Union and China compete with each other for the support of local Communists.

It is possible that the overriding ideological agreement of the Soviet Union and China, particularly *vis-à-vis* the West (an agreement in which Yugoslavia also joins), may ultimately bridge the gap between these two giants both within the Communist camp and internationally. It is also possible, however, that their violent criticism of each other may lead to an open break. Neither prospect should offer the West any justification for relaxing its efforts to keep its own democratic ways of life strong and to aid the developing states.

3. INTERNATIONAL RELATIONS

Since World War II, an almost continuous series of international meetings between the Soviet Union and the Western powers has sought to devise joint decisions on a vast variety of international issues. Some of these have taken place through the United Nations, some through more temporary bodies established to draw up the peace treaties or for other specific purposes.

The most wearing feature of postwar diplomacy has been the difficulty of persuading the Russians to agree to anything. The European Advisory Committee, set up during the war to coordinate the postwar policies of the Big Three, met over five hundred times without reaching any important decisions. The Council of Foreign Ministers, set up at Potsdam in 1945 to prepare for the peace settlements, met a hundred and twenty-two times over a period of fifteen months before securing agreement on the peace treaties with Italy, Bulgaria, Rumania, and Hungary. Even then it could not settle such controversial

issues as the future of the Italian colonies—
which was ultimately dealt with by the United
Nations General Assembly. The Security Council of the United Nations has been blocked over
and over again by the Soviet Union's use of the
veto. Even now, disarmament discussions drag
on endlessly without noticeable results.

Soviet Diplomacy

Experience has shown that the Russian technique of diplomacy and understanding of compromise differ from those of the Western powers. Negotiations are tightly controlled by the
Party Politburo. The main objective is to secure
full acceptance of every Soviet proposal and to
say "no" to all other suggestions, at least at first.
When the Soviets accept a compromise, it is
not looked on as a solution but merely as a step
toward securing their original goal. Various
other means are then tried to secure the first
objective.

International diplomacy, like international
policies, is a reflection of domestic methods and
aims. Within their totalitarian structure the Russians have no parallel to the constant process of
negotiation and compromise that forms the pattern of life in a democratic country. Soviet trade
union leaders bring information to the directors
of industry, but they do not "negotiate" with
them as American trade unions negotiate with
their employers. The Five-Year Plans are drawn
up by experts on the basis of objectives laid
down by the Soviet leaders, not hammered out
through the give and take of voluntary associations and party and pressure groups. It is not
surprising therefore that in international negotiations the Russians adopt the same approach:
working by every means to achieve their particular objective, instead of adopting the typically Western approach of seeking an agreement
either by modifying details or devising a compromise.

It is true that since Stalin's death Soviet diplomats have been more flexible in negotiations
on international issues. Yet what settlements
have been secured have been, in fact, on Soviet
terms. At Panmunjom, for example, the Communists did not yield an inch of the Korean
territory they held. The only concessions they
can be said to have made were withdrawing

their troops from Austria, abandoning the Soviet base at Porkkala, and reducing their armed
forces, none of which weakened their overall
strategic position. Soviet diplomacy has often
been flexible and skillful, however, in seeking
its objectives in Europe. Fearing the revival of
a militarily dominant Germany, Soviet leaders
first proposed an enforced neutrality of a reunified Germany. Failing to secure this objective, the Soviet Union put major resources into
building up East Germany, both economically
and militarily, and maintains a closer hold on
its regime than any other in Eastern Europe
except Bulgaria. Soviet leaders have also encouraged France's withdrawal from NATO
and have thus weakened the key alliance aimed
at containing Soviet expansionism.

Soviet Overtures to Uncommitted States

A strong feature of Soviet foreign policy is
the drive to win the friendship of the uncommitted states of Asia, the Middle East, and Africa, either by selling arms or by offering long-
term economic development programs. In the
latter field, the Soviet Union is openly competing with Western countries that aid developing
states through their own agencies, like the
United States AID program, or cooperative arrangements, like the Colombo plan, or the
United Nations technical assistance program.

While the overall scale of aid offered by the
Soviet Union does not match that of the United
States or France, its agreements and offers have
nevertheless attracted much attention among
developing countries. Soviet aid is offered ostensibly without political strings; commonly it is
for spectacular projects or through long-term
loans at low interest that can be repaid through
export surpluses from the recipient countries.
The result is publicity and a sense of independence in the recipient countries.

Though the Soviet Union still needs most of
its production for its own or its allies' needs, it
spares an increasing quantity of capital goods
for economic aid to the uncommitted countries.
Moreover, the Soviet government has several
advantages in comparison with Western countries. It can fix the terms and interest rates of
its loans without reference to economic returns;
determine their timing by political advantage,

without reference to popular support; absorb almost any kind of imports in return for the aid it provides; and offer stable prices for years in advance, whereas Western prices for raw materials fluctuate. Naturally enough, the Soviet Union does not encourage the free enterprise institutions that Western countries favor, but they are not always suitable for developing countries. Thus, though its economic aid program may seem modest, it is an important factor to reckon with in the competition to win influence in the uncommitted third of the world.

Conclusion

Any realistic appraisal of Soviet foreign policy must take two factors into consideration.

First, Soviet leaders enjoy a freedom and flexibility in the conduct of policy unparalleled in Western countries. To convince the American public of the importance of recognizing Communist China or admitting it to the United Nations is a major operation. But the Soviet Union can alternate its approval or disapproval of a regime such as Nasser's, or Tito's, without public opposition. What matters in the Soviet Union are the objectives and tactics that dominate the thinking of its leaders.

Second, the Soviet leaders are convinced that communism will ultimately triumph throughout the world and that capitalism will be overcome and disappear. They accept the fact that this victory may be long delayed, but they believe the transition is already under way.

The controversy within the Communist camp is not over this fact but over the leadership and the tactics that will best facilitate the transition to ultimate and full Communist control everywhere. Soviet leaders are unlikely to precipitate a contest of strength until they are certain that they can win it. So long as the Western powers are strong, not only militarily but morally, there will be every reason for delay. Since the Soviet leaders are convinced that the capitalist world will ultimately decay and disintegrate, they can well afford to wait.

The challenge the Soviet Union raises for Western countries is twofold. First, capitalism is challenged to prove that it can provide and maintain prosperity. On the face of things, the West is much stronger materially than the Soviet Union and its allies. The United States, Great Britain, France, and Germany have far higher standards of living than the Soviet Union. Every measure bolstering economic stability in the world today is a practical denial of the Soviet assumption of the impending collapse of capitalism. If, however, economic crisis and depression (which Marxists believe are inevitable under capitalism) cause mass unemployment and social discontent—that is, if capitalist strength decays from within—the time may appear more propitious for Soviet action. In this sense, then, economic prosperity is the West's surest guarantee of peace.

The second, and even more basic, challenge is to the democratic faith of the Western peoples. Can democratic states provide the internal cohesion and degree of external cooperation that will enable them to match the unity of purpose that the Soviet government can enforce upon its people and its satellites? Moreover, can the democratic countries maintain their unity, even if the menace of Soviet aggression appears to fade?

Beyond this, will democratic states accept sacrifices for the sake of external purposes such as the economic development of other countries? Will they aid the developing countries in ways that yield no immediate return in commitments or privileged positions?

These questions must be faced if American foreign policy is to be constructive and effective. No one should suppose that the Soviet Union has any intention of effectively reducing its armed strength in relation to that of the Western countries, or of giving up its ultimate objective of the world-wide victory of communism. Thus it would be irresponsible to reduce the military power of the free world except in response to carefully calculated mutual concessions. But still more important than actual striking power is the solidarity of the free world; and for this the United States, as its strongest member, has a particular responsibility. The success of the British Commonwealth's technique of prior consultation suggests that the more powerful a state is, the more it needs to have regard for the sensitivities of its allies.

Though the West should guard against overoptimism regarding Soviet tactics or intention, it should also respond to whatever openings the

Soviet Union may provide. Trade, exchange of nonmilitary information, and freer travel to and from the Soviet Union should be encouraged to its utmost, for constant and open contacts are the lifeblood of democracy. Moreover, whatever the provocation, the free world in general and the United States in particular must use democratic methods in international affairs, even when they are dealing with authoritarian or totalitarian states.

In considering policies toward the uncommitted countries of Asia, the Middle East, and Africa, it is well to remember that they are inevitably far more interested in their own development than in great-power politics. Thus they think of economic aid in terms of its current usefulness, not in terms of its international implications. They are exceedingly sensitive, however, to any apparent interference with their national independence. Moreover, they are not unaware that it is often easier to secure economic or military aid from the United States when there is a Communist threat to their security or an alternative offer of Soviet help. Such maneuvers undercut the impact of American aid. Thus, there is all the more reason to provide aid to developing countries because of a genuine interest in their well-being and not as a move in an international chess game.

It is the pride of democracy that when its people recognize the need for forward-looking action, they contribute initiative, self-reliance, and freely willed sacrifices to its achievement. In the trial of moral strength to which the Soviet Union challenges the Western world, the decisive factors may well be the foresight and steadiness of Western peoples and the vitality of their democratic beliefs and practice, not only at home but also in their relations with other countries.

Conclusion

A final judgment of the Soviet government depends on the view of what objectives are most important and also of the order in which these objectives can be achieved. If the most important consideration is the freedom of the individual to develop his talents and potentialities and if the good life is inconceivable without freedom to question, to challenge, to choose for oneself, and even to make mistakes, then one condemns the uniformity of thought imposed by the Soviet government, the control of speech and of the press, the political absolutism, and the always possible, if now restrained, use of terror, forced labor, and the political police. If the most important objectives are a great increase in industrial productivity and security against unemployment, then there is more sympathy with the Soviet system. Particularly in developing areas, there is no easy way of achieving both objectives at the same time.

It would be infinitely simpler for the foreign observer if political absolutism went hand in hand with technical backwardness; it is now all too apparent, however, that economic and technical progress may be achieved by the use of coercion. Thus the dilemma can be stated in terms of means and ends: the Soviet supporter maintains that rapid industrialization justifies the (perhaps temporary) use of force and suppression of political and intellectual liberty, and the Western critic insists that nothing can justify the use of means that are inherently evil.

Actually, the disagreement is more profound. The problem may be called not one of means and ends, but of means and consequences. The prolonged existence of all-pervasive controls and the lack of any guaranteed privacy inevitably produces a particular kind of society. The consequence, then, may be a different type of human being, one who is better fed or clothed but whose intellectual and spiritual growth may be stunted or distorted.

The obvious changes that have occurred in the Soviet Union since Stalin's death have led some observers to suggest that the USSR is moving toward a situation more comparable to that of Western countries, not only in terms of improved standards of living but also in terms of greater respect for individuals and organized groups, and even of greater influence by the people over the regime. What has been most encouraging has been the shift from indiscriminate terror and compulsory labor to milder incentives and persuasion as a means of achieving public response to the purposes of the government. It is clear that the instruments of coercion still exist and that there is no agency, not even the judiciary, that can prevent their use. Nonetheless the major techniques by which Stalin enforced his will have been noticeably absent since his death.

In the second place, there has been a marked increase in popular participation in the work of government. While the Supreme Soviet retains its monotonous unanimity, its commissions and the lesser soviets engage in discussion and may even influence decision. Although the encouragement of "popular justice" is disturbing, the greater activity of local soviets and their sections suggests a direct contact with the everyday business of government that can hardly help but stimulate thought about its processes and effects.

But does this mean a trend toward popular control or toward more effective dictatorship? The organs of the party now meet with more regularity, and their proceedings are more publicized (even occasionally those of the Central

Committee). Moreover, the party's membership has been made more representative of the population as a whole by increasing the percentage of workers and peasants as well as by adding members of the smaller nationalities. But there is no evidence that this greater representativeness has brought with it any greater degree of effective participation in the making of decisions. Officials and secretaries still control the agencies of the party and are themselves appointed from above. It is likely that the leaders share responsibilities among themselves and that they take more account of public feeling than was true under Stalin. They do so, however, within the context of totalitarian autocracy.

There may even be increasing interference in the life of the individual. Legally no sphere is protected from such encroachments, but in practice not everything can be controlled all the time. The very emphasis on voluntarism, people's militias, and antiparasitical measures suggests that over and beyond what the party and the state can do to influence aspects of life, the Soviet people are being encouraged to involve themselves in their neighbors' lives—to the purpose of making them "think socially."

The key to the character of the Soviet Union is the nature and aims of the men who run it. There is a kind of natural selection that brings to the highest positions in the Soviet government not those who are skilled in democratic leadership but those who are adept in running the dictatorial institutions that at present exist. There is considerable naïveté, then, in expecting such men, at the appropriate hour, to introduce a regime of political liberty and democratic action in which they have had no experience, for which they lack the necessary skills, and which they do not desire. That the people of the Soviet Union could respond to the opportunities of

democracy is much more likely. The framework of representative institutions exists, and the experience of the Hungarian revolt suggests that there is more yearning for self-expression behind totalitarian façades than we used to think. But to make democratic processes meaningful in the Soviet Union would require an acceptance of the fact that to criticize and even oppose the policies of the party's leaders is acceptable. Proposals for change are being made and even accepted in the interests of a more dynamic economic system but not of a more open-ended political system. Indeed, for the present rulers of the Soviet Union to yield their power and to submit themselves to the judgment and directives of their people would constitute a sacrifice of authority for which history provides almost no precedent and for which the training and heritage of the leaders provide no basis.

But can the Western countries themselves make possible the desired synthesis of individual liberty, social and racial equality, and economic productivity not only for themselves but also for the developing uncommitted third of the world? There are many millions of people— perhaps the majority of mankind—to whom meaningful participation in political institutions may be of little importance in comparison with the rapid achievement of industrial power. If they are convinced that it is necessary to choose between these objectives, Asians and even Africans may choose the authoritarian path. In this sense, the attempt of the Western democracies to achieve the good material life for themselves through free consent and without the sacrifice of civil liberties and also to aid the developing countries to achieve the same synthesis may well be of decisive importance in determining which direction the latter will follow.

Conclusion

1. PATTERNS OF GOVERNMENT IN THE MODERN WORLD

Our examination of four major powers and the comparisons we have made between them and the United States make evident several patterns of political organization and governmental systems. Democracy and totalitarianism seem to form polar points on the spectrum of political alternatives. But in order to distinguish more clearly between actual and potential forms of polities, we might cast our analysis in terms of a twofold dichotomy, depending upon which one of two fundamental questions is posed.

Four Basic Patterns

The first of these questions concerns the subject, or bearer, of political power: Who governs? To this the answer may be: the many, or the few. If the totality of the adult members of a particular political community—that is, the people—hold ultimate political power, we call this form of government *democracy*. The rule of a minority—whether an aristocratic elite, or another oligarchy, or, in the extreme event, a one-man absolutist monarchy or a one-man dictatorship—we call *authoritarianism*.

The second, quite different, basic question concerns the sphere controlled by political authority (whether the latter be organized democratically or in an authoritarian fashion): How wide is this sphere? How much in the life of society and its members falls under government direction? If political authority extends in principle over everything in the life of the people, the regime is *totalitarian*. If government is limited, leaving certain, often large, spheres of individual and group life protected by convention or law against government intervention, we call the regime *liberal*.

Definitions such as these, of course, are subject to historical change and qualification. The definition of *democracy,* for instance, depends greatly on what, at a particular point of historical development, is defined as *the people*. Athenian democracy would today be considered oligarchy, since its citizens lorded it over a majority of slaves, noncitizens, and women who at that time were not included in *the people*. By the same token, the rule of the white minority in South Africa cannot be characterized as democratic. In reference to the other dichotomy, a laissez faire liberal of the mid-nineteenth century type might have termed *totalitarian* the degree of government regulation and government intervention, especially in the fields of economy and industrial relations, which obtains today in

615

"liberal"-democratic countries such as the United States. Today those countries, with their broad realms of protected individual and group liberties and freedoms, appear genuinely liberal in contrast to totalitarian dictatorships.

The natural correlates among these four concepts are liberal democracy and totalitarian authoritarianism, or totalitarian dictatorship. Indeed, when talking of *democracy* and *totalitarianism,* we used these two terms as shorthand versions of the above. However, it is also possible to correlate the concepts crosswise—that is, democracy with totalitarianism, and authoritarianism with liberalism. There have been examples of these latter types in history, some of which we have encountered in our study of foreign powers. In the initial stages of a popular revolution (as in the French Revolution), democracy may tend to disregard limitations on popular control and thus become totalitarian. And obversely, a ruling minority may accept limitations on its authoritarian rule, as witness the early nineteeth-century monarchical-aristocratic "constitutionalism" of Continental European countries, out of which grew the German *Rechtsstaat,* or England before it became fully democratic. De Gaulle's France has some aspects of this combination.

Much more common, however, both historically and organizationally, are the other pairings. In fact, experience suggests that totalitarian democracy, as in the French Revolution, turns into small-group or one-man rule, while liberal authoritarianism tends to give way to full-fledged liberal democracy. The combination of liberalism and democracy characterized political developments in the Western countries in the era of the rising middle classes and the first industrial revolution. In the twentieth century, however, the impact of unsolved social and international questions created a reaction that turned many societies into totalitarian ones, a development that reached its acme in the fascism of the German-Nazi variety and the Stalinist and Maoist versions of Communism. In some of the new states, the trend has recently been away from democracy (to the degree this existed) toward the authoritarianism of military regimes.

Thus between the polar types there are many gradations of in-between systems approximat-

ing more or less liberal democracy or totalitarian dictatorship. Regimes characterized by oligarchic or dictatorial controls may lack some or most of the characteristics of totalitarianism. In fact, the standard, traditional forms of "rule from above," as they are inherited from the predemocratic, more or less authoritarian past, still prevail in many countries of the not-yet-modernized variety, as, for example, in traditional Latin-American junta rule. Even fascist dictatorships showed significant variation, ranging from the extreme of Nazi totalitarianism over less complete Italian fascist control to such protofascist regimes as those in Spain and Portugal, which in fact are quite similar to traditional predemocratic authoritarian regimes based on social and economic conservatism. One overall problem facing such regimes is whether their political conservatism can withstand the winds of change which modernization—the aim of all or most countries—carries with it. A predemocratic climate of attitudes, especially in the relationship of governors to governed, is ill suited to the antipaternalistic tendencies of modern man in the modernized, technically oriented machine world.

Communist regimes, on the other hand, make social change a major objective. Thus they are more in line with the trend toward modernization. But even they (as China, the Soviet Union, and such former satellites as Poland clearly indicate) differ markedly in revolutionary fervor, in type of leadership, in organization of social and economic structures, and, as has become increasingly clear in recent years, in the range of their controls. Indeed, the latter variation may be the most significant one. In some cases there appears to be a transformation from totalitarianism to a more or less liberal authoritarianism. In Poland and some other Eastern European countries, the "thaw" in the realm of culture has allowed a degree of experimentation in literature, in style of arts, and in related fields that equals cultural freedom in the West. If such trends should in due course be accompanied by more liberalism in the area of the political rights of individuals and group freedoms, the development might even presage a moderation of dictatorship and authoritarian controls. In the light of the trend in liberal democracies toward the concentration of power in the executive and the increasing difficulty of maintaining popular control over such power, we might foresee an era in which democracy and totalitarianism might no longer form such polar contrasts.

For the time being, however, liberal democracy and totalitarian dictatorship are sufficiently meaningful opposites to provide the basic distinction for our final discussion of overall issues of present-day government and politics. The Soviet type of communism will serve as the prototype of totalitarian dictatorship (or whatever other designation this still half-totalitarian group oligarchy should be given). Liberal democracies vary greatly, but the Soviet pattern will be compared with the two major types: the parliamentary democracy of the European countries, and the presidential-congressional system of the United States.

Parliamentary and Presidential Systems

The prime characteristic of a parliamentary system, as we have seen, is the fusion of executive and legislature. The executive becomes the governing group not because of a direct vote by the electorate, as in the presidential system, but because it comprises the leaders of one or several parties represented in the legislature who command sufficient support within that body to pass the legislation they desire. Technically, this system revolves around the institution of expressing or denying confidence in the executive. Where parliament can force the government (in the sense of the executive) to resign by voting "nonconfidence" in it—or at least compel the executive to dissolve parliament in such a case and appeal to the electorate—the parliamentary system is operating in its classical form. Systems such as those of present-day France and West Germany, which render difficult such expressions of confidence or nonconfidence, are thus of questionable parliamentary nature.

The presidential pattern of government is the other great type of representative democracy. Its distinctive feature, in contrast to parliamentary government, is that the chief executive holds office whether or not he is supported by the majority in the legislature. In the United States, the voters may even elect a President from one party and give the majority in Congress to the other. Under these circumstances there is an extreme example of a constant give-and-take between executive and legislature. Even when the President's party dominates the legislature, the President has less assured control over the passage of laws than has even a weak British Prime Minister. Yet at the same time, there are great resources at the disposal of an American President. In guaranteed possession of office for four years, he is leader of his party, controls the administration, and can appeal directly to the people to support his program.

On the other hand, the presidential system is one of built-in restraints. The constitutional provisions for dividing and balancing authority—the bicameralism of two more or less equally powerful chambers, federalism, judicial review, staggered elections, the presidential veto, and the power inhering in the necessities for legislative consent—all combine to prevent or to impede major changes in policy until public pressures have built up on a broad scale. Where the parliamentary system responds quickly to popular majorities, the American presidential system reinforces the position of powerful minorities, which traditionally have been most strongly represented in the committees of the legislature.

Having briefly sketched the prime features of these systems, we must now consider those questions that we raised in the Introduction, and above all those that concern limited government, the factor that chiefly distinguishes liberal democracy from totalitarian dictatorship. Thus we will first consider the means, and their effectiveness, for keeping government limited. Second, we will examine how the channels of political action—elections, parties, and parliaments—operate under different systems. And, finally, we will discuss the functions that political and administrative leadership fulfill.

2. CONSTITUTIONALISM: FUNCTION AND PROBLEMS

The function of constitutions is to define, and thereby to limit, public power. A constitutional framework provides that governmental powers shall be exercised in accordance with known procedures. Moreover, it protects certain areas of personal and group life from governmental interference.

Only in nontotalitarian countries do constitutions provide such limitations. Formal appearances notwithstanding, totalitarian regimes do not have them. Whatever rules exist there—and they may even be called "constitutions"—either lack assured political impact and meaning (as in relation to parliamentary legislation or to individual liberties in the Soviet Union), or are forever provisional—and changeable at the whim of the party or leader. Therefore, as was also so under the Nazi regime, they lack the generality, reliability, and thus calculability that the rules of law can be expected to possess. Genuine constitutionalism is likewise absent where constitutions are forever made and remade, changed and abolished, so as to fit the political needs of the respective power-holders, as is all too often true in some Latin American countries.

Even regimes that we commonly call totalitarian, however, may show the beginnings of limitations that, in time, might develop into something like constitutionalism. It is problematic as to whether this is the case in regard to certain "rights" that have been more widely respected in the Soviet Union since the demise of Stalinism (for example, a much lower incidence of arbitrary arrest and detention). But in Poland a number of seats in parliament have been reserved, as if by customary law, to representatives of Catholicism, who are permitted genuine criticism, a practice that constitutes more restraint than does the presence of "stooge" parties in the East German People's Chamber.

What counts in nontotalitarian countries is not only the existence of written constitutions as such but the degree to which there is adherence to known and established practices. The British constitution, as we have seen, is largely composed of custom. And although formulation and formalization of rules have been the hallmark of modern government, it is clear that even in the United States there are certain rules of prime importance (such as those referring to presidential nominations or to the organization and procedures in Congress) that are either customary or without constitutional force, while the Constitution itself contains many provisions that do not serve any constitutional (that is, any limiting or delimiting) function.

Constitutions may originate in "pact" or "compact." Historically, they usually derived from pact, as in the Continental European constitutional monarchies of the nineteenth century, where the previously unlimited power of the crown was restrained by a compromise between crown and people, or crown and estates, and was formalized in a written constitution. Originally, the American Constitution was a pact between the founding states. But in the United States and Great Britain, limitations on political power that had their origin in pact subsequently turned into compacts, that is, commonly agreed-upon rules under which the people want to live. A constitution then serves less the function of delimiting the spheres of classes, groups, or territorial subdivisions than of reflecting a popular consensus on the basic governmental and political framework and of being the symbol of the nation's integration into one political unit. This has been so in the most soundly based democracies, such as the United States. In Germany and France, on the other hand, the basis for the original pact has disappeared, and later constitutions have failed to attain the symbolical and integrating character that the Constitution has in the United States. The underpinning of these limitations therefore remains fragile.

The wide variations in the origin, function, and strength of constitutionalism can be illustrated by some of its most common characteristics: its system of rights and liberties, constitutional jurisdiction, the independence of the judiciary, and territorial (geographical) division, that is, deconcentration of power.

Basic Rights and Liberties Today

The "classical" type of fundamental rights and liberties as embodied in the American Bill of Rights has been criticized in this century as being too individualistic and too little concerned with the needs of groups. Catalogues of social and similar rights—such as the right to education, to work, and to decent payment for work, etc.—have been inserted not only in spurious documents such as the Stalin Constitution but also in modern democratic constitutions, for example, the Weimar Constitution of Germany and the preamble to the Constitution of the Fourth French Republic.

But the classical rights and freedoms have gained new luster where people have had the bitter experience of losing them. Life under totalitarian lawlessness teaches people the importance of such blessings as legal security in its most elementary sense of freedom from arbitrary arrest and detention. It is significant that the post-Nazi Bonn Constitution, while dropping most of the Weimar catalogue of economic and social rights, gives the traditional bill of rights new emphasis.

There are also new advances in the sphere of the classical freedoms themselves. In an age of mass society, in which the standards of mass organization weigh increasingly on the individual person, we need to protect the right to creativity and also to nonconformity in areas that have not yet been invaded by the state or other big organizations. Technological progress, for example, in the area of electronic devices for invading the most intimate spheres of privacy, makes protection imperative. Thus in the United States there has of late been interesting debate concerning the rights of creative expression in the arts, literature, and the entertainment fields; of the right to be protected against the noise of one's environment; of the right of audiences to refuse to become captive victims of advertising; and of the right of the citizen, in a shrinking and integrated world, to move freely not only within his own country but in the world abroad, that is, freely to leave and reenter his country.

But the chief field of basic rights remains that of the classical bills of rights. Through these, from the time of "the mother of them all," the English Bill of Rights, there have been established not only the basic boundary lines of freedom but also a bridge between liberalism and democracy, since without guarantees of some fundamental political rights (for example, freedom of the press and of association), genuine democracy, in the sense of rule of the people, would be impossible.

In examining the present status of these rights and liberties in the major countries, let us start with the Soviet Union. Up to and through the Stalin era it would have been ludicrous to talk about protected rights in any meaningful sense in view of the pervasive terror machinery of the regime. The famous Bill of Rights of the Stalin Constitution was merely a fig leaf to cover up a dictatorship which, like most modern nondemocratic regimes, seemed unable to dispense with pseudodemocratic trappings. In the post-Stalin period, however, while there has not yet been evidence of meaningful freedom of opinion and genuine guarantees of political rights, it is difficult to imagine that a legally unchecked secret police or indefinite detentions in concentration camps could be reintroduced in a nation now accustomed to at least a minimal degree of security. In the area of social and economic rights, free education and free health services have prevailed so widely and over so long a period that they would seem for all intents and purposes irrevocable. These illustrations serve to show that even under dictatorship, lip-service and paper promises may turn into restraints on rulers who cannot afford to disregard the expectations of their people in a modernized or modernizing society.

The way in which rights and liberties are protected in the United States—their elaborate listing in federal and state constitutions, their protection not only against executive but also against legislative infringement, and their enforcement by effective independent courts—seems to lie at the opposite pole. But even here, reality does not always come up to potentialities. First of all, the enforcement machinery of the state—that is, the local and state police authorities—has often been woefully inadequate in the protection of individual and group rights and liberties. This has been true both in general and in regard to particular groups, such as Negroes or those groups battling on their behalf. Indeed, on occasion—especially in the South—the police have even turned against those needing protection, and the courts have been unavailable or ineffective in the face of such abuse of power. Moreover, under the impact of the cold war erosion of liberties has been permitted in two ways: by recognizing legal limitations on political liberties, in particular through a broad construction of the "clear and present danger" test; and, still more dangerous, through extralegal social pressures for conformity. The results of the latter influences show how dependent formal guarantees are on public support.

Yet, if such danger of curtailment has arisen in one democratic country, Great Britain offers encouraging evidence that continued respect for freedom is in itself the best guarantee of basic rights. The preservation of traditional liberties in that country provides a prime illustration of the force of tradition and the prevailing spirit of a nation as contrasted with the impact of formal rules and institutions. Even though no higher law of a written constitution protects the basic rights of an Englishman, they are safely guarded through the application of the rule of law; and while Parliament, by legislation, or the Cabinet, by delegated power, clearly has the power to tamper with these rights, the danger is remote that they would do so more than temporarily, and then only during genuine emergencies. So closely is Britain integrated as a nation of free men mutually tolerant and respectful of their differences that, in Churchill's words, they can "lump" the most unpleasant of such divergencies.

In contrast to the British, the French since the age of the Enlightenment and the Great Revolution have raised the battle cry of the "rights of man" rather than the rights of Frenchmen. But the trouble has been that it was the battle cry of only one group of Frenchmen in the perennial French conflict of opposing ideologies. Many a glorious legal and political battle has been fought over these rights and their protection, and some of them have been decisive for the liberal democratic development of the country—as witness the Dreyfus affair. But it can hardly be said that these rights are as safely anchored in France as they are in Britain. The French system is at its best in the protection of individual liberties it offers through its system of administrative jurisdiction, but these procedures protect personal rights, such as property rights, against an entrenched and solid bureaucracy, rather than political freedoms. It would be gratifying to infer from the broad freedoms enjoyed in France by political movements of even the most radical sort, including communism, a British-type agreement on "lumping it" in the interests of freedom and diversity. What seems more likely, however, is that freedom in France has been the result of dissent and the past weakness of the public power that has so often asserted itself with difficulty in the face of warring factions.

In Germany, as in France, liberalism has not been unsuccessful in the realm of personal security and property rights; these were clearly protected by that Central European marriage of freedom and authoritarianism known as the *Rechtsstaat*. But political rights prior to Weimar meant little. If the Weimar regime distinguished —and perhaps extinguished—itself through an overly broad grant of political freedoms, the Bonn Constitution also experiments in two novel and interesting ways. First, it declares that certain especially fundamental rights are unamendable (Article 19), a provision that raises the difficult problem of whether there can and should be limits to the power of constitutional amendment; and second, it sets out limits upon the exercise of political rights when used "in order to attack the liberal-democratic order" (Articles 18, 21). It was under these provisions that the neo-Nazis and later the Communist party were suppressed.

This problem of what democratic states should do about organized Communist activity in politics and in the trade unions is one of the most intricate with which they are confronted. The range of reactions has gone from complete outlawry to complete toleration. The dilemma is whether to grant freedom to those who would use it to destroy freedom for others, or whether to restrict freedom and thereby risk a too far-reaching curtailment of liberties in general. It has been obvious from innumerable instances of the second type that nothing is more easy and more tempting than to use provisions supposedly directed against a specific group or movement, such as communism, for attacking any unwanted, nonconformist, or merely opposition group, party, or opinion. South Africa's Suppression of Communism Act, under which anybody advocating economic or social change can be charged with the offense of "statutory communism," constitutes one of the most glaring cases of such abuse. Under the guise of defending a free system against communism, such a policy can threaten to transform this same free system into a noxious "rightist" totalitarianism. Moreover, there is little evidence that a ban on the Communist party does much more than drive its activities underground. In few areas is it more necessary to combine restraint on the part of government with constant alertness by the governed if individual rights are to be safeguarded.

Constitutional Jurisdiction

Constitutional jurisdiction means court action to secure the observance of the rules of a constitution. It may be concerned not only with the protection of individual and group rights but also with keeping state action within constitutional limits. Thus it may attain political importance far beyond that of other judicial action.

Constitutional jurisdiction has been particularly important in countries with a federal structure in which the powers of member units are delimited in relation to those of the federal (national) government. It took a civil war in the United States to establish the principle that a judicial organ of the federal government, rather than an individual state (or states) is the final arbiter. As resistance to the Supreme Court's decision on school desegregation points up, this principle has to be reestablished again and again. Ultimately, as history has shown, such delimitations of power that have significant social effects depend not only on judicial interpretation but also on persuading the most powerful forces in a community to accept the decisions that have been made.

Constitutional jurisdiction has assumed major importance in both West Germany and the United States. There are three chief areas in which courts may undertake to guarantee the functioning of a constitutional system. In the first place, the courts may act to keep in balance both the powers of, and the relations among, the organs of government, for example, the spheres of the legislature and executive, the rights of majorities and minorities in parliament, or the jurisdictions of the federal government and the member states. A second important sphere is the relation between ordinary legislation and the law of the constitution. The third relates to the individual or group rights and liberties that a constitution protects. Thus, constitutional jurisdiction may deal with any or all of the following: (a) "organ conflicts," that is, conflicts between the organs of the state or government; (b) judicial review of the constitutionality of laws; and/or (c) conflicts between the state and individuals or groups over whether there has been a violation of basic rights or liberties.

The new German system is perhaps most interesting in providing for legal settlement of organ conflicts (point a). The idea of offering political groups and governmental authorities a chance to fight out constitutional conflicts in court reflects a typically German legalistic approach to political problems. Even under the German Empire (when the Bundesrat had jurisdiction) and later under Weimar (when a constitutional tribunal was established) provision had been made for the resolution of certain types of organ conflicts. But only now has full "juridification" of the system been attained, with the Bonn Constitution allotting to the federal Constitutional Court the power to decide even those conflicts that arise among the highest federal organs and agencies. This, for a country with strong authoritarian traditions, is an important new venture.

The American judicial system is not concerned with this particular aspect of organ conflicts, but it hears suits regarding encroachment by the executive or the legislature in the sphere of the other and, of course, also those concerning the territorial-federal division of power. In addition, American courts are concerned with the protection of rights and liberties (point c). The distinctive function of the American judicial system, however, is judicial review (point b), that is, the maintenance of the superiority of the Constitution over all state action, including ordinary lawmaking. This reflects an ingrained American feeling that the Constitution is the higher law, to be preserved against the changing and possibly transitory will of the people.

What about constitutional jurisdiction in other countries and systems? Totalitarian regimes, of course, cannot permit procedures for the effective limitation of power; they avoid even the make-believe appearance of such jurisdictions, asserting that to give courts powers of judicial review, for instance, would hamstring the sovereign legislature. But the same argument is used by the French, who traditionally have believed that sovereignty rests inalienably in the people and those on whom they bestow it. To them the idea of a higher law of the constitution is foreign. Their unitary system leaves no room for federal-state conflicts, while once parliamentary and now executive supremacy have long ruled out the possibility of judicial review of national legislation as well as a judicial decision of organ conflicts. But it would be strange, indeed, to have no institutional protection of individual rights in the very country of *les droits de l'homme et du citoyen;* such protection does reside in the system of administrative jurisdiction.

The British system of parliamentary supremacy, like the French system, operates without judicial review or judicial settlement of organ conflicts. It is typically British in avoiding the institutionalization of protection. It relies instead on such general provisions and traditions as the rule of law, the independence of the judiciary, the recognition of implied restraints upon state power, and the application of the rule of reason to any and all of the system's manifestations. And since constitutionalism is hardly anywhere more safely anchored than in that country, Britain again illustrates the fact that national tradition can be a more important safeguard of rights than constitutional procedures and institutional devices.

Independence of the Judiciary

Constitutional jurisdiction is not the only device for safeguarding constitutionalism. There is also an essential relationship between constitutionalism and the judicial function in general. The decisive factor here is judicial independence. In contrast to police states, where the courts are looked on as instruments of the regime in carrying out its political and general purposes, courts in constitutional systems are separate, independent agencies bound by their own rules of procedure and determining cases according to publicly known law.

It is through judicial independence (usually guaranteed by the appointment for life and the irremovability of judges) that Montesquieu's device for the limitation of power has found its last redoubt even in countries such as Great Britain and France, where little else remains of the separation of power. Under modern conditions of the welfare state and of government regulations, the separation between the lawmaking and the executive branches may no longer be as feasible or even as desirable as it used to be; but the separation of an independent judiciary from both seems to be the irreducible minimum required for an effective system of limitation of power. The more modern government interferes, administers, and regulates, the more urgent is the need to preserve a check on the way these activities affect individuals and groups. The helplessness of the individual in the absence of such control is all too obvious in systems where the judiciary is either dependent or powerless, whether they be modern totalitarian systems with their knock on the door in the dead of night or premodern ones with their *lettres de cachet.*

Strong as the feeling may be for judicial independence, there can still be problems. Equal justice under law must, after all, be dispensed by men. And men, however strong their feeling of security and their insistence on independence, possess ideals and predilections, and even preconceived ideas and prejudices. An aging judiciary may be behind the times; a judiciary drawn from certain strata or classes may reflect class or caste bias. Moreover, the substantive law itself necessarily reflects class interest where there is class rule, economic interests where such interests prevail in a given society, religious interests where particular denominations or churches predominate. The remedy here, if one is desired, is not a change in the judicial system but a change in the laws through democratic processes. As for class, personal, or any other bias of the judicial personnel, the remedy is not in rendering the judiciary more dependent but in bringing about reforms that render such shortcomings less likely—for example, selecting the German and even the British judiciary from a less narrow base, and protecting the American judiciary, especially in the states, from undue party influence.

Further problems arise if courts are entrusted with overly political tasks. When, as in the United States, courts have to make decisions in such significant and controversial areas as free enterprise vs. governmental regulation, or racial segregation vs. integration, through the interpretation of broad terms such as "due process of law" or "equal protection of the laws," their decisions are bound to involve elements of policymaking. Many countries consider certain political issues (such as foreign policy decisions in American practice, or *actes de gouvernement* in France) to be nonjusticiable. Since decisions in such cases have to be made somewhere, however, it seems to be a matter of convenience whether ultimate control is given to a judicial body or to the more political part of the government.

The more encompassing the range of what is considered justiciable, however, the greater the danger that in a conflict involving basic issues of policy or fundamentally opposed forces in state and society, normative judgment will prove unenforceable. It is the crises of a regime or country that test the very bases of its institutions and put constitutionalism to its real test. Only a civil war, and not the Supreme Court, could solve the issues of slavery and of state sovereignty in the United States. And, as we have seen, the Constitutional Court of Weimar Germany was equally unable to enforce its verdict (compromise decision though it was) when antidemocratic forces undertook to destroy the last stronghold of Weimar democracy. Everything depends in such cases on whether judicial bodies are backed up by public determination sufficiently strong to uphold the rule of law in this broader sense.

Deconcentration of Power

A further way of limiting the authority of the central government is through deconcentration of power. Providing local or larger geographical subdivisions of a country with important jurisdictions gives citizens additional spheres of participation in government and also restrains government through diversification. As elsewhere, however, the trend toward big and comprehensive government has tended to limit, if not eliminate, genuine autonomy and self-government at these lower levels.

Traditionally, one of the counterweights against too much centralized government was found in local self-government. It is often said, and with some justice, that the grassroots, the essential training ground of democracy, is to be found at the local level. It is there that people deal with problems of immediate and direct importance to themselves—problems, moreover, that are intelligible to them in terms of their personal experience. Significantly, local government in Germany developed and was able to gain genuine importance at a time when German state institutions were still authoritarian; again, after the German collapse at the end of World War II, self-government first reasserted itself at the local level. Local self-governing institutions have shown stubborn vitality in times of stress. They can also provide a healthy counterbalance to overcentralization by restraining the "apoplexy at the center and the anaemia at the extremities," both of which are dangers in the highly organized, bureaucratic state of today.

Even in countries with long traditions of local self-government, however, there is a marked trend toward centralized supervision, financing, and even control. In Great Britain, for instance, activities such as education and public health that used to be locally oriented are now organized nationally. Yet there is still a major difference between the functions and functioning of local government in Britain and the United States and those in France, where the prefect is the political agent of the central administration. The most serious evidence of decline in the vitality of local government is the lack of interest in local issues. In France, Britain, and Germany, for instance, local elections are increasingly looked on as trials of strength for the national parties, which interject national issues into local contests. This may increase public interest, but it entails a danger that such contests are without firm roots in local needs.

There is a further problem that may yet pose the gravest threat to meaningful local government: the trend not only toward urbanization but toward the formation of huge metropolitan areas, encompassing tens of millions of people and covering territory that overlaps local government areas or even the boundaries of higher political units. The problem then is, how to make even local issues meaningful to individuals who are mere atoms in huge communities and how to coordinate the affairs of a megalopolis whose government and administration are cut up among so many units. Such urgent problems facing urbanized mankind as traffic and transportation, housing and education, public health and the pollution of the environment demand a new appoach to these new-style problems of local government.

Similar problems are found where federalism provides an intermediary level of government between local and central affairs. Of the major powers treated in this book, only two present even the appearance of federalism. Federalism in Germany is of long duration and is comparatively strong, because the nation arose from formerly independent units and some tradition of sectionalism (or particularism) has remained. In the Soviet Union, by contrast, as in any dictatorial regime, federalism is more apparent than real, since, as the Nazi experience also demonstrated, the concentration of power in one man or a small ruling group heading a nation-wide single party stands in sharp contradiction to the limitation on central power that federalism involves.

But even in such classical federal systems as the United States, Canada, Australia, Germany, and Switzerland, there is now a serious question of whether units below the national government that are not mere administrative subdivisions of that government can effectively carry out more than strictly local functions in a period when so many activities are necessarily nation-wide, if not even broader. Both national planning and national security belong naturally to the national government; these activities tend to become ever more encompassing. The fact that, ordinarily, only the national government commands the resources to finance large-scale tasks and programs has meant that there is a marked trend toward centralization even in the established federal systems of the world.

In the face of this development, students of federalism have given much thought to its inherent constitutional and political problems. Should the federal or state sphere possess what unspecified residual powers there are? Should the administration of national laws be entrusted to national executive agencies, as in the United States, or left in the main to state bureaucracies under federal supervision, as in Germany and Switzerland? And how should the body be organized that represents the member states on the federal level? Should it be composed of representatives of the people in the states, on the American senatorial pattern, or, as in Germany, of delegates representing state governments?

But experience shows that however these problems are met technically, what really counts are underlying social trends and the viability of the member units. Thus, in the United States, terms such as *interstate commerce* were used to enhance central power at the expense of member units despite the vesting of residual powers in the latter. Member-state viability is determined today by two main factors: the financial and the political. Financial viability depends on the distribution of the chief financial resources, especially taxes. Even systems such as the German, which reserved most of the sources of income to the states, have ended by giving the federal government the major share of power and resources. In the United States, where there is free competition among levels of government in tapping resources, the balance has likewise shifted overwhelmingly to the national level.

Even more relevant to the survival of federalism is whether strong sentiments of regionalism exist or whether sectional interests, backed by regionally concentrated nationality, linguistic, or religious groups, seek protection from centralization through reinforcing states' rights. In contrast to the new countries of the world, federalism in the older systems seems to survive chiefly through the latter factor, interest, rather than through true regionalist sentiment. Indeed, as distances shrink in the air age, as metropolitan areas cut through state lines and people move like latter-day nomads from place to place, such traditionalist, partly nonrational, regional sentiment tends to atrophy.

It is nevertheless true in the older federal countries that certain interests that by themselves have little to do with regionalism have tried to underpin federal divisions. Thus in Germany, national political parties find their control of state governments a vantage point from which to influence national policies. In the United States, mining, gas, oil, or similar interests, by their dominant position in particular states and a consequent influence on those states' senators in Washington, may become more strongly entrenched and thus more ardent supporters of federalism. The American party system as such, of course, is still built on local and regional organization. But none of this evidences strong regional feelings among the people at large— feelings that do not in fact exist except for white sectionalism in the South. And, as in other industrialized countries, the interests and organizations of the chief social and economic groups (in labor, trade, and industry) are nation-wide and thus counteract whatever regional interests and sentiments remain.

Thus the outlook for federalism in the older systems is none too good. But this does not necessarily provide a danger for liberalism. It is far from sure that smaller units of government are more sensitive to the rights and liberties of individuals and groups than are larger ones. Moreover, against the pressure of nongovernmental power, such as that of "big business" or any other big interest group, central government sometimes provides more effective protection. In any event, some kind of administrative decentralization will undoubtedly be retained in many spheres of activity in order to lessen the load on national administrations.

Federalism might well have gained fresh importance in the world today as new countries come into existence. Indeed, federalism may be the only way by which otherwise too small or economically weak units can group themselves into viable entities. Canada and Australia earlier took this middle way between the fragmentation of large areas of the world into splinter units and excessive centralization. Indian and Malayan experience suggests that when large units organized as one under colonial administration gain their independence from colonial rule, federalism may be the best way to prevent their disintegration into ever smaller linguistic or similar fragments. Yet despite its obvious advantages, federalism has seemed to most of the newer countries less attractive—and less manageable—than centrally directed state unity. Thus the most definite regionalist trends in Africa as in Western Europe are in the economic rather than the political sphere.

3. CHANNELS OF POLITICAL ACTION

In the Introduction we posed questions about whether and how, in our modern mechanized society, popular control can be maintained through channels of political action. We also pointed out how dependent popular action is on certain preinstitutional requirements, such as the ability to secure accurate information and the freedom to express opinion. Under constitutionalism, we have considered to what extent these and other freedoms are still meaningful today and how they are safeguarded in different countries and systems. We now turn to the institutionalized means of political action: to elections, parties, and parliaments.

Such devices and institutions are essential in modern times because populations are far too large and too dispersed for direct action, even though the device of a plebiscite is occasionally used, as in France and Switzerland. Modern government thus is representative government. But this very fact raises a vast number of other questions: How are representatives to be chosen so that they will be responsible to their constituents? How can they make their influence effective on the executive? In other words, how can the vast variety of often opposing groups in a modern community be linked effectively with the process of government in such a way that policy-making can be carried on speedily and decisively and yet with due regard to the consent of the governed?

In Totalitarian Regimes

To talk of elections, parties, and representative bodies as "channels" or means to enable the people at large to participate actively in government and politics seems utterly inappropriate in the case of totalitarian dictatorships. What, indeed, is the meaning of elections in which voters have a choice neither between candidates nor between programs? How can "party" be an instrument for exercising popular power or control if there exists only one party which in practice exercises power and control over the people? How can assemblies be "representative" where they are merely permitted to voice an occasional acclaim of members and policies of the ruling group?

It is true that to one raised in the Western tradition of self-government and limited powers such institutions must seem ineffectual and merely a façade. Their chief function appears to be to create the illusion of popular control and consent where it does not exist. But we should not overlook the fact that at least in the ideology of communism things appear somewhat different. For a regime whose leaders, for all we know, may be honestly convinced that socialism means the emancipation of man and mankind, such restrictions or denials of popular control assume the character of necessary but temporary transition measures. During a period in which partly because of the "ideological backwardness" of the masses, partly because of a hostile international environment, the vanguard must still lead, it cannot give free rein to deviating policies and opinions. But neither can it rule in a vacuum, since its doctrine is predicated on the assumption that what the vanguard does is merely the fulfillment of what history wills and that the masses, if enlightened, must of necessity will this same thing. Thus, its policy toward and in regard to the masses of the people is education and "enlightenment." Election campaigns, the discussion of issues within and by the party, and debates in assemblies all have this function. In addition, however, they serve that purpose of engineering of consent that also underlies the often frantic efforts of the regime to mobilize the masses in any and all other fields of life. As we have seen from our study of East German government, this may be a matter of establishing constantly changing "points of concentration" for economic or social efforts, or of organizing "operating brigades" of volunteers for various changing purposes. It may be a call to the people to engage in criticism (within carefully defined limits) or of trying, sometimes almost desperately, to engage in discussion of problems close to "the basis," that is, in the enterprises, at the lowest level of administration, in neighborhood units, and the like. The term *close to the basis* is itself significant. It reflects the yearning of a group that somehow feels that its basis for ruling is not democratically legitimate yet wants to be recognized in a more than make-believe way. Thus, what appears to the outside observer to be phony and deceptive remains for the true believer something real, necessary, and vital—a means of maintaining contact between the masses and their vanguard.

These facts apply above all to the totalitarian party. In the doctrinal sense, this party constitutes the primary embodiment of "historical reason" and therefore the "real" will of the (presumed) revolutionary majority of the people. Rather than comparing such a party to parties in nontotalitarian systems, it should be compared with the other chief organizations in totalitarian regimes. Significantly these are referred to as "mass organizations" and are supposedly the real representatives of the masses in the particular fields of industry (trade unions), agriculture, culture, or in men's, youth, or women's groups. Trade unions, under communism, are not considered as means of representing one group *against* another, as we have seen, but rather as organs for coordinating a common purpose. In a similar fashion, the party is not supposed to emphasize diversity and criticism but to be the body of the faithful dedicated to the maintenance of one truth and to seeing it prevail throughout government and society. Thus it must operate on the principle of "democratic centralism": Comments may be offered in the early stages of a proposal, but once a decision has been made everyone must accept it. Thus also it must sift its membership carefully to ensure conformity to the doctrine and policy lines set by the leadership acting as the vanguard. The purge of the unfaithful and of deviators inevitably constitutes a permanent feature of such regimes. In a way, the role of the totalitarian party may be likened to that of the clergy in Calvinist-Puritan doctrine: While it does not directly govern (except in cases of personal identity between party leaders and governmental office-holders), it is the source of those standards and precepts which, as they make a commonwealth a Christian one under Puritanism, similarly render it genuinely socialist under the controls of the Communist party.

Despite the fundamental difference between parties and other institutions under democracy and totalitarianism, liberal democrats may feel a slight measure of encouragement even from purposes for which these institutions are used under dictatorship. Ideas and institutions often have their own way of deceiving or betraying those who hold and use them. The use of elections and parliaments for "educational" purposes may turn out to be truly educational by telling people something about the ways of exercising genuine influence. Authoritarian rulers may eventually be compelled or see fit to permit some measure of such influence. Moreover, a constant urge to keep "close to the basis" may ultimately render leaders more amenable to the opinions, wishes, and needs of the masses than dictators ruling by terror and intimidation would be. Such "thawing" of regimes depends, of course, on so many other factors (such as foreign-political ones, for instance) that any expectations or predictions of liberalization are premature. But as the case of Yugoslavia and, to some extent, of some of the former satellites has shown, such a development is not impossible.

Elections and Parties in Liberal Democracies

In the light of the totalitarian use, or abuse, of institutions such as elections and parties, we see still more clearly their great significance as channels of political action in nontotalitarian systems. Yet we should not forget the antidemocratic criticism of the type we referred to in the Introduction that is leveled by spokesmen of authoritarianism and conservatism against liberal-democratic institutions. What about elections where the choice is only between two very similar programs? What about parties that are influenced or even controlled by special interests that finance their activities?

Electoral Problems

There are also more technical questions referring, for example, to the procedural details of voting systems, which have serious political implications. For instance: Should elections be held in single-member districts where the decision · is always clear, or in multimember constituencies, where the results, through proportional allocation of seats, more closely reflect the popular attitudes? Single-member districts have the advantage that there is a clear-cut contest and that usually one party emerges as the majority group capable of forming a stable government and carrying out a coherent program; they have the disadvantage of possibly disenfranchising the minority party or parties and of weighting power too much in favor of what may be only a relative majority representing less than 50 percent of the electorate. Proportional representation, on the other hand, while facilitating the effective voicing of a larger number of different opinions and lines of policy, may split the electorate, and therewith the legislature, into so many groups that stable and effective government becomes difficult.

There are other issues related to the aim of equal representation. Mathematical equality can hardly be expected to prevail even under proportional representation. But to draw election districts in such a way that they contain markedly unequal numbers of voters or so that their boundaries contribute to the advantage of specific groups (gerrymandering) may make a mockery of democracy in the sense of equality in sharing influence. Thus, some American districts had not been redistricted for over a century while the rural population was generally vastly overrepresented in Congress as well as in state legislatures to the disadvantage of urban dwellers. Only recently, under Supreme Court mandate, has "redistricting" begun to make representation more equitable in the House of Representatives and in the state chambers.

There are two still more fundamental problems concerning elections: the one regarding "real freedom of choice"; the other the influence of powerful "interests." Marxist-Leninist doctrine maintains that no real alternative is offered voters under capitalism, since a capitalistic system permits only those candidates and parties defending that system to compete. Thus, it asserts, there is no meaningful choice between American Republicans and Democrats, or British Conservatives and Laborites. To the non-Communist, however, there is a difference, and possibly a vital one, between the representatives of big business and of trade unions, of farmers and of urban people, of advocates of free enterprise and those of the welfare state. What may from time to time be true, on the other hand, is that one or the other of these groups lacks the "equal opportunity" to compete, either because certain technical regulations work against it or because there is an atmosphere of fear or intimidation. Such an atmosphere can be not unlike that which prevails in totalitarian systems, be it for political reasons (for example, intimidation of Negro voters in the South) or for economic ones (employee voters in a company town).

Equally serious may be the overbearing influence of powerful vested interests, especially during a campaign. Under modern conditions, an election is a vastly expensive business both for the candidates and the parties concerned. Those who can lavish huge sums of money on press, radio, and television campaigns may enjoy an undue advantage. If the subsidies come from a few special interest groups rather than from a large number of small contributors, there is a very real danger that candidates and parties will become beholden to these interests. And while here again we can hardly expect mathematical equality or proportionality for all groups, democracy suffers when there is too high a degree of inequality in this respect. It then remains exposed to charges that wealthy or other powerful interests are in control behind an egalitarian façade.

Political Parties

This issue of finance in campaigns leads us to problems that concern political parties as such. Basic to the process of choice in an election is the role of parties in formulating issues, presenting candidates, and providing the chief means through which individual and group interests can organize to secure and exercise political power. One of the major problems of the mass party, which is the natural product of universal suffrage and of the need to appeal broadly to different groups, is that it tends to be highly organized with large numbers of often full-time and salaried functionaries, and, like all "big" organizations, to be controlled in an "oligarchic" manner by "bosses" or self-perpetuating top party bureaucrats. This does not imply that the trend is necessarily always toward a nation-wide centralism of such mass parties, as has been the case in Britain and Germany. In the United States, on the contrary, except at short periods during presidential campaigns, the parties tend to disintegrate into frequently feuding regional and local groupings. Even so, the oligarchic tendencies that are characteristic of modern party organization are noticeable at the local, county, or state level.

This trend raises the problem of how the internal structure and operations of parties can be kept or made more democratic—that is, how to have meaningful interaction between party members and leaders. In this regard such technicalities as devising the right kind of intraparty regulations and arranging the nominations of candidates and elections of party officials in such a manner that there is free debate, open competition, and less wirepulling behind the scene can play as important a role as do such institutions as primary elections, provisions for recall, and so forth. But beyond these devices is the necessity of securing the active interest and participation of the people at large in party life. "Mass party"

does not automatically imply either mass participation or mass membership; only where such active public concern and participation prevail is there hope of transforming parties from oligarchic or otherwise managed groups into genuinely democratic institutions.

While a one-party system is characteristic of totalitarianism or at least authoritarianism, there are cases, especially in new states, where the one ruling party is so organized as to allow for intraparty wings and groupings that provide chances of debate and of give-and-take somewhat akin to those of a plural-party system.

When combined, as in Tanzania, with popular choice between locally nominated candidates, there can also be effective mass participation.

Besides the problems of intraparty democracy there are those involving the relations between parties. Ordinarily, this is a question of two-party vs. multiparty systems. Here the problems involved are similar to those raised in the discussion of single-member district systems of election vs. proportional representation. Indeed, there is often a correlation, although no absolute causality, between single-member districts and two-party setups, and between proportional representation and multiparty systems.

Two-party systems, especially where the two parties are strongly centralized, provide, as in Great Britain, for that "classical" contrast of, and alternation between, majority and opposition that is the heart of genuine parliamentary government. At the same time, this system may force the voter to support a party because it has a chance to be effective rather than because it reflects his point of view. Moreover, unless there is a good deal of diversification and give-and-take within each of the two main groups, it may also involve the rigid and possibly protracted rule of one single powerful class, group, or interest to the exclusion of all others.

In a multiparty system, on the other hand, the process of compromise that may go on within the major parties in a two-party system is transferred to the floor of the assembly or to the rooms where party leaders meet to hammer out the composition and program of a coalition government. The advantages are the more genuine discretion and influence of small groups or party deputies in the assembly and of the assembly itself vis-à-vis the executive. The shortcomings are equally obvious: the likelihood of executive instability, the excessive influence of often insignificant but strategically placed groups, continuous "horse-trading" even over matters of principle, and the uncertainty for the voter in knowing whether the party for which he votes is going to form the central part of a government coalition or not (for example, a group gaining a relative majority may even find itself in opposition).

The choice between the two systems is not, of course, a free one. Whether a two-party or multiparty system exists in a given country is usually a matter of historical development and of existing social, national, racial, or ideological cleavages. Americans have a general preference for two-party structures; but where the two parties represent two radically opposed groups of people, such as, for instance, the extreme right and the radical left, the system tends either to destroy the community or to lead to authoritarian control by one of the two. In such circumstances, multiparty "anarchy" may well be the lesser evil.

Lastly, there is a problem that involves not so much the number of parties as their programs and policies. The old charge, already referred to, that parties do not offer a real choice was based on the Marxist assumption that in a bourgeois society, both parties or all parties reflect the interests of the ruling class to the exclusion of the ruled. The rise of labor parties and similar groups disproved this interpretation. However, largely because of the increased share of workers and other formerly proletarianized groups in the affluence of modernized society, there has been of late a trend, especially in European parties, toward what the late Otto Kirchheimer called "catch-all" parties and away from those that constitute meaningful alternatives (even where they did not constitute an "opposition of principle" such as socialist, Communist, or fascist). In the Introduction we noted that international bloc formations and the influence of a superpower tend to make for a foreign policy consensus and for hesitancy to deviate from foreign policy "orientations." Where, in addition, the affluent society creates a broad middle class to which all major parties appeal, attitudes on domestic issues may become blurred, party

distinctions may lose their color, and the role of the opposition may dwindle.

Doubtlessly such a situation lessens the internecine warfare of parties, especially doctrinally divided ones, and diminishes the concomitant threat of deeply dividing a nation, as in the Germany of the Weimar Republic, in the French Third and Fourth Republics, and as is threatened in Italy today. But it also involves dangers: Public interest in real issues, formerly promoted by parties that differed in meaningful ways, may be translated into "popularity contests" of the respective party leaders, as was evident in recent West German and British elections. Moreover, if all major parties concentrate their interest on a broad, more or less affluent majority, the minorities that are still economically or otherwise disadvantaged or simply have different ideas may find themselves without political advocates and will tend to be forgotten. Thus in the United States, poverty groups and some racial minorities were disregarded for a long time as political parties appealed to the majority strata. But recent developments there have shown that this is by no means inevitable even in an age of modernization and affluence. It all depends on the minorities' ability to assert themselves forcefully and on the moral sense of responsibility of the members of the majority for the interests of all, including the minorities.

A chief reason for parliament's decline, paradoxically, has been the victory of democracy. In many European countries—in England after the Glorious Revolution and in France and other countries in the nineteenth century—parliament was the fighting force of the middle classes against authoritarian executives (the crown, and so forth); as such, its members developed a spirit of their own and a sense of their distinctive task, in legislation, budget-making, and criticism of the administration. As separate authoritarian forces disappeared from the political scene the executive has been drawn from the majority party (or parties) which tends to feel that it is not its job to embarrass an executive that represents the same political force as itself. If, then, as in Britain and West Germany, the executive actually turns out to be the more powerful of the two, and if, as we have observed before, there is a trend for even the opposition party to play a weaker role in providing opposition, parliament could be in danger of becoming a rubber stamp. In lawmaking, then, it takes second place to the initiating functions of the administration or of interest groups; in addition, the executive's decree-making and rule-making functions grow. And parliamentary debate, while occasionally approximating the idealized "contest for truth," more often turns out to be a contest among representatives of interests or among the leaders of parties who keep the ordinary deputies under tight control.

The Role of Parliament in Liberal Democracies

The operations of modern government have largely disproved or discounted the ideology of early liberalism, which placed the representative assembly in the center of political action. This view held that the "truth" would emerge from a battle of wits and a competition of ideas and would form the basis of agreed-upon decisions and actions in all fields, in particular in determining the basic and general rules and standards of the community through lawmaking. Parliament is still an important center of political action in liberal democracies, but it is neither *the* main one (for big and comprehensive government has shifted more and more weight to the executive) nor do its debates sway decisions as earlier periods expected them to do.

There are, in fact, two extremes of parliamentary development into which the modern system of representative government may degenerate. At one end rigid party discipline, especially where the two-party system prevails, may render parliament wholly subservient to the executive; this has been one by-product of the British parliamentary system where, as in South Africa, it is not counterbalanced by the self-restraint of the party in power. At the other end, it is possible to find parliament not only dominating the executive but also endlessly wrangling, and thus causing that inefficiency, instability, and log-rolling that discredited the systems of the French Third and Fourth Republics and of Weimar Germany. Moreover, under a system of separate powers, as in the United

States, executive stability may be combined with a legislative pattern of divided parties or interests whose concentration on their own concerns may lead to the neglect of the "commonweal."

While, in contrast to the British Parliament, Congress and the state legislatures in the United States have effective power over the process of law- and budget-making, they also illustrate the more technical difficulties of modern assemblies in regard to organization and procedures. To carry the crushing burden of modern parliamentary work loads requires labor-dividing procedures through devices such as committees, allocation of time for debate, and so on. But these devices may develop into a brake on action rather than initiate and promote it (as we have seen in filibusters in the Senate, or in the role of the Rules Committee in the House), or make laws reflect the power of entrenched groups rather than the majority will in the assembly. Thus modern government must seek to find a middle way between overriding the rights of individuals and groups of deputies and yielding too easily to their demands. With the latter, there is the danger of making the body either ineffective or the instrument of its most influential members and the interests behind them.

Under a system of separation of powers, the assembly serves as an important means to limit power. Bicameralism is a further means of checking power with power, its chief advantage when there are no additional reasons for having a second chamber, such as representing the member units in a federal system. Even then, however, the second chamber is warranted only where there remains genuine sectional sentiment, which, as we have seen, is dwindling in modern federalism, at least in the longer-established countries. The United States Senate today represents states' rights and interests hardly more than does the House, which in any event is strongly controlled by sectional interests. Paradoxically, the national interest often has a better chance to prevail in the former than in the latter. Occasionally, however, bicameralism serves a particular purpose as, for example, in West Germany, where the Federal Council successfully coordinates federal lawmaking with the administration of the laws in the states.

But despite all this criticism, a modern democratic assembly has an enduring value in certain realms. To expect any large and varied group of nonspecialized representatives to frame the laws of a complex society or to coordinate the government's far-flung activities is to impose a burden no assembly can be expected to bear. What a well-organized assembly can do—and do well—is to analyze, criticize, and judge the policies and proposals of the government; to voice the desires and anxieties of the mass of the citizens; to protect their liberties against abuse of power by the government; to educate public opinion through its debates; and, finally, to participate in the process of lawmaking to the extent this is still possible in an area that relies so much on the expert and the administrator.

In some ways, the legislature is particularly suited to these tasks. If its members lack the expert knowledge necessary to frame technical legislation, they possess a different kind of knowledge that the experts themselves are not likely to have; the legislators, taken in the mass, represent a range of experience in terms of class and geographical origin and have an intimate knowledge of their constituents that should make them exceptionally good judges of public opinion and of the acceptability and workability of laws. As protector of individual liberties against abuse of governmental power, the House of Commons is unexcelled; for educating the public on important issues its debates are remarkably effective, as is the opposition as critic of proposed legislation. Thus it is in its scrutinizing, supervising, and criticizing function that the democratic parliament, at its best, comes into its own.

4. POLITICAL LEADERSHIP

In the Introduction we emphasized how almost all trends in modern society—the growth in the functions of government, the oligarchic tendencies within any big organization, and especially the chronic crises and emergencies in international affairs—have contributed to a proportionate increase in the power of the executive. It is here, at the top level, rather than in legislatures or other institutions, that leadership now rests. This situation confronts democratic government with a twofold imperative: To see that such leadership provides strong, determined, and forceful direction to the community while at the same time it remains ultimately responsible to the people.

Dictatorial or otherwise authoritarian regimes do not know this dilemma. Their all-too-forceful leadership considers itself responsible not to any institutionally expressed popular will but to a cause, or to the "welfare of the community" as interpreted solely by the leader. Fascist doctrine states this frankly, while Communist theory proclaims responsibility to the masses whom the leaders are not supposed to leave too far behind. But in the absence of institutionalized criticism and control, who holds the vanguard to its task? Even though Stalin's rule was indicted as deviationist by his successors, there is little evidence that effective procedures for the enforcement of responsibility have since been devised or observed by Soviet leaders.

In democracies, on the other hand, the decisive constitutional rules and procedures—direct popular election of a chief executive or voting for a party whose leader then becomes head of the government—aim at providing responsible leadership through conferring a mandate limited in time. Democratic leadership means, in fact, power with a time limit. Although this leadership may possess, during its mandate, power that appears uncomfortably large and comprehensive—especially when it includes special "martial-law" powers to cope with emergencies—it is understood that it will periodically revert to the people.

Still, such leadership confronts two dangers of opposite natures. One danger is that in order to be and stay responsible, the leaders look too anxiously for, and follow too closely, whatever appears to be the mood of the people or their representatives at the moment. Modern executive leadership must develop initiative as the most important motive power in government. If it is weak or pliant, leadership falls nowhere, or elsewhere. The opposite problem is illustrated by the dilemma that President Franklin Roosevelt faced when, with a largely isolationist public opinion, he realized that America had to intervene against Nazi fascism. Should he then, as a responsible leader, have yielded to the pressure of opinion against his own better knowledge, or have gone ahead? In doing the latter, he was accused of acting "dictatorially," but history showed that intervention was necessary to save the democratic forces in the world. Similarly, Prime Minister Wilson forced stringent economic restraints on a far-from-willing British people in 1966 to improve Britain's economic position. Everything in such instances depends on whether such a "broad" interpretation of mandate is still in line with ultimate democratic objectives and attitudes. Thus democratic leadership today involves not only initiative and broad powers but also a deep sense of responsibility to the basic purposes of the people.

Selection, Succession, Access

All of this underlines the tremendous role of personality and thus the problems of selection, succession, and access. Various nontotalitarian systems differ widely concerning the prerequisites for top leadership and the ways to achieve it. In parliamentary systems leaders usually go through a lengthy period of political apprenticeship in a party organization and parliament; in presidential systems this is not necessarily the case. The somewhat haphazard nomination system of the two major American parties provides no guarantee that the choice will fall on a man with previous experience and qualifications in the most decisive areas of statesmanship.

In regard to succession, on the other hand, it is dictatorship that faces the more serious problems. In systems where law determines what happens in government, succession will proceed in prescribed ways. A system where rule is based on the person of the unique and infallible leader is put to its greatest test with his demise or overthrow. Totalitarian leaders have been loath to designate successors in order not to endanger their own power while they still exercise it. A lack of clear designation, however, usually leads to strife among contestants. "Collective leadership," as events in the Soviet Union showed after Stalin's death, and even after Khrushchev's ouster is difficult to maintain and it is generally the toughest and most ruthless who emerge as the fittest in this process of natural selection.

However great the trend toward concentration of power at the top and however strong the top leader may be, he must delegate work even of the most decisive nature in order to cope with his task. Moreover, all leaders inevitably listen to lieutenants and similar official and unofficial advisers. The greater the impact of the top leadership, the more vital therefore the problem of access to leadership. To whom does the chief executive listen? With whom does he associate both inside and outside the formal office structure? Where, and how, does he get his information? It is here that informal channels of access may prove as important as formal ones, or even more so. Unofficial aides or friends may turn out to wield vast, and often hidden, influence, and their existence may raise real problems for maintaining responsible leadership. Moreover, the very fact of a chief executive's limited time points up another problem. An appointment secretary, deciding whom the leader sees and for how long, may be more influential than top government aides.

Since for security and related reasons the top level of policy-making has necessarily to be conducted in secrecy, responsible democratic government depends greatly on whether and how the decision makers are held to account for their decisions, especially by parliament and by the mouthpieces of public opinion. In particular do they avoid, wherever possible, confronting the public with *faits accomplis?* Internal checks may be provided by organizational means, such as the cabinet system, but even there the ultimate decision must lie with someone. Where a decision is made by majority vote, it is likely to weaken the top leadership, as was the case with earlier French and German regimes. Cabinets that consist of party coalitions may provide the individual minister with much more independent authority than that enjoyed by a British cabinet minister since in a multiparty system he is probably the representative of a party whose support is needed to keep the coalition together. Cabinet solidarity, on the other hand, may render even ministers subservient to the top leader—as witness the West German system under Adenauer. In their different ways the British and American systems have generally proved more successful at combining effective action with responsibleness.

Leadership and Administration

Under any circumstances, the top leadership must subdelegate powers, and it is this fact that creates the political role of the bureaucracy, and in particular of that higher level of the service that participates in policy-making. And since the administration carries the responsibility of executing the laws and of seeing that they fulfill the purposes for which they were designed, the way in which the bureaucracy functions, and especially whether it considers itself responsible to the people as a genuine civil service, are decisive factors in the functioning of democratic government.

In modern government the civil service is supposed to implement impartially the directives of the government (cabinet, minister, and so forth); but in practice much depends on the history, the traditions, and the general structure of bureaucracy and administration in a given country. Where, as in Prussia-Germany, the officialdom antedates representative and democratic institutions, or where, as in the French Third and Fourth Republics, unstable government made the civil service the dominant permanent force in the state, its political influence is likely to surpass the limits of mere executive-administrative action. If its members are selected from specific classes or come to constitute a caste of their own, this type of bureaucracy may color a nation's entire government and politics, as has been not uncommon in some Continental European countries.

In the Anglo-American systems, on the other hand, the modern civil service was established in a more democratic environment that by and large avoided or eliminated special social selectivity. In England this has produced generally felicitous results; and in the United States the cross-fertilization between public service and other occupations, such as business, has had much to do with keeping the service free from any pronounced caste spirit. On the other hand, the turnover among officeholders in the United States causes a good deal of inefficiency and waste of manpower. Moreover, lack of permanence may open the way to the substantial or even corrupting influences of special interests. "Patronage"—that is, the system in which public office is used to reward often unqualified persons to whom party leaders are obligated politically or possibly financially (for example, for contributions to campaign funds), or to appoint those who, in turn, will be beholden to the person or party making the appointment for their jobs—was long the bane of the American system (as it is the bane of any genuine civil service system) and still occasionally leads to highly unsuitable appointments.

Leadership and Pressure Groups

While a responsible civil service must feel itself beholden to the people and their main needs and desires, it must by the same token avoid becoming an instrument, or mouthpiece, of specific interests. Especially in a country such as the United States where entire branches of the administration are often considered, and even consider themselves, to be "representing" specific groups (for example, agriculture, commerce, or labor), this danger is very real. And if a capitalistic society wants to escape the Marxist indictment of being an instrument in the hands of dominant economic interests, modern government must possess in its administrative machinery an organization that is able and willing to counter the pressures of special interest groups.

Inevitably, in any open society, a large number of varied interest groups exercise pressure on government and politics whenever lawmaking or the application of law affects them. If a country's larger and smaller interest groups, themselves organized democratically, operate freely and compete with each other on an equal footing, this is not a danger to, but an expression of, democracy. There have been periods in American history (as in that of other countries), however, when the influence of big business was so much stronger than any other that government appeared a mere reflection of such interests; there are other countries, notably certain of the Scandinavian countries, where organized labor has had more influence on government than any other group has had; in other cases an agricultural or even a feudal interest may prevail. But even so, much depends on how the public power reacts. The Marxist view that the relation between interests and government is automatically one of unilateral influence, of cause and effect as it were, is oversimplified and overmechanical. A strong public power may react to these influences without necessarily becoming the mere mouthpiece and representative of one or several of them. But even where influence groups balance each other, it should not be the task of the public power merely to register the compromises and deals of opposed interests. The public interest may well be different from such solutions. Management and labor, for example, might agree on wage increases in what appears to both sides to be their mutual interest, but such an agreement might yet run counter to the common good (in this instance, the interest of consumers) because of consequent price increases and inflationary effects on a nation's economy.

This is not to say that interest groups and their representatives should be excluded from the policy-making and administrative process altogether. Lobbying has its legitimate functions. Provided pressure groups are not permitted to usurp a political function, and that administrators remain mindful that they represent the national interest vis-à-vis such groups, the latter's specialized knowledge of attitudes and facts may even serve as an important link between government and the people to whom it is responsible.

It is here that the type and attitude of leadership will be decisive. Especially in a country such as the United States, where the parties are the chief representatives of competing interests, the national mandate of the presidency is of utmost importance. If there is no integration of the plurality of groups and interests at this point, there will be none at all. Still, the American system, where interests, although working in and through parties, are not organized *as* parties, seems to be at an advantage compared with systems where coalition governments made up from interest parties have a hard time rising above a mere dividing up of the commonwealth in their own favor.

Quite generally, the type of party and governmental system prevailing in a country determines to a large extent the degree of pressure group influence and the way the pressures operate. Where, as in such parliamentary systems as those of Great Britain or West Germany, or as in France today, basic decisions are made at the top level of the executive rather than in parliament, lobbyists are more likely to besiege the executive and administration than members of parliament. Where, as previously in France and now in Italy, the legislature predominates at least in lawmaking, deputies bear the brunt. Under a separation of powers, as in the United States, pressures are likely to affect both branches equally. Moreover, the way in which parties represent particular interests has a bearing on how pressures will be applied and on their chances of success. Where, as in the United States, both parties appeal to all major strata, pressures operate on and within both parties, and it then is of particular importance whom an individual legislator represents, how susceptible he is to influence, and so forth. Where, as in Britain, the two major parties still represent to a considerable degree two distinct classes, in a way they function as interest groups, as witness the number of trade unionists among Labor M.P.'s or of businessmen among Conservatives. Where, as in Germany (and Japan), members of interest groups, such as industrialists or farmers, tend to leave the representation of their interests to professionals, one finds many officials of interest organizations serving as deputies in parliament. Such infiltration of parliament by the lobby tends to make it a social and economic council rather than a body representing the people.

The importance of forceful, disinterested, and responsible leadership in the democracies is thus obvious. It is heightened by two current developments. In the domestic sphere, the advent of the affluent society has shifted the urgency of governmental functions to the much neglected public sector of life. But since it is now a minority rather than, as in the past, a majority, which is likely to be economically underprivileged and disadvantaged, it may be more difficult, though no less necessary, to marshal support for it in a framework of majority procedures. Internationally, the democracies are confronted with a somewhat comparable situation. Here the developed nations constitute the affluent few who must help the vast masses of the developing world. Democratic leadership, in both situations, must convince the people to act on behalf of the interests of others; if they fail to do so, the democracies will not only be defeated morally and politically by their chief opponents, but will also deny their own basic values.

5. DEMOCRACY IN THE MODERN WORLD

What chances has democracy in a world beset with the threats of totalitarianism, the uncertainties of an emerging world of developing new nations, and its own trends toward oligarchism and an erosion of liberties? As we look over our list of the weaknesses and shortcomings of liberal democracy, we may feel discouraged. Does it not add up to a deficient rather than efficient system, one in which professed ideals and promises are contradicted more often than not by the facts? Has the ideal of a freely debating, freely deciding, and freely consenting "sovereign" people yielded, in practice, to the actuality of manipulated opinion-making, of parties and legislatures controlled by oligarchs or special interests, of administrations lording it over helpless citizens, and of leaders weak and influenced or so powerful that little distinguishes them from dictators?

Before we make a judgment, however, let us note that democratic theory has always been inclined to measure realities with the yardstick of an ideal that has never been realizable. The belief of eighteenth-century Enlightenment and nineteenth-century Progressivism in a mankind that would come ever closer to a state of internal and external peace, a harmony of interests, and a community of the free and equal has yielded under the impact of the cruel experiences of our century to the more realistic insight that the ideal must forever remain unobtainable. Yet it can still serve as a guiding star for unending efforts to measure up to it. And this is where democracy has a value far beyond anything that nondemocratic belief systems and regimes can offer. As long as there remains the possibility of debate, the competition of opinion and policy groups, and changes of procedures and institutions, democracy will continue to be an open system in which experimentation is the means of remedying insufficiencies and providing reform. The very fact of

criticism like ours points up this basic asset. And it has always been one of the greatest strengths of democracy that it possesses an abundant variety of devices that can be used to move closer to the ideal of free, representative, responsible, and efficient government. Electoral systems can be used for the worse, but also for the better. So can the procedures of legislatures, or systems for the recruitment of public officials. Novel institutions such as the public corporation can be invented to cope with problems of government ownership; or an institution like that of the ombudsman can be taken over for better protection against executive arbitrariness. New types of court systems or procedures can be adopted to cope with the increasing number and importance of those cases where the citizen clashes with public authorities.

Best of all, democracy allows people to learn from experience. Institutions that have proved successful in one country can be introduced in another. Each democracy is a laboratory for others. Here, it is true, we must again beware of overoptimism. Every country develops its institutions in terms of its own historical heritage, its social and economic framework, its own ideal of a "way of life." We have seen that overambitious experiments in reeducation may fail. But we also can find successful imitation and adaptation as broad as that of the general parliamentary pattern and as specific as in such institutions and practices as administrative courts and judicial review.

Thus democratic self-analysis is neither fair nor valid if it overlooks the successes and potentialities of democracy or if it is more critical of democratic than of totalitarian shortcomings. Some of those observers who have been most ruthless in their assessment of the political ineptitude of the people have been rather credulous in their willingness to attribute qualities of wisdom and integrity to the leaders and administrators of authoritarian states. Yet revelations of Hitler and his "court" disclose a degree of folly of which no democracy has shown itself capable. Similarly, it would be hard to think of a more devastating indictment of Soviet leadership than the revelations about Stalin made by the Soviet's own top leadership.

There remains one problem. The devices and institutions of liberal democracy are operational.

They leave open the question of the objective of government—that is, the type of community to be established by free discussion and consent. Even though the devices may be unimpeachably democratic, the people using them may be at sea as to their ultimate aims. It is then that *anomie* and frustration may beset them. Certainly, the greatest strength of totalitarianism is its belief in a cause, and its attempt and frequent success in providing people with certain and appealing aims.

But there is no reason why democracy cannot likewise avoid emptiness. We have no shortage of worthwhile objectives, ranging all the way from ensuring peace and genuine peaceful co-existence to aiding the advance of the under-developed majority of the human race. Indeed, it is becoming clearer every day that the democracies must unite on these aims if they are to survive and to fulfill themselves.

It is especially in the area of advancing the underdeveloped South of the globe that the fate of liberal democracy is likely to be decided. Democracy flourishes best where there is a feeling of economic well-being and security. The absence of these economic requirements makes the fulfillment of democratic requirements, such as detached, reasonable judgment of public affairs and consideration for the interests and rights of others, extremely difficult. The rising and rapidly multiplying masses of the world's South, the agricultural and subsistence proletariat of the present-day world, can hardly achieve the maturity liberal democracy requires without a rapid improvement in living standards; unless the poor nations are helped in their present struggle to meet their own and their peoples' aspirations, their governments, whether democratically inclined or not, are likely to fall prey to anarchy, radicalism, or militant forces, and the great powers may be pulled into the vortex. Coupled with the tasks still facing the democracies at home—such as wiping out their own areas of discrimination and poverty, this external challenge is enough to provide them with worthwhile objectives for the remainder of this century.

The democratic way of life is not an easy one, but its rewards are great. No form of government is simpler than that of one man ruling over others; yet history stands as a record of the abuse of power so concentrated. Democracy requires from its citizens a level of political intelligence, experience, maturity, public spirit, and self-restraint lacking in large parts of the world; it also demands the exercise of ingenuity in finding solutions and developing the political machinery appropriate for a system that desires freedom and responsibility as well as efficiency. The great strength of democracy is that its way of life fosters and encourages these very qualities. It is in the democracies that no one attitude or solution is orthodox, that diversity and experiment are considered natural and desirable. And as one looks at the great variety of devices that have in practice been developed for the realization of democratic aims, it would be rash to conclude that in imaginativeness, willingness to experiment, and social idealism, the democracies yield in any way to other forms of government.

Bibliography

PREPARED BY LOUISE W. HOLBORN

Radcliffe Institute for Independent Study, Cambridge, Mass.

The steady output of new books on many aspects of the governments and politics of the major foreign powers has made it necessary to cull with care those listed in the previous bibliographies. A high proportion of the books included in this bibliography were published from 1961 on; books that appeared earlier are not listed unless they are of particular importance. Articles have been included only when they form a major source of information on a particular subject.

For those who want a more detailed survey of earlier material, attention is drawn to the comprehensive bibliographies in earlier editions of *Major Foreign Powers* and to the supplementary bibliography, prepared by Miss Holborn in 1959, issued by Harcourt, Brace & World.

In keeping with the practice in earlier bibliographies, this compilation has been confined to publications in English. The wealth of material on foreign governments available in this language is a reflection of the vastly increased concern of the English-speaking world to understand the peoples and policies of other countries.

Except in rare instances, government publications are not included. They can be secured from the following information centers:

United States: Superintendent of Documents, Government Printing Office, Washington, D.C. 20025
United Kingdom of Great Britain: British Information Services, 845 Third Avenue, New York, N.Y. 10021
France: French Embassy, Press and Information Services, 972 Fifth Avenue, New York, N.Y. 10021
Federal Republic of West Germany: German Information Center, 410 Park Avenue, New York, N.Y. 10022
For USSR Material in English: Publishing House, Moscow, through Four Continent Book Co., 156 Fifth Avenue, New York, N.Y. 10010

For obtaining material on the British parties, the following addresses in the United Kingdom will be useful:

Conservative Party: Conservative and Unionist Central Office, 32 Smith Square, Westminster, London, S.W. 1; Bow Group, 60 Berners Street, London, W. 1.
Labour Party: The Labour Party, Transport House, Smith Square, London, S.W. 1; Fabian Society, 11 Dartmouth Street, London, S.W. 1.
Liberal Party: The Liberal Party, 36 Smith Square, London, S.W. 1.

ABBREVIATIONS

AHR: American Historical Review, New York, quarterly.
AJCL: American Journal of Comparative Law, Ann Arbor, Mich., quarterly.
AJES: American Journal of Economics and Sociology, New York, quarterly.
AJIL: American Journal of International Law, Washington, D.C., quarterly.
AJS: American Journal of Sociology, Chicago, bimonthly.
Annals: The Annals of the American Academy of Political and Social Science, Philadelphia, bimonthly.
APSR: American Political Science Review, Washington, D.C., quarterly.
ASEER: The American Slavic and East European Review, Columbia U., New York, quarterly.
ASR: American Sociological Review, New York, bimonthly.
B: Bulletin.
BAS: Bulletin of the Atomic Scientists, Chicago, monthly.
BBC: British Broadcasting Corporation, London.
BIS: Bulletin of the Institute for the Study of the USSR, Munich, monthly.
BJES: British Journal of Educational Studies, London, semiannually.
BJS: British Journal of Sociology, London, quarterly.
CDSP: The Current Digest of the Soviet Press, Joint Committee on Slavic Studies, New York, weekly.

CER: Comparative Education Review, New York, 3 issues annually.
CH: Current History, Philadelphia, monthly.
CJEPS: Canadian Journal of Economics and Political Science, Toronto, quarterly.
CLR: Columbia Law Review, New York, monthly.
Cmd: Command Paper, HMSO, London.
COI: Central Office of Information, London.
CPC: Conservative Political Centre, London.
CR: Contemporary Review, London, monthly.
CS: Commonwealth Survey, London, fortnightly.
CSM: Christian Science Monitor, Boston, daily.
CSSH: Comparative Studies in Society and History, The Hague, quarterly.
DSB: Department of State, Bulletin, Washington, D.C., biweekly.
E: The Economist, London, weekly.
EJ: Economic Journal, London & New York, quarterly.
FA: Foreign Affairs, New York, quarterly.
Fabian: Fabian Society, London.
For. Lang. Pub.: Foreign Language Publications, Moscow.
Hansard: Hansard Society for Parliamentary Government, London.
HICOG: High Commission for Germany.
HLR: Harvard Law Review, Cambridge, Mass., monthly (Nov.–June).
HMSO: Her Majesty's Stationery Office, London.
IA: International Affairs, London, monthly.
IC: International Conciliation, New York, monthly, except July and August.
ICFTU: International Confederation of Free Trade Unions.
ICLQ: International and Comparative Law Quarterly, London, quarterly.
IJ: International Journal, Toronto, quarterly.
ILO: International Labor Office, Geneva.
ILR: International Labour Review, Geneva & Washington, D.C., monthly.
Ind. LJ: Indiana Law Journal, Bloomington, Ind., quarterly.
Inst.: Institute.
Int.: International.
IO: International Organization, Boston, quarterly.
IPSA: International Political Science Abstracts, Oxford, quarterly.
ISSJ: International Social Science Journal, Paris, quarterly.
J: Journal.
JCEA: Journal of Central European Affairs, Boulder, Colo., quarterly.
JCH: Journal of Contemporary History, London, quarterly.
JCPS: Journal of Commonwealth Political Studies, Leicester U.P., monthly (Nov.–June).
JIA: Journal of International Affairs, Columbia U., New York, 3 issues annually.
JICJ: Journal of the International Commission of Jurists, Geneva, monthly.
JMH: Journal of Modern History, Chicago, quarterly.
JP: The Journal of Politics, Gainesville, Fla., quarterly.

JPC: Journal of the Parliaments of the Commonwealth, London, quarterly.
JPE: Journal of Political Economy, Chicago, bimonthly.
JRSS: Journal of the Royal Statistical Society, London, 3 issues annually.
JSP: Journal of Social Psychology, Provincetown, Mass., quarterly.
LIB: Labor and Industry in Britain, British Information Services, New York, quarterly.
Lib: Library.
Lib. Cong.: Library of Congress, Washington, D.C.
LJ: Law Journal.
LR: Law Review.
MIT: Mass. Institute of Technology, Cambridge, Mass.
MJPS: Midwest Journal of Political Science, Wayne State University Press, Detroit, quarterly.
MLR: Modern Law Review, London, quarterly.
NPA: National Planning Association, Washington.
Oceana: Oceana Publications, New York.
P: Press.
Pbk: paperback.
PAR: Public Administration Review, Chicago, quarterly.
Parl. Aff.: Parliamentary Affairs, London, quarterly.
PEP: Political and Economic Planning, London.
Pers. Ad.: Personnel Administration, Washington, D.C., bimonthly.
Phil. Lib.: Philosophical Library, New York.
Pol. Sc.: Political Science, Wellington, N.Z., biannually.
POQ: The Political Opinion Quarterly, Princeton, quarterly.
PQ: Political Quarterly, London, quarterly.
Problems: Problems of Communism, Washington, D.C., bimonthly.
PS: Political Studies, Oxford, 3 issues annually.
PSQ: Political Science Quarterly, New York, quarterly.
Pub.: Publisher.
Pub. Ad.: Public Administration, London, quarterly.
Pub. Aff.: Public Affairs Press, Washington, D.C.
Pub. Pers. Rev.: Public Personnel Review, Chicago, quarterly.
Q: Quarterly.
QJE: Quarterly Journal of Economics, Cambridge, Mass., quarterly.
R: Review.
Ref. Pamph.: Reference Pamphlet.
RES: Review of Economics and Statistics, Cambridge, Mass., quarterly.
RIIA: Royal Institute of International Affairs, London.
SAQ: South Atlantic Quarterly, Durham, quarterly.
SR: Social Research, New York, quarterly.
SS: Soviet Studies, Oxford, quarterly.
U: University.
USGPO: United States Government Printing Office, Washington, D.C.
WP: World Politics, Princeton, quarterly.
WPQ: The Western Political Quarterly, Salt Lake City, quarterly.
WT: The World Today, London, monthly.
YBE: The Yearbook of Education, London, annually.
YLR: Yale Law Review, New Haven, quarterly.
YR: Yale Review, New Haven, quarterly.

COMPARATIVE WORKS

Abraham, Henry J., *Courts and Judges, An Introduction to the Judicial Process*, Oxford UP, 1959, 58 pp.

——, *The Judicial Process, An Introductory Analysis of the Courts of the United States, England, and France*, Oxford UP, 1962, 349 pp, pbk.

Adinow, Joseph, "The Constitutional and Judicial Organization of France and Germany and Some Comparisons of the Civil Law and Common Law Systems," *Ind. LJ*, 37, 1961:1–50.

Alford, Robert R., *Party and Society, The Anglo-American Democracies*, Murray, 1964, 419 pp.

Almond, Gabriel A. and James S. Coleman, eds., *The Politics of the Developing Areas*, Princeton UP, 1960, 591 pp.

—— and G. Bingham Powell, Sr., *Comparative Politics, A Developmental Approach*, Little, Brown, 1966, 348 pp.

—— and Sidney Verba, *The Civic Culture, Political Attitudes and Democracy in Five Nations*, Little, Brown, 1965, 379 pp, pbk.

Andrews, William George, ed., *Constitution and Constitutionalism*, 2nd ed., Van Nostrand, 1963, 201 pp.

Arendt, Hannah, *The Origins of Totalitarianism*, new rev. ed., Harcourt, Brace & World, 1966, 526 pp.

Barker, Sir Ernest, *Essays on Government*, 2nd ed., Oxford UP, 1951, 304 pp.

——, *Reflections on Government*, Oxford UP, 1942, 424 pp.

Basset, R., *The Essentials of Parliamentary Democracy*, 2nd rev. ed., Cass, London, 1964, 214 pp.

Becker, Carl L., *Modern Democracy*, Yale UP, 1941, 100 pp.

Beloff, Max, "The Federal Solution in Its Application to Europe, Asia and Africa," *PS*, 1(2), June 1953: 114–31.

Benn, S. I. and R. S. Peters, *Social Principles and the Democratic State*, Allen & Unwin, London, 1959, 403 pp.

Bernstein, Marver J., *The Job of the Federal Executive*, Brookings, 1958, 241 pp.

Bowie, Robert R. and Carl Joachim Friedrich, eds., *Studies in Federalism*, Little, Brown, 1954, 88 pp.

Brimmell, F. H., *Communism in South-East Africa, A Political Analysis*, Oxford UP, 1959, 415 pp.

Brogan, Denis W., *Citizenship Today, England, France, the United States*, U North Carolina P, 1960, 116 pp.

Bryce, James, Viscount, *Modern Democracies*, Macmillan, 1924, 2 vols, 567 and 757 pp.

Brzezinski, Zbigniew and Samuel P. Huntington, *Political Power, USA/USSR, Similarities and Contrasts, Convergence or Evolution*, Viking, 1964, 461 pp.

Burmeister, Werner, ed., *Democratic Institutions in the World Today*, Praeger, 1958, 157 pp.

Butler, David E., ed., *Elections Abroad*, St Martin's, 1959, 280 pp.

Campion, Lord and D. W. S. Lidderdale, *European Parliamentary Procedure, A Comparative Handbook*, Allen & Unwin, London, 1955, 270 pp.

Carnell, Francis, comp., *The Politics of the New States, A Select Annotated Bibliography with Special Refer-ence to the Commonwealth*, Oxford UP, 1961, 171 pp.

Carter, Gwendolen M., ed., *National Unity and Regionalism in Eight African States*, Cornell UP, 1966, 565 pp.

—— and John H. Herz, *Government and Politics in the Twentieth Century*, rev. enl. ed., Praeger, 1965, 231 pp, pbk.

—— and Alan F. Westin, eds., *Politics in Europe, 5 Cases in European Government*, Harcourt, Brace & World, 1965, 205 pp.

Cassinelli, C. W., *The Politics of Freedom, An Analysis of the Modern Democratic State*, U Washington P, 1961, 214 pp.

Castberg, Freda, *Freedom of Speech in the West, A Comparative Study of Public Law in France, the United States and Germany*, Allen & Unwin, London, 1961, 475 pp.

Chapman, Brian, *The Profession of Government, The Public Service in Europe*, 3rd ed., Allen and Unwin, 1966, 352 pp.

Clegg, H. A., *A New Approach to Industrial Democracy*, Blackwell, Oxford, 1960, 140 pp.

Cole, George D. H., *A History of Socialist Thought*, St Martin's, 5 vols: *The Forerunners, 1789–1850*, 1953, 345 pp; *Marxism and Anarchism, 1850–1890*, 1954, 481 pp; *The Second International, 1889–1914*, 1956, 1042 pp; *Communism and Social Democracy, 1914–1931*, 1959, 940 pp; *Socialism and Fascism, 1931–1939*, 1960, 350 pp.

Coleman, James Smoot, ed., *Studies in Political Development*, Princeton UP, 1965, 620 pp.

Corry, J. A. and J. E. Hodgetts, *Democratic Government and Politics*, 4th ed., Oxford UP, 1964, 842 pp.

Dahl, Robert A., ed., *Political Oppositions in Western Democracies*, 2 vols., Yale UP, 1966, 458 pp and 477 pp.

Dietze, Gottfried, "America and Europe, Decline and Emergence of Judicial Review," *Virginia LR*, 44(8), Dec. 1958:233–72.

——, "Judicial Review in Europe," *Michigan LR*, 55(4), Feb. 1957:539–66.

Drachkovitch, Milorad M., ed., *Marxism in the Modern World*, Stanford UP, 1965, 293 pp.

Duverger, Maurice, *Political Parties, Their Organization and Activity in the Modern State*, trans. by Barbara and Robert North, Wiley, 1954, 439 pp.

——, *The Political Role of Women*, UNESCO, Paris, 1955, 221 pp.

Ehrmann, Henry W., ed., *Democracy in a Changing Society*, Praeger, 1964, 210 pp, pbk.

——, ed., *Interest Groups on Four Continents*, U Pittsburgh P, 1958, 316 pp.

Einaudi, Mario and François Goguel, *Communism in Western Europe*, Cornell UP, 1951, 239 pp.

Einzig, Paul, *The Control of the Purse, Progress and Decline of Parliament's Financial Control*, Secker & Warburg, London, 1959, 344 pp.

Evans, Roger Warren, "French and German Administrative Law, with Some English Comparisons," *ICLQ*, 14(4), Oct. 1965:1089–1103.

Farrell, R. Barry, ed., *Approaches to Comparative and International Politics*, Northwestern UP, 1966, 368 pp.

Fesler, James W., "Approaches to the Understanding of Decentralization," *JP*, 27(3), Aug. 1965:536–66.

Finer, Herman, *The Theory and Practice of Modern Government*, 4th ed., Methuen, London, 1961, 982 pp.

Finer, S. E., *The Man on Horseback, The Role of the Military in Politics*, Pall Mall, London, 1962, 268 pp.

Fogarty, Michael P., *Christian Democracy in Western Europe, 1820–1953*, U Notre Dame P, 1957, 461 pp.

"Foreign Policy in a Polycentric World," *Survey*, No. 58, Spec. Issue, Jan. 1966.

Friedmann, Wolfgang, ed., *The Public Corporation, A Comparative Symposium*, Carswell, Toronto, 1954, 612 pp.

Friedrich, Carl Joachim, *Constitutional Government and Democracy, Theory and Practice in Europe and America*, rev. ed., Ginn, 1950, 688 pp.

——, ed., *Totalitarianism*, Harvard UP, 1954, 386 pp.

—— and Zbigniew K. Brzezinski, *Totalitarian Dictatorship and Autocracy*, 2nd ed., Praeger, 1966, 427 pp, pbk.

Galenson, Walter, *Trade Union Democracy in Western Europe*, U California P, 96 pp, pbk.

Gellhorn, Walter, *Ombudsmen and Others, Citizens' Protectors in Nine Countries*, Harvard UP, 1967, 448 pp.

Gregoire, Roger, "The French Fonction Publique and the British Civil Service," *Can. Pub. Ad.*, 8(4), Dec. 1965:457–69.

Gulick, Charles A. et al., *History and Theories of Working-Class Movements, A Select Bibliography*, U California P, 1955, 364 pp.

Heckscher, Gunnar, *The Study of Comparative Government and Politics*, Macmillan, 1957, 172 pp.

Herz, John H., *International Politics in the Atomic Age*, Columbia UP, 1962, 360 pp, pbk.

——, *Political Realism and Political Idealism*, U Chicago P, 1951, 275 pp.

Hicks, Ursula K., *Development from Below, Local Government and Finance in Developing Countries of the Commonwealth*, Oxford UP, 1961, 564 pp.

"Housing in Britain, France and West Germany," PEP, Aug. 1965:217–65.

"International Fascism 1920–45," *JCH*, 1(1), 1966.

IPI Survey, *The Press in Authoritarian Countries*, Int. P Inst., Zurich, 1959, 201 pp.

Joelson, Mark R., "Legal Problems in the Dismissal of Civil Servants in the United States, Britain and France," *AJCL*, 12(1), 1963:149–71.

Kandel, I. L., *The New Era in Education, A Comparative Study*, Houghton Mifflin, 1955, 388 pp.

Kersell, John E., *Parliamentary Supervision of Delegated Legislation, The United Kingdom, Australia, New Zealand and Canada*, Stevens, London, 1960, 178 pp.

Kirchheimer, Otto, "Majorities and Minorities in Western European Government," *WPQ*, 12(2), June 1959:492–510.

——, *Political Justice*, Princeton UP, 1961, 452 pp.

——, "The Waning of Opposition in Parliamentary Regimes," *SR*, 24(2), Summer 1957:127–56.

Kolarz, Walter, *Communism and Colonialism*, St Martin's, 1964, 147 pp.

Kornhauser, William, *The Politics of Mass Society*, Free P, 1959, 256 pp.

Landauer, Carl et al., *European Socialism*, U California P, 2 vols, 1959, 1894 pp.

La Palombara, Joseph, ed., *Bureaucracy and Political Development*, Princeton UP, 1963, 487 pp.

—— and Myron Weiner, eds., *Political Parties and Political Development*, Princeton UP, 1966, 495 pp.

Leys, Colin, "Models, Theories, and the Theory of Political Parties," *PS*, 7(2), June 1959:127–46.

Lindsay, Alexander D., *The Modern Democratic State*, Oxford UP, Vol. 1, 1943, 286 pp.

Livingstone, William S., *Federalism and Constitutional Change*, Oxford UP, 1956, 386 pp.

Lorwin, Lewis L., *The International Labor Movement, History, Policies, Outlook*, Harper, 1953, 366 pp.

MacIver, Robert M., *The Web of Government*, Macmillan, 1947, 498 pp.

Mackenzie, W. J. M., *Free Elections*, Rinehart, 1958, 184 pp.

Macmahan, Arthur W., ed., *Federalism Mature and Emergent*, Doubleday, 1955, 550 pp.

Macridis, Roy L., *The Study of Comparative Government*, Random House, 1955, 77 pp.

—— and Bernard E. Brown, *Comparative Politics, Notes and Readings*, Dorsey, 1964, 705 pp.

——, ed., *Foreign Policy in World Politics*, 2nd ed., Prentice-Hall, 1962, 374 pp.

Mannheim, Karl, *Freedom, Power and Democratic Planning*, Oxford UP, 1950, 384 pp.

Moody, Joseph, ed., *Church and Society, Catholic Social and Political Thought and Movements, 1789–1950*, Arts, 1953, 914 pp.

Moore, Russell F., *Modern Constitutions with Brief Commentaries*, Littlefield, Adams, 1957, 305 pp.

Morstein, Marx Fritz, *The Administrative State, An Introduction to Bureaucracy*, U Chicago P, 1957, 202 pp.

Mueller, Bernard, *Western Europe, Canada and the United States, A Statistical Handbook of the North Atlantic Area*, Twentieth Century, 1965, 239 pp.

Myrdal, Gunnar, *Beyond the Welfare State, Economic Planning and Its International Interpretation*, Yale UP, 1960, 287 pp.

——, *An International Economy, Problems and Prospects*, Harper, 1956, 381 pp.

Neumann, Sigmund, "Comparative Politics, A Half-Century Appraisal," *JP*, 19(2), May 1957:369–90.

——, "The Comparative Study of Politics," *CSSH*, 1(2), Jan. 1959:105–12.

——, ed., *Modern Political Parties, Approaches to Comparative Politics*, U Chicago P, 1956, 460 pp.

Nollan, Gunther, *International Communism and World Revolution*, Hollis & Carter, London, 1961, 372 pp.

Nolte, Ernst, *Three Faces of Fascism, Action Française, Italian Fascism, National Socialism*, Holt, Rinehart & Winston, 1966, 561 pp, pbk.

Normanton, E. L., *The Accountability and Audit of Governments*, Praeger, 1966, 470 pp.

"Our Invisible Government, Pressure Groups and Lobbies," *Annals*, 319, Sept. 1958, entire issue.

Peaslee, Amos J., *Constitutions of the Nations*, 3 vols, 2nd ed., Justice House, 1956, 2752 pp.

Plamenatz, John, *On Alien Rule and Self-Government*, Longmans, London, 1960, 224 pp.

Political Handbook of the World, ed., Walter H. Mallory, Harper, published annually.

Pye, Lucian W., ed., *Communications and Political Development*, Princeton UP, 1963, 381 pp.

—— and Sidney Verba, *Political Culture and Political Development*, Princeton UP, 1965, 584 pp.

Radice, Giles, *Democratic Socialism, A Short Survey*, Longmans, London, 1966, 173 pp.

Retzlaff, Ralph A., "The Use of Aggregate Data in Comparative Political Analysis," *JP*, 27(4), Nov. 1965:797–917.

Richardson, G. Henry, *Economic and Financial Aspects of Social Security, An International Survey*, Allen & Unwin, London, 1960, 270 pp.

Ridley, F. F., "French Technocracy and Comparative Government," *PS*, 14(1), Feb. 1966:34–52.

Robinson, Kenneth et al., *Five Elections in Africa*, Oxford UP, 1960, 496 pp.

Rogger, Hans and Eugen Weber, eds., *The European Right, A Historical Profile*, U California P, 1965, 589 pp.

Rose, R. and A. J. Heidenheimer, eds., "Symposium on Comparative Political Finance," *JP*, 25(4), 1963:643–811.

Ross, Murray G., ed., *New Universities in the Modern World*, St Martin's, 1966, 190 pp.

Rowat, Donald C., ed., *The Ombudsman Citizen's Defender*, Allen & Unwin, London, 1965, 348 pp.

Schwartz, Bernard, ed., *The Code Napoleon and the Common-Law World*, New York UP, 1956, 448 pp.

Seton-Watson, Hugh, *The East-European Revolution*, Praeger, 1961, 412 pp.

——, *Nationalism and Communism*, Praeger, 1964, 253 pp.

Shonfield, Andrew, *Modern Capitalism, the Changing Balance of Public and Private Power*, Oxford UP, 1965, 456 pp.

Siffin, William J., ed., *Toward the Comparative Study of Public Administration*, Indiana UP, 1957, 331 pp.

Smith, T. E., *Elections in Developing Countries*, St Martin's, 1960, 278 pp.

Stewart, Michael, *Modern Forms of Government, A Comparative Study*, Praeger, 1961, 284 pp, pbk.

Strauss, E., *The Ruling Servants: Bureaucracy in Russia, France and Britain*, Praeger, 1961, 308 pp.

Strong, C. F., *A History of Modern Political Constitutions: An Introduction to Comparative Study of Their History and Existing Form*, Capricorn, 1964, 389 pp, pbk.

Talmon, Jacob Lieb, *The Origins of Totalitarian Democracy*, Praeger, 1960, 377 pp, pbk.

——, *Political Messianism, the Romantic Phase*, Praeger, 1961, 607 pp.

Thompson, James D., ed., *Comparative Studies in Administration*, U Pittsburgh P, 1960, 224 pp.

Tickner, F. J., *Technical Cooperation*, Hutchinson U Lib., 1965, 206 pp.

Ulich, Robert, *The Education of Nations, A Comparative Treatise in Historical Perspective*, Harvard UP, 1960, 352 pp.

Verney, Douglas V., *The Analysis of Political Systems*, Routledge, London, 1959, 239 pp.

Wheare, Kenneth C., *Federal Government*, 4th ed., Oxford UP, 1964, 266 pp, pbk.

——, *Legislatures*, Oxford UP, 1963, 247 pp, pbk.

——, *Modern Constitutions*, Oxford UP, 1963, 247 pp.

Wolf-Phillips, Leslie, *Constitutions of Modern States*, Pall Mall, London, 1966.

GREAT BRITAIN

GENERAL WORKS

"After the Election," *PQ*, 35(2), Apr.-June, 1964, entire issue.

Bagehot, Walter, *The English Constitution*, Introduction by R. H. S. Crossman, full bibliography, Cornell UP, 1966, 310 pp.

Bailey, Sidney D., *British Parliamentary Democracy*, 3rd ed., Harrap, London, 1964, 181 pp.

Boyd, Francis, *British Politics in Transition, 1945–1963*, Praeger, 1964, 253 pp.

Brasher, N. H., *Studies in British Government*, St Martin's, 1965, 178 pp.

Butler, David and Jennie Freeman, *British Political Facts, 1900–1960*, St Martin's, 1963, 245 pp.

Campion, Sir Gilbert et al., *British Government Since 1918*, Macmillan, 1950, 232 pp.

Crossman, Richard H. S., *The Charm of Politics and Other Essays in Political Criticism*, Harper, 1959, 243 pp.

Greaves, Harold R. G., *The British Constitution*, new ed., Allen & Unwin, London, 1960, 263 pp.

Gwyn, William B., *Democracy and the Cost of Politics in Britain*, Athlone, London, 1962, 256 pp.

Harrison, Wilfred, *The Government of Britain*, 6th ed., Hutchinson, London, 1960, 176 pp.

Jennings, Sir Ivor, *The British Constitution*, 5th ed., Cambridge UP, 1966, 210 pp, pbk.

——, *Cabinet Government*, 3rd ed., Cambridge UP, 1959, 587 pp.

——, *The Law and Constitution*, 5th ed., U London P, 1959, 354 pp.

——, *The Queen's Government*, Pelican, 1954, 158 pp.

Laski, Harold J., *Parliamentary Government in England, A Commentary*, Viking, 1938, 383 pp.

Macfarlane, L. J., *British Politics, 1918–1964*, Pergamon, 1966, 175 pp, pbk.

Moorhouse, Geoffrey, *Britain in the Sixties, The Other England*, Penguin, 1964, 189 pp.

Morrison, Herbert Stanley, *Government and Parliament, A Survey from the Inside*, 3rd ed., Oxford UP, 1964, 386 pp, pbk.

Muir, Ramsay, *How Britain Is Governed*, 4th ed., Constable, London, 1940, 335 pp.

Robson, William A., *The Governors and the Governed*, Allen & Unwin, London, 1964, 68 pp, pbk.

Rose, Richard, *Politics in England*, Little, Brown, 1964, 266 pp, pbk.

Rose, Richard, *Studies in British Politics,* Little, Brown, 1966, 352 pp.

Sampson, Anthony, *Anatomy of Britain Today,* new enl. ed., Harper, 1966, 720 pp.

Stewart, Michael, *The British Approach to Politics,* 5th ed., Allen & Unwin, London, 1966, 310 pp, pbk.

Wedgewood Benn, Anthony, *The Regeneration of Britain,* Gollancz, London, 1965, 144 pp.

Wheare, Kenneth C., *Government by Committee, An Essay on the British Constitution,* Oxford UP, 1955, 264 pp.

White, Leslie William and William Douglas Hussey, *Government in Great Britain, the Empire and the Commonwealth,* 4th ed., Cambridge UP, 1965, 298 pp.

Wilkinson, Rupert Hugh, *The Prefects, British Leadership and the Public School Tradition,* Oxford UP, 1964, 243 pp.

Chapter 1. THE BRITISH PEOPLE AND THEIR POLITICS

LAND AND PEOPLE

Banton, Michael, *White and Coloured, The Behavior of British People Toward Coloured Immigrants,* Cape, London, 1959, 223 pp.

Barker, Sir Ernest, *Britain and the British People,* 2nd ed., Oxford UP, 1955, 186 pp.

———, ed., *The Character of England,* Oxford UP, 1948, 607 pp.

Brockway, Fenner and Norman Pannell, *Immigration—What Is the Answer? Two Opposing Views,* Routledge, London, 1965, 120 pp, pbk.

Brogan, Denis W., *The English People, Impressions and Observations,* Knopf, 1945, 295 pp.

Cole, George D. H., *Studies in Class Structure,* Routledge, London, 1956, 202 pp.

——— and Raymond Postgate, *The British Common People,* Barnes & Noble, 1961, 742 pp, pbk.

Coupland, Sir Reginald, *Welsh and Scottish Nationalism,* Collins, London, 1954, 448 pp.

Davison, R. B., *Commonwealth Immigrants,* Oxford UP, 1964, 87 pp.

Deakin, Nicholas, ed., *Colour and the British Electorate, 1964, Six Case Studies,* Pall Mall, London, 1965, 172 pp.

Fletcher, Ronald, "Social Change in Britain," *PQ,* 34(4), Oct.–Dec. 1963:399–410.

Foot, Paul, *Immigration and Race in British Politics,* Penguin Special, 1965, 254 pp.

Freedman, Maurice, ed., *A Minority in Britain, Social Studies of the Anglo-Jewish Community,* Mitchell, London, 1955, 304 pp.

Gaus, John Merriman, *Great Britain, A Study in Civic Loyalty,* U Chicago P, 1929, 329 pp.

Glass, Ruth and Harold Pollins, *London's Newcomers, the West Indian Migrants,* Harvard UP, 1961, 278 pp.

Guttsman, W. L., *The British Political Exile,* MacGibbon & Kee, London, 1963, 398 pp.

Hackett, John W. and A. M., *The British Economy, Problems and Prospects,* Allen & Unwin, London, 1967, 221 pp.

Henderson, Patrick Donald, ed., *Economic Growth in Britain,* Weidenfeld & Nicolson, London, 1966, 296 pp.

Hooper, Richard, ed., *Colour in Britain,* BBC, London, 1965, 239 pp.

Huxley, Elspeth, *Back Street New Worlds, A Look at Immigrants in Britain,* Morrow, 1965, 190 pp.

Isaac, Julius, *British Postwar Migration,* Cambridge UP, 1955, 329 pp.

Jones, J. Mervyn, *British Nationality Law,* rev. ed., Oxford UP, 1956, 306 pp.

Lewis, Ray and Angus Maude, *The English Middle Classes,* Knopf, 1950, 386 pp.

Mansergh, Nicholas, *The Irish Question, 1840–1921, A Commentary on Anglo-Irish Relations and on Social and Political Forces in Ireland in the Age of Reform and Revolution,* Toronto UP, 1966, 316 pp.

Morgan, Kenneth O., *Wales in British Politics, 1868–1922,* U Wales P, 1963, 353 pp.

Parry, Clive, *British Nationality, Including Citizenship of the United Kingdom and Colonies and the Status of Aliens,* Stevens, London, 1955, 216 pp.

Richmond, Anthony H., *The Colour Problem, A Study of Racial Relations,* Pelican, 1955, 370 pp.

Rowntree, B. Seebohm and G. R. Lavers, *English Life and Leisure: A Social Study,* Longmans, London, 1937, 719 pp.

Stacey, Margaret, *Tradition and Change, A Study of Banbury,* Oxford UP, 1960, 231 pp.

Stamp, Lawrence Dudley, *The Land of Britain—Its Use and Misuse,* 3rd ed., Longmans, London, 1962, 546 pp.

——— and S. H. Beaver, *The British Isles, A Geographic and Economic Survey,* 4th ed., Longmans, London, 1954, 780 pp.

Thompson, E. P., *The Making of the English Working Class,* Pantheon, 1964, 845 pp.

Thornberry, Cedric, *Stranger at the Gate, A Study of the Law on Aliens and Commonwealth Citizens,* Fabian, London, Aug. 1964, 27 pp.

Wickenden, James, *Colour in Britain,* Oxford UP, 1959, 46 pp.

Willmott, Peter and Michael Young, *Family and Class in a London Suburb,* Humanities P, 1960, 187 pp.

Wilson, Thomas, ed., *Ulster Under Home Rule, A Study of the Political and Economic Problems of Northern Ireland,* Oxford UP, 1956, 253 pp.

Youngson, A. J., *The British Economy, 1920–1957,* Harvard UP, 1960, 258 pp.

CHURCHES

Facts and Figures About the Church of England, 1959, Church House, London, 1959.

Garbett, Cyril, *Church and State in England,* Hodder & Stoughton, London, 1950, 320 pp.

Heubel, E. J., "Church and State in England, The Price of Establishment," *WPQ,* 18(3), Sept. 1965:646–55.

Hill, Clifford S., *West Indian Migrants and the London Churches,* Oxford UP, 1963, 89 pp.

Hunter, Leslie S., *The English Church, A New Look,* Penguin, 1966, 176 pp.

Lloyd, R., *The Church of England in the Twentieth Century,* 2 vols, Longmans, London, 1946–50, 270 pp.

Mayfield, Guy, *The Church of England, Its Members and Its Business*, 2nd ed., Oxford UP, 1963, 211 pp.

TRADE UNIONS AND INDUSTRIAL RELATIONS

Allen, V. L., *Trade Unions and the Government*, Longmans, London, 1960, 326 pp.

Bailey, Jack, *British Cooperative Movement*, Hutchinson, London, 1955, 178 pp.

Bonner, A., *British Co-operation*, Co-operative Union, Manchester, 1961, 540 pp.

Brown, E. H. Phelps, *The Growth of British Industrial Relations*, Macmillan, 1960, 451 pp.

Burn, Duncan, *The Structure of British Industry*, Cambridge UP, 1958, 2 vols, 403 and 499 pp.

Citrine, Lord, *Men and Work, Autobiography*, Hutchinson, London, 1964, 384 pp.

Clegg, H. A., Alan Fox, and E. F. Thompson, *A History of British Trade Unions Since 1889*, Vol. 1. *1889–1910*, Oxford UP, 1964, 514 pp.

Clements, Richard, *Glory Without Power, A Study of Trade Unionism in Our Present Society*, Morrison & Gibbs, London, 1959, 143 pp.

Hobsbawn, Eric John, *Labouring Men, Studies in the History of Labour*, Weidenfeld & Nicolson, London, 1964, 401 pp.

Hutt, G. Allen, *British Trade Unionism: A Short History*, 5th ed., Lawrence & Wishart, London, 1962, 200 pp.

ILO, *The Trade Union Situation in the United Kingdom*, 1961, 123 pp.

Jenkins, Olive and J. E. Mortimer, *British Trade Unions Today*, Pergamon, 1965, 125 pp.

Macdonald, D. F., *The State and the Trade Unions*, St Martin's, 1961, 119 pp.

Pelling, Henry, *A History of British Trade Unionism*, Penguin, 1963, 287 pp.

Pollard, Sidney, *Cooperatives at the Crossroads*, Fabian, London, 1965, 44 pp.

Potter, Allen, *Organized Groups in British National Politics*, Faber, London, 1961, 396 pp.

Roberts, B. C., *Trade Union Government and Administration in Great Britain*, Harvard UP, 1956, 570 pp.

Trades Union Congress, *Annual Reports*, London.

Webb, Sidney and Beatrice, *The History of Trade Unionism*, 2nd ed., Longmans, London, 1920, 784 pp.

Welton, Henry, *Trade Unions, the Employer and the State*, Pall Mall, London, 1960, 177 pp.

Wigham, Eric L., *Trade Unions*, Oxford UP, 1956, 276 pp.

———, *What's Wrong with the Unions?* Penguin, 1961, 233 pp.

Williams, Francis, *Magnificent Journey, The Rise of the Trade Unions*, Odhams, London, 1954, 448 pp.

Wootton, Graham, *The Official History of the British Legion*, Macdonald & Evans, London, 1956, 348 pp.

Zweig, Ferdynand, *The Worker in an Affluent Society, Family Life and Industry*, Heinemann, London, 1961, 268 pp.

PRESS, BROADCASTING, AND TELEVISION

Andrews, Sir Linton, *The Autobiography of a Journalist*, Benn, London, 1964, 262 pp.

Annual Reports and Accounts of the British Broadcasting Corporation, HMSO.

Annual Reports and Accounts of the Independent Television Authority, HMSO.

BBC Handbook, BBC, London, published annually.

Braddon, Russell, *Roy Thomson of Fleet Street*, Collins, London, 1965, 396 pp.

Briggs, Asa, *The History of Broadcasting in the United Kingdom*, Oxford UP, 2 vols: *The Birth of Broadcasting*, 1961, 415 pp; *The Golden Age of Wireless*, 1965, 688 pp.

The British Broadcasting Corporation Act, Cmd. 9138 and Cmd. 9196, HMSO, 1954.

Christiansen, Arthur, *Headlines All My Life*, Heinemann, London, 1961, 306 pp.

Christoph, J. B., "The Press and Politics in Britain and America," *PQ*, 34(2), Apr.–June 1963:137–50.

Crozier, Mary, *Broadcasting, Sound and Television*, Oxford UP, 1958, 236 pp.

Cudlipp, Hugh, *At Your Peril*, Weidenfeld & Nicolson, London, 1963, 400 pp.

General Council of the Press, *Annual Reports*, since Oct. 1954, The Council, London.

Howard, Peter, *Beaverbrook, A Study of Max the Unknown*, Hutchinson, London, 1964, 164 pp.

Moorhouse, Geoffrey, *The Press*, Ward Lock, London, 1964, 94 pp.

Paulu, Burton, *British Broadcasting in Transition*, U Minnesota P, 1962, 250 pp.

Political and Economic Planning, *Balance Sheet of the Press*, PEP, 1955, 200 pp.

———, *Ownership of the Press*, PEP, 1955, 200 pp.

———, *Television in Britain*, PEP, 1958.

Report of the Broadcasting Committee, 1949 (Beveridge Committee), *Cmd. 8116*, HMSO, 1951, 327 pp.

Report of the Royal Commission on the Press, 1947–1949, Cmd. 7700, HMSO, 1949, 363 pp.

Taylor, Henry Archibald, *The British Press*, Barker, London, 1961, 176 pp.

Trenaman, Joseph and Denis McQuail, *Television and the Political Image, A Study of the Impact of Television on the 1959 General Election*, Methuen, London, 1961, 287 pp.

Williams, Raymond, *Britain in the Sixties, Communications*, Penguin Special, 1963, 134 pp.

Wilson, H. H., *Pressure Groups, The Campaign for Commercial Television in England*, Rutgers UP, 1961, 232 pp.

Windlesham, Lord, *Communication and Political Power*, Cape, London, 1966, 288 pp.

Chapter 2. THE BRITISH POLITICAL HERITAGE

HISTORY AND CONSTITUTION

Amery, Leopold, *Thoughts on the Constitution*, 2nd ed., Oxford UP, 1964, 195 pp, pbk.

Anson, Sir William R., *Law and Custom of the Constitution*, 4th ed. Oxford UP, 1922–35, 2 vols, 404 pp.

Birch, A. H., *Representative and Responsible Government*, Allen & Unwin, London, 1964, 252 pp.

Brose, Olive J., *Church and Parliament: The Reshaping*

of the Church of England, 1828–1960, Stanford UP, 1959, 239 pp.

Churchill, Sir Winston S., *The Great Democracies, A History of the English-Speaking Peoples,* Dodd, Mead, 4 vols: *The Birth of Britain* (to 1485), 1956, 521 pp; *The New World* (1485–1688), 1956, 433 pp; *The Age of Revolution* (1688–1815), 1957, 402 pp; *The Great Democracies* (1815–1900), 1958, 403 pp.

Dicey, Albert V., *Introduction to the Study of the Law of the Constitution,* 10th ed., Macmillan, 1959, 837 pp., 1961, 535 pp, pbk.

Harvey, Jack and L. Bather, *The British Constitution,* St Martin's, 1964, 572 pp.

Jennings, Sir Ivor, *Magna Carta and Its Influence in the World Today,* HMSO, 1965, 43 pp.

Keir, Sir David Lindsay, *The Constitutional History of Modern Britain Since 1485,* 7th ed., Cornell UP, 1964, 591 pp.

Kidd, Ronald, *British Liberty in Danger, An Introduction to the Study of Civil Rights,* Lawrence & Wishart, London, 1941, 270 pp.

Laski, Harold J., *Reflections on the Constitution, the House of Commons, the Cabinet, the Civil Service,* Viking, 1951, 220 pp.

LeMay, G. H. L., *British Government, 1914–1953, Select Documents,* Methuen, London, 1955, 416 pp.

Maitland, Frederic William, *The Constitutional History of England,* Macmillan, 1961, 548 pp, pbk.

Marshall, Geoffrey and Graeme C. Moodie, *Some Problems of the Constitution,* rev. ed., Hutchinson, London, 1961, 201 pp.

Pelling, Henry, *Modern Britain, 1885–1955,* Nelson, London, 1961, 212 pp.

Phillips, Owen Hood, *The Constitutional Law of Great Britain and the Commonwealth,* 2nd ed., Sweet & Maxwell, London, 1957, 835 pp.

Smellie, Kingsley Bryce, *Great Britain Since 1688,* Michigan UP, 1964, 488 pp.

Taylor, Alan John Percival, *English History, 1914–1945,* Oxford UP, 1965, 736 pp.

Thomson, David, *England in the Nineteenth Century, 1815–1914,* rev. bibliography, Penguin, 1964, 251 pp.

———, *England in the Twentieth Century,* Penguin, 1965, 304 pp.

Trevelyan, George M., *Illustrated History of England,* Longmans, London, 1956, 758 pp.

The United Kingdom, The Development of Its Laws and Constitution, Part I, *England, Wales, Northern Ireland and the Isle of Man,* ed. by G. W. Keeton and D. Lloyd; Part II, *Scotland,* by T. B. Smith, and *The Channel Islands,* by L. A. Sheridan, Stevens, London, 1955, 523 and 603 pp.

Williams, Lord Francis, *A Pattern of Rulers,* Longmans, London, 1965, 272 pp.

Woodward, E. L., *History of England,* Methuen, London, 1948, 273 pp.

POLITICAL IDEAS

Anderson, Perry and Robin Blackburn, *Towards Socialism,* Fontana Lib., London, 1965, 397 pp, pbk.

Bennett, George, ed., *The Concept of Empire, Burke to Attlee, 1774–1947,* Black, London, 1953, 434 pp.

Brinton, Crane, *English Political Thought in the Nineteenth Century,* Benn, London, 1933, 311 pp.

Bullock, Alan Louis C. and Maurice Shock, eds., *The Liberal Tradition from Fox to Keynes,* New York UP, 1957, 288 pp.

Canavan, Francis P., *The Political Reason of Edmund Burke,* Duke UP, 1960, 222 pp.

Cecil, Lord Hugh, *Conservatism,* Butterworth, London, 1912, 254 pp.

Cobban, Alfred, *Edmund Burke and the Revolt Against the Eighteenth Century,* Allen & Unwin, London, 1960, 280 pp.

Cole, George D. H., *Fabian Socialism,* Allen & Unwin, London, 1943, 172 pp.

Cole, Margaret, *The Story of Fabian Socialism,* Stanford UP, 1962, 366 pp.

Davidson, W. L., *Political Thought in England, The Utilitarians from Bentham to J. S. Mill,* Oxford UP, 1947, 196 pp.

Fremantle, Anne, *This Little Band of Prophets, The British Fabians,* Mentor, 1960, 320 pp, pbk.

Gooch, G. P., *Political Thought in England, Bacon to Halifax,* Oxford UP, 1946, 108 pp.

Gray, Alexander, *The Socialist Tradition from Moses to Lenin,* Longmans, London, 1948, 523 pp, pbk.

Hearnshaw, F. J. C., *Conservatism in England, An Analytical, Historical and Political Survey,* Macmillan, 1935, 322 pp.

Hobhouse, Leonard T., *Liberalism,* Holt, 1911, 254 pp.

Letwin, Shirley Robin, *The Pursuit of Certainty, David Hume, Jeremy Bentham, John Stuart Mill, Beatrice Webb,* Cambridge UP, 1965, 391 pp.

Maccoby, S., ed., *The English Tradition, 1763–1914,* Kaye, London, 1952, 236 pp.

———, *English Radicalism, The End?* Allen & Unwin, London, 1961, 640 pp.

McDowell, R. R., *British Conservatism, 1832–1914,* Faber, London, 1960, 191 pp.

Morris, C., *Political Thought in England, Tyndale to Hooker,* Oxford UP, 1953, 220 pp.

Plamenatz, J. P., *The English Utilitarians,* Macmillan, 1949, 228 pp.

———, ed., *Readings from Liberal Writers, English and French,* Barnes & Noble, 1965, 228 pp.

St. John-Stevas, Norman, *Walter Bagehot, A Study of His Life and Thought Together with a Selection from His Political Writings,* Indiana UP, 1959, 485 pp.

Sheean, Timothy P., *Reflections with Edmund Burke,* Vantage, 1960, 288 pp.

The Autobiography of John Stuart Mill, Dolphin, Oxford, 1962, 240 pp, pbk.

Tsuzuki, Chūshichi, *H. M. Hyndman and British Socialism,* Oxford UP, 1961, 304 pp.

Ulam, Adam B., *Philosophical Foundations of English Socialism,* Harvard UP, 1951, 173 pp.

Chapter 3. BRITISH PARTIES AND ELECTIONS

GENERAL

Beer, Samuel H., *British Politics in the Collectivist Age,* Knopf, 1964, 384 pp.

Blondel, Jean, *Voters, Parties and Leaders: The Social Fabric of British Politics*, Penguin, 1963, 272 pp.

Bulmer-Thomas, Ivor, *The Growth of the British Party System*, Baker, London, 1966, 672 pp.

———, *The Party System in Great Britain*, Macmillan, 1953, 328 pp.

Cross, Colin, *The Fascists in Britain*, St Martin's, 1963, 214 pp.

Guttsman, Wilhelm L., *The British Political Elite*, Basic Books, 1964, 398 pp.

Jennings, Sir Ivor, *Party Politics*, Cambridge UP, 3 vols: *Appeal to the People*, 1960, 387 pp; *The Growth of Parties*, 1961, 404 pp; *The Stuff of Politics*, 1962, 504 pp.

Jones, Charles O., "Inter-Party Competition in Britain, 1950–1959," *Parl. Aff.*, 17(1), Winter 1963–1964:50–56.

McKenzie, Robert T., *British Political Parties, The Distribution of Power Within the Conservative and Labour Parties*, 2nd ed., Praeger, 1963, 694 pp, pbk.

Mullaly, Frederic, *Fascism Inside England*, Morris, London, 1946, 100 pp.

Northedge, F. S., "British Foreign Policy and the Party System," *APSR*, 54(3), Sept. 1960:635–47.

Rose, Richard, "Parties, Factions and Tendencies in Britain," *PS*, 12(1), Feb. 1964:33–46.

Thayer, George, *The British Political Fringe*, Blond, London, 1965, 256 pp.

CONSERVATIVE PARTY

Berrington, Hugh, "The Conservative Party, Revolts and Pressures, 1955–1961," *PQ*, 32(4), Oct.–Dec. 1961:363–73.

Birch, Nigel, *The Conservative Party*, Collins, London, 1949, 49 pp.

Block, Geoffrey D. M., *Conservative and Unionist Onwards: A Source Book*, CPC, 1964, 96 pp.

"The Conservative Party," *PQ*, 32(3), July–Sept. 1961, special issue.

Dickie, John, *The Uncommon Commoner, A Study of Sir Alec Douglas-Home*, Praeger, 1964, 224 pp.

Griffiths, Eldon, ed., *Peaceful Change, A Selection of Speeches by Sir Alec Douglas-Home*, Baker, London, 1964, 131 pp.

Hailsham, Viscount (Quintin M. Hogg), *The Conservative Case*, Penguin, 1959, 176 pp.

———, *The Left Was Never Right*, Faber, London, 1945, 206 pp.

———, *Science and Politics*, Faber, London, 1963, 110 pp.

———, *Science and Society*, CPC, 1962, 94 pp.

Hoffman, J. D., *The Conservative Party in Opposition, 1945–51*, MacGibbon & Kee, London, 1964, 288 pp.

Kilmuir, 1st Earl of (David Maxwell Fyfe), *Political Adventure, Memoirs*, Weidenfeld & Nicolson, London, 1964, 356 pp.

Nicholson, Sir Godfrey, "The Conservative Party 1965," *QR*, 648, Apr. 1966:107–20.

The One Nation Group of MPs, *The Responsible Society*, CPC, 1959, 63 pp.

Petrie, Sir Charles, *The Carlton Club*, Eyre & Spottiswoode, London, 1955, 221 pp.

Punnett, R. M., "The House of Lords and Conservative Governments 1951–1964," *PS*, 13(1), Feb. 1965:85–88.

Raison, Timothy, *Why Conservative?* Penguin, 1964, 144 pp.

Sparrow, Gerald, *Rab, Study of a Statesman, The Career of Baron Butler of Saffron Walden*, Odhams, London, 1965, 253 pp.

White, Reginald James, ed., *The Conservative Tradition*, Black, London, 1955, 276 pp.

Wood, John, *A Nation Not Afraid, The Thinking of Enoch Powell*, Batsford, London, 1965, 156 pp.

LABOR PARTY

Abrams, Mark and Richard Rose, *Must Labour Lose?* Penguin, 1960, 127 pp.

Alderman, R. K., "The Conscience Clause of the Parliamentary Labour Party," *Parl. Aff.*, 19(2), Spring 1966:224–32.

———, "Discipline in the Parliamentary Labour Party, 1945–1951," *Parl. Aff.*, 18(1), Summer 1965:293–305.

Attlee, Clement Richard, 1st Earl, *The Labour Party in Perspective—and Twelve Years Later*, Longmans, London, 1949, 199 pp.

Bealey, Frank and Henry Pelling, *Labour and Politics, 1900–1906*, Macmillan, 1958, 314 pp.

Bevan, Aneurin, *In Place of Fear*, Simon & Schuster, 1952, 213 pp.

Brand, Carl F., *The British Labour Party, A Short History*, Stanford UP, 1964, 340 pp.

Briggs, Asa and John Saville, ed., *Essays in Labour History*, Macmillan, 1960, 364 pp.

Bullock, Alan, *The Life and Times of Ernest Bevin, Trade Union Leader, 1881–1940*, Heinemann, London, 1960, 685 pp.

"Cassandra" (William Connor), *George Brown, A Profile*, Pergamon, 1964, 96 pp.

Cole, George D. H., *British Working Class Politics, 1832–1914*, Routledge, London, 1941, 220 pp.

———, *A History of the Labour Party from 1914*, Routledge, London, 1948, 517 pp.

———, *Short History of the British Working Class Movement, 1789–1947*, rev. ed., Allen & Unwin, London, 500 pp.

Collins, Henry and Chimer Abramsky, *Karl Marx and the British Labour Movement, Years of the First International*, Macmillan, 1965, 356 pp.

Crosland, C. A. R., *The Conservative Enemy, A Programme of Radical Reform for the 1960's*, Cape, London, 1963, 251 pp.

Crossman, Richard H. S., ed., *New Fabian Essays*, Praeger, 1952, 215 pp.

———, *Planning for Freedom*, Hamish Hamilton, London, 1965, 252 pp.

———, *The Politics of Socialism*, Atheneum, 1965, 252 pp.

"Demos," *The Go Ahead Year, Labour in Power*, Book Distributors, Leicester, 1966, 160 pp.

Dowse, Robert E., "The Parliamentary Labour Party in Opposition," *Parl. Aff.*, 13(4), Autumn 1960:520–29.

Epstein, Leon D., "New MPs and the Politics of the PLP," *PS*, 10(2), June 1962:121–29.

Fabian Essays in Socialism, 6th ed., Allen & Unwin, London, 1962, 322 pp.

Foot, Michael, *Harold Wilson: A Pictorial Biography,* Pergamon, 1964, 100 pp.

Gaitskell, Hugh, *In Defence of Politics,* Birkbeck College, London, 1954, 14 pp.

Hall, Peter Geoffrey, *Labour's New Frontiers,* Deutsche, London, 1964, 180 pp, pbk.

Hanson, A. H., "The Labour Party and House of Commons Reform," Parts I and II: *Parl. Aff.,* 10(4), Autumn 1957:454–68; 11(1), Winter 1957–58:39–56.

Harrison, Martin, *Trade Unions and the Labour Party Since 1945,* Wayne State UP, 1960, 360 pp.

Howard, Anthony and Richard West, *The Road to Number 10,* Macmillan, 1965, 317 pp.

Hughes, Emrys, *Keir Hardie,* Allen & Unwin, London, 1956, 252 pp.

Hunter, L., *The Road to Brighton Pier,* Barker, London, 1959, 224 pp.

Jay, Douglas, *Socialism in the New Society,* Longmans, London, 1962, 358 pp.

Jenkins, Roy, *The Labour Case,* Penguin, 1959, 146 pp.

Loewenberg, Gerhard, "The Transformation of British Labour Party Politics Since 1945," *JP,* 21(2), May 1959:234–57.

MacKenzie, Norman, ed., *Conviction,* MacGibbon & Kee, London, 1958, 237 pp.

McKenzie, Robert T., "The Wilson Report," *PS,* 4(1), Feb. 1956:93–97.

Middlemas, Robert Keith, *The Clydesiders, A Left Wing Struggle for Parliamentary Power,* Hutchinson, London, 1965, 307 pp.

Miliband, Ralph, *Parliamentary Socialism, A Study in the Politics of the Labour Party,* Merlin, London, 1964, 356 pp, pbk.

Murphy, J. T., *Labour's Big Three, A Biographical Study of Clement Attlee, Herbert Morrison and Ernest Bevin,* John Lane, London, 1949, 266 pp.

Noel, G. E., *Harold Wilson and the "New Britain," The Making of a Modern Prime Minister,* Campion, London, 1965, 143 pp.

Northcott, Jim, *Why Labour?* Penguin, 1964, 192 pp.

Pelling, Henry, *The Origins of the Labour Party, 1880–1900,* 2nd ed., rev., Clarendon P, Oxford, 1965, 256 pp.

———, *A Short History of the Labour Party,* St Martin's, 1961, 135 pp, pbk.

Phillips, Morgan, *Labour in the Sixties,* Labour Party, London, 1960, 24 pp.

Poirier, Philip P., *The Advent of the British Labour Party,* Columbia UP, 1958, 288 pp.

Rodgers, W. T., ed., *Hugh Gaitskell 1906–1963,* Thames & Hudson, London, 1964, 167 pp.

——— and Bernard Donoughue, *The People into Parliament, A Concise History of the Labour Movement in Britain,* Viking, 1966, 191 pp.

Rose, Saul, "Labour's Pax Britannica," *PQ,* 36(2), Apr.–June 1965:131–41.

Shinwell, Emanuel, *The Labour Story,* Macdonald, London, 1963, 222 pp.

Shore, Peter, *Entitled to Know,* MacGibbon & Kee, London, 1966, 160 pp.

Sissons, Michael and Philip French, eds., *Age of Austerity, 1945–1951,* Hodder & Stoughton, London, 1963, 349 pp.

Smith, Dudley, *Harold Wilson, A Critical Biography,* Hale, London, 1964, 224 pp.

Smith, Leslie, *Harold Wilson, The Authentic Portrait,* Scribner's, 1965, 231 pp.

Tawney, R. H., *The Radical Tradition,* Allen & Unwin, London, 1964, 240 pp.

Towards Socialism: Essays, Fontana Lib, 1965, 397 pp, pbk.

Tracey, Herbert, ed., *The Labour Party, Its History, Growth, Policy and Leaders,* Caxton, London, 1948, 3 vols.

Webb, Beatrice, *Our Partnership,* Longmans, London, 1948, 543 pp.

Wedgewood Benn, Anthony et al., *Where? Five Views on Labour's Future, Together with an Analysis of the Election Results,* Fabian, London, 1959, 36 pp.

Williams, Francis, *Fifty Years' March, The Rise of the Labour Party,* Odhams, London, 1949, 379 pp.

Wilson, Harold, *The New Britain, Labour's Plan, Selected Speeches 1964,* Penguin, 1964, 134 pp.

———, *Purpose in Politics, Selected Speeches, 1956–1963,* Weidenfeld & Nicolson, London, 1964, 270 pp.

———, *The Relevance of British Socialism,* Weidenfeld & Nicolson, London, 1964, 115 pp.

LIBERAL PARTY

Bonham-Carter, Victor, *In a Liberal Tradition, A Social Biography, 1700–1959,* Constable, London, 1960, 272 pp.

Cowie, Harry, *Why Liberal?* Penguin, 1964, 155 pp.

Cross, Colin, *The Liberals in Power, 1905–1914,* Barrie & Rockliff, London, 1963, 198 pp.

Fulford, Roger, *The Liberal Case,* Penguin, 1959, 175 pp.

Fyfe, Hamilton, *The British Liberal Party, An Historical Sketch,* Allen & Unwin, London, 1928.

Grimond, Joseph, *The Liberal Challenge, Democracy Through Participation,* Hollis & Carter, London, 1965, 320 pp.

———, *The Liberal Future,* Faber, London, 1960, 197 pp.

Lort-Phillips, Patrick, "The British Liberal Revival," *FA,* 38(1), Oct. 1959:121–31.

Pope-Hennessy, James, Lord Crewe, *The Likeness of a Liberal,* Constable, London, 1955, 205 pp.

Rasmussen, Jorgen Scott, *The Liberal Party, A Study of Retrenchment and Revival,* Constable, London, 1965, 316 pp.

Stansky, Peter, *Ambitions and Strategies, The Struggle for the Leadership of the Liberal Party in the 1890's,* Oxford UP, 1965, 328 pp.

Vincent, John, *The Formation of the Liberal Party, 1857–1868,* Constable, London, 1966, 281 pp.

Watkins, Alan, *The Liberal Dilemma,* MacGibbon & Kee, London, 1966, 158 pp.

Watson, George, ed., *Radical Alternative, Essays in Liberalism by the Oxford Liberal Group,* Eyre & Spottiswoode, London, 1962, 190 pp.

———, *The Unservile State, Essays in Liberty and Welfare,* Macmillan, 1957, 324 pp.

Wilson, Trevor, *The Downfall of the Liberal Party,
1914–1935,* Collins, 1966, 416 pp.

COMMUNIST PARTY

Darke, Bob, *The Communist Technique in Britain,* Penguin, 1952, 159 pp.
Gallacher, William, *The Case for Communism,* Penguin, 1949, 208 pp.
Laski, Harold J., *The Secret Battalion, An Examination of the Communist Attitude to the Labour Party,* London, 1946, 30 pp.
MacFarlane, L. J., *The British Communist Party, Its Origin and Development Until 1929,* MacGibbon & Kee, London, 1966, 338 pp.
Pelling, Henry, *The British Communist Party, A Historical Profile,* Macmillan, 1958, 204 pp.
Wood, Neal, *Communism and British Intellectuals,* Columbia UP, 1959, 256 pp.
Zilliacus, Konni, *Why I Was Expelled, Bevinism v. Election Pledges, Socialism and Peace,* Narod, London, 1949, 72 pp.

ELECTIONS

Allen, A. J., *The English Voter,* English UP, 1964, 258 pp, pbk.
Benney, Mark et al., *How People Vote, A Study of Electoral Behaviour in Greenwich,* Routledge, London, 1956, 227 pp.
Birch, A. H., *Small-Town Politics, A Study of Political Life in Glossop,* Oxford UP, 1959, 199 pp.
Bealey, Frank et al., *Constituency Politics: A Study of Newcastle-Under-Lyme,* Faber, London, 1965, 440 pp.
Bonham, John, *The Middle Class Vote,* Faber, London, 1954, 210 pp.
Bromhead, Peter, "The General Election of 1966," *Parl. Aff.,* 19(3), Summer 1966:332-45.
Butler, David E., *The British General Election of 1951,* Macmillan, 1952, 288 pp.
———, *The British General Election of 1955,* Macmillan, 1956, 236 pp.
———, *The Electoral System in Britain Since 1918,* 2nd ed., Clarendon P, Oxford, 1963, 232 pp.
——— and Anthony King, *The British General Election of 1964,* St Martin's, 1965, 410 pp.
——— and Anthony King, *The British General Election of 1966,* St Martin's, 1967, 320 pp.
——— and Richard Rose, *The British General Election of 1959,* St Martin's, 1960, 203 pp.
Chrimes, S. B. et al., *The General Election in Glasgow, February 1950,* Jackson, Glasgow, 1950, 202 pp.
Comfort, George O., *Professional Politicians, A Study of British Party Agents,* Pub. Aff., 1958, 69 pp.
Daudt, H., *Floating Voters and the Floating Vote: A Critical Analysis of American and English Election Studies,* Stenfert Kroise N.V., Leyden, 1961, 171 pp.
Fulford, R., *Votes for Women, The Story of a Struggle,* Faber, London, 1957, 343 pp.
Hanham, H. J., *Elections and Party Management,* Longmans, London, 1959, 485 pp.
McCallum, Ronald B. and Alison Readman, *The British General Election of 1945,* Oxford UP, 1947, 311 pp.
Martin, Laurence W., "The Bournemouth Affair, Britain's First Primary Election," *JP,* 22(4), Nov. 1960: 654-81.
Milne, R. S. and H. C. MacKenzie, *Marginal Seat, 1955, A Study of Voting Behaviour in the Constituency of Bristol North-East at the General Election of 1955,* Hansard, London, 1958, 210 pp.
———, *Straight Fight, A Study of Voting Behaviour in the Constituency of Bristol North-East at the General Election of 1951,* Hansard, London, 1954, 174 pp.
Mitchell, Brian R. and Klaus Boehm, *British Parliamentary Election Results, 1950–1964,* Cambridge UP, 1966, 135 pp.
Nicholas, H. G., *The British General Election of 1950,* Macmillan, 1951, 353 pp.
Ranney, Austin, "Inter-Constituency Movement of British Parliamentary Candidates, 1951–1959," *APSR,* 36(1), 1964:36-45.
———, *Pathways to Parliament, Candidate Selection in Britain,* Wisconsin UP, 1965, 298 pp.
Richards, Peter G., *Patronage in British Government,* Allen & Unwin, London, 1963, 284 pp.
Rose, Richard, *Influencing Voters, A Study of Campaign Rationality,* St Martin's, 1967, 330 pp.
Schofield, A. Norman, *Parliamentary Elections,* 3rd ed., Shaw, London, 1959, 1021 pp.
Trenaman, Joseph and D. McQuail, *Television and the Political Image, A Study of the Impact of Television on the 1959 General Election,* Methuen, London, 1961, 287 pp.

Chapter 4. THE BRITISH PARLIAMENT

Abraham, L. A. and S. C. Hawtrey, *A Parliamentary Dictionary,* 2nd ed., Butterworth, London, 1965, 241 pp.
Advisory Committees in British Government, A PEP Report, Allen & Unwin, London, 1960, 228 pp.
Allen, Sir Carleton Kemp, *Law and Orders,* 3rd ed., Stevens, London, 1965, 412 pp.
Bailey, Sydney D., ed., *The Future of the House of Lords,* Praeger, 1954, 180 pp.
———, "Parliamentary Diplomacy," *Parl. Aff.,* 16(3), Summer 1963:308-14.
Barker, Anthony, "Parliamentary Studies 1961–1965, A Bibliography and Comment," *PQ,* 36(3), July–Sept. 1965:347-59.
Boardmann, Harry, *The Glory of Parliament,* Allen & Unwin, London, 1960, 208 pp.
Body, Richard, "Unofficial Committees in the House of Commons," *Parl. Aff.,* 11(3), Summer 1958:295-320.
Bossom, Alfred C., Lord Bossom of Maidstone, *Our House, An Introduction to Parliamentary Procedure,* rev. ed., Barrie-Rockliff, London, 1965, 207 pp, pbk.
Bromhead, Peter A., *The House of Lords and Contemporary Politics, 1911–1957,* Routledge, London, 1958, 283 pp.
———, "Mr. Wedgewood Benn, the Peerage and the Constitution," *Parl. Aff.,* 14(4), Autumn 1961:493-506.
———, "Parliament and the Press," *Parl. Aff.,* 16(3), Summer 1963:279-92.
———, *Private Members' Bills in the British Parliament,* Routledge, London, 1956, 216 pp.

Campion, Lord, *An Introduction to the Procedure of the House of Commons*, 3rd ed., St Martin's, 1958, 350 pp.

Cawthorne, Graham, *Mr. Speaker, Sir*, Cleaver-Hume, London, 1952, 164 pp.

Chester, D. N. and Nona Bowring, *Questions in Parliament*, Oxford UP, 1962, 335 pp.

Chilston, Viscount, *The Political Life and Times of Aretas Akers-Douglas, First Viscount Chilston*, Routledge, London, 1961, 383 pp.

Chubb, Basil, *The Control of Public Expenditure, Financial Committees of the House of Commons*, Oxford UP, 1952, 291 pp.

Conference on the Reform of the Second Chamber, 1918 (The Bryce Report), *Cmd. 9038*, HMSO, 1918.

Coombes, David, *The Member of Parliament and the Administration, The Case of the Select Committee on Nationalized Industries*, Allen & Unwin, London, 1966, 221 pp.

Crick, Bernard, *The Reform of Parliament, The Crisis of British Government in the 1960's*, Weidenfeld & Nicolson, London, 1964, 274 pp.

De Smith, S. A., "Reform of the Lords. Report of the Joint Committee on House of Lords Reform," *MLR*, 26(3), May 1963:288–92.

Eaves, John, Jr., *Emergency Powers and the Parliamentary Watchdog, Parliament and the Executive in Great Britain, 1939–1951*, Hansard, London, 1957, 208 pp.

Finer, Samuel Edward et al., *Backbench Opinion in the House of Commons, 1955–1959*, Pergamon, London, 1961, 219 pp.

Ford, P. and G., *A Breviate of Parliamentary Papers*, Blackwell, Oxford, 3 vols: *The Foundation of the Welfare State, 1900–1916*, 1957, 470 pp; *Inter-War Period, 1917–1939*, 1951, 571 pp; *War and Reconstruction, 1940–1954*, 1961, 515 pp.

———, *A Guide to Parliamentary Papers, What They Are, How to Find Them, How to Use Them*, new ed., Blackwell, Oxford, 1956, 79 pp.

———, *Select List of British Parliamentary Papers, 1833–1899*, Blackwell, Oxford, 1953, 165 pp.

Goldsworthy, David, "The Debate on a Parliamentary Committee for Colonial Affairs," *Parl. Aff.*, 19(2), Spring 1966:191–207.

Gordon, Strathearn, *Our Parliament*, 6th ed., Cassell, London, 1964, 256 pp.

Hampton, William, "Parliament and the Civil Service," *Parl. Aff.*, 17(4), Autumn 1964:430–38.

Hanson, A. H., *Parliament and Public Ownership*, Cassell, London, 1961, 248 pp.

——— and H. V. Wiseman, *Parliament at Work, A Case-Book of Parliamentary Procedure*, Stevens, London, 1962, 358 pp.

Heasman, D. J., "Parliamentary Paths to High Office," *Parl. Aff.*, 16(3), Summer 1963:315–30.

Herbert, Sir Alan Patrick, *The Ayes Have It*, Methuen, London, 1937, 240 pp.

———, *Independent Member*, Doubleday, 1951, 363 pp.

Hill, Andrew and Anthony Wichelow, *What's Wrong with Parliament?* Penguin, 1964, 102 pp.

House of Commons, issued after each election, The Times, London.

Howarth, Patrick, *Questions in the House, The History of a Unique British Institution*, Lane, London, 1956, 220 pp.

Humberstone, Thomas Lloyd, *University Representation*, Hutchinson, London, 1951, 128 pp.

Ilbert, Sir Courtenay, rev. by Sir Cecil Carr, *Parliament, Its History, Constitution and Practice*, Oxford UP, 1956, 230 pp.

James, Robert Rhodes, *An Introduction to the House of Commons*, Collins, London, 1961, 160 pp.

Jennings, Sir Ivor, *Parliament*, 2nd ed., Cambridge UP, 1959, 587 pp.

Johnson, N., *Parliament and Administration, the Estimates Committee, 1945–1965*, 1966, 200 pp.

Justice, *The Citizen and the Administration, The Redress of Grievances* (The Whyatt Report), Stevens, London, 1961, 104 pp.

Keeton, G. W., *The Passing of Parliament*, 2nd ed., Benn, London, 1954, 218 pp.

Kersell, John E., *Parliamentary Supervision of Delegated Legislation*, Stevens, London, 1960, 178 pp.

King, Horace M., *Parliament and Freedom*, new ed., Murray, London, 1962, 144 pp.

Laundy, Philip, *The Office of Speaker*, Cassell, London, 1964, 488 pp.

MacKenzie, Kenneth R., *The English Parliament*, rev. ed., Penguin, 1959, 208 pp.

Mann, Jean, *Women in Parliament*, Odhams, London, 1962, 256 pp.

Manual of Procedure in Public Business, 8th ed. (only official work on parliamentary procedure), HMSO, 1951.

May, Sir Thomas Erskine, *Treatise on the Law, Privileges, Proceedings and Usage of Parliament*, 17th ed., Butterworth, London, 1964, 1145 pp.

Milne, R. S. and H. C. MacKenzie, *Marginal Seat, 1955*, Hansard, London, 1958, 210 pp.

Minney, Rubeigh James, *Viscount Addison, Leader of the Lords*, Odhams, London, 1958, 256 pp.

Morrison, Lord of Lambeth, Herbert Stanley, *Government and Parliament, A Survey from the Inside*, 3rd ed., Oxford UP, 1964, 384 pp, pbk.

"An Ombudsman and Parliamentary Reform," *PQ*, 37(1), Jan.–Mar. 1966:1–7.

Palmer, John, *Government and Parliament in Britain, A Bibliography*, 2nd ed. rev. and enl., Hansard, London, 1964, 51 pp.

Parliamentary Reforms, A Survey of Suggested Reforms Covering the Period from 1933–1960, Cassell, London, 1961, 193 pp.

Pring, David, "Standing Committees in the House of Commons," *PA*, Summer 1958:303–17.

Report from the Select Committee on *Delegated Legislation*, HMSO, 1953, 183 pp.

Richards, Peter G., *Honourable Members, A Study of the British Backbencher*, new ed., Faber, London, 1964, 294 pp.

Ross, James F. S., *Parliamentary Representation*, Yale UP, 1944, 245 pp.

Roth, Andrew, *The Business Background of MPs*, Parliamentary Profile Services, 1965, 420 pp, pbk.

Seymour-Ure, Colin, "Parliamentary Privilege and

Broadcasting," *Parl. Aff.*, 16(4), Autumn 1963:411–18.

Seymour-Ure, Colin, "The Misuse of the Question of Privilege in the 1964–1965 Session of Parliament," *Parl. Aff.*, 18(4), Autumn 1965:380–88.

Taylor, Eric, *The House of Commons at Work*, 5th ed., Penguin, 1964, 256 pp.

Utley, Thomas Edwin, *Occasion for Ombudsman, Is a Grievance Man Necessary for Britain?* Christopher Johnson, London, 1961, 160 pp.

Walkland, S. A., "Science and Parliament, The Origins and Influence of the Parliamentary and Scientific Committee," *Parl. Aff.*, 17(3), Summer 1964:308–20 and 17(4), Autumn 1964:389–402.

———, "Science and Parliament, The Role of the Select Committees of the House of Commons," *Parl. Aff.*, 18(3), Summer 1965:266–78.

Weare, Vincent, "The House of Lords, Prophecy and Fulfilment," *Parl. Aff.*, 18(4), Autumn 1964:422–33.

Weston, Corime C., *English Constitutional Theory and the House of Lords*, Routledge, London, 1965, 304 pp.

Wheare, Kenneth C., *Government by Committee, An Essay on the British Constitution*, Oxford UP, 1955, 264 pp.

Wilding, Norman and Philip Laundy, *An Encyclopedia of Parliament*, rev. ed., Praeger, 1961, 797 pp.

Winterton, Lord, *Orders of the Day*, Cassell, London, 1954, 369 pp.

Wiseman, H. V., *Parliament and the Executive, An Analysis with Readings*, Routledge, London, 1966, 271 pp, pbk.

———, "Procedure: The House of Commons and the Select Committee," *Parl. Aff.*, 13(2), Spring 1960: 236–48.

Wolf-Phillips, Leslie, "Parliamentary Divisions and Proxy Voting," *Parl. Aff.*, 18(4), Autumn 1965:415–21.

Yardley, D. C. M., "The Work and Status of the Parliamentary Agent," *Parl. Aff.*, 18(2), Spring 1965: 162–66.

Young, Roland, *The British Parliament*, Faber, London, 1962, 259 pp.

PRESSURE GROUPS

Christoph, James B., *Capital Punishment and British Politics, The British Movement to Abolish the Death Penalty, 1955–1957*, Allen & Unwin, London, 1962, 202 pp.

Eckstein, H., *Pressure Group Politics, The Case of the British Medical Association*, Allen & Unwin, London, 1960, 168 pp.

Finer, S. E., *Anonymous Empire, A Study of the Lobby in Great Britain*, rev. ed., Pall Mall, London, 1966, 173 pp, pbk.

Potter, A. M., *Organised Groups in British National Politics*, Faber, London, 1961, 396 pp.

Stewart, J. D., *British Pressure Groups, Their Role in Relation to the House of Commons*, Oxford UP, 1958, 273 pp.

Wilson, H. H., *Pressure Group, The Campaign for Commercial Television*, Secker & Warburg, London, 1961, 232 pp.

Wootton, Graham, *The Politics of Influence, British Ex-Servicemen, Cabinet Decisions and Cultural Change, 1917–1957*, Routledge & Kegan Paul, London, 1963, 301 pp.

Chapter 5. THE BRITISH CABINET, PRIME MINISTER, AND MONARCH

Altrincham, Lord et al., *Is the Monarchy Perfect?* Calder, London, 1958, 151 pp.

Attlee, Clement R., *As It Happened*, Heinemann, London, 1954, 227 pp.

Baldwin, A. W., *My Father, The True Story*, Essential, London, 1956, 360 pp.

Bardens, Dennis, *Portrait of a Statesman, The Personal Life Story of Sir Anthony Eden*, Phil. Lib., 1956, 326 pp.

Beaverbrook, Lord, *The Abdication of King Edward VIII*, ed. by Allan John Percival Taylor, Hamilton, London, 1966, 122 pp.

Benemy, F. W. G., *The Elected Monarch, The Development of the Power of the Prime Minister*, Harrap, London, 1965, 284 pp.

———, *The Queen Reigns, She Does Not Rule*, Harrap, 1963, 182 pp.

Beveridge, Lord, *Power and Influence*, Hodder & Stoughton, London, 1953, 448 pp.

Birkenhead, 2nd Earl of, *The Life of Lord Halifax*, Hamilton, London, 1965, 626 pp.

Bowle, John, *Viscount Samuel*, Gollancz, London, 1957, 367 pp.

Brandon, Henry, *Full Circle, The Memoirs of Anthony Eden*, Houghton Mifflin, 1960, 676 pp.

Brome, Vincent, *Clement Attlee*, Lincolns-Praeger, London, 1949, 92 pp.

Bromhead, Peter, "The Peerage Act and the New Prime Minister," *Parl. Aff.*, 17(1), Winter 1963–64:57–64.

Bullock, Alan Louis C., *The Life and Times of Ernest Bevin*, Vol. 1, *Trade Union Leader 1881–1940*, Heinemann, London, 1960, 685 pp.

Campbell-Johnson, Alan, *Eden, The Making of a Statesman*, Ives Washburn, 1939, 362 pp.

———, *Sir Anthony Eden, A Biography*, McGraw-Hill, 1955, 272 pp.

Carter, Byrum E., *The Office of Prime Minister*, Princeton UP, 1956, 364 pp.

Carter, Lady Violet Bonham, *Winston Churchill, An Intimate Portrait*, Harcourt, Brace & World, 1965, 413 pp.

Chester, D. N., "Who Governs Britain?" *Parl. Aff.*, 15(4), Autumn 1962:511–18.

Churchill, Randolph S., *They Serve the Queen*, Hutchinson, London, 1953, 68 pp.

Cooke, Colin, *The Life of Richard Stafford Cripps*, Hodder & Stoughton, London, 1957, 414 pp.

Daalder, Hans, *Cabinet Reform in Britain, 1914–1963*, Stanford UP, 1963, 381 pp.

Dalton, Hugh, *Memoirs*, Muller, London, 3 vols: *Call Back Yesterday, 1887–1931*, 1953, 330 pp; *The Fateful Years, 1931–1945*, 1957, 493 pp; *High Tide and After, 1945–1960*, 1962, 453 pp.

De Mendelssohn, Peter, *The Age of Churchill, Heritage and Adventure, 1874–1911*, Knopf, 1961, 676 pp.

Eden, Sir Anthony (Earl of Avon), *Memoirs*, Houghton Mifflin, 2 vols: *Full Circle, 1951–1957*, 1960, 676 pp; *The Reckoning*, 1965, 704 pp.

Ehrman, John, *Cabinet Government and War, 1890–1940*, Cambridge UP, 1958, 138 pp.

Feiling, Keith, *The Life of Neville Chamberlain*, Macmillan, 1946, 475 pp.

Fletcher, Ifan Kyrle, *The British Court, Its Traditions and Ceremonial*, Cassell, London, 1953, 131 pp.

Forsey, Eugene A., *The Royal Power of Dissolution in the British Commonwealth*, Oxford UP, 1943, 316 pp.

Gash, Norman, *Mr. Secretary Peel*, Longmans, London, 1961, 707 pp.

Halifax, Earl of, *Fullness of Days*, Collins, London, 1957, 319 pp.

Heasman, D. J., "The Prime Minister and the Cabinet," *Parl. Aff.*, 15(4), Autumn 1962:461–84.

Hughes, Emrys, *Macmillan, Portrait of a Politician*, Allen & Unwin, London, 1962, 256 pp.

James, Robert Rhodes, *Rosebery*, Weidenfeld & Nicolson, London, 1963, 548 pp.

Jenkins, Roy, *Asquith, Portrait of a Man and an Era*, Chilmark P, 1965, 572 pp.

———, *Mr. Attlee*, Heinemann, London, 1948, 266 pp.

Jennings, Sir Ivor, *Cabinet Government*, 3rd ed., Cambridge UP, 1959, 587 pp.

———, *Constitutional Laws of the Commonwealth*, Vol. 1, *The Monarchies*, Oxford UP, 1957, 496 pp.

Jones, G. W., "The Prime Minister's Power," *Parl. Aff.*, 18(2), Spring 1965:167–85.

Jones, Thomas, *A Diary with Letters, 1931–1950*, Oxford UP, 1954, 582 pp.

———, *Lloyd George*, Harvard UP, 1951, 330 pp.

Keith, A. Berriedale, *The British Cabinet System*, 2nd ed., rev. by H. H. Gibbs, Stevens, London, 1952, 466 pp.

King, Mark M., *Aneurin Bevin, Cautious Rebel*, Thomas Yoseloff, London, 1961, 316 pp.

Mackintosh, John P., *The British Cabinet*, Stevens, London, 1962, 546 pp.

Macleod, Iain, *Neville Chamberlain*, Atheneum, 1962, 319 pp.

Macmillan, Harold, *Winds of Change, 1914–1939*, Harper, 1966, 584 pp.

Magnus, Philip, *King Edward the Seventh*, Dutton, 1964, 528 pp.

Martin, Kingsley, *The Crown and the Establishment*, Penguin, 1963, 192 pp.

Morrah, Dermont, *The Work of the Queen*, Kimber, London, 1958, 191 pp.

Morrison, Herbert, Lord of Lambeth, *An Autobiography*, Odhams, London, 1960, 336 pp.

Nicolson, Sir Harold G., *Curzon, The Last Phase, 1919–1925*, Harcourt, Brace & World, 1939, 416 pp.

———, *King George the Fifth, His Life and Reign*, Doubleday, 1953, 570 pp.

———, *Monarchy*, Weidenfeld & Nicolson, London, 1962, 335 pp.

Norwich, Alfred Duff Cooper, Viscount, *Old Men Forget, An Autobiography*, Hart-Davis, London, 1953, 399 pp.

Owen, Frank, *Tempestuous Journey, Lloyd George, His Life and Times*, McGraw-Hill, 1955, 756 pp.

Petrie, Sir Charles Alexander, *The Modern British Monarchy*, Eyre & Spottiswoode, London, 1961, 228 pp.

———, *The Powers Behind the Prime Ministers*, MacGibbon & Kee, London, 1958, 190 pp.

Pope-Hennessey, James, *Queen Mary*, Allen & Unwin, London, 1960, 685 pp.

Ratcliff, Edward C., *The Coronation Service of Her Majesty Queen Elizabeth II*, Cambridge UP, 1953, 79 pp.

Report of the Machinery of Government Committee, Cmd. 9230, HMSO, 1918 (Haldane).

Salter, Sir Arthur, *Personality in Politics*, Faber, London, 1947, 253 pp.

Shinwell, Emanuel, *Conflict Without Malice, An Autobiography*, Odhams, London, 1955, 252 pp.

Shrimsley, Anthony, *The First Hundred Days of Harold Wilson*, Praeger, 1965, 162 pp.

Southgate, Donald, *"The Most English Prime Minister," The Policies and Politics of Palmerston*, Macmillan, 1966, 647 pp.

Templewood, Viscount, *Nine Troubled Years*, Collins, London, 1954, 448 pp.

Wheeler-Bennett, Sir John W., *King George VI, His Life and Reign*, Macmillan, 1958, 891 pp.

Whitehall and Beyond, Conversations of Norman Hunt with Jo Grimond, Enoch Powell and Harold Wilson, BBC, 1964, 71 pp.

Williams, Sir Francis, *A Prime Minister Remembers, The War and Post-War Memoirs of the Rt. Hon. Earl Attlee*, Heinemann, London, 1961, 264 pp.

Willson, F. M. G., "The Routes of Entry of New Members of the British Cabinet, 1868–1958," *PS*, 7(3), Oct. 1959:222–32.

Wilson, Harold, *Purpose in Politics*, Houghton Mifflin, 1965, 270 pp.

Young, Kenneth, *Arthur James Balfour*, Bell, London, 1963, 542 pp.

Chapter 6. THE BRITISH ADMINISTRATION: NATIONAL AND LOCAL

NATIONAL ADMINISTRATION

The Accountability of Government Departments, rev. ed., Administrative Staff College, 1963.

The Administrators, Fabian, London, June 1964, 45 pp.

Beer, Samuel H., *Treasury Control, The Coordination of Financial and Economic Policy in Great Britain*, 2nd ed., Oxford UP, 1957, 138 pp.

Beveridge, Sir William Henry, *Full Employment in a Free Society*, Norton, 1945, 429 pp.

British Public Administration, Select Bibliography, RIPA, London, 1963, 22 pp.

Brittain, Sir Herbert, *The British Budgetary System*, Macmillan, 1959, 320 pp.

Brittan, Samuel, *The Treasury Under the Tories, 1951–1964*, Penguin, 1964, 374 pp.

Chapman, Brian, *British Government Observed, Some European Reflections*, Allen & Unwin, London, 1963, 64 pp, pbk.

Clarke, John Joseph, *Outlines of Central Government, Including the Judicial System of England*, 14th ed., Pitman, London, 1965, 275 pp.

Coatman, John, *Police*, Oxford UP, 1959, 248 pp.

Control of Public Expenditure, Plowden Report, *Cmd. 1432*, HMSO, June 9, 1961.

Economic Survey, Annual since 1947, *Cmd.*, HMSO.

Gladden, Edgar N., *The Essentials of Public Administration*, 3rd ed., Staples, London, 1964, 288 pp.

————, *An Introduction to Public Administration*, 4th ed., 1966, 260 pp.

Gowing, Margaret M., *Britain and Atomic Energy, 1939–1945*, St Martin's, 1964, 464 pp.

"Indicative Planning," *PQ*, 36(2), Apr.–June 1965:125–30.

Johnson, Franklyn A., *Defence by Committee, The British Committee of Imperial Defence, 1885–1959*, Oxford UP, 1960, 416 pp.

"The Machinery for Economic Planning," *Pub. Ad.*, 44, Spring 1966:1–72.

Mitchell, Joan, "The Functions of the National Economic Development Council," *PQ*, 34(4), Oct.–Dec. 1963:354–65.

Peacock, Alan T. and Jack Wiseman, *The Growth of Public Expenditure in the United Kingdom*, Princeton UP, 1962, 244 pp.

Political and Economic Planning, *French Planning, Some Lessons for Britain*, PEP, 1963, 75 pp.

————, *Advisory Committees in British Government*, Allen & Unwin, London, 1960, 228 pp.

Robinson, Howard, *Britain's Post Office, A History of Development from Beginning to Present Day*, Oxford UP, 1953, 299 pp.

Rowley, C. K., *The British Monopolies Commission*, Allen & Unwin, London, 1966, 394 pp.

Shonfield, Andrew, *British Economic Policy Since the War*, Penguin, 1958, 288 pp.

Sisson, C. H., *The Spirit of British Administration and Some European Comparisons*, Faber, London, 1959, 162 pp.

Walker, Gilbert, *Economic Planning by Programme and Control in Great Britain*, Heinemann, London, 1957, 175 pp.

————, *The Organization of British Central Government, 1914–1965*, Allen & Unwin, London, 1957, 457 pp.

Williams, Alan, *Public Finance and Budgetary Policy*, Allen & Unwin, London, 1963, 283 pp, pbk.

Willson, F. M. G., "The Organization of British Central Government, 1955–1961," *Pub. Ad.*, 40(2), Summer 1962:156–206.

Wiseman, H. Victor, "Regional Government in the United Kingdom," *Parl. Aff.*, 19(1), Winter 1965–66:56–82.

Zupnick, Elliot, *Britain's Postwar Dollar Problem*, Columbia UP, 1957, 256 pp.

New Whitehall Series, under the auspices of the RIPA, studies of individual departments by senior civil servants, Allen & Unwin, London:

The Home Office, Sir Frank Newsam, 1954, 224 pp.

The Foreign Office, Lord Strang, 1955, 226 pp.

The Colonial Office, Sir Charles Jeffries, 1956, 222 pp.

The Ministry of Works, Sir Harold Emmerson, 1956, 171 pp.

The Scottish Office and Other Scottish Government Departments, Sir David Milne, 1957, 232 pp.

The Ministry of Pensions and National Insurance, Sir Geoffrey King, 1958, 163 pp.

The Ministry of Transport and Civil Aviation, Sir Gilmour Jenkins, 1959, 231 pp.

The Ministry of Labour and National Service, Sir Godfrey Ince, 1960, 215 pp.

The Ministry of Agriculture, Fisheries and Food, Sir John Winnifrith, 1962, 224 pp.

Her Majesty's Customs and Excise, Sir James Crombie, 1962, 208 pp.

The Department of Scientific and Industrial Research, Sir Harry Melville, 1962, 196 pp.

The Treasury, Lord Bridges, 1964, 248 pp.

The Inland Revenue, Alexander Johnston, 1965, 201 pp.

PUBLIC ENTERPRISE

Baldwin, George B., *Beyond Nationalization, The Labour Problems of British Coal*, Harvard UP, 1956, 348 pp.

————, "Nationalisation in Britain, A Sobering Decade," *Annals*, 310, March 1957:39–54.

Barry, Eldon E., *Nationalization in British Politics*, Stanford UP, 1965, 396 pp.

Chester, D. N., *The Nationalised Industries, An Analysis of the Statutory Provisions*, 2nd ed., Allen & Unwin, London, 1951, 93 pp.

Dow, J. C. R., *The Management of the British Economy, 1945–1960*, Cambridge UP, 1966, 462 pp.

Goodman, Edward, *Forms of Public Control and Ownership*, Christophers, London, 1952, 142 pp.

Grove, J. W., *Government and Industry in Britain*, Longmans, London, 1962, 514 pp.

Hanson, A. H., *Managerial Problems in Public Enterprise*, Asia Pub. House, 1962, 148 pp.

————, *Parliament and Public Ownership*, 2nd ed., Cassell, London, 1962, 248 pp.

————, *Nationalisation, A Book of Readings*, Allen & Unwin, London, 1963, 475 pp.

Henriques, F. N. Dennis and C. Slaughter, *Coal Is Our Life*, McClelland, London, 1956, 256 pp.

Keeling, B. S. and A. E. G. Wright, *The Development of the Modern British Steel Industry*, Longmans, London, 1965, 210 pp.

Kelf-Cohen, Reuben, *Nationalisation in Britain, The End of a Dogma*, 2nd ed., St Martin's, 1961, 380 pp.

Labour Research Dept., *The Case for Nationalisation and Control*, Transport House, London, 1945, 61 pp.

Management Under Nationalisation: Studies in Decentralisation, Acton Society, London, 1953, 79 pp.

Monopolies and Restrictive Practices Commission, *Collective Discrimination*, Cmd. 9504, HMSO, 1955.

Nationalised Industry, Nos. 1–12, ed. by G. R. Taylor, Acton Society, London, 1950–52.

Pritchard, E. P., "The Responsibility of the Nationalised Industries to Parliament," *Parl. Aff.*, 17(4), Autumn 1964:439–49.

Robson, William A., *Nationalized Industry and Public Ownership*, rev. ed., Allen & Unwin, London, 1962, 567 pp.

Rogow, Arnold A., with assistance of P. Shore, *The*

Labour Government and British Industry, 1945–51, Cornell UP, 1955, 204 pp.

Saxena, S. K., *Nationalisation and Industrial Conflict, Example of British Coal Mining,* Nijhoff, The Hague, 1955, 185 pp.

Self, Sir Albert Henry and Elizabeth M. Watson, *Electricity Supply in Great Britain,* Allen & Unwin, London, 1952, 219 pp.

Shanks, Michael, ed., *Lessons of Public Enterprise,* Fabian, London, 1963, 314 pp.

Spero, Sertling D., *Labor Relations in British Nationalized Industry,* New York UP, 1955, 83 pp.

Weiner, Herbert E., *British Labor and Public Ownership,* Pub. Aff., 1960, 111 pp.

LOCAL GOVERNMENT

Benham, H., *Two Cheers for the Town Hall,* Hutchinson, London, 1964, 288 pp.

Bentwich, Helen, *Our Councils, The Story of Local Government,* Routledge, London, 1962, 136 pp.

Birch, A. H., *Small-Town Politics,* Oxford UP, 1959, 199 pp.

Clarke, John Joseph, *A History of Local Government of the United Kingdom,* Jenkins, London, 1955, 303 pp.

———, *The Local Government of the United Kingdom,* 15th ed., Pitman, London, 1956, 684 pp.

———, *Outlines of Local Government of the United Kingdom,* 19th ed., Pitman, London, 1960, 347 pp.

Cole, Margaret, *Servant of the Country,* Dobson, London, 1956, 200 pp.

Drummond, J. M. (rev. by W. A. C. Kitching), *The Finance of Local Government (England and Wales),* 2nd rev. ed., Allen & Unwin, London, 1962, 206 pp.

Eyre, Frank and E. C. R. Hadfield, *The Fire Service,* 2nd ed., Oxford UP, 1953, 156 pp.

Griffith, J. A. G., *Central Departments and Local Authorities,* Allen & Unwin, London, 1966, 574 pp.

Hart, Sir William Edward, *Introduction to the Law of Local Government and Administration,* 7th ed., Butterworth, London, 1962, 727 pp.

Headrick, T. E., *The Town Clerk in English Local Government,* Allen & Unwin, London, 1962, 232 pp.

Jackson, Richard Meredith, *The Machinery of Local Government,* new ed., Penguin, 1959, 222 pp.

Jackson, William Eric, *Local Government in England and Wales,* 3rd ed., Pelican, 1963, 222 pp.

Jennings, Sir Ivor, *The Principles of Local Government Law,* 4th ed., U London P, 1960, 316 pp.

"Local Government in Great Britain, Symposium," *PQ,* 37(2), Apr.-June 1966:121–205.

"Local Government Today and Tomorrow," *PQ,* Apr.–June 1966, special issue.

Lofts, Dudley, ed., *Local Government Today and Tomorrow,* Municipal Journal, London, 1963, 128 pp.

Marshall, A. H., *Financial Administration in Local Government,* Allen & Unwin, London, 1960, 392 pp.

———, *Local Government in the Modern World,* Athlone, London, 1965, 28 pp.

Maud, Sir John and S. E. Finer, *Local Government in England and Wales,* 2nd ed., Oxford UP, 1953, 230 pp.

Morrison, Herbert, *How London Is Governed,* 2nd ed., Barrie, London, 1949, 191 pp.

Redlich, Josef and Francis W. Hirst, *The History of Local Government in England,* ed. by Brian Keith-Lucas, St Martin's, 1959, 261 pp.

Report of the Royal Commission on Local Government in Greater London, Cmd. 1164, HMSO, 1960.

Richards, Peter G., *Delegation in Local Government,* Allen & Unwin, London, 1957, 184 pp.

Robson, William A., *The Government and Misgovernment of London,* Macmillan, 1958, 518 pp.

———, *Local Government in Crisis,* Allen & Unwin, London, 1966, 160 pp, pbk.

Self, Peter, "The Herbert Report and the Values of Local Government," *PS,* 10(2), June 1962:146–62.

Smallwood, Frank, *Greater London, The Politics of Metropolitan Reform,* Bobbs-Merrill, 1965, 324 pp, pbk.

Warren, John Herbert, *The English Local Government System,* 7th ed., Allen & Unwin, London, 1963, 192 pp.

———, *Municipal Administration,* Pitman, London, 1958, 254 pp.

Webb, Sidney and Beatrice, *The Development of English Local Government, 1689–1835,* Oxford UP, 1963, 194 pp.

PUBLIC SERVICE

Abramovitz, Moses and Vera Eliasberg, *The Growth of Public Employment in Great Britain,* Princeton UP, 1957, 151 pp.

Bontecou, Eleanor, "The English Policy as to Communists and Fascists in the Civil Service," *CLR,* 51(5), May 1951:564–86.

Bridges, Lord, *Portrait of a Profession, The Civil Service Tradition,* Cambridge UP, 1953, 33 pp.

Brown, R. Douglas, *The Battle of Crichel Down,* Lane, London, 1955, 192 pp.

Burns, Sir Alan Cuthbert, *Colonial Civil Servant,* Allen & Unwin, London, 1949, 339 pp.

Campbell, G. A., *The Civil Service in Britain,* 2nd ed., Duckworth, London, 1965, 256 pp.

Committee on the Political Activities of Civil Servants, Cmd. 7718, HMSO, June 1949, 717 pp.

Craig, Sir John, *A History of Red Tape,* Macdonald & Evans, London, 1955, 221 pp.

Dale, Harold E., *The Higher Civil Service,* Oxford UP, 1941, 232 pp.

Denning, Lord, *The Profumo–Christine Keeler Affair, Report to Parliament,* Popular Lib., 1963, 174 pp, pbk.

Dunnill, Frank, *The Civil Service, Some Human Aspects,* Allen & Unwin, London, 1956, 226 pp.

Fabian Society, *The Reform of the Higher Civil Service, A Report by a Special Committee,* Gollancz, London, 1947, 60 pp.

Foot, M. R. D., *SOE in France,* HMSO, 1966, 578 pp.

Gladden, Edgar N., *British Public Service Administration,* Staples, London, 1961, 328 pp.

———, "The Estimates Committee Looks at the Civil Service," *Parl. Aff.,* 19(2), Spring 1966:233–40.

Great Britain, Treasury, *Political Activities of Civil Servants, Cmd. 8783,* HMSO, 1953.

Grunbaum, Werner F., "The British Security Program, 1948–1958," *WPQ*, 8(3), Sept. 1960:764–80.

Hampton, William, "Parliament and the Civil Service," *Parl. Aff.*, Autumn 1964:430–38.

Heussler, Robert, *Yesterday's Rulers: The Making of the British Colonial Service*, Syracuse UP, 1963, 260 pp.

Irving, Clive, Ron Hall and Jeremy Wallington, *Scandal '63, A Study of the Profumo Affair*, Heinemann, London, 1963, 227 pp, pbk.

Kelsall, R. K., *Higher Civil Servants in Britain, from 1870 to the Present Day*, Routledge, London, 1955, 233 pp.

Kingsley, John D., *Representative Bureaucracy, An Interpretation of the British Civil Service*, Allen & Unwin, London, 1938, 218 pp.

Ministry of Agriculture and Fisheries, *Public Inquiry into the Disposal of Land at Crichel Down*, Cmd. 176, HMSO, 1954, 33 pp.

Richards, Peter G., *Patronage in British Government*, Toronto UP, 1963, 285 pp.

Robinton, Madeline R., "The Lynskey Tribunal, The British Method of Dealing with Political Corruption," *PSQ*, 68(1), Mar. 1953:109–24.

Robson, William A., ed., *The Civil Service in Great Britain and France*, Hogarth, London, 1956, 191 pp.

Salter, Lord, *Memoirs of a Public Servant*, Faber, London, 1961, 355 pp.

Scott, Sir Harold, *Your Obedient Servant*, Deutsch, London, 1959, 192 pp.

Walker, N., *Morale in the Civil Service, A Study of the Desk Worker*, Edinburgh UP, 1961, 302 pp.

Wheare, Kenneth D., *The Civil Service in the Constitution*, Athlone, London, 1956, 34 pp.

White, L. D., *Whitley Councils in the British Civil Service, A Study in Conciliation and Arbitration*, U Chicago P, 1933, 375 pp.

Willson, F. M. G., *Administrators in Action*, Vol. 1, Allen & Unwin, London, 1961, 350 pp.

Wilson, H. H., *The Problem of Internal Security in Great Britain, 1948–1953*, Doubleday, 1954, 86 pp.

Young, Wayland, *The Profumo Affair, Aspects of Conservatism*, Penguin, 1963, 117 pp.

Chapter 7. ENGLISH LAW AND COURTS

Allen, Sir Carleton Kemp, *Law in the Making*, 6th ed., 1958, 684 pp., Oxford UP, 1961, 645 pp, pbk.

———, *The Queen's Peace*, Stevens, London, 1953, 192 pp.

Bow Group Report, *Scales of Justice*, CPC, London, 1962, 61 pp.

Cross, Rupert and P. Asterley Jones, *An Introduction to the Criminal Law*, 4th ed., Butterworth, London, 1959, 472 pp.

Denning, Sir Alfred, *The Road to Justice*, Stevens, London, 1955, 118 pp.

Devlin, Lord Patrick, *The Criminal Prosecution in England*, Yale UP, 1958, 150 pp.

———, "The Enforcement of Morals," *Proceedings of the British Academy*, 45, 1960:129–51.

———, *Trial by Jury*, Stevens, London, 1956, 187 pp.

Dicey, Albert V., *Law and Public Opinion in England*, Macmillan, 1962, 600 pp, pbk.

Evans, Peter, *Law and Disorder*, Secker & Warburg, London, 1956, 308 pp.

Fellman, David, *The Defendant's Rights Under English Law*, U Wisconsin P, 1966, 137 pp.

Friedmann, Wolfgang, *Law and Social Change in Contemporary Britain*, Stevens, London, 1951, 322 pp.

Gardiner, Gerald, *Capital Punishment as a Deterrent, and the Alternative*, Gollancz, London, 1956, 95 pp.

Geldart, William Martin et al., *Elements of English Law*, 6th ed., Oxford UP, 1959, 222 pp.

Giles, Francis T., *Criminal Law, A Short Introduction*, 3rd ed., Penguin, 1963, 300 pp.

Ginsberg, Morris, ed., *Law and Opinion in England in the Twentieth Century*, Stevens, London, 1959, 407 pp.

Goodhart, Arthur L., *English Law and the Moral Law*, Stevens, London, 1953, 151 pp.

Hanbury, Harold G., *Modern Equity*, 7th ed., Stevens, London, 1957, 683 pp.

Heuston, R. F. V., *Essays in Constitutional Law*, Stevens, London, 1961, 187 pp.

Holmes, Oliver Wendell, *Introduction to the Common Law*, rev. ed., Little, Brown, 1923, 422 pp.

James, Philip S., *Introduction to English Law*, 4th ed., rev. by K. J. LeDavies, Butterworth, London, 1959, 486 pp.

Jennings, Sir Ivor, *The Law and the Constitution*, 5th ed., U London P, 1959, 354 pp.

Keeton, George W. and G. Schwarzenberger, eds., *Current Legal Problems*, published annually, Stevens, London.

MacDermott, Lord, *Protection from Power Under English Law*, Stevens, London, 1957, 196 pp.

Pound, Roscoe, *Introduction to the Philosophy of Law*, 2nd ed., 1954, pbk.

———, *The Spirit of the Common Law*, Jones, 1921, 224 pp.

The United Kingdom, The Development of Its Laws and Constitutions, Part 1, *England, Wales, Northern Ireland, and the Isle of Man*, ed. by G. W. Keeton and D. Lloyd; Part 2, *Scotland*, by T. B. Smith, and *The Channel Islands*, by L. A. Sheridan, Stevens, London, 1955, 523 and 603 pp.

Vinogradoff, Sir Paul, *Common Sense in Law*, 3rd ed., Oxford UP, 1959, 192 pp.

Wade, E. C. S. and G. Godfrey Phillips, *Constitutional Law, An Outline of the Law and Practice of the Constitution, Including Central and Local Government and the Constitutional Relations of the British Commonwealth*, 6th ed., Longmans, London, 1960, 725 pp.

Watson, J. A. F., *British Juvenile Courts*, Longmans, London, 1950, 44 pp.

Williams, Glanville, *The Proof of Guilt, A Study of the English Criminal Trial*, Stevens, London, 1958, 326 pp.

Yardley, D. C. M., *Introduction to British Constitutional Law*, Butterworth, London, 1960, 151 pp.

———, "Parliament and Law Reform," *Parl. Aff.*, 18(1), Winter 1964–65:40–52.

JUDGES AND THE COURT SYSTEM

Archer, P., *The Queen's Courts,* Hamondsworth, London, 1956, 289 pp.

Edwards, J. Ll. J., *The Law Officers of the Crown, A Study of the Offices of Attorney-General and Solicitor-General of England with an Account of the Office of the Director of Public Prosecutions of England,* Sweet & Maxwell, London, 1964, 425 pp.

Fellman, David, *The Defendant's Rights Under English Law,* U Wisconsin P, 1966, 137 pp.

Fox, Lionel W., *English Prison and Borstal Systems,* Routledge, London, 1952, 479 pp.

Fry, Margery, *Arms of the Law,* Gollancz, London, 1951, 255 pp.

Giles, Francis T., *The Juvenile Courts, Their Work and Problems,* Allen & Unwin, London, 1946, 131 pp.

————, *The Magistrate Courts, What They Do, How They Do It and Why,* rev. ed., Penguin, 1955, 222 pp.

Hanbury, Harold G., *English Courts of Law,* 3rd ed., Stevens, 1963, 250 pp.

Heuston, R. F. V., *Lives of the Lord Chancellors, 1885–1940,* Oxford UP, 1964, 632 pp.

Hyde, H. Montgomery, *The Life of Lord Birkett of Ulverston,* Hamilton, London, 1964, 624 pp.

Jackson, Richard M., *The Machinery of Justice in England,* 4th ed., Cambridge UP, 1964, 455 pp.

Martienssen, Anthony, *Crime and the Police,* Penguin, 1953, 256 pp.

Page, Leo, *Justice of the Peace,* 2nd ed., Faber, London, 1947, 276 pp.

Radcliffe, G. R. Y. and Geoffrey Cross, *The English Legal System,* 4th ed., Butterworth, London, 1964, 460 pp.

Rubinstein, Ronald, *John Citizen and the Law,* 3rd ed., Penguin, 1952, 379 pp.

Shawcross, Lord, *Contempt of Court, A Report,* Stevens, London, 1959, 42 pp.

————, "The Office of the Attorney-General," *Parl. Aff.,* 7(4), Autumn 1954:380–92.

Slesser, Sir Henry, *The Administration of the Law,* Longmans, London, 1948, 244 pp.

Watson, John Arthur Fergus, *British Juvenile Courts,* rev. ed., Longmans, London, 1950, 40 pp.

Whitaker, Ben, *The Police,* Penguin, 1965, 224 pp.

Zander, Michael, "Reforming the English Legal Profession," *PQ,* 37(1), Jan.–March 1966:33–45.

ADMINISTRATIVE LAW AND TRIBUNALS

Allen, Sir Carleton Kemp, *Law and Orders, An Inquiry into the Nature and Scope of Delegated Legislation and Executive Powers in England,* 3rd ed., Stevens, London, 1965, 412 pp.

Griffith, John Aneurin Gran and Harry Street, *Principles of Administrative Law,* 3rd ed., Pitman, London, 1963, 339 pp.

Hewart, Lord George Gordon, *The New Despotism,* Cosmopolitan Book, 1945, 311 pp.

Phillips, O. Hood, *Constitutional and Administrative Law,* 3rd ed., Sweet & Maxwell, London, 1962, 855 pp.

Street, Harry, *Freedom, Individual and the Law,* Penguin, 1963, 316 pp.

Wade, Henry William Rawson, *Administrative Law,* Oxford UP, 1961, 290 pp.

Wheare, Kenneth C., *The Citizen and the Administration,* Stevens, London, 1961, 104 pp.

Chapter 8. GREAT BRITAIN: A NEW SOCIETY?

EDUCATION

Alexander, Sir William Picken, *Education in England, The National System, How It Works,* Newnes, London, 1964, 163 pp.

Armfelt, Roger, *The Structure of English Education,* Cohen & West, London, 1955, 207 pp.

Armstrong, Michael and Michael Young, *New Look at Comprehensive Schools,* Fabian, London, Jan. 1964, 19 pp.

Banks, Olive, *Workers and Technical Change,* Liverpool UP, 1960, 152 pp.

Baron, George A., *A Bibliographical Guide to the English Educational System,* enl. ed., Athlone, London, 1960, 97 pp.

Berdahl, Robert O., *British Universities and the State,* U California P, 1959, 229 pp.

Brand, John A., "Ministry Control and Local Autonomy in Education," *PQ,* 36(2), Apr.–June 1965:154–63.

Brogan, Colm, *The Educational Revolution,* Muller, London, 1955, 192 pp.

Butler, Lord, *The Education Act of 1944 and After,* Longmans, London, 1966, 24 pp.

Curtis, Stanley James, *History of Education in Great Britain,* 4th ed., U Tutorial P, London, 1957, 655 pp.

Dent, Harold Collett, *British Education,* rev. ed., Longmans, London, 1966, 70 pp.

————, *The Education Act, 1944, Regulations, Circulars, Later Acts,* 7th ed., U London P, 1958, 144 pp.

————, *The Educational System of England and Wales,* London UP, 1961, 224 pp.

————, *Universities in Transition,* Cohen & West, London, 1961, 176 pp.

Dodd, H. W., L. M. Hacker, and L. Rogers, *Government Assistance to the Universities in Great Britain,* Columbia UP, 1952, 133 pp.

15 to 18, Report of the Central Advisory Council for Education in England, The Crowther Report, 2 vols, HMSO, 1959 (reprinted 1962), 759 pp.

Half Our Future, Report of the Central Advisory Council for Education in England, The Newsom Report, HMSO, Aug. 1963, 299 pp.

Higher Education, Government Statement on the Robbins Report, Cmd. 2165, HMSO, 1963, 5 pp.

Higher Education, The Robbins Report, Cmd. 2154, HMSO, Oct. 1963, 335 pp.

Kamm, Josephine, *Hope Deferred, Girls' Education in English History,* Methuen, London, 1964, 332 pp.

Kelly, Thomas, *A History of Adult Education in Great Britain,* Liverpool UP, 1962, 352 pp.

Kneller, George F., *Higher Learning in Britain,* U California P, 1955, 300 pp.

Logan, Sir Douglas, *Universities: The Years of Challenge,* Cambridge UP, 1963, 40 pp.

Lowndes, G. A. N., *The British Educational System,* Hutchinson, London, 1960, 183 pp.

New Patterns for Primary Schools, Fabian, London, Sept. 1964, 25 pp.

Partridge, John, *Middle School, The Secondary Modern School,* Gollancz, London, 1966, 176 pp.

Payne, George Louis, *Britain's Scientific and Technological Manpower,* Stanford UP, 1960, 466 pp.

Pedley, Robin, *The Comprehensive School,* Penguin, 1963, 222 pp.

Peers, Robert A., *Adult Education,* Routledge, London, 1958, 365 pp.

Robbins, Lord, *The University in the Modern World,* Macmillan, London, 1966, 170 pp.

Simon, Brian, *Education and the Labour Movement, 1870–1920,* Lawrence & Wishart, London, 1965, 387 pp.

Smith, William Owen Lester, *Education in Great Britain,* 3rd ed., Oxford UP, 1958, 217 pp.

———, *Education, An Introductory Survey,* rev. ed., Penguin, 1965, 240 pp.

The Structure of Higher Education, Fabian, London, Oct. 1961, 20 pp.

Wells, M. M. and P. A. Taylor, *The New Law of Education,* 4th ed., Butterworth, London, 1954, 70 pp.

The Years of Crisis, Report of the Labour Party's Study Group on Higher Education, Transport House, 1963, 47 pp.

SOCIAL SERVICES

Abel-Smith, Brian and Kathleen Gales, *British Doctors at Home and Abroad,* Codicote, Herts, 1964.

——— and Richard M. Titmuss, *The Cost of the National Health Service in England and Wales,* Cambridge UP, 1955, 196 pp.

Beveridge, Janet, *Beveridge and His Plan,* Hodder & Stoughton, London, 1954, 239 pp.

Beveridge, Sir William Henry, *The Pillars of Security,* Macmillan, 1943, 248 pp.

The Beveridge Report, Social Insurance and Allied Services, Cmd. 6404, Macmillan, 1942, 249 pp.

Carter, Alan M., *The Redistribution of Income in Postwar Britain,* Yale UP, 1955, 229 pp.

Cartwright, Ann, *Human Relations and Hospital Care,* Routledge, London, 1964, 272 pp.

Choice in Welfare, Inst. Ec. Aff., 1965.

Clegg, Hugh Armstrong and Theodore Edward Chester, *Wage Policy and the Health Service,* Blackwell, London, 1957, 150 pp.

Eckstein, Harry, *The English Health Service, Its Origins, Structure and Achievements,* Harvard UP, 1959, 289 pp.

Farndale, W. A. J., *Trends in the National Health Service,* Pergamon, 1964, 423 pp.

The Field Work of the Family Doctor, The Gillie Report, HMSO, 1964.

Gemmill, Paul F., *Britain's Search for Health,* U Pennsylvania P, 1960, 170 pp.

Goldman, Peter, *The Welfare State,* Michael Joseph, London, 1964, 77 pp.

Hall, Mary Penelope, *The Social Services of Modern England,* 4th rev. ed., Routledge, London, 1946, 224 pp.

Harris, Robert W., *National Health Insurance in Great Britain, 1911–1946,* Allen & Unwin, London, 1946, 224 pp.

Jefferys, Margot, *An Anatomy of Social Welfare Services,* Michael Joseph, London, 1966, 371 pp.

Jewkes, John and Sylvia, *The Genesis of the British National Health Service,* Blackwell, Oxford, 1961, 68 pp.

Lindsey, Almont, *Socialized Medicine in England and Wales, The National Health Service, 1948–1961,* North Carolina UP, 1963, 561 pp.

Marsh, David C., *The Future of the Welfare State,* Penguin, 1965, 140 pp.

Marshall, T. H., *Social Policy,* Hutchinson, London, 1965, 192 pp.

Medical Staffing Structure in the Hospital Service, The Platt Report, HMSO, 1964.

Morris, Mary, *Voluntary Organizations and Social Progress,* Gollancz, London, 1955, 224 pp.

National Health Service, The "Guillebaud" Report, Cmd. 9663, HMSO, 1956.

Nelson, F. J. R., "The Machinery for Complaints in the National Health Service," *Pub. Ad.,* 43, Spring 1965:59–70.

Owen, David, *English Philanthropy, 1660–1960,* Harvard UP, 1965, 610 pp.

Pavitt, Laurie, *The Health of the Nation,* Fabian, London, 1964, 37 pp.

Raynes, Harold E., *Social Security in Britain, A History,* 2nd ed., Pitman, London, 1962, 272 pp.

Rowntree, B. Seebohm and G. R. Lavers, *Poverty and the Welfare State,* Longmans, London, 1951, 104 pp.

Shenfield, Barbara E., *Social Policies for Old Age,* Routledge, London, 1957, 236 pp.

Titmuss, Richard M., *Essays on "The Welfare State,"* Allen & Unwin, London, 1958, 232 pp.

Vaizcy, John, *The Cost of Social Service,* Fabian, London, Sept. 1954, 200 pp.

Wootton, Barbara, *The Social Foundations of Wage Policy,* Allen & Unwin, London, 1955, 200 pp.

TOWN AND COUNTRY PLANNING

Abercrombie, Sir Patrick, *Town and Country Planning,* 3rd ed., Oxford UP, 1960, 291 pp.

Ashworth, Herbert, *Housing in Great Britain,* Skinner, London, 1957, 157 pp.

Ashworth, William, *The Genesis of Modern British Town Planning,* Routledge, London, 1955, 259 pp.

Best, Robin H. and J. T. Coppock, *The Changing Use of Land in Britain,* Faber, London, 1962, 353 pp.

Change and Challenge, Next Steps in Town and Country Planning, CPC, 1962, 64 pp.

Coppock, J. T. and Hugh C. Prince, eds., *Greater London,* Faber, London, 1964, 378 pp.

Glass, Ruth et al., *London, Aspects of Change,* MacGibbon & Kee, London, 1964, 342 pp.

Greve, John, *The Housing Problem,* Fabian, London, 1961, 40 pp.

Hall, Peter Geoffrey, *London 2000,* Faber, London, 1963, 220 pp.

Heap, Desmond, *An Outline of Planning Law,* 3rd ed., Sweet & Maxwell, London, 1960, 213 pp.

Keeble, Lewis, *Principles and Practice of Town and*

Country Planning, 2nd ed., Estates Gazette, London, 1959.

Olson, Donald J., *Town Planning in London, The Eighteenth and Nineteenth Centuries*, Yale UP, 1965, 264 pp.

Rodwin, Lloyd, *The British New Towns Policy*, Harvard UP, 1956, 252 pp.

Chapter 9. GREAT BRITAIN AND THE WORLD

EMPIRE TO COMMONWEALTH

Apter, David E., *The Gold Coast in Transition*, Princeton UP, 1956, 355 pp.

Ayearst, M., *The British West Indies, The Search for Self-Government*, New York UP, 1960, 258 pp.

Barker, Sir Ernest, *The Ideas and Ideals of the British Empire*, 2nd ed., Macmillan, 1951, 177 pp.

Burns, Sir Alan, *In Defence of Colonies, British Colonial Territories in International Affairs*, Macmillan, 1957, 338 pp.

Carrington, C. E., *The British Overseas, Exploits of a Nation of Shopkeepers*, Cambridge UP, 1950, 1082 pp.

Carr-Saunders, M. A., *New Universities Overseas*, Allen & Unwin, London, 1961, 260 pp.

Cohen, Sir Andrew, *British Policy in Changing Africa*, Northwestern UP, 1959, 116 pp.

Coupland, R., *The Durham Report, An Abridged Version with an Introduction and Notes*, Oxford UP, 1945, 186 pp.

Furnivall, J. S., *Colonial Policy and Practice*, New York UP, 1956, 568 pp.

Hancock, William K., *Empire in the Changing World*, Penguin, 1943, 186 pp.

———, *Wealth of Colonies*, Cambridge UP, 1950, 81 pp.

Hinden, Rita, *Empire and After, A Study of British Imperial Attitudes*, Essential, London, 1949, 196 pp.

———, ed., *Fabian Colonial Essays*, Allen, London, 1945, 261 pp.

Jeffries, Sir Charles, *The Transfer of Power, Problems of the Passage to Self-Government*, Pall Mall, London, 1960, 148 pp.

Jennings, Sir Ivor, *The Approach to Self-Government*, Cambridge UP, 1956, 204 pp.

Johnson, Franklyn Arthur, *Defence by Committee, The British Committee of Imperial Defence, 1885–1959*, Oxford UP, 1960, 416 pp.

Jones, Arthur Creech, ed., *New Fabian Colonial Essays*, Hogarth, London, 1959, 271 pp.

Kirkman, W. P., *Unscrambling an Empire, A Critique of British Colonial Policy, 1956–1966*, Chatto & Windus, London, 1966, 214 pp.

Labour Party, *Labour's Colonial Policy, The Plural Society*, Transport House, London, 1950, 47 pp.

———, *The Smaller Territories*, Transport House, London, 1957, 29 pp.

Madden, A. F., *Imperial Constitutional Documents, 1765–1952, A Supplement*, Blackwell, Oxford, 1953, 91 pp.

Nicholson, Marjorie, *Self-Government and the Com-* *munal Problem, A Study of Colonial Constitutional Problems Arising in Plural Societies*, Gollancz, London, 1948, 45 pp.

"The Passing of Colonialism," *PS*, July–Sept. 1958, 112 pp., Special No.

Perham, Margery, ed., *Colonial Government, Annotated Reading List on British Colonial Government with Some General and Comparative Material upon Foreign Empires*, Oxford UP, 1950, 80 pp.

Problems of Parliamentary Government in Colonies, Hansard, London, 1952.

Stokes, E., *The Political Ideas of English Imperialism*, Oxford UP, 1960, 38 pp.

Strachey, John, *The End of Empire*, Random House, 1960, 351 pp.

Thornton, A. P., *The Imperial Idea and Its Enemies, A Study in British Power*, St Martin's, 1959, 370 pp.

Walker, Eric A., *The British Empire, Its Structure and Spirit, 1497–1953*, 2nd ed., Harvard UP, 1956, 353 pp.

White, L. H. and W. D. Hussey, *Government in Great Britain, the Empire and the Commonwealth*, Cambridge UP, 1959, 295 pp.

Wight, Martin, *The Development of the Legislative Council, 1606–1945*, Faber, London, 1946, 187 pp.

THE COMMONWEALTH OF NATIONS

Attlee, Clement, Earl, *Empire into Commonwealth*, Oxford UP, 1961, 53 pp.

Austin, Dennis, *West Africa and the Commonwealth*, Penguin, 1957, 124 pp.

Bell, Philip W., *The Sterling Area in the Postwar World, Internal Mechanism and Cohesion, 1946–1952*, Oxford UP, 1956, 478 pp.

Benham, Frederick, *The Colombo Plan and Other Essays*, Oxford UP, 1956, 478 pp.

Bradley, Kenneth, ed., *The Living Commonwealth*, Hutchinson, London, 1961, 543 pp.

Brady, Alexander, *Democracy in the Dominions, A Comparative Study in Institutions*, 3rd rev. ed., U Toronto P, 1958, 614 pp.

Brookes, Edgar H., *The Commonwealth Today*, Pietermaritzburg, U Natal P, 1959, 70 pp.

Carter, Gwendolen M., *The British Commonwealth and International Security, The Role of the Dominions, 1919–1939*, Ryerson, Toronto, 1947, 326 pp.

———, "The Commonwealth and the United Nations," *IO*, 4(2), May 1, 1950:247–60.

———, "The Expanding Commonwealth," *FA*, 35(1), Oct. 1956:131–43.

The Commonwealth and Europe. The Economist Intelligence Unit, London, 1960, 606 pp.

The Commonwealth Relations Conference, 1959, Oxford UP, 1959, 64 pp.

Conservative Political Center, *Wind of Change, The Challenge of the Commonwealth*, London, 1960, 63 pp.

Dawson, Robert MacGregor, ed., *The Development of Dominion Status, 1900–1936*, Oxford UP, 1937, 466 pp.

De Smith, S. A., *The New Commonwealth and Its Constitutions*, Stevens, London, 1964, 312 pp.

Eayrs, J., ed., *The Commonwealth and Suez: A Documentary Survey*, Oxford UP, 1964, 483 pp.

Elman, Russell, *Asian Experiment,* Ryerson, Toronto, 1961, 110 pp.

Fawcett, J. E. S., *The Inter Se Doctrine of Commonwealth Relations,* Athlone, London, 1958, 48 pp.

Foot, Hugh (Lord Caradon), *A Start in Freedom,* Hodder & Stoughton, London, 1964, 256 pp.

Frost, Richard, ed., *British Commonwealth and World Society,* RIIA, London, 1947, 204 pp.

Gardner, Richard N., *Sterling-Dollar Diplomacy, Anglo-American Collaboration in the Reconstruction of Multilateral Trade,* Oxford UP, 1956, 423 pp.

Hancock, William K., *Survey of British Commonwealth Affairs,* Oxford UP, 2 vols in 3 parts: *Problems of Nationality, 1918–1936,* 673 pp; *Problems of Economic Policy, 1918–1939, 1937–1942,* 324 and 355 pp.

Harvey, Heather J., *Consultation and Co-operation in the Commonwealth, A Handbook on Methods and Practice,* Oxford UP, 1951, 411 pp.

Hollander, Barnett, *Colonial Justice, The Unique Achievement of the Privy Council's Committee of Judges,* Bowes & Bowes, London, 1961, 115 pp.

Ingram, Derek, *The Commonwealth Challenge,* Allen & Unwin, London, 1962, 291 pp.

Jennings, Sir Ivor, *The British Commonwealth of Nations,* 4th ed., Hutchinson, London, 1961, 224 pp.

———, *The Commonwealth in Asia, A Discussion of the Problems of Pakistan, India and Ceylon,* Oxford UP, 1950, 124 pp.

———, *Problems of the New Commonwealth,* Duke UP, 1957, 104 pp.

McHenry, Dean E., "Formal Recognition of the Leader of the Opposition in the Parliaments of the British Commonwealth," *PSQ,* 69(3), Sept. 1954:438–52.

Mansergh, Nicholas, *The Commonwealth and the Nations, Studies in British Commonwealth Relations,* Oxford UP, 1948, 229 pp.

———, ed., *Documents and Speeches on British Commonwealth Affairs, 1931–1952,* Oxford UP, 2 vols, 1954, 604 and 690 pp; and *1952–1962,* 1963, 775 pp.

———, *The Multi-Racial Commonwealth,* Oxford UP, 1955, 175 pp.

———, *Survey of British Commonwealth Affairs, Problems of External Policy, 1931–1939,* Oxford UP, 1952, 481 pp.

———, *Survey of British Commonwealth Affairs, Problems of Wartime Co-operation and Post-war Change, 1939–1952,* Oxford UP, 1958, 469 pp.

——— et al., *Commonwealth Perspectives,* U Durham P, 1958, 214 pp.

Marshall, Geoffrey, *Parliamentary Sovereignty and the Commonwealth,* Oxford UP, 1957, 277 pp.

Mendelsohn, Ronald, *Social Security in the British Commonwealth,* Athlone, London, 1954, 390 pp.

Milburn, Josephine F., "Trade Unions in Politics in the British Commonwealth," *WPQ,* 17(2), June 1964: 273–93.

Miller, J. D. B., *The Commonwealth in the World,* 3rd ed., Harvard UP, 1965, 304 pp, pbk.

Olawale, Elias Taslim, *British Colonial Law,* Sweet & Maxwell, London, 1962, 323 pp.

Parry, Clive, *Nationality and Citizenship Laws of the Commonwealth and the Republic of Ireland,* Stevens, London, 2 vols, 1957 and 1960, 1021 and 1285 pp.

Perham, Margery Freda, *The Colonial Reckoning, The End of Imperial Rule in Africa in the Light of British Experience,* Knopf, 1962, 203 pp.

Political and Economic Planning, *Britain and Commonwealth Migration,* PEP, London, 1957.

Polk, Judd, *Sterling, Its Meaning in World Finance,* Harper, 1956, 286 pp.

Roberts-Wray, Kenneth, *Commonwealth and Colonial Law,* Stevens, London, 1966, 1062 pp.

Scott, F. R., "The End of Dominion Status," *AJIL,* 38(1), Jan. 1944:34–49.

Somervell, D. C. and Heather Harvey, *The British Empire and Commonwealth,* rev. ed., Christophers, London, 1959, 444 pp.

Soper, Tom, *Evolving Commonwealth,* Pergamon, 1966, 150 pp.

Taylor, Don, *The Years of Challenge, The Commonwealth and the British Empire, 1945–1958,* Praeger, 1960, 255 pp.

Underhill, Frank H., *The British Commonwealth, An Experiment in Cooperation Among Nations,* Duke UP, 1956, 127 pp.

United Kingdom, Colombo Plan for Cooperative Economic Development in South and Southeast Asia, Annual Reports of the Consultative Committee, HMSO, annually since 1957.

Watts, R. L., *New Federations, Experiments in the Commonwealth,* Oxford UP, 1967.

Wheare, Kenneth C., *The Constitutional Structural of the Commonwealth,* Oxford UP, 1961, 201 pp.

———, *The Statute of Westminster and Dominion Status,* 5th ed., Oxford UP, 1953, 347 pp.

Williamson, James A., *Great Britain and the Commonwealth,* 3rd ed., rev. enl. ed., Black, London, 1965, 242 pp.

Wilson, Dick, "The Future of Hong Kong," *WT,* 20(9), Sept. 1964:395–402.

Wiseman, H. V., *Britain and the Commonwealth,* Allen & Unwin, London, 1966, 157 pp, pbk.

———, *The Cabinet in the Commonwealth, Post-War Developments in Africa, the West Indies, and South-East Asia,* Praeger, 1959, 364 pp.

Young, C. M., *Constitutional Laws of the Commonwealth,* rev. ed., Oxford UP, 1952, 520 pp.

Zimmern, Sir Alfred Eckhard, *The Third British Empire,* 3rd ed., Oxford UP, 1934, 192 pp.

INTERNATIONAL RELATIONS

Allen, Harry Cranbrook, *The Anglo-American Predicament, the British Commonwealth, the United States and European Unity,* St Martin's, 1960, 241 pp.

———, *Great Britain and the United States, A History of Anglo-American Relations, 1783–1952,* Odhams, London, 1955, 1024 pp.

Anderson, J. N. D., ed., *Changing Law in Developing Countries,* Allen & Unwin, London, 1963, 269 pp.

Barker, A. J., *Suez, The Seven-Day War,* Faber, London, 1964, 223 pp.

Beloff, Max, *New Dimensions in Foreign Policy, A Study in British Administrative Experience, 1947–1959,* Macmillan, 1961, 208 pp.

"British Defence Policy," *PQ,* 31(1), Jan.–Mar. 1960, special issue.

British Interests in the Mediterranean and Middle East, Oxford UP, 1958, 123 pp.

Brown, Neville, "Some Features of the British Defence Review," *WT,* 22(4), Apr. 1966:171–76.

Butler, Rohan and J. P. T. Bury, eds., *Documents on British Foreign Policy, 1919–1939,* first series, Vol. 10, *German Affairs and Plebiscite Problems, 1920,* HMSO, 1960, 896 pp.

Camps, Miriam, *Britain and the European Community, 1955–1963,* Princeton UP, 1964, 547 pp.

Carter, W. Horsfall, *Speaking European, The Anglo-Continental Cleavage,* Allen & Unwin, London, 1966, 223 pp.

Catlin, George, *The Grandeur of England and the Atlantic Community,* Pergamon, Oxford, 1966, 217 pp.

Crosby, Gerda Richards, *Disarmament and Peace in British Politics, 1914–1919,* Harvard UP, 1957, 192 pp.

Epstein, Leon D., *British Politics in the Suez Crisis,* U Illinois P, 1964, 220 pp.

Fitzsimons, M. A., *The Foreign Policy of the British Labour Government, 1945–1951,* U Notre Dame P, 1953, 182 pp.

Fleming, Danna Frank, *The Cold War and Its Origins, 1917–1960,* 2 vols, Doubleday, 1961, 1158 pp.

Franks, Sir Oliver S., *Britain and the Tide of World Affairs,* Oxford UP, 1955, 80 pp.

Gaitskell, Hugh, *The Challenge of Coexistence,* Harvard UP, 1957, 114 pp.

Glubb, John Bagot, *Britain and the Arabs, 1908–1958,* Hodder & Stoughton, London, 1958, 496 pp.

Gladwyn, Lord, *The European Idea,* Weidenfeld & Nicolson, London, 1966, 171 pp.

Goodhart, Philip, *Fifty Ships That Saved the World,* Heinemann, London, 1965, 278 pp.

Goodwin, Geoffrey L., *Britain and the United Nations,* new ed., Manhattan, 1957, 478 pp.

Johnston, Franklyn A., "Politico-Military Organization in the United Kingdom, Some Recent Developments," *JP,* 27(2), May 1965:339–50.

Kenen, Peter B., *British Monetary Policy and the Balance of Payments, 1951–1957,* Harvard UP, 1960, 325 pp.

Kitzinger, U., *Britain, Europe and Beyond,* Sythoff, Leyden, 1965, 222 pp.

Luard, Evan, *Britain and China,* Chatto & Windus, London, 1962, 256 pp.

Mally, Gerhard, *Britain and European Unity,* Hansard, London, 1966, 156 pp.

Meehan, Eugene J., *The British Left Wing and Foreign Policy, A Study of the Influence of Ideology,* Rutgers UP, 1961, 201 pp.

Monroe, Elizabeth, *Britain's Moment in the Middle East, 1914–1956,* Johns Hopkins P, 1963, 254 pp.

Moulton, James Louis, *Defence in a Changing World,* Eyre & Spottiswoode, London, 1964, 191 pp.

Nicholas, H. G., *Britain and the United States,* Chatto & Windus, London, 1963, 180 pp.

Northedge, F. S., *British Foreign Policy, The Process of Readjustment, 1945–1961,* Allen & Unwin, London, 1962, 341 pp, pbk.

Pinder, John, *Britain and the Common Market,* Cresset, London, 1961, 134 pp.

Robertson, Terence, *Crisis, The Inside Story of the Suez Conspiracy,* Hutchinson, London, 1965, 365 pp.

Second Thoughts on Aid, BBC, 1966.

Strang, Lord, *Britain in World Affairs, The Fluctuation in Power and Influence from Henry VIII to Elizabeth II,* Praeger, 1961, 426 pp.

Taylor, Alan John Percival, *The Trouble Makers, Dissent over Foreign Policy, 1792–1939,* Indiana UP, 1958, 207 pp.

Walker, Patrick Gordon, *The Commonwealth,* Secker & Warburg, London, 1963, 408 pp.

Ward, Barbara and P. T. Bauer, *Two Views on Aid to Developing Countries,* Inst. of Economic Affairs, 1966, 58 pp.

Watkins, K. W., *Britain Divided, The Effect of the Spanish Civil War on British Political Opinion,* Nelson, London, 1963, 270 pp.

Watt, Donald Cameron, *Personalities and Policies, Studies in the Formulation of British Foreign Policy in the Twentieth Century,* Longmans, London, 1965, 277 pp.

Wint, Guy, *The British in Asia,* rev. ed., Inst. for Pacific Rel., 1954, 244 pp.

Wiseman, H. V., *Britain and the Commonwealth,* Allen & Unwin, London, 1965, 157 pp.

Wolfers, Arnold and Laurence W. Martin, eds., *The Anglo-American Tradition in Foreign Affairs,* Yale UP, 1956, 286 pp.

Woodhouse, C. M., *British Foreign Policy Since the Second World War,* Hutchinson, London, 1961, 255 pp.

Younger, Kenneth, *Changing Perspectives in British Foreign Policy,* Oxford UP, 1965, 147 pp.

FRANCE

GENERAL WORKS

Aron, Raymond, *France, The New Republic,* Oceana, 1959, 114 pp.

Brogan, Denis W., *The French Nation, from Napoleon to Pétain, 1814–1940,* Harper, 1957, 328 pp, pbk.

Cairns, John Campbell, *France,* Prentice-Hall, 1965, 180 pp, pbk.

Furniss, Edgar S., Jr., *France, Troubled Ally, de Gaulle's Heritage and Prospects,* Praeger, 1960, 559 pp, pbk.

Guérard, Albert Léon, *France,* Michigan UP, 1964, 616 pp.

Hoffmann, Stanley S. et al., *In Search of France,* Harvard UP, 1965, pbk.

Laponce, J. A., *The Government of the Fifth Republic, French Political Parties and the Constitution,* U California P, 1961, 415 pp.

Macridis, Roy C. and Bernard E. Brown, *The de Gaulle Republic, Quest for Unity,* Dorsey, 1960, 400 pp.

———, *Supplement to the de Gaulle Republic,* Dorsey, 1963, 141 pp.

Pickles, Dorothy, *The Fifth Republic, Institutions and Politics,* 3rd ed., Praeger, 1965, 261 pp, pbk.

Thomson, David, *Democracy in France Since 1870,* 4th ed., Oxford UP, 1964, 350 pp, pbk.

Williams, Philip M., *Crisis and Compromise*, 3rd ed., Anchor, 1964, 546 pp.

Wright, Gordon, *France in Modern Times, 1760 to the Present*, Rand-McNally, 1962, 621 pp.

Chapter 1. THE FRENCH PEOPLE AND THEIR POLITICS

Aron, Raymond, *France, Steadfast and Changing, The Fourth to the Fifth Republic*, trans. by T. J. Irwin and Luigi Einaudi, Harvard UP, 1960, 201 pp.

Bosworth, William, *Catholicism and Crisis in Modern France, French Catholic Groups at the Threshold of the Fifth Republic*, Princeton UP, 1961, 408 pp.

Brogan, Denis W. and the editors of *Life, France*, Time, 1960, 176 pp.

Camp, Wesley D., *Marriage and the Family in France Since the Revolution, An Essay in the History of Population*, Bookman, 1961, 203 pp.

Curtius, Ernst Robert, *The Civilization of France, An Introduction*, Allen & Unwin, London, 1932, 247 pp.

Earle, Edward Mead, ed., *Modern France, Problems of the Third and Fourth Republics*, Princeton UP, 1959, 522 pp.

Fauvet, Jacques, *The Cockpit of France*, trans. by Nancy Pearson, Harvill, London, 1960, 159 pp.

Hayes, Carlton J. H., *France, A Nation of Patriots*, Columbia UP, 1930, 487 pp.

Joll, James, *Intellectuals in Politics*, Weidenfeld & Nicolson, London, 1960, 217 pp.

Luethy, Herbert, *France Against Herself*, trans. from German by Erich Mosbacher, Praeger, 1955, 476 pp.

McKay, Donald C., *The United States and France*, Harvard UP, 1951, 334 pp.

Metraux, Rhoda and Margaret Mead, *Themes in French Culture, A Preface to a Study of French Community*, Stanford UP, 1954, 120 pp.

Morazé, Charles, *The French and the Republic*, Cornell UP, 1958, 214 pp.

Park, Julian, ed., *The Culture of France in Our Time*, Cornell UP, 1954, 345 pp.

Peyre, Henri, *The Contemporary French Novel*, Oxford UP, 1955, 363 pp.

Schram, Stuart R., *Protestantism and Politics in France*, Corbière & Jugain, Alençon, 1954, 288 pp.

Sieburg, Friedrich, *Who Are These French?* Macmillan, 1932, 303 pp.

Siegfried, André, *France, A Study in Nationality*, Yale UP, 1930, 122 pp.

Valery, Paul, *Dialogues*, trans. by William McCausland Stewart, Pantheon, 1964, 195 pp.

Wright, Gordon, "Catholics and Peasantry in France," *PSQ*, 68(4), Dec. 1953:526–51.

———, *Rural Revolution in France, The Peasantry in the Twentieth Century*, Stanford UP, 1964, 271 pp.

INTEREST GROUPS

Ambler, John Steward, *The French Army in Politics, 1945–1962*, Ohio State UP, 1966, 427 pp.

Brown, Bernard E., "Alcohol and Politics in France," *APSR*, 51, Dec. 1957:976–94.

———, "The Army and Politics in France," *JP*, 23(2), May 1961:262–78.

Brown, Bernard E., "Pressure Politics in the Fifth Republic," *JP*, 25(3), Aug. 1963:509–25.

———, "Pressure Politics in France," *JP*, 18, Nov. 1956:702–19.

Domenach, Joan-Marie, "The French Army in Politics," *FA*, 39(2), Jan. 1961:85–95.

Ehrmann, Henry W., "Bureaucracy and Interest Groups in the Decision-Making Process of the Fifth Republic," Festschrift für Ernst Fraenkel, Berlin, 1963.

———, *French Labor from Popular Front to Liberation*, Oxford UP, 1947, 342 pp.

———, "The French Trade Associations and the Ratification of the Schuman Plan," *WP*, 6(4), July 1954: 453–81.

———, *Organized Business in France*, Princeton UP, 1957, 514 pp.

Kelly, George Armstrong, *Lost Soldiers, The French Army and Empire in Crisis, 1947–1962*, MIT P, 1965, 404 pp.

Lorwin, Val R., *The French Labor Movement in Postwar France*, Harvard UP, 1931, 346 pp.

Chapter 2. THE FRENCH POLITICAL HERITAGE

THE THIRD REPUBLIC AND BEFORE

Armstrong, Hamilton Fish, *Chronology of Failure, The Last Days of the French Republic*, Macmillan, 1940, 202 pp.

Barthélemy, Joseph, *The Government of France*, Allen & Unwin, London, 1924, 222 pp.

Brogan, Denis W., *France Under the Republic*, Harper, 1940, 744 pp.

———, *The French Nation, from Napoleon to Pétain, 1814–1940*, Harper, 1958, 328 pp.

Chapman, Guy, *The Dreyfus Case, A Reassessment*, Viking, 1955, 400 pp.

Cobban, Alfred, *The Decline of the Third Republic*, Chatto & Windus, London, 1960, 127 pp.

———, *A History of Modern France*, Penguin, 3 vols: *Old Regime and Revolution, 1715–1799*, 1957, 287 pp; *From the First Empire to the Fourth Republic, 1799–1945*, 1961, 287 pp; *France of the Republics, 1871–1962*, 1965, 272 pp.

———, *The Social Interpretation of the French Revolution*, Cambridge UP, 1964, 178 pp.

Colton, Joel, *Léon Blum, Humanist in Politics*, Knopf, 1966, 512 pp.

Darby, Louise Elliott, *Léon Blum, Evolution of a Socialist*, Yoseloff, London, 1963, 447 pp.

De Tocqueville, Alexis, *The Old Regime and the French Revolution*, trans. by Stuart Gilbert, Doubleday, 1955, 300 pp.

Gooch, Robert K., *Parliamentary Government in France, Revolutionary Origins, 1789–1791*, Cornell UP, 1960, 253 pp.

Graham, B. D., "Theories of the French Party System Under the Third Republic," *PS*, 12(1), Feb. 1964:21–32.

Guérard, Albert Léon, *France, A Modern History*, U Michigan P, 1959, 563 pp.

Halasz, Nicholas, *Captain Dreyfus, The Story of a Mass Hysteria*, Simon & Schuster, 1956, 274 pp.

Jackson, J. Hampden, ed., *A Short History of France from Early Times to 1958*, Cambridge UP, 1959, 222 pp.

Joll, James, ed., *The Decline of the Third Republic*, Praeger, 1959, 127 pp.

Maurois, André, *A History of France*, rev. ed., Farrar, Straus, 1957, 598 pp; Grove, 1960, pbk.

Micaud, Charles A., *The French Right and Nazi Germany, 1933–1939*, Duke UP, 1943, 255 pp.

Paul-Boncour, Joseph, *Recollections of the Third Republic*, Vol. 1, trans. by George Marion, Jr., Speller, 1958, 269 pp.

Pinkney, David H., *Napoleon III and the Rebuilding of Paris*, Princeton UP, 1958, 245 pp.

Romier, Lucien, *A History of France*, trans. and completed by A. L. Rowse, Macmillan, 1953, 487 pp.

Seignobos, Charles, *The Evolution of the French People*, Knopf, 1932, 382 pp.

Weber, Eugen, *Action Française, Royalism and Reaction in Twentieth-Century France*, Stanford UP, 1966, 594 pp.

———, *The Nationalist Revival in France, 1905–1914*, U California P, 1959, 237 pp.

Werth, Alexander, *France in Ferment*, Harper, 1935, 309 pp.

———, *France and Munich*, Harper, 1939, 447 pp.

———, *The Twilight of France, 1933–1940*, Harper, 1942, 368 pp.

———, *Which Way France?* Harper, 1937, 414 pp.

Zeldin, Theodore, *The Political System of Napoleon III*, Macmillan, 1958, 196 pp.

THE VICHY REGIME AND THE FREE FRENCH

Aron, Robert, *De Gaulle Triumphant, The Liberation of France, August 1944–May 1945*, Putnam, 1964, 360 pp.

———, *France Reborn, The History of the Liberation, June 1944–May 1945*, trans. by Humphrey Hare, Scribner's, 1964, 490 pp.

——— and George Elgey, *The Vichy Regime, 1940–1944*, trans. by Humphrey Hare, Macmillan, 1958, 536 pp.

Blum, Léon, *Léon Blum Before His Judges*, Routledge, London, 1943, 159 pp (a transcript of Blum's statement at the Riom Trial).

Brogan, Denis W., *French Personalities and Problems*, Knopf, 1947, 241 pp.

Cole, Hubert, *Laval, A Biography*, Putnam, 1963, 314 pp.

Géraud, André (Pertinax), *The Gravediggers of France*, Doubleday, 1944, 612 pp.

Hytier, Adrienne Doris, *Two Years of French Foreign Policy, Vichy 1940–1942*, Drosz, Geneva, 1958, 402 pp.

Langer, William L., *Our Vichy Gamble*, Knopf, 1947, 412 pp.

Laval, Pierre, *The Diary of Pierre Laval*, Scribner's, 1948, 240 pp.

Maurois, André, *Tragedy of France*, Harper, 1940, 255 pp.

Paxton, Robert O., *Parades and Politics at Vichy, The French Officer Corps Under Marshal Pétain*, Princeton UP, 1966, 432 pp.

Pickles, Dorothy M., *France Between the Republics*, Love & Malcolmson, London, 1946, 247 pp.

Reynaud, Paul, *In the Thick of the Fight, 1930–1945*, trans. by James L. Lambert, Cassell, London, 1955, 694 pp.

Spears, Edward, *Assignment to Catastrophe*, A. A. Wyn, 2 vols: *Prelude to Dunkirk, July 1939–May 1940*, 332 pp; *The Fall of France, June 1940*, 336 pp; 1954–55.

Tissier, Pierre, *The Government of Vichy*, Harrap, London, 1942, 347 pp.

Viorst, Milton, *Hostile Allies, FDR and Charles de Gaulle*, Macmillan, 1964, 280 pp.

White, Dorothy Shipley, *Seeds of Discord, De Gaulle, Free France, and the Allies*, Syracuse UP, 1964, 471 pp.

THE FOURTH REPUBLIC

Duverger, Maurice, *The French Political System*, U Chicago P, 1958, 227 pp.

Friedrich, Carl Joachim, "The Political Theory of the New Constitutions," *RP*, 12(2), Apr. 1950:215–24.

Goguel, François, *France Under the Fourth Republic*, Cornell UP, 1952, 198 pp.

Matthews, Ronald, *The Death of the Fourth Republic*, Praeger, 1954, 318 pp.

Meisel, James J., *The Fall of the Republic, Military Revolt in France*, U Michigan P, 1963, 320 pp.

Mendès-France, Pierre, "The Crisis of France, 1945–1959," *IA*, 35(3), July 1959:285–94.

Pickles, Dorothy M., *French Politics, The First Years of the Fourth Republic*, Oxford UP, 1953, 302 pp.

Romains, Jules, *A Frenchman Examines His Conscience*, Essential, London, 1956, 118 pp.

Schoenbrun, David, *As France Goes*, Harper, 1957, 341 pp.

Taylor, O. R., *The Fourth Republic of France, Constitution and Political Parties*, Oxford UP, 1951, 216 pp.

Werth, Alexander, *France, 1940–1956*, Holt, 1956, 764 pp.

Wright, Gordon, *The Reshaping of French Democracy*, Reynal, 1948, 277 pp.

———, *France in Modern Times, 1760 to the Present*, Rand McNally, 1960, 621 pp.

THE FIFTH REPUBLIC

Aron, Robert, *An Explanation of de Gaulle*, Harper, 1966, 202 pp, pbk.

Campbell, Peter and Brian Chapman, *The Constitution of the Fifth Republic, Translation and Commentary*, Blackwell, Oxford, 1958, 60 pp, pbk.

The French Constitution Adopted by Referendum of Sept. 28, 1958, and Promulgated on Oct. 4, 1958, French text and English trans., French Embassy, Press and Information Division, 1958, 75 pp.

Friedrich, Carl Joachim, "The New French Constitution in Political and Historical Perspective," *HLR*, 72(5), Mar. 1959:801–37.

Harrison, Martin, "The Constitution of the Fifth Republic, A Commentary," *PS*, 7(1), Feb. 1959:41–62.

Hoffmann, Stanley H. and Nicholas Wahl, "The French Constitution," Part 1, "The Final Text and

Its Prospects," Part 2, "The Initial Draft and Its Origin," *APSR*, 53(2), July 1959:332–82.

Johnson, D., "The Political Principles of General de Gaulle," *IA*, 41(4), Oct. 1965:650–62.

Kirchheimer, Otto, "France from the Fourth to the Fifth Republic," *SR*, 26(4), Winter 1958:379–414.

Loewenstein, Karl, "The Constitution of the Fifth Republic, A Preliminary Report," *JP*, 21(2), May 1959: 211–33.

Werth, Alexander, *The de Gaulle Revolution*, Hale, London, 1960, 404 pp.

Williams, Philip M. and Martin Harrison, *De Gaulle's Republic*, 2nd ed., Longmans, London, 1961, 279 pp.

POLITICAL IDEAS

Becker, Carl L., *The Heavenly City of the Eighteenth Century Philosophers*, Yale UP, 1932, 168 pp.

Binion, Rudolph, *Defeated Leaders, The Political Fate of Callou, Jouvenal and Tardieu*, Columbia UP, 1960, 425 pp.

Buthman, William C., *The Rise of Integral Nationalism in France*, Columbia UP, 1939, 355 pp.

Caute, David, *Communism and the French Intellectuals 1914–1960*, Macmillan, 1964, 413 pp.

Charlton, D. G., *Positivist Thought in France During the Second Empire, 1852–1870*, Oxford UP, 1959, 251 pp.

Curtis, Michael, *Three Against the Third Republic, Lorel, Barres, and Maurras*, Princeton UP, 1959, 313 pp.

Elbow, Matthew H., *French Corporative Theory, 1789–1948, A Chapter in the History of Ideas*, Columbia UP, 1954, 222 pp.

Graham, B. D., *The French Socialists and Tripartisme, 1944–1947*, Toronto UP, 1965, 299 pp.

Hayes, Carlton J. H., *The Historical Evolution of Modern Nationalism*, R. R. Smith, 1931, 327 pp.

Howell, Ronald F., "The Philosopher Alain and French Classical Radicalism," *WPQ*, 18(3), Sept. 1965:594–614.

Lichtheim, George, *Marxism in Modern France*, Columbia UP, 1966, 212 pp.

Manuel, Frank E., *The New World of Henri Saint-Simon*, Harvard UP, 1956, 423 pp.

Martin, Kingsley, *The Rise of French Liberal Thought, A Study of Political Ideas from Bayle to Condorcet*, 2nd ed., ed. by J. P. Mayer, New York UP, 1954, 316 pp.

Micaud, Charles A., *Communism and the French Left*, Weidenfeld & Nicolson, London, 1963, 308 pp.

Muret, Charlotte, *French Royalist Doctrines Since the Revolution*, Columbia UP, 1933, 326 pp.

Pierce, Roy, *Contemporary Political Thought*, Oxford UP, 1966, 288 pp, pbk.

Rémond, René, *The Right Wing in France, from 1815 to de Gaulle*, trans. by James M. Laux, U Pennsylvania P, 1966, 425 pp.

Soltau, Roger, *French Political Thought in the Nineteenth Century*, Yale UP, 1931, 500 pp.

Soucy, R. J., "The Nature of Fascism in France," *JCH*, 1(1), Jan. 1966:27–55.

Chapter 3. FRENCH PARTIES AND ELECTIONS

Almond, Gabriel A., "Political Ideas of Christian Democracy," *JP*, 10(4), Nov. 1948:734–63.

Andrews, William, "By-Election System of the Fifth Republic," *WPQ*, 17(2), June 1964:690–702.

Barnes, Samuel H., "The Politics of French Christian Labor," *JP*, 21(1), Feb. 1959:105–22.

Blum, Léon, *For All Mankind*, Viking, 1946, 186 pp.

Bouscaren, Anthony, "The European Christian Democrats," *WPQ*, 2(1), Mar. 1949:59–75.

Cairns, John C., "Notes and Comment, France, December 1965, End of the Elective Monarchy," *IJ*, 21(1), Winter 1965–66:93–100.

Campbell, Peter, *French Electoral Systems and Elections Since 1789*, 2nd ed., Faber, London, 1965, 155 pp.

Cantril, Hadley, *The Politics of Despair*, Basic Books, 1958, 269 pp.

Cook, Geoffrey C., "De Gaulle and the R.P.F.," *PSQ*, 65(3), Sept. 1950:335–52.

DeTarr, Francis, *The French Radical Party from Herriot to Mendès-France*, Oxford UP, 1961, 264 pp.

Ehrmann, Henry W., "Direct Democracy in France," *APSR*, 57(4), Dec. 1963:883–901.

Einaudi, Mario and François Goguel, *Christian Democracy in Italy and France*, U Notre Dame P, 1952, 229 pp.

"The French Election of 1956," *PS*, 4(2), June 1956: 139–75; 4(3), Oct. 1956:250–82.

Godfrey, E. Drexel, Jr., "The Communist Presence in France," *APSR*, 50(2), June 1956:321–38.

———, *The Fate of the French Non-Communist Left*, Doubleday, 1955, 79 pp.

Goldey, David B., "The French Presidential Election of 5 and 19 December, 1965, Organization and Results," *PS*, 14(2), June 1966:208–15.

———, "The French Referendum and Elections of 1962, The National Campaigns," *PS*, 11(3), Oct. 1963:287–307.

Harrison, Martin and Uwe Kitzinger, "The French General Election, 1958, Two Constituencies: (1) Paris 5: Safe Seat; (2) Personal, Regional, and Religious Factors: Strasbourg Nord-Sud," *PS*, 7(2), June 1959:147–73.

Larmour, Peter J., *The French Radical Party in the 1930's*, Stanford UP, 1964, 327 pp.

Laponce, Jean A., *The Government of the Fifth Republic, French Political Parties and the Constitution*, U California P, 1961, 415 pp.

Lichtheim, George, "The Stranded Whale, On the French Communist Left," *Encounter*, 23(5), 1964: 31–35.

McLellan, David S., "The French and Italian Communist Parties and the Decisions of the Twentieth Congress, C.P.S.U.," *WPQ*, 10(2), June 1957:446–47.

MacRae, Duncan, Jr., "Religious and Socio-economic Factors in the French Vote, 1946–1956," *AJS*, 64(3), Nov. 1958:290–98.

Marcum, John A., "French Party Literature," *WPQ*, 12(1), Part 1, Mar. 1959:168–77.

Marcus, John T., *French Socialism in the Crisis Years, 1933–1936, Fascism and the French Left,* Praeger, 1958, 216 pp.

Nicholas, H. G. and Philip M. Williams, "The French Election of 1956, I. Electoral Law and Machinery; II. The Campaign," *PS,* 4(2), June 1956:139–75.

Noland, Aaron, *The Founding of the French Socialist Party, 1893–1905,* Harvard UP, 1956, 248 pp.

Osgood, Samuel M., *French Royalism Under the Third and Fourth Republics,* Nijhoff, The Hague, 1960, 228 pp.

Pierce, Roy, "De Gaulle and the RPF—A Post Mortem," *JP,* 16(1), Feb. 1954:96–119.

Rieber, Alfred, "Communist Tactics in France, 1945–1953," *JP,* 16(1), Spring 1954:73–85.

Rossi, Angelo, *A Communist Party in Action, An Account of the Organization and Operations in France,* Yale UP, 1949, 301 pp.

Schlesinger, Joseph A., "The French Radical Socialist Party and the Republican Front of 1956," *WPQ,* 11(1), Mar. 1958:71–85.

Thorez, Maurice, *France Today and the People's Front,* Intern. Pub., 1936, 255 pp.

Williams, Philip M., "The French Presidential Election of 1965," *Parl. Aff.,* 19(1), Winter 1965:14–30.

———, "The French Referendum, 1960," *Parl. Aff.,* 14(3), Summer 1961:335–52.

———, "The French Referendum and Election of October–November 1962," *Parl. Aff.,* 16(2), Spring 1963:165–73.

———, "Party, Presidency and Parish Pump in France," *Parl. Aff.,* 18(3), Summer 1965:257–65.

——— and Martin Harrison, "The French Referendum of April, 1962," *Parl. Aff.,* 15(3), Summer 1962: 294–306.

Zariski, Raphael, "Problems and Prospects of Democratic Socialism in France and Italy," *JP,* 18(2), May 1956:254–80.

Zartman, I. William, "French Communist Foreign Policy, 1952–1954, A Propaganda Analysis," *WPQ,* 9(2), June 1956:344–62.

Chapter 4. THE FRENCH PARLIAMENT

Gooch, Robert K., *The French Parliamentary Committee System,* Appleton-Century-Crofts, 1935, 259 pp.

Howard, John E., *Parliament and Foreign Policy in France,* Cresset, London, 1948, 172 pp.

King, Jere Clemens, *Generals and Politicians, Conflict Between France's High Command, Parliament and Government,* U California P, 1951, 294 pp.

Leites, Nathan, *On the Game of Politics in France,* Stanford UP, 1959, 190 pp.

Lidderdale, D. W. S., *The Parliament of France,* Hansard, London, 1951, 296 pp.

Mavrinac, Albert, *Organization and Procedure of the National Assembly of the Fifth French Republic,* Hansard, London, 1960, 39 pp.

Chapter 5. THE FRENCH EXECUTIVE

Aron, Robert, *An Explanation of de Gaulle,* trans. by Marianne Sinclair, Harper, 1966, 210 pp.

Barrés, Philippe, *Charles de Gaulle,* Doubleday, 1941, 260 pp.

Burgess, W. Randolph, "The Economic and Political Consequences of General de Gaulle," *PSQ,* 78(4), 1963:537–47.

Campbell, Peter, "The Cabinet and the Constitution in France," *Parl. Aff.,* 5(3), Summer 1951:341–61.

———, "The Cabinet and the Constitution in France, 1951–1956," *Parl. Aff.,* 9(3), Summer 1956:206–306.

Deferre, Gaston, "De Gaulle and After," *FA,* Apr. 1966:434–45.

De Gaulle, Charles, *The Edge of the Sword,* Criterion, 1960, 128 pp.

———, *Speeches,* Oxford UP, 1944, 189 pp.

———, *War Memoirs,* Simon & Schuster, 3 vols: *The Call to Honor,* 1940, 1942, 319 pp; *Unity, 1942–1944,* 1959, 378 pp; *Salvation, 1944–1946,* 1960, 404 pp.

De Lamothe, A. Dutheillet, "Ministerial Cabinets in France," *Pub. Ad.,* 43, Winter 1965:365–81.

Funk, Arthur Layton, *Charles de Gaulle, The Crucial Years, 1943–1944,* U Oklahoma P, 1959, 336 pp.

Furniss, Edgar S., Jr., *De Gaulle and the French Army, An Appraisal of a Civil Military Crisis,* Twentieth Century Fund, 1964, 331 pp.

———, *The Office of the Premier in French Foreign Policy-Making, An Application of Decision-Making Analysis,* Princeton UP, 1954, 67 pp.

Gaudemet, P. M., "The Relationship Between the President and the Prime Minister in France," *Scots Law Times,* Edinburgh, July 22, 1961:117–20.

Harrison, Martin, "The French Experience of Exceptional Powers, 1961," *JP,* 25(1), Feb. 1963:139–58.

Hayward, J. E. S., "Presidentialism and French Politics," *Parl. Aff.,* 18(1), Winter 1964–65: 23–39.

Herriot, Edouard, *In Those Days Before the First World War,* trans. by Adolphe de Milly, Old and New World Pub., 1952, 276 pp.

Hoffmann, Stanley, "De Gaulle's Memoirs, The Hero as History," *WP,* 8(1), Oct. 1960:140–55.

———, "Succession and Stability in France," *JIA,* 18(1), 1964:86–103.

Johnson, Douglas, "The Political Principles of General de Gaulle," *IA,* 41(4), Oct. 1965:650–62.

Lacouture, Jean, *De Gaulle,* New Amer. Lib., 1966, 188 pp.

McCormick, Donald, *Mr. France, The Life and Times of France's Dynamic Postwar Premier,* Jarrolds, London, 1955, 240 pp.

Macridis, Roy C., ed., *Implacable Ally,* Harper, 1966, 248 pp.

Mauriac, Francois, *De Gaulle,* Doubleday, 1966, 229 pp.

Melnik, Constantin and Nathan Leites, *The House Without Windows, France Selects a President,* trans. by Ralph Manheim, Row, Peterson, 1958, 358 pp.

Mendès-France, Pierre, *The Pursuit of Freedom: An Autobiography,* Longmans, London, 1956, 256 pp.

Mengin, Robert, *No Laurels for de Gaulle,* trans. by Jay Allen, Farrar, Straus & Giroux, 1966, 402 pp.

Merle, Marcel, "The Presidency of the Fourth Republic," *Parl. Aff.,* 3, Summer 1954:287–302.

Pickles, William, "Making Sense of de Gaulle," *IA,* 42(3), July 1966:410–20.

Pickles, William, "Special Powers in France, Article 16 in Practice," *Pub. Law,* Spring 1963:23–50.

Schoenbrun, David, *The Three Lives of Charles de Gaulle,* Atheneum, 1966, 373 pp.

Thomson, David, *Two Frenchmen, Pierre Laval and Charles de Gaulle,* Cresset, London, 1951, 256 pp.

Viansson-Ponte, Pierre, *The King and His Court (Les Gaullistes),* Houghton Mifflin, 1965, 250 pp.

Werth, Alexander, *De Gaulle, A Political Biography,* Penguin, 1966, 391 pp.

———, *Lost Statesman, The Strange Story of Pierre Mendès-France,* Abelard-Schuman, 1958, 428 pp.

Wright, Gordon, *Raymond Poincaré and the French Presidency,* Stanford UP, 1942, 271 pp.

Chapter 6. THE FRENCH ADMINISTRATION: NATIONAL AND LOCAL

NATIONAL ADMINISTRATION

Baum, Warren C., *The French Economy and the State,* Princeton UP, 1958, 391 pp.

Brown, J. C., "Education of the New French Administrative Class," *Pub. Pers. Rev.,* 16(1), Jan. 1955:17–27.

Clough, Shepard C., "Economic Planning in a Capitalist Society, France from Monnet to Hirsh," *PSQ,* 71(4), Dec. 1956:539–68.

Cohen, Stephen, *French Economic Planning,* Weidenfeld & Nicolson, London, 1965.

Crozier, Michel, *The Bureaucratic Phenomenon,* U Chicago P, 1964, 320 pp.

De Vries, Henry P. and Berthold H. Hoeniger, "Post Liberation Nationalizations in France," *CLR,* May 1950:629–56.

Einaudi, Mario et al., *Nationalization in France and Italy,* Cornell UP, 1955, 260 pp.

Feyzioglue, T., "The Reforms of the French Higher Civil Service," *Pub. Ad.,* 33(1), Spring 1955:69–93 and 33(2), Summer 1955:173–89.

Grégoire, Roger, *The French Civil Service,* trans. from French, rev. ed., Intern. Inst. Admin. Sciences, Brussels, 1965, 363 pp, pbk.

Hackett, John and Anne-Marie, *Economic Planning in France,* Harvard UP, 1963, 418 pp.

Mendès-France, Pierre and Gabriel Ardan, *Economics and Action,* Columbia UP, 1955, 222 pp.

Parris, Henry, "Twenty Years of l'Ecole Nationale d'Administration," *Pub. Ad.,* 43, Winter 1965:395–411.

Perroux, Francois, *The IVth French Plan, 1962–65,* trans. by Bruno Leblanc, Nat. Inst. Ec. and Social Res., London, 1965, 84 pp, pbk.

Peterson, Wallace C., *The Welfare State in France,* U Nebraska Studies, Lincoln, 1960, 115 pp.

Piquard, Michel, "Organization and Planning of the Paris Region," *Pub. Ad.,* 43, Winter 1965:383–93.

Ridley, F. and J. Blondel, *Public Administration in France,* Routledge, London, 1964, 336 pp.

Robson, William, ed., *The Civil Service in Britain and France,* Macmillan, 1965, 191 pp.

Sheahan, John B., *Promotion and Control of Industry in Postwar France,* Harvard UP, 1963, 301 pp.

Sturmthal, Adolf, "The Structure of Nationalized Enterprises in France," *PSQ,* 67(3), Sept. 1952:357–78.

Sweetman, L. T., "Prefects and Planning, France's New Regionalism," *Pub. Ad.,* 43, Spring 1965:15–30.

Waline, Marcel, "The Constitutional Council of the French Republic," *AJCL,* 12, Autumn 1963:483–93.

Wilson, John Stuart Gladstone, *French Banking Structure and Credit Policy,* Harvard UP, 1957, 453 pp.

LOCAL ADMINISTRATION

Blondel, Jean, "Local Government and the Local Offices of Ministries in a French Department," *Parl. Aff.,* 37(2), Spring 1959:65–74.

Chapman, Brian, *Introduction to French Local Government,* Allen & Unwin, London, 1953, 238 pp.

Kaminsky, Elija Ben-Zion, "The Reorganization of Metropolitan Paris," *Pub. Aff. Bull.,* Arizona State U, 4(1), 1965, 4 pp.

Marshall, A. H., "Wide Powers Vested in Prefects and Mayors, Aspects of Central Administration and Local Government in France," *Mun. J,* Nov. 23, 1956:2273–74 and Dec. 7, 1956:2878–79.

Chapter 7. FRENCH LAW AND COURTS

CIVIL LAW AND COURTS

Amos, Sir Maurice Sheldon and F. P. Walton, *Introduction to French Law,* Oxford UP, 1935, 393 pp.

David, René and Henry P. de Vries, *The French Legal System, An Introduction to Civil Law Systems,* Oceana, 1958, 152 pp.

King, Jerome B., "Constitutionalism and the Judiciary in France," *PSQ,* 80(1), March 1965:62–87.

Lewy, Claude et al., *Essays on French Law,* Washington Law Society, 1958, 96 pp.

Rabel, Ernst, "The French Civil Code," *Louisiana LR,* 1949–50:107–19.

ADMINISTRATIVE LAW AND COURTS

Alibert, Ralph, "French Conseil d'État," *Modern LR,* London, Apr. 1940:257–71.

Chapman, Brian, "The French Conseil d'État," *Parl. Aff.,* 12(2), Spring 1959:164–73.

Colliard, C. A., "Comparison Between English and French Administrative Law," *Grotius Society Transactions,* London, 1940:119–33.

Diamant, Alfred, "The French Council of State, Comparative Observations on the Problem of Controlling the Bureaucracy of the Modern State," *JP,* 13(4), Nov. 1951:562–88.

Freedman, Charles E., *The Conseil d'État in Modern France,* Columbia UP, 1961, 205 pp.

Garner, James W., "Judicial Control of Administrative and Legislative Acts in France," *APSR,* 9(4), Nov. 1915:637–65.

Hamson, C. J., *Executive Discretion and Judicial Control, An Aspect of the French Conseil d'État,* Stevens, London, 1954, 222 pp.

Koch, Gerald L., "The Machinery of Law Administration in France," *U Pennsylvania LR,* 108, 1959–60: 366–86.

Schwartz, Bernard, *French Administrative Law and the Common-Law World*, New York UP, 1954, 367 pp.

Chapter 8. FRENCH SOCIETY IN CHANGE

EDUCATION

Aron, Raymond, "Some Aspects of the Crisis in the French Universities," *Minerva*, 2, Spring 1964:477–83.

Fraser, W. R., *Education and Society.in Modern France*, Humanities, 1963, 140 pp.

"French Education, Why Jeannot *Can* Read," Yale French Studies, 22, Winter–Spring 1958–59.

Hoyt, N. Deming, "Educational Reform in France," *Harvard Educ. R*, 18(4), Fall 1948:220–27.

Ridley, F., "The French Educational System, Policy and Administrative Aspects," *PS*, 11(2), June 1963:178–202.

Weber, Eugen, "Current Control of French Education," *CH*, 40(238), June 1961:327–33.

SOCIAL POLICY

Galant, Henry C., "France, A Comprehensive Health Plan," *CH*, 44(262), June 1963:351–58, 368.

Lorwin, Val R., "Collective Bargaining in Postwar France," *Annals*, 310, Mar. 1957:66–74.

Mares, V. E., "The French New Deal," *CH*, 45(267), Nov. 1963:276–82, 303.

Peterson, Wallace C., *The Welfare State in France*, Nebraska UP, 1960, 115 pp.

Rodgers, Barbara, "Social Security in France," *Pub. Ad.*, 31(4), Winter 1953:377–98 and 32(1), Spring 1954:99–116.

Social Security in France, Ministry of Labor and Social Security, Paris, 1965, 79 pp.

Chapter 9. FRANCE AND THE WORLD

FROM EMPIRE TO COMMUNITY

Andrews, William G., *French Politics and Algeria, The Process of Policy Formation 1954–1962*, Appleton-Century-Crofts, 1962, 217 pp, pbk.

Beloff, Nora, *The General Says No, Britain's Exclusion from Europe*, Penguin, 1963, 181 pp.

Berg, Elliot J., "The Economic Basis of Political Choice in French West Africa," *APSR*, 54(2), June 1960: 391–405.

Brace, Richard M. and Joan, *Ordeal in Algeria*, Van Nostrand, 1960, 450 pp.

Cady, John F., *The Roots of French Imperialism in Eastern Asia*, Cornell UP, 1956, 322 pp.

Camps, Miriam, *What Kind of Europe? The Community Since de Gaulle's Veto*, Oxford UP, 1965, 140 pp, pbk.

Catroux, Georges, "The French Union," *IC*, 495, Nov. 1953:193–256.

Clark, Michael, *Algeria in Turmoil, A History of the Rebellion*, Praeger, 1960, 480 pp.

Delavignette, Robert, *Freedom and Authority in French West Africa*, Oxford UP, 1950, 152 pp.

Fisher, Sidney Nettleton, ed., *France and the European Community*, Ohio State UP, 1964, 176 pp.

Gillespie, Joan, *Algeria, Rebellion and Revolution*, Praeger, 1960, 208 pp.

Gordon, David C., *The Passing of French Algeria*, Oxford UP, 1966, 265 pp.

Grosser, Alfred, *Foreign Policy of the Fifth Republic*, Little, Brown, 1966, 189 pp.

———, "France and Germany, Divergent Outlooks," *FA*, 44(4), Oct. 1965:26–36.

Hammer, Ellen J., *The Struggle for Indo-China*, Stanford UP, 1954, 342 pp.

———, *The Struggle for Indo-China Continues, Geneva to Bandung*, Stanford UP, 1955, 40 pp.

Hodgkin, Thomas and Ruth Schachter, "French-Speaking West Africa," *IC*, 528, 1960.

Kraft, Joseph, *The Struggle for Algeria*, Doubleday, 1961, 263 pp.

Pickles, Dorothy, *Algeria and France, from Colonialism to Co-operation*, Methuen, London, 1963, 215 pp.

Robinson, Kenneth, "Alternative to Independence," *PS*, 4(3), Oct. 1956:225–49.

———, "The End of Empire: Another View," *IA*, 30(2), Apr. 1954:186–95.

———, "A Survey of the Background Material for the Study of Government in French Tropical Africa," *APSR*, 50(1), Mar. 1956:179–98.

Sulzberger, Cyrus Leo, *The Test, de Gaulle and Algeria*, Harcourt, Brace & World, 1962, 228 pp.

Thompson, Virginia and Richard Adloff, *French Equatorial Africa*, Stanford UP, 1961, 595 pp.

———, *French West Africa*, Stanford UP, 1958, 626 pp.

Tillon, Germaine, *Algeria, The Realities*, Knopf, 1958, 128 pp.

———, *France and Algeria, Complementary Enemies*, Knopf, 1961, 184 pp.

Willis, F. Roy, *France, Germany, and the New Europe, 1945–1963*, Stanford UP, 1965, 397 pp.

INTERNATIONAL RELATIONS

Aron, Raymond and Daniel Lerner, eds., *France Defeats EDC, Studies in an International Controversy*, Praeger, 1957, 225 pp.

Cowan, Laing G., *France and the Saar, 1680–1948*, Columbia UP, 1950, 247 pp.

Deniau, J. F., *The Common Market, Its Structure and Purpose*, Barrie-Rockliff, London, 1960, 143 pp.

France and Britain, A Report by a Chatham House Study Group, RIIA, London, 1945, 110 pp.

France and the European Community, PEP, London, 1961, 41 pp.

Furniss, Edgar S., Jr., *Weaknesses in French Foreign Policy-Making*, Princeton UP, 1954, 52 pp.

Gooch, G. P., "Franco-German Coexistence at Last?" *FA*, 37(3), Apr. 1959:432–42.

Heckscher, August and Raymond Aron, *Diversity of Worlds*, Viking, 1957, 178 pp.

Hoffmann, Stanley S., "De Gaulle, Europe, and the Atlantic Alliance," *IO*, 18(1), Winter 1964:1–28.

Jordan, W. M., *Great Britain, France, and the German Problem, 1918–1939, A Study of Anglo-French Relations in the Making and Maintenance of the Versailles Settlement*, Oxford UP, 1944, 235 pp.

Lauret, René, *France and Germany, the Legacy of Charlemagne*, trans. by Wells Chamberlin, Regnery, 1964, 272 pp.

Lieber, Robert J., "The French Nuclear Force, A Strategic and Political Evaluation," *IA*, 42(3), July 1966:421–31.

Marcus, John T., *Neutralism and Nationalism in France*, Bookman, 1959, 207 pp.

Reynaud, Paul, *The Foreign Policy of Charles de Gaulle, A Critical Assessment*, Odyssey P, 1964, 160 pp.

———, *Unite or Perish*, Simon & Schuster, 1951, 214 pp.

Salvin, Marina, "Neutralism in France and Germany," *IC*, 472, June 1951:283–318.

Wolfers, Arnold, *Britain and France Between Two Wars, Conflicting Strategies of Peace Since Versailles*, Harcourt, Brace & World, 1940, 467 pp.

GERMANY

GENERAL WORKS [1]

Chapter 1. GERMAN PEOPLE AND POLITICS

Butz, Otto, *Modern German Political Theory*, Doubleday, 1955, 72 pp.

Davison, W. Phillips, "The Mass Media in West German Political Life," in Hans Speier and W. Phillips Davison, eds., *West German Leadership and Foreign Policy*, Row, Peterson, 1957:242–81.

Dickinson, Robert E., *Germany, A General and Regional Geography*, Dutton, 1953, 700 pp.

Dill, Marshall, Jr., *Germany*, Michigan UP, 1964, 504 pp.

Eich, Hermann, *The Unloved Germans*, trans. by Michael Glenny, Stein & Day, 1965, 255 pp.

Fliess, Peter J., *Freedom of the Press in the German Republic, 1918–1933*, Louisiana State UP, 1955, 147 pp.

Friedrich, Carl Joachim, "The Political Thought of Neo-Liberalism," *APSR*, 40(2), June 1955:509–25.

Gimbel, J., "The 'Spiegel Affair' in Perspective," *MJPS*, 9(3), Aug. 1965:282–97.

Janowitz, Morris, "Social Stratification and Mobility in West Germany," *AJS*, 64(1), July 1958:6–24.

Klemperer, Klemens von, *Germany's New Conservatism, Its History and Dilemma in the Twentieth Century*, Princeton UP, 1957, 268 pp.

Krieger, Leonard, *The German Idea of Freedom, History of a Political Tradition*, Beacon, 1957, 540 pp.

[1] General works are listed under Chapters 1, 2, and 8. For a comprehensive treatment of the governmental structure of each of the two Germanies, in the German language, see:

Ellwein, Thomas, *Das Regierungssystem der Bundesrepublik Deutschland*. 2nd ed., Westdeutscher Verlag, Cologne, 1965, 718 pp.

Richert, Ernst, *Macht ohne Mandat, Der Staatsapparat in der sowjetischen Besatzungszone Deutschlands*, 2nd ed., Westdeutscher Verlag, Cologne, 1963, 305 pp.

Lowie, Robert H., *The German People, A Social Portrait to 1914*, Farrar & Rinehart, 1945, 143 pp.

Mosse, George L., *The Crisis of German Ideology, The Intellectual Origins of the Third Reich*, New U Lib, 1964, 373 pp.

Pounds, Norman J. G., *The Ruhr, A Study in Historical and Economic Geography*, Indiana UP, 1952, 283 pp.

Stern, Fritz, *The Politics of Cultural Despair, A Study in the Rise of the Germanic Ideology*, U California P, 1961, 367 pp.

Veblen, Thorstein, *Imperial Germany and the Industrial Revolution*, Viking, 1939, 324 pp.

Wallich, Henry C., *Mainsprings of the German Revival*, Yale UP, 1955, 401 pp.

Wohlrabe, Raymond A. and Werner Krusch, *The Land and People of Germany*, Lippincott, 1957, 118 pp.

Chapter 2. THE GERMAN POLITICAL HERITAGE

GENERAL HISTORY

Balfour, Michael, *The Kaiser and His Times*, Houghton Mifflin, 1964, 524 pp.

Barraclough, G., *The Origins of Modern Germany*, 2nd ed., Blackwell, Oxford, 1949, 481 pp.

Bryce, James, *The Holy Roman Empire*, rev. ed., Macmillan, 1932, 575 pp.

Eyck, Erich, *Bismarck and the German Empire*, Allen & Unwin, London, 1950, 327 pp.

Flenley, Ralph, *Modern German History*, rev. ed., Dent, London, 1964, 491 pp.

Holborn, Hajo, *A History of Modern Germany*, Knopf, 2 vols: *The Reformation*, 1959, 374 pp; *1648–1840*, 1964, 531 pp.

Passant, Ernest James et al., *A Short History of Germany, 1815–1945*, Cambridge UP, 1959, 255 pp, pbk.

Pinson, Koppel S., *Modern Germany*, 2nd ed., Macmillan, 1966, 682 pp.

Pollock, James K. and Homer Thomas, *Germany in Power and Eclipse*, Van Nostrand, 1952, 661 pp.

Ritter, Gerhard, *The German Problem, Basic Questions of German Political Life, Past and Present*, Ohio State UP, 1966, 233 pp.

Simon, W. M., *Germany, A Brief History*, Random House, 1966, 358 pp.

Snyder, Louis L., *Basic History of Modern Germany*, Van Nostrand, 1957, 192 pp.

Taylor, Alan John Percival, *The Course of German History*, rev. ed., Methuen, London, 1961, 271 pp.

WEIMAR REPUBLIC

Blachley, Frederick F. and Miriam E. Oatman, *The Government and Administration of Germany*, Johns Hopkins P, 1928, 770 pp.

Brecht, Arnold, *Prelude to Silence, The End of the German Republic*, Oxford UP, 1944, 156 pp.

Carsten, Francis L., *The Reichswehr and Politics, 1918–1933*, Oxford UP, 1966, 435 pp.

Dorpalen, Andreas, *Hindenburg and the Weimar Republic*, Princeton UP, 1964, 506 pp.

Eyck, Erich, *A History of the Weimar Republic*, trans. by H. P. Hanson and R. G. L. Waite, Harvard UP,

2 vols: *From the Collapse of the Empire to Hindenburg's Election*, 1962, 373 pp; *From the Locarno Conference to Hitler's Seizure of Power*, 1964, 535 pp.

Hertzman, Lewis, *DNVP, Right-Wing Opposition in the Weimar Republic, 1918–1924*, U Nebraska P, 1964, 263 pp.

Hunt, Richard N., *German Social Democracy, 1918–1933*, Yale UP, 1964, 292 pp, pbk.

Rosenberg, Arthur, *A History of the German Republic*, Methuen, London, 1936, 350 pp.

Schorske, Carl E., *German Social Democracy, 1905–1917, The Development of the Great Schism*, Wiley, 1965, 358 pp.

Vermeil, Edmond, *Germany in the Twentieth Century, A Political and Cultural History of the Weimar Republic and the Third Reich*, trans. by L. J. Ludovici, Praeger, 1956, 288 pp.

NAZI PERIOD

Allen, William Sheridan, *The Nazi Seizure of Power, The Experience of a Single German Town, 1930–1935*, Quadrangle Books, 1965, 345 pp.

Bramsted, Ernest K., *Goebbels and National Socialist Propaganda, 1925–1945*, Michigan State UP, 1965, 488 pp.

Bullock, Alan L. C., *Hitler, A Study in Tyranny*, rev. ed., Harper, 1964, 848 pp, pbk.

Delarue, Jacques, *The Gestapo*, Morrow, 1964, 384 pp.

Hale, Orono J., *The Captive Press in the Third Reich*, Princeton UP, 1964, 353 pp.

Heiden, Konrad, *Der Fuehrer, Hitler's Rise to Power*, Houghton Mifflin, 1944, 788 pp.

Hitler, Adolf, *Hitler's Secret Book*, trans. by Salvator Attanasia, Grove, 1961, 230 pp.

——, *Mein Kampf*, Reynal & Hitchcock, 1941, 1003 pp.

International Military Tribunal, *The Trial of German Major War Criminals*, HMSO, London, 1946–47, 15 vols.

Lewy, Guenter, *The Catholic Church and Nazi Germany*, McGraw-Hill, 1964, 416 pp.

Mau, H. and H. Krausnick, *German History, 1933–1945*, Oswald Wolff, London, 1959, 157 pp.

Mosse, George L., *Nazi Culture, Intellectual, Cultural, and Social Life in the Third Reich*, Grosset & Dunlap, 1966, 386 pp.

Neumann, Franz L., *Behemoth, The Structure and Practice of National Socialism 1933–1944*, 2nd ed., Oxford UP, 1944, 649 pp.

Prittie, Terence, *Germans Against Hitler*, Hutchinson, London, 1964, 292 pp.

Rauschning, Hermann, *The Voice of Destruction*, Putnam's, 1940, 295 pp.

Reitlinger, Gerald, *The Final Solution, The Attempt to Exterminate the Jews of Europe, 1938–1945*, Valentine, Mitchell, London, 1953, 622 pp.

Ritter, Gerhard, *The German Resistance*, trans. by R. T. Clark, Praeger, 1959, 330 pp.

Romoser, George, "The Politics of Uncertainty: The German Resistance Movement," *SR*, 31(1), Spring 1964:73–93.

Rothfels, Hans, *The German Opposition to Hitler*, Wolff, London, 1961, 166 pp.

Schoenbaum, David, *Hitler's Social Revolution, Class and Status in Nazi Germany 1933–1939*, Doubleday, 1966, 336 pp.

Schweitzer, Arthur, *Big Business in the Third Reich*, Indiana UP, 1964, 739 pp.

Shirer, William L., *The Rise and Fall of the Third Reich, A History of Nazi Germany*, Simon & Schuster, 1960, 1245 pp; Fawcett World Lib., 1962, pbk.

Toynbee, Arnold and Veronica M., eds., *Survey of International Affairs, Hitler's Europe*, Oxford UP, 1954, 730 pp.

Trevor-Roper, Hugh R., ed., *Hitler's Secret Conversations, 1941–44*, Farrar, Straus, 1953, 597 pp.

Zeman, Z. A. B., *Nazi Propaganda*, Oxford UP, 1964, 226 pp.

POSTWAR RECONSTRUCTION

Adenauer, Konrad, *Memoirs, 1945–1953*, trans. by Beate Ruhm von Oppen, Regnery, 1966, 478 pp.

Balfour, Michael and John Mair, *Four Power Control in Germany and Austria, 1945–1946*, Oxford UP, 1956, 390 pp.

Bishop, Joseph W., "The 'Contractual Agreements' with the Federal Republic of Germany," *AJIL*, 49(2), Apr. 1955:125–47.

Byrnes, James F., *Speaking Frankly*, Harper, 1947, 324 pp.

Clay, Lucius D., *Decision in Germany*, Doubleday, 1950, 522 pp.

Davidson, Eugene, *The Death and Life of Germany, An Account of the American Occupation*, Knopf, 1959, 422 pp.

Ebsworth, Raymond, *Restoring Democracy in Germany, The British Contribution*, Praeger, 1961, 215 pp.

Freymond, Jacques, *The Saar Conflict 1945–1955*, Praeger, 1960, 395 pp.

Gimbel, John, *A German Community Under American Occupation, Marburg, 1945–52*, Stanford UP, 1961, 259 pp.

Golay, John F., *The Founding of the Federal Republic of Germany*, U Chicago P, 1958, 256 pp.

Grosser, Alfred, *The Colossus Again, Western Germany from Defeat to Rearmament*, Praeger, 1955, 249 pp.

Herz, John H., "The Fiasco of Denazification in Germany," *PSQ*, 43, 1948:569–94.

Litchfield, Edward H. et al., *Governing Germany*, Cornell UP, 1953, 661 pp.

McInnis, Edgar, R. Hiscocks, and R. Spencer, *The Shaping of Postwar Germany*, Praeger, 1961, 195 pp.

Merkl, Peter H., *The Origin of the West German Republic*, Oxford UP, 1963, 269 pp.

Montgomery, John D., *Forced to Be Free, The Artificial Revolution in Germany and Japan*, U Chicago P, 1957, 209 pp.

Oppen, Beate Ruhm von, ed., *Documents on Germany Under Occupation 1945–1954*, Oxford UP, 1955, 660 pp.

US Department of State, *Germany 1947–1949, The Story in Documents*, Pub. No. 3556, USGPO, 1950, 631 pp.

US Office of Military Government, *Documents on the*

Creation of the German Federal Constitution, Sept. 1, 1949, 154 pp.

US Office of Military Government, *Documents on Germany, 1944–61*, USGPO, 1961, 833 pp.

Willis, F. Roy, *The French in Germany, 1945–1949*, Stanford UP, 1961, 308 pp.

Zink, Harold, *The United States in Germany, 1944–1955*, Van Nostrand, 1957, 374 pp.

BONN REPUBLIC

Boelling, Klaus, *Republic in Suspense, Politics, Parties, and Personalities in Postwar Germany*, Praeger, 1964, 276 pp.

Bracher, Karl Dietrich, "Problems of Parliamentary Democracy," in *A New Europe?* ed. by Stephen R. Graubard, Houghton Mifflin, 1964:245–64.

Duebber, Ulrich and Gerard Braunthal, "West Germany," *JP*, 25(4), Nov. 1963:774–89.

Epstein, Klaus, *Germany after Adenauer*, For. Pol. Ass., Headline Series no. 164, Apr. 1964, 63 pp.

Erler, Fritz, *Democracy in Germany*, Harvard UP, 1965, 139 pp.

"Germany," *Encounter*, 22(4), Apr. 1964, special issue.

"Germany, Today and Tomorrow," *Survey* (61), Oct. 1966, entire issue.

Grosser, Alfred, *The Federal Republic of Germany*, Praeger, 1964, 150 pp, pbk.

Hiscocks, Richard, *The Adenauer Era*, Lippincott, 1966, 271 pp.

Johnson, Nevil, "The Era of Adenauer and After," *Parl. Aff.*, 17(1), Winter 1963–64:31–49.

Leonhardt, Rudolf Walter, *This Germany, The Story since the Third Reich*, New York Graphic Society, 1964, 275 pp.

Mason, John Brown, "Government, Administration, and Politics in West Germany, A Selected Bibliography," *APSR*, 52(2), June 1958:313–30.

Merkl, Peter H., *Germany, Yesterday and Tomorrow*, Oxford UP, 1965, 366 pp.

Plischke, Elmer, *Contemporary Government of Germany*, Allen & Unwin, London, 1964, 248 pp.

Pollock, James K. and J. C. Lane, *Source Materials on the Government and Politics of Germany*, Wahr, 1964, 403 pp.

Stahl, Walter, ed., *The Politics of Postwar Germany*, Praeger, 1963, 480 pp.

Chapter 3. GERMAN PARTIES AND ELECTIONS

Barnes, S. H. et al., "The German Party System and the 1961 Election," *APSR*, 56(4), Dec. 1962:899–914.

Braunthal, Gerard, "The Free Democratic Party in West Germany," *WPQ*, 13(2), June 1960:332–48.

Chalmers, Douglas A., *The Social Democratic Party of Germany, From Working-Class Movement to Modern Political Party*, Yale UP, 1964, 258 pp, pbk.

Childs, David, "SPD at Dortmund, Ulbricht Sets the Pace," *WT*, 22(7), July 1966:285–92.

Cromwell, Richard S., "Rightist Extremism in Postwar West Germany," *WPQ*, 17(2), June 1964:284–93.

Culver, Lowell W., "Land Elections in West German Politics," *WPQ*, 19(2), June 1966:304–36.

Edinger, Lewis J., "Electoral Politics and Voting in Western Germany," *WP*, 13, Apr. 1961:471–84.

——, *Kurt Schumacher, A Study in Personality and Political Behavior*, Stanford UP, 1965, 390 pp.

Frye, Charles E., "Parties and Pressure Groups in Weimar and Bonn," *WP*, 17(4), July 1965:635–55.

Heidenheimer, Arnold J., *Adenauer and the CDU, The Rise of the Leader and the Integration of the Party*, Nijhoff, The Hague, 1960, 259 pp.

——, "German Party Finance: The CDU," *APSR*, 51, 1957:369–85.

——, "Succession and Party Politics in West Germany," *JIA*, 18(1), 1964:32–42.

Johnson, Nevil, "State Finance for Political Parties in Western Germany," *Parl. Aff.*, 18(3), Summer 1965: 279–92.

Kitzinger, Uwe, *German Electoral Politics, A Study of the 1957 Campaign*, Oxford UP, 1960, 365 pp.

——, "The West German Electoral Law," *Parl. Aff.*, 11(2), Spring 1958:220–37.

Lidtke, Vernon L., *The Outlawed Party, Social Democracy in Germany, 1878–1890*, Princeton UP, 1966, 376 pp.

Path to Dictatorship, 1918–1933, Ten Essays by German Scholars, introd. by Fritz Stern, trans. by John Conway, Doubleday, 1966, 217 pp, pbk.

Pulzer, P. G. J., "Western Germany and the Three Party System," *PQ*, 33(4), Oct. 1962:414–26.

Romoser, George K. and Charles R. Foster, "Safety First, The West German Election," *Parl. Aff.*, 19(1), Winter 1965–66:31–36.

Schellenger, H. Kent, "The German Social Democratic Party After World War II, The Conservatism of Power," *WPQ*, 19(2), June 1966:251–65.

Schneider, Carl J., "Political Parties and the German Basic Law of 1949," *WPQ*, 10(3), Sept. 1957:527–40.

Stiefbold, R. P., "The Significance of Void Ballots in West German Elections," *APSR*, 59(2), June 1965: 391–407.

Tauber, Kurt B., "Nationalism and Social Restoration, Fraternities in Postwar Germany," *PSQ*, 78(1), Mar. 1963:66–85.

Chapter 4. GERMAN PARLIAMENTARY INSTITUTIONS

Johnson, Nevil, "Questions in the Bundestag," *Parl. Aff.*, 16(1), Winter 1962:22–34.

King-Hall, Stephen and Richard K. Ullmann, *German Parliaments*, Praeger, 1954, 162 pp.

Kirchheimer, Otto, "Germany, The Vanishing Opposition," in Robert A. Dahl, ed., *Opposition in Western Democracies*, Yale UP, 1966:237–59.

Loewenberg, Gerhard, *Parliament in the German Political System*, Cornell UP, 1966, 464 pp.

Lohse, Egon, "West Germany's Military Ombudsman," in Donald C. Rowat, ed., *Ombudsman, Citizen's Defender*, Allen & Unwin, London, 1965:119–26.

Neunreither, Karlheinz, "Politics and Bureaucracy in the West German *Bundesrat*," *APSR*, 53(3), Sept. 1959:713–31.

Pinney, Edward L., *Federalism, Bureaucracy, and Party*

Politics in Western Germany, The Role of the Bundesrat, U North Carolina P, 1963, 268 pp.

Ridley, F., "The Parliamentary Commissioner for Military Affairs in the Federal Republic of Germany," PS, 12(1), Feb. 1964:1–20.

Rueckert, George L. and W. Crane, "CDU Deviance in the German Bundestag," JP, 24(3), Aug. 1962:477–88.

Trossmann, Hans, The German Bundestag, Organization and Operation, Neue Darmstaedter Verlagsanstalt, 1965, 156 pp, pbk.

Chapter 5. EXECUTIVE AND ADMINISTRATION

EXECUTIVE AND CIVIL SERVICE

Herz, John H., "Political Views of. the West German Civil Service," in Speier-Davison, op. cit., pp. 96–135.

Jacob, Herbert, German Administration Since Bismarck, Central Authority Versus Local Autonomy, Yale UP, 1963, 224 pp.

Lukomski, Jess M., Erhard and Germany, Praeger, 1965, 240 pp.

Merkl, Peter H., "Equilibrium, Structure of Interests and Leadership, and Adenauer's Survival as Chancellor," APSR, 56(3), Sept. 1962:634–50.

Neunreither, Karlheinz, "Federalism and the West German Bureaucracy," PS, 7(3), Oct. 1959:233–45.

Rosenberg, Hans, Bureaucracy, Aristocracy and Autocracy, The Prussian Experience, 1660–1815, Harvard UP, 1958, 247 pp.

Wighton, Charles, Adenauer, A Critical Biography, Coward-McCann, 1963, 389 pp.

STATE AND LOCAL GOVERNMENT

Braunthal, Gerard, "Federalism in Germany, The Broadcasting Controversy," JP, 24(3), Aug. 1962: 545–61.

Brecht, Arnold, Federalism and Regionalism in Germany, Oxford UP, 1945, 202 pp.

Chaput de Saintonge, R. A. A., Public Administration in Germany: A Study in Regional and Local Administration in Land Rheinland-Pfalz, Weidenfeld & Nicolson, London, 1961, 371 pp.

Culver, Lowell W., "Land Elections in West German Politics," WPQ, 19(2), June 1966:304–36.

Merkl, Peter H., "Executive-Legislative Federalism in West Germany," APSR, 53(3), Sept. 1959:732–41.

Wells, Roger H., German Cities, Princeton UP, 1932, 283 pp.

——, The States in West-German Federalism, A Study in Federal-State Relations, 1949–1960, Bookman, 1961, 148 pp.

Chapter 6. GERMAN LAW AND ADMINISTRATION OF JUSTICE

Baade, Hans W., "Social Science Evidence and the Federal Constitutional Court of West Germany," JP, 23(3), Aug. 1961:421–61.

Cole, Taylor, "Three Constitutional Courts, A Comparison," APSR, 53(4), Dec. 1959:963–84.

"German Administrative Law with Special Reference to the Latest Developments in the System of Legal Protection," ICLQ, 2(3), July 1953:368–82.

Loewenstein, Karl, "Law and the Legislative Process in Occupied Germany," Yale LJ, 57, Mar.–Apr. 1958: 724–60.

McWhinney, Edward, Constitutionalism in Germany and the Federal Constitutional Court, Sythoff, Leyden, 1962, 71 pp.

——, "The German Federal Court and the Communist Party Decision," Indiana LJ, 32(3), Spring 1957:295–312.

Müller, Gebhard, "The Federal Constitutional Court of the Federal Republic of Germany," JICJ, 6(2), Winter 1965:191–218.

Naumann, Bernd, Auschwitz, A Report on the Proceedings Against Robert Karl Ludwig Mulka and Others Before the Court at Frankfurt, Praeger, 1966, 433 pp.

Reich, Donald R., "Court, Comity and Federalism in West Germany," MJPS, 7, Aug. 1963:197–228.

Rheinstein, Max, "Approach to German Law," Indiana LJ, 34(4), Summer 1959:546–58.

Rosenne, S., Constitutionalism in Germany and the Federal Constitutional Court, Oceana, 1962, 72 pp.

Rupp, Hans G., "Judicial Review in the Federal Republic of Germany," AJCL, 9(1), 1960:29–47.

Schmertzing, Wolfgang P. von, trans. and ed., Outlawing the Communist Party, A Case History, Bookmailer, 1957, 227 pp.

Wunderlich, Frieda, German Labor Courts, U North Carolina P, 1946, 252 pp.

Chapter 7. PROBLEMS OF GERMAN SOCIETY

EDUCATION

"Education in Transition, The Schools in Germany," in Contemporary Education, J. F. Cramer and G. S. Brown, Harcourt, Brace & World, 1956:432–73.

Educational Yearbook, Teachers College, Columbia UP (Vols. 1924ff. contain articles on German education).

Stahl, Walter, Education for Democracy in West Germany, Praeger, 1961, 356 pp.

LABOR AND SOCIAL SECURITY

Bunn, Ronald F., "Codetermination and the Federation of German Employers' Organization," MJPS, 2(3), Aug. 1958:278–97.

Kirchheimer, Otto, "West German Trade Unions, Their Domestic and Foreign Policies," in Speier-Davison, op. cit.:136–94.

Reich, Nathan, Labor Relations in Republican Germany 1918–1933, Oxford UP, 1938, 293 pp.

Schuchman, Abraham, Codetermination, Labor's Middle Way in Germany, Pub. Aff., 1957, 247 pp.

Spiro, Herbert J., The Politics of German Codetermination, Harvard UP, 1958, 180 pp.

Wunderlich, Frieda, Farm Labor in Germany, Princeton UP, 1961, 390 pp.

BUSINESS AND AGRICULTURE

Almond, Gabriel A., "The Politics of German Business," in Speier-Davison, op. cit.:195–241.

Braunthal, Gerard, *The Federation of German Industry in Politics*, Cornell UP, 1965, 389 pp.

Bruck, W. F., *Social and Economic History of Germany from William II to Hitler, 1888–1938*, Oxford UP, 1938, 292 pp.

Erhard, Ludwig, *Prosperity Through Competition*, trans. and ed. by Edith Temple Roberts and John B. Wood, Praeger, 1958, 272 pp.

Hartmann, Heinz, *Authority and Organization in German Management*, Princeton UP, 1959, 318 pp.

Hirsch-Weber, Wolfgang, "Some Remarks on Interest Groups in the German Federal Republic," in Henry W. Ehrmann, ed., *Interest Groups on Four Continents*, U Pittsburgh P, 1958:96–116.

Martin, James Stuart, *All Honorable Men*, Little, Brown, 1950, 326 pp.

Muhlen, Norbert, *The Incredible Krupps*, Holt, 1959, 308 pp.

Stolper, Gustav, *German Economy, 1870–1914*, Reynal & Hitchcock, 1940, 295 pp.

Chapter 8. BERLIN AND THE SOVIET ZONE

BERLIN

Davison, W. Phillips, *The Berlin Blockade*, Princeton UP, 1958, 446 pp.

Fleming, D. F., "The Future of West Berlin," *WPQ*, 14(1), Mar. 1961:27–48.

Frei, Otto, "The Barrier Across Berlin and Its Consequences," *WT*, 17(11), Nov. 1961:459–70.

Galante, Pierre, *The Berlin Wall*, Doubleday, 1965, 277 pp.

Gottlieb, Manuel, *The German Peace Settlement and the Berlin Crisis*, Paine-Whitman, 1960, 275 pp.

Hangen, Welles, *The Muted Revolution, East Germany's Challenge to Russia and the West*, Knopf, 1966, 231 pp.

Plischke, Elmer, *Government and Politics of Contemporary Berlin*, Nijhoff, The Hague, 1963, 119 pp.

———, "Integrating Berlin and the Federal Republic of Germany," *JP*, 27, Feb. 1965:35–65.

Smith, Bruce L., "The Governance of Berlin," *IC*, 525, 1959, 230 pp.

Speier, Hans, *Divided Berlin, The Anatomy of Soviet Political Blackmail*, Praeger, 1961, 201 pp.

Von der Gablentz, O. M., ed, *Documents on the Status of Berlin, 1944 bis 1959*, Oldenbourg, Munich, 1959, 240 pp.

THE SOVIET ZONE

Abel, Paul, "Relations Between the German Federal Republic and the German Democratic Republic in Matters of Criminal Law," *ICLQ*, 10(2), Apr. 1961: 346–57.

Bendix, Reinhard, "Managerial Ideologies in the Soviet Orbit," *Work and Authority in Industry*, Wiley, 1956:341–433.

Brant, Stefen, *The East German Uprising, 17th June 1953*, trans. and adapted by Charles Wheeler, Praeger, 1955, 202 pp.

Epstein, Fritz T., *East Germany, A Selected Bibliography*, Lib. Cong., 1959, 55 pp.

Friedrich, Carl Joachim, ed., *The Soviet Zone of Germany*, Human Relations Area Files, 1956, 646 pp.

Grothe, Peter, *To Win the Minds of Men*, Pacific Books, 1958, 241 pp.

Hamel, Johannes, *A Christian in East Germany*, trans. by Ruth and Charles West, SCM Press, London, 1960, 126 pp.

Hangen, Welles, *The Muted Revolution, East Germany's Challenge to Russia and the West*, Knopf, 1966, 231 pp.

———, "New Perspectives Behind the Wall," *FA*, 45(1), Oct. 1966:135–47.

Herz, John H., "East Germany, Progress and Prospects," *SR*, 17(2), Summer 1960:139–56.

Kirchheimer, Otto, *Political Justice*, Princeton UP, 1961: 259–303.

Lyon, Peyton V., "A Case for the Recognition of East Germany," *IJ*, 15(4), Autumn 1960:337–45.

Mason, John Brown, "Government, Administration and Politics in East Germany, A Selected Bibliography," *APSR*, 53(2), June 1959:507–23.

Nettl, J. P., *The Eastern Zone and Soviet Policy in Germany, 1945–1950*, Oxford UP, 1951, 324 pp.

Shell, Kurt, "Totalitarianism in Retreat, The Example of the DDR," *WP*, 18(1), Oct. 1965:105–16.

Skilling, H. Gordon, *The Governments of Communist East Europe*, Crowell, 1966, 256 pp.

Stern, Carola, *Ulbricht, A Political Biography*, Praeger, 1965, 231 pp.

Stolper, Gustav, Karl Häuser, and Knut Borchardt, *The German Economy: 1870 to the Present*, trans. by Toni Stolper, Harcourt, Brace & World, 1967, 353 pp.

Stolper, Wolfgang F. and Karl Roskamp, *The Structure of the East German Economy*, Harvard UP, 1960, 478 pp.

Wagner, Helmut R., "The Cultural Sovietization of East Germany," *SR*, 24(4), Winter 1957:395–426.

The Worldmark Encyclopedia of Nations, Harper, 1960:356–65.

Wunderlich, Frieda, *Farmer and Farm Labor in the Soviet Zone of Germany*, Twayne, 1958, 162 pp.

Chapter 9. GERMANY AND THE WORLD

Bathurst, M. E. and J. L. Simpson, *Germany and the North Atlantic Community, A Legal Survey*, Praeger, 1956, 217 pp.

Bracher, Karl Dietrich, "The Foreign Policy of the Federal Republic of Germany," in Joseph E. Black and Kenneth W. Thompson, *Foreign Policies in a World of Change*, Harper, 1963:115–47.

Brandt, Willy, *The Ordeal of Coexistence*, Harvard UP, 1963, 112 pp.

Craig, Gordon A., *From Bismarck to Adenauer, Aspects of German Statecraft*, rev. ed., Harper, 1965, 136 pp.

Deutsch, Karl W. and Lewis J. Edinger, *Germany Rejoins the Powers, Mass Opinion, Interest Groups and Elites in Contemporary German Foreign Policy*, Stanford UP, 1959, 320 pp.

Dyck, Harvey L., *Weimar Germany and Soviet Russia 1926–1933, A Study in Diplomatic Instability*, Columbia UP, 1966, 279 pp.

Freund, Gerald, *Germany Between Two Worlds,* Harcourt, Brace & World, 1961, 296 pp.

Gass, Oscar, "German Unification, Prospects and Merits," *Commentary,* 40, July 1965:25–38.

Grosser, Alfred, "France and Germany: Divergent Outlooks," *FA,* 44(1), Oct. 1965:26–36.

Hartmann, Frederick H., *Germany Between East and West, The Reunification Problem,* Prentice-Hall, 1965, 181 pp, pbk.

Holbik, Karel and Henry Myers, *Post-War Trade in Divided Germany, The Internal and International Issues,* Johns Hopkins P, 1964, 138 pp.

Kaplan, Lawrence S., "NATO and Adenauer's Germany, Uneasy Partnership," *IO,* 15(4), Autumn 1961: 618–29.

Kirchheimer, Otto, "The Problem of the East German Republic," *Salmagundi,* 1(1), Fall 1965:88–95.

Meyer, Henry Cord, *Mitteleuropa in German Thought and Action, 1815–1945,* Nijhoff, The Hague, 1955, 378 pp.

Neal, Fred Warner, *War and Peace and Germany,* Norton, 1962, 166 pp.

Rhode, Gotthold and Wolfgang Wagner et al., comps. and eds., *The Genesis of the Oder-Neisse Line, Sources and Documents,* Brentano, Stuttgart, 1959, 287 pp.

Richardson, James L., *Germany and the Atlantic Alliance, The Interaction of Strategy and Politics,* Harvard UP, 1966, 403 pp.

Schlamm, William S., *Germany and the East-West Crisis,* McKay, 1959, 237 pp.

Schroeder, Gerhard, "Germany Looks at Eastern Europe," *FA,* 44(1), Oct. 1965:15–25.

Schütz, Wilhelm W., "German Foreign Policy, Foundations in the West—Aims in the East," *IA,* 35(3), July 1959:210–15.

———, "New Initiatives for a New Age, A German View," *FA,* 36(3), Apr. 1958:460–71.

Snell, John L., *Wartime Origins of the East-West Dilemma over Germany,* Hauser, 1959, 268 pp.

Speier, Hans, *German Rearmament and Atomic War, The Views of German Military and Political Leaders,* Row, Peterson, 1957, 272 pp.

Strauss, Franz Josef, *The Grand Design, A European Solution to German Reunification,* Praeger, 1966, 105 pp.

Von der Gablentz, O. M., *Documents on the Status of Berlin, 1944–1959,* Oldenbourg, Munich, 1959, 240 pp.

Wagner, Wolfgang, *The Genesis of the Oder-Neisse Line, A Study in the Diplomatic Negotiations During World War II,* Brentano, Stuttgart, 1957, 167 pp.

Wahrhaftig, Samuel L., "The Development of German Foreign Policy Institutions," in Speier-Davison, *op. cit.*:7–56.

White, John, *German Aid, A Survey of the Sources, Policy, and Structure of German Aid,* The Overseas Inst., London, 1965, 221 pp.

———, "West German Aid to Developing Nations," *IA,* 41(1), Jan. 1965:74–88.

Willis, F. Roy, *France, Germany and the New Europe 1945–1963,* Stanford UP, 1965, 387 pp.

Wiskemann, Elizabeth, *Germany's Eastern Neighbors, Problems Relating to the Oder-Neisse Line and the Czech Frontier Regions,* Oxford UP, 1956, 309 pp.

SOVIET UNION

GENERAL WORKS

The American Bibliography of Russian and East European Studies, Indiana UP, published annually since 1957.

The Anatomy of Terror, Khrushchev's Revelations About Stalin's Regime, introduction by Nathaniel Weyl, Pub. Aff., 1956, 73 pp.

Andrews, William G., ed., *Soviet Political Institutions and Policies, Inside Views,* Van Nostrand, 1965, 411 pp, pbk.

Armstrong, John A., *Ideology, Politics and Government in the Soviet Union,* Praeger, 1962, 160 pp, pbk.

Bauer, Raymond A. et al., *How the Soviet System Works,* Knopf, 1960, 312 pp, pbk.

Burch, Betty Brand, ed., *Dictatorship and Totalitarianism: Selected Readings,* Van Nostrand, 1964, 210 pp, pbk.

Braham, Randolph L., ed., *Readings in Soviet Politics and Government,* Knopf, 1965, 615 pp, pbk.

Conquest, Robert, *Power and Policy in the USSR, The Study of Soviet Dynastics,* St Martin's, 1961, 485 pp.

———, *Russia After Khrushchev,* Praeger, 1965, 267 pp.

Crankshaw, Edward, *Khrushchev's Russia,* Penguin, 1960, 175 pp.

Dallin, Alexander and Alan F. Westin, *Politics in the Soviet Union: 7 Cases,* Harcourt, Brace & World, 1966, 320 pp, pbk.

Deutscher, Isaac, *Russia in Transition,* rev. ed., Grove, 1960, 265 pp, pbk.

Diamond, Sigmund, ed., "The Soviet Union Since Khrushchev, New Trends and Old Problems," *Proc. Ac. Pol. Sc.,* 28(1), Apr. 1965, 116 pp.

East, W. Gordon, *The Soviet Union,* Princeton UP, 1964, 136 pp.

Ehrenberg, Ilya, *The Thaw,* trans. by Manya Harari, with an essay, "The Death of Art," by Russell Kirk, Regnery, 1955, 230 pp.

Fainsod, Merle, *How Russia Is Ruled,* 2nd ed., Harvard UP, 1963, 684 pp.

———, *Khrushchev's Russia,* Australian Inst IA, Melbourne, 1963:233–59.

Fisher, Harold H., *The Communist Revolution, An Outline of Strategy and Tactics,* Stanford UP, 1955, 89 pp.

Gunther, John, *Inside Russia Today,* rev. ed., Pyramid Books, 1962, 604 pp, pbk.

Hammond, Thomas T., ed., *Soviet Foreign Relations and World Communism, Bibliography,* Princeton UP, 1966, 1240 pp.

Hazard, John N., *The Soviet System of Government,* 3rd ed., Chicago UP, 1964, 304 pp, pbk.

Hendel, Samuel, ed., *The Soviet Crucible, Soviet Government in Theory and Practice,* 2nd ed., Van Nostrand, 1963, 706 pp.

Holt, Robert T. and John E. Turner, eds., *Soviet Union, Paradox and Change*, Holt, 1962, 240 pp, pbk.

Horecky, Paul L., ed., *Russia and the Soviet Union, A Bibliographic Guide to Western Language Publications*, U Chicago P, 1965, 473 pp.

Kochan, Lionel, *The Making of Modern Russia*, Cape, London, 1962, 320 pp.

Koestler, Arthur, *The Yogi and the Commissar*, Macmillan, 1945, 247 pp.

Kolarz, Walter, ed., *Books on Communism, Bibliography*, rev. ed., Allen & Unwin, London, 1964, 453 pp.

Kingsbury, Robert C. and Robert N. Taaffe, *An Atlas of Soviet Affairs*, Praeger, 1965, 150 pp.

Kravchenko, Victor, *I Chose Freedom, The Personal and Political Life of a Soviet Official*, Scribner's, 1946, 496 pp.

Kulski, Wladyslaw W., *The Soviet Regime, Communism in Practice*, 3rd ed., Syracuse UP, 1959, 524 pp.

McClosky, Herbert and John E. Turner, *The Soviet Dictatorship*, McGraw-Hill, 1960, 657 pp.

Maichel, Karol, *Guide to Russian Reference Books*, Vol. II, *History, Auxiliary Historical Sciences, Ethnography and Geography*, ed. by J. S. G. Simmons, Stanford UP, 1964, 297 pp.

Mandel, William, *Russia Re-examined, the Law, the People, and How They Live*, Hill & Wang, 1964, 244 pp.

Meisel, James and Edward S. Kozers, *Materials for the Study of the Soviet System*, 2nd ed., Wahr, 1953, 613 pp.

Meyer, Alfred G., *The Soviet Political System, An Interpretation*, Random House, 1965, 494 pp.

Miller, Wright, *The USSR*, Oxford UP, 1963, 126 pp, pbk.

Moore, Barrington, Jr., *Soviet Politics, The Dilemma of Power, A Study of the Role of Ideas in Social Change*, Harvard UP, 1950, 503 pp.

——, *Terror and Progress, USSR, Some Sources of Change and Stability in the Soviet Dictatorship*, Harvard UP, 1954, 261 pp.

Mosely, Philip E., ed., *The Soviet Union, 1922–1962*, Praeger, 1963, 497 pp, pbk.

Riha, Thomas, ed., *Readings in Russian Civilization*, Chicago UP, 1964, 801 pp.

Salisbury, Harrison E., *Russia*, Atheneum, 1965, 144 pp, pbk.

Schapiro, Leonard, *The Government and Politics of the Soviet Union*, Random House, 1965, 191 pp.

Schuman, Frederick L., *Government in the Soviet Union*, Crowell, 1961, 190 pp, pbk.

——, *Russia Since 1918, Four Decades of Soviet Politics*, Knopf, 1957, 490 pp.

Schwartz, Harry, ed., *The Many Faces of Communism*, Berkley-Medallion, 1962, 254 pp, pbk.

Ulam, Adam B., *The New Face of Soviet Totalitarianism, An Essay on the Sources of Influence of Marxism and Communism*, Praeger, 1965, 233 pp.

Webb, Sidney and Beatrice, *Soviet Communism, A New Civilization?* Scribner's, 1936, 2 vols.

Whiting, Kenneth R., *The Soviet Union Today, A Concise Handbook*, Praeger, 1962, 350 pp.

Woytinsky, W. S., *Stormy Passage, A Personal History Through Two Russian Revolutions to Democracy and Freedom, 1905–1960*, Vanguard, 1961, 535 pp.

Chapter 1. SOVIET PEOPLE AND POLICIES

COMMUNISM

Acton, H. B., *The Illusion of the Epoch, Marxism-Leninism as a Philosophical Creed*, Cohen & West, London, 1955, 278 pp.

Anderson, Thornton, *Masters of Russian Marxism*, Appleton-Century-Crofts, 1964, 296 pp, pbk.

Balabanoff, Angelica, *Impressions of Lenin*, Michigan UP, 1964, 152 pp.

Beer, Samuel, ed., *The Communist Manifesto with Selections from the Eighteenth Brumaire of Bonaparte and Capital*, Appleton-Century-Crofts, 1955, 96 pp.

Berdyaev, Nickolai A., *Russian Revolution*, U Michigan P, 1961, 91 pp, pbk.

Berlin, Isaiah, *Karl Marx, His Life and Environment*, 3rd ed., Oxford UP, 1963, 295 pp.

Brzezinski, Zbigniew K., *Ideology and Power in Soviet Politics*, Praeger, 1962, 188 pp.

Bukharin, Nikolai, *Historical Materialism*, Intern. Pub., 1926, 318 pp.

Cole, George D. H., *The Meaning of Marxism*, Gollancz, London, 1948, 302 pp.

Dan, Theodore (Fedore Ilich), *The Origins of Bolshevism*, Secker & Warburg, London, 1964, 469 pp.

Daniels, Robert V., ed., *A Documentary History of Communism*, 2 vols, Random House, 1960, 391 and 393 pp.

——, *Marxism and Communism, Essential Readings*, Random House, 1965, 178 pp.

——, *The Nature of Communism*, Random House, 1962, 398 pp.

Deutscher, Isaac, ed., *The Age of Permanent Revolution, A Trotsky Anthology*, Dell Laurel, 1964, pbk.

——, *The Prophet Outcast, Trotsky, 1929–1940*, Oxford UP, 1963, 543 pp.

Fischer, Louis, *The Life of Lenin*, Harper, 1964, 703 pp.

Garthoff, Raymond L., *The Soviet Image of Future War*, Pub. Aff., 1960, 137 pp.

Haimson, Leopold H., *The Russian Marxists and the Origins of Bolshevism*, Harvard UP, 1955, 272 pp.

Hook, Sidney, *Marx and Marxists, The Ambiguous Legacy*, Van Nostrand, 1955, 254 pp.

Howe, Irving, ed., *The Basic Writings of Trotsky*, Random House, 1963, 427 pp.

Hunt, R. N. Carew, ed., *Books on Communism, A Bibliography*, Oxford UP, 1960, 333 pp.

——, *A Guide to Communist Jargon*, Macmillan, 1957, 169 pp.

——, *The Theory and Practice of Communism*, Penguin, 1963, 315 pp.

Jacobs, Dan N., *The New Communist Manifesto and Related Documents*, Row, Peterson, 1961, 217 pp.

Kautsky, Karl, *Dictatorship of the Proletariat*, National Labour P, Manchester, 1919, 149 pp.

Khrushchev, Nikita S., *The International Situation and Soviet Foreign Policy*, Crosscurrents, 1960, 36 pp.

Khrushchev, Nikita S., "On Peaceful Coexistence," *FA*, 38(1), Oct. 1959:1–18.

———, *USSR Victory in Peaceful Competition with Capitalism*, Dutton, 1960, 784 pp.

Labedz, Leopold, ed., *Revisionism, Essays on the History of Marxist Ideas*, Allen & Unwin, London, 1962, 404 pp.

——— and Walter S. Laqueur, eds., *The Future of Communist Society*, Praeger, 1961, 202 pp.

Laski, Harold J., *Communism*, Holt, 1927, 256 pp.

Lenin, Vladimir, *Letters*, ed. by Elizabeth Hill and Doris Mudie, Harcourt, Brace & World, 1937, 499 pp.

———, *Selected Works of V. I. Lenin*, Intern. Pub., 1935–39, 12 vols.

———, *What Is to Be Done?* ed. by and introduction and notes by S. V. Utechin, trans. by S. V. and Patricia Utechin, Clarendon P, Oxford, 1963, 213 pp.

Lewis, John, *Life and Teaching of Karl Marx*, Intern. Pub., 1965, 286 pp, pbk.

Lichtheim, George, *Marxism, An Historical and Critical Study*, Praeger, 1961, 412 pp.

Lindsay, Alexander D., *Karl Marx' Capital, An Introductory Essay*, Oxford UP, 1947, 128 pp.

Low, Alfred D., *Lenin on the Question of Nationality*, Bookman, 1958, 193 pp.

McKenzie, Kermit E., *Comintern and World Revolution, 1928–1943, The Shaping Doctrine*, Columbia UP, 1964, 368 pp.

McNeal, Robert H., *Lenin, Stalin, Khrushchev*, Prentice-Hall, 1963, pbk, 2 vols: *Voices of Bolshevism*, 180 pp, *The Bolshevik Tradition*, 181 pp.

Marcuse, Herbert, *Soviet Marxism, A Critical Analysis*, Columbia UP, 1958, 271 pp.

Marx, Karl, *Capital, the Communist Manifesto, and Other Writings*, Modern Lib., 1932, 429 pp.

Marx-Engels-Lenin Inst., *Joseph Stalin*, Intern. Pub., 1949, 128 pp.

Mayo, Henry B., *Introduction to Marxist Theory*, Oxford UP, 1960, 334 pp.

Mehring, Franz, *Karl Marx, The Story of His Life*, trans. by Edward Fitzgerald, U Michigan P, 1962, 575 pp, pbk.

Meyer, Alfred G., *Communism*, Random House, 1960, 217 pp.

———, *Leninism*, Praeger, 1962, 336 pp.

———, *Marxism, The Unity of Theory and Practice*, U Michigan P, 1963, 181 pp, pbk.

Page, Stanley W., *Lenin and World Revolution*, New York UP, 1959, 252 pp.

Payne, Robert, *The Life and Death of Lenin*, Simon & Schuster, 1964, 672 pp.

Plamenatz, John, *German Marxism and Russian Communism*, Longmans, London, 1954, 356 pp.

Possony, Stefan T., *Lenin, The Compulsive Revolutionary*, Regnery, 1964, 418 pp.

Sabine, George H., *Marxism*, Cornell UP, 1958, 60 pp.

Seton-Watson, Hugh, *Nationalism and Communism Essays, 1946–1963*, Methuen, London, 1964, 288 pp.

Shub, David, *Lenin, A Biography*, New Am. Lib., 1966, 496 pp, pbk.

Simmons, Ernest J., ed., *Continuity and Change in Russian and Soviet Thought*, Harvard UP, 1955, 563 pp.

Stalin, Joseph, *Collected Works*, For. Lang. Pub., Moscow, 1953.

———, *Economic Problems of Socialism in the U.S.S.R.*, Intern. Pub., 1952, 71 pp.

———, *The Great Patriotic War of the Soviet Union*, Intern. Pub., 1945, 167 pp.

———, *Leninism*, Intern. Pub., 1928–33, 2 vols.

———, *Leninism, Selected Writings*, Intern. Pub., 1942, 479 pp.

———, *Marxism and the National and Colonial Question*, Intern. Pub., 1936, 304 pp.

———, *Selected Writings*, Intern. Pub., 1945, 479 pp.

Swearer, Howard R. and Richard P. Longaker, eds., *Contemporary Communism, Theory and Practice*, Wadsworth, 1963, 384 pp, pbk.

Tertz, Abram (pseud.), *On Socialist Realism*, Pantheon, 1961, 95 pp.

Triska, Jan R., ed., *Soviet Communism, Programs and Rules*, Chandler, 1961, 196 pp.

Trotsky, Leon, *The Case of Leon Trotsky*, Harper, 1937, 617 pp.

———, *Lenin*, Putnam-Capricorn, 1962, 216 pp, pbk.

———, *Lessons of October*, Pioneer, 1937, 1925 pp.

———, *My Life*, Scribner's, 1930, 613 pp.

———, *The Real Situation in Russia*, Harcourt, Brace & World, 1928, 364 pp.

———, *The Revolution Betrayed*, Doubleday, 1937, 308 pp.

———, *Stalin*, Harper, 1946, 516 pp.

———, *Terrorism and Communism*, U Michigan P, 1961, 191 pp, pbk.

Tucker, Robert C., *The Soviet Political Mind, Studies in Stalinism and Post-Stalin Change*, Praeger, 1963, 251 pp, pbk.

Two Communist Manifestoes, Washington Center of Foreign Policy Research, 1961, 108 pp.

Ulam, Adam B., *The Unfinished Revolution, An Essay on the Sources of Influence of Marxism and Communism*, Random House, 1961, 307 pp.

Utechin, S. V., *Russian Political Thought*, Praeger, 1963, 320 pp, pbk.

Wetter, Gustav A., *Dialectical Materialism, A Historical and Systematic Survey of Philosophy in the Soviet Union*, Praeger, 1959, 609 pp.

Wiles, P. J. D., *The Political Economy of Communism, A Critical Study of Communist Theory and Practice*, Harvard UP, 1963, 404 pp.

LAND AND PEOPLE

Armstrong, John A., *Ukrainian Nationalism, 1939–1945*, Columbia UP, 1955, 322 pp.

Barghoorn, Frederick C., *Politics in the USSR, A Country Study*, Little, Brown, 1966, 418 pp, pbk.

Barnier, Lucien, trans., *The Secrets of Soviet Science*, Wingate, London, 1959, 165 pp.

Bauer, Raymond A., *Nine Soviet Portraits*, MIT P, 1965, 187 pp, pbk.

Berg, Lev S., *Natural Regions of the USSR*, trans. by Olga Adler Titelbaum, ed. by John A. Morrison and C. C. Nikiforoff, Macmillan, 1950, 436 pp.

Bilinsky, Yaroslav, *The Second Soviet Republic, The Ukraine After World War II*, Rutgers, 1964, 539 pp.

Black, Cyril E., ed., *The Transformation of Russian Society, Aspects of Change Since 1861*, Harvard UP, 1960, 695 pp.

Braham, Randolph L., *Jews in the Communist World, A Bibliography, 1945–1960*, Bookman, 1961, 64 pp.

Cole, J. P. and F. C. German, *A Geography of the USSR, The Background to a Planned Economy*, Butterworth, London, 1961, 290 pp.

Conquest, Robert, *Common Sense About Russia*, Gollancz, London, 1960, 175 pp, pbk.

———, *The Courage of Genius, The Pasternak Affair, A Documentary Report on Its Literary and Political Significance*, Collins, London, 1961, 191 pp.

———, *The Soviet Deportation of Nationalities*, Macmillan, 1960, 203 pp.

Cressey, George B., *Soviet Potentials, A Geographic Appraisal*, Syracuse UP, 1962, 256 pp.

Dodge, Norton T., *Women in the Soviet Economy, Their Role in Economic, Scientific, and Technical Development*, Johns Hopkins P, 1966, 331 pp.

Dudintsev, Vladimir, *Not by Bread Alone*, trans. by Edith Bone, Dutton, 1957, 512 pp.

Goldberg, B. Z., *The Jewish Problem in the Soviet Union*, Crown, 1961, 374 pp.

Grossman, Gregory, *Soviet Statistics of Physical Output of Industrial Commodities*, Princeton UP, 1960, 151 pp.

Hare, Richard, *The Art and Artists of Russia*, Methuen, London, 1965, 295 pp.

Hayward, Max and Edward L. Crowley, eds., *Soviet Literature in the Sixties: An International Symposium*, Praeger, 1964, 232 pp.

Hula, Erich, "The Nationalities Policy of the Soviet Union in Theory and Practice," *SR*, 10, May 1944: 168–201.

Inkeles, Alex and Raymond A. Bauer, *The Soviet Citizen, Daily Life in a Totalitarian Society*, Harvard UP, 1959, 540 pp.

Johnson, Priscilla, *Khrushchev and the Arts, The Politics of Soviet Culture, 1962–1964*, MIT P, 1965, 300 pp.

Jorré, Georges, *The Soviet Union, The Land and Its People*, trans. and rev. by E. D. Laborde, Longmans, London, 1961, 392 pp.

Keep, J. H. L., *The Rise of Social Democracy in Russia*, Clarendon P, Oxford, 1963, 334 pp.

Kluckhohn, Clyde K. M., Raymond A. Bauer, and Alex Inkeles, *The Soviet System, Cultural, Psychological and Social Themes*, Harvard UP, 1956, 274 pp, pbk.

Kolarz, Walter, *The Peoples of the Soviet Far East*, Praeger, 1955, 194 pp.

———, *Russia and Her Colonies*, 3rd ed., Praeger, 1955, 350 pp.

Krypton, Constantine, *The Northern Sea Route and the Economy of the Soviet North*, Praeger, 1956, 219 pp.

Lasky, Victor, *The Ugly Russian*, Trident, 1965, 313 pp.

Levine, Isaac Don, *I Rediscover Russia*, Duell, Sloan & Pearce, 1964, 216 pp.

Mace, David and Vera, *The Soviet Family*, Doubleday, 1963, 367 pp.

Mehnert, Klaus, *Soviet Man and His World*, trans. from German by Maurice Rosenbaum, Praeger, 1961, 310 pp.

Mihajlov, Mahajlo, *Moscow Summer*, Farrar, Straus & Giroux, 1965, 220 pp.

Miller, Margaret, *Rise of the Russian Consumer*, Inst. Ec. Aff., London, 1965, 254 pp, pbk.

Miller, Wright, *Russians as People*, Dutton, 1961, 205 pp.

Novak, Joseph (pseud.), *The Future Is Ours, Comrade, Conversations with the Russians*, Doubleday, 1960, 286 pp.

Pasternak, Boris, *Dr. Zhivago*, trans. by Max Hayward and Manya Harari, Pantheon, 1958, 558 pp.

Paustovsky, Konstantin, *Story of a Life*, Vol. 1, Pantheon, 1964, 661 pp.

Pietromarchi, Luca, *The Soviet World*, trans. by Lovett F. Edwards, Allen & Unwin, London, 1965, 462 pp.

Pipes, Richard, ed., *The Russian Intelligentsia*, Columbia UP, 1961, 234 pp.

Pitcher, Harvey J., *Understanding the Russians*, Allen & Unwin, London, 1964, 168 pp.

Schlesinger, Rudolf, ed., *The Nationalities Problem and Soviet Administration, Selected Readings on the Development of Soviet Nationalities Policies*, trans. by W. W. Gottlieb, Routledge, London, 1956, 294 pp.

Schwarz, Solomon M., *The Jews in the Soviet Union*, Syracuse UP, 1951, 380 pp.

Shimkin, Dmitri, *Minerals, A Key to Soviet Power*, Harvard UP, 1953, 452 pp.

Sholokhov, Mikhail A., *Harvest on the Don*, trans. by H. C. Stevens, Putnam, 1960, 399 pp.

Simmons, Ernest J., ed., *Through the Glass of Soviet Literature, Views of Russian Society*, Columbia UP, 1953, 301 pp.

Stillman, Edmund, ed., *Bitter Harvest, The Intellectual Revolt Behind the Iron Curtain*, Praeger, 1959, 313 pp, pbk.

Vakar, Nicholas P., *A Bibliographical Guide to Belorussia*, Harvard UP, 1956, 63 pp.

Wheeler, Geoffrey, *Racial Problems in Soviet Muslim Asia*, Oxford UP, 1960, 66 pp.

Zenkovsky, Serge A., *Pan-Turkism and Islam in Russia*, Harvard UP, 1960, 345 pp.

PROPAGANDA AND THE CONTROL OF IDEAS

Aczel, Tamas and Tibor Meray, *The Revolt of the Mind*, Praeger, 1960, 449 pp.

Buzek, Antony, *How the Communist Press Works*, Praeger, 1964, 287 pp.

Gibian, George, *Interval of Freedom, Soviet Literature During the Thaw, 1954–1957*, U Michigan P, 1960, 180 pp.

Gorokhoff, Boris I., *Publishing in the USSR*, Indiana UP, 1959, 306 pp.

Huxley, Julian, *Heredity, East and West, Lysenko and World Science*, Shuman, 1949, 246 pp.

Inkeles, Alex, *Public Opinion in Soviet Russia, A Study in Mass Persuasion*, Harvard UP, 1950, 379 pp.

Khokhlov, Nikolai, *In the Name of Conscience*, Muller, London, 1960, 356 pp.

Kirkpatrick, Evron M., *Year of Crisis, Communist Propaganda Activities in 1956*, Macmillan, 1957, 414 pp.

Keep, John, ed., *Contemporary History in the Soviet Mirror*, Praeger, 1964, 331 pp.

Lysenko, Trofim D., *The Science of Biology Today*, Intern. Pub., 1948, 62 pp.

Pálóczi-Horváth, George, *The Writer and the Commissar*, Bodley Head, London, 1960, 112 pp.

Stillman, Edmund, ed., *Bitter Harvest, The Intellectual Revolt Behind the Iron Curtain*, Praeger, 1959, 313 pp, pbk.

Struve, Gleb, *Soviet Russian Literature, 1917–1950*, U Oklahoma P, 1951, 414 pp.

Vucinich, Alexander, *The Soviet Academy of Sciences*, Stanford UP, 1956, 157 pp.

SUPPRESSION OF OPPOSITION

Brzezinski, Zbigniew K., *The Permanent Purge, Politics in Soviet Totalitarianism*, Harvard UP, 1956, 256 pp.

Deriabin, Peter et al., *The Secret World*, Doubleday, 1959, 334 pp.

Koestler, Arthur, *Darkness at Noon*, Macmillan, 1941, 267 pp.

Leites, Nathan and Elsa Bernaut, *Ritual of Liquidation, The Case of the Moscow Trials*, Free P, 1954, 515 pp.

Lipper, Elinor, *Eleven Years in Soviet Prison Camps*, Regnery, 1951, 310 pp.

Penkovsky, Oleg, *The Penkovsky Papers*, trans. by Peter Deriabin, Doubleday, 1966, 411 pp.

Schapiro, Leonard, *Origin of the Communist Autocracy, Political Opposition in the Soviet State, First Phase, 1917–1922*, Harvard UP, 1955, 397 pp.

Tucker, Robert C. and Stephen Cohen, eds., *The Great Purge Trial*, Grosset & Dunlap, 1965, 725 pp, pbk.

Wolin, Simon and Robert S. Slusser, eds., *The Soviet Secret Police*, Praeger, 1957, 408 pp.

RELIGION

Ciszed, Walter J. and Daniel J. Flaherty, *With God in Russia*, Peter Davies, London, 1964, 302 pp.

Curtiss, John S., *The Russian Church and the Soviet State, 1917–1950*, Little, Brown, 1953, 387 pp.

Fletcher, William C., *A Study in Survival, The Church in Russia, 1927–1943*, Macmillan, 1965, 169 pp.

Kolarz, Walter, *Religion in the Soviet Union*, St Martin's, 1961, 518 pp.

Scott, Richenda C., *Quakers in Russia*, Michael Joseph, London, 1964, 302 pp.

Spinka, Matthew, *The Church in Soviet Russia*, Oxford UP, 1956, 192 pp.

Szczesniak, Bolislaw, ed. and trans., *The Russian Revolution and Religion*, U Notre Dame P, 1960, 289 pp.

Chapter 2. THE SOVIET POLITICAL HERITAGE

Baron, Samuel H., *Plekhanov, The Father of Russian Marxism*, Stanford UP, 1964, 400 pp.

Black, C. E., ed., *Rewriting Russian History, Soviet Interpretations of Russia's Past*, Praeger, 1956, 420 pp.

Carr, Edward Hallett, *A History of Soviet Russia*, Macmillan, 6 vols: *The Bolshevik Revolution, 1917–1923*, 1951, 430 pp; *The Struggle for Power, 1923–1928*, 1952, 400 pp; *The Economic Order and Soviet Russia and the World*, 1953, 614 pp; *The Interregnum, 1923–1924*, 1954, 392 pp; *Socialism in One Country, 1924–1926*, 1958 and 1960, 557 pp.

Carr, Edward Hallett, "Russia and Europe as a Theme of Russian History," in *Essays Presented to Sir Lewis Namier*, ed. by R. Pares and Alan John Percival Taylor, Macmillan, 1956:357–93.

Clarkson, Jesse D., *A History of Russia*, Random House, 1962, 857 pp.

Dallin, David J., *From Purge to Coexistence*, Regnery, 1964, 289 pp.

Daniels, Robert V., ed., *Documentary History of Communism*, 2 vols, Vintage, 1960, 321 and 393 pp, pbk.

Deutscher, Isaac, *Ironies of History*, Oxford UP, 1966, 278 pp.

———, *The Prophet Armed, Trotsky, 1879–1921*, Oxford UP, 1954, 540 pp.

———, *The Prophet Unarmed, Trotsky, 1921–1929*, Oxford UP, 1959, 490 pp.

———, *The Prophet Outcast: Trotsky, 1929–1940*, Oxford UP, 1963, 543 pp.

Ehrenburg, Ilya, *Men, Years, Life, The War, 1941–1945*, Vol. 5, MacGibbon & Kee, London, 1964, 198 pp.

Fainsod, Merle, *Smolensk Under Soviet Rule*, Harvard UP, 1958, 484 pp.

Hill, Christopher, *Lenin and the Russian Revolution*, Macmillan, 1950, 245 pp.

Kennan, George, *Soviet-American Relations, 1917–1920*, Princeton UP, 2 vols: *Russia Leaves the War*, 1956, 544 pp; *The Decision to Intervene*, 1958, 524 pp.

Kerensky, Alexander, *The Crucifixion of Liberty*, Day, 1934, 406 pp.

Lawrence, John, *A History of Russia*, Grove, 1961, 372 pp, pbk.

Levin, Alfred, *The Second Duma*, Yale UP, 1940, 414 pp.

Masaryk, Thomas G., *The Spirit of Russia*, 2nd ed., Macmillan, 2 vols, 1955, 480 and 664 pp.

Mazour, Anatole G., *Modern Russian Historiography*, rev. enl. ed., Van Nostrand, 1958, 260 pp.

Moorehead, Alan, *The Russian Revolution*, Harper, 1958, 301 pp.

Pares, Sir Bernard, *A History of Russia*, 3rd rev. ed., Knopf, 1953, 674 pp.

Pavlov, Dimitri, *Leningrad 1941, The Blockade*, U Chicago P, 1965, 186 pp.

Pipes, Richard, *The Formation of the Soviet Union, Communism and Nationalism, 1917–1923*, rev. ed., Harvard UP, 1964, 365 pp.

Seton-Watson, Hugh, *The Decline of Imperial Russia, 1855–1914*, Praeger, 1953, 406 pp.

———, *The Pattern of Communistic Revolution, A Historical Analysis*, rev. enl. ed., Methuen, London, 1961, 432 pp.

Tarulis, Albert N., *Soviet Policy Toward the Baltic States, 1918–1940*, U Notre Dame P, 1959, 276 pp.

Trotsky, Leon, *The History of the Russian Revolution*, Gollancz, London, 1965.

———, *The Russian Revolution*, condensed, Doubleday, 1959, 524 pp.

Vernadsky, George, *A History of Russia*, 4th ed., Yale UP, 1961, 512 pp, pbk.

Vernadsky, George, *Russia at the Dawn of the Modern Age*, Yale UP, 1959, 347 pp.

Von Laue, Theodore H., *Why Lenin? Why Stalin? A Reappraisal of the Russian Revolution 1900–1930*, Weidenfeld & Nicolson, London, 1966, 242 pp.

Von Rauch, Georg, *A History of Soviet Russia*, 4th rev. ed., Praeger, 1964, 528 pp.

Walsh, Warren Bartlett, *Russia and the Soviet Union, A Modern History*, U Michigan P, 1959, 640 pp.

Werth, Alexander, *Russia at War, 1941–1945*, Barrie & Rockliff, London, 1964, 1100 pp.

Wolfe, Bertram D., *Three Who Made a Revolution, A Biographical History*, Dial, 1964, 659 pp, pbk.

Chapter 3. THE COMMUNIST PARTY

Armstrong, John A., *The Politics of Totalitarianism, The Communist Party of the Soviet Union from 1934 to the Present*, Random House, 1961, 458 pp.

Avtorkhanov, A., *Stalin and the Communist Party*, Stevens, London, 1960, 379 pp.

Borys, Jurij, *The Russian Communist Party and the Sovietization of Ukraine*, Norstedt & Sonel, Stockholm, 1960, 374 pp.

Daniels, Robert Vincent, *The Conscience of the Revolution, Communist Opposition in Soviet Russia*, Harvard UP, 1960, 526 pp.

Embree, G. D., *The Soviet Union Between the 19th and 20th Party Congresses, 1952–1956*, Nijhoff, The Hague, 1959, 365 pp.

Fainsod, Merle, "The 22nd Party Congress," *Problems*, 10(6), Nov.–Dec. 1961:11, special supplement.

Gruliow, Leo, ed., *Current Soviet Policies*, Vol. 1, *The Documentary Record of the 19th Communist Party Congress and the Reorganization After Stalin's Death*, Praeger, 1953, 270 pp.

———, *Current Soviet Policies*, Vol. 2, *The Documentary Record of the 20th Communist Party Congress and Its Aftermath*, Praeger, 1957, 247 pp.

———, *Current Soviet Policies*, Vol. 3, *The Documentary Record of the Extraordinary 21st Congress of the Communist Party of the Soviet Union*, Columbia UP, 1961, 230 pp.

History of the Communist Party of the Soviet Union (Bolsheviks), Short Course, ed. by a commission of the Central Committee of the CPSU, Intern. Pub., 1939, 487 pp.

Jacobs, Daniel Norman, ed., *The New Communist Manifesto, And Related Documents*, Harper, 1962, 250 pp, pbk.

Kenney, Charles D., "The Twentieth CPSU Congress, A Study in Calculated Moderation," *APSR*, 50(3), Sept. 1956:764–86.

Khrushchev, Nikita S., *Report of the Central Committee of the Communist Party of the Soviet Union to the 20th Party Congress*, For. Lang. Pub., Moscow, 1956, 145 pp.

Klatt, Werner, "The Twenty-Third CPSU Congress (2)," *Survey*, 60, July 1966:85–93.

Malenkov, G., *Report to the Nineteenth Party Congress on the Work of the Central Committee of the CPSU*, Collet's Holdings, London, 1952, 147 pp.

Meissner, Boris, ed., *The Communist Party of the Soviet Union*, Praeger, 1956, 276 pp.

Mosely, Philip E., "The Nineteenth Party Congress," *FA*, 31(2), Jan. 1953:238–57.

Mote, Max E., *Soviet Local and Republic Elections*, Stanford UP, 1965, 123 pp.

Pethybridge, Roger, *A Key to Soviet Politics, The Crisis of the "Anti-Party" Group*, Allen & Unwin, London, 1962, 207 pp.

Popov, Nikolai N., *Outline History of the Communist Party of the Soviet Union*, Intern. Pub., 2 vols, 1934.

Reshetar, John S., Jr., *A Concise History of the Communist Party of the Soviet Union*, rev. ed., Praeger, 1964, 372 pp, pbk.

Schapiro, Leonard, *The Communist Party of the Soviet Union*, Random House, 1960, 631 pp.

———, "The Twenty-Third CPSU Congress (1)," *Survey*, 60, July 1966:72–85.

———, ed., *The USSR and the Future, An Analysis of the New Program of the CPSU*, Praeger, 1962, 324 pp, pbk.

"The 23rd Congress of the CPSU, Problems and Auguries," *WT*, 22(4), Apr. 1966:135–41.

Wheeler, Marcus, "Political Aspects of the 23rd Congress of the CPSU," *WT*, 22(7), July 1966:307–14.

Wolfe, Bertram D., *Khrushchev and Stalin's Ghost, The Text, Background and Meaning of Khrushchev's Secret Address*, Praeger, 1956, 322 pp.

Chapter 4. THE SOVIETS

Carson, George Barr, Jr., *Electoral Practices in the USSR*, Praeger, 1955, 151 pp.

Karpinsky, V., *The Social and State Structure of the USSR*, For. Lang. Pub., Moscow, 1950.

Rigby, Thomas H., "Changing Composition of the Supreme Soviet," *PQ*, 24(3), July–Sept. 1953:307–16.

Chapter 5. SOVIET POLITICAL LEADERSHIP

Alexandrov, Victor, *Khrushchev of the Ukraine*, Phil. Lib., 1957, 216 pp.

Armstrong, John A., *The Soviet Bureaucratic Elite, A Case Study of the Ukrainian Apparatus*, Praeger, 1959, 174 pp.

Crankshaw, Edward, *Khrushchev, A Career*, Viking, 1966, 311 pp.

Deutscher, Isaac, *Heretics and Renegades*, Hamilton, London, 1955, 288 pp.

———, *Stalin, A Political Biography*, Vintage, 1960, 600 pp, pbk.

Ebon, Martin, *Malenkov, Stalin's Successor*, New York UP, 1953, 284 pp.

Frankland, Mark, *Khrushchev*, Penguin, 1966, 213 pp.

Institute for the Study of the USSR, *Who's Who in the USSR*, 2nd ed., Scarecrow, 1965, 1189 pp.

Kellen, Konrad, *Khrushchev; A Political Portrait*, Praeger, 1961, 271 pp.

Khrushchev, Nikita S., *Disarmament and Colonial Freedom, Speeches and Interviews at the 15th UN Assembly*, Lawrence & Wishart, London, 1961, 300 pp.

Khrushchev, Nikita S., *For Victory in Peaceful Competition with Capitalism*, Dutton, 1960, 784 pp.

——, *Raising the Soviet Standard of Living, A Report to the Supreme Soviet, May 5, 1960*, Crosscurrents, 1960, 101 pp.

Khrushchev in America, Crosscurrents, 1960, 231 pp.

Khrushchev in New York, A Documentary Record of K's Trip to New York, Sept. 19–Oct. 13, 1960, Crosscurrents, 1960, 286 pp.

Let Us Live in Peace and Friendship, The Visit of N. S. Khrushchev to the USA, Sept. 15–17, 1959, For. Lang. Pub., Moscow, 1959, 406 pp.

Linden, Carl A., *Khrushchev and the Soviet Leadership, 1957–1964*, Johns Hopkins P, 1966, 270 pp, pbk.

Nicolaevsky, Boris, *Power and the Soviet Elite*, ed. by Jane Zagoria, Praeger, 1965, 275 pp.

Pálóczi-Horváth, George, *Khrushchev, The Making of a Dictator*, Little, Brown, 1960, 304 pp.

Payne, Robert, *The Rise and Fall of Stalin*, Simon & Schuster, 1965, 767 pp.

Pistrak, Lazar, *The Grand Tactician, Khrushchev's Rise to Power*, Praeger, 1961, 296 pp.

Randall, Francis B., *Stalin's Russia*, Free P, 1965, 328 pp.

Rigby, T. H., ed., *Stalin*, Prentice-Hall, 1966, 182 pp.

Rush, Myron, *Political Succession in the USSR*, Columbia UP, 1965, 223 pp.

Schueller, George K., *The Politburo*, Stanford UP, 1951, 79 pp.

Whitney, Thomas P., *Khrushchev Speaks, Selected Speeches, Articles and Press Conferences*, 1963, 466 pp.

Chapter 6. ADMINISTRATION IN THE USSR: PLANNING AND CONTROLS

THE PLANNED ECONOMY

Baykov, Alexander, "Some Observations on Economic Development in the USSR," in J. Tinbergen et al., *Economic Planning*, Mouton, The Hague, 1963:21–44.

Belov, Fedor, *The History of a Soviet Collective Farm*, Praeger, 1955, 237 pp.

Bergson, Abram, *The Economics of Soviet Planning*, Yale UP, 1964, 394 pp, pbk.

——, *The Real National Income of Soviet Russia Since 1928*, Harvard UP, 1961, 472 pp.

Campbell, Robert W., *Soviet Economic Power, Its Organization, Growth and Challenge*, Houghton Mifflin, 1960, 209 pp, pbk.

Central Statistical Administration, *The National Economy of the USSR, A Statistical Collection*, Moscow, 1956, 262 pp.

Chapman, Janet G., "Real Wages in the Soviet Union, 1928–1952," *RES*, 36(2), May 1954:134–56.

Davies, R. W., *The Development of the Soviet Budgetary System*, Cambridge UP, 1959, 372 pp.

Degras, Jane, ed., *Soviet Planning*, Praeger, 1965, 224 pp.

Dinerstein, Herbert S. and Leon Goure, *Two Studies in Soviet Controls, Communism and the Russian Peasant, and Moscow in Crisis*, Free P, 1955, 254 pp.

Erlich, Alexander, *The Soviet Industrialization Debate, 1924–1928*, Harvard UP, 1960, 214 pp.

Granick, David, *The Red Executive, A Study of the Organization Man in Russian Industry*, Doubleday, 1960, 334 pp.

Griffiths, Sir Percival, *The Changing Face of Communism*, Bodley Head, London, 1961, 223 pp.

Grossman, Gregory, *Soviet Statistics of Physical Output of Industrial Commodities*, Princeton UP, 1960, 151 pp.

——, ed., *Value and Plan: Economic Calculation and Organization in Eastern Europe*, U California P, 1960, 370 pp.

Hardt, John P. et al., *The Cold War Economic Gap, The Increasing Threat to American Supremacy*, Praeger, 1961, 128 pp.

Hodgkins, Jordan A., *Soviet Power, Energy Resources, Production and Potentials*, Prentice-Hall, 1961, 190 pp.

Hodgman, Donald R., *Soviet Industrial Production, 1928–1951*, Harvard UP, 1954, 241 pp.

Holzman, Franklyn D., *Soviet Taxation, The Fiscal and Monetary Problems of a Planned Economy*, Harvard UP, 1955, 376 pp.

Ingram, David, *The Communist Economic Challenge*, Praeger, 1965, 168 pp.

Jasny, Naum, *Khrushchev's Crop Policy*, Glasgow U, 1965, 243 pp.

——, *The Socialized Agriculture of the USSR, Plans and Performance*, Stanford UP, 1949, 837 pp.

——, *Soviet Industrialization, 1928–1952*, U Chicago P, 1961, 488 pp.

Karcz, Jerzy F. and V. P. Timoshenko, *Soviet Agricultural Policy, 1953–1962*, Stanford UP, 1964.

Kaser, Michael, "Kosygin, Liberman, and the Pace of Soviet Industrial Reform," *WT*, 21(9), Sept. 1965: 375–88.

Kazakov, George, *The Soviet Peat Industry, A Descriptive Study*, Praeger, 1956, 245 pp.

Khrushchev, Nikita S., *Target Figures for the Economic Development of the Soviet Union, 1959–1965, Report to the Special Twenty-First Congress of the Communist Party of the Soviet Union, January 27, 1959, and Reply to Discussion*, Soviet News, London, 1959, 116 pp.

——, "Theses of the Seven-Year Plan, I & II," *CDSP*, Dec. 1958 and Jan. 1959.

Laird, Roy D., *Collective Farming in Russia, A Political Study of the Soviet Kolkhozy*, U Kansas P, 1958, 176 pp.

Miller, Margaret et al., *Communist Economy Under Change, Studies in the Theory and Practice of Markets and Competition in Russia, Poland, and Yugoslavia*, Deutsche, London, 1963, 272 pp.

Nove, Alec, *Economic Rationality and Soviet Politics, or Was Stalin Really Necessary?* Praeger, 1964, 316 pp.

——, *The Soviet Economy, An Introduction*, Praeger, 1961, 328 pp.

Nutter, G. Warren, *The Growth of Industrial Production in the Soviet Union*, Princeton UP, 1962, 733 pp.

Opdahl, Roger W., "Soviet Agriculture Since 1953," *PSQ*, 75(1), Mar. 1960:47–65.

Ploss, Sidney I., *Conflict and Decision-Making in Soviet Russia, A Case Study of Agricultural Policy, 1953–1963*, Princeton UP, 1965, 312 pp.

Preobazhensky, E., *The New Economics*, trans. by Brian Pearce, Oxford UP, 1965, 310 pp.

The Soviet Seven-Year Plan, A Study of Economic Progress and Potential in the USSR, Phoenix, London, 1960, 126 pp.

Schwartz, Harry G., *The Soviet Economy Since Stalin*, Lippincott, 1965, 256 pp, pbk.

Shaffer, Harry G., *The Soviet Economy, A Collection of Western and Soviet Views*, Appleton-Century-Crofts, 1964, 465 pp, pbk.

Wiles, P. J. D., *The Political Economy of Communism*, Blackwell, Oxford, 1962, 404 pp.

Zhukov, Victor, *A Plan for the People*, Soviet Booklets, London, 1959, 26 pp.

LOCAL ADMINISTRATION

Cattell, David T., "Leningrad, Case Study of Soviet Local Government," *WPQ*, 17(2), June 1964:188–99.

Rigby, Thomas H., "Soviet Local Government and Democracy," *Australian Outlook*, 8(1), Mar. 1954: 19–31.

Wesson, Robert G., *Soviet Communes*, Rutgers UP, 1963, 275 pp.

LABOR, TRADE UNIONS, AND MANAGEMENT

Barker, G. Russell, *Some Problems of Incentives and Labour Productivity in Soviet Industry*, Blackwell, Oxford, 1956, 130 pp.

Berliner, Joseph S., *Factory and Manager in the USSR*, Harvard UP, 1957, 386 pp.

Dewar, Margaret, *Labour Policy in the USSR, 1917–1928*, Oxford UP, 1956, 294 pp.

Granick, David, *Management of the Industrial Firm in the USSR, A Study in Soviet Economic Planning*, Columbia UP, 1954, 346 pp.

Schwarz, Solomon M., *Labor in the Soviet Union*, Praeger, 1952, 364 pp.

Chapter 7. SOVIET LAW AND COURTS

Berman, Harold J., "The Comparison of Soviet and American Law," *Indiana LJ*, 34(4), Summer 1959: 558–70.

——, *Justice in the USSR, An Interpretation of Soviet Law*, rev. ed., Harvard UP, 1963, 450 pp.

——, "Soviet Law Reform, Dateline Moscow 1957," *Yale LJ*, 66(8), July 1957:1191–1215.

—— and James W. Spindler, trans. and introduction by, *Soviet Criminal Law and Procedure, the RSFSR Codes*, Harvard UP, 1966, 501 pp.

Feifer, George, *Justice in Moscow*, Simon & Schuster, 1964, 353 pp.

Gsovski, Vladimir and Kazimierz Grzybowski, eds., *Government, Law and Courts in the Soviet Union and Eastern Europe*, Praeger, 2 vols, 1960, 2067 pp.

Guins, George C., *Soviet Law and Soviet Society*, Nijhoff, The Hague, 1954, 457 pp.

Hayward, Max, ed. and trans., *On Trial, The Soviet State Versus "Abram Tertz" and Nikolai Arzhak*, Harper, 1966, 183 pp, pbk.

Hazard, John N., *Law and Social Change in the USSR*, Carswell, Toronto, 1953, 310 pp.

——, *Settling Disputes in Soviet Society, The Formative Years of Legal Institutions*, Columbia UP, 1960, 534 pp.

——, ed., *Soviet Legal Philosophy*, Harvard UP, 1952, 520 pp.

—— and Isaac Shapiro, *The Soviet Legal System, Post-Stalin Documentation and Historical Commentary*, Oceana, 1962, 186 pp.

Kelsen, Hans, *The Communist Theory of Law*, Praeger, 1955, 203 pp.

La Fave, Wayne, ed., *Law in the Soviet Society*, Illinois UP, 1965, 297 pp, pbk.

Margolis, Emanuel, "Soviet Views on the Relationship Between National and International Law," *ICLQ*, Jan. 1955:116–28.

Morgan, Glenn G., *Soviet Administrative Legality, The Role of the Attorney General's Office*, Stanford UP, 1962, 281 pp.

Szirmai, Z., ed., *Law in Eastern Europe*, Vol. 3, *The Federal Criminal Law of the Soviet Union*, Sijthoff, Leyden, 1959, 157 pp.

Vyshinsky, Andrei Y., *The Law of the Soviet State*, Macmillan, 1948, 749 pp.

Chapter 8. THE USSR: A WORKERS' SOCIETY?

EDUCATION

Alt, Herschel and Edith, *Russia's Children*, Bookman, 1959, 240 pp.

Benton, William, *This Is the Challenge, The Benton Report on the Nature of the Soviet Threat*, Associated College P, 1958, 254 pp.

Bereday, George Z. F. and Joan Pennar, eds., *The Politics of Soviet Education*, Praeger, 1960, 217 pp.

Boiter, Albert, *The Khrushchev School Reform*, American Committee for Liberation, 1959, 26 pp.

Counts, George S., *The Challenge of Soviet Education*, McGraw-Hill, 1957, 330 pp.

——, *Khrushchev and the Central Committee Speak on Education*, U Pittsburgh P, 1959, 66 pp.

Fisher, Ralph Talcott, *Pattern for Soviet Youth, A Study of the Congresses of the Komsomol, 1918–1954*, Columbia UP, 1959, 452 pp.

Kline, George L., ed., *Soviet Education*, Columbia UP, 1957, 192 pp.

Korol, Alexander G., *Soviet Education for Science and Technology*, Wiley, 1957, 494 pp.

Levin, D., *Soviet Education Today*, Staples, London, 1959, 170 pp.

Meek, Dorothea L., ed. and trans., *Soviet Youth, Some Achievements and Problems*, Routledge, London, 1957, 251 pp.

Meyer, Frank S., *The Molding of Communists, The Training of the Communist Cadre*, Harcourt, Brace & World, 1961, 214 pp.

Moos, Elizabeth, "The Changes in Soviet Schools in September 1964," *CER*, Dec. 1964:264–68.

Redl, Helen B., *Soviet Educators on Soviet Education*, Free P, 1964, 252 pp.

Report of the Second Seminar on Education in the Soviet Union, Inst. of Intern. Educ., 1959, 78 pp.

Rosen, Seymour, *Education in the USSR*, USGPO, 1957, 226 pp.

——, *Significant Aspects of Soviet Education*, USGPO, 1965, 22 pp.

LABOR AND SOCIAL SECURITY

Bergson, Abram, "The Concept of Social Welfare," *QJE*, 68(2), May 1954:233–52.

Brown, Emily Clark, *Soviet Trade Unions and Labor Relations*, Harvard UP, 1966, 394 pp.

Chapman, Janet G., *Real Wages in Soviet Russia Since 1928*, Harvard UP, 1963, 395 pp.

DeWitt, Nicholas, *Education and Professional Employment in the USSR*, Nat. Science Found., 1962, 856 pp.

——, *Soviet Professional Manpower, Its Education, Training and Supply*, Nat. Science Found., 1955, 400 pp.

Field, Mark G., *Doctor and Patient in Soviet Russia*, Harvard UP, 1957, 266 pp.

Laird, Roy D., ed., *Soviet Agricultural and Peasant Affairs*, Kansas UP, 1963, 335 pp.

Principal Current Soviet Labor Legislation, A Compilation of Documents, US Dept. of Labor, 1962, 135 pp.

A Report on Social Security Administration in the Soviet Union, US Social Security Administration, 1960, 157 pp.

A Report on Social Security Programs in the Soviet Union, US Dept. of Health, Education, and Welfare, 1960, 157 pp.

Sasnovy, Timothy, *The Housing Problem in the Soviet Union*, Praeger, 1954, 300 pp.

Chapter 9. THE SOVIET UNION AND THE OUTSIDE WORLD

SOVIET RELATIONS WITH
OTHER COMMUNIST COUNTRIES

Bain, Leslie B., *The Reluctant Satellites, An Eyewitness Report on East Europe and the Hungarian Revolution*, Macmillan, 1960, 233 pp.

Ballis, William B., "The Political Evolution of a Soviet Satellite, The Mongolian People's Republic," *WPQ*, 9(2), June 1956:293–321.

Benes, Valclav L., Robert F. Brynes, and Nicolas Spulber, eds., *The Second Soviet-Yugoslav Dispute*, Indiana UP, 1939, 272 pp.

Borsody, Stephen, *The Triumph of Tyranny, The Nazi and Soviet Conquest of Central Europe*, Macmillan, 1960, 285 pp.

Brown, J. F., *The New Eastern Europe, The Khrushchev Era and After*, Praeger, 1966, 306 pp.

Brzezinski, Zbigniew K., *The Soviet Bloc, Unity and Conflict*, rev. ed., Praeger, 1967, 575 pp.

Burks, R. V., *The Dynamics of Communism in Eastern Europe*, Princeton UP, 1961, 244 pp.

Carlisle, Donald S., "The Changing Soviet Perception of the Development Process in the Afro-Asian World," *MJPS*, 8(4), Nov. 1964:385–407.

Carlton, Richard R., ed., *Forced Labor in the People's Democracies*, Praeger, 1955, 256 pp.

Dewar, Margaret, *Soviet Trade with Eastern Europe, 1945–1959*, RIIA, 1951, 123 pp.

Duchacek, Ivo, "The Strategy of Communist Infiltration in Czechoslovakia, 1944–1948," *WP*, 2(3), Apr. 1950:345–72.

Gordon, J., ed., *The Jews in the Soviet Satellite Countries*, Cornell UP, 1953, 500 pp.

Gripp, Richard C., "Eastern Europe's Ten Years of National Communism, 1948–1958," *WPQ*, 13(4), Dec. 1960:934–50.

Gsovski, Vladimir, ed., *Church and State Behind the Iron Curtain*, Praeger, 1955, 270 pp.

Halasz, Nicholas, *In the Shadow of Russia*, Ronald, 1959, 390 pp.

Hiscocks, Richard, *Poland, Bridge for the Abyss, An Interpretation of Developments in Postwar Poland*, Oxford UP, 1963, 359 pp.

Ionescu, Ghita, *Soviet Empire in Eastern Europe*, Penguin, 1965, 168 pp.

Kertesz, Stephen D., *Diplomacy in a Whirlpool, Hungary Between Nazi Germany and Soviet Russia, A Study of Soviet Penetration and Domination of Hungary*, Notre Dame UP, 1966, 273 pp.

——, ed., *East Central Europe and the World, Developments in the Post-Stalin Era*, U Notre Dame P, 1966, 350 pp.

Korbel, Josef, *The Communist Subversion of Czechoslovakia, 1938–1948, The Failure of Coexistence*, Princeton UP, 1959, 270 pp.

Seton-Watson, Hugh, *The East European Revolution*, Praeger, 1961, 435 pp.

Skilling, Harold Gordon, *The Governments of Communist East Europe*, Crowell, 1966, 256 pp.

Stehle, Hansjakob, *The Independent Satellite, Society and Politics in Poland Since 1945*, Praeger, 1965, 361 pp.

Tarulis, Albert N., *Soviet Policy Toward the Baltic States, 1918–1940*, U Notre Dame P, 1959, 276 pp.

Váli, Ferenc A., *Rift and Revolt in Hungary, Nationalism Versus Communism*, Harvard UP, 1961, 590 pp.

Wszelaki, Jan, *Communist Economic Strategy, The Role of East-Central Europe*, Oxford UP, 1959, 132 pp.

FOREIGN POLICY

Adams, Arthur E., *Readings in Soviet Foreign Policy*, Heath, 1961, 420 pp.

Allen, Robert Loring, *Soviet Economic Warfare*, Pub. Aff., 1960, 293 pp.

Aspaturian, Vernon-V., *The Union Republics in Soviet Diplomacy, A Study of Soviet Federalism in the Service of Soviet Foreign Policy*, Yale UP, 1960, 228 pp.

Barghoorn, Frederick C., *The Soviet Cultural Offensive, The Role of Cultural Diplomacy in Soviet Foreign Policy*, Princeton UP, 1960, 353 pp.

Beloff, Max, *The Foreign Policy of Soviet Russia, 1929–1941*, Oxford UP, 2 vols: *1929–1936*, 1947, 261 pp; *1936–1941*, 1949, 434 pp.

——, *Soviet Policy in the Far East, 1944–1951*, Oxford UP, 1954, 278 pp.

Berliner, Joseph S., *Soviet Economic Aid, The New*

Aid and Trade Policy in Underdeveloped Countries, Praeger, 1958, 232 pp.

Berman, Harold J., introduction by, *The Trial of the U2,* Translation World, 1960, 158 pp.

Carr, Edward H., *German-Soviet Relations Between the Two World Wars, 1919–1939,* Johns Hopkins P, 1951, 146 pp.

Clemens, Walter C., *Soviet Disarmament Policy, 1917–1963,* Stanford UP, 1965, 151 pp, pbk.

Cornell, Margaret, *Russia and the Western Powers in the Post-War World, A Chronology of Events,* RIIA, London, 1960, 50 pp.

Dallin, Alexander F., comp., *Soviet Conduct in World Affairs,* Columbia UP, 1960, 318 pp.

———, *Soviet Foreign Policy After Stalin,* Lippincott, 1961, 543 pp.

———, *The Soviet Union at the United Nations, Inquiry into Soviet Motives and Objectives,* Praeger, 1962, 250 pp, pbk.

Deane, John R., *The Strange Alliance, The Story of Our Efforts at Wartime Co-operation with Russia,* Viking, 1947, 344 pp.

Degras, Jane, ed., *Soviet Documents on Foreign Policy,* Oxford UP, 3 vols: *1917–1924,* 1951, 501 pp; *1925–1932,* 1952, 560 pp; *1933–1941,* 1953, 522 pp.

Dennett, Raymond and Joseph E. Johnson, eds., *Negotiating with the Russians,* World Peace Found., 1951, 322 pp.

Embree, George D., ed., *The Soviet Union and the German Question, Sept. 1958–June 1961,* Nijhoff, The Hague, 1963, 331 pp.

Fischer, Louis, *Russia, America and the World,* Harper, 1961, 244 pp.

———, *The Soviets in World Affairs, A History of the Relations Between the Soviet Union and the Rest of the World, 1917–1929,* Princeton UP, 1951, 2 vols, 960 pp.

Gibney, Frank, *The Khrushchev Pattern,* Duell, Sloan & Pearce, 1960, 280 pp.

Goldwin, Robert A. and Marvin Zetterbaum, eds., *Readings in Russian Foreign Policy,* Oxford UP, 1959, 775 pp, pbk.

Horelick, Arnold L. and Myron Rush, *Strategic Power and Soviet Foreign Policy,* Chicago UP, 1966, 225 pp.

Jacobson, Harold Karan, *The USSR and the UN's Economic and Social Activities,* U Notre Dame P, 1963, 309 pp.

Jados, Stanley S., *Documents on Russian-American Relations, Washington to Eisenhower,* Catholic U America P, 1965, 416 pp.

Joy, Admiral C. Turner (chief negotiator for the UN in Korea), *How the Communists Negotiate,* Macmillan, 1956, 178 pp.

Kennan, George F., *On Dealing with the Communist World,* Harper, 1964, 57 pp, pbk.

———, *Russia, the Atom and the West,* Oxford UP, 1958, 120 pp.

———, *Russia and the West Under Lenin and Stalin,* Little, Brown, 1961, 411 pp.

Kovner, Milton, *The Challenge of Coexistence,* Pub. Aff., 1961, 130 pp.

Kulski, Wladyslaw W., *Peaceful Co-existence, An Analysis of Soviet Foreign Policy,* Regnery, 1959, 662 pp.

Laqueur, Walter, *Russia and Germany, A Century of Conflict,* Weidenfeld & Nicolson, London, 1965, 367 pp.

———, *The Soviet Union and the Middle East,* Praeger, 1959, 366 pp.

Lederer, Ivo J., ed., *Russian Foreign Policy, Essays in Historical Perspective,* Yale UP, 1964, 620 pp.

Lenczowski, George, *Russia and the West in Iran, 1918–1948, A Study in Big-Power Rivalry,* Cornell UP, 1949, 393 pp.

Lippmann, Walter, *The Coming Tests with Russia,* Little, Brown, 1961, 37 pp.

Lukacs, John, *A History of the Cold War,* Doubleday, 1961, 288 pp.

Mackintosh, John Malcolm, *Strategy and Tactics of Soviet Foreign Policy,* Oxford UP, 1962, 332 pp.

Moore, Harriet, *Soviet Far Eastern Policy, 1931–1945,* Princeton UP, 1945, 284 pp.

Morrison, David, *The USSR and Africa,* Oxford UP, 1964, 124 pp.

Mosely, Philip E., *The Kremlin and World Politics, Studies in Soviet Policy and Action,* Vintage, 1960, 557 pp.

Neal, Fred Warner, *US Foreign Policy and the Soviet Union,* Center for the Study of Democratic Institutions, 1961, 60 pp.

Nove, Alec and Desmond Donnelly, *Trade with Communist Countries,* Hutchinson, London, 1960, 183 pp.

Pryor, Frederic L., *The Communist Foreign Trade Systems,* Allen & Unwin, London, 1963, 296 pp.

Roberts, Henry L., *Russia and America,* Mentor, 1960, 215 pp, pbk.

Rubinstein, Alvin Z., ed., *The Foreign Policy of the Soviet Union,* 2nd ed., Random House, 1966, 478 pp, pbk.

———, *The Soviets in International Organizations, Changing Policy Towards Developing Countries, 1953–1963,* Princeton UP, 1964, 380 pp.

Schapiro, Leonard, comp. and ed., *Soviet Treaty Series,* Vol. 1, *1917–1928,* Georgetown UP, 1950, 406 pp.

Seton-Watson, Hugh, *The New Imperialism,* Bodley Head, London, 1961, 136 pp.

Sharp, Samuel L., *Soviet Foreign Policy, A 50-Year Perspective,* Atherton, 1966.

Shulman, Marshall, *Beyond the Cold War,* Yale UP, 1966, 111 pp, pbk.

Slusser, Robert M., ed., *The Meaning of Yalta, Big Three Diplomacy and the New Balance of Power,* Louisiana UP, 1956, 239 pp.

——— and Jan F. Triska, *A Calendar of Soviet Treaties, 1917–1957,* Stanford UP, 1959, 530 pp.

Stalin's Correspondence with Churchill, Attlee, Roosevelt and Truman, 1941–1945, Lawrence & Wishart, London, 1958, 2 vols, 401 and 302 pp.

Thornton, Thomas Perry, ed., *The Third World in Soviet Perspective, Studies by Soviet Writers on the Developing Areas,* Princeton UP, 1964, 355 pp.

Triska, Jan F. and Robert M. Slusser, *The Theory, Law and Policy of Soviet Treaties,* Stanford UP, 1962, 593 pp.

Yemelyanov, V. S., "Atomic Energy for Peace, The U.S.S.R. and International Cooperation," *FA*, 38(3), Apr. 1960:465–75.

Zyzniewski, Stanley J., "The Soviet Bloc and the Underdeveloped Countries," *WP*, 15(3), Apr. 1959:378–99.

ARMED FORCES

Dinerstein, Herbert S., *War and the Soviet Union, Nuclear Weapons and the Revolution in Soviet Military and Political Thinking*, Praeger, 1959, 268 pp.

Erickson, J., "The 'Military Factor' in Soviet Policy," *IA*, 39(2), Apr. 1963:214–26.

Garthoff, Raymond L., *Soviet Strategy in the Nuclear Age*, Praeger, 1962, 320 pp, pbk.

Gilzin, K., *Sputniks and After*, Macdonald, London, 1959, 285 pp.

Hart, Basil Henry Liddell, ed., *The Soviet Army*, Weidenfeld & Nicolson, London, 1957, 480 pp.

Kilmarx, Robert A., *A History of Soviet Air Power*, Faber, London, 1962, 366 pp.

Lee, Asher, ed., *The Soviet Air and Rocket Forces*, Praeger, 1959, 311 pp.

O'Ballance, Edgar, *The Red Army*, Faber, London, 1964, 237 pp.

Saunders, M. G., ed., *The Soviet Navy*, Praeger, 1958, 340 pp.

Shternfeld, Ari, *Soviet Space Science*, Basic Books, 1959, 361 pp.

Sokolovski, Marshal Vasilii Danilovich, ed., *Military Strategy, Soviet Doctrine and Concepts*, Praeger, 1963, 396 pp.

Stockwell, Richard E., *Soviet Air Power*, Pageant, 1956, 238 pp.

INTERNATIONAL COMMUNISM

Alexander, Robert J., *Communism in Latin America*, Rutgers UP, 1957, 449 pp.

Almond, Gabriel, *The Appeals of Communism*, Princeton UP, 1954, 415 pp.

The Anti-Stalin Campaign and International Communism, A Selection of Documents, ed. by the Russian Inst., Columbia UP, 1956, 342 pp.

Bialoguski, Michael, *The Case of Colonel Petrov, How I Weaned a High MVD Official from Communism*, McGraw-Hill, 1955, 238 pp.

Borkenau, Franz, *World Communism, A History of the Communist International*, Norton, 1939, 442 pp.

Bromke, Adam, ed., *The Communist States at the Crossroad, Between Moscow and Peking*, Praeger, 1965, 270 pp, pbk.

Cronyn, George W., *A Primer on Communism*, rev. ed., Dutton, 1962, 192 pp, pbk.

Dallin, David J., *Soviet Espionage*, Yale UP, 1955, 558 pp.

Degras, Jane, ed., *The Communist International 1919–1943, Documents*, Oxford UP, 3 vols: *1919–1922*, 1956, 479 pp; *1923–1928*, 1960, 584 pp; *1929–1943*, 1965, 494 pp.

Doolin, Dennis J., *Territorial Claims in the Sino-Soviet Conflict*, Stanford UP, 1965, 80 pp.

Fainsod, Merle, *International Socialism and the World War*, Harvard UP, 1935, 238 pp.

Finley, David D., "A Political Perspective of Economic Relations in the Communist Camp," *WPQ*, 17(2), June 1964:294–316.

Footman, David, ed., *International Communism*, Southern Ill. UP, 1961, 151 pp.

Goodman, Elliott R., *The Soviet Design for a World State*, Columbia UP, 1960, 512 pp.

Griffith, William E., *The Sino-Soviet Rift*, MIT P, 1964, 512 pp, pbk.

Hammond, Thomas Taylor, ed., *Soviet Foreign Relations and World Communism, A Selected, Annotated Bibliography of 7,000 Books in 30 Languages*, Princeton UP, 1965, 1240 pp.

Heilbrunn, Otto, *The Soviet Secret Services*, Praeger, 1956, 216 pp.

Hudson, G. F. et al, *The Sino-Soviet Dispute*, Praeger, 1961, 234 pp.

Kirkpatrick, Evron M., ed., *Target, the World, Communist Propaganda Activities in 1955*, Macmillan, 1956, 362 pp.

Labedz, Leopold, ed., *International Communism After Khrushchev*, MIT P, 1965, 232 pp.

Lowenthal, Richard, *World Communism, The Disintegration of a Secular Faith*, Oxford UP, 1964, 296 pp.

Mamatey, Victor S., *Soviet Russian Imperialism*, Van Nostrand, 1964, 191 pp.

Mehnert, Klaus, *Peking and Moscow*, trans. by Leila Venewitz, Putnam's, 1963, 522 pp.

Nollau, Guenther, trans. by Victor Anderson, *International Communism and World Revolution, History and Methods*, Praeger, 1961, 357 pp.

Seton-Watson, Hugh, *From Lenin to Khrushchev, The History of World Communism*, rev. ed., Praeger, 1960, 447 pp, pbk.

Sino-Soviet Conflict, Report on the Sino-Soviet Conflict and Its Implications, US 89th Cong. 1st Sess., House Doc. No. 237, May 14, 1965.

Skilling, Harold Gordon, *Communism National and International, Eastern Europe After Stalin*, U Toronto P, 1965, 168 pp, pbk.

The Soviet Empire, A Study in Discrimination and Abuse of Power, USGPO, 1965, 197 pp.

Sworakowski, Witold S., *The Communist International and Its Front Organizations, Research Guide and Check List of Holdings in American and European Libraries*, Stanford UP, 1966, 493 pp.

World Communism, A Selected Annotated Bibliography, US 88th Cong. 2nd Sess., Senate Doc. No. 69, 1964.

Index